Securities Regulation

ASPEN CASEBOOK SERIES

Securities Regulation

Cases and Materials

Ninth Edition

James D. Cox
Brainerd Currie Professor of Law
Duke University

Robert W. Hillman
Professor of Law and Fair Business Practices and Investor Advocacy Chair
University of California, Davis

Donald C. Langevoort
Thomas Aquinas Reynolds Professor of Law
Georgetown University

Ann M. Lipton
Michael M. Fleishman Associate Professor in Business Law & Entrepreneurship
Tulane University

William K. Sjostrom
Professor of Law
University of Arizona

Published by Wolters Kluwer in New York.

Wolters Kluwer Legal & Regulatory U.S. serves customers worldwide with CCH, Aspen Publishers, and Kluwer Law International products. (www.WKLegaledu.com)

To contact Customer Service, e-mail customer.service@wolterskluwer.com, call 1-800-234-1660, fax 1-800-901-9075, or mail correspondence to:

Wolters Kluwer
Attn: Order Department
PO Box 990
Frederick, MD 21705

Printed in the United States of America.

1 2 3 4 5 6 7 8 9 0

ISBN 978-1-5438-1064-6

Library of Congress Cataloging-in-Publication Data

Names: Cox, James D., 1943- author. | Hillman, Robert W. (Robert William), 1949- author. | Langevoort, Donald C., author. | Lipton, Ann, author. |
Sjostrom, William K., Jr., author.
Title: Securities regulation: cases and materials / James D. Cox, Brainerd Currie Professor of Law, Duke University; Robert W. Hillman, Professor of Law and Fair Business Practices and Investor Advocacy Chair, University of California, Davis; Donald C. Langevoort, Thomas Aquinas Reynolds Professor of Law, Georgetown University; Ann M. Lipton, Michael M. Fleishman Associate Professor in Business Law & Entrepreneurship, Tulane University; William K. Sjostrom Professor of Law, University of Arizona.
Description: Ninth edition. | New York: Wolters Kluwer, [2020] | Includes
index. | Includes bibliographical references and index. | Summary:
"Securities Regulation casebook for law students"– Provided by
publisher.
Identifiers: LCCN 2019040123 | ISBN 9781543810646 (hardcover) |
ISBN 9781543816846 (ebook)
Subjects: LCSH: Securities—United States. | LCGFT: Casebooks (Law)
Classification: LCC KF1439.C69 2020 | DDC 346.73/0922—dc23
LC record available at https://lccn.loc.gov/2019040123

About Wolters Kluwer Legal & Regulatory U.S.

Wolters Kluwer Legal & Regulatory U.S. delivers expert content and solutions in the areas of law, corporate compliance, health compliance, reimbursement, and legal education. Its practical solutions help customers successfully navigate the demands of a changing environment to drive their daily activities, enhance decision quality and inspire confident outcomes.

Serving customers worldwide, its legal and regulatory portfolio includes products under the Aspen Publishers, CCH Incorporated, Kluwer Law International, ftwilliam.com and MediRegs names. They are regarded as exceptional and trusted resources for general legal and practice-specific knowledge, compliance and risk management, dynamic workflow solutions, and expert commentary.

To Bonnie, Olympia, Joni, Estelle, and Nancy

Summary of Contents

Contents

▌ 2 ▌

▍ 3 ▍

▍ 4 ▍

▮ 5 ▮

Exempt Transactions **239**

|| 6 ||

Secondary Distributions   **321**

‖ 7 ‖

❘ 8 ❘

Exempt Securities 417

❚ 9 ❚

❚ 10 ❚

▌ 11 ▌

Financial Reporting: Mechanisms, Duties, and Culture 553

‖ 12 ‖

Inquiries into the Materiality of Information   591

‖ 13 ‖

Fraud in Connection with the Purchase or Sale of a Security   669

‖ 14 ‖

The Enforcement of the Securities Laws   753

‖ 15 ‖

The Regulation of Insider Trading   867

‖ 16 ‖

‖ 17 ‖

‖ 18 ‖

‖ 19 ‖

‖ 20 ‖

Preface

For this Ninth Edition of *Securities Regulation: Cases and Materials,* the number of co-authors increases from the original three to five. The two newcomers, Ann Lipton and Bill Sjostrom, are both prolific thinkers and writers who bring new thoughts and perspectives to the ever-challenging study of securities regulation. The first generation authors could not be more pleased.

This edition keeps its content up-to-date with new cases, notes, and problems that reflect the changes that keep happening in Congress, the courts, and at the SEC. Notable developments in the litigation realm examined here are the implications of *Salman, Lorenzo,* and *Halliburton II,* in addition to the many lower court decisions the last few years that harbor new dimensions for the public and private enforcement of the securities laws. On the regulatory front, the most notable shifts have been along the ever-vexing line between public offerings and public company status on the one hand and a more deregulated world of capital and issuers on the private side on the other. This movement began in earnest with the JOBS Act in 2012 and, as of the publication of this edition in 2020, shows no sign of ceasing: As of this writing, the SEC has just issued a concept release that looks toward the possibility of even more extensive reform. Meanwhile, significant developments have occurred in other domains as well, including private securities litigation, the disclosure infrastructure put in place by Sarbanes-Oxley, the Dodd-Frank reforms, and new broker-dealer responsibilities. As always, we have tried to bring clarity to these teaching materials in the face of (and without hiding) the complexities and nuances that challenge all who enter the field of securities law.

Once again, we are grateful to those who teach from our book and help us out with suggestions for the things we could do better and matters that need correction. As with all editions of our casebook, occasional case and statute citations have been omitted from quoted material without indication. Most footnotes have been omitted from cases and other cited materials, also without indication, but those that remain retain original numbering.

October 2019

James D. Cox
Robert W. Hillman
Donald C. Langevoort
Ann M. Lipton
William Sjostrom

Acknowledgments

Committee on the Federal Regulation of Securities, Report of the Task Force on Regulation of Insider Trading—Part II: Reform of Section 16, 42 Bus. Law 1087 (1987). Reprinted with permission from the American Bar Association. Copyright © 1987. All rights reserved.

Campbell, Rutherford B., Jr., The Impact of NSMIA on Small Issuers, 53 Bus. Law. 575, 582-583 (1998). Copyright © 1998 by the American Bar Association. Reprinted with permission of The Business Lawyer and the author.

Cox, James, D., Insider Trading Regulation and the Production of Information: Theory and Evidence, 64 Wash. U. L.Q. 475, 493-495 (1986). Copyright © 1986 by the Washington University Law Quarterly. Reprinted with permission.

Easterbrook, Frank and Daniel Fischel, Mandatory Disclosure and the Protection of Investors, 70 Va. L. Rev. 669, 682-684 (1984). Copyright © 1984 by the Virginia Law Review Association. Reprinted with the permission of the Virginia Law Review Association and Fred B. Rothman & Co.

Lowenstein, Louis, Shareholder Voting Rights: A Response to SEC Rule 19c-4 and to Professor Gilson, 89 Colum. L. Rev. 979-1014 (1989). Copyright © 1989 by the Directors of the Columbia Law Review Association, Inc. All rights reserved. Reprinted by permission.

Poliakoff, Abba, SEC Review: Comfort or Illusion, 17 U. Balt. L. Rev. 40, 43-47 (1987). Copyright © 1987 by Abba David Poliakoff and Gordon, Feinblatt, Rothman, Hoffberger & Hollander. Reprinted with the permission of the University of Baltimore Law Review and the author.

Schneider, Carl, Joseph Manko, and Robert Kant, Going Public: Practice, Procedure and Consequences, 22-23 (Bowne & Co, 1999). Copyright © 1999 by Carl Schneider, Joseph Manko, and Robert Kant. Reprinted with permission of the authors.

Sjostrom, Jr., William K., PIPEs, 2 Entrepreneurial L. J. 381, 383-389 (2007). Copyright © 2007 The Ohio State University Entrepreneurial Business Law Journal. Reprinted with permission.

‖1‖
The Framework of Securities Regulation

A. Securities Transactions

The securities laws exist because of the unique informational needs of investors. Unlike cars and other tangible products, securities are not inherently valuable. Their worth comes only from the claims they entitle their owner to make upon the assets and earnings of the issuer, or the voting power that accompanies such claims. Deciding whether to buy or sell a security thus requires reliable information about such matters as the issuer's financial condition, products and markets, management, and competitive and regulatory climate. With this data, investors can attempt a reasonable estimate of the present value of the bundle of rights that ownership confers.

Securities are bought and sold in two principal settings: issuer transactions and trading transactions. As we shall see, the federal securities laws are structured differently for each of these settings.

1. Issuer Transactions

Issuer transactions are those involving the sales of securities by the issuer to investors. They are the means by which businesses raise capital—to develop, to grow, or simply to survive. The successful business is one that grows. Growth in sales, assets, and earnings can occur without the issuance of additional securities that would add new claimants to the firm's assets and earnings beyond those of its founders, but, frequently, in order to grow a firm must expand its ownership base. The sole proprietorship may take on a partner, the partnership may add partners, the close corporation may become publicly owned, and the public corporation may issue more stock or bonds to become an even larger company or to acquire another company.

By far the most expedient form of issuer transaction is the private placement of securities. This entails the issuer selling securities to a select number of investors. On the small scale, a private placement includes a partnership or closely held corporation adding new owners. Large public corporations also

1

engage in private placements when they raise large sums of capital through negotiated sales of securities to one or more financial institutions, such as an insurance company. In either case, special exemptions exist under the securities laws that enable private placements to escape the rigors of regulation.

On the other hand, the firm may not be able to raise all the capital it needs from a small number of investors. In this case, it must make a public offering of securities to a large number of diverse investors. We shall refer to such a public offering as a *primary distribution*. Whenever a large amount of securities is to be offered to the public, the selling effort usually occurs through a syndicate of broker-dealers, known as *underwriters*. An offering on behalf of a company going public for the first time is called an *initial public offering* (IPO).

2.   Trading Transactions

a.   *Introduction to Trading*

In contrast to primary distributions, *trading transactions* are the purchasing and selling of outstanding securities among investors. Resales of securities may either be privately negotiated or occur through public markets. Those who hold securities in a small firm for which no public market exists generally can only dispose of their shares by privately negotiating with an interested buyer. An exception to this statement occurs when the amount of securities to be resold is so great as to support a public offering. This is called a *secondary distribution* and most frequently occurs when individuals who control the securities' issuer wish to sell some of their shares.

Resales of outstanding securities are much more easily accomplished when there is a preexisting public market for those securities. The facilities through which outstanding securities are publicly traded are known as *securities markets*. Trading activity on U.S. markets is immense; in 2018 average daily trading volume on all U.S. public markets was 7.3 billion shares ($347 billion). By way of comparison, the total equity raised through all forms of public offerings in 2018 was $221 billion. SIFMA U.S. Stock Average Trading Volume by Exchange (2019). It should be apparent that investors engaged in trading transactions are in need of information just as are those who purchase securities in a primary distribution. The considerations of whether and at what price to purchase IBM common shares on an exchange are identical to the considerations investors ponder when offered IBM shares in a primary distribution. As will be seen, the mechanics, practices, and rules for disclosure, as well as other activities, differ significantly for primary distributions and trading transactions.

American securities markets can be roughly divided among bond, equity, and derivative/options markets. Traders in bond markets are primarily large financial institutions. Although trading in corporate debt instruments is in absolute amounts significant, all trading in such instruments is dwarfed by the magnitude of trading in U.S., state, and municipal bonds. Even though trading in government securities, as well as original issues of government securities, involves significantly larger amounts than trading in and offerings of business issuers, government securities are exempt from the disclosure regulations.

Regulation of government securities focuses upon those who sell government securities. Corporate bond issuances dwarf the issuance of stocks: In 2018, offerings of corporate bonds were nearly $1.3 trillion, whereas public offerings of equity involved $221 billion (IPOs represented only $49.8 billion). SIFMA Equity Underwriting Activity and Issuances in the U.S. Bond Market.

b. The Structure of Trading Markets

The trading of a security begins with a customer instructing her representative, a broker, to purchase or sell a security either at the best available market price ("market order") or at a stated price ("limit order"). With a limit order, the broker is not to execute the trade until the shares reach (or surpass) the price specified by the customer. Since 2007, all U.S. equity market transactions are executed at penny ($0.01) increments, more commonly referred to as decimalization of pricing. The broker first will seek to match the customer's order with that of another customer within the firm; if this is not possible, the broker may take the other side of the transaction so that the firm becomes a principal in the transaction—for example, buying from a selling customer. If the broker does not act as a principal and the order is not matched internally with another customer's order, the order is routed to the floor broker at the *exchange* or to a *market maker.*

Securities trade on one or more competitive markets in the United States. By far the largest U.S. equity market is the New York Stock Exchange; indeed, NYSE listed shares represent nearly 80 percent of the capitalization of all U.S. equity markets. The next largest market is Nasdaq. There are many other exchanges that are registered with the Securities and Exchange Commission (SEC). Because securities listed on one market, such as NYSE, can also be traded in another of these markets, such as the BATS Exchange, competition among the markets is keen. For example, only about 25 percent of the securities listed on NYSE or Nasdaq are traded on their respective exchange.

Shares not "listed" on an exchange can be traded in the over-the-counter market. At the core of the over-the-counter market is an electronically connected network of broker-dealers who publicly and regularly publish "bid" and "ask" prices for a security. They are therefore referred to as "market makers," as they attract investors' orders. The orders are handled either on a principal or agency basis. If the market maker purchases for its inventory, or sells the security from its inventory, it is deemed to be acting as a principal; in contrast, if a market maker simply matches the willing buyer with a willing seller, it is acting as an agent. In either case, the commission derived by the market maker is the "spread" between the bid and the asked price. Nasdaq, although technically today an exchange as defined in the Exchange Act, evolved from this over-the-counter structure; it is a computer network that links brokers and market makers (and, more importantly, their bid and ask quotes).

Of special note is how limit orders can pose a particular challenge since the requested price may depart materially from the present market price. For example, a customer limit order may call for the purchase of a security at $15 when the most recent transaction in that security occurred at $16. Since the market professional can be expected to avoid selling personal inventory shares at a price below the then market price, the broker can leave the order in the limit order book. Thus, an alternative function of the intermediary is to maintain a limit order book in which unfilled orders are recorded and later filled by the intermediary as market conditions permit. In the preceding example, if the price of the security in the limit order book declines to $15, the intermediary will execute the order for the customer—receiving, of course, a commission on the trade.

We should take a moment to reflect on the multiple social benefits provided by public securities markets:

> The modern regulated exchange has several roles. Its transparency provides a price discovery mechanism and liquidity so that investors, speculators, and hedgers can quickly create and liquidate positions at current market prices. . . . The exchange clearinghouses provide clearing and settlement functions that assure the smooth processing and confirmation of trades . . . within three days on the securities exchanges. . . .
>
> The stock exchanges and Nasdaq impose minimum listing requirements as quality control mechanisms. . . .
>
> One service, and revenue source, for exchanges is fulfilling the demand for market data. . . . The exchanges' profitability from the dissemination of trade data is large; according to some researchers, market data fees accounted for 50% of the NYSE Group's total revenues in 2006 while those same fees represented about 80% of Nasdaq's total revenues. . . .
>
> [Exchanges] are uniquely qualified to act as gatekeeper for membership, resolve disputes, establish codes for acceptable trading practices, and implement other policies that are applicable to the industry and its trading requirements and standards. . . .

Markam, For Whom the Bell Tolls: The Demise of Exchange Trading Floors and the Growth of ECNs, 33 J. Corp. L. 865, 882-885 (2008).

B.   *The Legal Framework of Securities Regulation*

Before learning more about the various legislative and administrative initiatives that have produced the American securities laws, consider the following regarding the challenges policymakers face in formulating sound regulation:

> Investing is a choice; people can do many different things with their money. If people choose not to invest (or invest less), the capital markets—and the financial community—suffer. Given the inevitability and repeated salient examples of opportunism, the level of investment should vary based on how confident investors feel that they will not be exploited when parting with their hard-earned money. The standard economic justification for investor protection regulation is that some public commitment to fight marketplace abuses is necessary to offset fear of exploitation and instill investor confidence. Regulation at this base-line level can be cost-efficient and justifiable even to the most ardent free-marketeer, promoting the conservative trilogy (now baked into the law) of "efficiency, competition and

capital formation." But where that sweet spot is, no one knows. Economists, by and large, think we have too much—or at least too much of the wrong kind—of securities regulation.

As you read on, I want you to put yourself in the role of a securities regulator, perhaps the SEC chair. Here is the mental image with which to begin: There are more than a hundred million investor households in the United States, all making difficult financial choices. There are tens of thousands of businesses and entrepreneurs seeking capital from investors. There are competing stock exchanges and electronic trading platforms facilitating the secondary trading of hundreds of millions of shares every day, and thousands of large institutional investors like mutual funds, hedge funds, pension funds that now dominate these financial markets, with massive conflicts of interest. Legions of brokers and investment advisers engage in a never-ending effort to get deeply into their clients' wallets. Much of this takes place globally, often outside the reach of any one domestic regulator. Imagine that you were asked to make this wide-open territory "safe" for investors, many of whom seem habitually disinclined toward prudence, and also to promote robust capital formation. How would you do it? How much in the way of resources would you insist on as a condition for taking the job and doing it well? How would you know whether you are succeeding or failing, or being used?

What does investor protection even mean?

D.C. Langevoort, Selling Hope, Selling Risk: Corporations, Wall Street, and the Dilemmas of Investor Protection 2-3 (2016).

1.   The Federal Securities Laws

a.   *The Securities Act of 1933*

Debate on the merits of a mandatory disclosure system began early in the twentieth century, but it was the Great Depression and the market collapse in October 1929 that provided the political momentum for congressional action that would over the course of a decade produce a collection of acts known as the federal securities laws. The first of the federal securities laws enacted was the Federal Securities Act of 1933 ('33 Act), which regulates the public offering and sale of securities in interstate commerce. The abuses prompting the legislation were legion:

> During the postwar decade some 50 billion of new securities were floated in the United States. Fully half or $25,000,000,000 worth of securities floated during this period have been proved to be worthless. These cold figures spell tragedy in the lives of thousands of individuals who invested their life savings, accumulated after years of effort, in these worthless securities. The flotation of such a mass of essentially fraudulent securities was made possible because of the complete abandonment by many underwriters and dealers in securities of those standards of fair, honest, and prudent dealing that should be basic to the encouragement of investment in any enterprise.
>
> Alluring promises of easy wealth were freely made with little or no attempt to bring to the investor's attention those facts essential to estimating the worth of any security. High pressure salesmanship rather than careful counsel was the rule in this most dangerous enterprise.

H.R. Rep. No. 85, 73d Cong., 1st Sess. 2 (1933).

Disclosure is the remedy the Securities Act embraces for this malady. The '33 Act and much of the federal securities laws are influenced by the regulatory philosophy championed by Justice Brandeis: "Sunlight is said to be the best of disinfectants: electric light the most efficient policeman." L.D. Brandeis, Other People's Money 62 (1914). The Act's disclosure demands apply to public offerings of securities that occur through the process of "registering" such an offering with the SEC. The following is a broad overview of the Securities Act's registration process; a much closer examination of that process occurs in Chapter 4.

Through the preparation of a registration statement, the Securities Act seeks to assure full and fair disclosure in connection with the public distribution of securities. The information issuers are compelled to disclose in their registration statements is set forth in the SEC regulations and covers all significant aspects of the issuer's business. The precise disclosure requirements are somewhat industry sensitive. In general, the registration statement must provide a thorough description of the issuer's business, property, and management. Extensive financial information must be disclosed, including certified financial statements for the current and several previous years as well as revenues and earnings for each significant product line. Management must also provide its analysis and review of the issuer's capital needs, solvency, and financial performance, including analysis of any variances in revenues or profits from the preceding year. A detailed description of the rights, privileges, and preferences of the offered security, as well as the existing capital structure of the firm, must be set forth in the registration statement.

Paternalism toward investors is evident throughout the SEC's instructions and guides to its disclosure regulations as it seeks to paint a somber picture of the issuer's prospects. This dimension of the '33 Act disclosure process is underscored by information appearing in the first section of the registration statement, where any "risk factors" that make the offering speculative must be described. Examples of such special risks are that there is no preexisting market for the security (i.e., it is an IPO), that the issuer has recently experienced substantial losses, and that the nature of the business the issuer is engaged in or proposes to engage in poses unusual risks. The information filed by an "unseasoned" issuer with the SEC undergoes several drafts and reviews under the watchful and demanding eye of the SEC's Corporation Finance staff. Most of the registration statement's substantive information is also required to be disclosed in the *prospectus*. The need for care and honesty in the preparation of the registration statement is underscored by the exposure of the issuer's underwriters, officers, directors, and certain experts to civil liability for omissions and misstatements in the registration statement.

As can be seen from the above, the objective of the registration process is the production of a prospectus that includes most of the information disclosed in the registration statement. The prospectus is designed to provide all material information necessary for investors to fully assess the merits of their purchase of the security; the prospectus is the vehicle for stationing investors on as nearly an equal footing with the issuers and their underwriters as possible, with the hope their purchase is neither worthless nor overpriced.

The underwriters' selling efforts cannot commence until the registration statement has been filed with the SEC, and no sales or deliveries of securities may occur until the registration statement is effective. Nevertheless, extensive selling efforts commence after the registration statement is filed, at which time investor interest is orally solicited. Written offers during this period can be made through a preliminary prospectus that embodies all the substantive information then contained in the registration statement as well as through other materials if certain conditions, reviewed later in Chapter 4, are satisfied. Once the registration statement becomes effective, actual sales can be made, and the purchased securities can be delivered. The Securities Act's objective of full disclosure for public offerings of securities occurs through the registration process and the Act's compulsion for a prospectus to be available to investors.

As will be seen in later chapters, Section 3 exempts numerous categories of securities from the Act's registration requirements, the most significant being those issued by governmental bodies, banks, and insurance companies, and Section 4 exempts securities sold in certain types of transactions. Importantly, the Act provides both private and public remedies to assure compliance with its provisions. Thus, Section 11 provides a private right of action for materially false statements in the registration statement, and Section 12 imposes civil liability upon those who sell securities in violation of Section 5's registration requirement as well as upon anyone who sells any security in a public offering by means of a materially misleading statement. The SEC's enforcement powers include the power to issue administrative cease-and-desist orders under Section 8A as well as to prosecute violations civilly in the federal courts under Section 20.

b. The Securities Exchange Act of 1934

History and Philosophy. The disastrous market effects of the Great Depression were, of course, not borne solely by the purchasers of new issues. The decline in value of outstanding securities was dramatic and painful. For example, the total value of all New York Stock Exchange listed securities declined from a pre-crash 1929 high of $89 billion to $15 billion in 1932. Investor interest and confidence in markets evaporated overnight, and for many stocks, trading halted completely.

The causes of the crash were many, and most were unrelated to abusive practices. The pre-crash market was driven not by fundamentals, but by speculative frenzy. Speculating in stocks was something of a national pastime. For example, 55 percent of all personal savings were used to purchase securities. E.R. Willet, Fundamentals of Securities Markets 211 (1968). A significant amount of all investment was on margin, in which an investor borrowed most of the stock's purchase price. There was no limit on the amount of credit that could be extended to an investor for margin trading. Typically, the lender was the brokerage firm, which in turn borrowed the funds from a bank. So long as the stock price did not decline, substantial margin trading posed no harm to the investor or markets generally. However, once steam began to run out of the market in late 1929, lenders began making calls upon the investor to cover the amount that the securities' market value had declined below its purchase price. This produced a chain reaction as margin calls triggered sales of securities owned by overextended customers; sales made in response to margin calls further depressed stock prices, so that even more margin calls were made upon other investors, and so on.

A good deal of the content of the Depression Era securities laws, and particularly the collage of provisions that would become the Exchange Act, was shaped by the sensational hearings of the Senate Committee on Banking and Currency, whose chief investigator, Ferdinand Pecora, presented in riveting detail the abuses visited on public investors. *See* Michael Perino, The Hellhound of Wall Street: How Ferdinand Pecora's Investigation of the Great Crash Forever Changed American Finance (2010). Much of the hearings leading up to Congress' enactment of the securities laws was devoted to accounts of trading practices by unscrupulous market manipulators. The hearings produced reports that the bull market of the 1920s was the heyday of the crooked stock pools. These were devices used by brokers and dealers to create a false appearance of trading activity by simultaneously buying the same security they were selling. Innocent investors were attracted to the manipulated stock by its price and volume changes. Eventually, unwitting investors' orders provided all the upward momentum to the stock's price. And, as the price rose, the brokers and dealers behind the scheme dumped their holdings at the higher price created by the unwitting investors' interest. More recent examination of market practices in the 1920s suggests that the congressional hearings greatly exaggerated the effect and existence of such abusive schemes, perhaps doing so for political purposes. *See* Mahoney, The Stock Pools and the Securities Exchange Act, 51 J. Fin. Econ. 343 (1999).

There also was plenty of evidence that stock prices were adversely affected by false and misleading information and that corporate insiders took advantage of their access to confidential inside information to further their own trading profits. Related to this was the absence of legal compulsion for publicly traded firms to make timely disclosures of material information or to publish even annual financial reports. A further problem was the belief that public corporations were not sufficiently responsive to their owners due to weaknesses in the proxy solicitation process.

An inventory of these market abuses is summarized in Section 2 of the Securities Exchange Act ('34 Act), which captures the popular and congressional view that stock prices reflected the actions of speculators, manipulators, and inside traders, as well as the gullible, but not the astute and the sophisticated. *See* Thel, The Original Conception of Section 10(b) of the Securities Exchange Act, 42 Stan. L. Rev. 385, 409 (1990). One of the great ironies of securities regulation is that, even though Congress when it enacted the '34 Act had a dim view of the overall sophistication of market participants, today many of the Commission's regulatory initiatives under the '34 Act are premised on the assumption that trading markets are dominated by sophisticated, resourceful investors. The irony of this underscores the breadth and flexibility of the '34 Act's provisions.

There is an important difference in style between the Securities Act and the Exchange Act. In the Securities Act, Congress empowered the Federal Trade Commission (FTC) to discharge a specific and well-defined task: the registration of public offerings of securities not otherwise exempt from the Act. The means, as well as the end result, are clearly and unequivocally defined in the Securities Act. In contrast, the Exchange Act is in large part a laundry list of problems for which Congress articulated neither the means nor the end objective. Instead, Congress, through Section 4 of the Act, created the Securities and Exchange Commission and delegated to it the task of grappling with the problem areas.

The contrast in style between the two acts bears witness to the fact that compromises were necessary to assure passage of the Exchange Act whereas that was not the case for the Securities Act. Recall that the Congress that enacted the Securities Act also enacted in those heady first hundred days of Roosevelt's first term other legislative packages that greatly centralized the federal government's control over the economy, the most prominent piece being the National Recovery Act. Many of Roosevelt's advisers were urging upon him a similar approach to the regulation of securities practices. For example, then-Professor William O. Douglas, who would later become the third Chairman of the SEC before being appointed to the Supreme Court, was one who openly counseled Roosevelt that a disclosure-oriented approach was inadequate and that legislation was needed that directly involved the federal government in identifying the firms that should be permitted to approach investors with their public offerings and thus gave it an active role in channeling capital into industries the government preferred to nurture. *See, e.g.*, Douglas, Protecting the Investor, 23 Yale L.J. (N.S.) 521 (1934).

Despite the willingness of the New Dealers to embrace modes of direct government involvement in the economy's private sector, the Securities Act's exclusive orientation was disclosure, a clear victory for those who embraced a less intrusive federal role in capital markets. Landis, The Legislative History of The Securities Act of 1933, 28 Geo. Wash. L. Rev. 29 (1959). On the other hand, the Exchange Act as originally proposed envisioned strong federal control of the trading markets as well as important structural changes for the securities industry and its participants. The radicalism of these proposals energized the securities industry, and its representatives came to Washington with their own proposals. In the end, the '34 Act reflects the many compromises necessary to assure its passage. Indeed, the creation of the Securities and Exchange Commission itself was a concession to the industry, which felt it would fare better under an agency whose energies were focused exclusively on capital markets and the securities industry—the industry had found the leading regulators at the FTC to be formidable and devoted regulators.[1] In the end, many of the pressing regulatory issues were unresolved in the '34 Act and were instead dumped into the lap of the newly created Commission, where the debate and compromise would continue. *See generally* J. Seligman, The Transformation of Wall Street, chs. 2 & 3 (3d ed. 2003).

---

1. The industry believed the creation of a separate commission would shield it from individuals such as James M. Landis, then an FTC commissioner and a strident proponent for regulation. With the creation of the SEC, the industry saw one of its own, Joseph Kennedy, appointed as its first chairman, but also found to its horror that Landis became one of its members and succeeded Kennedy as chair when Kennedy was appointment ambassador to Britain. When Landis left to become Dean of Harvard Law School, William O. Douglas, later Justice Douglas, became its third chairman.

Continuous Disclosure and Other Disclosure Provisions.   Whereas the Securities Act grapples with the protection of investors in primary distributions of securities, the Exchange Act's concern is trading markets and their participants. An important contribution to efficient trading markets is the '34 Act's system of continuous disclosure for companies required to register under its provisions. Three categories of companies are subject to the '34 Act's continuous disclosure requirements: companies that have a class of securities listed on a national securities exchange (Section 12(b)); companies that have assets in excess of $10 million and that have a class of equity securities held by at least 2,000 record holders (Section 12(g) and Rule 12g-1—prior to 2012, continuous reporting was required for firms with 500 or more record holders); and companies that have filed a '33 Act registration statement that has become effective (Section 15(d)). A company that meets any one of these requirements is called a *reporting company.*

Reporting companies are required to register with the SEC and thereafter make timely filings of reports required by Section 13 of the '34 Act. Unlike the '33 Act's disclosure requirements, there is no additional requirement that '34 Act filings be forwarded to investors or market professionals. All registrants (domestic and foreign) are required to file with the SEC their '33 Act registration statements and their periodic reports under the '34 Act in electronic format (i.e., submissions occur through e-mail or the physical delivery of diskettes or magnetic tapes). The present system is called EDGAR (Electronic Data Gathering, Analysis, and Retrieval System). In its quest for facilitating investor decisionmaking, since 2009 the SEC has required filings to be pursuant to its Interactive Data Electronic Applications (IDEA), which itself builds on a software program, XBRL (Extensible Business Reporting Language), by which information is "tagged" by reporting companies so that users can thereafter sort information according to the pretagged codes. The XBRL system allows investors to compare discrete reporting items (e.g., research and development expenditures) across a range of companies without the necessity of serially accessing the forms of individual companies. Information filed with the SEC is available to anyone through its web site (*www.sec.gov*).

The most significant of the compelled reports is the annual report on Form 10-K, which is required to include an extensive description of the company's business, audited financial statements for the fiscal year, and management's discussion and analysis of the position and performance of the company. Quarterly reports on Form 10-Q are also required to be filed with the SEC. The disclosures on Form 10-Q include unaudited interim financial statements for the company as well as management's analysis of financial operations and conditions. A further report compelled by Section 13 is Form 8-K, which must be filed within a few days of the occurrence of a material development of the type specified in the form, for example, a change in control, credit downgrade, the acquisition or disposition of a significant amount of assets, the commencement of insolvency proceedings, a change in auditors, or the resignation of a director in a dispute over policy.

The SEC in the early 1980s adopted the process of "integrated disclosure," whereby certain companies registering securities under the Securities Act could fulfill many of the '33 Act's disclosure demands by incorporating into the Securities Act registration statement information from their Exchange Act (e.g., Form 10-K) filings. As we see in Chapter 4, following sweeping reforms adopted by the SEC in 2005, today integrated disclosure is available to seasoned issuers, which is defined as a company that has filed an annual report with the SEC and is current in its filings. Integrated disclosure was the first step toward melding the Securities Act and Exchange Act so that their disclosure demands are complementary and their registrants' burdens lightened. Under integrated disclosure, issuers are required to file a registration statement with the SEC in advance of their offering, and for most issuers there is a period of delay before the issuers can sell the registered securities. As will be seen, integrated disclosure reduces greatly the delay and costs that normally accompany registering securities.

The Act also requires those companies that are subject to the continuous reporting requirements because they fall within either Exchange Act Section 12(b) or Section 12(g), discussed above, to make full and fair disclosure whenever soliciting their stockholders' proxies and to otherwise comply with the numerous proxy rules the Commission has promulgated under Section 14(a). Through the Williams Act Amendments in 1968, disclosure by an outsider is required when more than 5 percent of a class of registered equity securities is or will be owned as a result of a tender offer or purchase. Other tender offer practices are also regulated as a consequence of the Williams Act Amendments.

Regulation of Exchanges, Broker-Dealers, and Market Abuses. Continuing its emphasis on regulating trading markets, the Exchange Act embraces a strong, active role for a variety of self-regulatory organizations (SROs). Two important types of SROs are each of the national securities exchanges and the Financial Industry Regulatory Authority (FINRA). As discussed in section B.3 below, the SROs' regulatory role is played under the Commission's watchful eye. Later, in Chapter 18, we examine the regulatory authority of FINRA and the SEC over brokers and dealers. The Exchange Act also seeks to protect the integrity of capital markets and investors by arming the SEC, as well as private litigants, with its antifraud and anti-manipulation provisions. Both the public and the private enforcement of the antifraud and anti-manipulation rules are closely examined later in this book.

c.   Federal Regulation Beyond Disclosure: The Sarbanes-Oxley Act of 2002 and Dodd-Frank Wall Street Reform and Consumer Protection Act of 2010

In July 2002, the Sarbanes-Oxley Act was enacted and ushered in a new era of financial regulation for U.S. capital markets. As is seen throughout this book, many of the provisions Congress included in Sarbanes-Oxley depart radically from the securities laws' historical preoccupation of addressing investor protection via disclosure. Among other features, the Act sets forth broad prescriptions for corporate governance, authorizes the SEC to develop rules for professional conduct for lawyers, and regulates areas that have always been the province of the states, such as loans to officers and directors. The events that prompted Congress to act were many and are collectively referred to as the accounting and financial scandals of 2002. The scandals actually began in 2001 with the sudden collapse of Enron Corporation, the seventh largest American corporation.

Enron was a high-flying energy trading company whose aggressive management style consistently impressed Wall Street with ever-increasing profits and reports of an even brighter future. For five consecutive years before its collapse Fortune 500 executives had voted Enron as one of America's most innovative companies. But all that glitters is not gold. In early December 2001, Enron filed for bankruptcy protection, at that time the largest bankruptcy filing in American history. It was soon revealed that Enron's profits were fabricated by its executives, that its Big Five accounting firm, Arthur Andersen, had acquiesced in clear violations of accounting and reporting principles, that it appeared that two national law firms that advised it had not appropriately advised their clients of possible misconduct by senior management, and that financial analysts were co-opted by pressures from their investment banking colleagues to support Enron with "strong buy" recommendations as a means to garner lucrative investment banking business from Enron. *See generally* Report of the Staff to the Senate Committee on Governmental Affairs, Financial Oversight of Enron: The SEC and Private-Sector Watchdogs (Oct. 8, 2002). More information regarding the financial reporting frauds and other market abuses committed by Enron and others in the months leading up to Sarbanes-Oxley is presented in later chapters.

Sarbanes-Oxley would not have been enacted if Enron had been an isolated event. Enron's bankruptcy was soon followed by the financial collapse of approximately a dozen large public companies where there was also strong evidence of reporting violations and audit failures even more egregious than that which occurred in Enron. Moreover, over the course of the five preceding years the number of earnings restatements by public companies quadrupled. The final culminating event propelling the enactment of Sarbanes-Oxley was the revelation in late June 2002 that WorldCom's chief financial officer had overstated earnings over several quarters by several billions of dollars. Soon after making its own earnings restatements, WorldCom itself entered bankruptcy, supplanting Enron for the honor of the largest company ever to seek the protection of the bankruptcy laws. With the enactment of Sarbanes-Oxley the focus of the securities laws and the SEC is today significantly broader than disclosure. Sarbanes-Oxley does not alter the core features of the U.S. securities laws, but the Act introduces important procedural and substantive requirements for public companies as additional safeguards to protect investors. It is also apparent from this book's review of the regulatory initiatives ushered in by Sarbanes-Oxley that important areas of corporate governance are no longer solely a matter controlled by state law.

Just as the Great Depression ushered in various New Deal regulators such as the SEC, the financial crisis that began in 2008 led to the enactment of the Dodd-Frank Wall Street Reform and Consumer Protection Act in 2010. The seeds of this crisis can be traced to the housing bubble that had reached full bloom by mid-2005. As a result of extraordinarily low interest rates and questionable predatory lending practices, home mortgages were granted against what quickly became artificially heightened real estate values. Many of these mortgages were denoted "subprime" because their borrowers posed serious credit risks. Through the alchemy of asset-backed securitization, the mortgages were bundled together, given questionable "investment-grade" ratings, and then sold to financial institutions. When the bubble burst, which is a nasty tendency of bubbles, the financial institutions found that their investment-grade securities were hardly that, and many institutions failed or teetered at the edge of failure. Fear gripped all sectors of the financial markets. In fall 2008, the Dow Jones Industrial Average plunged dramatically, banks became unwilling or unable to lend to one another, and the once highly liquid and low-risk commercial paper market evaporated. This was followed by massive government bailouts of commercial banks, investment banks, and other financial institutions that on a worldwide basis exceeded $2 trillion.

There were many culprits behind the credit crisis. Most of Dodd-Frank is aimed at the regulation of depositary institutions, derivatives, and consumer finance. These areas are not covered in this book as they involve institutions and regulatory paradigms that are outside the realm of securities regulation. However, Dodd-Frank does contain numerous provisions that impact the scope and content of U.S. securities laws such as mandatory disclosure related to "conflict minerals," authorization for the SEC to adopt rules providing shareholders with a means to nominate directors of public companies, and clarification of the SEC enforcement authority with respect to foreign issuers. Each of these provisions, as well as many other Dodd-Frank securities-related provisions, are studied later. In broad overview, what is notable about Dodd-Frank's interface with the securities laws is that many of its securities-related provisions, like those of Sarbanes-Oxley, transcend disclosure. One question is whether the strong bipartisan support the SEC and securities regulation has historically enjoyed is weakened by the content of U.S. securities laws that no longer focuses exclusively on disclosure and fraud, but includes as well procedures by which public companies govern themselves and their need to disclose information that is politically and socially sensitive, e.g., trafficking in conflict minerals or CEO pay versus pay of the average employee. In this sense, Congress through Sarbanes-Oxley and Dodd-Frank has moved the SEC into new and unfamiliar terrain.

d.   The Regulation of Investment Advisers and Investment Companies

The bulk of the securities regulation course materials focus on the provisions of the Securities Act and the Securities Exchange Act. As is seen in Chapter 19, the SEC has an important regulatory role with respect to investment advisers and investment companies.

The Investment Company Act of 1940 and the Investment Advisers Act of 1940 were the culmination of a comprehensive four-year SEC investigation of investment companies and their advisers. *Investment companies,* simply defined, are companies formed for the purpose of buying, selling, and holding a portfolio of securities for investment, rather than for control purposes. Common versions of investment companies are money market funds and mutual funds. The Investment Company Act regulates the independence of the company's board of directors; requires annual review of any management contract between the investment company and its investment adviser; conditions transactions between the company and its officers, directors, or affiliates upon approval by the SEC; and regulates the capital structure of investment companies. Even though investment companies are required to register under the Investment Company Act, they remain subject to the registration and prospectus requirements of the

Securities Act when they engage in a public offering of their securities. They also are subject to the reporting requirements of the Exchange Act.

An *investment adviser* is one engaged in the business of rendering investment advice to others for compensation. The Investment Advisers Act of 1940 requires advisers to register with the SEC, establishes a few minimum requirements for fair dealings by investment advisers, and prohibits fraudulent and deceptive practices by investment advisers.

e. The Organizational Structure of the SEC

The SEC is an independent, nonpartisan agency created by the Securities Exchange Act of 1934; the '33 Act, until the creation of the Commission, was administered by the FTC. The Commission is composed of five commissioners appointed by the President to five-year terms. The terms are staggered so that one expires each June, and not more than three commissioners may be of the same party as the President. One of the commissioners is designated by the President to serve as the chairman of the Commission. The commissioners meet frequently as a deliberative body to resolve issues raised by the staff. The Commission's staff is organized into divisions and offices.

The SEC operates through four principal divisions. The Division of Corporation Finance has overall responsibility for administering the federal securities laws' disclosure requirements through its review of the registration statements for public offerings, quarterly and annual reports, proxy statements, tender offer statements, and other documents required to be filed with it. The Division of Trading and Markets has responsibility to oversee the operation of secondary trading markets, including the registration and behavior of exchanges and broker-dealers as well as rating agencies. Responsibility for administering the Investment Company Act and the Investment Advisers Act is with the Division of Investment Management. The Division of Enforcement is to the general public the most visible of all the divisions because of the publicity that frequently accompanies its investigations and prosecutions. Enforcement actions can occur via an administrative proceeding or in the courts. Criminal prosecutions, however, are within the exclusive authority of the Department of Justice attorneys, usually through the appropriate U.S. Attorney's Office, with assistance of the SEC enforcement staff. In 2009, the newest part of the SEC was established, the Division of Economic and Risk Analysis, which draws on a variety of disciplines to assist the SEC in policymaking, rulemaking, enforcement, and examinations.

f. The Mediums Through Which the SEC Speaks

The Commission and its staff's views on regulatory issues are communicated in a variety of mediums. Through the exercise of its broad rulemaking power, the Commission formally makes its position known on regulatory issues. In the releases that accompany its proposals and adoption of regulations, the SEC goes to great lengths to provide guidance regarding the content of the regulations it is considering. SEC releases are essentially press releases and invariably accompany the proposal, adoption, or modification of rules. The Commission, through its enforcement staff, plays an important role in expanding and refining the law through the enforcement actions it chooses to initiate and the theories under which the suits are maintained. The classic illustration of the Commission's impact in this regard was its success in proscribing insider trading through its early administrative proceedings, *see* Cady, Roberts & Co., 40 S.E.C. 907 (1961), and judicial proceedings, *see SEC v. Texas Gulf Sulphur Co.,* 401 F.2d 833 (2d Cir. 1968). The Commission's positions are also presented in private litigation through amicus briefs the staff files on important issues.

Extensive guidance is provided through the SEC web site in its "Compliance and Disclosure Interpretations." These staff interpretations are focused on distinct regulatory topics or rules and provide a good deal of guidance into how the provisions are administered by the staff. An especially important source of guidance occurs through the staff's issuance of *no-action letters.* Since the SEC's creation, its staff has been willing to respond to individual inquiries regarding the staff's interpretation of the federal securities laws' application to a specific transaction. The staff's responses to such inquiries are known as no-action letters because the key expression in a favorable response to an inquiry states that the staff "will recommend *no action* to the Commission" if the transaction is carried out as stated in the letter. Because the no-action letters express the views only of the staff involved with the day-to-day responsibility of administering that provision of the law, they do not represent the official view of the Commission. 17 C.F.R. §202.1(d). No-action letters are compliance oriented and designed to provide some measure of certainty to those planning securities transactions. Even though the Commission will not challenge that transaction as a violation of the law if the transaction is completed as represented in the no-action letter request, Securities Act Release No. 4553 (Nov. 6, 1962), a no-action letter is not binding on private parties, who can challenge the transaction. Also, the predictive value of relying on a no-action letter obtained by another is seriously weakened by the power of the Commission or its staff to reconsider the position it took in the earlier no-action letter.[2] In any case, there is a somewhat lengthy list of items the staff refuses to offer an opinion on through the no-action letter process. Securities Act Release No. 6253 (Oct. 28, 1980). Among those areas so excluded is the availability of a statutory exemption from registration, whether novel real estate interests are a security, and hypothetical questions. *See* Nagy, Judicial Reliance on Regulatory Interpretations in SEC No-Action Letters: Current Problems and Proposed Framework, 83 Cornell L. Rev. 921 (1998) (examining the conditions when it is appropriate for courts to defer to SEC no-action letters).

The SEC's web site, *www.sec.gov,* also contains a good deal of guidance on regulatory issues. Found there are desk guides addressing commonly asked questions, recent speeches of commissioners and agency personnel, enforcement releases, and other helpful publications.

Further guidance through the uncharted waters of the securities laws and regulatory discretion occurs informally by individual commissioners, division

---

2.   SEC no-action letters are not judicially reviewable because they are not *orders* of the Commission. *Board of Trade of the City of Chicago v. SEC,* 883 F.2d 525 (7th Cir. 1989).

and office heads, and their assistants expressing their views and describing prevailing practices within the SEC in their speeches and during participation in securities programs. This medium also nurtures a professional bond between the regulators and the securities bar.

g.   The SEC: Some Critical Perspectives

The SEC has long held a reputation for quality and vigor that sets it apart from many of its regulatory peers. This reputation is of considerable importance: It aids in the recruitment of new personnel and serves as a form of psychic compensation to the staff to help offset some of the financial sacrifices of government service. It also gives to the Commission a considerable level of public support from which to draw when it takes action.

The Commission is not without its critics, however. Much of the criticism comes from the perspective of economic theory and charges that the SEC has substantially over-regulated areas such as disclosure policy, with excessive and paternalistic focus on "investor protection" to the exclusion of equally compelling notions of cost justification and allocative efficiency. To state this concern, however, does not help explain *why* it is that the Commission might behave in a way that, in substance, seems short of optimal.

One explanation that has achieved a good deal of currency draws from the body of literature of public choice theory, as articulated by such notable economists as George Stigler and Sam Peltzman. Public choice theory posits that far from seeking some independent conception of the "public good," regulators rationally seek simply to maximize their own level of political support and thus frequently allocate wealth (in the form of regulatory subsidies and/or restraints on competition) to those groups that offer the most in terms of such support. Often, this means regulation that actually favors some segment of the industry that the agency is supposed to control (sometimes referred to as the "capture" hypothesis), since that special interest is likely to be the best organized and most effective "rent-seeker." Here we may ask whether securities lawyers and financial accountants, among others, who earn their livelihood through providing the compliance efforts related to mandatory disclosure requirements have a significant stake in the status quo. For a public choice perspective on the SEC, *see* Coates, Private vs. Political Choice of Securities Regulation: A Political Cost Benefit Analysis, 41 Va. J. Int'l L. 531 (2001); Macey, Administrative Agency Obsolescence and Interest Group Formation: A Case Study of the SEC at Sixty, 15 Cardozo L. Rev. 909 (1994).

There has long been concern with regulatory agencies regarding the "revolving door" whereby civil servants migrate from the regulator to the regulated. There indeed is a good deal of movement of staff of the SEC to the private sector, no doubt reflecting the valuable experience garnered by working with the Commission. But does it reflect more? Studies of SEC enforcement personnel who thereafter are retained by law firms reflect that the individuals moving to the private sector during their tenure at the SEC were associated with successful, even aggressive, enforcement efforts that involved more complex matters. *See* de Haan, Kedia, Koh & Rajgopa, The Revolving Door and the SEC's Enforcement Outcomes: Initial Evidence of Civil Litigation, 60 Acct. & Econ. 65

(2015); Choi & Pritchard, SEC Enforcement Attorneys: Should I Stay or Should I Go?, ___ J.L. & Econ. ___ (2019) (forthcoming). A very different dimension of the revolving door is examined in Cox & Thomas, Revolving Elites: The Unexplored Risk of Capturing the SEC, 107 Geo. L.J. 845 (2019), reporting that during the first 50 plus years of its existence SEC division heads were selected from the existing SEC staff; however, beginning in the mid-1990s, the prevalent practice shifted so that division heads were recruited from outside the agency, generally from law firms who represent clients before the Commission. Thus, over the past 20 years nearly three-fourths of all directors came from outside the SEC. What might be the regulatory benefits sought by wooing outsiders to become SEC division heads?

Separate from the industry capture concerns expressed above are complaints of the SEC's disinclination to adopt or endorse bright-line rules, notwithstanding the value of such an approach in promoting, planning, and reducing the incidence of litigation. Inevitably claiming that such an approach provides a "blueprint for fraud," the Commission jealously seems to preserve the largest degree of discretion to sanction conduct that it determines, after the fact, to have been improper. One sees this in the Commission's preference for making policy through no-action letters or enforcement, rather than through rulemaking, and in its cautious approach to the development of safe-harbor rules in areas of considerable statutory ambiguity (such as the non-public offering exemption under the '33 Act). *See* R. Karmel, Regulation by Prosecution (1981). A further concern is that the agency tends to be "siloed"—referring to complaints that there is not sufficient communication and collaboration among divisions.

A final source of criticism focuses on the dominance of lawyers in policy-making roles at the SEC. Indeed, an overwhelming number of SEC commissioners and high-level staff persons have been attorneys. It has frequently been said that regulators have a natural bias toward the presence (or enhancement) of complex regulation, rather than its absence (or reduction),[3] a function of institutional and personal self-esteem as well as economic self-interest. In many ways, this same bias is held by lawyers generally and is hence reinforced when lawyers assume the function of regulators. For a more detailed analysis of these issues, *see* Langevoort, The SEC as Lawmaker: Choices About Investor Protection in the Face of Uncertainty, 84 Wash. U. L. Rev. 1591 (2006).

h.   Judging SEC Rulemaking

The rulemaking authority the SEC enjoys under each of the securities laws is subject to the statutory mandate that "the Commission shall . . . consider, in addition to the protection of investors, whether the action will promote efficiency, competition, and capital formation."[4] In 2011, the SEC's modest rule

---

3. A. Downs, Inside Bureaucracy (1967), referred to this as the "Law of Increasing Conservatism."

4. Each of the four major securities laws administered by the SEC now contains the same review standard. Securities Act of 1933 §2(b), 15 U.S.C. §77b(b); Securities Exchange Act of 1934 §3(f), 15 U.S.C. §78c(f); Investment Company Act of 1940 §2(c), 15 U.S.C. §80a-c(c); and Investment Advisers Act of 1940 §202(c), 15 U.S.C. §80b-2(c).

authorizing stockholders to nominate a limited number of directors was struck down for failure to satisfy what the D.C. Circuit said was required in meeting this review standard:

> Here the Commission inconsistently and opportunistically framed the costs and benefits of the rule; failed adequately to quantify the certain costs or to explain why those costs could not be quantified; neglected to support its predictive judgments; contradicted itself; and failed to respond to substantial problems raised by commenters.

Business Roundtable v. SEC, 647 F.3d 1144 (D.C. Cir. 2011). This defeat for the SEC comes on the heels of similar reversals the SEC has faced when its actions were challenged for their failure to consider a rule's impact on "efficiency, competition and capital formation." *See American Equity Investment Life Insurance Co. v. SEC*, 613 F.3d 166 (D.C. Cir. 2010); *Chamber of Commerce v. SEC*, 412 F.3d 133 (D.C. Cir. 2005). While neither the express statutory language nor the legislative history call for rigorous cost-benefit analysis, until the Supreme Court speaks, SEC rulemaking proceeds with a healthy respect that there is now ample precedent before the court where challenges to its rules most likely will occur. *See* Cox & Baucom, The Emperor Has No Clothes: Confronting the D.C. Circuit's Usurpation of SEC Rulemaking Authority, 90 Tex. L. Rev. 1811 (2012). The SEC has therefore entered a most uncertain area in its history.

In *Business Roundtable*'s wake, the SEC has provided guidance to the staff calling for future rulemaking to include the following four elements: (1) a statement of the need for proposed action; (2) a definition of a baseline against which to measure the likelihood of economic consequences of the proposed regulation; (3) the identification of alternative approaches; and (4) an evaluation of the benefits and costs, both quantitative and qualitative, of the proposed action and the main alternatives identified in the analysis. SEC, Current Guidance on Economic Analysis in SEC Rulemaking (Mar. 16, 2012). In an important article, Professor John Coates characterizes cost-benefit analysis in the context of financial regulation as "guesstimating" due to the degree of complexity and interconnectedness of financial regulation being deeply integrated so that the result depends on casual inferences, problematic data, and contestable assumptions. Coates, Cost-Benefit Analysis of Financial Regulation: Case Studies and Implications, 124 Yale L.J. 882 (2015); Coates & Srinivasan, SOX after Ten Years: A Multidisciplinary Review, 28 Acct. Horizon 627 (2014) (illustrating why it is easier to identify and measure the *direct* cost of a regulatory initiative than the measure's benefits and *indirect* costs).

In an earlier era, the SEC did not face the level of scrutiny in adopting rules that it faces today. Hence, as you progress through the course material and study specific rules consider the difficulty the SEC would have confronted if, when it adopted the rule, it was compelled to estimate the rule's likely compliance costs and expected benefits. Query, might this force the SEC to regulate via enforcement, since enforcement actions are not subject to the before mentioned review standard?

2. Blue Sky Laws

Sharp promoters and questionable investment opportunities have been a fixture of markets throughout their existence. State regulation of securities and their promoters began in the nineteenth century with requirements for registration of securities offerings by public utilities and companies engaged in the exploration and extraction of minerals, each being a fertile area of abusive practices. Kansas in 1911 enacted the first comprehensive system of registering securities brokers and offerings of securities of all types of enterprises. Similar reforms soon swept across America as part of the legislative agenda of the populist movement. At the time of the Great Crash, nearly all states embraced some form of regulation of brokers and securities. These laws reflected the prevalent view that hardworking common men and women were frequently the victims of not just confidence men, but also slick investment bankers from Wall Street. *See generally* M.E. Parrish, Securities Regulation and the New Deal 5-20 (1970). A recent reexamination of the history of the causes leading to the states' enactment of their securities laws found they were driven by the interests of "state banking regulators, interested in protecting and expanding their regulatory turf and in advancing the financial interests of banks under their supervision . . . [as well as] farmers and small business owners who saw the suppression of securities sales as a useful means for increasing their own access to bank credit." Macey & Miller, Origin of the Blue Sky Laws, 70 Tex. L. Rev. 347, 351 (1991). *See also* Mahoney, The Origins of the Blue Sky Laws: A Test of Competing Hypotheses, 46 J.L. & Econ. 229 (2003) (concluding that the impact of blue sky laws adopted by states in 1911-1930 was to increase the profits of small banks).

State securities laws are generally referred to as *blue sky laws*, an expression rooted in their initial objective of curbing promoters who would sell interests having no more substance than "so many feet of blue sky." *Hall v. Geiger-Jones Co.*, 242 U.S. 539, 550 (1917) (upholding the constitutionality of blue sky laws under the Fourteenth Amendment and finding no burden on interstate commerce). The original author of the Kansas legislation explained that the term referred to rainmakers who promised rain but produced nothing but blue sky. *See* Fleming, 100 Years of Securities Laws: Examining a Foundation Laid in the Kansas Blue Sky, 50 Washburn L.J. 583 (2011).

As is discussed in Chapter 4, an important difference between the federal and the state approaches to securities regulations is that the former is exclusively disclosure oriented, whereas many state jurisdictions include within their blue sky laws a so-called merit regulation standard whereby qualification depends on convincing the state blue sky administrator of the substantive merits of the offering. Most state laws embrace some form of merit review. *See* SEC Report on the Uniformity of State Regulatory Requirements for Offerings of Securities That Are Not "Covered Securities," 8 (1997).

The lack of uniformity among the states is a problem, if not a nightmare, for the attorney "blue skying" an offering that will be made in several states. The Uniform Securities Act was promulgated by the National Conference of Commissioners on Uniform State Law in 1956. The current version of the Act was adopted in 2002 (with some revisions in 2005). *See* Seligman, The New Uniform Securities Act, 81 Wash. U. L. Rev. 244 (2003). Most states have some version of the Uniform Securities Act. But there are two important caveats: Two notable non-adopting states are New York and California and in crafting their own blue sky laws, individual states vary widely in their deviations from the Uniform Securities Act.

The North American Securities Administrators Association (NASAA), a group composed of blue sky law administrators, has worked diligently to coordinate the approach and interpretations followed in each of the states. Nonetheless, the lack of uniformity remains a constant concern. A further blow to uniformity is that the budgets of blue sky regulators vary widely from state to state, with the individual state's population only partially explaining the different levels of funding and more of the resulting variance being accounted for by the importance a state's legislature places on the regulation of securities transactions. Some relief for the attorney facing multiple states in which an offering will occur is the 1996 enactment of the National Securities Market Improvement Act that amends Section 18 of the Securities Act to exempt from the states' registration procedures several categories of securities, called "covered securities," including those that are listed (or that will be listed) on the New York Stock Exchange or Nasdaq's national market system. As a result of the 1996 legislation (National Securities Market Improvement Act), the power of the states to compel registration of offerings under their blue sky laws is now restricted to relatively small offerings that are not made to sophisticated investors. Chapter 4 examines the extent of the challenges that await the securities lawyer involved in an offering that falls outside the preemptive scope of the 1996 legislation.

Blue Sky regulators maintain enforcement activities with a substantial focus on prosecuting fraudulent practices. *See* Rose & LeBlanc, Policing Public Companies: An Empirical Examination of the Enforcement Landscape and the Role Played by State Securities Regulators, 65 Fla. L. Rev. 395 (2013) (states whose blue sky head is elected account for 80 percent of all state investigations and enforcement actions disclosed in SEC filings; 68 percent of state enforcement actions target out-of-state firms).

3. Self-Regulatory Organizations

The Securities Exchange Act is unique to the extent it prescribes a cooperative regulatory effort by the SEC and industry-sponsored groups called self-regulatory organizations (SROs). Currently, there are four types of SROs embraced by the Exchange Act: the national securities exchanges, the national securities association, registered clearing agencies, and the Municipal Securities Rulemaking Board (MSRB). Later, in Chapter 18, a closer review is made of the pattern of regulatory power the SEC exercises over each SRO as well as the disciplinary powers and standards they impose on their members. The following provides a brief description of the regulatory framework that applies to the two most important SROs, the exchanges and the National Association of Securities Dealers.

Section 5 requires all exchanges to register as "national securities exchanges." While in the public's eye there are two exchanges that are well known—the New York Stock Exchange (NYSE) and Nasdaq—as will be seen in Chapter 10 there are many other trading centers that are also registered exchanges. In addition to registering, a national securities exchange must satisfy Section 6, which requires just and adequate rules to ensure fair dealing and to protect investors.

The securities industry and the SEC joined forces in 1938 to convince Congress to add Section 15A to the Exchange Act and thereby call for the creation of a "national securities association" whose task is to prevent fraudulent and manipulative acts and to promote just and equitable trade practices among over-the-counter broker-dealers. The only such association is the Financial Industry Regulatory Authority (FINRA), to which most brokers belong. FINRA is the largest of the SROs. The scope of FINRA's responsibility is broad and includes overseeing the operation of the over-the-counter market and establishing and enforcing rules for its efficient and fair operation. Under Section 15(a)(1), brokers or dealers must register with the SEC if they offer, sell, or purchase securities. Section 15(b)(8)-(9) makes it unlawful for any registered broker or dealer who is not a member of a national securities association to make any security transaction unless those transactions occur solely on an exchange in which he is a member. FINRA was formed in 2007 by the merger of the National Association of Securities Dealers (NASD) with the member regulation, enforcement, and arbitration functions of the NYSE (even after the merger the NYSE retains several regulatory functions).

The alliance between the SEC and SROs may be symptomatic of the "hot potato" phenomenon endemic to the Exchange Act, in which Congress, after lengthy hearings, identified a parade of horrors in securities markets that needed remedying. As seen, Congress granted to the SEC broad discretionary powers over problem areas, but it specified neither the ends nor the means for their resolution. The SEC in turn has been most willing to defer to the SROs in a host of subject areas, and especially in the development of procedures for the functioning of securities markets.

The listing requirements of the NYSE and Nasdaq contain significant provisions regarding both good disclosure practices and corporate governance. For example, it is among the listing requirements that we find requirements for boards of public companies to have a critical mass of their directors be individuals who are independent of management, and also where we find affirmative commands that companies should adhere to a course of promptly disclosing significant financial events. In later chapters we will see that the initial response to the financial frauds of 2000 and 2001 were initiatives by the NYSE and Nasdaq to tighten their corporate governance requirements, particularly with respect to strengthening the role and independence of audit committees.

C. *Financing Startups*

We can think of companies passing through four different stages in their financial development:

    I.   Seed Stage—company has little more than a business plan and perhaps a prototype of its product

   II.   Startup Stage—while not generating any revenues, company has a product and an initial organization

  III.   Growth and Expansion Stage—company has revenues, but is not yet profitable

  IV.   Later Stage—company is profitable

Investing occurs at each of these stages. Certainly we expect the promoters/ entrepreneurs, as well as their friends and family, to provide funding during the first two stages. Angel investors can appear at any of the stages, but most frequently appear during the Startup and Growth/Expansion stages. Venture capital firms are more dominant in the Later Stage. As seen in the following excerpt, angel investors are the lifeline that connects the new venture to when the venture capitalist arrives. And, in most instances, access to the VC is pivotal for the business' survival.

▌▎ **Ibrahim, The (Not So) Puzzling Behavior of Angel Investors**
▌▎ 61 Vand. L. Rev. 1405, 1410-1419 (2008)

II.   The Venture Capital Investment Model

Venture capital has been the financial engine driving most successful start-up companies over the past several decades. . . .

It is almost axiomatic to observe that a start-up's chances for success will increase if it can attract venture capital. Paul Gompers and Josh Lerner attempted to quantify the venture capital effect. They found that ninety percent of start-ups that were unable to attract venture capital within the first three years failed, while the failure rate dropped to thirty-three percent for those that did attract venture capital. In addition to financial capital, venture capitalists provide crucial value-added services. They use their networking skills to recruit professional managerial talent, and they can provide seasoned expertise for decisionmaking, such as determining the most profitable exit strategy.

Infusions of venture capital are coupled with investment contracts that set forth the venture capitalists' rights and obligations in the start-up. . . . [V]enture capital investment contracts are necessarily incomplete, which gives rise to problems of uncertainty, information asymmetry, and agency costs in the form of potential opportunism by entrepreneurs. . . . Start-ups have little or no operating history or tangible assets with which to predict future performance, and scientific or technological novelty like that found in the typical Silicon Valley start-up adds another layer of uncertainty. This uncertainty provides entrepreneurs with significant informational advantages over venture capitalists and increases agency costs by making it more difficult for venture capitalists to sort between good and bad entrepreneurs and monitor investments.

Although it is impossible for venture capitalists to eliminate these problems, they mitigate them by syndicating their investments with other venture capitalists and investing in a portfolio of start-ups. Venture capitalists also use incentive-aligning compensation arrangements with entrepreneurs, such as stock options and stock grants that vest over time. And, . . . venture capitalists mitigate unforeseeable problems by designing comprehensive investment contracts that give venture capitalists far more control than their percentage ownership warrants, which, under the conventional wisdom, cash-strapped entrepreneurs are forced to accept.

. . . First, the contract provides for the disbursement of funds to the entrepreneur in stages. Staged financing reduces uncertainty by delaying funding until the entrepreneur proves herself by achieving performance milestones set by the venture capitalist. Venture capitalists can cut their losses by refusing to fund entrepreneurs who do not reach these milestones. Staging reduces information asymmetry and agency costs by allowing venture capitalists to more effectively screen their investments and spend less time monitoring in between financings. Screening of potential investments is facilitated through signaling. The theory is that good entrepreneurs will signal their quality by agreeing to condition funds upon entrepreneurial performance while bad entrepreneurs will not. Venture capitalists also have less need to monitor entrepreneurs because staging strongly aligns entrepreneurs' interests with venture capitalists' interests. The entrepreneur who needs the next cash infusion to survive has a strong performance incentive and is unlikely to shirk or seek private benefits at the expense of the venture capitalist, which reduces agency costs. . . .

Second, venture capitalists take convertible preferred stock in exchange for their cash infusions, in contrast to the common stock taken by entrepreneurs and friend-and-family investors. The use of preferred stock offers several advantages for venture capitalists. For starters, it provides downside protection: the preferred stock is paid first in the event of a liquidation or sale of the start-up—a common end result for new start-ups. The liquidation preference also facilitates entrepreneurial signaling on the theory that entrepreneurs who are willing to grant a venture capitalist the first payout signal their belief that the start-up will be worth more than the venture capitalist's preference. . . .

The third and fourth common features of investment contracts are intended to allocate decisionmaking control to venture capitalists, which reduces the potential for opportunistic behavior by entrepreneurs (who otherwise would have such opportunities due to their majority ownership). Venture capitalists secure board seats in increasing numbers with each round of investment. Control of the board entitles a venture capitalist to significant control of the start-up because of the board's broad authority under corporate law. . . .

Another allocation of control comes from negative covenants. Negative covenants require venture capitalist approval for major decisions. . . . For instance, the venture capitalist probably has only a minority of board seats after its first round of investment, but negative covenants prevent the entrepreneur from acting opportunistically during that time (e.g., by issuing additional preferred stock that dilutes the venture capitalist's share).

Finally, investment contracts provide venture capitalists with specific exit rights, which are important in private corporations with illiquid shares. These exit rights include redemption (or put) rights, demand registration rights, and conversion rights. . . . As a general rule, venture capitalists require earlier exits due to the short life of venture funds and the need to make distributions to fund investors, while entrepreneurs wish to delay exit in order to extend private benefits such as a steady salary. Redemption and other specific exit rights address these potential conflicts by allocating the exit decision to venture capitalists.

III.   The Angel Investment Model: A Departure from Financial Contracting Theory?

A.   THE NEED FOR ANGELS

Venture capital is crucial to a start-up's success, but it is not immediately available to most start-ups. Most venture capitalists fund start-ups that have survived their earliest stages and are expanding, for instance by delivering products and services to customers, or are preparing for an IPO or private sale. Nor is venture capital readily available in the smaller amounts that might be appropriate for very young companies. A typical venture round averages between $2 million and $10 million, although it can be much higher. Therefore, venture capitalists leave a critical funding gap that has both time and capital components. The time gap is present during the earliest stage of a start-up's life, which commonly lasts at least one year. The capital gap exists for funding in amounts less than $2 million. Of course, friends, family, and the entrepreneur's own efforts may provide some funding (up to $100,000 or so), but this is hardly enough to sustain the rapid-growth start-up for very long.

. . . The funding gap poses a serious problem for start-ups. Without financial and nonfinancial assistance during their first year, many start-ups fail to develop to the point of attractiveness for venture capitalists. This early point is where angels are so critical. Angels fill the funding gap as to both time and capital, functioning as a "conveyor belt" that moves young start-ups toward waiting venture capitalists.

First, angels fill the time gap by investing when venture capitalists will not. . . . [Therefore,] angels and venture capitalists mostly serve complementary rather than competitive functions.

Second, angels fill the capital gap by providing appropriate amounts of funding to early-stage start-ups. A typical angel round ranges from $100,000 to $1 million or even $2 million at the high end—the very size of the capital gap. This financing allows early-stage companies to accomplish a variety of objectives that will make them attractive to venture capitalists including marketing, securing customers, and obtaining patent protection. The aggregate angel capital market is estimated to be as large as, or even larger than, the venture capital market. But because each angel round is smaller, angels fund significantly more start-ups than venture capitalists—perhaps thirty to forty times more. Therefore, while angels provide a filtering function for venture capitalists, they do not use too fine a filter, which reduces the chance that a promising start-up will fail prematurely.

Finally, angels provide value-added services to entrepreneurs. . . . Most angels are ex-entrepreneurs themselves, which allows them to offer seasoned advice on and empathy with the many difficulties faced in advancing an early-stage venture. Angels typically invest in companies that are a short drive away to facilitate regular interactions with entrepreneurs and active participation in the venture's growth. . . .

NOTES AND QUESTIONS

1. Angel Groups. Increasingly, angels are ceasing to act independently and act as part of a local or regional group of investors. While investments are individual (not pooled) the investors identify investment opportunities collectively. There is some reason to believe that angels who operate through a group are somewhat more sophisticated than non-group angels. However, angel groups still represent a small percentage of overall angel investing, but the practice is growing. *See generally* Ibrahim, Financing the Next Silicon Valley, 87 Wash. U. L. Rev. 717, 752 (2010) (angel groups, because of their overall greater sophistication and being repeat players much like venture capitalist signal the quality of the funded startup).

2. Venture Capital Firms. Venture capital (VC) firms typically are formed as limited partnerships; the general partner is a company made up of investment professionals and operates successive limited partnerships and the limited partners are institutional investors. The general partner's investment is rarely greater than 1 percent of the fund's total capital. What it brings to the VC is its experience and talent to identify, nurture, and ultimately exit the startups in which the VC invests. The general partner receives a management fee, usually in the range of 2-2.5 percent of the capital managed, plus the "carried interest," i.e., 20 percent of the profits ultimately realized when the partnership is liquidated. A ten-year life is common for the VC partnership. Exit from individual startups that comprise the VC portfolio occur via the startup going public (an IPO) or by the startup's acquisition by an existing company. While extraordinary gains have been harvested by those investing in VC partnerships, the gains usually are derived from a very small percentage of the VC's portfolio investments. *See, e.g.,* Gilson, Engineering a Venture Capital Market: Lessons from the American Experience, 55 Stan. L. Rev. 1067, 1076 (2003) (reporting that two studies reflect that about half the returns enjoyed by VC are from merely 6.8 percent of the portfolio companies and one-third of the portfolio companies result in partial or total losses).

3. Small Business Investment Companies. Various provisions in the securities laws provide important dispensations when the investor is a "small business investment company" (SBIC). *See, e.g.,* Rules 144A(a)(1)(C) (defining "qualified institutional investor") and 501(a)(1) (defining "accredited investor"). An SBIC is privately owned, but obtains part of its financial support from the Small Business Administration (today mostly in the form of loan guarantees) and in return is restricted to investing in small businesses; typically such investments fall in the $100,000-$250,000 range. There are about 300 SBICs. In 2010, SBICs provided about $1.6 billion in funds to small business, many of them startups.

4. The Puzzle of Unicorns. Unicorns are nonpublic companies, startups, that have a value greater than $1 billion. In early 2015, there were over 200 such companies, with about a score of them with values in excess of $10 billion ("decacorns"). Airbnb, SpaceX, and WeWork are each decacorns. So, why do such highly valued firms remain private?

Avoiding the multiple costs and burdens of being a public company is part of the answer. Why go public if the startup can obtain venture financing via private markets and the IPO market is at best tepid? Indeed, in 2015, the height of unicorn valuations, many startups and particularly unicorns were flush with cash from recent eye-popping rounds of venture funding and were also being pursued by late-stage investors, such as mutual funds, and cash-rich tech companies, such as Google, SoftBank, and Alibaba, who purchased substantial interests in the private firm.

But good times do not continue indefinitely. The slowdown in the global economy rocked the venture financing world and soon institutions were reporting substantial write-downs in the carrying value of their unicorn investments. The global economic decline led to wide retrenchment across the startup community; laid-off employees exercised their options and dumped their shares, causing further imbalances between buyers and sellers with resulting downward pressure on valuations. These developments were met with a chorus of "I told you so" by commentators' long-standing critiques that unicorn valuations were untested and were based on overly optimistic venture capital financings. *See* R.P. Bartlett, A Founder's Guide to Unicorn Creation: How Liquidation Preferences in M&A Transactions Affect Startup Valuation, in Research Handbook on Mergers and Acquisitions, ch. 6 (2016).

Even though the music for over-valuing firms may have stopped, or at least slowed down, unicorns still exist. Why have their owners not rushed to realize their large values through a liquidation event, such as an IPO or acquisition by a public company? For some firms, such as Airbnb whose revenue growth is eye-popping, investors may wisely choose to be patient. Consider also that there is some liquidity for large investors' holdings via private sales to other institutional holders, a topic examined in Chapter 6. How important, therefore, is liquidity to the owners of unicorns or hope-to-be unicorns?

‖2‖
The Definition of a Security

A. Introduction

The definition of a *security* represents the gateway to federal securities regulation. When this status is accorded a financial instrument, the full weight of the securities laws—including the registration and prospectus requirements, as well as the antifraud provisions—is brought to bear on the transactions underlying its marketing and sale. Although continuing debates over the definition of a security are often rarefied and esoteric, the issue is of great practical importance. A conclusion that a transaction involves a security not only introduces significant regulatory forces, but also may provide the investor disappointed by the returns of a business venture with a potent weapon in the quest to recover invested capital.

The '33 Act and the '34 Act have substantially similar definitions of a *security*. These provisions are a lawyer's dream. They begin with a circumscribing phrase limiting applicability of the definition if "the context otherwise requires," which has provided an important basis for the exercise of judicial discretion concerning the proper scope of the securities laws. There follows a laundry list of examples, some of which seem, at first glance, straightforward (notes, stock, bonds, debentures, and certificates of deposit), and others of which are elusive and therefore susceptible to expansive interpretation (investment contracts, certificates of interest in profit sharing agreements, and interests commonly known as securities). Each of these features of the definition—the clause limiting coverage if the "context" so requires, the seemingly obvious examples of securities, and the more equivocal instruments included in the list—has contributed to a body of case law that is both vast and disorderly. That this has occurred may prove unsettling for the student of securities regulation, but should not be surprising, for the seeming completeness of the definitional sections masks an essential question of statutory interpretation: To what types of capital transfers should the federal securities laws be applied? Given the infinite number of ways that capital is transferred and the boundless creativity of those who seek the use of other people's money, the task of providing a definitive answer to this question is hopeless.

The complexity of the definitional problem is illustrated by examining those parts of the definitions that seem straightforward. The casual observer, for example, should have little difficulty with the notion that "stock" is a security. But should distinctions be drawn between the stock of publicly held and that of closely held corporations? And is the label put on an instrument dispositive, so that "stock" issued by a noncommercial enterprise is subject to the securities laws, while an instrument with similar characteristics, but a different name is not, even though it is issued by a corporation listed on the New York Stock Exchange? Similarly, a "note" is a rather straightforward type of financial instrument, but did Congress really intend to make "any note" a security? The question is of some importance, since concluding that all notes are securities would bring transactions such as consumer purchases on an installment basis and purchases of homes under the federal securities law scheme.

If items like stock and notes raise questions, the more elusive instruments listed in the definitions are even more baffling. What exactly is meant by a "profit sharing agreement"? Does this cover general partnership interests, which do not otherwise appear in the definition? What is "evidence of indebtedness"? How does this differ from other debt instruments listed in the definitions, and why was it included in the '33 Act's definition, but omitted from the '34 Act's counterpart provision? The definitions would be problematic enough if they stopped at this point. They go on to include, however, the "investment contract," a catchall phrase that is sufficiently imprecise as to defy categorization as a financial instrument. Most of the decades-old debate over the definition of a security has centered on the meaning of the investment contract abstraction. This has led to a body of law that is both unsettled and evolving, particularly as applied to recent innovations such as cryptocurrencies, initial coin offerings (ICOs), and related virtual instruments.

This chapter explores some of these important questions regarding the types of investment products that are subject to federal securities laws.

B.   The Development of a Framework for Defining an Investment Contract

The first Supreme Court case interpreting the breadth of the statutory definition, and therefore the scope of the federal securities laws, was *SEC v. C.M. Joiner Leasing Corp.*, 320 U.S. 344 (1943), where the promoter sold assignments of oil leases and committed to drill test wells. The Court held that the definition's inclusion of "fractional undivided interest in oil, gas or other mineral rights" and failure to reference *divided* interests in oil rights of the type marketed in the case did not preclude the Court from treating the offering as within the more general, catchall provisions of the definition:

> [T]he reach of the Act does not stop with the obvious and commonplace. Novel, uncommon, or irregular devices, whatever they appear to be, are also reached if it be proved as matter of fact that they were widely offered or dealt in under terms or courses of dealing which established their character in commerce as "investment contracts" or as "any interest or instrument commonly known as a security."

Id. at 351.

At the time of *Joiner*, virtually every state had enacted blue sky laws covering the offering and sale of securities. Rather than borrowing from existing state law on the meaning of "investment contract," *Joiner* seemed content with offering vague but potentially expansive notions of the breadth of the concept. The Court provided a more precise framework for dealing with this important definitional question three years later in the landmark case of *SEC v. W.J. Howey Co.*

Securities and Exchange Commission v. W.J. Howey Co.
328 U.S. 293 (1946)

MURPHY, J. This case involves the application of §2(1) of the Securities Act of 1933 to an offering of units of a citrus grove development coupled with a contract for cultivating, marketing and remitting the net proceeds to the investor.

The Securities and Exchange Commission instituted this action to restrain the respondents from using the mails and instrumentalities of interstate commerce in the offer and sale of unregistered and non-exempt securities in violation of §5(a) of the Act. . . .

Most of the facts are stipulated. The respondents, W.J. Howey Company and Howey-in-the-Hills Service, Inc., are Florida corporations under direct common control and management. The Howey Company owns large tracts of citrus acreage in Lake County, Florida. . . . Howey-in-the-Hills Service, Inc. is a service company engaged in cultivating and developing many of these groves, including the harvesting and marketing of the crops.

Each prospective customer is offered both a land sales contract and a service contract, after having been told that it is not feasible to invest in a grove unless service arrangements are made. While the purchaser is free to make arrangements with other service companies, the superiority of Howey-in-the-Hills Service, Inc., is stressed. Indeed, 85% of the acreage sold during the 3-year period ending May 31, 1943, was covered by service contracts with Howey-in-the-Hills Service, Inc.

The land sales contract with the Howey Company provides for a uniform purchase price per acre or fraction thereof, varying in amount only in accordance with the number of years the particular plot has been planted with citrus trees. Upon full payment of the purchase price the land is conveyed to the purchaser by warranty deed. Purchases are usually made in narrow strips of land arranged so that an acre consists of a row of 48 trees. . . . These tracts are not separately fenced and the sole indication of several ownership is found in small land marks intelligible only through a plat book record.

The service contract, generally of a 10-year duration without option of cancellation, gives Howey-in-the-Hills Service, Inc. a leasehold interest and "full and complete" possession of the acreage. For a specified fee plus the cost of labor and materials, the company is given full discretion and authority over the cultivation of the groves and the harvest and marketing of the crops. The company is well established in the citrus business and maintains a large force of skilled personnel and a great deal of equipment. . . . Without the consent of the company, the land owner or purchaser has no right of entry to market the crop, thus there is ordinarily no right to specific fruit. The company is accountable only for an allocation of the net profits based upon a check made at the time of picking. All the produce is pooled by the respondent companies, which do business under their own names.

The purchasers for the most part are non-residents of Florida. They are predominantly business and professional people who lack the knowledge, skill and equipment necessary for the care and cultivation of citrus trees. They are attracted by the expectation of substantial profits. . . . Many of these purchasers are patrons of a resort hotel owned and operated by the Howey Company in a scenic section adjacent to the groves. The hotel's advertising mentions the fine groves in the vicinity and the attention of the patrons is drawn to the groves as they are being escorted about the surrounding countryside. They are told that the groves are for sale; if they indicate an interest in the matter they are then given a sales talk. . . .

The legal issue in this case turns upon a determination of whether, under the circumstances, the land sales contract, the warranty deed and the service contract together constitute an "investment contract" within the meaning of §2(1). An affirmative answer brings into operation the registration requirements of §5(a), unless the security is granted an exemption under §3(b). The lower courts, in reaching a negative answer to this problem, treated the contracts and deeds as separate transactions involving no more than an ordinary real estate sale and an agreement by the seller to manage the property for the buyer.

The term "investment contract" is undefined by the Securities Act or by relevant legislative reports. But the term was common in many state "blue sky" laws in existence prior to the adoption of the federal statute and, although the term was also undefined by the state laws, it had been broadly construed by state courts so as to afford the investing public a full measure of protection. Form was disregarded for substance and emphasis was placed upon economic reality. An investment contract thus came to mean a contract or scheme for "the placing of capital or laying out of money in a way intended to secure income or profit from its employment." *State v. Gopher Tire & Rubber Co.*, 146 Minn. 52, 56, 177 N.W. 937, 938. This definition was uniformly applied by state courts to a variety of situations where individuals were led to invest money in a common enterprise with the expectation that they would earn a profit solely through the efforts of the promoter or of some one other than themselves.

By including an investment contract within the scope of §2(1) of the Securities Act, Congress was using a term the meaning of which had been crystallized by this prior judicial interpretation. It is therefore reasonable to attach that meaning to the term as used by Congress, especially since such a definition is consistent with the statutory aims. In other words, an investment contract for purposes of the Securities Act means a contract, transaction or scheme whereby a person invests his money in a common enterprise and is led to expect profits solely from the efforts of the promoter or a third party, it being immaterial whether the shares in the enterprise are evidenced by formal certificates or by nominal interests in the physical assets employed in the enterprise. [Such a definition] permits the fulfillment of the statutory purpose of compelling full and fair disclosure relative to the issuance of "the many types of instruments that in our commercial world fall within the ordinary concept of a security." H.R. Rep. No. 85, 73d Cong., 1st Sess., p.11. It embodies a flexible rather than a static principle, one that is capable of adaptation to meet the countless and variable schemes devised by those who seek the use of the money of others on the promise of profits.

The transactions in this case clearly involve investment contracts as so defined. The respondent companies are offering something more than fee simple interests in land, something different from a farm or orchard coupled with management services. They are offering an opportunity to contribute money and to share in the profits of a large citrus fruit enterprise managed and partly owned by respondents. They are offering this opportunity to persons who reside in distant localities and who lack the equipment and experience requisite to the cultivation, harvesting and marketing of the citrus products. Such persons have no desire to occupy the land or to develop it themselves; they are attracted solely by the prospects of a return on their investment. Indeed, individual development of the plots of land that are offered and sold would seldom be economically feasible due to their small size. Such tracts gain utility as citrus groves only when cultivated and developed as component parts of a larger area. A common enterprise managed by respondents or third parties with adequate personnel and equipment is therefore essential if the investors are to achieve their paramount aim of a return on their investments. Their respective shares in this enterprise are evidenced by land sales contracts and warranty deeds, which serve as a convenient method of determining the investors' allocable shares of the profits. The resulting transfer of rights in land is purely incidental.

Thus all the elements of a profit-seeking business venture are present here. The investors provide the capital and share in the earnings and profits; the promoters manage, control and operate the enterprise. It follows that the arrangements whereby the investors' interests are made manifest involve investment contracts, regardless of the legal terminology in which such contracts are clothed. The investment contracts in this instance take the form of land sales contracts, warranty deeds and service contracts which respondents offer to prospective investors. And respondents' failure to abide by the statutory and administrative rules in making such offerings, even though the failure results from a bona fide mistake as to the law, cannot be sanctioned under the Act.

This conclusion is unaffected by the fact that some purchasers choose not to accept the full offer of an investment contract by declining to enter into a service contract with the respondents. The Securities Act prohibits the offer as well as the sale of unregistered, non-exempt securities. Hence, it is enough that the respondents merely offer the essential ingredients of an investment contract.

We reject the suggestion of the Circuit Court of Appeals . . . that an investment contract is necessarily missing where the enterprise is not speculative or promotional in character and where the tangible interest which is sold has intrinsic value independent of the success of the enterprise as a whole. If the test [outlined in this opinion] be satisfied, it is immaterial whether the enterprise is speculative or non-speculative or whether there is a sale of property with or without intrinsic value. . . .

Howey applied the securities acts to investments in a form (units of a citrus grove coupled with servicing contracts) not ordinarily traded on the organized securities markets. Contrast with *Howey* the later decision of the Court in *Marine Bank v. Weaver,* 455 U.S. 551 (1982), where the Weavers pledged a bank certificate of deposit to secure a bank loan to the Columbus Packing Company, owned by the Piccirillos. In return, the Weavers received a share of Columbus' net profits together with the right to use the company's pasture and barn and the right to veto further borrowing by Columbus. Columbus went into bankruptcy and the bank attempted to claim the pledged certificate of deposit. In opposition, the Weavers asserted the bank's complicity in fraudulent misrepresentations had induced their investment, which they claimed was a "security" under the criteria outlined in *Howey*. The Court concluded the Weavers had not purchased a security:

> The unusual instruments found to constitute securities in prior cases involved offers to a number of potential investors, not a private transaction as in this case. In *Howey*, for example, 42 persons purchased interests in a citrus grove during a 4-month period. . . . In *C.M. Joiner Leasing*, offers to sell oil leases were sent to over 1,000 prospects. . . . In *C.M. Joiner Leasing*, we noted that a security is an instrument in which there is "common trading." . . . The instruments involved in *C.M. Joiner Leasing* and *Howey* had equivalent values to most persons and could have been traded publicly.
>
> Here, in contrast, the Piccirillos distributed no prospectus to the Weavers or to other potential investors, and the unique agreement they negotiated was not designed to be traded publicly. The provision that the Weavers could use the barn and pastures of the slaughterhouse at the discretion of the Piccirillos underscores the unique character of the transaction. Similarly, the provision that the Weavers could veto future loans gave them a measure of control over the operation of the slaughterhouse not characteristic of a security. . . . Accordingly, we hold that this unique agreement, negotiated one-on-one by the parties, is not a security.

Id. at 559-560.

To be sure, the arrangement between the Weavers and the Piccirillos was "unique" in that it would have different values to various investors and therefore was not suitable for public trading. What would the result in *Marine Bank* have been if the pasture privileges were not part of the transaction? Were the veto rights concerning future financing sufficient to remove the interests from the realm of investment contracts? If so, what result if both the veto and the pasture rights were eliminated? Would the privately negotiated (but nonunique) nature of the transaction be dispositive? On what basis would the Court distinguish *Howey*?

Apart from the investment contract analysis concerning the deal struck between the Weavers and the Piccirillos, *Marine Bank* also concluded that the bank certificate of deposit was not a security because "the holders of bank certificates of deposit are abundantly protected under the federal banking laws." This aspect of *Marine Bank* will be considered in a later portion of this chapter.

NOTES AND QUESTIONS

1. Private Versus Public Actions. The SEC initiated the *Howey* litigation seeking to enjoin the marketing of securities without compliance with the registration provisions of the '33 Act. There were no allegations of fraud or misrepresentation by the promoters, nor was there any evidence investors had lost money. More often, it is the investor who initiates a private cause of action asserting the existence of a security that should have been registered. *See* Securities Act §12(a)(1). This claim is typically advanced in the hope of recovering capital invested in a bad business deal or as the basis of a defense asserting the invalidity of a contractual obligation to pay money. Some of the cases involve obvious fraud by promoters, while others simply represent ventures that failed to meet investors' original expectations.

2.   The Howey Company's Checkered Past.   Although the SEC did not allege fraudulent activities, the W.J. Howey Company was no stranger to litigation. In 1930, the company was sued by a retired schoolteacher who claimed the defendant fraudulently induced her to purchase an interest in an orange grove. *See Pepple v. Rogers*, 104 Fla. 462, 140 So. 205 (1932). A few years later, similar allegations were made in a suit filed by a purchaser of grapefruit orchards. The plaintiff alleged the Howey Company had represented "that the grapefruit grown upon said land would cure diabetes and possess other medicinal qualities and properties not common to grapefruit grown upon other lands in Florida." *See Brite v. W.J. Howey Co.*, 81 F.2d 840 (5th Cir. 1936). A third suit was prompted by a disgruntled investor seeking to enforce a repurchase agreement. *See Cowan v. Orange Belt Securities Co.*, 142 Fla. 194, 194 So. 489 (1940).

3.   Optional Service Contracts.   Was it relevant that purchasers were not required to enter into service contracts with Howey? Nine of the 51 purchasers made other service arrangements, and 15 percent of the acreage sold was not serviced by Howey. Presumably, the purchasers who did not contract with Howey engaged one of seven other companies in the area offering similar service contracts. Did their purchases also involve investment contracts?

4.   The Relevance of Risk.   Should the degree of risk be relevant in determining whether a security exists? The concluding paragraph of *Howey* suggests that it is not. In reviewing subsequent decisions, consider the extent to which courts have departed from this aspect of *Howey* and explicitly or implicitly consider the degree of investor risk in evaluating whether a transaction involves a security.

5.   Investment of "Money."   For the purpose of applying *Howey*'s investment of money standard, "money" may be interpreted broadly to include media of exchange other than traditional hard currencies. An investment of "Bitcoin" or other digital currencies, for example, should satisfy the *Howey* standard. *Cf. SEC v. Shavers*, 2013 U.S. Dist. LEXIS 110018, at *2 (E.D. Tex. Aug. 6, 2013) (concluding Bitcoin is "a currency or form of money"). And there is little question that the requisite investment under *Howey* may be in forms of value other than real or digital currencies, such as goods or services. *See, e.g., Int'l Bhd. of Teamsters v. Daniel*, 439 U.S. 551, 560 n.12 (1979).

6.   Varying Approaches—State Regulation and the Risk Capital Test.   *Howey* and subsequent federal cases have influenced the development of state law on the meaning of investment contract and other definitional issues affecting coverage of securities regulation at the state level. Responding to the perceived rigidities of *Howey*, however, a number of states employ an alternative approach in the form of the *risk capital* test. The impetus for the risk capital alternative was provided by Justice Traynor in *Silver Hills Country Club v. Sobieski*, 55 Cal. 2d 811, 361 P.2d 906, 13 Cal. Rptr. 186 (1961), where country club developers had financed improvements through sale of club memberships. The price of memberships was to increase as additional facilities were developed. Members had no rights in the assets or income of the club, but they could transfer their memberships to individuals approved by the board of directors. Concluding that the memberships were securities, Justice Traynor observed:

> We have here nothing like the ordinary sale of a right to use existing facilities. Petitioners are soliciting the risk capital with which to develop a business for profit. The purchaser's risk is not lessened merely because the interest he purchases is labeled a membership. Only because he risks his capital along with other purchasers can there be any chance that the benefits of club membership will materialize.

55 Cal. 2d at 815. For a contrasting example of the status of a country club membership under federal law's investment contract analysis, *see* Coral Beach & Tennis Club, SEC No-Action Letter (Jan. 25, 2012) (membership interest is not a security).

Silver Hills has prompted many state courts to define investment contracts for state law purposes under a risk capital analysis. A state following the risk capital approach may offer the test as the exclusive means of defining an investment contract or as an alternative to the *Howey* test. *See, e.g., Greentree Real Estate, LLC v. Bridger Commer. Funding, LLC*, 2009 U.S. Dist. LEXIS 57055 (S.D. Ind. July 1, 2009) (alternative tests). Risk capital means different things to different courts, however, and one of the major problems with the test is its ambiguity, particularly relating to risk assessment. Generally, a security will not exist under the risk capital test unless capital provided by investors is at substantial risk. The existence of collateralization or other security may negate the possibility that a transaction involves a security. For an economic analysis of risk and framework for defining a security based upon risk, *see* Corgill, Securities as Investments at Risk, 67 Tul. L. Rev. 861 (1993).

Interpretive difficulties aside, the risk capital test may differ from the test outlined in *Howey* in a number of respects. First, the risk capital test does not necessarily require a common enterprise among investors. Second, the test avoids the requirement that profits be derived "solely" from the efforts of others, although circuit court interpretations of this element of *Howey* have softened its apparent inflexibility. More importantly, the risk capital test accommodates an analysis based upon the degree of risk assumed by the investor. If that risk is minimal because of the issuer's strong balance sheet or adequate collateralization, the likelihood that an investment contract will be found is lessened.

C. Howey *Applied*

1. Investment Versus Consumption

Howey requires that there be an investment of money. A particularly interesting issue arises when there is some element of consumption that motivates the investment. *Howey* presented little difficulty in this regard because the investors were motivated by the prospect of profits rather than an unending and inexpensive supply of oranges. But what if the expected returns are not in the usual form of dividends and price appreciation and instead involve some other benefits to be derived from use or enjoyment of the underlying assets? The distinction between investment and consumption goals is an important part of the following case.

▌ United Housing Foundation, Inc. v. Forman
421 U.S. 837 (1975)

POWELL, J. The issue in these cases is whether shares of stock entitling a purchaser to lease an apartment in Co-op City, a state subsidized and supervised nonprofit housing cooperative, are "securities." . . .

I

Co-op City is a massive housing cooperative in New York City. Built between 1965 and 1971, it presently houses approximately 50,000 people on a 200-acre site containing 35 high-rise buildings and 236 town houses. . . . In order to encourage private developers to build low-cost cooperative housing, New York provides them with large long-term, low-interest mortgage loans and substantial tax exemptions. Receipt of such benefits is conditioned on a willingness to have the State review virtually every step in the development of the cooperative. The developer also must agree to operate the facility "on a nonprofit basis," . . . and he may lease apartments only to people whose incomes fall below a certain level and who have been approved by the State.

The United Housing Foundation (UHF), a nonprofit membership corporation . . . , was responsible for initiating and sponsoring the development of Co-op City. . . . UHF organized the Riverbay Corporation (Riverbay) to own and operate the land and buildings constituting Co-op City. Riverbay, a nonprofit cooperative housing corporation, issued the stock that is the subject of this litigation. UHF also contracted with Community Services, Inc. (CSI), its wholly owned subsidiary, to serve as the general contractor and sales agent for the project.

To acquire an apartment in Co-op City an eligible prospective purchaser must buy 18 shares of stock in Riverbay for each room desired. . . . The sole purpose of acquiring these shares is to enable the purchaser to occupy an apartment in Co-op City; in effect, their purchase is a recoverable deposit on an apartment. The shares are explicitly tied to the apartment: they cannot be transferred to a nontenant; nor can they be pledged or encumbered; and they descend, along with the apartment, only to a surviving spouse. No voting rights attach to the shares as such: participation in the affairs of the cooperative appertains to the apartment, with the residents of each apartment being entitled to one vote irrespective of the number of shares owned.

Any tenant who wants to terminate his occupancy, or who is forced to move out, must offer his stock to Riverbay at its initial selling price of $25 per share. . . .

Riverbay circulated an Information Bulletin seeking to attract tenants for what would someday be apartments in Co-op City. After describing the nature and advantages of cooperative housing generally and of Co-op City in particular, the Bulletin informed prospective tenants that the total estimated cost of the project, based largely on an anticipated construction contract with CSI, was $283,695,550. Only a fraction of this sum, $32,795,550, was to be raised by the sale of shares to tenants. The remaining $250,900,000 was to be financed by a 40-year low-interest mortgage loan from the New York Private Housing Finance Agency. After construction of the project the mortgage payments and current operating expenses would be met by monthly rental charges paid by the tenants. . . . [T]he 1965 Bulletin estimated that the "average" monthly cost would be $23.02 per room, or $92.08 for a four-room apartment. . . .

. . . Ultimately the construction loan was $125 million more than the figure estimated in the 1965 Bulletin. As a result, while the initial purchasing price remained at $450 per room, the average monthly rental charges increased periodically, reaching a figure of $39.68 per room as of July 1974.

These increases in the rental charges precipitated the present lawsuit. Respondents, 57 residents of Co-op City, sued in federal court on behalf of all 15,372 apartment owners, and derivatively on behalf of Riverbay, seeking upwards of $30 million in damages, forced rental reduction, and other "appropriate" relief. Named as defendants (petitioners herein) were UHF, CSI, Riverbay, several individual directors of these organizations, the State of New York, and the State Private Housing Finance Agency. The heart of respondents' claim was that the 1965 Co-op City Information Bulletin falsely represented that CSI would bear all subsequent cost increases due to factors such as inflation. Respondents further alleged that they were misled in their purchases of shares since the Information Bulletin failed to disclose several critical facts. On these bases, respondents asserted two claims under the fraud provisions of the federal Securities Act of 1933, as amended, §17(a); the Securities Exchange Act of 1934, as amended, §10(b), and [Rule 10b-5]. . . .

[The Second Circuit reversed the District Court's grant of a motion to dismiss, resting] its decision on two alternative grounds. First, the court held that since the shares purchased were called "stock" the Securities Acts, which explicitly include "stock" in their definitional sections, were literally applicable. Second, the Court of Appeals concluded that the transaction was an investment contract within the meaning of the Acts and as defined by *Howey*. . . .

II

A

We reject at the outset any suggestion that the present transaction, evidenced by the sale of shares called "stock," must be considered a security transaction simply because the statutory definition of a security includes the words "any . . . stock." . . .

The primary purpose of the Acts of 1933 and 1934 was to eliminate serious abuses in a largely unregulated securities market. The focus of the Acts is on the capital market of the enterprise system: the sales of securities to raise capital for profit-making purposes, the exchanges on which securities are traded, and the need for regulation to prevent fraud and to protect the interest of investors. Because securities transactions are economic in character Congress intended the application of these statutes to turn on the economic realities underlying a transaction, and not on the name appended thereto. . . .

In holding that the name given to an instrument is not dispositive, we do not suggest that the name is wholly irrelevant to the decision whether it is a security. There may be occasions when the use of a traditional name such as "stocks" or "bonds" will lead a purchaser justifiably to assume that the federal securities laws apply. This would clearly be the case when the underlying transaction embodies some of the significant characteristics typically associated with the named instrument.

In the present case respondents do not contend, nor could they, that they were misled by use of the word "stock" into believing that the federal securities laws governed their purchase. Common sense suggests that people who intend to acquire only a residential apartment in a state-subsidized cooperative, for their personal use, are not likely to believe that in reality they are purchasing investment securities simply because the transaction is evidenced by something called a share of stock. These shares have none of the characteristics "that in our commercial world fall within the ordinary concept of a security." H.R. Rep. No. 85, supra, at 11. Despite their name, they lack what the Court in *Tcherepnin* deemed the most common feature of stock: the right to receive "dividends contingent upon an apportionment of profits." . . . Nor do they possess the other characteristics traditionally associated with stock: they are not negotiable; they cannot be pledged or hypothecated; they confer no voting rights in proportion to the number of shares owned; and they cannot appreciate in value. In short, the inducement to purchase was solely to acquire subsidized low-cost living space; it was not to invest for profit.

B

The Court of Appeals . . . concluded that a share in Riverbay was also an "investment contract" as defined by the Securities Acts. Respondents further argue that in any event what they agreed to purchase is "commonly known as a 'security'" within the meaning of these laws. In considering these claims we again must examine the substance—the economic realities of the transaction— rather than the names that may have been employed by the parties. We perceive no distinction, for present purposes, between an "investment contract" and an "instrument commonly known as a 'security.'" In either case, the basic test for distinguishing the transaction from other commercial dealings is "whether the scheme involves an investment of money in a common enterprise with profits to come solely from the efforts of others." *Howey*, 328 U.S., at 301.[16] This test, in shorthand form, embodies the essential attributes that run through all of the Court's decisions defining a security. The touchstone is the presence of

---

16. This test speaks in terms of "profits to come *solely* from the efforts of others." (Emphasis supplied). Although the issue is not presented in this case, we note that the Court of Appeals for the Ninth Circuit has held that "the word 'solely' should not be read as a strict or literal limitation on the definition of an investment contract, but rather must be construed realistically, so as to include within the definition those schemes which involve in substance, if not form, securities." *SEC v. Glenn W. Turner Enterprises*, 474 F.2d 476, 482, *cert. denied*, 414 U.S. 821 (1973). We express no view, however, as to the holding of this case.

an investment in a common venture premised on a reasonable expectation of profits to be derived from the entrepreneurial or managerial efforts of others. By profits, the Court has meant either capital appreciation resulting from the development of the initial investment . . . or a participation in earnings resulting from the use of investors' funds. . . . In such cases the investor is "attracted solely by the prospects of a return" on his investment. . . . By contrast, when a purchaser is motivated by a desire to use or consume the item purchased—"to occupy the land or to develop it themselves," as the *Howey* Court put it—the securities laws do not apply. . . .

In the present case there can be no doubt that investors were attracted solely by the prospect of acquiring a place to live, and not by financial returns on their investments. . . .

The Court of Appeals recognized that there must be an expectation of profits for these shares to be securities, and conceded that there is "no possible profit on a resale of [this] stock." . . . The court correctly noted, however, that profit may be derived from the income yielded by an investment as well as from capital appreciation, and then proceeded to find "an expectation of 'income' in at least three ways." Two of these supposed sources of income or profits may be disposed of summarily. [The Court concluded that tax deductions associated with the investment benefits in the form of below-market value rents were not profits sufficient to find a security]. . . .

The final source of profit relied on by the Court of Appeals was the possibility of net income derived from the leasing by Co-op City of commercial facilities, professional offices and parking spaces, and its operation of community washing machines. The income, if any, from these conveniences, all located within the common areas of the housing project, is to be used to reduce tenant rental costs. Conceptually, one might readily agree that net income from the leasing of commercial and professional facilities is the kind of profit traditionally associated with a security investment. . . . But in the present case this income—if indeed there is any—is far too speculative and insubstantial to bring the entire transaction within the Securities Acts. . . .

There is no doubt that purchasers in this housing cooperative sought to obtain a decent home at an attractive price. But that type of economic interest characterizes every form of commercial dealing. What distinguishes a security transaction—and what is absent here—is an investment where one parts with his money in the hope of receiving profits from the efforts of others, and not where he purchases a commodity for personal consumption or living quarters for personal use. . . .

Reversed.

NOTES AND QUESTIONS

1. Howey's Relevance to Cases Not Involving Investment Contracts. The Court's comment that the *Howey* test "embodies the essential attributes that run through all of the Court's decisions defining a security" prompted many lower courts to test under the *Howey* criteria even those instruments specifically included in the statutory definition. Under this reasoning, instruments such as stock and notes specifically delineated in the statutory definition might not be securities if they fail to meet *Howey*'s investment contract criteria. Subsequent Supreme Court decisions, however, have undermined the breadth accorded the *Howey* analysis by the Court in *Forman*. *See, e.g., Landreth Timber Co. v. Landreth,* infra (*Howey* framework inappropriate when stock has the normal attributes of stock). Apart from the issue of whether the *Howey* factors should be applied to all instruments included in the statutory definition, how did *Forman* change the *Howey* criteria for an investment contract?

2. *The Relevance of Profit Potential.* *Forman* illustrates that the traditional dividend and capital appreciation allure of stock may not be the primary motivations of stockholders in some types of corporations with unique purposes. Consider the National Football League's Green Bay Packers, which is unique in its status as the only publicly owned major league sports franchise. From time to time since 1923, the Green Bay Packers, Inc., which operates as a nonprofit corporation, has offered stock to the public. The most recent sale of 250,000 shares at $250 per share commenced in 2011 to fund renovations at the team's Lambeau Field facilities. The stock essentially is nontransferable and will not receive dividends, and the Prospectus makes clear that investors in the Packers are not protected by the federal securities laws and should not expect a profit: "It is virtually impossible for anyone to realize a profit on a purchase of common stock or even to recoup the amount initially paid to acquire such common stock." Stockholders are assured, however, that they will "become part of the Packer's great tradition as a community-owned team." *See also* LA Fan Club, Inc., Membership Program, SEC No-Action Letter (May 19, 2017) (LA Rams fan club memberships involving personal seat licenses and ticket-related member benefits not securities even though they may be transferred for profit under limited circumstances, presumably in part because purchasers represented they made purchases to attend events and enjoy benefits rather than in anticipation of selling for profits).

3. *Social Enterprises and Muted Profit Objectives.* Recent years have seen the development of new associational forms for businesses in which profits are not the sole or even the principal objective of the enterprises. A number of states now recognize social enterprises formed to pursue some blend of altruistic and profit objectives. Should the financial instruments issued when these firms raise capital from investors be treated as securities (investment contracts, stock, or bonds, depending on the type of instrument), or should application of the securities laws be tailored to reflect the fact that investors in social enterprises simply have different objectives and expectations than investors in profit-driven business enterprises?

As will be discussed in Chapter 8, securities of nonprofit issuers are exempt from the registration provisions of the '33 Act. But social enterprises exist to pursue multiple objectives, one of which may be the generation of profits. Does the existence of a (partial) profit objective justify the imposition of regulatory costs and burdens that may make the altruistic goals of the social enterprise more difficult to achieve? For an excellent discussion of this issue, *see* Heminway, To Be or Not to Be (a Security): Funding for-Profit Social Enterprises, 25 Regent U. L. Rev. 299 (2013).

PROBLEMS

2-1. A few years ago, Reuters carried a story describing Jaguar's plans to develop the XJ220, a 200-mph sports car, to be sold for $587,000. The story continued:

> Jaguar unveiled a prototype of the XJ220 last year, but executives feared it would never go on sale because flagging profits would prevent production.

> Customers are being asked to put down a deposit of [$80,000] but will have to wait [three years] before the first models roll off the production line.

> The wait could be worth it. The Times newspaper estimated that collectors would be prepared to pay [$1.6 million] for one of the cars.

Under U.S. law, was Jaguar selling investment contracts?

2-2. Jackson is a 15-year old athlete who shows great promise. His parents are intrigued by the idea of monetizing his future so that he could have current income based on his future prospects. To this end, they propose to sell to investors interests in Jackson's future income. They are still working on a formula, but the idea is that for a $100,000 investment today the investor would be entitled to a specified percentage of all Jackson's future earnings (including income from endorsements). Is this arrangement an investment contract? Does the existence of multiple investors affect your analysis? What if Jackson is part of a pool of promising athletes, with investors purchasing undivided interests in a portion of the income stream generated by the athletes? For an excellent discussion of investing in people as if they were corporations and the myriad forms taken by such investments (including education loans), *see* Schwartz, The Corporatization of Personhood, 2015 Ill. L. Rev. 1119.

2. Common Enterprise and Profits Solely from the Efforts of Others

Securities and Exchange Commission v. Edwards
540 U.S. 389 (2004)

Justice O'CONNOR delivered the opinion of the Court.

"Opportunity doesn't always knock . . . sometimes it rings." And sometimes it hangs up. So it did for the 10,000 people who invested a total of $300 million in the payphone sale-and-leaseback arrangements touted by respondent under that slogan. The Securities and Exchange Commission (SEC) argues that the arrangements were investment contracts. . . . In this case, we must decide whether a moneymaking scheme is excluded from the term "investment contract" simply because the scheme offered a contractual entitlement to a fixed, rather than a variable, return.

I

[ETS Payphones, Inc.] sold payphones to the public via independent distributors. The payphones were offered packaged with a site lease, a 5-year lease-back and management agreement, and a buyback agreement. All but a tiny fraction of purchasers chose this package, although other management options were offered. The purchase price for the payphone packages was approximately $7,000. Under the leaseback and management agreement, purchasers received $82 per month, a 14% annual return. Purchasers were not involved in the day-to-day operation of the payphones they owned. . . . *[handwritten: ⟶ fixed return]*

The payphones did not generate enough revenue for ETS to make the payments required by the leaseback agreements, so the company depended on funds from new investors to meet its obligations. In September 2000, ETS filed for bankruptcy protection. The SEC . . . alleged that respondent and ETS had violated the [registration and antifraud provisions of the '33 and '34 Acts]. The Court of Appeals . . . held that respondent's scheme was not an investment contract, on two grounds. First, it read this Court's opinions to require that an investment contract offer either capital appreciation or a participation in the earnings of the enterprise, and thus to exclude schemes, such as respondent's, offering a fixed rate of return. Second, it held that our opinions' requirement that the return on the investment be "derived solely from the efforts of others" was not satisfied when the purchasers had a contractual entitlement to the return. We conclude that it erred on both grounds. . . .

II

[W]hen we held [in *Howey*] that "profits" must "come solely from the efforts of others," we were speaking of the profits that investors seek on their investment, not the profits of the scheme in which they invest. We used "profits" in the sense of income or return, to include, for example, dividends, other periodic payments, or the increased value of the investment.

There is no reason to distinguish between promises of fixed returns and promises of variable returns for purposes of the test, so understood. In both cases, the investing public is attracted by representations of investment income, as purchasers were in this case by ETS' invitation to "watch the profits add up." Moreover, investments pitched as low-risk (such as those offering a "guaranteed" fixed return) are particularly attractive to individuals more vulnerable to investment fraud, including older and less sophisticated investors. . . .

We hold that an investment scheme promising a fixed rate of return can be an "investment contract" and thus a "security" subject to the federal securities laws. The judgment of the [Eleventh Circuit] is reversed, and the case is remanded for further proceedings consistent with this opinion.

On remand, the Eleventh Circuit concluded the sale-and-leaseback arrangements were investment contracts. It noted the investors' dependence on the managerial efforts of the promoters, who had sole discretion over where to place the phones as well as full maintenance responsibility. *See SEC v. ETS Payphones, Inc.*, 408 F.3d 727 (11th Cir. 2005).

a. The Meaning of Common Enterprise

The Supreme Court did not avail itself of the opportunity provided by *Edwards* to refine or clarify the common enterprise component of *Howey*. The circuits have taken varying approaches in determining the existence of a common enterprise. Some courts look to *vertical commonality* in evaluating the presence of a common enterprise. Under this approach, which emphasizes the relationship between the investors and the promoter, the principal inquiry is whether the activities of the promoter are the controlling factor in the success or failure of the investment, and a common enterprise may exist even though there is no pooling of investors' funds or interests. Cases applying the vertical commonality standard have varied somewhat in the expansiveness of their interpretations.

Under an approach labeled *broad vertical commonality*, some courts look to the uniformity of the impact of the promoter and require only a connection between the efforts of the promoter and the collective successes or losses of the investors. *See, e.g., SEC v. ETS Payphones, Inc.*, 408 F.3d 727 (11th Cir. 2005) (returns to investors are dependent on the expertise or efforts of the promoters). Mere dependency on the continued solvency of the promoter has been sufficient for some courts to find the presence of a common enterprise under broad vertical commonality. *See, e.g., Living Bens. Asset Mgmt., L.L.C. v. Kestrel Aircraft Co. (In re Living Bens. Asset Mgmt., L.L.C.)*, 916 F.3d 528, 536 (5th Cir. 2019) (recognizing the overlap between (broad vertical) commonality and the reliance on the efforts of others prongs of *Howey*).

Other courts have opted for *strict vertical commonality* and require a direct relationship between the success (as opposed to the efforts) of the promoter and that of the investors; this requires the promoters and investors to share the risks of a venture. *See, e.g., Marini v. Adamo*, 995 F. Supp. 2d 155, 186 (E.D.N.Y. 2014) (commissions paid to promoter on sale of investor's coins sufficient to establish strict vertical commonality), *aff'd on other grounds*, 2016 U.S. App. LEXIS 5611 (2d Cir. Mar. 23, 2016). *But cf. Gugick v. Melville Capital, LLC*, 2014 U.S. Dist. LEXIS 12234 (S.D.N.Y. Jan. 31, 2014) (strict vertical commonality not satisfied when promoter received commissions even when investor incurred losses; a different result would be reached if commissions were paid only when the investor booked gains). Under either the broad or strict approach to vertical commonality, a common enterprise arguably may exist even if there is only a single investor.

A more restrictive approach looks to the presence of *horizontal commonality* and requires a pooling of investors' funds. Although this typically will involve a pro rata distribution of profits or sharing of losses among investors, horizontal commonality may exist when promised returns are fixed rather than variable provided there is the requisite pooling of investor funds. *See SEC v. Infinity Group Co.*, 212 F.3d 180 (3d Cir. 2000) (common enterprise existed even though investors were promised fixed rates of return ranging from 138 to 181 percent). In contrast to the vertical commonality tests, this approach emphasizes the common enterprise among investors, rather than the common enterprise between a promoter and investors.

Because horizontal commonality presupposes multiple investors, it may seem reasonable to conclude that a common enterprise is not present if there is a single investor. But consider the treatment of the issue in *SEC v. Lauer*, 52 F.3d 667 (7th Cir. 1995), where the investment involved a program in high-yield securities and contemplated multiple investors. As things developed, however, there was only one investor. In response to the argument that horizontal commonality cannot exist with a single investor, the court reasoned:

> [I]t is the character of the investment vehicle, not the presence of multiple investors, that determines whether there is an investment contract. Otherwise, a defrauder who was content to defraud a single investor . . . would have immunity from the federal securities laws. That would not make any sense, and is not contemplated by any of the cases that require horizontal commonality.

Id. at 670. The court was influenced by the original intention to involve multiple investors and the communication of that intention to the investor. But if it was clear from the beginning that there would be a single investor, how could there be the requisite pooling—planned or actual—that the Seventh Circuit seems to require for a common enterprise? *See generally* Gordon, Defining a Common Enterprise in Investment Contracts, 72 Ohio St. L.J. 59 (2011) (arguing a common enterprise requires multiple investors).

PROBLEMS

2-3. Harold, a dealer of rare coins, maintains a widely followed blog discussing alternative investments such as rare coins and precious metals. Impressed by what he read on the blog, Rocco approached Harold and requested help in structuring a diversified portfolio of rare coins. Harold was more than happy to oblige. He represented to Rocco that the coins he would recommend and sell to Rocco "were the top 1 percent of 1 percent, very rare, and those weren't the kind of coins that he has ever seen go down in value." He also offered to repurchase at current value any coins Rocco previously bought from him. Rocco was comforted by Harold's reassurances that Rocco could "cash out in 24 to 48 hours," that the coins were rare and "couldn't go down in value," and that Rocco was getting in "at the dirt bottom." The clincher for Rocco was Harold's representation that he would only recommend coins that he (Harold) held in his own personal portfolio. Assured that their interests were aligned because Harold "was eating his own cooking," Rocco bought $5 million in coins over the next five years; during this period, he sold a few of the coins back to Harold.

Rocco has learned the coins he purchased from Harold were priced far in excess of fair value. He would like to pursue a fraud claim against Harold. Assuming their two coin portfolios were substantially the same (though not identical), was there a common enterprise? *See Marini v. Adamo*, 812 F. Supp. 2d 243 (E.D.N.Y. 2011) aff'd on other grounds, 644 Fed. App'x 33 (2d Cir. 2016).

2-4. Magnificent Properties, Inc. (MPI) is in the business of managing commercial real estate. It has sold $90 million in debt securities to 20 investors; the proceeds will be used by MPI to acquire eight suburban shopping centers that it will renovate and manage. To raise an additional $10 million needed to complete the acquisition, MPI has entered into an agreement with Handsome Trust. Under the agreement, Handsome will invest $10 million and will have the right to a substantial percentage of the net profits of the eight properties if and when a certain income threshold has been passed. Has Handsome purchased an investment contract? Does the answer depend upon which theory of common enterprise is employed?

2-5. SG Trading Company maintains a web site allowing individuals to play a game called "StockGeneration." The lure of this game is easy money, or as is stated on the web site, "Would you like your money to double each month? Then welcome to the Virtual Stock Exchange SG." The game allows participants to purchase shares in 11 different "virtual companies" listed on the web site's virtual stock exchange. Although the companies are fantasy companies that exist only in cyberspace, participants invest real money in this game. SG arbitrarily sets the purchase and sale prices of each of the virtual companies (adjusted biweekly) and guarantees that investors can buy or sell any quantity of shares at the posted prices. Invested funds are pooled in a single account used to settle participants' online transactions. SG believes that the system will work as long as the base of investors continues to grow. To ensure that condition, SG promises to pay StockGeneration participants who recruit new participants bonuses equal to 20 percent of the new recruits' payments.

SG also promises that the share price for one "privileged company" will continuously rise and that investors in that company will enjoy a 10 percent per month return. To make sure that this happens, SG pledges that it will allocate a portion of its profits derived from its web site operations to a special reserve fund designed to support the price of the privileged company's shares.

Does this game involve an investment contract? *See SEC v. SG Ltd.*, 265 F.3d 42 (1st Cir. 2001).

b. *Profits from the Managerial Efforts of Others*

Interpreted strictly, *Howey*'s notion that an investment contract will exist only if profits are to be derived *solely* from the managerial efforts of the promoter or third parties suggests that promoters may circumvent application of the securities laws by merely requiring investors to nominally participate in the management of their ventures. In *SEC v. Glenn W. Turner Enterprises, Inc.*, 474 F.2d 476, 482 (9th Cir.), *cert. denied*, 414 U.S. 821 (1973), however, the court stated that the critical inquiry is "whether the efforts made by those other than the investor are the undeniably significant ones, those essential managerial efforts which affect the failure or success of the enterprise." *See also SEC v. Scoville*, 913 F.3d 1204 (10th Cir. 2019) (sale of "Adpacks" providing specified levels of traffic to purchasers' web site, combined with allowing purchasers to generate revenue for each Adpack purchased through small levels of clicking on the web sites of other purchasers, involved investment contracts because the efforts of the purchasers amounting to at most a few minutes a day were not "significant" when compared to those of the promoter).

In *United Housing Foundation, Inc. v. Forman,* supra, the Supreme Court noted the *Turner* restatement of the *Howey* test but declined to pass on its validity; at the same time, the Court proceeded to reaffirm the *Howey* formulation in a way that eliminated the troublesome qualifier "solely": "The touchstone is the presence of an investment in a common venture premised on a reasonable expectation of profits to be derived from the entrepreneurial or managerial efforts of others." 421 U.S. at 852. Although *Forman's* mixed signals on "solely" confused rather than clarified the issue, most lower courts have followed the lead of *Turner* and *Koscot* and have concluded an investment contract may exist even though there is some investor participation in a venture. In these cases, the problem is one of determining how active investors may be without undermining the character of their investments as investment contracts.

For example, in *Miller v. Cent. Chinchilla Grp., Inc.,* 494 F.2d 414 (8th Cir. 1974). Investors were told that only minimal care was required to raise chinchillas, and the promoters agreed to purchase the offspring at above-market prices. The venture could return the promised profits only if the promoters were successful in marketing the repurchased offspring at inflated prices to new investors. In fact, chinchillas are difficult to raise and have a high mortality rate. Plaintiffs initiated a class action asserting that the sale of chinchillas involved the offering of investment contracts in violation of both Section 5's registration requirements and the antifraud provisions of the '33 and '34 Acts. In evaluating the nature of the investors' efforts, the Eighth Circuit disregarded the efforts actually expended and focused instead upon the promoters' representations to potential investors that only minimal efforts would be required. Relying upon *Turner,* the court concluded that the "undeniably significant" efforts were those of the promoters in persuading additional persons to invest in the enterprise (i.e., buy additional chinchillas at inflated prices). Security status may also arise from breeding programs involving silver foxes, *e.g., SEC v. Payne,* 35 F. Supp. 873 (S.D.N.Y. 1940) (predates *Howey*), and beavers, *e.g., Continental Mktg. Corp. v. SEC,* 387 F.2d 466 (10th Cir. 1967), *cert. denied,* 391 U.S. 905 (1968). For a more down-to-earth case involving earthworms, *see Smith v. Gross,* 604 F.2d 639 (9th Cir. 1979).

Problems associated with such promotional schemes are not limited to the United States. Investors using the sword of the federal securities laws generally fare poorly when attacking traditional types of franchise or distributorship arrangements. In these cases, the level of activity required of the franchisees is generally sufficient to defeat classification of their investments as investment contracts. For example, in *Creative Am. Educ., LLC v. Learning Experience, LLC,* 2015 U.S. Dist. LEXIS 61307 (S.D. Fla. May 11, 2015)), *aff'd,* 668 Fed. App'x 883 (11th Cir. 2016), the court held that the purchase of a childcare franchise by foreign investors did not involve an investment contract because the investors intended to operate the franchise. The fact that subsequent to this agreement the investors' arrival in the United States was delayed and necessitated their entry into a management agreement with the seller did not change this result.

Is the *timing* of the efforts of others relevant to the investment contract analysis? The issue was addressed in *SEC v. Life Partners, Inc.,* 87 F.3d 536 (D.C. Cir. 1996), which dealt with viatical settlements whereby investors acquire an interest in the life insurance policy of a terminally ill person (typically an AIDS patient). The purchase is at a discount to the face value of the policy and provides the insured individual with immediate cash and the investor with a return measured by the difference between the discounted purchase price of the interest and the death benefit later collected. Life Partners, Inc., acted as an intermediary in arranging the transactions. Most of its efforts occurred *prior* to the point the investments actually were made. Following the investments, Life Partners' efforts were substantially reduced and related primarily to monitoring the status of the insured and attending to the details of the insurance policies (i.e., making sure premiums are paid when due and overseeing the disbursement of funds). The court concluded the arrangements did not involve investment contracts because the major "efforts of others" (i.e., Life Partners) occurred *before* purchasers made their investments.[1]

The distinction drawn by *Life Partners* between pre-investment and post-investment promoter services was rejected in a later decision of the Eleventh Circuit, which concluded there is no basis for excluding pre-purchase managerial activities from the investment contract analysis. *See SEC v. Mutual Benefits Corp.*, 408 F.3d 737 (11th Cir. 2005). Most courts have found *Mutual Benefits* persuasive. *See, e.g., Living Bens. Asset Mgmt., L.L.C. v. Kestrel Aircraft Co. (In re Living Bens. Asset Mgmt., L.L.C.)*, 916 F.3d 528, 538 (5th Cir. 2019) ("With rare exceptions, federal district courts and state courts have sided with the Eleventh Circuit's analysis over the D.C. Circuit's analysis."). *See generally* Albert, The *Howey* Test Turns 64: Are the Courts Grading This Test on a Curve?, 2 Wm. & Mary Bus. L. Rev. 1 (2011).

PROBLEMS

2-6. Belmont Reid needs funds to develop its gold mines. It offers to sell gold, in the form of coins, directly to investors. The coins are sold in sets of 12. The price is at a substantial discount to the world market price of gold at the time of the offering. Delivery of the coins will be in the future, and purchasers are advised that the gold required to mint the coins has not yet been extracted. In the event the world market price of gold declines to a level below the prepayment price, Belmont Reid promises to refund the difference to the purchasers. To secure both its guarantee and its performance, Belmont Reid puts the deed to one of its mines in a trust account. Is Belmont Reid selling a security? Does your answer depend upon whether the sales are made during a period in which the price of gold is rising? *See SEC v. Belmont Reid & Co.*, 794 F.2d 1388 (9th Cir. 1986); *SEC v. R.G. Reynolds Enterprises, Inc.*, 952 F.2d 1125 (9th Cir. 1991).

2-7. McSushi Inc. has been formed to develop Japanese fast food restaurants. Its initial capitalization is very small, and the plan is to raise funds to promote

---

1. Life Partners may have enjoyed early success in its skirmishes with the SEC but, ultimately, the Commission prevailed in its efforts to rein in the viatical settlement business. It sued Life Partners and certain of its top executives and in 2014 secured a judgment of $46 million for misrepresentations of investors. The company is now bankrupt.

the concept and gain public recognition by selling franchises to operate specific restaurants. For an investment of $35,000 plus a percentage of the gross receipts, McSushi will train franchisees in the preparation of Japanese food, provide equipment needed in the restaurants, engage in extensive advertising to promote the McSushi label, and supervise the restaurants to ensure quality control and uniformity of operation. Both food and uniforms must be purchased from McSushi. The franchisees are expected to work as on-site managers. They may, however, establish menu prices and engage in local promotions. Are these franchises securities?

3. Cryptocurrencies, ICOs, and Beyond

The highly volatile markets for cryptocurrencies, initial coin offerings (ICOs), and related virtual instruments have challenged the traditional structure of securities regulation because of uncertainties surrounding application of the securities laws. In evaluating potential application of the securities laws, begin with the simplest of cases. Is a cryptocurrency that purports to be nothing more than a store of value and medium of exchange a security? Traditionally, true currencies have not been regulated as securities even though they may fluctuate in value. If this seems surprising, review the statutory definitions of a security in the '33 and '34 Acts and attempt to locate "currency." There remains, of course, the investment contract catchall, but few would argue that traditional currencies fit neatly within the criteria outlined in *Howey*.

The same *may* be true for true cryptocurrencies that function purely, or even largely, as currencies. Many different types of coins and tokens comprise the cryptocurrency market. One of the simplest and most popular is the *stored value coin*, a notable example of which is Bitcoin, though some may argue with characterizing Bitcoin in this fashion on the theory that it offers more than stored value. Stored value coins represent interests in blockchain networks (distributed databases that generate lists of records called blocks). For present purposes, the issue is whether stored valued coins may fit within *Howey*'s investment contract framework.

Consider *Howey*'s common enterprise requirement. Horizontal commonality may be satisfied because the networks receive funding from a pool of investors. But the vertical commonality analysis is less clear. Stored value coins often lack a vertical structure and instead are governed by a diffuse group of miners and developers. Although the fortunes of lay investors are tied to those of miner-investors, they are not relying on an identifiable promotional entity or foundation.

A further issue in the investment contract analysis concerns the extent to which "investors" rely on the efforts of others for profits. Although to some extent purchasers may rely on the efforts of miners and developers, the miners and developers are just influential investors and do not have coordinated activities or an official hierarchy. Further, past market fluctuations raise the likelihood that coin-holders are looking for profits from market forces, like investors in gold, rather than innovations by miners or developers. *Cf. SEC v. Belmont Reid & Co.*, 794 F.2d 1388 (9th Cir. 1986) (holding that investors in gold coins during a period of high inflation looked for profits from market forces rather than the efforts of the promoters). Along this line, the Commodities Futures Trading Commission has concluded Bitcoin should be regulated as a commodity, not a security, and the Chair of the CFTC has observed that Bitcoin has some similarities with gold (even though it leaves much to be desired as a medium of exchange).

Stored value coins may be purchased as an investment or for purposes of consumption, an important distinction discussed earlier in this chapter. Along this line, some retailers accept Bitcoin as payment. To the extent that it gains wide acceptance primarily as a unit of exchange, the likelihood of treating Bitcoin as an investment contract diminishes. But the day is still young, and huge fluctuations of value, such as those experienced by Bitcoin, may cut against the "consumption" characteristics of an instrument and increase its investment profile. *See, e.g.*, Colesanti, Trotting Out the White Horse: How the S.E.C. Can Handle Bitcoin's Threat to American Investors, 65 Syracuse L. Rev. 1 (2014) (early analysis perceptively noting "in the five years of its formal existence, Bitcoin's use as an alternative to 'PayPal' or Western Union has likely been overridden by its utility as an aggressive mutual fund").

As noted, stored value coins are just one type of virtual instrument, and the investment contract analysis will vary depending on the characteristics of the unit involved. ICOs and tokens, for example, may be used as a way to raise capital, and purchasers of these units may be seeking profits rather than just stores of value. Not surprisingly, as virtual instruments become more than pseudo-currencies, the risk that they will be treated as securities increases. Consider, for example, the tokens created by Munchee, which developed an iPhone app for reviewing restaurants. The tokens could be used to buy goods and services through a not-yet-developed "ecosystem." Going beyond the simplest of stored value pseudo-currency coins, Munchee consistently emphasized the lure of profits in touting its tokens to potential purchasers and committed to take steps to increase the value of tokens in circulation. First and foremost, Munchee stated it would limit the number of tokens sold. It would "burn" tokens (take out of circulation) when restaurants paid for advertising with tokens. It also offered a "tiered" program allowing restaurants to pay reviewers in tokens, with the level of payment depending on the number of tokens already owned by the purchaser. And Munchee promised to promote the development of a secondary market for trading tokens.

Munchee planned to sell $15 million in tokens, with the proceeds to be used to fund its business and build the promised ecosystem. It never happened, however, because the SEC issued a cease-and-desist order. *See* Securities Act Release No. 10445 (Dec. 11, 2017). The order followed from its conclusion that the tokens were investment contracts: "Purchasers would reasonably believe they could profit by holding or trading MUN tokens, whether or not they ever used the Munchee App or otherwise participated in the MUN 'ecosystem,' based on Munchee's statements in its MUN White Paper and other materials. Munchee primed purchasers' reasonable expectations of profit through statements on blogs, podcasts, and Facebook that talked about profits."

This was consistent with the approach taken by the Commission a few months earlier in 2017 in "The DAO Report," which essentially laid down regulatory markers and served notice that the SEC intended to assert regulatory authority over a broad swath of cryptocurrency and blockchain transactions. *See*

Report of Investigation Pursuant to Section 21(a) of the Securities Exchange Act of 1934: The DAO, Exchange Act Release No. 81207 (July 25, 2017). The Report's introduction clearly signaled significant SEC involvement is to come, noting: "The automation of certain functions through this technology, 'smart contracts,' or computer code, does not remove conduct from the purview of the U.S. federal securities laws." On smart contracts, *see generally* Werbach & Cornell, Contracts Ex Machina, 67 Duke L.J. 313 (2017) (discussing how smart contracts fit within traditional contract law); Rodrigues, Law and the Blockchain, 104 Iowa L. Rev. 680 (2019) (discussing contract gaps and law's inability to supply default terms in blockchain smart contracts).

The Commission has enjoyed some early court successes in bringing cryptocurrency arrangements under the investment contract framework. *See, e.g., SEC v. Blockvest, LLC,* 2019 U.S. Dist. LEXIS 24446 (granting preliminary injunction blocking promoters of Blockvest ICO from proceeding with an allegedly fraudulent securities offering); *United States v. Zaslavskiy,* 2018 U.S. Dist. LEXIS 156574, 2018 WL 4346339 (E.D.N.Y. 2018) (upholding an indictment relating to fraudulent misrepresentations in two virtual currency investment schemes and related ICOs). *See also* Securities Act Release No. 10445, 2017 WL 10605969 (Dec. 11, 2017) (administrative proceeding finding ICO centering on iPhone app for restaurant reviews involved securities in part because tokens sold could appreciate in value, even though no dividends or profit distributions were forthcoming). Private actions litigants are enjoying similar successes in applying the *Howey* framework to ICOs. *See, e.g., Balestra v. ATBCOIN LLC,* 2019 U.S. Dist. LEXIS 55972, 2019 WL 1437160 (S.D.N.Y. 2019) (sustaining class action complaint alleging ICO was sale of unregistered securities).

In late 2018, SEC announced the launch of the agency's Strategic Hub for Innovation and Financial Technology (FinHub), which serves as a resource for public engagement on the SEC's FinTech-related issues and initiatives and builds on the work of several internal working groups at the SEC that have focused on similar issues. In 2019, FinHub published a framework, excerpted below, presenting its plain English views of digital assets as investment contracts. Although this is not a rule binding on the Commission itself, it will prove influential.

Framework for "Investment Contract" Analysis of Digital Assets
Strategic Hub for Innovation and Financial Technology (FinHub) (2019)

I. INTRODUCTION

If you are considering an Initial Coin Offering, sometimes referred to as an "ICO," or otherwise engaging in the offer, sale, or distribution of a digital asset, you need to consider whether the U.S. federal securities laws apply. . . .

The U.S. Supreme Court's *Howey* case and subsequent case law have found that an "investment contract" exists when there is the investment of money in a common enterprise with a reasonable expectation of profits to be derived from the efforts of others. . . .

II.   APPLICATION OF *HOWEY* TO DIGITAL ASSETS

A.   THE INVESTMENT OF MONEY

The first prong of the *Howey* test is typically satisfied in an offer and sale of a digital asset because the digital asset is purchased or otherwise acquired in exchange for value. . . .

B.   COMMON ENTERPRISE

Courts generally have analyzed a "common enterprise" as a distinct element of an investment contract. In evaluating digital assets, we have found that a "common enterprise" typically exists.[11]

C.   REASONABLE EXPECTATION OF PROFITS DERIVED FROM EFFORTS OF OTHERS

Usually, the main issue in analyzing a digital asset under the *Howey* test is whether a purchaser has a reasonable expectation of profits (or other financial returns) derived from the efforts of others. . . . When a promoter, sponsor, or other third party . . . (each, an "Active Participant" or "AP") provides essential managerial efforts that affect the success of the enterprise, and investors reasonably expect to derive profit from those efforts, then this prong of the test is met. . . .

1.   *Reliance on the Efforts of Others*

The inquiry into whether a purchaser is relying on the efforts of others focuses on two key issues:

- Does the purchaser reasonably expect to rely on the efforts of an AP?
- Are those efforts "the undeniably significant ones, those essential managerial efforts which affect the failure or success of the enterprise,"[14] as opposed to efforts that are more ministerial in nature?

Although no one of the following characteristics is necessarily determinative, the stronger their presence, the more likely it is that a purchaser of a digital asset is relying on the "efforts of others":

---

11.   Based on our experiences to date, investments in digital assets have constituted investments in a common enterprise because the fortunes of digital asset purchasers have been linked to each other or to the success of the promoter's efforts. *See SEC v. Int'l Loan Network, Inc.*, 968 F.2d 1304, 1307 (D.C. Cir. 1992).

14.   *SEC v. Glenn W. Turner Enter., Inc.*, 474 F.2d 476, 482 (9th Cir.), *cert. denied*, 414 U.S. 821, 94 S. Ct. 117, 38 L. Ed. 2d 53 (1973) ("*Turner*").

- An AP is responsible for the development, improvement (or enhancement), operation, or promotion of the network. . . .[16]
  - Where the network or the digital asset is still in development and the network or digital asset is not fully functional at the time of the offer or sale, purchasers would reasonably expect an AP to further develop the functionality of the network or digital asset (directly or indirectly). . . .
- There are essential tasks or responsibilities performed and expected to be performed by an AP, rather than an unaffiliated, dispersed community of network users (commonly known as a "decentralized" network).
- An AP creates or supports a market for, or the price of, the digital asset. . . .
- An AP has a lead or central role in the direction of the ongoing development of the network or the digital asset. . . .
- An AP has a continuing managerial role in making decisions about or exercising judgment concerning the network or the characteristics or rights the digital asset represents. . . .
- Purchasers would reasonably expect the AP to undertake efforts to promote its own interests and enhance the value of the network or digital asset, such as where:
  - The AP has the ability to realize capital appreciation from the value of the digital asset. This can be demonstrated, for example, if the AP retains a stake or interest in the digital asset. In these instances, purchasers would reasonably expect the AP to undertake efforts to promote its own interests and enhance the value of the network or digital asset.
  - The AP distributes the digital asset as compensation to management or the AP's compensation is tied to the price of the digital asset in the secondary market. To the extent these facts are present, the compensated individuals can be expected to take steps to build the value of the digital asset.
  - The AP owns or controls ownership of intellectual property rights of the network or digital asset, directly or indirectly.
  - The AP monetizes the value of the digital asset, especially where the digital asset has limited functionality. . . .

---

16. We recognize that holders of digital assets may put forth some effort in the operations of the network, but those efforts do not negate the fact that the holders of digital assets are relying on the efforts of the AP. That a scheme assigns "nominal or limited responsibilities to the [investor] does not negate the existence of an investment contract." *SEC v. Koscot Interplanetary, Inc.*, 497 F.2d 473, 483 n.15 (5th Cir. 1974) (citation and quotation marks omitted). If the AP provides efforts that are "the undeniably significant ones, those essential managerial efforts which affect the failure or success of the enterprise," and the AP is not merely performing ministerial or routine tasks, then there likely is an investment contract. *See Turner*, 474 U.S. at 482; *see also The DAO Report* (although DAO token holders had certain voting rights, they nonetheless reasonably relied on the managerial efforts of others). Managerial and entrepreneurial efforts typically are characterized as involving expertise and decision-making that impacts the success of the business or enterprise through the application of skill and judgment.

2.   *Reasonable Expectation of Profits*

An evaluation of the digital asset should also consider whether there is a reasonable expectation of profits. . . .   Price appreciation resulting solely from external market forces (such as general inflationary trends or the economy) impacting the supply and demand for an underlying asset generally is not considered "profit" under the *Howey* test.

The more the following characteristics are present, the more likely it is that there is a reasonable expectation of profit:

- The digital asset gives the holder rights to share in the enterprise's income or profits or to realize gain from capital appreciation of the digital asset. . . .
- The digital asset is transferable or traded on or through a secondary market or platform, or is expected to be in the future.[19]
- Purchasers reasonably would expect that an AP's efforts will result in capital appreciation of the digital asset and therefore be able to earn a return on their purchase.
- The digital asset is offered broadly to potential purchasers as compared to being targeted to expected users of the goods or services or those who have a need for the functionality of the network.
  - The digital asset is offered and purchased in quantities indicative of investment intent instead of quantities indicative of a user of the network. For example, it is offered and purchased in quantities significantly greater than any likely user would reasonably need, or so small as to make actual use of the asset in the network impractical.
- There is little apparent correlation between the purchase/offering price of the digital asset and the market price of the particular goods or services that can be acquired in exchange for the digital asset.
- There is little apparent correlation between quantities the digital asset typically trades in (or the amounts that purchasers typically purchase) and the amount of the underlying goods or services a typical consumer would purchase for use or consumption.
- The AP has raised an amount of funds in excess of what may be needed to establish a functional network or digital asset.
- The AP is able to benefit from its efforts as a result of holding the same class of digital assets as those being distributed to the public.
- The AP continues to expend funds from proceeds or operations to enhance the functionality or value of the network or digital asset. . . .

---

19.   Situations where the digital asset is exchangeable or redeemable solely for goods or services within the network or on a platform, and may not otherwise be transferred or sold, may more likely be a payment for a good or service in which the purchaser is motivated to use or consume the digital asset. . . .

3. Other Relevant Considerations

When assessing whether there is a reasonable expectation of profit derived from the efforts of others, federal courts look to the economic reality of the transaction. In doing so, the courts also have considered whether the instrument is offered and sold for use or consumption by purchasers.[21]

Although no one of the following characteristics of use or consumption is necessarily determinative, the stronger their presence, the less likely the *Howey* test is met:

- The distributed ledger network and digital asset are fully developed and operational.
- Holders of the digital asset are immediately able to use it for its intended functionality on the network, particularly where there are built-in incentives to encourage such use.
- The digital assets' creation and structure is designed and implemented to meet the needs of its users, rather than to feed speculation as to its value or development of its network. For example, the digital asset can only be used on the network and generally can be held or transferred only in amounts that correspond to a purchaser's expected use.
- Prospects for appreciation in the value of the digital asset are limited. For example, the design of the digital asset provides that its value will remain constant or even degrade over time, and, therefore, a reasonable purchaser would not be expected to hold the digital asset for extended periods as an investment.
- With respect to a digital asset referred to as a virtual currency, it can immediately be used to make payments in a wide variety of contexts, or acts as a substitute for real (or fiat) currency. . . .
- If it is characterized as a virtual currency, the digital asset actually operates as a store of value that can be saved, retrieved, and exchanged for something of value at a later time. With respect to a digital asset that represents rights to a good or service, it currently can be redeemed within a developed network or platform to acquire or otherwise use those goods or services. . . .
- Any economic benefit that may be derived from appreciation in the value of the digital asset is incidental to obtaining the right to use it for its intended functionality.
- The digital asset is marketed in a manner that emphasizes the functionality of the digital asset, and not the potential for the increase in market value of the digital asset.
- Potential purchasers have the ability to use the network and use (or have used) the digital asset for its intended functionality.

---

21. *See Forman*, 421 U.S. at 852-53 (where a purchaser is not "'attracted solely by the prospects of a return' on his investment . . . [but] is motivated by a desire to use or consume the item purchased . . . the securities laws do not apply.").

- Restrictions on the transferability of the digital asset are consistent with the asset's use and not facilitating a speculative market.
- If the AP facilitates the creation of a secondary market, transfers of the digital asset may only be made by and among users of the platform.

Digital assets with these types of use or consumption characteristics are less likely to be investment contracts. . . .

For a sampling of the growing literature on regulation of cryptocurrencies, *see* Brummer & Yadav, Fintech and the Innovation Trilemma, 107 Geo. L.J. 235 (2019) (discussing difficulties in applying traditional regulatory approaches to the exponential growth of financial technology); Chaffee, The Heavy Burden of Thin Regulation: Lessons Learned from the SEC's Regulation of Cryptocurrencies, 70 Mercer L. Rev. 615 (2019) (arguing for narrowly focused tailored regulation of cryptocurrencies); Cohney et al., Coin-Operated Capitalism, 119 Colum. L. Rev. 591 (2019) (excellent discussion of ICOs built around a survey of 50 ICOs in 2017).

PROBLEM

2-8. TurnKey Jet, Inc. (TKJ) provides interstate air charter services. It proposes to launch a Token membership program and develop a Token platform to facilitate Token sales for air charter services via a private blockchain network ("Network"). Desiring to avoid financial and regulatory issues with traditional payment methods utilizing wire transfers or credit cards, TKJ proposes to allow consumers of their services to purchase Tokens via a private blockchain network, which offers cost and speed efficiencies for both TKJ and its customers. TKJ will sell Tokens at a fixed ratio of $1 for 1 token.

Consumers interested in chartering aircraft may purchase tokens through the blockchain network managed by TKJ. TKJ will utilize smart contracts establishing that the Tokens are prepayment of the future consumption of air charter services and there will be no return of principal or interest on the monies that are prepaid. Further, TKJ will use the smart contracts to execute the consideration for TKJ Token redemptions.

When a Token enters circulation, TKJ consumers may freely trade or exchange the Tokens in their possession with other consumers enrolled in the Network. Since TKJ itself will continuously sell Tokens for $1 each, the market for tokens is likely to remain stable at around $1, rendering it unlikely that anyone could sell tokens for a profit. Moreover, TKJ requires token purchasers to agree that they are purchasing tokens solely for prepaid air charter services and not with the intention of reselling for investment gains.

Are the Tokens securities? *See* TurnKey Jets, SEC No-Action Letter (Apr. 3, 2019). Would your answer change if the Network does not presently exist and will not be operational for three years, so Token purchasers would be pre-purchasing charter services that would not be provided for several years?

D. Associational Formalities: Interests in Corporations, Partnerships, and LLCs as Securities

1. Stock as a Security

Although the statutory definitions of a security include "stock" among the types of securities listed, *United Housing Foundation v. Forman*, supra, concluded that some types of stock (in that case, stock in a nonprofit housing cooperative) are not securities. The case also suggested that the *Howey* criteria for an investment contract provided a common base linking all types of securities. Lower courts, seemingly following the *Forman* lead eschewing literalism in favor of a functional approach, began considering when a *Howey*-type analysis might remove transactions in more conventional stock from regulation under the federal securities law. This gave rise in a number of circuits to the "sale of business" doctrine exempting from the federal securities laws sales of all or substantially all of the stock in closely held corporations.

The sale of business doctrine was laid to rest in *Landreth Timber Co. v. Landreth*, 471 U.S. 681 (1985), which involved the sale of all of the stock in the family owned lumber business. Dissatisfied with their investment, the purchasers sought rescission of the sale and $2,500,000 in damages. In accepting the purchasers' claims that the stock was a security and that the sale of business doctrine should not be followed, the Court adopted a literal approach to the issue of when stock is a security:

> As we also recognized in *Forman*, the fact that instruments bear the label "stock" is not of itself sufficient to invoke the coverage of the Acts. . . . We identified those characteristics usually associated with common stock as (i) the right to receive dividends contingent upon an apportionment of profits; (ii) negotiability; (iii) the ability to be pledged or hypothecated; (iv) the conferring of voting rights in proportion to the number of shares owned; and (v) the capacity to appreciate in value. . . .
>
> Under the facts of *Forman*, we concluded that the instruments at issue there were not "securities" within the meaning of the Acts. . . .
>
> In contrast, it is undisputed that the stock involved here possesses all of the characteristics we identified in *Forman* as traditionally associated with common stock. . . . Moreover, unlike in *Forman*, the context of the transaction involved here—the sale of stock in a corporation—is typical of the kind of context to which the Acts normally apply. It is thus much more likely here than in *Forman* that an investor would believe he was covered by the federal securities laws. Under the circumstances of this case, the plain meaning of the statutory definition mandates that the stock be treated as "securities" subject to the coverage of the Acts. . . .
>
> Under other circumstances, we might consider the statutory analysis outlined above to be a sufficient answer compelling judgment for petitioner. Respondents

urge, however, that language in our previous opinions, including *Forman*, requires that we look beyond the label "stock" and the characteristics of the instruments involved to determine whether application of the Acts is mandated by the economic substance of the transaction. . . .

[Respondents] argue that our cases require us in every instance to look to the economic substance of the transaction to determine whether the *Howey* test has been met. According to respondents, it is clear that petitioner sought not to earn profits from the efforts of others, but to buy a company that it could manage and control. Petitioner was not a passive investor of the kind Congress intended the Acts to protect, but an active entrepreneur, who sought to "use or consume" the business purchased just as the purchasers in *Forman* sought to use the apartments they acquired after purchasing shares of stock. Thus, respondents urge that the Acts do not apply.

We disagree with respondents' interpretation of our cases. First, it is important to understand the contexts within which these cases were decided. All of the cases on which respondents rely involved unusual instruments not easily characterized as "securities.". . . *Forman* does not, however, eliminate the Court's ability to hold that an instrument is covered when its characteristics bear out the label. . . .

Second, we would note that the *Howey* economic reality test was designed to determine whether a particular instrument is an "investment contract," not whether it fits within *any* of the examples listed in the statutory definition of "security." . . .

Finally, we cannot agree with respondents that the Acts were intended to cover only "passive investors" and not privately negotiated transactions involving the transfer of control to "entrepreneurs." The 1934 Act contains several provisions specifically governing tender offers, disclosure of transactions by corporate officers and principal stockholders, and the recovery of short-swing profits gained by such persons. . . . Furthermore, although §4(2) of the 1933 Act exempts transactions not involving any public offering from the Act's registration provisions, there is no comparable exemption from the antifraud provisions. Thus, the structure and language of the Acts refute respondents' position.

Id. at 686-692. Should the literal approach reflected in the opinion extend to other types of instruments included in the statutory definitions of a security, most importantly notes? On this important point, the Court cautioned that stock may be distinguishable from notes and that it would "leave until another day" the question of whether notes are securities.

NOTES AND QUESTIONS

1. *Consistency?*   *Landreth* involved a sale of all of the stock of a family business where the sellers and purchasers had an opportunity to negotiate the transaction on a face-to-face basis. Yet in *Marine Bank v. Weaver*, supra, decided only three years earlier, the Court held a "unique agreement, negotiated one-on-one by the parties, is not a security." 455 U.S. at 560. Are these cases consistent? Can they be distinguished adequately on the basis that *Landreth* involved stock while *Marine Bank* involved an investment contract?

2. *Is Partial Satisfaction of the* **Landreth** *Criteria Sufficient to Foreclose Further Inquiry?*   In light of *Landreth*'s list of five characteristics of stock and the fact that

all were present in the case, how should a court proceed when some but not all of the characteristics are present? Most courts are still content to rest on the label. For example, in *Gilmore v. Gilmore*, 2011 U.S. Dist. LEXIS 99441 (S.D.N.Y. Sept. 1, 2011), the defendants argued that contractual limits on negotiability (negating the second and third *Landreth* criteria) necessitated a broader inquiry into the economic realities underlying the instrument. The court rejected the argument, noting simply that stock in a for-profit corporation is "the paradigm of a security." But what if the requisite label is missing? In a case involving a promise to transfer a 5 percent interest in a business, the court concluded that failure to reference "stock" in the agreement is a basis for distinguishing *Landreth* because both the label "stock" and the attributes of stock must be present. *See D.R. Mason Constr. Co. v. GBOD, LLC*, 2018 U.S. Dist. LEXIS 41236 (S.D. Cal. 2018) (a more persuasive basis for distinguishing *Landreth* is that the subject business apparently was an LLC, not a corporation).

   3. Reining in **Howey.** There was certain logic to the now-defunct sale of business doctrine if one accepts *Forman*'s assumption that *Howey*'s definition of an investment contract captures the essence of all securities covered by the Acts. *Landreth*, however, left little doubt that it was rejecting this aspect of *Forman*: "[W]e would note that the *Howey* economic reality test was designed to determine whether a particular instrument is an 'investment contract,' not whether it fits within *any* of the examples listed in the statutory definition of 'security.'" 471 U.S. at 691.

PROBLEMS

2-9. Sam has agreed to purchase Hillary's real estate brokerage business, Vistas, Inc. The parties are exploring alternative ways to structure the transaction. Hillary would like for Sam simply to purchase her stock in Vistas, but Sam would prefer to use a corporation he owns to purchase all of the assets and assume all of the liabilities of Vistas. In either case, Sam (or a corporation wholly owned by Sam) winds up owning Hillary's business. How does the structure of the transaction affect the analysis of whether it involves a security?

2-10. Championship Auto Racing Teams, Inc. (CART) organizes auto races, most notably the Indianapolis 500. A share of stock in CART makes the holder a member of CART, which is a condition to participating in the races. No owner may enter a car in a race without the membership that is linked to CART stock ownership. Transfer of any CART shares requires approval of CART's board, which may be had only if CART determines that the buyer is fit to race. Failure of a CART shareholder to participate in races may lead to a redemption of the shareholder's stock. CART shareholders elect the board. They also are entitled to dividends, although historically CART's profit distributions have been minimal and the stock's major attraction is the opportunity it provides to generate income from racing and consequent endorsements. Is stock in CART a security? Do you need additional information? *See Giuffre Org., Ltd. v. Euromotorsport Racing, Inc.*, 141 F.3d 1216 (7th Cir. 1998).

2. Partnership and Limited Liability Company Interests as Securities

It should not be surprising that investors disgruntled with the performances of business ventures often seek "security" status for their interests. Because interests in the various unincorporated associations such as partnerships are not among the items enumerated in the statutory definition of a security, the issue in these cases centers generally on the presence of an investment contract and specifically on whether investors are dependent for their profits on the efforts of others.

Prior to the emergence of limited liability partnerships (LLPs) and limited liability companies (LLCs), the investment contract issue for unincorporated associations arose almost exclusively in the context of general partnerships and limited partnerships. On the surface, bringing general partnership interests under *Howey*'s investment contract framework may seem a stretch given the active role partners often take in the management of their businesses. But as the Ninth Circuit recently observed, "Dressing an investment contract in the trappings of a general partnership interest does not immunize that interest from the federal securities laws." *SEC v. Schooler*, 905 F.3d 1107, 1110 (9th Cir. 2018).

The leading case on partnership interests as securities is *Williamson v. Tucker*, 645 F.2d 404 (5th Cir.), *cert. denied*, 454 U.S. 897 (1981), which offered the framework that continues to be widely used:

> A general partnership or joint venture interest can be designated a security if the investor can establish . . . that (1) an agreement among the parties leaves so little power in the hands of the partner or venturer that the arrangement in fact distributes power as would a limited partnership; or (2) the partner or venturer is so inexperienced and unknowledgeable in business affairs that he is incapable of intelligently exercising his partnership or venture powers; or (3) the partner or venturer is so dependent on some unique entrepreneurial or managerial ability of the promoter or manager that he cannot replace the manager of the enterprise or otherwise exercise meaningful partnership or venture powers.

Id. at 424. For a recent extensive discussion of the *Williamson* framework and application of its factors, *see SEC v. Arcturus Corp.*, 912 F.3d 786 (5th Cir. 2019) (discussing, among many other matters, how investors' ability to communicate with each other affects the analysis of their power, whether cold calling as a means of gathering investors is probative of their lack of experience and dependence on managers, and why the structure of the partnership's contractual relationships may bear on the replaceability of the managers).

Although in recent years associational options have expanded to include LLPs, LLCs, and their variations, the following case illustrates that the core investment contract issue—the controls investors have over the management of their investments—remains constant.

United States v. Leonard
529 F.3d 83 (2d Cir. 2008)

KATZMANN, Circuit Judge:

Over sixty years ago, the Supreme Court established the test for whether a given financial instrument or transaction constitutes an "investment contract"—and, therefore, a security—for purposes of the federal securities laws. *SEC v. W.J. Howey Co.*, 328 U.S. 293, 66 S. Ct. 1100, 90 L. Ed. 1244 (1946). We write today to underscore that, in applying the *Howey* factors, courts can (and should) look beyond the formal terms of a relationship to the reality of the parties' positions to evaluate whether "the reasonable expectation was one of significant investor control." *SEC v. Aqua-Sonic Prods. Corp.*, 687 F.2d 577, 585 (2d Cir. 1982).

Appellants Dickau and Silverstein were two of twenty-five individuals indicted for criminal fraud for their role in marketing investment interests in film companies. Following a jury trial, they were each convicted of securities fraud and conspiracy to commit securities and mail fraud. On appeal, they challenge their convictions, claiming, *inter alia*, that insufficient evidence supported the determination that the interests at issue were securities. . . .

BACKGROUND

[Dickau and Silverstein] each operated an independent sales office ("ISO") selling interests in companies formed to finance the production and distribution of motion pictures. Dickau's ISO sold interests in Little Giant, LLC, an entity created to produce the film *Carlo's Wake*. The ISOs solicited investments in Little Giant and Heritage over the phone, calling potential investors to generate interest in the film projects. The film's promoters would then mail potential investors offering materials, including a brochure, operating agreement, subscription agreement, risk disclosure sheet, and instruction sheet. If the potential investor decided to participate in the investment, he or she would send the subscription agreement, along with a check, directly to the film's promoters.

When an ISO succeeded in selling an interest in Little Giant or Heritage, it would receive a commission. . . . Dickau's company sold a combined total of $520,000 worth of Little Giant and Heritage units and retained $210,376 in commissions. Silverstein's company sold $90,000 in interests in Heritage, pocketing $32,939 in commissions.

The government charged Dickau with four counts [of securities and mail fraud]. All counts centered around the failure to disclose accurately the sales commission that the ISOs would be taking on the investment units. Following a trial in the Eastern District of New York, the jury returned a verdict of guilty on all counts against Dickau and Silverstein. . . .

DISCUSSION

I.   WHETHER SUFFICIENT EVIDENCE SUPPORTED THE FINDING THAT THE UNITS WERE SECURITIES

. . . [T]he parties agree that the only category that potentially applies to this case is "investment contract." . . . Appellants suggest that the Little Giant and Heritage units cannot constitute securities because investors never expected profits "solely from the efforts" of the promoters or others.

Following the Ninth Circuit's lead, *see SEC v. Glenn W. Turner Enterprises*, 474 F.2d 476, 482 (9th Cir. 1973), we have held that the word "solely" should not be construed as a literal limitation; rather, we "consider whether, under all the circumstances, the scheme was being promoted primarily as an investment or as a means whereby participants could pool their own activities, their money and the promoter's contribution in a meaningful way." *SEC v. Aqua-Sonic Prods. Corp.*, 687 F.2d 577, 582 (2d Cir. 1982). . . .

Our consideration of whether the investors in Little Giant and Heritage viewed the units primarily as a passive investment is complicated by the fact that Little Giant and Heritage were each structured as an LLC—a relatively new, hybrid vehicle that combines elements of the traditional corporation with elements of the general partnership while retaining flexibility for federal tax purposes. Although "common stock is the quintessence of a security," [citations omitted] and "[n]ormally, a general partnership interest is not considered a 'security,'" [citation omitted] because of the sheer diversity of LLCs, membership interests therein resist categorical classification. Thus, an interest in an LLC is the sort of instrument that requires "case-by-case analysis" into the "economic realities" of the underlying transaction, *Reves*, 494 U.S. at 62.

One of the original promoters of Little Giant and Heritage, Russell Finnegan, testified at trial that the LLCs were structured so as to minimize the possibility that the investment units would constitute securities—"to get into . . . the gray areas of the securities law." Indeed, were we to confine ourselves to a review of the organizational documents, we would likely conclude that the interests in Little Giant and Heritage could not constitute securities because the documents would lead us to believe that members were expected to play an active role in the management of the companies. For example, the sheet titled "Summary of Business Opportunity: Heritage Film Group, LLC" explains:

> Each Member is required to participate in the management of the Company retaining one (1) vote for each Unit acquired. Each important decision relating to the business of the Company must be submitted to a vote of the Members.
>
> The purchase of interests in the Company is not a passive investment. While specific knowledge and expertise in the day to day operation of a film producing and distributing company is not required, Members should have such knowledge and experience in general business, investment and/or financial affairs as to intelligently exercise their management and voting rights. . . . Further, each Member is required to participate in the management of the Company by serving on one or more committees established by the Members.

The summary further states that a manager may be chosen to perform certain "ministerial functions," such as keeping books and records, keeping the members informed, and circulating ballots to members, but the members retain the right to replace the manager and appoint his successor upon majority vote. Likewise, the operating agreement for Heritage provides that the "Company shall be managed by the Members. . . . [E]ach Member shall have the right to act for and bind the Company in the ordinary course of its business." Thus, on the face of the documents, Heritage and Little Giant appear to provide for too much investor control to allow the jury to conclude that the units were securities.

In actuality, however, the Little Giant and Heritage members played an extremely passive role in the management and operation of the companies. At trial, members testified that they voted, at most, "a couple of times." [Although the organizational documents provided for the formation of a number of committees, very few investors served on committees.] Thus, the vast majority of investors in both companies did not actively participate in the venture, exercising almost no control.

Record evidence allowed the jury to conclude that—notwithstanding the language in the organizational documents suggesting otherwise—from the start there could be no "reasonable expectation" of investor control. . . .

For one, under the organizational documents, the members' managerial rights and obligations did not accrue until the LLCs were "fully organized." [S]o-called "interim managers" initially held legal control rights, and they decided almost every significant issue prior to the completion of fundraising: "The script, the director, the cast, the crew, scoring of it, editing. The entire picture was pretty well preproduced. . . ." Thus, the jury could reasonably have found the managerial rights contained in the organizational documents were hollow and illusory.

The jury was also entitled to consider the fact that the members appear not to have negotiated any terms of the LLC agreements. Rather, they were presented with the subscription agreements on a take-it-or-leave-it basis. . . .

Moreover, the members had no particular experience in film or entertainment and therefore would have had difficulty exercising their formal right to take over management of the companies after they were fully organized. . . . And their number and geographic dispersion left investors particularly dependent on centralized management. . . . In sum, upon consideration of the totality of the circumstances, we conclude that the jury could have determined that, notwithstanding the organizational documents drafted to suggest active participation by members, the defendants sought and expected passive investors for Little Giant and Heritage, and therefore the interests that they marketed constituted securities. . . .

[The court affirmed the convictions but found that the district court improperly calculated losses for purposes of sentencing guidelines. It vacated the sentences and remanded for resentencing.]

NOTES AND QUESTIONS

1. Limited Versus General Partnerships. Consider the degree to which limited partners are permitted to participate in management without losing the shield of limited liability. Section 303 of the Revised Uniform Limited Partnership Act provides that a limited partner does not take part in the control of the business solely by engaging in one or more enumerated activities. These include, in part, acting as an agent or employee of the limited partnership; consulting with or advising the general partner; requesting or attending a meeting of the partners; and voting on (1) the dissolution of the partnership, (2) the sale or mortgaging of substantially all of the partnership assets, (3) the borrowing of money other than in the ordinary course of business, (4) any amendment to the limited partnership agreement, or (5) the removal of a general partner.

When partnership agreements give these powers to limited partners, the limited partners may have a significant say in how their businesses are run. Nevertheless, courts typically find that limited partners are the types of passive investors in need of the protections of the federal securities laws. So strong is the inclination to treat limited partnership interests as securities that one court found security status even though the holders of limited partnership interests also indirectly participated in management of the trustee general partner. The court emphasized that profits were dependent on others involved in management. *See Liberty Prop. Trust v. Republic Properties Corp.*, 577 F.3d 335 (D.C. Cir. 2009).

A notable exception is *Steinhardt Group, Inc. v. Citicorp*, 126 F.3d 144 (3d Cir. 1997), where the court concluded that a limited partner may have too much control to be a passive investor under *Howey* even though the limited partner's powers did not exceed those permitted under the state's limited partnership statute.

2. *LLC Interests as Securities.* As *Leonard* noted, the limited liability company is a comparatively new alternative to the corporate and partnership forms of organization. Something of a hybrid, the LLC offers its members the benefits of limited liability (a corporate attribute) and a pass-through of tax income and losses (a partnership attribute). Generally, management of the LLC is vested in its members in much the same way as in a general partnership. The statutes, however, typically allow members to opt out of the member-managed default form in favor of centralized management in a manager-managed LLC. Accordingly, member-managed LLCs resemble general partnerships, while manager-managed LLCs approximate limited partnerships, at least insofar as the attribute of centralized management is concerned.

Leonard illustrates that in evaluating whether LLC interests are investment contracts, the analysis parallels that of general and limited partnerships. In contrast with the result reached in *Leonard*, an investment contract was not present in *Robinson v. Glynn*, 349 F.3d 166 (4th Cir. 2003), where an investor sat on his LLC's board of managers and executive committee and served as its treasurer. These positions did not give the investor direct control over management, but they did enable him to oversee his interests to ensure that other managers did not harm his investment. Although the investor lacked the technical experience of the managers, the court noted he was a savvy and experienced businessman who negotiated for significant management rights, and for this reason it concluded his LLC interest was not an investment contract. Similar reasoning was outlined in *Endico v. Fonte*, 485 F. Supp. 2d 411 (S.D.N.Y. 2007), where though the investor was a "babe in the real estate woods" his control of the checking account and his ability to veto a mortgage of partnership assets were sufficient to rebut his claim that because he was a passive investor, the LLC interest he purchased was a security. *See also Iguaçu, Inc. v. Filho*, 2016 U.S. App. LEXIS 3218

(9th Cir. Feb. 24, 2016) (investments in limitadas, the Brazilian equivalent of an LLC, were not securities because investors were actively engaged in management). Yet another case, however, concluded that a requirement that checks be signed by a particular member does not in itself justify a conclusion that the member had significant management authority. *See Sudo Properties, Inc. v. Terrebonne Parish Consol. Gov't*, 2008 U.S. Dist. LEXIS 50559 (E.D. La. July 2, 2008) (involving investment in an arena football team).

3.   Is the Agreement Dispositive?   Should a court look beyond the four corners of an agreement to assess control issues, and at what point is the determination concerning the powers of partners to be made? For both partnerships and LLCs, the issue frequently becomes whether the investors' control options are more theoretical than real. One of the better treatments of the issue is found in *SEC v. Merchant Capital, LLC*, 483 F.3d 747 (11th Cir. 2007), where the court took a hard look at the extent to which investors actually were able to exercise any meaningful control:

> [I]n arguing that the partners did not function as limited partners, Merchant relies primarily on the allegedly substantial powers reserved to the partners through the partnership agreement. The partnership materials informed partners that they were expected to take an active role in the business, and the agreement gave partners certain rights and powers. Partners had the ability to call meetings and hold regular quarterly meetings; the ability to participate in committees; the ability to elect the [Managing General Partner, "MGP"]; the ability to remove the MGP for cause upon a certain vote; the ability to inspect books and records; the ability to approve additional funding; the ability to amend the agreement or to dissolve the partnership upon a two-thirds vote; and the exclusive authority to approve obligations exceeding $5000.
>
> In the first place, the power to name the MGP was not a significant one in this case. Partners were required to turn in their ballots with their capital contribution, before their partnerships had even been formed. The power therefore reveals nothing about the partners' ability to control the business after their initial investment. . . .
>
> The partners also did not have the practical ability to remove Merchant once it was installed as MGP. First, the agreement provided for removal only for cause. . . .
>
> Compounding the legal difficulty in removing Merchant, the investors in an individual partnership were geographically dispersed, with no preexisting relationships. . . . [I]n this case, the lack of face-to-face contact among the partners exacerbated the other difficulties and rendered the supposed power to remove Merchant illusory.[8] . . .
>
> The next power reserved to the partners was the ability to approve all obligations over $5,000. If this power was real, it was a substantial one. . . . However, as shown by Merchant's tenure as MGP, the ballot right also did not give the partners meaningful control over their investment.
>
> First, Merchant controlled how much information appeared in the ballots, and did not submit sufficient information for the partners to be able to make

---

8. For these same reasons, the power to amend or dissolve the partnership agreement was also illusory. Such a move would have required a two-thirds vote of geographically distant, unacquainted partners. This power therefore did not cure the lack of other powers. No amendments were ever made, and no partnerships were ever dissolved.

meaningful decisions to approve or disapprove debt purchases. . . . Second, . . . the partners had no way to force Merchant to heed the results of the process. . . . Merchant repeatedly abused the balloting process [by purchasing more debt than the partners authorized]. . . . Finally, the voting process was tilted in Merchant's favor from the very start. The partnership agreement provided that unreturned and unvoted ballots were voted in favor of management. [T]he ballots always contained insufficient information for investors to make informed decisions. The levers of the voting process were thus in Merchant's hands from the very beginning. . . . We therefore conclude that the voting process was a sham and did not give partners meaningful control over their investment.

Id. at 757-760.

As to whether a court should look beyond the four corners of the agreement, the court looked to "[p]ost-investment events . . . as evidence of how much power partners reserved at the inception." Id. at 760. How relevant are the post-formation activities of partners in evaluating whether the interests they purchased were securities? Should capacity to participate in control be measured only as of the time of the investment? Or should subsequent events inform the inquiry? For a recent application of *Williamson* and endorsement of *Merchant Capital*'s consideration of post-formation developments in determining the original intent of the parties, *see SEC v. Shields*, 744 F.3d 633 (10th Cir. 2014). For recent cases discussing information available to investors as a control factor, *see SEC v. Sethi*, 910 F.3d 198 (5th Cir. 2018) (giving investors "little to no information" is evidence they could not use their legal powers); *SEC v. Arcturus Corp.*, 912 F.3d 786 (5th Cir. 2019) (distinguishing *Merchant Capital* and noting that the fact managers were the sole source of information does not mean investors lacked control, particularly when they were free to communicate with each other).

PROBLEMS

2-11. Hibbert and Hubbert is a law firm headquartered in New York. The firm has more than 400 partners and branch offices in eight cities. Because of the departure of a probate lawyer in the Los Angeles office, Hibbert made an offer of partnership last year to Slickperson, a senior associate in another firm. Under the terms of the offer, Slickperson will make a modest capital contribution of $35,000. Slickperson's income from the partnership will be set by a compensation committee on the basis of Slickperson's productivity (measured by billable hours collected and clients brought to the firm). Slickperson was given only abbreviated financial statements on the firm and was led to believe it would be unseemly to push for more information. No disclosures were made that the partners in the Miami, Washington, D.C., and San Francisco offices were about to leave and establish their own firms. Now the partners have left, leaving the firm in dire financial straits. Is Slickperson's partnership interest a security? Would it make any difference if the firm was a professional corporation, rather than a partnership?

2-12. Venezia Holding, LLC, is organized by three individuals as a member-managed limited liability company to own and manage the Venezia Resort in Florida. Notwithstanding the member-managed designation, the operating agreement designates Bernard Favret as managing member and vests in Favret all day-to-day management authority. Favret has considerable experience in the management of resort properties. The three members of the LLC have equal voting rights, and each member has the right to inspect the books and records at any time. A two-thirds vote is required to remove Favret as manager and designate a substitute. Are the non-manager members purchasing securities? *See Venezia Amos, LLC v. Favret*, 2008 U.S. Dist. LEXIS 10452 (N.D. Fla. Feb. 12, 2008). What if the agreement provided that any check over $1,000 had to be cosigned by one of the two non-manager members?

3. The Policy Question: Should Investment Contract Status Be Elective?

The above discussion of stock, partnership interests, and LLC interests illustrates how the associational form may affect the question of whether a given investment involves a security. Keying application of the securities to the form of business association selected gives rise to an important, and controversial, private ordering opportunity. If corporate stock, limited partnership interests, and interests in manager-managed LLCs generally are securities, while general partnership interests and interests in member-managed LLCs generally are not securities, promoters may control application of the securities acts through the expedient of choosing one form of association over another. Normally, one would expect promoters to attempt to discourage litigation by disgruntled investors through the technique of organizing the business venture under a form that does not involve application of the securities acts (or so they hope). Some investors will resist this effort or otherwise discount investments not under the securities acts, but others may lack the sophistication to fully appreciate the consequences of associational form. In either case, the opt-out possibilities suggested here are difficult to square with the anti-waiver provisions of the securities acts.

The issue has not escaped the attention of scholars. Professor McGinty has proposed that LLC investors be allowed to opt out of securities law coverage, provided they are notified in advance of their investments that the securities laws will not apply. *See* McGinty, The Limited Liability Company: Opportunity for Selective Securities Law Deregulation, 64 U. Cin. L. Rev. 369 (1996). Professor Ribstein favored the "bright-line" approach (outlined above) allowing investors to effectively waive securities law coverage through the choice of their associational form; under this approach, investments in corporate stock and limited partnership interests would be securities, while investments in general partnership and limited liability company interests would not be securities. *See* Ribstein, Form and Substance in the Definition of a "Security": The Case of Limited Liability Companies, 51 Wash. & Lee L. Rev. 807 (1994). *See also* Welle, Freedom of Contract and the Securities Laws: Opting Out of Securities Regulation by Private Agreement, 56 Wash. & Lee L. Rev. 519, 570-571 (1999) (doubting that either approach would achieve its intended goals because promoters would act opportunistically to circumvent the application of securities law).

E. Real Estate as Securities

The standard real estate transaction in the form of a sale or lease of property does not involve the offer of a security. When the seller or its affiliates offer collateral arrangements promising post-acquisition income to the buyer, however, an investment contract may be present.

The presence of a security may be asserted in real estate promotions that emphasize appreciation based upon property development efforts of the promoters or others. Particularly common are cases involving sales of residential lots promoted with representations concerning future development activities. Unless those development activities will be accomplished by the promoters, however, it is unlikely that the sale of undeveloped real estate will involve securities. This point is aptly illustrated by *Rodriguez v. Banco Central Corp., Inc.*, 990 F.2d 7 (1st Cir. 1993), where the land was Florida swamp. In finding that the purchasers (who for the most part had intended to build homes on their lots) had *not* purchased investment contracts, the court emphasized that the promoters never promised to develop the community themselves:

> [T]he most that can be said is that the promoter left the distinct, and distinctly false, impression that a community was going to develop through natural forces. Many buyers were told that Disney World's presence nearby would spur growth. . . . Accordingly, . . . there is no pretence of a "common enterprise" managed by the promoter and hence no "security."

Id. at 11-12.

Issues involving real estate as securities often arise in the context of resort condominiums that will not be full-time residences of the purchasers. The leading case is *Hocking v. Dubois*, 885 F.2d 1449 (9th Cir. 1989) (en banc), *cert. denied*, 494 U.S. 1078 (1990), where Gerald Hocking, a Nevada resident, purchased a condominium in a resort complex in Hawaii. Although many of the units in the complex were short-term rentals, the sellers in this case had occupied their unit (hence this was a resale transaction). Hocking was shown the condominium by Dubois, a real estate broker, who explained to him that the condominium could be put in an optional rental pool operated by a third party unaffiliated with the sellers and the agent.

The key feature of a rental pool is that income and expenses of all units in the pool are divided pro rata among the investors (recall this type of pooling structure was present in *Howey*). Pooling is to be contrasted with a separate accounting arrangement in which income and expenses would not be pooled and instead would be separately assigned to the specific units. Hocking calculated the likely cash flow from rentals based on information on the daily rental rate provided by Dubois. He liked the look of these numbers, purchased the condo, and put it in the rental pool.

Had he heeded the sage advice of Alexander Pope ("Blessed is he who expects nothing, for he shall never be disappointed."), Hocking would have accepted the unexpectedly low cash flow from rentals and the eventual foreclosure on his condo. But Hocking was indeed disappointed rather than sanguine. So Hocking sued the broker for securities fraud.

Applying *Howey*'s investment contract analysis, the Ninth Circuit noted that Hocking made an investment of money in a *package* that included the condominium and the rental pool arrangement. This likely satisfied the Ninth Circuit's horizontal commonality standard. But was Hocking looking solely to the efforts of others as the source of his profits? Here, Hocking's inability to control the rental management is the relevant inquiry going forward:

> [H]ocking's investment is a unit in a resort condominium . . . with many investors pooling their units together. In order for Hocking to replace HCP, he would have to gain the votes of 75 percent of participating investors. These facts alone create a real question whether Hocking was stuck with HCP as a rental manager. Had Hocking purchased a residential condominium for investment purposes, to be rented out to long-term tenants, then it would have been a relatively easy matter to switch rental agents. Managing a resort operated as a hotel . . . may be a much more difficult service to replace than that of a long-term leasing agent. The commercial viability of a one-room hotel does not strongly argue for separate management. . . .

Id. at 1461.

The lesson of *Hocking* is that the "package" may be crucial to the question of whether the transaction involves a security. The simple purchase of a condominium is not a transaction under the federal securities laws. When something is added, like putting the condominium under the long-term control of a third party charged with renting the purchased unit as well as other units in the complex, then things may change. But what is a package? The more recent case below, also from the Ninth Circuit, explores this important nuance.

Salameh v. Tarsadia Hotel
726 F.3d 1124 (9th Cir. 2013)

GOULD, Circuit Judge:

A transaction that looks nothing like a sale of stock and involving such diverse items as citrus groves and vacation homes may qualify as a sale of a security under federal law. . . . Here, we must decide whether Plaintiffs-Appellants have alleged the sale of a security based on their purchase of condominiums in the Hard Rock Hotel San Diego. . . .

The Hotel is a twelve-story, mixed-use development with commercial space and 420 condominium units. Through television and print advertising, the public was offered the opportunity to buy condominiums in the Hotel. Plaintiffs each did so and later signed a rental-management agreement. Plaintiffs complain that the Purchase Contract they executed with 5th Rock, LLC not only sold them their condominiums but also obligated them to enter into the Rental Management Agreement with Tarsadia Hotels. Even though these contracts were executed with distinct entities eight to fifteen months apart, Plaintiffs allege that these contracts together form an investment contract because Plaintiffs have no control over their units and expect a profit only through the efforts of the Hotel developer and operator. For example, Plaintiffs were not issued keys to their units but had to obtain keys from the Hotel operator when staying in their units. The units had to be operated as part of the Hotel, and certain Defendants were responsible for daily management, operation, and marketing of the units. Plaintiffs also note that a local zoning ordinance prohibited them from occupying their units for more than 28 days per year. . . .

The crux of Plaintiffs' claims is that the sale of the hotel condominiums and the later Rental Management Agreement together constituted the sale of a security. We disagree and hold that the transactions did not constitute the sale of a security. . . .

What matters is the economic reality of the transaction. So long as money is invested in a common enterprise with profits anticipated by virtue of others' work, there may be an investment contract.

In *Hocking v. Dubois*, [885 F.2d 1449 (9th Cir. 1990),] sitting en banc, we held that there was a genuine issue of material fact whether the sale of a condominium along with a rent-pooling arrangement constituted a security. Hocking worked with real-estate agent Dubois to find a condominium that he could use as an investment. *Hocking*, 885 F.2d at 1452. Dubois found a condominium in a resort complex and told Hocking that if he would buy the condominium, a rent-pooling arrangement [where each owner receives a pro rata share of the rental income, whether or not his individual unit has actually been rented] would be available. . . . The record showed and we emphasized "that but for the availability of the rental pool arrangement [Hocking] would not have purchased the condominium." Id. at 1453, 1455, 1458; *see also* id. at 1466 (Norris, J., dissenting).

We held that there was a genuine issue of material fact as to whether Dubois had offered Hocking the sale of a security. . . .

Closely examining what had induced the sale, we held that there was a fact issue where Hocking had "put forward numerous facts concerning whether the condominium sale and rental agreements were presented to him as parts of one transaction." Id. at 1458. "We also cannot ignore the fact that . . . these agreements were entered into immediately following the purchase of the condominium." Id. We stressed that these facts "distinguish this case from a situation where, after a purchase and separate from any inducement to purchase, a [broker] arranges for a rental pool." Id. We then applied the *Howey* factors to the package of contracts and held that there was a genuine issue of material fact as to whether Dubois offered Hocking a security.

Here, by contrast, Plaintiffs' allegations are not sufficient to show that a security was sold when the condominiums were transferred. Plaintiffs allege no facts showing that the Purchase Contracts and the Rental Management Agreements were offered as a package. They do not allege that the Rental Management Agreement was promoted at the time of the sale. They do not allege that Defendants told them that the Rental Management Agreement would be forthcoming. They do not allege that they were told that the Rental Management Agreement would result in investment-like profits. . . .

Plaintiffs allege that representations in the Hotel Guide and the Rental Management Agreement FAQs show that the Purchase Contract and Rental Management Agreement were a package, but they plead no facts establishing when the Guide and the FAQs were given to them. . . . A large time gap between the real-estate purchase and the execution of a rental-management agreement may not be dispositive in every case. . . . Yet here, where Plaintiffs did not allege that the contracts were presented at the same time, the large time gap underscores our holding that Plaintiffs were not offered a security.

Plaintiffs' strongest argument that the two contracts, signed about a year apart, form a single transaction is their assertion that the "economic reality" shows that the two transactions are part and parcel of one scheme. They contend that the Purchase Contract, combined with external factors, such as the zoning ordinance, gave them no choice but to sign the Rental Management Agreement when it was later presented. This argument has some force. But to accept this argument, we not only would have to ignore the large time gap between the two transactions that were executed with different entities, but also the fact that Plaintiffs' complaint is void of any allegation that they were induced to buy the condominiums by the Rental Management Agreement. The economic reality as we see it is that these two transactions were distinct. . . .

Taking all non-conclusory facts alleged in the complaint as true, we hold that Plaintiffs have not alleged the sale of a security and thus have not stated claims for relief under federal or state securities law. . . .

NOTES AND QUESTIONS

1.   *Residential Condominiums as Common Enterprises.* *Hocking* found the pooling of rents sufficient to satisfy the horizontal common enterprise standard applied by the Ninth Circuit (which also accepts the alternative of strict vertical commonality). Pooling may be a critical factor, as is evident in the decisions of other courts reaching contrary conclusions on common enterprise grounds. In *Revak v. SEC Realty Corp.*, 18 F.3d 81 (2d Cir. 1994), the Second Circuit found that the lack of a pooling of rents defeated horizontal commonality and rejected broad vertical commonality as sufficient to satisfy *Howey* (leaving to another day the question of whether strict vertical commonality would be sufficient). In *Wals v. Fox Hills Development Corp.*, 24 F.3d 1016 (7th Cir. 1994), the Seventh Circuit held that the timeshare interest before it was not a security because there was no pooling of profits necessary to meet horizontal commonality under *Howey*. On the other hand, in *Baroi v. Platinum Condo. Dev., LLC*, 2012 U.S. Dist. LEXIS 95724 (D. Nev. July 10, 2012), the court looked to federal law in determining whether an investment contract existed under Nevada law and found that a condominium sale and rental agreement package satisfied the common enterprise standard even though rents would not be pooled; the sharing of rental profits by the promoters and investors established strict vertical commonality sufficient to establish an investment contract.

2.   *Are State Law Remedies Inadequate?* Why isn't the state law of fraud an adequate basis of relief for those able to establish fraud in real estate transactions? *Cf. Rodriguez v. Banco Cent. Corp., Inc.*, 990 F.2d 7 (1st Cir. 1993) (concluding defrauded Puerto Rican real estate purchasers had not purchased securities, but had ample remedies under Puerto Rican law).

PROBLEMS

(handwritten margin notes:
don't think
so, still
passes risk-
capital test
Still vertical
Commonality ⊢
broad variation
commonality
↓
Still need
Production)

2-13. Purchasers of condominiums in a resort complex are invited to put their units in a rental program with a simulated pooling feature. Rather than generally pooling the income and expenses of units available for rental, as was the case in *Hocking*, income and expenses are allocated to the units actually rented for the periods of their rentals. Through an automated unit assignment system, however, renters are assigned to available units in a way that assures a fair allocation of rental income among the owners, so the net effect approximates that of pooling even though separate accounting is employed. Does the simulated rather than real pooling sufficiently distinguish the rental program from that present in *Hocking* to justify a different result in this case? *See* One Central Park West, SEC No-Action Letter (Nov. 2, 1995).

2-14. Some utilities have developed a "net metering" program that allows customers to offset electricity they consume with electricity they are able to generate on their properties through use of solar panels (typically roof-top). To accommodate property owners who are unable to install solar panels where they live, CommunitySun, LLC proposes to offer and sell real estate interests in a solar facility. Each interest will be dubbed a "SolarCondo" and for state law purposes will be regulated as a condominium.

The purchaser of a SolarCondo will be offered a net metering arrangement under which the owner's portion of the electric energy generated at the solar facility will be transmitted to the utility's grid, and that energy will be offset by the utility against the energy consumed by the SolarCondo owner at her residence or business, the same as if it were produced on-site through rooftop solar panels. The only benefit a SolarCondo owner will enjoy through net metering is a reduction in her utility bills. If she consumes no electricity, she receives no benefit.

Although SolarCondos do not have separate meters because individual metering is not cost effective, the owners of SolarCondos will be credited individually with output based on their proportionate share of the aggregate output of the entire facility. CommunitySun will make reasonable efforts to ensure that the amount credited to each owner matches the output of that owner's SolarCondo. For example, the credit will be adjusted to reflect the number of days that a particular SolarCondo is not producing due to maintenance or other reasons.

SolarCondos will be marketed as investment opportunities. Although a SolarCondo may be resold for a profit (but only to a purchaser who lives in the service area), the lifespan of the solar panels is only 20 years, which means fairly rapid depreciation in the asset value is likely to limit any profit upside.

Is the purchaser of a SolarCondo buying a security? *See* CommunitySun LLC, SEC No-Action Letter (Aug. 29, 2011).

F.   Notes as Securities

The '33 Act and '34 Act differ slightly in their treatment of notes. Section 2(1) of the '33 Act includes in the statutory definition of a security "any note," but Section 3(a)(3) then exempts from the registration requirements a note that "arises out of a current transaction or the proceeds of which have been or are to be used for current transactions" and that will mature within nine months; Section 17(c) makes it clear that this exemption does not extend to the '33 Act's antifraud provisions. In contrast, the '34 Act's relevant inclusion and exclusion occur within the definitional section: Section 3(a)(10) describes as a security "any note," but then proceeds to exclude from coverage of the statute those notes with maturities of less than nine months. At least in theory, the differing treatment means that short-term notes are exempt altogether from the '34 Act, but are still subject to the provisions of the '33 Act other than those dealing with registration.

Although some short-term notes fall outside the statutes, any note with a maturity exceeding nine months would seem to come squarely within the statutory definitions of a security. Most courts and commentators, however, have been unwilling to conclude that transactions such as home mortgages, consumer installment purchases, and ordinary commercial financing involve securities. As one exasperated court observed, "If it had intended, in legislation entitled the 'Securities Exchange Act,' to extend federal jurisdiction to transactions of this type, Congress most certainly would have given a real indication of such an intent." *Lino v. City Investing Co.*, 487 F.2d 689, 695 (3d Cir. 1973). *But see* Rosin, Historical Perspectives on the Definition of a Security, 28 S. Tex. L. Rev. 575, 584-585 (1987) (arguing the legislative history reveals Congress did so intend).

Initially, courts began using the "context clause" qualification on the definition of a security to develop more discriminating approaches toward the coverage of notes under the securities laws. Methodologies varied among the circuits, however, and the Supreme Court's grant of certiorari in the case below prompted some optimism that the Court might develop a cohesive theory for determining the circumstances under which notes are subject to regulation as securities.

Reves v. Ernst & Young
494 U.S. 56 (1990)

MARSHALL, J. This case presents the question whether certain demand notes issued by the Farmer's Cooperative of Arkansas and Oklahoma are "securities" within the meaning of §3(a)(10) of the Securities Exchange Act of 1934. We conclude that they are.

I

The Co-op is an agricultural cooperative that [had] approximately 23,000 members. In order to raise money to support its general business operations, the Co-op sold promissory notes payable on demand by the holder. Although the notes were uncollateralized and uninsured, they paid a variable rate of interest that was adjusted monthly to keep it higher than the rate paid by local financial institutions. The Co-op offered the notes to both members and nonmembers, marketing the scheme as an "Investment Program." . . . Despite [assurances that investments were safe], the Co-op filed for bankruptcy in 1984. At the time of the filing, over 1,600 people held notes worth a total of $10 million.

After the Co-op filed for bankruptcy, petitioners, a class of holders of the notes, filed suit against Arthur Young & Co., the firm that had audited the Co-op's financial statements (and the predecessor to respondent Ernst & Young). . . . Petitioners maintained that, had Arthur Young properly treated the plant in its audits, they would not have purchased demand notes because the Co-op's insolvency would have been apparent. . . .

II

A

This case requires us to decide whether the note issued by the Co-op is a "security" within the meaning of the 1934 Act. . . .

In defining the scope of the market that it wished to regulate, Congress painted with a broad brush . . . [and] enacted a definition of "security" sufficiently broad to encompass virtually any instrument that might be sold as an investment. . . .

[In] discharging our duty, we are not bound by legal formalisms, but instead take account of the economics of the transaction under investigation. . . . Congress' purpose in enacting the securities laws was to regulate investments, in whatever form they are made and by whatever name they are called.

[S]ome instruments are obviously within the class Congress intended to regulate because they are by their nature investments. In *Landreth Timber Co. v. Landreth*, 471 U.S. 681 (1985), we held that an instrument bearing the name "stock" that, among other things, is negotiable, offers the possibility of capital appreciation, and carries the right to dividends contingent on the profits of a business enterprise is plainly within the class of instruments Congress intended the securities laws to cover. . . . [T]he public perception of common stock as the paradigm of a security suggests that stock, in whatever context it is sold, should be treated as within the ambit of the Acts.

We made clear in *Landreth Timber* that stock was a special case, explicitly limiting our holding to that sort of instrument. . . . While common stock is the quintessence of a security . . . the same simply cannot be said of notes, which are used in a variety of settings, not all of which involve investments. Thus, the phrase "any note" should not be interpreted to mean literally "any note," but must be understood against the backdrop of what Congress was attempting to accomplish in enacting the Securities Acts.

Because the *Landreth Timber* formula cannot sensibly be applied to notes, some other principle must be developed to define the term "note." A majority of the Courts of Appeals that have considered the issue have adopted, in varying forms, "investment versus commercial" approaches that distinguish, on the basis of all of the circumstances surrounding the transactions, notes issued in an investment context (which are "securities") from notes issued in a commercial or consumer context (which are not). . . .

The Second Circuit's "family resemblance" approach begins with a presumption that any note with a term of more than nine months is a "security." *See, e.g., Exchange Natl. Bank of Chicago v. Touche Ross & Co.*, 544 F.2d 1126, 1137 (CA2 1976). Recognizing that not all notes are securities, however, the Second

Circuit has also devised a list of notes that it has decided are obviously not securities. Accordingly, the "family resemblance" test permits an issuer to rebut the presumption that a note is a security if it can show that the note in question "bear[s] a strong family resemblance" to an item on the judicially crafted list of exceptions . . . or convinces the court to add a new instrument to the list. *See, e.g., Chemical Bank v. Arthur Andersen & Co.*, 726 F.2d 930, 939 (CA2 1984).

In contrast, the Eighth and District of Columbia Circuits apply the test we created in *SEC v. W.J. Howey Co.*, 328 U.S. 293 (1946), to determine whether an instrument is an "investment contract" to the determination whether an instrument is a "note." . . . *See also Underhill v. Royal*, 769 F.2d 1426, 1431 (CA9 1985) (setting forth what it terms a "risk capital" approach that is virtually identical to the *Howey* test).

We reject the approaches of those courts that have applied the *Howey* test to notes; *Howey* provides a mechanism for determining whether an instrument is an "investment contract." The demand notes here may well not be "investment contracts," but that does not mean they are not "notes." To hold that a "note" is not a "security" unless it meets a test designed for an entirely different variety of instrument "would make the Acts' enumeration of many types of instruments superfluous," *Landreth Timber*, 471 U.S., at 692, and would be inconsistent with Congress' intent to regulate the entire body of instruments sold as investments.

The other two contenders—the "family resemblance" and "investment versus commercial" tests—are really two ways of formulating the same general approach. Because we think the "family resemblance" test provides a more promising framework for analysis, however, we adopt it. The test begins with the language of the statute; because the Securities Acts define "security" to include "any note," we begin with a presumption that every note is a security. We nonetheless recognize that this presumption cannot be irrebuttable. . . . Congress was concerned with regulating the investment market, not with creating a general federal cause of action for fraud. In an attempt to give more content to that dividing line, the Second Circuit has identified a list of instruments commonly denominated "notes" that nonetheless fall without the "security" category. *See Exchange Natl. Bank*, supra, at 1138 (types of notes that are not "securities" include "the note delivered in consumer financing, the note secured by a mortgage on a home, the short-term note secured by a lien on a small business or some of its assets, the note evidencing a 'character' loan to a bank customer, short-term notes secured by an assignment of accounts receivable, or a note which simply formalizes an open-account debt incurred in the ordinary course of business (particularly if, as in the case of the customer of a broker, it is collateralized)"); *Chemical Bank*, supra, at 939 (adding to the list "notes evidencing loans by commercial banks for current operations").

We agree that the items identified by the Second Circuit are not properly viewed as "securities." More guidance, though, is needed. It is impossible to make any meaningful inquiry into whether an instrument bears a "resemblance" to one of the instruments identified by the Second Circuit without specifying what it is about those instruments that makes them non-securities.

An examination of the list itself makes clear what those standards should be. In creating its list, the Second Circuit was applying the same factors that this Court has held apply in deciding whether a transaction involves a "security." First, we examine the transaction to assess the motivations that would prompt a reasonable seller and buyer to enter into it. If the seller's purpose is to raise money for the general use of a business enterprise or to finance substantial investments and the buyer is interested primarily in the profit the note is expected to generate, the instrument is likely to be a "security." If the note is exchanged to facilitate the purchase and sale of a minor asset or consumer good, to correct for the seller's cash-flow difficulties, or to advance some other commercial or consumer purpose, on the other hand, the note is less sensibly described as a "security." *See, e.g., Forman,* 421 U.S., at 851 (share of "stock" carrying a right to subsidized housing not a security because "the inducement to purchase was solely to acquire subsidized low-cost living space; it was not to invest for profit"). Second, we examine the "plan of distribution" of the instrument, *SEC v. C.M. Joiner Leasing Corp.,* 320 U.S. 344, 353 (1943), to determine whether it is an instrument in which there is "common trading for speculation or investment," id., at 351. Third, we examine the reasonable expectations of the investing public: The Court will consider instruments to be "securities" on the basis of such public expectations, even where an economic analysis of the circumstances of the particular transaction might suggest that the instruments are not "securities" as used in that transaction. . . . Finally, we examine whether some factor such as the existence of another regulatory scheme significantly reduces the risk of the instrument, thereby rendering application of the Securities Acts unnecessary. *See, e.g., Marine Bank,* 455 U.S., at 557-559, and n.7.

We conclude, then, that in determining whether an instrument denominated a "note" is a "security," courts are to apply the version of the "family resemblance" test that we have articulated here: a note is presumed to be a "security," and that presumption may be rebutted only by a showing that the note bears a strong resemblance (in terms of the four factors we have identified) to one of the enumerated categories of instrument. If an instrument is not sufficiently similar to an item on the list, the decision whether another category should be added is to be made by examining the same factors.

B

Applying the family resemblance approach to this case, we have little difficulty in concluding that the notes at issue here are "securities." Ernst & Young admits that "a demand note does not closely resemble any of the Second Circuit's family resemblance examples." Nor does an examination of the four factors we have identified as being relevant to our inquiry suggest that the demand notes here are not "securities" despite their lack of similarity to any of the enumerated categories. The Co-op sold the notes in an effort to raise capital for its general business operations, and purchasers bought them in order to earn a profit in the form of interest. Indeed, one of the primary inducements offered purchasers was an interest rate constantly revised to keep it slightly above the rate paid by local banks and savings and loans. From both sides, then, the transaction is most naturally conceived as an investment in a business enterprise rather than as a purely commercial or consumer transaction.

As to the plan of distribution, the Co-op offered the notes over an extended period to its 23,000 members, as well as to nonmembers, and more than 1,600 people held notes when the Co-op filed for bankruptcy. To be sure, the notes were not traded on an exchange. They were, however, offered and sold to a broad segment of the public, and that is all we have held to be necessary to establish the requisite "common trading" in an instrument. . . .

The third factor—the public's reasonable perceptions—also supports a finding that the notes in this case are "securities." . . . The advertisements for the notes here characterized them as "investments," and there were no countervailing factors that would have led a reasonable person to question this characterization. . . .

Finally, we find no risk-reducing factor to suggest that these instruments are not in fact securities. The notes are uncollateralized and uninsured. Moreover, unlike the certificates of deposit in *Marine Bank,* which were insured by the Federal Deposit Insurance Corporation and subject to substantial regulation under the federal banking laws, and unlike the pension plan in *Teamsters v. Daniel* which was comprehensively regulated under the Employee Retirement Income Security Act of 1974, the notes here would escape federal regulation entirely if the Acts were held not to apply.

The court below found that "[t]he demand nature of the notes is very uncharacteristic of a security," on the theory that the virtually instant liquidity associated with demand notes is inconsistent with the risk ordinarily associated with "securities." This argument is unpersuasive. Common stock traded on a national exchange is the paradigm of a security, and it is as readily convertible into cash as is a demand note. The same is true of publicly traded corporate bonds, debentures, and any number of other instruments that are plainly within the purview of the Acts. The demand feature of a note does permit a holder to eliminate risk quickly by making a demand, but just as with publicly traded stock, the liquidity of the instrument does not eliminate risk all together. . . . We therefore hold that the notes at issue here are within the term "note" in §3(a)(10).

III

Relying on the exception in the statute for "any note . . . which has a maturity at the time of issuance of not exceeding nine months," respondent contends that the notes here are not "securities," even if they would otherwise qualify. Respondent cites Arkansas cases standing for the proposition that, in the context of the state statute of limitations, "[a] note payable on demand is due immediately." . . . Respondent concludes from [this] rule that the "maturity" of a demand note within the meaning of §3(a)(10) is immediate, which is, of course, less than nine months. . . .

Petitioners counter that the "plain words" of the exclusion should not govern. Petitioners cite legislative history of a similar provision of the 1933 Act [§3(a)(3)] for the proposition that the purpose of the exclusion is to except from the coverage of the Acts only commercial paper—short-term, high quality instruments issued to fund current operations and sold only to highly sophisticated investors. . . . If petitioners are correct that the exclusion is intended to cover only commercial paper, these notes, which were sold in a large scale offering to unsophisticated members of the public, plainly should not fall within the exclusion.

We need not decide, however, whether petitioners' interpretation of the exception is correct, for we conclude that even if we give literal effect to the exception, the notes do not fall within its terms. . . .

If it is plausible to regard a demand note as having an immediate maturity because demand could be made immediately, it is also plausible to regard the maturity of a demand note as being in excess of nine months because demand could be made many years or decades into the future. Given this ambiguity, the exclusion must be interpreted in accordance with its purpose. [W]e will assume for argument's sake that petitioners are incorrect in their view that the exclusion is intended to exempt only commercial paper. Respondent presents no competing view to explain why Congress would have enacted respondent's version of the exclusion, however, and the only theory that we can imagine that would support respondent's interpretation is that Congress intended to create a bright-line rule exempting from the 1934 Act's coverage all notes of less than nine months' duration, because short-term notes are, as a general rule, sufficiently safe that the Securities Acts need not apply. As we have said, however, demand notes do not necessarily have short terms. In light of Congress' broader purpose in the Acts of ensuring that investments of all descriptions be regulated to prevent fraud and abuse, we interpret the exception not to cover the demand notes at issue here. Although the result might be different if the design of the transaction suggested that both parties contemplated that demand would be made within the statutory period, that is not the case before us.

IV

For the foregoing reasons, we conclude that the demand notes at issue here fall under the "note" category of instruments that are "securities" under the 1933 and 1934 Acts. We also conclude that, even under a respondent's preferred approach to §3(a)(10)'s exclusion for short-term notes, these demand notes do not fall within the exclusion. . . .

Justice STEVENS, concurring. While I join the Court's opinion, an important additional consideration supports my conclusion that these notes are securities notwithstanding the statute's exclusion for currency and commercial paper that has a maturity of no more than nine months. *See* §3(a)(10) of the Securities Exchange Act of 1934. The Courts of Appeals have been unanimous in rejecting a literal reading of that exclusion. They have instead concluded that "when Congress spoke of notes with a maturity not exceeding nine months, it meant commercial paper, not investment securities." *Sanders v. John Nuveen & Co.*, 463 F.2d 1075, 1080 (CA7 1972), *cert. denied*, 409 U.S. 1009 (1972). . . .

The legislative history of §3(a)(3) of the 1933 Act indicates that the exclusion was intended to cover only commercial paper, and the SEC has so construed it. . . . As the Courts of Appeals have agreed, there is no apparent reason to construe §3(a)(10) of the 1934 Act differently. . . .

Chief Justice REHNQUIST, with whom Justice WHITE, Justice O'CONNOR, and Justice SCALIA join, concurring in part and dissenting in part. I join Part II of the Court's opinion, but dissent from Part III and the statements of the Court's judgment in Parts I and IV. In Part III, the Court holds that these notes were not covered by the statutory exemption for "any note . . . which has a maturity at the time of issuance of not exceeding nine months." . . .

In construing any terms whose meanings are less than plain, we depend on the common understanding of those terms at the time of the statute's creation. . . . Pursuant to the dominant consensus in the case law, instruments payable on demand were considered immediately "due" such that an action could be brought at any time without any other demand than the suit. . . .

Accordingly, in the absence of some compelling indication to the contrary, the maturity date exemption must encompass demand notes because they possess "maturity at the time of issuance of not exceeding nine months."

Petitioners and the lower court decisions cited by Justice Stevens rely, virtually exclusively, on the legislative history of §3(a)(3) of the 1933 Act for the proposition that the terms "any note" in the exemption of §3(a)(10) of the 1934 Act encompass only notes having the character of short-term "commercial paper" exchanged among sophisticated traders. I am not altogether convinced that the legislative history of §3(a)(3) supports that interpretation even with respect to the terms "any note" in the exemption in §3(a)(3), and to bodily transpose that legislative history to another statute has little to commend it as a method of statutory construction.

The legislative history of the 1934 Act—under which this case arises— contains nothing which would support a restrictive reading of the exemption in question. . . .

The plausibility of imputing a restrictive reading to §3(a)(10) from the legislative history of §3(a)(3) is further weakened by the imperfect analogy between the two provisions in terms of both phraseology and nature. Section 3(a)(10) lacks the cryptic phrase in §3(a)(3) which qualifies the class of instruments eligible for exemption as those arising "out of [] current transaction[s] or the proceeds of which have been or are to be used for current transactions. . . ." While that passage somehow may strengthen an argument for limiting the exemption in §3(a)(3) to commercial paper, its absence in §3(a)(10) conversely militates against placing the same limitation thereon.

The exemption in §3(a)(3) excepts the short-term instruments it covers solely from the registration requirements of the 1933 Act. The same instruments are not exempted from the 1933 Act's anti-fraud provisions. . . . By contrast, the exemption in §3(a)(10) of the 1934 Act exempts instruments encompassed thereunder from the entirety of the coverage of the 1934 Act including, conspicuously, the Act's anti-fraud provisions. . . .

In sum, there is no justification for looking beyond the plain terms of §3(a)(10), save for ascertaining the meaning of "maturity" with respect to demand notes. That inquiry reveals that the co-op's demand notes come within the purview of the section's exemption for short-term securities. I would therefore affirm the judgment of the Court of Appeals, though on different reasoning.

NOTES AND QUESTIONS

1. The Commercial Paper Exemption in the '33 Act. Chapter 8 will explore in some depth the exemption contained in Section 3(a)(3) of the '33 Act for notes the proceeds of which are to be used for "current transactions" and the maturities of which do not exceed nine months. Although *Reves* involved the definition of a security under Section 3(a)(10) of the '34 Act and not the scope of the

Section 3(a)(3) exemption under the '33 Act, the '34 Act's exclusion from the coverage of the statute of notes with maturities of less than nine months raises the issue of whether the '33 Act's exemption parallels the '34 Act's definition.

Prior to *Reves*, it generally was assumed that the '33 Act exemption and '34 Act definition excluded the same types of notes. The SEC and the courts have treated the '33 Act exemption as available only for "commercial paper," which is a generic term used to describe the unsecured promissory notes issued in large denominations by very large, financially sound companies and purchased by institutional investors. *See, e.g., SEC v. Tee to Green Golf Parks, Inc.*, 2011 U.S. Dist. LEXIS 4388 (W.D.N.Y. Jan. 18, 2011) (short-term notes sold by issuer that could not be described as high quality are not commercial paper); *Fox v. Dream Trust*, 743 F. Supp. 2d 389, 401 (D.N.J. 2010) (short-term notes issued to finance real estate activities of borrower with serious cash flow problems are not commercial paper).

The notes in *Reves* clearly were not commercial paper. Only Justice Stevens, however, concluded that Section 3(a)(3) of the '33 Act and Section 3(a)(10) of the '34 Act should not be construed differently. Four dissenting Justices were unwilling to construe the sections in a parallel fashion and went so far as to imply that limiting the Section 3(a)(3) exemption to commercial paper might be inappropriate.

2.   Demand Notes.   What is the maturity of a note payable on demand? The *Reves* majority concluded that the demand notes issued by Co-op did not have immediate maturities, presumably because the parties did not contemplate that demand would be made within nine months. If the character of demand notes is to turn on the parties' intent, how will the requisite states of mind be determined? Along this line, consider a case involving short-term loans to National Football League prospects awaiting signing bonuses. As in *Reves*, the notes were demand notes, but the fact that they did not accrue additional interest after five months was an important factor in the court's conclusion that the notes were short term and not securities. *See Asset Prot. Plans, Inc. v. Oppenheimer & Co.*, 2011 U.S. Dist. LEXIS 68959 (M.D. Fla. June 27, 2011).

Should courts examine the intent of each purchaser? Or should they assess a "collective" state of mind? If the latter, will past practices be determinative, so that, if the majority of noteholders did not demand payment within nine months, the notes will be treated as securities? And if that is the case, why is past practice determinative of the character of an instrument when the '33 and '34 Acts speak of maturity *at the time of issuance*?

3.   The Relevance of Risk.   The *Reves* majority rejected the Ninth Circuit's risk capital test as a basis for determining which notes are securities. Yet risk remains relevant under the four-factor test outlined in the opinion. Is risk of the same importance in the investment contract definition? If not, why is risk relevant to the issue of whether notes are securities? For an economic analysis of risk and a framework for defining a security based upon risk, *see* Corgill, Securities as Investments at Risk, 67 Tul. L. Rev. 861 (1993).

4.   Regulation as a Risk-Reduction Factor.   One of the more intriguing aspects of *Reves* is the Court's discussion of risk reduction through alternative regulatory schemes. *Reves* is not the first Supreme Court decision treating regulation as relevant to the definition of a security analysis. In *International Brotherhood of Teamsters v. Daniel*, 439 U.S. 551, 559 (1979), the Court pointed to the existence of the Employee Retirement Security Act of 1974 to support its conclusion that interests in pension plans are not securities. Similarly, in *Marine Bank v. Weaver*, 455 U.S. 551, 559 (1982) (supra), the Court found that a bank certificate of deposit was not a security because "the holders of bank certificates of deposit are abundantly protected under the federal banking laws."

What type of regulatory scheme should reduce risk to an extent sufficient to affect whether the transaction involves a security? The bankruptcy laws, which exist to protect the interests of creditors, are insufficient as a regulatory scheme to satisfy this risk reduction factor, a point that should be obvious in light of the bankruptcy of the issuer in *Reves*. *See also Delgado v. Ctr. on Children, Inc.*, 2012 U.S. Dist. LEXIS 97251, at *5 (E.D. La. July 13, 2012) ("Although state law relief for breach of the promissory notes or relief through federal bankruptcy law may be available to Plaintiffs, this relief falls short of the comprehensive regulatory schemes that have exempted notes from classification as *securities* in other cases.").

Post-*Reves* decisions have been reluctant to equate regulation with risk reduction, at least for purposes of determining whether notes are securities. In *Holloway v. Peat, Marwick, Mitchell & Co.*, 900 F.2d 1485 (10th Cir. 1990), for example, the Tenth Circuit concluded that state regulation of the transaction should not be a factor governing application of the remedial securities laws, but hinted that federal banking regulation would be a risk-reducing factor under *Reves*. *See also Banco Espanol de Credito v. Sec'y Pac. Nat'l Bank*, 973 F.2d 51 (2d Cir. 1992), *cert. denied*, 509 U.S. 903 (1993) (Comptroller of the Currency regulations render application of securities laws unnecessary). Other courts have suggested that federal banking regulation is designed to protect the stability of banks, rather than to protect investors, and, accordingly, is not a risk-reducing factor under *Reves*. *See, e.g., Procter & Gamble Co. v. Bankers Trust Co.*, 925 F. Supp. 1270 (S.D. Ohio 1996) (somewhat equivocal, but still skeptical of banking regulation as a risk-reducing factor).

Banking regulation seems to have had a somewhat greater influence in the *Marine Bank* line of cases involving bank certificates of deposit. *See, e.g., Dubach v. Weitzel*, 135 F.3d 590, 592 (8th Cir. 1998) (drawing no distinction between federal and state law and concluding a certificate of deposit of a credit union is not a security because "[t]o apply federal securities law would 'double-coat' the transaction"); *Tafflin v. Levitt*, 865 F.2d 595 (4th Cir. 1989), *aff'd on other grounds*, 493 U.S. 455 (1990) (certificates of deposit were not securities because of state regulation even though the regulation proved to be totally inadequate). Not all courts, however, would defer to state regulation. Most notably, the Tenth Circuit observed, "[O]ur focus must be on federal regulation; state regulatory schemes cannot displace the acts." *Holloway v. Peat, Marwick, Mitchell & Co.*, 900 F.2d 1485, 1488 (10th Cir. 1990). Also, courts are unwilling simply to defer to the label of an instrument as a "certificate of deposit." *See, e.g., United States v. Sumeru*, 449 Fed. App'x 617 (9th Cir. 2011) (whether purported certificates of deposit were in reality investment contracts is a question for the jury).

What of regulation by foreign governments? In *Wolf v. Banco Nacional de Mexico, S.A.*, 739 F.2d 1458 (9th Cir. 1984), *cert. denied*, 469 U.S. 1108 (1985), a U.S. purchaser of a peso-denominated certificate of deposit issued by a Mexican bank sought recovery of his devalued investment on the ground the bank had sold an unregistered security. The court found Mexican banking regulation to provide the same degree of protection from insolvency as U.S. regulation and, applying *Marine Bank*, concluded the certificate of deposit was not a security.

5. ***Collateralization or Personal Guarantee as a Risk-Reduction Factor.*** *Reves'* comment that the loans in the case were "uncollateralized and uninsured" raises the possibility that adequate collateralization may be an alternative mode of risk reduction to that provided by a regulatory system. Often, risk is reduced through private contracting in loan transactions. Common practices in this regard include obtaining third-party guarantees or securing the obligation with the assets of the borrower.

Something short of full and sufficient collateral, however, likely will not defeat the finding of a security. One court has cited the absence of "real, valuable collateral" in concluding *Reves* risk reducing factors were not present. *SEC v. Smart*, 2011 U.S. Dist. LEXIS 61134 (D. Utah June 6, 2011). Securing notes with a life insurance policy is an insufficient risk reduction measure when the proceeds of the policy are available only on the death of the issuer and, in any event, would be inadequate to cover the $60 million owed under the notes. *See SEC v. Zada*, 787 F.3d 375 (6th Cir. 2015). Partial collateralization, of course, is not the equivalent of full collateralization. *See United States v. McKye*, 638 Fed. App'x 680, 215 U.S. App. LEXIS 21810 (10th Cir. 2015) ("Even assuming McKye is correct that the evidence . . . showed that 29% of the investment notes were collateralized, that would mean that 71% of the invested funds were at full risk of loss. Thus, the Government's evidence . . . amply showed the actions allegedly taken by McKye to collateralize the investment notes did not meaningfully reduce the risk of loss to investors."), *cert. denied, McKye v. United States*, 136 S. Ct. 2522 (2016).

6. ***Contractual Remedies as a Risk-Reduction Factor.*** May risk reduction within the meaning of *Reves* be accomplished through artful drafting by the lawyer? Suppose, for example, that an agreement provides for substantial and immediate penalties for the slightest default and includes a provision that if a required principal or interest payment is even one day late, the entire balance of the loan becomes immediately due. Such provisions may reduce risk, but do they do so in a way that should affect the definition of a security analysis? *See Stoiber v. SEC*, 161 F.3d 745, 751-752 (D.C. Cir. 1998) ("We think these are significantly less valuable than collateral or insurance and not by our thinking an adequate substitute for the protection of federal law. . . . Unlike collateral and insurance, acceleration provisions and the like in the notes do not guarantee recovery by the note holders. . . .").

7. ***Investment Perceptions.*** Compare *Reves* with the more recent case of an English company proposing to issue notes to philanthropic endowments, cooperatives, and development agencies worldwide. The funds are to be used to support investment in developing countries where credit conditions restrict loans. The notes, which are not transferable, bear no interest. In its request for a no-action letter from the SEC, the company argued "noteholders could not reasonably believe the Notes are securities and will not be acquiring the Notes

for investment purposes or with an expectation of receiving any benefit of any kind." The SEC responded favorably. *See* Global Development Co-operative, SEC No-Action Letter (Oct. 19, 2011). Is this conclusion affected by the interest rate environment in which the notes are issued (i.e., no interest at a time when interest rates are at historic lows)? *See also* Poplogix, SEC No-Action Letter (Nov. 5, 2010) (no security is involved when web site is created to facilitate loans to artists when lenders will not receive interest on the loans and the loans are not transferable). *Compare SEC v. Thompson*, 732 F.3d 1151, 1162 (10th Cir. 2013), where the Tenth Circuit concluded that a relatively high interest rate provided "strong evidence" that the noteholders were interested primarily in profits and that the notes should be treated as securities.

    8. *Plan of Distribution.* The likelihood of notes being treated as securities increases dramatically when they are sold to large groups of investors, especially when many or all of those investors are unsophisticated. Consider along this line the Tenth Circuit's quick rejection of a promoter's argument that he sold notes only to his family and friends, a distribution network too narrow to justify classification of the instruments as securities:

> [T]hompson's own sworn statements leave us with the firm conviction that, while Novus's first holders may have been Thompson's "family and friends," Novus sought to expand its distribution to anyone interested who had $100,000 to invest—even if that meant unsophisticated investors obtaining the money by liquidating home equity—and it made its Instruments available to anyone willing to pay.

SEC v. Thompson, 732 F.3d 1151, 1165 (10th Cir. 2013). Similar reasoning was offered in *Tripodi v. Welch*, 810 F.3d 761, 765 (10th Cir. 2016), where selling to large numbers of unsophisticated investors was a factor supporting treating the investments as purchases of securities. Although a large number of investors is a factor favoring treating notes as securities, the participation of only a handful of investors does not require a contrary conclusion. *See, e.g., Tripodi v. Capital Concepts, LLC*, 2014 U.S. Dist. LEXIS 90440, at *5 (D. Utah 2014) ("Even a small number of holders is not dispositive in determining that a note is not a security, as a debt instrument may be distributed to but one investor, yet still be a security.").

    9. *The Syndicated Loan Market and the Frontiers of* Reves. Classically, business borrowed in two distinct fashions: issuing bonds or taking a loan from a bank. Bonds are subject to the securities laws, a fact that drives many borrowers to their banks. But banks are heavily regulated, particularly after the financial crisis. Loans involving borrowers with a good deal of debt pose regulatory concerns for lending banks if they hold the loans. Hence, banks increasingly are syndicators of such loans.

    Loan syndications involve a structure in which a large loan is made to a single borrower and assigned to a number of institutional lenders by one or more banks acting as "arrangers." The syndicated loan market, sometimes called the leveraged loan market because the borrowers have high levels of debt, now exceeds $1 trillion. Loan documents are standardized, and covenants by borrowers are minimal or even nonexistent.

Matters were quiet on the securities law front until 2019, when investors in a 2014 $1.8 billion loan that JP Morgan had arranged for Millennium Health LLC sought to recover their losses after Millennium filed for bankruptcy following disclosures of improper billing practices. They argue that JP Morgan knew of federal investigations of Millennium at the time of the syndication and that the failure to make appropriate disclosures constituted securities fraud. But of course, this assumes the syndicated loans involved securities.

Industry participants warn that applying the securities laws to the leveraged loan market would not only severely impede the ability of borrowers to access needed funding but would also wreak havoc as banks and other financial institutions divest themselves of "securities" they are restricted or prohibited from holding.

As to the *Reves* factors, the arrangers argue that the loans were commercial rather than investment in nature, the plan of distribution involves only institutional investors as lenders, the perceptions of the participants is that the transactions are loans and not investments, and the involvement of various federal agencies in regulating leveraged lending obviates the need to apply the securities laws.

But now consider the arguments the lenders may advance for treating their loans as securities. May they find some support in *Reves*? What additional facts do you need? Is *Reves* adequate to resolve this issue one way or the other?

For an excellent discussion of the convergence of the corporate bond and the leveraged loan markets and the disparate securities law treatment of each, *see* de Fontenay, Do the Securities Laws Matter? The Rise of the Leveraged Loan Market, 39 J. Corp. L. 725-768 (2014).

PROBLEMS

2-15.　Karla is a broker with an addiction to gambling known only to her family. To pay some overdue debts, she borrows money from ten of her clients, issuing each a promissory note bearing 8 percent interest and payable on demand. The clients, who are not terribly sophisticated in financial matters, are happy with this arrangement because the return it offers is much higher than they had been receiving in their money market accounts. Are Karla's notes securities? Would your analysis change if each of the clients was highly sophisticated in financial matters? *See McNabb v. SEC*, 298 F.3d 1126 (9th Cir. 2002).

2-16.　Bradford Custom Homes intends to finance its homebuilding activities by borrowing money from qualified individuals. Each transaction is specific to a particular property and the lender's funds are earmarked for an identified home. Bradford plans to have as many as 25 lenders for each parcel. This mode of financing departs from the industry practice of creating pools of funds available for financing multiple homes. Under the Bradford plan, each lender will receive a note with a maturity date nine months from the closing of the loan with one renewal option. The note will be secured by a deed of trust on the property for the benefit of the lenders. The lenders will not participate in Bradford's profits and are motivated solely by the desire to earn interest on reasonably short-term loans. Is Bradford selling a security? Do you need additional information? *See* Bradford Homes, Inc., SEC No-Action Letter (Dec. 11, 1997).

2-17.   Same company as above. To finance its expansion into new regions, Bradford would like to issue $10 million in 10-year, 11 percent bonds. The bonds will be collateralized by zero coupon U.S. Treasury securities (i.e., government debt instruments that do not pay interest and are issued at deep discounts). Under this arrangement, Bradford will take 20 cents of every dollar raised in the bond offering and purchase the zero coupon securities. The maturity of the securities will coincide with that of the Bradford bonds. As their maturity shortens, the discount on the government securities lessens and is eventually eliminated at maturity. Accordingly, purchasers of Bradford bonds are assured sufficient funds will be available to pay principal on the bonds when they mature in ten years. Is Bradford selling a security?

G.   Separate Securities and Pass-Throughs

The materials in this chapter illustrate that not all income-producing instruments constitute securities. The bank certificate of deposit and the note issued in a consumer transaction, to name just two examples, are not securities. The activities of an intermediary in packaging financial instruments, however, may create a security out of something that is not. For example, in *Gary Plastic Packaging Corp. v. Merrill Lynch, Pierce, Fenner & Smith, Inc.,* 756 F.2d 230 (2d Cir. 1985), Merrill Lynch offered its customers bank certificates of deposit. The brokerage firm claimed to offer a number of services in this program, including screening banks to determine which offered the most competitive yields, negotiating with the banks, monitoring the creditworthiness of the banks, and maintaining a secondary market to promote the liquidity of investments through this program. Applying *Howey,* the Second Circuit concluded Merrill Lynch was selling securities:

> Merrill Lynch is engaged in activity that is significantly greater than that of an ordinary broker or sales agent. Since Merrill Lynch possesses significant economic power, it is able to negotiate with the issuing banks to obtain a favorable rate of interest. Pursuant to defendants' scheme, the banks create new CDs that carry interest rates lower than those they pay their direct customers. From this differential, Merrill Lynch receives a commission for its services, which include providing a secondary market and cultivating a large group of banks that desire to borrow money. Therefore, a significant portion of the customer's investment depends on Merrill Lynch's managerial and financial expertise.
>
> The customers rely on the skill and financial stability of Merrill Lynch for a number of reasons. First, resale in the secondary market created and maintained by Merrill Lynch is crucial to the investor. . . . Ordinary CDs purchased directly from the issuing bank are not freely redeemable prior to maturity. Those redeemed before maturity are subject to a substantial withdrawal penalty. . . . [B]y purchasing through the CD program the investor has the option of selling its CD

back to Merrill Lynch if prevailing interest rates drop, thereby realizing profits from capital appreciation. . . .

Second, the investor relies on Merrill Lynch's implicit promise to maintain its marketing efforts. The success of the secondary market and the availability of CDs at competitive rates hinge on Merrill Lynch's success in finding new buyers of CDs and developing strong working relationships with issuing banks. . . .

Finally, investors rely on Merrill Lynch's ongoing monitoring of the issuing banks. If an issuing bank becomes insolvent, the FDIC or FSLIC will pay the investor the principal due under the terms of the certificate of deposit. Here investors are buying something more than an individual certificate of deposit. They are buying an opportunity to participate in the CD Program and its secondary market. And, they are paying for the security of knowing that they may liquidate at a moment's notice free from concern as to loss of income or capital, while awaiting for FDIC or FSLIC insurance proceeds.

Id. at 240-241.

The transaction in *Gary Plastic* is slightly different from pass-through arrangements that give the investor an undivided interest in a pool of diversified assets. Almost any kind of income-producing instrument with standardized terms and common elements may be pooled and packaged for sale as a pass-through:

> In securitization, a company partly "deconstructs" itself by separating certain types of highly liquid assets from the risks generally associated with the company. The company can then use these assets to raise funds in the capital markets at a lower cost than if the company, with its associated risks, could have raised the funds directly by issuing more debt or equity. The company retains the savings generated by these lower costs, while investors in the securitized assets benefit by holding investments with lower risk.

Schwarcz, The Alchemy of Asset Securitization, 1 Stan. J.L. Bus. & Fin. 133, 134 (1994).

Real estate mortgages, government securities, bank CDs, and corporate accounts receivable have been particularly popular subjects for securitization. Most notably, real estate mortgage-backed securities (MBS) significantly altered the role of institutions in residential real estate financing and expanded the availability of financing for real estate purchases. Rather than acting as a long-term lender to the home purchaser, the institution originating the mortgage develops a pool of mortgages, transfers the mortgages to a trust, and causes the trust to sell undivided interests in itself to large numbers of investors. Because the mortgages are pooled and packaged together, the risks of defaults on the mortgages are spread across the entire pool. Furthermore, because securitization allows hedge funds, mutual funds, and other institutions to access the mortgage market, mortgage lending is no longer limited to commercial banks, who scrutinized home-buyers to mitigate the probability of default. As securitizations became more popular, investor demand for higher risk (and higher interest payouts) prompted a relaxing of borrowing requirements.

Government-sponsored entities (GSEs), such as the Government National Mortgage Association (GNMA, or Ginnie Mae), the Federal Home Loan Mortgage Corporation (FHLMC, or Freddie Mac), and the Federal National

Mortgage Association (FNMA, or Fannie Mae), played a large role in contributing to the proliferation of mortgage-backed securities. As GSEs, they have had a mandate from the government to promote home ownership, particularly in underserved populations. Loans guaranteed by Fannie Mae and Freddie Mac have the implicit backing of the federal government, and therefore there is an inherent reduction in risk of default.

Fannie Mae and Freddie Mac were instrumental in relaxing qualification standards for borrowers as a means of dramatically expanding home ownership in the years leading up to the 2008 financial crisis. With the approval of Fannie Mae and Freddie Mac, banks and other firms originating mortgages steadily reduced borrowing standards and combined mortgages into ever larger pools of loans with higher risk profiles. In addition to issuing guarantees, Freddie Mac and Fannie Mae purchased mortgage pools as a way of injecting liquidity into the mortgage market and encouraging financing of home purchases. Such liquidity led to further lending by other institutions, which in turn created even more mortgage pools. By 2008, loans guaranteed or owned by the GSEs accounted for approximately half of the U.S. mortgage market.

The subprime lending problems that became apparent in late 2007, leading to a federal takeover of Fannie Mae and Freddie Mac in 2008 in an effort to stem severe liquidity problems, have prompted some commentators to question the wisdom of a securitization process that allows the original lenders to escape consequences for poor lending decisions. Dodd-Frank addresses the moral hazard problem by requiring the "securitizer" to retain at least 5 percent of the credit risk of assets it puts in a securitization package. The retention threshold, which is codified in Section 15G of the '34 Act, may be lowered under certain circumstances and, significantly, does not apply to "qualified residential mortgages" if specified conditions are met. The SEC, the Office of the Comptroller of the Currency, the FDIC, and other enforcement agencies jointly have issued proposed rules for implementing the credit risk requirement. *See* Release No. 34-64148 (Mar. 30, 2011).

It should be noted at this point that Section 3 exempts from registration securities issued or guaranteed by a domestic governmental entity or a bank. Many pass-throughs have such guarantees (e.g., GNMA, Fannie Mae, and Freddie Mac mortgage pools) and therefore need not be registered. Along a somewhat similar line, the packaging of corporate accounts receivable (i.e., pooling the receivables and selling undivided interests in the pool) is sometimes accompanied by bank guarantees of timely payment, which will exempt the security (if such exists) from registration requirements. The use of bank guarantees with pass-throughs will be explored more fully in Chapter 8, and regulatory responses to the development of new techniques for securitization will be discussed in Chapter 10.

PROBLEM

2-18.   Fidelity Deposits is in the business of selling insurance and annuities. To attract customers, Fidelity advertises "FDIC federally insured" certificates of deposit with more attractive interest rates than those offered by banks. In fact,

Fidelity does not offer CDs. Anyone who expresses interest in a Fidelity CD is asked to make an appointment with a Fidelity representative. At the appointment, the representative will try to convince the individual to purchase an annuity instead of a CD. If the investor insists on a CD, Fidelity will provide a list (updated daily) of banks offering high interest rates on federally insured CDs. In response to the investor's objection that the bank interest rates are lower than those promised in the advertisement, Fidelity promises to make up the difference between the rate it advertised and the rate actually paid on the bank CD. To collect, the investor need only supply Fidelity with proof of purchase of the bank CD. Note that investors who purchase CDs invest no money with Fidelity.

Is Fidelity selling a security? What if Fidelity serves as a broker and places investors' funds with the bank of its choice? *See Reiswig v. Dep't of Corporations,* 144 Cal. App. 4th 327, 50 Cal. Rptr. 3d 386 (2006).

||3||
Understanding Investors

A. The Efficient Market Hypothesis: Implications and Limitations

Of all recent developments in financial economics, the efficient capital market hypothesis (ECMH) has achieved the widest acceptance by the legal culture. It now commonly informs the academic literature on a variety of topics; it is addressed by major law school casebooks and textbooks on business law; it structures debate over the future of securities regulation both within and without the Securities and Exchange Commission; it has served as the intellectual premise for a major revision of the disclosure system administered by the Commission; and it has even begun to influence judicial decisions and the actual practice of law. In short, the ECMH is now *the* context in which serious discussion of the regulation of financial markets takes place.

Gilson & Kraakman, The Mechanisms of Market Efficiency, 70 Va. L. Rev. 549-550 (1984).

Though the above quote is now approaching its 40th year, it remains prescient in observing that the efficient market hypothesis is a powerful descriptive theory of the relationship between the disclosure of financially significant information and changes in securities market prices. As is true with such sweeping theories, its precise meaning, as well as whether and to what extent it does describe how securities markets *in fact* function, has not been accepted in all quarters and continues to undergo close scrutiny. Nevertheless, the efficient market hypothesis is the intellectual framework within which current disclosure policies are formulated and their operation assessed.

1. The Meaning and Mechanisms of Market Efficiency

The puzzle regarding the rationality of share prices is worth pondering, for its solution has much to say about the appropriate thrust of securities regulation. If the future payouts of a corporation to its shareholders could be predicted with certainty and were not subject to any appreciable level of risk, there would be little basis for disagreement about the present value of a share of stock. But such prediction is far from certain: Forecasting earnings involves a large element of crystal ball gazing (as does the assessment of the proper level of risk associated with the predictions). Corporate histories are full of surprising twists and turns. Reasonable investors will disagree, probably dramatically, as to fundamental value, and there is no reason to expect that any of their predictions will turn out to be correct. Against these uncertainties and their related imperfections in discerning ex ante the intrinsic value of a security, the conventional view simply argues that the consensus of an *efficient market* will be the *best* possible measure of value at the moment, usually falling somewhere in the middle between extreme optimism and pessimism.

The statement that securities markets are efficient raises further questions as to what is meant by efficiency, and even within one meaning, there are degrees of efficiency. A workable definition of an efficient market focuses on the relationship between price and information. A security's price can be seen as being established in an efficient market if, with respect to specific information, the price that exists for the security is the same as the price it would have if everyone had the same information. Beaver, Market Efficiency, Acct. Rev. 23 (1981). Market efficiency does not mean that all market participants have the same opinion as to the security's price; rather, an efficient market is the result of their collective investment decisions, even if participating investors hold varying beliefs as to the information's impact.

Traditionally, market efficiency has been thought of as possibly occurring in three different levels: the weak form, the semi-strong form, and the strong form of market efficiency. The weak form of market efficiency exists when security prices reflect all the information embodied in the past prices of that security. That is, if securities markets are efficient in the weak form, investors cannot extrapolate a security's future price from a series of past prices. The weak form of market efficiency was the first to be investigated; with great consistency researchers found that successive stock prices are independent of one another, i.e., they are randomly distributed, that a stock's future price cannot be extrapolated from only its past price changes. Such studies spawned a popular pseudonym for market efficiency, "the random walk theory." Evidence that stock price changes follow a random walk, however, is not inconsistent with the belief that stocks have an intrinsic value and that an individual stock's market value reflects, and is responsive to, financially significant events and information. Inquiry into the relationship between stock prices and such events and information focuses on testing whether securities markets are efficient in the semi-strong form of market efficiency.

The semi-strong form of market efficiency exists if security prices reflect all publicly available information. A logical explanation of why stock prices follow a random walk is that stock prices quickly reflect successive pieces of new information as that information becomes available. If stock prices responded slowly to new information, it would be expected that stock price changes would be dependent, not independent. But a useful theory about the formulation of stock prices can be formed, if we hypothesize that information changes daily, that such changes are independent of one another in the sense that one cannot forecast perfectly tomorrow's information from what is known today, and that stock prices respond quickly to new information. These essentially are the core features of the semi-strong form of market efficiency.

Here we should consider the variety of forces that would cause the market for a particular security to be considered efficient in the semi-strong form. Should it matter if the company files periodic reports pursuant to the Exchange Act, that it is followed closely by several investment analysts, and that it counts many institutional investors among its stockholders? And, consider as well whether there is a paradox at play here. A central tenet of the semi-strong form of market efficiency is that financially significant information (e.g., an increase in earnings) is rapidly impounded in a security's price upon the public release of that information. A correlative point is that if this indeed is the case, then investors cannot generally "beat the market" by examining publicly available information for the purpose of determining which stocks are undervalued and which are overpriced in light of publicly available information. What then are the incentives for the sophisticated investor to closely analyze a company's news releases and financial reports? Vital to the thesis that securities markets are efficient in the semi-strong form is the belief that sophisticated investors and analysts will indeed examine public information to identify undervalued and overvalued stocks. But if markets are indeed efficient in the semi-strong form, why would they do this? And if this does not occur, can a market be efficient in the semi-strong form?

the most realistic?

The strong form of market efficiency occurs when security prices reflect all information, whether that information is publicly available or not. There is no significant empirical evidence supporting the view that markets are efficient in the strong form.   → insider trading

The three forms of market efficiency are counter to well-recognized trading strategies. The weak form of market efficiency is inconsistent with the efforts of chartists who plot past stock price movements to shed light on tomorrow's market play; the semi-strong form of market efficiency rejects the notion that securities are under- or overpriced in the market; and if the strong form of market efficiency were true, then a lot of effort has been misspent recently prosecuting individuals for insider trading.

Today, the true battleground is whether securities markets are efficient in the semi-strong form. Studies examining whether markets are efficient in the semi-strong form customarily are event studies where the researcher studies stock price behavior before and after a financially significant event or announcement. Such event studies have with great consistency reflected not only that stock prices respond to such information, but they do so rapidly. But the debate now is not whether stock prices are following quickly after a public announcement, but whether the resulting price seems to be one reflecting the stock's fundamental value. That is, as research methodologies have become more sophisticated, they have investigated whether stock markets are *fundamentally* efficient, meaning not only that investors process information rapidly, but also that their trading prices reflect accurate estimates of a security's intrinsic value. It is in this area of inquiry that the greatest disagreements have arisen over the market's efficiency. *See* Fama, Efficient Capital Markets: II, 46 J. Fin. 1575 (1991). As is seen in the materials below, there is much in the nature of stock markets that is inconsistent with the view that markets are *fundamentally* efficient (defined to mean that prices reflect the security's intrinsic value). One area of concern is evidence suggesting there is excessive volatility in stock markets. *See, e.g.,* Campbell & Shiller, The Dividend-Price Ratio and Expectations of Future Dividends and Discount Factors, 1 Rev. Fin. Stud. 192 (1988). And much of the evidence on stock price behavior suggests that the markets commonly overreact to announcements and that security prices reach their equilibrium point not rapidly, but over a long period of time through a process that appears to have mean-reverting tendencies (meaning prices periodically drift, then reverse course, and ultimately stabilize). *See generally* Ball & Brown, Ball and Brown 1968: A Retrospective, 89 Acct'g Rev. 1 (2014). Should U.S. disclosure mechanisms be built solely on an empirical foundation supporting the view that stock prices respond quickly to financial announcements, or should disclosure mechanisms also be premised on evidence that markets are fundamentally efficient? For the view that the efficient market hypothesis offers too simplified a view of the price-setting process of securities markets, *see* Stout, The Mechanisms of Market Inefficiency: An Introduction to the New Finance, 28 J. Corp. L. 635 (2003).

NOTES AND QUESTIONS

1. Information Costs and Market Efficiency. An important relationship exists between information costs and market efficiency. Information costs include market participants' cost to acquire information, their expense to decipher and understand its significance to the firm's risk and return potential, and their cost to verify the information's validity. Professors Gilson and Kraakman explain the three forms of market efficiency in terms of their relative information costs. They explain that markets are not efficient in the strong form because the costs to acquire nonpublic information (e.g., through industrial espionage) are high. Such information requires more processing and entails additional efforts to verify its accuracy. On the other hand, the semi-strong state of market efficiency uses information that is "publicly available," for which market professionals incur much lower information costs. Efforts either by government directives, such as mandatory disclosure rules, or by issuers' voluntary announcements, greatly minimize information acquisition costs for market participants. Gilson and Kraakman emphasize that publicly available information also has lower processing and verification costs due to the presence of third-party verifiers, such as certified public accountants. And for the weak form of market efficiency, the examination of stock prices poses the lowest acquisition, processing, and verification costs of all. Gilson & Kraakman, The Mechanisms of Market Efficiency, 70 Va. L. Rev. 549 (1984). In the wake of the 2008-2010 financial crisis, the utility of the efficient market hypothesis was doubted by many who argued that public awareness that there was an ongoing housing bubble was inconsistent with high values contemporaneously being accorded various financial products that were backed by home mortgages. To this charge, Gilson and Kraakman argue that the reasoning in their original article was right. Building on their thesis that pricing inefficiency is the product of information costs, they observe that a central feature

[handwritten margin notes: lack of transparency of MBS ↓; higher information costs ↳ market inefficiencies]

of the various financial products that depended on home mortgages was their opacity. Because extraordinary effort and cost was therefore needed to assess their value, pricing inefficiencies naturally arose. Gilson & Kraakman, Market Efficiency After the Financial Crisis: It's Still a Matter of Information Cost, 100 Va. L. Rev. 313 (2014).

2. *Informational and Allocational Efficiency: Which Should Guide Public Policy?* At several points in succeeding chapters, we find various regulatory positions supported in part by the belief that the action is desirable because markets are efficient. On close inspection, there are really two distinct aspects of market efficiency: informational efficiency and allocational efficiency. *Informational efficiency* describes the speed with which market prices adjust to new information. *Allocational efficiency* concerns the allocation of resources to their best or highest use. Those who take exception to the usefulness of the efficient market hypothesis do so principally because the evidence is weak that markets are fundamentally efficient, meaning they do not yield prices that reflect the intrinsic value of the security. Notwithstanding this criticism, many believe that secondary markets do affect resource allocation because they capture the relationship between risk and return gleaned from securities traded in an efficient market, which informs those engaged in making loans to business enterprises or purchasing the shares of companies that are going public. *See, e.g.,* Dow & Gorton, Stock Market Efficiency and Economic Efficiency: Is There a Connection?, 52 J. Fin. 1087 (1997). In the design of optimal disclosure policies, does it matter whether markets are fundamentally efficient if we recognize they are informationally efficient?

Policy justification for regulation

3. *Darts, Analysts, and Market Efficiency.* If you accept the tenets of the semi-strong form of market efficiency, are you well advised to follow the advice of investment analysts, or should you select stocks for your portfolio by periodically throwing darts at the financial pages? For many years, the Wall Street Journal pitted the expertise of a changing group of investment analysts against dart throwers. One study comparing the performance of these two groups in a two-year period found that the analysts won 24 times and the dart throwers 17 times, with the pros netting an average gain of 8.4 percent against the dart throwers' 3.3 percent. However, after close analysis, two finance professors concluded that, adjusting for the greater risk of the securities selected by the analysts over those randomly struck by the darts, the analysts produced only a 0.4 percent greater return. Moreover, what effect do you give to the fact that the analysts' recommendations once made are publicized, but the stocks selected by the dart throwers are never disclosed? *See* Barber & Loeffler, The "Dartboard" Column: Second-Hand Information and Price Pressure, 28 J. Fin. & Quant. Analysis 273 (1993). The experiment was repeated in 2019, with the dart throwers whipping the analysts by a whopping 27 percentage points over a 12-month period. Jakob, The Darts Beat the Experts in Investing, Wall St. J., May 6, 2019, at B-10. *But see* Jasen, A Brief History of Our Contest, Wall St. J., Oct. 7, 1998, at C-1 (over the course of 100 six-month contest periods, invited analysts garnered an average return of 10.8 percent, dart throwers showed a

6.8 percent return, and the Dow Jones Industrial Average yielded an average return of 6.8 percent).

   4.   *Criteria for Securities Traded in an Efficient Market.*   As we will see, securities regulatory issues frequently depend on whether the market for a particular security is deemed to be an efficient one. *Cammer v. Bloom*, 711 F. Supp. 1264 (D.N.J. 1989), is by far the most influential opinion on this subject. *Cammer* identifies the following factors as indicative of a security likely to be so traded: (1) percentage of shares traded weekly, (2) analysts following, (3) presence of market makers and arbitrageurs, (4) eligibility to take advantage of the SEC's integrated disclosure procedures pursuant to Form S-3 for engaging in public offerings, and (5) responsiveness of security's price to new information. As in any factor analysis, the courts tend not to require all factors to be present, and some courts have added considerations such as the market capitalization of the firm (i.e., number of shares outstanding multiplied by their market price), bid-ask spreads, percentage of stock held by insiders, and institutional share ownership. *See* Fisher, Does the Efficient Market Theory Help Us Do Justice in a Time of Madness?, 54 Emory L.J. 843, 859-866 (2005). Why are these factors consistent with market efficiency?

PROBLEMS

3-1.   To illustrate some of the mechanisms that contribute to market efficiency, assume Alpha common shares and Beta common shares are each currently trading at $15 per share. Christine just discovered some "bad" news regarding Alpha and some "good" news regarding Beta. If Christine is a rational investor, what actions should she take? What must we know about the meaning of "good" and "bad" news before answering this question? What must we know about Christine's resources or the information's availability to determine whether her activities will affect in any way the market price for either Alpha or Beta shares? Under what circumstances will the price of Alpha and Beta shares be affected by Christine's discovery if she is an analyst for a research department of an investment banking firm, rather than the holder of a portfolio of stocks?

3-2.   Bob believes his day has started out on a good note. Over his morning coffee he is intrigued by a story in his local newspaper, the San Jose Mercury, reporting on local rumors that Omega Company, a large pharmaceutical company, is expected to file that day a request for the Food and Drug Administrations (FDA) to enter the final stage of human testing of a drug that reduces significantly the adverse effects of asthma. Wasting little time, Bob called his cousin, Carol, who works in Omega's research department. Carol confirmed the rumor. Bob could hardly contain himself. He called his broker, leaving a message on the broker's voice mail to purchase 1,000 Omega shares. The order was executed later in the day, approximately six hours after the Omega application was publicly filed with the FDA in Washington, D.C. In an insider trading prosecution against Bob, how likely is it that the SEC will be able to establish that Bob benefited financially by purchasing Omega shares?

2. The Debate over Efficiency of the Market

Though it is a cornerstone on which much of securities law has recently been built, the efficient market hypothesis continues to be surrounded by controversy as scholars from the fields of economics, finance, and psychology seriously question whether the model fully captures investor behavior that causes stock price changes or, for that matter, whether the model can ever be validated or discredited. Leading the assault on the hypothesis is an eminent group of theorists who believe that "noise"—pricing influences not associated with rational expectations about asset values—plays a significant role in stock market behavior.[1] In essence, noise theory offers approaches for understanding possible causes and mechanisms of market *in*efficiency. But how and to what extent do the insights from the social sciences impact the efficient market hypothesis as guidepost for policy?

> ### Young, Brief of Financial Economists as *Amici Curae* in Support of Respondents, Halliburton, Inc. v. Erica P. John Fund, Inc., U.S. Supreme Court (2014)

Because economists disagree about the extent to which securities markets are efficient, it is crucial to be clear about the precise economic propositions at issue. . . .

Professional economists have debated for decades the extent to which the securities markets actually conform to the SSEMH [the semi-strong version of the efficient market hypothesis]. . . .

The SSEMH is based on two propositions: (1) that most investors rationally invest on the basis of available information; and (2) to the extent that some investors act irrationally, their investments do not affect prices because well-funded, highly sophisticated investors can drive the prices back to fundamentals in a process known as "arbitrage."

Authors writing in the field of behavioral economics disagree with both propositions. First, they argue that investor irrationality is pervasive rather than occasional or limited. Second, they argue that because of the costs and risks of arbitrage—the arbitrager must typically borrow money in anticipation of the market correcting itself, which may not happen quickly enough—arbitrage does not always drive prices back to fundamentals.[4] As one critic puts it, "real-world arbitrage is risky and therefore limited," and its effectiveness depends "on the availability of close substitutes for securities whose price is potentially affected by noise trading."[5] SSEMH proponents disagree about the magnitude

---

1. The expression "noise" is a euphemism for *irrational* investor behavior and was coined by the renowned economist Fischer Black. ". . . [by him] renaming irrational trading avoided the I-word, thereby sanitizing irrationality and rendering it palatable to many analysts. . . ." Leroy, Efficient Capital Markets and Martingales, 27 Econ. Lit. 1583, 1612 (1989).

4. *See, e.g.*, Andrei Shleifer, *Inefficient Markets: An Introduction to Behavioral Finance* 10-12 (2000). . . .

5. Shleifer, *Inefficient Markets*, at 13.

of the limits on arbitrage and argue that any anomalies are quickly eliminated in the market.[6]

The debate has played out through a series of empirical studies. In the 1980s, for example, Robert Shiller published stock market data that in his view showed that stock market prices were considerably more volatile than the SSEMH could account for. Other scholars found that stock prices tended to overreact to news—good news about a company might cause the price to increase in the short term and then fall in the long term as the market digested the information more carefully. Other findings include superior performance of small companies and predictability of returns according to market to book ratios. As Professor Shleifer points out, "this evidence points to excess returns based on stale information, in contrast to semi-strong form market efficiency."[10] Defenders of the SSEMH, however, have argued that the data can be explained on the basis of hidden factors that are consistent with investor rationality. Or they argue that the anomalies are trivial, and tend to disappear after they are identified as rational investors take advantage of them.

We have outlined these debates in some detail because it is important to understand what is and is not in dispute. Economists disagree about the ability of arbitrage to compensate for investor irrationality; the possibility of "beating the market" through investment strategies based on either value investing or exploiting irrational tendencies of investors; the importance of non-information-based factors to stock prices; and the speed and completeness of the market's ability to incorporate material information about a stock.

But economists generally do *not* disagree about whether markets respond to material information. . . .

The SSEMH, as stated by Professor Fama and other proponents of efficient markets, does not simply say that stock prices move in response to information; rather, it holds that the market completely digests all public information about the stock, so that security prices fully reflect all available information (or at least that prices reflect information to the point where the marginal benefits of acting on information do not exceed the marginal costs of doing so) and that prices are a function *only* of that relevant information.

Critics of SSEMH, on the other hand, insist that this dynamic is not the whole story. Sometimes markets incorporate information slowly or incompletely, and sometimes stock prices display volatility that *cannot* be explained by changes in the available information about stocks.

The focus of these debates is on whether stock prices reflect fundamental value—that is, the actual value of the company—not on whether stock prices can be counted on to move up or down in response to information. That is why so much of the literature criticizing the SSEMH refers to fundamental value and fundamental efficiency. That literature goes far beyond the question of whether markets respond in a predictable direction and reasonably promptly to material information.

---

6.   *See, e.g.,* id. at 4 (summarizing arguments by Milton Friedman and Eugene Fama that "[t]he process of arbitrage brings security prices in line with their fundamental values even when some investors are not fully rational and their demands are correlated, as long as securities have close substitutes").

10.   Id. at 18.

Economists have tested the SSEMH empirically primarily by testing whether it is, in fact, possible to earn excess returns through particular trading strategy. The results are disputed; Andrei Schleifer and Lawrence Summers, for example, have argued that it *is* possible to make excess returns—that is, to "beat the market"—under certain circumstances.

The critical point, however, is that this debate about excess returns has little to do with the modest assumption that prices move reasonably promptly in a predictable direction in response to favorable or unfavorable public information. The excess returns debate goes to whether stock prices are fundamentally *accurate*, not whether they move in response to information. Moreover, behavioral economists do not dispute that market prices generally remain the best available indicia of share value, and their advice to investors generally dovetails with that offered by proponents of the SSEMH. Professor Shiller, for example, has acknowledged that it is "unlikely that the average amateur investor can get rich quickly by trading in the markets based on publicly available information. . . . I personally believe this, and in my own investing I have avoided trading too much, and have a high level of skepticism about investing tips."[17]

The supporters and critics of the SSEMH also debate the extent of any need for regulation of the market. But there is a general consensus that fraudulent misrepresentations harm market participants and should not be condoned; the SSEMH, after all, depends on the availability of public and *truthful* information to drive prices. Nor do skeptics of market efficiency dispute that information *affects* prices—they simply assert that other things affect prices, too. Because the market responds to public statements, there is a substantial public interest in ensuring that those statements are truthful.

The economic proposition that prices move reasonably promptly in a predictable direction in response to favorable or unfavorable public information does not require that markets be anywhere near perfectly efficient. Nor does it require that one take any position on whether particular trading strategies might "beat the market" or whether government regulation is appropriate. . . .

3. Passive Investing and Market Efficiency

Active investors are central to efficient markets because they fund market research and engage in trading that causes security prices to reflect information.

> Grossman and Stiglitz's . . . classic article "On the Impossibility of Informationally Efficient Markets" [70 Am. Econ. Rev. 393 (1980)] illuminates the key mechanism [of market efficiency]. . . . [I]nformed traders invest money and resources in acquiring information on an asset's fundamental value. These informed traders then exploit this information by selling high and buying low, and in the process of doing so they push prices toward their fundamental level.
>
> But, if informed traders are selling high and buying low, other traders—uninformed or "noise" traders (which can include actively managed funds without an informational advantage)—must be taking the other side of those trades,

---

17. Robert J. Shiller, *Sharing Nobel Honors, and Agreeing to Disagree*, N.Y. Times, Oct. 26, 2013,

meaning that they are selling low and buying high. Selling low and buying high is a losing strategy relative to a buy-and-hold passive strategy (though of course uninformed investors will still on average earn a positive return in absolute terms). So, on average, uninformed traders lose money to informed traders. The losses of the uninformed traders are the profits of the informed traders, and it is the possibility of trading profitably against uninformed traders that creates the incentive for informed traders to invest the effort and resources needed to become informed in the first place.

James, Mittendorf, Pirrone & Robles-Garcia, Does the Growth of Passive Investing Affect Equity Market Performance? A Literature Review, FCA Research Note at 5 (Feb. 2019), available at *www.fca.org.uk.*

On reflection, active trading may be thought of as a *negative* sum game because (i) the trading gain of one active investor derives from the trading loss of another investor; and (ii) each bears some cost, e.g., commissions, value of effort, etc. for their respective trades. In light of these considerations, it is not surprising that studies reflect that active institutional investors underperform the market when fees are taken into account. *See, e.g.,* Susko & Turner, The Implications of Passive Investing for Securities Markets, BIS Quarterly Rev. 113 (Mar. 2018). This has been a major explanation for the massive shift of investors from active to passive investment funds such as indexed mutual funds or index exchange traded funds. Passive investment funds enable investors to garner a return close to the market return by holding a diversified portfolio without expending money to become informed whether a particular security is overvalued or undervalued.

In combination, overt passive investment funds now hold approximately 43 percent of equity funds and this represents 20 percent of all publicly traded equity. Id. And, the percentage continues to grow. Moreover, about 70 percent of the money flowing into passive funds in the past decade has gone to the three largest fund managers, reflecting the advantages of scale that enable large funds to compress fees offered to their investors as a result of allocating their high fixed costs to adhere to an indexing strategy over a growing portfolio. It should also be noted that there is a good deal of evidence that many funds pursue an indexing strategy, at least for a substantial portion of their portfolio, but do not openly profess to doing so (generally referred to as "closet indexing"). Thus, equity holdings within passively managed portfolios are higher than 20 percent.

The dramatic shift toward such passive investment strategies raises concern whether insights gleaned from the past regarding stock price formation in public markets, namely empirical observations consistent with the efficient market hypothesis, carry forward to markets with increasing investor passivity. First, consider that as more and more investors migrate to passive investment funds, the active investors enjoy less competition, but the competition they encounter is likely from fellow informed traders, and not the noise/uninformed traders who have been in the vanguard of dumping active funds. It thus may well be that on average the rewards of informed traders will not be so ample as to justify their search and trading costs. Will this in fact reduce materially the amount of informed trading that in the past has caused stock prices to respond quickly to new information?

A second basis for concern is that index fund managers are locked into their referent index so that trading is driven by their quest to regularly rebalance the portfolio so that its composition mirrors the referent index, e.g., the S&P 500; managers of passive investment funds have no interest in firm-specific developments that impact the value of a particular company. Passive managers buy and sell the securities making up the referent index and do so in response to fund inflows and outflows. Awareness of the limited narrow focus of such managers frames the concern that their preoccupation with "mechanical investment rules" may cause distortions in the pricing of individual securities. Thus, with not less than 43 percent of U.S. public equity guided by this strategy, what impact does such a narrow trading focus have on security prices? For example, studies reflect a great deal of co-movement among securities within indexes with the consequential effect of magnifying pricing differences with securities not within indexes; a correlative effect is that prices for securities commonly held in passively managed funds reflect less of the impact of firm-specific information. *See* Sushko & Turner, *supra* at 119-121.

4.   Considering Algorithmic Trading

About 70 percent (and for very large firms the level approaches 85 percent) of transactions on exchanges is algorithmic trading; this refers to orders being initiated by computers pursuant to pre-set programs built upon highly stylized models. The speed of computerized trading is measured in milliseconds or microseconds; trades not only occur rapidly but more importantly the computers are able to digest and respond to ever-changing information with equal speed so that algorithmic traders can thereby garner gains anticipated in their underlying model. The computers receive their data from a variety of sources, such as news reports, social media, regulatory announcements, etc. Algorithmic trading includes at least two forms.

First, algorithmic arbitrage trading refers to computer programs built on various proprietary valuation models that when interfaced with ongoing current macroeconomic data and firm-specific information execute trades to capture gains by buying shares of companies the model predicts are selling cheaply and selling shares of firms that are believed to be overpriced. Such trading is consistent with the "informed trader" discussed earlier, as each entails arbitrage trading that drives so much of the semi-strong form of market efficiency.

The other large category of algorithmic trading is so-called high frequency trading (HFT). The important difference between the two types is the former's focus is on how the current trading price compares to the price predicted by the computer's model, whereas the latter is focused on anticipated changes in a security's price in light of forecasts of the future price change based on trading patterns captured, observed, and analyzed in the model. Moreover, HFT generally has another distinguishing characteristic—roughly 90 percent of the orders placed by HFT programs are cancelled; the HFT order generally is exploratory in nature, being designed to detect possible future volume and direction of trading. These are sometimes referred to as "phantom orders."

Like the corner grocery store, algorithmic traders make their profits on volume, lots of volume. With relatively small amounts of capital they engage in large numbers of transactions, buying and selling batches, rapidly. At first glance, there are some readily identifiable social benefits of algorithmic trading: it provides arbitrage trading that is consistent with the forces that underlie market efficiency and it provides desirable liquidity in securities markets. So, what could be the concern?

At the heart of algorithmic trading is the model that guides the trades. This appears to be the fount of much of the concern. First, the social value of arbitrage trading is premised on driving a security's price to its fundamental value. Weaknesses in the model used by the computer or in an understanding of the information on which the model bases its trading necessarily weaken the positive contribution the resulting trade has on the reasonableness of the resulting price. Furthermore, the models may well place too much weight on some factors and not enough on others. Thus, model risk is a concern. Moreover, there is a fear that algorithmic traders necessarily have a short-term bias in their modeling. Because so many more variables can influence long-term performance of a firm's model, modelers can more easily and cheaply focus the model on examining short-term variables that can cause equally short-term swings in a security's price. If this is true, the forest is missed by focusing on individual trees (saplings), with the result that algorithmic trading may retard the security's price moving quickly to a better equilibrium price. A further concern is that the nimbleness and growing prevalence of algorithmic trading may well drive many traditional informed traders from the markets as the speedier computer deflects more and more gains of arbitrage away from slow and deliberate human traders. *See generally* Yadav, How Algorithmic Trading Undermines Efficiency in Capital Markets, 68 Vand. L. Rev. 1607 (2015).

B. *Behavioral Economics and Decisions by Individual Investors*

The controversy about noise trading discussed in the previous section comes down to the question of whether individual trading decisions exhibit *systematic* departures from rationality that could influence stock prices and whether corrective forces such as "smart money" arbitrage will effectively counter those biases. Whatever the outcome of that debate about market prices, there is little doubt that many investors make decisions that fall far short of the economist's rational ideal. These decisions will have a considerable personal financial impact, often costly, even if they have no market-wide reverberations.

Securities regulation has always assumed that there are many unsophisticated investors in need of the protection of the securities laws, but until recently there was little systematic study of what kinds of cognitive errors investors make or exactly how pervasive those errors are. Research in behavioral economics seeks to fill some of these gaps, although that work is largely still in its infancy.

"Loss aversion" is one commonly cited bias—the tendency to be somewhat more willing to take on risk to avoid a loss than to pocket a gain. *See, e.g.*, Odean, Are Investors Reluctant to Realize Their Losses?, 53 J. Fin. 1775 (1998). People become more aggressive gamblers when trying to get back to the status quo ante than when confronting a risky chance initially. A stockbroker trying to coax a customer into more risky securities might try to encourage the sense that the customer has fallen behind some benchmark (e.g., how other customers have done with their investments) and needs to catch up. While this framing is often artificial, it can have an impact.

One of the most robust findings in research on investor behavior is that most people are overconfident in their ability to choose stocks, even in the absence of solid information. A study of online brokerage accounts showed that investors given initial positive feedback (i.e., the stocks they choose go up in price) become more and more aggressive in their trading, even though the costs of active trading more than wipe out any abnormal positive returns. Barber & Odean, Trading Is Hazardous to Your Wealth: The Common Stock Investment Performance of Individual Investors, 55 J. Fin. 773 (2000) (examination of trading in over 66,000 accounts of a discount brokerage firm for 1991-1996 found that the average return of those that traded the most was 11.4 percent whereas the average for the entire sample was 16.4 percent and return for the market was 17.9 percent).

Research has also examined the role of emotions in investment decision-making. Curiously, there is evidence that things as simple as the weather have an impact on investment decisions, even among professionals. Hirshleifer & Shumway, Good Day Sunshine: Stock Returns and the Weather, 58 J. Fin. 1009 (2003).

So what? We might consider the above-described behavioral insights in light of two distinct, albeit related, questions. First, what are their implications for the efficient market hypothesis? *See* Gilson & Kraakman, The Mechanisms of Market Efficiency Twenty Years Later: The Hindsight Bias, 28 J. Corp. L. 715, 738 (2003) ("three conditions must be met for psychological distortions to affect share prices: (1) cognitive biases must be pervasive, . . . (2) they must be correlated (because otherwise they are offsetting), . . . and finally, (3) the arbitrage mechanism must fail with respect to their effects"). The second concern is how effective is securities regulation's dominant strategy—mandatory disclosure—if investors' choices are more influenced by social or emotional factors than by rational study and analysis. If excitement leads someone considering whether to buy in the aftermarket of an IPO to have a diminished sensitivity to risk probabilities, how useful is a list of risk factors in the prospectus? Will the investor even be interested enough to read it?

Indeed, if individual investment decisionmaking is heavily influenced by bias and emotions, should effective securities regulation take a completely different approach—investor education designed to counteract the influence techniques of Wall Street, the issuer community, and the financial media, perhaps going so far as to throw cold water on the idea that investing heavily in stocks is the most profitable way to plan for one's financial future? *See* Hu, Faith and Magic: Investor Beliefs and Government Neutrality, 78 Tex. L. Rev. 777 (2000).

C. Institutionalization

Who owns America? This is not an irrelevant question in securities regulation. Ownership of American securities arises through their acquisition in either a primary distribution or a trading transaction. Insight into the composition of investors in each type of transaction will improve the fairness and efficiency of regulatory choices. Certainly the regulatory choices should be assessed differently if the bulk of trading investors are widowers and orphans and, worse yet, unsophisticated in the world of finance, than if most investment is by financially robust, sophisticated, and resourceful financial institutions.

Consider the distribution of ownership of equities as set forth in the following excerpt:

> In the 1950s, institutional investors held less than 10 percent of the stock of the largest 1,000 public companies. Certain types of institutional investors (mutual funds, pension funds, insurance companies, foundations and savings institutions) together now hold more than 50 percent of US equities. Among the top 1,000 companies in the United States, ownership of these institutions is even higher— representing more than 70 percent of equity holdings. Individual shareholders are the direct beneficial owners of approximately 32 percent of US public company stock. Most of these individual owners hold their shares through brokers or bank custodians. As of mid-2013, approximately 52 percent of Americans—a 15-year low—reported owning stock, either directly or indirectly through a mutual fund or self-directed retirement account.

The Conference Board, What Is the Optimal Balance in the Relative Roles of Management, Directors, and Investors in the Governance of Public Corporations? 9-10 (2014).

Eighty percent of the total market value of the S&P 500 is held by financial institutions and as the companies' size increases so does the ownership held by institutions (institutions own slightly more than 85 percent of large companies such as Apple, Microsoft, and Facebook). McGrath, Pensions & Investing (Apr. 25, 2017). Another study of public companies found that among a random, albeit statistically representative, sample of public companies, 96 percent of the firms had a holder of at least 5 percent of the voting securities and on average such a blockholder owned 26 percent (average ownership of among all blockholders per firm being 39 percent). Holderness, The Myth of Diffuse Ownership in the United States, 22 Rev. Fin. Studies 1377 (2009) (observing an inverse relationship between firm size and blockholder ownership concentration).

Table 3-1 reports the securities holdings of the most relevant types of American financial institutions. On the basis of the data, how would you answer the question "Who owns America?"

Institutionalization is the product of a set of forces—social, political, and economic. See generally M.J. Roe, Strong Managers, Weak Owners (1994); Clark, The Four Stages of Capitalism, 94 Harv. L. Rev. 561 (1981). American society has evolved to the stage where retirement funds are provided through a pension plan, which like the weekly paycheck is a feature of the employee-employer relationship. Our tax laws favor this arrangement, and our society has come to expect such from socially responsible employers. Even the self-employed

TABLE 3-1
U.S. Holdings of Equities by Type of Holder—Value and Percentage 2017

	Market Value (Billions)	Share of Total (Percentage)
Total U.S. Holdings	**45,824.6**	**100%**
Households	17,877.3	39.0%
Institutions	27,947.4	61.0%
Mutual funds	10,829.2	23.6%
Foreign	7,079.7	15.4%
Exchange-traded funds	2,775.6	6.1%
State and local government retirement funds	2,668.1	5.8%
Private pension funds	2,662.9	5.8%
Life insurance companies	508.7	1.1%
Property casualty companies	390.8	0.9%
Federal government retirement funds	323.8	0.7%
Broker/dealers	224.0	0.5%
State and local governments	210.5	0.5%
U.S. chartered depository institutions	131.7	0.3%
Closed-end funds	109.2	0.2%
Federal government	33.2	0.1%

Note: Households include nonprofit organizations.

Source: SIFMA Fact Book for 2018 extracted from Federal Reserve Flow of Funds, L.223.

person's retirement depends on funds that are committed to either an insurance company or a mutual fund. Add to this the proliferation of consumer-oriented financial products, such as "cash management accounts," variable annuities, and universal life insurance investment programs, which further accelerate the flow of funds to financial institutions. Moreover, the mutual fund has replaced the savings account as the typical family's major source of savings. A further consideration is the economies of scale that are available for investment activities, which cause an ever-increasing number of households to rely upon institutional intermediaries, rather than carrying out this activity themselves. Theoretical developments have also nurtured institutionalization. Under the influence of portfolio theory, investors seek the kind of professional diversification they can obtain through mutual funds, whether they prefer the more passive investment of an "index fund" or the aggressive pursuit of a certain niche of the economy in a "sector fund." Though investors could construct their own portfolios, the transaction and opportunity costs in doing so are considerably higher than those incurred in pursuing their objective through a financial institution.

D.   Globalization

Institutionalization is not the only force shaping the participants in and character of American capital markets. Willie Sutton is immortalized for answering, "That's where the money is," when questioned why he robbed banks. Things have changed since Sutton's laconic reply. Fiber optics and satellite technology now allow money to move quickly throughout the world, so that raising capital and investing can happen anywhere and in fact does happen everywhere. By making the world smaller, technology has contributed mightily to the globalization of capital markets. With respect to the rapid changes taking place because of such globalization, consider the following data on cross-border capital flows. As a measure of such cross-border activity, consider that in 2017, U.S. investors owned $8.9 trillion of stock (trading $10 trillion in foreign equity in that year) in foreign companies (and $2.8 trillion of their bonds); in the same year, foreign investors held $7 trillion of U.S. stocks and $4 trillion of U.S. corporate bonds. SIFMA 2018 Fact Book 61, 62 & 66. The rising level of global trading reflects a growing appetite on the part of both U.S. and foreign investors to diversify their holdings across countries. As we will see, this poses a challenge to securities regulators around the globe as they grapple with the complexities of globalized securities offerings and trading.

An attractive feature of U.S. markets for foreign investors and foreign issuers that choose to have their companies' shares traded in the United States is the greater depth of U.S. capital markets compared with most foreign markets (the major exception being London). U.S. regulators cannot claim sole responsibility for this attractive feature. An important consideration is that the predominant characteristic of U.S. and U.K. public companies is that their ownership is widely dispersed among numerous shareholders. In contrast, a central characteristic of companies in most countries is that they are controlled by a family or the State. *See* LaPorta, Lopez-de-Silanes & Shleifer, Corporate Ownership Around the World, 54 J. Fin. 471 (1999). A further consideration here is the ease with which those in control of the foreign company can, under their home country laws, act opportunistically vis-à-vis the controlled company or the minority owners. *See* LaPorta, Lopez-de-Silanes, Shleifer & Vishny, Law and Finance, 106 J. Pol. Econ. 1113 (1998) (least-developed capital markets were found in countries providing the weakest protection to investors and minority owners); LaPorta, Lopez-de-Silanes, Shleifer & Vishny, Legal Determinants of External Finance, 52 J. Fin. 1131 (1997) (same). What, then, do foreign issuers gain by listing their securities in the United States? Consider here that when a foreign issuer's shares are listed on an exchange in the United States or on Nasdaq it must comply with most U.S. disclosure requirements; however, internal governance questions, including the existence and scope of fiduciary obligations, are determined by the laws of its home country. Should a U.S. investor be neutral between investing in a French company traded on the Paris Bourse and a French company listed on the NYSE? What issues arise in assessing the risks of a French company and a U.S. company if each is traded on the NYSE?

One aspect of globalization is the increasing interconnectedness of capital markets, a characteristic that was dramatically illustrated by events in October 1987. On "Black Monday," October 19, 1987, the Dow Jones Industrial Average (an index of 30 NYSE stocks) plunged 508 points or 22.6 percent. This began a financial tsunami, as when trading began in Tokyo on October 20 (October 19 in New York due to the International Date Line), nearly 21 percent of the stocks were unable to open because of order imbalances on the sell side, and the market declined overall 14.7 percent, a record one-day decline. Nervousness next reached the London market, which immediately fell 19 percent and was off

12.2 percent for the day. In the words of the SEC staff, "it does appear that a cataclysmic market event such as that which occurred on October 19 can be expected to have worldwide repercussions." SEC, The October 1987 Market Break, 11-7, 11-8 (1988).

That the world is shrinking means more than that economic events have worldwide repercussions; it poses serious regulatory concerns, especially for the United States, whose level of securities regulation is unrivaled. For example, outside of the United States, many industrialized countries do not require public corporations to issue quarterly earnings reports, and their annual financial reports are not nearly as detailed or comprehensive as those required for American publicly traded corporations. Moreover, most industrialized countries do not maintain the level of enforcement staff regularly policing American securities markets, and the deterrence and disciplining influence of private causes of action are nearly nonexistent because of the absence of class action and contingency fee devices. In later chapters, we will see how U.S. securities laws have responded to the realities posed by increasing globalization of securities distributions and trading.

4

The Public Offering

This chapter examines the demands Section 5 of the Securities Act makes on those involved in distributing a security when neither the security nor the transaction is exempt from Section 5's registration and prospectus delivery requirements. The ultimate regulatory objective is a registration statement that is filed with the SEC that sets forth material facts bearing on the issuer and the offered security. The expectation is that information in a registration statement will reach sophisticated market participants, so that even any secondary market in which the registered security is traded will be equally informed by information contained in the registration statement and prospectus for the registered security. As will be seen, much of the former paper-based disclosures mandated by the Securities Act now occur through the Internet. This reflects not only that information can be distributed more broadly, cheaply, and reliably through electronic media, but also that the dissemination of information can be better controlled and timed through electronic media than under the paper-based system. The power and the ubiquity of the Internet are largely responsible for prompting the sweeping reforms examined in this chapter that the SEC adopted in June 2005 for regulating the public offering process.

A later section of this chapter provides an overview of the type of information customarily included in a registration statement. For now, it should be observed that the type and content of disclosures are guided by many considerations, starting with the express requirements set forth in the Commission's rules for completing registration statements. But these rules merely set forth the minimal disclosures required. Of great importance here is Section 11 of the Securities Act, which imposes liability upon the issuer, its principal officers, its directors, and its underwriters for any material omissions or misstatements in the registration statement when it became effective. The issuer's outside accountants are also liable if they have certified materially misleading financial statements that are included in the registration statement. Each of these parties therefore has significant liability exposure when preparing material for the registration statement, and this factor further drives the form and content of the disclosures made.

Because public offerings customarily occur through underwriters, the first section of this chapter describes common underwriting arrangements as well as the culture of underwriters (or, more particularly, investment bankers) and some of the conflicts of interest they commonly face when underwriting securities. Later sections examine the many aspects of the registration process under both the Securities Act and the state blue sky laws. Particularly close attention is given to the severe limitations Section 5 imposes on the timing and manner of soliciting investors through the use of a prospectus. The special regulatory problems that arise under Section 5 in connection with multinational offerings are also examined later in this chapter along with a comparative review of securities regulations practices of selected developed and developing countries.

A. Underwriting and Underwriters

1. Methods of Underwriting

> **In re National Association of Securities Dealers, Inc., Exchange Act Release No. 17371**
> Securities and Exchange Commission (Dec. 12, 1980)

III. THE FIXED PRICE UNDERWRITING SYSTEM

. . . A corporation may acquire needed funds in several ways. It may, for example, borrow money from a bank. It may also sell securities in either a public offering or a private one. If the corporation decides to offer securities, it may engage the services of broker-dealers to sell the securities to the public in either "firm commitment" or "best efforts" underwritings. In a firm commitment underwriting, one or more investment banking firms agree to purchase the securities from the issuer for resale to the public at a specified public offering price. In a best efforts underwriting, broker-dealers do not purchase the securities from the issuer but instead agree for a fee to use their best efforts to sell the securities on behalf of the issuer at the offering price.

In a typical firm commitment offering of securities, investment banking firms organize an underwriting syndicate. Each member of the syndicate agrees to purchase from the issuer a specified amount of the securities and to resell those securities at a specified public offering price. The syndicate is managed by a managing underwriter who, on behalf of the syndicate, executes with the issuer an "underwriting agreement." The underwriting agreement spells out the terms of the offering and the amount of securities that each syndicate member is committed to buy or underwrite.

The syndicate members also execute an "agreement among underwriters" that establishes the obligations of each member. Typically, the agreement grants to the managing underwriter (or underwriters) broad discretionary authority to conduct the offering. Pursuant to that agreement, the managing underwriter may be authorized, among other things, to buy and sell in the open market and for the account of the underwriters the securities being offered, to charge each underwriter for expenses incurred by the manager and to terminate the agreement. The managing underwriter may also select additional broker-dealers to assist the syndicate in selling the securities. Those dealers, who may also be syndicate members (the "selling group"), will sign a "selected dealer agreement," setting forth their rights and obligations, including their agreement to sell the securities at the public offering price.

Both the underwriters and the selected dealers agree to sell the securities to the public[15] at a fixed public offering price. The difference between that price and the amount received by the issuer is known as the "gross spread." The spread may range in size from a fraction of 1 to 10% or more of the public offering price depending upon a number of factors, including the characteristics of the security, the risk to the underwriters, the amount of selling effort required and the costs of distributing the security.

The spread normally is composed of three parts: (i) the management fee for the managing underwriter, (ii) the underwriting compensation received by the underwriters, and (iii) the "selling concession" received for any securities sold to the public by any broker-dealer participating in the distribution. Usually, the amount of the selling concession is set in advance by the managing underwriter and may be as much as 60 to 65% of the spread depending upon the effort required to sell the security. The selling concession has increased as a percentage of the spread in recent years.[16]

In connection with some fixed price offerings, the underwriters may elect to "stabilize" the market for the offered security during the distribution. The managing underwriter places in the primary market for the security a syndicate bid to purchase the security that is being underwritten. The bid price is usually set at or just under the public offering price. Stabilization is intended to facilitate an orderly distribution of securities by preventing or retarding a marked decline in the price of the offered security.[17]

As described above, the amount of securities underwritten by each syndicate member is set by agreement. Typically, however, each syndicate member retains control over and directly places only a portion of the securities it agrees to underwrite. This portion is known as its "retention." The remainder of the underwritten securities is placed in a general syndicate account, often called

---

15.   Usually, the syndicate and selling group members are also permitted to sell the underwritten securities to one another and to any other NASD member at the public offering price less a dealer reallowance that does not exceed a stated percentage of the selling concession.

16.   Witnesses testified at the hearings that the spread negotiated by the issuer and the underwriters is often smaller in an offering that will be sold primarily to institutional purchasers since offerings of that type usually require less selling effort than offerings sold primarily to individuals. Testimony of Goldman Sachs & Co.; Sanford C. Bernstein & Co., Inc.

17.   The syndicate's stabilizing activities during the offering must be conducted in accordance with the provisions of Rule [104] under the Act. Witnesses at the hearings testified that stabilization frequently occurs in offerings of equity securities, but almost never in offerings of debt securities. *See* testimony of the NASD; McCarthy, Ried, Crisanti & Maffei, Inc.

the "pot," under the control of the managing underwriter. During the course of the distribution, the managing underwriter allocates and reallocates securities among syndicate and selling group members for a variety of reasons, particularly the ability of the member to sell the securities. As explained below, the "pot" also provides institutional customers with the convenience of centralized billing and delivery.

Purchasers that buy large amounts of a security, such as institutions, frequently may place their orders directly with the managing underwriter. Customarily, the managing underwriter will deliver the securities and confirm the transaction, but the purchaser may direct that the sale be credited to the account of one or more dealers that are syndicate or selling group members ("designated orders"). The preference of some customers to place designated orders with the managing underwriter has caused some dealers to be included in the selling group at the request of prospective purchasers in cases where the dealers might not otherwise have been asked to participate.

NOTES AND QUESTIONS

1. Issuer Meets Underwriter. In most cases, the relationship between the issuer and the managing underwriter for an upcoming public offering begins months before the public offering is commenced. As is seen in later materials, the managing underwriter renders advice over wide-ranging issues pertinent to preparing the issuer for the public offering. The advice touches on matters such as the type and amount of security to be sold, the offering's timing, and the steps the issuer can take before the offering to put itself in as attractive a light as possible. Not to be overlooked here is the assistance the underwriter can provide in helping the issuer to arrange its own financial affairs in preparation for the disclosure that must be made in its upcoming registration statement. These various steps are much easier, of course, for the company that is already public, especially if it is already a reporting company, than they are for the company considering an initial public offering (IPO).

The reputation of the lead underwriter affects nearly every aspect of an offering, whether it be an IPO, seasoned equity offering, or bond offering. Evidence consistently reflects that offerings headed by more highly reputed underwriters command higher prices, receive more price support during the offering, and overall perform better relative to the market. These benefits give rise to higher demand for the services of blue-chip underwriters, who garner more in fees and market share than lower-reputation underwriters. *See* Fang, Investment Bank Reputation and the Price and Quality of Underwriting Services, 60 J. Fin. 2729 (2005). Not surprisingly, offering/issuer risk corresponds to underwriter reputation.

The risks of a firm commitment underwriting include being left with a sticky issue—an offering for which investor interest is so weak that the underwriters require a much longer time to sell the entire issue than expected or, worse, they cannot sell the entire amount. In such a case, the managing underwriter's reputation suffers greatly by having misjudged the issuer and the market for its securities. Such a misjudgment also harms its co-underwriters. Furthermore, to the extent the shares underwritten cannot be sold, the underwriters' capital is tied up in what is likely to be a losing or somewhat illiquid investment and cannot be used for more lucrative purposes. Hence, the managing underwriter, and all underwriters generally, do not approach the issuer cavalierly. In this respect, it is worth considering whether the quality of an offering is signaled not only by the quality of the underwriters involved with its distribution, but also by whether the arrangement is a best efforts or firm commitment underwriting. *See* Bae et al., Determinants of Underwriter Participation in Initial Public Offerings of Common Stock: An Empirical Study, 26 J. Bus., Fin. & Acct. 595 (1999).

   2.   Best Efforts Underwriting and Underwriting Hierarchies.   There are in fact three types of best efforts underwriting, each with different degrees of risk for the underwriter: the "straight," the "mini/maxi," and the "all or none." The difference among these three is the threshold number of shares that must be sold before the offering can close and the underwriter can earn its commission. In a *straight* best efforts offering, any securities sold to investors remain sold; there is no minimum amount that must be sold as a condition to the deal closing. Under the *mini/maxi* arrangement, a stipulated minimum amount of all the shares to be sold must be sold during a specific period of time before the offering can close: Proceeds of all sales are placed in escrow until the minimum number of shares is sold. If the minimum number is not sold, the deal falls through, and the money held in escrow is returned to the potential purchasers. Finally, in an *all or none* offering, all the securities must be sold before the deal is completed.
   When a best efforts underwriting collapses because the underwriter has failed to sell the minimum, the temptation is sometimes irresistible to "fudge," so that the issuer can receive the proceeds and the underwriter, its commission. *See, e.g., SEC v. Manor Nursing Centers, Inc.*, 458 F.2d 1082 (2d Cir. 1972). Exchange Act Rule 15c2-4 deems it "fraudulent, deceptive or manipulative" to close out an offering before satisfying its stated conditions. Rules 10b-9 and 15c2-2 contain other requirements, such as that the time period and price must be specific and the escrow agreement must be in writing. *See SEC v. First Pacific Bancorp*, 143 F.3d 1186 (9th Cir. 1998).
   Does the precise type of best efforts underwriting signal to the investment public the relative risk of the project? One study found that the average offering price for securities promoted through a best efforts arrangement was $1.45 per share as compared with $8.74 per share for firm commitment underwritings. Moreover, the average best efforts offering raised $2.8 million per offering, whereas the average firm commitment offering raised $9 million. Johnson & Miller, Going Public: Information for Small Businesses, J. Small Bus. Mgmt. 39 (Summer 1988); D'Amico, In the End, Are Best Efforts Your Best Buy?, Venture, July 1985, at 20 (two-thirds of the best efforts IPOs had lost money one year after their sale versus only one-half of the firm commitment IPOs and, more ominously, of the 25 underwriters who sponsored the best efforts underwriting in the study, only 18 were still in business one year later).

   3.   Screening.   When a company is considering going public, the initial question is whether the issuer is ready to go public.

   The most important function performed during origination is the selection of candidates for public investment. The decision to underwrite a particular issue is normally made only after careful investigation of the issuer and evaluation of its prospects. Not all corporations are able to win sponsorship . . . and prestigious underwriters reject many more candidates than they accept. . . . [T]he screening and investigative processes employed in origination should weed out those prospective issuers least likely to make productive use of publicly invested funds and should identify elements of risk in those issues which are selected and presented to the public.

Dooley, The Effects of Civil Liability on Investment Banking and the New Issues Market, 58 Va. L. Rev. 776, 785-787 (1972). While the underwriter does approach this question with a view of preserving its reputation, it also is true that competition for underwriting commissions is keen and, therefore, a serious consideration. On this point, what impact would you expect regulatory developments that enhanced competitive bidding to have on the eagerness of investment bankers to underwrite risky issuers?

When seeking an underwriter, issuers also have their priorities. Today, venture capital firms (VCs) are prevalent holders of shares in companies contemplating a public offering. Typically, VCs dispose of their shares in a follow-on offering that occurs 6-12 months after the IPO. Similarly, insiders eagerly contemplate the post-IPO period as they customarily agree not to sell for 180 days after the IPO. Hence, insiders and VCs hope that the ardor for the issuer created by the underwriter's promotional efforts in connection with the IPO will not only push the IPO out the window, but that there will be analyst coverage in the post-IPO period that will sustain investor interest so they can later exit and perhaps even at a price higher than the IPO price. This most likely occurs if the underwriter provides "all-star" analyst coverage of the issuer in the post-IPO period. Thus, during the "beauty contest" in which issuers interview underwriters, there is a good deal of focus on analyst coverage. *See* Liu & Ritter, Local Underwriter Oligopolies and IPO Underpricing, 102 J. Fin. Econ. 579 (2011).

We can now understand some of the forces that contribute to the oligopoly-like structure that exists among lead underwriters. Underwriters offer a variety of things: underwriter quality/reputation, industry expertise, and analyst coverage. Because there are a limited number of firms who can provide *all* of these services, an oligopoly ensues.

    4. The Certification Function of Other Professionals. The public offering of securities poses a classic information asymmetry problem where the issuer enjoys much greater knowledge regarding the offered security's value than do outside investors. The issuer's pitch that "this is a great investment" can be received with skepticism by the investor who expects all issuers to make such a claim, valid or otherwise. Certainly such a boast made by the seasoned company with a solid financial history is met with less skepticism than when made by the issuer contemplating an IPO. As seen above, issuers seek high-reputation underwriters as one of the strategies they pursue to signal the security's quality. Can the quality of the law firm that prepares the opinion letter stating the offered security has been validly authorized under the laws of the issuer's domicile also be a means for issuers to signal the quality of the offering? *See* Barondes, Nyce & Sanger, Law Firm Prestige and Performance in IPOs: Underwriter's Counsel as Gatekeeper or Turnstile, 2 Cap. Markets L.J. 164 (2007); Okamoto, Reputation

and the Value of Lawyers, 74 Or. L. Rev. 15, 31 (1995). What about the quality
of the accounting firm that audits the issuer's financial statements? A further
question here is the certification function provided by the VC that has provided financing to the issuer prior to its IPO. How should investors interpret
the VC selling within the public offering a significant portion of its stake in the
issuer? *See* Gompers & Lerner, Conflicts of Interest in the Issuance of Public
Securities: Evidence from Venture Capital, 42 J.L. & Econ. 1, 18 (1999) (collecting data supporting the conclusion that the greater the stake the VC sells to the
public the greater the likelihood of the issuer's long-term success).

    5.   *Rights Offerings and the Accompanying Paradox.*   A small percentage of all
offerings registered with the SEC are "rights offerings," in which the issuer's
existing stockholders are granted the opportunity (i.e., right) to purchase the
new offering of shares, usually at a discount below their current market price.
It is common practice for the issuer to enter into a "standby agreement" with
an investment banker (or syndicate of investment bankers) under which the
banker agrees to purchase any of the offering's shares that are not subscribed
for by the existing shareholders exercising their rights. Because the issuer's
shareholders usually have several weeks in which to exercise their rights, the
underwriters incur non-trivial market risks during this time as they stand by to
acquire whatever shares remain unsold. This risk is partially reduced by purchasing the issued "rights" from the shareholders and selling the shares they
acquire through those rights; in this case, they need not wait until the rights
portion of the offering closes to complete the distribution of the shares.
    The finance literature identifies a paradox posed by rights offerings.
Evidence consistently demonstrates that issuers who finance themselves through
rights offerings incur significantly lower underwriting costs than under the standard firm commitment underwriting arrangement; the cost savings are present
even after taking into account the discounted purchase price of the issuer's
shareholders. Paradoxically, rights offerings by U.S. issuers occur rarely. Why
then don't more corporate issuers employ rights offerings? One possible answer
is suggested by the fact that companies that employ rights offerings are those
in which a significant amount of the stock is owned by a few shareholders or by
the current management. *See* Cronqvist, The Choice Between Rights Offerings
and Private Equity Placement, 78 J. Fin. Econ. 375 (2005) (corporate control
considerations have an important effect on the decision to undertake a rights
offering). Another explanation is that U.S. rights offerings typically occur without affording non-participating shareholders the types of protection against
dilution that are common in Europe. *See* Holderness & Pontiff, Shareholder
Nonparticipation in Valuable Rights Offerings, 120 J. Fin. Econ. 252 (2016)
(finding U.S. shareholder participation averaged 64 percent and results in
wealth transfer from nonparticipating shareholders to participating shareholders equal to about 7 percent of the offering's value).

    **6.   *The Shrinking Role of the Middleman: First the "Bought Deal" and Now the
Internet.***   As is examined later in this chapter, the cumbersome and time-
consuming registration procedures were greatly reduced in 1982 for most large
publicly traded companies when the SEC instituted its integrated disclosure
system and authorized shelf registration procedures (each discussed later in

this chapter) that allow large issuers to tap capital markets more quickly. These developments substantially shortened the regulatory process so that issuers no longer faced "market risk" related to the earlier long-term preregistration consultation and preparation process. Consequentially, competitive bidding among underwriters (generally referred to as the "bought deal") thereafter became the norm for large-seasoned companies. A tandem development was the rapid rise of institutional investors who became dominant purchasers in registered offerings by large issuers eligible to take advantage of the SEC's integrated disclosure and shelf registration procedures. Thus, for many high-grade issuers, the presence of institutional buyers and the ability to satisfy the registration requirements quickly through use of the Commission's integrated disclosure system have led to competitive bidding among underwriters so that lower underwriting commissions resulted. Because the bought deal forecloses the type of pre-selling efforts that accompany the traditionally underwritten offering, the bought deal flourishes for those issuers where there are ready purchasers for the shares among the financial institutions. Why don't those issuers, who customarily rely on competitive bidding to sell their securities, simply eliminate the underwriter by dealing directly with financial institutions?

     7.   *Dutch Auctions.*   Under the Dutch auction technique, the issuer solicits bids from institutions and broker-dealers for any amount of securities each bidder wishes to acquire; the bidder states the amount of securities it wishes to purchase and the amount it will pay for those securities. All bids are irrevocable offers to purchase that amount of securities (unless withdrawn before the preset time for closing all bids). At closing, the bids are arrayed with the highest bid price first and the lowest bid price last. The issuer first accepts the bid with the highest price for the amount of securities covered in that bidder's bid; other bids are accepted at successively lower prices for the amount of securities covered in each bid until the issuer has placed all the registered securities. The lowest price accepted by the issuer through this process is the price paid by *all* bidders whose bids were accepted through the process. To illustrate, assume the managing underwriter learns the following in response to a Dutch auction to sell 8 million shares:

Number of Shares Investors Will Purchase at = Price

Shares	Price
4 million	$15
5 million	14
9 million	13
11 million	12

What is the sale price? What in the above information suggests it is likely that open market trades immediately following the offering will be higher than the offering price?

     Recently, the Dutch auction has been married to the Internet. Certain online underwriting firms conduct Dutch auctions over the Internet and compete for underwritings by offering commissions of 3-5 percent instead of the more common 7 percent charged by established firms.

The Dutch auction has its critics. *See* Oh, The Dutch Auction Myth, 42 Wake Forest L. Rev. 853 (2007) (Dutch auctions are susceptible to fraud and manipulation in ways that offerings via traditional underwriting are not). When Google went public in 2007, it created quite a stir with its decision to do so via a Dutch auction. For the view that Google's choice of an underwriting method was not driven by a desire to reduce its underwriters' commissions, but by a strategic marketing decision to underscore its public image as an innovative, independent spirit, *see* Fleischer, Brand New Deal: The Branding Effect of Corporate Deal Structures, 104 Mich. L. Rev. 1581 (2006).

8. *Direct Listing.* With a direct listing, instead of selling newly issued securities to the public, an issuer simply makes previously issued shares available on a trading market. These shares were likely distributed in private sales — possibly, though not necessarily, with the assistance of an investment banking firm — but now will be available for wider trading. Spotify Technology S.A. effected the most well-known direct listing in April of 2018. Below is a transcript of a video Spotify posted in March 2018 explaining why it pursued a direct listing instead of a traditional underwritten IPO.

> Many people have speculated about why Spotify is pursuing a Direct Listing. We think it is best that you hear directly from us why we think this is the right approach for the people at Spotify.
>
> From where we sit, there are five key reasons. First, to list without the Company having to sell shares. Second, to offer liquidity for shareholders. Third, to provide equal access to all buyers and sellers. Fourth, to conduct the process with radical transparency. And fifth, is to enable market-driven price discovery through the New York Stock Exchange.
>
> So, let's take a look at each one individually. Spotify is not selling any shares. There is no underwritten offering and there are no underwriters. Why? Because there's no reason to dilute our existing shareholders to raise money we don't need. We are already well capitalized, with over one-point-five billion euro in cash and cash equivalents as of year-end, have no debt after the exchange of our Convertible Notes, and have positive Free Cash Flow.
>
> As a publicly listed company, Spotify's private investors and employee shareholders will be able to sell their shares on the New York Stock Exchange, instead of the private market. They will also be able to sell their shares at a time of their choosing, subject to securities laws. And as a publicly listed company, new investors will be able to purchase Spotify shares should they wish, provided there is a willing seller.
>
> Our third reason is to provide equal access to buyers and sellers. Any investor who wants to buy Spotify shares will be able to do so on the Exchange. There's no underwriting syndicate, no limited float, no IPO allocations, and no preferential treatment for any investor. Unlike the traditional IPO, it's a completely level playing field with no built in "pop" for anyone. Our shareholders and employees will not be subjected to any underwriter mandated lockups, so supply will not be unnaturally constrained and price will not be distorted by market stabilization activities or short sellers gaming a lock-up expiration.

Our fourth reason is to ensure that we conduct the Direct Listing process with radical transparency. Spotify has filed a [registration statement] with the SEC that provides full financial disclosure, just like we would have if we had conducted a traditional underwritten IPO. Instead of a traditional roadshow process focused on a relatively small group of U.S. based institutional investors, we are hosting an Investor Day presentation which will be streamed live and viewable around the world. A recording will be made available for subsequent and unrestricted playback and reference. And our entire leadership team will be participating so that investors can hear directly from the management team running the company.

Finally, just like a publicly traded company, Spotify will be issuing guidance to the market, prior to the commencement of trading on the New York Stock Exchange.

And lastly, we believe that market forces should drive price discovery, like they do for the majority of publicly traded stocks where supply and demand find equilibrium through a transparent process, without the friction created by traditional lock-ups and a limited float.

It is our belief that the wisdom of crowds trumps expert intervention, and that the market price for Spotify will find equilibrium through natural market forces.

We set out to reimagine the IPO process, because we believe we can. Why? Because . . . Our brand is well known and well liked. We have global scale. We have an easy to understand business model. We have a transparent company culture. And we have a belief that the stock price will take care of itself if we build a great company.

Thank you for your time and interest.

Note that Spotify engaged Goldman Sachs, Morgan Stanley, and Allen & Company to advise it on the listing, including consulting with the NYSE designated market maker for its shares in setting the opening trading price for its shares. Spotify's registration statement lists $35 million as "Other advisers' fees," which it presumably paid to these firms. Additionally, Spotify filed a Securities Act registration statement with the SEC to register the resale of shares Spotify previously issued to Spotify affiliates and employees. Details about registering resales of securities are covered in Chapter 6.

9.   *Self-Underwritten Offerings.* In a self-underwritten offering, also called a direct public offering or DPO, an issuer markets and sells its securities to the public itself without the aid of an underwriter. These deals are normally undertaken only by issuers who are unable to attract an underwriter. While the issuer in a self-underwritten offering saves on underwriting commissions and fees, it will have a hard time attracting investors for the offering. Many potential investors will be turned off by the lack of screening, certification, and post-offering support an underwriter brings to a deal. Further, potential investors will assume that the only reason the issuer is going the self-underwriting route is because every underwriter, if there are any, that considered taking on the offering passed.

10.   *Switching Underwriters.* A public company can be expected to engage in many securities offerings during its existence. A common reason for a public company changing underwriters in connection with an equity offering (known as a "seasoned equity offering") is to obtain the services of a higher-reputation underwriter and/or to acquire influential analyst support. Issuers need-ing neither—they are with a high-reputation underwriter and enjoy analyst coverage—experience lower issuing costs staying with their existing under-writer than switching. *See* Burch et al., Does It Pay to Be Loyal? An Empirical Analysis of Underwriting Relationships and Fees, 77 J. Fin. Econ. 673 (2006). On the other hand, when issuing bonds, issuers incur higher underwriting costs by staying loyal and average fees do not rise when bond underwriting is shifted for reasons of obtaining analyst coverage. Why would issuers have such a differ-ent experience with respect to bonds?

2.   Underwriters: Their Culture and Their Industry

a.   *Cultural Hierarchy*

The securities industry consists of firms engaged in many activities, which can be divided roughly into two broad categories: retail brokerage and invest-ment banking. The cyclical nature of revenues from the firms' brokerage business is partially offset by the somewhat steadier revenues from investment banking. Investment banking is of particular interest to us in this chapter, for investment banking includes the underwriting of securities offerings and refers to the wide range of financial planning and assistance services that investment banking firms render in connection with mergers, acquisitions, and recapital-izations. Underwriting is important to securities firms for several reasons. While it represents no more than about 10 percent of the total revenues of major investment banking houses, it nevertheless is one of the most profitable areas of their business. Furthermore, underwriting has the added benefit of establishing a relationship between the issuer and investment banker that leads to additional consulting and financial services by the investment banker.

The securities industry is characterized by its concentration, even though there are thousands of firms engaged in one or more of these activities. For example, fewer than a dozen firms have nationwide brokerage offices, and these firms account for most of the brokerage activities in secondary markets. Investment banking activities are particularly concentrated among a few firms, i.e., BofA Merrill, Citigroup, Goldman Sachs, JP Morgan Chase, and Morgan Stanley.

The concentration within investment banking is best indicated by a quick perusal of the list of underwriters at the bottom of the outside front cover page of a prospectus for a high-profile IPO. Below is the listing from Uber's May 2019 IPO:

Morgan Stanley	Goldman Sachs & Co. LLC	BofA Merrill Lynch
Barclays	Citigroup	Allen & Company LLC
RBC Capital Markets	SunTrust Robinson Humphrey	Deutsche Bank Securities
HSBC	SMBC	Mizuho Securities
Needham & Company	Loop Capital Markets	Siebert Cisneros Shank & Co., L.L.C.

Academy Securities	BTIG	Canaccord Genuity	CastleOak Securities, L.P.	Cowen	Evercore ISI	JMP Securities	Macquarie Capital
Mischler Financial Group, Inc.		Oppenheimer & Co.	Raymond James	William Blair	The Williams Capital Group, L.P.	TPG Capital BD

The listing reveals much more than industry concentration; it reveals an important social and financial hierarchy. The name or names appearing at the top of the list of syndicate members is the managing underwriter or underwriters for the offering. Being a manager underwriter is a favored position because it earns added commissions, selects the other houses that will be invited to participate in the offering, and establishes each participant's allotment. Larger offerings often have co-managers.

After the manager line is the *special bracket.* Being a member of this special bracket is a highly visible report of the firm's standing among its peers—a signal not missed by captains of industry considering whom to retain for investment banking services. It cannot be overemphasized that stature and prestige are what investment bankers build and retain their business on and the most tangible symbol of that standing is a firm's acceptance and standing among its fellow investment bankers. It should also be observed that, while competition for clients is keen among investment bankers, there is a good deal of mutual back scratching; those who are members of the special bracket in one offering, when they are later the manager of an offering, will include in that offering's special bracket the manager of the earlier offering.

Following the special bracket is the *major bracket,* the beginning of which is indicated by the beginning of a new alphabetical order. The members of this group are less well established in the industry than those that regularly appear in the special bracket. One's position in the bracket is important not just because it is hard to explain to your spouse and mother why you are not higher up, but also because the underwriting allotment for participants in the major bracket customarily is about 20 percent smaller than that allotted to participants in the special bracket. There are also several sub-brackets after the major bracket, with diminishing allotments. The firms in these sub-brackets are customarily included in the underwriting syndicate for their retailing efforts.

b. The Industry over Time

Investment banking did not take hold in America until the great capital needs of the railroads arose in the middle of the nineteenth century as the formerly agrarian nation industrialized. In the early 1900s, when the resources of banks, insurance companies, and trust companies expanded significantly, alliances, interconnections, and cross-ownership between these financial institutions and investment bankers became common. It was common that funds used for a firm-commitment underwriting were provided by a bank, an insurance company, or a trust company. In the aftermath of the Great Depression, Congress passed the Glass-Steagall Act, which separated the functions of banking from those of investment banking. Among the concerns of Glass-Steagall was that the solvency of banks were threatened if they were permitted to underwrite securities; moreover, banks may be tempted to make unwise loans to aid their investment bankers to underwrite questionable offerings. Furthermore, a bank affiliated with a broker-dealer would be tempted to steer its customer to the offering that that broker-dealer was underwriting and would advance their customers the funds with which to purchase the shares. As a result of Glass-Steagall, commercial banks were compelled to sever their relationships with investment bankers.

Conflicts of interests

The overall effect of Glass-Steagall was to assure there would be *no* profound changes in underwriting, or for that matter in the investment banking industry. It would continue the pyramidal syndicate design with management and allotments of offers being concentrated among the few. In sum, Glass-Steagall did not bring new entrants to investment banking; its bar to commercial banks engaging in investment banking assured that practices common to the industry for over 100 years would continue. And so the comfortable life of underwriters remained unchallenged until the early 1970s.

One notable development in the early 1970s was the regular appearance of Merrill Lynch and Salomon Brothers within the special bracket. Their good and steady service over half a century was finally rewarded. Merrill Lynch broke into the group by operating a highly efficient and effective retail operation servicing individual investors (it now also has a large institutional client base, a result of its enhanced prestige). Salomon Brothers won acceptance through its close relationship with its institutional clients. Both signaled the important market events: the return of retail customers to the marketplace and the rising influence of institutional investors.

However, the 1970s also ushered in rumblings within both the Congress and the SEC over the industry's adherence to fixed commission rates for brokerage. For decades, brokers charged all their customers—financial institutions and the proverbial small investor—the same flat percentage commission regardless of the size of the order and any accompanying economies of scale. The end of fixed commission rates for brokerage business came on May 1, 1975 ("May Day" to those in the industry), causing brokerage revenues to drop by 40 percent. The industry promptly began to change. Small and even medium-sized brokerage houses that were not viable after the monopolistic rate structure was lifted failed. Many other firms merged and combined, so that the industry became even more concentrated. The bright side of most of this activity was that revenues and profits from underwriting continued to be excellent. Also, in the 1970s, investment bankers began to introduce new products that overall boosted their earnings. From the highly popular money market funds to various asset-backed securities offerings to other novel investment devices, the investment bankers cushioned the blows deregulation otherwise had dealt their brokerage and underwriting business. And the merger and takeover frenzy of the 1980s, followed by corporate restructurings and positioning in the 1990s, produced astronomical fees for investment bankers involved in the "deals."

The 1970s introduced two other significant developments. The broad use of computers enabled investment banks to expand their proprietary trading operations. No longer were they just advising others how to invest; computing power enabled investment banks to be players. Trading, however, requires capital, and the more capital the better. Thus, investment banks ceased being intimate partnerships; they incorporated, went public, deployed the cash raised into their proprietary trading operations and, as seen above, went on an acquisition binge of acquiring lesser rivals. The big got bigger. We might wonder whether the rising importance of trading to their overall performance as well as incorporation caused reputation to assume a subsidiary purpose in their business? *See* Wilhelm & Morrison, Trust, Reputation and Law: The Evolution of Commitment in Investment Banking, 7 J. Leg. Analysis 1 (2015).

Overall, history has treated investment bankers well, and they have responded to this by doing well. *See* Carosso, Investment Banking in America (1970). However, we have moved into a very different regulatory environment that poses new challenges to investment bankers. First, in 1999, Congress enacted the Graham-Leach-Bliley Act (GLBA) and thereby repealed Glass-Steagall. GLBA permits insurance, merchant banking, underwriting, and banking to be conducted under a common holding company. Following GLBA, a holding company can be made up of several financial service affiliates, with each affiliate regulated by its own "functional regulator." The insurance affiliate is regulated by a state insurance commissioner, banking affiliates are regulated by a state or federal banking regulator, and the securities affiliate is subject to SEC regulation. Though the Federal Reserve retains "umbrella" supervisory powers for financial holding companies that include a bank, it generally defers to the examinations and reports of the functional regulator. For a negative view of GLBA, *see* Shivdasani et al., Breaking Down the Barriers: Competition, Syndicate Structure, and Underwriting Incentives, 99 J. Fin. Econ. 581 (2011) (GLBA observed to have led to more competition so that screening incentives were reduced for underwriters with consequential effect of increasing level of misrepresentations made in offerings during boom markets); Wilmarth, The Transformation of the U.S. Financial Services Industry, 1975-2000: Competition, Consolidation, and Increased Risks, 2002 Ill. L. Rev. 215 (GLBA does not facilitate efficiency but quests for market power and empire building through financial conglomeration). One effect of GLBA has been mergers between the once independent investment banks and commercial banks, so that the commercial bank's lending clout could be used to secure lucrative underwriting business for their underwriting (i.e., investment bank) subsidiary. *See* Druker & Puri, On the Benefits of Concurrent Lending and Underwriting, 60 J. Fin. 2763 (2005). Commercial banks use their lending-generated proprietary information to lower issuance costs, but address investor concerns of self-interest flowing from their position as a creditor by enlisting a high-reputation underwriter to serve as co-manager. Narayanan et al., The Role of Syndicate Structure in Bank Underwriting, 72 J. Fin. Econ. 555 (2004).

The biggest regulatory change is prompted by the "credit crisis" that began in early 2008. With the collapse of the housing market bubble, investment banks suffered substantial losses flowing from their significant derivative holdings that were backed by home mortgages. This caused the firms' credit ratings to plummet. Since investment banks had become highly leveraged and dependent on short-term borrowing to feed their cash needs, as credit sources dried up they became starved for cash and began to perish. The failure of Bear Stearns in March 2008 was soon followed by the bankruptcy of Lehman Brothers. Even mighty Merrill Lynch was not immune from the financial calamity; its financial problems led to its quick acquisition by Bank of America. In a quest for cash, the last two major investment banks, the legendary Goldman Sachs and Morgan Stanley, opted to transform themselves into bank holding companies to avail themselves of future customer deposits as a resource for meeting their regulatory minimum capital requirements. The credit crisis raised fears regarding the systemic risk that financial institutions, particularly large banks which combined commercial and investment banking operations, posed to the world economy.

Congress' response to the credit crisis was enactment of the Dodd-Frank Wall Street Reform and Consumer Protection Act of 2010. While Dodd-Frank has multiple foci, among its most significant initiatives addresses the systemic risks posed by the proprietary trading of investment banks. A key provision of Dodd-Frank, the Volcker Rule, examined later in Chapter 18, authorizes various regulators, including the SEC, to prohibit proprietary trading by financial institutions that have federally insured deposits. Thus, while the Act does not restore the broad prohibitions of Glass-Steagall, we can think of the Volcker Rule as having a similar aim: to reduce risk-taking activities of commercial banks. It remains to be seen how the industry will adjust to not just the Volcker Rule, but to multiple changes introduced by Dodd-Frank. But, if past is prologue, we can expect that the industry will adapt, endure, and likely thrive. *See generally* Davidoff, Morrison & Wilhelm, The SEC and Goldman Sachs: Reputation, Trust, and Fiduciary Duties in Investment Banking, 37 J. Corp. L. 529 (2012); Lo, The Gordon Gekko Effect: The Role of Culture in the Financial Industry, 22 NYFRB Pol'y Rev. 17 (2016).

3.   Underwriting Agreements: Contracting to Reduce Risk

a.   *Agreement with the Issuer*

A series of documents precedes any public offering of securities. In combination, they provide an interesting contractual web that binds the underwriting syndicate and the issuer together. The first such document is the *letter of intent,* which more or less represents the culmination of the preliminary negotiations and tentative understandings between the managing underwriter and the issuer. Tentative is an apt description because the underwriter in drafting the letter of intent studiously avoids any commitments to the issuer. The letter of intent reflects little more than the underwriter's interest in assisting the issuer in its proposed offering; however, it is the only document purporting to set forth the relationship between the issuer and its underwriter until shortly before the registration statement becomes effective, at which point the issuer and underwriter sign an underwriting agreement.

The formal underwriters' agreement with the issuer is executed immediately before the registration statement becomes effective. In addition to setting forth the amount and type of securities to be underwritten (augmented by any "greenshoe option" discussed below), the agreement includes the price to be paid the issuer, the identification of the syndicate members, the power of the managing underwriter to substitute one or more underwriters if any underwriter defaults, and provisions related to time of payment of the issuer as well as the obligations of the issuer to pay for printing and other expenses of furnishing investors a prospectus. The agreement between the issuer and the underwriter has several features designed to reduce the underwriters' risks.

The "Shoe." *Over-allotments* occur when more shares are distributed than the underwriting syndicate was obligated to purchase from the issuer. Over-allotments therefore entail the syndicate members' selling more shares than required by their firm commitment agreement with the issuer. This can occur because investor interest is unexpectedly strong for the issue, so that both the issuer and the underwriting syndicate benefit by tapping that interest through distributing more shares than originally planned. (When over-allotments are handled by purchasing additional shares from the issuer, it is usually pursuant to an option to do so in the agreement with the issuer; the option is known as a *greenshoe* option because it was first used in an offering by the Green Shoe Company.)

Over-allotments also arise because of stabilizing purchases carried out by the managing underwriter. As we will see in a later section, the managing underwriter sometimes purchases the distributed securities in the aftermarket so as to support their price. Such purchases by the lead underwriter provide liquidity for those who purchased the security from the syndicate, but those shares purchased for stabilization purposes have to be resold. Currently, FINRA limits the amount of over-allotments to 15 percent of the shares the underwriters are obligated to purchase. Agreements among underwriters customarily further limit their members' exposure to over-allotments by stating precisely how many shares can be purchased either in the market or from the issuer beyond those the syndicate is obligated to purchase and establishing a short time (e.g., 30 days) after which such purchases cannot be made.

The agreement between the issuer and the underwriters has several features designed to reduce the underwriters' risks.

Insider Lock-ups.   In IPOs, the underwriters customarily extract from the senior management of the issuer a promise by the managers not to sell any of their shares during the 180 days following the public offering. The managing underwriter can, however, approve earlier resells by the insiders. Why do the underwriters impose such lock-ups? *See generally* Brav & Gompers, The Role of Lock-ups in Initial Public Offerings, 16 Rev. Fin. Stud. 1 (2003) (insiders of firms with VCs or higher-quality underwriters are more likely to be released from their lock-up restrictions).

Market Out Clause.   A common feature of the firm commitment underwriters' agreements with the issuer is a clause that permits the underwriters to withdraw any time prior to the public offering and/or the settlement date (i.e., when the syndicate must pay for the securities purchased) if one of several exigent changes in circumstances develops: (1) The government or a self-regulatory organization (SRO) has imposed restrictions on the trading of securities in general; (2) there is a war or other national calamity; (3) there has been a material adverse change in markets (either generally or for the distributed security); or (4) there has been a material adverse event affecting the issuer. While the clause exists, it is considered poor form to exercise it, and, hence, it is rarely exercised. Why? Are syndicate members acting in their best interests not to exercise the clause when a change in market conditions assures the offering cannot easily be sold?

At what point does the market out clause convert the underwriting arrangement from being a firm commitment to a best efforts underwriting? In a no-action letter, the Commission's staff states:

> [M]arket out clauses . . . [that] permit the underwriter to terminate its obligations to purchase the offered securities from the issuer based upon (1) the occurrence of

nonmaterial events affecting the issuer or the securities markets in general, or (2) an inability to market the securities, are inappropriate in the context of a firm commitment underwriting. Such clauses place the risk of the success of the offering upon the issuer and result in the underwriter participating upon a "best efforts" basis.

First Boston Corp., SEC No-Action Letter, [1985-1986 Transfer Binder] Fed. Sec. L. Rep. (CCH) ¶78,152 (Sept. 2, 1985). *See Walk-In Medical Centers, Inc. v. Breur Capital Corp.*, 818 F.2d 260, 266 (2d Cir. 1987) (invoking the First Boston no-action letter position, and concluding that a decline in the price of an issuer's stock could not, under a fair interpretation of the clause, be considered an "adverse market condition").

Indemnification Provisions. Another risk underwriters face is liability under Section 11 of the Securities Act if, at the time the registration statement becomes effective, it contains an omission or misstatement of material fact. As discussed in Chapter 9, the underwriters can avoid liability if they can demonstrate they "had, after reasonable investigation, reasonable ground to believe and did believe" that the registration statement was not materially misleading. *See* Sections 11(a)(5), 11(b)(3). This "due diligence" defense imposes nontrivial investigation costs on underwriters participating in registered offerings; worse yet, there is always the fear that an underwriter's investigation will not in the particular case satisfy this statutory standard. In response to this fear, underwriters place in their agreement with the issuer various provisions designed to shift ultimate responsibility away from themselves and onto others.

A standard provision in the agreement with the issuer requires the issuer to indemnify the underwriters for any liability they may incur under federal or state laws because the registration statement or prospectus is materially misleading. The effect of indemnification is to *shift* the cost of liability to another—in this case, from the underwriters to the issuer. The standard indemnification clause, however, makes an exception for omissions and misstatements of matters peculiarly within the knowledge of the underwriters. As is examined later in this book, indemnification of securities violations generally has been viewed by the courts as inconsistent with the broad purpose of the civil liability provisions—that is, to assure compliance with the disclosure requirements of the federal securities laws. Interestingly enough, the Commission has not opposed the inclusion of indemnification clauses, although the Commission takes a much less charitable view of the issuer's agreement to indemnify its officers and directors. *See* Item 512(i) of Regulation S-K.

Contribution Provisions. If the underwriters cannot shift their liability by indemnification or opinion and comfort letters, discussed next, their fallback position is their provision for contribution among those liable under the registration statement. Contribution under Section 11 is examined in Chapter 9; it is sufficient at this point to observe that contribution clauses are valid and enforced because, unlike indemnification, which shifts responsibility to another party, contribution is a means for its burdens to be shared among equal wrongdoers.

Opinion, 10b-5, and Comfort Letters. The underwriters' further attempts at shifting any Section 11 losses to others are demonstrated by the requirement in the underwriting agreement that issuer's counsel provide the underwriter with an *opinion letter* at closing, stating various legal conclusions related to the offering, subject to qualifications and assumptions specified in the letter. Among other things, the letter will normally state that the issuer has the power and authority to execute and deliver the underwriting agreement and perform its obligations under it; consummating the securities offering and entering into the underwriting agreement does not violate the issuer's organizational documents, material agreements, or applicable laws; the sections of the registration statement describing the issuer's organizational documents fairly summarizes those documents; the issuer is not subject to litigation or, to counsel's knowledge, that no litigation is threatened that might affect the issuer's business materially; and the registration statement and the prospectus comply as to form in all material respects with the requirement of the Securities Act.

The underwriting agreement will likely also require issuer's counsel to deliver what is commonly known as a *10b-5 letter*. This letter states that nothing came to counsel's attention leading it to believe that the offering documents contain any materially misleading statements or omit to make any statements without which the offering documents would be materially misleading.

Underwriters' counsel usually provides the underwriters with an opinion letter and a 10b-5 letter.

Additionally, the underwriting agreement will require the issuer's outside auditor to give the underwriters a *comfort letter* immediately prior to the registration statement becoming effective and at closing providing assurances about financial information contained in the registration statement. To be sure, the outside accountants are already exposed to liability for any material misrepresentations in the financial statements they certify that are part of the registration statement. *See* Section 11(a)(4). But the underwriters will also ask the accountants to opine on a wide array of financial information that appears in charts and text in other portions of the registration statement, even though that information is not part of the financial statement formally certified by the accountants. Thus, through the comfort letter, the underwriters create a device by which they can recover on a theory of negligent or fraudulent preparation of the comfort letter for any liability the underwriters incur to investors, provided the sued-upon misrepresentations were also the subject of a comfort letter.

Obviously, opinion, 10b-5, and comfort letters are something counsel and accountants prefer not to provide, and, thus, the precise undertakings of their respective letters to the underwriters are a subject of extensive negotiation. Are these letters consistent with the likely purposes behind Congress' imposing Section 11 upon underwriters? Does your answer depend on whether Section 11's goal is compensation or deterrence?

Akin to the comfort letter extracted from counsel and accountants are various warranties and representations the issuer makes in its agreement with the underwriter, including warranties that the registration statement is free of materially misleading statements.

b. Agreement Among the Underwriters

As has been seen, the managing underwriter begins assembling the underwriting syndicate soon after being approached by the issuer. The formal understandings among the members of the syndicate are embodied in an *agreement among the underwriters*. The agreement has many important aspects, but only a few are emphasized here. The agreement among the underwriters solidifies the managing underwriter's authority to represent the syndicate in negotiations with the issuer. It does this by granting the managing underwriter a power of attorney over all aspects of its dealings with the issuer. Included within this broad grant is the power to determine with the issuer the offering price of the securities, the underwriting commission, and the concession/commission provided to dealers participating in the selling group.

Many investment banks have signed a master agreement among underwriters with the firms that often serve as managing underwriters. The master is typically based on the model form provided by the Securities and Financial Markets Association and applies to all offerings managed by the particular firm in which the investment bank participates as an underwriter.

A few days prior to the date the registration statement becomes effective, the managing underwriter informs all the syndicate members of the precise number of shares to be underwritten and their respective allotments. This notice also informs the syndicate members of the time by which their previous grant of a power of attorney (POA) can be revoked; after that time, non-revoking members are bound by the agreements signed by the manager on behalf of the syndicate members. The agreement among the underwriters also sets forth the compensation for managing, underwriting, and selling efforts in connection with the offering.

Many practices common to underwriting reflect the cartel-like qualities that have long characterized the industry, but these are beyond the reach of the antitrust laws. *Credit Suisse Securities (USA) LLC v. Glen Billings*, 127 U.S. 2383 (2007), held that underwriting enjoys implied immunity from the antitrust laws, reasoning that to apply the antitrust laws to underwriting would be "clearly incompatible" with the regulatory oversight Congress had lodged with the SEC.

Allotments. The amount of each underwriter's allotment is important for several reasons. Firm commitment underwriters are separately compensated for absorbing the risk of reselling the security. The amount of such underwriting risk so absorbed, and hence the compensation paid for absorbing that risk, is based on each underwriter's relative allotment. For example, if Underwriter Y's allotment is 100,000 shares of the 10 million shares to be sold, Underwriter Y is entitled to 1 percent of the commission paid for underwriting the security. To carry the illustration further, let's assume that the shares will be purchased from the issuer at $9 per share and resold to the public at $10 per share, and that the percentage of this spread allocated to compensation for underwriting is 30 percent (along traditional lines, the balance is allocated 20 percent to the manager and 50 percent as a selling commission). Under these assumed facts, the compensation to Underwriter Y for its underwriting the issue will be $30,000 (i.e., 1 percent of 30 percent × $1 spread × 10 million shares). If it sells all the shares within its allotment, Underwriter Y will receive an additional $50,000 for its selling efforts.

The individual underwriter's allotment also has important liability limitations. Section 11(e) of the Securities Act limits the liability of each underwriter to "the total price at which the securities underwritten by him and distributed to the public were offered to the public." Hence, Underwriter *Y* would have no greater liability under Section 11 than 1 percent of the total damages recoverable by the plaintiff investors. The individual underwriter's allotment also guides the amount it will be assessed if one of the syndicate members defaults by failing to purchase its agreed share of the offering.

Anti-Flipping Clause.   *Flipping* occurs when shares in an IPO are quickly resold ("flipped") in the market at a profit. Flipping places downward pressure on the distributed security's price and therefore impedes the syndicate in quickly distributing the offering. The agreement among the underwriters frequently imposes a penalty on syndicate members if flipped shares are traced to their allotment. The purpose of the penalty is to provide an incentive for each underwriter to place the shares with investors who are likely to hold them for an extended period of time. The penalty is normally restricted to the selling commission and sometimes is as high as 150 percent of the commission. FINRA Rule 5131 bars the discriminatory application of the penalty, i.e., the managing underwriter may impose the sanction only if the penalty is imposed upon all syndicate members whose clients flipped shares. When the offering is oversubscribed, managing underwriters are not likely to impose any sanction for flipped shares. Indeed, they frequently ask their institutional clients to resell the shares to the underwriter should they wish to flip their shares; the underwriters then resell (at the market price) the reacquired shares to retail customers who were unable to acquire the shares initially. Who are the winners under such an arrangement? "Spinning" is a variation of flipping, arising when the underwriting has allocated some of the scarce IPO shares to an executive of a company that may be planning to go public. The executive then flips the shares and thereby usually harvests a nice gain. Through spinning, the underwriter seeks to garner favor so as to win future underwriting business.

4. Underwriters' Compensation

a. Review by FINRA

FINRA Rule 2010 requires its members to comply with the "high standards of commercial honor and just and equitable principles of trade." Through this broad and lofty command, FINRA reviews all public offerings of underwritten securities to assure that member broker-dealers do not receive unfair or unreasonable compensation for their underwriting activities. Prior to making any offer to the public of securities, the managing underwriter files with FINRA the underwriting documents, as well as the offering prospectus, and the FINRA staff then applies its years of experience and the broad interpretative guidelines to determine the fairness and reasonableness of the proposed underwriter compensation. It should be noted that these procedures must be followed with any offering to the public, even if the offering is otherwise exempt from registration with the SEC because, for example, it falls within the intrastate exemption. However, certain high-quality offerings, such as shelf-registered offerings on Form S-3, discussed later, as well as nonconvertible debt or preferred stock rated "B" or better, are exempt from FINRA review. *See* FINRA Rule 5110(7).

After its review of the filed documents, FINRA informs the managing underwriter of its approval or disapproval of the compensation arrangement. If FINRA disapproves of the compensation, the managing underwriter may agree with the issuer to reduce its compensation to a level that FINRA will approve. Members who violate the FINRA requirements for fair and reasonable underwriting compensation can be sanctioned by FINRA.

Underwriter compensation can and does generally take a combination of different forms. In the firm commitment underwriting, there is the spread, the difference between the offering price and the amount paid to the issuer. The equivalent for a best efforts underwriting is a stated percentage of the offering proceeds. In addition to these amounts, it is common for underwriters to obtain warrants to acquire the issuer's shares, either of the same class as that being distributed or of an entirely different class. In lieu of warrants, the underwriters may have the option to purchase the issuer's stock at a stated discount, so-called cheap stock. Finally, the underwriters may have an expense allocation for a stated percentage of the offering against which they charge various out-of-pocket costs to organize and carry out the distribution, such as phone, travel, and publicity.

In overview, the FINRA interpretations offer a few objective guidelines as to appropriate levels of compensation. The guidelines are most precise with respect to warrants, cheap stock, and over-allotments. Underwriters may not purchase securities of the issuer within a 12-month period prior to the distribution at a price significantly below its offering price; underwriters may not receive warrants for the issuer's securities in excess of 10 percent of the amount of securities to be offered, and the exercise price of such warrants cannot be less than the distributed securities' offering price or extend for a period longer than five years; and any over-allotment option cannot exceed 15 percent of the offering. Furthermore, warrants and cheap stock received as compensation cannot be sold until one year after the public offering.

With respect to the notions of the overall compensation, as well as spreads or commissions that are deemed fair and reasonable, the guidelines are not as concrete. It is suspected that the FINRA staff operates in this area pursuant to unpublished guidelines that in any case assure the staff has fairly broad discretion in determining what is fair and reasonable compensation. In general, gross compensation for offerings under $1 million is reasonable if it constitutes no more than 15 percent of the offering for a best efforts underwriting; a slightly lower percentage appears to apply for firm commitment underwritings of similar amounts. An inverse relationship exists between the size of the offering and the underwriters' gross compensation, so that for offerings in the range of $10 million average underwriter compensation is around 11 percent of the offering amount. *See generally* 3A H.S. Bloomenthal & Samuel Wolf, Securities and Federal Corporate Law §8.66 (2d ed. 2008).

b. The Problems of Fixed Price Offerings

The cornerstone of the underwriting syndicate is that all members must sell the offered security to the public at a fixed price that is stated in the registration statement and accompanying prospectus. In the vernacular of the antitrust laws, the underwriting syndicate thereby "establishes a system of resale price maintenance in the public distribution of securities. Under this system the price per share or unit of securities is the same whether the purchaser buys 100 or 100,000 shares or units." Gerla, Swimming Against the Deregulatory Tide: Maintaining Fixed Prices in Public Offerings of Securities Through the NASD Antidiscounting Rules, 36 Vand. L. Rev. 9, 11 (1983). We may ponder whether the syndicate's interest in avoiding price competition among its members is reinforced by the Securities Act. Current rules require that the offering price be stated in the prospectus. It would seem possible, however, that the disclosure could state, for example, that sales above a certain level would be discounted to reflect the economies of scale of such large lot transactions. The real prohibition here is FINRA Rule 5141, forbidding discounts in public offerings. As a result, any economies of scale due to the size of a particular investor's purchase are not, and cannot be, passed on to that purchaser by the underwriter's discounting the shares to the investor. Broker-dealers who are members of FINRA can, however, purchase from syndicate members the offered securities at a price less than the offering price, the discount being the usual selling commission for such offerings.

An earlier government antitrust attack on this system was unsuccessful. *See United States v. Morgan*, 118 F. Supp. 21 (S.D.N.Y. 1953). In light of the increasing role of institutions in the public offerings, the fixed price offering continues to strike many as seriously out of step with the times.

But one should never underestimate the ability of the sophisticated and resourceful to overcome an arbitrary rule. Professor Gerla, supra, at 14-16, identifies three common circumventions. First, under the so-called designated order technique, the distributing underwriter agrees to provide the purchasing institutions with a set amount of free goods or research services as a form of discount for the institution's large purchase. The second technique is the *overtrade* or *swap*, under which the institutional buyer swaps securities in its portfolio for the security being distributed by the underwriter. An indirect discount appears when the value of the security given up by the institution is less than that of the securities acquired from the underwriter. A third technique is the *recapture*, under which the motto is "If you can't beat 'em, join 'em." The institution will form a broker-dealer subsidiary that upon joining FINRA can purchase the offered securities from the underwriting syndicate at the customary dealer discount. The subsidiary then resells the purchased securities to its parent institution at the fixed offering price. The subsidiary reaps the selling spread on the transaction, but since it is wholly owned by the parent institution, profits are in fact the equivalent of a discount for the institution. The frequency of such circumventions has increased as financial institutions, especially mutual funds, have become the major outlet for such offerings. What is the social utility of permitting FINRA to enforce its bar to discounting of fixed price offerings? Who benefits from this rule? Do issuers? Do investors? Does the public interest? Finally, it should be observed that some of the heat over this issue has been ventilated through SEC initiatives, for example, integrated disclosure and shelf registrations (examined infra), which in combination allow large, well-established issuers to more frequently distribute their securities through competitive bidding.

B. The Market for Initial Public Offerings

1. Irrational or Contrived Exuberance

IPOs are an important component of our economy. By meeting the capital needs of emerging companies, production capacity is expanded, significant numbers of new jobs are created, and the continued expansion of the economy is fueled by IPOs. At the same time, it must be noted that the volume of IPOs is trivial in amount in comparison with that of other types of public offerings. The volume of IPOs, nevertheless, is a visible sign of both the health of the economy and investor optimism. Some see "hot" IPO markets as visible evidence of investor gullibility.

The IPO market is a cyclical one. The new issues market is something of a bewitching hour, coming frequently at the closing moments of a bull market that has energized the small investor and made them feel that their chance for financial security is at hand. *See* Lowry & Schwert, IPO Market Cycles: Bubbles or Sequential Learning, 57 J. Fin. 1171 (2002). Many nonpublic firms rush to take advantage of this window of opportunity. The feeding frenzy that results makes one wonder if the chief obstacle facing the underwriters is not the Securities Act of 1933, but rather their inability to print share certificates fast enough to meet the investors' seemingly insatiable appetite.

Empirical studies fire a warning shot across the bow of investors sailing toward the troubled IPO waters. Data supports the view that IPOs are a good buy in the extremely short term, but a lousy purchase in the long run. Consider that a study of thousands of IPOs between 1980 and 2001 found that the average price gain for an IPO in the first day of trading is 18.8 percent, suggesting that serious mispricing is being committed by the IPO underwriters. Ritter & Welch, A Review of IPO Activity, Pricing, and Allocations, 57 J. Fin. 1795 (2002). However, in the years following their sale to the public, the IPO shares provide substantially lower returns to their owners than comparable investment (matched by industry and size) in a non-IPO firm.

Anecdotal evidence paints an equally compelling image of the psychology that prevails in the roaring IPO market. Consider the experience of Boston Chicken's IPO. Though offered to the public at $20 a share, investor interest in the stock was so keen that the first sale on Nasdaq was at $45 per share. During this frenzy, investors sought any piece of the chicken action they could obtain, with the effect that other chicken restaurant stocks rose significantly. Boston Chicken shares closed trading that day at $48 per share, meaning that the company had a market value of $800 million—not bad for a company whose revenues the preceding year were $8.3 million, yielding a net loss of $5.9 million. Power, Boston Chicken Soars by 143% on Its IPO Day, Wall St. J., Nov. 10, 1993, at C-1. Is this an efficient market? In October 1999, Boston Chicken traded at $0.50 and filed for bankruptcy protection.

> Some of the imperfections in the IPO market that account for this grim record are well known. We need not dwell on them at length:
>
> 1. The new issue market, far from being an easy, two-sided market, is a complex three-sided one. Investors are the only ones who systematically lose.

The investment bankers who are at the center of the process, between the issuer and the public, wear two very different hats. Customers are important, but when the moon is full and new issues are hot—in short, when new issues are most easily sold—they compete much more avidly for corporate clients than for investors. Each new issue represents not just a profitable piece of business but an added corporate client for the future. . . .

2. As they say on Wall Street, new issues are sold, not bought. The engine driving those sales are commissions that average several times the commissions in the secondary trading market. . . . Underwriters' discounts for IPOs average about 7 percent, even though commissions in the secondary market have shrunk dramatically and shelf registrations have cut the discounts for other public offerings. The underwriters account for much of that 7 percent spread, but enough is left for the salespeople manning the telephones to produce commissions three times the usual.

3. New issues are overpriced and underpriced all at the same time, but it is the overpricing that determines the ultimate outcome. The underpricing is a selling technique, one that highlights the very short-term incentives that drive this market.

How can a stock be over- and underpriced all at once? Strong new issue markets are a creature of the late stages of bull markets when investors' wits are dulled, and their appetites whetted, by the prospect of easy money. . . .

Alas, the answer is no more complicated than watching a pitchman playing "three card monte" on the sidewalks of New York. Try it sometime. Watch the fellow working the cards—an investment banker sans necktie—allowing the patsy to win a hand or two. It's a good lesson in new issue economics.

If new issues seem to be "bargains," it is because they have been consciously priced as such. The salesperson . . . can pull out his spreadsheet and show that this or that new issue is "cheap." And he is right—in some very myopic sense. Almost by magic, many a new issue moves to a premium price the very day of the offering. This "found money" whets appetites, of course, and refuels the process. But eventually the bull market in stocks as a whole dies, bringing even greater losses in these "bargain" new issues.

4. It has been said that if the federal securities laws had been in effect, the West would not have been won. Don't believe it. The West would have been developed, but many more pine trees would have been felled and financial printers would have prospered mightily. A 1933 Act prospectus does contain detailed and meticulously crafted disclosure, so well crafted as to be almost unreadable at times, but it is more a defense against litigation than a selling document. IPOs are a promotional process, one designed to create a demand for stock many times the eventual, normal trading volume. And the prospectus is not what moves it.

Lowenstein, Shareholder Voting Rights: A Response to SEC Rule 19c-4 and to Professor Gilson, 89 Colum. L. Rev. 979, 997-999 (1989).

The much anticipated 2012 public offering by Facebook illustrates another risk related to investor frenzy that can accompany a hotly anticipated IPO. Due to glitches in the computers that link the Nasdaq market on which Facebook shares were listed for nearly two hours many investors and market makers were in the dark regarding their positions and orders for Facebook.[1] For 41 days

---

1. Ironically, a computer glitch also befell BATS Global Markets in March 2012 when it launched its IPO with trading to occur on its *own* exchange. The IPO was withdrawn after computer problems interrupted trading in BATS shares on the BATS market.

after the Facebook offer, the IPO market was silent. When the market returned, underpricing increased, but with most of the observed increase being associated with offerings by the lead underwriters who had earlier participated in the Facebook offering, suggesting they may have been compensating their clients in the earlier Facebook debacle. Facebook's computer hiatus likely contributed to the volatility of the first day's trading. From the IPO price of $38, the stock traded as high as $45 on its first day, but closed that day 23 cents above its offering price. The next day the shares closed below its offering price. Facebook's share price was not helped by the announcement near the offering that a major advertiser had concluded that Facebook was not an effective medium to reach would-be consumers. *See* Krigman & Jeffus, IPO Pricing as a Function of Investment Bank's Past Mistakes: The Case of Facebook, 38 J. Corp. Fin. 335 (2016).

Practices common to underwriting, some of which are condoned by the securities laws, contribute to an IPO security's share price increasing in the market after its public offering. As studied later in this chapter, underwriters are permitted to "stabilize" the offered security's price so as to retard its decline during the distribution period. Also, members of the underwriting syndicate are penalized by the syndicate if they sell to a *flipper*, a person who quickly resells the IPO security. Flippers are not a favored species because their resale puts downward pressure on the offered security's price and thereby complicates the task of the syndicate in pushing the fixed price offering out the window. Abuses in the IPO process also contribute to the problem and include allocating shares in hot IPOs to purchasers willing to purchase additional shares in the aftermarket (called "laddering"), and sometimes at a higher than normal commission rate (called "quid pro quo arrangements"), as well as allocating hot IPO shares to senior executives of companies from whom the underwriter wished to obtain future investment banking business (called "spinning"). Finally, buoyant recommendations by analysts affiliated with the underwriting feed the euphoria that accompanies an IPO. Cook et al., On the Marketing of IPOs, 82 J. Fin. Econ. 356 (2006). *See also In re eBay, Inc.*, 2004 WL 253521 (Del. Ch. 2004) (spinning gives rise to a breach of fiduciary duty on the part of the recipient executive). Practices such as the above spawned 309 class action suits on behalf of investors who lost billions of dollars in IPOs whose shares later collapsed. *See In re Initial Public Offering Securities Litigation*, 241 F. Supp. 2d 281 (S.D.N.Y. 2003). Such abuses gave rise to a multi-agency $1.4 billion settlement by ten leading investment banking firms with several governmental agencies. *See* SEC Press Release: SEC, NY Attorney General, NASD, NASAA, NYSE and State Regulators Announce Historic Agreement to Reform Investment Practices (Dec. 20, 2002).

The truly dismal performance of so many companies that went public in the hot IPO market in 1999-2000 can also be attributed to the heightened competition for underwriting. High-reputation underwriters in the face of losing participation in, or management of, an IPO over time seriously relaxed their financial performance criteria for taking companies public. *See* Ip et al., The Internet Bubble Broke Records and Bank Accounts, Wall St. J., July 14, 2000, at A-1 (reporting that CS First Boston reduced its criteria for taking a company public from $10 million in revenue for the prior 12 months to $2.5 million for the prior quarter). And what are the effects of the prevalent practice among underwriters to allocate most of the offered shares to institutional investors?

A common view is that underwriters' allocating a significant portion (frequently as much as 85 percent) of any IPO to financial institutions has the effect of driving up the post-offering price of IPOs; proponents of this view reason that institutions are less likely to flip their shares so that their getting shares constricts the supply of tradable shares in the aftermarket. However, recent data reflects that institutions do not always have the "strong hand," as in both strong or weak markets institutions are far more likely to resell their shares than are retail investors. *See* Aggarwal, Allocation of Initial Public Offerings and Flipping Activity, 68 J. Fin. 111 (2003) (institutions flip nearly 48 percent of the shares allocated to them versus almost 28 percent on the part of retail customers in hot IPO setting); Boehmer et al., Do Institutions Receive Favorable Allocations in IPOs with Better Long Run Returns?, 41 J. Fin. Q. Analysis 809 (2006) (finding institutions retain shares in better firms that have better long-term performance and flip others). Should managers, underwriters, or regulation decide who should obtain allocations of an IPO? *See* Levy, The Law and Economics of IPO Favoritism and Regulatory Spin, 33 Sw. L. Rev. 185 (2004).

2. Underpricing of Initial Public Offerings

Corporate America has left a record $23 billion on the table from IPOs this year—but no one's going hungry. The number represents the staggering gain generated in the first day trading for all initial public stock offerings . . . through October.

McGough & Smith, IPO Issuers Don't Mind Money Left on the Table, Wall St. J.,
Nov. 3, 1999, at C-1

When the very prominent head of a major investment banking house called a meeting of his New York brokers a few years back, the brokers figured he wanted to apologize [for putting] customers into a large new stock offering that collapsed within a week of issue. . . . Instead of apologizing, . . . however, he said, "the client is delighted."

Stern & Bartlett, But the Client Is Delighted, Forbes, Apr. 3, 1989, at 130

Who are the clients of the multi-service investment banking firm? Its clients are both the corporate issuers whose securities it underwrites, and from whom it earns sizable commissions, and the many customers to whom it sells the underwritten securities. Remember, no sales means not only that there are no commissions, but also that in the case of a firm commitment underwriting some of the investment banker's capital continues to be tied up for its portion of the undistributed shares. Consider, then, the conflicting tugs on the investment banker when pricing the IPO. The issuer wants as high a price as possible to maximize the proceeds it receives from the offering; the firm commitment underwriter wants to minimize its risks, so it wishes a price that will assure that the offering "goes out the window." And in the case of the IPO, there is no ready benchmark to determine what price will fulfill each party's desires because there is no pre-existing market for the issuer's securities.

A troubling phenomenon of IPOs is *underpricing*, which occurs when the immediate trading market price for IPOs is significantly higher than their initial offering price. For example, one representative study found an average price increase of 18.8 percent during the first day of trading following the IPO offerings. *See* Ritter & Welch, A Review of IPO Activity, Pricing, and Allocations, 57 J. Fin. 1795 (2002); *see also* Loughran & Ritter, Why Don't Issuers Get Upset About Leaving Money on the Table in IPOs?, 15 Rev. Fin. Stud. 413 (2002) ($27 billion left on table between 1990 and 1998, which was twice the amount of underwriting commissions for the IPOs, compared to $8 billion the same issuers earned the year before going public).

Issuers attuned to the underpricing could demand that the underwriters receive a lower commission. But the managing underwriter will see that a lower commission offers less incentive to syndicate members and others whose selling efforts are being relied on to move the underwritten securities. Thus, a lower commission can actually increase the risk, rather than lower it. Consider the allegations in *EBC 1, Inc. v. Goldman Sachs & Co.*, 936 N.Y.S.2d 92 (N.Y. App. Div. 2011), *leave to appeal granted*, 19 N.Y.3d 810 (N.Y. 2012). On the advice of its lead underwriter, eToys set the price of its IPO at $20; the stock closed at $77 after its first day of trading. Two years later, eToys declared bankruptcy and its creditors alleged that its underwriter had intentionally underpriced the IPO so that it could allocate shares from the offering to customers who were obligated to return to the underwriters some of the profits they made when reselling the shares. The creditors further alleged that had the shares not been underpriced, eToys would have had the funds to weather the financial headwinds that drove it into bankruptcy. While appealing from a holding that the confidence eToys placed in Goldman Sachs did not rise to the level of trust needed to create a fiduciary duty, Goldman Sachs settled the matter, paying $7.5 million. *See http:// www.chicagotribune.com/business/sns-rt-us-goldmansachs-etoys.*

One strategy pursued by some issuers—most notably Google when it went public in 2004—to address fears of underpricing is the use of a Dutch auction process to establish the offering price. As discussed earlier, with a Dutch auction the offering price is set on the basis of bids submitted by investors, with the ultimate offering price being the price by which the issuer can dispose of all the offering's shares.

Studies report an inverse relationship between the relative prestige of the issuer's underwriter and the amount of mispricing for IPOs. That is, studies have consistently demonstrated that the difference between an IPO's aftermarket price and its offering price increases as the level of prestige of the issuer's investment banker decreases. *See, e.g.*, Lewellen, Risk, Reputation, and IPO Price Support, 61 J. Fin. 613, 641 (2006) (elite banks engage in more aftermarket support than lower-reputation firms). However, VC-backed IPOs have greater underpricing when the underwriter provides "all-star" analyst coverage in the post-IPO period; this is believed indicative that VC support underpricing as a means to attract and sustain investor interest in the issuer, at least long enough for the VC to exit. Liu & Ritter, Local Underwriter Oligopolies and IPO Underpricing, 102 J. Fin. Econ. 579 (2011). *See also* Lee et al., Grandstanding, Certification and the Underpricing of Venture Capital Backed IPOs, 73 J. Fin. Econ. 375 (2004) (the greater the underpricing, the larger the inflows of capital into VC funds).

Why should initial offering prices consistently be lower than such offerings' aftermarket prices? *See generally* Griffith, A Legal and Economic Analysis of the Preferential Allocation of Shares in Initial Public Offerings, 69 Brook. L. Rev. 583 (2004) (linking underpricing and spinning to the underwriters' desire to establish a currency by which it can obtain future investment banking business); Aggarwal et al., Strategic IPO Underpricing, Information Momentum and Lockup Expiration Selling, 66 J. Fin. Econ. 105, 120-123 (2002) (managers prefer underpricing, as it attracts attention to the firm's security, driving up prices later when they are allowed to sell their personal stakes in the firm); Krigman et al., The Persistence of IPO Mispricing and the Predictive Power of Flipping, 54 J. Fin. 1015, 1042 (1999) (underwriters' claim that irrational retail investors account for most significant price run-ups that occur, which later collapse, is supported by empirical data showing inverse relationship between incidence of flipping by institutions and the long-term performance of the security); Tinic, Anatomy of Initial Public Offerings of Common Stock, 43 J. Fin. 789 (1988) (underpricing is a form of implicit insurance against potential liability under Section 11 for misstatements in registration statement—i.e., investors seldom sue over a good buy). What do you believe causes IPOs to be systematically underpriced? Why are they favored by investors if, in the long run, on average, they perform significantly less well than the market as a whole?

But, in view of the long-term performance of IPOs, does underpricing exist? On closer analysis, concern for market imperfections is not limited to IPOs. Professors Loughran and Ritter examined the five-year performance of stocks of both IPOs and seasoned equity offerings (SEOs) following their sale to the public and found that both categories underperformed a matched sample of stocks of firms that did not make a public offering of their equity securities.

> Investing in firms issuing stock is hazardous to your wealth. Firms issuing stock during 1970 to 1990, whether an IPO or an SEO, have been poor long-run investments for investors. The average annual return during the five years after issuing is only 5 percent for firms conducting IPOs, and only 7 percent for firms conducting SEOs. Investing an equal amount at the same time in a nonissuing firm with approximately the same market capitalization, and holding it for an identical period, would have produced an average compound return of 12 percent per year for IPOs and 15 percent for SEOs. The magnitude of the underperformance is large: it implies that 44 percent more money would need to be invested in the issuers than in non-issuers to be left with the same wealth five years later.

Loughran & Ritter, The New Issues Puzzle, 50 J. Fin. 23, 46 (1995). The authors' data suggests that an important factor in the IPOs' underperformance is that not only do firms time their public offerings to take advantage of surges in investor interest in public offerings, but also the individual firm's aberrational surges in profitability cause markets to overreact in the sense that the markets systematically overestimate the likelihood that the firm will be able to maintain the rate of increase in its profitability. *See also* McLaughlin et al., The Information Content of Corporate Offerings of Seasoned Securities: An Empirical Analysis, 27 Fin. Mgmt. 31 (1998) (operating performance of firms declines following their securities offerings and greater decline occurs if they sold equity securities).

3.   Reforming the IPO Process

The numerous abuses during the hot IPO market in the late 1990s prompted reform efforts on a variety of fronts. *See* NYSE and NASD IPO Advisory Committee, Report and Recommendations to the Securities and Exchange Commission 10-11 (2003). The most visible abuses flowed from the close connection between the analysts and the underwriting group who worked for the same investment banking firm. *See* Cliff & Denis, Do Initial Public Offering Firms Purchase Analyst Coverage with Underpricing?, 59 J. Fin. 2871 (2004) (finding strong correlation among lead underwriter with all-star analyst providing post-IPO coverage and degree of underpricing). Too frequently underwriters involved their firm's analysts in making pitches to prospective underwriting clients, such as promising that the analyst would provide "buy" and "strong buy" recommendations for the underwritten firm's securities during and after the IPO. Analysts' compensation frequently was linked to their reports generating or otherwise supporting investment banking transactions. Moreover, there was a good deal of evidence that analysts were disciplined if they issued unflattering reports of companies that were, or were being wooed to become, investment banking clients. In the years following the .com market collapse, FINRA, the SEC, and Congress each responded to some of the abuses.

FINRA bars investment banking departments from supervising or controlling analysts. *See* FINRA Rule 2711 & NYSE Rules 351 and 472. The rules also prohibit analysts' compensation being linked to investment banking transactions. The rules further bar firms from issuing research reports on an issuer until ten days after the IPO if the firm managed the offering; the bar does not, however, apply to research reports addressing the effects of significant news or events on the subject company. As discussed more fully later in this chapter, the JOBS Act, enacted in 2012, lifts certain SRO and SEC restrictions on the participation of security analysts in connection with the IPO of "emerging growth companies" (as we will see, this term includes all but the very biggest IPOs). For example, the ten-day mandate for a "quiet period" does not apply to such an issuer. Nonetheless, FINRA's other prohibitions, e.g., the linking analysts' compensation to successful underwriting, are not affected by the JOBS Act. An interesting item of the rule is the requirement that all research reports must disclose the distribution of "buy," "sell," and "hold" recommendations among the issuers covered by the firm—a regulation spawned by the overwhelming percentage of the ratings by sell-side analysts being "buy" recommendations and that the percentage of "buy" recommendations is even greater when the investment banking firm has a relationship with the issuer. At the time of making their recommendation, analysts must disclose any conflicts of interest, including whether the analyst owns securities in the company that is the subject of the report. Query, is it consistent with the First Amendment to bar analysts from speaking to financial journalists who as a matter of custom will not include in their columns the analyst's conflict of interest disclosures?

The SEC adopted Regulation A-C, which requires that analysts certify that their recommendations—including those made in public appearances—accurately reflect their personal views regarding the issuer's performance and prospects, and requires disclosure whether the analyst's compensation is dependent on the views expressed about the issuer. The Sarbanes-Oxley Act adds Section 15D to the Exchange Act to strengthen the independence of analysts. The provision calls for structural safeguards to ensure that analysts are independent from the investment banking activities of the firm and to protect analysts from retaliation for unpopular recommendations.

Recall the practice of "spinning," where those engaged in underwriting direct IPO allocations to senior executives of corporations, with the expectation that the executives will in the future guide their firm's investment banking business to the underwriters. Spinning is now addressed in FINRA Rule 5131, which broadly prohibits the allocation of IPO shares in the expectation of future investment banking business.

FINRA also has acted to introduce greater transparency vis-à-vis the issuer in the pricing of IPOs. As discussed later in this chapter, before the offering's price is set and shares are sold to the public, the underwriters solicit investors and thereby test the waters for an appropriate offering price. FINRA Rule 5131 requires the lead underwriter to report to the issuer the names of institutions (including their respective number of shares) that have indicated interest in the offering as well as the aggregate interest among retail investors. Following the offering, the lead underwriter must disclose to the issuer the specific allocations that were made for the completed offering.

C. A Panoramic View of the Registration Statement

The central objective of the Securities Act is the preparation of a registration statement for securities offered to the public. We provide here a description of the information required to be included in the typical registration statement. By being familiar with the registration statement's contents, you are better able to understand not only what steps are involved in its preparation, but also how the registration statement serves the overall objectives of the Securities Act. But first a word about the SEC's authority over the registration statement's contents.

In Section 7, Congress sets the tenor of disclosure by providing that the registration statement "shall contain the information, and be accompanied by the documents specified in Schedule A" of the Act. Recognizing its own lack of expertise and the obvious need for flexibility, Congress softened its own reference to Schedule A by granting the Commission broad rulemaking authority in Section 7 to delete or increase the information or documents specified in Schedule A. The Commission enjoys equally broad rulemaking authority under Section 19(a), wherein it has the power to adopt, amend, and rescind "such rules and regulations as may be necessary to carry out the provisions of" the Act, including the contents of registration statements and prospectuses, as well as "defining accounting, technical and trade terms" used in the Act. Even though the Commission's authority under Section 19(a) extends as well to accounting standards and principles used in the preparation of financial statements appearing in the registration statements, the Commission has rarely invoked its authority to establish accounting principles and standards; the Commission has deferred to the private sector, particularly the Financial Accounting Standards

Board, with respect to the metrics for accounting-based disclosures. Under Section 10, the Commission has the power to decide what portion of the information that appears in the registration statement must be included in the prospectus. Thus, through Section 10, the Commission regulates the contents of the prospectus. In sum, there is little cause to doubt the Commission's power over the form and content of '33 Act registration statements and prospectuses.

The information that must be included in a registration statement can roughly be divided into four categories: information bearing on the registrant, information about the distribution and use of its proceeds, a description of the securities of the registrant, and various exhibits and undertakings that must be filed as part of the registration statement. Only information within the first three categories must be reproduced in the prospectus.

As is true with any document that must be filed with the SEC, the first step in determining what must be disclosed begins by determining the precise "form" that is to be filed with the SEC. As will be seen, in the registration of securities the standard forms are Forms S-1 and S-3 (Form S-2 was subsumed by changes to Form S-1 in 2005 so no longer exists). Form S-1 is the default form because it applies when the issuer cannot meet the eligibility requirements of Form S-3 (discussed later in this chapter). Each SEC form identifies the disclosures that must be made for specific items and directs the form's preparer to Regulation S-K for detailed guides for what precisely must be disclosed with respect to that item. Thus, the second step in the disclosure process is to consult Regulation S-K with respect to the specific item called for by the form, for example, Form S-1. Regulation S-K performs this same function for the Exchange Act's periodic disclosure requirements, such as those on Forms 10-K and 10-Q.

Information with Respect to the Registrant. The disclosures in this part of the registration statement entail a fairly penetrating and detailed description of the registrant's business, property, and management (its directors and executive officers). For example, the executive officers' compensation and security ownership must be disclosed, and for each class of the registrant's outstanding common stock, the registration statement must set forth the high and low prices within the two most recent fiscal years, the number of their holders, and the frequency and amount of dividends for each class. As will be seen in our examination of materiality standards in Chapter 12, registrants must disclose legal proceedings involving the issuer or certain individuals affiliated with the registrant.

The extensive, detailed disclosures about the issuer pose a daunting task to the typical small investor. Therefore, the first and last glimpse of the prospectus for many investors is likely to be its most user-friendly parts: the summary and risk factor sections. In the summary, the issuer is required by Item 501(c) of Regulation S-K to set forth the terms of the offering and to identify the page where risk factors are discussed. The risk factors portion of the registration statement is governed by Item 503(c), which requires the registrant to identify the principal factors that make the offering speculative or one of high risk. Rule 421(d) requires both of these sections to be written in "plain English." Though the plain English requirement is mandated for only the front and back cover pages, the summary, and risk factors sections of the prospectus, the SEC encourages registrants to make the prospectus a less forbidding document by making it clear, concise, and easy to read rather than filled with dense, turgid, and

hard-to-read legalese. Rule 421(d)(2) specifies six minimum plain English principles for registrants: short sentences, everyday language, active voice, tabular
presentation of complex material, no legal jargon, and no multiple negatives.

Example of No Multiple Negatives

Before	After
No clause can become valid unless approved by both parties.	A clause can become valid only if both parties approved it.

Example of Active Voice

Before	After
No person has been authorized to give any information or make any representation other than those contained or incorporated by reference in this joint proxy statement/prospectus, and if given or made, such information or representation must not be relied upon as having been authorized.	You should rely only on the information contained in this document or incorporated by reference. We have not authorized anyone to provide you with information that is different.

The core of the registration statement's information about the issuer is the
various financial statements required by Regulation S-X. These include audited
balance sheets for the end of each of the two preceding fiscal years as well as
audited income statements and statements of changes in financial position for
each of the three fiscal years preceding the date of the most recent audited
balance sheet. As will be seen, the requirement is two years if the registrant is
an "emerging growth company." If the registrant has been in existence for a
shorter period than two or three years, the requirements are shortened accordingly. The position and performance of the registrant for the period between
the last audited balance sheet and the filing of the registration statement must
be disclosed through interim financial statements whenever the registration
statement is filed more than 135 days after the date of the last audited balance
sheet. Interim statements, however, are not required to be audited.

Items 301 and 302 of Regulation S-K require the registrant to disclose a
wide array of other financial information about itself that supplements and
emphasizes the information in its audited financial statements. A crucial portion of the registration statement is Item 303's requirement with respect to management's discussion and analysis of the registrant's financial condition and
results of operations. This section forces management to identify trends and
developments that it has reason to believe will affect the registrant and reflects
the Commission's attempt to encourage registrants to go beyond the bare disclosure of historical information so that the registration statement is even more
relevant to the information needs of investors.

The mandated disclosures are sometimes guided by a desire to curb abusive
conduct. For example, certain transactions between the registrant and its executive officers, affiliates, and promoters must be disclosed. Similarly, registrants

must disclose any changes in or material disagreements with its outside accountants over accounting or financial disclosures. The latter is intended to discourage registrants from "shopping" for accounting opinions for the purpose of improving their financial reports by an artful use of accounting principles.

The Distribution and Its Proceeds.   Underwriters in privity with the registrant must disclose the general terms of their agreement and their compensation (both in the aggregate and on a per share basis). The net expected proceeds of the offering must be disclosed, and if the registrant has plans for the proceeds, those plans must be disclosed. More detailed disclosure about the proceeds' use is required when they are to be used in connection with other funds to accomplish a specified purpose. For example, a more detailed disclosure of the proceeds' use is required if the proceeds will be used to discharge indebtedness, acquire assets other than in the ordinary course of business, or to engage in acquisitions of other businesses.

Securities of the Registrant.   The registration statement must set forth the rights, privileges, and preferences of the security being offered, including any provision that would subordinate the holder's rights to other security holders or restrict the registrant's ability to incur indebtedness or the payment of dividends. Whenever there is a substantial disparity between the public offering price for an equity security and the price certain insiders acquired the security for within the past five years (or at which the insiders currently can acquire such security), this disparity must be highlighted in the registration statement if the registrant is not a reporting company prior to filing the registration statement.

Exhibits and Undertakings.   Numerous exhibits must be filed as part of the registration statement, including the registrant's articles of incorporation, bylaws, attorney's opinion as to the legality of the securities registered, and any 10-K or 10-Q reports incorporated by reference into the registration statement. As will be seen in later materials, the Commission's procedures frequently require registrants to undertake certain obligations to perform specified tasks after the effective date of the registration statement. For example, when a security is to be offered on a delayed basis, we will see in our discussion of shelf registration procedures that the registrant must undertake to update the registration statement by filing post-effective amendments. This undertaking and others that may be imposed on the registrant must be filed with the registration statement. The registrant must also include in its registration statement information regarding all unregistered securities sold during the past three years.

Filings via EDGAR.   The Electronic Data Gathering, Analysis, and Retrieval System (EDGAR) facilitates the electronic submission of filings with the SEC. Submissions occur through e-mail transmission or the physical delivery of diskettes or magnetic tapes. All registrants, domestic and foreign, are required to file their '33 Act registration statements and periodic reports under the '34 Act pursuant to EDGAR. The manner and protocol for making electronic filings are set forth in Regulation S-T. Filed information is protected against tampering through confidential passwords assigned to registrants and is usually available within 30 minutes of filing with the SEC. Interested parties may access EDGAR filings through the Internet at *http://www.sec.gov.*

D. Registration of the Unseasoned Issuer

This section discusses the many steps involved in the preparation and review of the registration statements for companies not eligible to use the SEC's integrated disclosure system, discussed later, which is available for established publicly held firms. It should be noted that the effort and expense of an IPO are far greater than for an offering by a company that already is publicly traded, especially one that is already subject to the reporting requirements of the '34 Act. The accounting records and reports of a registrant contemplating its first public offering may never have been audited or certified by outside accountants, its internal records may not be in sufficient form to support the disclosures in the detail required by Regulation S-K, and management will surely have to be educated not just on the openness solicited by the registration statement, but also on the overall disclosure requirements for public companies. Once the company goes public, many facts about the company and its officers that previously were confidential will be disclosed in Commission filings. The CEO's salary will now be known not just by her mother and spouse, but also by anyone who cares to review the company's filings with the Commission. This openness is mandated minimally by Section 15(d) of the '34 Act, which requires any issuer who has filed a registration statement, regardless of the size of its assets or the number of its shareholders, to comply with the periodic reporting requirements of Section 13 of the '34 Act for at least the fiscal year in which the registration statement became effective. A close examination of how issuers become reporting companies is provided in Chapter 11.

As we discuss in a later section of this chapter, Section 5 imposes restrictions on the freedom the issuer and underwriters have to promote the offering until the registration statement is filed. Although the SEC has recently expanded the scope of permissible communications, activities likely to produce investor interest in the offering may violate Section 5, at least until the registration statement is filed. Thus, the period leading up to the filing of the registration statement is for the issuer and its underwriters a quiet time, but not necessarily a serene time. As discussed above, a good deal of work goes into the preparation of the registration statement and, at points, tension develops among the issuer, its underwriters, and the attorney quarterbacking the preparation of the registration statement. There are deadlines, disclosure problems, and the gnawing uncertainty about the market's appetite when the registration statement becomes effective.

Once the registration statement is filed and the Commission's staff begins its review, a different role is assumed by the underwriters because now efforts to promote the registered offering can commence. With the filing of the registration statement, underwriters can sample investor interest by aggressively soliciting their offers to buy. As we examine more closely later, Section 5 bars any sales until the registration statement becomes effective. But in the period between the filing of the registration statement and its becoming effective (called the *waiting period*), when the registration statement is being reviewed by the Commission's staff, significant efforts are afoot to promote the offering.

1.   Preparing the Registration Statement for Filing

The burden of assuring that the registration statement is prepared in accordance with the Commission's regulations falls squarely on the shoulders of the registrant's attorney, who must grapple not only with whether all the information sought by Regulation S-K's directives has been provided, but also with whether other information must be disclosed to assure that no material omission or half-truth is committed. *See* Rule 408. In making these judgments, the securities lawyer is torn between putting his client's best foot forward and providing a candid view of the risks the issuer and the offering face. Even disclosing in the registration statement the registrant's great successes sometimes places the attorney at odds with the registrant's management, as reflected by the remarks of one company's officer: "We were proud of our profitability, but we would rather have had competitors underestimate us. We also knew that the success we were having could attract other competitors." Phillips & Ayala, Headaches as Well as Riches Result from Going Public, Wall St. J., Oct. 9, 1989, at B-2.

An overarching consideration is to whom the disclosures are directed; the content, form, and emphasis given to an item are very much dependent on the intended target of the disclosures. The following excerpt discusses other concerns that face the attorney, such as maintaining a professional relationship with the registrant, establishing and following an orderly schedule for taking the offering to market, and being sensitive to the costs of the offering. For the large, well-established company, these concerns are mitigated by the availability of registration pursuant to the SEC's integrated disclosure system, discussed in the next section of this chapter. But for the less seasoned and less well-heeled registrant who registers its offering without being able to make use of integrated disclosure on its Form S-1, timing and costs are important concerns.

> ## Schneider, Manko & Kant, Going Public: Practice, Procedure, and Consequences
> 22-23, 40-43 (Bowne & Co. 1999)

PREPARING THE REGISTRATION STATEMENT

The "quarterback" in preparing the registration statement is normally the attorney for the company. Drafts are circulated to all concerned. Company counsel is principally responsible for preparing the non-financial parts of the registration statement. The managing underwriters and their counsel generally play an active role in drafting various sections of the prospectus, particularly those that will assist in marketing the shares. There are normally at least a few "all hands" drafting sessions prior to filing the registration statement, attended by management personnel of the company, counsel for the company, the company's auditors, representatives of the managing underwriters, and underwriters' counsel. . . . Close cooperation is required among [all of them] . . . and the printer. . . .

It is essential for the issuer and all others involved in the financing to perceive correctly the role of company counsel. Counsel normally assists the company and its management in preparing the document and in performing their "due diligence" investigation to verify all disclosure for accuracy and completeness. Counsel often serves as the principal draftsperson of the registration statement. Counsel typically solicits information both orally and in writing from a great many people, and exercises judgment in evaluating the information received for accuracy and consistency. Experience indicates that executives often overestimate their ability to give accurate information from their recollections without verification. It shows no disrespect, but merely the professionally required degree of healthy skepticism, when the lawyer insists on backup documentation and asks for essentially the same information in different ways and from different sources.

. . . The normal scope of a professional engagement does not contemplate that the lawyer will act as the ultimate source to investigate or verify all disclosures in the registration statement or to assure that the document is accurate and complete in all respects. Indeed, in many cases the lawyer would lack the expertise to assume that responsibility. In some instances, the lawyer may lack the technical background even to frame the proper questions and must depend upon the client for education about the nature of the business. Counsel does not routinely check information received against books of original entry or source documents, as auditors do, nor does counsel generally undertake to consult sources external to the client to obtain or verify information supplied by the client. . . .

Preliminary Preparation

For the average first offering, a very substantial amount of preliminary work is required that does not relate directly to preparing the registration statement as such. To have a vehicle for the offering, the business going public normally must be conducted by a single corporation or a parent corporation with subsidiaries. In most cases, the business is not already in such a neat package when the offering project commences. It often is conducted by a number of corporations under common ownership, by partnerships, by limited liability companies, or by combinations of business entities. Considerable work must be done in order to reorganize the various entities by mergers, liquidations and capital contributions. Even when there is a single corporation, a recapitalization almost always is required so that the company will have an appropriate capital structure for the public offering. A decision must be made regarding the proportion of the stock to be sold to the public. . . .

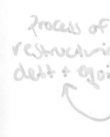

Among other common projects in preparing to go public, it is often necessary to enter into, revise, or terminate employment agreements, adopt stock option plans and grant options there-under; transfer real estate; revise leases; rewrite the corporate charter and by-laws; engage a transfer agent and registrar;

rearrange stockholdings of insiders; draw, revise or cancel agreements among shareholders. . . .

TIMETABLE

Although businesspersons find it difficult to believe, the average first public offering normally requires two to three months of intensive work before the registration statement can be filed. One reason so much time is required is the need to accomplish the preparatory steps just referred to at the same time the registration statement is being prepared. There are many important and often interrelated business decisions to be made and implemented, and all of these questions rarely are decided definitively at the outset. . . . Furthermore, drafting of the prospectus normally begins before the financial statements are available. Almost inevitably, some rewriting must be done in the non-financial parts of the prospectus after the financial statements are distributed in order to blend the financial and non-financial sections together. As the filing deadline approaches, companies frequently have the frustrating feeling that everything is hopelessly confused. They are quite surprised to see that everything falls into place at the eleventh hour.

After the registration statement is filed with the Commission, the waiting period begins. . . . The Commission reviews the registration statement and finally issues its letter of comments. There is a wide variation in the time required for the SEC to process a registration statement. . . .

The SEC's current policy calls for the issuance of an initial letter of comments within 30 days. The delay is longer and at times has exceeded 100 days but at certain times the wait is less than 30 days. Delays occur despite various initiatives by the SEC, including the adoption of various "short-form" registration statements for certain types of companies and transactions, increases in the dollar amount of securities which could be sold without registration and an allocation of SEC resources to initial public offerings. . . .

The overall time lapse between the beginning of preparation of a company's first registration statement and the final effective date may well exceed six months. Rarely will it be less than three months. . . .

Lawyers prepare the registration statement. In doing so the lawyer relies on reports and summaries provided by the client's personnel that are usually accompanied by further discussions with the client's personnel. While the lawyer does not independently verify the information provided by the firm—so in this regard the lawyer's role is fundamentally different from that of the auditor of the financial statements included in the registration statement—the lawyer critically reviews the material to assure there are no disclosure issues posed.

There is one area where the lawyer does in fact opine on the validity of a fact represented in the registration statement—namely, that the securities being offered have been validly authorized. Obviously, opinions of attorneys may be solicited for other reasons in certain instances, such as the opinion of tax counsel for the offering of a tax-sheltered investment or patent counsel for a research and development offering.

2. Regulatory Dispensations for Emerging Growth Companies

a. Emerging Growth Companies

The "on ramp" initiative of the 2012 JOBS Act provides relaxation of several reporting requirements for "emerging growth companies." Congress acted because it believed the securities laws unduly regulated startups and their quest for capital. Section 2(a)(19) of the Securities Act defines an emerging growth company as a registrant with less than $1 billion in total annual revenues (provided the issuer does not have a public float above $700 million); as a practical matter this category encompasses all but the very largest issuers in their initial years after an IPO.

The overall objective of the on-ramp initiative is to make registered public offerings more attractive to entities meeting the emerging growth company definition by relieving them (for up to five years) of a list of specific obligations that follow from their becoming a reporting company after an IPO. To be precise, the dispensations terminate on the earlier of: (1) the issuer's revenues reaching $1 billion; (2) the issuer having a public float of at least $700 million; (3) issuing more than $1 billion in non-convertible debt (within a three-year period); or (4) the passage of five years since going public.

On ramp provides a host of dispensations that fall into one of two broad categories:

Corporate Governance. Emerging growth companies are exempt during their incubation period from several Dodd-Frank mandated provisions, such as an advisory stockholder vote on executive compensation (a.k.a. "say on pay"), detailed disclosures related to how compensation relates to firm performance, and comparative disclosures of executive pay and median employee pay.

Disclosure. The on-ramp provisions reduce from three to two years the required audited financial reports for emerging growth companies and lift during the incubation period the Sarbanes-Oxley requirement that the auditor opine on management's assessment of internal controls. The on-ramp provisions also remove during the incubation period compliance with any new accounting standards, any future mandate that firms rotate auditors, or that their auditors provide supplemental reports to investors beyond the current limited audit opinion.

b. Is It a Supply or a Demand Problem?

Support for deregulatory efforts such as those embraced in the JOBS Act is premised on strong empirical evidence that over the past two decades there has been a precipitous decline in IPOs. Particularly noticeable here has been the near disappearance of the "small IPO," those involving about $50 million. A natural focus for what is causing a dearth of IPOs is to characterize the problem as a *supply* problem whereby the volume of prospective firms going public is reduced by the regulatory burdens and their associated costs that must be overcome for the IPO to occur. Hence, Congress' initiatives, such as the JOBS

Act, that lighten or remove the regulatory burdens are taken in the belief this will stimulate IPOs and capital formation generally.

A very different perspective on the causes for the decline in IPOs is provided by Professors Bartlett, Rose, and Solomon, What Happened in 1998? The Demise of the Small IPO and the Investing Preferences of Mutual Funds, Working Paper (May 2016). Their focus is on forces that constrict the *demand* for small IPOs. As seen earlier, financial institutions are a dominant player in issuer transactions. Indeed, mutual funds have become major purchasers of IPOs. Mutual funds face significant liquidity concerns since their investors enjoy unfettered redemption rights: If a fund investor wishes to exit the fund, the fund must redeem the shares, which can mean disposing of portfolio assets, e.g., shares in a company that were acquired in an IPO. Bartlett et al. document that starting with a series of international financial shocks that began in 1998, mutual funds fled small IPO holdings out of concerns for their illiquidity. They conclude that the withdrawal of funds from this sector set in motion a chain of events whereby "illiquidity-bred-illiquidity," with the consequence that small IPOs as a practical matter were not attractive to anyone. Does the direction that reform may take depend on whether the disappearance of the small IPO is a supply or a demand problem?

3. Review by the SEC's Staff: The Letter of Comment

Upon filing the registration statement with the SEC and paying the filing fees, under Section 8(a) the registration statement can, barring any other actions, become effective 20 days after filing. The next excerpt describes the SEC staff practices in reviewing registration statements. Today, due to this review, unseasoned issuers and other problem companies can expect a much longer wait than 20 days before their registration statements become effective.

Poliakoff, SEC Review: Comfort or Illusion?
17 U. Balt. L. Rev. 40, 43-47 (1987)

B. REVIEW OF REGISTRATION STATEMENTS

In practice, after the registration statement has been filed with the Commission, the registration statement is assigned to one of the operating branches of the Commission's Division of Corporation Finance. The Commission's staff reviews the registration statement to determine its compliance with the informational requirements of the 1933 Act and the forms, regulations and policies of the staff. After commenting on (or determining not to review) the registration statement, and determining that any amendment filed complies with the staff's comments, the staff, on behalf of the Commission, will issue an order declaring the registration statement effective, and the company will commence the public offering.

The 1933 Act does not specifically provide for this type of review of registration statements filed with the Commission. In fact, section 8(a) of the 1933

Act provides that a registration statement will become effective automatically twenty days after it is filed with the Commission, or twenty days after any amendment to the registration statement is filed with the Commission. The 1933 Act expressly envisions formal proceedings in the event the disclosure in a registration statement is deficient or misleading. Under section 8(b) of the 1933 Act the Commission may issue an order refusing to permit the effectiveness of a registration statement if the registration statement appears to the Commission to be incomplete or inaccurate in any material respect. After the registration statement has become effective, section 8(d) of the 1933 Act provides that the Commission may issue a stop order suspending the effectiveness of an effective registration statement if the Commission determines that the registration statement includes an untrue statement of a material fact or fails to state a material fact required to be stated or necessary to make the statements in the registration statement not misleading.

The Commission learned, however, in its early years soon after the enactment of the 1933 Act, that the formal process of challenging the registration statement was not the best method of policing disclosure. Because of the overwhelming number of registration statements which were filed with the Commission each year, the Commission devised the "letter of deficiencies" review method, later renamed the "letter of comment" method, to effectuate the statutory aims of assuring full and fair disclosure without invoking the unduly harsh consequences of formal process under section 8. Under this method of operation, the Commission's staff reviewed the initial filing of a registration statement and issued a detailed letter of comment advising the issuer's counsel of any deficiencies in the registration statement that the staff believed needed correction.[21] This revised method of operation, adopted for the review of registration statements subject to the 1933 Act, offered a distinct advantage to all parties, including the Commission's staff and public investors. The new technique was so successful that it received explicit congressional approval by incorporation in the Investment Company Act of 1940.[22] . . .

In the course of the review process, registration statements are usually amended at least once in response to a letter of comment from the Commission's

---

21.   The Commission's comments are not necessarily limited to the specific material disclosure items contained in or omitted from the registration statement, but also may refer to the form and readability of the registration statement. Expediting Registration Statements Filed under the Act, Securities Act Release No. 4970, [1961 Transfer Binder] Fed. Sec. L. Rep. (CCH) ¶77,705 (May 1, 1969). *See generally* Orlanski, SEC Comments on the Offering Prospectus, 17 Rev. Sec. Reg. 887 (1984). Although there are no legal consequences for failing to respond to a letter of comment, the issuer's failure to respond to the letter of comment carries with it the implied threat of a formal stop order proceeding. Accordingly, rather than risk the adverse consequences of formal action, issuers will comply readily with the staff's comments contained in the letter of comment.

22.   . . . Receipt of a letter of comment, however, is not a "right" which may be demanded or enforced. When a registration statement is grossly deficient or when the deficiencies appear to stem from a careless disregard of the statutory and regulatory requirements, the staff is not obligated to pinpoint each alleged inadequacy. "[T]o require it to do otherwise would unduly interfere with administrative efficiency and delay the processing of other filings that do not present comparable disclosure problems." *Boruski v. Division of Corp. Fin.*, 321 F. Supp. 1273, 1276 (S.D.N.Y. 1971). In such cases, a brief letter usually is sent which merely highlights some of the major areas of deficiency.

staff recommending corrections or clarifications. In order to prevent the registration statement from becoming effective in deficient form automatically after the twenty-day statutory period, issuers include a legend, referred to as the "delaying amendment," on the facing page of the initial filing of the registration statement.[24] The delaying amendment postpones the automatic effective date of the registration statement until the issuer has amended the registration statement to comply with the comments of the Commission's staff.

C. ACCELERATION OF EFFECTIVENESS AND POST-EFFECTIVE AMENDMENTS

When the issuer has finally amended the registration statement to the satisfaction of the Commission's staff and is ready to initiate the public offering, the issuer will then request that the Commission "accelerate" the effective date of the registration statement. Under Section 8 of the 1933 Act, the Commission has authority to set the effective date of a registration statement earlier than the twentieth day after filing of a registration statement or any pre-effective amendment. The Commission is authorized also to fix the effective date of an amendment to the registration statement filed after the registration statement has become effective. In practice, the effective date is accelerated to a date specified by the issuer by letter to the Commission received at least two days before the requested effective date.

Section 8 of the 1933 Act articulates the standards to be met in order for the Commission to accelerate the effective date of a registration statement and to fix the effective date of a post-effective amendment. Section 8(a) provides that the Commission may accelerate the effective date of a registration statement, "having due regard to the adequacy of the information respecting the issuer theretofore available to the public . . . and to the public interest and the protection of investors." Applying similar standards, Section 8(c) empowers the Commission to fix the effective date of a post-effective amendment "if such amendment, upon its face, appears to the Commission not to be incomplete or inaccurate in any material respect . . . , [the Commission] having due regard to the public interest and the protection of investors." In this context, the Commission has delineated, in SEC Rules 460 and 461, some of the factors which must be considered in determining whether the Section 8 standards have been met, principally relating to the adequacy of the disclosure and the

---

24. The delaying amendment is a notation on the cover of a registration statement pursuant to Rule 473 that "amends" the registration statement every twenty days, preventing it from becoming effective automatically by lapse of time, until the Commission, the issuer and underwriters are prepared to permit the offering to commence. *See* 17 C.F.R. §230.473 (1987). The delaying amendment consists of the following language:

> The registrant hereby amends this registration statement on such date or dates as may be necessary to delay its effective date until the registrant shall file a further amendment which specifically states that this registration statement shall thereafter become effective in accordance with Section 8(a) of the Securities Act of 1933 or until the registration statement shall become effective on such date as the Commission acting pursuant to said Section 8(a), may determine.

17 C.F.R. §270.473 (1987).

dissemination of information regarding the issuer by means of distributing the preliminary prospectus.

NOTES AND QUESTIONS

1. Confidential Pre-Registration Filings.   How public should the registrant's responses to the SEC review be? When online coupon company Groupon, Inc. went public in 2010, the very public revisions it made to the draft registration statement filed with the SEC raised investor eyebrows. For example, the first draft filed in June 2010 reported revenue of $713.4 million. In response to questions raised by the SEC's staff, Groupon revised its revenue figures, reporting revenues of $312.9 million. The change drew attention to certain risks flowing from its business model as well as questionable practices that Groupon used when measuring its revenue. Despite the benefits of such transparency to the investor community, the incident nonetheless stirred controversy about whether so much transparency with respect to the early versions of the registration statement has a chilling effect on the company's IPO or the willingness to undertake an IPO. Section 6(e) of the Securities Act now allows "emerging growth companies" (EGCs) undertaking an IPO to file drafts of their registration statement with the SEC on a confidential basis; their filings do not become public until 15 days before the registrant launches its first "road show" (road shows are discussed in the next section but generally the term refers to gatherings where issuers and their underwriters pitch the offering to selected investors before the registration statement becomes effective). If there is no road show, the veil is lifted 15 days before the expected effective date of the registration statement.

In 2017, the SEC expanded the types of draft registration statements that an issuer can file confidentially to the following:

- a registration statement in connection with an IPO (i.e., no more EGC limitation);
- an initial registration statement for the listing of a class of securities under Exchange Act Section 12(b); and
- a registration statement for a follow-on offering within one year after the effective date of an IPO or initial Section 12(b) registration statement.

2. Acceleration Requests and Indemnification.   Section 11 imposes liability on certain persons if the registration statement contains a material misrepresentation when it becomes effective. Among those exposed to liability are the directors and certain officers of the issuers. The issuer may attempt to lighten their concerns for Section 11 liability by agreeing to indemnify them for such losses. If such an agreement exists and the issuer requests its offering to be accelerated, Item 512(i) of Regulation S-K extracts an undertaking from the registrant that, in the event that a claim for indemnification is made of a director, an officer, or a controlling person, the registrant will submit the propriety of such indemnification for approval by a court unless its counsel opines that the propriety of such indemnification is settled by controlling precedent. If disclosure is the object of the Securities Act, why is this undertaking necessary? *See also* Item 702 of Regulation S-K.

3. The Pricing Amendment. The last piece of information filed is the price amendment; to have filed this information months or even days earlier would have subjected the underwriters to the unbearable risk that the market may turn against them before the effective date of the registration statement. Historically, a request was made for the registration statement to become effective with the filing of the pricing amendment. The underwriters' contract with the issuer is also conditioned on the registration statement's becoming effective on a specified date and hour. As a consequence of Rule 430A, these practices have changed for *cash* offerings because the rule eliminates the need for a pre-effective amendment to the registration statement for the sole purpose of disclosing the price of the offering, names of the underwriters syndicate, underwriter compensation, amount of the proceeds, and other information dependent on the offering price.

Rule 430A allows the registration statements covering an offering of securities for cash to become effective without price-related information, provided such information is made available by a supplement to the *prospectus* within 15 business days of the effective date. Price-related information provided more than 15 days after the effective date requires the filing of an amendment to the registration statement. As will be seen later in this chapter, a costly consideration for any post-effective amendment to the registration statement is that it resets the liability clock under Section 11. Thus, any information that was accurate when the registration statement initially became effective, but that is rendered false by a supervening event, can be the basis for liability under Section 11 if a post-effective amendment is made to the registration statement without correcting the information rendered false by the supervening event. Even though Rule 430A permits the price to be excluded from the registration statement for some offerings, the registration statement's cover page is required to set forth a range within which the security will be sold when priced.

Rule 430A also allows changes in the amount of securities being offered to be disclosed through a supplement to the prospectus, provided the change does not materially affect the disclosures in the registration statement. A decrease or increase of no more than 20 percent of the total amount of the offering is not material. Rule 430A's permission to report price or volume changes (falling within the 20 percent range) in the prospectus, rather than by an amendment to the registration statement, substantially reduces the burdens of reporting these changes and encourages issuers to "go effective" even before their marketing process is completed. However, does the 20 percent limit also encourage underpricing of IPOs?

4. Why Is Everyone So Cooperative? One may wonder where the source of the Commission's power over the registrant is to elicit changes in the filed registration statement in response to its deficiency letter. One answer may be that a certain cooperative spirit is part of the culture that surrounds the registration process, and it is fed by the belief that the dispassionate eye of the Division of Corporation Finance staff may indeed shield the issuer from liability under Section 11 of the Act. *See* Barker, SEC Registration of Public Offerings Under the Securities Act of 1933, 52 Bus. Law. 65 (1996). And there is the realization that bucking the staff's deficiency letter may result in a more formal response, such as a refusal order under Section 8(b), or, more likely, a stop order under

Section 8(d). Certainly, a formal proceeding is not the type of publicity the issuer wishes to precede its distribution.

Also, the importance to the issuer and the underwriters of the staff's power to accelerate the effective date of the registration statement itself fosters a cooperative spirit on the issuer's part. Rules 460 and 461 set forth the many considerations for granting the registrant's request to accelerate. Overall, Rule 460 focuses on whether there has been sufficient circulation of the preliminary prospectus (the prospectus that is used after the registration statement is filed and before the registration statement becomes effective) among underwriters and dealers and also on the adequacy of the information in the preliminary prospectus. A review of Rule 461 reveals a good deal of discretionary power over whether to grant the registrant's request to accelerate. Rule 461 conditions acceleration upon among other factors, the prospectus's being "reasonably concise and readable." Other bases to deny acceleration under Rule 461 are that the misleading effects of a preliminary prospectus circulated earlier have not been sufficiently overcome by the issuer's distribution of corrected materials to underwriters and dealers; the issuer, its underwriter, or a person controlling the issuer is currently being investigated by the Commission; any of the proposed underwriters of the offering cannot meet their regulatory minimum capital requirements; anyone connected with the offering has artificially affected the market price of the security to be distributed; and the compensation to the underwriters, after review by FINRA, has not been approved by it. Are Rule 461's bases for denying acceleration an ultra vires exercise of authority by the Commission?

   5.   Real and Imputed Costs of Going Public.   Going public is not cheap. The average costs between 2015-2017 for an IPO of $100 million to $250 million in proceeds were $2.0 million in legal fees, $1.1 million for the auditor, underwriter commissions of typically 7 percent of the offering amount, $400,000 in printing costs, and $800,000 for various filing fees (SEC, blue sky, FINRA, and exchange listing), and miscellaneous costs. In addition, the company should be aware of the distraction costs; during the registration, some 75 percent of the CFO's time, about 40 percent of the CEO's time, and 20 percent of other senior officers' time will be devoted to matters related to the offering. *See* PricewaterhouseCoopers, Considering an IPO to Fuel Your Company's Future Growth? Insight into the Costs of Going Public and Being Public, at 6 (Nov. 2017).

   There are other concerns, indeed risks, of going public. Bringing in other stockholders through a common stock offering means control must be shared with outsiders. If a controlling block of stock is not retained by management, there is always the potential for the managers to be displaced through the ballot or the takeover. These concerns are frequently addressed by issuing supervoting shares to the founders and adopting other defensive measures prior to going public. Other concerns are that once public, the firm incurs the burden of complying with the periodic reporting requirements of the '34 Act. While out-of-pocket costs may be trivial in relation to the registrant's assets or net income, the more significant costs are those associated with the consciousness of operating in the public eye. In sum, the vast majority of small closely held companies eschew going public because remaining private is cheaper, ensures the company is simpler to operate, and assures greater freedom in managing the company. *See* Brau & Fawcett, Initial Public Offerings: An Analysis of

Theory and Practice, 61 J. Fin. 399 (2006) (a large survey of CFOs finds that the decision to remain private is driven by their wish to preserve decision-making control and ownership. Thus, it is not surprising that many firms raise needed capital by using one of the exemptions from registration provided in Sections 3 and 4 of the Securities Act, discussed in Chapter 5, or by simply borrowing the needed funds. Those whose capital needs cannot be so satisfied move into the big leagues, where their ticket to capital markets is the registration statement.

6.   *Small Business Issuer System.* For "smaller reporting companies," defined as issuers whose "public float" does not exceed $75 million, the SEC provides 12 user-friendly disclosure guidelines in Regulation S-K, called "scaled disclosures." *See* Regulation S-K Item 10(f). These guidelines are written in plain English and call for more abbreviated disclosure than the side-by-side guidelines for larger issuers. Nonetheless, about two-thirds of Regulation S-K's disclosure guidelines are the same regardless of an issuer's size, but now the SEC is engaged in a long-term effort to further revise Regulation S-K with a view toward eliminating or further scaling mandated disclosures.

7.   *Other Registration Forms.* Several specialized '33 Act registration forms exist. For example, Form S-4 applies to securities issued in business combinations, and Form S-8 covers securities offered through employee stock purchase and savings plans. In its series F (Forms F-1 through F-6), the SEC has developed a hierarchy of registration forms for foreign issuers that mirrors the requirements for domestic issuers. Similarly, an array of registration forms exists for investment companies on Forms N-1 to N-5 and N-14.

8.   *Blank Check Offerings.* Pursuant to its authority under Section 7(b)—added to the Securities Act in 1990—the Commission prescribes through Rule 419 special protective requirements that apply to offerings by so-called blank check companies, defined as companies that lack any specific business plan or purpose or whose plan is to engage in "acquisition" of an unidentified company (what the layman would likely refer to as a "pig in the poke"). The investors' acquire shares in a special purpose acquisition company (SPAC) that will, after raising funds from investors, seek suitable companies to acquire. The vast bulk of their acquisitions are private companies. *See generally* Rodrigues & Stegemoller, Exit, Voice, and Reputation: The Evolution of SPACs, 37 Del. J. Corp. L. (2012). The requirements of Rule 419 transcend mere disclosure. The proceeds the SPAC raises from the public offering are required to be kept in a financially secure escrow account. Once an agreement is made to acquire a business or assets for the conduct of a business in an amount equal to 80 percent of the offering proceeds, the registrant is required to disclose to all its investors extensive information about the business or assets acquired. After receiving disclosure of how at least 80 percent of the offering's proceeds will be used, purchasers have the option of retaining their investment in the blank check company or receiving their share of the funds in the escrow account. Only after these steps are taken can the registrant access the funds remaining in the escrow account to engage in the proposed purchase of a business or assets. In no case can the blank stock registrant retain escrow funds for longer than 18 months after the effective date of the initial registration statement.

9. *The Ethics of Taking Stock.* When PC vendor VA Linux went public in 1999, the law firm that guided its IPO had special cause to celebrate the 698 percent price increase during the first day of trading: The 102,584 VA Linux shares owned by the law firm were then worth $24.5 million. It is not unusual for law firms to own stock in their clients. Indeed, the law firm representing VA Linux held stock in 33 of the 53 companies it took public in 1999. *See* Baker, Who Wants to Be a Millionaire, 86 A.B.A. J. 36, 37 (Feb. 2000). Such ownership is not prohibited by professional standards. *See* ABA Ethics Opinion 00.418 (July 17, 2000). Model Rule of Professional Conduct 1.8, as amended in 2002, requires that the lawyer's dealings with his client be fair, reasonable, and accompanied by full disclosure, and further requires that the client consent in writing to transactions after being warned of desirability of obtaining independent counsel for equity-for-fees transaction. Does ownership of stock in a company making a public offering pose special conflicts of interest on the part of the lawyer of a type not contemplated by drafters of professional standards? *Compare* McAlpine, Getting a Piece of the Action: Should Lawyers Be Allowed to Invest in Their Client's Stock?, 47 UCLA L. Rev. 549 (1999) (seeing a community of interest among the lawyer, VC, and the client that will discourage attorney overreaching), *with* Dzienkowski & Peroni, The Decline in Lawyer Independence: Lawyer Equity Investments in Clients, 81 Tex. L. Rev. 405 (2002) (listing many concerns posed by equity ownership by attorneys).

E. *Gun-Jumping Concerns for the IPO*

The linchpin of the Securities Act is Section 5, whose regulatory reach begins before the registration statement is filed with the SEC, continues through the period between the filing of the registration statement and the time when the registration statement becomes effective, and extends even after the registration statement is effective. The materials in this section closely examine Section 5's regulatory demands at each of these three stages, more commonly referred to as the *pre-filing period,* the *waiting period,* and the *post-effective period.* By way of a quick overview, Section 5(c) prohibits any offer to sell or offer to buy prior to the filing of a registration statement. Under Section 5(a), no sales or deliveries of registered securities can occur until the registration statement is effective. After the registration statement is filed and even after it is effective, Section 5(b)(1) requires that all written offers to sell be in connection with a prospectus that complies with Section 10 of the Act. This provision is designed to assure a wide distribution via the prospectus of the most salient portions of the registration statement so that investors have reliable information when considering their purchase of the registered security. Per Section 5(b)(2), a final prospectus must accompany any transportation of the securities to investors.

The jurisdictional reach of each of the provisions in Section 5 is the same, namely, the use of any means or instruments of transportation or communication *in interstate commerce or the mails.* Certainly, none of the provisions of Section 5 applies if all activities are on a face-to-face basis with no use of the mail, phone, or other commercial medium to arrange or carry out the sale.

At the same time, if the money for the purchase is mailed by the buyer to the seller or the security is mailed by the seller to the buyer after all negotiations occurred on a face-to-face basis, the jurisdictional requirements of the statute are met. This is the import of the "directly or indirectly" language of each provision. At the same time, there is cause to doubt that the language reaches purely *intrastate* activities where the mails are not used. On this point, consider the definition of *interstate commerce* in Section 2(a)(7), and contrast the manner in which the 73d Congress expressed the jurisdictional reach of Section 5 with how that same Congress articulated the jurisdictional requirement one year later for Section 10(b) of the '34 Act. For example, under Section 10(b) of the '34 Act, a purely intrastate phone call constitutes the "use of an instrumentality of interstate commerce."

In the following review of Section 5 and its supporting regulations, observe the delicate balance between attempting to protect the investor and at the same time accommodating various commercial considerations. Moreover, all that is said below is subject to the substantial qualification that certain types of securities and specific transactions are, as discussed in later chapters, exempt. If either the security is exempt or the transaction qualifies for an exemption, the regulatory demands of Section 5 do not apply. For present purposes, the most important exemption appears in Section 4(a)(1), which exempts from Section 5 transactions by everyone other than "an issuer, underwriter, or dealer." Each of these nonexempt parties is defined in Section 2: *Issuer* is defined in Section 2(a)(4), the term *underwriter* is broadly defined in Section 2(a)(11), and *dealer* is defined in Section 2(a)(12) to include brokers. The effect of Section 4(a)(1) is to subject to Section 5 those actively involved in the issuer's distribution—the issuer itself as well as its underwriters and certain dealers (many dealers have an exemption discussed at the end of this section).

In 2005, the SEC introduced sweeping reforms for the public offering of securities so that today a greater range of communications are permitted during the offering process. *See* Securities Act Release No. 8591 (July 19, 2005). Although the 2005 reforms liberalize the range of communications, it is important to understand that the reforms are embodied in a series of safe harbors. Each safe harbor conditions its protection on certain technical requirements, which are specified. Hence, a communication that does not meet the conditions of a safe harbor must be examined in accordance with the general principles outside the 2005 reforms that define an "offer" or "offer to sell" and a "prospectus." These principles and their related safe harbors are examined in the materials that follow. For a critique of the 2005 reforms, *see* Morrissey, Rhetoric and Reality: Investor Protection and the Securities Regulation Reform of 2005, 56 Cath. U. L. Rev. 561 (2007).

1. The Pre-Filing Period

Under Section 5(c), it is unlawful "to offer to sell or offer to buy" any security unless a registration statement has been filed for that security. Even after a registration statement is filed, the constraints of Section 5(c) reappear if that registration statement "is the subject of a refusal order or stop order or (prior to the effective date of the registration statement) any public proceeding or examination under section 8." The breadth of this prohibition is assured by Section 2(a)(3)'s definitions of "offer to sell," "offer for sale," and "offer," which include "every attempt or offer to dispose of, or solicitation of an offer to buy, a security or interest in a security, for value." The meaning of "offer" is potentially even broader than that set forth in Section 2(a)(3) because the statute merely states that "'offer' shall *include*" the items there listed; Section 2(a)(3) thus provides a nonexclusive list of activities that constitute an offer to sell, and it remains possible that other actions may under the circumstances constitute an offer to sell.

a. Conditioning the Market

Historically, the Commission has maintained an expansive view of the meaning of "offer for sale" to assure that Section 5's broad remedial purposes are carried out. It justified this position out of concern that issuers, underwriters, and dealers would otherwise attempt to condition the public and arouse public interest in the issuer and its securities as a prelude to undertaking a public offering. The following excerpt reflects this historical prohibition against nonfactual releases of information that could have the effect of conditioning investor interest in a forthcoming offering. Although the 2005 reforms have provided several useful safe harbors, regulatory issues nonetheless require that you understand how the statutory term *offer* is construed.

> ### Securities Act Release No. 3844
> **Securities and Exchange Commission (Oct. 8, 1957)**

Questions frequently are presented to the . . . Commission and its staff with respect to the impact of the registration and prospectus requirements of Section 5 . . . on publication of information concerning an issuer. . . . Some of the more common problems which have arisen in this connection and the nature of the advice given by the Commission and its staff are outlined herein for guidance. . . .

The terms "sale," "sell," "offer to sell," and "offer for sale" are broadly defined in Section 2[a](3) of the Act and these definitions have been liberally construed by the Commission and the courts.

It follows from the express language and the legislative history of the Securities Act that an issuer, underwriter or dealer may not legally begin a public offering or initiate a public sales campaign prior to the filing of a registration statement. It apparently is not generally understood, however, that the publication of information and statements, and publicity efforts, generally, made in advance of a proposed financing, although not couched in terms of an express offer, may in fact contribute to conditioning the public mind or arousing public interest in the issuer or in the securities of an issuer in a manner which raises a serious question whether the publicity is not in fact part of the selling effort.

EXAMPLE NO. 1

. . . An underwriter-promoter is engaged in arranging for the public financing of a mining venture to explore for a mineral which has certain possible potentialities for use in atomic research and power. While preparing a registration statement for a public offering, the underwriter-promoter distributed several thousand copies of a brochure which described in glowing generalities the future possibilities for use of the mineral and the profit potential to investors who would share in the growth prospects of a new industry. The brochure made no reference to an issuer or any security nor to any particular financing. It was sent out, however, bearing the name of the underwriting firm and obviously was designed to awaken an interest which later would be focused on the specific financing to be presented in the prospectus shortly to be sent to the same mailing list.

The distribution of the brochure under these circumstances clearly was the first step in a sales campaign to effect a public sale of the securities and as such, in the view of the Commission, violated Section 5 of the Securities Act. . . .

EXAMPLE NO. 6

. . . The president of a company accepted, in August, an invitation to address a meeting of a security analysts' society to be held in February of the following year for the purpose of informing the membership concerning the company, its plans, its record and problems. By January a speech had been prepared together with supplemental information and data, all of which was designed to give a fairly comprehensive picture of the company, the industry in which it operates and various factors affecting its future growth. Projections of demand, operations and profits for future periods were included. The speech and the other data had been printed and it was intended that several hundred copies would be available for distribution at the meeting. In addition, since it was believed that stock-holders, creditors, and perhaps customers might be interested in the talk, it was intended to mail to such persons and to a list of other selected firms and institutions copies of the material to be used at the analysts' meeting.

Later in January, a public financing by the company was authorized, preparation of a registration statement was begun and negotiation with underwriters was commenced. It soon appeared that the coming meeting of analysts, scheduled many months earlier, would be at or about the time the registration statement was to be filed. This presented the question whether, in the circumstances, delivery and distribution of the speech and the supporting data to the various persons mentioned above would contravene provisions of the Securities Act.

It seemed clear that the scheduling of the speech had not been arranged in contemplation of a public offering by the issuer at or about the time of its delivery. In the circumstances, no objection was raised to the delivery of the speech at the analysts' meeting. However, since printed copies of the speech might be received by a wide audience, it was suggested that printed copies of the speech and the supporting data not be made available at the meeting nor be transmitted to other persons.

EXAMPLE NO. 7

. . . Two weeks prior to the filing of a registration statement the president of the issuer had delivered, before a society of security analysts, a prepared address which had been booked several months previously. In his speech the president discussed the company's operations and expansion program, its sales and earnings. The speech contained a forecast of sales and referred to the issuer's proposal to file with the Commission later in the month a registration statement with respect to a proposed offering of convertible subordinated debentures. Copies of the speech had been distributed to approximately 4,000 security analysts.

The Commission denied acceleration of the registration statement and requested that the registrant distribute copies of its final prospectus to each member of the group which had received a copy of the speech. . . .

A few years after issuing Release No. 3844, the Commission in *In re Carl M. Loeb, Rhoades & Co.*, 38 S.E.C. 843 (1959), considered whether the blurred line between releasing newsworthy information and conditioning the market had been crossed. The focus of the action was whether, because of their participation in the publication of the two following press releases, Carl M. Loeb, Rhoades & Co. (Loeb Rhoades) and Dominick & Dominick (Dominick) had violated Section 5, so that their broker-dealer registration should be revoked, and whether they should also be expelled from membership in the NASD.

Arthur Vining Davis entered into an arrangement with Loeb Rhoades and Dominick for financing the development of his extensive real estate holdings. Two press releases were prepared by Stanley R. Grant, a Loeb Rhoades partner. The July release appeared in several Florida newspapers, and by calling the reporters at three prominent New York newspapers, as well as the major wire services, Grant assured that the September press release was widely circulated.

The July press release announced that Arthur Vining Davis ("noted industrialist") was "entering into a new phase" in his Florida real estate business, for he would begin developing new communities, industrial parks, and recreational areas on his holdings. The release further announced that the vehicle for these activities would be Arvida Corporation, which would hold title to the major portion of Mr. Davis' property and would "launch a full scale program for the orderly development of the lands." The release concluded: "Arrangements are being made to provide a large amount of new capital to implement the program."

The longer September release provided more details about Arvida's financial situation and the developmental efforts. It announced that Arvida "will be provided $25 to $30 million of additional capital through an offering of part of its new common stock to the public." The release continued: "The public offering, scheduled for some time in the next 60 days, will be conducted through a nationwide group of investment banking firms to be headed by Carl M. Loeb, Rhoades & Co. and Dominick & Dominick, both of New York." It announced that the offering's registration statement was being prepared.

The September release described some of the properties held by Arvida and the plans for their development: the properties were "largely undeveloped but sizable tracts of acreage . . . suitable for immediate use as residential and commercial sites."

The Commission held that both releases were solicitations of offers to sell in violation of Section 5. But what were the facts that could have been provided according to Release No. 3844? Furthermore, as you review the Commission's reasoning in the next two excerpts, do you get the impression that its concerns extend beyond mere conditioning of the market?

> We . . . find that such release and publicity was of a character calculated, by arousing and stimulating investor and dealer interest in Arvida securities and by eliciting indications of interest from customers to dealers and from dealer to underwriters, to set in motion the processes of distribution. In fact it had such an effect. It contained descriptive material concerning the properties, business, plans and management of Arvida, it included arresting references to "assets in excess of $100,000,000," and "over 100,000 acres, more than 155 square miles, in an area of the Gold Coast." Reporters were furnished with price data, and registrants were named as the managing underwriters thus permitting, if not inviting, dealers to register their interest with them. We find that such activities constituted part of a selling effort by the managing underwriters.
>
> The principal justification advanced for the September 19 release and publicity was the claim that the activities of Mr. Davis, and specifically his interests in Florida real estate, are "news" and that accordingly Section 5(c) should not be construed to restrict the freedom of the managing underwriters to release such publicity. We reject this contention. Section 5(c) is equally applicable whether or not the issuer or the surrounding circumstances have, or by astute public relations activities may be made to appear to have, news value.

38 S.E.C. at 851-852.

> Comparison of the September publicity with the final prospectus of Arvida illustrates the wisdom of the congressional prohibition against pre-filing publicity. Wholly omitted from the release and withheld from reporters were the essential financial facts of capitalization, indebtedness and operating results which are so material to any informed investment decision. The great acreage owned by Arvida was stressed without disclosing that the bulk of it was in areas remote in time and distance from the development which was also stressed. Obscured also was the probable use of much of the proceeds of the financing, not to develop the properties but rather to discharge mortgage debt. . . . From the publicity investors could, and no doubt many did, derive the impression that the risk and financing requirements of this real estate venture had been substantially satisfied by Davis and that the public was being invited to participate in reaping the fruits through early development. In fact, as clearly appears from the final prospectus, much of the risk remains to be taken and much of the financing essential to the issuer's business remains to be carried out.

Id. at 854.

The regulatory concerns of whether a communication conditions the market arise when the issuer is "in registration." This moment has never been precisely defined by the SEC, which rather broadly has stated that being "in registration . . . mean[s] the entire process of registration, at least from the time the issuer reaches an understanding with the broker-dealer, which is to act as a managing underwriter until the completion of the offering and the period of

40 or 90 days during which dealers must deliver a prospectus." Securities Act Release No. 5009, n.4 (Oct. 7, 1969).

Consider the ironies of Section 5 vis-à-vis the overall operation of the securities laws. Many provisions and regulations of the securities laws have as their goal encouraging the release of information. As will be seen in Chapter 12, Congress has even enacted safe harbors for the release of "forward-looking" information for the purpose of encouraging corporations to more frequently make voluntary disclosures, particularly of internally generated predictions, appraisals, and forecasts. Indeed, the Management Discussion and Analysis section of the registration statement is an attempt to elicit more information from management concerning the company's future prospects and challenges. In Chapter 1, we saw how the continuous disclosure provisions of the Exchange Act are designed to assure a steady flow of information to trading markets, a flow that was not so steady, reliable, or broadly available across publicly traded firms before the Exchange Act. Against these aspirations and commands, Section 5 reaches the anomalous result of discouraging the release of many types of highly useful information once a company is in registration. Does this make sense? Are the gains of avoiding conditioning the market overcome by the harm of withholding such information from markets where the issuer's outstanding shares are regularly traded? Should concern for conditioning the market apply equally to firms undertaking an IPO and firms with shares that already are publicly traded? Just how great is the threat to investors if issuers do condition the market? A further consideration is the fact that a dominant part of registered offerings, whether they be an IPO or made by a seasoned issuer, are placed with financial institutions. In the "bookbuilding" process in which their interest is first solicited, and the underwriters are therefore assessing the market for the security, a good deal information is shared with institutions that is not otherwise public. *See* Langevoort & Thompson, IPOs and the Slow Death of Section 5, 102 Ky. L. Rev. 891 (2013-2014). There is also evidence that the informational advantages garnered by the institutions stimulate interest among retail investors that contributes to post-IPO price surges discussed earlier. *See* Da, Engleberg & Gao, In Search of Attention, 66 J. Fin. 1461 (2011) (finding correlation between volume of Google searches for information about companies in registration and their underpricing). Pondering these questions sheds some light on the reasoning of the SEC's 2005 reform efforts, reviewed below, identifying communications that can occur during the offering process.

As you review the following material, observe that the SEC has created important safe harbors for certain types of communications; however, a communication that falls outside the safe harbor must still be assessed by the triple considerations of whether the communication was by someone other than an "issuer, underwriter or dealer," "conditioned the market," and was made when the issuer was "in registration."

b. Safe Harbors for Permissible Communications

Capital markets are not alone in their insatiable thirst for information. Customers, suppliers, and employees are eager for information about a firm's operations, prospects, products, and the like. Because much of the information sought by these groups is relevant to investors as well, a company "in registration" frequently finds itself torn between legitimate commercial needs to release information about itself and the command of Section 5(c) not to condition the market. As you review the following protective safe harbors, consider how successful the SEC has been in balancing these conflicting forces.

30-Day Bright-Line Exclusion.   Rule 163A provides *all* issuers a bright-line time period, ending 30 days prior to the filing of a registration statement, during which the issuer or those acting on its behalf can communicate without violating Section 5. However, this protection is not without important qualifications. First, the communication must be made "by or on behalf of the issuer," so that communications by other distribution participants are not shielded by Rule 163A, even if made more than 30 days prior to the filing of a registration statement. Second, the communication cannot make any reference to the securities offering. Third, the issuer must take reasonable steps to prevent further distribution or publication of the communication during the 30-day period immediately before filing of the registration statement. The 30-day exclusion does not apply to certain types of offerings, such as blank check offerings or business combinations (the latter are subject to special safe harbor provisions discussed in Chapter 7).

Rule 135.   Rule 135 provides that it is not an offer to sell securities if the issuer (as well as those acting on its behalf) releases certain information about its operations and activities, even though the issuer is in registration. For example, under paragraph (a) of Rule 135, an issuer can disclose its intention to make a public offering and can announce such information as the amount and type of security as well as the manner and purpose of the offering. On the other hand, Rule 135 prohibits the identification of the prospective underwriters or the security's offering price in the pre-filing release. What purpose is served by withholding the underwriters' identity in the release? How likely is it that the underwriters' identity or the probable offering price cannot be discovered by a resourceful financial columnist? By a resourceful investor? *Chris-Craft Industries, Inc. v. Bangor Punta Corp.*, 426 F.2d 569 (2d Cir. 1970) (en banc), *rev'd on other grounds*, 430 U.S. 1 (1977), held that Rule 135 provides limited authorization of what issuers may include in pre-filing announcements of offers. Piper Aircraft was the target of a hostile tender offer by Chris-Craft Industries when a friendly second suitor, Bangor Punta Corp., announced it would soon file a registration statement for an offer to the Piper shareholders of a package of Bangor securities valued at "$80 or more" for each Piper share.[2] The court held that Section 5 was violated because disclosing the value of the securities went beyond the information permitted by Rule 135.

Factual Information.   Non-reporting issuers enjoy a limited safe harbor in Rule 169 for their communication of "regularly released" "factual business information." However, this type of communication by a non-reporting company is protected only if the intended audience is not investors but others, such

---

2.   Since the *Chris-Craft* decision, the Commission has amended the disclosure requirements for tender offers to require disclosure of such information, even if a registration statement has not yet been filed. *See* Exchange Act Release No. 14699 (Apr. 24, 1978).

as customers and suppliers. *See* Chemmanur & Yan, Product Market Advertising and New Equity Issues, 92 J. Fin. Econ. 40 (2009) (companies increase market advertising in advance of IPO).

Qualified Institutional Buyers and Accredited Institutional Investors. The JOBS Act added Section 5(d) to the Securities Act to permit emerging growth companies prior to (or after) filing a registration statement to communicate with "qualified institutional buyers" or institutions that are "accredited investors" to determine whether such investors may have an interest in the security to be offered or being offered. This practice is known as "testing the waters." The definition of qualified institutional investor (QIB) is set forth in Rule 144A, a topic examined closely in Chapter 6; broadly speaking, QIBs are financial institutions with a large (for most $100 million) investment portfolio. The topic of accredited investors is studied more closely in Chapter 5, where we will find that institutions such as certain banks, insurance companies, and broker-dealers are deemed accredited investors. In February 2019, the SEC proposed Securities Act Rule 163B, which would extend testing the waters to all issuers, not just EGCs.

Analyst and Broker Communications. The JOBS Act amended Section 2(a)(3) of the Securities Act and added Section 15D(c) to the Exchange Act. The amendment to the Securities Act exempts research reports regarding emerging growth companies by brokers from the definition of offer to sell and Section 15D(c) prohibits any FINRA and SEC rules and regulations that restrict communication or participation by analysts in an IPO by an emerging growth company. This part of the on-ramp initiative was intended to reintroduce the financial analysts to the underwriting process. Research coverage of IPOs is a matter that has some recent history going back to a series of abuses that occurred in connection with the dot.com market bubble in 1999-2000. One of the abuses chronicled during that era was the underwriters' use of analysts to promote stock offerings.[3] As a result of those abuses, multiple regulatory steps were taken to separate analysts from the underwriters. Then, in 2012, fearing that research had dried up for initial public offerings, and believing that such research is a desideratum for public offerings, Congress in the JOBS Act provided an exemption from the definition of "offer to sell" and "offer for sale" by amending Section 2(a)(3). As now amended, Section 2(a)(3) states that a "research report" (which is broadly defined) published or distributed *by brokers* in connection with an emerging growth company's equity offering does not violate Section 5(c). In considering the scope of the exemption for brokers' research reports, think about how this provision impacted the broker in *Loeb, Rhoades.*

c. Arrangements with and Among Underwriters

Section 2(a)(3) excludes from the definitions of "sale," "offer to sell," and "offer to buy" both the negotiations and the agreements that the issuer has with its underwriter, as well as the negotiations and agreements among

---

3. *See, e.g.,* SEC Press Release: SEC, NY Attorney General, NASD, NASAA, NYSE and State Regulators Announce Historic Agreement to Reform Investment Practices (Dec. 20, 2002).

the underwriters, provided they are or will become parties to the underwriting agreement with the issuer. Just what negotiations and agreements are so protected depends on whether the person is an *underwriter,* a term defined in Section 2(a)(11) so as to exclude those "whose interest is limited to a commission *from the underwriter* not in excess of the usual and customary distributors' or sellers' commission." The parties obviously excluded by this language are members of the selling group who absorb none of the offering's risk.

[handwritten: ↳ help underwriters but not responsible for unsold securities]

PROBLEMS

Omega Company manufactures fiber-optic switches and is located in Cupertino, California, just south of San Francisco. Omega was formed about seven years ago and now desperately needs to expand its manufacturing capacity as well as pursue certain new product development possibilities. For this, it needs to raise about $50-$70 million through a public offering of common shares. Omega contemplates that a registration statement covering the offering will be filed May 1st. For each of the problems that follow, consider whether Section 5 of the Securities Act has been violated. Omega is not a reporting company, has not previously engaged in a public offering of its security, and is an emerging growth company.

4-1.   On February 10th, Bob, Omega's vice president of marketing, places an advertisement to appear in nine upcoming issues of *Business Week.* The advertisement previously had run for several months in *Tech World,* a computer trade magazine, and in addition to listing the full range of products manufactured by Omega, it carried a quote from a trade magazine that "Omega is the emerging industry leader in the development and design of fiber-optic switches."

4-2.   On February 14th, Alice, Omega's vice president of finance, invites five representatives of San Francisco investment banking firms to meet with her to explore each firm's possible interest in underwriting Omega's forthcoming offering. As a result of these discussions, she asks one of the firms, Hedley, Hadley Inc., to serve as Omega's underwriter. On February 15th, they execute a draft agreement calling for Hedley, Hadley to head a firm commitment underwriting syndicate for 4 million Omega shares to be sold for approximately $15 per share. All discussions were conducted in San Francisco solely with Hedley, Hadley's California-based staff.

[handwritten: ↳ participants deal yet]

4-3.   Bob, the head of Hedley, Hadley's San Francisco office, on February 16th faxes the underwriting agreement to his supervisors in New York City, where the agreement is signed there on behalf of Hedley, Hadley.   *[handwritten: OK → underwriter?]*

4-4.   From its San Francisco offices, Hedley, Hadley circulates a letter inviting 80 national and regional brokerage houses to participate as underwriters in the upcoming Omega offering.   *[handwritten: Pre-nego docs protected § 2(a)(3)]*

4-5.   A few of the smaller firms invited by Hedley, Hadley to join in the underwriting have stated that they are not in a position to underwrite any part of the Omega offering. Hedley, Hadley responded with an offer to pay them their usual commission rate for any shares they sold in the Omega offering.

[handwritten margin notes: until April 30th; OK under 163A; emerging may be too forward looking under R. 163, should edit to be claim toks are OK, firm syndicate OK, draft agreement; OK → underwriter?; deal the wears principin & ESGs; not allowed, would make them selling group unit; violates S.5 ← not buy firing]

5.5 viewed as "offer to sell"

4-6. On March 15th, Omega's public relations team prepared a brochure highlighting the company's rapid development and innovative products for distribution to the financial media. Copies will also be distributed to lawyers, accountants, investment advisers, and other localities where Omega's name is likely to be recognized. The brochure indicates that Omega intends to make a public offering in the near future and includes estimates of its future production capacity as a result of the forthcoming offer. What if the brochure would only be directed to certain large institutional investors?

OK if testing the waters provision to QIBs doesn't sell

under 169A cuz it mentions offering, not 135 because it's promotional

or 169

4-7. On April 5th, Omega invites journalists and others to tour its production facilities as a prelude to its "big expansion plans." No mention is made of the forthcoming public offering, but company officials take the occasion to exhibit the first prototypes of some unusual new products. Articles in the press begin to appear and are picked up by some wire services. The business section of a number of newspapers around the country print stories about a particularly intriguing product that Omega highlighted. Does resolving this problem depend on what kind of journalists Omega invited to join its tour?

no 30 day safe harbor depends on if they normally hold tours, still forward-looking

? evidence isn't conv

(168) Maybe OK if technical journalists about the offering

4-8. In late April, Hedley, Hadley issues on its letterhead an announcement that is carried over the various financial wire services disclosing that Omega will soon undertake a public offering through a syndicate of underwriters of about 4 million common shares. The announcement further discloses that the <u>proceeds of the offering</u> will be used to expand Omega's production capabilities as well as to broaden its research base. Omega obtains a copy of the announcement and posts it to its web site.

would be OK as an IPO announcement under 135 if H

why it was doing it — can't be forward looking / promotional

4-9. On April 27th, Omega mails its <u>annual report</u> to its shareholders. In the report, Diane, Omega's CEO, blandly states that "Omega's management is optimistic that the company can continue its growth, especially in light of an expected augmentation of its production facilities and product lines with the proceeds of the upcoming public offering." The annual report is a glossier rendering of prior reports: The current report is filled with high-quality color photos of the company's products, and regal graphics are used to portray the company's earnings and sales progress since its formation. The report also includes bouncy biographical sketches of its cadre of distinguished outside directors, one of the most recently appointed being a former adviser to President Clinton.

dividend talk doesn't matter / legend

can't name underwriter

glossier, probably not OK, needs to be like PSA ads, again

shouldn't be forward looking, instead should just have a simple announcement of IPO

4-10. On April 28th, Omega placed on its web site a digital recording of Alice's recent presentation to a gathering of investment analysts. The analysts' invitation to Alice was made before Omega had begun its discussions with Hedley, Hadley. At the meeting, Alice volunteers that management fully expects that the proceeds of the new offering will make a substantial contribution to earnings within a year or two. In response to a financial columnist's question asking for Alice's reaction to rumors that the new offering is likely to boost earnings by $.25 per share, Alice observed that "$.25 was certainly in the ballpark."

shouldn't be forward looking w/ legend

not w/in 30 day safe harbor; scheduled in advance is fine

4-11. In late April, Carl, a broker in St. Louis, heard of the Omega offering and wrote to Hedley, Hadley offering to purchase 1,000 shares for his personal account.

but take it off website can't be forward looking can't mention offering

violates 5.5 if they don't reject it can't have selling group until filing 2(a)(3)

2.   The Waiting Period

With the filing of a registration statement, Section 5(c)'s broad prohibitions against offers to sell and offers to buy disappear, and the registrant enters the waiting period. Even though a registration statement has been filed, Section 5(a) continues to bar sales until the registration statement becomes effective; but with the filing of the registration statement, selling efforts can commence. The form of all such selling efforts, however, is shaped significantly by Section 5(b)(1). At first reading, Section 5(b)(1) appears to pose no formidable regulatory burdens because it simply renders it "unlawful . . . to carry or transmit any *prospectus* relating to any security with respect to which a registration statement has been filed . . . unless such *prospectus* meets the requirements of section 10." To the uninitiated, it would appear that you could elude Section 5(b)(1) so long as the document used is not formally labeled a prospectus. But Section 5(b)(1) does not stand on narrow formalities because *prospectus* is defined broadly in Section 2(a)(10), so that any written communication, as well as radio and television transmissions, is deemed to be a prospectus whenever a communication through such medium offers a security for sale or confirms such a sale. On the other hand, *oral* offers to sell are not within the definition of a prospectus. As will be seen, the tandem operation of Sections 5(b)(1) and 2(a)(10) significantly shapes the solicitation efforts during the waiting period.

a.   The Preliminary and Summary Prospectus

As initially enacted, the Securities Act provided that written offers could only occur after the registration statement had become effective, and then, only in connection with a final prospectus whose contents are governed by Section 10(a). This early vision soon gave way to the industry's request that the Commission permit investors to be solicited during the waiting period through a prospectus that embodied most of what was then in the issuer's registration statement. The Commission accommodated the industry by taking the position that a written communication that included the information then on file as the issuer's registration statement was not an offer to sell. This regulatory flexibility thus permitted written offers to be made during the waiting period using a prospectus popularly known as a "red herring," an expression reflecting the legend printed in red on the cover page of the prospectus giving notice that the red herring was not an offer to sell a security, that the security described therein was not registered, and that no sales could occur until the registration statement became effective. In sum, the Commission nimbly sidestepped Section 5 by rationalizing that distribution of the red herring was not a solicitation, but solely informational.

The use of the red herring was legitimized with the 1954 Amendments to the Securities Act, so that today Section 10(b) expressly empowers the Commission to adopt rules for prospectuses that either do not include all the information found in a final prospectus or summarize such information. Section 10(b), however, confines the use of the prospectus so authorized to one satisfying the prospectus requirements of Section 5(b)(1). Hence, a Section 10(b)-authorized prospectus cannot be used to fulfill Section 5(b)(2)'s requirement that a prospectus meeting the requirements of Section 10(a), a final prospectus, accompany or precede the delivery of certificates. Pursuant to Section 10(b), the Commission has adopted Rules 430 and 431.

Rule 430 embraces the practices that existed prior to 1954 for the red herring prospectus. It provides that prior to the effective date of a registration statement, Section 5(b)(1) is satisfied by the use of a prospectus that includes substantially the same information that will ultimately appear in the final prospectus under Section 10(a), except the preliminary prospectus may exclude the offering price, underwriter and dealer compensation, amount of the proceeds, and conversion rates, call prices, and other matters dependent on the offering price. This prospectus is called a *preliminary prospectus* and bears a legend much like that of the old red herring as well as the caption "Preliminary Prospectus," each printed in traditional Commission red.

Also tracing its efficacy to Section 10(b) is Rule 431, which authorizes the summary prospectus for use in meeting the requirements of Section 5(b)(1). Rule 431 is conditioned on, among other factors, the issuer having been a reporting company for 36 months. The summary prospectus is something of a relic of the past since it is rarely used in connection with today's public offerings. The preliminary and summary prospectuses are increasingly in electronic format and made available to investors through e-mail or accessing the issuer's or underwriter's web site.

b. Tombstone Ads and Identifying Statements

Once a registration statement is filed, publicity can be given through an announcement commonly known as a "tombstone ad"—this not-too-reassuring name reflects the announcement's unadorned contents. There are in fact two distinct forms for such announcements: the tombstone ad and the identifying statement. The tombstone ad traces its authority to the original language of Section 2(a)(10), which exempts any communication with respect to a security "if it states from whom a written prospectus meeting the requirements of Section 10 may be obtained and, in addition, does no more than identify the security, state the price thereof, [and] state by whom orders will be executed." Boston Beer Co., the brewer of Samuel Adams, made a creative use of the tombstone ad in connection with its public offering; it placed a tombstone ad on the neck of its beer bottle and thereby reached what turned out to be natural buyers for its stock. Rosenberg, Boston Beer Stock Leaps 40%, The Boston Globe, Nov. 22, 1995, at 69.

The tombstone ad is not used much today, appearing more frequently after the successful completion of a public offering where the lead underwriter is in fact advertising its marketing prowess, and not therefore for its intended purpose of informing potential investors where a prospectus can be obtained. More frequently used is an "identifying statement" that is authorized by Rule 134, which lists 22 categories of information that may be included in an announcement. The most distinctive feature of an announcement issued under Rule 134 as contrasted with the classic tombstone ad is that under Rule 134, in addition to the information appearing in the tombstone ad, a brief description of the issuer's business may appear as well as information about the securities being offered, underwriting information, and even information about the procedures investors are to follow to express their interest in the offering. The expanded Rule 134 announcements are likely to be more useful to the syndicate. Rule 134 permits communication of details about the mechanics and anticipated schedule of the offering, including marketing events such as road shows as well as procedures investors can follow for submitting expressions of interest. Rule 134 announcements can take the form of e-mails or web site postings so long as their content conforms to the matters covered by Rule 134.

c.   Free Writing

Those involved in the distribution frequently desire to circulate among potential investors information that is not contained in the registration statement. An example of such information is the "term sheet," a document that sets forth details related to the security being offered such as its price and features as well as salient information about its issuer. Supplementary information is generally referred to as free writing. Prior to the SEC's adoption in 2005 of Rules 164 and 433, free writing was possible only after the registration statement had become effective and even then it was subject to fairly tight conditions. The former restrictions on free writing arose from Sections 5(b)(1) and 2(a)(10). As we have seen, Section 2(a)(10) deems any written communication to be a prospectus and Section 5(b)(1) mandates that distribution participants can only use a prospectus that meets the requirements of Section 10 (i.e., a preliminary or final prospectus or a summary prospectus). Absent any other exemptive language, this forecloses distribution participants from using any written communications to supplement the statutorily mandated prospectus.

Now under Rules 164 and 433 free writing is possible during the waiting period for most issuers, provided certain conditions are satisfied. Rules 164 and 433 refer to such supplementary written material, including electronic communications, as a "free writing prospectus" and provide that if the Rules' conditions are satisfied that the free writing prospectus will itself be deemed a Section 10(b) prospectus. The alchemy of deeming the supplementary offering material to be a Section 10(b) prospectus means that circulation of the free writing prospectus is the circulation of the very type of document permitted by Section 5(b)(1). Hence, this new regulatory flexibility is accomplished not so much by an exemption as by broadening the definition of what is a Section 10 prospectus.

Rule 433 is complex. Its dissection for the IPO begins with paragraph 433(b)(2), which authorizes free writing by the issuer and the distribution participants in connection with offerings of securities for a non-reporting issuer or unseasoned issuer. An "unseasoned issuer" is not directly defined by the SEC; this term refers to issuers who cannot avail themselves to free writing via subparagraph (b)(1). Thus, an unseasoned issuer is a firm that is neither a "well-known seasoned issuer" nor one that is eligible to use Form S-3 or F-3. This would include non-reporting companies and reporting companies that are relegated to the default Form S-1 when registering shares (i.e., non-seasoned reporting company).

Preliminary Prospectus.   For the IPO or non-seasoned reporting company, free writing can commence provided that a registration statement has been filed with the SEC and that the free writing prospectus is accompanied or preceded by a prospectus that satisfies Section 10 (i.e., a preliminary prospectus during the waiting period) and also provided it includes the security's price range. Note that the need for a statutory prospectus to precede or accompany the free writing prospectus can be satisfied via an active hyperlink to the statutory prospectus so that underwriters can actively engage in electronic free writing even for IPOs. Once the required statutory prospectus is provided to an investor, additional materials can be provided without the need to provide an additional statutory prospectus, unless there is a material change in the most recent statutory prospectus.

Legend.   There is the universal condition that any free writing prospectus must include a legend indicating where the prospectus is available from the underwriters through a toll-free number and advising investors that registration materials can be accessed through the SEC's web site. Rule 164 provides a means to cure any unintentional or immaterial failure to include the required legend.

Filing.   Rule 433 has some rather convoluted rules regarding when and who must file a copy of the free writing prospectus with the SEC. In broad overview, in many instances there is no condition that the underwriters or dealers must file with the SEC the free writing prospectus that they prepare, use, or refer to. For example, if the free writing prospectus reflects only information provided by the issuer, the issuer has a duty to file the free writing prospectus. If the supplementary material is assembled by a distribution participant and not from information provided it by the issuer, for example, the information came from publicly available sources, whether the distribution participant must file the material depends on the breadth of its circulation. Under Rule 433(d)(1)(ii), when the free writing prospectus is used by an offering participant in a manner reasonably designed to lead to its broad unrestricted dissemination (e.g., inclusion on its web site), the offering participant must file it with the SEC. And if the supplementary material describes the final terms of the securities or the offering, the issuer must file this information with the SEC within two days of which such terms have been established, regardless of whether the issuer prepared this information. Finally, there is a universal requirement that issuers and offering participants retain for three years any free writing prospectuses.

Although the information in the free writing prospectus can be different from and supplementary to that in the registration statement, it cannot conflict with information in the registration statement.

While Rules 164 and 433 have expanded the range of information that can be circulated during the waiting period, we might want to consider why it took so many years for this liberalization to occur. One place to begin in answering this question is to understand that very different liability standards apply to free writing materials than apply to materials included in the registration statement. These differences will be studied in detail in Chapter 9. But accepting that an issuer and its agents are more easily held liable for misrepresentations appearing in the registration statement than for misrepresentations committed in free writing, would we not expect that, all else being equal, issuers and others may not devote the same attention and resources to assure the accuracy of a free writing prospectus as they will for information set forth in the registration statement itself? Should this difference justify constricting the range of information that can be disseminated outside the registration statement?

d.   Hyperlinks to the Prospectus

Companies increasingly make use of their web sites to promote their commercial image. The ubiquity of the information placed on a firm's web site poses serious questions under Section 5 if it is in registration. As we have seen earlier, during the pre-filing period, web sites pose the classic gun-jumping concern of conditioning the market prior to filing the registration statement. During the waiting period, the issue is whether information on a web site is a "prospectus" because it conditions the market; if so, Section 5(b)(1) is violated if the web site information does more than replicate the information in the Section 10 prospectus. Placing the preliminary prospectus on the issuer's or underwriter's web site does not *itself* import the web site's other information into the prospectus or render that information a part of the offering process. However, hyperlinks between the prospectus and other web site information bundles the documents together so that for regulatory purposes they will be seen as an offer to sell the distributed security. Absent a hyperlink, the outcome turns on the murky inquiries as to whether the web site's content is an "offer to sell" and whether the prospectus and other materials are in "close proximity" to one another. The latter inquiry has come to be called the *envelope theory*, because outcomes turn on analogies to the paper-based setting, where such questions are resolved by the prospectus and other forwarded information sharing the same delivery vessel. When the web site contains both a prospectus and other information about the issuer, the SEC envisions a virtual envelope by admonishing that "the web site content must be reviewed in its entirety to determine whether it contains impermissible free writing." Securities Act Release No. 7856 (Apr. 28, 2000). This position is now embodied in Rule 433(e) so that the linked information is a free writing prospectus subject to the filing requirements of Rule 433(d). However, pursuant to Rule 433(e)(2), historical information about the issuer that is so identified and appears in a separate section of the web site is not considered to be an offering of the security so that this information is not considered free writing.

e.   Road Shows

Initially, road shows were gatherings attended by potential underwriters, selling group members, the managing underwriter, and the issuer. The function of the meeting was to provide potential distribution participants an opportunity to understand the proposed offering and an opportunity to satisfy some elements of the "due diligence" defense provided by Section 11 of the Securities Act. Over time, road shows expanded to include institutional investors. With advancements in communication techniques, video and audio recordings of the road shows were distributed to those who could not be physically present.

For many years, the SEC deemed such communications not to be a "prospectus," on the grounds that video or audio tapes directed to specific persons did not constitute a broadcast medium; hence, it did not involve the use of "radio or television" that is referenced in Section 2(10), *see, e.g.*, Exploration, Inc., SEC No-Action (Oct. 9, 1986), especially if the communication was available only to pre-qualified investors with a password. *See, e.g.*, Charles Schwab & Co., Inc., [1999-2000 Transfer Binder] Fed. Sec. L. Rep. (CCH) ¶77,650 (Nov. 15, 1999) (underwriter permitted to make road shows available through its web site to individuals who either had *significant trading experience*—defined as 24 trades annually—or a household equity position of at least $500,000). Following the reforms of 2005, described below, the road show audience no longer must be limited in any way or otherwise have limits on the viewer's ability to copy or rebroadcast the road show.

Road shows are now regulated by Rule 405's definition of "graphic communication" and Rule 433(d)(8). If deemed a graphic communication, a road show is a form of free writing and its regulation is through the requirements for a free writing prospectus. Thus, the threshold consideration is whether the communication is deemed graphically communicated. The transmission of a "real-time presentation to a live audience" that does not originate from a recorded form is not a graphic communication, and hence, is not a prospectus. Even visual aids, such as a power point presentation, and other written communications used during such a live road show are not deemed to be a written communication. On the other hand, if the broadcast is not in real time and to a live audience (e.g., it is prerecorded and shown to a group of investors), this is clearly a "graphic communication." As such, Rule 433(d)(8) comes into play and treats the communication as a free writing prospectus. This means that the electronic road show must include specified legends. However, the full reach of Rule 433 does not come into play in all cases; a road show that is a free writing prospectus need only be filed with the SEC if the issuer is offering an equity security, is not a reporting company, and has not made at least one version of the road show publicly available. What appears to be the purpose of this filing requirement?

f. Dealing with the Media

The financial media is a valuable source of information to investors. The financial reporter can also be a tool employed by the issuer's executives to woo investors to its offering. If the issuer or those acting on its behalf prepares, pays, or gives consideration for the preparation of a communication in the media, this is treated as a free writing prospectus and must satisfy all the conditions of Rule 433 (to the extent the information exceeds that permitted by Rule 134). By contrast, if the communication is not so prepared or paid for—as would be the case where the issuer simply grants an interview to a journalist who then writes a story for publication—Rule 433(f) does not require that there be delivery of a statutory prospectus and provides that the filing requirements of the Rule are satisfied if a copy of the story is filed with the SEC within four business days after becoming aware of the publication. Alternatively, the issuer can file a transcript of the interview with the reporter or file all the information that was provided in the interview. An example of the issues here is the statement by Mr. Ermotti, CEO of the lead underwriter for Ferrari's IPO, that he made in fall 2015 in a Bloomberg report observing that it was "almost impossible to think that the Ferrari IPO can't be successful" (in the Italian press he cooed "un grande momento"). The statements were issued during the waiting period and prompted Ferrari to file a free writing prospectus clarifying that Ermotti's statements were focused on the offering itself and "were not intended to refer to the company's business." Ex ante, how should this statement have been handled?

g.   Bookbuilding: Selling Practices During the Waiting Period

As seen, Section 5(b)(1) does not reach oral selling efforts, except in the unlikely event they occur via radio or television. Consequently, during the waiting period, significant promotional efforts occur outside the regulatory reach of Section 5. One may ponder a bit on what exactly is being solicited from the customer at this point in light of Section 5(a)'s bar of any sale of a security prior to the registration statement's becoming effective. It may well be that what is solicited is the customer's offer to buy, which the parties understand cannot be accepted until the registration statement becomes effective. Another approach is that only an expression of interest is being sought during the waiting period, with an understanding that no offer to buy will be made until the registration statement becomes effective. The distinction between these two choices is that the former gives rise to a contract automatically upon the registration statement's becoming effective, whereas the latter would require subsequent agreement by the customer. There are other variations that the arrangement may take between the customer and the broker-dealers promoting the offering. But for all possible configurations, there is the important constraint in Section 5(a)(1) that their arrangement or understanding cannot constitute the sale of a security prior to the registration statement's becoming effective.

It should be observed that Rule 134(d) does permit, subject to a few formal conditions, a *written* communication to be sent during the waiting period to any investor asking them to express an interest in the distributed security by, for example, completing a card or form. This device is conditioned on the communication being accompanied or preceded by a prospectus satisfying Section 10. It also needs to contain a statement that, among other things, warns the investor that no offer to buy can be accepted and that no payment toward the purchase price can be received until the registration statement is effective, and that further informs the customer that their offer can be withdrawn anytime before acceptance is given after the effective date.

The commercial benefit of permitting oral offers to sell is that this allows significant sampling of investor interest in the offering. This overall process is referred to as "book building." It provides important information regarding investor interest that will affect decisions such as the offering price, amount of the security that can be sold, and level of underwriting risk. Furthermore, a modicum of discipline is imposed on the broker's behavior during this process through the antifraud provisions, the most significant in this context being Section 12(a)(2) of the '33 Act, which exposes sellers to liability for omissions or misstatements of a material fact unless they can prove they did not know and in the exercise of reasonable care could not have known of the omission or misstatement. But consider the following:

> [I]n 2005, the SEC deregulated in ways that made hyping publicity easier. And brokers have always been able to work the phones and do face-to-face meetings to push the stock in the month or so before sales begin, a freedom that now (within some technical limitations) extends to email and social media. Academic research shows fairly convincingly a link between hype and underpricing, including some subtle means. Earnings management (the self-serving use of accounting discretion) increases. Companies also engage in greater product advertising in anticipation of an IPO, suggesting that the brand message is directed at potential investors as well as potential customers. And it seems to work.
>
> Whether this bothers you or not is a good test of your gut feelings about investor protection. Hype and earnings management are not necessarily fraudulent, even if they play on emotions and trust. On the other hand, the marketing effort is designed to stimulate in the brain the image of a winning lottery ticket in the investor's hands, burying the reality that if those inside the company believed the shares were worth so much, they probably wouldn't be selling at the chosen offering price. Which is worse, opportunism or gullibility? When you choose gullibility, or even just sigh and say there is nothing to be done to help the gullible except make them learn from experience, Wall Street smiles. Hope often triumphs over experience in the waves of sentiment when IPO windows are wide open.

D.C. Langevoort, Selling Hope, Selling Risk: Corporations, Wall Street and the Dilemmas of Investor Protection 121 (2016).

h. *Gap Filling with Exchange Act Rule 15c2-8*

At this point, it is necessary to stand back and reflect on the "gap" Section 5 has created for the waiting period. During the waiting period, intense oral selling efforts are permitted, and there is no requirement at this stage that the targets of these efforts be provided with a preliminary prospectus. The Commission's efforts in tailoring the circulation of the preliminary prospectus are designed, with the exception discussed below, to assure that those involved in the distribution receive the preliminary prospectus, not that the investors to whom they speak on the phone get the preliminary prospectus. The Commission's good efforts in reviewing the prospectus and commenting on its contents appear to produce a document that reaches those involved in the registered security's distribution. In sum, there is a good deal of dependence throughout the distribution process on the filtration of the registration statement's information through broker-dealers to their clients.

Those who hold less than undying obeisance to the belief in the filtration process must wonder if the '33 Act renders a disservice to its overall mission by excluding oral communications from its definition of a prospectus. An investor whose offer to buy was solicited orally and whose offer can be accepted upon the registration statement's becoming effective may receive or access a final prospectus when the confirmation of the sale is mailed or when the purchased securities are delivered. But absent some other regulatory steps, this prospectus may serve no greater purpose than to document the foolishness of the investor's offer to buy—the commercial equivalent to shutting the barn door after the horse has departed. In response to these concerns, the Commission has once again demonstrated its resourcefulness, not to mention its good sense, by its practice of not accelerating the effective date of a registration statement for an issuer that is not subject to the Exchange Act's reporting requirements unless copies of the preliminary prospectus have been or are being distributed to all persons to whom the underwriters expect to send a confirmation not less than 48 hours prior to the time such confirmation is expected to be mailed. *See* Exchange Act Rule 15c2-8(b). There is an additional condition that copies of the preliminary prospectus be distributed to underwriters and dealers who it is reasonably anticipated will be invited to participate in the distribution of the security to be offered or sold. *See* Securities Act Release No. 4968 (Apr. 24, 1969).

The Commission's position in Securities Act Release No. 4968 is further supported by Exchange Act Rule 15c2-8, under which it is a deceptive act or practice for a broker or dealer participating in a distribution, among other items, to fail to deliver a copy of a preliminary prospectus 48 hours prior to the mailing of a confirmation if the issuer is not previously a reporting act company. Rule 15c2-8 also focuses on the broker's and dealer's obligation to provide a prospectus in response to a customer's written request and to make the prospectus available to its associates who will be soliciting customers and on the managing underwriter's obligation to take steps to assure that all brokers and dealers involved in the distribution have sufficient copies of the prospectus. The Internet, of course, greatly reduces the burdens of satisfying Rule 15c2-8's requirements.

Separate from the customary concerns for circulating a preliminary prospectus to those to whom a confirmation will be sent is the issue of whether a recirculation of the preliminary prospectus is required because the earlier circulated preliminary prospectus was so incomplete or at odds with the information in the more recent prospectus as to be materially misleading. Here, the problem is that absent recirculation, the issuer or its underwriters may incur liability under Section 12(a)(2) to those who acquired the security on the basis of the earlier materially misleading prospectus. *See* Jenkins, Recirculation of the Preliminary Prospectus: Statutory Basis and Analytical Techniques for Resolving Recirculation Issues, 55 Bus. Law. 135 (1999).

PROBLEMS

Recall the earlier background information regarding Omega's pending IPO that was discussed at the end of the materials focused on the pre-filing period. On May 1st, after several weeks of intense work by Omega, its lawyers and the staff from Hedley, Hadley, Omega files a registration statement with the SEC covering 4 million of its common shares. Each of the following activities occurs during the waiting period. For each of the following problems, resolve whether Section 5 of the Securities Act has been violated (assuming Omega is an emerging growth company).

4-12.   Ethan, a broker with H.T. Gaines, one of the underwriters for the Omega offering, telephones Gail and strongly recommends that she purchase some of the upcoming Omega offering. Gail says she is mildly interested, and Ethan sends her a preliminary prospectus to review.

4-13. Because Ethan has not heard from Gail for several days and his phone messages are not being returned, Ethan mails Gail a form that asks her to indicate how many shares of the offering she would like to purchase. Ethan attaches his business card to the form, with the note "This is still a good buy."

[handwritten: written offer, but already sent prelim prospectus]
[handwritten: → broker's card but needs legend → 5.5 violation]

4-14. Gail responds to Ethan's communication by sending him a check in the amount of $1,500, penning the note "Put me down for 100 shares. Thanks for your thoughtfulness. Gail."

[handwritten: broker card confirm sale during waiting period → need to send back check]

4-15. Florence is a new broker with Hedley, Hadley and has yet to develop a solid clientele. As a step toward developing some rapport with prospective clients, she e-mails a preliminary prospectus to the entire membership of her health club, a total of 438 addressees. A few days later, she follows up with a phone call to each person to whom she earlier mailed the prospectus.

[handwritten: Abel / OK]

4-16. Hedley, Hadley publishes an <u>advertisement</u> in all of the leading financial newspapers announcing that it <u>is the lead underwriter</u> for a public offering of 4 million Omega common shares. <u>The advertisement</u> also identifies the other underwriters and states that a prospectus can be acquired from any of the underwriters listed in the advertisement.

[handwritten: Tombstone ad exception]

4-17. Various underwriters associated with the offering prepare and distribute their own sales brochures to brokers and potential customers. These are not shared with other underwriters in the offering and are <u>not</u> filed with the SEC. Also, consider how your approach to this question is changed if Omega is not an emerging growth company.

[handwritten: FWP—needs legend / any special exception? → if EGC ok UBS Act / → only need to be filed if broad dissemination / need prospectus delivery]

4-18. Omega's registration statement lists its web site address and states "Our SEC filings are also available to the public from our web site." Among the items on its web site is a hyperlink to a trade publication touting Omega's most recent product. *See* Baltimore Gas & Electric Co., SEC No-Action Letter (Jan. 6, 1997).

4-19. Alice, Omega's vice president of finance, undergoes a one-hour interview with some of the underwriters for the forthcoming offering. Also in attendance are several potential investors who will be approached by the underwriters. The interview is digitally recorded and placed on Hedley, Hadley's web site, where it is generally available to the public.

[handwritten: FWP—need legends accompanied by PP, filed]

4-20. In the wake of news reports critical of Omega's recent performance, Alice, Omega's vice president of finance, sent an e-mail to pep up the company's 334 employees. The memo spoke optimistically about Omega's future. Somehow a copy of the e-mail message was posted on a popular online chat room.

[handwritten: email to employees / FWP? not an offer or solicitation to buy]
[handwritten: chat room → try to take it down / "market report" — didn't supply it, maybe file to be safe]

3. The Post-Effective Period

Recall that in most cases the registration statement becomes effective after the Commission's staff has agreed to accelerate its effectiveness, usually just after the last amendment has been filed. In any case, once the registration statement is effective, Section 5(a)(1) no longer prohibits closing sales of the registered security, and under Section 5(a)(2), the security can be delivered to its purchaser. As a pure statutory matter, whenever such a security is delivered, Section 5(b)(2) requires that it be "accompanied or preceded by a prospectus that meets the requirements of subsection (a) of section 10." This means a final prospectus. Comparing the final prospectus with the preliminary prospectus discussed in the preceding section, we find that the final prospectus includes all the information normally contained in a preliminary prospectus plus information on the offering price, underwriter compensation, amount of the proceeds, and other information that is dependent on the offering price, such as the terms of any conversion feature of the security. This reflects the enacting Congress' belief that the purchasing investor should receive a final prospectus. The problem with this view is that the final prospectus comes after the investor is committed.

In June 2005, the SEC liberated much of the capital formation process from the necessity of distribution participants *physically delivering* a final prospectus to investors. The rules now embrace the view that "access equals delivery." To be sure, a final prospectus still emerges from the registration process; however, its physical delivery is not the medium for widely circulating information among investors. The most notable change is Rule 172(a) exempting from Section 5(b)(1) written confirmations (as well as notices of allocations that will be made from a registered offering). Absent this exemption, a written confirmation or allocation notice would have to be accompanied or preceded by a final prospectus. Now brokers can confirm a sale or inform an investor of the exact number of shares they will be allocated in a distributed security without having to provide the investor with a final prospectus. At the same time, despite the sweeping nature of the recent reforms, Exchange Act Rule 15c2-8(b) still requires that underwriters deliver a preliminary prospectus to buyers at least 48 hours before sending confirmation of sale.

The next significant change is Rule 172(b)'s relaxation of the prospectus delivery requirements when the registered securities are to be transferred. Recall that after a registered offering has become effective that Section 5(a) permits sales of registered securities to be consummated and that Section 5(b)(2) provides that registered securities cannot be carried in interstate commerce unless accompanied or preceded by a final prospectus. One can ponder the benefits of an investor receiving a prospectus at this point: "A prospectus that comes with the security does not tell the investor whether or not he or she should buy; it tells the investor whether he has acquired a security or a lawsuit." L. Loss & J. Seligman, I Securities Regulation 430 (4th ed. 2007). Rule 172(b) provides that Section 5(b)(2)'s obligation to forward a final prospectus when delivering securities is satisfied if the issuer has filed with the Commission a prospectus meeting the requirements of Section 10(a)—provided also that the registration statement is not then subject to an administrative enforcement action.

As we have seen before, Rule 433 broadly authorizes distribution participants to use a free writing prospectus during both the waiting period and post-
effective period. Distribution participants who circulate supplementary written
materials in the post-effective period can assure that those materials are a permissible "free-writing prospectus" if Rule 433's legend and filing requirements,
earlier discussed, are satisfied. Alternatively, Section 2(a)10(a) permits free writing in the post-effective period conditioned only upon the free writing material
being accompanied or preceded by a final prospectus.

NOTES AND QUESTIONS

1.   Duration of Section 5's Requirements.   By virtue of Section 4(a)(1), the
burdens of Section 5 extend only to issuers, underwriters, and dealers. Anyone
not falling within any of these three classes is free of the many demands of
Section 5, such as the provision of a prospectus. How long therefore are the
issuer, its underwriters, and dealers subject to the prospectus delivery requirements of Section 5(b)? The answer to this question as to the issuer is relatively
easy to state, but for the others, the answer takes a bit more development.
   Issuers continue to be subject to the restrictions of Section 5 (e.g., free writing)
as long as they are offering the security to the public. Under Section 4(a)(3)(C),
underwriters and dealers are subject to the prospectus requirements as long as
their allotment or subscription in the distribution is unsold. However, by virtue
of Rules 172 and 174 the scope of this obligation is much reduced. As we have
seen, written confirmations and notices of allocations are excluded by Rule
172(a) from the type of written document that is a prospectus under Section
5(b)(1). And, under Rule 172(c)(4), dealers are not required to deliver a prospectus in connection with their transporting the distributed security. However,
pursuant to Rule 173, issuers, underwriters, and dealers who are not otherwise
exempt by Section 4(a)(3) or Rule 174, discussed below, must provide a final
prospectus not later than two business days following completion of the sale;
alternatively, notice can be given that the sale was made pursuant to a registration statement. This written notice is itself exempt from being deemed a prospectus that must comply with Section 5(b)(1). Interestingly, failure to comply
with Rule 173 does not prevent the dealer or underwriter from invoking the
benefits of Rule 172 when confirming a sale or transporting the security.
   We might ponder about the continuing import, if any, of one of the most
convoluted provisions of the Securities Act, Section 4(a)(3), the so-called dealer
exemption. What separates a dealer from a broker is that the former solicits the
investor's interest in a security. Absent a solicitation, the "broker's transaction"
exemption of Section 4(a)(4) applies, provided the broker is not acting as an
underwriter. The import of Section 4(a)(3) is that at one time even dealers
not participating in the distribution were required to deliver a prospectus. In
crafting Section 4(a)(3), it was clearly Congress' intent to conscript dealers,
even though not participants in the underwriting syndicate, into the social mission of widely distributing the final prospectus. Thus, a broker who solicited an
investor to purchase in the secondary market a security of a company whose
registration statement had just recently become effective was required to deliver
in connection with that sale a final prospectus. This result occurred, first,

because dealers are not exempt under Section 4(a)(1), and second, because Section 4(a)(3) provides that "section 5 shall not apply to . . . transactions by a dealer . . . except. . . ." The important exception for a dealer not participating in a registered offering appears in paragraph (B), which requires such a nonparticipating dealer to deliver a prospectus during the 40 days after the later of the registration statement becoming effective or the security being offered to the public. *See P. Stolz Family Partnership L.P. v. Baum*, 355 F.3d 92 (2d Cir. 2004). This requirement is extended to 90 days for IPOs. As will be seen, today Rules 153, 172, and 174 substantially lift the requirement for a dealer to make available a prospectus.

Rule 153 is similar to Rule 172(b) in that it excuses the need for a dealer to deliver a prospectus in connection with the delivery of securities sold through an exchange. Of broader application is Rule 174, which provides further relief for dealers. Under Rule 174, a dealer that is not an underwriter is completely relieved of the need to make available a prospectus within the 40- or 90-day period specified in Section 4(a)(3) if the issuer, prior to filing its registration statement, was a reporting company under the '34 Act. Even if the issuer is not a reporting company, Rule 174(d) dispenses with the prospectus provision requirement by dealers beginning 25 days after the offering date if the security is either listed on a national exchange or authorized for inclusion in an interdealer quotation system of a registered SRO. Even if the dealer does not enjoy an exemption in Rule 174 (e.g., the company is neither a reporting company nor listed on an exchange), Rules 172(c)(4) and 174(h) excuse the delivery of a prospectus when transporting the securities provided the issuer's registration statement is not then the focus of an SEC administrative enforcement proceeding. However, a dealer who is not excused by either Section 4(a)(3) or Rule 174 must, under Rule 173, within two days of the sale provide either a final prospectus or notice that the security is covered by a registration statement.

The broker who does not solicit her client's interest in a registered security falls literally within the broker's transaction exemption provided in Section 4(a)(4). In such a case, the broker is merely an agent to her client's objective in buying the registered security. For such a transaction, the exemption afforded in Section 4(a)(4) appears unnecessary to exempt the broker from Section 5(b)(1); that provision's operative language depends on the transmission of a prospectus that under Section 2(a)(10) applies only if the written communication "offers any security for sale or confirms the sale of any security," but is necessary for Section 5(b)(2).

2.   What If the Final Prospectus Is Misleading?   As will be seen in Chapter 9, the Securities Act imposes serious liability on the issuer, underwriters, and specified others if the registration statement contains a material misrepresentation as of the time it becomes effective. Are there other consequences if the prospectus used to satisfy Section 5's delivery requirements is materially misleading? *SEC v. Manor Nursing Centers, Inc.*, 458 F.2d 1082 (2d Cir. 1972), held that Section 5(b)(2) was violated because the prospectus used to deliver the securities was materially misleading. *See also A.J. White & Co. v. SEC*, 556 F.2d 619 (1st Cir. 1977). *Contra SEC v. Southwest Coal & Energy Co.*, 624 F.2d 1315, 1318 (5th Cir. 1980) (criticizing *Manor Nursing* for supplanting remedies directed toward misleading disclosures with remedy designed to compel registration and distribution of materials). Note that, if a court follows *Manor Nursing* in a private suit, the investors get rescission under Section 12(a)(1), in contrast to the lesser sum that is usually available in damages in a misrepresentation-based action. *See Jeffries & Co. v. Arkus-Duntov*, 357 F. Supp. 1206 (S.D.N.Y. 1973). However, in light of the treatment of confirmations and delivery of securities in Rules 172 and 173, is there much opportunity for the *Manor Nursing* issue to arise today?

PROBLEMS

Omega's registration statement covering 2 million common shares with an offering price of $15 became effective on July 1st of this year, shortly after the meeting with all the underwriters' representatives. After its IPO, Omega's shares will trade on Nasdaq. Consider whether any of the following activities violate the federal securities laws. Assume that Omega is an emerging growth company.

4-21. Hedley, Hadley e-mails copies of an article from the Wall Street Journal to many of its customers. The article paints a very positive picture of Omega's performance and discusses the likely effects of its forthcoming public offering, including several bits of information about Omega that are not in the documents filed with the SEC (e.g., a quote from its CFO forecasting a 15 percent jump in earnings for the next fiscal year). The e-mail contains a hyperlink to Hedley, Hadley's web site, where a final prospectus for Omega can be obtained.

4-22. Before the registration statement became effective, Omega's CFO meets with several members of the financial press to discuss how proceeds from the forthcoming public offering would enhance its profitability in the near future. Shortly after the registration statement became effective, several major newspapers provided very glowing analyses of Omega and optimistic views regarding its future.

4-23. Hedley, Hadley e-mails confirmations for sales to all its customers who had made offers to purchase during the waiting period. Each customer had earlier been given a preliminary prospectus and most have consented to the electronic delivery of information via e-mail. The confirmation informs the customer that by accessing Hedley, Hadley's web site the customer can obtain a "term sheet" that sets forth information about the offering's price, amount, and underwriter commissions that was omitted from the preliminary prospectus.

4-24. C.T. Gaines, one of the underwriters in the Omega offering, sold its entire allotment by July 5th. On July 10th, Nida, one of the brokers with C.T. Gaines, recommended that Oscar purchase a block of Omega common stock on Nasdaq. Oscar agrees. Must C.T. Gaines forward a final prospectus to Oscar when it confirms the sale and delivers the shares to Oscar? What result if C.T. Gaines had not sold its entire allotment?

4-25. Tom, a longtime customer of Polly's and a very independent sort, instructs Polly to purchase 300 Omega shares on the market. Polly purchases the shares through the Nasdaq system, even though Hedley, Hadley still has not sold its allotment for the Omega public offering. Hedley, Hadley does not include a prospectus with the confirmation it mails to Tom.

4-26.   Hedley, Hadley learns that not all the brokers with C.T. Gaines have been provided with copies of the term sheet for the Omega offering. It posts a copy of the term sheet on its web site and gives notice of the posting to C.T. Gaines. Has Hedley, Hadley fulfilled its obligations with respect to this member of the syndicate?

F. *Public Offers by Seasoned and Well-Known Seasoned Issuers*

1.   Integrated Disclosure for the Seasoned Company

Because the '33 Act is oriented toward protecting offerees in public distributions of securities, whereas the '34 Act is directed toward protecting secondary market trading, it is not surprising that during the first four decades of its existence the SEC administered the disclosure requirements of the two Acts with strict obeisance to the view that their dissimilar objectives precluded any common disclosure requirements. The format and content of disclosure the SEC prescribed developed separately for each act, so that the disclosure of an event varied depending on whether it appeared in a '33 or a '34 Act filing. That is, investors considering the purchase of an issuer's securities would find that for a given item—for example, management compensation—quite different information was provided in the issuer's '33 Act registration statement than in its filing made under the '34 Act, and the information appeared in a different format.

Commentators have long called not only for melding disclosure policies for the two acts, but more important, for bringing the two reporting mechanisms into a single integrated disclosure system.[4] The evolution of the current integrated disclosure system began modestly in 1967, gained speed in the 1970s with the increasing acceptance of the efficient market hypothesis's description of the functioning of American securities markets, had its first iteration beginning the early 1980s, and reached its current state in 2005. The overall objective of the SEC's integrated disclosure program is to eliminate overlapping and unnecessary disclosure and dissemination requirements without compromising

---

4.   The slowness of integrating the disclosure mechanisms for the two acts may be something of a historical accident.

The combined disclosure requirement of these statutes would have been quite different if the 1933 and 1934 Acts . . . had been enacted in opposite order, or had been enacted as a single, integrated statute—that is, if the starting point had been a statutory scheme of continuous disclosures covering issuers of actively traded securities and the question of special disclosures in connection with public offerings had been faced in this setting.

Cohen, "Truth in Securities" Revisited, 79 Harv. L. Rev. 1340, 1341-1342 (1968).

the information needs of investors so that the regulatory burdens on issuers are reduced.

First Step: "The Basic Information Package."   An important first step in the design of an integrated disclosure system was the SEC's development of a "basic information package" that includes the type of company-specific information useful to investors assessing the financial performance, position, and prospects of the firm. Briefly, this included, first, audited financial statements consisting of balance sheets for the end of the two most recent fiscal years as well as an income statement and statement of changes in financial position for each of the three most recent fiscal years; second, selected financial information for the last five years highlighting trends in such important items as sales, income/loss, total assets, long-term obligations, and dividends paid per common share; third, management's discussion and analysis of the issuer's financial condition and operations, with emphasis on any apparent trends in its business; and, finally, information about the trading market for the issuer's stock.

The basic information package appears in: (1) the issuer's annual report to its stockholders, which accompanies each proxy statement; (2) its Form 10-K; and (3) all registration statements under the '33 Act. Form 10-K includes information beyond that appearing in the basic information package, with a detailed description of the issuer's business, properties, and legal proceedings as well as certain information about officers and directors.

Information pertinent to assessing a specific transaction, as distinguished from registrant-oriented information, is disclosed in connection with that transaction. An example of transaction-specific information in connection with a public offering of securities is information about the type and features of the security being sold, the planned use of the proceeds from the offering, and the compensation and understandings with the securities underwriter.

Once the SEC sorted out the information needs of investors in their differing contexts, and with the religious salve of the efficient market hypothesis to soothe any unease related to its newfound boldness, the SEC moved to embrace the two distinctive features of today's integrated disclosure system. First, the SEC adopted uniform disclosure requirements for documents filed under the '33 and '34 Acts. The requirements for all financial items appear in Regulation S-X and the requirements for all non-financial items appear in Regulation S-K.

The second feature involves the coordination of disclosure required by the '33 and '34 Acts so that large publicly traded companies can satisfy the '33 Act registration statement requirements for company-specific information by incorporating by reference such information from their current '34 Act filings.

Classes of Issuers.   The content of a registration statement is prescribed by the specific form that the issuer is eligible to use. Today there are two principal forms for registering securities under the '33 Act for domestic issuers: Form S-1 and Form S-3. The eligibility requirements for Form S-3 are set forth in the form itself. The differences between Forms S-1 and S-3 reflect the Commission's determination as to (1) when this required information must be presented in full in the prospectus delivered to investors, and (2) when certain information may be incorporated into the registration statement from documents in the Exchange Act continuous reporting system without delivery to investors. For such issuers, the registrant-oriented portion of their registration statement, as opposed to the transaction-specific information, is the same as that which they have included in annual reports to the Commission on Form 10-K and in annual reports to security holders, as well as in quarterly and current reports on Forms 10-Q and 8-K, respectively. Thus, they can satisfy their '33 Act disclosure requirements for this type of information by the fiat of incorporating into their registration statement the relevant portions of their '34 Act filings. Information about the offering (e.g., amount and type of security as well as the manner of distribution), however, will not have been reported in any other disclosure document or otherwise publicly disseminated, and thus is required to be presented in the registration statement. Generally, the Form S-3 prospectus will present the same transaction-specific information as presented in a Form S-1 prospectus, but information regarding the Form S-3 registrant itself is incorporated by reference from Exchange Act reports. Also, any prospectus that may be required does not present any information incorporated by reference, unless there has been a material change in the registrant's affairs that has not been reported in an Exchange Act filing or the Exchange Act reports.

A reporting issuer that cannot meet the specific transaction eligibility requirements of Form S-3, and is thereby relegated to the residual Form S-1, nevertheless can opt for integrated disclosure on Form S-1, provided it has filed at least one annual report, is otherwise current with the '34 Act filings, and makes the incorporated information readily available on a web site maintained by or for the issuer.

In 2005 the SEC created a super-subset of issuers eligible to use Form S-3, called the "well-known seasoned issuer" (WKSI). Falling into this group are any issuers with a common stock market capitalization (excluding shares held by affiliates) of $700 million or, in the case of a debt or non-convertible preferred stock offering, issuers that in the prior three years have offered $1 billion in non-convertible securities other than common stock. You can also be a WKSI eligible to use Form S-3 for a common stock offering if you meet the $1 billion non-convertible securities test and have common stock float of $75 million. For such issuers, the SEC provides the most flexible registration procedures, which it refers to as an "automatic shelf registration process." The SEC reports that issuers with a market capitalization of at least $700 million that carried out public offerings between 1997 and 2004 had 52 percent of their shares held by institutions and accounted for 70 percent of all 1997-2004 equity offerings (although they represent only 30 percent of listed companies). Issuers meeting the debt portion of the definition, although representing only 17 percent of the issuers that registered public debt offerings, account for 65 percent of the dollar amount of all debt and preferred stock offerings, and none of their debt was rated less than investment grade.

Via the new "automatic shelf registration process," discussed later in this chapter, the issuer's "base" registration statement is composed of information incorporated from the issuer's Exchange Act filings. The transaction-specific information (e.g., offering price, detailed description of the securities, identity of the underwriters or selling security holders, and the plan of distribution) is provided *after* the securities are sold. This is analogous to the treatment of price-related information under current Rule 430A, discussed earlier, which permits such information to be supplied via a prospectus supplement. The SEC rules permit eligible WKSIs to register unspecified amounts of different securities on Form S-3 that will become automatically effective. By allowing the registration statement to become effective on its base, with the missing price-related information and even type of security registered being provided after the transaction, issuers are better able to take advantage of "market windows." Note also that the registration statement for WKSIs is automatically effective when filed, independent of SEC staff review. Automatic shelf registration statements have a three-year life; at the end of that period, issuers can re-submit their current statement and amend it as they deem appropriate. The automatic shelf registration process is available for primary (excluding mergers and exchange transactions) as well as secondary offerings of securities of WKSIs.

As you reflect on the material in this chapter, observe that the applicability of the SEC's forms and regulatory requirements frequently depends on which of four distinct classes of issuers applies to the issuer:[5]

1. Well-known seasoned issuers (WKSIs);
2. Seasoned issuers (those that are not WKSIs but can avail themselves of Form S-3, namely those with 12 months of timely Exchange Act reports);
3. Unseasoned issuers (reporting issuers that fail to meet the eligibility requirements of Form S-3); and
4. Non-reporting issuers (issuers that are not required to file Exchange Act reports).

The reforms for the offering process also refer to "ineligible issuers," which include blank check companies (those with no specifically identified business), shell companies, penny stock issuers (issuers with non-listed securities that trade under $5), and certain bad actors (those not current in filing their '34 Act reports, or the subjects of SEC enforcement proceedings in the prior three years). Most of the reforms discussed below do not extend to ineligible issuers.

NOTES AND QUESTIONS

1. Form S-3 Eligibility Requirements. The integrated disclosure format embodied in Form S-3 was initially justified on the insights drawn from the efficient market hypothesis. Now, three decades and many iterations of Form S-3 later, we might pause and consider whether the efficient market hypothesis underlies much of Form S-3. To investigate this, consider that Form S-3 is conditioned on meeting both the issuer eligibility requirements set forth in Item I.A of the form's General Instructions and one of the listed transaction requirements in I.B. Which of the requirements found in I.A.1 to 5 appear driven by

---

5. As a technical matter, an issuer could be an emerging growth company, as defined in Section 2(a)(19), and also fall within any of the latter three above classes of issuers. This is because when Congress, in 2012, created the concept of the emerging growth company it did so without linking the JOBS Act's "on ramp" initiatives to any of the terminology of above issuer categories that had already been established by the SEC with its offering reforms in 2005.

paternalism and which appear to be informed by the efficient market hypothesis? Of special note is the contrast between the transaction requirements in I.B.1 and I.B.6. In 2007, the SEC greatly liberalized the availability of Form S-3 by adding I.B.6 so that even if the issuer has a common stock float below $75 million (and thus cannot avail itself of the transaction requirement set forth in I.B.1), it nonetheless can use Form S-3 provided: (a) the offering is for cash; (b) the offering amount during any 12-month period does not exceed one-third of the market value of the common held by non-affiliates (the float); and (c) the issuer has one class of common listed on a national exchange. Does the relaxation of eligibility embodied in I.B.6 appear to be guided by the efficient market hypothesis? Do you believe the eligibility requirement in I.B.1 is guided by the efficient market hypothesis? Are the transaction requirements in I.B.2, for secondary offerings by the issuer's control persons, or I.B.5, covering offerings of investment-grade asset-backed securities, guided by the efficient market hypothesis?

2. *Incongruence of '33 Act and '34 Act Liability Standards.* The integration concept assumes, plausibly enough, that the *content* of issuer disclosure that investors need in order to make an informed decision is the same regardless of whether the transaction occurs in the primary or the secondary marketplace. It does not necessarily follow, however, that one can say the same about the *quality* of issuer disclosure. Presumably, based on the belief that the incentive for the issuer to misrepresent its financial condition and prospects is greatest when it will enjoy a direct pecuniary benefit in terms of a higher offering price, the '33 Act imposes strict liability on issuers in shareholder suits involving misrepresentations in a registration statement and requires certain others associated with the distribution (e.g., underwriters) to exercise due diligence to assure the accuracy of the registration statement to avoid sharing that liability. Registration statements are prepared with a level of care reflecting this exposure.

In contrast, significant liability under the continuous disclosure scheme of the '34 Act follows for all practical purposes only from intentional or reckless conduct, and 10-Ks and annual reports no doubt reflect some lesser degree of diligence in their preparation. As a result, one cannot assume that "off the rack" use of '34 Act disclosure forms necessarily results in the same quality of disclosure as that in a '33 Act setting. Moreover, underwriters who are selected through competitive bidding near the offering date have little time to review adequately the issuer's SEC filings. *See, e.g., Shaw v. Digital Equipment Corp.,* 82 F.3d 1194, 1204, 1208-1209 (1st Cir. 1996).

3. *Integrated Disclosure for the S-1 Registrant.* Integrated disclosure is not limited to issuers eligible for Form S-3. Form S-1 permits reporting companies that have filed at least one annual report to incorporate a good deal of information required for registration from reports the issuer has filed with the SEC. *See* Part VII of Form S-1.

4. *Ratings—Can't Live Without Them, Can You Live With Them?* Credit ratings are an important source of information to investors in debt instruments such as bonds and asset-backed securities. There are multiple reasons ratings are important. State and federal laws sometimes link the type of security in

which a financial institution may invest to the security holding a certain rating. *See, e.g.,* Investment Company Rule 2a-7 defining mutual funds. Investors, particularly when considering complex financial products such as asset-backed securities, rely on ratings as a simplifying heuristic to judge the security. Following the financial crisis, the SEC has reduced, but not eliminated, the link between ratings and certain regulatory dispensations. For example, earlier the eligibility criteria for Form S-3 included certain types of securities enjoying an "investment grade" rating; that was replaced by current provision I.B.2 that focuses on the amount of debt the issuer has outstanding. Nonetheless, the "investment grade" criteria still persists in various SEC regulations, such as Form S-3's eligibility criteria for registering asset-backed securities. *See* Form S-3, I.B.5. For a critique of credit rating agencies, *see* Partnoy, The Siskel and Ebert of Financial Markets? Two Thumbs Down for the Credit Rating Agencies, 77 Wash. U. L.Q. 619, 711 (1999) ("Credit rating agencies have not survived for six decades because they produce credible and accurate information. . . . Instead, the credit rating agencies have thrived, profited, and become exceedingly powerful because they have begun selling licenses, i.e., the right to be in compliance with regulation."). The regulation of credit rating agencies (Moody's, Standard & Poor's, and Fitch dominate the industry) is discussed later in Chapter 18.

2.   Gun-Jumping Concerns for the Seasoned Issuer

As seen earlier in our discussion of Section 5's impact on the IPO, the regulatory thrust, at least at the time of enactment, was to identify the registration statement as the dominant source of information about the offering and to assure broad delivery of information through various prospectus delivery requirements. Notwithstanding the difficulties these objectives visit upon the non-reporting company, the problems are even greater when it is a reporting company that is in registration. Public companies by definition have stockholders who have ongoing needs for current information about the issuer. Hence, public corporations not only have formal obligations, imposed by the exchanges where their shares are listed, to make timely disclosures of newsworthy information, but they also have more broad-based obligations to inform their stockholders, customers, and other constituencies of newsworthy developments affecting the company. Moreover, any delay in the release of material information increases the potential for abusive practices, such as insider trading. Finally, the ubiquity of the Internet has greatly enriched the information environment for all companies so that unbending obeisance to classical concerns for conditioning the market is no longer a workable approach. In response to this concern, the SEC has adopted a series of safe harbors to better balance the regulatory objectives of Section 5 with the ongoing information needs of investors.

a.   *Issuer Safe Harbors*

Well-Known Seasoned Issuers.   As can be expected, the greatest freedom from the prohibitions against gun-jumping is provided in the WKSI: Rule 163 permits such issuers to engage in unrestricted oral and written offers *before* a registration statement is filed. However, the exclusion is subject to several important conditions. First, it applies only to communications "by or on behalf of" the issuer; thus it does not shield communications by other distribution participants such as underwriters. Second, to invoke Rule 163, if an offer prior to the issuer's filing a registration statement is made in writing, that written communication must be filed "promptly" with the Commission when the registration statement is ultimately filed and must bear the legend required by subsection (b)(1) of Rule 163. If the issuer has filed a registration statement, the written offer is treated as a "free writing prospectus," discussed below, and must be filed with the Commission. Rules 163(b)(1)(iii) and (b)(2)(iii) excuse "immaterial or unintentional" failure to include the specified legend or the failure to file the communication with the SEC, respectively. The excuse is conditioned on there being a "good faith and reasonable effort . . . to comply."

Reporting Issuers: Factual Business Information and Forward-Looking Statements.   Rule 168 provides that announcements by *reporting issuers* that have engaged in the regular release of "factual business information or forward-looking information" will not be treated as offers to sell a security. The Rule defines *factual business information* as including factual information about the issuer, its business, or financial developments, as well as product advertisements. *Forward information* refers to such items as forecasts or discussions of future business plans. Rule 168 is also conditioned on the information being of the type the issuer has previously released in the ordinary course of its business, and that the manner of its dissemination should correspond to past releases of that type of information. The protection for forward-looking information concerns such items as earnings forecasts, statements of management's plans or objectives, and statements about future economic performance. Rule 168 applies only to statements issued by or on behalf of the issuer; it does not protect communications issued by the issuer's underwriters or other participants in the distribution. Expressly excluded from the safe harbor is any communication of information about the registered offering itself, although some information about the offering is permitted under Rules 134 and 135, discussed earlier.

b. Free Writing Prospectus

A free writing prospectus can be used by well-known seasoned issuers and their distribution participants at any time; other issuers and their distribution participants can use a free writing prospectus after a registration statement has been filed. The conditions for being able to use a free writing prospectus depend on the nature of the issuer.

For seasoned issuers, Rule 433 permits a free writing prospectus to be used after the filing of a registration statement (and as discussed above, well-known seasoned issuers pursuant to Rule 163 can engage in free writing even before filing a registration statement) and such free writing is not conditioned on providing a prospectus in advance or simultaneous with the free writing prospectus. Instead, the user of a free writing prospectus must notify the recipient through a required legend of the filing of a registration statement and the uniform resource locator (URL) for the SEC web site where the recipient can access or hyperlink the prospectus. And, after the registration statement has become effective, Section 2(a)(10) permits free writing with the condition only that the material be accompanied or preceded by a final prospectus.

The same guidelines of Rules 433(d)(8) and (f) apply to seasoned issuers as apply to unseasoned issuers with respect to road shows and issues that arise when the issuer's representatives speak to the press.

c. *Research Reports*

On reflection, it should be apparent that the breadth of Section 5 threatens a destructive impact on the creation and dissemination of financial/investment information in securities markets. When the issuer already has outstanding publicly traded securities, too tight a lid on the publication of information about the issuer or its securities impedes the mechanisms that contribute to the efficient pricing of its outstanding securities in their public markets and also operates to the disadvantage of purchasers, sellers, and holders of those securities. Investment professionals, such as those that publish research reports and investment newsletters, and broker-dealers who regularly circulate investment recommendations among their clientele, should be wary of Section 5 when the object of their recommendation or analysis is a company in registration. The Commission in its Rules 137, 138, and 139 alleviates some of the concern in this area.

As seen earlier, the JOBS Act lightens regulation for "emerging growth companies" when conducting an IPO; Exchange Act Section 15D(c) provides that the SEC and FINRA rules may not restrict analyst communications in connection with an IPO by an emerging growth company. And, Section 2(a)(3) provides that research reports regarding the equity security of an emerging growth company published or distributed by brokers are not an offer to sell per either Section 2(a)(10) or Section 5(c). The general fraud provisions, of course, continue to apply to such communications.

The Commission's rules sometimes use the expression "participant in a distribution" to identify whether such a person can make use of the safe harbor provided by the rule. Who exactly is or is not a "participant in a distribution" is not separately defined in any of the Commission's rules. It would seem quite clear that the issuer, its underwriters, and members of the selling group are all "participants in the distribution." On the other hand, brokers who receive their compensation from their customers and not from the underwriter are not participating in the distribution. Should an underwriter that has sold its allotment continue to be viewed as a "participant in a distribution"?

Rule 137. Rule 137 clarifies the status of persons not participating in a distribution. It permits nonparticipating brokers and dealers to publish or distribute, in the regular course of their business, information, opinions, and recommendations regarding securities of an issuer in registration. The exemption provided by Rule 137 is lost if the broker or dealer receives for the particular research report compensation or has a special arrangement with the issuer, a selling security holder, or any participant in the distribution. The Rule applies to all issuers and is not, as are the other rules dealing with research reports, applicable only to reporting companies.

Rule 138. This Rule applies to reporting issuers that are current in their periodic Exchange Act filings, as well as to certain large foreign issuers that are not reporting companies. A broker or dealer, whether or not a participant in such a registrant's distribution of non-convertible preferred stock or non-convertible debt security, may publish opinions or recommendations for that registrant's common stock; correlatively, the broker-dealer, whether or not a participant in the distribution of the registrant's common stock, can publish opinions or recommendations for that registrant's non-convertible preferred stock or non-convertible debt security. Rule 138 is based on the Commission's recognition that the market for senior securities is largely institutional and that there is little danger of creating investor interest in a senior non-convertible security by promoting its issuer's common stock, and vice versa. This exemption is nonetheless conditioned on the broker or dealer having previously published or distributed in the regular course of its business research reports on similar types of securities, although these reports need not have included the securities of the particular issuer.

Rule 139. Rule 139 deals with two types of research reports: focused reports and industry reports. It permits a broker or dealer, whether or not participating in the issuer's distribution, to publish opinions and recommendations focused solely on the issuer, provided the issuer meets the eligibility requirements of Form S-3 or F-3. For this group of issuers, there is the broad requirement that the broker or dealer must, at the time of reliance upon Rule 139, have previously distributed or published a report in the regular course of its business (as well that such publication does not represent the initiation or re-initiation after discontinuance of a report about the issuer). This Rule also applies to certain large non-reporting foreign issuers.

Rule 139 also extends to "industry reports" by brokers and dealers participating in the distribution by a reporting company. This exemption is conditioned on the report's containing similar information with respect to a substantial number of other issuers in the issuer's industry or including a comprehensive list of securities currently recommended by the broker or dealer. Also, the issuer is given no greater prominence in the publication of the industry report's analysis than other issuers, and the report must have been issued in the regular course of the broker's or dealer's business.

The importance of Rule 139's technical demands was illustrated when, before Chrysler Corporation's registration statement became effective, its lead underwriter for a $1 billion offering circulated a research report to its clients about the deal's structure. Fearing that Bear Stearns had overstepped Rule 139, several of its co-underwriters withdrew from the syndicate, so Chrysler withdrew the public offering and sold only $600 million of the securities privately to financial institutions. Siconolfi, Bear Stearns Muffs Chrysler Financial $1 Billion Offering, Wall St. J., Feb. 4, 1992, at C-13.

The last two sentences of Section 2(a)(3) were added in 2012 by the JOBS Act. Certainly it was the intent of Congress that offerings by emerging growth companies would not be subject to the so-called quiet period of FINRA that bars the managing underwriter from issuing an investment report about the underwritten offering until 40 days after the offering. *See* FINRA Manual NASD Rule 2711(f). And, in light of the breadth of the language in Section 2(a)(3), we can surmise that the restrictions in Rules 137, 138, and 139 do not apply to equity offerings by emerging growth companies.

PROBLEMS

For the problems that follow, assume that Omega is a reporting company eligible to use Form S-3 for its offering and, unless otherwise stated, is neither an emerging growth company nor a well-known seasoned issuer. The registration statement was filed on May 1st and became effective July 1st.

4-27. Reprise of Problem 4-6. On April 15, just a couple of weeks before Omega was planning to file a registration statement for an offering of common shares, the public relations staff prepared a brochure highlighting the company's rapid development and innovative products for distribution to the financial media. Copies would also be distributed to lawyers, accountants, and investment advisers, and to other localities where Omega's name is likely to be recognized. The brochure indicates that Omega intends to make a public offering in the near future and includes estimates of its future production capacity as a result of the forthcoming offer. The brochure does not include any statement disavowing an offer of a security. Is Omega in violation of Section 5 of the Security Act?

4-28. What result in Problem 4-27 if Omega is a well-known seasoned issuer?

4-29. What result in Problem 4-27 if Omega is a well-known seasoned issuer and the brochure was prepared independently by Langman, Hillvort, a regional brokerage firm that has agreed to participate in the Omega offering and on May 2 circulated the brochure to its institutional clients?

4-30. What result in Problem 4-29 if Omega is a reporting company but not eligible to use Form S-3?

4-31. On May 1, immediately after filing its registration statement, Omega placed on its web site, in the section labeled "Historical Developments," a glowing report of Omega that was prepared by Wickersham & Dibble, a brokerage firm that is not participating in the offering of Omega's common shares. Does this violate Section 5? Does your analysis change if Omega qualifies as an emerging growth company?

4-32. Omega's key executives met with journalists and other members of the media on July 1, just minutes before the registration statement was to become effective. They talked up the company and indicated their satisfaction with how well the offering was going. Stories to that effect appear in a number of newspapers and on some financial web sites. Omega provides hyperlinks to some of those stories on its own web site. Advise Omega on the issues these actions raise.

4-33. Hedley, Hadley made plans to send to each of several institutional clients an e-mail on July 2 confirming its purchase of Omega shares. What requirements must it satisfy with respect to delivering a prospectus to these clients?

G.   *Shelf Registration Under Rule 415*

1.   The Regulatory Concerns and the "Traditional" Shelf Registration

The typical registered offering covers all the shares the registrant intends to make available for sale when the registration statement becomes effective. Consider that the issuer of debt securities, being aware that interest rates are volatile, will definitely find it is to its advantage to register its bonds and then wait for a beneficial dip in interest rates before offering them for sale. Through such wise timing, the issuer reduces its cost of capital. Similarly, an issuer may wish to have a reservoir of registered common stock so that it can quickly accomplish a series of acquisitions through the issuance of those shares. A slightly different situation is posed in those cases where, even though a security is being presently offered for sale, it is not reasonable to believe the security will be sold at this time. Such would be the case when, for example, the terms of a new issue of preferred stock sold for $50 per share permits its holder at any time to convert one share of preferred stock into one share of common stock; under the fifth sentence of Section 2(a)(3), this constitutes both an offer to sell the preferred stock and an offer to sell the common stock. This is so even if the common stock's present market value is well below that of the preferred shares that must be given up when those shares are converted, and therefore it is not realistic to believe that a sale of the common stock will presently occur because conversion in this situation would entail the holder exchanging a valuable security for a less valuable one. In any event, there are other situations that exist in which an issuer will find it desirable to register securities that either it does not presently intend to offer for sale or that it is presently offering for sale, but there is reason to believe that a sale is not likely to occur. Registration of such securities to be offered on a delayed or continuous basis is commonly referred to as a *shelf registration.*

The necessity for some sort of shelf registration authorization can be traced to the Commission's heavy regulatory hand in the formative years of the '33 Act. The last sentence of Section 6(a) of the Securities Act provides that "[a] registration statement shall be deemed effective only as to the securities specified therein as proposed to be offered." Nothing in the legislative history of the Securities Act reveals what Congress intended this sentence to mean. Hodes, Shelf Registration: The Dilemma of the Securities and Exchange Commission, 49 Va. L. Rev. 1106, 1108-1111 (1963). The Commission filled this void in Shawnee Chiles Syndicate, 10 S.E.C. 109 (1941), reasoning, "The policy behind the last sentence of section 6(a) is to assure investors that the registration statements and prospectuses on which they rely, so far as is reasonably possible, provide current information." Id. at 113. The SEC further reasoned it was misleading to register more securities than the registrant presently intended to offer. Thus, the Commission's initial position was that only securities intended to be sold immediately could be registered. *See also* United Combustion Corp., 3 S.E.C. 1062 (1938).

The SEC soon began to bend with the winds of commercial necessity, not to mention various legislative efforts to amend Section 6(a), so that over the years there evolved a number of situations in which the Commission as a matter of practice permitted registrations for the shelf. So-called traditional shelf offerings are now expressly authorized in paragraphs (a)(1)(i) through (a)(1)(ix) of Rule 415. The Commission's earlier concern that shelf registrations disserved investors by providing them only with a stale prospectus is met by the shelf registrant's undertaking to file post-effective amendments to the registration statement for the purpose of preserving the currency of the disclosures in its registration statements and prospectus. This undertaking, which is pursuant to paragraph (a)(3) of Rule 415, is set forth in Item 512(a) of Regulation S-K. Thus, under Item 512(a)(1)(i), the registrant must file a post-effective amendment covering any prospectus required by Section 10(a)(3). This in effect means that the registrant must update its financial statements annually. Any acts or events arising after the effective date of the registration statement that individually or in the aggregate represent a *fundamental* change in the information set of the registration statement are required by Item 512(a)(1)(ii) to be disclosed in a post-effective amendment to the registration statement. Use of "fundamental," rather than "material," reflects the Commission's general position that post-effective amendments are required for major or substantial changes. Securities Act Release No. 6334 (Aug. 6, 1981). Nevertheless, Item 512(a)(1)(iii) requires a registrant to file a post-effective amendment for any material change with respect to the distribution.

2. Catching Market Windows

When it was adopted in 1981, Rule 415 went a big step beyond the "traditional" forms of shelf registration that were mainly exceptions to the basic norm of immediate commencement to the distribution. In an effort to streamline the capital raising process for larger capitalization companies (i.e., those eligible to use form S-3 or F-3 for a primary offering), such issuers were permitted to register securities for the shelf, with minimal limitations, so long as they expected to sell them within two years. Because these issuers can use incorporation by reference of their '34 Act filings (including filings after the effective date, which is called "forward incorporation"), the registration statement itself was largely limited to information about the securities and plan of distribution. Gradually, shelf registration became the public offering mechanism of choice for blue-chip issuers. This was especially so after the SEC amended its rules to allow the filing of a shelf registration statement without even designating the specific kind of securities to be offered, the "universal shelf" filing discussed below. The SEC also became increasingly permissive on what changes in the distribution-related disclosures could be made by prospectus supplement rather than a post-effective amendment. By the late 1990s, shelf "takedowns" by large issuers were truly high velocity transactions. Assuming that no post-effective amendment was needed, the issuer could decide that the time was ripe for the takedown, obtain bids from underwriters and sell the securities, all within a day or two. The paperwork was easy: Under Rule 424(b)(2), the filing of a prospectus supplement was not required until two days later, to accompany confirmation or delivery of the security. In other words, there was nary a "speed bump" in the entire process.

But are speed bumps necessarily a bad thing? Underwriters were not enthusiastic supporters of this aspect of the shelf registration rule. Among their concerns was the fear that the speed with which the issuer's securities could reach the market would seriously erode the underwriters' ability to fulfill their due diligence review of the issuer's registration statement as required by Section 11. They accordingly cautioned the Commission that Rule 415 would ultimately erode the quality of the shelf registrant's disclosures. The SEC partially addressed this concern by limiting paragraph (a)(1)(x) to issuers qualified to use S-3 (F-3).

There is no evidence that Rule 415 has cut the underwriters out of the game, but it has reduced their share of the pot because paragraph (a)(1)(x) of Rule 415 leads to more competition among underwriters and consequentially lower underwriting fees are incurred than are experienced outside of the shelf registration rule. *See* Report of the Advisory Committee on the Capital Formation and Regulatory Processes, app. A, tbl. 4 (SEC 1996) (median underwriting commission for public offering of common stock on Form S-1 was 7.0 percent; on Form S-2, 6.0 percent; on Form S-3 (nonshelf), 5.0 percent; and on Form S-3 (shelf), 4.6 percent in 1993-1995).

Since Rule 415 was adopted, the dominance of institutional investors in capital markets has increased, there has been further concentration among underwriters and also increased competition among them for underwriting business, and underwriting fees for established public companies have declined. But as seen earlier, many of these developments were occurring well before Rule 415 was even in the proposal stage. The industry's trend toward concentration began in the late 1960s and was accelerated by the abolishment of fixed brokerage fees in 1975. At the heart of all concerns about Rule 415's impact on the industry and markets is the bought deal. The bought deal, however, is not the child of Rule 415, but was first introduced in America by the availability of foreign financing. That is, beginning in the 1970s, American firms were increasingly placing their securities abroad, particularly in Europe, because through such off-shore financing money could be raised more quickly and cheaply than it could by compliance with the '33 Act's registration process. Later, the registration process for large American issuers was shortened significantly through the development of integrated disclosure procedures. Developments such as these introduced the possibility of negotiated underwriting commissions; in a sense, it truly brought the bought deal home. To abolish the regulatory innovations of the integrated disclosure system, including Rule 415(a)(1)(x), may achieve no more than to further drive American corporations to foreign markets for their capital needs. Thus, it may be wiser to view Rule 415 and the entire integrated disclosure system as affording a medium within which American underwriters can compete more effectively with international capital markets, rather than as a pernicious development that has driven some underwriters from the marketplace.

3.   Automatic Shelf Registration for Well-Known Seasoned Issuers

In the 2005 offering reforms, the SEC substantially amended the capital raising process for well-known seasoned issuers by creating "automatic" shelf registration.

Securities Offering Reform, Securities Act Release No. 8591
Securities and Exchange Commission (2005)

In addition to the updating of the shelf registration process described above, we are adopting rules to establish a significantly more flexible version of shelf registration for offerings by well-known seasoned issuers. This version of shelf registration, which we refer to as "automatic shelf registration," involves filings on Form S-3 and Form F-3. . . .

For well-known seasoned issuers, we believe that the modifications we are adopting will facilitate immediate market access and promote efficient capital formation, without at the same time diminishing investor protection. Most significantly, the rules will provide the flexibility to take advantage of market windows, to structure securities on a real-time basis to accommodate issuer needs or investor demand, and to determine or change the plan of distribution of securities as issuers elect in response to changing market conditions. . . .

Under our automatic shelf registration process, eligible well-known seasoned issuers may register unspecified amounts of different specified types of securities on immediately effective Form S-3 or Form F-3 registration statements. Unlike other issuers registering primary offerings on Form S-3 or Form F-3, the automatic shelf registration process allows eligible issuers to add additional classes of securities and to add eligible majority-owned subsidiaries as additional registrants after an automatic shelf registration statement is effective. They also can freely accommodate both primary and secondary offerings using automatic shelf registration. Thus, these issuers have significant latitude in determining the types and amounts of their securities or those of their eligible subsidiaries that can be offered without any potential time delay or other obstacles imposed by the registration process. . . .

Our rules as adopted will allow well-known seasoned issuers using automatic shelf registration statements to omit more information from the base prospectus in an automatic shelf registration statement than is the case currently or than is the case in a regular shelf registration statement under Rule 430B. A base prospectus included in an automatic shelf registration statement can, as today, omit information pursuant to Securities Act Rule 409 that is unknown or not reasonably available and, as adopted, can omit the following additional information:

- whether the offering is a primary or secondary offering;
- the description of the securities to be offered other than an identification of the name or class of the securities;
- the names of any selling security holders; and
- the disclosure regarding any plan of distribution. . . .

The rules provide issuers with automatic shelf registration statements the ability to add omitted information to a prospectus by means of:

- a post-effective amendment to the registration statement;
- incorporation by reference from Exchange Act reports; or
- a prospectus or prospectus supplement that would be deemed to be part of and included in the registration statement. . . .

The base prospectus in the initial registration statement must identify in general terms the names and classes of securities registered. . . . [However, there is no requirement for] allocating the mix of securities registered between the issuer, its eligible subsidiaries, or selling security holders. . . .

[And,] a well-known seasoned issuer can add new classes of securities or securities of an eligible subsidiary to an automatic shelf registration statement at any time before sale of those securities . . . [but to do so] the issuer must file a post-effective amendment, which will be immediately effective, to register an unspecified amount of securities of a new class of security. . . .

Under the automatic shelf registration statement rules we are adopting today, all automatic shelf registration statements and post-effective amendments thereto will become effective immediately upon filing . . . [and will have a duration of three years].

4.   Can Disclosure Be a Bad Thing?

Though Rule 415 has a favorable impact on the issuer's cost of capital, *equity* shelf offerings rarely occurred prior to the SEC's authorization in 1993 of a "universal registration statement," discussed below. *See* Denis, Shelf Registration and the Market for Seasoned Equity Offerings, 64 J. Bus. 189, 190-195 (1991). To understand management's former reluctance to resort to a shelf registration for equity securities, consider that a stock's price customarily drops on announcement that the company has filed a registration statement to sell additional shares; this is attributed to the market's belief that managers sell additional shares when the stock price has peaked. *See* Barclay & Litzenberger, Announcement Effects of New Equity Issues and the Use of Intraday Price Data, 21 J. Fin. Econ. 71 (1988). The price drop, however, is greater with the filing of a shelf registration statement. What explains this phenomenon? As seen earlier in this chapter, underwriters back the offering's price with both their capital and their reputations, so that the decline is moderated to some extent by the market's belief that underwriters will not participate in an offer that is overpriced. This certification process, however, is not present with equity shelf registrations whose purpose is to catch windows of opportunity. There is greater uncertainty, and hence a greater discounting in the market, in connection with shelf-registered equities than with non-shelf-registered equities. Issuers understanding this process may well conclude that the savings in issuance costs provided by Rule 415 for their equity offerings are smaller than the discounting such a registration will subject their shares to in the market. This explanation was sufficient to cause the SEC in 1993 to amend its procedures to eliminate specifying the number of common shares to be registered and to authorize an unallocated shelf registration statement (also known as a "kitchen sink" or "universal" registration statement) on which only the identity of *classes* of securities being registered and the aggregate proceeds of all classes need be disclosed. The SEC justified the rule's change as an effort to encourage greater use of Rule 415 for equity offerings. Rule 430B(a)'s treatment of what information can be omitted from the base prospectus carries forward this development. Does such a change serve the public interest? Is the notion of "windows of opportunity" for equity offerings consistent with market efficiency? Since the change was introduced in 1993, there has been a significant increase in the use of shelf registrations for common shares. *See* Report of the Advisory Committee on the Capital Formation and Regulatory Processes, app. A, tbl. 3 (SEC 1996).

NOTES AND QUESTIONS

1.   How Shelf Offerings Can Be Conducted.   There are three primary ways S-3 eligible issuers carry out offerings under Rule 415(a)(1)(x). An *at-the-market* offering is an offering of securities into an existing market that occurs with the issuer's underwriter selling the shares through ordinary trading transactions. A *direct offering* is marketed much like a private placement to interested investors, typically financial institutions. Each of these two manners of distribution requires an effective registration statement. The third method, an *over-the-wall* transaction, relies on Rule 163 so that this method is only available to a WKSI. Typically, underwriters contact prospective institutional investors about a potential offering, but without identifying the issuer. If an institution expresses interest, it is then brought "over the wall" by being provided with detailed information about the issuer. Under Rule 163, this information is deemed a "free writing prospectus" and thereby subject to a legend and filing requirement. The promotional efforts, pricing of the security, filing of the registration statement, and closing of the sale occur quickly, frequently overnight. With an over-the-wall offering, the issuer can test the waters, avoid large marketing efforts, and even moderate disclosure price effects associated with the market's reaction to the issuance.

2.   Updating the Base Prospectus via Rules 430B and 430C.   Earlier we saw that Rule 430A permits certain price-related information in offerings to be filed after the registration statement became effective. Shelf registrations enjoy even greater liberality for what information can be omitted from a registration statement before it becomes effective. As discussed above, the shelf registration procedures contemplate that certain information regarding the distributed security will not be known until after the registration statement has become effective. When this occurs, the information that is filed with the SEC and forms the registration statement when it becomes effective is known as the "base" or "core" prospectus. Thereafter, the SEC's rules set certain time limits for the missing information to be provided. Understanding the regulatory process for shelf registrations begins with Rule 430B, which broadly authorizes omission from the base prospectus of information that is unknown or not reasonably available to the issuer (e.g., the price), as well as omitting details pertaining to the securities that will be sold via the base prospectus. In the case of seasoned issuers, the base prospectus can omit the identity of any selling security holders as well as the amounts they propose to sell; this information can be provided via a later filing after the effective date. The base prospectus that omits information in accordance with Rule 430B is not a final prospectus; it is nevertheless a prospectus that can be used in any case other than when a final prospectus is required.

When the supplemented information is combined with the base prospectus they constitute a final prospectus. Under Rule 430B(d), the information authorized to be omitted from the base prospectus is later included via a post-effective amendment, a prospectus filed with the SEC pursuant to Rule 424, or in certain instances through the issuer's periodic reports that are incorporated by reference. Rule 430B provides that a prospectus supplement must be prepared and filed pursuant to Rule 424 when the information omitted from the base prospectus is later provided via an amendment to the issuer's Exchange Act filings; however, this requirement is satisfied if the prospectus supplement merely identifies the report in which the amendment has been made. Rule 430B(e) expressly provides that when the earlier omitted information is subsequently included in the prospectus that this information becomes part of the registration statement so that the liability under Section 11 attaches to the supplemented information. Rule 430B applies to all offerings by well-known seasoned issuers, shelf offerings pursuant to Rule 415(a)(1)(x) (discussed below), certain secondary offerings, and offerings of mortgage-backed securities. For information supplemented in other offerings Rule 430C provides that the supplemented information thereby becomes part of the registration statement.

    3. Prospectus Requirements Revisited.   Rule 415 has a limited purpose: It sets forth specific instances in which securities can be registered for the shelf, thus overcoming the SEC's earlier narrow reading of the Securities Act. Rule 415 does not prescribe on what form the securities are to be registered. Whether the securities are to be registered on Form S-1, S-3, or some other form is determined by the offering's ability to satisfy a particular form's eligibility requirements. Note also that the specific requirements for the contents of the prospectus that must be made available in connection with the securities offering are also guided by the registration form that applies to that issuer. Compare Part I of Form S-3 with Part I of Form S-1. Of special note here is the requirement in Item 12 of Form S-3 that the registrant identify in the prospectus (and hence the registration statement) the Exchange Act reports that are incorporated by reference, that it state that all Exchange Act reports subsequently filed (up to completion of the offering) are also incorporated, and set forth that reports incorporated by reference will be provided upon request.

    Consider how slender the prospectus is that must be made available to investors in connection with a Form S-3 offering, especially if that offering is a firm commitment offering for cash. As seen earlier, absent a request from the investor, the distribution participants in a Form S-3 offering do not have to make available much of the basic information package, most notably information about the issuer's business, management, financial statements, or management discussion and analysis. However, any material change in this information from that set forth in the Exchange Act reports that are incorporated by reference must be provided to the investor. What must be disclosed via the prospectus delivery requirements is the information set forth in Part I of Form S-3, but this is where Rule 430A has an important impact. Price-based information, such as the price of the security and the amount of the underwriter's commission that are omitted under Rule 430A, is omitted from the package of information sent to the customer if that information is filed with the SEC pursuant to Rule 424(b) on or prior to the mailing of a confirmation. Thus, the investor must be content with the cover page setting forth a price range for the security. Other information called for by Form S-3 for the prospectus is a brief summary of the offering, any risk factors, proposed use of the proceeds, how the offering price will be determined, dilutive effects if an equity offering, identification of selling shareholders, if any, and identity of the underwriters and their obligations to acquire the securities. Notice here how little information about the issuer is contained in the prospectus.

PROBLEMS

4-34. Thorprods, Inc., common stock is listed on the New York Stock Exchange and satisfies the listing requirements of Form S-3, but it is not a well-known seasoned issuer. Thorprods common shares currently trade at $15 per share. Thorprods proposes to register $100 million of bonds to be issued in $1,000 denominations bearing a face rate of interest of 11 percent, payable each quarter. Each bond is convertible at any time into 50 Thorprods common shares. Bonds of the same risk classification as Thorprods currently carry an effective rate of interest of about 12 percent. Thorprods is not desperate for the cash from the offering and hopes to be able to place the bonds when there is a decline in interest rates, which it hopes will be in the near future. Can the securities Thorprods proposes to offer be registered for the shelf?

4-35. Assume BetaChem, Inc., is considering raising capital. It is uncertain whether it will do so via issuing 1 to 2 million additional shares or via a senior security, such as preferred stock or even bonds. It would prefer not to issue common shares but is concerned that rising interest rates may make bonds or even preferred shares carry too high an interest or dividend, respectively. BetaChem believes it needs to move forward in satisfying its regulatory requirements so that it can be in a position to move quickly to take advantage of any positive developments in capital markets. What regulatory flexibility is available for it to register the offering without identifying the amount and type of security it proposes to offer, assuming it must register the security on Form S-1? What flexibility does it enjoy if it is eligible to use Form S-3, but is not a well-known seasoned issuer? How does your answer change if BetaChem is a well-known seasoned issuer?

4-36. Tavist Company, a small company whose shares are traded in the over-the-counter market, has been a reporting company for less than one year. Its controlling stockholder, Alice, wishes to sell a significant amount of her stock. Because Tavist stock is quite volatile, Alice is contemplating registering 100,000 shares for the shelf and selling as many shares as she can whenever the stock price is above $15 or $16 per share. Can Alice's shares be registered for the shelf?

4-37. Ralston Purina Co. is a large and highly successful corporation and a well-known seasoned issuer. To foster strong relations with its employees, the firm's management embarked on a concentrated effort to encourage "key employees" at all levels to become owners of the company's shares. This could occur by the employees devoting some of their personal retirement accounts to the purchase of Ralston shares or using a payroll deduction plan. As an incentive, Ralston offers to match (up to 5 percent of the employee's annual gross salary) the individual employee's purchase with an incremental increase in the employee's salary. Shares will be sold to the employees at the closing market price on the day the employee's order is received. An elaborate process was established to identify key employees who would become the beneficiaries of this program. What information must Ralston make available to the key employees singled out pursuant to this program and how should it proceed with registering the securities?

H.   Updating and Correcting the Registration Statement

The regulatory hand of the federal securities laws is exercised throughout the distribution process. In an earlier section, we saw how Section 5's prospectus delivery requirements reach all those who are distributing the securities. In this section, we examine the issuer's obligations to update its prospectus and in turn the registration statement. To focus the analysis of the material that follows, consider the issues that flow from the following problem.

PROBLEM

4-38.   Alpha Company's registration statement became effective on July 12th, and reported that Alpha owned 900,000 acres of uncut Oregon timberland and that the company would soon obtain permits to log the timberland. On July 18th, with less than one-half of the Alpha offering sold, 350,000 acres of Alpha's Oregon timberland was lost to forest fires then ravaging the Pacific Northwest. On the basis of the readings that follow, consider the source of Alpha's duty to amend its registration statement as well as the SEC's power to compel such an amendment. Consider how your response is altered if the registration statement's initial figure was inflated by an error made by the company's surveyor and the actual amount of timberland is 350,000 acres.

1.   Refusal Orders and Stop Orders

Deficiencies and problems with a filed registration statement are generally handled through the letter of comment practices described earlier. Occasionally, the defects in the registration statement are of such a character and so extensive that they cannot in the Commission's judgment be dealt with informally. Specifically, the Commission's Rule 3, 17 C.F.R. §202.3, provides that it will not use the informal procedures to address deficiencies in a registration statement that appear to stem from a careless disregard of its disclosure requirements or entail a deliberate attempt to conceal or mislead, or otherwise where the Commission believes the public interest requires it to proceed formally against the registrant. It nevertheless is a rare case when the Commission decides to proceed formally through either a refusal order under Section 8(b) or a stop order under Section 8(d).

Without much debate, the weakest weapon in the Commission's '33 Act arsenal is its authority to issue a "refusal order" under Section 8(b) barring a filed registration statement from becoming effective. By its terms, the Section 8(b) refusal order is of limited use because it reaches only patent misstatements and omissions in a filed registration statement. Section 8(b) does not apply where the misleading feature of the registration statement is not apparent on its face; that is, it does not apply where the misleading character can only be discerned from conditions or facts not appearing in the registration statement. Furthermore, Section 8(b) requires that the Commission give notice of a hearing within ten days of the statement's filing and that the hearing occur within ten days of said notice, a level of alacrity not common to the Commission. Moreover, the refusal order must be issued before the registration statement becomes effective. Recall that Section 8(a) provides that the registration statement becomes effective within 20 days of its filing, so there is a very small window of time to initiate a refusal order proceeding. However, the Commission's procedure in Rule 473 for a permanent delaying amendment that continuously tolls the commencement of the 20-day period mitigates somewhat the problems Section 8(a) poses to the timely use of a refusal order.

Because of the restrictions on the refusal order, the Commission more frequently proceeds under Section 8(d) to issue a stop order that broadly empowers it to act "if it appears . . . at any time that the registration statement includes any untrue statement of a material fact." *See, e.g., In the Matter of Cross Research Corp.*, 1992 LEXIS 703 (1992) (misrepresentation of the company's officers and directors as the firm's founders). In a sense, the stop order is broader than simply correcting material omissions and misstatements that appear in the registration statement. The Commission views the stop order as serving an important informational role to investors, so that it uses the procedure even when the offering has been completely sold; in such a case, the stop order serves notice to the investing public that the Commission has found the issuer's registration statement disclosures materially misleading. Under Section 8(e), the Commission can also issue a stop order *solely* on the basis of the registrant's or underwriter's failure to cooperate in the Commission's investigation or their obstruction of the staff's investigation.

Even though Section 8(d) refers to a registration statement that *includes* (rather than "included") a misrepresentation and permits this to be determined "at any time," the Commission's authority under Section 8(d) extends to material misrepresentations that appear in the registration statement *prior* to its becoming effective, *and* allows enforcement after the effective date for material misrepresentations in the registration statement as of the effective date.

However, Section 8(d) does not reach situations where post-effective developments render a previously accurate registration statement misleading. Therefore, the Commission must proceed under Section 8A, which authorizes a cease-and-desist order, or in the federal courts under the antifraud provisions of Section 17(a) of the Act.

Recall that Section 5(c) bars offers to buy or offers to sell when a refusal or stop order has been issued against a registration statement; this provision is interpreted to apply upon the bare initiation of an investigation under Section 8(e).

An important consequence of a refusal or stop order against an issuer's registration statement is that each triggers the "bad boy" disqualifiers that prevent the issuer's use of certain exemptions, discussed in Chapter 5, from full registration. These collateral sanctions are important considerations to the Commission in deciding whether to proceed with a stop order in the face of a registrant who wishes to withdraw its registration statement with a view toward proceeding with its offer under exemptions that would be denied it if the Commission were to proceed with a stop order. For a sympathetic view of the Commission's prerogatives under Section 8, *see* McLucas, Stop Order Proceedings Under the Securities Act of 1933: A Current Assessment, 40 Bus. Law. 515 (1985).

2.   Post-Effective Amendments

a.   *Correcting Material Inaccuracy*

The registration statement can be amended after it has become effective, and under Section 8(c), a post-effective amendment "shall become effective on such date as the Commission may determine." The principal, but by no means the sole, purpose of a post-effective amendment is to correct any material inaccuracy appearing in the registration statement when it became effective. However, the Commission has expanded the duty to file post-effective amendments by relying on Section 10(a)'s linkage of the contents of the registration statement with the contents of the prospectus; Section 10(a) provides that "a prospectus . . . shall contain the information in the registration statement." As seen above, sales of securities made by means of a materially deficient prospectus expose their sellers to liability under Section 12(a)(2) of the '33 Act as well as the '34 Act's antifraud provision. Thus, those involved in the offer must constantly assess whether the prospectus used in the distribution must be updated or otherwise changed so as not to be materially misleading. *See* Jenkins, Recirculation of the Preliminary Prospectus: Statutory Basis and Analytical Techniques for Resolving Recirculation Issues, 55 Bus. Law. 135 (1999).

A material change can arise in the post-effective period that renders the registration statement misleading (e.g., the company's plant described in the prospectus has been destroyed by an act of God), or there may be a post-effective development on a matter not discussed at all in the registration statement (e.g., a materially adverse judgment in a suit not discussed in the registration statement because the adverse outcome was, when the registration statement became effective, believed to be too remote to even be mentioned). In each case, concerns for fraud will drive those involved with the offering to amend the prospectus used in the offering. Deciding whether they are also bound to file the amended prospectus as a post-effective amendment to the registration statement begins with an analysis of Section 10(a), which requires the prospectus to "contain the information contained in the registration statement." In practice, this language is interpreted to require a post-effective amendment of the registration statement only when the post-effective information is to be *substituted* for, but not *added* to, information appearing in the registration statement. Such fine distinctions are no doubt in the eye of the beholder, and the Commission's perception on this is blurred by its preoccupation that any material change merits a post-effective amendment to the registration statement. Securities Act Release No. 6276, 21 S.E.C. Dock. 1052, 1075 (Dec. 23, 1980). On the other hand, information that does not portend the type of substantive change or addition referred to in Rule 424(a) can occur without filing an amendment to the registration statement. In the case of a paper-based prospectus, such an addition occurs by placing a sticker containing the new information on the prospectus. The stickers are affixed to the cover page or sometimes other appropriate pages in the prospectus. The procedures for filing the stickered prospectus with the Commission are set forth in Rule 424(b)(3)-(5), and such a filing does not constitute an amendment to the registration statement.

A couple of important points need to be considered about the consequences that flow from a post-effective amendment to understand why the registrant is not neutral about the question of whether the post-effective changes are handled as an amendment to the registration statement or treated as a filing of the stickered (amended) prospectus under Rule 424(b)(3)-(5). Post-effective amendments to the registration statement do not become effective without action by the Commission's staff. While waiting for the staff to declare the amendment effective, the distribution efforts can continue using the stickered prospectus because the filing of a post-effective amendment does not disturb or suspend the effectiveness of an earlier effective registration statement. When the post-effective amendment is declared effective, it reaffirms all that then appears in the registration statement, and under Section 11(a), the entire registration statement, not just the amendment, is deemed to speak as of the date the amendment became effective. Therefore, if matters true when the registration statement first became effective are no longer true and are not corrected in the post-effective amendment, the post-effective amendment provides subsequent purchasers with a means to sue under Section 11 that they would not have had if no post-effective amendment had been made.

b. Supplementing Information That Is Permitted to Be Omitted Prior to Effectiveness

As seen earlier, Rule 430A permits a registration statement to become effective despite the omission of certain price-related information, and Rules 430B and 430C permit a good deal of information to be omitted from the base prospectus for shelf registration offerings. Each of these rules requires filing the omitted information with the SEC. One means of providing the information is by filing with the SEC an amendment to the prospectus that includes the missing information. Rule 424(b)(2) requires that within two business days of the sale, the information permitted to be omitted by Rule 430B in connection with a shelf registration must be filed with the SEC. Under the SEC's rules, such a post-effective amendment to the prospectus becomes part of the registration statement. As we examine later in Chapter 9, what information is in a registration statement and when that statement becomes effective is significant under Section 11 because this provision imposes absolute liability on issuers for misrepresentations that exist in a registration statement when it became effective. Directors, those who sign the registration statement, and underwriters are also liable, unless they establish, among other facts, that the misrepresentation could not have been discovered via a "reasonable investigation." Therefore, the information filed later poses interesting Section 11 issues because both the supplemental information and the originally filed information may be tested for their truthfulness as of a date later than when the registration statement first became effective.

To consider the operation of the rules, assume a well-known seasoned issuer whose registration statement broadly covers an unspecified amount of equity and debt securities. The registration statement is filed in January and in September, as part of the "takedown" by the underwriter, a prospectus supplement is filed with the SEC disclosing that its underwriter has sold 1 million common shares. Assume further that between January and September that a patent that is a major source of the issuer's income has been declared invalid, that this is a material fact, and that it was never disclosed. Rule 430B(f)(1) provides that the registration statement is amended as of the earlier date the newly filed prospectus was first used or the first sale subsequent to filing the prospectus. This essentially resets the Section 11 liability clock to September; under subsection (f)(2), this change applies only for the issuers and underwriters. In the hypothetical, this means that the issuer and its underwriter are responsible under Section 11 for the failure of the registration statement in connection with the September takedown to disclose the patent's invalidity. However, because subsection (f)(2) applies only to the issuers and underwriters, the issuer's directors' (as well as any non-issuer signer's) liability under Section 11 is not affected by the post-effective amendments to the registration statement; their responsibility under Section 11 is based on when the registration statement initially became effective in January when there was no misrepresentation of the information set forth at that time. Also to be noted is that the registration statement is deemed amended only as to those parts that pertain to the transaction involving *that* underwriter. For example, under the preceding hypothetical, post-effective developments peculiar to the issuance of *debt* would not become the responsibility of the underwriter who sold only common shares. Thus, if after the effective date the tax laws changed to increase the tax rate for interest payments to bondholders and the prospectus supplement failed to disclose this change, the underwriter of *only common* shares is not responsible for this omission (but if bonds were instead sold, the underwriter of the bonds would be responsible).

3.   Undertakings to Update

An important, if not indispensable, component of the shelf registration provision in Rule 415 is the undertaking extracted through Item 512(a) that the registrant will file as a post-effective amendment to its registration statement:

1. Any prospectus required by Section 10(a)(3) (hence, even though the general rule is that registrants need not file the more current prospectus being used more than nine months after the registration statement became effective, such an amendment is necessary if the offering is being made on a continuous or delayed basis under Rule 415);
2. To reflect any change in facts or events after the registration statement became effective that individually or in the aggregate represent a *fundamental* change in the registration statement's information; or
3. To include any material information with respect to the plan of distribution or material change in such information from that in the registration statement.

In the case of a shelf registration conducted through Form S-3, the above post-effective undertakings can be satisfied through filings made pursuant to such issuer's '34 Act reports. Changes other than those required by Item 512(a) can be made by "stickering" the change to the prospectus. Such a stickered change is not an amendment to the registration statement; thus, the sticker does not expose anyone to liability under Section 11. Furthermore, the stickered information need not await any decision from the Commission or its staff regarding its becoming effective.

4. Withdrawal of the Registration Statement

Rule 477 provides that an issuer may withdraw its registration statement or any amendment or exhibit thereto; the withdrawal is effective immediately, unless the Commission objects within 15 days of the withdrawal application being filed. As will be seen in Chapter 5, Rule 477 complements Rule 155's safe-harbor provision that facilitates an issuer abandoning its efforts to undertake a public offering and pursuing its need for capital through an exemption from registration (subject to a 30-day cooling-off period). Why would an issuer abandon steps taken toward making a public offering?

The Commission has successfully denied the withdrawal of a registration statement in cases where the registrant has sold securities covered by the deficient registration statement, *Columbia General Investment Corp. v. SEC*, 265 F.2d 559 (5th Cir. 1959), and where the registrant has previously sold securities of the same class, *SEC v. Hoover*, 25 F. Supp. 484 (N.D. Ill. 1938). Even when it allows a registration statement to be withdrawn, the Commission frequently publishes its opinion setting forth the statement's deficiencies in the belief that publicity has some benefit to investors, should the same registrant seek to sell securities in the future.

I. *The Trading Practice Rules*

By far the most accurate reflection of a security's value is its price in a free and efficient market. And in a sense, the market provides the world with a crisp image of how traders perceive the issuer and its securities. If the issuer's security is falling in value in the market at the same time the underwriters are distributing a new offering of that security, the underwriter's life is not an easy one. In contrast, it is far easier and quicker to distribute a security whose price is rising in the market; such an issue "goes out the window." It can therefore be seen that there are substantial temptations by the issuer and its underwriters, as well as their associates, to influence the secondary trading market for the security being distributed so that the distribution occurs more quickly and perhaps at a higher price (if the offering is being made at market). To such possible abuses, the so-called trading practice rules discussed below apply.

1. Purchases During a Distribution

Acting pursuant to its authority under Section 10(b) of the Exchange Act to proscribe "manipulative or deceptive devices or contrivances" in connection with the purchase or sale of securities, the Commission has, since 1955, pro-scribed bids and purchases of a distributed security by the key participants in its distribution. The Rule is intended to prevent those involved in the distribution of securities from artificially conditioning the market for securities to facilitate the distribution. Purchases during a distribution formerly were regulated by Rule 10b-6, but since 1997 are regulated by Rules 100-102 of Regulation M.

Bids or purchases during a distribution by the issuer or other person on whose behalf the distribution is being made are regulated by Rule 102, and Rule 101 reaches bids and purchases by: (1) the distribution's underwriter (and even prospective underwriters); and (2) a broker, dealer, or other person who has agreed to participate or is participating in the distribution. Purchases by "affiliated purchasers"—those who are acting in concert with any of the above-named participants in the distribution or who control or are under the control of a distribution participant—are also reached. Rule 100 contains definitions of *underwriter, prospective underwriter,* and *affiliated purchaser,* and defines the cir-cumstances under which a person shall be deemed to have completed his par-ticipation in the distribution.

In general, the prohibition against bids and purchases during a distribu-tion applies until the regulated person has completed his participation in the distribution. *Distribution* is defined so that it reaches offerings, whether or not they are registered under the '33 Act, so long as the offering "is distinguished from ordinary trading transactions by the magnitude of the offering and the presence of special selling efforts and selling methods."

NOTES AND QUESTIONS

1.   *The Cooling-off Period.*   An important regulatory question is *when* Rules 101 and 102's prohibitions of bids and purchases commence. This can be an especially ticklish question for the issuer or other distribution participants when sales of a security are being made or about to be made off the shelf under Rule 415. Both Rule 101 and Rule 102 prohibit purchases and bids only during the "restricted period," which is either one business day or five business days before the security's price is determined or when the person becomes a distribution par-ticipant. The choice between these two numbers is guided by the "average daily trading value" of the security to be distributed and different commencement time applies to IPOs and acquisitions. *See* Rule 100's definition of "restricted period."

2.   *Notable Exemptions.*   Regulation M exempts certain transactions on the ground that they are unlikely to affect the market price of the distributed secu-rity. For example, purchases among the underwriting syndicate's members or by an underwriter from the issuer are exempt, as are odd-lot purchases. Rule 101(b)(3) and (8). And there are exemptions that are justified because the situations they reach pose no potential for abuse. For example, any purchase on behalf of a customer where the customer's order was not solicited (i.e., the classic broker's transaction) is exempt. Rule 101(b)(5). There is also a broad exemption for actively traded securities meeting certain volume requirements as well as investment-grade securities. Rules 101(c) and 102(d). Regulation M provides more exemptions for "distribution participants" than to the issuers, selling securities holders, or their affiliated purchasers. For example, they have

a transaction exemption for *de minimis purchases,* defined as those not exceeding 2 percent of the security's average daily trading value. Rule 101(b)(7).

3. *Laddering Revisited.*   Recall that earlier in this chapter's discussion of abuses that may occur during IPOs we discussed "laddering." This occurs when an underwriter conditions the allocation of shares in an IPO to an investor upon the investor agreeing to purchase in the after market a certain amount of the distributed security. Such practices have been identified in an SEC interpretive release as likely violating Regulation M. *See* Securities Act Release No. 8565 (Apr. 7, 2005).

PROBLEMS

4-39.   First Bank recently announced it would acquire Watchoveru Bank by issuing its shares to the Watchoveru shareholders. First Bank has filed a registration statement covering the shares to be issued in the merger. Soon after First's announcement, Sun Bank announced it would soon formally announce an offer to acquire all the outstanding shares of Watchoveru by offering its shares to the Watchoveru stockholders. After Sun's announcement, but well before it filed a registration statement covering the shares it will offer for the Watchoveru shares, the Federal Reserve Board increased substantially the net capital requirements that apply to national banks such as First and Sun. Fearing that the Fed's actions will depress the market value of their shares, both First and Sun propose to support their stock's value by engaging in substantial market purchases of their company's shares. Can they do this? *See* Tyson Foods, Inc. SEC No-Action Letter, Fed. Sec. L. Rep. (CCH) ¶78,155 (Sept. 24, 2001).

4-40.   Tempco, a large multinational corporation, earlier filed a registration statement for the shelf for a $150 million offering of its 10 percent, 20-year debentures that became effective January 10th; it sold $30 million of the registered debentures at that time. The debentures are not rated as investment grade by any rating agency. Tempco soon began to plan for another $40 million of the registered debentures to be sold through competitive bidding on or about March 15th, if market conditions were favorable. On March 10th, Tempco's vice president of finance called the leading underwriting firms asking them to submit bids for the $40 million of debentures. One of the firms so approached, Hedley, Hadley Ltd., just after it submitted its bid, on March 12th purchased in the market $600,000 of the Tempco offering for its trading account. Tempco opened all the submitted bids after the market closed on March 15th and accepted Hedley, Hadley's bid, and Hedley, Hadley made its first sale of the purchased securities on March 16th. Has Hedley, Hadley committed a violation? What if the $600,000 purchase had been on March 17th for the account of one of Hedley, Hadley's partners? What if Hedley, Hadley had not submitted the winning bid?

2. Stabilization

Stabilization is the pegging or fixing of a security's market price through purchases or bids for the limited purpose of preventing or retarding a decline in the security's price during a public offering of the security. Even though stabilizing purchases are by definition artificial and thus manipulative, they nevertheless are seen as beneficial in connection with the security's distribution. Certainly, excessive selling in the market of the distributed security makes it more difficult for the underwriters to dispose of their unsold allotments, and doubly so if such selling pressure causes the price of the distributed security to decline below its offering price. If the pressures of such selling efforts are alleviated by members of the underwriting syndicate purchasing the security in the market, this improves their ability to sell their allotments. Furthermore, a large amount of sell orders at the same time a security is being distributed has a destabilizing effect on the distribution as a whole. Not only do purchases by the underwriting syndicate allay these concerns and thus reduce somewhat the underwriting risk of the offering, but also their presence can provide some assurance of liquidity for investors who may find it necessary to sell their shares soon after they acquire them. Such considerations prompted Congress to equivocate in its response to stabilization, for, rather than rendering stabilizing purchases and bids unlawful outright, Section 9(a)(6) of the Exchange Act proscribes only "pegging, fixing, or stabilizing the price of such security" that contravenes the Commission's rules on the subject. Congress therefore placed the ball firmly in the Commission's court, where over time a complex set of rules for stabilization has evolved, first under Rule 10b-7 and now under Rule 104 of Regulation M.

Compliance with the SEC's stabilization rule has two effects: The purchases are not deemed to be manipulative or deceptive as those terms are used in Section 10(b) of the Exchange Act, and furthermore, purchases and bids that so comply do not violate the bar to purchases during a distribution. *See* Rule 101(b)(2). When stabilizing is likely to occur, Item 508(l) of Regulation S-K requires that appropriate disclosures be made in bold type in the inside cover page of the prospectus. Stabilization is not permitted for offerings that are made "at market."

Rule 104 regulates stabilizing in connection with securities offerings. The Rule greatly liberalizes stabilizing practices over those of its predecessor, Rule 10b-7 of the Exchange Act, by allowing underwriters to initiate and change stabilizing bids based on the distributed security's current market price in its principal market (whether U.S. or foreign). More specifically, Rule 104(f)(2)(i) and (4) allows underwriters to initiate and change stabilizing bids based on the current (independent) price in the principal market (whether U.S. or foreign) as long as the bid does not exceed the offering price. Underwriters can maintain, reduce, and raise their bids to follow the independent bids for the security so long as they do not exceed that bid or the offering price of the stabilized security. Where there is no independent market price, stabilizing is limited only by the offering price. Rule 104(f)(2)(iii). The Rule imposes disclosure and record-keeping obligations with respect to the underwriters' stabilization activities.

An intriguing gap within the regulatory framework exists because both Section 9(a)(6) and Section 10(b) of the Exchange Act render unlawful only stabilizing activity that is proscribed as unlawful in the Commission's rules. The only direct rule on this point is Rule 104, and that Rule only applies to purchases and bids that stabilize "the price of a security to facilitate an offering of any security." Does this mean that pegging, fixing, or otherwise stabilizing the price of a security for other purposes does not violate the antifraud rules, such as Rule 10b-5?

PROBLEM

4-41. Hedley, Hadley Ltd. is the lead underwriter of Tecto Company common stock. Tecto common shares are currently quoted on Nasdaq, and Hedley, Hadley has maintained a bid to purchase Tecto common at $9 for several days prior to Tecto's registration statement becoming effective. The last quoted price before Hedley, Hadley entered its $9 bid was $9.25. Just before it filed the pricing amendment, the last sale price of Tecto common stock was $9.50. Tecto filed its pricing amendment, setting an offering price of $9.50, and the Commission's staff permitted acceleration of that amendment, so that the registration statement became effective at 10 A.M. that day. Hedley, Hadley then increased its bid to $9.50. Do Hedley, Hadley's actions constitute lawful stabilization?

NOTES AND QUESTIONS

1. *Global Offerings and the Distribution Rules.* The Commission's position is that Section 10(b) and hence the trading practice rules apply to distribution participants and their affiliates whenever part of a global offering occurs within the United States. This has posed serious problems for the market making activities of foreign distribution participants because many foreign exchanges require market makers to stand ready to buy and sell securities at all times. Since a security's major market makers are logical participants in any global offering of that security, a strict application of the Commission's distribution rules poses serious conflicts with such participants' local market making obligations. Also, with worldwide trading in a security, there is the additional concern that the price at which a security closes in New York may not be an appropriate price for stabilization when that security opens in London, and vice versa. The Commission has attempted to ameliorate the adverse international effects of the distribution rules through granting exemptions and no-action letters. Much of the regulatory thrust of Regulation M is to reduce conflict that the trading practice rules pose for participants in global offerings. This is accomplished by exempting from Rule 101's proscription of purchases during a distribution securities that have an average daily trading volume of $1 million issued by a company whose common equity has a public float value of at least $150 million. *See* Rule 101(c)(1). Rule 104 also provides relief for the global offering by allowing stabilization prices to be determined not solely by the price in the security's principal market when that market is closed. *See* Rule 104(f)(ii) (may use lower of closing price in principal market or the most recent independent price in the market where stabilization is to occur). Adjustments also are permitted in the stabilizing price to reflect exchange rate fluctuations. *See* Rule 104(f)(5). Finally, Rule 104(g) provides that stabilizing purchases in connection with a global offering do not violate Rule 104 provided that no stabilizing purchases occur in the United States and the stabilizing purchases that do occur in a foreign market are in compliance with regulatory provisions that the SEC by rule or order deems comparable to Rule 104.

2. *Stabilization and Increasing the Rewards of Underwriting.* The underwriters' agreement with the issuer commonly includes an over-allotment option (OAO),

which allows the underwriters to distribute up to 15 percent more shares than registered in the official offering; there usually is a 30-day period during which the underwriter can exercise the option. Consider how this option can increase the underwriters' income. If the underwriters sell the full 115 percent of the official offering, they then have a short position in the issuer's security, which they can meet either through exercising their OAO or repurchasing shares in the market. Shares purchased pursuant to stabilization activities can, therefore, serve dual purposes: to facilitate the rapid distribution of the offering by retarding any decline in the security's price below the offering amount and to maximize the underwriters' income. The latter occurs by underwriters deftly timing their stabilization purchases so that they occur at below the security's offering price so that the underwriters garner a gain for the difference between their market repurchases and their sales of the distributed security. The ability of the underwriters to so increase their income is further facilitated by the time period they have to deliver securities sold pursuant to established rules:

> The settlement procedure for delivery of stock (by the company) and the proceeds (by the underwriter) is very important in determining the importance of the OAO to the underwriter. In most cases, official shares, or the number of shares listed in the final registration statement, must be delivered by the company within a few days (usually within three days) after issuance. . . .
>
> The OAO shares, however, need not be settled within three days. The underwriter may deliver these shares to investors who bought the shares at issuance up to thirty calendar days after issuance. This allows the underwriter to initiate price stabilization activities in the days after issuance by repurchasing shares in the open market (or purchasing securities after the stock has fallen below the offer price), and to wait until weeks later before deciding whether and how much of the OAO to exercise.

Cotter & Thomas, Firm Commitment Underwriting Risk and the Over-Allotment Option: Do We Need Further Legal Regulation?, 26 Sec. Reg. L.J. 245, 252-253 (1998) (finding price stabilization is inversely correlated to exercise of OAO). One study even found that underwriters rarely undertake market purchases for the purpose of stabilizing the offering price, but instead carry out their market purchases to cover their short positions in the distributed security. Indeed, the study finds that there is an inverse relationship between the size of the underwriters' short position and the strength of investor demand for the distributed security. See Aggarwal, Stabilization Activities by Underwriters after Initial Public Offerings, 55 J. Fin. 1075, 1089 (2000).

J.   The International Public Offering

Investors increasingly include the shares of foreign issuers in their investment portfolio. Thus, at the end of 2011, foreign ownership of U.S. stocks was in excess of $3 trillion and U.S. holdings of foreign stocks was $4.1 trillion. The numbers are somewhat lower for bonds; foreign ownership of U.S. company bonds was nearly $2.9 trillion and U.S. ownership of foreign firm's bonds was nearly $1.8

trillion. U.S. Dept. Commerce, The International Investment Position of the United States at Yearend 2011 (July 2012). Foreign issuers have not been blind to the U.S. investors' appetite and frequently offer their securities in the United States. Such globalization of capital raising and investing has been nurtured by the cooperative efforts of government regulators. As is seen in the following materials, the global offering poses serious challenges to defining the scope of Section 5 of the Securities Act as well as the content of the registration statement for foreign issuers offering their securities in the United States.

1.   Accommodating Foreign Issuers' Offerings in the United States

Absent one of the standard exemptions provided in Sections 3 and 4 of the '33 Act, the foreign issuer that offers its securities in the United States must register its offering under Section 5. Registration potentially is a more burdensome undertaking for a foreign issuer whose local accounting and disclosure practices can be expected to diverge greatly from those that apply to U.S. issuers. The most sweeping accommodation to foreign issuers occurred with the Commission's adoption in 1991 of a collection of rules, forms, and schedules to facilitate cross-border offerings and continuous reporting by specified Canadian issuers. Securities Act Release No. 6902 (June 21, 1991). In broad overview, the changes, known as the multi-jurisdictional disclosure system (MJDS), permit eligible Canadian issuers to satisfy SEC registration and reporting requirements by filing disclosure documents that satisfy Canadian requirements. Concurrently, Canada undertook changes in its own securities laws to permit U.S. issuers to satisfy its laws by filing documents prepared in accordance with SEC requirements. MJDS applies only to "substantial issuers," an expression that refers to the total market value of the issuer's equity stock (a minimum float of $75 million held by non-affiliates generally applies) and the issuer must also have been subject to Canada's reporting system for 12 months. The Commission has not developed reciprocal registration statements with any country other than Canada, so that a foreign issuer contemplating an offer in the United States must consider registration on Form F-1 or F-3.

Forms F-1 and F-3 parallel the hierarchy of registration forms available to U.S. issuers (i.e., Forms S-1 and S-3). Form F-3 is limited to issuers who have been subject to the '34 Act's reporting provisions for one year and all of whose filings under that Act have been made in a timely manner during the 12 months preceding the filing of its registration statement. Moreover, the issuer must not have failed to pay a fixed dividend, interest, debt, or rental payment since the end of the fiscal year for which it has filed certified financial statements. Finally, Form F-3 is limited to issuers whose worldwide float of common stock held by non-affiliates must at least equal $75 million. Firms that cannot meet Form F-3 eligibility requirements must use Form F-1. Non-U.S. issuers registering securities in the United States generally are concerned whether they will be successful in coordinating their efforts in both the United States and their home markets. For example, time sensitive transactions, such as rights offerings in their home country, can be very tricky if there is uncertainty in the timing of the U.S. offering due to SEC regulatory requirements. The challenges faced by foreign issuers in this respect are now at least easier for the foreign issuer who meets the SEC's

"well-known seasoned issuer" classification for Form F-3 issuers, since its registration statement now is effective immediately upon filing. And foreign issuers,
just like their domestic counterparts, enjoy the relaxation of rules that occurred
with the SEC's 2005 reforms for the regulation of public offerings.

In adopting these forms, the Commission has in many areas lightened
the foreign issuer's disclosure burdens. For example, foreign issuers' financial
statements can be prepared according to the body of comprehensive accounting principles of their local country, provided the registration statement discusses any material variations from U.S. GAAP. In their annual reports filed
with the SEC, foreign issuers must present a schedule reconciling their financial
statements with U.S. GAAP. However, reflecting the increasing convergence of
International Financial Reporting Standards (IFRS) issued by the Europe-based
International Accounting Standards Board and U.S. GAAP, since 2008 the SEC
has waived reconciliation for foreign private issuers whose financial statements
are prepared in accordance with IFRS as adopted by the IASB; the reconciliation requirement continues for foreign issuers whose financial statements are
prepared in accordance with their home country accounting principles or some
modified version of IFRS. *See* Securities Act Release No. 8879 (Dec. 21, 2007).
Embracing the value of a single set of high-quality accounting standards, the
SEC has proposed a time schedule whereby all reporting companies, domestic
and foreign, must prepare their financial statements in accordance with IFRS.
Foreign issuers have much lower disclosure obligations with respect to certain
items, such as management compensation and their material transactions with
the issuer than customarily apply to U.S. issuers by virtue of Items 402-404 of
Regulation S-K. As a further accommodation to foreign issuers, the SEC has
tailored Form 20-F so that it closely mirrors the disclosure standards established
by the International Organization of Securities Commissioners in 1998. Form
20-F is filed annually by non-Canadian firms that are listed on a U.S. exchange.

Also to be considered in this delicate balance is that relaxing the disclosure
obligations for foreign issuers and not their American counterparts may not
play very well in Peoria. What justifications are there for imposing disclosure
costs on U.S. issuers that are not borne by foreign issuers when they are accessing U.S. capital markets? Consider further that a fundamental objective of the
Commission's basic information package is comparability among issuers; is this
objective seriously compromised when an important segment of issuers—that
is, foreign issuers—is not subject to the same disclosure standards as apply to
domestic issuers?

2. Offerings Outside the United States

a. *Regulation S*

A different regulatory problem is posed by securities offerings that take
place outside the United States. As a threshold matter, it should be observed
that Section 5's jurisdictional reach is potentially quite broad. *Interstate commerce*
is defined in Section 2(a)(7) to include "trade or commerce in securities or
any transportation or communication relating thereto . . . between any foreign
country and any State, Territory, or the District of Columbia." Under a literal

reading of this provision, it would appear that any offering by a U.S. issuer would fall within Section 5 if in the process of selling the security abroad there was the use of the U.S. mails or telephone calls into the United States. Similarly, a European offering by a French issuer whose securities soon are traded among American investors in the U.S. over-the-counter market can also be seen as triggering Section 5's jurisdictional provision by failing to control the flow of unregistered securities into U.S. trading markets.

In view of Section 5's overbreadth and the increasing importance of international securities offerings, the Commission has taken a series of interpretative and regulatory steps to lighten seriously the concerns over Section 5's application. The Commission's initial foray into the area was through Securities Act Release No. 4708 (July 9, 1964), which rather imprecisely took the position that an offering sold in a manner reasonably designed to preclude distribution or redistribution within or to nationals of the United States did not require registration under Section 5. There then ensued 25 years of frequently inconsistent and always uncertain standard setting through no-action letters. A much more definitive position is now set forth in Regulation S, adopted by the Commission in 1990. Regulation S, which embodies Rules 901-905, provides safe harbors for offshore distributions and resales of unregistered securities of U.S. and foreign issuers.

Regulation S is territorially oriented. Rule 903 provides three different categories for the issuer safe harbor. Each of the three is unavailable if, in connection with an offering, an offer or sale is made to a person in the United States, or if there have been selling efforts within the United States. Extensive planning and preparation can, however, occur inside the United States without jeopardizing the Regulation S safe harbors. Whether there are additional requirements for the safe harbor depends on the nature of the issuer.

Rule 903(b) divides issuers into three categories according to the relative likelihood that securities of that category of issuer will enter American trading markets. The three categories are:

903(b)(1):   foreign issuers for which there is no substantial U.S. market interest in their securities, or foreign issuers that direct their offering to residents of a single country other than the United States;

903(b)(2):   U.S. issuers that are '34 Act reporting companies offering debt securities, foreign issuers that are reporting companies offering equity securities, foreign issuers whether or not a reporting company offering debt securities; and

903(b)(3):   all other issuers.

The least demanding safe harbor requirements apply to Category 1 issuers, described in Rule 903(b)(1). Offerings falling within this category need only meet the basic requirement that all offers and sales be "an offshore transaction" and there being no "directed selling efforts" in the United States. In contrast, offerings falling within Category 2 or 3 have additional restrictions that regulate the manner in which the offering is conducted and impose restrictions regarding the transfer of the security during the "distribution compliance period." For example, the distribution compliance period is one year for an equity security offered under Category 3, but 40 days for securities offered pursuant to Category 2. Table 4-2 on page 209 sets forth the requirements for each category of issuer safe harbors. The important aspects of these requirements are discussed in the release that follows.

Rule 904 provides a safe harbor that applies to resales of securities. The Rule 904 safe harbor addresses the question of whether one who purchased an unregistered security abroad violates Section 5 if that security is resold to an American. As will be seen, further restrictions on resale occur by virtue of Rule 905 treating Regulation S securities as "restricted" securities.

Regulation S, Securities Act Release No. 6863 (Apr. 24, 1990)
Securities and Exchange Commission

. . . Regulation S as adopted includes two safe harbors. One safe harbor applies to offers and sales by issuers, securities professionals involved in the distribution process pursuant to contract . . . (the "issuer safe harbor"), and the other applies to resales by persons other than the issuer, securities professionals involved in the distribution process pursuant to contract . . . (the "resale safe harbor"). An offer, sale or resale of securities that satisfies all conditions of the applicable safe harbor is deemed to be outside the United States within the meaning of the General Statement and thus not subject to the registration requirements of Section 5.

Two general conditions apply to the safe harbors. First, any offer or sale of securities must be made in an "offshore transaction," which requires that no offers be made to persons in the United States and that either: (i) the buyer is (or the seller reasonably believes that the buyer is) offshore at the time of the origination of the buy order, or (ii) for purposes of the issuer safe harbor, the sale is made in, on or through a physical trading floor of an established foreign securities exchange, or (iii) for purposes of the resale safe harbor, the sale is made in, on or through the facilities of a designated offshore securities market, and the transaction is not pre-arranged with a buyer in the United States. Second, in no event could "directed selling efforts" be made in the United States in connection with an offer or sale of securities made under a safe harbor. "Directed selling efforts" are activities undertaken for the purpose of, or that could reasonably be expected to result in, conditioning of the market in the United States for the securities being offered. Exceptions to the general conditions are made with respect to offers and sales to specified institutions not deemed U.S. persons, notwithstanding their presence in the United States. . . .

The Regulation adopted today is based on a territorial approach to Section 5 of the Securities Act. The registration of securities is intended to protect the U.S. capital markets and investors purchasing in the U.S. market, whether U.S. or foreign nationals. Principles of comity and the reasonable expectations of participants in the global markets justify reliance on laws applicable in jurisdictions outside the United States to define requirements for transactions effected offshore. The territorial approach recognizes the primacy of the laws in which a market is located. As investors choose their markets, they choose the laws and regulations applicable in such markets. . . .

Regulation S relates solely to the applicability of the registration requirements of Section 5 of the Securities Act, and does not limit the scope of extraterritorial application of the antifraud or other provisions of the federal securities laws or provisions of state law relating to the offer and sale of securities. . . . It is generally accepted that different considerations apply to the extraterritorial application of the antifraud provisions than to the registration provisions of the Securities Act. . . .

2.   ISSUER SAFE HARBOR

The issuer safe harbor is available [in Rule 903] for issuers, distributors, their respective affiliates, and persons acting on behalf of any of the foregoing. The issuer safe harbor distinguishes among three classes of securities, with varying procedural safeguards imposed to have the securities offered come to rest offshore. The criteria used to divide securities into three groups, such as nationality and reporting status of the issuer and the degree of U.S. market interest in the issuer's securities, were chosen because they reflect the likelihood of flowback into the United States and the degree of information available to U.S. investors regarding such securities. . . .

A.   CATEGORY 1: FOREIGN ISSUERS WITH NO SUBSTANTIAL U.S. MARKET INTEREST; OVERSEAS DIRECTED OFFERINGS; SECURITIES BACKED BY THE FULL FAITH AND CREDIT OF A FOREIGN GOVERNMENT; EMPLOYEE BENEFIT PLANS

The first issuer safe harbor category is available for offers and sales of securities of foreign issuers with no "substantial U.S. market interest" for their securities, securities offered and sold in "overseas directed offerings," securities backed by the full faith and credit of a foreign government, and securities offered and sold pursuant to certain employee benefit plans. Securities issued by foreign entities that do not have a substantial U.S. interest in their securities may be expected to flow back or remain in their major or home market, and are not likely to flow into the United States following an offshore offering. Flowback concerns also are limited where securities of a foreign issuer, even with a substantial U.S. market, are offered and sold in an offering directed at residents of a single foreign jurisdiction and conducted in accordance with local laws, and customary local practices and documentation. . . .

Offers and sales of securities included in this category may be made in reliance on the safe harbor without any limitations or restrictions other than the general conditions that the transaction be off-shore and that no directed selling efforts be made in the United States. Offers and sales of securities to U.S. investors who are overseas at such time will not preclude reliance on the safe harbor for securities in this category. Of course, trading of a substantial amount of such securities in the United States shortly after they had been offered offshore may indicate a plan or scheme to evade the registration provisions; where a transaction is part of such a plan or scheme, Regulation S is not available.

TABLE 4-2
Issuer Safe Harbors

903(b)(1) Qualifications	903(b)(2) Qualifications	903(b)(3) Qualifications
(i) A foreign issuer that has no "substantial U.S. market interest" or (ii) A foreign issuer engaged in an "overseas directed offering"	(i) A domestic or foreign Issuer offering debt; (ii) A foreign issuer subject to Exchange Act's reporting requirements offering equity	All other issuers
903(b)(1) Conditions to Be Satisfied	**903(b)(2) Conditions to Be Satisfied**	**903(b)(3) Conditions to Be Satisfied**
Must be (a) "Offshore transaction" and (b) No "directed selling efforts" in United States	Same as 903(b)(1)	Same as 903(b)(1)
Offering restrictions: None	Offering restrictions: During the distribution compliance period (a) Each distributor agrees to conform efforts to requirements of safe harbor; and (b) All offering material will bear a legend that securities have not been registered in the U.S. without either registration or an exemption	Offering restrictions: Same as 903(b)(2)
None	During the 40-day distribution compliance period, (a) No sales to the account of a "U.S. person," and (b) Distributors during the period must inform securities professionals of the restrictions on sale to U.S. persons	Distribution compliance period is 40 days for debt and one year for equity (a) Purchasers during period must certify they are not a U.S. person and are not purchasing for such person; (b) Equity purchasers during restricted period must agree only to sell or hedge in accordance with Regulation S, a '33 Act registration or an exemption therein; (c) Shares of domestic issuer must bear legend barring transfer except in accordance with Regulation S; and (d) All issuers must have a provision in bylaws or elsewhere empowering it to bar transfers not in accordance with Regulation S

(1)   *"Substantial U.S. Market Interest"*

A "substantial U.S. market interest" in a class of a foreign issuer's equity securities is defined to exist where at the commencement of the offering (a) the securities exchanges and inter-dealer quotation systems in the United States in the aggregate constitute the single largest market for such securities in the shorter of the issuer's prior fiscal year or the period since the issuer's incorporation or (b) 20 percent or more of the trading in the class of securities took place in, on or through the facilities of securities exchanges and inter-dealer quotation systems in the United States and less than 55 percent of such trading took place in, on or through the facilities of securities markets of a single foreign country in the shorter of the issuer's prior fiscal year or the period since the issuer's incorporation. . . .

[Substantial U.S. market interest for debt securities is measured differently, determined in part by 20 percent or more being held by 300 or more U.S. persons, provided the amount so held is at least $1 billion.]

Foreign issuers with no "substantial U.S. market interest" are eligible to rely on the first category of the issuer safe harbor, whether or not they are reporting under the Exchange Act, have securities listed on a U.S. exchange or quoted on Nasdaq, or sponsor an American depositary receipt ("ADR") facility. . . .

(2)   *"Overseas Directed Offerings"*

. . . Of particular importance in the concept of "overseas directed offering" is the requirement that such offerings be "directed" at a single country. Where the foreign issuer, a distributor, any of their respective affiliates, or a person acting on behalf of any of the foregoing, knows or is reckless in not knowing that a substantial portion of the offering will be sold or resold outside that country, the offering will not qualify as an overseas directed offering. . . .

B.   CATEGORY 2: REPORTING [U.S.] ISSUERS' [DEBT SECURITIES]; . . . FOREIGN ISSUERS' DEBT SECURITIES; . . . REPORTING FOREIGN ISSUERS' EQUITY SECURITIES

[Debt] securities of all domestic issuers that file reports under the Exchange Act are subject, under the second safe harbor category, both to the general conditions that an offer or sale be an offshore transaction and that no directed selling efforts may be made in the United States, and to specified selling restrictions. [Equity] securities of foreign reporting issuers with substantial U.S. market interest are subject to the same restrictions [if they did not have a substantial U.S. market interest, Category 1 would be available]. The selling restrictions applicable to the second category are designed to protect against an indirect unregistered public offering in the United States during the period the market is most likely to be affected by selling efforts offshore. In the event flowback of reporting issuers' securities does occur after the restricted period, the information relating to such securities publicly available under the Exchange Act generally should be sufficient to ensure investor protection.

The second category also applies to offerings of debt securities of any . . . [foreign issuer, even if not a reporting company]. The inclusion of those offerings in this category reflects the view that offering restrictions applicable to the category provide adequate protection against an indirect U.S. distribution because of the generally institutional nature of the debt market and the trading characteristics of debt securities. . . .

Two types of selling restrictions exist for securities in the second category—"transactional restrictions" and "offering restrictions."

(1) Transactional Restrictions

Transactional restrictions require that the securities sold under the safe harbor prior to the expiration of a . . . [distribution compliance] period not be offered or sold to or for the benefit or account of a U.S. person. Persons relying on the second issuer safe harbor category are required to ensure (by whatever means they choose) that any non-distributor to whom they sell securities is a non-U.S. person and is not purchasing for the account or benefit of a U.S. person. Transactional restrictions also require a distributor selling securities to certain securities professionals to send a confirmation or notice to such purchasers advising that the purchaser is subject to the same restrictions on offers and sales that apply to a distributor.

(a) *U.S. Person.* Rule 902 (o) contains a definition of the term "U.S. person." . . . U.S. residency rather than U.S. citizenship is the principal factor in the test of a natural person's status as a U.S. person under Regulation S. Thus, for example, a French citizen resident in the United States is a U.S. person. . . .

(b) *Measurement of the . . . [Distribution Compliance] Period.* The . . . [distribution compliance] period begins to run on the later of the date of the closing of the offering or the date the first offer of the securities to persons other than distributors is made. . . .

(2) Offering Restrictions

"Offering restrictions" are procedures that must be adopted with regard to the entire offering by the issuer, distributors, their respective affiliates, and all persons acting on behalf of any of the foregoing, in order for a transaction to be in compliance with the second or third categories of the issuer safe harbor. . . . In effect, offering restrictions are procedures set up by such persons to ensure compliance with the transactional restrictions, particularly the restrictions on offer or sale of the securities to or for the account or benefit of U.S. persons. . . . The offering restrictions require distributors, who by definition are participating in the distribution pursuant to a contractual arrangement, to contract that all their offers and sales of the securities will be made in accordance with the safe harbor (or pursuant to registration under the Securities Act or an exemption therefrom).

The issuer, distributors, or their respective affiliates, and persons acting on behalf of any of the foregoing, must ensure that certain materials disclose that the securities have not been registered and may not be offered or sold in the United States or to a U.S. person (other than a distributor), unless registered or an exemption from registration is available. Disclosure of the restrictions must appear in any prospectus, offering circular or other document (other than a press release) used in connection with the distribution prior to the expiration of the restricted period. All advertisements relating to the securities are subject to that requirement. . . .

C. CATEGORY 3: . . . [ALL OTHER ISSUERS]

All securities not covered by the prior two categories fall into this residual category, which is subject to procedures intended to protect against an unregistered U.S. distribution where there is little (if any) information available to the marketplace about the issuer and its securities and there is a significant likelihood of flowback. This category includes [debt] securities of non-reporting U.S. issuers, [equity securities of all U.S. issuers] and equity securities of non-reporting foreign issuers with substantial U.S. market interest in their equity securities.

As in the case of securities of reporting issuers, offerings of securities in this category are subject to the two general conditions and to offering and transactional restrictions. Offering restrictions that must be adopted for offerings of these securities are the same as for offerings of securities of reporting issuers. In contrast to offerings in the second category, more restrictive transactional restrictions to prevent flowback are applicable. . . .

Prior to the expiration of the . . . [distribution compliance] period, the securities may not be sold to U.S. persons or for the account or benefit of U.S. persons (other than distributors). Purchasers of the [equity] securities (other than distributors) are required to certify that they are not U.S. persons and are not acquiring the securities for the account or benefit of a U.S. person other than persons who purchased securities in transactions exempt from the registration requirements of the Securities Act. Such purchasers are also required to agree only to sell the securities in accordance with the registration provisions of the Securities Act or an exemption therefrom, or in accordance with the provisions of the Regulation.

With respect to equity securities of domestic issuers, the safe harbor requires that a legend be placed on the shares stating that transfer is prohibited other than in accordance with the Regulation. The safe harbor further requires that any issuer, by contract or a provision in its bylaws, articles, charter or comparable document, refuse to register any transfer of equity securities not made in accordance with the provisions of the Regulation. Where bearer [equity] securities are being sold, or foreign law prevents an issuer from refusing to register securities transfers, use of reasonable procedures, such as a legend, will suffice to satisfy the requirement designed to prevent transfer of equity securities other than in accordance with the Regulation.

Purchasers of debt securities offered under the third issuer safe harbor category (other than distributors) are subject to different restrictions than equity purchasers under this category. Prior to the expiration of the forty day restricted period, the securities may not be sold to U.S. persons or for the account or benefit of U.S. persons (other than distributors). . . .

4. SAFE HARBOR PROTECTIONS

If an issuer, distributor, any of their respective affiliates (other than officers and directors relying on the resale safe harbor), or any person acting on behalf of any of the foregoing: (1) fails to comply with the offering restrictions; or (2) engages in a directed selling effort in the United States, the Rule 903 safe harbor is unavailable to any person in connection with the offering of securities. If the issuer, a distributor, any of such respective affiliates, or any person acting on behalf of any of the foregoing, fails to comply with any other requirement of the issuer safe harbor, the safe harbor is not available for any offer or sale in reliance thereon made by the person failing to comply, its affiliates or persons acting on their behalf. The availability of Rule 903 for other persons' offers and sales of securities is unaffected. . . .

The availability of the Rule 904 resale safe harbor generally is unaffected by the actions of the issuer, distributor, their respective affiliates (other than certain officers and directors relying upon Rule 904), or persons acting on behalf of any of the foregoing. An offer or sale of securities made in compliance with the provisions of Rule 904 is within the safe harbor, notwithstanding non-complying offers or resales by other unaffiliated persons not acting on behalf of the seller. . . .

C. INTERACTION WITH OTHER SECURITIES ACT PROVISIONS

(1) Contemporaneous U.S. and Offshore Offerings

Offshore transactions made in compliance with Regulation S will not be integrated with registered domestic offerings or domestic offerings that satisfy the requirements for an exemption from registration under the Securities Act, even if undertaken contemporaneously. . . .

Statement of the Commission Regarding Use of Internet Web Sites to Offer Securities . . . Offshore
Securities Act Release No. 7516 (Mar. 23, 1998)

. . . The purpose of this interpretation is to clarify when the posting of offering or solicitation materials on Internet Web sites would not be considered activity taking place "in the United States." . . .

Under this interpretation, application of the registration provisions of the U.S. securities laws depends on whether Internet offers, solicitations or other communications are targeted to the United States. . . .

This interpretation does not address the anti-fraud and anti-manipulation provisions of the securities laws, which will continue to reach all Internet activities that satisfy the relevant jurisdictional tests.[5] Even in the absence of sales in the United States, we will take appropriate enforcement action whenever we believe that fraudulent or manipulative Internet activities have originated in the United States or placed U.S. investors at risk. . . .

II. BACKGROUND

. . . The posting of information on a Web site may constitute an offer of securities or investment services for purposes of the U.S. securities laws. Our

---

5. The courts have recognized U.S. jurisdiction over fraudulent conduct where substantial conduct or effects occur in the United States. . . .

discussion of these issues will proceed on the assumption that the Web site contains information that constitutes an "offer" of securities or investment services under the U.S. securities laws. Because anyone who has access to the Internet can obtain access to a Web site unless the Web site sponsor adopts special procedures to restrict access, the pertinent legal issue is whether those Web site postings are offers in the United States that must be registered.

III. OFFSHORE OFFERS AND SOLICITATIONS ON THE INTERNET

A. GENERAL APPROACH

. . . We believe that our investor protection concerns are best addressed through the implementation by issuers and financial service providers of precautionary measures that are reasonably designed to ensure that offshore Internet offers are not targeted to persons in the United States or to U.S. persons. . . .

B. PROCEDURES REASONABLY DESIGNED TO AVOID TARGETING THE UNITED STATES

When offerors implement adequate measures to prevent U.S. persons from participating in an offshore Internet offer, we would not view the offer as targeted at the United States and thus would not treat it as occurring in the United States for registration purposes. What constitutes adequate measures will depend on all the facts and circumstances of any particular situation. We generally would not consider an offshore Internet offer made by a non-U.S. offeror as targeted at the United States, however, if:

- The Web site includes a prominent disclaimer making it clear that the offer is directed only to countries other than the United States. . . .
- The Web site offeror implements procedures that are reasonably designed to guard against sales to U.S. persons in the offshore offering. For example, the offeror could ascertain the purchaser's residence by obtaining such information as mailing addresses or telephone numbers (or area code) prior to the sale. This measure will allow the offeror to avoid sending or delivering securities, offering materials, services or products to a person at a U.S. address or telephone number.

These procedures are not exclusive. . . . Regardless of the precautions adopted, however, we would view solicitations that appear by their content to be targeted at U.S. persons as made in the United States. Examples of this type of solicitation include purportedly offshore offers that emphasize the investor's ability to avoid U.S. income taxes on the investments. . . .

C. EFFECT OF ATTEMPTS BY U.S. PERSONS TO EVADE RESTRICTIONS

We recognize that U.S. persons may respond falsely to residence questions. . . .

In our view, if a U.S. person purchases securities . . . notwithstanding adequate procedures reasonably designed to prevent the purchase, we would not view the Internet offer after the fact as having been targeted at the United States, absent indications that would put the issuer on notice that the purchaser was a U.S. person. This information might include (but is not limited to): receipt of payment drawn on a U.S. bank; provision of a U.S. taxpayer identification or social security number. . . .

IV. ADDITIONAL ISSUES UNDER THE SECURITIES ACT . . .

A. OFFSHORE OFFERINGS BY FOREIGN ISSUERS

1. *Regulation S*

When a foreign issuer is making an unregistered offshore Internet offer and does not plan to sell securities in the United States as part of the offering, it should implement the general measures outlined in Section III.B. to avoid targeting the United States. . . .

B. OFFSHORE OFFERINGS BY U.S. ISSUERS

. . . For the following reasons, additional precautions are justified for Web sites operated by domestic issuers purporting not to make a public offering in the United States:

- The substantial contacts that a U.S. issuer has with the United States justifies our exercise of more extensive regulatory jurisdiction over its securities-related activities;
- There is a strong likelihood that securities of U.S. issuers initially offered and sold offshore will enter the U.S. trading markets; and
- U.S. issuers and investors have a much greater expectation that securities offerings by domestic issuers will be subject to the U.S. securities laws.

Our experience with abusive practices under Regulation S indicates that we should proceed cautiously when giving guidance to U.S. issuers in the area of unregistered offshore offerings. As a result, we would not consider a U.S. issuer using a Web site to make an unregistered offer to have implemented reasonable measures to prevent sales to U.S. persons unless, in addition to the general precautions discussed above in Section III.B., the U.S. issuer implements password-type procedures that are reasonably designed to ensure that only non-U.S. persons can obtain access to the offer. Under this procedure, persons seeking access to the Internet offer would have to demonstrate to the issuer or intermediary that they are not U.S. persons before obtaining the password for the site.[35]

---

35. *See* Securities Act Release No. 7392 at n.31 (Feb. 28, 1997) [62 FR 9258] (issuer cannot accept at face value representations by investors regarding their residence).

C. CONCURRENT U.S. REGISTERED OFFERING

A registered offering in the United States that takes place concurrently with an unregistered offshore Internet offer presents concerns because of the Securities Act's restrictions on making offers prior to the filing of a registration statement or, in the case of written or published offers, outside of the statutory prospectus. Consistent with these requirements, therefore, premature posting of offering information must be avoided. Existing Commission rules that provide a safe harbor for announcements of anticipated offerings provide guidance in this respect. The Commission is considering whether to provide further guidance or to make further changes concerning concurrent U.S. registered offerings and offshore Internet offers in the context of broader Securities Act reforms.

D. UNDERWRITERS

Just as an issuer must take reasonable steps to avoid offers of unregistered securities in the United States, so too must persons acting on behalf of the issuer, such as underwriters or distributors. . . . Thus, regardless of whether the underwriter is foreign or domestic, what constitutes measures reasonably designed to prevent sales to U.S. persons will depend on the status of the issuer. . . .

NOTES AND QUESTIONS

1. *Abuses of Regulation S.*   The Commission has initiated several enforcement actions against sham Regulation S offerings. The Commission's enforcement efforts have targeted transactions where the investment risk never left the United States. Clearly this occurs when offshore sales are made pursuant to an arranged resale into the United States. *See SEC v. Softpoint, Inc.,* [1997 Transfer Binder] Fed. Sec. L. Rep. (CCH) ¶99,450 (S.D.N.Y. 1997). Other examples include securities purchased abroad through nonrecourse notes, or through recourse notes by an entity with nominal assets, where the purchase notes will be satisfied by selling the securities in the United States after the applicable restricted period has passed. A similar concern arises with the simultaneous overseas purchase of shares and short selling in the United States of shares of the same class of stock. *See generally* Note, Evasion and Flowback in the Regulation S Era: Strengthening U.S. Investor Protection While Promoting U.S. Corporate Offshore Offerings, 17 Fordham Int'l L.J. 806, 850-851 (1995). In one instance, Primerica sold 7 million shares in a Regulations S offering. Because of the restrictions on resale, the shares were sold at a 9 percent discount to the U.S. market price. Primerica's domestic price fell from $46⅛ to $42¾ on rumors on the offshore offering. Later, it was learned that European investors had used their Regulation S shares to cover their short sales in the United States. Note here Rule 903(b)(3)(iii)(2)'s requirement that purchasers of equity securities offered pursuant to the Category 3 agree to conform any hedging of the purchase to the Securities Act.

2. *Resale Safe Harbor Rule 904.* The resale safe harbor in Rule 904 is available for the resale of any security regardless of whether it was acquired in an offshore transaction under Regulation S. The safe harbor distinguishes between resales by securities professionals (dealers or others who receive a selling commission for the securities being offered) and other sellers (e.g., individual investors). Resales by the latter fall within the safe harbor, provided their resale occurs in an "offshore transaction" and without "directed selling efforts" within the United States. Securities professionals similarly must limit their resales to offshore transactions and avoid directed selling efforts in the United States. In addition, throughout the distribution compliance period for an offering falling within the safe harbor provided in Rule 903(b)(2) or (3), the securities professionals must not resell to any buyer known to be a "U.S. person." Further, if a securities professional knows the purchaser is also a securities professional, the seller is required to send a confirmation or other notice appraising the purchaser of the restrictions that apply during the distribution compliance period.

3. *Restrictions Beyond the Distribution Compliance Period.* Rule 905 deems *equity* securities of U.S. issuers to be restricted. The import of this is that resales even after the one-year distribution compliance period must conform to the general requirements that apply to resales of unregistered securities, a topic examined more closely in Chapter 6. In broad overview, Rule 905 imposes serious limits on any resales into the United States for one year *after* the expiration of distribution compliance. The restrictions that so apply are set forth in Rule 144, the subject of Chapter 6, which conditions resale upon the securities having been outstanding for one year, requires there be certain publicly available information about the issuer, limits the number of shares that can be sold, and conditions the resale on the buyer not being solicited, that is, a broker's transaction.

4. *Press Coverage for Foreign Issuers.* Some foreign countries, unlike the United States, permit companies offering securities for sale to conduct press conferences, issue press releases, and meet with members of the press during the offering. Though they typically exclude U.S. journalists, the information ultimately is reported in the U.S. press, albeit usually later than in the foreign press. Because the SEC believed U.S. investors were placed at a competitive disadvantage by the exclusion of U.S.-based journalists from such conferences, the SEC adopted Rule 135e. The Rule provides it is not an offer to sell a security if a *foreign* issuer or its representatives permit journalists to attend press conferences or meetings with the issuer or its representatives where information related to a present or proposed public offering of securities will be released. The exemption is conditioned on the press conference being held outside the United States and that the security offering will not occur *solely* in the United States. Is Rule 135e consistent with the position taken in Securities Release No. 7516, supra? Is Rule 135e fair to a U.S. issuer who contemplates selling its shares in the United States and England?

5. *Research Reports.* Rules 138 and 139 include a provision that research reports that otherwise comply with either Rule 138 or 139 will not be deemed to constitute directed selling efforts for the purpose of Regulation S. Does such a report put added pressure on those engaged in the "off shore" offering to make sure their purchasers are not U.S. residents?

6. *Are Regulation S Offerings Harmful?* Professor Stephen Choi has found that announcement of an offshore Regulation S offering has a statistically significant adverse impact on the domestic market price of the issuer's security. He isolates the cause of this to the dilutive effects of the Regulation S offering (which is sold at a discount due to the resale restrictions that apply during the distribution compliance period) and the risk that the securities are overvalued, a fear arising in part due to there being less disclosure that surrounds the offering. *See* Choi, The Unfounded Fear of Regulation S: Empirical Evidence on Offshore Securities Offerings, 50 Duke L.J. 663 (2000) (finding sample of Regulation S securities were sold at a 14 percent net discount). If Regulation S offerings yield harmful effects to domestic shareholders, why would the firm's managers undertake the offering?

PROBLEMS

4-42. Textron, Ltd., a British textile company, plans to raise $20 million by selling common stock in London and Toronto. Textron's common stock is traded on the London Stock Exchange and also on the American Stock Exchange (approximately one-half of its weekly trading volume occurs on each exchange). The offering circular has been prepared essentially by its New York counsel in close cooperation with its Canadian and British underwriters. Textron expects that all arrangements for the offering will be such that sales can commence on January 15th. Can the Textron common shares be sold to Americans working or traveling in Canada or Great Britain? What steps must the underwriters take to assure that the offering does not flow back to the United States? Is it likely that these steps will cause the offering price to be less than the price quoted on the American Stock Exchange?

4-43. Is Regulation S still available in Problem 4-42 if some of the Textron shares are sold to Ira Blue, a U.S. citizen who heads up the London office of a major New York law firm?

4-44. Assume in Problem 4-42 that Textron was incorporated in Delaware. What steps then must its underwriters take to assure the offering does not flow back to the United States?

4-45. Assume Textron's management in the problem above wishes to inform its U.S. stockholders that the company is raising capital by issuing additional shares at a discount from their quoted market price and that the offering's proceeds will be used to modernize Textron's facilities. Will this announcement jeopardize the Regulation S safe harbor? *See* Longstreth & Prager, "Gun Jumping" Revisited: A Proposal to Prevent False Starts in Private Offerings, 21 Sec. Reg. L.J. 235, 237 (1993); Rule 135c.

4-46. MoneyConnections.com operates a European-based financial bulletin board service through its web site. Approximately 20 percent of the bulletin board's subscribers are residents of the United States. In return for a modest commission paid by the underwriter representing Textron in Problem 4-42,

MoneyConnections has placed on the bulletin board offering materials for the Textron offering. MoneyConnections' web site and the offering materials placed on the bulletin board clearly warn that the offering is not available to U.S. residents. Does this render Regulation S unavailable for the Textron offering?

b.   Offerings Falling Outside Regulation S

Europe and Overseas Commodity Traders, S.A. v. Banque Paribas London
147 F.3d 118 (2d Cir. 1998)

[Carr, the sole shareholder and agent of EOC, a Panamanian company with a mailing address in Monaco, commenced discussions in London with Arida, a U.K. national, regarding a substantial investment EOC could make through Arida. Carr then departed to Florida for some much needed rest. There he had further communications with Arida both by phone and fax. The court found that while he was in Florida, Carr approved the purchase by EOC of shares from Arida. Carr, believing that Arida had lied to him, sued under the Exchange Act's antifraud provision and for rescission under Section 12(a)(1), alleging Arida had sold a security in the United States in violation of Section 5. The Second Circuit had no trouble concluding that the offer failed to satisfy any Regulation S safe harbor because of the communications that occurred while Carr was in Florida.]

Through mandatory disclosure, Congress sought to promote informed investing and to deter the kind of fraudulent salesmanship that was believed to have led to the market collapse of 1929. . . . The registration provisions are thus prophylactic in nature. Seen in this light, the registration provisions also can be said to aim at certain conduct with the potential for discernible effects. Specifically, the registration provisions are designed to prevent the offer of securities in the United States securities markets without accompanying standardized disclosures to aid investors, a course of conduct. The conduct, in turn, has the effect of creating interest in and demand for unregistered securities. To avoid this result . . . the registration provisions should apply to those offers of unregistered securities that tend to have the effect of creating a market for unregistered securities in the United States; and by "creating a market" we do not mean that the conduct must be directed at a large number of people. . . .

The nearly *de minimis* U.S. interest in the transactions presented in the instant case precludes our finding that U.S. jurisdiction exists under the more limited conduct and effect standard appropriate under the registration provisions of the 1933 Act. Under the facts as alleged by EOC, there was conduct in the United States because Arida called Carr here and Carr executed his order here. However, the conduct was not such as to have the effect of creating a market for those securities in the United States. Carr's presence here was entirely fortuitous and personal and the actual purchaser of shares . . . was an offshore corporation without a place of business here.

As will be seen in Chapter 20, *Morrison v. National Australian Bank, Ltd.*, 561 U.S. 247 (2010), held Congress intended that the Exchange Act's antifraud provision would reach "only transactions in securities listed on domestic exchanges, and domestic transactions in other securities. . . ." Is the approach taken in *Banque Paribas* consistent with *Morrison*? Is Regulation S, i.e., Rule 902(c) & (h), consistent with *Morrison*?

3. How the Public Offering Is Regulated Elsewhere: Contrasting Examples

A full appreciation of the regulatory challenges posed by the internationalization of securities offerings requires some understanding of just how substantial the differences are across major industrialized countries in their own regulation of public offerings. As any student of comparative law knows, the differences are informed by each country's culture, and in the case of the regulation of the public offering, vastly different regulatory responses also reflect differences in distribution methods used within each country.

There is now developing a body of empirical data that supports the favorable impact that strong corporate and securities laws have on the vitality of a nation's capital markets and, more specifically, the effect regulation has in reducing the cost of capital for firms raising funds in those markets. *See, e.g.*, LaPorta, Lopez-De-Silanes, Shleifer & Vishny, Legal Determinants of External Finance, 52 J. Fin. 1131 (1997). Needless to say, all countries seek to nurture robust securities markets as a means to foster growth of their productive resources. This quest is especially strong for developing countries. Here we might well benefit from the lessons learned from the Czech Republic, which undertook a massive privatization effort as a means to spur economic growth, but unfortunately did so without providing important protections for investors in the privatized firms:

> In 1995, the Prague Stock Exchange had 1716 listings. Blessed with relatively low inflation and nearly full employment, the Czech Republic's strong macroeconomic position made it seem the country in Central or Eastern Europe most likely to make a smooth transition into a market-oriented economy. Yet by early 1999, the number of listings on the Prague Stock Exchange had fallen by more than 80% to 301, and observers estimated that fewer than a dozen of these enjoyed any liquidity. Correspondingly, over the same period, the value of an investment in an index of the leading 50 stocks on the Prague Stock Exchange fell by over 60%. Trading dried up, and the viability of the Prague Stock Exchange was itself threatened. . . .
>
> What happened? The fundamental fallacy in Czech privatization was that securities markets would develop spontaneously, simply because voucher privatization would create an initially dispersed ownership structure. By widely distributing the stock in privatized companies to a broad segment of the Czech adult population, Czech planners expected that an active secondary market would develop naturally. The militantly laissez-faire attitude of the initial Czech government also made it highly resistant to any regulation of this market.
>
> . . . [F]or an initial period of high optimism . . . share prices did rise. But then, after a series of scandals, the Czech bubble began to burst. First, foreign portfolio investors began to flee the Czech market. . . .

Behind this massive disinvestment in the Czech market lay a pervasive loss of investor confidence, as small, dispersed owners witnessed widespread looting of Czech investment funds and the systematic exploitation of the remaining minority shareholders in Czech firms once any faction acquired a controlling position. In consequence, small shareholders systematically divested their shares and moved savings to other forms of investment. . . .

Coffee, Privatization and Corporate Governance: The Lessons from Securities Market Failure, 25 J. Corp. L. 1, 9-10 (1999). *See also* Richter, Tunnelling: The Effect—and the Cause—of Bad Corporate Law, 17 Colum. J. Eur. L. 23 (2011).

From the Czech experience, and the studies of the relationship between regulation and a country's cost of capital, we could do worse than draw the conclusion: law matters. To this end, consider the social, political, and economic conditions that explain the differences in the regulatory approaches taken by the following two countries.

a.   The United Kingdom

British laws view full disclosure as the investor's best protection. To effectuate full disclosure, the British public offering must (1) obtain *admission for listing* by winning the approval of its listing particulars by the Financial Conduct Authority (FCA), (2) secure *admission for trading* with either the London Stock Exchange or another recognized investment exchange, and (3) publish its listing particulars.

To achieve admission for listing, the issuer must file completed listing particulars with the FCA. Because the United Kingdom is/was a member of the European Union (EU) (depending on what happens with Brexit, currently slated for October 31, 2019 but delayed numerous times as of this writing), the touchstone for the U.K. approach to both the offering prospectus and the listing particulars is the EU Prospectus Directive, which requires issuers to publish an approved prospectus in connection with either a public offering or an admission for trading of securities on an EU market. "Public offering" is broadly defined, but the breadth of regulation is nonetheless limited by a series of exemptions, such as offers to fewer than 100 persons in each member state or offers of a minimum denomination of €50,000. Once a prospectus is approved by the issuer's "home member state," the Prospectus Directive establishes a "single passport" concept whereby the prospectus is valid for any public offer or admission for trading of those securities throughout the EU. The home member state of an EU issuer is usually the state of its registered office (greater discretion is accorded foreign issuers and EU issuers of non-equity securities, e.g., debt, for whom the home member state is based on where the security will be listed for trading). The Prospectus Directive mandates "maximum harmonization," in which each member state's requirements must at least meet the disclosure requirements set forth in the Prospectus Directive. The competent authority in the U.K. is the FCA.

Complementing the Prospectus Directive is the Transparency Directive, which imposes requirements for annual and semi-annual financial reports. However, the Transparency Directive is guided by a philosophy of "minimum harmonization," which means that individual member states can employ differing approaches regarding both the content and mechanisms for satisfying the mandated periodic disclosures. The Prospectus Directive follows the American scheme of permitting incorporation by reference of periodic disclosures filed with the competent authority, provided that the information is of the same detail as called for by the Prospectus Directive. Since the Transparency Directive entails only minimum harmonization, so that the disclosures it calls for need not be as particularized as required by the Prospectus Directive, and because the Transparency Directive can be satisfied by filings at locations other than with the competent authority, incorporation by reference is not always smooth in member states whose compliance with the Transparency Directive is not aligned with the more demanding requirements of the Prospectus Directive. Finally, the Prospectus Directive permits shelf registration. However, this process does not provide the same flexibility as the U.S. system because the competent authority (i.e., the FCA) must approve the amendments filed with it at the takedown moment; this approval can prove problematic for issuers attempting to catch "market windows."

In the U.K., admission to trading requires the sponsorship of an underwriter that is a member of the exchange for which trading privileges are sought. The overall function is to impose an obligation on the sponsoring member to ensure that an issuer is in compliance with minimum standard and fulfills a due diligence in assuring the disclosure requirements have been met. Although under the single-passport philosophy of the Prospectus Directive disclosures for admission for listing on the London Stock Exchange are mandated by the directive, exchanges still have the freedom to mandate non-disclosure-oriented conditions for listing, such as governance requirements.

Publication is the final component of the regulatory process. Once the listing particulars and the listing application have been approved, the listing particulars are published in the financial press. This formally commences the public offering and is known as "Impact Day." Those engaged in the distribution must ensure the availability of the prospectus. This is done formally by filing it with the Register of Companies and stating in the publication of the listing particulars where those interested can obtain a prospectus.

A common distribution technique is the "offer for sale" method whereby the underwriter that sponsored the issuer's listing acquires the entire offering from the issuer, but is joined in that underwriting risk by sub-underwriters, many of which are institutional investors who acquire the security for their own accounts. There also is the U.S. version of the underwriting syndicate, known in the United Kingdom as the "intermediaries offer." The requirement to offer up to 25 percent of any equity securities to the public leads to there being a two-week period after Impact Day before the underwriters know just how many shares they must acquire. The "invitation to tender" is akin to the Dutch auction technique, where subscribers are allowed to indicate how many shares they wish to purchase and at what price; the underwriter then sells the shares at the price at which all shares would be subscribed; finally, there are "placings," offerings that are limited to a limited number of the underwriter's clients.

Post-Brexit, it is expected that the FCA will continue to use the EU Prospectus Directive as its content requirements for prospectuses. In other words, U.K. disclosure requirements likely will not change following Brexit, at least for now.

b. The People's Republic of China

Chinese securities regulation presently is highly paradoxical both in its origins and function—it represents on the one hand the state's effort to develop an efficient capital market, yet on the other hand it seeks to sustain what presently are large state-owned enterprises that are visible legacies of socialist planning. Beginning with a series of economic reforms in the 1970s, China began to develop securities markets that had been cast aside with the 1949 founding of the P.R.C. In 1999, China adopted a comprehensive national securities law that consolidated most of the regulatory authority in the China Securities Regulatory Commission (CSRC).

The procedure for conducting a public offering involves merit review. An application must be filed with the CSRC and the offer cannot occur without its approval, a process that customarily takes three months. The application requires a good deal of information about the issuer and its managers. Even though the statute clearly calls on the CSRC to carry out a merit review, there has also been substantial movement toward a disclosure-based system of securities regulation. Nonetheless, delays plague the system, so many successful Chinese startups bypass the difficult IPO system by going public via a backdoor process in which they merge into a publicly held or dormant public company. Xie & Hong, Test Case Looms for "Backdoor" Listings, Wall St. J., May 24, 2016, at C-3.

At one time, before making application to the CSRC, the issuer was required to obtain approval from local, provincial, or ministerial authorities. These various approvals are no longer necessary. Today, the decision to go public is one that begins with an application to the CSRC supported by the recommendation of an investment bank and, frequently, that of a local or central government ministry; the CSRC's approval comes in response to a recommendation from its IPO Audit Committee, which is composed of financial experts, lawyers, and CSRC officials. A final requirement is that the documents filed with the CSRC, including its accounting report, must be made publicly available.

Underwriting occurs through either the Chinese version of a firm commitment underwriting (the "sole agency basis") or a best efforts underwriting (the "agency basis"). The underwriting efforts cannot extend beyond 90 days.

K. Registration Under State Blue Sky Laws

As mentioned in Chapter 1, all states historically required the registration of any primary public offering to be made in the state. Thus, an issuer that intended to market its public offering nationwide would have to register it with the SEC and all 50 states. However, this situation changed in 1996 when, as mentioned in Chapter 1, Congress enacted the National Securities Market Improvement Act (NSMIA). Among other things, NSMIA amended Section 18 of the Securities Act to establish various categories of "covered securities." Section 18, as amended, prohibits a state from requiring registration or qualification (discussed below) of any offering of covered securities or securities that will be covered securities upon completion of the offering. Covered securities include securities that are listed or are authorized for listing on the New York Stock Exchange, Nasdaq Global Market, Nasdaq Global Select Market, or the Nasdaq Capital Market, among others. Given that an offering of any significance will be of securities already listed or authorized for listing on one of these markets, state registration requirements are functionally limited to offerings by small issuers, i.e., companies that do not meet the listing requirements for their securities to be traded on the Nasdaq Capital Market (the market with the least stringent listing requirements among the four mentioned).

Smaller companies do pursue public offerings of non-covered securities (i.e., securities that will be traded on the OTC Bulletin Board, OTCQX Best Market, OTCQB Venture Market, or Pink Open Market. Hence, such an offering will need to be registered, or "blue skyed," in the states in which the offering will be marketed. This process occurs under one of three distinct procedures: notification, coordination, and qualification. Notification is available for certain seasoned, quality issuers. Under the Uniform Securities Act, notification can be used by firms that have been in operation for at least five years, have not defaulted within the current or preceding three years on fixed interest or dividend payments, and have earned at least 5 percent on their capital during the preceding three fiscal years. Notification entails filing a statement demonstrating the issuer is eligible to register through notification, some basic information about the offering, and a copy of the offering prospectus. The state registration through notification becomes effective in the afternoon of the second full day after its filing. Registration by notification occurs infrequently, in part because the earnings requirements are sufficiently rigorous that notification is available to few issuers who are otherwise not exempt. While there are numerous exemptions under the blue sky laws, an important one in this context is the exemption of securities issued by financial institutions.

Registration by coordination is only available for issuers that have filed a registration statement with the SEC under the '33 Act. Coordination usually entails filing a copy of the federal registration statement and any amendments to it with the state administrator. Subject to certain conditions, the state registration statement for an offering registered through coordination becomes effective automatically when the federal registration statement becomes effective. As under the federal rules, offers to sell the security can occur prior to the registration statement becoming effective, but actual sales within the state cannot occur until after the statement has become effective.

The most extensive review occurs for issuers whose offerings are not eligible for registration by notification or coordination. Such an offering must be registered in the state by qualification. Qualification entails filing a registration statement in each state where the offering will be made. The disclosure elicited through qualification is quite extensive. For example, the Uniform Securities Act requests 16 different categories of information. The individual states vary greatly in this area, so that the attorney can expect to encounter several different state filings involving different disclosure requirements. As discussed in the next excerpt, many state administrators have authority not only to review the adequacy of the issuer's disclosures but also to carry out a merit review whereby qualification depends on satisfying the administrator on the substantive merits of the offering.

Securities and Exchange Commission, Report on the Uniformity of State Regulatory Requirements for Offerings of Securities That Are Not "Covered Securities"
8-9 (1997)

. . . [A]pproximately 40 states undertake a "merit review" of the filing. A merit review of a filing involves a substantive review of the issuer and the offering and is intended to "prevent promotion of fraudulent or inequitable issues." Common merit review provisions relate to the following matters:

Cheap stock—limiting sales of stock to insiders and promoters that are proximate to the offering at a significantly discounted price;

Loans to and other affiliate transactions—requiring all insider loans to be repaid before the public offering; other material transactions must be on similar terms available from unaffiliated third parties and be ratified by a majority of the independent directors;

Debt securities—requiring cash flow in the past fiscal year that is sufficient to cover fixed charges, meet debt obligations as they become due and service the debt being offered; . . .

Impoundment of proceeds—subjecting the proceeds from any offering (especially best efforts and minimum/maximum offerings) to impound;

Options and warrants—limiting stock underlying such securities, at the time of the public offering, to, for example, 15 percent of the outstanding common stock; . . .

Preferred stock—requiring net income in the past fiscal year that is sufficient to cover fixed charges, preferred stock dividends and redemption requirements of the preferred stock being offered, and requiring the establishment of redemption provisions;

Promoters' equity investment—with respect to development stage companies, requiring the promoters' equity interest to be more than 10 percent of the aggregate public offering;

Promotional shares—requiring escrow of shares or the reduction of the offering price where equity securities of a development stage company have been issued to promoters for a value of less than 85 percent of the proposed public offering price;

Selling expenses and selling security holders—limiting expenses to a percentage of the offering amount; requiring selling security holders to pay a pro rata share of the additional expense due to the inclusion of their shares in the public offering;

Unequal voting rights—prohibiting these, unless accompanied by preferential dividend or liquidation provisions;

Capitalization requirements—prohibiting the issuance of any security except common equity where the issuer is "unseasoned"; and

Specifying offering price—requiring such prices to relate to book value, earnings history and/or industry price/earnings multiples where there is no established market for the security; requiring the price to be no lower than, e.g., $2 in any event, or no more than 25 times earnings; and forbidding certain types of offerings such as ones with a planned "step-up" pricing mechanisms.

When the state registration occurs through qualification, there is no automatic effectiveness of the state registration statement. It becomes effective when the state administrator so orders. Offers that are registered by qualification are those that have escaped registration with the SEC because of an exemption provided by the '33 Act.

Several developments have reduced the friction that blue sky laws introduce into the issuer's movement toward the investor's wallet. At one time the complaints regarding merit review—the application of "hip pocket" standards and the opaqueness and slowness of the process—were more prevalent than they are today. One step has been the development by the North American Securities Administrators Association (NASAA) of model merit standards that many blue sky administrators follow. The frequency of merit reviews is also limited by an expanding array of exemptions, discussed in the next chapter, as well as administrative interpretations that provide "presumptive merit" for offerings on such criteria as having an offering price that exceeds $5 per share and being accomplished through a firm commitment underwriting arrangement. *See* Sargent, A Future for Blue Sky Law, 62 U. Cin. L. Rev. 471 (1993).

In most states, the many registration burdens have been greatly lifted for small offerings because of their adoption of the Small Corporate Offerings Registration (SCOR), which was developed by the NASAA. SCOR differs from the ordinary registration form because it uses a question-and-answer, fill-in-the-blanks format. The form is limited to offerings that do not exceed $1 million (thus, complementing the SEC's safe harbor Rule 504 discussed in Chapter 5). Most states do not permit SCOR to be used if the shares' offering price is less than $5 or the offering is by an issuer that cannot describe either the business it will engage in or the property it will acquire (the so-called blind pool investment). SCOR is of great benefit to small companies that have designed their offerings to fit within one of the exemptions of the '33 Act and for whom any regulatory compliance cost is a significant consideration.

Nearly all states participate in a cooperative effort, Coordinated Equity Review, to address the problem of the issuer having to deal separately with reviewers in each of the states where the security will be distributed.

Coordinated Equity Review (CER) is a new program to facilitate the review of multi-state public offerings of corporate equity securities. It is available for corporate equity offerings filed . . . on SEC Forms . . . S-1 and F-1. It was developed by NASAA to streamline state review of initial public offerings of corporate equity securities of small-cap companies [becoming operational in April 1997].

Mechanically, an issuer files a Uniform Application to Register Securities, a copy of its SEC registration statement, and a filing fee with all the states in which it desires to offer securities. . . . A similar filing is made with the Arizona Securities Division (even if the issuer is not offering securities in Arizona) because Arizona is acting as the CER administrator. Arizona assigns the offering to one "lead" state for disclosure issues and one "lead" state for merit issues and advises all states in which the issuer has filed of the lead-state designations. States have ten business days to relay comments to the lead states. Promptly, after the ten-business day period, the lead states send a comment letter to the issuer covering all disclosure and merit issues. . . .

All CER-participating states have agreed that CER offerings will be reviewed using the uniform NASAA CER SOPs, which address (i) Loans and Other Material Affiliated Transactions; (ii) Preferred Stock; (iii) Underwriting Expenses; (iv) Options and Warrants; (v) Promoter's Equity Investment; (vi) Promotional Shares; (vii) the Impoundment of Proceeds; (viii) Specificity in Use of Proceeds; (ix) Unsound Financial Condition; (x) Corporate Securities Definitions; and (xi) Unequal Voting.

The issuer works directly with the lead states to resolve all regulatory issues. When all issues have been resolved, the lead states "clear" the offering and CER-participating states have agreed to grant simultaneous effectiveness of the offering in their jurisdiction. . . .

Rutledge, NSMIA . . . One Year Later: The States' Response, 53 Bus. Law. 563, 571-572 (1998). In response to the JOBS Act, the coordinated review procedures were streamlined so that, in the absence of a deficiency, an offer can be cleared in 21 days.

PROBLEMS

4-47. Assume your firm has been retained by Tecto Enterprises, Inc. to assist it in raising $5 to $8 million for oil exploration efforts at a yet-to-be-determined location in the United States through a public offering of Tecto common stock that will be made in California and Texas and traded on the OTC Bulletin Board. The senior partner has just learned that four months ago senior officers purchased Tecto common shares at $10 per share and that the broker-dealer that will assist Tecto in the offering has an option to acquire 10,000 common shares at $10 per share. Tecto proposes to offer the Tecto common shares to the public at around $14 per share. You have been asked to prepare a memorandum outlining the problems likely to be encountered in blue skying the Tecto offering.

4-48. Assume that Tecto in Problem 4-47 purported to carry out its offering pursuant to a private offering exemption authorized by Section 4(2) of the Securities Act. However, its attorney failed to assure that all the conditions of that exemption were satisfied so that as a technical matter the offering did not satisfy the federal exemption's requirements. If shares were sold in California and Texas, has Tecto violated the laws of these states? *See Brown v. Earthboard Sports USA*, 481 F.3d 901 (6th Cir. 2007).

L. *The Debate over Mandatory Disclosure*

1. How Strong Are the Incentives to Disclose Voluntarily?

The mandatory disclosure requirements of the '33 and '34 Acts have not escaped the criticism of those who prefer Adam Smith's invisible hand to the heavy regulatory hand of the federal securities laws. The necessity of mandatory disclosure rules has been questioned in light of the natural incentives managers have to disclose information. The traditional pro-regulation view is that reporting requirements are necessary because managers lack sufficient incentives to disclose trustworthy corporate information. Further underscoring the necessity of mandatory disclosure rules is the widely held fear that managers will disclose material information only after they have exploited its value for their private gain by insider trading. Thus, mandatory disclosure can be seen as a means to break the managers' monopoly over corporate information. The rejoinder to this view begins with a consideration of the varied positions of owners and managers.

Owners and managers each seek to maximize their own utility. In the publicly traded corporation, utility maximization is an interesting problem because owners and managers are different sets of individuals. In general, the owners' utility is maximized by increasing their wealth through the combined appreciation in the value of their shares as well as dividends. The managers' interest in maximizing their utility is not always coincident with their stockholders' desire that the firm's value should be maximized. This indeed is the classic problem of the separation of ownership from control, for it suggests natural forces exist in the public corporation that can cause managers to maximize their own utility at the stockholders' expense. For example, consider that a manager who owns 0.5 percent of her company's stock gains only $50 by locating and directing a new business opportunity worth $10,000 to the company. If she appropriates the advantage exclusively for herself, her personal wealth will increase by $9,950 above what she would enjoy had she acted to increase the firm's value.

A highly influential article, Jensen & Meckling, Theory of the Firm: Managerial Behavior, Agency Cost and Ownership Structure, 3 J. Fin. Econ. 305 (1976), discusses how such deviations can be optimally dealt with by the owners and managers. Because investors ex ante cannot precisely measure the amount or frequency of their managers' deviations, reasonable investors will discount the price at which they are willing to purchase the firm's stock by the average amount of misbehavior expected of *all* firms. Jensen and Meckling argue that this will stimulate managers whose deviations are less than the average for all firms to signal this message to securities markets or bond their reliability and trustworthiness. Their incentive to do so is to reduce the discounting and thus to increase the value of their firm's stock because the managers benefit in some direct or indirect way from such an increase.

In this regard, it is natural that owners and managers contract so as to provide incentives necessary for managers to act in an optimal manner—that is, the managers' discretionary choices will, as a result of these incentives, be stimulated to have a favorable impact on the firm's value. Stock options, bonus arrangements, and other modes of compensation linked to changes in the value of the firm's stock are classic devices used to more closely align the managers' interests with those of the owners. The managers' willingness to have a significant percentage of their earnings be so determined itself is a type of bonding arrangement that effectively signals to capital markets the managers' belief in their reliability and trustworthiness.

Even more direct action to curb management departures from the owners' wealth-maximizing goals can occur through monitoring the managers' behavior. Outside directors and certification of accounting reports by independent accountants are two prevalent forms of monitoring. Markets also provide their own incentives for managers to maximize the firm's value. A management team that seriously underperforms is vulnerable to being removed, perhaps by a proxy contest or hostile takeover. We should also consider the possible effects of the market for managers: Incumbent managers and their subordinates may be driven to receive good "report cards" to enhance their value to their firm as well as their currency in the managerial market. Thus, there are several market-based incentives for managers to maximize the value of their firm. *See* S.A. Ross, Disclosure Regulation in Financial Markets: Implications of Modern Finance Theory and Signaling Theory in Issues in Financial Regulation 177 (F.R. Edwards ed., 1979).

Consider for a moment what incentives the firm's managers have to voluntarily disclose information. Can the connection between disclosure and management incentives be relied on to replace mandatory disclosure rules? By way of background, empirical data supports the view that financial disclosures reduce the riskiness that surrounds the pricing of securities in the marketplace because they remove the uncertainty regarding the firm's financial position and performance—that is, firms that voluntarily disclose financial information can be expected to have lower risks and thus higher share prices than if they did not so disclose. Consider this question further after you have read the following.

PROBLEM

4-49.   Assume that there are six firms contemplating going public. The firms and the intrinsic value of each firm are as follows:

Firm	Intrinsic Value
A	$80
B	$70
C	$60
D	$40
E	$36
F	$20

Assume there are no mandatory disclosure requirements and that investors know the combined intrinsic value of all six firms is $306 but do not know the intrinsic value of any particular firm. They are aware that when purchasing a security there is an equally likely chance that the value of the firm they purchase will be $80, $70, $60, $40, $36, or $20; however, they otherwise do not know the intrinsic value of what they are going to purchase. Under these assumptions, and assuming no additional information is available to investors, how much can Firm C expect to receive if it goes public? Under these conditions, will Firm E go public? What strategies should Firm A follow if it wished to go public?

Easterbrook & Fischel, Mandatory Disclosure and the Protection of Investors
70 Va. L. Rev. 669, 682-684 (1984)

If disclosure is worthwhile to investors, the firm can profit by providing it. . . . [T]he Coase Theorem suggests that firm and investors can strike a mutually beneficial bargain. A decision by the firm effectively "coordinates" the acts of many investors who could not bargain directly.

To see how this works, take a simple example of a firm that wants to issue new securities. The firm has a project (say, the manufacture of a new computer) that it expects to be profitable. If the firm simply asked for money without disclosing the project and managers involved, however, it would get nothing. Investors would assume the worst, because, they would reason that if the firm had anything good to say for itself it would do so. Silence means bad news. A firm with a good project, seeking to distinguish itself from a firm with a mediocre project (or no project at all), would disclose the optimal amount of information. That is, it would disclose more and more so long as the cost of disclosure (both direct costs of dissemination and indirect costs of giving information to rivals) was worthwhile to investors as a whole. . . .

The process works for bad news as well as for good. Once the firm starts disclosing it cannot stop short of making any critical revelation, because investors always assume the worst. It must disclose the bad with the good, lest investors assume that the bad is even worse than it is. And the firm cannot stand on its say-so alone. Mere disclosure would be enough if the rule against fraud were perfectly enforced, but it is not. Thus the firm uses . . . verification and certification devices. . . . Given these devices, a rule compelling disclosure seems redundant, and if the fraud penalty and verification devices do not work, a rule compelling disclosure is not apt to be enforceable either.

The principle of self-induced disclosure as a solution to the lack of property rights in information applies to trading in the secondary market as well as to the initial issuance of stock. The firm's investors always want to be able to sell their stock in the aftermarket for the highest price. Their ability to do so depends on a flow of believable information (otherwise potential buyers reduce the bid prices, assuming the worst). For most information about a firm, the firm itself can create and distribute the knowledge at less cost than the shareholders, and the firm's decision, because it reflects the value to all shareholders, will be correct at the margin. A firm that wants the highest possible price when it issues stock must take all cost-justified steps to make the stock valuable in the aftermarket, so it must make a believable pledge to continue disclosing.

Among the arguments in support of mandatory disclosure rules is that issuers have the lowest costs of providing the information. Furthermore, those who support mandatory disclosure rules are skeptical not only whether managers will provide information with the same promptness and detail as are compelled currently by the securities laws, but also whether issuers will engage in the optimal level of verification of the information they provide. Finally, there is a good deal of doubt whether employment contracts can ever sufficiently align the managers' interests with the shareholders' interest in maximizing the firm's value. On this point, consider the capacity of managers to circumvent even the most thorough compensation incentives through inside trading or even a leverage buyout led by the firm's managers. *See* Coffee, Market Failure and the Economic Case for a Mandatory Disclosure System, 70 Va. L. Rev. 722-723 (1984).

Judge Easterbrook and Professor Fischel respond to those who are skeptical about a voluntary disclosure system by outlining various steps that could be taken under a voluntary disclosure system to address the paramount justification for the current mandatory disclosure rules—the informational asymmetries between investors and managers, in which the managers know the position and performance of the firm and outside investors do not. As seen above, they envision a disclosure hierarchy developing in which higher-quality firms will engage in more disclosure than lower-quality firms. But they also recognize that the world is neither perfect nor filled by those who abide by the rules, so that one can reasonably expect in such a perfectly laissez-faire environment that disclosures by high-quality firms will be mimicked by some low-quality firms, such that investors would not be able ex ante to distinguish the two sets of disclosures. Easterbrook and Fischel counsel that the high-quality firms may wish to distinguish themselves from low-quality reporting firms through a number of devices, including: using outside auditors to certify their financial statements; selling their securities through reputable investment bankers who will have assessed the firm's prospects; having insiders purchase a substantial quantity of the firm's stock; promising to pay dividends, thereby forcing managers to return to capital markets repeatedly in order to expand operations; and leveraging the firm itself to underscore management's optimistic view of the firm's prospects. These are all nontrivial bonding, monitoring, and signaling costs. The authors further suggest that a rule against fraudulent reporting, while not necessary, nevertheless would serve to reduce the reporting costs of high-quality issuers.

Obviously, not all issuer-released information is a result of the mandatory disclosure rules. Issuers frequently provide information not required to be disclosed by the securities laws. The best illustration of this is management's announcement of earnings forecasts. Consider the correctness of Easterbrook and Fischel's description of the world they envision (i.e., a laissez-faire environment, in which all corporate disclosures are voluntary) in light of the following synthesis of the numerous studies of firms that voluntarily release earnings forecasts:

All studies of financial forecasts have found that investors alter their assessments of the firm's worth in response to financial forecasts thus confirming the informational value of management forecasts. . . . Significant price and volume changes are associated with a forecast announcement. The price change is positive, even though the forecasted amount is below that anticipated by investors prior to management's announcement.

The cause for the abnormally positive change in return associated with a forecast's announcement is not known, but may be attributed to the usual information content involved with the *act* of issuing a forecast, as distinguished from the forecasted amount. Because companies are not required to offer financial forecasts, the self-selecting feature of forecasting ensures that those that do forecast have unique characteristics. These characteristics support the belief that the act of forecasting is an important form of signaling engaged in by managers to increase their firm's market value. This value enhancement occurs importantly by reducing the firm's riskiness in the eyes of analysts. In this regard forecasts are most frequent among firms which enjoy low fluctuations in year-to-year earnings. Higher risk firms, i.e., those with great earnings variability, are less likely to proffer a forecast. Also, forecasting firms have lower earnings variability in the fiscal period after their forecast than do comparable non-forecasting firms. Moreover, managers are more likely to forecast if earnings are increasing than when earnings are declining.

Thus, there is a greater frequency of forecasting during periods of growth in the national economy than where there is a recession. In sum, the forecast is a means for managers to communicate their optimism of the firm's position and future operations in a way that causes investors to associate the forecasting firm in a less risky category than if the same firm did not engage in forecasting. . . .

In what some may call resourcefulness, managers appear to have systematically developed their own compensation schedule when forecasting. . . . In a study of insider trading activity before and after forecast announcements, insiders were found systematically to time their purchases and sales in relation to forecast announcements. They were able to earn abnormal returns on their trading. Moreover, the strength of the correlation between the frequency of insider purchases and their forecasts was directly related to the forecast's ultimate impact on the security's market price. Insiders, therefore, not only are privileged in their ability to know when a forecast will be announced, but also are excellent judges of whether an upcoming forecast announcement will cause a material increase in the stock's price.

Cox, Insider Trading Regulation and the Production of Information: Theory and Evidence, 64 Wash. U. L.Q. 475, 493-495 (1986).

Is there reason to believe that all firms will engage in voluntary disclosures as Easterbrook and Fischel suggest? Will the managers of a firm with "good" news sometimes be tempted not to disclose this information? In this regard, consider the disclosure incentives of managers contemplating a management buyout of the stockholders. And what are the incentives to release "bad" news? Here, consider the insights gathered by Professors Arlen and Carney in their analysis of a large sample of securities fraud class actions involving public companies that issued misleading reports. Arlen & Carney, Vicarious Liability for Fraud on Securities Markets: Theory and Evidence, 1992 U. Ill. L. Rev. 691. Nearly all of the misrepresentations in these cases arose in instances where managers used public misrepresentations to conceal declines in earnings or other bad news that would cause the managers' continued employment by the firm to be placed in jeopardy if the truthful reports had been issued. Simply stated, "managers of ailing firms commit Fraud on the Market in an attempt to save their jobs, by using the period of the fraud to turn the firm around." Id. at 701. *See also* Langevoort, Organized Illusions: A Behavioral Theory of Why Corporations Mislead Stock Market Investors (and Cause Other Social Harms), 146 U. Pa. L. Rev. 101, 133 (1997) (examining the strong organizational and psychological forces that bias managers to misperceive events and risks such that corporate disclosures do not reflect an objective perception but what someone embedded in a particular culture perceives); Seligman, The Historical Need for a Mandatory Corporate Disclosure System, 9 J. Corp. L. 1 (1983) (reviewing wealth of evidence documenting rampant problems of excessive underwriter commissions and fraudulent disclosure practices prior to the enactment of the federal securities laws).

2. Regulatory Competition and Issuer Choice

With the globalization of securities markets, the debate on the desirability of mandatory disclosure rules has shifted its focus to *what* regulatory body should control the disclosure requirements that must be met by issuers. The prevailing orthodoxy is that the host country's law applies. Hence, SEC-mandated disclosures apply to all issuers, foreign and domestic, who offer securities for sale in the United States or whose shares trade in U.S. markets. Many of today's commentators champion departing from the present-day territorially oriented approach. Professor Paul Mahoney argues that disclosure should be set by the exchange on which the securities are listed. Mahoney, The Exchange as Regulator, 83 Va. L. Rev. 1453 (1997). Professors Merritt Fox and Roberta Romano defer to the nation and state, respectively, of the issuer's domicile. Fox, Securities Disclosure in a Globalizing Market: Who Should Regulate Whom, 95 Mich. L. Rev. 2498 (1997); Romano, Empowering Investors: A Market Approach to Securities Regulation, 107 Yale L.J. 2359 (1998). The most sweeping approach is that advanced by Professors Choi and Guzman, who favor a system of "portable reciprocity" whereby issuers could select the regulatory regime that will govern their offerings and continuous disclosure requirements. Choi & Guzman, Portable Reciprocity: Rethinking the International Reach of Securities Regulation, 71 S. Cal. L. Rev. 903 (1998).

At the heart of the approaches taken by Professors Mahoney and Fox is the belief that standard setters of the exchange and issuer's domicile, respectively, are in a better position to balance the costs and benefits of disclosure requirements.

> The efficient market hypothesis assures us that an issuer's share price will be discounted in the market to reflect the investor welfare effects of its applicable disclosure regime. This fact means that the primary function of disclosure is promotion of efficiency in the real economy, not investor protection. . . . [A]n appropriate level of disclosure by a country's issuers can, through its positive effects on managerial motivation and the choice of real investment projects, increase the returns generated by capital-raising enterprises. . . .
>
> The United States thus has a strong interest in the disclosure level of all U.S. issuers. . . . By the same token, the United States has little interest in the disclosure behavior of foreign issuers, even those issuers whose shares are sold to or traded among U.S. residents.

Fox, Retaining Mandatory Securities Disclosure: Why Issuer Choice Is Not Investor Empowerment, 85 Va. L. Rev. 1335, 1415-1416 (1999).

Professors Choi, Guzman, and Romano emphasize that regulatory competition will ultimately foster optimal disclosure requirements. They believe that competition for incorporations, listings, and offerings among jurisdictions will lead to improved disclosure standards.

> The argument for regulatory competition's strength in producing optimal rules is fairly easy to state. It is essentially a market approach toward regulation by which demand and supply influence the state's regulatory choices. Investors contemplating a transaction in two competing markets will not be neutral to otherwise equal reported financial risks and returns of the security if they recognize that the incidence of fraud, manipulation, unfairness or untrustworthiness of information is significantly greater in one market than it is in the other. The rational investor, ex ante, will discount the price of the security in each market by the combined value of the average likelihood and magnitude of the feared misconduct posed by all securities in that market. The securities traded in the market with the greater

likelihood of such abuses will, all else being equal, trade at a greater discount than under a more regulated and more trustworthy regime. This effect is not limited to the investor's ex ante assessment. Issuers will quickly note that any penalty investors impose through their ex ante assessment translates to a higher cost of capital than the issuer will encounter if it offered its securities in the more regulated market. Issuers will therefore gravitate to markets whose disclosure standards offer the optimal cost of capital.

Obeisance to the view that regulatory competition will provide discipline adequate to insure an optimal disclosure regime rests on a series of classic assumptions that underlie any market approach. Among the critical assumptions relevant to disclosure standard setting is the existence of a large number of competing regulators, the size of each regulatory jurisdiction being such that it can compete with its rivals, perfect information being available regarding the benefits and costs of disclosure, and the absence of externalities or monopolies that will distort the effects of inter-jurisdictional competition.

Cox, Regulatory Duopoly in U.S. Securities Markets, 99 Colum. L. Rev. 1200, 1230-1232 (1999). Consider just what conditions, including social, political, and economic forces, are likely to guide a country's promulgation of disclosure standards and whether those forces are likely to lead to a race among regulators to develop disclosure standards. If there is a race, is it one toward the top or the bottom?

3. Global Competitiveness of U.S. Capital Markets

A final dimension of the debate is whether U.S. capital markets are at a competitive disadvantage to more lightly regulated foreign markets.

> . . . A leading indicator of the competitiveness of U.S. public equity markets is the ability of the U.S. market to attract listings of foreign companies engaging in initial public offerings—so-called global IPOs. During the 1990s the number of foreign companies listed on the NYSE increased from 100 to almost 400. NASDAQ enjoyed similar fortunes, while the European exchanges, including London, lost market share. In the new millennium the trend seems to have reversed. . . .
>
> During 2000, one of every two dollars raised globally was raised in the United States, while, in 2005, approximately one in every 20 dollars was raised in the United States. Similarly, during the same period the percentage of global IPOs that chose to list in the United States declined from 37 percent to 10 percent. . . . Twenty-four of twenty-five of the largest IPOs in 2005 and nine of the ten largest IPOs in 2006 to date took place outside the United States. . . . The loss of market share exists in both the high-tech and non-high-tech sectors.

Interim Report of the Committee on Capital Markets Regulation (Dec. 2006). The Committee on Capital Market Regulation applauds the lighter regulation practiced by foreign markets—particular in the U.K. through the Financial Services Authority, which in place of a heavy reliance on enforcement follows a more advisory, prudential form of regulation. Another advantage of the FSA is that market participants face a single regulator rather than multiple regulators as occurs in the United States, where conduct frequently is the purview of SROs or state and federal regulators. Others sound a more sanguine note concerning the U.S. regulatory environment's impact on domestic capital markets, believing the increase in IPOs and listings enjoyed recently by non-U.S. markets reflects both the improved quality of foreign markets (rather than the unattractiveness of U.S. markets), weaknesses in the dollar, and a strategic need on the part of foreign issuers to list near their home countries. *See, e.g.,* Goldman Sachs Global Economics Weekly, No. 07/06 (Feb. 14, 2007); Doidge, Karolyi & Stulz, Has New York Become Less Competitive in Global Markets? Evaluating Foreign Listing Choices over Time, Ohio State Working Paper (April 2007) (observing steady decline in secondary listings on London and NYSE explained by firm characteristics but noting a listing premium persists for firms obtaining secondary listing on NYSE).

There continues to be a lively debate on whether and to what extent securities laws foster larger and more liquid capital markets. An important component of this inquiry is not just the law a country may have on its books, but rather the actual resources as well as the mechanisms devoted to enforcement. An important cross-national study of this question finds that countries that spend more in public enforcement have better capital market outcomes. *See* Jackson & Roe, Public and Private Enforcement of Securities Laws: Resource-Based Evidence, 93 J. Fin. Econ. 207 (2009).

4.   Implications of Vanishing Listings

Because of the inherent conflict between absent owners and wealth-seeking managers, Professor Michael Jensen famously declared that public firms are inefficient and can be expected to join unicorns as a vanishing species, or at least become endangered species. Jensen, Eclipse of the Public Corporation, 67 Harv. Bus. Rev. 61 (1989). In an important study, Professors Doidge, Karolyi, and Stulz provide support for Jensen's forewarning. They report that at least in the United States, public listings have seriously declined such that they are 39 percent lower than when Jensen wrote his classic article. Since robust capital markets are widely believed to signal economic vitality, is the decline in listings to be seen as the canary in the mine? Can the decline in listings over the past 23 years relative to the experience in other markets be attributed to over-regulation?

> The U.S. has experienced a dramatic decrease in the number of publicly-listed firms whereas listings increased in the rest of the world. As a result, the U.S. has developed a listing gap compared to other countries and this gap has become large, exceeding 5,000 firms. . . . The listing gap does not arise because there are fewer firms or startups. Though the size of the smallest listed firms is larger at the end of our sample than at the listing peak, all listed firms have generally become larger. While these changes indicate that the exchanges have become less hospitable to the smallest firms, the probability that a firm is listed has fallen for all firm sizes, albeit less so for the very largest firms. We conclude that firm size alone cannot explain the listing gap.
>
> Before the listing peak in 1996, the net new list rate in the U.S. was positive. After 1996, it was negative because the delist rate increased and the new list rate fell. We show that if the new list and delist rates from the pre-peak period applied after 1996, there would be no gap today. Similarly, the net new list rate in

non-U.S. countries was positive and sufficiently large after 1996 that there would be no gap if the U.S. had had new list and delist rates similar to these countries.

The listing gap cannot be explained by just the decrease in the new list rate. We show that the U.S. would still have a listing gap if the new list rate had not fallen. To explain the gap, one has to explain *both* the fall in the new list rate *and* the rise in the delist rate. We show that the delist rate rose because of an increase in merger activity involving publicly-listed targets. After 1996, the percentage of firms delisted for cause did not increase, but the percentage of firms delisted because of a merger did. Much has been made of the increase in firms going dark or going private after SOX. We show that the percentage of firms delisting voluntarily is too small to explain the listing gap or even to contribute meaningfully to closing the gap.

Doidge et al., The U.S. Listing Gap, NBER Working Paper No. 21181 (May 2015). Note that the authors reflect that the percentage of "startup" firms going public has steadily declined over the years and that the percentage of startup firms going public has similarly declined. How does this data match with the discussion of unicorns in Chapter 1? Are we seeing the impact of institutionalization of markets whereby a dynamic market for capital formation and investment exists outside the regulatory framework for being public? As you reflect on the regulatory premises that underlie the breadth of Section 5 of the Securities Act studied in this chapter, and as you learn about the many recent initiatives to deregulate capital formation outside Section 5 that are studied in Chapter 5, consider whether the listing gap is further evidence of an increasing "privateness" in our securities markets. *See generally* Thompson & Langevoort, Redrawing the Public-Private Boundaries in Entrepreneurial Capital Raising, 98 Cornell L. Rev. 1573 (2013).

NOTES AND QUESTIONS

1. Is More Always Better?   Consider whether arguments favoring mandatory disclosure rules premised on the economies inherent in the issuer producing the information, rather than numerous independent investors and financial intermediaries, run a serious risk of *overproviding* information. For users of information, more is always better, especially if the cost of acquiring it is borne by another—the issuer. Thus, disclosure policies and rules that are driven exclusively by the information demands of users lack natural constraints on the burdens to be imposed on issuers who must internalize all the costs of responding to the insatiable appetite of investors and financial intermediaries. The SEC bears responsibility for striking a healthy balance in this equation, but do historical inertia and political forces within and without the SEC impede its ability to discharge this task? The total costs of mandatory disclosure rules include more than the expense of gathering and disseminating the information. An important concern to issuers is the possible damage to a firm's competitiveness by requiring disclosure of otherwise confidential information about its business strategies. And with disclosure, there is the ever-present litigation risk, particularly in the case of forward-looking information, such as forecasts or appraisals. *See* Kitch, The Theory and Practice of Securities Disclosure, 61 Brook. L. Rev. 763 (1995).

   2.   *Empirical Inquiries into the Benefits of Disclosure.*   Two important critics of the utility of mandatory disclosure are Professors George Stigler and
George Benston, each of whom sought to demonstrate empirically that the '33
and '34 Acts neither enriched the information environment nor significantly
reduced the riskiness of investing. *See, e.g.,* Benston, The Value of the SEC's
Accounting Disclosure Requirements, 44 Acct. Rev. 515 (1969); Stigler, Public
Regulation of Securities Markets, 37 J. Bus. 117 (1964). Contrary to his hypothesis, Stigler's data reveals that stock prices were less volatile for the post-'33/
'34 Act firms he investigated than they were for the pre-'33/'34 Act firms in
his study. Undaunted, Stigler concludes that the overall effect of the securities
laws is to close capital markets to riskier firms. Benston supports his thesis that
adequate incentives exist for firms to voluntarily disclose financial information
with evidence that 62 percent of firms listed for trading on the New York Stock
Exchange voluntarily disclosed financial information prior to the '34 Act's disclosure requirements. What is the probative value of this when we consider that
after the '34 Act *all* exchange-traded firms had to make even more extensive disclosure than Benston found? On the value of additional disclosure, consider the
impact of the 1964 extension of periodic disclosure requirements to large over-
the-counter securities. Professor Allen Ferrell found that following this change,
the affected over-the-counter securities experienced significant declines in
volatility and positive abnormal returns. *See* Ferrell, Mandatory Disclosure and
Stock Returns: Evidence from the Over-the-Counter Market, 36 J. Legal Stud.
213 (2007). For a close analysis of the empirical studies that have framed much
of the mandatory disclosure debate, *see* Fox, Retaining Mandatory Securities
Disclosure: Why Issuer Choice Is Not Investor Empowerment, 85 Va. L. Rev.
1335, 1369-1394 (1999).

‖5‖
Exempt Transactions

A. Introduction

Not every transfer of capital involving a security will fully activate the 1933 and 1934 Acts. In many types of transactions, the disclosure requirements of the securities acts may seem less than compelling when balanced against other considerations, such as the sophistication of a given set of purchasers, the actual or theoretical likelihood of adequate state regulation, and the needs of businesses to raise comparatively small amounts of capital without the burdens of registration.

Accordingly, Sections 3 and 4 of the '33 Act set forth a series of exemptions relieving those involved in securities transactions of the need to comply with the registration provisions of the Act and, to a limited extent, the antifraud provisions of the '33 and '34 Acts. The exemptions are of critical importance. In 2018 alone, exempt offerings totaled nearly $3 trillion. This compares with $1.4 trillion raised in registered offerings. *See* Securities Act Release 33-10649 (June 18, 2019).

The exemptions fall into two classes. *Transaction exemptions* provide an exemption only from the registration provisions of Section 5 of the '33 Act. Securities placed under one of these exemptions remain subject to both the '33 and the '34 Acts and, importantly, cannot be resold unless either they are registered or another exemption is available. *Exempt securities,* on the other hand, need not be registered, but also may be resold free of registration burdens. Determining that a security is exempt, however, does not negate application of the securities acts in their entirety, for exempt securities remain subject (to varying degrees) to the antifraud provisions of the '33 and '34 Acts.

This chapter focuses on the more important of the transaction exemptions that may be available to issuers and, to a lesser extent, other sellers of securities. Chapter 6 covers the difficult terrain of exemptions for sales by underwriters, control persons, and dealers; Chapter 7 explores exemptions available in the case of corporate reorganizations and recapitalizations; and Chapter 8 treats some of the more important classes of exempt securities.

Although the various exemptions are often technical and complex in nature, keep in mind the "big picture" as you study each. Specifically, identify at the earliest possible point the *reason* a particular exemption exists. Then, evaluate the degree to which the law has developed to effectuate the *purpose* of the exemption. Finally, consider the problem of *indeterminacy* by evaluating whether standards found in cases, safe harbor rules, or other sources permit the seller (usually the issuer) to structure a transaction with the confidence that it can comply with the exemption and thereby not run afoul of Section 5's prohibitions against offers and sales of unregistered securities. As to the latter point, remember that the burden of proof will fall on the seller to establish that all of the conditions of the exemption have been satisfied.

Also keep in mind the provisions of the National Securities Markets Improvement Act of 1996 relevant to registration and exemptions. Specifically, the legislation added Section 28 to the '33 Act authorizing the Commission to exempt persons, securities, or transactions from all or part of the Securities Act. Section 28 potentially represents a significant expansion of administrative authority over that contained in Section 3(b)(1), which authorizes the Commission to exempt (from registration) issuances that do not exceed an aggregate amount of $5 million. Although the Commission has been slow in utilizing its expanded authority, recent initiatives reveal a willingness to utilize Section 28. Also, the 2012 Jumpstart Our Business Startups Act (JOBS Act) expanded SEC exemptive authority through a new Section 3(b)(2) directing the Commission to develop a new exemption for offerings not exceeding an aggregate offering amount of $50 million (the intention being that the higher offering amount will be used to revitalize the Regulation A exemption, discussed later).

In part due to changes in exemptions stemming from the JOBS Act, the overall framework for exempt offerings has changed significantly in recent years. Recognizing that the capital markets, issuers, and investors would benefit from a review and updating of the existing framework, the SEC has issued the Concept Release on Harmonization of Securities Offering Exemptions, which seeks comments on ways that the exemptions may be improved and harmonized. *See* Securities Act Release 33-10649 (June 18, 2019). As appropriate, the comments and questions posed in this release will be noted in the following discussion of the '33 Act's exemptions.

B.   The Private Offering Exemption: Section 4(a)(2)

Section 4(a)(2) of the '33 Act exempts "transactions by an issuer not involving any public offering."

The notion that certain types of discrete, face-to-face transactions between an issuer and a sophisticated investor should not be subject to the time and expense problems of the registration process is uncontroversial and is a premise accepted by all of the Western world's securities regimes. The easiest cases are those in which institutional investors, such as insurance companies and pension funds, are the purchasers in private placements. In such cases, the concern over information asymmetry (i.e., one party to the transaction is in possession of relevant information not known by the other party) is obviated to a considerable extent. Most institutional investors, we may assume, are sophisticated investors who know what to ask and are capable of protecting their own interests. Accordingly, the protections afforded by the registration process are unnecessary because the purchasers have the requisite expertise and bargaining leverage to obtain relevant information and negotiate concessions necessary to protect their investments.

Institutional investors are the important players in the private placement market, but they are not the only players. Individual investors with varying degrees of financial acumen and bargaining leverage are common targets of issuers seeking to sell securities under the private offering exemption. In these cases, the problem becomes one of defining the types of "private offerings" for which the protections of registration are unnecessary to correct any informational asymmetry that may exist between the parties.

As is often the case with exemptions, we have the problem under Section 4(a)(2) of defining the scope of a terse statutory exemption. This task is not made easier by sparse legislative history indicating, simply, the exemption is needed to "permit an issuer to make a specific or an isolated sale of its securities to a particular person, but if a sale of the issuer's stock should be made generally to the public that transaction would come within the purview of the Act." Between the isolated sale of securities to a particular person and the public sale of securities lies an infinite variety of transactions that have provided ample fodder for the development of the confusing and complicated law of private placements.

1.   Mapping the Scope of the Exemption

The first meaningful guidance on the circumstances under which the private offering exemption would be available came in the form of a letter by the general counsel of the SEC published in a 1935 release. *See* Securities Act Release No. 285, 1 Fed. Sec. L. Rep. (CCH) ¶2741-2744 (Jan. 24, 1935). The opinion identified four factors of particular importance:

1.   *The Number of Offerees and Their Relationship to Each Other and to the Issuer.* The number of offerees—not purchasers—is the critical inquiry.
2.   *The Number of Units Offered.* The issuance of securities in a large number of units of small denominations is an indication the issuer anticipates subsequent public trading in the securities.
3.   *The Size of the Offering.* The exemption was intended to apply chiefly to small offerings.
4.   *The Manner of Offering.* Transactions effectuated through direct negotiations are more likely to be private offerings than those effected through the use of the machinery of public distribution (such as advertising).

For nearly two decades, the general counsel's opinion was the authoritative statement on the private offering exemption. Although courts continue to cite the factors outlined by the general counsel in 1935, the focus of the inquiry shifted with the 1953 decision of the Supreme Court in *SEC v. Ralston Purina Co.*, which follows.

Securities and Exchange Commission v. Ralston Purina Co.
346 U.S. 119 (1953)

CLARK, J. . . . We must decide whether Ralston Purina's offerings of treasury stock to its "key employees" are within [the private offering exemption]. On a complaint brought by the Commission under §20(b) of the Act seeking to enjoin respondent's unregistered offerings, the District Court held the exemption applicable and dismissed the suit. The Court of Appeals affirmed. The question has arisen many times since the Act was passed; an apparent need to define the scope of the private offering exemption prompted certiorari. . . .

Ralston Purina manufactures and distributes various feed and cereal products. Its processing and distribution facilities are scattered throughout the United States and Canada, staffed by some 7,000 employees. At least since 1911 the company has had a policy of encouraging stock ownership among its employees; more particularly, since 1942 it has made authorized but unissued common shares available to some of them. Between 1947 and 1951, the period covered by the record in this case, Ralston Purina sold nearly $2,000,000 of stock to employees without registration and in so doing made use of the mails.

In each of these years, a corporate resolution authorized the sale of common stock "to employees . . . who shall, without any solicitation by the Company or its officers or employees, inquire of any of them as to how to purchase common stock of Ralston Purina Company." A memorandum sent to branch and store managers after the resolution was adopted, advised that "The only employees to whom this stock will be available will be those who take the initiative and are interested in buying stock at present market prices." Among those responding to these offers were employees with the duties of artist, bakeshop foreman, chow loading foreman, clerical assistant, copywriter, electrician, stock clerk, mill office clerk, order credit trainee, production trainee, stenographer, and veterinarian. The buyers lived in over fifty widely separated communities. . . . The lowest salary bracket of those purchasing was $2,700 in 1949, $2,435 in 1950 and $3,107 in 1951. The record shows that in 1947, 243 employees bought stock, 20 in 1948, 414 in 1949, 411 in 1950, and the 1951 offer, interrupted by this litigation, produced 165 applications to purchase. No records were kept of those to whom the offers were made; the estimated number in 1951 was 500.

The company bottoms its exemption claim on the classification of all offerees as "key employees" in its organization. Its position on trial was that

broad def.

> A key employee . . . is not confined to an organization chart. It would include an individual who is eligible for promotion, an individual who especially influences others or who advises others, a person whom the employees look to in some special way, an individual, of course, who carries some special responsibility, who is sympathetic to management and who is ambitious and who the management feels is likely to be promoted to a greater responsibility.

That an offering to all of its employees would be public is conceded.

The Securities Act nowhere defines the scope of §[4(a)(2)'s] private offering exemption. Nor is the legislative history of much help in staking out its boundaries. . . .

Decisions under comparable exemptions in the English Companies Acts and state "blue sky" laws, the statutory antecedents of federal securities legislation, have made one thing clear—to be public, an offer need not be open to the whole world. . . .

Exemption from the registration requirements of the Securities Act is the question. The design of the statute is to protect investors by promoting full disclosure of information thought necessary to informed investment decisions. . . . Since exempt transactions are those as to which "there is no practical need for [the bill's] application," the applicability of §[4(a)(2)] should turn on whether the particular class of persons affected needs the protection of the Act. An offering to those who are shown to be able to fend for themselves is a transaction "not involving any public offering."

The Commission would have us go one step further and hold that "an offering to a substantial number of the public" is not exempt under §[4(a)(2)]. We are advised that "whatever the special circumstances, the Commission has consistently interpreted the exemption as being inapplicable when a large number of offerees is involved." But the statute would seem to apply to a "public offering" whether to few or many. It may well be that offerings to a substantial number of persons would rarely be exempt. Indeed nothing prevents the commission, in enforcing the statute, from using some kind of numerical test in deciding when to investigate particular exemption claims. But there is no warrant for superimposing a quantity limit on private offerings as a matter of statutory interpretation.

The exemption, as we construe [it], does not deprive corporate employees, as a class, of the safeguards of the Act. We agree that some employee offerings may come within §[4(a)(2)], e.g., one made to executive personnel who because of their position have access to the same kind of information that the act would make available in the form of a registration statement. Absent such a showing of special circumstances, employees are just as much members of the investing "public" as any of their neighbors in the community. . . .

Keeping in mind the broadly remedial purposes of federal securities legislation, imposition of the burden of proof on an issuer who would plead the exemption seems to us fair and reasonable. . . . Agreeing, the court below thought the burden met primarily because of the respondent's purpose in singling out its key employees for stock offerings. But once it is seen that the exemption question turns on the knowledge of the offerees, the issuer's motives, laudable though they may be, fade into irrelevance.

The focus of inquiry should be on the need of the offerees for the protections afforded by registration. The employees here were not shown to have access to the kind of information which registration would disclose. The obvious opportunities for pressure and imposition make it advisable that they be entitled to compliance with §5.

Reversed.

PROBLEM

5-1.   Ralston decides to reestablish its stock plan in conformity with the Supreme Court's opinion. It limits participation in the plan to officers at the level of vice president or higher, directors, and plant managers. Does the access to information these individuals may have raise questions regarding improper insider trading because of the use of the information? Moreover, does a vice president of personnel necessarily have the kind of access to information the Court in *Ralston* had in mind? Does a plant manager?

2.   The Relevance of Numbers

The general counsel's 1935 opinion suggested that an offering to not more than 25 individuals is presumably not a public offering. Prior to *Ralston*, some issuers viewed this as a rule of thumb and concluded they could safely proceed with an offering directed to 25 or fewer people.

Although *Ralston* has had the effect of negating any numerically based guidelines for determining the scope of the statutory exemption (as opposed to the legitimacy of an SEC safe harbor), it may be read only as rejecting a quantity limit *above* which an offering is necessarily public in nature. That is, the *Ralston* Court rejected the SEC's argument that the large number of individuals given the opportunity to participate in the stock purchase plan was in and of itself conclusive proof the offering was not private. The Court did not say, however, that the use of a number below which an offering will be deemed private is not permissible.

In any event, *Ralston* eventually prompted the SEC to terminate the use of numerical tests either to set a ceiling above which an offering would be deemed public or to establish a floor below which it would be considered private. Nevertheless, courts continue to view a large number of offerees as indicative of a public rather than a private offering. *See, e.g., SEC v. Earthly Mineral Solutions, Inc.*, 2011 U.S. Dist. LEXIS 36767 (D. Nev. Mar. 23, 2011) (exemption not available when issuer conducted general solicitations through newspaper advertisements, raised over $18 million, and offered and sold the securities to more than 100 investors). As the number of offerees increases, the issuer's burden of proof that all offerees had the requisite access to information becomes more difficult to carry. A small number of offerees, on the other hand, does not negate the possibility of a public offering. *See, e.g., Butler v. Phlo Corp.*, 2001 U.S. Dist. LEXIS 10809 (S.D.N.Y. July 31, 2001) (two offerees may constitute a public offering).

3.   Offeree Qualification: Sophistication and Access to Information

PROBLEM

5-2.   Nolotek is an oil and gas operation that would like to make a private placement of unsecured debentures to Herb, a high school dropout who recently won $5 million in the state lottery. There are no other offerees, and resale of the securities will be restricted to prevent the possibility of a public distribution. Because it feels an offering limited to one person is, by definition, a private offering, Nolotek does not intend to incur the expense of preparing a disclosure document for Herb; it is willing, however, to answer any of his questions. Under *Ralston*, is Nolotek safe?

Much of the post-*Ralston* litigation concerning the private offering exemption has centered on identifying the types of persons in need of the protections afforded by registration and therefore ineligible subjects of private offerings. *See, e.g., SEC v. Trujillo,* 2010 U.S. Dist. LEXIS 99208, 18-19 (D. Colo. Sept. 22, 2010) ("Mere acknowledgment by [investors] that they had the opportunity to ask questions and evaluate the merits and risks of the investment is not sufficient to demonstrate that they had access to the information that would be disclosed in a registration statement.").

Although the Supreme Court in *Ralston* emphasized *access to information* as the critical inquiry, it also commented that an offering is not public when limited to those who are "able to fend for themselves." This raises a number of questions. What constitutes access to information? Do only insiders of an issuer have access? What is the relevance of sophistication, and is this enough to obviate inquiries into access? Is the lack of sophistication on the part of the offerees relevant when they have been given access to information? Can a private offering ever be directed at unsophisticated investors? What is sophistication?

A line of cases from the Fifth Circuit provides the most systematic attempt to deal with issues underlying the private placement exemption. In the first of the cases, *Hill York Corp. v. American International Franchises, Inc.,* 448 F.2d 680 (5th Cir. 1971), stock in a nationwide franchise operation was offered to an undetermined number of sophisticated investors, none of whom had a prior relationship with the issuer. Thirteen purchased the stock. The relationship of the offerees to each other and the issuer was not sufficient, the Fifth Circuit concluded, to justify treating this offering as private rather than public in scope. The offerees knew neither the issuer nor its business, and they lacked a *privileged relationship* with the issuer. Without access to information and the information itself, the offerees were in need of the protections of registration. The fact that they were sophisticated, and therefore were arguably able to fend for themselves, was irrelevant. In short, sophistication of the purchasers is no substitute for information. *See also In re Enron Corp. Sec., Derivative & ERISA Litig.,* 761 F. Supp. 2d 504, 551 (S.D. Tex. 2011) (the *Ralston* standard "is based more on access to information than a party's sophistication and wealth. Where a party has no ability to obtain the vital, material information about the investment, the exemption should not apply.").

The next year, the Fifth Circuit considered whether gratuitously giving offerees information equivalent to that provided in a registration statement could salvage a private offering when the offerees lacked the type of "privileged relationship" that would ensure them access to the same information. In *SEC v. Continental Tobacco Co.,* 463 F.2d 137 (5th Cir. 1972), the issuer was a manufacturer of a product that, at the time, was quite innovative—a low-tar and low-nicotine cigarette. The offering was conducted through group meetings with 38 prospective investors, some of whom had previously purchased unregistered debentures of the company. The SEC argued it is not enough to merely provide information tantamount to that which would have been made available through the registration process:

> [T]he issuer must affirmatively demonstrate by "explicit, exact" evidence that *each* person to whom unregistered securities were offered was able to "fend" for himself—in other words, that each offeree had a *relationship* to the company *tantamount* to that of an "insider" in terms of his ability to know, to understand and to verify for himself all of the relevant facts about the company and its securities.

This rather startling position that insider status was a condition precedent to offeree qualification prompted one commissioner to distance himself from the staff and publicly repudiate the argument advanced in the SEC's brief.

In reasoning the private exemption was unavailable, the Fifth Circuit said both a little and a lot. The court concluded that Continental had not carried its burden of showing that all offerees had received information about the company, and it also summarily observed that the prospectus used did not include all of the information that would be provided in a registration statement. Since the issuer relied heavily upon the information it had provided as a basis of satisfying the "access" requirement, this aspect of the opinion is unexceptional. The court went on to add, however, that supplying information equivalent to that in a registration statement would not have been enough, for not only must the offerees have been provided with the opportunity to obtain *additional* information, but also each offeree must have had personal contact with the officers of the issuer. Although the court did not embrace explicitly the SEC's position that insider status is a condition precedent to a private offering, it could be read to stand for just that proposition. *See, e.g., Butler v. Phlo Corp.,* 2001 U.S. Dist. LEXIS 10809 (S.D.N.Y. July 31, 2001) (individual who was issuer's founder and a former officer and director did not have access to information following his resignation).

A private offering exemption conditioned on the status of each offeree as an insider would sharply curtail use of this important method of financing, and it was not long before the Fifth Circuit began to reconsider the implications of *Continental.* Its first opportunity came in *Woolf v. S.D. Cohn & Co.,* 515 F.2d 591 (5th Cir. 1975), *vacated and remanded on other grounds,* 426 U.S. 944 (1976), where the court rather cryptically commented that those who have read *Continental* to require insider status are incorrect. A fuller analysis was offered in *Doran v. Petroleum Management Corp.,* 545 F.2d 893 (5th Cir. 1977), where the investor in an oil drilling limited partnership had previously invested in 26 oil and gas properties and had a net worth in excess of $1 million that included holdings in 26 oil and gas properties (not to mention a petroleum engineering degree from Texas A&M). Although the Fifth Circuit acknowledged the investor was sophisticated, it cautioned a finding of sophistication does not end the inquiry:

> In short, there must be a sufficient basis of accurate information upon which the sophisticated investor must be able to exercise his skills. Just as a scientist cannot be without his specimens, so the shrewdest investor's acuity will be blunted without specifications about the issuer. For an investor to be invested with exemptive status he must have the required data for judgment.

Id. at 903.

Sophistication, in short, does not eliminate the need for information. As to how an information standard is to be satisfied, *Doran* concluded that availability of information means "either disclosure of or effective access to the relevant information." If the *disclosure* option is exercised, the absence of a relationship between the issuer and the offeree would not preclude a finding that offering was private. If *access* to information is the measure, on the other hand, the relationship between the issuer and the offeree becomes the critical question:

> Such access might be afforded merely by the position of the offeree or by the issuer's promise to open appropriate files and records to the offeree as well as to answer inquiries regarding material information. In either case, the relationship between the offeree and issuer now becomes critical, for it must be shown that the offeree could realistically have been expected to take advantage of his access to ascertain the relevant information. Similarly, the investment sophistication of the offeree assumes added importance, for it is important that he could have been expected to ask the right questions and seek out the relevant information.

Id. at 904-905. In this way, *Doran* rejected a reading of *Continental Tobacco* that would condition the private placement exemption on the status of offerees as insiders. The court observed that "any such requirement would inhibit the ability of business to raise capital without the expense and delay of registration under circumstances in which the offerees did not need the protection of registration." Id. at 908.

❙❙ Securities and Exchange Commission v. Kenton Capital, Ltd.
69 F. Supp. 2d 1 (D.D.C. 1998)

[Kenton Capital, LTD (Kenton) is an entity incorporated in the Cayman Islands, British West Indies. Donald Wallace is Kenton's president. Wallace arranged for Jeffrey Carter, who knew a number of potential investors, to act as a consultant for Kenton. Carter arranged for Atlantic Pacific Guarantee Corporation (AP) to issue surety bonds as insurance for investors even though AP was not licensed to engage in this activity. From a hotel room in Little Rock, Arkansas, Carter contacted prospective investors about providing capital to Kenton so that the firm could run a "trading program." Carter sent agreements to investors describing trading programs with projected returns of 3750 percent per week for 40 weeks. Wallace signed these agreements, but he did not monitor Carter's representations to investors. Wallace has since stated that the projected profits were "not achievable," and that he had "no basis" for representing that they were achievable. On the basis of these representations, over 40 investors pledged to invest approximately $1,700,000 in Kenton's trading program. The SEC initiated this action alleging, in part, violations of the registration provisions of the '33 Act.]

1.   SECTION 4[(A)](2) EXEMPTION FOR "PRIVATE OFFERINGS"

. . . Defendants assert, and the SEC does not dispute, that the number of offerees was limited, and that the manner of the offering was not a general solicitation. The SEC does dispute, however, Defendants' claims regarding the sophistication of Kenton's offerees, and the offerees' access to information. The Court will consider these two factors in turn.

Defendants support their allegation that their offerees were sophisticated by evidence that they screened their offerees. Wallace testified that he developed a checklist of information that was required of all investors, which was included in the material that Kenton sent to investors. Closer examination of this list, however, reveals that the information requested therein consisted of a photocopy of the investor's passport, a copy of the investor's driver's license or social security card, and a bank reference showing the investor to be in good standing with a bank. This information is wholly irrelevant to the sophistication of the offerees. The Court is equally unimpressed by Wallace's contention that Kenton's minimum investment requirement provided any safeguard of investor sophistication.

Even if the Court were to find that Defendants had created an issue of material fact with respect to investor sophistication, "sophistication is not a substitute for access to the information that registration would disclose." *Doran v. Petroleum Management Corp.*, 545 F.2d 893, 902-903 (5th Cir. 1977) (holding that an engineering degree, investment experience, and large net worth were insufficient to show a private offering exemption absent a "sufficient basis of accurate information upon which the sophisticated investor may exercise his skills"). With respect to the offerees' access to information, Defendants claim that "investors were given the names and telephone numbers of [Kenton] officials and sales agents of whom they could ask questions" and that "at least some investors" received copies of AP's financial statements. Defendants have offered no evidence, however, that Kenton even possessed the kind of information that would normally be disclosed in a registration statement. Absent any evidence that Defendants provided sophisticated investors with meaningful access to information equivalent to that which would have been provided in a registration statement, the Court concludes that Defendants do not qualify for an exemption from section 5's registration requirements.

NOTES AND QUESTIONS

1. Protecting Offerees. As *Ralston* and virtually every other case on Section 4(a)(2) make clear, the critical inquiry concerning the private offering exemption is the need of the *offerees*—not just the purchasers—for protection. This places a significant burden on the issuer not only to prequalify offerees, but also to keep careful records to permit later substantiation of their backgrounds. The task is not made easier through the use of salespersons more motivated in closing deals than complying with the niceties of the federal securities laws.

In addition to prequalifying offerees by requiring them to complete information sheets concerning their background and experience, cautious issuers number all informational materials sent to offerees. This is so they can later provide convincing information on the qualifications of *all* offerees. *See, e.g., SEC v. StratoComm Corp.*, 2 F. Supp. 3d 240 (N.D.N.Y. 2014) (issuer's failure to provide evidence on the exact number and identities of offerees supports denial of exemption).

What is the justification for tying the exemption to the needs of the offerees rather than the purchasers? Why are offerees who never become purchasers in need of the protections of the federal securities laws? May Section 4(a)(2) be construed in a way to emphasize the positions of purchasers rather than offerees?

2. *The Quality of Disclosures.*   *Kenton Capital* and other cases speak of disclosures tantamount to that which would have been provided in a registration statement. *See, e.g., SEC v. Empire Dev. Group, LLC,* 2008 U.S. Dist. LEXIS 43509 (S.D.N.Y. May 30, 2008) (exemption not available because investors were not given the "same" information a registration statement would have provided). The point of reference for making such disclosures is Schedule A of the '33 Act, which sets forth a list of 32 matters that should be disclosed in any registration statement. The cautious issuer will make the disclosures in connection with a private offering by means of a carefully prepared (and lengthy) document known as the offering circular. Although some practitioners favor more abbreviated disclosures, including less than Schedule A type disclosures in the offering circular may prove risky. For example, in *Direct Benefits, LLC v. TAC Fin. Inc.,* 2014 U.S. Dist. LEXIS 20941 (D. Md. Feb. 20, 2014), the court concluded that failing to provide even sophisticated investors with the same financial information they would receive through a registration statement negates the argument they had access to information under the *Ralston* standard. Along a similar line, the court in *SEC v. Alternate Energy Holdings, Inc.,* 2014 U.S. Dist. LEXIS 66401 (D. Idaho May 13, 2014), pointedly observed that providing investors with a company's annual report is not the same as providing them with the detailed information that would be available in a registration statement.

Apart from the risk that a court will later determine that inadequate disclosures undermined a purported private offering, what are the dangers in use of an abbreviated disclosure document?

3. *Unsophisticated Offerees.*   Assuming the requisite access to information exists and disclosures tantamount to those of a registration statement are made, may an issuer make a private offering to a small group of unsophisticated offerees? There are differences of opinion on this question. In *Lively v. Hirschfeld,* 440 F.2d 631 (10th Cir. 1971), the Tenth Circuit suggested only "persons of exceptional business experience" would be qualified offerees in a private placement transaction. Yet in later cases this same circuit indicated sophistication of offerees is a relevant, but not necessarily essential condition to the availability of the exemption. *See, e.g., Cowles v. Dow Keith Oil & Gas, Inc.,* 752 F.2d 508 (10th Cir. 1985), *cert. denied,* 479 U.S. 816 (1986). The Ninth Circuit treats sophistication as one of four factors (the others being the number of offerees, the size and manner of the offering, and the relationship of the offerees to the issuer), forming parts of "flexible tests" used to distinguish public from private offerings. *See, e.g., SEC v. Murphy,* 626 F.2d 633 (9th Cir. 1980). The Fifth Circuit seems to place greater emphasis on disclosures than sophistication and admits that evidence of offeree sophistication is not required in all cases in which the availability of the private offering exemption is asserted. *See, e.g., Doran v. Petroleum Management Corp.,* supra. And the Eighth Circuit seems not to require sophistication and emphasizes the offerees' access to information, *e.g., Van Dyke v. Coburn Enters.,*

Inc., 873 F.2d 1094, 1098 (8th Cir. 1989) ("[T]he appellants had the economic bargaining power to demand any information necessary to make an informed investment decision.").

    4. Who's Sophisticated? Even though many cases have tied the availability of the private placement exemption to the sophistication of offerees, there is little in the cases to suggest exactly what is meant by sophistication. Courts sometimes avoid the issue by simply stating the exemption was not satisfied because the defendant was unable to produce evidence that *all* the offerees were sophisticated. *See, e.g., Mark v. FSC Sec. Corp.*, 870 F.2d 331, 335-336 (6th Cir. 1989). More frequently, sophistication either is not at issue or is assumed away by the court. *See, e.g., Acme Propane, Inc. v. Tenexco, Inc.*, 844 F.2d 1317, 1321 (7th Cir. 1988) ("the complaint does not portray the buyers as tenderfeet"). In between these polar approaches, there is only an occasional glimpse of what factors support a finding of sophistication. *See, e.g., Lively v. Hirschfeld,* 440 F.2d 631, 633 (10th Cir. 1971) (all offerees must have "exceptional business experience"). Notwithstanding the tendency of some courts to label offerees as either sophisticated or unsophisticated, sophistication is best viewed as a matter of degree rather than an all-or-nothing proposition.

    The elusiveness of sophistication as a standard is aptly illustrated by *Hedden v. Marinelli,* 796 F. Supp. 432 (N.D. Cal. 1992), where one of the investors had a bachelor's degree in economics from Stanford as well as a law degree from Hastings; he also was the founding director of a bank and trust company. The other investor had invested in many stock transactions involving sums exceeding $50,000 and had been the CEO of the company the stock of which he was purchasing. Yet the court refused to conclude for summary judgment purposes that "these individuals were sufficiently sophisticated to not require the protections of the 1933 Act."

    Irrespective of the standard of sophistication, how is the issuer to measure the sophistication of a *prospective* offeree before having the types of contacts with the offeree that might constitute offers? Consider *Feldman v. Concord Equity Partners, LLC,* 2010 U.S. Dist. LEXIS 49613 (S.D.N.Y. May 19, 2010), where Feldman, a purchaser in a purported private placement, had originally been approached by Schulte with the idea of creating an investment firm that would be headed by Feldman:

> The evidence indicates that Schulte was simply soliciting participation and financial support for a start-up business. Feldman agreed to invest because Schulte said that principals would be expected to contribute capital to the new venture, not because he was offered securities by one of the Defendants. To hold that such preliminary discussions trigger securities law registration requirements would create a severe impediment to the creation of small businesses. Second, even if the Court were to consider those discussions an "offer" within the meaning of securities laws, Feldman . . . agreed to become an executive officer of the firm before he was "offered" securities by Schulte. . . . As an executive officer and initial member who played an integral role in starting the business, there is no indication that Feldman was not privy to all material information and the risks of investment when he purchased equity in the company. The law does not contemplate that executive officers such as Plaintiff, with his level of access to information, be able to avail themselves of Section 12(a)(1).

Do you agree that in the context of enticing an individual to invest in and manage a startup firm, "preliminary discussions" are not offers of securities?

5. *Sophistication in Other Contexts.* Oddly enough, more guidance on the meaning of sophistication is provided in other areas of securities law where the investor's sophistication is of pivotal importance. As will be seen in Chapter 6, the ability of a control person of an issuer to resell that issuer's securities frequently turns on whether the buyer is sophisticated. For example, in *Ackerberg v. Johnson*, 892 F.2d 1328 (8th Cir. 1989), the court concluded the control person's buyer was sophisticated because his net income was $200,000, his net worth was in excess of $1 million, and his trading account totaled around $500,000. While these facts do suggest a level of comfort and perhaps even success generally, do they necessarily bespeak sophistication?

The *Ackerberg* court emphasized that the purchaser had signed a subscription agreement acknowledging that he had experience and knowledge in investing and was able to evaluate the merits and risks of the purchase. To what extent should this type of self-serving statement be sufficient to establish sophistication? *Cf.* Securities Act Section 14 ("Any condition, stipulation, or provision binding any person to waive compliance with any provision of this title or the rules and regulations of the Commission shall be void.").

Far greater insight into the meaning of sophistication may be gleaned from the so-called suitability cases, in which plaintiffs allege brokers failed to disclose that the securities they were recommending were too risky to be suitable for plaintiffs' brokerage accounts. Where plaintiffs understand that devices and investments such as "puts," "calls," and "junk bonds" entail unusual levels of risk, disclosures as to suitability are unnecessary. In a leading suitability case, the plaintiff was deemed sophisticated because he had a college degree in accounting, could read and understand financial reports, and was a regular reader of investment advisory literature. *See Follansbee v. Davis, Skaggs & Co.*, 681 F.2d 673 (9th Cir. 1982). In contrast, the proverbial retired schoolteacher recovered against her broker for his failure to disclose that "junk bonds" were unsuitable for her account. *See Clark v. John Lamula Investors, Inc.*, 583 F.2d 594 (2d Cir. 1978). *See also SEC v. Trujillo*, 2010 U.S. Dist. LEXIS 99208 (D. Colo. Sept. 22, 2010) (evidence investors signed subscription agreements affirming they had opportunities to ask questions actually suggests they are the very type of investors who need the protections of the registration provisions).

All of this leads to the following paradox:

> [T]he SEC's and Congress's attempts to exempt securities offered and sold to sophisticated investors have created a legal paradox: the scheme requires registration of securities offered to *unsophisticated* investors, thus ensuring that people who do not read prospectuses receive copies of them, but exempts securities offered to *sophisticated* investors who would read and benefit from prospectuses if they received them. A legal structure that creates such anomaly demands reconsideration.

Fletcher, Sophisticated Investors Under the Federal Securities Laws, 1988 Duke L.J. 1081, 1125-1126. Do you agree? And, consider the oddity of requiring sophistication of investors for some types of transactions but not others:

> Regulation has, until recently, greatly limited [unsophisticated] investors' access to new offerings. The irony of this regulatory choice is that investors who fall into this group are permitted to purchase, with abandon, securities sold on public markets, including the unregulated Pink Sheet Market where issuers that do not comply with SEC reporting requirements trade. They are not, however, permitted

to acquire unregistered securities offered by the issuer. Thus, their protection depends not on what they purchase, but the medium with which they pursue the investment.

Cox, Who Can't Raise Capital?: The Scylla and Charybdis of Capital Formation, 102 Ky. L.J. 1, 5 (2013-2014).

6.   The Relevance of Risk.   Outside the safe harbor of Rule 506, the ability of offerees to assume that risk has not emerged as a factor in assessing the availability of the private offering exemption. What are the policy considerations for and against considering elements of risk and risk-bearing ability?

PROBLEMS

5-3.   Two physicians recently sold their interests in a medical center for a sizable profit. Flush with cash and in urgent need of a tax shelter, they commence negotiations with a promoter experienced in developing and operating oil and gas limited partnerships. The physicians have <u>no experience with oil and gas ventures</u>, but they have made a number of past investments in real estate ventures. Over the next three months, the physicians and the promoter work on developing a limited partnership custom tailored to meet the physicians' needs. In the view of the physicians, this is an educational process, and by the time the agreement is struck and they make an investment of $700,000, they are quite confident about their own level of expertise on the oil and gas business. How sophisticated are these investors? How easy will it be for them in a subsequent suit to establish their lack of sophistication? What level of disclosures is required in order for the promoter to protect itself? *Cf. Bayoud v. Ballard,* 404 F. Supp. 417 (N.D. Tex. 1975).

5-4.   Same facts as above, but the physicians have also hired a lawyer to review the documents. How active must the lawyer be before her involvement is relevant to the question of the offeree's sophistication? Is the lawyer's background in practice relevant, or are lawyers conclusively presumed to be sophisticated? Have you received the training necessary to represent the physicians in this oil and gas private offering? Will you before you graduate from law school?

4.   Resales of Securities Acquired in a Private Offering

Because Section 4(a)(2) is transactional in nature, the private offering cannot be used as a subterfuge for a public offering by making a private placement to a small group of individuals who then proceed to sell the securities to the public. The issuer is vitally concerned with the effect of resales, for a determination that supposed investors were actually acting as conduits in a public offering will retroactively negate the validity of the original transaction as a private placement.

Of course, this does not mean securities acquired in a private offering can never be resold. As is discussed more fully in Chapter 6, the critical question is whether any of the purchasers acquired the securities with a view to their distribution, rather than as investment (an intent to hold for the long term). Issuers commonly take three steps to avoid the problem of initial purchasers' acting as conduits in the public distribution of securities. First, they require purchasers to sign statements of investment intent. Although these types of statements are somewhat self-serving, they do serve to make sure the investors are aware that they are receiving unregistered securities the transfer of which is restricted. Second, issuers normally inscribe securities placed in a private offering to disclose that the securities are unregistered and a transfer may take place only if specified conditions (such as an opinion of counsel that an exemption from registration is available) are satisfied. Finally, issuers customarily put into effect stop-transfer orders instructing the transfer agent not to process any transfers of restricted securities without the consent of the issuers. Although the statutory exemption is not conditioned on the presence of any or all of these devices to restrict transferability, the absence of such corrective measures is difficult to explain and may lead to the denial of the exemption. *See, e.g., United States v. Hill*, 298 F. Supp. 1221 (D. Conn. 1969).

C.   *Regulation D and the Limited Offering Exemptions*

Regulation D provides two exemptions that together cover the vast majority of offerings exempt from registration.[1] Although the exemptions under Rules 504 and 506 coexist within a single regulation and contain many common conditions, the limited offering exemptions of Regulation D rest upon two distinct statutory foundations. Rule 504 was promulgated on the basis of Section 3(b)(1) of the '33 Act, which authorizes the SEC to develop exemptions covering offerings up to $5 million in amount when registration is not necessary to protect the public interest or investors. Rule 506, on the other hand, represents a nonexclusive safe harbor for the private offering exemption of Section 4(a)(2).

Regulation D offers the most important exemptions from the registration requirements. In 2017, there were 37,785 Regulation D offerings accounting for more than $1.8 trillion in new capital raised by issuers. *See* Baguess, Gullapalli & Ivanov, Capital Raising in the U.S.: An Analysis of the Market for Unregistered Securities Offerings, 2009-2017 2 (SEC White Paper, Aug. 2018). Regulation D is especially important both to pooled fund issuers (e.g., hedge funds and venture capital funds) and to newer nonfinancial businesses formed within three years of their offerings (the median size of offerings by nonfinancial issuers is less than $1 million). Id. at 2.

---

    1. 2016 amendments to Regulation D pared the exemptions from three to two. Rule 505 has been eliminated, and Rule 504 has been broadened to fill the void.

1.   An Overview of Regulation D

Rules 504 and 506 must be read in conjunction with Rules 500-503 and 507-508, which provide conditions applicable, for the most part, to both exemptions. The principal conditions of each of the exemptions are:

> **Rule 504**—Maximum aggregate offering price of $5 million (increased from $1 million in 2016); not available for reporting companies or investment companies; no limitations on the number of purchasers; no affirmative disclosure obligations; resale of securities is restricted except under limited circumstances.
>
> **Rule 506**—No limitation on the maximum aggregate offering price; no more than 35 purchasers; certain classes of individuals, including accredited investors, not counted in computing the number of purchasers; affirmative disclosure obligations applicable when there are non-accredited investors; nonaccredited investors or their representatives must meet sophistication standards; resale of securities is restricted; not subject to state regulation through registration.

Note that the exemptions of Regulation D are available on a sliding-scale basis. Rule 506, available for offerings of any size, imposes the more serious constraints by establishing a sophistication standard, imposing an affirmative disclosure requirement, and permitting no more than 35 purchasers (accredited investors are not counted for purposes of this limitation). Rule 504 eliminates the disclosure and sophisticated purchaser requirements as well as limitations on the number of purchasers, but it is available only for offerings up to $5 million. Given the relationship between the restrictions of the exemptions and the limitations on aggregate offering price, Regulation D offers clear choices for issuers, but demands careful attention in structuring transactions to comply with the exemptions.

The harsher requirements of Rule 506 are ameliorated to some extent when purchasers are accredited. In those cases, the sophistication and affirmative disclosure standards are lifted, and there is no limitation on the number of accredited purchasers. The concept of accredited investors is discussed below.

Regulation D offerings historically have been subject to broad prohibitions on general solicitation and advertising. Revisions in 2013 to Rule 506 now give issuers the choice of either structuring their offerings under existing Rule 506(b) (with prohibitions on general solicitation and advertising) or proceeding under a new Rule 506(c) (with no prohibitions on general solicitation and advertising), if all purchasers are accredited and the issuer takes steps to verify that each investor meets the standards for an accredited investor. *See* Securities Act Release No. 33-9415 (July 10, 2013). Rule 506(c) is discussed more fully in the section on Limitations on the Manner and Scope of an Offering, below.

A major advantage of Rule 506 over Rule 504 is that securities issued under the former are "covered securities" under the National Securities Markets Improvement Act of 1996 and, accordingly, not subject to state regulation through registration. The same benefit does not extend to offerings under Rule 504. A study by Professor Rutherford B. Campbell reveals that companies raising relatively small amounts of capital under Regulation D have been opting to make their offerings under the more exacting standards of Rule 506 rather than Rule 504 simply to avoid state regulation of their offerings. *See* Campbell, The Wreck of Regulation D: The Unintended (and Bad) Outcomes for the SEC's Crown Jewel Exemptions, 66 Bus. Law. 919 (2011). More recent data confirm Professor Campbell's findings. *See* Bauguess, Gullapalli & Ivanov, Capital Raising in the U.S., supra, at 2 ("During 2009-2017, [Rule 506 accounted] for 99.9% of the amounts reported sold through Regulation D, including 93% of capital raised in offerings with maximum offer size of $1 million and 98% of capital raised below the amended Rule 504 offering limit threshold ($5 million), suggesting that issuers continue to value the preemption of state securities laws provided for offerings conducted pursuant to Rule 506").

PROBLEM

5-5. Assume a pool of 60 offerees, half of whom qualify as accredited investors. Each offeree is willing to invest $100,000 in a Regulation D offering. The issuer would like to structure the offering in a way that minimizes the expense of preparing a disclosure document. It also has reason to believe some of the offerees are not terribly sophisticated and wants to assume no risk in this regard. Advise the issuer on its options and the trade-offs with each of the Regulation D exemptions.

2. Accredited Investors

The status of purchasers as accredited investors is important under Rule 506. The rule limits availability of the exemption to offerings in which there are no more than 35 purchasers; accredited investors, however, are not included when computing the number of purchasers. *See* Rule 501(e). Accordingly, there may be an unlimited number of accredited investors in a 506 offering without jeopardizing the exemption. Accredited investor status is also important in determining the disclosure obligations imposed by Rule 506. If all purchasers are accredited investors, the exemption is not conditioned upon affirmative disclosures by the issuer.

Moreover, a determination of whether an investor is accredited is important in assessing the obligations of an issuer under the private placement safe harbor of Rule 506 to assess the sophistication of purchasers. Accredited investors are conclusively presumed to be sophisticated, and it is only when a purchaser does not satisfy the standards of accreditation that an issuer must undertake the difficult, and risky, task of evaluating the sophistication of the purchaser.

Note under recent rule changes referenced above and discussed more fully below, issuers who wish to engage in a general solicitation or general advertising (previously prohibited) have the option of doing so by structuring their offering under a new Rule 506(c), which must be limited to accredited investors.

Rule 501(a) defines *accredited investor*. The following are the more important classes of accredited investors.

Financial Institutions.   This category includes banks, savings and loan associations, registered brokers or dealers, insurance companies, and investment companies.

Pension Plans.   Accredited investor status is accorded to the trusts of employee retirement plans managed by an institutional trustee or registered investment adviser, retirement plan trusts with assets in excess of $5 million without regard to the qualifications of plan managers, and retirement plan trusts that permit participants to direct the manner in which funds credited to their accounts will be invested if investment decisions are made solely by accredited investors.

Venture Capital Firms.   A venture capital firm provides capital and loans to businesses that have significant growth potential, but are not yet large enough to have a public offering of their securities.

Although Rule 501 eschews use of the term *venture capital,* two categories of accredited investors—private business development companies and small business investment companies—are financing entities typically associated with the concept. Private business development companies satisfying the requirements of Section 202(a)(22) of the Investment Advisers Act of 1940 are accredited investors for purposes of Regulation D. To qualify under the Advisers Act, the business development company must make available "significant managerial assistance" to the issuers of the securities it purchases.

To be distinguished from the typical venture capital firms described above are so-called angel investors, who invest at the earliest stages in the development of rapid-growth startup companies. Typically, startup issuers reach out to the angel market at very early stages in their development and seek smaller amounts of funding than would be attractive to venture capital investors. Angel investors tend to be individuals (who often prefer to remain anonymous) who qualify as accredited investors under the threshold wealth standards described below. For good discussions of the angel finance market, *see* Ibrahim, Financing the Next Silicon Valley, 87 Wash. U. L. Rev. 717 (2010); Orcutt, Improving the Efficiency of the Angel Finance Market: A Proposal to Expand the Intermediary Role of Finders in the Private Capital Raising Setting, 37 Ariz. St. L.J. 861 (2005).

Corporations and Other Organizations Exceeding a Certain Size.   Any corporation, partnership, or tax-exempt organization with assets exceeding $5 million is an accredited investor, as is any trust with assets exceeding that same amount if the trust is directed by a person with knowledge and experience in business and financial matters and capable of evaluating the merits and risks of the prospective investment.

Insiders of the Issuer.   Certain insiders of the issuer and its affiliates are accredited investors. These include a director, executive officer, or general partner of either the issuer or its affiliates. *Executive officer* is defined to include the president, vice president in charge of a principal business unit, and any other person who performs a policymaking function for the issuer.

Natural Persons with Wealth or Income Exceeding Threshold Standards. A natural person whose net worth exceeds $1 million qualifies as an accredited investor. Similarly, an individual whose annual income exceeds $200,000 (or $300,000 when combined with spousal income) for each of the last two years may be an accredited investor if the current year's income is likely to be above this level.

Entity Owned by Accredited Investors. An entity in which all of the owners are accredited investors is deemed to have the same status.

NOTES AND QUESTIONS

1. Why Consider Wealth? What are the justifications for considering wealth or income in according the status of an accredited investor to a purchaser? Does this reflect an assumption that individuals qualifying on this basis are able to evaluate and understand the risks and merits of an investment? If so, is it sensible to set up a conclusive presumption that a wealthy, but possibly inept individual is able to protect himself? Or does accreditation based upon these factors assume the purchaser is able to bear the economic risk of loss? Consider the following comments on the premise underlying wealth as a basis for accreditation.

> Rule 506 thus departs from the *Ralston Purina* line of cases. Whereas before, private placement purchasers had to be smart, now they need only be rich. Such a departure raises an important, and unanswered, question: should the law presume that wealthy investors, who can bear investment risks, are sophisticated investors, and treat them as such, no matter how financially naive they may be? Conversely, should the law treat poor, but financially sophisticated investors, who cannot bear investment risks, like other sophisticated investors? In short, what role should wealth and sophistication play in the determination of whether an issuer must undertake 1933 Act registration?

Fletcher, Sophisticated Investors Under the Federal Securities Laws, 1988 Duke L.J. 1081, 1123-1124. *See also* Friedman, On Being Rich, Accredited, and Undiversified: The Lacunae in Contemporary Securities Regulation, 47 Okla. L. Rev. 291, 299 (1994) ("It may seem odd that an agency supposedly committed to the protection of investors has created an exception whereby unsophisticated investors are encouraged to invest in mispriced securities, on the ground that they can afford to lose money. But this oddity has been embraced as a method of encouraging capital formation.").

2. How Many Potential Investors Are Accredited? The SEC estimates that about 11.2 million households, or about 8.9 percent of all households, meet the accreditation standard under the individual income threshold ($200,000), while 5.8 million households, or 4.6 percent of all households, meet the standard under the joint income threshold ($300,000). As to net worth ($1 million), 11.8 million households, or 9.4 percent of all households, meet the standard. *See* Securities Act Release No. 33-10649 (June 18, 2019).

3. Possible Changes in the Accredited Investor Definition. The accredited investor definition has changed little over the years. Section 413 of Dodd-Frank, however, directs the SEC to review periodically (every four years beginning in 2014) the accredited investor definition as applied to natural persons to determine whether the standards should be revised for the protection of investors and the public interest. Commentators and even the current Chair of the SEC have argued for a fresh examination of how accredited investors are defined.

Along this line, in late 2015 the SEC staff issued a report recommending consideration of revising the financial standards for an accredited investor to require, for example, indexing the standards for inflation. More broadly, the report discussed possibly expanding the definition to permit accredited investor status to be obtained under broader standards than those available under present law, including allowing individuals with a minimum amount of investments to qualify as accredited investors and permitting individuals with certain professional credentials to qualify as accredited investors. *See* Report on the Review of the Definition of "Accredited Investor" (SEC Staff Report, Dec. 18, 2015).

Commenters on the staff report overwhelmingly favored expanding standards for accreditation beyond financial criteria. In its 2019 Concept Release on Harmonization of Securities Offering Exemptions, Securities Act Release No. 33-10649 (June 18, 2019), the Commission has solicited comments on ways that the definition of accredited investors may be expanded. It has identified some possible reforms, including revising the financial criteria; allowing individuals to qualify based on minimum investments, experience with exempt offerings, possession of professional credentials, or by passing an exam; and treating an investor represented by a financial professional as accredited.

4. Accredited Investors as Preferred Investors. Fewer than 10 percent of Regulation D offerings include nonaccredited investors. *See* Bauguess, Gullapalli & Ivanov, Capital Raising in the U.S.: An Analysis of the Market for Unregistered Securities Offerings, 2009-2017 2 (SEC White Paper, Aug. 2018). For offerings with only accredited investors, issuers can avoid inquiries into investor sophistication and affirmative disclosure obligations under Rule 502(b). Although excluding purchasers who are not accredited investors is a sensible method of reducing the risk to the issuer, business considerations may dictate inclusion of some nonaccredited investors. High-quality offerings by large issuers may be fully subscribed by accredited investors, but smaller issuers may be unable to attract the same degree of interest on the part of institutions and individuals qualifying as accredited investors. In that case, the issuer faces increased burdens in disclosure requirements and, if the offering is under Rule 506, sophistication requirements.

5. Hedge Funds. Hedge funds are private investment funds that not only buy and sell financial assets but also use more speculative trading strategies, most notably short selling (selling a security the fund does not own) and the use of borrowed funds to purchase securities. Hedge funds target wealthy investors. As Professor Booth succinctly put it, "Hedge funds do not want the money of small investors." Booth, The Buzzard Was Their Friend—Hedge Funds and the Problem of Overvalued Equity, 10 J. Bus. L. 879, 881 (2008). Although hedge funds often succeed in posting above-market returns, they do so by incurring greater risks. Occasional spectacular collapses of hedge funds do little to dampen the enthusiasm of wealthy investors attracted to the prospects of higher returns achieved through the assumption of greater risks.

Rule 506 is the exemption under which most hedge funds raise capital (nearly $400 billion in 2017). By limiting their offerings to accredited investors and otherwise complying with the requirements of Regulation D, the funds are able to limit disclosures and operate in an environment that critics contend lacks necessary transparency. The '33 Act registration exemption is to be distinguished from some recent regulatory efforts (discussed in later chapters) to require certain hedge fund advisers to register under the Investment Advisers Act.

6. Exclusion of Personal Residence from the Net Worth Calculation. Section 413 of Dodd-Frank directed the Commission to adjust the net worth standard for an accredited investor who is a natural person ($1 million) by excluding the value of the investor's primary residence. This reverses past SEC practice of allowing an investor to include the value of a primary residence in the net worth calculation. In her fascinating discussion of a Ponzi scheme involving thousands of investors (including many vulnerable seniors) in a purported private placement, Professor Jennifer Johnson commented on the change:

> The 2010 Dodd-Frank "do not count the house" rule may have impacted the MedCap offering. Many victims in MedCap were retired or hope-to-be-retired retail investors who were solicited by their stockbrokers. The brokers helped the investors add up the supposed value of their homes, furniture, cars, trucks, dogs and kids to get to the $1 million asset value to qualify them as accredited. One might hope that removing the house from the $1 million calculation will help protect Grandmas. On the other hand, one cannot underestimate the ingenuity of a motivated commissioned sales force. Far too many of these brokers behave like sea lions camped at the foot of Bonneville Dam gobbling up helpless salmon. For example, I have recently learned that some brokers are routinely using the present value of Grandma's social security and pension payments to get to the $1 million mark to qualify an investor as accredited.

Johnson, Fleecing Grandma: A Regulatory Ponzi Scheme, 16 Lewis & Clark L. Rev. 993, 1003 (2012).

In Securities Act Release No. 33-9297 (Sept. 21, 2011), the Commission amended Rule 501 to implement the legislative direction to exclude homes from the net worth calculation. Although the amended rule makes no attempt to define "primary residence," the Adopting Release notes the term has "a commonly understood meaning as the home where a person lives most of the time."

How, then, should the liability of a home mortgage be handled in the calculation of net worth? The amended rule directs that indebtedness up to the value of the personal residence and secured by the residence (i.e., a standard home mortgage) is not treated as a liability unless the borrowing occurred within 60 days prior to the purchase of securities in the Regulation D offering and is not in connection with the acquisition of the residence (i.e., a refinancing). The 60-day exception is designed to prevent a homeowner from manipulating net worth on the eve of purchasing securities by borrowing against home equity and inflating net worth with the proceeds of the borrowing. As the SEC noted in the adopting release, "If the rule does not address that issue, the population Congress intended to protect—individuals whose net worth is below $1 million unless their home equity is taken into account—may be incentivized (or urged by unscrupulous salespeople) to take on debt secured by their homes for the purpose of qualifying as accredited investors and participating in investments without the protection to which they are entitled."

For underwater mortgages where mortgage debt exceeds the value of the home, the amount in excess is considered a liability for purposes of the net worth calculation, without regard to whether the loan is nonrecourse.

PROBLEMS

5-6.   Sybil is the vice president in charge of governmental relations for Interg. Her principal functions are to coordinate the company's legislative lobbying and to disseminate information on important regulatory developments. Will she qualify as an accredited investor by virtue of her position as an officer of the company? *See* Rule 501(f).

5-7.   The financial statement of Mel, a prospective participant in a Regulation D offering, shows the following assets:

Checking and savings account	$25,000
Estimated value of art collection	250,000
U.S. Savings Bonds	125,000
Household furnishings/personal effects	50,000
Estimated value of house	600,000
Vested interest in retirement plan	350,000
Total Assets	$1,400,000
Liabilities (balance on home mortgage)	$245,000
Net Worth	$1,155,000

Will Mel qualify as an accredited investor? What if the week before the exempt offering Mel takes out a $250,000 second mortgage on his home and places the loan proceeds in his savings account (increasing the account balance to $275,000)? Will this help him qualify as an accredited investor? What if the borrowing occurred three months before the exempt offering?

5-8.   Three purchasers participate in a Rule 506 offering. The issuer was without legal counsel and made no attempt to assess whether the purchasers qualified as accredited investors or complied with the provisions of Regulation D applicable when purchasers are nonaccredited. In fact, each of the purchasers satisfied the accreditation standards at the time of the offering. The investment has soured, and the purchasers would now like to rescind. What is the relevance of the issuer's lack of reasonable belief that the investors were accredited? *See* Rule 501(a).

3. The Sophistication Standard of Rule 506(b)

|| **Mark v. FSC Securities Corp.**
870 F.2d 331 (6th Cir. 1989)

SIMPSON, J. [The Malaga limited partnership was formed to invest in the Spanish Arabian horse industry. FSC, a broker-dealer, sold partnership interests to plaintiffs in this action. Plaintiffs now seek to rescind the transactions on various grounds, including failure of the offering to come within the private placement safe harbor of Rule 506.]

... In order to come within the Rule 506 safe harbor, FSC is required to offer evidence of the issuer's reasonable belief as to the nature of *each* purchaser. ...

The only testimony at trial competent to establish the issuer's [reasonable] belief as to the nature of the purchasers was that of Laurence Leafer, a General Partner in Malaga. By his own admission, he had no knowledge . . . as to the purchasers' knowledge and experience in financial and business matters, as required by Rule 506. . . .

Q: Am I correct that, in order to sell under a federal exemption, that it's necessary to ensure that the investors are qualified investors, and able to determine the risks of the investment?

A: They should be reasonably sophisticated.

Q: What was done to determine . . . if investors were, in fact, reasonably sophisticated?

A: Well, there were two things. Number one, we had investor suitability standards that had to be met. You had to have a certain income, be in a certain tax bracket, this kind of thing. Then in the subscription documents themselves, they, when they sign it, they supposedly represented that they had received information necessary to make an informed investment decision, and that they were sophisticated. And if they were not, they relied on an offering representative who was, things of that nature.

Q: Did you review the subscription documents that came in for the Malaga offering?

A: No. . . .

Similarly, the only other witness that defendants offered on the issue was Christopher J. Moran, an attorney once employed by FSC. [Moran testified that he neither saw nor reviewed subscription documents from any of the investors.] . . .

FSC also offered as evidence plaintiffs' executed subscription documents, as well as a set of documents in blank, to establish the procedure it followed in the Malaga sales offering. The subscription documents included a "suitability letter" in which the purchaser was required to warrant, among other things, that his or her income met the conditions set by [the general partner], that the purchaser had an opportunity to request and examine supplemental information, and that the purchaser had sufficient knowledge and experience in business affairs to enable the purchaser to evaluate the risks of the investment. The subscription documents also included an "Offeree Questionnaire" in which the purchaser was to set forth his or her educational and investment background, in addition to information as to whether the purchaser was represented by an attorney or an accountant. . . .

Although the plaintiffs' executed subscription documents, along with their testimony, may have been sufficient to establish the reasonableness of any belief the issuer may have had as to the plaintiffs' particular qualifications, that does not satisfy the burden of proof imposed by Rule 506 of Regulation D. That burden could have been met by offering each of the twenty-eight purchasers' executed subscription documents into evidence for the jury to examine; then the jury might have determined what the issuer reasonably believed. The burden of proof might also have been satisfied if any [representative of the general partner] had testified that Malaga limited-partnership interests were sold *only* to persons whose offeree questionnaires indicated they qualified as the sort of purchasers contemplated by Rule 506. . . .

However, in the case sub judice, the documents offered no evidence from which a jury could conclude the issuer reasonably believed each purchaser was suitable so as to warrant a Rule 506 exemption. . . . The blank subscription document and offeree questionnaire simply do not amount to probative evidence, when it is the answers and information received *from* purchasers that determines whether the conditions of Rule 506 have been met. Because there was no evidence from which a jury could determine that the issuer had the requisite belief, nor from which a jury could conclude the reasonableness of any such belief, FSC has failed to sustain its burden of proving an exemption under Rule 506 of Regulation D. . . .

Rule 506 requires that either (1) each purchaser who is not an accredited investor, alone or with a representative, have such knowledge and experience in financial and business matters to be able to evaluate the merits and risks of the prospective investment; or (2) the issuer reasonably believe this is the case. As to the latter requirement, some courts find that a sufficient basis for the issuer's reasonable belief exists if the prospective investor simply represents in the subscription document that she is an accredited investor. *See, e.g., Supernova Systems, Inc. v. Great Am. Broadband, Inc.,* 2012 U.S. Dist. LEXIS 16182 (N.D. Ind. Feb. 9, 2012). But incomplete responses in a questionnaire to be completed by investors may require the issuer to take additional steps to verify the accredited status of investors. *See SEC v. Mahabub,* 343 F. Supp. 3d 1022, 1037 (D. Colo. 2018) ("Mattos would 'normally' contact an investor who did not provide the needed information on the questionnaire, but Mattos admittedly overlooked at least some of those incomplete questionnaires. Given this admission, it must necessarily follow that GenAudio cannot prove that it reasonably believed that *all* of the 2010 and 2011 Offering investors were accredited.") (emphasis in original). Do you believe that self-certification by investors should satisfy the reasonable belief standard, or should some independent investigation and verification by the issuer be required?

Requiring investor sophistication (a concept explored earlier in the private placement portion of this chapter) represents an interesting and debatable policy decision that the extensive disclosures prompted by Section 5's registration requirements need not be mandated when an offering is limited to the very investors most likely to consider carefully disclosures concerning a prospective investment. Along this line, there is reason to believe that sophisticated investors frequently may engage in suboptimal decisionmaking. *See* Langevoort, Selling Hope, Selling Risk: Some Lessons for Law from Behavioral Economics About Stockbrokers and Sophisticated Customers, 84 Cal. L. Rev. 627 (1996).

Conditioning the Rule 506 exemption on the sophistication of purchasers introduces elements of uncertainty that issuers will attempt to minimize or eliminate. The best tactic for an issuer seeking to eliminate any question about the exemption's availability is to limit an issuance to accredited investors. Some issuers are able to do just that, but others are forced to cast a wider net in their quest for capital. An issuer forced to include nonaccredited purchasers in an offering may, of course, negate the sophistication problem by structuring the offering to comply with Rule 504, rather than Rule 506. But the aggregate offering price limitations of Rule 504 may prove problematic and justify the costs and risks that arise when the sought-after exemption is conditioned on the sophistication of each purchaser or purchaser representative.

PROBLEMS

Rule 501(h) defines *purchaser representative*. Evaluate the following problems in light of that definition.

5-9. Marvella is interested in purchasing securities in a Rule 506(b) offering by Syntertech. Although Marvella lacks the requisite sophistication required by the exemption, she relies on her brother-in-law, George, for advice. Assuming George has the requisite experience to meet the sophistication standard, which of the following circumstances would disqualify George from acting as a purchaser representative?

    a. Marvella divorces her husband.
    b. George is an officer of Syntertech.
    c. George is an officer of Syntertech and does not tell Marvella of his position.
    d. George is planning to buy a substantial block of stock offered by Syntertech.

5-10. Assume Marvella decides not to rely upon George for advice. Instead, she consults Priscilla, her attorney, on the merits of the investment. Does the issuer need to take any steps to satisfy itself that Priscilla is sophisticated? What if Priscilla is a CPA, rather than an attorney? What if Priscilla is both a CPA and an attorney?

5-11. As an attorney, what risk of liability will Priscilla incur if she acts as a purchaser representative for Marvella? Is it likely that this liability is covered by her malpractice insurance policy?

5-12.   Suppose Marvella, who is thrifty and unwilling to pay high fees to any-one, refuses to hire a representative. May the issuer pay the fee of Marvella's representative?

4.   Calculating the Number of Purchasers

Rule 506 is available only if the number of purchasers does not exceed 35 or, alternatively, the issuer reasonably believes the number of purchasers does not exceed 35. Rule 501(e), however, provides that certain types of purchasers are excluded for purposes of this calculation. The excluded classes include accred-ited investors, trusts or estates in which purchasers have beneficial interests exceeding 50 percent, spouses and certain relatives of purchasers, and corpora-tions or other organizations in which purchasers are at least 50 percent benefi-cial owners. A corporation, partnership, or other entity that is not accredited is counted as a single purchaser unless it was formed for the purpose of purchas-ing securities in the offering.

PROBLEMS

5-13.   Priscilla is a California resident and a nonaccredited investor in a Rule 506(b) offering. Her father, a New York resident, is a nonaccredited investor in the same offering, as is a corporation in which Priscilla and her father each have 50 percent beneficial ownership interests. Assuming the corporation does not qualify as an accredited investor, will Priscilla, her father, and the corporation be counted as one, two, or three purchasers? *See* Rule 501(e)(1).

5-14.   A partnership not qualifying as an accredited investor has 10 partners. If the partnership purchases securities, will the transaction be regarded as one by a single purchaser, 10 purchasers, or 11 purchasers? Must the individual part-ners satisfy the accreditation standards? What if the partnership was formed for the purpose of acquiring the securities being offered? *See* Rule 501(e)(2).

5-15.   An individual who is a purchaser in a Rule 506 offering satisfies the net worth standards for accredited investor status. He lives in the same home with his wife and her brother, who is not an accredited investor, but who would like to purchase securities in the offering. Does the brother count for purposes of computing the number of purchasers?

5.   Limitations on the Manner and Scope of an Offering

a.   In General

The sophistication and number of purchaser standards of Rule 506 refer to purchasers rather than offerees. This might suggest that an issuer need not be concerned with the manner and scope of an offering so long as the limitations pertaining to purchasers are satisfied. Such a conclusion, however, is undermined by Rule 502(c), which limits the process by which purchasers are solicited by prohibiting an issuer, or any person acting on its behalf, from offering to sell securities by any form of general solicitation or general advertising.

Rule 502(c)'s restrictions apply to both of the Regulation D exemptions, with two exceptions. First, as will be discussed below, Rule 506(c) was added pursuant to a JOBS Act directive and eliminates the solicitation and advertising restrictions for a Rule 506 offering, provided that the offering is limited to accredited investors and the issuer takes reasonable steps to verify that all investors are accredited. Second, the restrictions do not apply to offerings under Rule 504(b)(1), which includes:

1.   Offerings exclusively in one or more states that provide for registration of securities and require a disclosure document;
2.   Offerings in one or more states that have no provision for the registration of the securities or the public filing or delivery of a disclosure document before sale, if the securities have been registered in at least one state that provides for such registration and disclosure document; or
3.   Offerings exclusively according to state law exemptions from registration that permit general solicitation and general advertising so long as sales are made only to accredited investors.

Even with these exceptions, the general solicitation and advertising restrictions represent important conditions applicable to most Rule 504 and those Rule 506 offerings in which some purchasers are not accredited investors or the issuer does not take reasonable steps to verify the status of each investor as an accredited investor.

b.   What Is "General Solicitation or General Advertising"?

When is a communication a general solicitation or general advertisement? In some cases, there is little doubt that the scope of solicitation or advertising exceeds the limitations of Rule 502(c). Mass mailings and cold calls are the easy cases. *See, e.g., Cobalt Multifamily Investors I, LLC v. Arden*, 2012 U.S. Dist. LEXIS 125278 (S.D.N.Y. Aug. 14, 2012) (cold calling and evidence that more than 300 investors from 30 states purchased securities); *In the Matter of Priority Access, Inc.*, Release No. 33-7904 (Oct. 3, 2001) (2 million spam e-mails attempting to attract investors); *Black Diamond Fund, LLLP v. Joseph*, 211 P.3d 727, 732 (Colo. Ct. App. 2009) (marketing of interests through free lunch and free dinner seminars). But some courts draw a distinction between cold calls generally to obtain clients and cold calls for the purpose of selling specific investments. *See, e.g., SEC v. Schooler*, 106 F. Supp. 3d 1157, 1166 (S.D. Cal. 2015) ("Schooler does not say that Western offered or sold GP units through cold calls or lead lists, rather he says that Western obtained clients through such methods. . . . [O]btaining clients through general solicitation or advertising and then offering those clients securities does not necessarily violate Rule 506(b)'s general solicitation and advertising prohibition.").

What is surprising is the extent to which Rule 502(c) reaches more targeted communications not commonly thought to be "general solicitations." Consider *In the Matter of Kenman Corp.*, [1984-1985 Transfer Binder] Fed. Sec. L. Rep. (CCH) ¶83,767 (Apr. 19, 1985), which involved administrative proceedings against a broker participating in a Rule 506 offering:

> Persons to whom Kenman and Kenman Securities sent materials were chosen from six sources. First, they utilized a list of persons who had participated in prior offerings by them. Second, they reviewed the annual reports of fifty "Fortune 500" companies and obtained the names of executive officers. The third source was a list of names of persons who had previously invested $10,000 or more in real estate offerings by issuers other than Kenman. . . . The fourth source was a list of physicians in the State of California. The fifth source was a list of managerial engineers employed by Hughes Aircraft Company or by similar companies. Sixth, Kenman obtained a copy of the Morris County, New Jersey Industrial Directory and selected names of the presidents of certain listed companies. . . .

The Commission concluded the broker had engaged in a general solicitation that defeated the availability of the exemption. *See also Black Diamond Fund,* supra (general solicitation existed because invitations to free meal seminars were addressed anonymously to "Dear Valued Client").

Staff interpretations have consistently emphasized the importance of a *preexisting relationship* between the issuer (or person acting on its behalf) and the offeree in establishing the limited nature of a communication. Requiring a preexisting relationship is a way of ensuring that issuers will have the opportunity to evaluate the suitability of offerees as purchasers. As discussed below, brokers may be an important means for issuers without the necessary relationships to reach prospective investors.

c. *Activities by Broker-Dealers*

Issuers in Regulation D offerings often solicit the marketing assistance of broker-dealers. In such cases, a preexisting relationship between a qualified offeree and the broker-dealer (rather than the issuer) will suffice to render communication limited under Rule 502(c).

Broker-dealers are constantly trying to expand their customer base, however, and efforts to identify and communicate with clients potentially interested in Regulation D offerings may create problems under Rule 502(c). *See, e.g., SEC v. Credit First Fund, LP,* 2006 U.S. Dist. LEXIS 96697, at *44 (C.D. Cal. Feb. 13, 2006) (cold calling potential investors to gather information on their background and following up one week later to discuss specific investments is "likely a form of general solicitation [because the] duration of one week is not sufficient time to establish a relationship . . .").

In a number of no-action letters, the staff has attempted to provide guidance to broker-dealers attempting to structure their sales programs in conformity with Rule 502(c). One of the more important of the letters is Bateman Eichler, Hill Richards, Inc., SEC No-Action Letter (Dec. 3, 1985). Bateman Eichler wished to underwrite private offerings and proposed to implement a program for establishing relationships with new clients it identified as prospective purchasers. Account executives would be allowed to send up to 50 letters (with enclosed questionnaires) a month to local professionals and business people. The account executives were to review the completed questionnaires and request additional personal and financial information when appropriate. The information provided would be used to assess the qualifications of prospective investors. New clients would not have the opportunity to purchase securities currently sold or scheduled to be sold at the time of recruitment, and under no circumstances would any offering materials be sent for a period of at least 45 days after the first mailing.

Noting in particular that (1) the initial solicitation would be generic in nature and would not identify specific investments the firm was offering or would be offering, and (2) the firm would implement procedures to ensure no persons solicited would be offered securities the firm was offering or contemplating offering at the time of the solicitation, the SEC staff concluded the program was not a general solicitation within the meaning of Rule 502(c). More recently, the staff has provided additional guidance in Citizen VC, Inc., SEC No-Action Letter (Aug. 6, 2015). Building on *Bateman Eichler*, the staff responded favorably to a no-action request from the sponsor of an online venture capital investment platform allowing direct investment by its members. Citizen VC requires prospective investors to complete an online questionnaire providing suitability information. Following completion of each questionnaire, there is a "relationship establishment period" during which Citizen VC evaluates the prospective investor's financial circumstances and sophistication. After clearing this hurdle, an investor gains access to password-protected sections of the web site. For each investor, the relationship that is satisfied by the screening must exist *prior* to the commencement of the relevant offering. Although *Bateman Eichler* had involved a 45-day waiting period, the staff concluded no minimum waiting period is required but emphasized the importance of not presenting investors with investment opportunities during the qualification process.

PROBLEM

5-16. A broker-dealer uses suitability questionnaires to prequalify potential investors in Regulation D offerings. Assume a client prequalifies (on the basis of net worth and annual income) on February 1. On July 1 of the following year, the firm would like to offer securities to the client. Need it be worried about the client's continuing qualification? If so, what should it do?

d. The Internet and General Solicitations

The SEC from the beginning made clear its concern over the use of the Internet as a means of general solicitation and general advertising. *See, e.g.,* Release No. 33-7233 (Oct. 6, 1995) (placing private placement offering materials on a web page would not be consistent with Rule 502(c)'s prohibitions against general solicitation or advertising).

The first no-action letter of significance involving the use of the Internet to reach potential investors was issued in 1996. *See* IPONET, SEC No-Action Letter (July 26, 1996). IPONET maintained a web site allowing investors to obtain information on Regulation D offerings. To obtain the information, investors first registered by completing an online questionnaire allowing the broker-dealer affiliated with IPONET to determine whether the investor was accredited within the meaning of Rule 501(a) or sophisticated for purposes of Rule 506. Once qualified and registered, the investor was given a password allowing access to a page where private offerings *posted subsequent* to the investor's registration were listed. Moreover, an investor could participate in an offering "only after a sufficient time has elapsed between the IPONET member's registration as an Accredited Investor and the inception of a private offering."

In concluding the arrangement did *not* involve a general solicitation or general advertising within the meaning of Rule 502(c), the staff emphasized that (1) the questionnaire was generic in nature and did not reference specific offerings; (2) the password-protected page could not be accessed before the broker prequalified the investor; and (3) investors could participate only in those offerings posted subsequent to the investor's qualification.

In 2000, the Commission issued a release on the use of electronic media cautioning against practices "that deviate substantially from the facts in the IPONET interpretive letter." *See* Release No. 33-7856 (Apr. 28, 2000). It expressed reservations over non-broker-dealer web site operators that prequalify investors and noted that the principal method of satisfying the pre-existing relationship requirement is through the use of a broker-dealer in a position to make an investment recommendation to a client it knows. The Commission also expressed concern over loose qualification standards often allowing investors "to certify themselves as accredited or sophisticated merely by checking a box."

PROBLEM

5-17. DSM maintains a web site that includes a number of Regulation D offerings. To obtain information on any of the offerings, an investor must first register with DSM. The registration form includes a "full access" option for an "accredited individual investor." This status can be achieved by checking one of two boxes that provide:

☑ I alone, or in combination with my spouse, have a net worth in excess of $1 million; or

☑ For each of the past two years, my annual income has been greater than $200,000 or the combined annual income of my spouse and I has been greater than $300,000.

Upon checking the box, the investor is registered and immediately has access to materials on the offerings. Do you see any problems with this structure? *See* Release No. 33-7856 (Apr. 28, 2000), *supra.*

e. Eliminating the Ban on General Solicitations: Rule 506 Offerings Limited to Accredited Investors

For years, commentators have criticized the SEC's broad ban on general solicitations. Although the SEC resisted revisiting the ban, reformers were able to partially secure their objectives through congressional action. The 2012 JOBS Act directed the Commission to amend Regulation D so that Rule 502(c)'s ban on general solicitations or general advertising does not apply to offers and sales under Rule 506, provided that all purchasers are accredited investors. The legislation, which does not address the applicability of Rule 502(c) to the exemptions under Rule 504, also directs the SEC to require that issuers take reasonable steps to verify the status of purchasers as accredited investors.

The relaxation of general solicitation restrictions generated considerable excitement in the investment community. Enthusiasm was dampened somewhat by the legislation's requirement that issuers must take reasonable steps to verify that all purchasers are accredited. As was discussed above, Regulation D's accredited investor definition is satisfied if either the investor satisfies the standards of Rule 501(a) or the issuer reasonably believes that the investor satisfies these standards. The JOBS Act mandate adds the additional and potentially more onerous requirement that issuers actually take steps to verify that investors are accredited.

Under new Rule 506(c), an issuer may employ a general solicitation or advertising to offer and sell securities in a Rule 506 offering if three conditions are satisfied: (1) the issuer takes reasonable steps to verify that purchasers are accredited investors; (2) all purchasers are accredited investors, either because they qualify under the criteria of Rule 501(a) or because the issuer reasonably believes they qualify; and (3) other applicable conditions of Regulation D are satisfied. Alternatively, an issuer pursuing a Rule 506 offering may opt to include investors who are not accredited investors and/or not take steps to verify that all investors are accredited, but in such a case the offering must proceed under Rule 506(b) where the restrictions on general solicitation and advertising continue to apply. For a discussion of impediments that will exist for issuers proceeding under Rule 506(c), including the danger that those who solicit for the issuers (including its employees) will be subject to regulation as brokers, *see* Sjostrom, Direct Private Placements, 102 Ky. L.J. 947 (2013-2014).

Note that even if all investors are in fact accredited, the exemption is available only if the issuer also takes steps to verify that investors are accredited. The steps that must be taken to verify the status of purchasers has been the issue of greatest concern to issuers. When it first proposed Rule 506(c), the SEC opted for a flexible approach keying on "principles-based methods of verification." To this end, the release accompanying the proposal suggested three factors (the list is nonexclusive) that may be relevant in evaluating the reasonableness of steps taken:

1. *The Nature of the Purchaser and the Type of Accredited Investor the Purchaser Claims to Be.* Steps necessary to verify the status of a broker-dealer (e.g., simply going to FINRA's BrokerCheck web site) differ from the steps

necessary to verify the assets and liabilities of a natural person claiming to be an accredited investor.

2. *The Amount and Type of Information That the Issuer Has About the Purchaser.* Examples of information an issuer may rely on include publicly available information (e.g., public filings revealing an individual is an executive officer) and third-party information providing "reasonably reliable" evidence that an individual falls within one of the categories of accredited investors (e.g., an industry publication that discloses annual compensation of an individual at a level exceeding the income threshold for an accredited investor).

3. *The Nature and Terms of the Offering.* An issuer that solicits investors through a web site accessible to the general public or through a widely disseminated e-mail or social media solicitation presumably must take greater measures to verify accredited investors than an issuer that solicits investors from a database of pre-screened accredited investors created and maintained by a reasonably reliable third party, such as a registered broker-dealer. As to the terms of the offering, imposition of a high minimum investment standard that could only be met by an accredited investor could be a relevant factor in verification of accredited investor status.

Some commentators were sharply critical of Rule 506(c) as proposed because it failed to provide sufficiently clear standards for issuers assessing the status of investors. At least in part, the SEC responded to this criticism in the final form of the Rule. In finalizing Rule 506(c), the SEC did retain the flexible principles-based methods of verifying accredited investor status summarized above. *See* Release No. 33-9415 (July 10, 2013). The final rule, however, adds nonexclusive safe harbors designed to give issuers greater certainty that they have done what is necessary to verify the status of an investor in offerings involving natural persons. *See* Rule 506(c)(2)(ii). For individuals claiming to be accredited on the basis of income, the steps include reviewing personal tax returns. For individuals claiming to qualify on the basis of net worth, the steps include reviewing recent bank and brokerage statements, appraisals by third parties, and tax assessments; verification of liabilities may be addressed by reviewing at least one credit report. Alternatively, the issuer may rely on written confirmation from a broker-dealer, investment adviser, attorney, or CPA that such person has taken reasonable steps to verify that the individual is an accredited investor and that the individual does, in fact, satisfy the requirements for an investor to be accredited.

Rule 506 is the most robust of all the exemptions, but the Rule 506(b) and Rule 506(c) alternatives are equally popular. The response to Rule 506(c) has been, in a word, underwhelming. In 2018, the $1.5 trillion raised in 506(b) offerings was larger than the $1.4 trillion raised in registered offerings. *See* Securities Act Release 33-10649 (June 18, 2019). But only a small proportion of capital raised under Rule 506 offerings (under 5 percent) has been via Rule 506(c). As to why issuers have shown such a strong preference for Rule 506(b), consider the following comments of the SEC:

One reason why Rule 506(b) continues to dominate the Regulation D market may be that issuers with pre-existing sources of financing and/or intermediation channels are accustomed to relying on Rule 506(b) and do not need the flexibility provided by Rule 506(c). Other issuers may become more comfortable with Rule 506(c) market practices as they develop over time. Some issuers may be reluctant to use general solicitation because they do not wish to share information publicly (through advertising materials) for competitive and general business reasons. There may also be concerns about the added burden or appropriate levels of verification of the accredited investor status of all purchasers and possible investor privacy concerns. Regulatory uncertainty has also been previously identified as a possible explanation for the relatively low level of the Rule 506(c) offerings.

Id.

f.   A Recap: The Two Tracks of Rule 506

The accredited investor verification requirements of Rule 506(c) will apply to Rule 506 offerings in which the issuer engages in a general solicitation or general advertising. In other cases, the issuer may proceed under Rule 506(b), which does not include the new verification standards or require that all purchasers be accredited investors. Rule 506(b) may be an attractive option for an issuer that has preexisting relationships with a small group of prospective investors or chooses to market the offerings to a select group of investors in a manner that is not a general solicitation.

If the offering is under Rule 506(b), there remain the conditions that no more than 35 of the investors are not accredited and any purchaser who is not an accredited investor must be sophisticated or have a sophisticated representative. Thus, although a Rule 506(b) offering may include investors who are not accredited, the numerical limit on such investors and the need to assess sophistication of investors who are not accredited means that whether or not an investor is accredited is a relevant inquiry even under Rule 506(b). Over time it is likely that the issuers in Rule 506(b) offerings will employ means of assessing the accredited status of an investor similar to those required under Rule 506(c).

PROBLEMS

5-18.   J.R. is a promoter of oil drilling ventures and a member of the Houston Petroleum Club. He has sent an offering circular to the Club's members (approximately 200 individuals) describing the "deal" he is now putting together and soliciting their interest in participation as investors. J.R. is confident that all of the Club's members are accredited investors for purposes of Regulation D, but to avoid any problems, he has stamped, in red, on the first page of the offering circular: "FOR ACCREDITED INVESTORS ONLY." If the offering is under 506(b), has J.R. engaged in a general solicitation? Does it make a difference if all of the offerees are in fact accredited investors? If the offering is under Rule 506(c), what steps does J.R. need to take to verify the qualifications of the purchasers?

5-19. Assume J.R. proceeds with an offering under Rule 506(c) but does nothing to verify that the purchasers are accredited. Assume further that all purchasers in fact are accredited. Is the exemption available? *no, needs to verify*

5-20. Assume J.R. does nothing in the Rule 506(c) offering to verify that the purchasers are accredited. He does, however, establish a minimum investment amount of $1 million. His belief is that anyone with $1 million to invest must satisfy the net worth standard for an accredited investor. He feels that by setting the $1 million investment minimum he has taken sufficient steps to verify that purchasers are accredited. Do you agree?

no, could be the 15 yr old lotto winner & would need production

6. Determining the Aggregate Offering Price in Offerings Under Rule 504

Rule 504 limits the aggregate offering price on offerings within any 12-month period. The maximum aggregate offering price on securities that can be sold in reliance upon the Rule during any 12-month period is $5 million. *See* Rule 504(b)(2). The aggregate offering price limitation is reduced by the aggregate offering price of securities sold within the previous 12 months in reliance of Rule 504 or in violation of the registration requirements of Section 5(a). Note that the aggregate offering price principles have an obvious component and more subtle, but equally important dimensions. The obvious component is the $5 million ceiling established for offerings under Rule 504. The more subtle aspects of the aggregate offering price principles concern the methods by which the offering price and time periods of the offering are calculated.

Aggregation is a principle often confused with integration, but the two are actually distinct. Integration means that two ostensibly distinct offerings will be treated as one for the purpose of determining the availability of an exemption from registration requirements. For example, assume an issuer completes two offerings over a relatively short period of time. The first issuance is in compliance with the Rule 147 safe harbor for the intrastate offering exemption; proceeds from the offering total $10 million, and there are 50 purchasers. The second offering is under Rule 504. The aggregate offering price is $5 million, and purchasers, which total 30 in number, include both residents and nonresidents. *If the two offerings are integrated and treated as one*, the availability of an exemption for either becomes problematic. The intrastate offering exemption will fail because of offers to nonresidents. Rule 504 will not be available for a number of reasons, including an aggregate offering price exceeding $5 million.

Assuming in this example that there is no integration of the two offerings, aggregation will not be a problem because we are dealing with only one offering (the second) made under Rule 504, with its offering cap.

a. Calculating the Aggregate Offering Price

Rule 501(c) defines *aggregate offering price* as the sum of all cash, services, property, notes, cancellation of indebtedness, and other consideration the issuer receives for the securities. Determining the aggregate offering price if consideration paid for shares is limited to cash presents little difficulty. If securities are offered for both cash and non-cash consideration, Rule 501(c) requires that the aggregate offering price be determined on the basis of the price at which the securities are offered for cash. For example, assume an offering involves 1,000 shares of preferred stock, half of which is issued for cash at $100 per share and half of which is issued for non-cash consideration (e.g., real estate). One possibility would be to value the real estate and add this amount to the cash consideration to yield the aggregate offering price. Rule 501(c), however, adopts a less circuitous approach by directing the determination of aggregate offering price on the basis of the price at which the securities are offered for cash. Thus, since half of the securities were offered for cash, the cash purchases are doubled to yield the aggregate offering price for the entire issuance.

If the securities are not offered for cash, valuation difficulties are unavoidable. In these cases, Rule 501(c) directs the calculation of aggregate offering price on the basis of the value of the consideration as determined by bona fide sales made within a reasonable time or, if there are no sales, "fair value as determined by an accepted standard." The latter standard is vague, and therefore troublesome, and a conservative approach would caution against running to the limits of the Rule 504 exemption in issuances involving only non-cash consideration.

b. Relevant Amount and Time Period

Recall that the maximum aggregate offering price is *lowered* by the amount of any other securities sold within specified time periods under Rule 504. With two Rule 504 offerings, sales under the first offering taking place within 12 months preceding the second offering will affect what may be sold in the second. To be more precise, two time periods are relevant in applying the aggregate offering limitations of Rule 504: (1) the 12-month period preceding the commencement of the offering under Rule 504, and (2) the period of time during which the offering is open. The second of the two relevant time-period limitations is needed to prevent an issuer with no offerings during a preceding 12-month period from commencing simultaneous $5 million Rule 504 offerings.

For example, assume an issuer commences a Rule 504 offering on April 1. By June 1, $3 million in securities has been sold, and the offering is terminated. Further assume the issuer had no sales under any other Rule 504 offering (1) in the 12-month period prior to April 1 and (2) between April 1 and June 1, the period during which the Rule 504 offering took place. After June 1, the issuer proceeds with another Rule 504 offering. For the second offering, however, the maximum aggregate offering price will be $2 million because of the Rule 504 sales occurring in the preceding 12-month period. Assuming the issuer is unaware of the aggregation rules and sells $5 million in securities in the second offering, the first Rule 504 offering will not be affected, but the second offering will fail under Rule 504.

Calculations aside, what policy objectives are advanced by the aggregation rules? Consider the following comment: "Assuming that there are no disclosure issues as to potential dilution, voting, control, or other concerns as a result of the multiple offerings, it is difficult to find a justification for the aggregation doctrine other than the doctrine itself." Cohn & Yadley, Capital Offense: The SEC's Continuing Failure to Address Small Business Financing Concerns, 4 N.Y.U. J.L. & Bus. 1, 53 (2007) (also pointing out that the aggregation rules provide special hardships for smaller issuers because they are the most likely issuers to be raising capital under one of the monetarily restricted exemptions).

PROBLEMS

5-21. *A, B,* and *X* form a business. *A* and *B* pay $10 per share and receive 200,000 shares each. *X* holds a patent that she has spent $1.5 million developing and patenting. She contributes the patent and receives 100,000 shares. Does this meet Rule 504? *See* Rule 501(c).

5-22. On January 1, an issuer commences an offering under Rule 504. By April 1, $5 million in securities has been sold, and the offering is terminated. When may the issuer commence a new offering under Rule 504? When may the issuer safely commence an offering of the same class of securities under Rule 506?

5-23. An issuer has not offered or sold securities in the preceding 12 months. On January 1, it begins a Rule 504 offering that remains open until June 1; it sells $4.5 million in securities in the offering. On May 1 of the same year, the issuer begins another Rule 504 offering; in this second offering, which is open for two months, the issuer sells $750,000 in securities. What is the effect of the aggregation rules on each of these offerings? *See* Rule 504(b)(2).

5-24. An issuer sells securities in a transaction structured to comply with Rule 504 and completes Form D claiming this exemption. It now determines that the earlier offering satisfied the conditions of Rule 506. In order to avoid aggregation with a new Rule 504 offering it would like to have, may the issuer now treat the earlier offering as a Rule 506 rather than a Rule 504 transaction? *See* Rule 500(c).

5-25. A limited partnership has been formed for the purpose of acquiring and developing real estate. A total of 40 units of the partnership will be sold to investors at a cash price of $10,000 per unit. An additional 10 units will be sold for non-cash consideration in the form of real estate. Given the mix of cash and non-cash consideration, how will the aggregate offering price be determined? What if the offering is structured so that all investors contributed real estate and there is no cash consideration?

7. Disclosure Obligations in Offerings Under Rule 506

Regulation D does not impose affirmative disclosure obligations *if* the only purchasers are accredited investors. Any nonaccredited investors in a Rule 506 offering, however, must be given specified information "a reasonable time prior to sale." Even sophisticated nonaccredited investors must be provided with this information. *See SEC v. Schooler*, 106 F. Supp. 3d 1157 (S.D. Cal. 2015). In addition to required disclosures, nonaccredited investors must be given "any material written information concerning the offering that has been provided by the issuer to any accredited investor." *See* Rule 502 (b)(2)(iv). Failure to provide the required disclosures to nonaccredited investors will negate the availability of the exemption. *See, e.g., SEC v. Empire Dev. Group*, 2008 U.S. Dist. LEXIS 43509 (S.D.N.Y. May 30, 2008).

The nature of disclosures required is specified in Rule 502(b) and depends upon the size of the offering and the nature of the issuer. If the issuer is a reporting company, the affirmative disclosure obligation may be satisfied by providing purchasers with designated filings made with the SEC pursuant to the '34 Act reporting requirements. *See* Rule 502(b)(2)(ii). If the issuer is not a reporting company, Rule 502(b)(2)(i) prescribes certain disclosures *to the extent material to an understanding of the issuer, its business, and the securities being offered.*

Non-reporting issuers must disclose both nonfinancial information and financial statement information. In general, disclosure of nonfinancial information is equivalent to that which would occur in a Regulation A exempt offering (if the issuer is eligible to use Regulation A) or through a registration statement. Disclosures of financial statements, on the other hand, vary depending upon whether the size of the offering is under $2 million, between $2 million and $7.5 million, or over $7.5 million. Not surprisingly, less is required for offerings up to $2 million, but even these small offerings may require financial statements that include balance sheets that are audited and dated within 120 days of the start of the offering.

From a policy perspective, the disclosure obligations represent a controversial aspect of the Rule 506 exemption. If indeed investor protection requires some type of mandated disclosures (a point many would argue), it is an exacting challenge to balance disclosure mandates with the need to provide smaller issuers with a cost-effective means of raising capital. Although in the past the SEC has proposed easing disclosure obligations for non-reporting issuers, it failed to adopt that proposal. The issue is again on the agenda, however, and the 2019 Concept Release on exemption harmonization signals a willingness on the part of the Commission to consider easing these burdensome disclosure requirements. *See* Securities Act Release 33-10649 (June 18, 2019).

NOTES AND QUESTIONS

1. ***The Decision Not to Disclose.*** The prescribed disclosures for non-reporting companies are required only "to the extent material to an understanding of the issuer, its business, and the securities being offered." Under what circumstances would this information not be necessary?

2. ***Disclosure Policies Discriminating Against Accredited Investors.*** Although the issuer need not provide accredited investors with copies of disclosures made to nonaccredited investors, Rule 506(b)(1) contains the following note: "When

an issuer provides information to [nonaccredited investors], it should consider providing such information to accredited investors as well, in view of the anti-fraud provisions of the federal securities laws."

Would it ever make sense for an issuer to withhold from accredited investors written information given to their nonaccredited counterparts? Note the other side of this coin in Rule 502(b)(iv), which requires the issuer to provide nonaccredited investors with a summary of "material written information" that has been given to any accredited investor.

3.   Voluntary Disclosures to Accredited Investors.   An issuer is proceeding with a Rule 506 offering. All of the investors are accredited. Although not required, should the issuer provide the investors with an offering circular?

4.   Any Questions?   Rule 502(b)(v) requires the issuer to give each purchaser the opportunity to "ask questions and receive answers" concerning the terms and conditions of the offering and to obtain additional information that the issuer can provide without unreasonable effort or expense. Is there a basis in case law for this requirement, and what purpose does it serve?

5.   Does Anybody Care?   Are nonaccredited investors likely to care about or understand the types of disclosures required by Rule 502?

8.   Additional Regulation D Requirements and Features

a.   Limitations on Resale

Because Regulation D is not intended to permit the issuer to effectuate a public offering by circumventing the registration requirements, the resale of securities acquired under its exemptions is restricted. Rule 504(b)(1) excepts from this resale restriction securities placed in Rule 504 offerings that occur (1) exclusively in states providing for the registration of securities and requiring the filing and use of a substantive disclosure document; (2) in states that have no provision for the registration of securities or the use of a disclosure document provided that the securities are registered in at least one state having these requirements and the disclosure document is delivered before sale to all purchasers (including purchases in states not requiring the document); *or* (3) exclusively under state law exemptions that permit general solicitation and advertising provided that sales are made only to accredited investors. If these exceptions sound familiar, that is because they also apply as exceptions to the prohibitions on general solicitations and advertising, discussed above.

To ensure resale is effectively restricted, Rule 502(d) originally required the issuer to use reasonable care to ensure that purchasers of the securities are not underwriters. At a minimum, the issuer was required (1) to make reasonable inquiry that the purchasers are acquiring the securities for their own accounts and not with an intention to resell; (2) to provide written disclosures to each purchaser that the securities are unregistered and cannot be sold unless registered or under an exemption; and (3) to place a legend on the securities identifying their status as restricted shares. A 1989 amendment to Rule 502(d), however, renders the above actions nonexclusive methods of ensuring that securities do not fall into the hands of underwriters.

Resales of restricted securities are discussed more fully in Chapter 6.

b.   "Bad Actor" Disqualifiers

For years, the now-defunct Rule 505 stood alone among the Regulation D exemptions in including "bad actor" disqualifiers. Section 926 of the Dodd-Frank Wall Street Reform and Consumer Protection Act of 2010 directed the Commission to develop bad actor disqualification rules applicable to Rule 506 offerings. In response, the SEC adopted a new Rule 506(d) implementing the disqualifiers, which include, in part, prior felony or misdemeanor convictions stemming from securities sales or false filings with the Commission. Persons covered by the disqualification provisions include, among others, directors, executive officers, 20 percent or greater shareholders, and promoters. The Rule includes a transition providing that disqualification will not apply if the disqualifying event occurred prior to the effective date of the final rule (Sept. 23, 2013). Moreover, the Rule includes a reasonable care exception that will protect the issuer from losing the exemption if it shows that it did not know and, in the exercise of reasonable care, could not have known of the disqualification. *See* Securities Act Release No. 33-9414 (July 10, 2013).

In the 2016 amendments, the Commission extended the bad actor disqualification provisions to Rule 504 offerings. On the advisability of disqualifying bad actors from Rule 504 offerings, *see* Brown, Seed Capital, Rule 504 and the Applicability of Bad Actor Provisions (Feb. 8, 2012) (online at SSRN: *http://ssrn .com/abstract=2001529*).

c.   Integration of Offerings: The Safe Harbor

Rule 502(a) of Regulation D provides a six-month look-forward and look-backward guideline for defining when another offering by the issuer will not be regarded as part of the same issue in measuring compliance with the conditions of the safe harbor. Securities offered less than six months before the *start* or six months after the *completion* of a Regulation D offering may be integrated with the offering (with the likely result that the conditions of the Regulation will not be satisfied) if it is part of the same issue. As will be developed more fully later in this chapter, a number of factors are relevant in determining, outside of a safe harbor, whether offerings are part of the same issue: (1) whether the sales are part of a single plan of financing, (2) whether the offerings involve the same class of securities, (3) whether the sales have been made at about the same time, (4) whether the same type of consideration is received, and (5) whether the sales are made for the same general purpose. *See* Securities Act Releases No. 4434 (Dec. 6, 1961), No. 4552 (Nov. 6, 1962).

Note that actions taken after completion of a Regulation D offering may result in the denial of the exemption for the offering because of integration. Consider, for example, *Risdall v. Brown-Wilbert, Inc.*, 753 N.W.2d 723 (Minn. 2008), where Funeral.com completed a private offering in apparent compliance with Rule 506. Two months later, the issuer attempted to raise additional funds through another private placement in which investors were sought through Internet postings and general e-mail solicitations. When informed that the solicitation tactics violated the ban on general solicitations, the issuer terminated the second offering. Although no sales had been made under the second offering, the court concluded the second offering could be integrated with the first, with the consequence that the solicitation activities subsequent to the completion of the first offering may result in the loss of the Regulation D exemption for that offering.

In 2007, the SEC proposed changes to Regulation D that included a shortening of the integration safe harbor to 90 days. *See* Securities Act Release No. 8828 (Oct. 9, 2007). The proposed changes, however, have not been adopted.

d. Form D

Rule 503 requires the electronic filing of Form D with the SEC no later than 15 days after the first sale of securities under Rule 504 or Rule 506. Originally, the availability of the Regulation D exemptions was conditioned on timely filing of the form, but this rather harsh aspect of the Rule was eliminated in 1989. At the same time, the Commission adopted Rule 507, which makes Regulation D unavailable to issuers that previously have been enjoined for failure to comply with the filing obligations of Rule 503. Although Rule 503 no longer conditions the exemptions upon timely filing of Form D, the issuance of the injunction contemplated by Rule 507 may preclude an issuer from use of the Regulation D exemptions in the future.

e. FINRA Filing

FINRA Rule 5123 requires FINRA members to file with FINRA certain offering documents (principally offering memoranda and term sheets) used in private placements or to notify FINRA if no such documents were used. Because private placement is broadly defined as a nonpublic offering of securities conducted in reliance on an available exemption from registration, the rule has applicability beyond Regulation D offerings. The FINRA filing must occur within 15 days of the first sale. The rule does not address the content of disclosure documents or otherwise require disclosures.

The information supposedly will provide FINRA with better information about the private placement activities of member firms and assist it in identifying "problematic terms and conditions." The rule includes a number of exemptions, the most important of which cover offerings limited to certain institutional accredited investors. The new rule substantially expands an earlier filing obligation that applied only when a FINRA member or affiliate was the issuer.

f. Substantial Compliance

The Commission and its staff have clashed over the question of whether tolerance should be shown toward innocent and immaterial ("I and I") violations of Regulation D. Important amendments to Regulation D were proposed in 1985. When the time came for the Commission to vote on adopting the amendments, it deferred action because the staff had opposed the development of an amendment for "I and I" violations where there was a good-faith effort to meet most of the requirements of Regulation D. In response to a comment that the staff felt "uncomfortable" with the prospect of courts interpreting such a vague standard, a commissioner retorted that he was "appalled at the notion this agency is uncomfortable with the courts interpreting its rules and regulations." After the staff developed Proposed Rule 508, the Commission adopted the other proposed amendments to Regulation D.

Securities Act Release No. 6825
Securities and Exchange Commission (Mar. 14, 1989)

. . . As reproposed in December, Rule 508 provided that failure to comply with a term, condition or requirement of Regulation D would not cause a loss of the exemption for any offer or sale to a particular individual or entity if the person relying on the exemption were to demonstrate that (1) the term, condition or requirement violated was not directly intended to protect the complaining party, (2) the failure to comply was insignificant to the offering as a whole, and (3) a good faith and reasonable attempt was made to comply with all of the regulation's terms, conditions, and requirements. In a separate provision, proposed Rule 508 indicated that any failure to comply would, nevertheless, be actionable by the Commission. With regard to significance to the offering as a whole, the Commission proposal specifically indicated that the conditions relating to dollar ceilings, numerical purchaser limits and general solicitation would always be deemed significant and therefore beyond the protection of the rule. The public comments supported the Commission proposal and Rule 508 has been adopted without change.

In excluding general solicitation from the ambit of the Rule 508 defense, the Commission reiterates its view, expressed in the 508 Release, that, inasmuch as general solicitation is not defined in Regulation D, the question of whether or not particular activities constitute a general solicitation must always be determined in the context of the particular facts and circumstances of each case. Thus, for example, if an offering is structured so that only persons with whom the issuer and its agents have had a prior relationship are solicited, the fact that one potential investor with whom there is no such prior relationship is called may not necessarily result in a general solicitation. . . .

Securities and Exchange Commission v. Ishopnomarkup.com, Inc.
2007 U.S. Dist. LEXIS 70684 (E.D.N.Y. Sept. 24, 2007)

HURLEY, District Judge:

[Ishop was formed as an Internet shopping mall offering products directly from manufacturers to consumers at no markup. In connection with three private placements of stock, Ishop distributed confidential offering memoranda ("COMs") to its investors. The COMs contained detailed information about each Ishop stock offering. In total, Ishop sold approximately 6,748,617 shares of stock to at least 355 investors residing in 21 different states. Ishop obtained proceeds of more than $2.3 million.

The SEC initiated this enforcement action alleging violations of the registration and antifraud provisions of the securities law. Presently the court is entertaining the SEC's motion for partial summary judgment on the Section 5 claims.]

DISCUSSION

[The court concluded the three offerings should be integrated and treated as a single offering.]

D.   THERE ARE GENUINE ISSUES OF MATERIAL FACT AS TO WHETHER THE OFFERINGS ARE EXEMPT UNDER RULE 506

[P]laintiff contends that Ishop sold securities to at least 20 unaccredited investors. Under Rule 502, if the issuer sells stock under Rule 506 to any purchaser who is not an accredited investor, it "shall furnish the information specified in paragraph (b)(2) . . . to such purchaser a reasonable time prior to sale." Paragraph (b)(2) requires an audited balance sheet, dated "within 120 days of the start of the offering." . . . Thus, the issues before the Court are: (1) whether Defendants sold securities to any unaccredited investors; and (2) if so, whether Defendants provided the requisite audited financial information.

1. *The Evidence Is Undisputed That Defendants Sold Securities to Unaccredited Investors*

[D]efendants . . . contend that all investors affirmed in writing that they were accredited, that they relied upon these representations, and that "if any investors did not meet this standard, they were fewer than 35 in number." Prescinding for a moment from the issue of Defendants' good faith in relying on these signed affirmations, the Court notes that for purposes of the disclosure requirements under the Rule 506 exemption, it is irrelevant that less than 35 purchasers may have been unaccredited. The disclosure requirement applies to *any* unaccredited purchasers and a failure to provide even one unaccredited purchaser with the requisite information may result in the forfeiture of the exemption. . . . Here, the evidence is undisputed that Defendants sold securities to unaccredited investors. . . .

2. *The Evidence Is Undisputed That Defendants Failed to Provide Unaccredited Investors with the Requisite Financial Information*

[D]efendants at no time suggest that they complied with the disclosure requirement of Rule 502(b)(2) [by providing auditing financial statements to nonaccredited purchasers].

3. *Whether Defendants' Failure to Comply with Rule 502 May Be Excused Pursuant to Rule 508*

Defendants argue that they prepared thorough and detailed COMs, that they limited stock issuance to investors who affirmed in writing that they met accreditation requirements, and that they relied upon the advice of counsel, who allegedly prepared all of the paperwork connected to the offerings, that all three offerings were exempt from registration. . . .

Defendants argue that their good faith reliance on counsel's advice, as well as on the signed representations of the purchasers that they met accreditation requirements, excuses their failure to comply with Rule 502's financial disclosure requirements. In support of their argument, Defendants cite cases which reference Rule 508. Rule 508 was adopted in 1989 and provides a safeguard for "insignificant" deviations from the express terms of Regulation D if the error was made in good faith. . . .

Defendants have produced evidence that they exerted a good faith attempt to comply with all of the strictures of Rule 506. [They] claim that only relatives and friends who met the accreditation requirements were contacted to become investors, that each purchaser signed a subscription agreement affirming his or her accreditation, and that they relied on the advice of counsel that all requirements of the exemption had been met. A review of the COMs and subscription agreements demonstrate that all purchasers were provided with detailed information regarding Ishop and the risks involved in investing.

In addition, the rule Defendants failed to comply with—Rule 502(b)(2) requiring the furnishing of an audited balance sheet to all unaccredited investors—is not one of the rules specifically deemed "significant" under Rule 508.[5] In fact, several cases have applied Rule 508 to facts similar to the ones at hand and have held either that defendant's good faith attempt to comply with this provision presented a genuine issue of material fact or warranted judgment for the defendant. . . .

[The SEC] does not address Rule 508 in its papers. Instead, [the SEC] argues that Defendants' "purported reliance on advice of counsel is not relevant to determine whether they violated Section 5 of the Securities Act because such violations do not require the [SEC] to prove scienter." Regardless of the accuracy of this statement, none of [the SEC's] cases addresses Rule 508.

After careful consideration of the above, the Court finds that, based on the papers submitted, [the SEC] is not entitled to summary judgment on its claim that the three offerings violated Section 5. There remain genuine issues of material fact as to whether these offerings qualify for an exemption under Rules 506 and 508.

Conclusion

For all of the above reasons, [the SEC's] motion for partial summary judgment is DENIED.

Rule 508 clearly applies to private actions in which compliance with Regulation D is at issue. Does the Rule extend to SEC enforcement actions? Subsection (b) provides that "[w]here an exemption is established only through reliance upon paragraph (a) of this section, the failure to comply shall

----

5.   The failure to comply with Rule 504(b)(2), which limits the aggregate offering price to $1 million [now $5 million—Eds.] for purposes of the Rule 504 exemption, is deemed significant, however. 17 C.F.R. §230.508(a)(2). Therefore, the Court will not apply Rule 508 to Defendants' failure to comply with Rule 504(b)(2).

nonetheless be actionable by the Commission," but the Eleventh Circuit has held that the protections of Rule 508 for innocent and immaterial violations nevertheless extend to SEC enforcement actions. *See SEC v. Levin*, 849 F.3d 995 (11th Cir. 2017). It reached this conclusion after finding ambiguity in the way the "failure to comply" language was used in the Rule. After reviewing both subsections (a) and (b) of Rule 508, do you agree with *Levin*?

PROBLEM

5-26.   An issuer has completed a $7 million private placement under Rule 506. The purchasers consist of nine pension trusts (each qualifying as an accredited investor) and one individual who purchased a relatively small amount of the securities offered. The individual had no preexisting relationship with the issuer or any of its agents, did not satisfy the standards of an accredited investor, is not sophisticated, and did not have a purchaser representative. Three of the pension trusts would now like to rescind the transaction, and the issuer claims substantial compliance under Rule 508. What result?

g. *Foreign Offerings, the Internet, and Regulation D*

Under what circumstances may an issuer proceed with a domestic Regulation D offering and treat it as independent of a simultaneous offshore offering of the same or a similar class of securities? Recall from Chapter 4 that Regulation S, adopted in 1990, provides a safe harbor for issuers engaged in offshore offerings. Rule 500(g) in turn recognizes that securities offered and sold outside the United States in accordance with Regulation S need not be registered under the '33 Act, even if the offshore offering is coincident with the domestic Regulation D offering. *See also* Rule 502(a), Note ("Generally, transactions otherwise meeting the requirements of an exemption will not be integrated with simultaneous offerings being made outside the United States in compliance with Regulation S."). Accordingly, foreign purchasers are not counted in computing the number of purchasers under Regulation D, and proceeds generated in the foreign offerings are not included in the aggregate offering price.

9.   A Comparative Perspective on Private Placements

As noted, private placements are not unique to the United States, and virtually every jurisdiction that regulates public offerings exempts offerings of a private rather than a public character. The differences, of course, lie in the varying approaches to defining "private."

For example, the European Union current regulations offer a number of exemptions for limited offerings. The more important of these include exemptions for offerings to qualified investors (generally institutional and professional investors), offerings to fewer than 150 persons per member state, and offerings of securities to the public with a total consideration of less than €1,000,000 (calculated over a 12-month period). *See* Comm'n Reg. L 168/26 EN O.J. 2017 (EU). Exemptions also are available for offerings of units in large denominations (at least €100,000 per unit) and offerings with large invest-ment minimums (€100,000). Id. For an in-depth overview of the regulation, *see* Fagernes et al., The Why and How of the New European Union Prospectus Regulation, 20 Bus. L. Int'l 5 (2019).

China offers a limited exemption for stock issued to specifically targeted indi-viduals, with a maximum of 200 offerees. *See* Securities Law of the P.R.C. (promul-gated by the Stand. Comm. Nat'l People's Cong., Oct. 27, 2005, effective Jan. 1, 2006). While similar to a private placement in the United States, the exempt offering must be approved by the China Securities Regulatory Commission. Moreover, no advertising is permitted. *See generally* Li, Comparison of the Legal Institutions of Enterprise Financing in China and the United States 3 (2009). China has yet to include wealth-based exemptions for qualified individual inves-tors. Apparently, this is due to an assumption that the large number of people who meet financial requirements to be qualified investors (many of whom are first generation wealthy investors) may lack the experience and financial sophis-tication to properly evaluate private offerings. For a discussion of "unsophisti-cated 'qualified investors'" in China and regulatory attempts to protect these investors, *see* Lin, Private Equity Investor Protection: Conceptualizing the Duties of General Partners in China, 15 Berkeley Bus. L.J. 43, 54-58 (2018).

Japan exempts private offerings limited to fewer than 50 persons, quali-fied institutional investors, or offers made exclusively to professional inves-tors. *See* Financial Instruments and Exchange Act, Law No. 25 of 1948 (Japan). Individuals with financial assets in excess of 300 million yen (approximately $2.75 million) and one year of relevant experience can request professional investor status from the Financial Services Agency (FSA) of Japan. Cabinet Office Ordinance, No. 52 of 2007, Art. 61-61 (Japan). In addition, a simpli-fied form of registration is available for offerings between 10 million yen and 100 million yen. For an in-depth look at Japanese securities transactions, *see generally* 3 Doing Business in Japan §8 (2018).

Brazil exempts private offerings, which in general are offerings to a very restricted group of offerees with whom the issuer has had a previous relationship. In addition, Brazil exempts certain offerings intended exclusively for profes-sional investors (financial assets of at least R$10 million, or about $2.5 million); there may be no more than 75 offerees and 50 actual investors, and advertising is not permitted. In 2017, an exemption for limited offerings by small busi-nesses was replaced by a new exemption for small businesses (annual revenues less than R$10 million, or about $2.5 million) in a crowdfunding offering. *See* CVM Instruction No. 588 (ICVM 588/2017). The offering cap is R$5 million ($1.25 million) over a 180-day period. Investors are limited in the amounts they may invest over a one-year period (R$10,000, or approximately $2,500), although exceptions are made for professional investors and angel investors.

10. Possible Reforms of Regulation D?

In its far-reaching Concept Release on Harmonization of Securities Offering Exemptions, the SEC has solicited comments on a number of possible reforms of the present framework for exemptions. *See* Release 33-10649 (June 18, 2019). The potential reforms of Regulation D include raising the $5 million offering limit under Rule 504, consolidating the exemptions under Rules 504, 506(b), and 506(c) into a single exemption, clarifying or re-defining the general solicitation and advertising restrictions, reducing the disclosure requirements, revising or expanding methods of verifying accredited investor status under Rule 506(c), and allowing nonaccredited investors to purchase securities in offerings involving general solicitations.

D.   The Crowdfunding Exemption: Section 4(a)(6)

Crowdfunding is the collective effort of a large number of individuals who pool their resources to support a third party's effort to achieve a stated goal or engage in a defined activity. The concept applies to a variety of actions ranging from disaster relief to raising legal fees incurred in advancing a social cause. The potential of crowdfunding is demonstrated by Kickstarter, a fundraising platform for numerous creative projects, the largest number of which involve film and video. The Kickstarter web site reports that in the first ten years of its existence the platform funded more than 160,000 creative projects with contributions by 16 million individuals. Those who contribute through Kickstarter contribute for reasons other than financial gain and do not acquire ownership interests in the projects they fund.

The crowdfunding model also applies to financing for emerging companies. Large numbers of people may be willing to contribute individually small sums each to support a startup company, receiving in return equity interests in the company. Although it may be tempting to compare investors in a crowdfunded offering to angel investors in a startup, there are meaningful distinctions in the greater degree of uncompensated risk assumed by crowdfunding investors. *See generally* Dorff, The Siren Call of Equity Crowdfunding, 39 J. Corp. L. 493 (2014). And on governance issues likely to arise in crowdfunded companies, *see* Edwards, The Big Crowd and the Small Enterprise: Intracorporate Disputes in the Close-But-Crowdfunded Firm, 122 Penn St. L. Rev. 411 (2018).

But crowdfunding investors may have objectives in addition to profit-seeking. For a discussion of the uses of crowdfunding to raise funds for pro-social benefit enterprises, *see* Hurt, Pricing Disintermediation: Crowdfunding and Online Auction IPOs, 2015 U. Ill. L. Rev. 217. *See also* Schwartz, The Nonfinancial Returns of Crowdfunding, 34 Rev. Banking & Fin. L. 565, 566 (2015) ("Legal scholars in particular have expressed concern that investors will lose any money they invest in crowdfunding companies. While this may be true from a purely financial perspective, these critics are missing an important point: Crowdfund investors with negative returns will not simply have lost their money, but rather they will have spent it (at least in part) on nonpecuniary benefits, including entertainment, political expression, and community building."). Moreover, venture capital rarely finds its way to rural areas, and crowdfunding may offer some promise for rural entrepreneurs, including farmers, to access venture and business capital. *See generally* Schwartz, Rural Crowdfunding, 13 U.C. Davis Bus. L.J. 283 (2013).

As a means of tapping funds from small investors for small businesses, crowdfunding is a global phenomenon. Crowdfunding sites exist in Great

Britain, Hong Kong, Brazil, Malaysia, Germany, the Netherlands, and sub-Saharan Africa, among other locales. For a comparative look at crowdfunding, *see* Pekmezovic & Walker, The Global Significance of Crowdfunding: Solving the SME Funding Problem and Democratizing Access to Capital, 7 Wm. & Mary Bus. L. Rev. 347 (2016).[2] A World Bank Report has highlighted the great potential for equity crowdfunding in the developing world, noting that "developing economies have the potential to drive growth by employing crowdfunding to leapfrog the traditional capital market structures and financial regulatory regimes of the developed world." World Bank, Crowdfunding's Potential for the Developing World 9 (2013).

Until recently, crowdfunding as a method for financing a U.S. business has not fit comfortably within the traditional exemptions discussed in this chapter. Crowdfunding was given a significant congressional boost in the JOBS Act, however, which amends the '33 Act by providing a new exemption in Section 4(a)(6) for startup companies seeking to raise capital through crowdfunding. The new exemption was adopted notwithstanding the concerns of the SEC and others with potential abuses of unsophisticated investors. For a perspective on the development of the exemption and a cautious assessment of its potential, *see* Heminway, How Congress Killed Investment Crowdfunding: A Tale of Political Pressure, Hasty Decisions, and Inexpert Judgments That Begs for a Happy Ending, 102 Ky. L.J. 865 (2013-2014).

The key requirements of new Section 4(a)(6) of the '33 Act include the following:

1.   The issuer's aggregate amount sold during a 12-month period cannot exceed $1.07 million (amounts are adjusted for inflation);
2.   If the purchaser's annual income or net worth is less than $107,000, the aggregate amount sold to the purchaser during any 12-month period cannot exceed the greater of $2,200 or 5 percent of the purchaser's annual income or net worth;
3.   If the purchaser's annual income or net worth exceeds $107,000, the applicable limitation is 10 percent of annual income or net worth (subject to a $107,000 "maximum aggregate amount" on the sale); and
4.   The transaction must be conducted through a broker or funding portal registered with the SEC.

The latter requirement of a broker or funding portal is designed to involve an intermediary that is charged under new Section 4A of the '33 Act with a variety of duties, including securing investors' affirmations that they understand the risks of loss and illiquidity and obtaining background information on officers, directors, and significant shareholders. The mandatory use of a broker or funding portal was added by the Senate to address a perceived lack of investor protection in the House bill. For a favorable view of the use of intermediaries,

---

2.   For an interesting comparison of crowdfunding in the United States and in New Zealand and a discussion of why offerings in New Zealand tend to be more successful, *see* Schwartz, The Gatekeepers of Crowdfunding, 75 Wash & Lee L. Rev. 885 (2018) (discussing the greater emphasis in the United States on "inclusive" crowdfunding giving entrepreneurs broad access to investors).

see Ibrahim, Crowdfunding Without the Crowd, 95 N.C. L. Rev. 1481 (2017) (arguing that true crowdfunding is a fantasy and participation of experts is needed for investors to make wise decisions about startups).

Consistent with the view of crowdfunding as a means of financing startup companies, the legislation provides that the new exemption is not available for reporting companies under the '34 Act. Section 4A(b)(2) limits promotional activities by providing that issuers may not advertise other than through notices directing investors to a broker or funding portal. Section 4A(e) requires purchasers to hold the securities for at least a year, although earlier transfer is allowed to accredited investors and family members. A security issued under the crowdfunding exemption is a "covered security" and not subject to state regulation through registration or qualification. *See* Securities Act Section 18(b)(4)(C).

Although the legislation established a number of very specific requirements for the new crowdfunding exemption, much of the detail required for implementation was left to SEC rulemaking. In a 686-page release, the Commission finalized the long-awaited crowdfunding rules. *See* SEC Release No. 33-9974 (Oct. 30, 2015). The following is a summary of the key features of Regulation Crowdfunding, which became effective in May of 2016.

Offering Size. A $1.07 million cap on the aggregate amount sold by the issuer in any 12-month period includes all amounts sold under the Section 4(a)(6) crowdfunding exemption but does not include amounts sold under another exemption. Moreover, a crowdfunded offering will not be integrated with another exempt offering made by the issuer. The Commission cautioned that "[a]n issuer conducting a concurrent exempt offering for which general solicitation is not permitted will need to be satisfied that purchasers in that offering were not solicited by means of the offering made in reliance on Section 4(a)(6)."

Holding Period. Securities purchased under the exemption must be held for one year prior to resale (subject to limited exceptions, including transfer to the issuer, to an accredited investor, to certain members of the purchaser's family, or in connection with the purchaser's death or divorce).

Investment Limitations. The rule addresses the statute's ambiguous investment limitations when an investor's annual income exceeds $107,000 but net worth does not, or vice versa. It employs a sliding scale metric keyed to net worth and income thresholds. Under this approach, if *either* annual income or net worth is less than $107,000, then a limit of the greater of (1) $2,200, or (2) 5 percent of annual income or net worth (whichever is less) applies. If *both* net worth and annual income exceed $107,000, the investment cap (not to exceed $107,000) is 10 percent of the lesser of the net worth or annual income. The issuer may rely on the intermediary to assess whether purchasers are within these limits.

Note that the investment limitations as to a particular investor are applied in the aggregate across all crowdfunding offerings in which the investor participates over a 12-month period.

Business Plan. The issuer must have a business plan, which need not be a formal document: "We understand that issuers engaging in crowdfunding transactions may have businesses at various stages of development in differing industries, and therefore, we believe that a specific 'business plan' could encompass a wide range of project descriptions, articulated ideas, and business models."

Disclosures.   The rules generally outline the types of disclosures an issuer must make, including information about officers, directors, and significant shareholders (and related parties transactions), description of business and business plan, use of proceeds, target offering amount and deadline, offering price and capital structure, and material risk factors, among other items. The disclosures are filed with the Commission on Form C.

Financial Statements.   To implement Section 4A(b)(1)(D)'s requirement of a description of the financial condition of the issuer, the rules outline a tiered framework based on aggregate amounts offered over a 12-month period:

1. For offerings of less than $107,000, the issuer must provide income and tax data from the issuer's tax return and financial statements certified by the chief executive officer.
2. For offerings between $107,000 and $535,000, the issuer must provide financial statements "reviewed" by a public accountant that is independent of the issuer.
3. For offerings exceeding $535,000, the first-time crowdfunding issuer must provide financial statements "reviewed" by a public accountant independent of the issuer. If the issuer has previously sold securities under the crowdfunding exemption, the financial statements must be audited by an independent accountant.

Ongoing Reporting Obligations.   An issuer that has completed a crowdfunded offering will be required to file a report on EDGAR annually. The required disclosures and financial statements would be similar to those required at the offering stage.

Intermediaries.   An issuer must use a single intermediary. In the SEC's view, multiple intermediaries would make it more difficult for "members of the crowd to effectively share information because, essentially, there would be multiple 'crowds.'" Moreover, a single intermediary will facilitate use of the intermediary in securing the issuer's compliance with the rules. The rules prohibit direct or indirect issuer advertising other than notices somewhat similar to "tombstone ads" identifying the intermediary and directing investors to that platform.

Any person acting as an intermediary must register with the SEC as a broker or as a funding portal, and in either case the intermediary must become a member of a registered national securities associations (currently, the only such association is FINRA).

The intermediary must have a reasonable basis for believing the issuer is in compliance with crowdfunding rules. Although the belief may be based on reasonable reliance on the issuer's representations, unless the intermediary has reason to question the truthfulness or reliability of the representations, there are lingering concerns over uncertainties associated with possible due diligence obligations for intermediaries.

'34 Act Reporting Triggers. To address the concern that a large number of small investors in a crowdfunding transaction may trigger '34 Act Section 12(g) reporting requirements (applicable when the issuer has a class of securities with more than 2,000 holders or more than 500 holders who are not accredited investors), Congress directed the SEC to exempt most securities issued under the crowdfunding exemption from Section 12(g)'s record holder count. The SEC has adopted Rule 12g-6 in response to this direction.

The above discussion illustrates that the development of a crowdfunding exemption requires a delicate balance of the competing goals of investor protection and facilitating access to capital by small businesses. Whether the rather hastily drafted crowdfunding exemption of Section 4(a)(6) strikes the right balance, however, remains to be seen, even with the more deliberate "fixes" accomplished through SEC rulemaking in Regulation Crowdfunding. Consider the comments of Professor Bradford:

> The new crowdfunding exemption is disappointing. It is poorly drafted, leaving many ambiguities and inconsistencies for the SEC or the courts to resolve. Its mandatory disclosure requirements are too complicated and expensive for the small offerings it is designed to facilitate. Its individual investment limits are too high, exposing investors to more risk than many of them can afford. Its regulation of crowdfunding intermediaries is haphazard, unnecessarily disadvantaging non-broker intermediaries, but failing to include a crucial investor protection provision. . . . The new exemption is not the regulatory panacea crowdfunding supporters hoped for, and it is unlikely to spawn a crowdfunding revolution.

Bradford, The New Federal Crowdfunding Exemption: Promise Unfulfilled, 40 Sec. Reg. L.J. 195, 198 (2012).

As presently constituted, the crowdfunding exemption appeals mostly to smaller issuers that have not previously had exempt offerings. The median offering has been by an issuer that has been incorporated for two years and employs three people. Over half the offerings have been by issuers with no revenues. A third of the offerings have been in California. *See* Securities Act Release No. 33-10649 (June 18, 2019).

Clearly, the regulatory response to equity crowdfunding is a work in progress. Commenting in 2019 on the present and future state of crowdfunded offerings, the SEC Director of Corporate Finance observed that there have been approximately 1,300 offerings under Regulation CF, and the offerings have raised about $110 million. He added, "So, relative to Reg D, or even Reg A, the amounts are modest, but the numbers are increasing and we hear a lot of interest when we go out and speak around the country. So this is something we will be keeping an eye on."[3]

---

3. SEC Director of CorpFin Bill Hinman Provides Crowdfunding Update at Small Business Capital Formation Advisory Committee Meeting, reported at *https://www.crowdfundinsider.com/2019/05/147241-sec-director-of-corpfin-bill-hinman-provides-crowdfunding-update-at-small-business-capital-formation-advisory-committee-meeting/*.

As noted, the SEC has requested comments on ways to update and harmonize the existing framework of exemptions. *See* Securities Act Release No. 33-10649 (June 18, 2019). Among the specific crowdfunding exemption issues raised by the Commission are whether the costs and burdens of the exemption may be reduced without compromising investor protection, whether the offering limit should be raised to $5 million, whether the investment limits should be increased, and whether the financial disclosure requirements should be relaxed.

PROBLEMS

5-27. Janet is interested in participating in an offering structured under the crowdfunding exemption. She is a part-time school teacher with an annual income of about $25,000. Janet has no debt, but her only assets are $10,000 in a savings account and $30,000 in a 401K retirement plan. How much may she invest in the offering? How much may she invest if the balance of her 401K account is $100,000?

5-28. Assume that five months after Janet purchased $1,000 of stock in the offering she needs cash to pay some expected dental expenses. May she sell her stock to Bill, a friend and co-worker? What if Bill is her brother?

5-29. Hannah owns the Rusty Bucket, a popular restaurant located near a marina. She would like to open a second restaurant in the area, and to this end she has published on her web site an artist's rendition of the new restaurant as well as an interview she recently gave to the local paper discussing her plans and her hopes for the new restaurant. In the interview, Hannah talked about the exciting new concept of crowdfunding and that she plans to solicit small investments (maximum of $100) from a large number of people. The web site allows interested parties to leave their contact information if they would like to receive more information about how to participate. Do you see any problems for Hannah under the crowdfunding exemption?

A dramatic development on the equity crowdfunding front has been the suddenness with which many states have developed crowdfunding exemptions as part of their own blue sky laws. Most states now have some type of exemption for crowdfunded offerings. The conditions for the exemptions vary widely, but the speed with which the concept has been embraced at the local (state) level illustrates that a crowdfunding exemption may exist more comfortably in a state regulatory structure than as part of the federal scheme of exemptions from registration.

This popularity of crowdfunding exemptions at the state level has not been lost on the SEC. In the face of mixed reactions to its final rules on the crowdfunding exemption, the SEC has expanded intrastate and regional offering exemptions designed to dovetail with offerings at the state level that are exempt under a *local* (not federal) crowdfunding exemption. Thus, the most common structure for a crowdfunded offering may be to bring the offering within a crowdfunding exemption under state law and within an intrastate/regional exemption under federal law. The intrastate/regional federal exemptions are discussed in the next section.

E. The Intrastate Offering Exemptions

Historically, there has been one intrastate offering exemption. That exemption is outlined in Section 3(a)(11) of the '33 Act, which exempts

> [a]ny security which is a part of an issue offered and sold only to persons resident within a single State or Territory, where the issuer of such security is a person resident and doing business within, or, if a corporation, incorporated by and doing business within, such State or Territory.

In spite of its apparent simplicity, the intrastate offering exemption of Section 3(a)(11) has proven to be one of the more problematic of the '33 Act's exemptions. Numerous interpretive issues (e.g., What is a local financing? What does *doing business* mean? How is *residency* to be defined?) have been addressed through Rule 147, a safe harbor for the statutory exemption. But even with the guidance of Rule 147 the exemption seems unnecessarily rigid for current times, especially in light of the fact that its availability is defeated by a *single* offer to a nonresident of the state in which the offering is to occur.

As noted above, most states have adopted crowdfunding exemptions. Initially, the state exemptions were used in combination with the federal intrastate offering exemption of Section 3(a)(11) rather than the much newer, and more cumbersome and controversial, federal crowdfunding exemption. Still, there are limitations on the intrastate offering exemption that cannot be addressed through rulemaking and restrict the usefulness of the exemption. For example, the statutory requirement that a corporate issuer be incorporated within the state eliminates Delaware corporations from using the exemption (except, of course, for offerings in Delaware). Similarly, the exemption's restrictions on the residency of offerees and purchasers seem rigid, particularly for issuers located in geographic areas where numerous states are in close proximity.

The SEC responded with a proposal "to modernize and expand Rule 147" to comport with modern business practices and technology. *See* Release No. 33-9973 (Oct. 30, 2015). Initially, it was inclined to move forward with a clean slate by abandoning the traditional Rule 147 safe harbor in favor of an entirely new exemption grounded in Section 28 of the '33 Act. The advantage of this approach is that the parameters of the new intrastate offering exemption would be defined exclusively by the SEC. The disadvantage of this approach, on the other hand, is that a number of states have developed crowdfunding exemptions under state law that are paired with the Section 3(a)(11) exemption and Rule 147 under federal law. To abruptly eliminate Rule 147 would be disruptive, at least in the short run. Ultimately, the Commission decided both to retain and modernize (somewhat) the existing Rule 147 safe harbor under Section 3(a)(11) *and* to adopt a new intrastate offering exemption, Rule 147A, based on the exemptive authority of Section 28. Over time, states will tie their exemptions to the new Rule 147A exemption and thus render Section 3(a)(11) and Rule 147 inconsequential.

The following release highlights the principal features of the amended Rule 147 and the new Rule 147A. Note that these reforms were implemented together with the Regulation D reforms discussed above.

Exemptions to Facilitate Intrastate and Regional Securities Offerings, Securities Act Release No. 10238
Securities and Exchange Commission (Oct. 26, 2016)

. . . Today we are amending Rule 147 and establishing a new Securities Act exemption, designated Rule 147A. . . . We believe the final rules will facilitate capital formation by smaller companies by increasing the utility of the current Securities Act exemptive framework for smaller offerings while maintaining appropriate protections for investors. The final rules complement recent efforts by the U.S. Congress, state legislatures, and state securities regulators to modernize existing federal and state securities laws and regulations to assist smaller companies with capital formation.

[W]e are retaining and modernizing Rule 147 under the Securities Act as a safe harbor for intrastate offerings exempt from registration pursuant to Securities Act Section 3(a)(11). These amendments will modernize the safe harbor, while keeping within the statutory parameters of Section 3(a)(11), so that issuers may continue to rely upon the rule for offerings pursuant to state law exemptions, including crowdfunding provisions, that are conditioned upon compliance with Section 3(a)(11) and Rule 147. . . .

We are adopting new Rule 147A pursuant to our general exemptive authority under Section 28 of the Securities Act, and therefore, new Rule 147A will not be subject to the statutory limitations of Section 3(a)(11). Accordingly, Rule 147A will have no restriction on offers, but will require that all sales be made only to residents of the issuer's state or territory to ensure the intrastate nature of the exemption. Rule 147A also will not require issuers to be incorporated or organized in the same state or territory where the offering occurs so long as issuers can demonstrate the in-state nature of their business, which we believe will expand the number of businesses that will be able to seek intrastate financing under Rule 147A, as compared to amended Rule 147. Certain provisions of existing Rule 147 concerning legends and mandatory disclosures to purchasers and prospective purchasers will apply to offerings conducted pursuant to amended Rule 147 and Rule 147A. . . .

II.   AMENDMENTS TO RULE 147 AND NEW RULE 147A

A.   EXPLANATION OF AMENDMENTS TO RULE 147 AND NEW RULE 147A

Numerous commenters and the 2015 Small Business Forum recommended retaining Rule 147 as a safe harbor under Section 3(a)(11). Many of these commenters also recommended adopting a substantially similar new exemption pursuant to the Commission's general exemptive authority under Section 28 as an alternative to the Section 3(a)(11) exemption and safe harbor for companies that wish to conduct intrastate offerings under slightly broader conditions than contemplated by Section 3(a)(11). After considering the comments, we are amending Rule 147 to modernize the rule to incorporate most of our proposed amendments, except for the two proposed amendments that do not fit within the statutory limits of Section 3(a)(11)—allowing issuers to make offers accessible to out-of-state residents and to be incorporated out-of-state. These two provisions are the distinguishing features of the new Rule 147A exemption that we are establishing pursuant to our general exemptive authority under Section 28. Aside from these two provisions, the remaining provisions of new Rule 147A are substantively the same as the provisions of amended Rule 147. . . .

1. *Manner of Offering*

[W]e are adopting new Rule 147A to allow issuers to make offers accessible to out-of-state residents, so long as sales are limited to in-state residents. We are also retaining amended Rule 147 as a safe harbor under Section 3(a)(11) to preserve the continued availability of existing state exemptive provisions that are specifically conditioned upon issuer reliance on Section 3(a)(11) and Rule 147. Issuers relying on amended Rule 147 as a safe harbor under Section 3(a)(11) must continue to limit all offers and sales to in-state residents.

We believe offers made over the Internet that can be viewed by a significant number of out-of-state residents are not consistent with Section 3(a)(11) and Rule 147, even if such offers include prominent disclosure stating that sales will be made only to residents of the same state or territory as the issuer. . . . [I]n 1937 the Commission released guidance on the nature of the Section 3(a)(11) exemption in the form of a letter from the Commission's General Counsel. The letter stated that securities exempt from registration pursuant to Section 3(a)(11) "may be made the subject of general newspaper advertisement (provided the advertisement is appropriately limited to indicate that offers to purchase are solicited only from, and sales will be made only to, residents of the particular state involved)." . . . We do not read the legislative history for Section 3(a)(11) and the prior Commission statements as envisioning widespread out-of-state offers, but rather as recognition that some media of communication, such as a local newspaper or periodical, could only be imperfectly targeted to residents of a particular state. The Internet, however, is not similarly targeted to residents of a particular state, making it difficult for issuers to keep the distribution of such offers local in nature.

Given the foregoing, we believe that the most appropriate means to permit the offer and sale of securities on Internet websites, or using any other form of mass media likely to reach significant numbers of out-of-state residents, is to adopt a new intrastate offering exemption pursuant to the Commission's general exemptive authority under Section 28. Accordingly, new Rule 147A will require issuers to limit sales to in-state residents, but will not limit offers by the issuer to in-state residents. New Rule 147A thereby will permit issuers to engage in general solicitation and general advertising of their offerings, using any form of mass media, including unrestricted, publicly-available Internet websites, so long as sales of securities so offered are made only to residents of the state or territory in which the issuer is resident.

Consistent with the proposal, both Rule 147A and amended Rule 147 will require issuers to include prominent disclosure with all offering materials stating that sales will be made only to residents of the same state or territory as the issuer. . . .

2. Elimination of Residence Requirement for Issuers

[W]e are retaining the requirement [under Rule 147] that an issuer shall be deemed a resident of a state or territory in which it is incorporated or organized for issuers that are incorporated or organized under state or territorial law, such as corporations, limited partnerships and trusts.

In addition, for consistency between the provisions of Rule 147 and new Rule 147A, throughout amended Rule 147, we are replacing the "principal office" requirement with the proposed "principal place of business" requirement. . . .

Under amended Rule 147, issuers that are incorporated or organized under state or territorial law will be deemed a "resident" of a particular state or territory in which they are both incorporated or organized and have their "principal place of business." . . . Similarly, issuers that are general partnerships, or in the form of another business organization not organized under any state or territorial law, shall be deemed to be a "resident" of the state or territory in which they have their "principal place of business."

[N]ew Rule 147A(c)(1) will rely solely on the principal place of business requirement to determine the state or territory in which the issuer shall be deemed a "resident," not only for corporate issuers, but for all issuers, including issuers that are not organized under any state or territorial law, such as general partnerships. . . . We continue to believe that, outside the statutory requirements of Section 3(a)(11), the jurisdiction of entity formation should not affect the ability of an issuer to be considered "resident" for purposes of an intrastate offering exemption at the federal level. . . .

To ensure an appropriate connection between the state, issuers and investors, amended Rule 147(d) and Rule 147A(d) will require an issuer to be a resident of the same state where purchasers are resident or where the issuer reasonably believes they are resident. Viewed together, paragraphs (c) and (d) of each of Rules 147 and 147A help to ensure the local intrastate character of the offering by requiring that both issuers and purchasers reside and have their principal place of business (for purchasers, the principal place of business requirement only applies to purchasers who are legal entities) in the same state or territory where the offering takes place. . . .

B. COMMON REQUIREMENTS OF THE AMENDMENTS TO RULE 147 AND NEW RULE 147A

Our amendments to Rule 147 and the provisions of new Rule 147A are substantially identical, except that, as discussed above, new Rule 147A allows an issuer to make offers accessible to out-of-state residents and to be incorporated or organized out-of-state. Under the rules we adopt today, both amended Rule 147 and new Rule 147A will include the following provisions:

- A requirement that the issuer satisfy at least one "doing business" requirement that will demonstrate the in-state nature of the issuer's business.
- A new "reasonable belief" standard for issuers to rely upon in determining the residence of the purchaser at the time of the sale of securities.
- A requirement that issuers obtain a written representation from each purchaser as to his or her residency. . . .
- A limit on resales to persons resident within the state or territory of the offering for a period of six months from the date of the sale by the issuer to the purchaser of a security sold pursuant to the exemption.
- An integration safe harbor that will include any prior offers or sales of securities by the issuer, as well as certain subsequent offers or sales of securities by the issuer occurring after the completion of the offering.
- Disclosure requirements, including legend requirements, to offerees and purchasers about the limits on resales.

1. Requirements for Issuers "Doing Business" In-State

[W]e are adopting, as proposed, updated and modernized "doing business" requirements in Rule 147 and new Rule 147A to comport with contemporary small business practices. . . . [W]e believe these issuer "doing business" requirements, identical for both amended Rule 147 and new Rule 147A, will provide issuers with greater flexibility in conducting intrastate offerings and expand the availability of these two intrastate offering provisions.

[W]e are adopting amendments to Rule 147(c)(2) and including provisions in new Rule 147A(c)(2) that will provide issuers with greater flexibility to satisfy the current "doing business" requirements by adding an alternative test based on the location of a majority of the issuer's employees while retaining the three 80% threshold tests in current Rule 147(c)(2). Furthermore, while the substance of the three 80% threshold requirements of current Rule 147(c)(2) is being retained in the final rules, compliance with any one of the 80% threshold requirements (or the additional test based on the majority of employees) will be sufficient to demonstrate the in-state nature of the issuer's business, as proposed. This is a change from current Rule 147(c)(2), which requires issuers to satisfy all three 80% threshold requirements. . . .

[W]e are adding an alternative requirement to the three modified 80% threshold requirements. This requirement, which relates to the location of a majority of the issuer's employees, will provide an additional method by which an issuer may demonstrate that it conducts in-state business sufficient to justify reliance on either Rule 147 or new Rule 147A. For these purposes, we are permitting an issuer to satisfy the "doing business" requirements by having a majority of its employees based in such state or territory. . . .

2. Reasonable Belief as to Purchaser Residency Status

[C]onsistent with the . . . determination of accredited investor status under Regulation D, we are adopting amendments to Rule 147 and a provision in new Rule 147A that will include a reasonable belief standard for the issuer's determination as to the residence of the purchaser at the time of the sale of the securities. . . . Under the final rules, an issuer will satisfy the requirement that the purchaser in the offering be a resident of the same state or territory in which the issuer is resident by either the existence of the fact that the purchaser is a resident of the applicable state or territory, or by establishing that the issuer had a reasonable belief that the purchaser of the securities in the offering was a resident of such state or territory. . . .

4. Limitation on Resales

[W]e are adopting a requirement in amended Rule 147 and new Rule 147A providing that for a period of six months from the date of the sale of the security by the issuer any resale of the security shall be made only to persons resident within the state or territory in which the issuer was resident at the time of the sale of the security by the issuer. We are persuaded . . . that a period of six months is adequate to establish that securities sold in an intrastate offering have "come to rest" in a state by analogizing to provisions of Rule 144, in which a six-month holding period is deemed sufficient to establish a requisite investment intent. . . .

[T]he resale limitation period for both amended Rule 147(e) and new Rule 147A(e) will relate back to the date of purchase by a resident investor from the issuer, in contrast to current Rule 147(e) that does not start the resale limitation period until the offering has terminated (i.e., until all offers and sales have ceased). . . .

[A]n issuer's ability to rely on the respective rules will not be conditioned on a purchaser's compliance with Rule 147(e) and Rule 147A(e). As discussed in the Proposing Release, the application of current Rule 147(e) in the overall scheme of the safe harbor can cause uncertainty for issuers. We continue to believe that removing the condition on purchaser compliance with Rule 147(e) will increase the utility of the exemption by eliminating the uncertainty created in the offering process for issuers under the current rules. . . .

5. Integration

[W]e are adopting amendments to the integration safe harbor under Rule 147 and providing an identical integration safe harbor provision in new Rule 147A. . . . The integration safe harbor will cover any prior offers or sales of securities by the issuer, as well as certain subsequent offers or sales of securities by the issuer occurring after the completion of an offering pursuant to Rule 147 or Rule 147A, as applicable. Accordingly, offers and sales made pursuant to Rules 147 and 147A will not be integrated with:

- Offers or sales of securities made prior to the commencement of offers and sales of securities pursuant to Rules 147 or 147A; or
- Offers or sales of securities made after completion of offers and sales pursuant to Rules 147 or 147A that are:
  - [Registered under the Securities Act or exempt under Regulation A, Rule 701, Regulation S, or Section 4(a)(6)]; or
  - Made more than six months after the completion of an offering conducted pursuant to Rules 147 or 147A.

[I]ntegration safe harbors provide issuers, particularly smaller issuers whose capital needs often change, with greater certainty about their eligibility to comply with an exemption from Securities Act registration. . . . The bright-line integration safe harbor we are adopting in amended Rule 147(g) and new Rule 147A(g) will assist issuers, particularly smaller issuers, in analyzing certain transactions, but will not address the issue of potential offers or sales that occur concurrently with, or close in time after, a Rule 147 or 147A offering. There is no presumption that offerings outside the integration safe harbors should be integrated. Rather, whether concurrent or subsequent offers and sales of securities will be integrated with any securities offered or sold pursuant to amended Rule 147 or new Rule 147A will depend on the particular facts and circumstances, including whether each offering complies with the requirements of the exemption that is being relied upon for the particular offering. For example, an issuer conducting a concurrent exempt offering for which general solicitation is not permitted will need to be satisfied that purchasers in that offering were not solicited by means of the offering made in reliance on Rule 147 or new Rule 147A. If an offer fails to comply with the requirements of the exemption, and the offer is not registered and no other exemption is available, that offer would be in violation of Section 5 of the Securities Act.

Amended Rule 147, as a safe harbor under Section 3(a)(11), will continue to prohibit out-of-state offers to any person not residing in the same state or territory in which the issuer is resident. Accordingly, an issuer conducting a concurrent exempt offering for which general solicitation is permitted across state lines would be unlikely to comply with the in-state offer restriction in Rule 147(b). . . .

An issuer relying on the new Rule 147A exemption, which permits multi-state offers, may conduct a concurrent exempt offering for which general solicitation is permitted, so long as the issuer complies with the legend and disclosure requirements of Rule 147A(f), as well as any additional restrictions on the general solicitation required by the other exemption concurrently being relied upon by the issuer. . . .

NOTES AND QUESTIONS

1. Testing the Premise. One of the arguments advanced in support of the intrastate offering exemptions (both old and new) is that state regulation of truly local issuances adequately protects investors. Is the premise sound? Consider the following comment:

> Any significant degree of out-of-state business could ruin the exemption, a limitation that is archaic in light of the increasingly interconnected national and global economies. One might be more sympathetic to the exemption's limitations if there were merit to the notions that local investors know management and understand the local business, and that local enforcement can quickly discover and respond to offering violations. But those concepts make sense only in the smallest communities. When applied in states with millions of dispersed citizens ranging over hundreds of miles, concepts based upon local knowledge and control are no longer justifiable.

Cohn, The Impact of Securities Laws on Developing Companies: Would the Wright Brothers Have Gotten Off the Ground?, 3 J. Small & Emerging Bus. L. 315, 355 (1999). Still, in the National Securities Markets Improvement Act of 1996, Congress *excluded* transactions under Section 3(a)(11) from the legislation's narrowing of state registration and qualification activities, leaving the states an important role to play in the regulation of intrastate securities offerings.

2.   *Easing Standards for Measuring the Level of Business Activity in a State.* A recurring problem under the Section 3(a)(11) exemption has been to define what constitutes "doing business" in the state. Early case law, though sparse, was consistent in requiring that a "predominant" amount of the issuer's business must be within the state. Rule 147 provided some clarification in setting three 80 percent thresholds (applied to revenues, assets, and use of proceeds), all three of which had to be met. The 2016 reforms apply the same thresholds to Rule 147 and Rule 147A but relax the standards considerably by providing, for both rules, that the doing business standard is met by satisfying any one of the three thresholds. Moreover, the reforms added an alternative test for meeting the doing business standard based on the location of a majority of the issuer's employees.

3.   *Resales.* When do securities "come to rest" such that they may be resold without jeopardizing the issuer's exemption? In a number of ways, the 2016 reforms make life easier for the issuer proceeding under either Rule 147 or 147A. First, the traditional holding period long in place under Rule 147 has been shortened from nine months to six months. Second, the earlier approach of Rule 147 that the holding period is measured for all purchasers from the date of the last sale in the offering has been changed so that, under both rules, the holding periods are calculated separately with reference to each resident purchaser. Finally, Rule 147 originally penalized the issuer by denying the exemption if a single improper resale took place, regardless of the efforts of the issuer to prevent this from happening. Now, Rule 147 and Rule 147A are no longer strictly conditioned on *purchaser* compliance with resale restrictions. An issuer, of course, is expected to otherwise meet the conditions of the applicable rule, which will include legends, stop transfer restrictions, and disclosures of resale restrictions to purchasers.

PROBLEMS

For each of the following problems, consider the application of both Rule 147 and Rule 147A.

5-30.   Two physicians plan to form a Massachusetts insurance company that will write medical malpractice insurance policies for Massachusetts physicians. They would like to make an offering of common stock in the company to all Massachusetts physicians. They propose to advertise the offering in the Boston Globe and include information on the offering on their web site. Are there any problems with the breadth of this offering? *See* Release No. 4434. They also propose a direct mailing to all physicians on a Blue Shield mailing list of Massachusetts doctors (providing the office addresses of Blue Shield doctors). Any problems? *See* Palmer & Dodge, SEC No-Action Letter (Aug. 11, 1975). What if the major marketing of the offering is accomplished through an Internet web site?

5-31. Promoters intend to form a Washington limited partnership for the purpose of investing in oil and gas drilling ventures. All of the general and limited partners will be Washington residents, all of the books and records of the partnership (including securities and similar evidences of ownership in the ventures) will be maintained in Washington, and the sole office of the partnership will be in Washington. Moreover, investments in the oil and gas ventures will be executed through Washington brokers. Almost all of the ventures in which the partnership will invest, however, will be outside of Washington. Will this partnership be doing business in Washington for purposes of the intrastate offering exemption? *See* Professional Consultants, Inc., SEC No-Action Letter (Dec. 19, 1980).

5-32. Minnesota Cablesystems is planning an intrastate offering of limited partnership interests. One of the potential investors recently accepted a job offer with a Chicago-based company. He has listed his Minneapolis home for sale, but it is likely to take several months to complete the sale. In the meantime, he will stay in a Chicago hotel during the week and return home on the weekends. May this investor participate in the Minnesota offering? *See* Rule 147(d)(2) and Rule 147A(d)(2).

5-33. Davis Hardware, Inc., is a Delaware corporation with the entirety of its business operations in California. It wishes to raise funds through an intrastate offering. In light of the 2016 reforms, is it free to do so under either Rule 147 or Rule 147A?

5-34. Valdosta will merge into a subsidiary of Omega Corporation, a Georgia corporation. Most of the Valdosta shareholders not electing to receive cash will be given common stock, for which a registration statement will be filed. Shareholders who are residents of Georgia, however, may elect instead to receive promissory notes issued by Omega. Omega would like to rely upon the intrastate offering exemption (using either Rule 147 or Rule 147A) and avoid registration of the notes. How does the common stock issuance affect the availability of this exemption for the notes?

5-35. The Money Cafe, Inc. is a California company in the business of making consumer loans. It has about 300 employees who work in the Los Angeles office (also the corporate headquarters) where all work relating to loan approvals and collections is done. Approximately 300 more employees work at various offices outside California. About 30 percent of the company's gross revenues is in the form of interest from loans made to out-of-state borrowers. Depending on valuation techniques used, the company's assets in California are about 75-85 percent of its total assets.

The company has operated for the past several years under financing provided by a Texas bank. It would like to refinance this debt by issuing debt securities to California residents and using the proceeds to pay down the bank debt. Is either Rule 147 or Rule 147A available even though (1) the company has substantial income from interest paid by out-of-state customers, and (2) the company will be sending the proceeds out of state to the Texas bank? *See* Master Financial, Inc., SEC No-Action Letter (May 27, 1999).

5-36. *X* Corp. commences a Rule 147 offering on January 1. *A* purchases shares on January 15. The final sale to *D* occurs on March 1. When may *A* resell the shares to a nonresident?

5-37. A Connecticut corporation plans to offer stock to Connecticut residents. In lieu of paying cash, investors may elect to purchase their stock on an installment plan calling for 36 easy monthly payments. At what point will Rule 147's holding period expire? *See* Opportunities Inv. Assocs., SEC No-Action Letter (June 14, 1978). What if before this point one of the purchasers moves to another state? What can be done to ensure the holding period expires at the earliest possible date? *See* Diplomat, Ltd., SEC No-Action Letter (Jan. 13, 1984).

F. Employee Benefit Plans and Contracts Relating to Compensation: Rule 701

Securities Act Release No. 33-7645
Securities and Exchange Commission (Feb. 25, 1999)

In 1988, we adopted Rule 701 . . . to allow private companies to sell securities to their employees without the need to file a registration statement, as public companies do. The rule provides an exemption from the registration requirements of the Securities Act for offers and sales of securities under certain compensatory benefit plans or written agreements relating to compensation. The exemptive scope covers securities offered or sold under a plan or agreement between a non-reporting ("private") company . . . and the company's employees, officers, directors, partners, trustees, consultants and advisors.

When we adopted the rule, we determined that it would be an unreasonable burden to require these private companies, many of which are small businesses, to incur the expenses and disclosure obligations of public companies when their only public securities sales were to employees. Further, these sales are for compensatory and incentive purposes, rather than for capital-raising. To accommodate these companies, we used the maximum extent of the authority we had at that time under Section 3(b) of the Securities Act to exempt offers and sales of up to $5 million per year.

Currently, the amount of securities subject to outstanding offers in reliance on Rule 701, plus the amount of securities offered or sold under the rule in the preceding 12 months, may not exceed the greatest of $500,000, or an amount determined under one of two different formulas. One formula limits the amount to 15% of the issuer's total assets measured at the end of the issuer's last fiscal year. The other formula restricts the amount to no more than 15% of the outstanding securities of the class being offered. Regardless of the formula elected, Rule 701 restricts the aggregate offering price of securities subject to outstanding offers and the amount sold in the preceding 12 months to no more than $5 million.

[T]he $5 million limit appears to have become unnecessarily restrictive in light of inflation, the increased popularity of equity ownership as a retention and incentive device for employees, and the growth of deferred compensation plans.

In October 1996, Congress enacted the National Securities Markets Improvement Act of 1996 ("NSMIA"), which, for the first time, gave us the authority to provide exemptive relief in excess of $5 million for transactions such as these. The legislative history of NSMIA stated specifically that we should use this new authority to lift the $5 million ceiling on Rule 701.

Today, we announce revisions to the rule that:

(1) remove the $5 million aggregate offering price ceiling and, instead, set the maximum amount of securities that may be sold in a year at the greatest of:
— $1 million (rather than the current $500,000);
— 15% of the issuer's total assets; or
— 15% of the outstanding securities of that class;
(2) require the issuer to provide specific disclosure to each purchaser of securities if more than $5 million worth of securities are to be sold [this threshold was raised to $10 million in a 2018 rule change—EDS.];
(3) do not count offers for purposes of calculating the available exempted amounts;
(4) harmonize the definition of consultants and advisors permitted to use the exemption to the narrower definition of Form S-8;
(5) amend Rule 701 to codify current and more flexible interpretations; and
(6) simplify the rule by recasting it in plain English.

Together, these changes will add greater flexibility for companies to compensate their employees with securities and, at the same time, will provide that essential information be delivered to employees in appropriate situations and in a timely manner. . . .

NOTES AND QUESTIONS

1. Compensatory Plans Versus Schemes to Raise Capital. Preliminary Note 5 to Rule 701 indicates the exemption is available for securities issued in "compensatory circumstances" and the Rule does not apply to "plans or schemes to circumvent this purpose, such as to raise capital." Is this distinction workable?

How does Rule 701 attempt to distinguish plans with a compensatory purpose from those designed to raise capital?

More broadly, are startup employees vulnerable when paid in stock rather than cash? Professor Cable argues that in an early stage startup, employees may be well positioned to evaluate and monitor a company's progress, but "a more advanced company with thousands of employees is a different creature than a raw startup in the founders' garage." Cable, Fools Gold? Equity Compensation and the Mature Startup, 11 Va. L. & Bus. Rev. 615, 618 (2017).

2.   *Consultants and Advisers.*   In its initial adoption of Rule 701, the Commission acquiesced to the suggestions of commenters that consultants and advisers should be allowed to participate in compensatory benefit plans under the exemption. Citing concern over potential overbreadth of these classifications, the 1999 amendments narrowly define consultants and advisers. To qualify, an individual must provide "bona fide services." Such services do not include for this purpose services relating to the sale of securities in capital-raising transactions.

3.   *Rule 701 and the "Gig Economy."*   The Internet has led to new types of contractual relationships between companies and individuals in the workplace that do not fall easily within such traditional categories as "employees" and "consultants." In a concept release seeking comment on how Rule 701 should be adapted to the proliferation of new types of relationships, the SEC noted:

> These can involve short-term, part-time or freelance arrangements, where the individual—rather than the company—may set the work schedule. Typically, this involves the individual's use of the company's Internet "platform" for a fee to find business, whether that involves the individual providing services to end users, or using the platform to sell goods or lease property. Platforms are available that offer end users such services as ride-sharing, food delivery, household repairs, dog-sitting, and tech support. . . . An individual who provides services or goods through these platforms may have similar relationships with multiple companies, through which the individual may engage in the same or different business activities.
>
> Individuals participating in these arrangements do not enter into traditional employment relationships, and thus may not be "employees" eligible to receive securities in compensatory arrangements under Rule 701. Similarly, they also may not be consultants or advisors, or de facto employees under Rule 701. As with traditional employees, however, companies may have the same compensatory and incentive motivations to offer equity compensation to these individuals. Accordingly, we solicit comment regarding these "gig economy" relationships to better understand how they work and determine what attributes of these relationships potentially may provide a basis for extending eligibility for the Rule 701 exemption.

Securities Act Release No. 10521 (July 18, 2018).

4.   *Limiting Rule 701 to Non-Reporting Companies.*   Rule 701 is not available for reporting companies. Why? Apart from the fact that the issuer was a reporting company, would the plan at issue in *Ralston* now qualify under Rule 701?

5.   *Rule 701 and '34 Act Reporting Obligations.* As will be discussed in Chapter 11, Section 12(g)(1) of the '34 Act imposes reporting obligations on companies with more than $10 million in assets and stockholders of record exceeding a specified minimum number. This creates a problem for rapidly growing private companies that have broad based Section 701 plans and rather quickly hit the '34 Act reporting thresholds. The 2012 JOBS Act provided relief by amending Section 12(g)(1) to raise the stockholders of record threshold from 500 to 2,000 (or more than 500 stockholders who are not accredited investors) and, more importantly for present purposes, to specify that holders of record do *not* include persons who received the securities pursuant to an employee compensation plan in transactions exempt from the '33 Act's registration requirements (principally Rule 701 plans).

6.   *Disclosure Issues.* Other than requiring the issuer to provide participants with a copy of the plan and any written contract relating to compensation, Rule 701 does not require affirmative disclosures about the issuer *unless* sales during any consecutive 12-month period exceed $10 million (raised from $5 million in 2018). When that threshold is exceeded, information that must be provided to all investors includes information about the risks associated with the securities and financial statements comparable to those that are required in Regulation A offerings.

Citing the confidentiality needs of private issuers, the 2006 report of the Advisory Committee on Smaller Public Companies recommended an increase in the disclosure threshold from $5 million to $20 million. The SEC has not acted on that recommendation.

7.   *Google Meets the SEC.* In the two years prior to its 2004 IPO, Google utilized Rule 701 to issue over $80 million in stock options to its employees. To its later regret, it failed to make the financial disclosures required by the Rule when sales during a 12-month period exceed $5 million. The lapse complicated Google's attempts to make its IPO registration statement effective and ultimately led to administrative action by the SEC in the form of a cease and desist order against the company as well as its lawyer. In the release accompanying the order, the Commission noted:

> Google far exceeded the $5 million disclosure threshold, yet failed to register the options or provide the required financial information to employees. According to the Commission, Google—which, at the time, was still a privately-held company—viewed the disclosure of the information to employees as strategically disadvantageous, fearing the information could leak to Google's competitors.
>
> The Commission's order further finds that Google's General Counsel David Drummond, 41, of San Jose, Calif., was aware that the registration and related financial disclosure obligations had been triggered, but believed that Google could avoid providing the information to its employees by relying on an exemption from the law. According to the Commission, Drummond advised Google's Board that it could continue to issue options, but failed to inform the Board that the registration and disclosure obligations had been triggered or that there were risks in relying on the exemption, which was in fact inapplicable. . . .
>
> Added Helane Morrison, District Administrator of the Commission's San Francisco District Office, "Attorneys who undertake action on behalf of their

company are no less accountable than any other corporate officers. By deciding Google could escape its disclosure requirements, and failing to inform the Board of the legal risks of his determination, Drummond caused the company to run afoul of the federal securities laws."

SEC Press Release 2005-06 (Jan. 13, 2005). These comments should be considered carefully for the insights they offer both on the importance of strict observance of the conditions of an exemption if securities are sold without registration and on the critical role that the attorney plays in ensuring that the client complies with the securities laws.

   8.   Aggregation and Integration.   Rule 701 is relatively isolated from the effects of other exempt offerings that may occur during the same time period. The exemption speaks of an "aggregate sales price" that is determined solely by reference to securities sold under the exemption during any consecutive 12-month period. Moreover, the amounts sold under Rule 701 do not affect the aggregate offering price limitations for other offerings that may occur under one of the Section 3(b) exemptions. As to integration, Rule 701(f) provides that sales exempt under the rule are "deemed to be part of a single, discrete offering and are not subject to integration with any other offers or sales. . . ."

PROBLEMS

5-38.   Issuer has outstanding 10,000 shares of common stock and 5,000 shares of preferred stock, convertible, on a one-to-one basis, into common stock. It now wishes to establish a stock option plan qualifying for the Rule 701 exemption. Assuming no securities have been sold in reliance on Rule 701 in the last 12 months, what limits does Rule 701 place on the size of the stock option plan? What if the convertible preferred stock had previously been sold in an offering exempt under Rule 701?

5-39.   Issuer wishes to have simultaneous Rule 505 and Rule 701 offerings. Will the two be combined for purposes of aggregate offering or sales price limitations for each?

5-40.   Omnicare is a designer, manufacturer, and worldwide distributor of orthopedic implant devices. Although some companies in this industry rely on their own employees to conduct their sales and marketing activities, Omnicare has chosen to have these services performed by independent sales representatives. Although they are independent, Omnicare's sales representatives are contractually prohibited from distributing or promoting products that are competitive with those manufactured and sold by the company.
   Omnicare would like to adopt an equity-based award plan to provide compensation and performance incentives to its sales force. As a condition of participating in the plan, each salesperson will be required to represent in writing that the marketing of Omnicare's products is that person's primary trade or business activity. Will Omnicare's plan qualify under Rule 701? *See* Rule 701(5)(c). Are the prohibition on the sale of competitive products and the

representation concerning primary business activity relevant to your analysis? *See* Wright Acquisition Holdings, Inc., SEC No-Action Letter (Aug. 2, 2000).

G.   *Regulation A: Mini-Registration*

Regulation A (Rules 251-263) is an administrative exemption promulgated under Section 3(b) of the Securities Act, which was substantially expanded by the JOBS Act through the addition of Section 3(b)(2) authorizing the SEC to exempt from registration a class of securities if the aggregate offering price of the issuance does not exceed $50 million. Regulation A results in unrestricted securities and is available for primary or secondary offerings. Originally limited to offerings by non-reporting companies, 2018 rule changes mandated by the Economic Growth, Regulatory Relief, and Consumer Protection Act extend the availability of the exemption to reporting companies as well.

Prior to the JOBS Act and the SEC's finalization of new Regulation A rules in 2015, the maximum offering under the exemption was $5 million. In the face of a continuing decline in the use of Regulation A, due largely to the relatively low offering ceiling and full blue sky regulation (in contrast with Rule 506), Congress moved to revitalize the exemption by raising the offering threshold to $50 million (prompting some to refer to the revised exemption as Regulation A+).

The Commission's 2015 rulemaking dramatically restructures Regulation A offerings into two tiers likely to prove far more popular than the prior iteration of the exemption. *See* Securities Act Release No. 33-9741 (Mar. 25, 2015).

Tier 1 Offerings. Tier 1 is available for offerings up to $20 million (including no more than $6 million on behalf of sellers who are affiliates of the issuer) over a 12-month period. There are no qualification requirements for investors or limits on the amount a person may invest. Compliance with state blue sky laws is required for Tier 1 offerings.

Tier 2 Offerings. Tier 2 is available for offerings up to $50 million (including no more than $15 million on behalf of sellers who are affiliates of the issuer) over a 12-month period. There are no investment limitations for accredited investors. For an investor who is a natural person but not accredited, the purchase limit is no more than 10 percent of the greater of the investor's annual income or net worth. The purchase limits do not apply to purchases of securities that will be listed on a national securities exchange. Tier 2 offerings are exempt from blue sky review.

Other features and requirements for Regulation A offerings (Tier 1 and Tier 2) include the following:

Resales. In contrast with offerings under Regulation D, securities sold under Regulation A are not restricted, which means they may be resold immediately (resales by affiliates of the issuer may create complications, discussed in Chapter 6).

Integration.   Rule 251(c) provides that Regulation A offerings will not be integrated with either (1) any *prior* offerings, or (2) *later* offerings that are registered, made in reliance upon Rule 701 (compensatory benefit plans) or pursuant to an employee benefit plan, made in reliance upon Regulation S, made in reliance upon the crowdfunding exemption or, importantly, made more than six months after the Regulation A offering. Rule 251(c) is particularly important in that it offers "two-sided" integration protection, rather than the "one-sided" protection more generally offered in safe harbors (such as Regulation D).

To illustrate, assume two offerings, separated by seven months. The first is under the intrastate offering exemption of Section 3(a)(11), and the second is under Rule 506 of Regulation D. Regulation D's safe harbor (Rule 502(a)) operates to protect only the Rule 506 offering from the effects of earlier sales under the Section 3(a)(11) offering; it does nothing to protect the Section 3(a)(11) offering from the effects of later sales under the Rule 506 offering. Rule 251(c) of Regulation A, on the other hand, offers two-sided protection—that is, if the second offering is under Regulation A, not only will it be protected from integration with the earlier Section 3(a)(11) offering, but also the earlier offers and sales will be protected from integration with the later Regulation A offering. The availability of two-sided protection is one of the more attractive features of Regulation A. For an excellent discussion of this point, as well as other aspects of integration under Regulation A, *see* Bradford, Regulation A and the Integration Doctrine: The New Safe Harbor, 55 Ohio St. L.J. 255 (1994).

Filing and Disclosure Requirements.   Rule 251(d) requires the filing of an Offering Statement (Form I-A) before a Regulation A offering may commence. Issuers that are first-time filers may file nonpublic drafts for review. The Offering Statement must be qualified by the SEC before any sales may be made.

It is the filing obligations with respect to the Offering Statement that give a Regulation A offering the character of a mini-registration. The content requirements of the Offering Statement are simpler than the counterpart requirements of a registration statement. For Tier 1 offerings, balance sheets and income statements for two years are required; audited financial statements are required only to the extent that they exist having been prepared for other purposes. For Tier 2 offerings, audited balance sheets and income statements for two years are required. Moreover, Tier 2 offerings are subject to ongoing reporting requirements, but by virtue of 2018 changes to Rule 257, this requirement is deemed satisfied for reporting companies that are in compliance with their reporting obligations under the '34 Act.

Testing the Waters.   For many years, Rule 254 has allowed Regulation A issuers to "test the waters" by soliciting interest from prospective investors prior to filing Offering Statements. In the Commission's words:

> [O]ne of the major impediments to a Regulation A financing for a small start-up or developing company with no established market for its securities, is the cost of preparing the mandated offering statement. The full costs of compliance would be incurred without knowing whether there will be any investor interest in the company.

Securities Act Release No. 6949 (July 30, 1992). Regulation A's testing the waters provision addresses this problem by allowing issuers to assess at an early stage investor interest in a proposed offering. This feature of Regulation A influenced 2012 legislative reforms streamlining public offerings for emerging growth companies (discussed in Chapter 4).

Rule 255 allows issuers in either Tier 1 or Tier 2 offerings to assess investor interest both before and after the Offering Statement is filed. The issuer must file with the SEC any existing testing the water materials together with the Offering Statement. Rule 255(b) specifies the content and required legends for the materials. If testing the water materials are used after the SEC filing, the issuer must include an Offering Circular (a somewhat abbreviated version of the Offering Statement) or information on where it may be obtained. The Division of Corporation Finance has indicated through Compliance and Disclosure Interpretations that waters may be tested by using hyperlinks in Twitter or similar platforms, provided that additional hyperlinks must be included to provide the information required by Rule 255.

Altering Course After Testing the Waters.   Suppose an issuer tests the waters and concludes before filing an Offering Statement that the Regulation A offering should not go forward. May the issuer then offer the securities under another exemption or as part of a registered offering? As to a registered offering, Rule 255(e) provides that, if the issuer in the abandoned Regulation A offering solicited interest only from qualified institutional buyers or institutional accredited investors, then the abandoned offering would not be integrated with the subsequent registered offering. If the issuer solicited more broadly, then integration will not occur if at least 30 days passes between the last solicitation of interest under Regulation A and the filing of the registration statement; if fewer than 30 days elapse, whether integration occurs will be evaluated under the general (and nebulous) integration factors applicable when a safe harbor is not available.

What if after testing the waters but before filing an Offering Statement the issuer decides to instead have a Regulation D offering? Because Rule 255(e) speaks to registered rather than exempt offerings, the issuer would look to the more general integration provisions of Rule 251(c) (discussed above). Although the Rule provides for non-integration of Regulation A offerings with certain other listed offerings, a subsequent Regulation D offering is not one of those specifically listed, which means the cautious issuer will probably choose to avoid integration problems by waiting six months before proceeding with the Regulation D offering.

Disqualification.   Rule 262 includes the so-called bad actor disqualifiers that deny the exemption when the issuer or those closely associated with it have engaged in certain types of misconduct.

Substantial Compliance.   Regulation A includes a substantial compliance provision similar to that of Regulation D. Under Rule 260, failure to comply with a requirement of Regulation A will not result in loss of the exemption as to a particular purchaser if the issuer acted in good faith, the deviation was insignificant in relation to the offering as a whole, and the requirement not observed was not intended to protect the purchaser complaining of the deviation.

NOTES AND QUESTIONS

1. State Regulation.   One reason for the limited use of Regulation A prior to its revitalization under the JOBS Act was that securities offered under the exemption were not covered securities and, therefore, were subject to state regulation. The final rules partially address this perceived problem by exempting Tier 2 offerings from state regulation through registration or the equivalent (treating *all* offerees and purchasers under the offerings as "qualified purchasers" of covered securities). As is true with all covered securities, states may require notice filings, consisting of copies of documents filed with the SEC, together with consents for service of process.

Not surprisingly, the North American Securities Administrators Association, the voice of state regulators, opposed the preemption of state law for Tier 2 offerings. Hoping to forestall the preemption, NASAA announced prior to the finalization of the Regulation A rules that its members had approved a streamlined multi-state review protocol that will allow a Regulation A filing to be made in one place and distributed electronically to all states. This move was to no avail, however, and it did not dissuade the SEC from exempting in the final rules Tier 2 offerings from state blue sky regulation. Massachusetts and Montana responded with a suit challenging the SEC's treatment of all purchasers in Tier 2 offerings as qualified purchasers with the consequent exclusion of the states from oversight of such offerings, but their challenge was unsuccessful. *See Lindeen v. SEC,* 825 F.3d 646, 653-654 ((D.C. Cir. 2016).

The disparate state regulation treatment of Tier 1 and Tier 2 offerings has prompted many issuers to structure their Regulation A offerings under Tier 2 solely to avoid state regulation. As the SEC's Director of Corporate Finance has noted, "We see a lot of folks doing tier 2 offerings at amounts that could have been raised under tier 1. So they are willing to go a little bit further in the disclosure and live with tier 2 standards to afford themselves the preemption protections."[4]

2. Is Regulation A Attractive?   Regulation A has become more competitive with other exemptions. For example, when compared with offerings under Rules 504 and 505, a Regulation A Tier 1 offering may test the waters and is not subject to the general solicitation restrictions or Rule 505's numerical limits on nonaccredited investors. The above-referenced 2018 rule change making Regulation A available to reporting as well as non-reporting companies enhances the importance of the exemption. Moreover, Regulation A results in unrestricted securities that are freely tradable.

Similarly, Regulation A Tier 2 offerings offer some advantages over Rule 506 offerings. Rule 506(b) offerings are subject to the ban on general solicitations and advertising, and the more lenient Rule 506(c) limits offerings to accredited investors. An issuer in a Regulation A Tier 2 offering may test the waters before

---

4. SEC Director of CorpFin Bill Hinman Provides Crowdfunding Update at Small Business Capital Formation Advisory Committee Meeting, reported at *https://www .crowdfundinsider.com/2019/05/147241-sec-director-of-corpfin-bill-hinman-provides-crowdfunding-update- at-small-business-capital-formation-advisory-committee-meeting/.*

filing, and the status of an investor as accredited is irrelevant (although nonac-credited purchasers are subject to the investment limits). As is the case with Tier 1, Tier 2 offerings result in unrestricted securities.

But there are some drawbacks to Regulation A when compared to the Regulation D exemptions. Regulation A requires an offering statement and a Form 1A filing, and audited financial statements are required for Tier 2 offerings (as well as Tier 1 offerings when the statements are otherwise available). Although issuers in Rule 506 offerings customarily provide some disclosures even when not required, issuers in Regulation A Tier 2 offerings are subject to initial and ongoing reporting requirements. These are among the reasons that Regulation D offerings occur much more frequently than Regulation A offerings.

Regulation A may offer an attractive alternative to an IPO. The costs for the Regulation A offering (including legal counsel and auditors) will be lower. Form IA is a simpler filing than a registration statement, and SEC review will be quicker. To date, however, only a few Regulation A offerings have listed on Nasdaq and the NYSE American, and for the most part the performance of these listings has been poor. Concerns over lower accounting and disclosure requirements than those applicable to registered offerings are part of the explanation for the lukewarm investor response. In response, NASDAQ has initiated "heightened review" procedures for listing of Regulation A offerings and also has proposed to implement (subject to SEC approval) a requirement that Regulation A listed companies have been in business for at least two years. *See generally* Osipovich, Exchanges Shy Away from Mini-IPOs After Fraud Concerns, Wall St. J., June 10, 2019 (available online).

For a generally positive discussion of the revitalized Regulation A tempered by cautionary concerns over the large numbers of nonaccredited investors (many of whom are unsophisticated) actually investing in startups and other risky offerings under the exemption, *see* Newman, Regulation A+: New and Improved After the JOBS Act or a Failed Revival?, 12 Va. L. & Bus. Rev. 243 (2018) (including data on Tier 1 and Tier 2 filings).

3. Possible Reform? The Advisory Committee on Small and Emerging Companies and the Department of Treasury have recommended raising the Tier 2 limits to a level higher than $50 million, but to date the SEC has not acted on these recommendations. In its Concept Release on harmonizing the exemptions, the Commission has raised the possibility of a number of reforms of Regulation A, including raising the limits for both tiers, changing or eliminating the investment limits in Tier 2 offerings, and modifying the financial reporting requirements. *See* Securities Act Release 33-10649 (June 18, 2019).

PROBLEMS

5-41. Brocon is proceeding with a Tier 1 Regulation A offering of common stock that will include a large number of investors who are not accredited. One of the likely investors is Carl, whose annual income as a high school teacher is $60,000. Carl is a friend of one of Brocon's officers. Carl has no investing experience but is interested in purchasing $20,000 of stock in the offering. Is there anything about Carl that should concern Brocon? What if it is a Tier 2 offering?

5-42.   On April 1, Limitbeat, Inc. begins testing the waters for a $15 million Regulation A offering. On May 1 (the date the last prospective purchaser was contacted), it decides to scrap the Regulation A offer and proceed with a registered public offering. What is the earliest point at which it may safely file a registration statement without concern that the earlier Regulation A solicitation activities would constitute "gun jumping"? What if Limitbeat decides instead to proceed with a Rule 506 offering? *See* Rules 251(c), 255(e).

5-43.   On March 1, Hightech, Inc. completed a $5 million Rule 505 offering. On November 1, it commences a Regulation A Tier 1 offering. How large may the Regulation A offering be? *See* Rule 251(a).

H. *Integration of Offerings*

Integration of two offerings by an issuer may destroy the availability of an exemption for either or both of the offerings. Earlier materials have discussed integration in the context of Regulation D, intrastate, and Regulation A offerings. Outside of these rules, the integration analysis typically begins, but rarely ends, with an application of factors outlined in Securities Act Releases No. 4552 and No. 4434. Relevant factors include whether the offerings are part of a single plan of financing, whether the offerings involve the issuance of the same class of security, whether the offerings are made at or about the same time, whether the consideration to be received is the same, and whether the offerings are made for the same general purpose.

> *Single Plan of Financing.*   The issue of whether multiple offerings are part of a single plan of financing is perhaps the most important part of the integration analysis. But what is a "single plan of financing"? Sometimes this is answered by reference to the presence or absence of the other four factors listed in Releases No. 4552 and No. 4434. *See, e.g.,* Property Inv., Inc., SEC No-Action Letter (Oct. 18, 1972) (the fact that two offerings had the same timing, purpose, and consideration indicates they were part of "one integrated scheme of financing"). In other cases, the inquiry has focused on the purposes of the offerings, and on this question, the intent of the issuer at the time of the offering may prove dispositive. *See, e.g., Risdall v. Brown-Wilbert, Inc.,* 759 N.W.2d 67, 72 (Minn. Ct. App. 2009) ("[T]he issuer can show that there was no single plan of financing by demonstrating that no subsequent offering was contemplated at the time of each offering."). Since the existence of a *plan* presupposes an intent, there is logical appeal to this approach. Focusing on the intent of the issuer, however, poses some problems, for in the absence of either an admission by the issuer or documentation establishing a plan, the evidentiary balance on the existence of a plan tilts sharply in favor of the issuer. On the other hand, a single plan

of financing may exist when multiple offerings are used to fund distinct but related projects. *See, e.g., SEC v. Alternate Energy Holdings, Inc.*, 2014 U.S. Dist. LEXIS 66401 (D. Idaho 2014) (single plan of financing existed for construction of nuclear power "projects" even though each offering related to a distinct project).

Same Class of Security.   Generally, an offering of debt instruments will not be integrated with an offering of common stock, even if the purposes, timing, and consideration received are the same. *See, e.g.,* SBT Corp., SEC No-Action Letter (Dec. 19, 1980). Moreover, multiple offerings of securities ostensibly of the same general class are sometimes not integrated because of distinctions within the class. In the case of debt instruments, for example, differences in maturities and interest rates, *see, e.g., SEC v. Dunfee*, [1966-1967 Transfer Binder] Fed. Sec. L. Rep. (CCH) ¶91,970 (W.D. Mo. 1966), or in the degree of underlying security, *see, e.g.,* Eastern Ill. Tel. Corp., SEC No-Action Letter (Mar. 14, 1975), may justify non-integration.

Timing of the Offerings.   Although Releases No. 4552 and No. 4434 indicate that two offerings occurring "at or about the same time" is a factor in favor of integration, in practice this factor is applied somewhat differently than the manner of its statement suggests. If offerings are separated by a substantial period of time, the spacing is sufficient to create a presumption against integration. *But cf. SEC v. Schooler*, 905 F.3d 1107 (9th Cir. 2018) (suggesting that a separation of offerings in time is not in itself sufficient to avoid integration when the other factors support integration). A six-month lapse appears sufficient to create a rebuttable presumption. The presumption may become irrebuttable if offerings are separated by at least a year. Conversely, the proximity in time of two offerings normally will not, of itself, create a conclusive presumption that the offerings should be integrated. *See generally* Deaktor, Integration of Securities Offerings, 31 U. Fla. L. Rev. 465, 533-535 (1979).

Type of Consideration.   Since the most common form of consideration is cash, the fact that two offerings involve cash is not a factor supporting integration. *See, e.g.,* LaserFax, Inc., SEC No-Action Letter (Aug. 15, 1985) (the staff concluded the offering should be integrated, but did not rebut issuer's argument that the use of cash in the offerings is not a factor favoring integration). The use of non-cash consideration in one offering and cash consideration in the other also suggests the offerings should not be integrated. Non-cash consideration of a similar type, on the other hand, increases the possibility that multiple offerings will be integrated.

Same General Purpose.   It is not entirely clear what function this factor is designed to perform and how it differs from the first factor (single plan of financing). One of the more revealing discussions of the factor was offered in a Seventh Circuit opinion involving multiple partnerships for the drilling of oil:

> The term "same general purpose" suggests a level of generality to the integration analysis that may be satisfied by the observation that purpose of each partnership was to drill for oil. . . . The important point here is that each drilling project was

designed to stand or fall on its own merits. It may have been to Ona's advantage that the wells were clumped together, since economies of scale would bring down drilling costs. But because the turnkey price was fixed, those savings were not passed on to the partnerships. Accordingly, there was no common enterprise, no single plan of financing and no single issuer attempting to evade Section 5's requirements.

Donohoe v. Consolidated Operating & Prod. Corp., 982 F.2d 1130, 1140 (7th Cir. 1992).

In the Matter of Kevin D. Kunz
Securities and Exchange Commission 1934 Release No. 45290 (Jan. 16, 2002), *aff'd*, 64 Fed. App'x 659 (10th Cir. 2003)

[This is an appeal from the NASD's imposition of sanctions against Kunz and Cline Investment Management, Inc. (K&C) and Kevin Kunz (collectively the Applicants).

VesCor Capital Corp. [VesCor] was in the business of originating, purchasing, and selling loans secured by real property. Prior to 1994, VesCor sold the VesCor investment products without registering them under federal or state securities laws. The state of Nevada concluded that the loans were "securities." Nevada and VesCor entered into a settlement agreement requiring VesCor to make rescission offers to current holders of the VesCor investment products in the state of Nevada.

In conjunction with the rescission offers, VesCor planned to simultaneously offer investors the opportunity to reinvest in either Vescor Notes or third-party mortgages (MLPs). The investors could select terms of 30, 45, or 60 months for either the Notes or the MLPs. The Notes were direct obligations of VesCor and were either Accrual Notes, with interest at the rate of 12 percent per annum accrued monthly and paid at the end of the term, or Monthly Notes, with interest at the rate of 10 percent per annum paid monthly. In contrast, MLP purchasers held interests in mortgages acquired by VesCor; although investors were told that the "target" interest rate was 12 percent, this amount was not guaranteed and their return was the interest actually received from mortgages in which their funds were invested. VesCor kept the funds from the sale of MLPs in money market accounts until they were actually allocated to specific mortgages.

VesCor created six Private Placement Memoranda (PPMs) to accompany the simultaneous rescission-reinvestment offers, providing two different PPMs for each of the three investment products (Accrual Notes, Monthly Notes, and MLPs). VesCor used one set of three PPMs for residents of Nevada, and the other set of three PPMs for non-Nevada residents. The PPMs shared a common description of the use of the proceeds, with each PPM stating:

> [VesCor] intends to provide general funding for the operations of the Company's expansion activities with respect to a series of mortgages made or purchased at a discount. The source of such funds would be the proceeds from the sale of [the particular securities] and the sale of [the two other securities] pursuant to other simultaneous private offering memoranda.

Kunz admitted that he personally delivered PPMs to 113 investors. Kunz also testified that he mailed PPMs to a number of K&C customers, and that he discussed the investments with some customers on the telephone. Kunz stated that neither he nor K&C attempted to verify the number of nonaccredited investors for any of the VesCor offerings until the NASD requested information in connection with its investigation in September 1995. In fact, sales were made to many more than 35 nonaccredited investors for the Accrual Notes and the Monthly Notes.

The Commission concluded that the Applicants offered and sold securities pursuant to PPMs that materially misrepresented VesCor's financial condition and omitted disclosure of material facts about Applicants and VesCor and that such conduct was inconsistent with high standards of commercial honor and just and equitable principles of trade, as required by NASD Conduct Rule 2110.]

OFFERING UNREGISTERED SECURITIES TO THE PUBLIC

[O]ur review of the record indicates that there were 138 nonaccredited investors in all three offerings. If the offerings are considered a single, integrated offering, then Applicants would not be entitled to a Regulation D exemption. Applicants argue that the three VesCor offerings should not be integrated, and that VesCor should be entitled to a Regulation D exemption.

We consider five factors in determining whether apparently separate offerings should be viewed as one, integrated offering: (a) whether the offerings are part of a single plan of financing; (b) whether the offerings are made for the same general purposes; (c) whether the offerings are made at or about the same time; (d) whether the same kind of consideration is to be received; and (e) whether the offerings involve issuance of the same class of securities. Applicants argue that the first and second factors militate against integration. With respect to the first factor, Applicants state that there was no coordination between the offerings as to amount or timing. They further argue that, with one exception, none of their customers purchased investments of different types. As to the second factor, Applicants state that, since money raised from the sale of the MLP Interests could not be used for VesCor's operating expenses, the MLP Interests were not offered for the same general purposes as the Notes. Applicants' arguments concerning both factors are unpersuasive. The PPMs make it clear that the offerings were all made for the same general purpose—to finance VesCor's mortgage lending and trust deed business—and were part of a single plan of financing those activities. Each of the PPMs also stated that VesCor's "principal business objective . . . in offering [the securities was] to invest the proceeds from the sale of such [securities] in loans secured by first Mortgages on real property."

The third and fourth factors are met because all of the offerings were made at or about the same time. Furthermore, the consideration for the securities was the same: the rejection of the right to rescind a prior investment and the election to credit accumulated interest to principal. If a new or additional investment was made, the consideration was cash.

Applicants argue that the MLP Interests and the Notes were different classes of securities, and thus do not conform to the fifth factor. They point out that the MLP Interests were not of the same class of securities as the Notes because they were equity securities, not debt. Applicants admit that the Notes were all the same type of security, but argue that the Notes were of a different class because they have different terms of payment, i.e., the Accrual Notes were paid when they mature, and the Monthly Notes were paid on a monthly basis. Even assuming the validity of these arguments, consideration of the remaining factors militates in favor of finding that the three offerings were integrated.

Thus, applying the factors to the undisputed facts here, we conclude that the offerings of the MLP Interests and the Notes should be integrated. We therefore find that the offerings are not exempt under Regulation D.

Despite numerous no-action letters and several reported decisions, the doctrine of integration remains ill-defined and, in the words of an ABA task force, "seriously needs rethinking." Committee on Federal Regulation of Securities, Integration of Securities Offerings: Report of the Task Force on Integration, 41 Bus. Law. 595, 596 (1986). As Professor Bradford observed:

> The uncertainty of the five-factor test is costly. It increases the risk to issuers, potentially chilling even offerings that should not be integrated. It increases the legal costs of issuers because issuers are more likely to need legal advice and because it is harder for lawyers to predict the SEC's position. It increases the possibility of mistakes by the SEC staff in particular cases and also the cost of administering the integration doctrine. Thus, although the five factors are relevant to the economic analysis of integration, using them may cost more than they are worth.

Bradford, Transaction Exemptions in the Securities Act of 1933: An Economic Analysis, 45 Emory L.J. 591, 669 (1996). The confusion surrounding integration makes the integration safe harbors of Regulation D and Regulation A all the more attractive. Outside of those safe harbors, the five factors enumerated in Releases No. 4552 and No. 4434 survive as the principal, and problematical, guideposts to integration. *See, e.g., SEC v. Ishopnomarkup.com, Inc.,* 2007 U.S. Dist. LEXIS 70684 (E.D.N.Y. Sept. 24, 2007) (summarily reviewing the factors and concluding with minimal explanation that three transactions should be treated as one).

Criticism of existing integration doctrine is not limited to indeterminacy of standards. The Report of the Advisory Committee on the Capital Formation and Regulatory Processes app. A at 25 (SEC 1996) questioned the policy underpinnings of integrating offerings and noted that the present framework unduly burdens companies that raise capital frequently. The report recommends a system of company registration for seasoned issuers that would eliminate the need for qualifying issuers to bring offerings within exemptions and, accordingly, would render integration of offerings irrelevant. Along a somewhat different line, Professor Bradford has argued for a weighted exemption system (based on the level of investor protection provided by each exemption) that would eliminate the integration doctrine and allow issuers to combine various registration exemptions for a single offering, subject to an overall dollar amount limitation. *See* Bradford, Expanding the Non-Transactional Revolution: A New Approach to Securities Registration Exemptions, 49 Emory L.J. 437 (2000). Professor Campbell joins in the call for an elimination of the integration doctrine altogether:

> [T]he integration doctrine makes no sense in any setting. The availability of an exemption should be entirely independent of the fact that other offers or sales have (or have not) been made by the issuer. Other such sales are irrelevant to the question of whether or not the policy bases for an exemption exist for a particular sale. Such other offers and sales are neutral events respecting the question of whether investment information should be mandated or be the subject of free bargaining between the parties.

Campbell, The Overwhelming Case for Elimination of the Integration Doctrine Under the Securities Act of 1933, 89 Ky. L.J. 289, 324 (2001-2002). More recently, Professor Cohn has sharply criticized the integration doctrine not only because of the indeterminacy and complexity of standards but also as contrary to the goal of investor protection (decreasing access to capital may actually harm existing investors in smaller, younger companies). *See* Cohn, Keep Securities Reform Moving: Eliminate the SEC's Integration Doctrine, 44 Hofstra L. Rev. 3 (2015). Reflecting these concerns in its Concept Release on harmonizing the exemptions, the SEC has requested comments on a number of possible reforms of the integration doctrine, the most significant of which is to have a single integration test that applies uniformly to all the exemptions. *See* Securities Act Release 33-10649 (June 18, 2019).

NOTES AND QUESTIONS

1. *Issuer Integration.* To be distinguished from integration of offerings, discussed above, is *integration of issuers*, which arises when offerings by ostensibly distinct and separate issuers are integrated and treated as an offering by a single issuer. *SEC v. Murphy*, 626 F.2d 633 (9th Cir. 1980), is the leading case on issuer integration. A promoter, Murphy, formed Intertie to sponsor limited partnerships formed to invest in cable television systems. Intertie would purchase a cable system, sell it to a limited partnership, lease it back from the partnership, and manage the operation. Intertie sold the systems to a number of partnerships and commingled the funds derived from the sales. The success of the scheme depended upon generating ever-increasing amounts of capital through continued partnership offerings. Without such capital, Intertie could not meet its obligations on systems sold to previous investors. Murphy was active in the offering of partnership interests and did not make Intertie's financial statements available to investors. The limited partnership interests were not registered and were offered under the private offering exemption of Section 4(a)(2).

Eventually, Intertie filed a petition for bankruptcy, and the SEC charged Murphy and various other defendants with violations of the registration and fraud provisions of the securities acts. As to the question of who was the issuer of the securities, the court reasoned:

Intertie clearly held the key to success or failure of the partnerships. Accordingly, Intertie was the entity about which the investors needed information, and, therefore, it is properly considered the issuer of the securities for purposes of determining the availability of a private offering exemption.

Id. at 643-644. Having concluded that Intertie, rather than the individual partnerships, was the issuer, the court then applied the factors of Release No. 4552. It concluded that all the factors other than the third (timing of the offerings) pointed to integration, and because the third factor was heavily outweighed by the others, it held the private offering exemption was not available.

2. *Private Followed by Public Offerings: Rule 152.* Suppose shortly after an issuer completes a private offering under Section 4(a)(2) it files a registration statement for a public offering. Whether the offerings will be integrated, of course, may be addressed through application of the general integration factors discussed in this section. Even if application of the factors points to integration, some relief may be offered by Rule 152, which provides:

The phrase "transaction by an issuer not involving any public offering" in section 4[(a)](2) shall be deemed to apply to transactions not involving any public offering at the time of said transactions although subsequently thereto the issuer decides to make a public offering and/or files a registration statement.

Recognizing that an issuer may need to raise capital privately around the time of a planned public offering, the Commission in 2007 addressed some of the ambiguities of the "subsequently thereto" language of Rule 152. *See* Securities Act Release No. 8828 (2007). It noted:

[W]hile there are many situations in which the filing of a registration statement could serve as a general solicitation or general advertising for a concurrent private offering, the filing of a registration statement does not, *per se*, eliminate a company's ability to conduct a concurrent private offering, whether it is commenced before or after the filing of the registration statement. Further, . . . the determination as to whether the filing of the registration statement should be considered to be a general solicitation or general advertising . . . should be based on a consideration of whether the investors in the private placement were solicited by the registration statement or through some other means that would otherwise not foreclose the availability of the Section 4[(a)](2) exemption. . . . For example, if a company files a registration statement and then seeks to offer and sell securities without registration to an investor that became interested in the purportedly private offering by means of the registration statement, then the Section 4[(a)](2) exemption would not be available for that offering. On the other hand, if the prospective private placement investor became interested in the concurrent private placement through some means other than the registration statement that did not involve a general solicitation and otherwise was consistent with Section 4[(a)](2), such as through a substantive, pre-existing relationship with the company or direct contact by the company or its agents outside of the public offering effort, then the prior filing of the registration statement generally would not impact the potential availability of the Section 4[(a)](2) exemption for that private placement and the private placement could be conducted while the registration statement for the public offering was on file with the Commission. . . .

It is not necessary that the second offering be a registered public offering in order for the earlier private offering to be protected under the Rule. An intrastate offering under Section 3(a)(11), for example, may be a subsequent "public offering" for purposes of the protection Rule 152 accords the earlier private offering.

Rule 152 provides protection for offerings under Section 4(a)(2), which, of course, includes Rule 506(b). It is not available for offerings based on other exemptions, including Rule 504.

    3. Integration of Abandoned Offerings: Rule 155. A different problem from that described in Note 2 arises when the issuer decides to abandon its private offering in favor of raising more capital through a registered offering to the public. Alternatively, the issuer may decide to abandon its efforts to sell its securities through a public offering and seek a more modest amount by privately placing the securities. Rule 155, adopted in 2001, provides safe harbors for a registered offering following an abandoned private offering, or a private offering following an abandoned registered offering, without integrating the registered and private offerings in either case. Note that for purposes of the rule, private offering includes offerings exempt under Section 4(a)(2) of the Securities Act or Rule 506 (but not Rule 504) of Regulation D.

Rule 155 permits an issuer that commenced a registered offering to withdraw the registration statement before any securities are sold and then begin a private offering. The safe harbor is conditioned upon there being a 30-day cooling-off period between the registration statement withdrawal and the commencement of the private offering.

Conversely, if an issuer pursues a registered offering after abandoning a private offering, Rule 155 offers a safe harbor from integration protecting the registered offering if the issuer has terminated all offering activity with respect to the private offering and the prospectus filed as part of the registration statement discloses that the private offering was abandoned. There is a 30-day cooling-off period between abandoning the private offering and filing the registration statement. However, there is no cooling-off period if all of the offerees were (or were reasonably believed to be) accredited or sophisticated investors.

PROBLEMS

5-44. Alice and Bob formed Aztec, Inc. on February 1 to manufacture and market a product they recently patented. Equipment and working capital to begin its operations were provided through an intrastate offering carried out under Section 3(a)(11) on February 14. In that offering, Aztec raised $4 million from family, friends, and associates through the issuance of 400,000 shares of common stock.

Aztec has carried out its business in a building leased for one year under terms permitting Aztec to apply the first year's rental payments toward the fixed purchase price. Suitable manufacturing space is in short supply. According to Aztec's projections, it will run out of cash and exceed its established credit lines within a year. In early July, Aztec consults you about the possibility of raising

$5 million through the sale of common stock to a group of sophisticated and experienced investors. The proceeds of this offering will be used for working capital and also will be added to the rental payments made thus far to satisfy the down payment required to purchase the building pursuant to the option's terms. If the offering is in July and under Rule 506, will it be integrated with the February offering? What if the offering is in September under Rule 506?

5-45. What additional concerns arise in the preceding problem if either a July or a September offering is under Rule 505, rather than Rule 506? And is Aztec in a better position with respect to its second offering if the first offering was pursuant to Rule 147?

5-46. In Problem 5-18, we met J.R., a promoter of oil drilling ventures. Suppose the deal being put together by J.R. was a registered offering. Following the filing of the registration statement, conflicts developed with the underwriter, and the offering was canceled. Two months later, J.R. revives the offering, this time seeking to bring it under Rule 506 in an offering that will include mostly accredited but a few nonaccredited purchasers. Will the earlier registration statement cause general solicitation problems for J.R.? *See* Rule 155.

I.   *State Exemptions*

Consider the plight of an issuer about to offer unregistered securities. Adherence to the strictures of a federal exemption is not enough, for the issuer must also contend with the matter of state regulation of securities issuances. If the offering will be interstate in character, the problems are compounded, and compliance with the federal scheme of exemptions is comparatively simple when contrasted with exemptions at the state level, which may prove complex and often conflicting. Whatever progress occurs in the area of streamlining federal exemptions may be undermined if there is a failure to coordinate state and federal regulatory schemes.

The National Securities Markets Improvement Act of 1996 (NSMIA) addresses these problems through preemption and exempts a wide range of offerings from traditional state registration requirements. In particular, the legislation amended Section 18 of the '33 Act largely to exempt from state registration or qualification requirements "covered securities," which include, in part, listed securities, securities sold to "qualified purchasers" (for which the Commission's proposed definition mirrors the definition of an accredited investor under Regulation D), and securities qualifying for an exemption under Rule 506 and the crowdfunding exemption of Section 4(a)(6). *See Brown v. Earthboard Sports USA, Inc.,* 481 F.3d 901 (6th Cir. 2007) (it is not enough that promoter attempted to qualify an offering under Rule 506 because covered security status is achieved through *actual* rather than attempted qualification).

Covered security status does not extend to securities sold in offerings under several key exemptions for small issuers, including Rules 504 and 505 and Regulation A (Section 3(b)(1)); offerings under these exemptions remain fully subject to state regulation. As to why NSMIA offers so little for the small issuer, Professor Campbell suggested public choice theory may offer some insight:

> [T]he millions of small issuers . . . received essentially nothing from the legislation. . . . Small issuers constitute a large, diffuse group; free-rider problems are enormous for such a group and thus make it difficult for the group to exercise effective influence over legislation. The transaction costs for that diffuse group were simply too high for them to be effective in getting their way in the matter.

Campbell, The Impact of NSMIA on Small Issuers, 53 Bus. Law. 575, 585 (1998).

At the direction of NSMIA, the Commission published a report on the extent to which uniformity of state regulatory requirements has been achieved for securities that are not covered securities. *See* Report on the Uniformity of State Regulatory Requirements for Offerings of Securities That Are Not "Covered Securities" (SEC 1997). The report applauded the progress that has been made towards achieving uniformity of standards but also highlighted many areas in which significant differences remain, even as to covered securities. For example, although securities sold under Rule 506 are covered securities and therefore exempt from state registration and qualification requirements, NSMIA allows each state to require an issuer to file certain notices and pay fees in connection with the offering. Variations from state to state require the issuer to undertake a survey of blue sky laws to determine which states have different notice, information, or fee requirements. For those conducting the survey, NSMIA's goal of uniformity may seem elusive at best.

Most states have adopted the Small Corporate Offering Registration (SCOR) form, which is available for certain offerings exempt under Rule 504 of Regulation D, Regulation A, or Section 3(a)(11). It allows use of a simple question-and-answer format for registration. Although it is not an exemption, SCOR offers simplified state registration and is discussed in greater detail in Chapter 4.

1.   The Uniform Limited Offering Exemption (ULOE)

The burden of conflicting federal and state regulation and problems arising from contradictory regulatory approaches among the states prompted Congress in 1980 to authorize the development of a uniform federal/state exemption system. *See* Securities Act Section 19(c). The federal half of the uniformity equation is reflected in Regulation D. The adoption of Regulation D was followed by NASAA approval in 1983 of the Uniform Limited Offering Exemption (ULOE). The ULOE incorporates Rules 501-503 of Regulation D and establishes an exemption for offerings made in compliance with Rule 505 (repealed by the SEC in 2016) and/or Rule 506.

Since NASAA is a voluntary organization of state securities administrators, it is powerless to compel adoption of the ULOE at the state level or ensure that adopting states do not introduce modifications and variables that undermine the uniformity of the exemption. Illustrative of the tendency of states to take diverse approaches on the applicability of the exemption are the variations introduced on the ULOE's suitability standard. The ULOE imposes a suitability requirement in that all sales to nonaccredited investors must satisfy either of the following conditions:

1. The investment is suitable for the purchaser upon the basis of the facts, if any, disclosed by the purchaser as to his other security holdings and as to his financial situation and needs. For the purpose of this condition only, it may be presumed that if the investment does not exceed 10 percent of the investor's net worth, it is suitable.
2. The purchaser either alone or with his/her purchaser representative(s) has such knowledge and experience in financial and business matters that he/she is or they are capable of evaluating the merits and risks of the prospective investment.

In adopting the ULOE, a number of states have modified the above suitability standards. Some apply the tests on a conjunctive rather than disjunctive basis. Other states apply minimum purchase requirements or define minimum levels of net worth. And the states are far from uniform on whether the safe harbor presumption (10 percent of net worth) is rebuttable. These are but a few examples of the degree to which the states have altered the ULOE and, in the process, undermined the goal of uniformity that drove its creation. *See generally* Cohn & Yadley, Capital Offense: The SEC's Continuing Failure to Address Small Business Financing Concerns, 4 N.Y.U. J.L. & Bus. 10 (2007) (criticizing lack of coordination between state and federal law); Campbell, The Insidious Remnants of State Rules Respecting Capital Formation, 78 Wash. U. L.Q. 407 (2000); Johnson, Private Placements: A Regulatory Black Hole, 35 Del. J. Corp. L. 151, 172 (2010) (proposing a return to state supervision of private placements).

2. Nonuniform State Exemptions

The eclectic pattern of state regulation is further aggravated by the existence of a wide variety of state exemptions not based upon the ULOE. A number of states exempt listed securities. California exempts sales to no more than 35 purchasers if all purchasers either meet sophistication standards or have a "pre-existing personal or business relationship" with the offeror or any of its partners, officers, directors, or controlling persons.[5] Other states require registration of intrastate offerings, exempt sales to no more than a designated number of persons over a 12-month period, or exempt "isolated transactions." This is only a sampling of the diversity of approaches to exemptions, but it should give some indication of why the task of ensuring blue sky compliance is taxing and most often assigned to the most junior associates in a law firm's securities department.

---

5. Cal. Corp. Code §25102(f).

||6||
Secondary Distributions

The focus of the materials to this point has been on Section 5's proscription of sales *by* issuers. In this chapter, we consider when sales of securities by non-issuers are within the reach of Section 5. As was seen in Chapter 1, issuer sales are known as *primary offerings*, and sales by others are referred to as either *trading transactions* or *secondary distributions*. As will be seen, trading transactions are exempt from Section 5, and secondary distributions are not.

As you examine the material in this chapter you should also keep in mind that the focus of Section 5 of the Securities Act is both transactional and universal—Section 5 literally requires that every sale be either registered or exempt. Thus, there is the burden on all who sell or even offer to sell a security to prove compliance with Section 5. In doing so, the focus customarily begins with Section 4(a)(1), a transaction exemption for everyone except transactions by an "issuer, underwriter or dealer." As we will see, because of the breadth of the definition of *underwriter* in Section 2(a)(11), much of the focus of whether a person falls within this transaction exemption depends entirely on whether he is an underwriter.

As developed in the first section of this chapter, *underwriter* is broadly defined. It reaches well beyond the common meaning of underwriter or underwriting as explored earlier in Chapter 4, so that many sellers of securities acquired from an issuer fall within the definition of underwriter.

Resales of nonexempt securities frequently pose serious problems under the Securities Act. The first type of problem concerns whether the resale destroys the exemption the issuer relied upon when it sold that security without registration. This would occur, for example, if the issuer relied upon the private offering exemption in Section 4(a)(2) and its sophisticated purchaser soon sold to someone who does not satisfy the *Ralston* criteria. Similarly, a resale to one whose residency is different from that of the issuer may disqualify an offering that initially was exempt under the intrastate exemption of Section 3(a)(11). As will be seen in the materials that follow, not all sales to a purchaser who does not meet the exemption's criteria will destroy the issuer's exemption. The critical inquiry is whether from the surrounding circumstances one can conclude that the issuer's offering had "come to rest" before the resale occurred.

A second problem arises from the special position "control persons" occupy under the Securities Act. Later, this chapter examines how the Securities Act regulates the public sales by control persons as it does public offerings by issuers. The reach of Section 5 is extended to control persons through the combined efforts of Section 4(a)(1), which exempts all transactions except those by an issuer, an underwriter or a dealer, and Section 2(a)(11), because the last sentence treats those who purchase from or sell for a control person as underwriters when that purchase or assistance is part of the control person's *distribution*. In this way, the control person's public offerings are caught within the regulatory reach of Section 5. For example, assume Alice, a control person of Beta Company, wishes to sell shares she acquired five years ago in an offering that was registered under the '33 Act. Because Alice is a control person, her proposed sales of Beta shares, even though previously registered, will trigger Section 5 if those sales are deemed a distribution. As we will see later in these materials, control persons, such as Alice, who resell shares customarily rely on the safe harbor provided in Rule 144.

A third problem posed by resales concerns the person in the middle, the broker. As examined in Chapter 4, brokers by virtue of Section 2(a)(12) are dealers for the purpose of the Securities Act and therefore do not enjoy the broad exemption accorded others by Section 4(a)(1). For example, dealers in some situations are under a Section 4(a)(3) duty to deliver a prospectus in connection with public offerings, even though they are not participating in that offering. Does this obligation extend as well when they are simply acting as agents who are carrying out their clients' instructions to "buy" securities being distributed? Also, consider the problem the broker has when selling shares for a control person. For example, in the case of Alice, who is reselling some of her control shares in Beta, her broker will be considered an underwriter if those resales constitute a distribution. Later materials in this chapter explore the broker's complex obligations with respect to resales of securities. Again, Rule 144 provides a safe harbor for brokers, provided all the safe harbor's conditions are met.

By far the most significant SEC safe-harbor provision is Rule 144, which applies to resales of restricted securities and to sales of securities on behalf of control persons. Rule 144 provides its own definition of *restricted securities*, so that it reaches securities that were not sold in a public offering or that are subject to limits on resale due to their being offered by their issuer under Regulation D, as well as several other types of exempt offerings. As will be seen, Rule 144 provides much-needed certainty in determining whether those involved in the resale of restricted or the control person's securities are underwriters. A more specialized safe harbor for resales is Rule 144A, which applies generally to resales to large financial institutions.

Finally, for those resales that cannot fit within Rule 144's strict requirements, Section 4(a)(7) authorizes resales to accredited investors and control persons can invoke the so-called 4(a)(1½) exemption, discussed later. And as will be seen, the regulation of resales is not exclusively the concern of the Securities Act; the blue sky laws also impose their restrictions upon the resale of certain types of securities. The states' own brand of regulation is also discussed in this chapter.

A. The Underwriter Concept and Sales for an Issuer

Section 4(a)(1) is the central transaction exemption of the Securities Act. It exempts transactions by *anyone* except an issuer, underwriter, or dealer. While the inquiry into whether someone is an issuer or dealer is fairly straightforward, as each is narrowly defined in the Act, the definition of *underwriter* in Section 2(a)(11) is much broader. Whether one is an underwriter is determined functionally in terms of a person's involvement in an offering. This greatly expands the underwriter classification under Section 2(a)(11) and restricts the reach of the Section 4(a)(1) exemption.

On close review, there are four broadly defined roles that qualify someone as an underwriter:

1. any person who purchases from an issuer with a view to the distribution of a security; or
2. any person who offers or sells for an issuer in connection with a distribution; or
3. any person who participates or has a direct or indirect participation in the activities covered by 1 or 2 above; or
4. any person who participates or has a participation in the direct or indirect underwriting of any such undertaking.

It should be apparent from a close reading of Section 2(a)(11) that one does not become an underwriter solely because one has purchased from an issuer, sold for an issuer, or otherwise acted in connection with a purchase or sale. A further requirement before one engaged in such acts will be deemed an underwriter is that the purchase, sale, or underwriting activity must be "in connection with a distribution." Regrettably for those who wish for certainty, no definition of distribution appears in the Act.

Members of a public offering's selling group are expressly excluded from the underwriter classification, provided the commission received from an underwriter or a dealer is "not in excess of the usual and customary distributors' or sellers' commission." This phrase separates a selling group dealer from a sub-underwriter in that the latter certainly receives a commission, for its undertaking to absorb its allotment if the offering is a sticky one. Rule 141 further refines the meaning of "usual and customary" to include not only a direct payment by an underwriter, but also the "spread" permitted the dealer who as principal purchases from the underwriter and resells at a higher price, so long as the payment or spread is not in excess of what is usual and customary. Rule 141, however, does not protect a dealer who manages the offering or performs functions normally performed by an underwriter.

The focus on whether someone is an underwriter is not limited to considerations germane to Section 4(a)(1). It is also important to determine if a participant in a distribution is an underwriter because, for example, under Section 2(a)(3), underwriters may enter into preliminary negotiations and agreements for the purchase of a security before its registration, special disclosures in the registration statement must be made with respect to arrangements and the compensation of underwriters, and underwriters are among those privileged to be defendants under Section 11(a) if the registration statement is misleading. Thus, the breadth of Section 2(a)(11)'s definition of underwriter is something of a mixed blessing for those fitting within it.

Securities and Exchange Commission v. Chinese Consolidated Benevolent Association
120 F.2d 738 (2d Cir.), *cert. denied*, 314 U.S. 618 (1941)

HAND, J. The Securities and Exchange Commission seeks to enjoin the defendant from the use of any instruments of interstate commerce or of the mails in disposing, or attempting to dispose, of Chinese Government bonds for which no registration statement has ever been made.

The defendant is a New York corporation organized for benevolent purposes having a membership of 25,000 Chinese. On September 1, 1937, the Republic of China authorized the issuance of $500,000,000 in 4 percent Liberty Bonds, and on May 1, 1938 authorized a further issue of $50,000,000 in 5 percent bonds. In October 1937, the defendant set up a committee which has had no official or contractual relation with the Chinese government for the purpose of:

(a)   Uniting the Chinese in aiding the Chinese people and government in their difficulties.
(b)   Soliciting and receiving funds from members of Chinese communities in New York, New Jersey and Connecticut, as well as from the general public in those states, for transmission to China for general relief.

All the members of the committee were Chinese and resided in New York City. Through mass meetings, advertising in newspapers distributed through the mails, and personal appeals, the committee urged the members of Chinese communities in New York, New Jersey and Connecticut to purchase the Chinese government bonds referred to and offered to accept funds from prospective purchasers for delivery to the Bank of China in New York as agent for the purchasers. At the request of individual purchasers and for their convenience the committee received some $600,000 to be used for acquiring the bonds, and delivered the moneys to the New York agency of the Bank of China, together with written applications by the respective purchasers for the bonds which they desired to buy. The New York agency transmitted the funds to its branch in Hong Kong with instructions to make the purchases for the accounts of the various customers. The Hong Kong bank returned the bonds by mail to the New York branch which in turn forwarded them by mail to the purchasers at their mailing addresses, which, in some cases, were in care of the defendant at its headquarters in New York. Neither the committee, nor any of its members, has ever made a charge for their activities or received any compensation from any source. The Bank of China has acted as an agent in the transactions and has not solicited the purchase of bonds or the business involved in transmitting the funds for that purpose.

No registration statement under the Securities Act . . . has ever been made covering any of the Chinese bonds advertised for sale. . . .

. . . [The court below granted defendants' motion and dismissed the complaint.]

Under Section 2(a)(11) an "underwriter" is defined as: "any person who has purchased from an issuer with a view to, or sells for an issuer in connection with, the distribution of any security, or participates or has a direct or indirect participation in any such undertaking. . . ."

We think that the defendant has violated Section 5(a) of the Securities Act when read in connection with Section 2(a)(3) because it engaged in selling unregistered securities issued by the Chinese government when it solicited offers to buy the securities "for value." The solicitation of offers to buy the unregistered bonds, either with or without compensation, brought defendant's activities literally within the prohibition of the statute. Whether the Chinese government as issuer authorized the solicitation, or merely availed itself of gratuitous and even unknown acts on the part of the defendant whereby written offers to buy, and the funds collected for payment, were transmitted to the Chinese banks does not affect the meaning of the statutory provisions which are quite explicit. In either case the solicitation was equally for the benefit of the Chinese government and broadly speaking was for the issuer in connection with the distribution of the bonds. . . .

Under Section 4[(a)](1) the defendant is not exempt from registration requirements if it is "an underwriter." The court below reasons that it is not to be regarded as an underwriter since it does not sell or solicit offers to buy "for an issuer in connection with, the distribution" of securities. In other words, it seems to have been held that only solicitation authorized by the issuer in connection with the distribution of the Chinese bonds would satisfy the definition of underwriter contained in Section 2(a)(11) and that defendant's activities were never for the Chinese government but only for the purchasers of the bonds. Though the defendant solicited the orders, obtained the cash from the purchasers and caused both to be forwarded so as to procure the bonds, it is nevertheless contended that its acts could not have been for the Chinese government because it had no contractual arrangement or even understanding with the latter. But the aim of the Securities Act is to have information available for investors. This objective will be defeated if buying orders can be solicited which result in uninformed and improvident purchases. It can make no difference as regards the policy of the act whether an issuer has solicited orders through an agent, or has merely taken advantage of the services of a person interested for patriotic reasons in securing offers to buy. The aim of the issuer is to promote the distribution of the securities, and of the Securities Act is to protect the public by requiring that it be furnished with adequate information upon which to make investments. Accordingly the words "[sell] for an issuer in connection with the distribution of any security" ought to be read as covering continual solicitations, such as the defendant was engaged in, which normally would result in a distribution of issues of unregistered securities within the United States. Here a series of events were set in motion by the solicitation of offers to buy which culminated in a distribution that was initiated by the defendant. We hold that the defendant acted as an underwriter.

There is a further reason for holding that Section 5(a)(1) forbids the defendant's activities in soliciting offers to buy the Chinese bonds. Section 4[(a)](1) was intended to exempt only trading transactions between individual investors with relation to securities already issued and not to exempt distributions by issuers. The words of the exemption in Section 4[(a)](1) are: "Transactions by any person other than an issuer, underwriter, or dealer"; . . . The issuer in this case was the Republic of China. The complete transaction included not only solicitation by the defendant of offers to buy, but the offers themselves, the transmission of the offers and the purchase money through the banks to the Chinese government, the acceptance by that government of the offers and the delivery of the bonds to the purchaser or the defendant as his agent. Even if the defendant is not itself "an issuer, underwriter, or dealer" it was participating in a transaction with an issuer, to wit, the Chinese Government. The argument on behalf of the defendant incorrectly assumes that Section 4[(a)](1) applies to the component parts of the entire transaction we have mentioned and thus exempts defendant unless it is an underwriter for the Chinese Republic. Section 5(a)(1), however, broadly prohibits sales of securities irrespective of the character of the person making them. The exemption is limited to "transactions" by persons other than "issuers, underwriters or dealers." It does not in terms or by fair implication protect those who are engaged in steps necessary to the distribution of security issues. To give Section 4[(a)](1) the construction urged by the defendant would afford a ready method of thwarting the policy of the law and evading its provisions. . . .

The decree is reversed with directions to the District Court to deny the defendant's motion to dismiss and to issue the injunction as prayed for in the bill of complaint. . . .

SWAN, Circuit Judge (dissenting).

I think the majority opinion has construed the statute more broadly than its language will permit. In my opinion section 5, as limited by section 4, forbids only conduct by an issuer, underwriter or dealer. Concededly the appellee is neither an issuer nor a dealer. The definition of an underwriter, section 2(a)(11), includes three classes: (a) "any person who has purchased from an issuer with a view to . . . the distribution of any security"; (b) "any person who . . . sells [solicits 'an offer to buy' per section 2(a)(3)] for an issuer in connection with, the distribution of any security"; and (c) "any person who . . . participates or has a direct or indirect participation in any such undertaking." The appellee can fall only within class (b). To include it within that class gives no meaning to the words "for an issuer." Concededly it has no relationship whatever with the Chinese Government, "the issuer." The extent or success of its solicitations cannot be material; a single solicitation of an offer to buy would be equally within the language. Hence, a single newspaper editorial, published without instigation by the Chinese government and merely urging the purchase of the bonds in the name of patriotism, would make the newspaper an "underwriter." I cannot believe the statute should be so interpreted. It is my opinion that the decree should be affirmed.

NOTES AND QUESTIONS

1. Officers, Directors, Promoters.   Those who actively promote the sale of unregistered securities certainly are not a favored species under the Securities Act. The sweeping definition of underwriter in Section 2(a)(11) assures this result. Courts in their zeal to reach the right result sometimes engage in strained constructions of key definitional concepts. This has been especially true when justifying the application of Section 5 to promoters, officers, or control persons who have actively promoted an unregistered offering. Anyone who has arranged for public trading of an unregistered security or has stimulated investor interest in such a security through advertisements, research reports, or other promotional efforts can easily be considered to have "participated" in the issuer's distribution. *SEC v. Allison*, [1982 Transfer Binder] Fed. Sec. L. Rep. (CCH) ¶98,774 (N.D. Cal. 1982). They are thus within the definition of an underwriter and well beyond the Section 4(a)(1) exemption. Some courts have instead characterized officers, promoters, or control persons as issuers when they actively promote the sale of unregistered stock. *See, e.g., United States v. Rachal*, 473 F.2d 1338 (5th Cir.), *cert. denied*, 412 U.S. 927 (1973). Indeed, there is a fairly substantial body of cases equating those who control or dominate the issuer with the issuer. *See, e.g., Western Fed. Corp. v. Erickson*, 739 F.2d 1439, 1443 (9th Cir. 1984); *SEC v. Holschuh*, 694 F.2d 130, 140 (7th Cir. 1982).

Deeming officers or promoters as issuers is at best a curious interpretation of Section 2(a)(4). That section defines an issuer as "every person who issues or proposes to issue any security." In a corporate offering, the issuer is traditionally the company whose stock is sold. The sounder view is to focus upon functional considerations when analyzing the responsibilities of individuals such as promoters, officers, and control persons. The definition of Section 2(a)(11) is particularly well suited to serve the Securities Act's purposes in this area. Also consider whether an expansive interpretation of issuer does not seriously obviate the definition of underwriter in Section 2(a)(11), not to mention Section 4(a)(1).

2. *"Participates in an Underwriting."* The breadth of "participates in an underwriting" was illustrated in *Harden v. Raffensperger*, 65 F.3d 1392 (7th Cir. 1995). The defendant was retained to perform due diligence on the offering of another investment banking firm's securities; FINRA rules require its members to retain an independent company, known as a *qualified independent underwriter*, to perform due diligence on the registration statement.[1] The defendant argued it was not an underwriter because it had neither purchased nor sold any of the distributed securities. The court held that the defendant fell within the "participates" and "has a participation" language of Section 2(a)(11), reasoning that Section 2(a)(11) is broad enough to encompass all persons who engage in steps necessary to the distribution of securities. *See also Geiger v. Securities and Exchange Commission*, 363 F.3d 481, 487 (D.C. Cir. 2004) (underwriter includes person who finds an intermediary who will acquire the shares and then resale the shares into the market); *SEC v. CMKM Diamonds, Inc.*, 2011 U.S. Dist. LEXIS 80987 (D. Nev. July 25, 2011) (attorney who prepared 440 opinion letters forwarded to stock transfer agents that falsely justified resale of restricted securities

---

1. While FINRA replaced the NASD, it carries forward many of its predecessor's rules. NASD Rule 2720 calls for a qualified independent underwriter when more than 5 percent of an offering's net proceeds will be directed to an underwriter or its affiliates; this most frequently occurs when some of the offering proceeds will be dedicated to satisfaction of a credit facility with its underwriter or its affiliate.

was a necessary participant in resale as well as were the transfer agents who relied on the letters since the facts indicated reliance was not in good faith).

Also included within the "participates" language is "old-fashioned underwriting," whereby a person agrees to purchase any shares that cannot be sold in the offering. Rule 142, however, provides a limited exemption for some of these arrangements. The exemption provided in Rule 142 applies only where the agreement is to purchase *for investment* and is not with the issuer; for example, an agreement between an institutional investor and underwriter whereby the institutional investor will purchase what is not sold to the public falls within Rule 142 if the purchase was for investment.

Perhaps the broadest application of the "participates" language in Section 2(a)(11) is *Byrnes v. Faulkner, Dawkins & Sullivan*, 550 F.2d 1303 (2d Cir. 1977). The plaintiffs, owners of unregistered shares in White Shield Corporation, exercised a contractual right to compel White Shield to include their shares in a registration statement filed by White Shield for a public offering of its securities. The registration statement identified the plaintiffs as potential statutory underwriters. After the registration statement became effective, the plaintiffs, through a broker, sold their shares to the defendants. The plaintiffs did not assist White Shield in its offering. The defendants rejected the sale, and the plaintiffs sued for breach of contract. The court upheld the defendants' argument that the sale violated Section 5 because the plaintiffs failed to include a statutory prospectus with the confirmation of the sale. The court reasoned that plaintiffs "arranged to have their stock included in one of the White Shield registration statements and were identified as putative underwriters. . . . [Plaintiffs] therefore became participants in the White Shield distribution and accordingly became underwriters." Id. at 1312. In contrast, other decisions interpreting the meaning of "participates" have emphasized whether the defendant has provided assistance that facilitated the issuer's distribution. *See, e.g., SEC v. North Am. Research & Dev. Corp.*, 424 F.2d 63 (2d Cir. 1970). One concern raised by *Byrnes* is whether institutional investors who acquire unregistered shares and subsequently exercise their contractual right to require registration of the shares will be deemed underwriters when they sell their registered shares. *See McFarland v. Memorex Corp.*, 493 F. Supp. 631, 644 (N.D. Cal. 1980), *modified on other grounds*, 581 F. Supp. 878 (N.D. Cal. 1984) (not liable as underwriter under Section 11 because did not "formally underwrite" the stock issuance). *See generally* O'Hare, Institutional Investors, Registration Rights and the Specter of Liability Under Section 11 of the Securities Act of 1933, 1996 Wis. L. Rev. 217.

PROBLEM

6-1.   Carl, as a favor to his cousin, Alice, assists her in drafting an offering brochure for securities of her new company, Birdseed.com. At the conclusion of the drafting process, Carl was so impressed with the venture that he provided Alice with e-mail addresses of 250 members of the local chapter of the National Audubon Society, for which he is secretary. Alice forwarded the offering brochure to the e-mail addresses and thereby sold a significant portion of the offering to 40 of the chapter's members. In gratitude to Carl, she gave him 500 shares of the offering stock. Is Carl an underwriter? *See SEC v. Cavanagh*, 1 F. Supp. 2d 337 (S.D.N.Y.), *aff'd*, 155 F.3d 129 (2d Cir. 1998).

B. *Purchase from an Issuer*

Among those included within Section 2(a)(11)'s definition of *underwriter* is one "who has purchased from an issuer with a view to . . . the distribution of any security." Obviously, this includes the firm commitment underwriter, and as will be seen, it reaches any purchaser of unregistered securities from an issuer who acquires the securities with the intent to resell them to the public, even though he is not an investment banker or even a full-time investor.

What constitutes a purchase is not directly addressed by the '33 Act, which provides only a definition of sale, but not purchase. One would believe that the terms *sale* and *purchase*, because they are reciprocals of one another, should share some basic elements. A central element of the definition of sale of Section 2(a)(3) is that the disposition of the security must be "for value." This indeed is a requirement for a purchase; hence, a donee is not an underwriter unless one can find as a condition of the gift an undertaking by the donee that would constitute the giving of "value." Thus, the loyal alumna who endows with unregistered securities a chair to be named in her honor may well have not only the gratitude of her alma mater, but the gratitude of a purchaser as well. And what of the thief of unregistered securities who sets them loose in the stream of commerce? Is the thief only a thief, or is he a thieving underwriter as well?

Recall that Section 5 is transactionally oriented, so that literally every seller of a security must consider her compliance with the Act. More particularly, the focus is whether the sale falls within the exemption afforded by Section 4(a)(1) to every transaction not by an "issuer, underwriter or dealer," which invariably leads the analysis back to whether the seller is engaged in an underwriting transaction. In most cases, the troubling question is whether the purchase was "with a view to . . . the distribution" of the security. The material that follows deals separately with the twin questions of the purchaser's *investment intent* and the meaning of *distribution*.

1. Investment Intent

The concept of investment intent arises from Section 2(a)(11)'s definition of an *underwriter* as one who has purchased from an issuer "with a view to" the security's distribution. The phrase suggests that underwriter status is assumed by one who acquires an unregistered security for other than long-term investment. To be sure, this is not a precise standard, as demonstrated in a leading case, *Gilligan, Will & Co. v. SEC*, 267 F.2d 461 (2d Cir. 1959), where the investor, Gilligan, sought an exemption under Section 4(a)(1) for his resale of unregistered debentures purchased ten months earlier. Gilligan conceded that, if his sales were contemplated at the time of his purchase of the unregistered debentures from the issuer, Crowell-Collier Publishing Company, he would have been an underwriter and beyond the exemption in Section 4(a)(1). However, Gilligan argued the sales were made only after a change in the issuer's circumstances as a result of which Gilligan, acting as a prudent investor, thought it wise to sell. The court dismissed Gilligan's change of circumstances argument:

> The catalytic circumstances were the failure, noted by Gilligan, of Crowell-Collier to increase its advertising space as he had anticipated it would. We agree with the

Commission that in the circumstances here presented the intention to retain the debentures only if Crowell-Collier continued to operate profitably was equivalent to a "purchased . . . with a view to . . . distribution" within the statutory definition of underwriters in 2(a)(11). To hold otherwise would be to permit a dealer who speculatively purchases in an unregistered security in the hope that the financially weak issuer had, as is stipulated here, "turned the corner," to unload on the unadvised public what he later determines to be an unsound investment without the disclosure sought by the securities laws, although it is in precisely such circumstances that disclosure is most necessary and desirable. The Commission was within its discretion in finding on this stipulation that petitioners bought "with a view to distribution" despite the ten months of holding.

Id. at 468. The length of time the purchaser held the shares before reselling them plays a pivotal role in determining whether the purchaser acquired the shares with a view to their distribution.

At one time, most practitioners believed investment intent is established if the shares have been held for three years. *See, e.g.,* Sommer, Considerations Leading to the Adoption of Rule 144, 67 Nw. U. L. Rev. 65, 69 (Supp. 1972). For holding periods less than three years, a less definitive answer is forthcoming: Consideration must then be given to the circumstances surrounding the shares' purchase as well as any change in the purchaser's circumstances after their purchase. In this area, there is something of a "bendpoint" at two years, so that the presumptions favor the conclusion that the shares were purchased with a view to distribute when the shares have been held for less than two years, but favor the opposite conclusion when they have been held for more than two years. If the holding period is less than two years, the factors of the purchaser's circumstance when he purchased the shares and a change in circumstance after their purchase must negate any intent to distribute. On the other hand, if the shares have been held for more than two years (but less than three years), these two factors should not support an inference of an intent to distribute. *See* Flanagin, The Federal Securities Act and the Locked-In Stockholder, 63 Mich. L. Rev. 1139 (1965). As will be seen later in this chapter, the SEC's resale safe harbor, Rule 144, once had among its requirements for restricted shares a minimum holding period of three years, and two years if the resale was made pursuant to certain other limitations. Under current Rule 144, the holding period is six months for reporting companies and one year for non-reporting companies. Should this development change the "bendpoint" for resales outside the Rule 144 safe harbor? *See* Notice of Adoption of Rule 144, Securities Act Release No. 5223 (Jan. 10, 1972), 1972 WL 125477, at *8 ("The definitive holding period provided in [Rule 144] may be relied on only in connection with sales made pursuant to the rule."); *but see SEC v. Luna,* 2014 U.S. Dist. LEXIS 28876 (D. Nev. 2014) (in light of two-year "rule of thumb" it is a question of fact whether resale of restricted security within three and a half months of purchase occurred with investment intent).

NOTES AND QUESTIONS

1.   Change in Circumstances.   What set of events can support the conclusion that the investor sold the unregistered shares much earlier than she contemplated when they were purchased? This is an important line of inquiry whenever the shares have been held for less than two years. In *G. Eugene England Foundation v. First Federal Corp.*, 663 F.2d 988 (10th Cir. 1973), the defendant, 13 months after he acquired stock in a private offering, began negotiations to exchange the shares for land held by the plaintiff. The exchange finally occurred in April 1969, approximately 16 months after the shares had been issued to the defendant. The shares thereafter declined in value, and the plaintiff sought to rescind under Section 12(a)(1). The Tenth Circuit held that the defendant's holding period was too short to establish investment intent, and, there being no change in circumstances to explain their resale so soon after their purchase, the defendant was deemed to be an underwriter. On the other hand, in *Neuwirth Investment Fund, Ltd. v. Swanton*, 422 F. Supp. 1187 (S.D.N.Y. 1975), unregistered shares were acquired in September 1969, and their purchaser then requested that they be registered. The issuer, however, refused to register the shares. The purchaser became insolvent in August 1970, and its liquidator was denied a no-action letter from the SEC for the sale of the shares without registration. In January 1971, the liquidator sold the shares without registration. The court held that the purchaser's 1969 request that the shares be registered was not the same as an intent to resell the shares, especially since no subsequent attempts were made by the purchaser to sell the shares. The court observed that thereafter the purchaser's circumstances had changed and it was this change in circumstances that caused the sale, not the lack of the purchaser's investment intent when he initially acquired the shares. *See also Leitman v. VTR, Inc.*, [1969-1970 Transfer Binder] Fed. Sec. L. Rep. (CCH) ¶92,707 (S.D.N.Y. 1970) (sale of unregistered shares to satisfy the unexpected call by bank of demand note was sufficient change in circumstances so as not to question purchaser's intent when he acquired the shares 21 months earlier).

The SEC's 1972 adopting release for Rule 144 included the following regarding change in circumstances:

> [T]he Commission hereby puts all persons including brokers and attorneys on notice that the "change in circumstances" concept should no longer be considered as one of the factors in determining whether a person is an underwriter. The Commission recognizes that this concept has been in existence in one form or another for a long period of time. However, administrative agencies as well as courts from time to time change their interpretation of statutory provisions in the light of new considerations and changing conditions which indicate that earlier interpretations of such provisions are no longer in keeping with the statutory objectives. Thus, the "change in circumstances" concept in the Commission's opinion fails to meet the objectives of the Act, since the circumstances of the seller are unrelated to the need of investors for the protections afforded by the registration and other provisions of the Act.

Courts, however, are not bound by such an SEC pronouncement. In that regard, several commentators have asserted that the change in circumstances doctrine is still viable. *See Berckeley Inv. Group, Ltd. v. Colkitt*, 455 F.3d 195, 214 n.21 (3d Cir. 2006).

2. *Letters of Intent.* The purchasers in *Gilligan, Will* each signed a "letter of intent" that provided: "I hereby confirm to you that said debentures are being purchased for investment and that I have no present intention of distributing the same." How much weight should be given to such an undertaking? How better can the issuer's counsel assure that the purchaser is taking with investment intent? Why is this a concern of the *issuer's* counsel?

3.   Sale of Pledged Shares.   The Supreme Court in *Rubin v. United States*, 449 U.S. 424 (1981), held that a pledge of stock as collateral is an "offer or sale" of a security within the meaning of Section 17(a) of the Securities Act. Consider the problems faced by a lender whose collateral is unregistered securities. If upon default of the loan the pledgee sells to the public unregistered shares, is the pledgee an underwriter? *See SEC v. Guild Films Co.*, 279 F.2d 485 (2d Cir.), *cert. denied*, 364 U.S. 819 (1960). Should the result depend upon whether it is a "bona fide" pledge, meaning that at the moment of the pledge there was a low probability the collateral would have to be sold? *See A.D.M. Corp. v. Thomson*, 707 F.2d 25 (1st Cir.), *cert. denied*, 464 U.S. 938 (1983).

PROBLEMS

6-2.   Sixteen months ago, Beatrice purchased 1,000 unregistered Chromium Mines, Inc. common shares through a private placement. Much to her surprise, Beatrice has just been admitted to the prestigious and expensive Padooka University graduate school. If Beatrice now sells her Chromium shares to pay the tuition deposit demanded by Padooka University, will she violate Section 5?

6-3.   Janice, in desperate financial shape, exchanged worthless desert real estate for 125,000 shares of Issuer unregistered common stock. Thereupon, Janice pledged all the shares to Bank as collateral for a loan. She obtained the loan through fraudulently prepared financial statements. Janice promptly left town. While Janice has demonstrated several important flaws in her character, can Bank nevertheless resell the shares to satisfy the outstanding loan? Is your advice different if the pledged shares represent a control block of stock that Janice had held for five years?

2.   Distributions and Trading Transactions Contrasted

Distribution is not defined in the Securities Act, even though it is the linchpin of Section 2(a)(11)'s definition of an underwriter. Courts have fairly consistently followed the lead of *Gilligan, Will & Co. v. SEC*, 267 F.2d 461 (2d Cir. 1959), in reasoning that the meaning of distribution is to be found in the Supreme Court's standard announced in *SEC v. Ralston Purina Co.*, 346 U.S. 119 (1953), for determining whether an issue is a public offering: A distribution exists if there are sales to those who cannot "fend for themselves." In *Gilligan, Will*, the court found the defendants had engaged in a distribution by selling unregistered securities not only through the American Stock Exchange, but also privately to a few investors who neither were provided nor had access to the type of information that would have been available through registration under the Securities Act. Others who have considered the meaning of "distribution" have emphasized the buyer's sophistication. *See, e.g., Wheaten v. Mathews Holmquist*

& Assocs., Inc., [1995 Transfer Binder] Fed. Sec. L. Rep. (CCH) ¶98,727 (N.D. Ill. 1994).

To be sure, there is a certain appeal to referring to the standards of the private offering exemption of Section 4(a)(2) for guidance in determining whether there is a distribution. To do so equates distribution with "public offering" so that the regulatory objective of Section 5 of full and fair disclosure in connection with public offerings is fulfilled. If this was the intention of Congress, why wasn't "public offering" used in Section 2(a)(11) as it is in Section 4(a)(2)? In any case, there is a good deal of confusion whether all the criteria of the private offering exemption, such as sophistication of all offerees, necessarily have to be satisfied to avoid the resale's being deemed a distribution. This concern is examined more closely later in connection with the so-called Section 4(a) (1½) exemption, where the issue is whether a resale by a *control person* is a distribution. For non-control persons, the question of whether a distribution has occurred by the resale of unregistered securities is in fact much simpler than it is for a resale by a control person.

Resales of securities by a non-control person pose Section 5 problems only when the security being resold has not been registered. This conclusion follows from the view that the issuer's registration statement satisfies the information needs of all subsequent purchasers of the distributed security. In this way, we can well understand that what is in fact registered is not the security itself but its overall distribution, including resales, of the registered security. Even a seller of unregistered securities is beyond Section 5 if she can establish investment intent. If she purchased her securities from the issuer with investment intent, then her resale cannot be regarded as being "with a view to" their distribution. The question of whether the resale implicates a distribution therefore only arises if the non-control person making the resale cannot establish investment intent when the securities were acquired. However, not every resale of an unregistered security by one who took *without* investment intent constitutes a distribution. As illustrated in the examples that follow, we can conclude that "distribution" includes an offering of a security that is required to be registered because the issuer's offering did not come to rest only with investors who satisfy the criteria of a single exemption from registration.

For example, assume Issuer offered its shares only to residents of New York and all of the proceeds, as well as Issuer's operations, were in New York. Without more, Issuer's offering is exempt under the intrastate offering exemption of Section 3(a)(11). If Alice, herself a New York resident, purchased 1,000 of Issuer's shares and immediately resold those shares to another New York resident, this does not violate the issuer's intrastate exemption; the objective of the intrastate exemption is not violated by allowing Alice to resell an unregistered security to a person who, like herself, satisfies the criteria of the exemption relied on by the issuer to avoid registration of the security. Thus, even though Alice lacked investment intent, her resale is exempt under Section 4(a)(1) because that sale was not pursuant to a "distribution" by the issuer. Her resale was made to a person who meets the criteria of the exemption relied on by Issuer to avoid registration. *See* Campbell, Resales of Securities Under the Securities Act of 1933, 52 Wash. & Lee L. Rev. 1333, 1352 (1995). However, if Alice sold the shares to a California resident, her resale falls outside the issuer's exemption because the issuer's offering did not come to rest in the hands of those who satisfy the intrastate exemption. Her resale has rendered the entire offering—by the issuer's being of the character referred to in *Gilligan, Will*—a public (i.e., nonexempt) offering that was not registered; hence, it is a "distribution." The same analysis applies if Issuer had sought the exemption available for private offerings in Section 4(a)(2) and Alice quickly resold her shares. If that resale was to one who possessed sophistication and information about Issuer, her resale does not involve a distribution; however, if her resale was to one who lacked sophistication and/or information about the issuer, the resale destroys Issuer's exemption, and there is a distribution.

Notice the above analysis focuses not upon the number of shares resold, but upon whether the resale destroys the exemption under which the issuer sought to qualify its offering. If the resale destroys the exemption, then there is an offering that has to be registered under Section 5, that is, a distribution.

PROBLEMS

6-4. A year ago, Burt acquired 1,000 shares of SunTech Inc. in a private placement. SunTech's annual report, which has just been released, reflects that earnings have quadrupled in the past year. Burt is both ecstatic and in need of cash for a new addition to his house and has approached his neighbor Carol, a broker-dealer, about possibly reselling the shares. Carol offers to contact several of her clients about their purchase of Burt's shares. Burt agrees. Before Carol actually begins soliciting her clients, she asks your advice. What would you tell Carol?

6-5. Assume in Problem 6-4 that, when Burt acquired his SunTech shares, there already existed trading in SunTech shares in the over-the-counter market. Nevertheless, SunTech had issued shares to selected purchasers in a private placement to raise funds quickly and cheaply. One year after purchasing his shares, Burt approaches Carol about selling the shares into the over-the-counter market. How would you advise Carol?

6-6. What results if the shares had been sold to Burt as part of a registered offering, and shortly after Burt purchased those shares he resold them through Carol in the over-the-counter market?

3. Private Investment in Public Equity (PIPEs)

Sjostrom, Jr., PIPEs
2 Entrepreneurial Bus. L.J. 381, 383-389 (2007)

A PIPE is a type of financing transaction undertaken by a public company, normally with a small number of sophisticated investors. In a typical PIPE, the company relies on an exemption from SEC registration requirements to issue investors common stock or securities convertible into common stock for cash. The company then registers the resale of the common stock issued in the private placement, or issued upon conversion of the convertible securities issued in the private placement, with the SEC. Generally, investors must hold securities issued in a private placement for at least one year [now six months for reporting companies as a result of the 2008 changes to Rule 144]. However, because the company registers the resale of the PIPE shares, investors are free to sell them into the market as soon as the SEC declares the resale registration statement effective (typically within a few months of the closing of the private placement).

A. TYPES OF PIPES

. . . PIPE securities may consist of common stock or securities convertible into common stock, such as convertible preferred stock or convertible notes, and may be coupled with common stock warrants. . . . With a traditional PIPE, the PIPE shares are issued at a price fixed on the closing date of the private placement. This fixed price is typically set at a discount to the trailing average of the market price of the issuer's common stock for some period of days prior to closing of the private placement. . . . [B]ecause the deal price is fixed, investors in traditional PIPEs assume price risk, which is the risk of future declines in the market price of the issuer's common stock during the pendency of the resale registration statement. Of the 1,343 PIPE deals closed in 2006, 1,111 (82.7%) involved traditional PIPEs.

With a structured PIPE, the issuance price of the PIPE shares is not fixed on the closing date of the private placement. Instead it adjusts (often, downward only) based on future price movements of the issuer's common stock. Hence, with a structured PIPE, investors do not assume price risk during the pendency of the resale registration statement. If the market price declines, so too does the conversion price, and therefore the PIPE securities will be convertible into a greater number of shares of common stock. . . .

B. REGISTRATION REQUIREMENT

The registration requirement of a PIPE transaction can be either concurrent or trailing. With a concurrent registration requirement, investors commit to buy a specified dollar amount of PIPE securities in the private placement, but their obligations to fund are conditional on the SEC indicating that it is prepared to declare the resale registration statement effective. If the SEC never gets to this point, the investors do not have to go forward with the deal. Thus, the issuer bears the registration risk, that is, the risk that the SEC will refuse to declare the resale registration statement effective.

With a trailing registration rights requirement, the parties close on the private placement and then the issuer files a registration statement. Consequently, the investors bear the registration risk. If the issuer never files or the SEC never declares the registration statement effective, the investors will not be able to sell their PIPE shares into the market for at least [six months for reporting companies]. As a result, PIPE deals that include such trailing registration requirements typically obligate the issuer to file the registration statement within 30 days of the private placement closing date and require that it be declared effective within 90 to 120 days of such date. If these deadlines are not met, the issuer is obligated to pay the investors a penalty of 1 percent to 2 percent of the deal proceeds per month until filing or effectiveness.

C.   PIPE ISSUERS

. . . [T]he large majority of PIPE deals are undertaken by small public companies. These companies generally pursue PIPEs not because they offer advantages over other financing alternatives but because the companies have no other financing alternatives. By and large, PIPE issuers are not only small in terms of market capitalization but have weak cash flow and poorly performing stocks. . . . Further, a majority of them will run out of cash within a year unless they obtain additional financing. Thus, traditional forms of financing are simply not an option. Few, if any, investment banking firms are willing to underwrite follow-on offerings for small, distressed public companies. . . . [T]hese companies lack the collateral and financial performance to qualify for bank loans and the upside potential to attract traditional private equity financing.

Given the distressed status of PIPE issuers, PIPE financing can, of course, be very expensive. Not only does the company typically issue common stock or common stock equivalents at a discount to market price, but PIPE deals often involve other cash flow rights such as dividends or interest (typically paid in kind not cash) and warrants . . . [which yields an overall purchase discount of 14.3 to 34.7 percent].

Not surprisingly, PIPE issuers continue to perform poorly following PIPE financings. . . . [T]he stock of 28 percent of issuers was delisted within twenty-four months following the PIPE financing.

D.   PIPE INVESTORS

This dismal post-PIPE performance of course raises the question of who is investing in PIPEs. The answer is hedge funds. They constitute nearly 80 percent of the investors in micro-cap PIPEs. Hedge funds invest for the obvious reason: their returns from PIPE investments meet or beat market benchmarks. . . .

Hedge funds are able to obtain these returns notwithstanding the poor performance of PIPE issuers through a relatively straightforward trading strategy. They sell short the issuer's common stock promptly after the PIPE deal is publicly disclosed. To execute a short sale, a fund borrows stock of the PIPE issuer from a broker-dealer and sells this borrowed stock into the market. The fund then closes out or covers the short sale at a later date by buying shares in the open market and delivering them to the lender. By shorting stock against the PIPE shares, the fund locks in the PIPE deal purchase discount. With a traditional PIPE, if the market price of the issuer's common stock drops below the discounted price following a PIPE transaction, the fund will take a loss on the PIPE shares, but this loss will be exceeded by gains realized when it closes out its short position because it will be able to buy shares in the market to cover the position at a lower price than it earlier sold the borrowed shares. If the market price of the issuer's common stock rises after the PIPE transaction, the fund will take a loss when closing out the short position because it will have to buy shares to cover the position at a higher price than it earlier sold the borrowed shares. This loss, however, will be exceeded by an increase in the value of the PIPE shares since they were purchased at a discount to the pre-rise market price. . . .

. . . [PIPEs] can be even more profitable for hedge funds in a structured PIPE deal with a floating conversion price. If the issuer's stock price drops, a fund profits on its short sales dollar for dollar. At the same time, it also profits on the PIPE shares because the conversion price of the PIPE securities is based on a discount to market price on the date of conversion, i.e., the conversion price floats down with the market price. Hence, the fund makes money on both sides of the trade, subject only to unwinding risk.

NOTES AND QUESTIONS

1. *A Problematic Booming Source of Capital?*   PIPEs are not an isolated or passing phenomenon. Over the years, their dollar volume has grown tremendously, exceeding $44 billion in 2018 for 875 PIPE offerings by U.S. companies. To what extent does the regulatory quilt explain their prevalence? Consider as well whether PIPEs functionally are just the reverse of the shelf registration procedure studied earlier. As we saw with shelf registrations, Rule 415 authorizes the separation of the regulatory step (filing a registration statement) from the act of raising capital (selling the registered securities). In the case of shelf registration, the registration statement is filed and later, as market conditions merit, the securities are sold. Contrast this with PIPEs, where the issuer receives the sought-after capital by placing a security through an exemption and later satisfies the formal regulatory requirement by filing a registration statement; upon the registration statement's becoming effective, the issuer's security, albeit one different from that initially sold through the exemption, is placed in the hands of public investors. From the position of investor protection, is there an important difference between these two approaches?

2. *Who's the Underwriter?*   In 2006, the SEC announced that PIPE investors in some cases will be deemed "underwriters," so that, for example, they assume the responsibilities underwriters have under Section 11 for material misrepresentations in the registration statement. While not a fixed guideline, the staff's position is that an important consideration in determining, for a PIPE-related transaction, whether the investors who will be converting their security to obtain the registered security must be identified as underwriters in the registration is whether the shares covering the PIPE constitute 33 percent or more of the issuer's "public float" (i.e., shares of that type held by non-affiliates). "The end result of the SEC's position on primary versus secondary offerings is essentially a cap on the size of PIPE deals. In terms of dollar amounts, the lower the dollar value of a company's public float, the less money it will be able to raise through a PIPE. Hence, the cap hits small companies hardest, the very companies that have few, if any, other financing options." Sjostrom, supra at 412. The SEC enforcement efforts have also impacted the structure of PIPE transactions. *See* Bengtsson, Dai & Henson, SEC Enforcement in the PIPE Market: Actions and Consequences, 42 J. Bank. & Fin. 213 (2014) (observing that following the enactment of the 2002-2004 enforcement initiatives, PIPEs shifted from structured to traditional form, with hedge funds negotiating steeper discounts from issuers whereas formerly a larger portion of their gain was reaped through short selling, although those gains still persist albeit at a lower portion of their overall gain).

3.   Primary or Secondary Offering? Gun Jumping?   As seen, the first leg of a PIPE is the private placement of a security convertible into the issuer's common shares that, when issued, will be registered. Essentially, the proponents of the PIPE view the common shares as being registered for resale on a continuous and delayed basis pursuant to the shelf registration Rule 415(a)(1)(i), studied earlier. But the authority to use Rule 415(a)(1)(i) assumes the offering is a secondary and not a primary offering. If a primary offering, then the transaction would have to satisfy another provision of Rule 415, namely paragraph (a)(1)(x) since it would be an "at the market offering." This form of shelf offering, however, is limited to issuers eligible to use Form S-3. Thus, it is important for PIPE transactions to be treated as secondary offerings, not as an issuer's shelf registration. Factors used by the SEC to conclude the offering is secondary and not primary are how long the selling shareholder has held the shares, the amount of shares, whether the seller is in the business of underwriting securities, and finally whether under all the circumstances it appears that the seller is a conduit for the issuer. Selling shareholders, however, need to be cognizant that qualifying to meet Rule 415(a)(1)(i) does not come with the burdens of being deemed an underwriter as discussed above in Note 2.

A further concern is gun jumping. If the hedge fund participating in a PIPE transaction engages in a short sell of the issuer's security expecting to cover its short position with the shares being registered by the issuer, should this be seen as essentially selling those shares prior to the registration statement becoming effective? The SEC has unsuccessfully argued that such "naked" short sales do violate Section 5. *See, e.g., SEC v. Edwin Buchanan Lyon,* 529 F. Supp. 2d 444, 459-460 (S.D.N.Y. 2008) ("the PIPE shares used to cover defendants' short positions cannot be considered sold or offered for sale pursuant to Section 5 at the time defendants sold short the PIPE issuer's publicly traded securities").

4.   Regulation M's Impact.   Rule 105 of Regulation M, studied in Chapter 4, prohibits a person from short selling within five business days of the pricing of a security sold and then covering the short position with securities purchased in a firm commitment underwriting.

5.   Perils of Short-Swing Profits.   Exchange Act Section 16(b) requires directors, officers and owners of more than 10 percent of a reporting company's equity securities to disgorge any profit made if such security is sold within six months of its purchase. Because of the short turnaround for most PIPE transactions, such short-swing liability can be a concern. Although Rule 16(b)(3) exempts officers and directors from short-swing profits in board-approved acquisitions, it does not exempt an owner of more than 10 percent. *See Huppe v. WPCS Int'l Inc.,* 670 F.3d 214 (2d Cir. 2012). *Huppe* is studied later in Chapter 15.

PROBLEMS

6-7.   Quick Buck Ltd. has earned significant profits by repeatedly carrying out the following investment strategy. It acquires from public companies via private placements preferred shares from the issuing company that at some later date are convertible into the issuer's common shares. Customarily the conversion is on a one-for-one basis. Because the preferred shares are restricted, Quick Buck is able to purchase them from the issuer at a discount vis-à-vis the publicly traded common shares into which the preferred is convertible. Following the announcement of the private placement, the issuer's common shares invariably decline in value, reflecting the dilutive effect of the convertible security that was issued at a discount vis-à-vis the common shares into which it will ultimately be converted. In advance of the issuer's announcement of its private placement of convertible securities, Quick Buck secretly engages in substantial short selling of the issuer's common shares. Upon registration of the issuer's common shares, Quick Buck covers its short position in an issuer's common shares by converting its restricted preferred shares into registered common shares, thereby pocketing substantial profits through its short selling. Has Quick Buck violated Section 5? *See, e.g., Securities and Exchange Commission v. Edwin Buchanan*, 529 F. Supp. 2d 444 (S.D.N.Y. 2008).

6-8. Assume in Problem 6-7 that the issuer is Logicon Devices Inc. and that it does not meet the issuer criteria for Form S-3. Why doesn't Quick Buck's resale to the public of the registered security nullify Logicon's exemption? *See* Rule 152. What results if the SEC views the Logicon–Quick Buck transaction not as a secondary distribution but as a primary offering that will be carried out on a delayed basis at a variable price as set forth in Rule 415(a)(x)? *See* SEC Staff Adopts New Approach to Convertible PIPEs Transactions, 39 BNA Sec. Reg. & L. Rep. 175 (Feb. 5, 2007).

C.   *Control Person Distributions*

The reach of Section 5 of the Securities Act is broadened significantly by the second sentence of Section 2(a)(11): "As used in this paragraph the term 'issuer' shall include, in addition to an issuer, any person directly or indirectly controlling or controlled by the issuer, or any person under the direct or indirect common control with the issuer." Thus, one who purchases from a control person, or sells for a control person, or otherwise participates, directly or indirectly, in a distribution of the control person's securities is an underwriter. With this broadened definition of underwriters under Section 2(a)(11) and its correlative narrowing of the exemption available in Section 4(a)(1), distributions by control persons are subject to regulation similar to that applied to issuers. The House committee report explained the purpose of regulating the control person's distributions as follows:

> All the outstanding stock of a particular corporation may be owned by one individual or a select group of individuals. At some future date they may wish to dispose of their holdings and to make an offer of this stock to the public. Such a public offering may possess all the dangers attendant upon a new offering of securities. Wherever such a redistribution reaches significant proportions, the distributor would be in the position of controlling the issuer and thus able to furnish the information demanded by the bill. This being so, the distributor is treated as equivalent to the original issuer and, if he seeks to dispose of the issue through

a public offering, he becomes subject to the act. The concept of control herein involved is not a narrow one, depending upon a mathematical formula of 51 percent of voting power, but is broadly defined to permit the provisions of the act to become effective wherever the fact of control actually exists.

Report of Committee on Interstate and Foreign Commerce, H.R. Rep. No. 85, 73d Cong., 1st Sess. 13-14 (1933).

Section 2(a)(11) provides that a control person is an issuer, but only for the purpose of determining whether the person who purchases from or sells for the control person is an underwriter. A control person is not an issuer for other purposes of the Act because the control person is not included within Section 2(a)(4)'s definition of an issuer. The control person therefore is not able to use the issuer-based exemptions established in Section 4(a)(2), 4(a)(5), 4(a)(6), Regulation D, or Rule 147.

There are two important areas where the control person is on the same footing as everyone else when approaching Section 5. First, the control person is in no different a position than any other holder of an exempt security; an exempt security can be sold by anyone without fear of violating Section 5. Second, the control person's resale of an unregistered security may occur under circumstances that are consistent with the criteria of the exemption from Section 5 that the issuer sought. For example, if the issuer relied upon the private offering exemption in selling the shares to the control person and others, the control person's immediate resale to a *Ralston Purina* qualified purchaser would not destroy the issuer's exemption. This is because Section 4(a)(2) is a transaction exemption, so that not only is the issuer exempt, but also anyone participating in that transaction is exempt. In a sense, this is the correlative holding of cases such as *Chinese Consolidated* that stress the transaction aspect of the exemptions in Sections 4(a)(1) and 4(a)(2).

Under the second possible exemptive approach above for the control person, it is significant whether the issuer's offering has come to rest. If it has not, the resale is evaluated in terms of its impact on the exemption the issuer relied on in offering the security. The person reselling the security, whether or not a control person, is simply an intermediary in the issuer's transactions; if the issuer's sales and the resales of others in combination satisfy the criteria of the exemption sought by the issuer, then all such sales are protected. *See, e.g., Fuller v. Dilbert,* 244 F. Supp. 196 (S.D.N.Y. 1965), *aff'd,* 358 F.2d 305 (2d Cir. 1966). A resale to an unqualified offeree, however, destroys the issuer's exemption and renders the selling control person an underwriter in the issuer's distribution. *See Securities and Exchange Commission v. Lybrand,* 200 F. Supp. 2d 384 (S.D.N.Y. 2002); *United States v. Hill,* 298 F. Supp. 1221 (D. Conn. 1969).

On the other hand, if the issuer's offering has come to rest, the control person's position is quite different from that of a non-control person. In this case, the non-control person who purchased with investment intent is not an underwriter, so that her resale is exempt under Section 4(a)(1). In contrast, the control person is not protected by her investment intent. The control person's burden is not judged by whether she purchased from the Section 2(a)(4) issuer with a view toward the distribution of that security. Instead, the regulatory focus is whether someone is purchasing from the control person or selling for the control person, or otherwise participating in a distribution for the control person. If so, the person so purchasing, selling, or participating is an underwriter. The twin inquiries are whether there is a control person and whether the sales constitute a distribution.

On close analysis, three significant control relationships are implicated in Section 2(a)(11)'s broad sweep: first, any person controlling the issuer; second, any person controlled by the issuer; and third, any person under common control with the issuer. The effect of this provision is to subject the distributions by such control persons to regulation similar to that applied to issuers.

❘❘ United States v. Wolfson
405 F.2d 779 (2d Cir. 1968), *cert. denied*, 394 U.S. 946 (1969)

WOODBURY, J. It was stipulated at the trial that at all relevant times there were 2,510,000 shares of Continental Enterprises, Inc., issued and outstanding. . . . [T]he appellant Louis E. Wolfson himself with members of his immediate family and his right hand man and first lieutenant, the appellant Elkin B. Gerbert, owned 1,149,775 or in excess of 40%. The balance of the stock was in the hands of approximately 5,000 outside shareholders. . . . [B]etween August 1, 1960, and January 31, 1962, Wolfson himself sold 404,150 shares of Continental through six brokerage houses. . . .

[A]s the largest individual shareholder [Wolfson] was Continental's guiding spirit in that the officers of the corporation were subject to his direction and control and that no corporate policy decisions were made without his knowledge and consent. Indeed Wolfson admitted as much on the stand. No registration statement was in effect as to Continental; its stock was traded over-the-counter.

The appellants do not dispute the foregoing basic facts. They took the position at the trial that they had no idea during the period of the alleged conspiracy, stipulated to be from January 1, 1960, to January 31, 1962, that there was any provision of law requiring registration of a security before its distribution by a controlling person to the public. On the stand in their defense they took the position that they operated at a level of corporate finance far above such "details" as the securities laws; as to whether a particular stock must be registered. They asserted and their counsel argued to the jury that they were much too busy with large affairs to concern themselves with such minor matters and attributed the fault of failure to register to subordinates in the Wolfson organization and to failure of the brokers to give notice of the need. Obviously in finding the appellants guilty the jury rejected this defense, if indeed, it is any defense at all. . . .

The appellants argue that they come within [§4(a)(1)] for they are not issuers, underwriters or dealers. At first blush there would appear to be some merit in this argument. The immediate difficulty with it, however, is that §4(a)(1) by its terms exempts only "transactions," not classes of persons, see *SEC v. Culpepper*, 270 F.2d 241, 247 (2d Cir. 1959), and ignores §2[a](11) of the Act, which defines an "underwriter" to mean any person who has purchased from an issuer with a view to the distribution of any security, or participates directly or indirectly in such undertaking unless that person's participation is limited to the usual and customary seller's commission, and then goes on to provide: "As used in this paragraph the term 'issuer' shall include, in addition to an issuer, any person directly or indirectly *controlling* or controlled by *the issuer*, or any person under direct or indirect common control with the 'issuer.'" (Italics supplied.) In short, the brokers provided outlets for the stock of issuers and thus were underwriters. Wherefore the stock was sold in "transactions by underwriters" which are not within the exemption of §4[(a)](1), supra.

But the appellants contend that the brokers in this case cannot be classified as underwriters because their part in the sales transactions came within §4[(a)]4, which exempts "brokers' transactions executed upon customers' orders on any exchange or in the over-the-counter market but not the solicitation of such orders."[1] The answer to this contention is that §4[(a)](4) was designed only to exempt the brokers' part in security transactions. Control persons must find their own exemptions.

There is nothing inherently unreasonable for a broker to claim the exemption of §4[(a)](4), supra, when he is unaware that his customer's part in the transaction is not exempt. Indeed, this is indicated by the definition of "brokers' transaction" in 17 C.F.R. §230.154, commonly known as Rule 154, which provides:

> (a) The term "brokers' transaction" in Section 4(4) of the act shall be deemed to include transactions by a broker acting as agent for the account of any person controlling, controlled by, or under common control with, the issuer of the securities which are the subject of the transaction where:

> (4) The broker is *not aware* of circumstances indicating . . . that the transactions are part of a distribution of securities on behalf of his principal.

And there can be no doubt that appellants' sale of over 633,000 shares (25% of the outstanding shares of Continental and more than 55% of their own holdings) was a distribution rather than an ordinary brokerage transaction. *See* Rule 154(6), which defines "distribution" for the purpose of paragraph (a) generally as "substantial" in relation to the number of shares outstanding and specifically as a sale of 1% of the stock within six months preceding the sale if the shares are traded on a stock exchange.

Certainly if the appellants' sales, which clearly amounted to a distribution under the above definitions, had been made through a broker or brokers with knowledge of the circumstances, the brokers would not be entitled to the exemption. It will hardly do for the appellants to say that because they kept the true facts from the brokers they can take advantage of the exemption the brokers gained thereby. . . .

In conclusion it will suffice to say that full consideration of the voluminous record in this rather technical case discloses no reversible error.

Affirmed.

NOTES AND QUESTIONS

1.　The Meaning of Control.　Control is not defined in the Securities Act, although Section 2(a)(11) broadly describes the types of control relationships that will cause a control person to be treated as an issuer for the purpose of

---

1.　It is undisputed that the brokers involved in this case did not solicit orders from the appellants.

considering whether another is an underwriter. The SEC in its Rule 405 offers a definition of control that is much more sweeping than that set forth in the earlier excerpt from the House committee report. Rule 405 defines control functionally in terms of a person's or group's influence over management and business policies, whereas the House committee report looks to whether one could obtain, if necessary, the signatures needed for the issuer to file a registration statement covering the control person's sales. Section 6 of the Securities Act sets forth who is required to sign the registration statement, including its principal executive officers and a majority of its board of directors. Clearly, of all the signatories over which control must be exercised, the most important in the corporate context are the members of the board of directors, since all other corporate personnel are subordinates to the board of directors. Restricting the meaning of control to one who can compel the filing of a registration statement not only sharpens the focus of inquiry when determining who is a control person, but also lightens Section 5's burdens on individuals who, though they are influential within the issuer, are unlikely to be able to cause the issuer to gather information and obtain the signatures required for a registration statement.

> [I]t seems apparent that Congress was willing to saddle a control person with the responsibility of registering his securities because he could furnish the information required by the registration statement. By contrast, it is not clear that one who has the power to direct the management and policies of a corporation necessarily possesses the power to obtain registration. . . . [S]election of the ability to obtain registration approach provides an understandable, albeit general, norm. A selling shareholder usually can determine whether he reasonably can force or persuade the corporation to gather the information required in the registration statement and reasonably can obtain the necessary signatures.

Campbell, Defining Control in Secondary Distribution, 18 B.C. L. Rev. 37, 40 (1976).

   2.   Shelf Registration and the Control Person.   Absent an exemption, the control person's resale must be registered. Recall from Chapter 4 that secondary distributions can be registered for the shelf (*see* Rule 415(a)(1)(i)) and that pursuant to Rule 430B a shelf registration statement can omit the identity of any selling security holder. The omitted information can be provided later by a prospectus supplement, amendment to the registration statement, or amendment to an Exchange Act filing that is incorporated into the registration statement. Also recall that for well-known seasoned issuers the base registration statement becomes effective immediately. In combination, these changes accomplish much of a 1996 blue-ribbon committee's recommendations to address sales by control persons as a disclosure matter. *See* SEC Report of the Advisory Committee on the Capital Formation and Regulatory Process 98 (1996).

   3.   Broker's Exemption.   A dealer is commonly understood to be a market professional who acts as a principal in a securities transaction—selling shares from, or buying for, the dealer's own inventory. On the other hand, a broker acts solely as the agent in carrying out his customer's purchase or sale.

A question arises as to both the dealer's and the broker's obligation under Section 5 when their customer purchases a security that is being distributed to the public. As was seen in Chapter 4, dealers who are not also acting as the issuer's underwriter generally look to Section 4(a)(3) and Rule 174 to determine whether they are under an obligation to deliver a prospectus with respect to a security that is being distributed to the public. They also find comfort in new Rule 172, which relaxes the dealer's obligation to deliver a prospectus; recall that Rule 172 dispenses with the necessity for the confirmation, notice of allotment, or delivery of the share certificates to be accompanied or preceded by a final prospectus. Moreover, those acting solely as a broker can look to Section 4(a)(4) for their exemption.

Section 4(a)(4) exempts "brokers' transactions executed upon customers' orders on any exchange or in the over-the-counter market but not the solicitation of such orders." With all brokers being swept within Section 2(a)(12)'s definition of dealer, it should be clear that brokers need never resort to Section 4(a)(4) if for a specific transaction the broker's conduct is already exempt under Section 4(a)(3), or Rule 172 or 174. For example, a broker who sells to his customer registered securities of a reporting company is already exempt under Rule 174. He need not further consider whether the transaction violates the anti-solicitation language of Section 4(a)(4). In sum, the broker's exemption of Section 4(a)(4) is needed only when the broker cannot otherwise invoke the exemption available under Section 4(a)(3) and Rule 174.

The broker's transaction exemption also requires more of the broker than his being an unwitting participant in his customer's distribution. The SEC has long maintained that those who wish to rely on Section 4(a)(4) must make a searching inquiry as to the character of the securities being offered for sale whenever a customer wishes to sell a substantial number of shares of a little-known company. For example, in *World Trade Financial Corp. v. SEC*, 793 F.3d 1243 (9th Cir. 2014), the Ninth Circuit emphasized that the broker ignored numerous red flags, such as that the issuer was a recently established development stage company, the issuer's stock had just began to trade publicly, the stock was thinly traded, and the issuer had recently undergone a stock split in connection with its reverse merger. The court reasoned:

> [W]here, as here, there are numerous red flags indicating suspicious circumstances, a more searching inquiry is required. *See Wonsover*, 205 F.3d at 415 (requiring a "searching inquiry" where unfamiliar shareholders offered the broker "a substantial block of little-known and thinly traded security" under questionable circumstances). Petitioners did not inquire into the origins of the iStorage stock despite the significant red flags that we have identified. The circumstances called for a more diligent inquiry, and Petitioners did not satisfy their duty.

4.   Is the Broker's Exemption Available in a Distribution?   The "brokers' transactions" exemption of Section 4(a)(4) protects only the broker executing the transaction; the broker's client must seek his own exemption for a resale. Interpreting the legislative history of this exemption, a leading opinion by the Commission explained the brokers' transaction exemption as follows:

> [I]t is apparent that transactions by an issuer or underwriter and transactions by a dealer during the period of *distribution* . . . must be preceded by registration and

the use of a prospectus. It is likewise apparent that Congress intended that, during this period, persons other than an issuer, underwriter, or dealer should be able to *trade* in the security without use of a prospectus. Since such persons would carry on their trading largely through the use of brokers (who are included in the general definition of dealers) [and hence subject to the prospectus delivery requirements prescribed in Section 4(a)(3)], such trading through brokers without the use of a prospectus could be permitted . . . only if there were a special exemption for dealers acting as brokers. The importance of this exemption is emphasized in the case where a stop order might be entered against a registration statement. For, although such a stop order was intended to and would operate to stop all *distribution* activities, it would also result in stopping all *trading* by individuals through dealers acting as brokers unless a special exemption were provided for brokers. It was in recognition of this fact and to permit a dealer to act as a broker for an individual's trading transactions, while the security is being distributed and during the period of a stop order, that Section 4[(a)](4) was enacted.

In re Ira Haupt & Co., 23 S.E.C. 589 (1946). In *In re Ira Haupt*, the controlling stockholders of a liquor distiller over a six-month period sold 93,000 shares on the New York Stock Exchange using the services of Ira Haupt & Co., a broker-dealer. Their sales were pursuant to a standing order with Ira Haupt & Co. to sell 200 or 300 shares for each quarter-point increase in the price of the company's shares. The sales were made after the company announced it would soon declare a dividend in kind, liquor from the company's warehouse; in wartime America, a drink was frequently needed, but often in short supply. Following the announcement, the stock took off like a rocket, moving from $5 to a high of $98 five months after the announcement. The Commission held the brokers' transaction exemption was not available for sales made on behalf of the controlling stockholders. That exemption applies only to trading transactions, and the Commission viewed this as a distribution on behalf of the control persons because of the large number of shares being sold to the public for the account of a control person. Accordingly, Ira Haupt & Co. was sanctioned for a willful violation of Section 5.

In *SEC v. Cavanagh*, 445 F.3d 105 (D.C. Cir. 2006), the defendants, who each owned 25 percent of a shell company, engineered a series of transactions that ultimately led to public ownership of the company and to the defendants' ceasing to control the former shell company. The court held that because their resales were part of a single transaction to distribute the securities, they would be deemed control persons throughout, even though many of their resales occurred when, as a practical matter, they were no longer in effective control of the company. And the D.C. Circuit held that whether a control person is engaged in a distribution depends on the needs of the shares' purchasers and not on the magnitude of the shares being disposed of by the control person. *Geiger v. Securities & Exchange Commission*, 363 F.3d 481, 484 (D.C. Cir. 2004) (Section 5 violated by unregistered sale into a market of shares that represented 0.5 percent of the 12 million outstanding shares).

PROBLEMS

6-9.   Orange Company, Inc. is a highly successful software company, its shares are traded on Nasdaq, and it has a six-member board of directors. Alice, who owns 18.3 percent of the outstanding Orange common shares and is Orange's largest shareholder, has asked Bob, a broker with Fedder Investments, Inc., to sell in the market approximately one-third of her Orange shares. Bob is aware that three of the six members of Orange's board of directors are Alice's nominees. Bob has also been asked by Carl, one of Alice's nominees, to sell his Orange shares. Advise Alice, Bob, and Carl whether they have any Section 5 concerns. Assume the shares held by Alice and Carl were issued four years ago pursuant to a registered public offering. *See* Barron, Control and Restricted Securities— Determining Whether a Particular Person Is an "Affiliate" of an Issuer, 32 Sec. Reg. L.J. 213 (2004).

6-10. Assume in Problem 6-9 that none of the other six Orange directors are the nominees of Alice and collectively the six directors own 22 percent of the outstanding voting shares of Orange. How do these changes in the facts alter your analysis of Alice's resale? Carl's resale?

6-11. Ipco Inc., which was not a reporting company prior to the filing of its registration statement, made its first public offering through a registration statement that became effective June 1. Its securities are now traded through the Over-the-Counter-Bulletin-Board. Arbitrage House & Co., on August 8, acquired 15,000 Ipco shares in the over-the-counter market for its trading account. Six days later, Arbitrage's account executives began recommending Ipco to their clients, identifying Arbitrage as a principal in such sales. Did Arbitrage violate Section 5 by failing to deliver a prospectus to its clients who purchased Ipco shares?

D. Rule 144—Safe Harbor for Resales of Control and Restricted Securities

The distinction between trading transactions and distributions is important because the former are exempt and the latter are not. Because neither term is defined in the '33 Act, a good deal of uncertainty surrounded the freedom, if any, a broker had to sell for the account of a control person. In 1954, the SEC adopted Rule 154, establishing concrete standards by which the availability of the broker's exemption could be determined when sales were made for a control person. This regulatory development, although removing much uncertainty surrounding sales for control persons, did nothing about the continuing uncertainty accompanying the non-control person's sale of "restricted securities." In broad overview, restricted securities are those acquired from an issuer in an unregistered offering. In 1969, a blue-ribbon panel of securities lawyers headed by Francis Wheat recommended the creation of a safe harbor that would apply to the resale of restricted securities. The Wheat Report[2] played an instrumental

---

2. Disclosure to Investors: A Reappraisal of Federal Administration Policies Under the '33 and '34 Acts (1969).

role in the SEC's formulation and ultimate adoption in early 1972 of Rule 144, and the rescission of Rule 154.

Rule 144 is widely viewed as one of the Commission's most successful undertakings. Its fixed requirements provide much-needed certainty in an area fraught with uncertainties. However, that certainty occurs through language exacting somewhat arbitrary requirements. Language is always amenable to differing interpretations, at least to those trained in the law, and any want of clarity can be the source of relief when otherwise a fixed requirement would operate harshly in the particular case. Thus, it should come as no surprise that the LEXIS database contains thousands of no-action letter requests regarding Rule 144. Nevertheless, Rule 144 is a solid illustration of how much-needed clarification and certainty of result can be provided through the Commission's exercise of its rulemaking power. Indeed, one can only speculate how much greater the number of no-action requests would have been if Rule 144 had never been adopted.

Revisions to Rule 144
Securities Act Release No. 8869 (Dec. 6, 2007)

I.   BACKGROUND . . .

Rule 144 regulates the resale of two categories of securities: restricted securities and control securities. Restricted securities are securities acquired pursuant to one of the transactions listed in Rule 144(a)(3). Although it is not a term defined in Rule 144, "control securities" is used commonly to refer to securities held by an affiliate of the issuer, regardless of how the affiliate acquired the securities. Therefore, if an affiliate acquires securities in a transaction that is listed in Rule 144(a)(3), those securities are both restricted securities and control securities. A person selling restricted securities, or a person selling restricted or other securities on behalf of the account of an affiliate, who satisfies all of Rule 144's applicable conditions in connection with the transaction, is deemed not to be an "underwriter," as defined in Section 2(a)(11) of the Securities Act, and therefore may rely on the Section 4[(a)](1) exemption for the resale of the securities. . . .

Rule 144 states that a selling security holder shall be deemed not to be engaged in a distribution of securities, and therefore not an underwriter, . . . if the resale satisfies specified conditions. The conditions include the following:

- There must be adequate current public information available about the issuer;
- If the securities being sold are restricted securities, the security holder must have held the security for a specified holding period;
- The resale must be within specified sales volume limitations;
- The resale must comply with the manner of sale requirements; and
- The selling security holder must file Form 144 if the amount of securities being sold exceeds specified thresholds.

Rule 144, as it existed before today's amendments, permitted a non-affiliate to publicly resell restricted securities without being subject to the above limitations if the securities had been held for two years or more, provided that the security holder was not, and, for the three months prior to the sale, had not been, an affiliate of the issuer. . . .

II. DISCUSSION OF FINAL AMENDMENTS . . .

B. AMENDMENTS TO HOLDING PERIODS FOR RESTRICTED SECURITIES

1. *Six-Month Rule 144(d) Holding Period Requirement for Exchange Act Reporting Companies* . . .

The purpose of Rule 144 is to provide objective criteria for determining that the person selling securities to the public has not acquired the securities from the issuer for distribution. A holding period is one criterion established to demonstrate that the selling security holder did not acquire the securities to be sold under Rule 144 with distributive intent. We do not want the holding period to be longer than necessary or impose any unnecessary costs or restrictions on capital formation. . . . [W]e believe that a six-month holding period for securities of reporting issuers provides a reasonable indication that an investor has assumed the economic risk of investment in the securities to be resold under Rule 144. Therefore, we are adopting a six-month holding period for reporting companies. . . . Most commenters agreed that shortening the holding period to six months for restricted securities of reporting issuers will increase the liquidity of privately sold securities and decrease the cost of capital for reporting issuers, while still being consistent with investor protection. By reducing the holding period for restricted securities, these amendments are intended to help companies to raise capital more easily and less expensively. For example, by making private offerings more attractive, the amendments may allow some companies to avoid certain types of costly financing structures involving the issuance of extremely dilutive convertible securities. . . .

Under the amendments that we are adopting, the six-month holding period requirement will apply to the securities of an issuer that has been subject to the reporting requirements of Section 13 or 15(d) of the Exchange Act for a period of at least 90 days before the Rule 144 sale. Restricted securities of a "non-reporting issuer" will continue to be subject to a one-year holding period requirement. A non-reporting issuer is one that is not, or has not been for a period of at least 90 days before the Rule 144 sale, subject to the reporting requirements of Section 13 or 15(d) of the Exchange Act.

We believe that different holding periods for reporting and non-reporting issuers are appropriate given that reporting issuers have an obligation to file periodic reports with updated financial information (including audited financial information in annual filings) that are publicly available on EDGAR, the Commission's electronic filing system. Although non-reporting issuers must make some information publicly available before resales can be made under Rule 144, this information typically is much more limited in scope than information included in Exchange Act reports, is not required to include audited financial information, and is not publicly available via EDGAR. For these reasons, we believe that continuing to require security holders of non-reporting issuers to hold their securities for one year is not unduly burdensome and is consistent with investor protection.

2. Significant Reduction of Conditions Applicable to Non-Affiliates

Before adoption of these amendments, both non-affiliates and affiliates were subject to all other applicable conditions of Rule 144, in addition to the Rule 144(d) holding period requirement, including the condition that current information about the issuer of the securities be publicly available, the limitations on the amount of securities that may be sold in any three-month period, the manner of sale requirements and the Form 144 notice requirement. . . .

Under the amendments, after the applicable holding period requirement is met, the resale of restricted securities by a non-affiliate under Rule 144 will no longer be subject to any other conditions of Rule 144 except that, with regard to the resale of securities of a reporting issuer, the current public information requirement in Rule 144(c) will apply for an additional six months after the six-month holding period requirement is met. Therefore, a non-affiliate will no longer be subject to the Rule 144 conditions relating to volume limitations, manner of sale requirements, and filing Form 144.

We believe that the complexity of resale restrictions may inhibit sales by, and imposes costs on, non-affiliates. Because Rule 144 is relied upon by many individuals to resell their restricted securities, we believe that it is particularly helpful to streamline and reduce the complexity of the rule as much as possible while retaining its integrity. We continue to believe that retaining the current public information requirement with regard to resales of restricted securities of reporting issuers for up to one year after the acquisition of the securities is important to help provide the market with adequate information regarding the issuer of the securities. In addition, we generally believe that most abuses in sales of unregistered securities involve affiliates of issuers and securities of shell companies. As discussed below, we are codifying the staff's current interpretive position that Rule 144 cannot be relied upon for the resale of the securities of reporting and non-reporting shell companies.

The final conditions applicable to the resale under Rule 144 of restricted securities held by affiliates and non-affiliates of the issuer can be summarized as follows:

	Affiliate or Person Selling on Behalf of an Affiliate	*Non-Affiliate (and Has Not Been an Affiliate During the Prior Three Months)*
Restricted Securities of Reporting Issuers	During six-month holding period—no resales under Rule 144 permitted. After six-month holding period—may resell in accordance with all Rule 144 requirements including: • Current public information, • Volume limitations, • Manner of sale requirements for equity securities, and • Filing of Form 144.	During six-month holding period—no resales under Rule 144 permitted. After six-month holding period but before one year—unlimited public resales under Rule 144 except that the current public information requirement still applies. After one-year holding period—unlimited public resales under Rule 144; need not comply with any other Rule 144 requirements.
Restricted Securities of Non-Reporting Issuers	During one-year holding period—no resales under Rule 144 permitted. After one-year holding period—may resell in accordance with all Rule 144 requirements, including: • Current public information, • Volume limitations, • Manner of sale requirements for equity securities, and • Filing of Form 144.	During one-year holding period—no resales under Rule 144 permitted. After one-year holding period—unlimited public resales under Rule 144; need not comply with any other Rule 144 requirements.

C.   AMENDMENTS TO THE MANNER OF SALE REQUIREMENTS APPLICABLE TO RESALES BY AFFILIATES

Before today's amendments, the manner of sale requirements in Rule 144(f) required securities to be sold in "brokers' transactions" or in transactions directly with a "market maker," as that term is defined in Section 3(a)(38) of the Exchange Act. Additionally, the rule prohibits a selling security holder from: (1) soliciting or arranging for the solicitation of orders to buy the securities in anticipation of, or in connection with, the Rule 144 transaction; or (2) making any payment in connection with the offer or sale of the securities to any person other than the broker who executes the order to sell the securities. . . .

[W]e are adopting amendments to the manner of sale requirements that apply to resales of equity securities of affiliates. . . . [T]he growth of technological and other developments directed at meeting the investment needs of the public and reducing the cost of capital for companies have led us to refine the rules governing the trading of securities. We believe that it is appropriate now to adopt two amendments to the manner of sale requirements so that the restrictions better reflect current trading practices and venues.

First, we are adopting a change to Rule 144(f) to permit the resale of securities through riskless principal transactions in which trades are executed at the same price, exclusive of any explicitly disclosed markup or markdown, commission equivalent, or other fee, and the rules of a self-regulatory organization permit the transaction to be reported as riskless. We believe that these riskless principal transactions are equivalent to agency trades. As with agency trades, in order to qualify as a permissible manner of sale under the revised rule, the broker or dealer conducting the riskless principal transaction must meet all the requirements of a brokers' transaction, as defined by Rule 144(g), except the requirement that the broker does no more than execute the order or orders to sell the securities as agent for the person for whose account the securities are sold. The broker or dealer must neither solicit nor arrange for the solicitation of customers' orders to buy the securities in anticipation of or, in connection with, the transaction, must receive no more than the usual and customary markup or markdown, commission equivalent, or other fee, and must conduct a reasonable inquiry regarding the underwriter status of the person for whose account the securities are to be sold.

Second, we are amending Rule 144(g), which defines "brokers' transactions" for purposes of the manner of sale requirements. Under the definition of brokers' transactions, a broker must neither solicit nor arrange for the solicitation of customers' orders to buy the securities in anticipation of, or in connection with, the transaction. However, certain activities specified in . . . subparagraphs of Rule 144(g)[3] are deemed not to be a solicitation. We are adding another subparagraph covering the posting of bid and ask quotations in alternative trading systems that will also be deemed not to be a solicitation. This new provision permits a broker to insert bid and ask quotations for the security in an alternative trading system, as defined in Rule 300 of Regulation ATS, provided that the broker has published bona fide bid and ask quotations for the security in the alternative trading system on each of the last 12 business days.

D.   CHANGES TO RULE 144 CONDITIONS RELATED TO RESALES OF DEBT SECURITIES BY AFFILIATES. . .

2. No Manner of Sale Requirements Regarding Resales of Debt Securities

We are adopting the amendments to eliminate the manner of sale requirements for resales of debt securities held by affiliates, as proposed. We agree that, as financial intermediaries, brokers serve an important function as gatekeepers for promoting compliance with Rule 144, and we are concerned that eliminating the manner of sale requirements for equity securities would lead to abuse. However, we do not believe that the fixed income securities market raises the same concerns about abuse, and are persuaded that the manner of sale requirements may place an unnecessary burden on the resale of fixed income securities. Combined with the changes that we are making to the Rule 144(e) volume limitations, these amendments will permit holders of debt securities to rely on Rule 144 to resell their debt securities in a way and amount that was not possible previously.

As proposed, our definition of debt securities in Rule 144 includes non-participatory preferred stock (which has debt-like characteristics) and asset-backed securities (where the predominant purchasers are institutional investors including financial institutions, pension funds, insurance companies, mutual funds, and money managers) in addition to other types of nonconvertible debt securities. This definition of debt securities is consistent with the treatment of such securities under Regulation S.

3. Raising Volume Limitations for Debt Securities . . .

Before the amendments that we are adopting, under Rule 144(e), the amount of securities [whether debt or equity] sold in a three-month period could not exceed the greater of: (1) one percent of the shares or other units of the class outstanding as shown by the most recent report or statement published by the issuer, or (2) the average weekly volume of trading in such securities, as calculated pursuant to provisions in the rule. . . .

Debt securities generally are issued in tranches. We agree that . . . [the earlier] volume limitations in Rule 144 constrained the ability of debt holders to rely on Rule 144 for the resales of their securities. For the same reasons that we are eliminating the manner of sale requirements for debt securities, we believe that it is appropriate to adopt an alternative volume limitation that is specifically applicable to the resale of debt securities. We are amending Rule 144(e) to permit the resale of debt securities in an amount that does not exceed ten percent of a tranche (or class when the securities are non-participatory preferred stock), together with all sales of securities of the same tranche sold for the account of the selling security holder within a three-month period. We believe that this new ten percent limitation provision will permit a more reasonable amount of trading in debt securities than the one percent limitation has permitted. These revised volume limitations also apply to resales of non-participatory preferred stock or asset-backed securities, which are defined as debt securities for purposes of Rule 144.

E. INCREASE OF THE THRESHOLDS THAT TRIGGER THE FORM 144 FILING REQUIREMENT FOR AFFILIATES. . .

We are adopting . . . increased Form 144 filing thresholds. . . . [W]e are raising the dollar threshold to $50,000 to adjust for inflation since 1972 . . . [and] we are raising the share threshold to 5,000 shares. . . .

NOTES AND QUESTIONS

1. Control Person Anomalies. Rule 144 provides much-needed guidance for resales of a control person's *non*restricted securities. Paragraph (b) of Rule 144 extends its coverage to the sales by or on behalf of control persons and non-control persons when they resell restricted securities. However, the second phrase of paragraph (b) limits the Rule's scope with respect to *non*restricted securities to "any person *who sells . . . for the account of* an affiliate of the issuer of such securities. . . . " Paragraph (b) does not otherwise refer to the protections with respect to sales of nonrestricted securities, so that Rule 144 literally extends not to the control person, but only to one who sells the control person's nonrestricted securities. This gap in the scope of Rule 144 may make sound regulatory sense. The transaction orientation of the Section 4(a)(1) exemption, so well illustrated in *Chinese Consolidated* and *Wolfson*, may well be a two-way street. The limited scope of Rule 144(b) can have the effect of encouraging control persons to use brokers in their sales of nonrestricted control securities. This encouragement arises because a broker acting within the various limits of Rule 144 is not an underwriter. Following the transaction orientation of the exemption, this could be seen as exempting the entire transaction, so that even the control person enjoys its benefits. After all, the last sentence of Section 2(a)(11) does not define the control person as an underwriter, but only provides a manner by which one who purchases from, or sells for, a control person may be deemed an underwriter. Thus, a control person seeking certainty in her resales, especially when contemplating sales to unsophisticated and remote offerees, may find that the strictures of Rule 144 provide an important safe harbor. To be sure, the control person does not enjoy an exemption automatically because her broker has satisfied Rule 144. For example, Mr. Wolfson arranged his sales through numerous brokers, each unaware of the others' sales for Wolfson. Individually, each broker was able to qualify his own trading under Rule 144. Wolfson, however, was not able to piggyback onto their ignorance immunity for what certainly was his own cunning distribution. Does Rule 144, particularly the language of paragraph (b)(2), change the result reached in *Wolfson?*

2. Defining Control. Rule 144(a)'s definition of affiliate focuses on whether a person stands in a control relationship to another. Control is not defined in Rule 144, but is defined in Rule 405. The breadth of the meaning of control is demonstrated in *SEC v. Platforms Wireless Int'l,* 617 F.3d 1072 (9th Cir. 2010), where determining if Section 5 was violated turned on whether the seller of the unregistered securities, Intermedia, was an affiliate of the issuer, Platform Wireless. Martin was chairman and CEO of Platform, but denied that he controlled Intermedia, since his controlling block of stock in Intermedia had been transferred by him to his former wife as part of a divorce settlement.

> *Rule 144* does not define "control." However, Rule 405 of Regulation C contains an identical definition of "affiliate" and defines "control." . . . "The term control (including the terms controlling, controlled by and under common control with) means the possession, direct or indirect, of the power to direct or cause the direction of the management and policies of a person, whether through the ownership of voting securities, by contract, or otherwise." 17 C.F.R. §230.405. "'Control' is not to be determined by artificial tests, but is an issue to be determined from the particular circumstances of the case. Under Rule 405 . . . it is not necessary that one be an officer, director, manager, or even shareholder to be a controlling person. Further, control may exist although not continuously and actively exercised." *Pennaluna & Co. v. SEC,* 410 F.2d 861, 866 (9th Cir. 1969) (citation omitted); *see also United States v. Corr,* 543 F.2d 1042, 1050 (2d Cir. 1976) (stating that control is "a question of fact which depends upon the totality of the circumstances including an appraisal of the influence upon management and policies of a corporation by the person involved").
>
> We agree with the district court that there is no genuine issue of material fact that Martin controlled Intermedia at the time of the transactions. These points, as we see from the record, are critical: It is undisputed that Martin was an officer of Intermedia at the time of the transfers, and that he then represented himself to be its President and CEO. The SEC also produced evidence to establish that Martin was not a mere titular officer of Intermedia after the ownership transfer to his former wife in January 2000. For example, in February 2000, Martin applied for a business Visa credit card on behalf of Intermedia and signed the document as Intermedia's "President & CEO." An October 2000 "Certification of Corporate Authorization to Transfer" document "authorize[s] and empower[s]" Martin "to transfer, convert, endorse, sell, assign, set over and deliver any and

all . . . securities . . . in the name of or owned by" Intermedia, and was executed by Martin in his capacity as "President" of Intermedia. In November 2000, Martin's personal assistant at Platforms, Kate Marshall, wrote checks to Intermedia from a checking account labeled "Intermedia Video Marketing Corp; Intermedia/Platforms Acct A." Also in November 2000, Martin sold Platforms stock from a brokerage account registered to "Intermedia Video Marketing Corp.; Attn: William C. Martin." . . .

Perhaps most importantly, Martin has never disputed that the specific transactions at issue in this case were orchestrated under his direction.

Id. at 1087-1088. As will be seen in Chapter 14, control also assumes importance under the control person liability provisions of Section 15 of the Securities Act and Section 20(a) of the Exchange Act. There, however, we will see the courts employ a different test to determine whether a person is a control person under the liability provisions.

3. Restricted Securities and Other Anomalies. A close reading of Rule 144(a)(3) reveals some rather curious features about an important dimension of its scope: the resale of restricted securities. While there is a distinct preoccupation in the definition of restricted securities with securities sold in a private offering, this is not wholly the case. The definition also includes securities acquired in a transaction or chain of transactions meeting the requirements of Rule 144A or one of safe harbors provided by Regulation S as well as "securities acquired from the issuer that are subject to the resale limitations of Regulation D or Rule 701(c)." This would include offers under Rule 504, as well as "failed" Regulation D or Rule 701(c) offers, so long as the shares were subject to a resale restriction. By way of contrast, consider that Rule 147(f) also requires restrictions on resales as a condition of invoking its protections for its intrastate offer. However, securities offered under Rule 147 are not deemed restricted securities for the purpose of Rule 144. On the other hand, Rule 147 limits resales to residents of the issuer's state for only nine months, whereas restricted securities under Rule 144 can be resold in as few as six months. Furthermore, are there any justifiable policy reasons for not including within Rule 144 securities issued pursuant to Rule 147 and for not demanding the same holding period for all nonregistered securities?

4. Exiting Startups. Historically, investors (e.g., angels and venture capitalist) exited the startup either through an IPO or more likely the startup's acquisition by another company. While the former provides a much greater return for all, IPO markets are unpredictable and episodic so that the latter occurs more frequently. In any case, the timing and manner of exit poses some serious conflicts between the venture capitalist and the entrepreneurs and angel investors. Acquisition by another company is likely to be more attractive to earlier investors, such as the entrepreneurs, their friends and family, and angel investors who acquired their shares earlier than the VC and, presumably, paid a lower price. To the extent the earlier investors paid a lower price than the VC, they reap a much greater return by an early exit via sale to another firm. Consider further that the VC maintains a portfolio of investments and many to most produce no return. The VC therefore may believe it is better to swing to the fences than to bunt. That is, the VC may well prefer the chance of a greater return through the IPO over the much more certain, but lower, return of selling to another company. Consider the extent that recent market developments, described below, not only take some steam out of this conflict but may well be a nurturing force in financing startups:

> In 2009, VC secondary markets got a significant boost. Two electronic marketplaces, SharesPost and SecondMarket, launched as platforms for intermediating secondary market transactions. . . . SharesPost is structured as an online bulletin board where potential buyers and sellers post buy and sell bids for shares in the world's leading start-ups. . . .
>
> SecondMarket also launched its venture capital operations in 2009, although it has been facilitating secondary sales in bankruptcy claims and other illiquid assets for longer. Within venture capital, SecondMarket intermediates transactions in both the direct and fund markets. While SharesPost's status as a passive bulletin board limits the amount of hands-on intermediations it may do, SecondMarket is structured as a broker-dealer and therefore provides active assistance to buyers and sellers. . . .
>
> By offering a central site, SharesPost and SecondMarket make it easier for buyers and sellers to find one another. . . . As electronic marketplaces, these intermediaries are harnessing the power of technology to facilitate secondary market growth. Once buyers and sellers are matched, the electronic marketplaces allow for efficient price discovery by posting recent buy-sell bids and the latest contract price (SharesPost) and by providing third-party research reports on private startups (SharesPost and SecondMarket). The electronic marketplaces also significantly reduce transaction costs in papering deals by offering standardized sales contracts, e-signature options, and escrow services for transferring funds. SharesPost and SecondMarket now allow secondary transactions to be closed for a fraction of the cost, time and hassle of traditional secondary transactions.

Ibrahim, The New Exit in Venture Capital, 65 Vand. L. Rev. 1, 36-39 (2012). What steps should the operators of each of these markets take to assure they are not assisting in the violation of Section 5?

Three other pre-IPO marketplaces have since been launched—Equidate, EquityZen, and Nasdaq Private Market. SecondMarket was acquired by Nasdaq Private Market in 2015 and so no longer exists.

5. Aggregation Rules. Observe that Rule 144(e)'s volume limits require aggregation of shares of two or more sellers in certain instances. In addition to shares sold by a person's donees, pledgees, trusts, or estates, there is aggregation of shares sold by two affiliates acting in concert. On the other hand, Rule 144(e)(3)(vii) provides that shares sold pursuant to a registered offering or Regulation A or pursuant to a Section 4 exemption that did not involve a public offering are not aggregated with resales of securities sought to be qualified under Rule 144. In the latter case, should principles of integration be applied to determine whether the Section 4 resale constituted a public offering?

6. Fungibility. The fungibility doctrine holds that, when an investor has purchased both restricted and nonrestricted securities of the same class (e.g., common stock), as an economic matter it is impossible to distinguish between the shares. They are fungible. As such, for the purpose of applying the holding period criterion, all shares of that same class are treated as restricted, so that all shares owned are viewed as having been acquired when the last restricted shares were purchased. In essence, the fungibility doctrine operates to taint all securities of the same class with the restricted status of the most recently acquired restricted security. The doctrine does not apply to resales under Rule 144,[3] but the Commission appears to continue to apply it to resales of restricted securities outside of the Rule. *See, e.g.,* In Touch Global LLC, SEC No-Action Letter, [Current] Fed. Sec. L. Rep. (CCH) ¶77,209 (Nov. 14, 1995). This makes perfect sense in view of the fact that the doctrine of fungibility is essential if the requirement of investment intent is to operate with any level of integrity.

    7. *Coping with the Friction of Stop Transfer Restrictions.*   Restricted securities commonly bear a legend and are accompanied by stop transfer instructions for the transfer agent that provide that no transfer of the restricted security will occur until "receipt of an opinion of counsel satisfactory to the issuer that registration is not required" to effect the resale in compliance with the Securities Act. Thus, to satisfy the transfer agent, the holder of restricted security or its agents must supply an opinion that the manner in which the resale was carried out met the requirements of Rule 144 or another exemption. This process customarily introduces at least a five- or six-day delay into the resale of a restricted security and thereby poses serious market risks to the holders of restricted securities who naturally wish to take advantage of today's market price and not speculate what tomorrow's price will be. The delay also raises regulatory concerns under Exchange Act Rule 15c6-1, which mandates that broker-dealers settle all market sales not later than three business days after the date of trade ("T+3"). In response to these considerations, the SEC permits transfer agents to rely upon so-called "we will" (as contrasted with "we did") representations by the broker when necessary to comply with the T+3 requirement. In the typical "we will" letter the broker represents in the future tense the steps to be taken to carry out the resale so as to assure compliance with Rule 144. *See* Smith Barney, SEC No-Action Letter, [1995 Transfer Binder] Fed. Sec. L. Rep. (CCH) ¶77,055 (June 20, 1995). Attorneys who provide false information that restrictions on resale are met, for example, representing falsely that the holding period is satisfied, violate Section 5 as a participant in a step necessary for the distribution. *See, e.g., SEC v. Greenstone Holdings, Inc.,* 954 F. Supp. 2d 211 (S.D.N.Y. 2013).

    8. *Holding Period Reductions?* As mentioned in Chapter 5, in June of 2019 the SEC put out a 211-page document entitled Concept Release on Harmonization of Securities Offering Exemptions. While the release largely focused on primary offering exemptions, it did include materials at the end pertaining to resale exemptions. In that regard, the document included the following request for comment on page 209:

> Should we revise the Rule 144 non-exclusive safe harbor? If so, how should we revise Rule 144? For example, should we, as recommended by the 2012 and 2016 Small Business Forums, reduce the Rule 144 holding period for securities of issuers meeting the current public information requirement from six months to three

---

    3. *See* Definition of Terms "Underwriter" and "Brokers' Transactions," Securities Act Release No. 5223 (Jan. 10, 1972), 1972 WL 125477, at *19 ("For the purpose of the rule, the doctrine of 'fungibility' will not apply.").

months? Should we, as recommended by the 2012 Small Business Forum, reduce the Rule 144 holding period for securities of issuers not subject to the current information requirements from 12 months to six months?

9. *The Peril of Relying on No-Action Letters.* Throughout the book, we have seen the valuable guidance attorneys and their clients obtain from the SEC's staff through its no-action letters. But caution is always in order with regard to no-action letters because each proceeds with the admonition that its protection is limited only to its addressee and to the facts set forth in the no-action request. Thus, consider the lessons learned by Morgan Stanley & Co. when it sold a customer's securities from a margin account to satisfy the account's collateral requirements. Though the customer controlled the issuer, so that normally the volume limitations of Rule 144 would apply, Morgan Stanley relied on a line of no-action letters that relaxed the volume limits in such margin-call situations. Arguing that Morgan Stanley did not meet the conditions that existed in the earlier no-action letters, the investment banker was charged with violating Section 5; the matter was eventually settled, with Morgan Stanley agreeing to review and reform its practices under Rule 144. Morgan Stanley & Co., Inc., Exchange Act Release No. 28,900 (Mar. 20, 1991). The securities bar was upset with the SEC's apparent eagerness to institute an enforcement action against broker-dealers who rely in good faith on general policies embodied in prior no-action letters, but whose particular facts deviated slightly from the earlier no-action letters. For example, a column coauthored by an attorney who later would become the SEC's chairman observes that the SEC's position is "reminiscent of the apocryphal story of a judge with a heavy criminal docket who was chafing under the constraints of the Supreme Court's decision in *Miranda v. Arizona*. . . . When an out-of-town lawyer appeared to argue a client's case, the judge warned that, 'In this jurisdiction we construe the *Miranda* very narrowly—is your client's name Miranda?'" *See* Pitt & Johnson, "No Action" Doesn't Mean "No Action" Any Longer, N.Y. L.J., Apr. 1, 1991, at 1. *See Perez v. Mortgage Bankers Ass'n*, 135 S. Ct. 1199 (2014) (agency not bound by APA's notice and comment requirements when changing its interpretation of law).

PROBLEMS

Consider whether any fact in each of the following problems disqualifies the resale from Rule 144.

6-12. Jeff is the owner of 10,000 unregistered Apex common shares that he purchased in a private offering. He now wishes to sell some of these shares.

6-13. Assume the shares Jeff owns in Problem 6-12 were initially issued to Jeff pursuant to the intrastate offering and that he wishes to resale the shares.

6-14. One and one-half years ago, Zeta, Inc. issued 2 million common shares pursuant to an offering under Rule 506. However, Zeta's attorney failed to keep track of the number of purchasers in that offer, so that there were about 47 non-accredited purchasers in that offer. Susan, one of those purchasers, now wishes to resell her shares.

6-15.   Bill, a control person of Omega Company, is negotiating to sell his control block to Alice. All discussions between Bill and Alice have been on a direct
personal basis so far.

6-16.   In Problem 6-15, Bill has grown restless with his negotiations with Alice.
He has hired Broker to sell a large amount of his shares through the New York
Stock Exchange.

6-17.   Alpha Company is 5 months late in filing with the SEC the 10-Q report
for its third quarter, which it is required to file under Section 13 of the Securities
Exchange Act. Carla, an owner of Alpha restricted stock for 7 months, wishes to
resell her shares. Consider also the result if Carla owned her shares for 6 months
but the shares had been issued by Alpha 14 months prior to the proposed sale.
What result if Carla was Alpha's CEO?

6-18.   Beta Inc. is a small publicly owned company with 150 stockholders, but is
not subject to the Exchange Act's reporting provisions. Beta recently mailed to
its stockholders its most recent annual report, which includes 3 years of comparative audited financial statements. Dave has owned his restricted Beta common
stock for 11 months and wishes to resell.

6-19.   Ellen, the chief executive officer of Ocean Enterprises, Inc., 5 months
ago purchased 10,000 Ocean Enterprises common shares on the New York
Stock Exchange. She now wishes to sell those shares.

6-20.   Three years ago, John acquired in a private offering Amalgamated
Company common shares in exchange for his personal note in the amount of
the shares' purchase price. The note is a full recourse note due on demand and
bears interest at the rate of 9 percent per annum. The shares are collateral for
the note. John now plans to sell the shares, expecting to receive enough after
payment of the note to have earned a small profit.

6-21.   Assume in Problem 6-20 that 17 months ago John pledged his shares with
National Bank, using the loan proceeds to pay Amalgamated. John is now hope-
lessly insolvent and has defaulted on the loan from the bank, so that National
Bank wishes to sell the Amalgamated shares. How does your answer change if
John is the Amalgamated CEO?

6-22.   Mary is a control person of Theta. She acquired her shares in a registered public offering. Theta shares are listed on Nasdaq, where the average
weekly trading volume for Theta common stock is 150,000 shares and there
are 18 million outstanding Theta common shares. During the first 3 months of
the current calendar year, Mary sold 150,000 of her Theta shares, 50,000 shares
each month. How many Theta shares may she sell on April 1st?

6-23.   Assume the facts of Problem 6-22 and that on January 3 Mary gave Cornell
University 120,000 shares. Assuming Mary continues to be a control person of
Theta, when can Cornell dispose of these shares in the market? If Cornell and
Mary each wish to sell Theta shares in April, how many shares can each sell in
April assuming Mary sold 50,000 Theta shares in each of the first 3 months of

the year? Assume that Cornell delays its sale until December. What restrictions does it face when it does sell? *See* Barron, Control and Restricted Securities, 37 Sec. Reg. L.J. 74 (2009).

6-24. Assume Theta common shares in Problem 6-22 are traded on Nasdaq and Mary retained Broker to dispose of some of her Theta shares. Broker wrote to Margin & Co., which makes a market in Theta common shares, to inquire if it had any unfilled orders for Theta shares at or near the current market price. What if the shares are instead traded on the OTC Bulletin Board?

6-25. Assume Mary in Problem 6-22 has retained Broker to dispose of a sizable amount of her Theta shares over time. Unbeknownst to Broker, Mary has entered into a similar arrangement with a dozen other brokers, all of whom are selling for Mary's account sizable amounts of Theta shares.

6-26. Assume Broker sold 250,000 Theta common shares for Sally who is a control person of Theta. A week after the sale, Broker discovers that neither Sally nor Broker has filed Form 144. In the meantime, the price of Theta shares has fallen significantly.

6-27. Assume Sally, in the preceding problems, will sell shares through the OTC Bulletin Board exclusively through Broker. Sally discloses to Broker that, at the same time Broker is selling Sally's control shares to the public, Sally will privately sell 60,000 shares to Tom. Tom is not a sophisticated buyer, but he and Sally have negotiated directly with one another without the assistance of any intermediary. Must Broker take account of Sally's sale to Tom when considering the number of shares Broker can sell? *See* Rule 144(e)(3)(vii).

E. Resales to Qualified Institutional Buyers (QIBs) and Accredited Investors

1. Facilitating an Institutional Market for Unregistered Securities with Rule 144A

As you read the following description of the operation of Rule 144A and its role in creating an institutional trading market for unregistered securities, consider what impact Rule 144A has on the ability of *issuers* to raise capital as well as making U.S. capital markets more welcome to foreign issuers.

Resale of Restricted Securities, Securities Act Release No. 6862
Securities and Exchange Commission (Apr. 23, 1990)

. . . The Commission is adopting Rule 144A, which provides a safe harbor exemption from the registration requirements of the Securities Act of 1933 for resales of restricted securities to "qualified institutional buyers" as defined in the Rule. . . .

The Commission views Rule 144A as adopted today as the first step toward achieving a more liquid and efficient institutional resale market for unregistered securities. . . .

A.   GENERAL

Rule 144A sets forth a non-exclusive safe harbor from the registration requirements of Section 5 of the Securities Act for the resale of restricted securities to specified institutions by persons other than the issuer of such securities. The transactions covered by the safe harbor are private transactions that, on the basis of a few objective standards, can be defined as outside the purview of Section 5, without the necessity of undertaking the more usual analysis under Sections 4[(a)](1) and 4[(a)](3) of the Securities Act. Each transaction will be assessed under the Rule individually. The exemption for an offer and sale complying with the Rule will be unaffected by transactions by other sellers. The Commission wishes to emphasize that Rule 144A is not intended to preclude reliance on traditional facts-and-circumstances analysis to prove the availability of an exemption outside the safe harbor it provides.

By providing that transactions meeting its terms are not "distributions," the Rule essentially confirms that such transactions are not subject to the registration provisions of the Securities Act. . . .

In the case of securities originally offered and sold under Regulation D of the Securities Act, a person that purchases securities from an issuer and immediately offers and sells such securities in accordance with the Rule is not an "underwriter" within the meaning of Rule 502(d) of Regulation D. Issuers making a Regulation D offering, who generally must exercise reasonable care to assure that purchasers are not underwriters, therefore would not be required to preclude resales under Rule 144A. Similarly, the fact that purchasers of securities from the issuer may purchase such securities with a view to reselling such securities pursuant to the Rule will not affect the availability to such issuer of an exemption under Section 4[(a)](2) of the Securities Act from the registration requirements of the Securities Act.

B.   ELIGIBLE SECURITIES

Rule 144A would not extend to the offer or sale of securities that, when issued, were of the same class as securities listed on a national securities exchange registered under Section 6 of the Exchange Act or quoted in an automated inter-dealer quotation system. Accordingly, privately-placed securities that, at the time of their issuance, were fungible with securities trading on a U.S. exchange or quoted in Nasdaq would not be eligible for resale under the Rule.

Where American Depositary Shares ("ADSs") are listed on a U.S. exchange or quoted in Nasdaq, the deposited securities underlying the ADSs also would be considered publicly traded, and thus securities of the same class as the deposited securities could not be sold in reliance on the Rule. . . . Under the Rule, a convertible security is to be treated as both the convertible and the underlying security unless, at issuance, it is subject to an effective conversion premium of at least 10 percent.

C.   ELIGIBLE PURCHASERS

1.   TYPES OF INSTITUTIONS COVERED

As discussed above, except for registered broker-dealers, to be a "qualified institutional buyer" an institution must in the aggregate own and invest on a discretionary basis at least $100 million in securities of issuers that are not affiliated with the institution.

a.   *Banks and Savings and Loan Associations*

Banks, as defined in Section 3(a)(2) of the Securities Act, and savings and loan associations as referenced in Section 3(a)(5)(A) of the Act, must, in addition to owning and investing on a discretionary basis at least $100 million in securities, have an audited net worth of at least $25 million, as demonstrated in their latest published annual financial statements. . . . As federally-insured depository institutions, domestic banks and savings and loans are able to purchase securities with funds representing deposits of their customers. These deposits are backed by federal insurance funds administered by the Federal Deposit Insurance Corporation ("FDIC"). In light of this government support, these financial institutions are able to purchase securities without placing themselves at risk to the same extent as other types of institutions. In this respect, banks and savings and loans effectively are able to purchase securities using public funds. Therefore, the amount of securities owned by a bank or savings and loan institution may not, on its own, be a sufficient measure of such institution's size and investment sophistication. . . . A combined securities ownership and net worth test would appear to be a better means of sophistication for banks and savings and loan institutions. . . .

b.   *Registered Broker-Dealers*

. . . Commenters stated that . . . if the $100 million test was retained for registered broker-dealers in all situations, significant segments of the registered broker-dealer community, whose participation was important to the efficient functioning of the market, would be excluded from participation in the market as principals.

In response to these comments, the Rule as adopted provides that a broker-dealer registered under the Exchange Act which in the aggregate owns and invests on a discretionary basis at least $10 million in securities of issuers that are not affiliated with the broker-dealer is a qualified institutional buyer. Additionally, the Rule provides that registered broker-dealers acting as riskless principals for identified qualified institutional buyers would themselves be deemed to be qualified institutional buyers. . . .

c.   *Others*

Any corporation or partnership (wherever organized) that meets the $100 million in securities threshold may purchase under the Rule, except for a bank or savings and loan institution which must also satisfy the net worth test. Eligible purchasers under the Rule include entities formed solely for the purpose of acquiring restricted securities, if they satisfy the qualifying test. . . .

D. INFORMATION REQUIREMENT

. . . As adopted, availability of the Rule is conditioned upon the holder and a prospective purchaser designated by the holder having the right to obtain from the issuer, upon the holder's request to the issuer, certain basic financial information, and upon which prospective purchaser having received such information at or prior to the time of sale, upon such purchaser's request to the holder or the issuer. This information is required only where the issuer does not file periodic reports under the Exchange Act, and does not furnish home country information to the Commission pursuant to Rule 12g3-2(b). . . . The holder must be able to obtain, upon request, and the prospective purchaser must be able to obtain and must receive if it so requests, the following information (which shall be reasonably current in relation to the date of resale under Rule 144A): a very brief statement of the nature of the issuer's business and of its products and services offered, comparable to that information required by sub-paragraphs (viii) and (ix) of Exchange Act Rule 15c2-11(a)(5); and its most recent balance sheet and profit and loss and retained earnings statements, and similar financial statements for such part of the two preceding fiscal years as it has been in operation. The financial information required is the same as that required by subparagraphs (xii) and (xiii) of Rule 15c2-11(a)(5). The financial statements should be audited to the extent audited financial statements are reasonably available.

The Commission does not believe that the limited information requirement should impose a significant burden on those issuers subject to the requirement. Many foreign issuers that will be subject to the requirement, which were the focus of the commenters' concern, will have securities traded in established offshore markets, and already will have made the required information publicly available in such markets. Even for domestic issuers, the required information represents only a portion of that which would be necessary before a U.S. broker or dealer could submit for publication a quotation for the securities of such an issuer in a quotation medium in the United States. . . . Financial statements meeting the timing requirements of the issuer's home country or principal trading markets would be considered sufficiently current for purposes of the information requirement of the Rule. . . .

The Rule does not specify the means by which the right to obtain information would arise. The obligation could be, inter alia, imposed in the terms of the security, by contract, by corporate law, by regulatory law, or by rules of applicable self-regulatory organizations.

E. OTHER REQUIREMENTS

Although the Rule imposes no resale restrictions, a seller or any person acting on its behalf must take reasonable steps to ensure that the buyer is aware that the seller may rely on the exemption from the Securities Act's registration requirements afforded by Rule 144A.

NOTES AND QUESTIONS

1. Is an Information Requirement Necessary? Consider for a moment the anomaly in subsection 144A(d)(4), which, for non-reporting issuers, conditions the safe harbor's availability on the purchaser's ability to obtain certain information from the security's issuer. Does it make sense to mandate any disclosure for non-reporting companies as a precondition to the Rule 144A safe harbor when QIBs are also accredited investors (under Section 4(a)(5) with assets of only $5 million) so that their purchase from the issuer pursuant to Rule 506 can occur with no mandated disclosure?

The market appears to impose its own information requirement for Rule 144A transactions. The typical Rule 144A placement commences with negotiations between the issuer and a broker-dealer; those negotiations customarily lead to the issuer making extensive disclosures in the Offering Memorandum that the broker-dealer then uses in its resales to QIBs. The Offering Memorandum frequently includes extensive warranties and other representations that are necessary to promote the offered security. Moreover, the broker-dealer's counsel often provides a so-called 10b-5 opinion that recites important financial facts, including risk factors, as well as the investigatory process used to review the Offering Memorandum, stating that no fact came to counsel's attention that would cause them to believe it was untrue. *See* Gans, The Mechanics of Rule 144A/Regulation S Underwritings, in Securities Offerings 385, 431-440 (PLI 1998). The prevalent practice among institutions engaged with the 144A market to obtain a 10b-5 opinion has led to similar disclosure demands for private placements *within* Europe equal to the disclosure and due diligence standards followed in comparable transactions conducted in the United States. *See* Jackson & Pan, Regulatory Competition in International Securities Markets: Evidence from Europe in 1999—Part 1, 56 Bus. Law. 653, 685-686 (2001). If institutions expect and receive extensive disclosures via the 10b-5 opinion, what advantage over registration does the issuer achieve by proceeding with a 144A offering?

2. Quibbling About QIBs. Why is QIB defined to limit 144A purchasers to essentially various types of financial institutions that meet certain financial requirements? Compare this with the scope of the safe harbor exemption provided by Rule 506, which excuses information and sophistication requirements for purchasers who are accredited investors. The accredited investors requirements are not nearly as demanding as the requirements to be a QIB. As we ponder the definition of a QIB, we should bear in mind the global competitive forces that drove the SEC to create Rule 144A, for the purpose of making U.S. markets for unregistered securities competitive with those in Europe. On this point, consider that both issuers and individuals in the EU can freely sell/resell to an unlimited number of "qualified purchasers," defined as those who are financially sophisticated with assets exceeding €500,000. *See* EU Prospectus Directive 2003/71 Art. 2(1)(d).

3. *Research Reports and Rule 144A Offerings.* Recall from Chapter 4 that Rules 138 and 139 are safe harbors for certain research reports. Research reports are used in connection with Rule 144A transactions. Rules 138 and 139 provide that research reports satisfying the safe harbor conditions of either Rule will not be considered offers or general solicitations or general advertisements in connection with offerings to institutions under Rule 144A.

4. *PORTAL and the Market for 144A Offerings.* To facilitate both issuer placements and secondary trading of securities issued by U.S. and foreign entities that qualify for Rule 144A, Nasdaq operates Private Offerings, Resales and Trading through Automated Linkages (PORTAL), a web-based trading platform. The computerized system is limited to securities that qualify for trading under Rule 144A, and before an investor can trade through PORTAL, it must have been approved by the Nasdaq as meeting Rule 144A's requirement that it be a "qualified institutional buyer." PORTAL includes surveillance and other procedures to protect against unregistered securities being released into U.S. retail markets. In 2006, more than 2,700 different securities traded via PORTAL, with volume exceeding $1 trillion. About 30 percent of the overall volume of 144A offerings is by foreign issuers. *See* Sjostrom, The Birth of Rule 144A Equity Offerings, 56 UCLA L. Rev. 409, 412 (2008) ("[I]n 2006 more money was raised in Rule 144A equity offerings ($162 billion) than the combined total raised that year in IPOs listed on the New York Stock Exchange, Nasdaq Stock Market, and the American Stock Exchange ($154 billion).").

5. *Finding QIBs.* What result if, while seeking QIB purchasers, an offer is made to someone who is not a QIB? In 2013, Rule 144A(d)(1) was amended to remove references to "offer" and "offeree" so that the exemption applies even if offers are made to investors who are not QIBs, so long as the securities are sold only to persons the seller reasonably believes are QIBs. In adopting the change, the SEC reasoned that general solicitation and general advertisements could be used in connection with Rule 144A and also such communications will not affect the availability of the Section 4(a)(2) exemption for the initial sale of securities by issuers to initial purchasers. Securities Act Release No. 9415 (July 10, 2013).

6. *A/B Exchange Offers.* When restricted securities are exchanged for registered securities, the exchanging security holders are named in the registration statement as selling shareholders and, consequently, are subject to the underwriter's reasonable investigation burdens, discussed in Chapter 9. Pursuant to a series of SEC no-action letters that began with Exxon Capital Holdings Corporation, SEC No-Action Letter, LEXIS 682 (May 13, 1988), the exchanging shareholder avoids underwriter status, however, if she is not otherwise a broker engaged in the distribution of a security. Such exchanges are called A/B exchanges, and the SEC's staff limits its position to nonconvertible debt, certain types of preferred stock, and foreign issuers' initial offerings in the United States. The exemption therefore is not available to U.S. issuers of common shares whereby a restricted security is exchanged for a registered security; it is this feature that distinguishes A/B exchanges from PIPEs, discussed earlier in this chapter. A/B exchanges occur increasingly in connection with transactions structured around Rule 144A, with the institutional buyers obtaining an agreement from the issuer to exchange at some later date the registered securities for the unregistered securities. *See* Bloomenthal & Wolff, 3B Securities and Federal Corporation Law §9.91 (2d ed. 2016). What regulatory protection is afforded investors who ultimately acquire the securities that are sold publicly after the A/B exchange? Is the investment bank that places the securities with a QIB in a 144A transaction in such an A/B exchange offer an underwriter subject to Section 11 liability in the later registered offer if the investment bank is not otherwise engaged in the distribution of the registered shares? *See American High-Income Trust v. Allied Signal,* [2004 Transfer Binder] Fed. Sec. L. Rep. (CCH) ¶92,889 (S.D.N.Y. 2004).

PROBLEMS

6-28.   Frumble Motors Acceptance Corporation (FMAC) needs to quickly raise $70 million by issuing five-year bonds carrying an 8 percent interest rate. FMAC common shares are traded over Nasdaq. With time being of the essence, a registered public offering is not practicable. Marge, FMAC's chief financial officer, has excellent ties to numerous financial institutions. She seeks your advice on which of the following strategies FMAC should pursue. What differences do you see between FMAC directly soliciting, by mail and phone, approximately 200 large financial institutions to buy the unregistered bonds versus FMAC first placing all the bonds with an investment banking firm with the understanding that the investment bank will resell the bonds to the same 200 large financial institutions? You are told that each of the financial institutions has an investment portfolio in excess of $100 million. Which of these two options do you recommend?

6-29.   Assume FMAC placed the bonds in reliance on Rule 144A using an investment bank, Silver Bags. Unbeknown to Silver Bags, one of the purchasing financial institutions, Guaranty Trust, was not purchasing for its own account, but for the accounts of about 50 clients, and some of the clients are not accredited investors. Thereafter, FMAC begins to suffer certain financial reverses and the bonds' value plummets. What exposure does Silver Bags have to the 50 clients? What is its exposure to the other institutions who purchased the bonds from Silver Bags?

6-30.   Assume Bancorp purchased 20 percent of the FMAC bonds in Problem 6-28 that were sold through the investment banker relying on Rule 144A. Three months after this purchase, Bancorp is in financial distress and simultaneously sells half the FMAC bonds to its cross-town rival, Citizens' Bank, and the remaining half to seven wealthy, albeit unsophisticated, individual investors. Does FMAC or its investment banker have any exposure under Section 5 because of Bancorp's resale? What are Bancorp's problems under Section 5?

6-31.   Partial Reprise of Problem 6-13. Thirteen months ago, Alice acquired 10,000 Apex common shares in an intrastate offering. After holding the shares for six months, she sold them to State Bank, a QIB. After holding the shares for seven months, State Bank sold the shares to Jeff. Can Jeff resell the shares in the over-the-counter market?

6-32.   Barney acquired 1,000 SolarTech, Inc. shares from the issuer pursuant to an offering carried out in compliance with Rule 147. SolarTech is a reporting company. Four months later, Barney sold the shares to a business acquaintance, Alice, who lives in another state. Barney made no investigation of Alice's financial position; had he inquired he would have learned that Alice's net worth exceeded $1 million. Has Barney violated Section 5?

6-33.   What result in the preceding problem if Barney learned of Alice's interest in SolarTech through a local broker with whom both Barney and Alice had long-standing accounts? The broker acted as an intermediary and received his usual commission in connection with his efforts.

6-34.   When Barney sold his shares to Alice in Problem 6-32, he genuinely believed SolarTech had complied with Rule 147. In fact, SolarTech's offering did not satisfy any exemption, so its offering violated Section 5. Does Barney's sale violate Section 5?

6-35.   Assume that Barney acquired 1,000 shares from MoonTech, a non-reporting company, pursuant to a Rule 506 offering. Barney was among the few accredited investors who purchased in that offering. Four months later, he sold his shares to Sally, an accredited investor. In their negotiations leading up to the sale, Sally e-mailed Barney asking for information about MoonTech. Barney replied that he had "not received any information about MoonTech" when he made his own purchase. He copied MoonTech's corporate secretary on his response to Sally, asking that "relevant information" be sent to Sally. The corporate secretary e-mailed Sally a pdf file containing MoonTech's most recent customer catalog. Sally was impressed by the array of products and immediately purchased Barney's shares. Has Barney violated Section 5? Has MoonTech violated Section 5?

F. The Section 4(a)(1½) Exemption

A control person may find that he is unable to bring his sale within Rule 144. For example, the number of shares to be sold may exceed the volume limit of subsection (e), or the issuer may not be current in its '34 Act reports, or the information publicly available about a non-reporting company may not be sufficient to satisfy subsection (c), or the sale may not occur through a "brokers' transaction" as required by subsection (f) of Rule 144. In such cases, consider the extent to which the so-called Section 4(a)(1½) exemption may provide some much-needed relief.

Ackerberg v. Johnson
892 F.2d 1328 (8th Cir. 1989)

BEAM, J. Ackerberg bought the Vertimag shares in March of 1984. Ackerberg bought 12,500 shares from Johnson, who, in addition to being the chairman of the board, was one of the founders of Vertimag and its largest individual stockholder. ! . . .

The Vertimag transaction began in October of 1983. . . . Petrucci [a senior vice president of Piper, Jaffray & Hopwood (PJH), a brokerage firm,] then gave Ackerberg a ninety-nine page private placement memorandum which contained detailed information about Vertimag.

On March 17, 1984, Ackerberg signed a subscription agreement, prepared by counsel for Vertimag. Ackerberg testified by deposition that he read and understood this document. Vertimag's counsel stressed to Ackerberg that no sale could be made without the subscription agreement, which agreement informed Ackerberg that the Vertimag securities were unregistered and not readily transferable. . . . Ackerberg also represented in the subscription agreement that his yearly income was in excess of $200,000, that his net worth was over $1,000,000, and that his liquid assets exceeded $500,000. Indeed, Ackerberg's account at PJH alone totaled around $500,000.[3] . . .

On appeal, then, Johnson argues that the district court erred in its order of August 23, 1988, in which it granted summary judgment in favor of Ackerberg by concluding that Johnson was not entitled to an exemption under §4[(a)](1) of the 1933 Act. We agree with Johnson that he is entitled, as a matter of law, to an exemption under §4[(a)](1), because Johnson is not an issuer, underwriter or dealer.

Johnson argues that he is entitled to an exemption under §4[(a)](1) of the 1933 Act, which provides that the registration requirements of the 1933 Act,

---

3.   . . . Ackerberg argues that because of the involvement of PJH, a broker and, therefore, a dealer within §4[(a)](1), the §4[(a)](1) exemption cannot be available for Johnson, even if Johnson is not an issuer, underwriter, or dealer. We disagree. While it is true that §4(1) exempts transactions and not individuals, *see, e.g., SEC v. Holschuh*, 694 F.2d 130, 137-138 (7th Cir. 1982), the mere involvement of a broker, qua broker, in a secondary transaction by persons other than an issuer, underwriter or dealer, is insufficient to vitiate the exemption. PJH's role as broker cannot convert the transaction into one "*by* someone who was an issuer, underwriter or dealer." *Holschuh*, 694 F.2d at 138 (emphasis added). PJH owned no Vertimag securities and sold none. Were its involvement enough to deny the §4[(a)](1) exemption to persons not issuers, underwriters or dealers, few secondary transactions involving the resale of restricted securities would be exempt under §4[(a)](1). Ackerberg has cited no persuasive authority that such is the law, and given that the purpose of the §4[(a)](1) exemption is to exempt trading as opposed to distributions, we cannot agree with Ackerberg's contention.

Nor can we agree that the exemption is not available to Johnson because PJH is an underwriter. The district court, as discussed infra, failed to find that any distribution occurred, and, as a matter of law, none did occur in this case. Absent a distribution, no party to the transaction can be an underwriter.

found in 15 U.S.C. §77(e), shall not apply to "transactions by any person other than an issuer, underwriter, or dealer."[4] . . .

The terms "issuer" and "dealer" are defined, respectively, in §§2[a](4) and (12). . . . The parties do not seriously argue that Johnson was an issuer or a dealer. Clearly he is neither. Rather, Ackerberg contends that Johnson is an underwriter within §4[(a)](1).

When considering whether Johnson is an underwriter, it is helpful to consider that the §4[(a)](1) exemption is meant to distinguish "between distribution of securities and trading in securities." L. Loss & J. Seligman, 2 Securities Regulation 627 (3d ed. 1989) (quoting H.R. Rep. No. 85, 73d Cong., 1st Sess. 15 (1933)).

The statutory definition of "underwriter" is found in §2[(a)](11). "The term 'underwriter' means any person who has purchased from an issuer with a view to, or offers or sells for an issuer in connection with, the distribution of any security." The congressional intent in defining "underwriter" was to cover all persons who might operate as conduits for the transfer of securities to the public. Thus, "underwriter" is generally defined in close connection with the definition and meaning of "distribution." See Eugene England, 663 F.2d at 989 ("An underwriter is one who has purchased stock from the issuer with an intent to resell to the public."). . . .

We begin by considering whether the securities were acquired by Johnson with a view to their distribution. The inquiry depends on the distinction between a distribution and mere trading; so long as Johnson initially acquired his shares from the issuer with an investment purpose and not for the purpose of reselling them, the acquisition was not made "with a view to" distribution. While this determination would at first seem to be a fact-specific inquiry into the security holder's subjective intent at the time of acquisition, the courts have considered the more objective criterion of whether the securities have come to rest. That is, the courts look to whether the security holder has held the securities long enough to negate any inference that his intention at the time of acquisition was to distribute them to the public. Many courts have accepted a two-year rule of thumb to determine whether the securities have come to rest. See United States v. Sherwood, 175 F. Supp. 480, 483 (S.D.N.Y. 1959). . . . This two-year rule has been incorporated by the SEC into Rule 144, which provides a safe harbor for persons

---

4. It is clear that the applicable and appropriate exemption to be applied in this case is §4[(a)](1). To the extent that Ackerberg argues that both Johnson and the PJH defendants rely on a "§4[(a)](1)" exemption, he misunderstands the nature of a §4[(a)](1) exemption. While the term "§4[(a)](1) exemption" has been used in the secondary literature, see, e.g., ABA Report, The Section "4[(a)](1)" Phenomenon: Private Resales of "Restricted" Securities, 34 Bus. Law. 1961 (July 1979) . . . , the term does not properly refer to an exemption other than §4[(a)](1). Rather, the term merely expresses the statutory relationship between §4[(a)](1) and §4[(a)](2). That is, the definition of underwriter, found in §2(a)(11), 15 U.S.C. §77(b)(11) (1988), depends on the existence of a distribution, which in turn is considered the equivalent of a public offering. Section 4[(a)](2) contains the exemption for transactions not involving a public offering. Any analysis of whether a party is an underwriter for purposes of §4[(a)](1) necessarily entails an inquiry into whether the transaction involves a public offering. While the term "4[(a)](1) exemption" adequately expresses this relationship, it is clear that the exemption for private resales of restricted securities is §4[(a)](1). We need not go beyond the statute to reach this conclusion.

selling restricted securities acquired in a private placement. Professor Loss has also noted that a three-year holding period is "well-nigh conclusive" that securities were acquired without a view to distribution. L. Loss & J. Seligman, 2 Securities Regulation at 672.

Johnson purchased his securities in 1979 or 1980, when Vertimag Systems was incorporated in California. He did not sell any of these shares to Ackerberg until 1984. . . . Thus, Johnson held his shares for at least four years before selling them to Ackerberg, a period well in excess of the usual two years required to find that the securities have come to rest.

Our second inquiry is whether the resale was made "for an issuer in connection with" a distribution. Whether the sale was "for an issuer" can also be determined by whether the shares have come to rest. That is, the best objective evidence of whether a sale is "for an issuer" is whether the shares have come to rest. *See* ABA Report, 34 Bus. Law. at 1975.

To determine whether the sale was made "in connection with" a distribution, however, requires that we consider directly the meaning of "distribution," and thus whether the resale involved a public offering. The definition of "distribution" as used in §2[a](11) is generally considered to be synonymous with a public offering. In *Gilligan, Will & Co. v. SEC*, 267 F.2d 461 (2d Cir.), *cert. denied*, 361 U.S. 896 (1959), the court explained the connection between "underwriter," "distribution," and "public offering." "Since §2[(a)](11) . . . defines an 'underwriter' as 'any person who has purchased from an issuer with a view to . . . the distribution of any security' and since a 'distribution' requires a 'public offering,' . . . the question is whether there was a 'public offering.'" Id. at 466 (quoting H.R. Rep. No. 1838, 73d Cong., 2d Sess. (1934)).

The case law is equally clear that a public offering is defined not in quantitative terms, but in terms of whether the offerees are in need of the protection which the Securities Act affords through registration. Thus, the Supreme Court held in *SEC v. Ralston Purina*, 346 U.S. 119 (1953) that the proper focus is on the need of the offerees for information.

> Since exempt transactions are those as to which "there is no practical need for [the bill's] application," the applicability of [the private placement exemption] should turn on whether the particular class of persons affected needs the protection of the Act. An offering to those who are shown to be able to fend for themselves is a transaction "not involving any public offering."

Id. at 125. This circuit has followed *Ralston Purina* by finding that a public offering "turns on the need of the offerees for the protections afforded by registration. . . . If the offerees have access to such information, registration is unnecessary, and the section 4[(a)](2) exemption should apply." *Van Dyke v. Coburn Enter., Inc.*, 873 F.2d 1094, 1098 (8th Cir. 1989).

That "distribution" should be read in terms of "public offering," and the need of the offerees for information, makes sense in light of the purpose of the 1933 Act as construed by this circuit. . . . [T]he parties in this case do not dispute that Ackerberg is a sophisticated investor, not in need of the protections afforded by registration under the 1933 Act. As earlier stated, Ackerberg read and signed a subscription agreement in which he represented that: he had the knowledge and experience in investing to properly evaluate the merits and risks of his purchase of Vertimag securities; he was able to bear the economic risk of the investment in Vertimag securities; he was given full and complete information regarding Vertimag Systems Corporation; he knew that the securities were not registered under the 1933 Act, and were being sold pursuant to exemptions from the 1933 Act; and he knew that the sale was being made in reliance on his representations in the subscription agreement. Ackerberg further represented that his net worth was substantial, and the record clearly shows that Ackerberg is, if not a conscientious investor, at least a prolific one. We, therefore, have no trouble finding that Ackerberg is a sophisticated investor and not in need of the protections afforded by registration under the 1933 Act. Hence, this case involves no public offering, and thus no distribution. Absent a distribution, Johnson cannot be an underwriter within §4[(a)](1), and is, therefore, entitled to that exemption. . . .

NOTES AND QUESTIONS

1. A View of the Section 4(a)(1½) Exemption. Consider for a moment which of the two analyses used in *Ackerberg* in fact involves the so-called Section 4(a)(1½) exemption. Once the court concluded Mr. Johnson had investment intent, why was it necessary to resolve whether Mr. Ackerberg could fend for himself? Furthermore, if Mr. Johnson had not been a control person of Vertimag, would it have been necessary for the court to concern itself with whether Mr. Ackerberg was sophisticated? Should the court have emphasized in its "second inquiry" that Mr. Johnson's sales occurred through a broker, PJH? Does a non-control person always have to be concerned with whether the buyer of his unregistered shares is able to fend for himself? Why was Rule 144 not available for Mr. Johnson's sale?

To answer these questions, consider how in Chapter 5 we approached the question of whether the *issuer* loses *its* exemption under Section 4(a)(2) if one of its purchasers resells the unregistered shares to someone who lacked sophistication, or did not have access to information about the issuer, or both. Recall the concern there was whether the shares sold by the issuer had come to rest in the hands of all those able to fend for themselves à la *Ralston Purina*. Sales after the offering has come to rest do not destroy the issuer's exemption. For example, would Vertimag have lost the exemption through which it originally sold the shares to Johnson if the court had concluded that Ackerman was not sophisticated?

On the other hand, control persons, as we have seen, are treated differently than non-control persons as a result of the last sentence of Section 2(a)(11). Those who buy from or sell for a control person are involved in an underwriting transaction if they are involved in a distribution. Courts, in resolving this question, continue to follow *Gilligan, Will & Co. v. SEC*, 267 F.2d 461 (2d Cir.), *cert. denied*, 361 U.S. 896 (1959), to the effect that the meaning of distribution is to be found in the criteria that must be satisfied for the private offering exemption afforded *issuers* by Section 4(a)(2). Recall that Section 4(a)(2) is only available to issuers who are such because of Section 2(a)(4); control persons are not so defined—control persons are treated as issuers for the limited purpose of determining who is an underwriter under Section 2(a)(11). As such, the reference that *Ackerberg* and *Gilligan, Will* make to Section 4(a)(2) is solely for guidance as to the possible meaning of "distribution" as used in Section 2(a)(11). The relevant areas of inquiry are much the same as we found in considering whether the issuer's offer is exempt under Section 4(a)(2): The concerns are offeree sophistication, number of offerees, manner of solicitation, and disclosure or access to information about the issuer. But the courts' references to Section 4(a)(2) are no more than by analogy, and no court has held that strict compliance with the demands of Section 4(a)(2) is necessary for the control person's resale to be exempt under Section 4(a)(1½). Indeed, it appears one can be off by at least a fraction.

2. *Buyer Sophistication.* One of the most uncertain areas under Section 4(a)(1½) is whether the control person's buyers must be sophisticated. In *Value Line Fund, Inc. v. Marcus*, [1964-1965 Transfer Binder] Fed. Sec. L. Rep. (CCH) ¶91,523 (S.D.N.Y. 1965), the court held the control person's resale was exempt under Section 4(a)(1) when all five offerees were mutual funds and one of those purchased the control person's shares. The court analogized to *Ralston Purina*, concluding that all the offerees were sophisticated and each enjoyed sufficient access to the type of information that registration would make available. On the other hand, the control person who had owned his stock for four years violated Section 5 when he resold those shares to a self-employed landscaper, a junior high school teacher, and several other individuals who had never invested before. *SEC v. Manus*, [1981-1982 Transfer Binder] Fed. Sec. L. Rep. (CCH) ¶98,307 (S.D.N.Y. 1981). Similarly, in *Hidden v. Marinelli*, 796 F. Supp. 432 (N.D. Cal. 1992), the court would not rule as a matter of law that a resale to a Stanford law graduate with some investment experience met the Section 4(a)(1½) exemption. Also, the control person's resales were held to violate Section 5 when he was unable to establish that all of his offerees were sophisticated and had knowledge or access to information about the issuer. *McDaniel v. Compania Minera Mar De Cortes*, 528 F. Supp. 152 (D. Ariz. 1981).

3. *Number of Offerees and Manner of Offer.* Broad solicitations and advertising are generally believed to be inconsistent with the Section 4(a)(1½) exemption. The exception to this is found in favorable no-action letters that have permitted public advertising of a large block of stock, provided the entire block will be sold to a single purchaser. *See generally* Schneider, Section 4(a)(1½)—Private Resales of Restricted or Control Securities, 49 Ohio St. L.J. 501, 507 (1988). In a similar light, the overall number of purchasers must be small, and steps are advised to assure that those few purchasers do not quickly resell their shares, so that the total number of purchasers soon explodes to a number that appears akin to a public offering. Also, what case authority there is that has upheld the exemption has invariably involved offers and sales to very few purchasers. *See, e.g., Value Line Fund, Inc. v. Marcus*, [1964-1965 Transfer Binder] Fed. Sec. L. Rep. (CCH) ¶91,523 (S.D.N.Y. 1965).

4. *Information Disclosure Requirements.* Generally, the view is that there is an information requirement for the Section 4(a)(1½) exemption, and commentators such as Mr. Schneider, supra, advise that the seller make available current '34 Act reports or information of the sort necessary to satisfy either Regulation D's or Section 4(a)(2)'s requirements. The amount and type of information required are clouded considerably by the cases that deal with either very sophisticated parties who have been given a lengthy offering circular, as occurred in *Ackerberg*, or very unsophisticated purchasers who received little information, as occurred in *Manus*, supra, and *United States v. Lindo*, 18 F.3d 353 (6th Cir. 1994).

5. *Status of Shares Acquired from Control Person.*   The Commission views securities acquired from a control person under the Section 4(a)(1½) analysis as being restricted securities. In this way, the Commission perceives the transaction as though the securities were acquired from the issuer in a nonpublic offering.

6. *How Might Control Person Resales Be Broader Than Issuer Section 4(a)(2) Sales?*   Recall that cases considering the scope of the private offering exemption in Section 4(a)(2) focus on the number of shares being offered for sale, the manner of their sale, the number of potential offerees, the information disclosed or available to offerees, and the offeree's sophistication. Overall, the inquiry is whether the offerees can "fend for themselves." On the other hand, in cases such as *In re Ira Haupt & Co.*, discussed earlier in this chapter, the issue is whether a control person's sales into a market are a distribution and the concern is the impact the overall quantity and manner of sale by the control person will have on normal trading in those shares. This emphasis also appears in Rule 144's preface, which states that the trading transactions exempted by Section 4(a)(1) involve neither the offer of such a large quantity of shares nor a manner of sale that will disrupt trading markets. In contrast with this, Section 4(a)(2) would never permit open market sales of even a limited quantity because unsophisticated offerees would be among the targets of those resales. Does the language or statutory scheme justify the dissonance between the meaning of distribution when applied to resales by control persons and the meaning when applied to an issuer's sale?

7. *Non-Control Persons and Section 4(a)(1½).*   Our focus has been on the application of the Section 4(a)(1½) exemption to resales by control persons. Can the exemption apply to a resale by a *non*-control person? Consider the following: Assume Issuer, a private company, offered its shares to accredited investors in reliance on Rule 506. Andy, an accredited investor, purchased 1,000 shares in the offering. Three months later, Bethany, also an accredited investor, offers to buy those shares from Andy. Andy accepts the offer and sells his shares to Bethany. Is this transaction exempt under Section 4(a)(1½)? Does it matter whether Bethany can fend for herself? Does your analysis change if the issuer relied instead on Rule 147A?

PROBLEMS

In each of the following problems, consider whether the resale violates Section 5.

6-36.   Candice is a control person of Amalgamated Dry Goods, Inc. She resold 1,000 of her Amalgamated shares to Devin two months after she acquired her control shares from Amalgamated in a private offering. Devin is Amalgamated's newly recruited chief financial officer.

6-37.   Assume Amalgamated issued the shares to Candice, its controlling stockholder, and others pursuant to the intrastate offering exemption of Section 3(a)(11). Two months later, Candice resold 1,000 of those shares to her brother, Edward, a sophisticated and experienced investor who lives in a neighboring state.

6-38.   Assume the same facts as Problem 6-37, except that Candice's resale to Edward occurs five years after she acquired the shares from Amalgamated and that her attorney negotiated the terms of the sale to Edward.

6-39.   Five years ago, Candice acquired her control shares as part of Amalgamated's intrastate offering. There is no active market in Amalgamated common stock. Candice wishes to sell some of her shares and proposes to fly to New York City, where, on a street corner outside the New York Stock Exchange, she will attempt to sell some of her shares to any and all pedestrian traffic. How would you advise her?

6-40.   Assume the facts of Problem 6-39, except that Candice is too busy to make the trip to New York. For a standard commission fee, she retains her broker of many years to carry out this selling effort for her.

6-41.   Candice has been a controlling stockholder of Amalgamated for eight years. Amalgamated common stock is traded in the over-the-counter market. She now wishes to diversify her investments and has retained Smith Baley and Co. to sell 30,000 of her 1 million shares in an orderly manner in the over-the-counter market. Candice has herself privately negotiated to sell 50,000 of her shares to Harrold, an unsophisticated and inexperienced, albeit wealthy, investor. Soon after Harrold's purchase, Amalgamated's market price declines sharply. Advise Harrold of his rights.

G.   *The Section 4(a)(7) Exemption*

Congress added Section 4(a)(7) to the Securities Act in 2015, providing a new resale transaction exemption. The exemption is available to any seller (except the issuer or its subsidiary) and is conditioned on each purchaser being accredited and there being no general solicitation or general advertisement in connection with the resale. Note the prohibition against general solicitation and advertisement parallels the same prohibition in Rule 502(c) of Regulation D. Thus, the extensive guidance the SEC has provided through its no-action letters in connection with the similar prohibition in Rule 502(c) of Regulation D applies to new Section 4(a)(7). Recall that in the context of Rule 502(c), the SEC has consistently emphasized the importance of a preexisting relationship between buyer and seller. See Chapter 5, section C.5, Limitations on the Manner and Scope of an Offering.

The exemption provided in Section 4(a)(7) is purchaser, not offeree, based; therefore, a selling shareholder does not violate Section 5 if she mistakenly offers, but does not sell, the security to a person who is not accredited, so long as those that do purchase are all accredited investors. When the issuer is not a reporting company, certain basic information about the issuer as well as financial statements prepared according to generally accepted accounting principles (IFRs in the case of foreign issuers) must be made available to the purchaser. There is no information requirement if the issuer is a reporting company.

Section 4(a)(7) is available regardless of the exemption the issuer relied upon when it issued the securities to the reseller. Furthermore, the exemption does not impose a holding period on the reseller. However, the exemption is limited to securities "of a class that has been authorized and outstanding for at least 90 days prior to the date of the transaction."

Securities acquired under the exemption are "deemed to have been acquired in a transaction not involving any public offerings." Hence, such securities fall within Rule 144(a)(3)(i)'s definition of "restricted security" and can be sold under that safe harbor's provisions. Section 4(a)(7) does not apply if the seller or its agent is a "bad actor" as defined in Rule 506(d)(1) and does not apply if the issuer is a shell, blank check, or blind pool company.

Consider the ways in which Section 4(a)(7) is narrower than Section 4(a) (1½). Recall that the Section 4(a)(1½), among other things, focuses on the buyer's sophistication, not the buyer's accreditation status. Also, SEC no-action letters surrounding the Section 4(a)(1½) exemption permit advertisements to be used to place controlling blocks of shares. Further, whereas Section 4(a)(7) does not apply to certain issuers and does not apply if the seller or its agent is a "bad actor," as defined in Rule 506(d)(1), these limitations do not apply in Section 4(a)(1½) transactions.

Recall *Ackerberg v. Johnson* from above. Could Johnson have structured his sale to Ackerberg to fall within Section 4(a)(7) had it existed at the time? What if Johnson had held his shares for only six months instead of at least four years before selling them to Ackerberg?

PROBLEM

6-42.   Liam, a control person of Chungus Inc. and accredited investor, passed away three months ago. Chungus is a non-reporting issuer. Liam's estate is seeking a buyer for Liam's block of Chungus stock, which Chungus issued to him five years ago. Thus, the estate bought an ad from Google that appears in various investment-related Google search results. The ad offers Liam's block for sale, briefly describes Chungus, and contains a link to a recent document that includes the information specified in Securities Act Section 4(d)(3). Piper, an accredited investor, learns of the Chungus offering from the Google ad, contacts Chungus, and buys Liam's block. Does this transaction violate Section 5?

H.   Registered Resales

As touched on in the PIPE materials above, a resale can be registered, in which case the resale would not have to be made in compliance with Rule 144 or another exemption. Registering an offering requires extensive issuer partic-ipation. Hence, it is common for private placement investors to insist that the issuer sign a registration rights agreement as part of the private placement that contractually obligates the issuer to register the resale under specified circum-stances. Both Forms S-1 and S-3 allow the registration of resale transactions, and they are often done as shelf registrations, as allowed by Securities Act Rule 415.

There are two types of registration rights that issuers grant to investors—demand and piggyback. Demand rights obligate an issuer to register a resale upon the demand of holders of a specified percentage of securities sold in the private placement. Oftentimes, demand registration rights apply only if the issuer is eligible to register the resale on Form S-3. An issuer is so eligible, if, among other things: (1) it has been subject to Exchange Act reporting require-ments for at least 12 months; (2) it has timely filed all required Exchange Act reports during the last 12 months (subject to limited exceptions); and (3) it has securities of the same class as those to be registered for resale listed on a national securities exchange or quoted on an automated quotation system of a national securities exchange (note that the $75 million minimum public float requirement applies only to a primary offering, not a resale, or secondary, offering). As to a private company, a Form S-3 eligibility requirement prevents investors from essentially forcing the company to go public.

Piggyback registration rights require an issuer to register the resale of a holder's securities as part of a registration statement the issuer plans to file for a primary offering or for other security holders. The registration rights agree-ment will require the issuer to notify the holders of such plans by the issuer so that the holders can decide whether they want to participate in the offering.

Issuers are willing to grant registration rights to make investing in a private placement more attractive to investors. Specifically, more investors may be will-ing to participate and those who would have regardless may be willing to pay a little more. Investors value registration rights because it means they may be able to resell sooner, and for control persons, easier, than relying on Rule 144/Section 4(a)(1) or another exemption.

In a different vein, recall the Spotify direct listing described in Chapter 4, sec-tion A.1. In connection with the direct listing, Spotify filed a resale shelf registra-tion statement on Form F-1 (F-1 instead of S-1 because Spotify is organized outside of the United States) for certain of its control persons and employees, presumably so they could sell into the newly established public market for Spotify's shares without having to comply with Rule 144/Section 4(a)(1) or another exemption.

I.   Resales Under the Blue Sky Laws

Historically, resales of securities had to be registered or exempt under federal law and the blue sky law of the state in which the sale was made. However, this situation changed in 1996 when Congress enacted the National Securities Market Improvement Act (NSMIA). Among other things, NSMIA amended Section 18 of the Securities Act to establish various categories of "covered secu-rities." Section 18, as amended, prohibits a state from requiring registration or qualification of any offer or sale of covered securities. Covered securities include: (1) securities offered and sold in reliance on Securities Act Section 4(a)(1) if the issuer is an Exchange Act reporting company; and (2) securities listed on the New York Stock Exchange, Nasdaq Global Market, Nasdaq Global Select Market, or the Nasdaq Capital Market, among others. Hence, the application of state registration/exemption requirements for resales is functionally limited to securities of private companies.

Trading in private company securities has undoubtedly increased in frequency in the last decade, with private companies remaining private for longer and the rise of the pre-IPO secondary trading markets discussed earlier in this chapter. Thus, state registration/exemption requirements remain relevant notwithstanding NSMIA. Overall, the scheme of the blue sky laws is very similar to the federal scheme in that resales require the security to be registered in the state in which it is offered and sold unless the resale falls within one of several possible exemptions. As is seen in the discussion that follows, the conditions that must be met to satisfy the federal exemptions for resale are generally more demanding than their counterparts under the blue sky laws. This is particularly true with respect to the federal exemptions afforded by either Rule 144 or Section 4(a)(1½). Because the federal exemptions for resale are more rigorous in their requirements than the state exemptions, it is frequently the case that satisfaction of, for example, Rule 144 is more than sufficient to qualify the resale for at least one of the exemptions for resales under an applicable state blue sky law.

The discussion that follows examines the non-issuer exemptions of the Uniform Securities Act. Section 401(h) of the Act defines *non-issuer* to mean "not directly or indirectly for the benefit of the issuer." A holder does not need a non-issuer exemption if the security to be sold is exempt from registration under the blue sky laws. In this respect, the most significant security exemption is Section 402(a)(8), which exempts from registration securities listed on certain specified national securities exchanges. In most states, the non-issuer exemptions are available to control persons just as they are to non-control persons. A few states—for example, New Hampshire,[4] Minnesota,[5] and New Jersey[6]—do not allow control persons to rely on the non-issuer exemptions. Only the basic exemptions are discussed below and provide a useful contrast to the regulatory focus of the '33 Act. There are several narrower non-issuer exemption possibilities, such as those available to estate administrators and pledgees or for sales to certain institutional investors. If no exemption is available for a non-issuer transaction, whether for a control person or a non-control person, registration is required before the sale may occur.

1.   Isolated Non-Issuer Resale

Section 402(b)(1) provides the following exemption: "Any isolated non-issuer transaction, whether effected through a broker-dealer or not." Within this exemption, the most troubling problem is what is meant by *isolated*, which, of

---

4.   N.H. Rev. Stat. Ann. §421-B:2(XIV).
5.   Minn. Stat. Ann. §80A.14(14).
6.   N.J. Stat. Ann. §49:3-49(o).

course, modifies *transaction*, a term posing its own ambiguity. Does the transaction referred to include only a sale, or does it include many offers to sell leading up to that sale? And if there is more than one sale, can the transaction still be viewed as isolated? Cases have interpreted *isolated* to be something of an antonym to "repeated and successive." *See Kneeland v. Emerton*, 280 Mass. 371, 388-389, 183 N.E. 155, 163 (1932) ("isolated" means standing alone, disconnected from any other, so that two sales made within a reasonable time of one another such that they appear to be actuated by one general purpose will be deemed as successive, not isolated). A few states have provided certainty to the exemption by definitively stating in their regulations how many sales and/or offers may occur within a 12-month period without destroying the isolated transaction exemption. For example, Minnesota permits 5 sales within 12 consecutive months.[7]

2. The Manual Exemption

The most readily available non-issuer exemption is the manual exemption under Uniform Securities Act §402(b)(2), which exempts

> [a]ny nonissuer distribution of an outstanding security if (A) a recognized securities manual contains the names of the issuer's officers and directors, a balance sheet of the issuer as of a date within eighteen months, and a profit and loss statement of either the fiscal year preceding that date or the most recent year of operation.

The type of manual referred to in the exemption is a publication containing financial and operating information about selected public corporations, which information is updated periodically. The accepted manuals are set forth in either the individual state's statute or the accompanying regulations; the most frequently accepted service is the manual published by Mergent's Investor Service (formerly known as Moody's Investment Service). Standard & Poor's used to publish a manual as well (e.g., Standard & Poor's Corporation Record) but discontinued it in 2016. It should be observed that the information this section requires the manual to contain for the individual issuer is not nearly as encompassing as the information Regulation D requires to be provided to non-accredited investors or the information that Rule 144 requires to be publicly available. Many states have made modest additions to the list of information the manual must include and have added other limitations to their manual exemption, such as a requirement that the exemption not be available to control persons (*see* Massachusetts Securities Rules 14.402(B)(3)(b)) or that the issuer has been in continuous operation for a stated number of years (*see, e.g.,* Mich. Comp. Laws §451.802(b)(2)(A) (requiring issuer to have been in continuous operation for five years)). Disquiet with this exemption is fed by the fact that, even though most companies listed on the New York and American Stock

---

7. Minn. Stat. Ann. §80A.15(2)(a).

Exchanges appear in the leading manuals, many companies are included in such manuals because they have paid a modest fee to be included.

3. Unsolicited Offer Exemption

Section 402(b)(3) of the Uniform Securities Act provides an exemption for "any non-issuer transaction effected by or through a registered broker-dealer pursuant to an unsolicited order or offer to buy. . . ." Unlike Section 4(4) of the '33 Act, which only protects the broker's participation in a trading transaction, Section 402(b)(3) extends its protection to the customer (provided the customer is not an issuer) as well as the broker. It should be noted that the exemption protects the broker whether acting as an agent or a principal. This is the import of the "by or through" language. As with Section 4(4), the unsolicited offer exemption requires that the buyer's order not be solicited. Just as Rule 144(g)(2) lists certain steps a broker may take that do not constitute solicitation, it would appear to be within the policy of the unsolicited offer exemption to permit these same activities to occur without jeopardizing the blue sky exemption. *See* L. Loss, Commentary on the Uniform Securities Act 120-121 (1976).

4. Small Offering Exemption

Section 402(b)(9) provides an exemption that is available to both the issuer and those who acquire securities from the issuer with investment intent who later wish to sell their shares.

> Any transaction pursuant to an offer directed by the offeror to not more than ten persons . . . [plus an unlimited number of certain types of institutional investors] in this state during any twelve consecutive months, whether or not the offeror or any of the offerees is then present in this state, if (A) the seller reasonably believes that all the buyers in this state are purchasing for investment, and (B) no commission or other remuneration is paid or given directly or indirectly for soliciting any prospective buyer in this state . . . [is exempt].

The small offering exemption should not be confused with the more recently developed and more carefully designed Uniform Limited Offering Exemption (ULOE), which permits sales to up to 35 individuals. Many states adopting the ULOE have retained their small offering exemption. In any case, the ULOE is available only for *issuer* transactions due to its dependence on the transaction's qualifying for one of the exemptions in Regulation D, which is limited to issuer transactions.

It may well be that "small offering" is a bit of a misnomer for the exemption authorized in Section 402(b)(9). In fact, the exemption limits only the number of offers that can occur within *that* state; it does not limit the number of offers that can be made to residents of a single state. Thus, an offer in Texas to ten Texans is within the exemption even though that issuer has also offered the security to ten Texans while on a ski trip to Colorado. The exemption permits only offers to ten different persons within a single state, but this would permit 500 offers to be made nationwide. In most states, there is no limit on the amount of securities that can be sold through the small offering exemption, and the exemption does not carry any minimal disclosure requirements. Moreover, the investment intent requirement is not absolute; the person relying upon the exemption does not lose the exemption if it turns out that one of his purchasers resold the securities soon after her purchase. The exemption does not require clairvoyance, only a reasonable belief that the purchaser takes with investment intent. Nevertheless, it would appear that more is required by this standard than the empty undertaking embodied in the standard investment intent letter. The requirement that there be no commission or remuneration for soliciting investors certainly rules out the standard underwriter, but it nevertheless underscores that there can be solicitation of buyers, albeit the solicitor must not be compensated.

PROBLEM

6-43.   Alice purchased 700,000 Tecto common shares about 18 months ago in an offering exempt from federal regulation under Rule 147 and from state regulation under the ULOE. As a result of her purchase, Alice held most of the outstanding Tecto shares. Alice then caused Tecto to register information regarding Tecto with Goody's Financial Blue Book, one of the financial manuals recognized by Tecto's state of incorporation. Alice hired Woody, a local broker, to find a purchaser for as many shares as he can. Woody has worked the phone, and after about four dozen calls he has found 15 willing purchasers, 6 of whom live in another state. Would you advise Alice to sell her Tecto shares to the individuals located by Woody?

‖7‖
Recapitalizations, Reorganizations, and Acquisitions

Up to this point, the securities transactions studied have involved orthodox financing transactions in which the issuer seeks fresh capital through the issuance of securities. Securities are also issued when a corporation declares a stock dividend, or senior security holders convert or exchange their shares to receive another security from the issuer, or one company acquires another company by issuing its securities to the acquired company's stockholders, or the rights, privileges, and preferences of an outstanding class of stock are altered through amendment of the articles of incorporation, or a company is reorganized in the bankruptcy courts to rehabilitate itself financially by exchanging securities for outstanding claims or securities. Each of these transactions is subject to unique regulatory treatment under the Securities Act.

A. The "For Value" Requirement

The expressions "sale" and "offer to sell" are of paramount importance in the operation of Section 5. Section 2(a)(3) defines these expressions as involving "every attempt . . . to dispose of . . . a security . . . *for value.*" This section examines the important role the "for value" requirement has in defining the scope of Section 5.

1. Value Is Not Always What It Seems

Free Stock. A gift of securities would appear to be the classic illustration of the type of disposition that would escape Section 2(a)(3)'s broad definition of sale. The Commission, however, has been quite resourceful in finding consideration to support a disposition made without a payment in the classic sense when it believes the issuer or its promoters are gifting securities as part of a plan that will lead to the distribution of securities. For example, in *In re*

Capital General Corp., [1993 Transfer Binder] Fed. Sec. L. Rep. (CCH) ¶85,223 (1993), the promoters were unsuccessful in their attempt to skirt Section 5 by arguing no value was given for the shares they distributed. After purchasing all the shares of some 69 private companies, the promoters made gifts to 275 to 900 persons throughout the United States and retained a controlling block of shares in each company, which they later sold for a handsome profit. The Commission found the respondents had violated Section 5, reasoning that "for value" depends "not only on whether the recipient of the security gives some-thing of value . . . but also on whether value is received from any other source." Id. at 84,425. The Commission concluded the respondents received value in the form of the public market their gifts of shares had fostered. And, when many Internet startup companies awarded free stock to individuals who visited the company's web page, the SEC concluded the companies were violating Section 5; the staff reasoned that the issuance of securities in consideration of a per-son's registration on or visit to an issuer's Internet site fell within the meaning of Section 2(a)(3). *See, e.g., Vanderkam & Sanders*, [1999 Transfer Binder] Fed. Sec. L. Rep. (CCH) ¶77,520 (Jan. 27, 1999). On the other hand, a no-action letter was granted where it was reasoned no sale was involved when an employer issued unregistered shares to a broad class of employees. UnionBanCal, SEC No-Action Letter (Nov. 3, 2010).

Stock Dividends.   Consider whether a company's issuance of a stock divi-dend is the "sale" of that security. The stock dividend arises when a corporation issues shares to its existing stockholders and receives nothing in return. Because there is no consideration from those who receive the stock dividend, the typical stock dividend does not involve the sale of a security. However, if stockholders are granted the opportunity to choose between receiving a cash dividend and a stock dividend, it would appear that the issuer has thereby offered to sell a secu-rity. Such a transaction, if disaggregated, could be viewed as involving, first, the stockholder's receiving a cash dividend and, second, the payment of that cash for the newly issued shares. The SEC, nevertheless, adheres to the reasoning of its former general counsel that a choice between cash or a stock dividend does not involve the sale of, or offer to sell, a security.

> . . . [E]ven though under ordinary circumstances the waiver of a right would in my opinion constitute "value," I do not believe that that term should be regarded as comprehending within its meaning the action of a stockholder, to whom alter-native rights have been granted without consideration, in electing to exercise one such right, even though, under the terms of the grant, such election will have the effect of causing the lapse of the right not exercised. Consequently, if a corpora-tion by simultaneous action of its board of directors, declares a dividend payable at the election of the stockholder in cash or in securities, neither the declaration of the dividend, nor the distribution of securities to stockholders who elect to take the dividend in that form, would in my opinion constitute a sale within the mean-ing of the Securities Act, and no registration of the securities so distributed would be required under the Act.
>
>   However, . . . it is well settled in general law that upon the public declaration of a cash dividend out of surplus, the holders of the stock in respect of which the dividend is declared acquire immediately the rights of creditors of the corpora-tion. . . . If, therefore, there is declared a cash dividend payable to all stockholders,

and if the board thereafter determines to grant to stockholders the opportunity to waive their preexisting and vested rights to payment of the dividend in cash, and to receive the dividend in the form of securities, the stockholders electing to take securities would in my opinion be regarded as giving value for the securities so received.

Securities Act Release No. 929 (July 29, 1936). On the other hand, dividend reinvestment programs, in which stockholders may by prior agreement have their dividends applied toward the purchase of additional shares from the corporation at current market prices, are subject to registration under the Securities Act.[1] How does a dividend reinvestment program differ from permitting stockholders the option between cash and shares?

Warrants and Convertible Securities. The fifth sentence of Section 2(a)(3) provides an answer to the question of how many different securities are being offered when the issuer solicits investors to purchase a senior security, such as a bond, that is convertible into a more junior security, for example, common stock. The same question can be posed with respect to the offer of a warrant or an option that entitles its holder to purchase the issuer's common stock at a stated price. Bonds, warrants, and options are each specifically identified as securities in Section 2(a)(1) and must be registered unless an exemption is available. Whether the underlying security—the security that may be acquired through conversion or the exercise of a warrant or option—must be registered depends upon *when*, by the instrument's terms, the holder can acquire the underlying security through conversion or exercise of the warrant or option. If the conversion features or the warrant's or the option's terms provide that it can be exercised immediately, two distinct securities are then being offered, so that each must be registered or qualify for an exemption from registration. On the other hand, if by the terms of the instrument the holder cannot convert or exercise the warrant or option until some future date, the underlying security is not "offered for sale" until that future date, and the underlying security's registration is not required at the time the convertible security, warrant, or option is being offered. The House Committee Report accompanying this provision explains this distinction as follows:

> [Section 2[(a)](3)] exempts from the concept of "sale" the giving to a holder of a security, at the time of the sale of such security to the holder, a right either to conversion or a warrant to subscribe, where neither of these rights are immediately exercisable. This makes it unnecessary to register such a security prior to the time that it is to be offered to the public, although the conversion right or the right to subscribe must be registered. When the actual securities to which these rights appertain are offered to the public, the bill requires registration as of that time.

---

1. An important exception arises when the dividend reinvestment program is structured so that an entity separate from the issuer purchases on behalf of participating stockholders the issuer's shares on the market, with the cash being the amount that the issuer would otherwise have distributed to those stockholders as a dividend. Under this structure, the SEC's position is that the issuer is not involved in the sale of its securities. Securities Act Release No. 5515 (Aug. 8, 1974).

This permits the holder of any such right of conversion or warrant to subscribe to judge whether upon all the facts it is advisable for him to exercise his rights.

H.R. Rep. No. 85, 73d Cong., 1st Sess. 12 (1933). Recall that the shelf registration procedure in Rule 415, discussed in Chapter 4, is available for any security that can be acquired by conversion or exercise of a warrant or option and that an important feature of the shelf registration rule is the registrant's undertaking to keep its registration statement current by filing amendments disclosing any material changes or events. This procedure enriches the information otherwise available to the holder considering whether to convert or exercise an option or warrant.

Amendments of Articles or Indentures and Reincorporations. The rights of security holders can be altered in many ways. The corporation's articles of incorporation set forth the rights, privileges, and preferences of each class of a corporation's stock. These rights can be altered through an amendment to the articles of incorporation; this usually requires approval by a majority of the outstanding shares of that class of stock. The amendment may involve an insignificant change, such as a reduction in the share's par value; on the other hand, the amendment may entail a significant economic change, such as alteration of the dividend rights of a senior class of stock. The rights of bondholders may also be altered. Their rights are set forth in the bond's indenture, which also prescribes the procedures that must be followed to alter the bondholders' rights. Generally, any alteration of the indenture requires the approval of both the bondholders and the indenture trustee. An indenture may, for example, be amended to change interest payments from semi-annual to quarterly, or the change may extend the debt's maturity.

Whether an amendment to the articles of incorporation or bond indenture is subject to Section 5 of the Securities Act is determined by resolving two separate questions: whether a sale of the security is involved and whether that sale involves the type of exchange of securities exempted under Section 3(a)(9). The discussion in the remainder of this section focuses upon the tools the courts and the SEC have used when addressing the first question. Later, in section C of this chapter, we examine the exemption provided by Section 3(a)(9) for such transactions.

SEC v. Associated Gas & Electric Co., 99 F.2d 795 (2d Cir. 1938), reached the unsurprising conclusion that the extension of the maturity date on a bond's indenture by one or five years at the individual bondholder's option is a sale under the Public Utility Holding Company Act of 1935's broad definition of sale, which is nearly identical to that in Section 2(a)(3) of the Securities Act. In *Associated Gas & Electric*, the court reasoned that lengthening the maturity date is functionally equivalent to surrendering the old security for a new one. Even though the certificates were never physically exchanged, the modification was deemed a sale of a security. Should the surrender analysis of *Associated Gas & Electric* have less impact when the alteration is of a type contemplated in the original instrument? This line of thinking was pivotal in *Browning Debenture Holders' Committee v. DASA Corp.*, [1974-1975 Transfer Binder] Fed. Sec. L. Rep. (CCH) ¶95,071 (S.D.N.Y. 1975). The corporation wished to sell most of its assets. However, before the sale could occur, the corporation had to obtain its bondholders' waiver of various protective covenants in their bond indenture. To obtain the waiver, the corporation proposed to sweeten the bondholders' conversion privilege. Bondholders who were dissatisfied with the proposed terms complained that the corporation's solicitation of the bondholders to obtain two-thirds approval, in which they were also asked to approve reducing the conversion price of their bonds by 50 percent, was an offer to sell a security. The court held that no substantial alteration of the bonds had occurred because the original bond indenture authorized alteration of the bondholders' rights and the proposed change was accomplished according to those procedures.

If *Browning* were the prevailing view, it would narrow considerably Section 2(a)(3); most bond indentures and all articles of incorporation are subject to their holders' latent power to alter the security's rights, privileges, or preferences through procedures prescribed in the debenture or governing corporate law. In fact, to pose the question of whether an alteration is a sale itself implies that there was a preexisting power to change the security's original terms. Accordingly, *Browning*'s reasoning is out of step with most other cases on the subject. For example, the SEC, in its response to no-action letter requests, is fairly consistent in viewing all material changes in a security's economic or voting rights as entailing the sale of a new security. *See* McGuigan & Aiken, Amendment of Securities, Rev. Sec. Reg. 935, 937-938 (1976). On the other hand, a sale is not involved if the change involves no economic consequences to the holders, such as altering the share's par value.[2]

Stockholders' rights are also altered through the entity's reincorporation in a jurisdiction whose corporate law accords security holders different sets of rights than in its former corporate domicile. To be sure, this changes the stockholders' rights in a less direct way than does an amendment of the articles of incorporation. Stockholders' rights vary across states on such questions as voting rights, dividend and share repurchase regulation, and a variety of corporate governance issues. Thus, reincorporation could be viewed as a surrender of shares in, for example, a California corporation, where cumulative voting is mandated by statute, for shares in a Delaware corporation that has not elected to have cumulative voting. Nevertheless, the SEC maintains in its no-action letters that registration is not required because a *domestic* reincorporation involves only a change in form, not substance.[3]

---

2. In INDRESCO, Inc., SEC No-Action Letter, [1996 Transfer Binder] Fed. Sec. L. Rep. (CCH) ¶77,123 (Oct. 31, 1995), no sale was involved when shareholders of an operating company received the same proportionate interest in a newly created holding company. And in Columbus and Southern Ohio Electric Co., SEC No-Action Letter (avail. Mar. 12, 1973) (WL Fed Sec file), the utility obtained a no-action letter supporting its view that no sale was involved where the issuer sought the alteration of its indenture obligation to comply with all federal laws. The issuer was concerned that it may not be able to comply fully with strict new environmental laws.

3. *See, e.g.*, Adolf Coors Co., SEC No-Action Letter, [2003 Transfer Binder] Fed. Sec. L. Rep. (CCH) ¶78,532 (Aug. 25, 2003). With the adoption of Rule 145, discussed later in this chapter, these questions are addressed initially by considering whether the transaction falls within Rule 145(a)(2). *See* Russell Corp. SEC No-Action Letter, [2004 Transfer Binder] Fed. Sec. L. Rep. (CCH) 78,771 (Mar. 18, 2004). Compare changes via reincorporation with the more direct alteration of shareholder governance rights posed in *Western Air Lines, Inc. v. Sobieski*, 191 Cal. App. 2d 399, 12 Cal. Rptr. 719 (1961), wherein California's commissioner of corporations successfully argued that a Delaware corporation's amendment of its articles

The Exchange Act does not expressly refer to "value" in its definitions of *purchase* or *sale*, gateway terms for provisions such as the antifraud rule, Rule 10b-5. Here the jurisprudence of Section 2(a)(3) of the Securities Act has proven helpful, as courts in construing these terms in Exchange Act cases approach their meaning in a manner similar to the "for value" inquiry under the Securities Act, treating transactions as a "purchase" or a "sale" when the transaction in question has caused such a significant change in the nature of the investment or investment risk as to amount to a new investment. *See Gelles v. TDA Indus.*, 44 F.3d 102 (2d Cir. 1994).

PROBLEMS

For each of the following problems, determine whether the transaction involves the "sale" of a security.

7-1. Ventures Corporation has 300,000 shares of preferred stock outstanding. The preferred shares carry a cumulative dividend of $2 per share, with a possibility of shareholders receiving an additional $1 per share annually if the board of directors so decides. Ventures' board resolved that the preferred shareholders should be entitled to choose between (1) receiving their regular dividend of $2 per share, or (2) forgoing that dividend and receiving for each ten preferred shares owned one share of common stock as a stock dividend. The common stock's current market price is $24 per share.

7-2. Assume in the preceding problem that the regular $2 per year dividends on the Ventures preferred shares were four years in arrears. Assume that Ventures' board of directors has resolved to permit three shares of preferred stock to be exchanged for one share of common stock; the common stock's current market value is $24 per share.

7-3. Assume in Problem 7-1 that Ventures' board of directors, in order to deal with the preferred stock dividends that are in arrears, proposes that Ventures' articles of incorporation be amended to make the Ventures preferred shares convertible into common shares at any time. If the preferred shareholders approve the amendment and many of the preferred shares are converted, has there been a sale?

7-4. Alpha is concerned that under the laws of its current corporate domicile it is vulnerable to a hostile takeover. It is exploring the possibility of reincorporating in Delaware to take advantage of its anti-takeover statute. The reincorporation also will remove cumulative voting and preemptive rights that are mandatory under the laws of Alpha's current corporate domicile. Alpha

---

of incorporation to abolish cumulative voting constituted the "sale" of a security in California where more than 30 percent of its shares were owned by California residents. The SEC, however, treats foreign reincorporations as a sale. *See generally* Fresenius Aktiengesellschaft, SEC No-Action Letter (Oct. 10, 2006).

envisions that the reincorporation can be accomplished by the merger of Alpha into a Delaware corporation created solely for the purpose of the transaction. The merger will, of course, require the approval of Alpha's stockholders.

2. Shells and Spin-offs: Creating "Value"

Corporate spin-offs have long been used to separate, divest, and liquidate businesses. Traditionally, spin-offs have been the device employed for various business purposes to sever a distinct operation from the enterprise. Motivations for a spin-off can include separating incompatible operations, complying with local or federal antitrust laws, segregating hazardous activities, and even settling shareholder disputes. The orthodox spin-off begins with a corporation transferring the assets to be shed to a newly formed company, all of whose stock is owned by the transferring corporation. At this stage, the newly formed company is technically a wholly owned subsidiary of the transferring corporation. The subsidiary's stock is next distributed pro rata among the parent corporation's shareholders. If the parent corporation does not thereafter retain a controlling interest in the newly formed corporation, the newly formed company emerges as an independent entity, and its first set of stockholders is the stockholders of the transferring corporation. Because the transferring corporation was a public corporation and the newly formed company's shares are held by the stockholders of the transferring corporation, the newly formed company has also become a publicly held corporation.

a. Spin-offs and the '33 Act

In the 1960s, the spin-off became a device to avoid the high cost of going public through traditional regulatory channels. As the next case demonstrates, the regulators' response to this phenomenon was swift, but not altogether complementary to the finely tuned provisions of the Securities Act.

Securities and Exchange Commission v. Datronics Engineers, Inc.
490 F.2d 250 (4th Cir. 1973), *cert. denied*, 416 U.S. 937 (1974)

BRYAN, J. The Securities and Exchange Commission in enforcement of the Securities Act of 1933, §20(b), . . . sought a preliminary injunction to restrain Datronics Engineers, Inc., its officers and agents, as well as related corporations, from continuing in alleged violation of the registration and antifraud provisions of the Acts. The breaches are said to have been committed in the sale of unregistered securities, §5 of the 1933 Act.

Summary judgment went for the defendants, and the Commission appeals. We reverse.

. . . Datronics was engaged in the construction of communications towers. Its capital stock was held by 1000 shareholders and was actively traded on the market. All of the spin-offs occurred within a period of 13 months—from

November 1, 1968 to December 31, 1969—and the spun-off stock was that of nine corporations, three of which were wholly owned subsidiaries of Datronics and six were independent corporations.

The pattern of the spin-offs in each instance was this: Without any business purpose of its own, Datronics would enter into an agreement with the principals of a private company. The agreement provided for the organization by Datronics of a new corporation, or the utilization of one of Datronics' subsidiaries, and the merger of the private company into the new or subsidiary corporation. It stipulated that the principals of the private company would receive the majority interest in the merger-corporation. The remainder of the stock of the corporation would be delivered to, or retained by, Datronics for a nominal sum per share. Part of it would be applied to the payment of the services of Datronics in the organization and administration of the proposed spin-off, and to Datronics' counsel for legal services in the transaction. Datronics was bound by each of the nine agreements to distribute among its shareholders the rest of the stock.

Before such distribution, however, Datronics reserved for itself approximately one-third of the shares. Admittedly, none of the newly acquired stock was ever registered; its distribution and the dissemination of the false representations were accomplished by use of the mails.

Primarily, in our judgment each of these spin-offs violated §5 of the Securities Act, in that Datronics caused to be carried through the mails an unregistered security "for the purpose of sale or for delivery after sale." Datronics was actually an issuer, or at least a co-issuer, and not exempted from §5 by §4[(a)](1) of the Act, 15 U.S.C. §77d as "any person other than an issuer."

Datronics and the other appellees contend, and the District Court concluded, that this type of transaction was not a sale. The argument is that it was no more than a dividend parceled out to stockholders from its portfolio of investments. A noteworthy difference here, however, is that each distribution was an obligation. Their contention also loses sight of the definition of "sale" contained in §2 of the 1933 Act, 15 U.S.C. §77b. . . .

As the term "sale" includes a "disposition of a security," the dissemination of the new stock among Datronics' stockholders was a sale. However, the appellees urged, and the District Court held, that this disposition was not a statutory sale because it was not "for value," as demanded by the definition. Here, again, we find error. *Cf. Securities and Exchange Commission v. Harwyn Industries Corp.,* 326 F. Supp. 943, 954 (S.D.N.Y. 1971). Value accrued to Datronics in several ways. First, a market for the stock was created by its transfer to so many new assignees—at least 1000, some of whom were stockbroker-dealers, residing in various States. Sales by them followed at once—the District Judge noting that "[i]n each instance dealing promptly began in the spun-off shares." This result redounded to the benefit not only of Datronics but, as well, to its officers and agents who had received some of the spun-off stock as compensation for legal or other services to the spin-off corporations. Likewise, the stock retained by Datronics was thereby given an added increment of value. The record discloses that in fact the stock, both that disseminated and that kept by Datronics, did appreciate substantially after the distributions.

This spurious creation of a market whether intentional or incidental constituted a breach of the securities statutes. Each of the issuers by this wide spread of its stock became a publicly held corporation. In this process and in subsequent sales the investing public was not afforded the protection intended by the statutes. Further, the market and the public character of the spun-off stock were fired and fanned by the issuance of shareholder letters announcing future spin-offs, and by information statements sent out to the shareholders.

Moreover, we think that Datronics was an underwriter within the meaning of the 1933 Act. Hence its transactions were covered by the prohibitions, and were not within the exemptions, of the Act. By definition, the term underwriter "means any person who has purchased from an issuer with a view to, or offers or sells for an issuer in connection with, the distribution of any security, or participates or has a direct or indirect participation in any such undertaking. . . ." §2[(a)](11) of the 1933 Act. Clearly, in these transactions the merger-corporation was an issuer; Datronics was a purchaser as well as a co-issuer; and the purchase was made with a view to the distribution of the stock, as commanded by Datronics' preacquisition agreements. By this underwriter distribution Datronics violated §5 of the 1933 Act. . . .

Vacated with directions.

WIDENER, Circuit Judge (concurring). . . .

In my opinion, the root of this case is the pre-existing agreement between Datronics and the various companies whose stocks it spun off with no apparent purpose other than the incidental benefits of creation of a public market for the stock. If the transactions were with a view to creating a public market for the stock which the various companies could not otherwise do absent compliance with the statute, then I think Datronics may be held to be an underwriter. The value requirement of a sale, 15 U.S.C. §77b(3), for the issuer (15 U.S.C. §77b(4)) . . . , I think, may be satisfied by the exchange of stock of the various companies with Datronics or by the exchange of stock of the various companies for services of Datronics. *See also* 58 Va. L. Rev. 1451.

NOTES AND QUESTIONS

1. Spin-offs in the Courts.   SEC v. Harwyn Indus. Corp., 326 F. Supp. 943 (S.D.N.Y. 1971), held that a company violated Section 5 by spinning off four of its subsidiaries through a series of stock dividends. Soon after each spin-off, trading developed in each subsidiary's shares. The court concluded that registration was required because each spin-off lacked a business purpose and, therefore, each was viewed as a scheme to create a public market for unregistered shares. The SEC also once counseled that registration is less likely if the spin-off implements a *proper* business objective. *See* Securities Act Release No. 4982 (July 2, 1969). However, as will be seen, the current regulatory focus is on the desired disclosure that accompanies the spin-off.

The Exchange Act's definition of *sale* in Section 3(a)(13) does not include a "for value" requirement, so that an early case involving the Exchange Act's anti-fraud provision did not have to employ a *Datronics*-style analysis to conclude that a spin-off involved the sale of securities. *See International Controls Corp. v. Vesco*, 490 F.2d 1334 (2d Cir.), *cert. denied*, 417 U.S. 932 (1974). Subsequent decisions,

however, have held that spin-offs that are accompanied by misleading disclosures do not involve the purchase or sale of a security. *See Isquith v. Caremark
International Inc.*, 136 F.3d 531 (7th Cir. 1998); *Rathborne v. Rathborne*, 683 F.2d
914, 919-920 (5th Cir. 1982) (sale arises only if "transaction wrought a fundamental change in the nature of the [shareholder's] investment," which does not
occur if after the transaction the plaintiff holds the same proportionate interest
in the parent and the spun-off subsidiary). Would the standard embraced in
Rathborne lead to a different result in *Datronics*?

2. ***Spin-offs and the SEC's Staff.*** The regulatory net the SEC's staff has
woven for spin-offs was formulated over a series of no-action letters and is now
set forth in SEC Staff Legal Bulletin No. 4 (Sept. 16, 1997). The staff, though
still concerned that the spin-off is pursuant to a proper business purpose, places
far greater emphasis upon whether the spin-off was accompanied by adequate
information available about the spun-off company.[4] The current staff position
focuses on whether the distributee-shareholders are provided an "information
statement" (a document that contains information similar to that found in a
registration statement, proxy statement, or annual report). When the spun-off
company is not a reporting company and will not soon become one, the staff has
conditioned its no-action letter on the shares being subject to a transfer restriction so that a public market does not soon develop for the spun-off shares. Id.
at note 5.

Currently, the staff requires all sales of spun-off shares by an affiliate to
comply with Rule 144 (generally the staff also requires that the spun-off company have been a reporting company for 90 days prior to the resale), and sales
by non-affiliates must also be pursuant to Rule 144 if the spun-off company is
not a reporting company. If the spun-off shares are those of a reporting company, non-affiliates may dispose of their shares without concern for Rule 144.

3. ***Spin-offs and the Imaginative Use of Form S-8.*** Another route employed to
take a company public without registration is the artful use of Form S-8. Form
S-8 is an abbreviated registration statement that is available to register securities offered exclusively to the issuers' employees and consultants. Because the
purchasers are essentially insiders, the information required to be disclosed on
Form S-8 is minimal. Promoters have abused Form S-8 by registering shares of
the shell company. In the first step, the entity issues shares to promoters, other
"employees," and "consultants." In the second step, the insiders use a portion
of their shares to acquire a private company. The shares the promoters have
retained are then dumped on the public with no information about the issuer
in either its '33 Act or '34 Act filing. To correct this problem, the SEC now bars
the use of Form S-8 by shell companies (defined as entities with no or nominal assets, or assets consisting solely of cash, or some combination of cash and

---

4. For example, in Genge Industries, Inc., SEC No-Action Letter (May 14, 1971) (WL
Fed Sec file), Genge proposed to spin off its wholly owned subsidiary, which it had formed ten
years earlier, which had continuously been engaged in active business, and which was being
spun off because its business was unrelated to that of Genge. The request for a no-action
letter was declined because there was no public information about the subsidiary available to
the shareholders or the markets.

nominal assets). As further protection to investors, Form 8-K requires filing of information by a shell company bearing on a transaction that causes it to cease being a shell company. Excluded from the definition of shell company is an entity created specifically to facilitate reincorporation or an acquisition by an operating company. *See* Securities Act Release No. 8587 (June 29, 2005).

b. The Regulation of Spin-offs Under the '34 Act

Does *Datronics* employ strained reasoning to reach a result it believes necessary to protect investors? What investors are protected as a result of its alternative conclusions that Datronics was (1) an issuer and (2) an underwriter of the private companies' distributions? The *Datronics* case is an excellent case to consider why Section 2(a)(3) requires "value" for there to be a sale or offer to sell. The objective of Section 5 is to assure that public offerings of securities are accompanied by full disclosure of all information pertinent to the issuer and the offering. In a macroeconomic sense, the '33 Act disclosure facilitates the allocation of capital among competing enterprises. In a microeconomic sense, it enables offerees to protect themselves by having a better set of information about the offering than if the '33 Act had not been enacted. When offerees do not pay cash or exchange property for the offered shares, it is difficult to envision how either of these '33 Act objectives is threatened. In this way, the "for value" requirement is an indispensable element in accomplishing the objectives of the '33 Act.

It cannot be said that Datronics' stockholders were separated from any portion of their personal wealth as a result of the spin-offs, and, accordingly, it appears strained to conclude that as a result of receiving the stock dividends the Datronics stockholders reduced their investment in competing investment alternatives. How then were the objectives of the '33 Act threatened by Datronics' spin-offs? To be sure, secondary trading in the spun-off companies' stocks that followed the spin-offs occurred without there being adequate information about those companies, so that trading in those stocks could not be viewed as reflecting informed trading choices. Such trading is disquieting because economists, regulators, and Congress have long believed that the risk-return relationships established by public *trading* in outstanding securities indirectly affect the allocation of capital among operating companies. Nevertheless, the protection, efficiency, and fairness of trading markets are the object of the '34 Act, not the '33 Act. This no doubt explains why the most significant regulatory initiative against abusive spin-offs is through the Commission's exercise of its rulemaking authority under the '34 Act in adopting Rule 15c2-11, discussed below, with the goal of providing information to *trading* markets. Does this salve our unease with the reasoning of *Datronics* and its progeny?

The abusive spin-off illustrated in *Datronics* is a variation on a much larger market manipulation problem endemic to public trading in shell corporations. More recently, this problem has been referred to as the manipulation of *penny stocks*. Typically, the shell corporation scheme begins with sharp promoters acquiring control, through one means or another, of a dormant company, preferably one with a large number of shareholders. Frequently, the sole asset of the company is a large number of stockholders and a few broker-dealers that previously made a market in the shell's stock. Each ultimately becomes an underwriting participant or victim in the scheme. The promoters next instigate optimistic rumors about the shell's properties, management's plans, and the like. Of course, the rumors are not factually grounded. The full flavor of the rumors is suggested by the following announcement that the Commission required one shell company to release in the face of such unfounded rumors:

> The following rumors concerning Santa Fe have been circulating, none of which are true. They are absolutely *false.* We do not have two former governors of Colorado on our board of directors. We are not operating a silver mine. We are not being taken over by an insurance company. We do not have the food and beverage concessions on the ship Queen Elizabeth. We are not contemplating building a ski lodge near Georgetown, Colorado. . . . As of February 1, 1968, the company . . . had current assets consisting of cash in the sum of $7.80.

Santa Fe International, Inc., Exchange Act Release No. 8284 (Mar. 27, 1968). But the promoters generally are more resourceful than to rely on rumors alone to whet the public's appetite for the shell corporation's stock. The promoters often engage in one or more traditional forms of stock price manipulation, such as launching a series of purchases of the shell stock at rising prices or entering fictitious quotations for the shell corporation's securities. The object of each step is to attract sufficient interest in the stock to raise its price so that the promoters can unload their holdings at a healthy profit. A key operator in the scheme generally is the broker-dealer who serves as a market maker for the shell corporation's fictitious bids designed to drive the shell's securities price upward; the market maker may enter arbitrary quotations for the shell's stock or unleash its force of salespeople to recommend the shell security to investors without adequate factual basis for a positive recommendation. Such are the market abuses that accompany trading in shell corporations, corporations whose characteristics are not much different from the spin-offs engaged in by Datronics.

The SEC adopted Rule 15c2-11 in 1971 in order to avoid the artificial distinction between conventional and modern spin-offs, to focus directly upon the real concerns posed by unregistered spin-offs, and also to deal with a wider array of other securities transactions giving rise to the same regulatory concern: public trading in securities about which there is little information publicly available.

Exchange Act Release No. 27247
Securities and Exchange Commission (Sept. 1989)

B. Operation of Current Rule 15c2-11

Rule 15c2-11 regulates the initiation or resumption of quotations in a quotation medium by a broker or dealer for certain over-the-counter securities. Adopted in 1971, the Rule was designed primarily to prevent certain manipulative and fraudulent trading schemes that had arisen in connection with the distribution and trading of unregistered securities issued by shell companies,[14] or other companies having outstanding but infrequently-traded securities. The Rule was intended to prevent brokers and dealers from furnishing initial quotations in the absence of any information about the issuer, an activity that was critical to the success of many of the unlawful schemes.[15] The Rule focuses on the fraudulent and manipulative potential of quotations. A violation of the Rule may occur regardless of whether the broker-dealer also is engaged in retail activity in the security, or whether any interdealer transactions have occurred.

Subject to certain exceptions,[19] the Rule prohibits a broker or dealer from submitting a quotation[20] for a security in a quotation medium unless it has in its records specified information concerning the security and the issuer and, in certain circumstances, furnishes the information to the interdealer quotation system two days before the publication of such quotation. Specifically, a broker or dealer that initiates or resumes a quotation for the securities of an issuer must have in its records: (1) in the case of an issuer that has conducted a recent public offering registered under the Securities Act of 1933 ("Securities Act") or effected pursuant to Regulation A under the Securities Act, a copy of the prospectus or offering circular; or (2) in the case of an issuer that must file with the Commission reports pursuant to Sections 13 or 15(d) of the Exchange Act or is an insurance company of the kind specified in Section 12(g)(2)(G) of the Exchange Act, the issuer's most recent annual report and any reports required to be filed at regular intervals thereafter; or (3) in the case of foreign issuers exempt from Section 12(g) of the Exchange Act, the information furnished to the Commission pursuant to Rule 12g3-2(b) under the Exchange Act. In order to submit a quotation for the security of an issuer that falls into none of the above categories, the broker or dealer must have in its records the sixteen items of information, including certain financial information, specified in paragraph (a)(5) of the Rule. This information must be reasonably current in relation to the day the quotation is submitted, the broker or dealer must have no reasonable basis for believing that the information is not true and correct or reasonably current, and such information must be obtained from sources that the broker or dealer has a reasonable basis for believing are reliable. In addition, paragraph (c) of the Rule requires a broker or dealer to maintain in

---

14. Rule 15c2-11 was intended to address a variety of questionable practices involving a "spin-off" or other distribution to the public of the securities of a shell corporation and the subsequent active trading of those shares at increasingly higher prices that bore no relation to the value of the securities. . . .

15. The Rule "seeks to guard against 'the fraudulent and manipulative potential inherent . . . when a . . . dealer submits quotations concerning any infrequently-traded security in the absence of certain information.'" Gotham Securities Corporation, 46 S.E.C. 723, 725 (1976), *citing* Release 34-9310.

19. The Rule excepts from its coverage publication or submission of a quotation in the over-the-counter market for a security admitted to trading on a national securities exchange (if traded on that exchange on the same day or on the day before submission or publication of the quotation), or . . . [is a Nasdaq security for which trading is not suspended, terminated or prohibited]. *See* paragraphs (f)(1) and (f)(5) of Rule 15c2-11. As a result, the Rule's focus is the residual over-the-counter market, principally reflected in the pink sheets. *See* n.2 supra.

20. "Quotation" is defined in paragraph (e)(3) of the Rule, to include any advertisement by a broker or dealer that he wishes to buy or sell a particular security at a specified price or otherwise. . . .

its records any other information (including adverse information) regarding the issuer that comes to its knowledge or possession before the publication or submission of the quotation. . . .

C.   IMPACT OF A TRADING SUSPENSION ON THE OPERATION OF THE RULE

Following the expiration of any trading suspension in a security, the broker-dealer must satisfy the Rule's information requirements before the initiation or resumption of quotations for the security in a quotation medium.

In order to understand accurately the basis for the trading suspension, the broker-dealer should obtain a copy of the trading suspension order, or a copy of the Commission release announcing the trading suspension. Before initiating or resuming a quotation for pink sheet securities that have been the subject of a trading suspension, the broker-dealer must conduct a careful review in a professional manner of the basis for the trading suspension to determine whether there is a reasonable basis for the broker-dealer to believe that the information about the issuer in the broker-dealer's knowledge or possession is true and correct.[47] The broker-dealer may need to obtain additional information to cure deficiencies in that information. . . .

In conducting its inquiry, the broker-dealer may have to obtain support for the accuracy of the information or the source's reliability by conducting an independent review or obtaining verification of information provided by the issuer or promoter. For example, an opinion of an independent accountant or attorney may be warranted.

A broker-dealer may have difficulty obtaining the necessary information about an issuer after the expiration of a trading suspension. This difficulty, however, does not relieve a broker-dealer of its responsibilities under the Rule. Without having a reasonable basis to believe that its information is true and correct and obtained from reliable sources, the broker-dealer should not submit quotations for the securities of the subject issuer for publication in a quotation medium.

As noted in Chapter 18, the Penny Stock Reform Act of 1990 expands both the Commission's powers over and private remedies against promoters and brokers of penny stocks. *See also* new Section 7(b) of the '33 Act, which empowers the Commission to develop special disclosure rules and rescission rights for *blank check offerings*—offerings where no specific business plan or purpose

---

47.   . . . For example, if the Commission issued a trading suspension because it had serious questions regarding the adequacy or accuracy of the issuer's financial statements, the broker-dealer may be unable to provide itself with a reasonable basis for relying on the questioned financial statements even if they otherwise satisfy the Rule's presumption of "reasonably current" information. *See* 15c2-11(g). The presumption that information is "reasonably current" is vitiated if the broker-dealer has "information to the contrary."

is identified in the registration statement—which frequently are the first step toward manipulation of the issuer's stock.

PROBLEMS

Alasko Inc. is an integrated oil company having both vast petroleum reserves and refinery and retail operations throughout the country. Its common stock is listed on the New York Stock Exchange, and there are over 7,000 Alasko common stockholders. Most of the Alasko directors are the nominees of the Perch family, which owns 27 percent of the Alasko common stock. As part of a major restructuring plan, Alasko proposes to transfer all of its petroleum reserves to a newly created subsidiary, Paydirt, in exchange for 100 million Paydirt common shares. The book value of the reserves per Alasko's financial statements is $250 million. Alasko will next distribute 60 percent of those shares to its stockholders, so that each Alasko stockholder will receive one share of Paydirt for each six shares of Alasko common stock they own. Alasko will retain working control of Paydirt.

7-5.   Must Alasko register the Paydirt shares before their distribution? If not, what should Alasko do to assure that its non-control stockholders may freely resell the Paydirt shares shortly after their receipt?

7-6.   Assume the transaction was completed on January 10 of this year. Aletha Perch wishes to sell 40,000 of her Paydirt shares in the over-the-counter market. When can Aletha sell her Paydirt shares, and what limitations are likely to apply to her resale?

7-7.   Cook will act as Aletha's broker in the resale of her shares. What must Cook do before submitting a quote for Ms. Perch's shares? Does your answer depend upon whether Aletha instructs her broker to submit a specific "asked" price or merely to submit them to the market? *See* Rule 15c2-11(a), (f)(2).

7-8.   Paydirt shares have been actively traded in the over-the-counter market for several weeks. Hunt and Hedge, a registered broker-dealer, makes a market in Paydirt shares. Its files include Paydirt's most recent Exchange Act filings, which reflect a dramatic decline in Paydirt's proven reserves. William, unaware of this information, placed an order through Hunt and Hedge to purchase 300 Paydirt shares. What obligation does Hunt and Hedge have under Rule 15c2-11 to share Paydirt's filings with William?

B.   Mergers, Acquisitions, and Recapitalizations

Business combinations and recapitalizations trigger Section 5 concerns whenever they involve the issuance of securities. Recapitalizations are studied later in connection with Section 3(a)(9) and overall involve any transactions that lead to a "reshuffling" of a firm's capital structure. Recall from your corporate law course that a business combination can take one of several basic forms (and there are an endless number of permutations within each of these forms). First, it may involve a straight merger under which, for example, Beta Corporation is acquired by Alpha Corporation. A second form of business combination is achieved through the sale of all or some of the selling corporation's assets to the purchasing corporation. For example, Alpha may purchase Beta's assets. A third method of combination is the tender offer, the subject of Chapter 17, whereby the acquiring company offers to acquire some or all of the outstanding shares of another company. Thus, Alpha may publish an offer to acquire all outstanding Beta common shares. For the sake of simplicity, the following assumes that in carrying out its acquisition of Beta, Alpha issues its securities as part of the consideration in the combination.

The corporate law procedures and effects for each transaction are different. Under the third method (i.e., the tender offer), an offer of securities of the acquiring company (Alpha) is made directly to the shareholders of the acquired company (Beta). If the acquisition takes the form of either a merger or a purchase of assets, on the other hand, a vote of the shareholders of the company to be acquired is required. Finally, recall that one consequence of a merger is that the acquired company is dissolved by operation of law and the securities issued as consideration for the merger are issued directly to the shareholders of the acquired company. In contrast, the stockholders' vote to sell all or substantially all of the firm's assets does not dissolve their corporation, so that a separate resolution dissolving the selling corporation is generally necessary to allow the consideration received in the sale to be distributed to the selling shareholders as a liquidating distribution.

1. Rule 145

Former Rule 133 provided that securities issued pursuant to combinations structured as either mergers or purchases of assets were beyond Section 5 because the submission of the acquisition transaction to a vote of the shareholders was not deemed to involve a "sale" or "offer to sell" the acquiring company's shares. The "no-sale" doctrine of Rule 133 applied only to the Securities Act; the courts and the Commission held that under the Exchange Act securities issued in mergers or purchases of assets did involve the "sale" as well as the "purchase" of securities so that the Exchange Act's antifraud rule applied. Rule 133 was rescinded in 1972, thus extending the regulatory reach of Section 5 to mergers and sales of assets. Today, Rules 145, 165, and 166 regulate much of the scope of Section 5 when securities are issued in connection with most business combinations. Rule 145 was adopted in 1972 to replace Rule 133, and Rules 165 and 166 are important components of the Commission's 1999 Regulation M-A, which introduced sweeping changes in the regulation not only for business combinations in general, but also, as will be seen in Chapters 16 and 17, reformed the rules that apply to proxy solicitations, tender offers, and going private transactions.

There are three types of Rule 145 transactions that are prescribed in paragraph (a) of the Rule, provided each involves a vote or consent of the stockholders: recapitalizations, mergers, and certain transfers of assets (e.g., where the selling company is required to dissolve or distribute the securities received from the transfer within one year). Whether a transaction falls within Rule 145 is important for two important reasons. First and foremost, Rules 165 and 166, discussed below, apply only to transactions that fall within Rule 145 (or arise in a tender offer in which the issuer's securities are exchanged for those held by the target company's stockholders). Thus, the definitions provided in Rule 145(a) are the gateway for the relaxed regulatory treatment provided by Rules 165 and 166. Second, Rule 145(c) expands the scope of *underwriter* to include a holder who was a control person of the acquired or recapitalized *shell* company prior to the Rule 145 transaction (such person is referred to as a "Rule 145 affiliate"). A shell company is defined in Rule 405 as a firm with no or nominal operations and with assets that are either only cash or nominal except for cash. This underwriter status applies even though after the acquisition the holder is not a control person of the acquiring company. Other (non-control) security holders of the acquired company who receive registered securities are not underwriters, so their resale of registered securities poses no Section 5 concerns; however, if the securities they received in the Rule 145 transaction were issued pursuant to an exemption, their resale of those securities must occur pursuant to the restrictions that apply to the particular exemption used to carry out the Rule 145 transaction.

2.   Jumping the Gun in Business Combinations

Before the adoption of Rules 165 and 166, those involved in mergers and other acquisitions were barred from releasing deal-related disclosures prior to filing a registration statement. Such disclosures when made outside the registration statement posed the classic gun-jumping considerations examined in Chapter 4. As seen in the following SEC release accompanying the SEC's adoption of Rules 165 and 166, Regulation M-A significantly lifts the heavy regulatory hand of Section 5 with respect to the release of deal-related information. The deregulatory steps the SEC took in adopting Regulation M-A forecast the broad reform it launched in 2005 for the public offering process. Despite the otherwise sweeping nature of the 2005 reforms, the importance of Regulation M-A continues because most of the communication reforms in 2005 do not apply to transactions falling within Regulation M-A.

| **Excerpt from the Release Adopting Regulation M-A**
Securities Act Release No. 7760 (Oct. 22, 1999)

A.   OVERVIEW

1.   INCREASED COMMUNICATIONS PERMITTED BEFORE FILING DISCLOSURE DOCUMENT

Today, merger and acquisition transactions are occurring at a faster pace, due in part to the rapid development of new technologies and advancements in communications. As a result of economic and regulatory pressures, many companies are releasing more information to the market before a registration, proxy or tender offer statement is filed publicly with us. In many cases, parties are releasing information on proposed transactions including pro forma financial information for the combined entity, estimated cost savings and synergies. . . .

Existing restrictions on [the release of] communications . . . [arise] primarily from the broad concepts of "offer" and "prospectus" under the Securities Act, "solicitation" under the Exchange Act proxy rules, and "commencement" under the Williams Act tender offer rules. We recognize that restricting communications to one document may actually impede, rather than promote, informed investing and voting decisions.

We are adopting, as proposed, non-exclusive exemptions under the Securities Act, proxy rules and tender offer rules that permit communications for an unrestricted length of time. . . . Written communications made in reliance on the exemptions must be filed [with the SEC]. . . .

[T]he rules adopted today are designed to reduce selective disclosure by permitting widespread dissemination of information through a variety of media calculated to inform all security holders about the terms, benefits and risks of a planned extraordinary transaction. . . . [However, the new rules do not require oral communications to be reduced to writing and filed.] The new regulatory scheme is not intended to be used as a means to substitute selective oral disclosure for written and oral disclosure that becomes public on a widespread basis. Although this release does not impose new requirements on oral communications, we remain extremely troubled by the selective disclosure of material information. . . .

2. ELIGIBILITY

Our proposals did not make distinctions based on size and seasoned status. Due to the extraordinary nature of business combination transactions, security holders and the markets need full and timely information regarding those transactions regardless of the size or seasoned status of the companies involved. . . . Therefore, the exemptions are adopted as proposed, without any eligibility requirements. . . .

3. WRITTEN COMMUNICATIONS WITH LEGEND FILED ON DATE OF FIRST USE

We are adopting . . . a condition to the communications exemptions that all written communications in connection with or relating to a business combination transaction be filed on or before the date of first use. In addition, all written communications must include a prominent legend advising investors to read the registration, proxy or tender offer statement, as applicable. We believe that a prompt filing requirement is necessary to protect security holders and assure that these communications are available to all investors on a timely basis. In most cases, this information will need to be filed electronically via the EDGAR System, and thus will be rapidly disseminated to the marketplace. . . .

We believe . . . that in most cases parties to business combination transactions will be able to time their communications so that it is possible to file them on the same day they are made. Also, Rule 13(d) of Regulation S-T permits communications that are made outside of the Commission's business hours to be filed electronically as soon as practicable on the next business day. Further, we have clarified that an immaterial or unintentional delay in filing will not preclude reliance on the Securities Act exemption.

The filing requirement applies to written communications that are made public or are otherwise provided to persons that are not a party to the transaction. As a general matter, this would include, for example, scripts used by parties to the transaction to communicate information to the public and other written material (e.g., slides) relating to the transaction that is shown to investors. In contrast, internal written communications provided solely to parties to the transaction, legal counsel, financial advisors, and similar persons authorized to act on behalf of the parties to the transaction would not need to be filed. Also, as explained in the Proposing Release, business information that is factual in nature and relates solely to ordinary business matters, and not the pending transaction, would not need to be filed. . . .

B. COMMUNICATIONS UNDER THE SECURITIES ACT

1. SECURITIES ACT EXEMPTION AND FILING RULES

. . . These new and amended rules permit parties to communicate freely about a planned business combination transaction before a registration statement is filed, as well as during the waiting period and post-effective periods, so long as their written communications used in connection with or relating to the transaction are filed beginning with the first public announcement and ending with the close of the proposed transaction. . . .

New Rules 165 and 166 are available only for business combination transactions. New Rule 165 defines a business combination transaction as a transaction specified in Rule 145(a) or an exchange offer. Thus, either the proxy rules or the tender offer rules must be applicable to the transaction. We have added a preliminary note to Rules 165 and 166 to state that the exemption is not available to communications that may technically comply with the rule, but have the primary purpose or effect of conditioning the market for a capital-raising or resale transaction.[56]

2. LIABILITY FOR COMMUNICATIONS

. . . [B]oth oral and written communications made in reliance on the Securities Act exemption would be offers subject to Section 12(a)(2) liability, based on the belief that this level of liability would adequately protect investors without chilling communications. . . .

---

56. For example, the exemption would not be available where a non-reporting issuer conducts an exchange offer primarily for the purposes of giving its investors freely tradable securities and creating a public market in, or manipulating the market for, those securities. Likewise, it would be inappropriate to rely on the exemptions in effecting a merger of a public "shell" company to take a private company public. These mergers commonly are used to develop a market for the merged entity's securities, often as part of a scheme to manipulate the market for those securities.

Several commenters . . . were concerned that a failure to timely file a written communication could result in a loss of protection under the exemption, resulting in a Section 5 violation that would give security holders a right of rescission. In proposing the filing requirement, we did not intend to provide security holders with an automatic right of rescission if a communication is either filed late or there is an unintentional failure to file. To clarify this issue, we are revising the filing requirement in new Rule 165 to state that an immaterial or unintentional failure to file or delay in filing will not result in a loss of the exemption from section 5(b)(1) or (c), so long as a good faith and reasonable attempt to file the written communication is made and the communication is filed as soon as practicable after discovery of the failure to file.[59] . . .

4. PUBLIC ANNOUNCEMENT

Under the terms of the exemptions, written communications must be filed beginning with the first public announcement of the business combination transaction. Today we are adopting a specific definition of "public announcement" that encompasses all communications that put the market on notice of a proposed transaction. For purposes of determining when a filing obligation is incurred under the exemptions, "public announcement" means any communication by a party to the transaction, or any person authorized to act on a party's behalf, that is reasonably designed to, or has the effect of, informing the public or security holders in general about the transaction.[66] . . .

NOTES AND QUESTIONS

1. Form S-4. Form S-4 is used to register securities issued not only in mergers and purchases of assets, but also in other forms of business combinations, such as share exchanges (i.e., offers of securities in connection with tender offers). Form S-4 builds upon the integrated disclosure practices of Form S-3, so that large, seasoned issuers who could use Form S-3 in a traditional public offering can in a business combination incorporate most issuer-oriented information by reference from its '34 Act filings. A further advantage of Form S-4 is that under Rule 14a-6 it doubles as the proxy statement when stockholder approval of the combination is sought.

There are four distinct sections to Form S-4. The first section presents information about the combination or exchange offer itself. Next, there is

---

59. New Rule 165(e). . . . Factors to be considered in determining whether a delay in filing is immaterial or unintentional include: the nature of the information, the length of the delay, and the surrounding circumstances, including whether a bona fide effort was made to file timely. If a written communication is made late in the day and the offeror attempts to file it, but experiences difficulty in filing electronically on EDGAR, and files as soon as practicable after business hours or the following business day, the exemption will continue to be available.

66. New Rule 165(f)(3). A similar definition of "public announcement" is included in revised Rules 13e-4(c) and 14d-2(b).

information about the issuer. The third section presents information about the company being acquired. The degree to which information in this section can be incorporated by reference is determined by whether the acquired company is eligible to avail itself generally of the integrated disclosure system when registering its securities (e.g., eligible to use Form S-3). The final section sets forth the requirements surrounding the combination's approval (e.g., appraisal remedy, revocability of proxy, etc.). Finally, it should be observed that offers in connection with business combinations are "continuing offers" and hence must comply with the shelf registration requirements of Rule 415(a)(1)(viii).

With the expansion of Regulation A to reporting companies, Regulation A may be more attractive for carrying out acquisitions that fit within its dollar limits. For example, registered offerings impose a strict liability standard on issuers per Section 11, whereas issuers and others under Section 12(a)(2) enjoy the defense of "did not know and in the exercise of reasonable care could not have known." Moreover, the disclosures mandated by Regulation A are not as burdensome.

2. Prospectus Delivery in Corporate Combinations.   Rule 153a defines the Section's expression "preceded by a prospectus." The Rule addresses the very real likelihood that those voting or consenting to the transaction may not be the same individuals who later receive the securities issued in connection with the transaction.

> The persons entitled to vote or consent to a Rule 145 transaction will usually be determined either: (1) by the fixing of a record date for shareholders so entitled or, (2) by the closing of the stock transfer records of the acquired company. The group of persons thus determined may, because of interim transfers, vary somewhat from the group of persons ultimately entitled to receive the securities issued the transaction. . . . [R]ule 153A provides that the delivery of the final prospectus to security holders entitled to vote on or consent to the transaction shall be deemed to satisfy the prospectus delivery requirements of Section 5(b)(2) of the Act.

Securities Act Release No. 5316 (Oct. 6, 1972).

3. Parsing the Scope of Underwriter in Rule 145(c).   Rule 145(c) defines who is an underwriter in a Rule 145 transaction in the narrow context of shell companies as defined in Rule 405. Rule 145 does not define who should be deemed an underwriter in a transaction beyond Rule 145 or, for that matter, outside of shell companies. Having carved out a fairly narrow, albeit rigid, test for who is an underwriter, should this be seen as the exclusive standard for determining who is an underwriter? For example, assume Beta (a shell company) is acquired by Alpha in a merger that falls within Rule 145(a)(2) and the Alpha shares were not registered because the offering to the Beta shareholders falls within the private offering exemption of Section 4(a)(2). Can the former Beta shareholders sell their newly acquired Alpha shares without concern for violating Section 5? *See* Campbell, Resales of Securities Under the Securities Act of 1933, 52 Wash. & Lee L. Rev. 1333, 1362-1376 (1995).

3.　Reverse Mergers

A reverse merger is a transaction in which a private company becomes public by merging with a public "shell company." The shell company can be either a newly formed company or a former operating company that has become dormant.

In the former, investors have been attracted by vague plans to use the investors' funds to acquire emerging technologies and the like. When this approach is taken, the formed entity is known as a "special-purpose acquisition company" (SPAC). One issue faced by the SPAC is Rule 419, discussed earlier in Chapter 4 with reference to "blank stock offerings." There we found that Rule 419 requires escrowing of funds and shares accompanying the registration of blank check offerings (with the escrow being lifted once certain conditions are satisfied). However, Rule 419 applies only to "penny stock" offerings; per Exchange Act Rule 3a51-1(g), plus a helpful SEC interpretation of the rule, the escrow requirement is avoided if the blank check offering is a firm commitment offering that raises more than $5 million. *See* Penny Stock Definition for Purposes of Blank Check Rule, Securities Act Release No. 7024 (Oct. 25, 1993). Thus, the funds raised through the firm commitment underwriting enable the SPAC to later acquire a private operating company. Due to the earlier public offering, the SPAC would be a reporting company at least for the fiscal year following that offering. SPACs represented 7 percent of the funds raised through new issues in 2006. Cowan, "Blank Checks" Generate New Interest, Wall St. J., Dec. 24, 2007, at C-1. *See generally* Sjostrom, The Truth About Reverse Mergers, Entrepreneurial Bus. L.J. 743 (2008).

In contrast to using a SPAC, the reverse merger may occur with a dormant shell. Most dormant shells are what remain of a former operating company that has since been stripped of its operating assets, perhaps through bankruptcy (in which some of its creditors were issued shares pursuant to the Bankruptcy Act exemption in Section 1145, discussed later in this chapter). Reverse mergers into a dormant shell rarely occur in isolation; they regularly are the first step toward raising capital, usually via a PIPE transaction as described in Chapter 6.

In the last decade, reverse mergers have been a more popular route for going public. They pose substantially lower costs than an IPO and can be accomplished more quickly. Thus, in 2008-2016 period there were 1007 companies going public through an IPO compared to 1,346 going public through a reverse merger. *See* Bayar, Liu & Mao, How Reverse Merger Firms Raise Capital in PIPEs: Search Costs and Placement Agent Reputation, 2019 working paper, *available at* https://ssrn.com/abstract=3410696 (30.6 percent of the reverse merger firms shortly after going public raised capital through a PIPE but much larger sums were raised by IPO firms).

The well-understood benefits of a reverse merger led to problems in 2011-2012 when reverse merger transactions became largely synonymous with Chinese companies accessing U.S. capital markets via the backdoor. The influx into U.S. markets of the small and newly created Chinese companies was due to their facing serious obstacles to raising funds in China. Non-state-owned Chinese companies have limited access to domestic bank financing and the rigorous merit form of regulation carried out by the Chinese Securities Regulatory Commission (CSRC) foreclosed most infant firms from their home country equity markets. To be sure, the still infant ChiNext market, launched by the CSRC in 2009, relaxes some restrictions for small firms to be accepted for trading on that market. However, many companies with operations in China are not formed under the laws of the PRC and, therefore, not available for listing on ChiNext or for that matter the Shanghai or Shenzhen Exchanges. Hence, we find the lure of foreign markets to Chinese firms.

Reverse mergers have not entirely escaped the watchful eyes of regulators. Even though a company that goes public through a reverse merger thereby avoids the lengthy review process of Securities Act registration as well as the threat of Section 11 liability of the '33 Act, it may nonetheless become subject to the Exchange Act's reporting requirements if the resulting entity either is listed or has 2,000 or more record holders. And, if the shell company was a reporting company prior to the reverse merger, Items 2.01(f) & 5.06 of Form 8-K require it to disclose material terms and certain financial information regarding the reverse merger transaction within four business days. The disclosures so mandated parallel those that a company must make on Form 10 when initially registering under Section 12 of the Exchange Act. An important part of the Form 8-K disclosure process is the provision of audited financial statements and certain pro-forma statements for the business acquired. Unfortunately, scores of Chinese companies who entered U.S. markets via reverse mergers took advantage of the laxer oversight of Exchange Act reports; beginning in 2010 they collapsed under the weight of their own fraudulent acts.

Among other developments, in late 2011 the NYSE and Nasdaq began requiring a one-year seasoning period following the reverse merger transaction, i.e., the company traded for at least a year in an over-the-counter market in the United States or a foreign exchange, and coupled with this a requirement that in the 30-60 days prior to listing in the United States the firm has maintained a stable minimum share price. An exception to this requirement exists if the company has engaged in a firm commitment underwriting of its securities. Additionally, remember that those in control of the shell company, pursuant to Rule 145(c), are deemed "Rule 145 affiliates" so that their resale of any unregistered security must occur pursuant to the limitations set forth in paragraph (d) of Rule 145. Hence the definition of a "shell company" and "control" in Rule 405 are important in the regulation of steps toward a reverse merger. Moreover, those who received shares from a Rule 145 affiliate need to be cautious as well. In *SEC v. M & A West, Inc.*, 538 F.3d 1043, 1051-1053 (9th Cir. 2008), a shell promoter who engaged in several reverse mergers in which he arranged for sales by the private companies and received *from their founders* shares as compensation for arranging the reverse merger was deemed to be an underwriter due to purchasing shares from an affiliate. This result was reached, even though upon the completion of the reverse merger, the founders no longer were affiliates of the surviving company. The majority of the panel reasoned:

> Where a single transaction accomplishes both a change in status from an affiliate to a non-affiliate and a transfer of stock from that person or entity, the transfer must be viewed as a transfer from an affiliate. . . . The Supreme Court has long instructed that securities law places emphasis on economic reality and disregards form for substance. *See SEC v. W.J. Howey Co.* . . . Where a single transaction accomplishes both a change in status from an affiliate to a non-affiliate and a transfer of

stock from that person or entity, the transfer must be viewed as a transfer from an affiliate for the purposes of determining *Rule 144(k)* eligibility. The existence of multiple agreements bears little effect when the agreements collectively constitute a single transaction.

The multiple regulatory tweakings for reverse mergers reflect the particularly bad experience of American investors with PRC reverse mergers. For example, Reuters in 2011 found an $18 billion market decline for 122 Chinese reverse merger companies. Other studies of reverse mergers during the same time period document that reverse mergers have produced dramatic losses for their investors and more so for those involving PRC companies. Consider here the policy conundrum for regulators: balancing the needs of investors through the costly IPO process against the benefits of enabling firms efficiently to raise capital.

PROBLEMS

Alpha, Inc., is a conglomerate with assets in excess of $60 million. Its 4 million outstanding common shares are traded in the over-the-counter market and it is a public company. On average, about 60,000 Alpha common shares are traded each week.

Beta Company is a biotechnology company and is publicly traded. Ruth owns 60 percent of the Beta common stock.

Examine the following transactions under the Securities Act.

7-9. On January 10, Beta's board of directors agreed to sell all of its assets to Alpha in exchange for Alpha common stock. The terms of the sale call for Beta to dissolve so that the Alpha shares will be distributed to its shareholders: Ten shares of Alpha common will be exchanged for each share of Beta preferred, and six shares of Alpha common will be exchanged for each share of Beta common. Beta plans to convene a special stockholders meeting so that its common stockholders can approve the sale as well as the company's dissolution and the preferred stockholders can approve an amendment of the articles of incorporation that will redefine their rights so that upon dissolution one Beta preferred share is entitled to ten Alpha shares. Soon after the Beta board approved the terms of the combination with Alpha, it proposes to send to each Beta stockholder a letter setting forth the terms of the various transactions and the opinion of its investment banker that the transaction is fair to the common and preferred shareholders. How would you advise Beta? Can Alpha circulate a similar communication among its stockholders?

7-10. Assume that instead of circulating a letter to stockholders, Beta's management conducted a series of meetings with representatives of financial institutions that held Beta shares. At the meetings, Beta management through their PowerPoint presentations set forth the terms of the combination with Alpha and extolled its virtues for its common and preferred stockholders. Later, when it filed its proxy statements, copies of the PowerPoint presentation were filed with the SEC. Has Beta violated Section 5?

7-11.   Assume the facts as stated in Problem 7-9 and that proxies soliciting the stockholders' approval were circulated on March 1 to the holders of record. Beta's bylaws provide that only holders of record 30 days in advance of any meeting may vote at any meeting. Alex acquired Beta common shares on March 15 and did not receive a copy of the proxy materials and did not vote at the meeting. The Beta stockholders approved the various resolutions at a special stockholders meeting on March 26. Must a prospectus be forwarded to Alex when the 10,000 Alpha shares are mailed to him?

7-12.   Assume the facts as stated in Problem 7-9. Immediately following Beta's dissolution, Ruth (who formerly owned 60 percent of Beta) plans to sell about 150,000 Alpha shares in the over-the-counter market. What instructions would you give her broker? What is the result if Alex wishes to dispose of the shares he acquired in Problem 7-11? What result if Ruth is instead a 60 percent owner of Alpha shares, and Alpha is a company that for several months had few assets and no material operations?

7-13.   What restrictions apply to the proposed resales by Ruth and Alex if Beta was closely held and both Ruth and Alex acquired their Alpha shares in a Rule 145 transaction that also satisfied the requirements of Rule 506 of Regulation D?

7-14.   In February, Sly paid $100,000 to the bankruptcy trustee for Zippo Inc. and received 1 million unissued Zippo shares. Zippo was then in the final stages of an orderly liquidation of its affairs. Indeed, the transaction with Sly was the last transaction in wrapping up the bankrupt estate, leaving its nearly 2,500 Zippo stockholders, of which Sly was the largest, with no operating assets and a bank account of slightly in excess of $100,000, and holding shares in what was left of Zippo. Thereafter, in late July, Zippo's board of directors approved the purchase of TsingWa Ltd. Fabricators, issuing 2 million common shares to acquire TsingWa. The transaction was approved by Zippos stockholders. Zippo relied on Regulation S to issue the shares. Tsing Wa's assets are fairly valued at $12 million, but its liabilities were nearly $5 million. Simultaneous with the TsingWa acquisition, Zippo privately raised $25 million with Fund4Few, issuing non-voting preferred shares that were convertible into common shares that Zippo undertook to register with the SEC within the next year. What disclosure requirements does Zippo face and when must the disclosures occur?

7-15.   In the preceding problem, what advice do you give to Sly if in September, just before the filing with the SEC of a registration statement for common shares, Sly wishes to sell most of his shares in the over-the-counter market?

C.   *Exchanges Under Section 3(a)(9)*

Section 3(a)(9) exempts "[a]ny security exchanged by the issuer with its existing security holders exclusively where no commission or other remuneration is paid or given directly or indirectly for soliciting such exchange." This exemption was stimulated by the economic necessities of the 1930s, a time when a large number of corporations were undergoing voluntary readjustments of their financial obligations. *See* H.R. Rep. No. 152, 73d Cong., 1st Sess. 25 (1933). The exemption, however, is not limited to issuers whose financial difficulties force them to exchange, for example, common stock for their outstanding and overdue debentures. The exemption applies to a wide range of corporate transactions without regard to the issuer's financial position.

The traditional format of the Section 3(a)(9) exchange involves the issuer's offer to swap a new security for its old security. The issuer may, for example, wish to relieve itself of the periodic demands its outstanding preferred stock makes on its cash flow by offering to exchange common shares for those preferred shares. Such recapitalizations were more prevalent in the aftermath of the Great Depression, when preferred stock was more frequently a financing device and corporations found themselves saddled with burdensome dividend arrearages due their preferred stockholders. When a corporation is seriously behind in its preferred stock dividends, an exchange reorganization is a useful, if not necessary, vehicle to take the corporation to a fresh start. An exchange can also be forced upon all holders of a class by an amendment of the corporation's articles of incorporation if a majority of the shares approve. More recently, corporations have used exchanges to take the company private or to issue "poison pills" in defense of a takeover.

Many exchanges occurring within Section 3(a)(9) are elective with the individual stockholder. For example, the standard conversion feature of a debenture when exercised can be an exchange under Section 3(a)(9), so that the conversion is exempt.

An interesting question under Section 5 is raised whenever a security is convertible into another security. Under Section 2(a)(3), there is no sale of the underlying security at the time the convertible security is sold, provided the convertible security's terms do not permit *immediate* conversion into the underlying security.

> Another problem . . . of the §3(a)(9) exemption is created by the provision in §2(a)(3) . . . to the effect that the issuance of a security pursuant to a delayed conversion privilege is not a *sale* until the privilege is exercised. In such a case . . . the §3(a)(9) exemption is available for future conversions. On the other hand, when a company issues preferred stock immediately convertible into common . . . there is a present *offer* of the common. What, then, is the status of the common under §3(a)(9)? In a sense, the consideration given for the common is simply the preferred stock. On the other hand, when a purchaser pays $100 for a share of convertible preferred that he or she immediately converts into common, it does not seem altogether realistic to consider that he or she did not have an eye in part on the common when he or she parted with his or her money. . . . [In such cases] the Commission has required registration of the common along with the preferred on the ground that the *initial offer* . . . is not an exchange transaction, while regarding the actual *sale* . . . as exempt. In other words, although §3(a)(9) is not considered to exempt the initial offer of the common stock from the *registration* provisions of §§5(a) and 5(c), it is considered to exempt its issuance from the *prospectus* provisions of §5(b). More than that, the exemption extends also to the *continuing* offer of the common inherent in the convertible securities once they have all been issued. . . .

L. Loss, J. Seligman & T. Paredes, 3 Securities Regulation 162-163 (5th ed. 2015).

Section 3(a)(9)'s scope is narrowed significantly by the dual emphasis the Commission accords the awkward placement of "exclusively" in the exemption. For an exchange to qualify for the exemption, it must be *exclusively* with the security holders of the issuer. The exemption is lost if the offering includes those who are not the issuer's existing security holders. Why should the exemption be lost if, as part of revitalizing a failing company, new shares of common stock are sold to venture capitalists at the same time the company is exchanging common shares for its outstanding preferred shares? The exclusivity requirement raises the now-familiar question of whether other security offerings by the issuer should be integrated with the exchange offer. For example, if at the same time the issuer is offering to exchange its newly authorized preferred stock for its outstanding debentures it is also offering the preferred stock to the public, the Section 3(a)(9) exemption will be lost if both preferred stock offerings are integrated. *See* Securities Act Release No. 2029 (Aug. 8, 1939).

The word "exclusively" also modifies the consideration permitted in the exchange transaction. The exemption is not available if the existing security holders must, as a condition of the exchange, pay any consideration in addition to their old securities. Therefore, if stockholders are required not only to give up their shares, but also to pay new consideration as part of the exchange offer, the Section 3(a)(9) exemption is unavailable. The limitation is relaxed somewhat by Rule 149, which provides that security holders can be required to make cash payments when "necessary to effect an equitable adjustment" in the dividends or interest for the exchanged securities as between the security holders accepting the exchange offer. The Commission interprets the exclusivity limitation as barring only *new* consideration being paid, so that the exemption is not lost because the security holders as part of the exchange offer's terms must surrender voting rights, accrued dividends or interest, or collateral for their debentures. And the holders' agreement as part of the exchange transaction to drop their securities fraud action against the issuer was not seen by the SEC's staff as a cause to lose the exemption. *See* First Pennsylvania Mortgage Trust, SEC No-Action Letter, 1977 WL 13863 (Feb. 4, 1977). In view of the fact that the regulatory concern of the '33 Act is consideration passing *from the public* to the issuer, is it surprising that Rule 150 permits additional consideration to pass *from the issuer* to its existing security holders?

The exemption also is conditioned upon "no commission or other remuneration" being paid, directly or indirectly, in soliciting the exchange. The prohibition does not prevent directors and officers from urging shareholders to accept the exchange offer, nor does it prevent the issuer from retaining someone to assist it in the mechanical aspects of implementing the exchange. But such a third-party provider cannot engage in solicitation activities. As seen in other contexts, the line between permissible professional services that are mechanical and those that constitute solicitation is not a bright one. For example, the SEC granted a no-action request to an issuer using its investment banker to negotiate with representatives of certain institutional holders the exchange terms acceptable to them. *See* Seaman Furniture Co., SEC No-Action Letter, [1989-1990 Transfer Binder] Fed. Sec. L. Rep. (CCH) ¶79,360 (Oct. 10, 1989).

NOTES AND QUESTIONS

1. ***Who Is the Issuer in a Section 3(a)(9) Exchange?*** A recurrent problem is the exemption's requirement that the exchange be "by the issuer with its existing security holders." In most cases, this can be resolved easily by asking whether the securities to be exchanged are of the same issuer. But this is not a strictly literal inquiry. For example, when the holding company structure is being eliminated by holders in the holding company obtaining the same proportionate interest in the operating company, the SEC's staff granted a no-action request indicating that Section 3(a)(9) was available. *See* Union Carbide Corp., SEC No-Action Letter, [1994-1995 Transfer Binder] Fed. Sec. L. Rep. (CCH) ¶76,910 (Sept. 6, 1994). And if Alpha in its acquisition of Beta assumes all the duties and obligations under Beta's outstanding debentures, Alpha in effect is Beta, so that a later offer to exchange Alpha common for the outstanding Beta debentures will fall within Section 3(a)(9). However, even slight differences between the successor and predecessor issuers' undertakings or form will prevent the equivalence of the former with the latter for the purposes of Section 3(a)(9).

2. ***Resales of Section 3(a)(9) Securities.*** Section 3(a)(9) is a transaction exemption. It exempts only the issuer's exchange;[5] the exchanging security holder must find her own exemption for any subsequent sale of a security received in the exempted exchange.[6] Thus, control persons who are considering resales of securities received in an exchange should consider whether their resale will involve an underwriter transaction under the last sentence of Section 2(a)(11). If so, that resale is beyond the exemption provided in Section 4(a)(1). If the security given up was acquired earlier in an exempt transaction, for example, in a private or an intrastate offering, the taint of the earlier owned security attaches to the newly acquired security. This is unaffected by whether the exchange is a "reclassification" that complies with Rule 145(a)(1) or not. *See* Campbell, Resales of Securities: The New Rules and the New Approach of the SEC, 37 Sec. Reg. L.J. 317, 331 (2009). Thus, any resale of the security acquired in the exchange is subject to the same resale restrictions that would have applied to the security given up in the exchange; such a holder's four options are to

---

5. *SEC v. Weed*, 315 F. Supp. 3d 667-679 (D. Mass. 2018) ("The plain text of Section 3(a)(9), however, exempts 'any security exchanged by the issuer with its existing securities holders' rather than any security that has ever been or once was exchanged by the issuer."). The exemption is in Section 3(a)(9) as something of a legislative accident according to Professor Loss, who reports that it was moved in 1934 from Section 4(a)(3) to underscore an early Federal Trade Commission interpretation that the dealer's obligation to deliver a prospectus under Section 4(a)(3) applies only to securities not otherwise exempt from registration. 3 L. Loss, J. Seligman & T. Paredes, 3 Securities Regulation 5 (5th ed. 2015).

6. Securities Act Release No. 646, 1 Fed. Sec. L. Rep. (CCH) ¶¶2136, 2137 (1936). In the same release, the general counsel for the SEC offered what is now a fairly standard caveat for exemptions, namely, that Section 3(a)(9) is applicable only to bona fide exchanges and not to transactions that are effected merely as a step toward evasion of the Act's registration requirements. Factors to be considered in determining whether a particular exchange is bona fide are the length of time the securities to be received by the issuer were outstanding, the number of holders of the originally outstanding securities, the marketability of such securities, and whether the exchange was dictated by the issuer's financial considerations and not just by the desire of a few of its security holders to distribute the shares. Id. ¶2136.

establish that the shares were not acquired with a view toward their distribution, to comply with Rule 144, a resale pursuant to Section 4(a)(7), or a resale in compliance with the Section 4(a)(1½) exemption. Tacking is generally available to assist the holder in meeting the appropriate holding period.

Commentators disagree whether securities acquired in an exchange falling within Section 3(a)(9) are restricted when the exchange is functionally a private exchange involving a small number of holders, even when the securities given up had been registered. *Compare* 7 J.W. Hicks, Exempted Transactions Under the Securities Act of 1933 §2.08[2][b] (reasoning from Rule 144's inclusion of securities acquired in a non-public offering within its scope of "restricted securities" as warning of Section 5 issues), *with* Campbell, Resales of Securities Under the Securities Act of 1933, 52 Wash. & Lee L. Rev. 1333, 1356-1369 (1995) (securities received in a Section 3(a)(9) transaction are restricted only if securities exchanged were restricted). Control persons who wish to sell securities received in a Section 3(a)(9) transaction, of course, are subject to the standard restrictions that any control person faces.

3.   Section 3(a)(9) and Protecting Investors.   Compare the exemption provided by Section 3(a)(9) with the private placement exemption in Section 4(a)(2). What assurances does Section 4(a)(2) provide that their offerees' investment choices are protected? Are there similar assurances for transactions qualifying under Section 3(a)(9)? Professor Hicks reasons that "[i]n view of the special needs of security holders in certain exchange transactions and the variety of uses that the exchange exemption affords, it is difficult to understand why Congress and the SEC permit Section 3(a)(9) to continue in its present form." Hicks, Recapitalizations Under Section 3(a)(9) of the Securities Act of 1933, 61 Va. L. Rev. 1057, 1112 (1975). On the other hand, does Section 3(a)(9) provide any less protection to offerees than does the intrastate offering exemption of Section 3(a)(11)?

PROBLEMS

Venture Sails, Inc., began its sailboat chartering business modestly in 1986 when Jacqueline Smith and Albert Jones pooled their funds to acquire a single 37-foot sloop. Venture Sails now has more than 100 boats available for chartering, a resort at its yacht harbor in Key West, and a very successful travel agency. Jacqueline died a year ago, leaving her 50 percent interest equally to her children, Irene and Karl.

Albert owns 10,000 Venture common shares, and Jacqueline's children each own 5,000 shares. Because Jacqueline's heirs have separate careers and therefore no interest in participating in the management of Venture, they approached Albert with a proposal to exchange their common shares for 40,000 preferred shares having a $4 per share cumulative dividend. Albert has tentatively agreed to their proposition. Now there are questions as to its implementation. Neither Irene nor Karl is sophisticated or an accredited investor. Assume that the appropriate amendment to the articles of incorporation authorizing the preferred stock has already occurred and that the board of directors has adopted a resolution allowing one share of common to be exchanged for four shares of the newly authorized preferred stock. Consider the securities issues posed under Sections 5 and 3(a)(9) for each of the following non-cumulative scenarios.

7-16.　Because Karl has questioned whether the exchange poses serious tax consequences for him, some members of Venture's outside law firm (which has been advising Venture on the exchange) meet with Karl and explain that the exchange is in his best interest and is not a taxable event.

7-17.　Venture's articles of incorporation provide that the dividend on the preferred shares will be paid on the calendar quarter. Because of the unforeseen delay in persuading Karl to participate in the exchange, the exchange will take place on November 15, rather than October 1 as planned. Because the preferred shares will not have been owned for a full quarter when the next dividend payment is made, the heirs each agree to pay $5,000 to Venture when they exchange their shares, the amount representing one-half of that quarter's preferred stock dividend.

7-18.　Albert has approached a couple of Key West investors with the view of raising $3 million for Venture by issuing $4 non-redeemable preferred stock. The funds will be used to expand the company's present docking facilities and will be issued about the same time as the exchange offer.

7-19.　Irene sold 100 of the preferred shares she received through the exchange to Ray. Ray's interest in the shares was piqued by Irene's stockbroker, Sara, who actively pushed the shares to her clientele in return for a substantial commission from Irene.

D.　*Reorganizations Under Section 3(a)(10)*

1.　Non-Bankruptcy Reorganizations

Section 3(a)(10) exempts the issuer's exchange of securities for outstanding securities, claims or property, provided the transaction's fairness has been approved, after a hearing by a court, agency, commission, or other governmental authority. The exemption's legislative history is very limited, so authoritative guidance is found in Staff Legal Bulletin No. 3A (2008) and numerous no-action letters. The most frequent users of Section 3(a)(10) today are financially sound issuers undergoing recapitalizations, or acquiring other firms, or issuing securities pursuant to a court-approved settlement of litigation.[7] For

---

7.　Securities distributed as part of a court-approved settlement of a class action fall within Section 3(a)(10). *See* SELLAS Life Sciences Group, Inc. SEC No-Action Letter, [2018 Transfer Binder] Fed. Sec. L. Rep. (CCH) ¶78,802 (June 6, 2018). The only case to discuss

example, the Florida banking authority's approval of the fairness of an acquisition of a bank falls within the exemption. Wachovia Corp., SEC No-Action Letter, 1998 WL 60783 (Feb. 10, 1998). The approving tribunal can also be a foreign court. *See* Nabi Biopharmaceuticals, SEC No-Action Letter, [2010 Transfer Binder] Fed. Sec. L. Rep. (CCH) ¶77,005 (June 20, 2010) (exemption available after fairness approval by an Australian court). And even lawyers can reap benefits via the exemption. *See* Sprint Corp., SEC No-Action Letter, [2003-2004 Transfer Binder] Fed. Sec. L. Rep. ¶78,533 (Aug. 25, 2003) (shares issued to derivative suit's attorney as part of court-approved settlement fall within the exemption). However, securities issued pursuant to Chapter 11 of the Bankruptcy Act enjoy special exemptions provided under the Bankruptcy Act, discussed in the next section.

Similar to Section 3(a)(9), the exemption cannot be used to raise cash; the provision's "partly for cash" language is seen by the SEC as very narrow, covering only instances where needed for flexibility in structuring the exchange. There is no requirement that the securities exchanged be of the same issuer. Thus, the exemption is available for a reorganization involving two or more companies and a court-approved plan that calls for common stock of Company *A* to be exchanged for preferred stock of Company *B*. Finally, Section 3(a)(10) permits remuneration to be paid in connection with any solicitation undertaken in connection with the exchange.

The exemption's justification lies in the fairness hearing it prescribes. In the eyes of Section 3(a)(10)'s drafters, the hearing substitutes for registration. Because it is important that there be a full exploration of the exchange's terms and conditions at the hearing, there has long been recognized an implicit requirement that the hearing be preceded by adequate notice to all persons to whom securities will be issued. Moreover, the issuer must advise the tribunal before the fairness hearing that it will rely on the Section 3(a)(10) exemption for any exchange it approves.

The SEC has been prickly in its administration of Section 3(a)(10), denying no-action letter requests when the agency or tribunal holding the hearing was not empowered by its enabling statute to hold a hearing on the exchange's fairness, even though a hearing was in fact held. Thus, a statute authorizing a state banking commission to consider the impact on competition of a bank's acquisition would be deficient, even though the commission inquired into and approved the fairness of the acquisition's exchange terms and conditions.

---

the review standards sufficient for a court-approved settlement to satisfy the Section 3(a)(10) exemption is *SEC v. Blinder Robinson & Co.*, 511 F. Supp. 799 (D. Colo. 1981). American Leisure Corporation settled an enforcement action brought by the SEC by offering to exchange notes and stock for securities earlier offered through a misleading prospectus. The court held that, since the settlement involved a public prosecution, Section 3(a)(10) did not require it to compare the value of the securities being exchanged. Hence, it did not value the securities that were exchanged or those being issued. The court focused instead upon the openness of the proceeding, the adversarial nature of the proceeding, the level of discovery, the broad intervention rights of the parties, and the completeness of the notice announcing the proposed settlement. Finally, the settlement was not binding upon any American Leisure stockholder who did not submit his shares for exchange.

Section 3(a)(10) exempts only the exchange transaction; it is not a securities exemption. Therefore, resales need their own exemption. *See In the Matter of IBC Funds, LLC,* Securities Exchange Act Release No. 77195 (Feb. 10, 2016). If the seller is neither an affiliate of the issuer nor a Rule 145 affiliate (i.e., affiliate of a shell company participating in the transaction), the securities received in a Section 3(a)(10) transaction can be resold without regard to Rule 144. The SEC's staff maintains that restrictions on resale apply to securities issued in a transaction exempt under Section 3(a)(10) only for securities held by those who either before or after that transaction are affiliates of any party to the transaction. Those who are affiliates before or after the transaction must resell their securities pursuant to Rule 144; in the case of a Rule 145 affiliate, the resale must conform to Rule 145(d).

A final legal issue surrounding Section 3(a)(10) is the section's interaction with Section 18 of the Securities Act. In 1996, Congress amended Section 18 to preempt the application of state blue sky laws to certain types of securities and offerings (referred to as "covered securities"). The breadth of the 1996 amendment to Section 18 included any state fairness hearings that related to securities. This posed a concern that Congress had unwittingly barred socially useful fairness hearings, such as those carried out by state bank or insurance regulators. Thus, in 1998, Congress again amended Section 18 to exclude from the definition of covered securities any security issued pursuant to a transaction exempt under Section 3(a)(10). The 1998 amendment would appear to restore matters to their pre-1996 state when blue sky administrators had the power to apply merit review to corporate combinations and recapitalizations, although this would mean a partial retreat by Congress from the principles that guided the broad preemptive steps taken in 1996. The SEC's staff concedes as much, interpreting the 1998 amendment: "As a result, an issuer now may rely upon a fairness hearing conducted *under state securities law* to perfect an exemption under Section 3(a)(10) for securities that otherwise would be deemed covered securities." Id. (emphasis added). *See, e.g.,* Maverick Networks, SEC No-Action Letter, 1999 LEXIS 80 (Jan. 26, 1999) (fairness determination by the California blue sky administrator satisfies Section 3(a)(10) and thus obviates preemption effects of Section 18).

2.　The Bankruptcy Act's Collision with the Securities Laws

The present Bankruptcy Act became effective October 1, 1979, and introduces a good many complexities to the issuance and resale of securities by debtors undergoing reorganization under Chapter 11 of the Act. The difficulties posed by the Bankruptcy Act are its poorly executed attempts to both complement and supplement the provisions of the Securities Act. The problems occur in three distinct areas: the disclosure required to accompany the issuance of the debtor's securities, the provision of exemptions in Section 364(f) or 1145(a), and the restrictions on resale of securities issued by a debtor undergoing reorganization under Chapter 11.

a.   Disclosure in Chapter 11 Reorganizations

The Bankruptcy Act, in Section 1125, requires that there be adequate disclosure accompanying the solicitation of the debtor's claimants' approval of the
reorganization plan. Section 1125 provides its own disclosure guidelines for the
issuance of securities in a Chapter 11 reorganization. The disclosure compelled
by Section 1125 occurs as part of the procedures designed to secure the various
claimants' approval of the plan of reorganization. The claimants range from
unsecured creditors to bondholders to equity participants. The resulting disclosure statement bears the imprimatur of the bankruptcy court that the statement is an "adequate disclosure" of the plan of reorganization. The Bankruptcy
Act's definition of *adequate information* has an interesting twist. It scrupulously
avoids referring to the securities laws' materiality standard,[8] and "adequacy"
determinations take into consideration the condition of the debtor's books and
records. Hence, the quality of disclosure is not driven exclusively by the holder's
informational needs, but also weighs the debtor's ability to make a disclosure.[9]
For a review of how the Securities Act disclosure standards (which apply to public solicitations prior to the filing of a "prepackaged" bankruptcy reorganization plan) aggravate the collective action problem of creditors and strengthen
the hand of the debtor in possession in such prepackaged reorganizations, *see*
Mendales, We Can Work It Out: The Interaction of Bankruptcy and Securities
Regulation in the Workout Context, 46 Rutgers L. Rev. 1211, 1264-1291 (1994).

b.   Exemption for Sale and Exchange of Securities

All the Securities Act's standard exemptions from registration are available
to debtors undertaking a reorganization under Chapter 11. A special Securities
Act exemption in Section 3(a)(7) applies only to trustee or receiver certificates
issued with the court's approval. The certificates are in effect debt instruments
and invariably are issued to raise cash to carry on the debtor's business. Section
364(f) of the Bankruptcy Act provides a parallel exemption from Section 5 for
debt securities, whether or not approved by the bankruptcy court.

A far broader exemption aimed at facilitating adjustments between the
debtor and its various claimants is provided by Section 1145 of the Bankruptcy
Act. Section 1145(a) exempts from Section 5 of the Securities Act any securities
issued under a Chapter 11 reorganization plan if they are issued *principally* in

---

8.   Section 1125(d) provides that adequacy "is not governed by any otherwise applicable nonbankruptcy law, rule or regulation." 11 U.S.C. §1125(d). The SEC does have standing
to express its views to the bankruptcy court on the adequacy of the disclosure statement.

9.   11 U.S.C. §1125(a)(1). Those who in good faith and pursuant to the reorganization
plan solicit sales or approvals on the basis of the disclosure document enjoy a safe harbor
from any securities law liability should that document turn out to have been materially misleading. 11 U.S.C. §1125(4). The terms of the provision are less than clear whether the safe
harbor applies only where securities are issued under a Bankruptcy Act exemption or also
where fresh capital is raised under the Securities Act.

exchange for the debtor's existing debts and securities.[10] While the exemption allows the debtor's claimants to pay cash for the new security, the consideration they pay must "principally" be their claim against, or interest in, the debtor. The exemption is not available if securities are sold to others to raise fresh capital. Why so limit the scope of this exemption from registration? The exemption in Section 1145(a) applies not only to the debtor but also to its affiliates that are joint participants in the reorganization and will issue the affiliates' securities in exchange for the claims and interests others have in the debtor.[11] Both Section 364(f) and Section 1145(a) are transaction exemptions. Is Section 3(a)(7) of the Securities Act a transaction or a security exemption?

c. Resales of Securities Received in a Chapter 11 Reorganization

Section 1145(b) sets forth highly complex provisions defining who is an underwriter of securities acquired in a reorganization. Even though the language of that section appears to apply to resales of all securities issued in Chapter 11 reorganizations, the structure of the Act and its legislative history support the view that the subsection applies only to securities issued pursuant to Section 1145(a). Resales of securities sold under the Securities Act exemptions or registered securities are governed by the provisions of the Securities Act. Thus, a control person's resale of securities received in the reorganization of the controlled debtor company or resales of securities issued in the reorganization through a private placement can be made in reliance upon Rule 144. On the other hand, if the securities were issued pursuant to Section 1145(a), their resales must comply with Section 1145(b).

Under Section 1145(b)(3), ordinary trading transactions in securities received in the reorganization may be made immediately upon their receipt by security holders who are not affiliates. In this respect, the Bankruptcy Act provides the same result as occurs under Section 4(4) of the '33 Act for ordinary trading transactions.[12]

Control persons of the debtor do not fare well under the Bankruptcy Act. Any Section 1145(a) securities they hold may be sold only through registration because they are deemed to be underwriters with respect to their Section 1145(a) securities. The control person may not rely upon the Section 4(a)(1½) exemption or Rule 144.[13]

---

10. Section 1145(a) also facilitates the use of convertible securities, warrants, options, and rights in reorganizations by extending the exemption not only to their issuance but also to any securities acquired by their exercise.

11. Section 1145(a) also applies to securities issued by a successor to the debtor, so that, if all the debtor's assets were to be transferred to a successor company in consideration of the successor's securities that are distributed to the debtor's claimants, the securities would be exempt from registration. 11 U.S.C. §1145(a)(1).

12. Such a sale would probably occur through a stockbroker, and Section 1145(a)(4) provides stockbrokers an exemption similar to that accorded dealers in Section 4(3) of the Securities Act. Under Section 1145(a)(4), stockbrokers must provide a disclosure statement only within 40 days of the bona fide offer of the security to the public. Thereafter, the stockbroker is under no obligation to provide a disclosure statement.

13. Section 1145(b)(1)(A)-(C) also includes those who provide classic underwriting functions as underwriters. Included within this group are those who purchase claims against

d.   Resales from Debtor's Portfolio

An entirely different resale question is posed when the debtor is considering the sale of securities it owns in *another* issuer. In making such a resale, the debtor may avail itself of the standard Securities Act exemptions, such as Section 4(a)(1) or Rule 144. If the resale cannot qualify under a Securities Act exemption, the debtor undergoing a reorganization may resell limited quantities of stock to certain qualified issuers pursuant to Section 1145(a)(3). The conditions that must be satisfied are that: (1) the debtor must have owned the security when the petition was filed; (2) the issuer must be a company subject to the reporting requirements of the Securities Exchange Act; (3) the issuer must be current in its filings under that Act; and (4) the debtor may sell only up to 4 percent of that class of security outstanding in the two years following the petition's filing and may sell an additional 1 percent every six months thereafter. Why is this additional exemption provided to debtors undergoing a reorganization?

An excellent analysis of the impact of the Bankruptcy Act on the securities laws appears in Morgan, Application of the Securities Laws in Chapter 11 Reorganizations Under the Bankruptcy Reform Act of 1978, 1983 U. Ill. L. Rev. 861.

---

the debtor or interests in the debtor with a view to distributing the securities to be exchanged for such claim or interest and those who approach the debtor's claimants and security holders with an offer either to purchase the reorganization securities with a view toward their distribution or to assist such claimants or interest holders in their own resales.

‖8‖
Exempt Securities

Unlike the exempt transactions discussed in Chapter 5, exempt securities are permanently exempt from the registration provisions of the '33 Act, which means not only that issuers of exempt securities are free of the burdens of registration, but also that owners of the securities need no exemption in order to resell their securities.[1] Securities are exempt under Section 3 for a number of reasons of varying validity. Some securities are exempt because the character of the issuer (e.g., the U.S. government) minimizes the need for mandated disclosures at either the time of issuance or the time of resale. Similarly, other securities find an exemption because of the existence of a regulatory regime that, at least in theory, adequately protects investors in the securities (e.g., securities issued or guaranteed by banks, as well as insurance and annuity contracts). Securities may be exempt because the instruments do not represent "investments" as that term is typically used (e.g., securities of not-for-profit issuers). And still other securities are accorded an exemption because political or constitutional considerations, or a combination of both, render regulation through the registration provisions of the '33 Act at the very least problematic (e.g., municipal securities).

In studying the exempt securities of Section 3, you should keep in mind two important qualifications. First, the section's exemptions do *not* exempt securities from the '33 and the '34 Acts in their entirety, and transactions in most exempt securities are subject to the antifraud provisions of Section 17 of the 1933 Act, Section 10(b) of the 1934 Act, and, to varying extents, Section 12(a)(2) of the 1933 Act.[2] Even sophisticated courts, however, sometimes confuse this point and assume the exemption affects applicability of the securities laws generally. *See, e.g., United States v. Wosotowsky,* 527 Fed. App'x 207 (3d Cir. 2013) (seemingly assuming that the Section 3(a)(8) exemption for insurance and annuity projects, if applicable, would exempt the transaction from application of Section 10(b)). Second, a number of Section 3's exemptions pertain to

---

1. In addition, the issuer of exempt securities is not subject to the periodic reporting requirements of the 1934 Act.

2. By its terms, Section 12(a)(2) does not apply to securities issued under the Section 3(a)(2) exemption.

the transaction, rather than the security; in these cases, the exemption does not extend to resales. Accordingly, Section 3 is best viewed as an amalgamation of exemptions for securities *and* for transactions.

A. *An Overview of Section 3*

Section 3(a)(2): Government Securities, Bank Securities, and Collective, Common, or Single Trust Funds

In what may be the longest sentence in the federal securities acts, Section 3(a)(2) exempts a range of securities that may be grouped roughly into the categories of government securities, bank securities, and interests in certain trust funds.

Government Securities. Section 3(a)(2) exempts securities issued or guaranteed by the United States or any of its territories, the District of Columbia, any state, any political subdivision or public instrumentality of a state or territory, or any person acting as an instrumentality of the U.S. government. The exemption of government securities arguably may be justified on a number of grounds, including the character of the issuer (governments do not lie), the character of the security (governments do not default on their debt obligations), political realities (a check on the power of the federal government to establish a regulatory regime covering the issuance of municipal securities), and constitutional restraints (the Tenth Amendment reserves to the states powers not delegated to the federal government, and the power accorded to Congress to regulate interstate commerce does not extend to dictating the means by which integral government functions will be performed).

In the case of securities issued by states and their political subdivisions, broadly termed *municipal securities*, the advisability of an exemption from the registration requirements is a matter of intense debate. Fuel for the debate was provided by the 1995 bankruptcy of Orange County, California, following its fraudulent sale of over $2 billion in municipal securities, and San Diego's 2002-2003 sales of $260 million in bonds without disclosure of the extent of the city's unfunded pension and retiree health care obligations. In 2010, New Jersey became the first state charged by the SEC with violating the federal securities laws. The action related to New Jersey's representations on the adequacy of funding for the teachers' pension plan and was settled with a commitment by the state to cease and desist from future violations of the securities laws. And in 2016, the Justice Department launched the first-ever municipal bond fraud prosecution with the indictment of two public officials of Ramapo, New York, who, the Department alleged, "kicked truth and transparency to the curb, selling over $150 million of municipal bonds on fabricated financials." For a discussion of increased enforcement efforts by the SEC, *see* Guidotti, Seeking "the SEC's Full Protection": A Critique of the New Frontier in Municipal Securities Enforcement, 82 U. Chi. L. Rev. 2045 (2015). Problematic disclosures in some municipal bond offerings have reinforced the view of many that the reasons for the registration exemption of the $3.7 trillion municipal securities market are no longer compelling.

On the regulatory front, the SEC in 1989 adopted Rule 15c2-12, which requires underwriters of many municipal offerings to obtain a disclosure document (called the *official statement*) from issuers and, except in competitive bid underwritings, make the document available on request to any prospective purchaser. Interestingly, the Rule directs disclosures under the authority given the SEC to regulate manipulative, deceptive, or fraudulent practices by broker-dealers, rather than through directly regulating the offering activities of municipal issuers. The 1994 and 2010 amendments to Rule 15c2-12 require underwriters to determine that an issuer has agreed to provide certain ongoing disclosures to the secondary markets, and in 2012 the SEC issued a "risk alert," highlighting certain due diligence measures it expects of underwriters. Offerings under $1 million and private placements are exempt from Rule 15c2-12.

In a GAO report mandated by the Dodd-Frank Wall Street Reform and Consumer Protection Act, the General Accounting Office concluded that the SEC needs to improve its oversight of SROs responsible for monitoring the municipal securities markets. The report also noted that the municipal securities market lacks transparency and institutional investors are able to trade at better prices than individual investors. *See* GAO, Municipal Securities: Overview of Market Structure, Pricing, and Regulation (January 2012). A second GAO report and an SEC report discussed options for improving disclosures in municipal offerings, some of which would require changes in the '33 Act. *See* GAO, Municipal Securities: Options for Improving Continuing Disclosure (July 2012); SEC, Report on the Municipal Securities Markets (July 2012).

Bank Securities.   In addition to exempting government securities, Section 3(a)(2) exempts securities issued or guaranteed by banks. *Bank* is defined to mean a national bank, or any banking institution organized under the laws of a state or the District of Columbia, "the business of which is substantially confined to banking and is supervised by the State or territorial banking commission or similar official." Although the legislative history behind this exemption is sparse, there is evidence that Congress felt that the existing bank regulatory structure provided "adequate" supervision over the activities of banks. *See* H.R. Rep. No. 85, 73d Cong., 1st Sess. 14 (1933). *See also SEC v. McDuffie*, 2014 U.S. Dist. LEXIS 128664 (D. Colo. Sept. 15, 2014) (exemption is not available for securities issued by a credit union not regulated by federal or state authorities).

With internationalization of capital markets, a number of foreign banks have established branches in the United States, which raises the not unsurprising question of whether the Section 3(a)(2) exemption extends to the issuance or guarantee of securities by branches of foreign banks. In a 1986 interpretive release, the SEC reasoned that a U.S. branch or agency of a foreign bank is a bank for purposes of the Section 3(a)(2) exemption, "provided that the nature and extent of Federal and/or State regulation and supervision of the particular branch or agency is substantially equivalent to that applicable to Federal or State chartered domestic banks doing business in the same jurisdiction." Release No. 33-6661 (Sept. 23, 1986).

The SEC once proposed repeal of the exemption for securities issued or guaranteed by banks on the ground that banking regulation is not a substitute for disclosures prompted by the registration provisions of the '33 Act or the continuous reporting requirements of the '34 Act. *See* Report by the Securities and Exchange Commission on the Financial Guarantee Market (1987). Congress never acted on that proposal.

Common, Collective, and Single Trust Funds.   Interests in common trust funds maintained by banks are exempt securities under Section 3(a)(2). A *common trust fund* is a fund maintained by a bank for investing assets given to the bank in its capacity as a trustee, executor, administrator, or guardian. The bank, however, must exercise "substantial investment authority," and the trust fund must not be used as a vehicle for general investment by the public. *See, e.g.,* The Howard Savings Bank, SEC No-Action Letter, [1979-1980 Transfer Binder] Fed. Sec. L. Rep. (CCH) ¶82,320 (Aug. 13, 1979) (no-action request denied for a bank offering to its customers of "mini-trusts" under which the bank, as trustee, would invest funds deposited in trust in various investment vehicles maintained by the bank). Section 3(a)(2) also exempts collective trust funds maintained by banks. A *collective trust fund* is a fund maintained as an investment vehicle for tax-qualified pension and profit sharing plans (other than certain Keogh plans for the self-employed). If they pertain to tax-qualified pension and profit sharing plans, single trust funds (which do not have bank trustees) and contracts issued by insurance companies are also exempt by the section.

Section 3(a)(3): Short-Term Notes

Section 3(a)(3) exempts any note, draft, bill of exchange, or banker's acceptance arising out of a current transaction if the maturity at time of issuance does not exceed nine months. This, the so-called commercial paper exemption, has been interpreted by the SEC to apply only to "prime quality negotiable commercial paper of a type not ordinarily purchased by the general public." Securities Act Release No. 4412, 1 Fed. Sec. L. Rep. (CCH) ¶2045 (Sept. 20, 1961). Courts have agreed with this interpretation. *See, e.g., SEC v. Thompson,* 732 F.3d 1151, 1158 n.6 (10th Cir. 2013). As so interpreted, the exemption may be justified because of both the character of the issuer (the prime quality requirement) and the characteristics of the security (the requirements that funds be used in current operations and that the maturity not exceed nine months lessen risk). Maturities on commercial paper range up to 270 days but average about 30 days. If instruments ostensibly within the Section 3(a)(3) exemption include automatic rollover provisions providing for the automatic reinvestment in new debt instruments at the maturity dates unless investors then direct to the contrary, the exemption may be lost. *See* Securities Act Release No. 4412, supra.

Section 3(a)(4): Nonprofit Issuers

Section 3(a)(4) exempts securities offered by issuers that are organized and operated exclusively for religious, educational, benevolent, fraternal, charitable, or reformatory purposes, provided that no part of the earnings of the organization inure to the "benefit" of any person. Various policy justifications may support this exemption. Arguably, individuals do not "invest" in eleemosynary organizations and therefore are not in need of extensive disclosures about the economic aspects of the operations of such issuers. Furthermore, to subject nonprofit organizations to the costs of registering securities offered to the public would severely limit the ability of the organizations to raise capital needed to achieve the purposes for which they were formed. *See* Heminway, To Be or Not to Be (a Security): Funding For-Profit Social Enterprises, 25 Regent U. L. Rev. 299, 324 (2013) ("Generally, these policy justifications reflect an 'unstated premise that the eleemosynary character of the issuer obviates the need for disclosure to investors' and a prioritization of the social good of nonprofits over the need for enhanced disclosure to investors—disclosure in excess of that required for not-for-profits under federal tax law, state entity law, and state charitable donation regulation (as applicable)") (citation omitted) (2013). Whatever the policy justifications, significant interpretive difficulties with the exemption arise because of its requirement that no part of the profits of the organization "inures to the benefit" of any individual. *See, e.g., SEC v. Children's Hosp.*, 214 F. Supp. 883 (D. Ariz. 1963) (exemption not available for the sale of bonds to construct a hospital because promoters were to receive a profit from the organization and promotion of the institution); *but cf.* Deutsche Bank Microcredit Development Fund, SEC No-Action Letter (Apr. 8, 2011) (responding favorably to a no action letter request proposing payment of fees for services but distinguishing *Children's Hospital* as a case in which the fees paid were substantial).

Section 3(a)(5): Securities Issued by Savings and Loans, Cooperative Banks, and Similar Institutions

Securities issued by savings and loan institutions, cooperative banks, homestead associations, and similar organizations are exempt, provided the issuers are supervised and examined by federal or state authorities having supervision over their operations. Without regard to supervision by governmental authorities, the exemption is also available for farmer cooperatives and certain corporations that are exempt from federal taxation. One commentator has observed that the exemption exists for "obvious political reasons." Landis, The Legislative History of the Securities Act of 1933, 28 Geo. Wash. L. Rev. 29, 39 (1959). This, however, may be something of an overstatement. Initially, the exemption was not keyed to the existence of an overseeing regulatory structure, but instead was available only for a savings and loan (or related institution) "substantially all of the business of which is confined to the making of loans to members." The limitation on business activity was consistent with the then-accepted view of thrifts as institutions that exist for the benefit of members, rather than stockholders. For this reason, the income of savings and loans and related institutions was exempt from taxation. *See, e.g., Perpetual Bldg. & Loan Ass'n*, 34 T.C. 694, 710 (1960), *aff'd sub nom. Estate of Cooper v. C.I.R.*, 291 F.2d 831 (4th Cir. 1961) ("Unlike a banking institution which operates primarily for the benefit of its investing stockholders, a building and loan association is, fundamentally, intended to be conducted for the benefit of its borrowing members as well as nonborrowers.").

The development of the industry, however, led to fundamental changes in the ways thrifts operated. Eventually, the tax exemption that thrifts had enjoyed was repealed. In 1970, Section 3(a)(5)'s condition that substantially all of the business of the savings and loan be confined to making loans to members was replaced with the condition that the institution be supervised by federal or state authorities. Accordingly, the present justification for the Section 3(a)(5) exemption as applied to savings and loans is the existence of a regulatory structure obviating, in theory, the need for mandated disclosures under the '33 Act.

Section 3(a)(8): Insurance Policies and Annuities

Insurance and annuity contracts are exempt securities if issued by a corporation subject to regulation by insurance regulators at the state or federal level. The existence of Section 3(a)(8) suggests that insurance and annuity contracts are securities and therefore subject to the antifraud provisions of the securities acts. This conclusion is a matter of some debate. *See, e.g.*, L. Loss & J. Seligman, Fundamentals of Securities Regulation 397-398 (6th ed. 2011). The exemption can be justified both because adequate state regulatory structures exist for monitoring insurance companies and because a "pure" insurance or annuity contract shifts the risk of asset mismanagement from the purchaser to the carrier. Testing the limits of their exemption, a number of insurance companies began offering variable annuities under which returns to the purchasers were keyed to the success with which the companies invested funds. Because the contracts shift the risk from insurance companies to purchasers of the annuities, the Section 3(a)(8) exemption was held not to apply to variable annuities in *SEC v. Variable Annuity Life Insurance Co. of America*, 359 U.S. 65 (1959). More recently, insurance companies have marketed so-called guaranteed investment contracts that typically include guarantees as to a minimum level of return, but also offer the possibility of higher returns based upon investment performance. Whether these types of contracts are within the Section 3(a)(8) exemption will depend upon the degree to which the insurer has assumed the risk. Rule 151 offers a safe harbor on this point.

Additional Section 3(a) Exemptions

A number of the exemptions contained in Section 3(a) do not extend to resales and thus have the character of transaction exemptions, rather than exemptions for securities. These exemptions, which are treated in other chapters of this book, include the Section 3(a)(7) exemption for certain certificates issued by trustees or receivers in bankruptcy (Chapter 7), the Section 3(a)(9) exemption for issuer exchanges with existing securities holders (Chapter 7), the Section 3(a)(10) exemption for securities issued in corporate reorganizations (Chapter 7), and the Section 3(a)(11) exemption for intrastate offerings (Chapter 5).

Sections 3(b), 3(c), and 28

Section 3(b)(1) authorizes the SEC to exempt a class of securities (up to an aggregate offering amount of $5 million) if it finds that enforcement of the '33 Act with respect to the securities is not necessary to protect the public interest because of either the small amount involved or the limited character of the offering. The more important of the administrative exemptions based in whole or in part on Section 3(b) are Rule 504 of Regulation D and Rule 701 (compensatory benefit plans and contracts). In an attempt to revive Regulation A offerings, the Jumpstart Our Business Startups Act added to the '33 Act a new Section 3(b)(2) authorizing the SEC to exempt offerings of up to $50 million during a 12-month period (resulting in the so-called Regulation A+ exemption). These exemptions are discussed in Chapter 5.

Section 3(c) authorizes the SEC to exempt securities issued by small business investment companies (SBICs) if registration is not necessary for the protection of investors. The administrative exemption for SBICs is set forth in Regulation E.

Finally, Section 28 of the '33 Act, added by the National Securities Markets Improvement Act of 1996, authorizes the Commission to exempt "any person, securities, or transactions," from all or part of the Act. For the '34 Act, a parallel provision was added in Section 36. The expanded exemptive authority gives the Commission "enhanced flexibility to more easily adopt new approaches to registration, disclosure, and related issues." *See* H.R. Rep. 104-622, 104th Cong., 2d Sess. 38 (1996).

The balance of this chapter examines in greater depth five of the more problematic Section 3(a) exemptions. These include exemptions for (1) municipal securities, (2) securities issued or guaranteed by a bank, (3) short-term commercial paper (4) securities issued by nonprofit organizations, and (5) insurance and annuity contracts.

B. Municipal Securities

Lack of proven abuses, the perceived sophistication of investors, and the desire to avoid the costs of regulation are the traditional justifications for exempting from registration requirements the securities issued or guaranteed by governmental entities. At the federal level, these justifications are persuasive, but they are more debatable when applied to securities of other governmental entities. Although municipal securities (the label somewhat loosely applied to the issuances of state, regional, local, and special district governmental entities) have a default rate lower than that of their corporate counterparts, the near-default by New York City in 1975, the defaults by the Washington Public Power Supply System in 1983 and Orange County, California, in 1995, San Diego's false and misleading financial statements in a series of bond offerings in 2002 and 2003, the bankruptcies of Detroit in 2013, Jefferson County, Alabama, in 2011, and several California cities in recent years, together with SEC charges in 2012 of fraud against New Jersey for problematic disclosures on pension liabilities, have prompted new efforts to regulate the issuances of municipal securities.

1.   The Market and the Players

Report on the Municipal Securities Market 1-7
Securities and Exchange Commission, July 31, 2012

. . .

Over the past 30 years, the municipal securities market has grown significantly and now represents an increasingly important part of the U.S. capital markets. The municipal securities market is also an extremely diverse market, with close to 44,000 state and local issuers, and with a total face amount of $3.7 trillion. . . .

The interest paid on municipal securities is typically exempt from federal income taxation and may be exempt from state income and other taxes. The municipal securities market is critical to building and maintaining the infrastructure of our nation. The municipal securities market raises hundreds of billions of dollars each year on behalf of states, localities, and other public and private entities. . . . Individual (or "retail") investors hold as much as 75% of outstanding municipal securities both directly and indirectly, through mutual funds, money market funds, and closed-end funds.

State and local governmental entities issue municipal securities to finance a variety of public projects, to meet cash flow and other governmental needs, and to finance nongovernmental private projects (through the use of "conduit" financings on behalf of private organizations that obtain lower-cost tax-exempt financing). Issuers of municipal securities consist of a diverse group of entities that includes states, their political subdivisions (such as cities, towns, counties and school districts), and their instrumentalities (such as housing, health care, airport, port, and economic development authorities and agencies). State and local laws, including state constitutions, statutes, city and county charters, and municipal codes govern these public bodies. Such constitutions, statutes, charters, and codes impose on municipal issuer's requirements relating to governance, budgeting, accounting, and other financial matters. The governing bodies of municipal issuers are as varied as the types of issuers, ranging from state governments, cities, towns, and counties with elected officials to special purpose entities with appointed members.

In 2011, there were over one million different municipal bonds outstanding compared to fewer than 50,000 different corporate bonds. These municipal bonds totaled $3.7 trillion in principal, while corporate (and foreign) bonds and corporate equities outstanding totaled $11.5 trillion and $22.5 trillion, respectively. . . .

Municipal entities primarily issue securities that are generally classified as either general obligation bonds or revenue bonds. General obligation bonds are backed by the taxing power and/or "full faith and credit" of the issuing entity. A holder of a general obligation bond may look for repayment to all sources of revenue received by the municipal entity that may legally be used for such payments or, for example, the receipts of unlimited ad valorem taxes levied for that purpose. Revenue bonds may be backed by specific non-ad valorem revenues, such as sales and use taxes or the revenues of the specific project or enterprise being financed (e.g., a utility system, a toll road, or an airport or port facility).

Conduit revenue bonds are issued by a municipality or an agency or instrumentality of a municipality on behalf of a third party (often called a "conduit borrower" or "obligated person"). If certain requirements in the federal Internal Revenue Code ("IRC") and Internal Revenue Service ("IRS") regulations are met, conduit revenue bonds may be tax-exempt. Tax-exempt conduit revenue bonds include industrial development bonds on behalf of private entities, as well as financings for both non-profit and for-profit borrowers: such as hospitals; colleges and universities; power and energy companies; resource recovery facilities; multi-family housing projects; hotels; and sports stadiums. In a conduit revenue bond financing, the bondholder cannot look to the municipal issuer for payment of the bonds but rather must rely on payment from the conduit borrower.

Tax increment financing ("TIF"), a variant on the general obligation bond, uses taxes generated by an enhancement in value resulting from land improvement as the source of funds for repayment of the bonds. That is, the issuer anticipates generating income from *increased* property taxes, which it then uses to pay back the borrowed funds. A common structure for TIF is to identify and freeze tax revenues existing on pre-developed property. Post-development tax revenues up to the frozen amount remain as general unrestricted revenues, while tax revenues in excess of the frozen amount are committed to repayment of principal and interest on the bonds that financed the development. Thus, only the incremental taxes generated by the improvement in the property are used to pay back the debt. *See generally* Eagle, *Kelo*, Directed Growth, and Municipal Industrial Policy, 17 Sup. Ct. Econ. Rev. 63, 78-79 (2009); Tomme, Tax Increment Financing, Public Use or Private Abuse, 90 Minn. L. Rev. 213, 216 (2005).

There are some similarities in the methods of municipal and corporate finance, but there are also significant differences. The more important of these pertain to the roles of attorneys and underwriters.

Bond Counsel.   In the second half of the nineteenth century, a number of railroad bond issuers disclaimed liability on their own bonds because of errors made in issuing the bonds. To provide investors with some assurance that bonds were properly issued, bond counsel was retained to opine on the validity and enforceability of obligations of municipal issuers. Today, the opinion of bond counsel is an integral part of any municipal financing, and defective disclosure documents and misleading legal opinions may be a basis for asserting securities law liability against bond counsel. *See, e.g., Weiss v. SEC*, 468 F.3d 849 (D.C. Cir. 2006) (sustaining the imposition of sanctions by SEC against bond counsel). *See generally* The Function and Professional Responsibility of Bond Counsel (2011) (published by the National Association of Bond Lawyers).

Underwriters. Underwriters are active in municipal as well as corporate offerings. They operate somewhat differently, however, in the two contexts. In the corporate market, underwriters generally participate in offerings on the basis of negotiated bids. The underwriter has an ongoing relationship with the issuer and, spurred in part by the threat of Section 11 liability for defective registration statements, takes great pains to verify the accuracy of information given to potential investors. Although underwriters often act in a similar role in "negotiated" municipal offerings (free of the Section 11 risks), a large number of offerings are marketed on the basis of competitive, rather than negotiated, bids by underwriters. In a competitive bid offering, neither the underwriter nor its counsel will be involved until the final stages of an offering and the publication by the issuer of a notice of sale. At that point, interested underwriters have an opportunity to do some limited due diligence on the issuer, although any investigation they perform pales in comparison to their activities in a corporate securities offering. They then submit sealed bids and await the outcome of the competitive bidding.

2. Credit-Enhancing Devices

Municipal bond offerings may be supported by credit-enhancing devices, the most important of which has been insurance. Because of the strength of the participating insurance companies and reinsurers, insured municipal securities may receive high credit ratings regardless of the condition of the underlying issuer. As the risk bearer, the insuring organization has the incentive to perform whatever due diligence on the issuer may be needed.

Insurance is most effective when underwritten by companies with the highest credit ratings. In 2008, the industry encountered difficult times because of investment losses of insurers stemming from their portfolios' exposures to subprime mortgages and other distressed assets. As a consequence, rating agencies lowered or threatened to lower the credit ratings of a number of insurers, many of which withdrew from the market. These developments sharply curtailed the use of insurance in municipal bond offerings. In 2005, more than half of the bond offerings were insured. By early 2012, insurance was rarely offered, although there are some recent signs of a revival in the use of this credit-enhancing device for municipal offerings.

3. Disclosure Considerations

Municipal disclosures are made by means of a document called the *Official Statement,* which is a very rough counterpart to the corporate prospectus. Standards for disclosures are outlined in the Government Finance Officers Association's Disclosure Guidelines for State and Local Government Securities, the table of contents of which includes the following headings: Cover Page of the Official Statement, Summary of the Official Statement, Securities Being Offered and Related Documentation, Description of Issuer and Enterprise, Debt Structure, Financial Information, and Legal Matters. The Disclosure

Guidelines expressly do not set standards of legal sufficiency, but they do provide important guideposts for those involved in preparing the official statement. Although the Disclosure Guidelines have not been revised since 1991, practitioners continue to rely on these standards when drafting Official Statements.

In negotiated, or noncompetitive, bid situations, the underwriter will take the lead in preparing the official statement. In competitive bidding offerings, underwriters enter the process too late, and bond counsel will assume greater responsibility for preparing the official statement. In either situation, defects in an official statement are redressable under Section 10(b) of the '34 Act and Section 17(a) of the '33 Act, but not Section 11 or Section 12(a)(2) of the '33 Act. The Securities Act Amendments of 1975 added municipalities to the class of persons covered by Section 10(b).

Accounting and financial reporting standards provide an important distinction between the municipal and private securities markets. The Governmental Accounting Standards Board has justified the differences as follows:

> Separate accounting and financial reporting standards are essential because the needs of users of financial reports of governments and business enterprises differ. . . . Although businesses receive revenues from a voluntary exchange between a willing buyer and seller, governments obtain resources primarily from the involuntary payment of taxes. Taxes paid by an individual taxpayer often bear little direct relationship to the services received by that taxpayer. Overall, taxpayers collectively focus on assessing the value received from the resources they provide to government. Governmental accounting and financial reporting standards aim to address this need for public accountability information by helping stakeholders assess how public resources were acquired and either used during the period or are expected to be used. Such reporting also helps users assess whether current resources were sufficient to meet current service costs or whether some costs were shifted to future taxpayers, and whether the government's ability to provide services improved or deteriorated from the previous year.
>
> The needs of the users of governmental financial reports are reflected in differences in the components of the conceptual framework for setting accounting and financial reporting standards and in specific accounting and financial reporting standards themselves. Although investors and creditors are important constituencies of every standards-setting organization, the Governmental Accounting Standards Board's (GASB) conceptual framework also places priority on addressing the informational needs of citizens and elected representatives, two constituencies not identified as users of business enterprise financial statements by the Financial Accounting Standards Board (FASB). Consequently, the GASB's financial reporting objectives consider public accountability to be the cornerstone on which all other financial reporting objectives should be built.

GASB White Paper: Why Governmental Accounting and Financial Reporting Is—and Should Be—Different (2006). For a critical assessment of the failure to conform the regulation of municipal securities to broader standards and themes of securities regulation, *see* Gabaldon, Financial Federalism and the Short, Happy Life of Municipal Securities Regulation, 34 Iowa J. Corp. L. 739 (2009).

4. Regulation of Offerings

Prior to 1975, trading in municipal securities and the conduct of municipal securities professionals were largely exempt from regulation, and the SEC's jurisdiction was limited to post hoc enforcement of the antifraud provisions of the federal securities laws. The rather relaxed regulatory environment reflected: (1) concern over the costs of regulation (which would be passed on to state and local issuers of securities); (2) an assumption that purchasers of municipal securities were, for the most part, sophisticated institutions able to fend for themselves; and (3) uncertainty concerning the constitutional basis for congressional regulation of municipal issuers.

In response to evidence of pervasive fraudulent trading practices in the municipal securities markets during the early 1970s, the Securities Act Amendments of 1975 expanded the definition of *person* in Section 3(a)(9) of the '34 Act to include a "government or political subdivision, or instrumentality of a government," thus bringing the issuance of municipal securities within Section 10(b) of that statute. The 1975 amendments also included provisions establishing the Municipal Securities Rulemaking Board (MSRB) and requiring the registration of municipal securities dealers. Fear that the MSRB or the SEC might utilize rulemaking power to require the registration of municipal securities, however, prompted the so-called Tower Amendment, *see* Securities Exchange Act Section 15B(b), which expressly negates the authority of either agency to develop rules requiring issuers of municipal securities to file information prior to securities sales.

a. *The SEC and Rule 15c2-12*

In 1989, the SEC adopted Rule 15c2-12 under the authority given it by Section 15(c) of the '34 Act to promulgate rules and regulations to prevent deceptive practices by brokers and dealers. *See* Exchange Act Release No. 26,985 (June 28, 1989). The Rule is directed largely to underwriters participating in a primary offering of municipal securities with an aggregate offering amount of $1 million or more.

Paragraph (b)(1) of the Rule requires underwriters participating in a primary offering to "obtain and review an official statement that an issuer of such securities deems final." The obligation to review the official statement arises, in the SEC's view, from the underwriter's implied recommendation on the securities arising from its participation in the offering: "This recommendation implies that the underwriter has a reasonable basis for belief in the truthfulness and completeness of the key representations contained in the official statement. Once the underwriter has received and reviewed the official statement, it will be in a better position to assess the accuracy of the disclosure and to make informed recommendations to investors." Exchange Act Release No. 26,100, 3 Fed. Sec. L. Rep. (CCH) ¶25,097 (Sept. 22, 1988).

In 2010, the Commission adopted amendments to Rule 15c2-12 and took advantage of the occasion to elaborate on underwriters' responsibilities:

> The Commission believes that, if the underwriter finds that the issuer or obligated person has on multiple occasions during the previous five years, failed to provide on a timely basis continuing disclosure documents, including event notices

and failure to file notices, as required in continuing disclosure agreements for prior offerings it would be very difficult for the underwriter to make a reasonable determination that the issuer or obligated person would provide such information under a continuing disclosure agreement in connection with a subsequent offering. In the Commission's view, it is doubtful that an underwriter could meet the reasonable belief standard without the underwriter affirmatively inquiring as to that filing history. The underwriter's reasonable belief should be based on its independent judgment, not solely on representations of the issuer or obligated person as to the materiality of any failure to comply with any prior undertaking. If the underwriter finds that the issuer or obligated person has failed to provide such information, the underwriter should take that failure into account in forming its reasonable belief in the accuracy and completeness of representations made by the issuer or obligated person.

Release No. 34-62184A (May 26, 2010). And in March 2012, the SEC issued a "risk alert" outlining examples of effective practices identified by the staff that will be relevant when underwriters are examined by the SEC to assess their compliance with due diligence obligations. These include the use of due diligence memoranda, outlines for due diligence calls, and recordkeeping checklists. Shortly thereafter, a FINRA official indicated the self-regulatory organization would be considering the same factors when assessing whether member firms fulfilled their due diligence obligations.

Paragraph (b)(2) of Rule 15c2-12 requires that, except in competitively bid offerings, underwriters provide any potential customers who so request with a copy of the issuer's most recent preliminary official statement. The Rule does not establish the content of a preliminary official statement or require the preparation of such a document, but if one has been prepared, it must be made available to interested investors. The requirements of paragraph (b)(2) do not apply when an offering is on the basis of competitive bidding.

Paragraph (b)(4) requires underwriters to make the official statement available for a period of 90 days following the "end of the underwriting period." This period is shortened, however, if the official statement is available to any person from a nationally recognized municipal securities information repository, which is a facility discussed in the release excerpted below.

Paragraph (b)(5), added in the 1994 amendments to the Rule and further modified in 2010 amendments, requires underwriters to ascertain that an issuer or other obligor under the instrument has undertaken to provide secondary market disclosure, including notices of material events designated in the Rule. Paragraph (c), also added in the 1994 amendments, requires brokers and dealers recommending municipal securities in the secondary markets to have procedures in place to obtain notices of material events from issuers or other obligors.

The Rule includes three *exemptions* available if the securities are sold in denominations of not less than $100,000. The exemptions are available for limited placements (not more than 35 sophisticated investors), short-term securities (maturities of less than nine months), and securities that investors may put to the issuer at least as frequently as every nine months.

Rule 15c2-12 traditionally has relied on decentralized, voluntary dissemination of information through intermediaries known as nationally recognized municipal securities information repositories (NRMSIRs). More recently, the

SEC announced its support for an MSRB plan to streamline municipal securities disclosure by creating a centralized filing venue (Electronic Municipal Market Access, or EMMA) similar to the SEC's EDGAR system. *See* MSRB Release, EMMA: Electronic Municipal Market Access (Mar. 28, 2008). EMMA replaces the existing reliance on competition among NRMSIRs and offers investors electronic access to a database of information on municipal securities. The Commission subsequently adopted rule changes implementing the objective of a centralized filing repository (the MSRB) responsible for maintaining EMMA. *See* Release No. 34-59062 (Dec. 5, 2008). On prospects for EMMA, *see* Stanley, Narrowing the Disclosure Gap: Is EMMA EDGAR for the Municipal Securities Market?, 7 J.L. Econ. & Pol'y 91 (2010).

In a series of releases that have accompanied proposals and amendments to Rule 15c2-12, the Commission has offered its interpretation of the responsibilities of underwriters and other professionals who deal in municipal securities. In particular, it has consistently reminded underwriters of their existing obligations under the general antifraud provisions of the securities acts and the necessity that they have a reasonable basis for any recommendations concerning municipal securities. In the Commission's words: "When the underwriter provides disclosure documents to investors, it makes an implied representation that it has a reasonable basis for belief in the accuracy and completeness of the key representations contained in the documents." Exchange Act Release No. 26,985 (June 28, 1989). *See also* Exchange Act Release No. 33,741 (Mar. 9, 1994); Exchange Act Release No. 26,100 (Sept. 22, 1988).

The Commission had an opportunity to give meaning to these words as it sorted through the rubble of the Orange County bankruptcy. Early in 1998, the SEC settled an enforcement action against Credit Suisse First Boston Corp. stemming from a 1994 underwriting of more than $110 million of Orange County bonds. Asserting that the offering statement used in the underwriting misrepresented and omitted material facts, the Commission proceeded against the firm on the theory that the underwriter cannot simply rely on statements from the issuer in determining the adequacy of disclosure. The head of the SEC's regional office pointedly commented that underwriters "can't just slap their names on an offering circular [without] a reasonable basis for belief" that the information it contains is accurate. *See* Pasztor, SEC Tightens Disclosure Rules in Settling Orange County Case, Wall St. J., Jan. 30, 1998, at C1. First Boston agreed to pay a fine of $800,000 to resolve the SEC claims. Subsequently, the firm settled claims brought by the county. *See* Credit Suisse First Boston Settles Orange County Suit for $52.5 Million, 30 BNA Sec. Reg. & L. Rep. 748 (May 15, 1998).

The Commission also settled an action against Merrill Lynch based on its failure to conduct a professional review of official statements used in Orange County bond offerings underwritten by the firm. It noted that the settlement represented the first time the SEC "has placed blame for misleading disclosure squarely on an underwriter for failing to convey vital information about an offering to the firm's investment bankers." *See* Merrill Agrees to Pay $2 Million in Orange County Settlement with SEC, 30 BNA Sec. Reg. & L. Rep. 1278 (Aug. 28, 1998). The information not conveyed included the importance of key interest rate assumptions on likely investment returns and potential loss of principal. The settlement followed Merrill's earlier settlement for $400 million of the county's lawsuit against it. Among other institutional casualties of the Orange County offerings are accounting firm KPMG Peat Marwick ($75 million settlement) and bond counsel LeBoeuf, Lamb, Greene & MacRae ($55 million settlement). *See* KPMG Peat Marwick Settles Orange County Lawsuits for $75 Million, 30 BNA Sec. Reg. & L. Rep. 801 (May 22, 1998).

Rule 15c2-12 was last amended in 2010. The SEC is under ongoing pressure to amend the Rule to expand disclosures. Of particular concern are existing standards that do not require full disclosure of bank loans to municipalities, often structured as private placements. The MSRB has issued a Concept Release soliciting comment on the advisability of enhancing disclosure of these transactions. *See* Request for Comment on a Concept Proposal to Improve Disclosure of Direct Purchases and Bank Loans, MSRB Notice 2016-11 (Mar. 28, 2016). It noted:

> [I]nvestors may not be able to fully appreciate the overall amount of indebtedness of an issuer in a timely fashion, and they may also lack knowledge of key terms of any undisclosed indebtedness, which could be material to their investment decisions. For example, some direct purchases and bank loans may have provisions that make creditors senior to bondholders or that provide creditors with more favorable remedies than bondholders in the event of default.

Id. at 2. More broadly, some commentators argue for a broader and much more aggressive approach to disclosures in municipal offerings. *See, e.g.,* Naughton & Spamann, Fixing Public Sector Finances: The Accounting and Reporting Lever, 62 UCLA L. Rev. 572 (2015) (particularly critical of existing financial reporting standards and arguing that ineffective reporting and accounting gimmicks have directly contributed to the dramatic decline of public sector finances).

b. *The MSRB and Rule G-17*

As noted, the 1975 amendments established the MSRB, which is unique as a self-regulatory organization in that it exists by order of Congress rather than by action of an industry segment. The MSRB is charged with the development of rules governing transactions in municipal securities by brokers and dealers. The MSRB's rules are not effective, however, unless approved by the SEC, and the Board lacks enforcement powers with respect to its own rules.

The MSRB has adopted a number of rules addressing responsibilities of brokers and dealers. The most important of these is Rule G-17, which simply provides that "[i]n the conduct of its municipal securities activities, each broker, dealer, and municipal securities dealer shall deal fairly with all persons and shall not engage in any deceptive, dishonest, or unfair practice." As interpreted by the Board, the obligation to "deal fairly" requires the broker or dealer to disclose "all material facts concerning the transaction" known or reasonably ascertainable by the dealer.

The Dodd-Frank Wall Street Reform and Consumer Protection Act of 2010 broadened the MSRB's mission to include the protection of municipal securities issuers. In keeping with this expanded mandate, the MSRB in 2012 issued an interpretive notice under Rule G-17 expanding underwriter obligations to their state and local government clients to include disclosures about risks of complex financial transactions, potential conflicts of interest, and compensation received from third-party providers of derivatives and investments. *See* MSRB Interpretive Notice Concerning the Application of Rule G-17 to Underwriters of Municipal Securities (eff. Aug. 2, 2012). Two Commissioners dissented from the SEC's approval of the MSRB's interpretive guidance on the ground that the approach

> discourage[s] underwriters from distinguishing between less sophisticated municipal issuers that may benefit from and prefer to receive more extensive disclosures and those issuers that may determine that the additional disclosures are unnecessarily costly with little or no corresponding benefit. [At] least a portion of the increased cost to underwriters, including the cost associated with having to manage the regulatory uncertainty the guidance creates, would likely be passed on to municipal entities and, accordingly, to taxpayers.

Subsequently, the MSRB issued a more comprehensive statement of fair practice duties brokers and dealers owe to issuers of municipal securities when acting as underwriters for issuers' new issues of municipal securities. *See* MSRB Notice 2012-38, Guidance on Implementation of Interpretive Notice Concerning the Application of MSRB Rule G-17 to Underwriters of Municipal Securities (July 18, 2012).

NOTES AND QUESTIONS

1. The $1 Million Threshold. Is it sound for Rule 15c2-12 to apply the disclosure requirements only when the aggregate offering price exceeds $1 million? Consider the comment of one professional on this point: "If you cannot provide sufficient information, you should not be borrowing in the public markets." Picker, The Disclosure Debate Gets Nasty, Institutional Investor (April 1988), at 169, 170. Do you agree? What is the relevance of the exemption of limited placements to this inquiry?

2. Rulemaking Authority. Rule 15c2-12 was promulgated under Section 15(c) of the '34 Act, which authorizes the SEC to develop rules and regulations defining manipulative, deceptive, or otherwise fraudulent devices or contrivances on the part of brokers and dealers. Why isn't Section 10(b) of the '34 Act sufficient to address the problem tackled in Rule 15c2-12, and why does the Rule focus on the duties of underwriters, rather than issuers? Could the SEC have extended the offering statement distribution duties to issuers? *See* Securities Exchange Act Section 15B(d) (the Tower Amendment).

3. Content of Disclosure Document. Rule 15c2-12 does not establish content requirements for "near final" official statements. A footnote in the release issued at the time of the Rule's adoption, however, noted that "efforts by the industry have produced disclosure guidelines that are widely followed in the preparation of municipal official statements." Specifically, the Government Finance Officers Association has published Disclosure Guidelines for State and Local Government Securities (GFOA Guidelines). The GFOA Guidelines have long influenced the content and structure of official statements. Yet the GFOA represents a discrete group within the industry and does not have the status of a self-regulatory organization. Why is the SEC unwilling or unable to dictate the content of the official statement? Would failure to comply with the GFOA Guidelines constitute a manipulation or fraud?

*4. **Do Public Servants Lie?*** It is comforting to assume that officials vested with the public interest are less likely than those more entrepreneurially inclined to mislead the investing public. That may or may not be the case, but consider the SEC's comments on San Diego's failure to disclose in connection with the sale of $260 million in municipal bonds the extent of the city's underfunding of pension and retiree health benefits:

> The City, through its officials, acted with scienter. City officials who participated in drafting the misleading disclosure were well aware of the City's pension and retiree health care issues and the magnitude of the City's future liabilities. Moreover, even though the City officials knew that the City's pension issues were of concern to the rating agencies, they failed to disclose material information regarding the City's pension and retiree health care issues. In light of the City's officials' detailed knowledge of the magnitude of the City's pension and retiree health care liabilities and of the rating agencies' interest in those liabilities, the City officials acted recklessly in failing to disclose material information regarding those liabilities.

In the Matter of the City of San Diego, Securities Act Release No. 8751, 2006 SEC LEXIS 2608 (Nov. 14, 2006). The SEC charged five former San Diego city officials with fraud in connection with the offerings. Earlier, comments highly critical of disclosure practices were set forth in staff reports on Orange County defaults and New York City near defaults. *See* Report of Investigation in the Matter of County of Orange, California as It Relates to the Conduct of the Members of the Board of Supervisors, Exchange Act Release No. 36,761, at 6 (Jan. 24, 1996); SEC Staff Report, Transactions in Securities of the City of New York 110-111 (1977).

On the potential fraud liability of public officials for misstatements to investors, *see* Huang, Are Investors Listening When Politicians Speak? Assessing the Securities Fraud Liability of Political Officials Who Manage Large Civic Works Projects, 39 Am. Crim. L. Rev. 147 (2002).

*5. **Repeal the Exemption?*** In the mid-1970s, Senator Eagleton introduced legislation that would repeal the exemption for securities issued by state and local governments. Nothing came of the proposal, and the current environment favors greater rather than less regulation of the municipal securities market. Nevertheless, the proposal raises an interesting policy question. How might some municipal issuers actually benefit from a repeal of the exemption?

*6. **Possible Reform?*** In a 2012 report on the municipal securities markets, the SEC recommended consideration of a number of possible reforms for improving market regulation and investor protection, including key legislative changes that would authorize the SEC to: (1) require use and dissemination of Official Statements; and (2) regulate the form and content of financial statements. *See* SEC, Report on the Municipal Securities Market (July 31, 2012). Note the SEC did *not* recommend eliminating the Section 3(a)(2) exemption (except for conduit borrowers that are private entities rather than municipal entities).

PROBLEMS

8-1.   In connection with a public offering of general obligation bonds, Newark has developed a preliminary official statement. The underwriter will be selected on the basis of competitive bidding. When must the preliminary official statement be made available to potential investors? When must the underwriters obtain and review the official statement deemed final by the issuer? When and for how long must the final statement be made available to potential customers? Which potential customers are entitled to receive copies of the final official statement?

8-2.   On April 1, Wichita completes an offering of general obligation bonds with an aggregate principal amount of $999,000. The issuance is through an underwriter. On June 1 of the same year, it commences an identical issuance through the same underwriter. Will either or both of these offerings come under Rule 15c2-12? (Note that the Rule does not address this issue.)

8-3.   Los Angeles intends to complete a private placement exempt from Rule 15c2-12. The underwriting syndicate it has engaged has lined up 50 investors, each of whom clearly meets the definition of an accredited investor set forth in Regulation D. Any problems?

5.   "Pay to Play" Practices and Rule G-37

To address concerns over campaign contributions by broker-dealers to public officials who award underwriting business, the MSRB adopted Rule G-37, which restricts "pay to play" practices in negotiated underwritings. The Rule became effective in 1994, following SEC approval. It prohibits a securities firm from engaging in municipal securities business with an issuer if the firm, any municipal finance professional associated with the firm, or any political action committee controlled by the firm has made political contributions to an official of the issuer within the previous two years. Minority and female-dealer firms opposed the Rule G-37 for fear that it would operate to the benefit of established financial firms with long-term ties to municipal issuers. *See* Altman, Minority Firms, Not "Pay to Play" Are G-37's Target, Treasurer Says, The Bond Buyer, Aug. 31, 1994, at 1. The Rule withstood an early constitutional challenge launched by William Blount, the chairman of the Alabama Democratic Party and a municipal securities dealer. *See Blount v. SEC*, 61 F.3d 938 (D.C. Cir. 1995), *cert. denied*, 517 U.S. 1119 (1996). In 2016, the MSRB expanded the reach of Rule G-37 to reach municipal advisers (defined by Section 15B of the '34 Act as persons advising municipal entities with respect to financial products or issuing municipal securities). On Rule G-37 generally, *see* Jordan, The Regulation of "Pay-to-Play" and the Influence of Political Contributions in the Municipal Securities Industry, 1999 Colum. Bus. L. Rev. 489; Opp, Ending Pay-to-Play in the Municipal Securities Business: MSRB Rule G-37 Ten Years Later, 76 U. Colo. L. Rev. 243 (2005).

In 1996, the MSRB adopted a second Rule, Rule G-38, dealing with the related problem of undisclosed finders fees and kickbacks paid by dealers. The Rule provides that all arrangements with "consultants" must be in writing and disclosed to the issuer and the MSRB.

In response to concerns raised by SEC examiners over compliance with pay to play restrictions, the SEC in 2012 issued a risk alert reminding broker-dealers of their obligations to maintain adequate records and supervision to ensure compliance. *See* SEC Office of Compliance Inspections and Examinations, "Pay to Play" Prohibitions for Brokers, Dealers and Municipal Securities Dealers Under MSRB Rules (Aug. 31, 2012).

6.   Secondary Markets

Although relatively liquid, historically the secondary market for municipal securities has lacked the transparency offered by the secondary market for private sector securities. The SEC and MSRB consistently have pushed for improved disclosures, particularly relating to the pricing of municipal securities traded in the secondary market. An important step in this direction came in 2005 with the transition from the Transaction Reporting System, which provided next-day information on trades, to the current Real-time Transaction Reporting System. A comprehensive study of 43 million secondary market trades in the 2003-2010 period revealed that real time transparency in trading information has had the intended effect of decreasing price differences in customer-to-customer trading. *See* Municipal Securities Rulemaking Board, Report on Secondary Market Trading in the Municipal Securities Market (2014).

7.   Public Financing for the Private Sector

In a simpler world, public financing would be used to fund public-sector projects, and private financing would be used to fund private-sector projects. In our more complex world, however, the line between public and private projects is blurred. In the 1960s, many local governments began to respond to rising unemployment rates by making available public funds to finance labor-intensive commercial and industrial development. Over the years, the range of projects financed through conduit revenue bonds expanded to include a wide variety of undertakings, from the development of sports facilities to the expansion of fast food chains. Typically, the governmental units would provide financing by offering to the public low-interest, tax-exempt industrial development bonds (IDBs). The project financed would then be sold to or leased by the private-sector operator. Alternatively, funds raised by the municipality might be "loaned" to a commercial operator for construction and operation of the project. The amounts needed to make principal and interest payments on the IDBs would come from revenues generated by the project (in the form of sales proceeds, lease payments, or principal and interest payments on the loan by the municipality). IDBs bear strong similarities to the revenue bonds described earlier, with one important exception. Revenue bonds finance projects owned and operated by a governmental unit. IDBs, on the other hand, finance projects often owned and invariably operated by a private-sector party. Since payments by the municipality on the IDB are dependent on the success of the private-sector party in operating a project, the issue arises as to whether the bond should be accorded exempt security status under Section 3(a)(2).

In the 1960s, the Internal Revenue Service (IRS) began asserting that some debt obligations of political subdivisions were obligations of private companies enjoying the subsidies of tax exemption and, accordingly, interest on IDBs was not tax exempt. Reflecting the close relationship between the exemption for municipal securities accorded by the securities laws and the tax-exempt status of those securities, the SEC in 1968 adopted Rule 131. The Rule provides that, if any part of a public debt obligation is payable from proceeds derived from a lease, sale, or loan arrangement with an industrial or commercial enterprise, the obligation of the private party will be deemed a "separate security" issued by that party. The Rule includes, however, important exceptions to the separate security treatment. The underlying obligation is not a security if: (1) the debt obligation on the municipal security is payable from the general revenues of the governmental unit; (2) the obligation relates to a public project owned and operated by or on behalf of and under the control of a governmental unit; or (3) the obligation relates to a facility leased to and under the control of a private party that is part of a public project that, as a whole, is owned by and under the control of a governmental unit.

Although the IRS and the SEC were engaged in something of an assault on IDBs, Congress was not similarly inclined. It rejected the Service's position by amending the IRC in 1968 to continue the tax exemption for IDBs. In 1970, Congress amended Section 3(a)(2) to extend the exemption to tax-exempt IDBs (as defined in the IRC). At least in theory, the addition of tax-exempt IDBs to Section 3(a)(2) thwarted the SEC's attempt to deny the exemption to some public financings structured for private benefit and rendered the separate security concept of Rule 131 largely irrelevant.

But the debate did not die. Indeed, as the use of IDBs expanded as a result of the congressional actions in 1968 and 1970, concerns increased over the propriety of according tax-exempt and exempt-security status to bond issuances used to fund private-sector development. Consider, for example, the issues presented when a fast food chain funded part of its expansion through this technique of public finance. In the late 1970s, McDonald's planned to acquire 13 sites and construct restaurants on the properties. McDonald's would then lease the "improved" parcels to its franchisees. To finance the acquisitions and development, various municipalities agreed to acquire the properties from McDonald's (subject to the leases to the franchisees). The purchases would be funded through the issuance to the public of IDBs. After the bond issuance, the municipalities would reconvey the properties to McDonald's in exchange for notes, the principal and interest payments on which were tied to (and the source of) the principal and interest payments on the IDBs. Thus, the bonds permitted McDonald's to develop its restaurants through public rather than private financing.

Projects such as those proposed by McDonald's raise a number of disclosure issues concerning the Section 3(a)(2) exemption for municipal securities and IDBs. Principal and interest payments on the bonds were dependent on the successful operation of the restaurants, and we would expect that disclosures about the restaurant business, McDonald's, and the franchisees would be of interest to potential investors. Since an exemption from registration would not have been available for a public bond offering by McDonald's itself, it seems somewhat incongruous to use the presence of a public intermediary to shield the true issuers from the disclosures normally incident to public offerings. However important these issues may be from a public policy perspective, Congress essentially foreclosed debate through its 1968 and 1970 amendments to the IRC and the '33 Act. Thus, McDonald's was able to secure a favorable no-action response on the availability of the Section 3(a)(2) exemption for its expansion program. See McDonald's Corp., SEC No-Action Letter, [1980 Transfer Binder] Fed. Sec. L. Rep. (CCH) ¶76,336 (Dec. 17, 1979).

Although the 1970s were a good decade for the proponents of the use of subsidies (i.e., tax-exempt bonds) for private development purposes, the 1980s saw a shift in congressional thinking on the issue. Tax reform legislation in 1982 and 1986 instituted wholesale revisions of the IRC's treatment of tax-exempt securities of municipal issuers. For the most part, IDBs as tax-exempt instruments of finance have been eliminated from the IRC. Under the IRC as amended in 1986, bonds issued by state or local governments fall into two classes: private activity bonds and governmental use bonds. The interest on private activity bonds is not tax exempt unless the bonds fall into limited classes of permitted uses, including bonds issued to finance multifamily rental housing, water facilities, airports, docks and wharves, mass commuting facilities, sewage disposal plants, and hazardous waste facilities; bonds issued to finance student loans to state residents; and small issues (less than $10 million) offered for the purpose of financing the construction of manufacturing facilities. Moreover, tax-exempt private activity bonds are subject to significant volume limitations through the imposition of ceilings on the amount of private activity bonds that can be issued by any state or its subdivisions. The net effect of these changes in the tax law is to limit sharply, but not eliminate, the use of public financing to fund private commercial or industrial projects. Interest on governmental use bonds, on the other hand, remains tax exempt. For good discussions of the use of tax-exempt bonds for private redevelopment projects, see Eagle, Kelo, Directed Growth, and Municipal Industrial Policy, 17 Sup. Ct. Econ. Rev. 63 (2009); Knepper, Eliminating the Federal Subsidy in Kelo: Restricting the Availability of Tax-Exempt Financing for Redevelopment Projects, 94 Geo. L.J. 1635 (2006).

Section 3(a)(2) continues to reference industrial development bonds even though changes in tax law have replaced these interests with private activity bonds. The section has been interpreted consistent with changes in tax law. See, e.g., Tooele County, Utah, SEC No-Action Letter (Aug. 30, 1989) (favorable response concerning exemption as industrial development bond for private activity bond under the IRC.

The SEC has recommended that Congress amend the Section 3(a)(2) exemption to deny its use to conduit borrowers that are private rather than municipal entities. *See* SEC, Report on the Municipal Securities Markets 135 (July 31, 2012).

PROBLEM

8-4. In order to induce a major airline to expand its service to the community, an airport authority (which you may assume is a political subdivision or public instrumentality for purposes of Section 3(a)(2)) would like to add a new hangar to its present airport facility. Construction would be funded through a long-term conduit revenue bond offering by the airport authority. The airline in turn would enter into a long-term lease of the hangar. What are the issues under Rule 131, and how are they likely to be resolved? *See* Securities Act Release No. 5055, [1969-1970 Transfer Binder] Fed. Sec. L. Rep. (CCH) ¶77,797 (Mar. 31, 1970).

C.   *Securities Issued or Guaranteed by a Bank*

1.   The Exemption in General

Legislative history supporting the Section 3(a)(2) exemption of securities issued or guaranteed by banks is sparse, although there is some indication that Congress felt the existing bank regulatory structure offered "adequate" supervision over securities issuances by banks. *See* H.R. Rep. No. 85, 73d Cong., 1st Sess. 14 (1933). One commentator has suggested the exemption was included on the mistaken belief that banks were already required to file information with banking authorities comparable to that which would be included in a registration statement. *See* Butera, Bank Exemption from the 1933 Securities Act, 93 Banking L.J. 432, 457 (1976).

For purposes of the exemption for securities issued or guaranteed by banks, Section 3(a)(2) defines *bank* to mean "any national bank, or any banking institution organized under the laws of any State, territory, or the District of Columbia, the business of which is substantially confined to banking and is supervised by the State or territorial banking commission or similar official." Securities issued or guaranteed by bank holding companies (which, relative to banks, are subject to minimal regulation) are not within the Section 3(a)(2) exemption. *See, e.g.,* Bankers Trust Co., SEC No-Action Letter, [1971-1972 Transfer Binder] Fed. Sec. L. Rep. (CCH) ¶78,474 (Sept. 22, 1971).

A somewhat closer call is presented by those institutions that, although not banks in the traditional sense of that term, operate as the functional equivalent of commercial banks. A number of no-action letters have addressed the question of whether securities issued or guaranteed by industrial loan companies qualify for the exemption. *Industrial loan company* is a generic term with a meaning that varies substantially from state to state. In general, these companies are depository institutions that make consumer and, in some cases, commercial and real estate loans. They typically are regulated at the state level as financial institutions, and in recent years, the line between industrial loan companies and banks has blurred. A number of industrial loan companies have been successful in securing favorable no-action responses on the availability of the exemption. *See, e.g.,* Morris Plan Co. of California, SEC No-Action Letter, 1990 SEC No-Act. LEXIS 777 (May 7, 1990) (exemption available to industrial loan company because of the scope of its banking powers in accepting deposits and making loans, the extent of regulation by the California commissioner of corporations, and the maintenance of FDIC insurance).

A related issue concerns the ability of U.S. branches of foreign banks to avail themselves of the Section 3(a)(2) exemption. Nondiscriminatory treatment of U.S. branches of foreign banks was mandated by the 1978 International Banking Act (IBA), which allows foreign banks to establish a "federal" branch or agency licensed and supervised by the comptroller of the currency. The purpose of the IBA was to establish parity of treatment between foreign and domestic banks in like circumstances. Prior to 1986, the SEC issued more than 100 no-action letters concerning securities issued or guaranteed by U.S. branches of foreign banks. Beginning in 1984, it conditioned a favorable no-action letter on receipt of a legal opinion "that the nature and extent of federal and state regulation and supervision of the branch or agency in question were substantially equivalent to that applicable to federal or state chartered domestic banks doing business in the same jurisdiction." In 1986, the Commission formalized this position in Securities Act Release No. 6661, 1 Fed. Sec. L. Rep. (CCH) ¶2024A (Sept. 29, 1986).

2. Collateralized and Pass-Through Securities

Section 3(a)(2) exempts securities "issued or guaranteed" by a bank. Few interpretive problems with the concepts of issuing and guaranteeing arise when a bank offers its securities (e.g., common stock or bonds) to the public or guarantees the debt of a third party. Contemporary finance techniques, however, go well beyond these relatively straightforward transactions and test the limits of the exemption for bank-issued or bank-guaranteed securities.

Consider, for example, the development of structured financing, a financing technique that permits a corporation to utilize its receivables as a means of immediately tapping the capital markets. A corporation with receivables from its customers may, of course, collect the receivables as they become due, but this would require it to defer receipt of cash that might be put to good use if immediately available. As a means of effectively converting the receivables to cash, the company might instead set up a shell corporation, transfer the receivables to the shell, and have the shell offer *its* debt obligations to the public. If this is all that is done, we have a securities issuance by the shell for which an exemption from the registration requirements would probably not be available. Add one more feature in the form of a bank guarantee of the receivables. Provided the guarantee is unconditional and covers in full principal and interest payments, the presence of the bank guarantee will mean that the Section 3(a)(2) exemption will be available and the debt obligations of the shell need not be registered.[3] *See generally* Report by the United States Securities and Exchange Commission on the Financial Guarantee Market: The Use of the Exemption in Section 3(a)(2) of the Securities Act of 1933 by Banks and the Use of Insurance Policies to Guarantee Debt Securities (Aug. 28, 1987). This result is sensible only to the degree the premise underlying the exemption for bank-guaranteed securities is valid (i.e., investors do not need the disclosures prompted by registration because the bank regulation regime adequately protects their interest).

Bank guarantees are not limited to structured financings and are used with some regularity in offerings of pass-through securities. Recall the earlier discussion of pass-throughs as separate securities in Chapter 2. As was noted, almost any kind of income-producing instrument with standardized terms is suitable for use in pass-throughs. In some pass-throughs, the underlying instruments are not securities (e.g., residential real estate mortgages) or are exempt securities (e.g., government securities), but the pooling and packaging of the instruments may create separate securities requiring registration before offers can be made. A guarantee of the pass-through by a governmental agency or bank, however, will exempt the securities from the registration requirements. Pooled residential real estate mortgages, for example, often are guaranteed by an instrumentality of the government (e.g., the Government National Mortgage Association) and need not be registered. Similarly, pass-throughs of residential real estate mortgages guaranteed by a bank are exempt.[4]

If a bank is unwilling to guarantee pass-throughs, such as residential mortgages, it may nevertheless seek to exempt the offering as one *issued* by the bank. In an important no-action letter request, Bank of America argued the exemption was available for the packaging of private-sector mortgages it had originated. The Bank intended to assign the mortgages to an unaffiliated bank as custodian for the benefit of the holders of the certificates and to service the mortgages in the pool for a monthly service fee. Moreover, the Bank would make to investors representations and warranties concerning the terms and quality of the mortgages and would be obligated to repurchase mortgages in the event of a breach of the representations and warranties. Although the Bank did not guarantee payment of principal and interest, it argued the Section 3(a)(2) exemption was available because it was the issuer (rather than the guarantor) of the mortgage-backed securities:

> No other entity, corporate or governmental, has an economic interest of any significance in the transactions here contemplated, and there is no "issuer" of the mortgage notes underlying the Certificates, other than the numerous individual mortgagors. We recognize that, in certain instances in which the Commission or its Staff has held the 3(a)(2) exemption was not available, the "issuer" has been

---

3. In many structured financings, guarantees of insurance companies, rather than banks, are used. Although the Section 3(a)(2) exemption does not extend to guarantees of insurance companies, the guarantee may permit use of the Section 3(a)(2) exemption for prime-quality commercial paper, as discussed infra.

4. In addition, Section 4(a)(5), which was added to the '33 Act in 1975, provides a transaction exemption for certain mortgage-backed securities originated by banks, savings and loan associations, or mortgagees approved by the Secretary of Housing and Urban Development. The exemption is available only if the minimum price for each purchaser of the securities is at least $250,000.

stated to be the separate "pool." . . . In these instances, however, the banks seeking to rely upon the 3(a)(2) exemption had at best a custodial function only and not the total identification with the pool or the assets underlying the security which the Bank here would have.

Without explanation, the Division of Corporation Finance declined to issue the requested no-action letter, noting, significantly and somewhat unusually, that "the Commission concurs in the Division view that the Certificates are not exempt from registration pursuant to Section 3(a)(2) of the Securities Act." Bank of Am. Nat'l Trust & Sav. Ass'n, SEC No-Action Letter, [1977-1978 Transfer Binder] Fed. Sec. L. Rep. (CCH) ¶81,193 (Apr. 19, 1977).

Bank of America's argument apparently failed because interests in the mortgage pools were "separate securities" neither issued nor guaranteed by the Bank. A 1981 release sheds some light on the concept of separate securities and the circumstances under which the packaging bank will be treated as an issuer and therefore entitled to avail itself of the Section 3(a)(2) exemption. The release addressed the status of retail repurchase agreements (repos). As a technique to raise short-term capital, a number of banks and savings and loan associations offered to the general public interests in their own debt obligations collateralized by income-producing (typically U.S. government) securities held in trust by a third-party financial institution. After the bank's debt obligations matured and were satisfied, the collateral securities would revert to the bank. The SEC indicated the pool of government securities used as collateral would not be a separate security because, in part, (1) the investor obtains none of the economic characteristics of ownership of the underlying government securities; (2) the investor is not subject to swings in the value of the pool of government securities over the term of the agreement (the debt obligations purchased by the investors were nontransferable); (3) the interest paid by the bank is not limited to or dependent on the interest earned by the pool of government securities; and (4) the maturities of the government securities were not coterminous with the maturities of the bank's debt obligations. *See* Securities Act Release No. 6351, 1 Fed. Sec. L. Rep. (CCH) ¶2024 (Sept. 25, 1981).

PROBLEMS

8-5. NationsBank proposes to offer interests in a pool of mortgages it has previously originated. It will not guarantee timely payments of principal and interest. Will the Section 3(a)(2) exemption be available?

8-6. NationsBank decides to guarantee timely payment of principal (but not interest) on mortgages in the pool. Is the Section 3(a)(2) exemption available?

8-7. Rather than offering interests in a pool of mortgages, NationsBank proposes to issue debt instruments (in its name) to the public. The debt instruments will be secured by the pool of mortgages. Is the Section 3(a)(2) exemption available?

D. *Commercial Paper*

Section 3(a)(3) exempts any security that is a "note, draft, bill of exchange, or banker's acceptance," the proceeds of which are to be used for "current transactions" and the maturity of which does not exceed nine months. As the Second Circuit has noted, there is much more to this exemption than meets the eye:

> It is inconceivable that Congress intended §3(a)(3) to exempt from registration a periodic public offering of the issuer's own notes to small investors simply because their maturity was less than nine months. It is almost equally unlikely that Congress meant that an issuer soliciting broad public investment in notes issued for general corporate purposes should be able to avoid the anti-fraud provisions of the 1934 Act simply by arranging that they should have "a maturity at the time of issuance of not exceeding nine months."

SEC v. American Board of Trade, 751 F.2d 529, 539-540 (2d Cir. 1984).

Today, the most significant issuers in the $1 trillion commercial paper (commonly called "CP" for short) market are bank holding companies, finance companies, and industrial corporations. The largest companies in the United States issue CP and often do so in direct transactions with investors that do not involve intermediary broker-dealers. Maturities range up to 270 days but average about 30 days. The market is not limited to corporate lenders, and individuals have become significant lenders in the CP market by means of their indirect participation through "money market" mutual funds.

The 2008 financial crisis put considerable strain on the CP market as issuers of CP encountered difficulty in rolling over their short-term debt. The problems were partially alleviated with Federal Reserve intervention in the form of a funding facility to provide a "liquidity backstop" for issuers. For a general description of the CP market, *see* the web site of the Federal Reserve Bank of New York (*www.ny.frb.org*). *See also* Anderson & Gascon, The Commercial Paper Market, the FED, and the 2007-09 Financial Crisis, Federal Res. Bank of St. Louis Rev., Nov./Dec. 2009 at 589 (available online).

As is true with most exemptions, the outer limits of the CP exemption are not defined sharply. Few would quarrel that a three-month note issued by Exxon-Mobil Corporation and purchased by a pension fund fits neatly within the exemption. But does the same conclusion apply to any short-term borrowing by a corporate or, for that matter, an individual borrower? The answer lies in both the wording of the exemption and the substantial administrative and judicial gloss it has acquired over the years.

1. The Contours of Section 3(a)(3)

The Current Operations Requirement.   By its terms, the exemption is available only if the proceeds of the borrowing have been or are to be used for *current operations*. In a 1961 release, the SEC commented:

[T]he current transactions standard is not satisfied where the proceeds are to be used for the discharge of existing indebtedness unless such indebtedness is itself exempt under section 3(a)(3); the purchase or construction of a plant; the purchase of durable machinery or equipment; the funding of commercial real estate development or financing; the purchase of real estate mortgages or other securities; the financing of mobile homes or home improvements; or the purchase or establishment of a business enterprise.

Securities Act Release No. 4412, 1 Fed. Sec. L. Rep. (CCH) ¶2045 (Sept. 20, 1961). In this same release, the SEC noted that the current operations requirement covers "assets easily convertible into cash and . . . comparable to liquid inventories of an industrial or mercantile company." In other words, proceeds should be invested only in those assets easily convertible to cash so that the possibility of issuer default on the CP is lessened.

Although seemingly strict, the current operations restriction has *not* barred the use of CP proceeds to make construction loans; purchase furniture, fixtures, and vehicles; and pay retirement benefits. The positions taken in some no-action letters are far more liberal than the guidelines set forth in Release No. 4412. *See, e.g.,* Ryder Truck Rental, SEC No-Action Letter, [1980 Transfer Binder] Fed. Sec. L. Rep. (CCH) ¶76,337 (Dec. 18, 1979) (no-action letter granted for the sale of notes to finance the purchase of trucks and tractors to be leased for average term of 52 months); First National State Bancorporation, SEC No-Action Letter, [1976-1977 Transfer Binder] Fed. Sec. L. Rep. (CCH) ¶80,917 (Nov. 9, 1976) (allowing the issuance of CP for the purpose of retiring nonexempt debt). The SEC's liberality in interpreting the scope of the exemption, including its failure to strictly require the tracing of CP proceeds to current expenses, prompted an attorney for the agency to comment that the current operations requirement "is honored more in theory than fact." *See* Lowenstein, The Commercial Paper Market and the Federal Securities Laws, 4 Corp. L. Rev. 128, 145 (1981).

Note that issuers are not required to trace funds from Section 3(a)(3) offerings to particular permitted uses. Under the CP capacity doctrine, the current operations requirement is considered satisfied so long as the issuer's total amount of outstanding CP does not exceed its total current operations expenditures.

The Prime Quality Requirement.   An important interpretive gloss on the exemption is that the CP be of "prime quality." Traditionally, this has meant the CP must receive a high rating (but not necessarily the top rating) for quality from one of the organizations that rate CP (the most important being Standard & Poor's and Moody's).

Ratings agencies have been criticized on a number of grounds, not the least of which concerns their slowness in responding to negative changes in issuers' financial circumstances. Enron and WorldCom, for example, continued to issue CP rated as "prime quality" long after their financial condition deteriorated to levels well below what should be expected to support such a rating. More recently, the financial crisis beginning in 2007 prompted the rapid downgrading of CP that had been highly rated at issuance. Given the short duration of these instruments, the rapidity with which the downgrades occurred called into question the adequacy of the initial high ratings. *See generally* Mulligan, From AAA to F: How the Credit Rating Agencies Failed America and What Can Be Done to Protect Investors, 50 B.C. L. Rev. 1275 (2009). The Credit Rating Agency Reform Act of 2006 gave the SEC greater oversight over ratings agencies, and the Dodd-Frank Wall Street Reform and Consumer Protection Act enhanced the SEC's enforcement mechanisms and imposed additional requirements on credit rating agencies. The Commission has made and proposed a number of reforms intended to improve the quality and transparency of ratings. *See, e.g.,* Release No. 34-57967 (June 16, 2008).

Continuing concerns over the adequacy and quality of credit ratings create some doubts as to whether the CP exemption will remain closely tied to prime quality ratings. In *In re Enron Corp.*, 388 B.R. 131 (S.D.N.Y. 2008), for example, defendant Goldman Sachs, which had acted as one of three dealers for Enron CP sought removal of a proceeding from the bankruptcy court on the ground that the case requires a substantial reconsideration of the contours of the CP exemption. Although the court seemingly acknowledged that the scope of the exemption requires further consideration, it declined to remove the matter from the bankruptcy court because the case may be decided on grounds other than the scope of the exemption, in which event the securities law issue would be rendered moot.

Manner of Offering. The Section 3(a)(3) exemption covers only those short-term notes "not ordinarily purchased by the general public." Securities Act Release No. 4412, 1 Fed. Sec. L. Rep. (CCH) ¶2045 (Sept. 20, 1961). This is enforced by requiring that short-term notes be issued only in large denominations (typically $100,000), prohibiting general advertising and solicitation, and requiring that any noninstitutional investors be sophisticated. *See, e.g.,* Prescient Markets, Inc., SEC No-Action Letter (Jan. 29, 2001) (no-action letter for Internet-based, electronic execution platform where access is limited to institutional investors); *SEC v. The Better Life Club of America, Inc.*, 995 F. Supp. 167, 174 (D.D.C. 1998), *aff'd*, 203 F.3d 54 (D.C. Cir. 2000) (notes were "clearly not CP [when] offered to small-scale investors in the general public [and] not to typical, sophisticated, experienced purchasers of commercial paper").

Duration of the Notes. Since Section 3(a)(3) is available only for those notes with maturities of less than nine months, the exemption is limited to short-term financings.

Read with the current operations and prime quality elements of the exemption, the limitation on duration of qualifying notes may be seen as an attempt to remove from the registration requirements of the '33 Act only those transactions in which the risk of investors is minimal because the issuer is precluded from capturing the borrowed capital and committing it to long-term and illiquid uses.

The contours of the Section 3(a)(3) exemption discussed above seemed reasonably well settled prior to the Supreme Court's decision in *Reves v. Ernst & Young*, 494 U.S. 56 (1990) (excerpted in Chapter 2). Recall that in *Reves* the controversy involved the marketing to the public of notes issued by an agricultural cooperative. The issue before the Court was whether the notes were securities under the '34 Act. Further, recall that Section 3(a)(10) of the '34 Act defines a *security* to include notes, but then excludes from the definition notes that have a maturity of less than nine months. Although the exemption provided by Section 3(a)(3) includes the additional requirement that the proceeds of the notes be used for current operations, the definition in the '34 Act and the exemption in the '33 Act have generally been viewed as coterminous. In *Reves*, however, Justice Marshall (joined by Justices Brennan, Blackmun, and Kennedy) dodged a construction of the '34 Act's definition as extending only to CP. Dissenting Chief Justice Rehnquist (joined by Justices White, O'Connor, and Scalia) not only refused to apply standards developed for the Section 3(a)(3) exemption to the Section 3(a)(10) definition, but also called into question whether the Section 3(a)(3) exemption is limited to CP exchanged among sophisticated traders:

> I am not altogether convinced that the legislative history of §3(a)(3) [of the '33 Act] supports that interpretation even with respect to the terms "any note" in the exemption in §3(a)(3), and to bodily transpose that legislative history to another statute has little to commend it as a method of statutory construction.

494 U.S. at 79. Justice Stevens, on the other hand, concluded that the legislative history of Section 3(a)(3) reveals the section extends only to CP and there is no reason to read Section 3(a)(10) any differently. The long and short is that the book is not closed on either the Section 3(a)(3) exemption or the Section 3(a)(10) definition.

PROBLEMS

8-8. Issuer proposes to sell nine-month notes carrying the highest ratings from Moody's and Standard & Poor's. Will the issuance qualify for the Section 3(a)(3) exemption if either: (1) the notes provide for automatic rollovers absent contrary instructions from the purchasers delivered to the issuer prior to the expiration of the nine-month terms; or (2) the automatic rollover feature is not part of the package, but noteholders may accomplish the same result by instructing the issuer they wish to reinvest payable proceeds in new notes? What if the notes are demand notes instead of term notes? *See* Securities Act Release No. 4412, supra.

8-9. Same facts as above. A downturn in the issuer's business causes a reduction in the ratings of the notes to "highly speculative." *See Franklin Sav. Bank v. Levy*, 406 F. Supp. 40, 43 (S.D.N.Y. 1975), *rev'd on other grounds*, 551 F.2d 521 (2d Cir. 1977). What is the effect of the rating shift on the availability of the exemption for subsequent rollovers or renewals?

2. Securitization and Section 3(a)(3)

In the discussion of the Section 3(a)(2) exemption for securities issued by a bank, we noted the importance of structured financing as a technique of corporate finance. Recall that this involves the forming of an entity for the purpose of issuing debt securities, the proceeds of which are used to purchase income-producing assets, such as mortgages, leases, and automobile loans. The obligations of the shell to its securities holders are then guaranteed by a bank or insurance company. In the case of a bank guarantee, the Section 3(a)(2) exemption negates the need to register the offering.

For further exploration of the CP exemption, *see* Hicks, Commercial Paper: An Exempted Security Under Section 3(a)(3) of the Securities Act of 1933, 24 UCLA L. Rev. 227 (1976); Schweitzer, Commercial Paper and the Securities Act of 1933: A Role for Registration, 63 Geo. L.J. 1245 (1975) (arguing that Congress assumed the exemption would cover only current transactions that would generate sufficient proceeds to retire the CP before it became due and that this assumption has proven incorrect); Lowenstein, The Commercial Paper Market and the Federal Securities Laws, 4 Corp. L. Rev. 128 (1981); Comment, The Commercial Paper Market and the Securities Acts, 39 U. Chi. L. Rev. 362 (1972).

3. Section 4(a)(2) Versus Section 3(a)(3)

Issuers can and do sell CP in reliance on the Section 4(a)(2) private offering exemption instead of Section 3(a)(3). The primary advantages of doing so are no restrictions on the issuer's use of proceeds and no limitation on the length of maturity.[5] The big disadvantage is that the CP notes will be restricted securities and therefore can be resold only in compliance with a resale exemption. This factor may negatively affect the marketability of the notes or require the issuer to offer a slightly higher interest rate.

E. *Securities of Nonprofit Issuers*

Section 3(a)(4) provides an exemption for securities "issued by a person organized and operated exclusively for religious, educational, fraternal, charitable, or reformatory purposes and not for pecuniary profit, and no part of the net earnings of which inures to the benefit of any person, private stockholder, or individual. . . ." Although the exemption is not particularly controversial, it is noteworthy both because of its importance to religious organizations, universities, and hospitals and because of its unstated premise that the eleemosynary character of the issuer obviates the need for disclosure to investors.

The exemption is available only for issuers who are not organized for profit and whose net earnings do not inure to the benefit of any individual. Following is the leading case interpreting this limitation.

---

5. Maturity length will be limited by CP market expectations and Rule 2a-7 of the Investment Company Act of 1940. This rule restricts money market funds, significant CP purchasers, from buying notes with maturities exceeding 397 days.

Securities and Exchange Commission v. Children's Hospital
214 F. Supp. 883 (D. Ariz. 1963)

DAVIS, J. [Action by the SEC to enjoin the sale of Children's Hospital bonds. The proceeds from the sale were to be used to construct a hospital. Jennings and Ross, the promoters, had previous experience in the development of hospitals. Until temporarily restrained by the court, Children's, Jennings, and Ross had been offering and selling 8 percent first mortgage bonds to residents of several states. From July 1961 to November 1962, they sold approximately $1,357,900 worth of the bonds.]

V.   PROMOTERS' ROLE IN DEVELOPMENT OF CHILDREN'S

A.   ORGANIZATION AND SOLICITATION

1. Jennings, assisted by Ross, has actively participated in the organization of Children's. Jennings and Ross caused Children's to be incorporated, and selected the members of its first board of directors. Thereafter they became the only salaried directors.

2. Jennings and Ross had planned to withhold 10% of the proceeds from the sale of the Children's bonds. That portion of the 10% so withheld and not expended on office overhead, promotion and cost of sales, was to be retained by Jennings and Ross as compensation for their services. Under this arrangement Jennings and Ross were to receive a profit of about $50,000.

B.   CONSTRUCTION OF CHILDREN'S

[The contract to construct the hospital was awarded without competitive bidding. Because of the contractor's financial difficulties, the contract was assigned to a contractor in which Jennings and Ross had a significant financial interest.]

C.   OPERATION

1. On July 8, 1962, Children's was opened to receive patients. From that date to the present, Jennings and Ross have held two of the three positions on the board of directors of Children's and each of them has drawn a salary of $1,000 per month.

2. Jennings and Ross control Children's. They constitute a majority of Children's three-member board of directors. . . .

[T]he Section 3(a)(4) exemption is not available for the Children's Hospital bond offering because a "substantial purpose" of the organization of the hospital is to enrich the promoters by providing them with large profits from the enterprise. . . .

It appears that a "charitable purpose" requires dedication to a general public purpose for the benefit of an indefinite number of persons who are not required to give adequate consideration for benefits received. However, a hospital corporation is not required to furnish free services to the indigent as a condition precedent to a "charitable" exemption, as long as the hospital is devoted to the care of the sick and injured, to aid in maintaining public health, and to making valuable contributions to the advancement of medical science. A hospital not conducted for the profit of anyone connected therewith can be a "charitable" institution irrespective of whether patients are required to pay for services rendered. . . .

Following is a comment on "charitable purpose" by an Arizona court:

> If the purpose . . . is . . . *charitable,* . . . and if it is not maintained for the private gain, profit, or advantage of its *organizers,* officers, or owners, *directly or indirectly,* we think the institution is . . . charitable . . . so long as its receipts are devoted to the necessary maintenance of the institution and the carrying out of the purpose for which it was organized. . . . [T]he test is . . . whether those charged with its operation were conducting it for their private profit or advantage. . . . [Emphasis added by the court.][10]

The charitable purpose must extend to both the organization of the hospital and to its operation. A person who purchases securities in a corporation that is being organized for charitable purposes has the right to expect that the character of the corporation and hence of the securities will remain the same. Indeed, if it be known that the character of a corporation and its securities will change from non-commercial to commercial, such securities should be registered immediately, for . . . the basic motive impelling the purchasers to invest in the securities will rest upon entirely different considerations. Investors in hospitals or other institutions not organized and maintained for strictly charitable purposes are entitled to the disclosures concerning the enterprise which must be made under the registration process. . . .

The "profit" mentioned in [Section 3(a)(4)] need not emanate from the operational net earnings of the hospital corporation after it commences to provide medical services to the public. Profit from net earnings is discussed in a subsequent clause of Section 3(a)(4), to wit: ". . . no part of the net earnings of which inures to the benefit of any person, private stockholder, or individual." In order to prevent this latter clause from constituting mere surplusage, the prior proscription that the organization be "not for pecuniary profit" must be given a liberal interpretation, and must be construed to encompass profit, not only from net earnings, but from any source, arrangement or manipulation, whether such profit inures to anyone directly or indirectly connected with the corporation. . . .

Measured by the foregoing standards, the securities of Children's Hospital are not entitled to exemption from registration under Section 3(a)(4) of the Securities Act. The non-charitable element which defeats the exemption is the

---

10. *Southern Methodist Hosp. and Sanitorium of Tucson v. Wilson* (Ariz. 1938), 51 Ariz. 424, 77 P.2d 458, 459.

promoters' anticipated profit from the organization and promotion of the institution and from the construction of the hospital facilities. . . .

[The court also found that Section 17(a) was violated because of manipulation and deception in the sales of the bonds.]

NOTES AND QUESTIONS

1. Scale of Offerings. Section 3(a)(4) offerings may be quite large in size. In one no-action letter, the staff indicated it would not recommend enforcement action if Kaiser Foundation Hospitals proceeded with a $175 million note and bond issuance designed to raise funds for construction, acquisition, and equipment of hospitals. *See* Kaiser Found. Hosps., SEC No-Action Letter, [1980 Transfer Binder] Fed. Sec. L. Rep. (CCH) ¶76,409 (Apr. 10, 1980). Kaiser was helped by its 501(c)(3) tax status and the concomitant requirement under the IRC that no part of its net earnings "inure to the benefit of any private shareholder or individual." Yet the staff refused to issue a no-action letter requested by a Christian ministry desiring to have a $1,102,000 bond offering to renovate buildings it owned. *See* Jesus People U.S.A. Full Gospel Ministries, SEC No-Action Letter, 1988 SEC No-Act. LEXIS 1411 (Oct. 13, 1988). A companion organization controlled by the ministry operated a drug abuse rehabilitation program, provided English language training for recent immigrants, and served hot meals to several hundred people each day. To facilitate their service activities, members of the organization lived on a communal basis. They received no salaries for their services, although they were provided free room and board by the ministry. The value of this "compensation" did not exceed $3,200 per member annually. The staff's negative position on the no-action request was based on its concern that income might inure to the benefit of members. The room and board was clearly a problem. A complicating factor was that the operations of the ministry are in part funded by ministry-owned businesses (thrift shops and the like).

If room and board in the Jesus People situation is a problem, why does not the same problem exist in the Kaiser context because of the income contracting doctors will receive as Kaiser expands its facilities?

2. Policy Justifications for the Exemption. What are the policy justifications supporting the exemption for securities of nonprofit organizations? How sound is the observation of the court in *Children's Hospital* that purchasers of securities issued by nonprofit organizations are not motivated by the same investment concerns as purchasers of securities issued by for-profit entities?

3. Benefit Versus Profit. Because it was a "bad facts" case, *Children's Hospital* did not need to explore the subtleties of the critical concepts of *profit* and *benefit*. It would be facile to suggest that an issuer with employees cannot utilize the Section 3(a)(4) exemption because proceeds from an offering may permit the issuer to function and thereby meet its payroll (a benefit to employees). One means of distinguishing permissible from impermissible benefits when there is compensation is to determine whether the compensation is reasonable in light of the services rendered. Was this a factor in

Children's Hospital? See Deutsche Bank Microcredit Development Fund, SEC No-Action Letter (Apr. 8, 2011) (favorable response to a no-action letter request when fees would be paid to a tax-exempt microcredit financing fund but not at the "substantial" levels present in *Children's Hospital*). The vagueness of the standards in this area makes it all the more important to seek a no-action letter before issuing securities in reliance on the Section 3(a)(4) exemption.

4. Social Enterprise Companies. Social enterprise companies are a relatively recent development allowing the establishment of enterprises that pursue both social and profit goals. Several states now allow the formation of such "businesses," which create interesting questions under the federal securities laws. Professor Heminway argues that these new associational forms create "a somewhat uncertain middle ground between charitable donations and traditional equity and debt investment interests." Heminway, To Be or Not to Be (a Security): Funding for-Profit Social Enterprises, 25 Regent U. L. Rev. 299, 304, 331 (2013). She concludes investments in social enterprise companies are like contributions to nonprofit organizations and should be afforded similar treatment under the securities laws. *See also* Murray, Social Enterprise Innovation: Delaware's Public Benefit Corporation Law, 4 Harv. Bus. L. Rev. 345, 367 (2014).

5. The Philanthropy Protection Act of 1995. Congress in 1995 enacted the Philanthropy Protection Act exempting charitable income funds from the registration requirements of the '33 Act and preempting application of state registration requirements to the funds. The Act clearly covers arrangements under which a group of nonprofit organizations pools their funds collectively for investment purposes. There is some uncertainty, however, over whether charitable income funds would include gift annuities and charitable trusts, which are arrangements under which individuals donate property (often to a pooled fund) in return for the promise of the recipient to pay the donors a specified level of income for their lives. On coverage of the Act, *see generally* Horner & Makens, Securities Regulation of Fundraising Activities of Religious and Other Nonprofit Organizations, 27 Stetson L. Rev. 473 (1997).

PROBLEM

8-10. Consider the following noncumulative variations on the facts of *Children's Hospital* to determine which, if any, might (or should) have changed the result in that case.

   a. Jennings and Ross had no financial interest in the contractor that constructed the hospital.
   b. Jennings and Ross had a financial interest in the contractor, but the contract was awarded as a result of competitive bidding.
   c. Jennings and Ross had no financial interest in the contractor and received no compensation for their efforts in selling the bonds.
   d. Jennings and Ross received no salaries, but their physician-spouses had visiting privileges at the hospital.

    e. Jennings and Ross were able to show that their compensation of $50,000 for services in the offering was less than that which would have been charged by an unrelated party performing the same services.

    f. Jennings and Ross were physicians in the community and had no prior experience in the development of hospitals.

F.   *Insurance and Annuities*

Premised on the notion that the task of regulating the insurance industry is best left with the states, Section 3(a)(8) exempts insurance and annuity contracts *issued* by insurance companies regulated at the state or federal level.

    Note that this is an area in which traditional lines between banking and insurance have blurred in recent years. Banks, for example, are increasingly active on the marketing front, often making available to their customers annuities issued by insurance companies. *See, e.g., Nationsbank of N.C. v. Variable Annuity Life Insurance Co.,* 513 U.S. 251 (1995) (upholding Comptroller of Currency decision to allow national banks to serve as agents in sales of annuities issued by insurance companies). Because the exemption keys on the nature of the issuer, which remains an insurance firm, the participation by banks in the marketing of the products does not affect the availability of the exemption.

    The exemption seems short and to the point. The problem comes in determining when insurance truly is insurance.

1.   Insurance and Annuity Products as Securities

As a preliminary matter, there is some question whether traditional insurance and annuity products are securities:

> As it is, §3(a)(8) seems on its face to create a negative implication that insurance policies *are* securities, which are exempt from the registration requirements but are subject to the antifraud provisions. Nevertheless, the Commission early took the position that insurance or endowment policies or annuity contracts issued by regularly constituted insurance companies were not intended to be securities, and that in effect §3(a)(8) is *supererogation.* This undoubtedly carries out the legislative intention; for the House report states that the purpose of the exemption "makes clear what is already implied in the act, namely, that insurance policies are not to be regarded as securities subject to the provisions of the act." It has been held under a number of the blue sky laws that orthodox annuity contracts issued by life insurance companies are not securities.

L. Loss & J. Seligman, Fundamentals of Securities Regulation 398 (5th ed. 2011) (emphasis added).

    The supererogation view of the Section 3(a)(8) exemption finds support in dicta in one Supreme Court opinion. *See Tcherepnin v. Knight,* 389 U.S. 332, 342 n.30 (1967) ("the exemption from registration for insurance policies was clearly supererogation"). *See also SEC v. Variable Annuity Life Insurance Co.,* 359 U.S. 65, 74 n.4 (1958) (Brennan, J., concurring) ("[I]t would appear that in the case of the ordinary insurance policy, the exemption would be just confirmatory of the policy's noncoverage under the definition of security."); *SEC v. Life Partners, Inc.*, 87 F.3d 536, 541 (D.C. Cir. 1996) (insurance contracts "are altogether exempt from coverage under the federal securities laws"). Although this reading of legislative *intent* may indeed be accurate, the supererogation theory does not comport with the structure of the exemptive provisions of the '33 Act. If ordinary insurance policies and annuities are not securities, the presence of an exemption covering these policies does real mischief, for the exemption by its terms is relevant only to the registration requirements of the '33 Act and does not extend to the statute's antifraud provisions.

2. Variable Annuities

Supererogation issues aside, at least for the moment, the creation of diverse insurance and "quasi-insurance" products poses difficult interpretive problems under Section 3 (a)(8). *See, e.g., Holding v. Cook*, 521 F. Supp. 2d 832, 836 (C.D. Ill. 2007) ("[C]alling something an annuity doesn't necessarily make it one."). The development of the "variable annuity" is a prime example. In an ordinary fixed annuity, the purchaser makes a lump sum payment or installment payments in exchange for an insurance company's commitment to make periodic fixed payments for the purchaser's life. The insurance company bears a risk in such a case because the annuitant might live longer than actuarial tables would indicate. As the following excerpt reveals, the variable annuity, which was developed in response to the loss of savings dollars to the mutual fund industry, is an entirely different creature.

> The variable annuity preserves all the features of a fixed annuity contract, except that the consideration paid for the annuity is allocated to a "separate account" and invested in equity securities. The installment payments of consideration by the contractholder (the pay-in period), and the payments of the annuity to the contractholder, at his option, are adjusted wholly or in part to reflect the investment performance of equity securities in the separate account. . . . The "cash value" of the contract at any particular time during this period can be calculated by multiplying the number of units credited to the contractholder by the then value of the units.

Frankel, Variable Annuities, Variable Insurance and Separate Accounts, 51 B.U. L. Rev. 177, 182-183 (1971).

Securities and Exchange Commission v. Variable Annuity Life Insurance Co. of America
359 U.S. 65 (1959)

DOUGLAS, J. This is an action instituted by the Securities and Exchange Commission to enjoin respondents from offering their annuity contracts to the public without registering them under the Securities Act of 1933. . . .

Respondents are regulated under the insurance laws of the District of Columbia and several other States. It is argued that that fact brings into play the provisions of the McCarran-Ferguson Act, . . . §2(b) of which provides that "No Act of Congress shall be construed to invalidate, impair or supersede any law enacted by any State for the purpose of regulating the business of insurance. . . ." It is said that the conditions under which that law is applicable are satisfied here. . . . The question common to the exemption provisions of the Securities Act and the Investment Company Act and to §2(b) of the McCarran-Ferguson Act is whether respondents are issuing contracts of insurance.

We start with a reluctance to disturb the state regulatory schemes that are in actual effect, either by displacing them or by superimposing federal requirements on transactions that are tailored to meet state requirements. When the States speak in the field of "insurance," they speak with the authority of a long tradition. For the regulation of "insurance," though within the ambit of federal power . . . , has traditionally been under the control of the States. . . .

. . . [The variable annuity] came into existence as a result of a search for a device that would avoid paying annuitants in depreciated dollars. The theory was that returns from investments in common stocks would over the long run tend to compensate for the mounting inflation. The holder of a variable annuity cannot look forward to a fixed monthly or yearly amount in his advancing years. It may be greater or less, depending on the wisdom of the investment policy. In some respects the variable annuity has the characteristics of the fixed and conventional annuity: payments are made periodically; they continue until the annuitant's death or in case other options are chosen until the end of a fixed term or until the death of the last of two persons; payments are made both from principal and income; and the amounts vary according to the age and sex of the annuitant. Moreover, actuarially both the fixed-dollar annuity and the variable annuity are calculated by identical principles. Each issuer assumes the risk of mortality from the moment the contract is issued. That risk is an actuarial prognostication that a certain number of annuitants will survive to specified ages. Even if a substantial number live beyond their predicted demise, the company issuing the annuity—whether it be fixed or variable—is obligated to make the annuity payments on the basis of the mortality prediction reflected in the contract. This is the mortality risk assumed both by respondents and by those who issue fixed annuities. It is this feature, common to both, that respondents stress when they urge that this is basically an insurance device.

The difficulty is that, absent some guarantee of fixed income, the variable annuity places all the investment risks on the annuitant, none on the company. The holder gets only a pro rata share of what the portfolio of equity interests reflects—which may be a lot, a little, or nothing. We realize that life insurance is an evolving institution. Common knowledge tells us that the forms have greatly changed even in a generation. And we would not undertake to freeze the concepts of "insurance" or "annuity" into the mold they fitted when these Federal Acts were passed. But we conclude that the concept of "insurance" involves some investment risk-taking on the part of the company. The risk of mortality, assumed here, gives these variable annuities an aspect of insurance. Yet it is apparent, not real; superficial, not substantial. . . . For in common understanding "insurance" involves a guarantee that at least some fraction of the benefits will be payable in fixed amounts. . . . There is no true underwriting of risks, the one earmark of insurance as it has commonly been conceived of in popular understanding and usage.

Reversed.

Mr. Justice BRENNAN, with whom Mr. Justice STEWART joins, concurring.

I join the opinion and judgment of the Court. However, there are additional reasons which lead me to the Court's result. . . . I will express these reasons separately.

First. [The Securities Act of 1933 and the Investment Company Act of 1940] were specifically drawn to exclude any "insurance policy" and any "annuity contract" . . . and any "insurance company." . . . Except for these exclusions, there is little doubt that these contracts and the companies issuing them would be subject to the Federal Acts.

Why these exclusions? . . . The point must have been that there then was a form of "investment" known as insurance (including "annuity contracts") which did not present very squarely the sort of problems that the Securities Act and the Investment Company Act were devised to deal with, and which were, in many details, subject to a form of state regulation of a sort which made the federal regulation even less relevant.

At the core of the 1933 Act are the requirements of a registration statement and prospectus to be used in connection with the issuance of "securities". . . . The emphasis is on disclosure. . . .

The regulation of life insurance and annuities by the States proceeded, and still proceeds, on entirely different principles. It seems as paternalistic as the Securities Act of 1933 was keyed to free, informed choice. [Contract clauses are prescribed, and solvency and adequacy of reserves are monitored.] The system does not depend on disclosure to the public, and, once given this form of regulation and the nature of the "product," it might be difficult in the case of the traditional life insurance or annuity contract to see what the purpose of it would be. . . .

. . . There is no reason to suppose that Congress intended to make an exemption of forms of investment to which its regulatory scheme was very relevant in favor of a form of state regulation which would not be relevant to them at all. . . .

[*Second.*] [W]hat the investor is participating in during [the period between pay-in and pay-out] is something quite similar to a conventional open-end management investment company, under a periodic investment plan. . . . In this sort of operation, examination by state insurance officials to determine the adequacy of reserves and solvency becomes less and less meaningful. The disclosure policy of the Securities Act of 1933 becomes, by comparison, more and more relevant. And the detailed protections of the 1940 legislation . . . all become relevant in an acute way here. These are the basic protections that Congress intended investors to have when they put their money into the hands of an investment trust; there is no adequate substitute for them in the traditional regulatory controls administered by state insurance departments, because these controls are not relevant to the specific regulatory problems of an investment trust. . . .

Mr. Justice HARLAN, whom Mr. Justice FRANKFURTER, Mr. Justice CLARK and Mr. Justice WHITTAKER join, dissenting. . . .

. . . The Court is agreed that we should not "freeze" the concept of insurance as it [once] existed. By the same token we should not proceed on the assumption that the thrust of state regulation is frozen. As the insurance business develops new concepts the States adjust and develop their controls. This is in the tradition of state regulation and federal abstention. If the innovation of federal control is nevertheless to be desired, it is for the Congress, not this Court, to effect. I would affirm.

Justice Brennan also saw risk as the basis for federal regulation, but his risk was that of the investor, rather than the risk (or more precisely, the lack thereof) of the company writing the policy. *See generally* Clark, The Regulation of Financial Holding Companies, 92 Harv. L. Rev. 787, 854-860 (1979) (supporting the Brennan opinion and arguing that it is the degree of investment risk borne by the policyholder, rather than the presence or absence of a fixed return, that is the appropriate regulatory inquiry).

3.   Beyond Variable Annuities

Reading *Variable Annuity Life Insurance Co.* (*VALIC*) to mean that some significant measure of risk must be borne by the insurance company if its contracts are to come within the Section 3(a)(8) exemption, insurance companies began packaging their variable annuity programs in a way that, they hoped, would avoid federal regulation. A good example is the so-called guaranteed investment contract. In these arrangements, purchasers are guaranteed principal payments and a certain level (usually low) of interest payments; in addition, they often are offered the promise of "excess" interest payments payable under certain conditions. In *SEC v. United Benefit Life Insurance Co.*, 387 U.S. 202 (1967), the contract at issue was dubbed a "flexible fund annuity." The purchasers of this annuity committed to make monthly premium payments for a fixed number of years ending at a specified maturity date. The funds were allocated by United to a separate fund invested largely in common stocks. Prior to the maturity date, a purchaser could withdraw from the fund an amount up to his proportionate interest in the fund. United also guaranteed a minimum cash value based upon a percentage of premiums paid. At maturity, the policyholder had the choice of taking cash (in an amount equal to the greater of the policyholder's interest in the fund or the minimum guarantee) or converting the interest into a traditional life annuity. In the latter case, the dollars in the policyholder's flexible fund account would be withdrawn and commingled with other assets in United's general reserve.

The minimum guarantee was the basis upon which United attempted to distinguish its flexible fund annuity from the variable annuity found not to be an exempt security in *VALIC*. United argued the minimum guarantee was a risk borne by it, not the policyholder. Since the policyholder would always be entitled to an amount at least equal to the minimum guarantee and since the flexible fund annuity could be converted into a fixed annuity at the maturity date, United reasoned the flexible fund and fixed annuity portions of the contract should be viewed as a whole and, from this perspective, constituted a contract with the character of insurance. The Supreme Court disagreed. After concluding that "the guarantee cannot be said to integrate the pre-maturity operation into the post-maturity benefit scheme," it rejected the notion that *VALIC* turned solely on the absence of any substantial risk taking on the part of the insurer:

> Approaching the [Flexible Fund] portion of this contract, in this light, we have little difficulty in concluding that it does not fall within the insurance exemption of §3(a) of the Securities Act. "Flexible Fund" arrangements require special modifications of state law, and are considered to appeal to the purchaser not on the usual insurance basis of stability and security but on the prospect of "growth" through sound investment management. And while the guarantee of cash value based on net premiums reduces substantially the investment risk of the contract holder, the assumption of an investment risk cannot by itself create an insurance provision under the federal definition. . . . The basic difference between a contract which is to some degree insured and a contract of insurance must be recognized.

Id. at 210-211. *See also Associates in Adolescent Psychiatry, S.C. v. Home Life Insurance Co.*, 941 F.2d 561 (7th Cir. 1991), *cert. denied*, 502 U.S. 1099 (1992) (suggesting a guarantee announced in advance and before the deadline for determining whether to withdraw funds is important in classifying an instrument as an annuity exempt under Section 3(a)(8), even if substantial contract penalties occur because of a withdrawal of funds).

4. Rule 151

In response to widespread marketing of insurance products with some investment features, the SEC in 1979 issued Securities Act Release No. 6051, which emphasized the manner of marketing as the critical factor in determining whether an insurance contract is an annuity. These guidelines in turn were replaced by an annuity safe harbor set forth in Rule 151, which was proposed in 1984 and adopted in 1986. Under the safe harbor, an annuity will be within the exemption of Section 3(a)(8) if it is issued by a bank or insurance company regulated at the state or federal level, it is not marketed primarily as an investment, and the issuer "assumes the investment risk under the contract." *See Luzerne County Ret. Bd. v. Makowski*, 2007 U.S. Dist. LEXIS 87246 (M.D. Pa. Nov. 27, 2007) (rejecting application of safe harbor because to some extent the value of the annuities fluctuated depending on investment performance). Investment risk is deemed assumed by the issuer if the value of the contract does not vary according to the investment experience of a separate account, the issuer guarantees principal and interest, and the issuer credits a specified rate of interest (at least equal to that required under the state's nonforfeiture law) that will not be changed more often than once a year. Rule 151 is discussed in the following case.

Otto v. Variable Annuity Life Insurance Co.
814 F.2d 1127 (7th Cir. 1986)

CUDAHY, J. . . .

I

[VALIC sells fixed and variable annuities to employees of certain tax-exempt organizations.]

Under the fixed annuity, VALIC guarantees the principal and an interest rate of 4 percent per year for the first ten years and 3 ½ percent thereafter. "Excess" interest over the guaranteed rate is paid to fixed annuity participants at the discretion of VALIC. Funds are held in VALIC's unsegregated general account and are invested primarily in long-term debt-type instruments such as mortgages and bonds.

Under the variable annuity, neither the principal nor the rate of return is guaranteed; both fluctuate with VALIC's investment performance. Funds are placed in what is known as a Separate Account, an account segregated from VALIC's general assets. The Separate Account's funds are invested in a diversified portfolio of common stocks and other equity-type investments.

[Otto purchased a fixed annuity from VALIC in 1975. In 1982, she initiated this class action.] Otto claims that VALIC failed to disclose the manner in which interest was calculated under the fixed annuity plan—specifically, that it used the "banding" or "new money" method for crediting "excess" interest to the fixed annuity account. Under the banding method, the current rate of excess interest is paid only on deposits made during the current period. All prior contributions continue to earn the rates of excess interest declared during the periods in which those contributions were made. Otto also claims that the defendants failed to disclose the method by which a participant in a fixed annuity plan could maximize his or her rate of return. . . . [She asserts in this action violations of the disclosure provisions of the 1934 Act as well as ERISA and RICO violations.] . . .

II

. . . The issue before us is whether the fixed annuity plan sold by VALIC is an "annuity" under Section 3(a)(8) or whether the plan is an "investment contract" subject to the requirements of the 1934 Securities Act. The district court held that VALIC's fixed annuity was more properly viewed as an insurance product than as an investment contract. Because we agree with the district court's determination . . . we hold that the district court properly granted summary judgment on the 1934 Securities Act claim. . . .

Unlike the plans evaluated in *Peoria Union, United Benefit,* and *VALIC,* the defendant VALIC's fixed annuity plan in the present case appealed to potential participants on the usual insurance bases of stability and security. . . . Regardless of the investment success of VALIC's general account, VALIC was required to pay a guaranteed rate of interest on all fixed annuity contributions of 4 percent during the first ten years and 3½ percent thereafter. Although this was a low rate of return, it was not so low that we can say it placed the investment risk on the policyholder in a way substantial enough to make the fixed annuity a security. VALIC advertised that, although the earning power of the participant in the fixed plan might not be as great as anticipated due to inflation, the participant had the peace of mind that the investment was guaranteed regardless of economic conditions. Although VALIC boasted that the company's funds were managed by experienced and trained investment managers, . . . investment management is the "life blood" of life insurance companies, and thus it was not inappropriate for VALIC to tout its investment experience even in relation to an insurance product. . . .

In addition, that VALIC promoted its fixed annuity as insurance is especially apparent when contrasted with its promotion of its variable annuity. VALIC advertised its variable annuity as having a principal objective of long-term capital growth of tax-deferred investments. . . .

Our view that VALIC's fixed annuity does not constitute a security is supported by the Securities and Exchange Commission's recent issuance of Rule 151, which establishes a "safe harbor" for certain types of annuity contracts by guaranteeing them exemption from the federal securities laws. . . . Although Rule 151 is not applicable in this case because its effective date is subsequent to the sale in question, an examination of the Rule is nevertheless helpful in determining the scope of the Section 3(a)(8) exclusion. . . .

VALIC's fixed annuity satisfies all the requirements of Rule 151. VALIC, the insurer, is subject to the insurance laws of Texas and to regulation by the Texas Commissioner of Insurance, . . . thereby satisfying the first prong, subsection (a)(1), of Rule 151. VALIC's fixed annuity also fulfills the requirement under the second prong, subsection (a)(2), that the insurer assume the investment risk. Contributions are not invested in a separate account and therefore the value of the contract is not tied to the investment experience of such an account. *See* Rule 151(b)(1). VALIC guarantees that a participant will receive the cash value of all premiums and a specified rate of interest of 4 percent for the first ten years and 3 ½ percent thereafter. These specified rates of interest are more than the 3 percent minimum required under the Rule. *See* Rule 151(b)(2)(ii). Under subsection (b)(3), the insurer must guarantee that its rate of excess interest will not be modified more than once per year. Although VALIC does not guarantee that it will leave the excess interest rate unchanged for a year, it does use the "banding" method of computing interest. Under this method, VALIC in effect guarantees the excess interest rate on every deposit for the life of the annuity contract. In its discussion of Rule 151 that was released with the Rule's enactment, the SEC made clear that it considered the banding method . . . as satisfying this second requirement of Rule 151. Finally, the Rule requires under its third prong, subsection (a)(3), that the contract not be marketed primarily as an investment. Although the award of discretionary excess interest and VALIC's investment experience were given some emphasis, the fixed annuity . . . was marketed *primarily* on the basis of its stability and security.

[Opinion on rehearing follows.]

CUDAHY, J. [Following the issuance of the opinion in *Otto v. Variable Annuity Life Insurance Co.*, VALIC filed a motion to modify the opinion, and Otto petitioned for a rehearing. VALIC for the first time informed the court that it had the right, in its unfettered discretion, to adjust interest "bands" paid on past contributions.]

. . . Upon reexamination in light of VALIC's newly asserted right to alter past interest bands, we hold that VALIC's fixed annuity plan is a security subject to the federal securities laws.

The amount of discretion retained by VALIC to alter the interest it paid under the fixed annuity is relevant to the level of the investment risk assumed by VALIC. As discussed in our previous opinion, the Supreme Court, this circuit and the Securities and Exchange Commission (the "SEC") all have found that the degree of investment risk assumed by the insurance company is an important factor in determining whether a particular annuity plan is an insurance product or a security. . . .

A claimed right to change established excess interest rates and to eliminate excess interest payments entirely *at any time* surely tends to shift the investment risk from VALIC to the plan participant. . . .

The SEC in adopting Rule 151 rejected VALIC's view that guaranteeing a low minimum interest rate is a sufficient assumption of the investment risk by the insurance company. . . . We find that on the facts of this case the minimum interest rates guaranteed under VALIC's fixed annuity plan, although somewhat in excess of those required by Rule 151, do not alone place the investment risk on VALIC sufficiently to exempt the plan from the federal securities laws. To find otherwise we would have to overlook entirely any requirement for a guarantee of excess interest. To do this would be to disregard completely one element contained in the investment risk test of the SEC's safe harbor Rule 151. Admittedly this is not an element relied on previously in court decisions distinguishing securities from insurance products. But it is an element that the SEC has insisted on over the objection of some commentators. Because Rule 151 was cited to us by VALIC as a relevant test, we are unwilling to ignore it to the degree urged by VALIC.

We do not say that Rule 151 defines the meaning of "security"; it is a safe harbor rather than a definitional rule. . . . But VALIC's argument directly under the statute depends on its assertion that the guaranty of return here requires calling the instrument insurance under §3(a)(8) even if the prospect of "excess" interest is a principal inducement to purchase this particular instrument. Because the contract actually leaves the investor with an investment risk significant enough to throw its status into doubt, VALIC's argument in this court effectively depended on its own analogy to the standards of Rule 151, which has not sufficed. We therefore find that VALIC's fixed annuity plan is a security. . . .

NOTES AND QUESTIONS

1. *Mortality Risk.* The SEC contends mortality risk is relevant in determining the degree of risk assumed by the insurer. Was it relevant in *Otto?*

*2. **Supererogation Revisited.*** Rule 151 implicitly reflects the super-erogation view of the Section 3(a)(8) exemption. Although the Rule pur-portedly establishes a safe harbor for the exemption, the release issued in connection with Rule 151's adoption suggests that annuities coming within the safe harbor are exempt from the Act *in its entirety*. See Securities Act Release No. 6645, [1986-1987 Transfer Binder] Fed. Sec. L. Rep. (CCH) ¶84,004 (May 29, 1986). Note the consecutive, but possibly contradictory, sentences in that release:

> [T]he rule simply defines a class of annuities that the Commission believes is clearly entitled to rely on the section. While compliance with rule 151 will assure "non-security status," failure to comply with the rule would not mandate "security status" for an annuity product.

Neither of the preceding *Otto* opinions addressed the important distinction between concluding that a product is not a security and concluding that it is an exempt security. Each opinion assumes that an annuity meeting the guide-lines of Rule 151 is exempt from even the antifraud provisions of the Act. The supererogation view of the '33 Act's coverage of insurance and annuity products may well be an accurate reading of legislative intent, but does it square with the structure of the statute? Assuming Rule 151 is unobjectionable insofar as it is a statement of administrative position, should the supererogation premise under-lying the safe harbor preclude a plaintiff from seeking relief for fraud through a private cause of action?

*3. **Risk Allocation.*** How sound is the argument that true insurance prod-ucts should be exempt because all of the risk is borne by the insurer? Is Rule 151's treatment of risk bearing adequate?

*4. **Variable Annuities as "Covered Securities."*** The Securities Litigation Uniform Standards Act of 1998 (SLUSA) provides for the removal and dis-missal of class actions filed in state courts relating to *covered securities*, which are defined in Section 18 of the '33 Act to include "a security issued by an investment company that is registered, or that has filed a registration state-ment, under the Investment Company Act of 1940." Although insurance companies are not investment companies, they may sell variable annuities only through separate investment accounts that must be registered with the SEC pursuant to the 1940 Act. Several courts have concluded that variable annuities are covered securities, with the consequence that class actions related to misrepresentations in the marketing of the annuities may be pur-sued only in federal courts. See, e.g., *Herndon v. Equitable Variable Life Ins. Co.*, 325 F.3d 1252 (11th Cir. 2003). *See also Ring v. AXA Fin., Inc.*, 483 F.3d 95 (2d Cir. 2007) (affirming that variable life insurance policies are covered securities but allowing disaggregation of other insurance products sold in combination with variable policies for the purpose of establishing that these additional products are not covered securities); *Montoya v. New York State United Teachers*, 754 F. Supp. 2d 466 (E.D.N.Y. 2010) (inclusion of a fixed annuity option within a variable annuity package does not change status of package as a covered security).

5. *Equity-Indexed Annuities.* Introduced in 1995, the equity-indexed annuity (EIA) is one of the fastest growing of the insurance products. The SEC estimates that more than $123 billion is invested in EIAs, which have proven to be particularly bad investments for seniors (many of whom are victims of abusive sales practices). An EIA will provide its holder with a return based on changes in a benchmark equity index (e.g., the S&P 500). In addition, the holder is guaranteed a minimum return if the contract is held to maturity. The guaranteed return makes the EIA attractive to risk-averse investors who desire some equity exposure and an opportunity to participate in market returns. The allocation of risk also may bear on the question of whether the EIA is a security. *See Malone v. Addison Ins. Mktg., Inc.*, 225 F. Supp. 2d 743 (W.D. Ky. 2002) (concluding that EIA is not a security in part because the greater risk is borne by the insurance company).

To address the continuing uncertainty over the application of the Section 3(a)(8) exemption to EIAs, the SEC in 2009 adopted Rule 151A. The Rule provided that EIAs do *not* fall within the exemption if the amounts payable by the insurer "more likely than not" will exceed the amounts guaranteed under the contract; this determination is to be made by the insurer at or prior to the issuance of the contract and is conclusive if the insurer has used a reasonable methodology and assumptions. When proposed, Rule 151A drew more than 4,800 comments, with critics arguing that annuities are regulated adequately at the state level and that the Rule will increase the costs of annuities and limit consumer choice. Critics notwithstanding, the Commission's final rule was substantially the same as the proposed rule.

Rule 151A was short-lived. In *American Equity Investment Life Insurance Company v. SEC*, 613 F.3d 166 (D.C. Cir. 2010), the D.C Circuit concluded the procedure the SEC employed in promulgating the Rule was flawed in that the Commission failed to consider the Rule's effects on efficiency, competition and capital formation as required by the Administrative Procedure Act. Although *American Equity* was a victory for the insurance industry in its long battle with the SEC over regulation of indexed annuities, the decision left the door open for new SEC rulemaking on the subject. That door was closed only nine days later, however, with the signing of the Dodd-Frank Wall Street Reform and Consumer Protection Act of 2010, which in Section 989J directs the SEC to treat most indexed annuities as exempt securities.

6. *Viatical Settlements.* Promoters have attempted to match investors with terminally ill individuals (generally AIDS patients) who have in force life insurance policies. The arrangements are called *viatical settlements*. In exchange for a cash payment of 50 to 80 percent of the face value of the policies, the investors (or the promoters on behalf of the investors) acquire ownership of the policies. The exchange gives the sellers needed cash and provides the investors with a return equal to the difference between what they paid and the face value of the policies. In concluding the Section 3(a)(8) exemption is unavailable to exempt such arrangements from registration, one court reasoned as follows:

> [There is no evidence] that the typical investor who buys an LPI viatical contract pools the financial risk that the seller will live longer than expected. To do so, the investor would have to acquire enough contracts to reduce the actuarial risk

associated with the life span of each individual seller. The record gives no indication, however, that LPI's investors systematically engage in the risk-pooling that is
the essential characteristic of insurance.

SEC v. Life Partners, Inc., 87 F.3d 536, 542 (D.C. Cir. 1996). The court went on to
conclude, however, that the viatical contracts before it were not securities. On
viatical settlements, *see* Levin, Killing Life Partners: Why Viatical Settlements
Are "Securities" in Light of SEC v. Mutual Benefits Corp. and Other Recent
Cases That Explicitly Reject SEC v. Life Partners, 6 J. Bus. & Sec. L. 71 (2005/
2006); Martin, Life Settlements: The Death Wish Industry, 64 Syracuse L. Rev.
91 (2014).

|9|
Liability Under the Securities Act

Earlier chapters introduced the most significant attributes of the civil liability scheme established under the Securities Act of 1933: rescission pursuant to Section 12(a)(1) at the option of any purchaser for any violation of Section 5 and the extensive damage liability imposed by Section 11 upon the issuer and—absent due diligence—those associated with a public distribution when there is a material falsity or omission in a registration statement. Additional liability provisions of the '33 Act are found in the antifraud provisions of Sections 12(a)(2) and 17. This chapter explores these four liability provisions in detail.

A. Section 11

The length and complexity of Section 11 prompted one court to agree with counsel's characterization of the provision as "tough" and "nasty." *See APA Excelsior III L.P. v. Premiere Technologies, Inc.*, 476 F.3d 1261, 1268 (11th Cir. 2007). That said, the major point of Section 11 is straightforward: A material misrepresentation or omission in a registration statement will subject the issuer and (subject to due diligence defenses) a variety of persons associated with either the issuer or the distribution to damages in a suit brought by any person who bought securities issued pursuant to that registration statement.

To the financial community, this statutory provision was the most notorious feature of the Securities Act, leading to claims that capital in America would dry up because investment bankers would refuse to continue in a business subject to such a severe risk of liability. But plainly, investment bankers and others associated with the public offering process do expect compensation for the additional liability risk they are forced to assume as well as the additional expenses incurred in carrying out their due diligence obligations beyond those called for by good business practice. In this respect, Section 11 imposes a significant regulatory cost upon the capital formation process, ultimately borne in large part by the investor. *See* Dooley, The Effects of Civil Liability on Investment Banking and the New Issues Market, 58 Va. L. Rev. 776 (1972).

Many of the recent controversies and reforms in the Securities Act context explored earlier—shelf registration, the free writing prospectus, Rule 144A—are at heart part of a more generic debate over the extent to which the benefit to investors that comes from the process underlying due diligence can be expected systematically to justify those costs, whether there may instead be more efficient means of making credible the accuracy of issuer disclosure, and whether due diligence continues to be either fair or workable in a technology-based, institution-dominated marketplace for securities. We return to these questions shortly, after considering the elements of a Section 11 case.

1. Persons Bringing Suit

Anyone who buys stock issued pursuant to a defective registration statement has standing to sue under Section 11. There is no requirement that the purchaser show any sort of reliance on the registration statement or the statutory prospectus—much less show reliance on the actual falsity or omission—except in the atypical case where a person has acquired the security after the issuer has made generally available an earnings statement covering a period of at least one year beginning after the effective date of the registration statement.

Nor is it the plaintiff's burden to show causation or injury. Even the buyer who was completely unaware that the securities were part of a public distribution, having tossed any prospectus received into the garbage, has standing. Deterrence, rather than just compensation, is a principal objective of the provision.

There are some limits. First, the plaintiff must not have been aware of the truth at the time he bought the securities. Second, the relatively strict statute of limitations found in Section 13 of the Securities Act is applicable to all express private actions under the Act: No action may be maintained unless brought within one year after discovery of the falsity or omission was or should have been made, and in any event no more than three years after the security was offered to the public.

Finally, while privity is not required, the plaintiff does have to show that the securities purchased were issued pursuant to the registration statement in question. The meaning of this requirement is explored in the following opinion.

Hertzberg v. Dignity Partners, Inc.
191 F.3d 1076 (9th Cir. 1999)

W. FLETCHER, Circuit J. This case arises out of alleged misstatements and omissions contained in Appellee Dignity Partners, Inc.'s ("Dignity's") registration statement . . . for an initial public offering of Dignity common stock. Dignity was in the business of buying the rights to life insurance proceeds from people with AIDS, paying a lump sum up front and taking over the responsibility for paying the premiums. Shortly after the offering, the fact that AIDS patients were living longer than expected because of new AIDS treatments became public knowledge. As a result of the longer lives of the insured, Dignity posted huge losses, and the stock plummeted.

Plaintiffs/appellants Hertzberg, Derosa, and Feinman ("Hertzberg") are investors who purchased Dignity stock on the open market more than 25 days after the initial offering but before the news of the longer life expectancy or large losses became public knowledge. They brought a class action for several violations of the securities laws by Dignity, including violation of Section 11 of the Securities Act of 1933. Hertzberg claims that Dignity knew of the longer life expectancy but failed to disclose it in the registration statement. The district court dismissed the Section 11 causes of action on the ground that, because appellants had not bought their stock in the initial public offering, or within 25 days thereof, they did not have standing to bring the claim. . . .

We reverse the district court's holding that the original named plaintiffs lacked standing under Section 11. . . .

DISCUSSION

. . . In determining the meaning of a statute, we look first to its text. . . . Section 11(a) provides that where a material fact is misstated or omitted from a registration statement accompanying a stock filing with the Securities and Exchange Commission, "any person acquiring such security" may bring an action for losses caused by the misstatement or omission. The district court read this phrase as if it had been written, "any person acquiring such security on the first day of an initial public offering or in the twenty-five day period thereafter." This reading adds a significant limitation not found in the original text.

The term "any person" is quite broad, and we give words their ordinary meaning. . . . According to Webster's Third New Int'l Dictionary (3d ed. 1986), "any" means "one, no matter what one"; "ALL"; "one or more discriminately from all those of a kind." . . .

The limitation on "any person" is that he or she must have purchased "such security." Clearly, this limitation only means that the person must have purchased a security issued under that, rather than some other, registration statement. *See Barnes v. Osofsky*, 373 F.2d 269 (2d Cir. 1967). While it might present a problem of proof in a case in which stock was issued under more than one registration statement, the only Dignity stock ever sold to the public was pursuant to the allegedly misleading registration statement at issue in this case. Thus, as long as Hertzberg is suing regarding this security, he is "any person purchasing such security," regardless of whether he bought in the initial offering, a week later, or a month after that.

Further, paragraph (e) of Section 11 uses "the amount paid for the security (not exceeding the price at which the security was offered to the public)" as the baseline for measuring damages. Such a provision would be unnecessary if only a person who bought in the actual offering could recover, since, by definition, such a person would have paid "the price at which the security was offered to the public." We will "avoid a reading which renders some words altogether redundant." *Gustafson v. Alloyd Co., Inc.*, 513 U.S. 561, 574, 131 L. Ed. 2d 1, 115 S. Ct. 1061 (1995). [The court concluded by distinguishing other aspects of *Gustafson*, a case you will study later in this chapter.]

NOTES AND QUESTIONS

1.   More on Tracing.   When the challenged offering is an IPO, there should be little question that a plaintiff who purchases securities in the open market is a "person acquiring such security" for purposes of Section 11 standing. Far more problematic are purchases on the open market sometime after a public distribution of additional securities of a class already outstanding. Often, the buyer never requests physical delivery of the security from his broker, and when that happens—that is, the securities are held in "street name" by or on account for the broker—it may well be that no particular securities are even assigned to the customer's account. Indeed, street name securities are often held in regional depositories, outside even the broker's possession. Even when there is delivery, how is the plaintiff to know whether the stock delivered to him was newly or previously issued? And in any event, why should it matter from a policy standpoint?

Practical difficulties and lack of conceptual sensibility notwithstanding, the courts have read Section 11 literally to impose a *tracing* requirement on the plaintiff in such a context. In cases unlike *Hertzberg*, where shares other than IPO shares may be in the market, the tracing of shares is likely to prove problematic for plaintiffs. For example, in *Krim v. pcOrder.com*, 402 F.3d 489 (5th Cir. 2005), the court made clear that high statistical probabilities are no substitute for actual tracing:

> Unquestionably, the statistics in this case indicate a high probability that a person purchasing a given number of shares will obtain at least one tainted share. However, these general statistics say nothing about the shares that a specific person *actually* owns and have no ability to separate those shares upon which standing can be based from those for which standing is improper. The task before the district court was to determine, by a preponderance of the evidence, whether and in what amount a plaintiff's shares are tainted, not whether the same number of shares drawn at random would likely include at least one tainted share. Understood in this light, statistical tracing is not up to the task at hand.

Id. at 502 (emphasis in original). Many of the problems associated with the tracing requirement reflect the somewhat outmoded system that exists for the clearance, settlement, and recording of securities transactions. A move to block-chain technology for these functions, which many see as sensible and practicable, would also make tracing easier. *See* Geis, Traceable Shares and Corporate Law, 113 Nw. U. L. Rev. 227 (2018).

2.   Pleading.   Tracing issues may be raised in motions on the pleadings. *See In re Century Aluminum Co. Sec. Litig.*, 729 F.3d 1104 (9th Cir. 2013) (motion to dismiss granted for failure to plead satisfaction with tracing requirement).

2.   The Defendants and Their Defenses

a.   *Registered Offerings Generally*

While it is common to think of Section 11 liability in terms of its emphasis on due diligence, that is only partly justified. For the most important defendant made subject to suit—the issuer—there is no defense at all with regard to culpability. The issuer is subject to "virtually absolute liability" for material misstatements or omissions in its registration statement. *See Lindsay v. Morgan Stanley*, 592 F.3d 347, 359 (2d Cir. 2010), *quoting Herman & MacLean v. Huddleston*, 459 U.S. 375, 382 (1983).

Beyond the strict liability of the issuer, due diligence is a defense available for the other persons specifically made subject to suit by Section 11(a): (1) the signatories of the registration statement; (2) the directors of the issuer at the time of filing, as well as persons named as about to become directors; (3) the accountants and other experts named in the registration statement who have prepared certain materials that form the basis of some part of the statement; and (4) the underwriters.

As to underwriters, recall from Chapter 6 the discussion of the breadth of the concept of underwriting, a result supported by an expansive definition of underwriters in Section 2(a)(11) that includes those who directly or indirectly participate in a distribution. Does this broad definition apply for purposes of Section 11 claims? For the most part, courts take a narrow view of "underwriter" in the Section 11 context. Along this line consider *Wyoming State Treasurer v. Moody's Investors Serv.*, 650 F.3d 167 (2d Cir. 2011), which rejected the argument that underwriter liability extends to "everyone playing a facilitating role in the eventual sale or offer of securities"; the court concluded that a ratings agency's participation in structuring an offering to achieve the desired rating did not make it an underwriter because the agency was not involved in the distribution of securities from the issuer. Similar reasoning was offered in *In re Refco, Inc. Sec. Litig.*, 2008 U.S. Dist. LEXIS 62543 (S.D.N.Y. 2008), which concluded that brokerage firms' assistance in preparation of a registration statement is not sufficient to create underwriter status for purposes of Section 11 liability when the firms did not hold themselves out as having evaluated the securities or otherwise endorsed the contents of the registration statement. *See also Employees' Ret. Sys. v. J.P. Morgan Chase & Co.*, 804 F. Supp. 2d 141 (S.D.N.Y. 2011) ("underwriter" under Section 11 should be construed as the term is commonly understood to include only those who purchase from the issuer with a view to distribution).

Section 11(b) draws a distinction between so-called expertised and other portions of the registration statement. An *expertised portion* of the registration statement is one prepared by or on the authority of an expert—the most familiar examples are accounting statements, engineers' or geologists' reports, and attorneys' opinions. Section 7 provides that when an expert is named as having prepared or certified a portion of the registration statement, the issuer must file with the registration statement the written consent of the expert.

Credit rating agencies such as Standard & Poor's and Moody's typically assign ratings to the debt securities of larger corporate issuers. Courts have rejected arguments that ratings facilitate the marketing of securities and, therefore, the ratings agencies should be treated as underwriters. *See, e.g., Public Employees' Retirement System of Mississippi v. Goldman Sachs Group, Inc.*, 2011 U.S. Dist. LEXIS 3267, 18-19 (S.D.N.Y. Jan. 12, 2011). But is this type of activity sufficient to create expert status for purposes of Section 11 liability? In the past, Rule 436(g) has protected the agencies by providing that their ratings would not be considered part of the registration statement prepared under the authority of an expert. The Dodd-Frank Wall Street Reform and Consumer Protection Act, however, repealed Rule 436(g) and thereby created the potential for Section 11 liability for the agencies. In response, the major agencies announced they will not consent to the inclusion of their ratings in registration statements and related filings. The practice has since evolved to include the ratings in materials outside the registration statement filed with the SEC (in so-called free writing prospectuses) or to allow the issuer to reference the rating in the Management Discussions and Analysis of liquidity considerations. Neither approach requires the rating agency to be identified as an expert.

With respect to an expertised portion of the registration statement, the expert is liable for misstatements or omissions unless "he had, after reasonable investigation, reasonable ground to believe and did believe, at the time such part of the registration statement became effective" that the statements therein were complete and accurate. All other non-issuer defendants may raise the defense that they "had no reasonable ground to believe, and did not believe" that there was any inaccuracy or omission. In other words, the burden of due diligence *investigation* lies solely upon the expert; the others have a qualified right to rely on his efforts.

With respect to non-expertised portions of the registration statement, the signatories of the registration statement, the directors, and the underwriters are all subject to the duty to investigate and are able to raise the defense of due diligence only if "after reasonable investigation" they had "reasonable ground to believe and did believe" that the statements therein were true and complete. Everyone must investigate, in other words, or risk the consequences. Note the two-step nature of the analysis. There must be investigation *and*, after such investigation, no reason to doubt the accuracy of the registration statement. Assuming a material misstatement or omission, a defendant can be liable simply for not investigating adequately. The defendant can also be liable, even if an investigation was done, for going forward with participation in the offering with doubts about the accuracy of the registration statement.

This bifurcated approach to due diligence liability raises two general sorts of questions. First, what does *expertised* mean? On the assumption that as a practical matter the attorneys for the issuer and the underwriter do most of the investigation and drafting of the registration statement, can a director or signatory argue that, since they are experts, her independent duty of inquiry is excused? With uniformity, as in the case that follows, courts have said no. While such persons may choose to rely upon the attorneys (and presumably will be able to invoke *their* diligence), they do so at their peril if it turns out that the attorneys were not sufficiently careful. In practice, counsel will normally hold a due diligence meeting with the board and other signatories to report on their investigation and give those in attendance an opportunity to satisfy themselves of its adequacy.

This leads to the second and more fundamental sort of question—what constitutes due diligence? Here the most intriguing question of policy arises, for the more stringent the standard, the greater the cost of the offering. Is there a recognizable point short of "fail-safe" at which investigators may stop? Unfortunately—and perhaps surprisingly—there are very few cases that have thoroughly explored this question. As a result, much of the advice that lawyers give on this question is born of caution, not certainty.

Escott v. BarChris Construction Co.
283 F. Supp. 643 (S.D.N.Y. 1968)

McLean, J. This is an action by purchasers of 5½ per cent convertible subordinated fifteen year debentures of BarChris Construction Corporation (BarChris) . . . brought under Section 11 of the Securities Act of 1933. . . .

At the time relevant here, BarChris was engaged primarily in the construction of bowling alleys, somewhat euphemistically referred to as "bowling centers." . . .

BarChris was an outgrowth of a business started as a partnership by Vitolo and Pugliese in 1946. . . .

The introduction of automatic pin setting machines in 1952 gave a marked stimulus to bowling. It rapidly became a popular sport, with the result that "bowling centers" began to appear throughout the country in rapidly increasing numbers. BarChris benefited from this increased interest in bowling. Its construction operations expanded rapidly. It is estimated that in 1960 BarChris installed approximately three per cent of all lanes built in the United States. . . .

In general, BarChris's method of operation was to enter into a contract with a customer, receive from him at that time a comparatively small down payment on the purchase price, and proceed to construct and equip the bowling alley. When the work was finished and the building delivered, the customer paid the balance of the contract price in notes, payable in installments over a period of years. BarChris discounted these notes with a factor and received part of their face amount in cash. The factor held back part as a reserve. . . .

BarChris was compelled to expend considerable sums in defraying the cost of construction before it received reimbursement. As a consequence, BarChris was in constant need of cash to finance its operations, a need which grew more pressing as operations expanded.

In December 1959, BarChris sold 560,000 shares of common stock to the public at $3.00 per share. . . .

By early 1961, BarChris needed additional working capital. The proceeds of the sale of the debentures involved in this action were to be devoted, in part at least, to fill that need.

The registration statement of the debentures, in preliminary form, was filed with the Securities and Exchange Commission on March 30, 1961. A first amendment was filed on May 11 and a second on May 16. The registration statement became effective on May 16. The closing of the financing took place on May 24. On that day BarChris received the net proceeds of the financing.

By that time BarChris was experiencing difficulties in collecting amounts due from some of its customers. Some of them were in arrears in payments due to factors on their discounted notes. As time went on those difficulties increased. Although BarChris continued to build alleys in 1961 and 1962, it became increasingly apparent that the industry was overbuilt. Operators of alleys, often inadequately financed, began to fail. Precisely when the tide turned is a matter of dispute, but at any rate, it was painfully apparent in 1962.

In May of that year BarChris made an abortive attempt to raise more money by the sale of common stock. It filed with the Securities and Exchange Commission a registration statement for the stock issue which it later withdrew.

In October 1962 BarChris came to the end of the road. On October 29, 1962, it filed in this court a petition for an arrangement under Chapter XI of the Bankruptcy Act. BarChris defaulted in the payment of the interest due on November 1, 1962 on the debentures.

THE DEBENTURE REGISTRATION STATEMENT

In preparing the registration statement for the debentures, [defendant] Grant acted [as attorney] for BarChris. He had previously represented BarChris in preparing the registration statement for the common stock issue. In connection with the sale of common stock, BarChris had issued purchase warrants. In January 1961 a second registration statement was filed in order to update the information pertaining to these warrants. Grant had prepared that statement as well.

Some of the basic information needed for the debenture registration statement was contained in the registration statements previously filed with respect to the common stock and warrants. Grant used these old registration statements as a model in preparing the new one, making the changes which he considered necessary in order to meet the new situation.

The underwriters were represented by the Philadelphia law firm of Drinker, Biddle & Reath. John A. Ballard, a member of that firm, was in charge of that work, assisted by a young associate named Stanton.

Peat, Marwick, BarChris's auditors, who had previously audited BarChris's annual balance sheet and earnings figures for 1958 and 1959, did the same for 1960. These figures were set forth in the registration statement. In addition, Peat, Marwick undertook a so-called "S-1 review," the proper scope of which is one of the matters debated here. . . .

The prospectus contained, among other things, a description of BarChris's business, a description of its real property, some material pertaining to certain of its subsidiaries, and remarks about various other aspects of its affairs. It also contained financial information. It included a consolidated balance sheet as of December 31, 1960, with elaborate explanatory notes. These figures had been audited by Peat, Marwick. It also contained unaudited figures as to net sales, gross profit and net earnings for the first quarter ended March 31, 1961, as compared with the similar quarter for 1960. In addition, it set forth figures as to the company's backlog of unfilled orders as of March 31, 1961, as compared with March 31, 1960, and figures as to BarChris's contingent liability, as of April 30, 1961, on customers' notes discounted and its contingent liability under the so-called alternative method of financing.

Plaintiffs challenge the accuracy of a number of these figures. They also charge that the text of the prospectus, apart from the figures, was false in a number of respects, and that material information was omitted. . . .

[The court then turned to a lengthy discussion of the registration statement and its alleged inaccuracies. On the assumption that only those facts "which have an important bearing upon the nature or condition of the issuing corporation or its business" are material, it found many material ones. Sales and operating net income were overstated for 1960 and the first quarter of 1961 due to BarChris's incorrectly including among its sales several alleys (e.g., Capitol

Lanes and Howard Lanes, discussed later) that BarChris had been unable to sell to an outsider and was itself operating through one of its wholly owned subsidiaries. The registration statement understated BarChris's contingent liability on customer notes sold to Talcott. BarChris's representations were based upon a former arrangement with the factor under which BarChris guaranteed 25 percent of the customers' notes, whereas under most later arrangements it was contingently liable for 100 percent of the customers' notes sold to Talcott. BarChris incorrectly listed among its "backlog" of orders several orders, all to corporations not then in existence, with the same party signed as purchaser on each of the contracts. The tentative nature of these was suggested by their stating that "specifications are attached" for the alley's construction, though no specifications were attached. Minutes of BarChris's executive committee identified all the jobs as ones for which there were "no written contracts with customers." The registration statement falsely represented that all loans to BarChris by its officers had been repaid, when in fact nearly $400,000 in officer loans was outstanding. The registration statement also falsely represented that the offering proceeds would be used for a new plant, development of new equipment, and working capital. In truth, most of the proceeds were used to pay off BarChris's existing indebtedness. The court also found material misstatements in the financial reports covering 1960, which had been audited by Peat Marwick. "For convenience," the court recapitulated the various falsities and omissions in a table, which is reproduced below. Then, after noting that BarChris was strictly liable for these inaccuracies, it turned to the joint and several liability of the non-issuer defendants.]

TABLE 9-1

1.	1960 Earnings		
	(a)	Sales	
		As per prospectus	$9,165,320
		Correct figure	8,511,420
		Overstatement	$653,900
	(b)	Net Operating Income	
		As per prospectus	$1,742,801
		Correct figure	1,496,196
		Overstatement	$246,605
	(c)	Earnings per Share	
		As per prospectus	$.75
		Correct figure	.65
		Overstatement	$.10
2.	1960 Balance Sheet Current Assets		
		As per prospectus	$4,524,021
		Correct figure	3,914,332
		Overstatement	$609,689
3.	Contingent Liabilities as of December 31, 1960 on Alternative Method of Financing		
		As per prospectus	$750,000
		Correct figure	1,125,795
		Understatement	$375,795
		Capitol Lanes should have been shown as a direct liability	$325,000

4.   Contingent Liabilities as of April 30, 1961
          As per prospectus $825,000
          Correct figure   1,443,853
          Understatement $618,853
          Capitol Lanes should have been shown as a direct liability $314,166
5.   Earnings Figures for Quarter Ending March 31, 1961
       (a)   Sales
              As per prospectus $2,138,455
              Correct figure   1,618,645
              Overstatement $519,810

       (b)   Gross Profit
              As per prospectus $483,121
              Correct figure   252,366
              Overstatement $230,755
6.   Backlog as of March 31, 1961
          As per prospectus $6,905,000
          Correct figure   2,415,000
          Overstatement $4,490,000
7.   Failure to Disclose Officers' Loans Outstanding and Unpaid on $386,615
       May 16, 1961
8.   Failure to Disclose Use of Proceeds in Manner Not Revealed in $1,160,000
       Prospectus Approximately
9.   Failure to Disclose Customers' Delinquencies in May 1961 and   Over $1,350,000
       BarChris's Potential Liability with Respect Thereto
10.   Failure to Disclose the Fact that BarChris Was Already Engaged,
       and Was About to Be More Heavily Engaged, in the Operation of
       Bowling Alleys

RUSSO

Russo was, to all intents and purposes, the chief executive officer of BarChris. He was a member of the executive committee. He was familiar with all aspects of the business. He was personally in charge of dealings with the factors. He acted on BarChris's behalf in making the financing agreements with Talcott and he handled the negotiations with Talcott in the spring of 1961. He talked with customers about their delinquencies. . . . He was thoroughly aware of BarChris's stringent financial condition in May 1961. He had personally advanced large sums to BarChris of which $175,000 remained unpaid as of May 16. In short, Russo knew all the relevant facts. He could not have believed that there were no untrue statements or material omissions in the prospectus. Russo has no due diligence defenses. . . .

KIRCHER

Kircher was treasurer of BarChris and its chief financial officer. He is a certified public accountant and an intelligent man. He was thoroughly familiar with BarChris's financial affairs. . . .

Kircher worked on the preparation of the registration statement. He conferred with Grant and on occasion with Ballard. He supplied information to them about the company's business. He read the prospectus and understood it. He knew what it said and what it did not say.

Kircher's contention is that he had never before dealt with a registration statement, that he did not know what it should contain, and that he relied wholly on Grant, Ballard and Peat, Marwick to guide him. He claims that it was their fault, not his, if there was anything wrong with it. He says that all the facts were recorded in BarChris's books where these "experts" could have seen them if they had looked. He says that he truthfully answered all their questions. In effect, he says that if they did not know enough to ask the right questions and to give him the proper instructions, that is not his responsibility.

There is an issue of credibility here. In fact, Kircher was not frank in dealing with Grant and Ballard. He withheld information from them. But even if he had told them all the facts, this would not have constituted the due diligence contemplated by the statute. Knowing the facts, Kircher had reason to believe that the expertised portion of the prospectus, i.e., the 1960 figures, was in part incorrect. He could not shut his eyes to the facts and rely on Peat, Marwick for that portion.

As to the rest of the prospectus, knowing the facts, he did not have a reasonable ground to believe it to be true. On the contrary, he must have known that in part it was untrue. Under these circumstances, he was not entitled to sit back and place the blame on the lawyers for not advising him about it.

Kircher has not proved his due diligence defenses. . . .

BIRNBAUM

Birnbaum was a young lawyer, admitted to the bar in 1957, who, after brief periods of employment by two different law firms and an equally brief period of practicing in his own firm, was employed by BarChris as house counsel and assistant secretary in October 1960. Unfortunately for him, he became secretary and a director of BarChris on April 17, 1961, after the first version of the registration statement had been filed with the Securities and Exchange Commission. He signed the later amendments, thereby becoming responsible for the accuracy of the prospectus in its final form.

Although the prospectus, in its description of "management," lists Birnbaum among the "executive officers" . . . , the fact seems to be that he was not an executive officer in any real sense. He did not participate in the management of the company. As house counsel, he attended to legal matters of a routine nature. Among other things, he incorporated subsidiaries, with which BarChris was plentifully supplied. . . .

Birnbaum examined contracts. In that connection he advised BarChris that the T-Bowl contracts were not legally enforceable. He was thus aware of that fact.

One of Birnbaum's more important duties, first as assistant secretary and later as full-fledged secretary, was to keep the corporate minutes of BarChris and its subsidiaries. This necessarily informed him to a considerable extent about the company's affairs. . . .

It seems probable that Birnbaum did not know of many of the inaccuracies in the prospectus. He must, however, have appreciated some of them. In any case, he made no investigation and relied on the others to get it right. . . .

[H]e was entitled to rely upon Peat, Marwick for the 1960 figures, for as far as appears, he had no personal knowledge of the company's books of account or financial transactions. But he was not entitled to rely upon Kircher, Grant and Ballard for the other portions of the prospectus. As a lawyer, he should have known his obligations under the statute. He should have known that he was required to make a reasonable investigation of the truth of all the statements in the unexpertised portion of the document which he signed. Having failed to make such an investigation, he did not have reasonable ground to believe that all these statements were true. Birnbaum has not established his due diligence defenses except as to the audited 1960 figures.

AUSLANDER

Auslander was an "outside" director, i.e., one who was not an officer of BarChris. He was chairman of the board of Valley Stream National Bank in Valley Stream, Long Island. In February 1961 Vitolo asked him to become a director of BarChris. . . . As an inducement, Vitolo said that when BarChris received the proceeds of a forthcoming issue of securities, it would deposit $1,000,000 in Auslander's bank. . . .

On March 3, 1961, Auslander indicated his willingness to accept a place on the board. . . . Auslander observed that BarChris's auditors were Peat, Marwick. They were also the auditors for the Valley Stream National Bank. He thought well of them.

Auslander was elected a director on April 17, 1961. The registration statement in its original form had already been filed, of course without his signature. On May 10, 1961, he signed a signature page for the first amendment to the registration statement which was filed on May 11, 1961. This was a separate sheet without any document attached. Auslander did not know that it was a signature page for a registration statement. He vaguely understood that it was something "for the SEC."

Auslander attended a meeting of BarChris's directors on May 15, 1961. At that meeting he, along with the other directors, signed the signature sheet for the second amendment which constituted the registration statement in its final form. Again, this was only a separate sheet without any document attached. Auslander never saw a copy of the registration statement in its final form.

At the May 15 directors' meeting, however, Auslander did realize that what he was signing was a signature sheet to a registration statement. This was the first time that he had appreciated that fact. A copy of the registration statement in its earlier form as amended on May 11, 1961 was passed around at the meeting. Auslander glanced at it briefly. He did not read it thoroughly.

At the May 15 meeting, Russo and Vitolo stated that everything was in order and that the prospectus was correct. Auslander believed this statement.

In considering Auslander's due diligence defenses, a distinction is to be drawn between the expertised and non-expertised portions of the prospectus. As to the former, Auslander knew that Peat, Marwick had audited the 1960 figures. He believed them to be correct because he had confidence in Peat, Marwick. He had no reasonable ground to believe otherwise.

As to the non-expertised portions, however, Auslander is in a different position. He seems to have been under the impression that Peat, Marwick was responsible for all the figures. This impression was not correct, as he would have realized if he had read the prospectus carefully. Auslander made no investigation of the accuracy of the prospectus. He relied on the assurance of Vitolo and Russo, and upon the information he had received in answer to his inquiries back in February and early March. These inquiries were general ones, in the nature of a credit check. The information which he received in answer to them was also general, without specific reference to the statements in the prospectus, which was not prepared until some time thereafter.

It is true that Auslander became a director on the eve of the financing. He had little opportunity to familiarize himself with the company's affairs. The question is whether, under such circumstances, Auslander did enough to establish his due diligence defense with respect to the non-expertised portions of the prospectus. . . .

Section 11 imposes liability in the first instance upon a director, no matter how new he is. He is presumed to know his responsibility when he becomes a director. He can escape liability only by using that reasonable care to investigate the facts which a prudent man would employ in the management of his own property. In my opinion, a prudent man would not act in an important matter without any knowledge of the relevant facts, in sole reliance upon representations of persons who are comparative strangers and upon general information which does not purport to cover the particular case. To say that such minimal conduct measures up to the statutory standard would, to all intents and purposes, absolve new directors from responsibility merely because they are new. This is not a sensible construction of Section 11, when one bears in mind its fundamental purpose of requiring full and truthful disclosure for the protection of investors.

I find and conclude that Auslander has not established his due diligence defense with respect to the misstatements and omissions in those portions of the prospectus other than the audited 1960 figures. . . .

GRANT

Grant became a director of BarChris in October 1960. His law firm was counsel to BarChris in matters pertaining to the registration of securities. . . .

Grant is sued as a director and as a signer of the registration statement. This is not an action against him for malpractice in his capacity as a lawyer. Nevertheless, in considering Grant's due diligence defenses, the unique position which he occupied cannot be disregarded. As the director most directly concerned with writing the registration statement and assuring its accuracy, more was required of him in the way of reasonable investigation than could fairly be expected of a director who had no connection with this work. . . .

Having seen [Grant] testify at length, I am satisfied as to his integrity. I find that Grant honestly believed that the registration statement was true and that no material facts had been omitted from it.

In this belief he was mistaken, and the fact is that for all his work, he never discovered any of the errors or omissions which have been recounted at length in this opinion, with the single exception of Capitol Lanes. He knew that BarChris had not sold this alley and intended to operate it, but he appears to have been under the erroneous impression that Peat, Marwick had knowingly sanctioned its inclusion in sales because of the allegedly temporary nature of the operation.

Grant contends that a finding that he did not make a reasonable investigation would be equivalent to a holding that a lawyer for an issuing company, in order to show due diligence, must make an independent audit of the figures supplied to him by his client. I do not consider this to be a realistic statement of the issue. There were errors and omissions here which could have been detected without an audit. The question is whether, despite his failure to detect them, Grant made a reasonable effort to that end.

Much of this registration statement is a scissors and paste-pot job. Grant lifted large portions from the earlier prospectuses, modifying them in some instances to the extent that he considered necessary. But BarChris's affairs had changed for the worse by May 1961. Statements that were accurate in January were no longer accurate in May. Grant never discovered this. He accepted the assurances of Kircher and Russo that any change which might have occurred had been for the better, rather than the contrary.

It is claimed that a lawyer is entitled to rely on the statements of his client and that to require him to verify their accuracy would set an unreasonably high standard. This is too broad a generalization. It is all a matter of degree. To require an audit would obviously be unreasonable. On the other hand, to require a check of matters easily verifiable is not unreasonable. Even honest clients can make mistakes. The statute imposes liability for untrue statements regardless of whether they are intentionally untrue. The way to prevent mistakes is to test oral information by examining the original written record.

There were things which Grant could readily have checked which he did not check. For example, he was unaware of the provisions of the agreements between BarChris and Talcott. He never read them. Thus, he did not know, although he readily could have ascertained, that BarChris's contingent liability on Type B leaseback arrangements was 100 per cent, not 25 per cent. He did not appreciate that if BarChris defaulted in repurchasing delinquent customers' notes upon Talcott's demand, Talcott could accelerate all the customer paper in its hands, which amounted to over $3,000,000.

As to the backlog figure, Grant appreciated that scheduled unfilled orders on the company's books meant firm commitments, but he never asked to see the contracts which, according to the prospectus, added up to $6,905,000. Thus, he did not know that this figure was overstated by some $4,490,000. . . .

As far as customers' delinquencies is concerned, although Grant discussed this with Kircher, he again accepted the assurances of Kircher and Russo that no serious problem existed. He did not examine the records as to delinquencies, although BarChris maintained such a record. [Grant was aware that the minutes of several executive committee meetings had not been typed, and he did not insist they should be. The court observed that had he ever examined Kircher's notes of those meetings, he would have learned the committee had had extended discussions about customer delinquencies.] Any inquiry on his part of Talcott or an examination of BarChris's correspondence with Talcott in April and May 1961 would have apprised him of the true facts.

The application of proceeds language in the prospectus was drafted by Kircher back in January. It may well have expressed his intent at that time, but his intent, and that of the other principal officers of BarChris, was very different in May. Grant did not appreciate that the earlier language was no longer appropriate. He never learned of the situation which the company faced in May. He knew that BarChris was short of cash, but he had no idea how short. He did not know that BarChris was withholding delivery of checks already drawn and signed because there was not enough money in the bank to pay them.

[The court then recounts that among the checks making up BarChris's "negative cash balance" at its bank was a check to Grant's firm, Perkins, Daniels, McCormack & Collins, in the amount of $8,711. This amount was also included in calculating BarChris's disclosure on its registration statement that Perkins, Daniels had "received fees aggregating $13,000 from BarChris." This then raised a question of just when Perkins, Daniels had received the check, for, as the court observed, if Grant deliberately forbore presenting that check until after the offering was completed, then he would be in the same position as Russo and Kircher, as one having knowledge that the registration statement falsely presented BarChris's financial position. The court concluded that the check had not been received before the registration statement became effective on May 16. Thus, the registration statement falsely represented that this amount had been paid to Perkins, Daniels, when in fact payment had not yet been made.] Grant was unaware of this. In approving this erroneous statement in the prospectus, he did not consult his own bookkeeper to ascertain whether it was correct. Kircher told him that the bill had been paid and Grant took his word for it. If he had inquired and had found that this representation was untrue, this discovery might well have led him to a realization of the true state of BarChris's finances in May 1961.

Grant was entitled to rely on Peat, Marwick for the 1960 figures. He had no reasonable ground to believe them to be inaccurate. But the matters which I have mentioned were not within the expertised portion of the prospectus. As to this, Grant was obliged to make a reasonable investigation. I am forced to find that he did not make one. After making all due allowances for the fact that BarChris's officers misled him, there are too many instances in which Grant failed to make an inquiry which he could easily have made which, if pursued, would have put him on his guard. . . . I conclude that Grant has not established his due diligence defenses except as to the audited 1960 figures.

THE UNDERWRITERS AND COLEMAN

The underwriters other than Drexel made no investigation of the accuracy of the prospectus. . . . They all relied upon Drexel as the "lead" underwriter.

Drexel did make an investigation. The work was in the charge of Coleman, a partner of the firm, assisted by Casperson, an associate. Drexel's attorneys acted as attorneys for the entire group of underwriters. Ballard did the work, assisted by Stanton.

On April 17, 1961 Coleman became a director of BarChris. He signed the first amendment to the registration statement filed on May 11 and the second amendment, constituting the registration statement in its final form, filed on

May 16. He thereby assumed a responsibility as a director and signer in addition to his responsibility as an underwriter. . . .

Like Grant, Ballard, without checking, relied on the information which he got from Kircher. He also relied on Grant who, as company counsel, presumably was familiar with its affairs. . . .

[It] is clear that no effectual attempt at verification was made. The question is whether due diligence required that it be made. Stated another way, is it sufficient to ask questions, to obtain answers which, if true, would be thought satisfactory, and to let it go at that, without seeking to ascertain from the records whether the answers in fact are true and complete?

I have already held that this procedure is not sufficient in Grant's case. Are underwriters in a different position, as far as due diligence is concerned?

The underwriters say that the prospectus is the company's prospectus, not theirs. Doubtless this is the way they customarily regard it. But the Securities Act makes no such distinction. The underwriters are just as responsible as the company if the prospectus is false. And prospective investors rely upon the reputation of the underwriters in deciding whether to purchase the securities.

There is no direct authority on this question, no judicial decision defining the degree of diligence which underwriters must exercise to establish their defense under Section 11.

There is some authority in New York for the proposition that a director of a corporation may rely upon information furnished him by the officers without independently verifying it. *See Litwin v. Allen*, 25 N.Y.S.2d 667 (Sup. Ct. 1940).

In support of that principle, the court in *Litwin* (25 N.Y.S.2d at 719) quoted from the opinion of Lord Halsbury in *Dovey v. Cory*, [1901] App. Cas. 477, 486, in which he said: "The business of life could not go on if people could not trust those who are put into a position of trust for the express purpose of attending to details of management."

Of course, New York law does not govern this case. The construction of the Securities Act is a matter of federal law. But the underwriters argue that *Litwin* is still in point, for they say that it establishes a standard of reasonableness for the reasonably prudent director which should be the same as the standard for the reasonably prudent underwriter under the Securities Act.

In my opinion the two situations are not analogous. An underwriter has not put the company's officers "into a position of trust for the express purpose of attending to details of management." The underwriters did not select them. In a sense, the positions of the underwriter and the company's officers are adverse. It is not unlikely that statements made by company officers to an underwriter to induce him to underwrite may be self-serving. They may be unduly enthusiastic. As in this case, they may, on occasion, be deliberately false.

The purpose of Section 11 is to protect investors. To that end the underwriters are made responsible for the truth of the prospectus. If they may escape that responsibility by taking at face value representations made to them by the company's management, then the inclusion of underwriters among those liable under Section 11 affords the investors no additional protection. To effectuate the statute's purpose, the phrase "reasonable investigation" must be construed to require more effort on the part of the underwriters than the mere accurate reporting in the prospectus of "data presented" to them by the company. It should make no difference that this data is elicited by questions addressed to the company officers by the underwriters, or that the underwriters at the time believe that the company's officers are truthful and reliable. In order to make the underwriters' participation in this enterprise of any value to the investors, the underwriters must make some reasonable attempt to verify the data submitted to them. They may not rely solely on the company's officers or on the company's counsel. A prudent man in the management of his own property would not rely on them.

It is impossible to lay down a rigid rule suitable for every case defining the extent to which such verification must go. It is a question of degree, a matter of judgment in each case. In the present case, the underwriters' counsel made almost no attempt to verify management's representations. I hold that that was insufficient.

On the evidence in this case, I find that the underwriters' counsel did not make a reasonable investigation of the truth of those portions of the prospectus which were not made on the authority of Peat, Marwick as an expert. Drexel is bound by their failure. It is not a matter of relying upon counsel for legal advice. Here the attorneys were dealing with matters of fact. Drexel delegated to them, as its agent, the business of examining the corporate minutes and contracts. It must bear the consequences of their failure to make an adequate examination.

The other underwriters, who did nothing and relied solely on Drexel and on the lawyers, are also bound by it. . . . [T]hey have not established their due diligence defense, except as to the 1960 audited figures.

The same conclusions must apply to Coleman. . . . He made no investigation after he became a director. When it came to verification, he relied upon his counsel to do it for him. Since counsel failed to do it, Coleman is bound by that failure. Consequently, in his case also, he has not established his due diligence defense except as to the audited 1960 figures. . . .

PEAT, MARWICK

. . . The part of the registration statement purporting to be made upon the authority of Peat, Marwick as an expert was, as we have seen, the 1960 figures. But because the statute requires the court to determine Peat, Marwick's belief, and the grounds thereof, "at the time such part of the registration statement became effective," for the purposes of this affirmative defense, the matter must be viewed as of May 16, 1961, and the question is whether at that time Peat, Marwick, after reasonable investigation, had reasonable ground to believe and did believe that the 1960 figures were true and that no material fact had been omitted from the registration statement which should have been included in order to make the 1960 figures not misleading. In deciding this issue, the court must consider not only what Peat, Marwick did in its 1960 audit, but also what it did in its subsequent "S-1 review." The proper scope of that review must also be determined. . . .

THE 1960 AUDIT

Peat, Marwick's work was in general charge of a member of the firm, Cummings, and more immediately in charge of Peat, Marwick's manager, Logan. Most of the actual work was performed by a senior accountant, Berardi, who had junior assistants, one of whom was Kennedy.

Berardi was then about thirty years old. He was not yet a C.P.A. He had had no previous experience with the bowling industry. This was his first job as a senior accountant. He could hardly have been given a more difficult assignment.

After obtaining a little background information on BarChris by talking to Logan and reviewing Peat, Marwick's work papers on its 1959 audit, Berardi examined the results of test checks of BarChris's accounting procedures which one of the junior accountants had made, and he prepared an "internal control questionnaire" and an "audit program." Thereafter, for a few days subsequent to December 30, 1960, he inspected BarChris's inventories and examined certain alley construction. Finally, on January 13, 1961, he began his auditing work which he carried on substantially continuously until it was completed on February 24, 1961. Toward the close of the work, Logan reviewed it and made various comments and suggestions to Berardi. . . .

Accountants should not be held to a standard higher than that recognized in their profession. I do not do so here. Berardi's review did not come up to that standard. . . . Most important of all, he was too easily satisfied with glib answers to his inquiries.

This is not to say that he should have made a complete audit. But there were enough danger signals in the materials which he did examine to require some further investigation on his part. . . . It is not always sufficient merely to ask questions.

. . . I conclude that Peat, Marwick has not established its due diligence defense. . . .

NOTES AND QUESTIONS

1. Insiders and Outsiders.   *BarChris* draws a distinction between corporate insiders (management) and outsiders (non-management directors), and in turn between outsiders who have special expertise or involvement in the distribution (e.g., directors who are the company's lawyers or investment bankers) and others. Among these, there seems to be a sliding scale of responsibility based on what can realistically be expected of the particular defendant. At one end of this scale, top managers of the issuer are held to the highest standard of diligence. Another illustration of the sliding-scale approach is found in *Feit v. Leasco Data Processing Equipment Inc.*, 332 F. Supp. 544, 578 (E.D.N.Y. 1971), where the court went so far as to suggest that insiders are virtual "guarantors" of the registration statement. For an expression of concern about how *BarChris* is generally read, especially with regard to underwriter responsibilities, *see* Leahy, The Irrepressible Myth of *BarChris*, 37 Del. J. Corp. L. 411 (2012).

At the other end of this scale, outside directors and other "peripheral" participants are judged in a more forgiving light—though their duty to investigate remains. Their exposure in turn varies depending upon particular expertise. Here, again, there is an intriguing conceptual question. Is it really consistent with the structure of Section 11(b) to say that for a non-expertised portion of the registration statement, director *A* may be liable for an inaccuracy because her special expertise (e.g., as an attorney) should have put her on notice that something was wrong, while director *B* is not liable? Or would it be more consistent to say that director *B* should nonetheless be held liable by virtue of his failure to assure that someone with the requisite expertise did in fact exercise the proper level of care? In other words, does the *BarChris* approach introduce out of whole cloth something of an "expertising" notion (i.e., a right to rely on others) with respect to the entire registration statement?

The sliding-scale approach to due diligence liability is codified in Rule 176, which says that in evaluating either reasonable investigation or reasonable grounds for belief, account should be taken of, for example, "[t]he presence or absence of another relationship with the issuer when the person is a director or proposed director" and "[r]easonable reliance on officers, employees and others whose duties should have given them knowledge of the particular facts (in light of the functions and responsibilities of the particular person with respect to the issuer and the filing)."

2.   *Who Assesses Diligence?* Whether a Section 11 due diligence defense may be established through summary judgment will significantly affect the settlement dynamic underlying the litigation. In *Software Toolworks Securities Litigation*, 789 F. Supp. 1489 (N.D. Cal. 1992), the court held that the adequacy of a due diligence investigation is a question for the judge, not a jury:

> First, the due diligence defense is a statutory standard; as such, its application to undisputed historical facts should normally be a matter for the judge. This ensures that the administration of the statutory defense benefits from consistency, uniformity and predictability. Second, a decision on the due diligence defense generally affects a class of persons (as opposed to one person), making it in the nature of judicial rule making. Third, knowledge of what constitutes due diligence does not fall within the common experience of jurors, making it instead a question better suited for the judge. Fourth, leaving the question of what constitutes due diligence to the jury will lead to a battle of experts. While this may be appropriate in some cases, with a question like due diligence, the inquiry does not lend itself to any objective standards. The experts, who basically become paid advocates, will simply express an opinion based on their own subjective viewpoints, which will be biased by their role. The jurors will then be forced to decide between these paid advocates. The resulting uncertainty will increase litigation against deep pocket defendants (such as underwriters) and encourage collusion between plaintiffs and the issuer, who will often be in a precarious financial situation already. These policy implications favor summary judgment as the preferred means of resolution. Finally, treating due diligence as a question of law, once the historical facts are undisputed, will apportion the risk more appropriately, encourage settlement at early stages and lead to more equitable and consistent results.

Id. at 1495-1496. On appeal, the Ninth Circuit agreed that due diligence could be decided as a matter of law (and by means of summary judgment) where the historical facts were undisputed, but only upon determining that no rational jury could find otherwise. It affirmed the lower court's findings for the under-writers as to some matters, but reversed as to others. *See In re Software Toolworks Securities Litigation,* 38 F.3d 1078 (9th Cir. 1994).

3.   Sounds in Fraud?   Because Section 11 creates strict liability for the issuer and due diligence liability for other offering participants, plaintiffs have no need to allege fraud. But many courts say that if plaintiffs choose to make allegations that "sound in fraud," then they have a heightened obligation to plead those facts "with particularity" under Rule 9(b) of the Federal Rules of Civil Procedure, and are thus subject to dismissal if the pleadings fall short. *See Rombach v. Chang,* 355 F.3d 164 (2d Cir. 2004). The same applies when plaintiffs are forced to claim intentional misrepresentation, for example, because a line item disclosure requirement on which they are relying is limited to facts "known" to management or because the alleged misstatement was forward-looking and thus subject to statutory protection absent actual knowledge of falsity. *TransEnterix Inv'r Grp. v. TransEnterix, Inc.,* 272 F. Supp. 3d 740, 757-758, 762 (E.D.N.C. 2017). There is a great deal of case law on how and when the height-ened pleading requirement applies, and what plaintiffs must do to avoid it. *E.g., Fresno Cty. Emp. Ret. System v. comScore,* 268 F. Supp. 3d 526 (S.D.N.Y. 2017) (plaintiffs successfully based claims on negligence and strict liability).

4.   Attorneys' Liability.   Given the central role that they play in the draft-ing of a registration statement, it seems curious that attorneys are not listed among the potential defendants in an action under Section 11 except to the extent that they are also officers or directors or otherwise treated as "experts." And the courts have held that attorneys are experts only with respect to the discrete portions of the registration statement that operate as legal opinions, for example, that the shares in question have been validly authorized and issued and are nonassessable under state law. *See, e.g., In re ZZZZ Best Securities Litigation,* Fed. Sec. L. Rep. (CCH) ¶94,485 (C.D. Cal. 1989); *Ahern v. Gaussoin,* 611 F. Supp. 1465 (D. Or. 1985). As a result, it is unlikely that the law firm that mistakenly fails to discover material information will be directly liable to inves-tors at all under Section 11. This does not mean, however, that the firm is safe from liability elsewhere under the securities laws, including Rule 10b-5. We will see more about attorney liability in Chapters 13 and 14. As an entirely separate matter, of course, the negligent firm may be liable under a variety of state law theories, including malpractice.

5.   Whistleblowing.   Section 11(b)(1) provides an "out" for an officer or a director who is named in the registration statement when it is filed, but who thereafter becomes dissatisfied with the disclosure. That person is not liable under Section 11 if, before the registration statement becomes effective, the required steps to resign the position with the issuer are taken and the SEC is advised that such action has occurred and that further responsibility for the accuracy of the registration statement will not lie. (Section 11(b)(2) provides a similar disavowal procedure when a registration statement becomes effective without a particular person's knowledge.) The resignation option, of course, is designed to alert the Commission that something is amiss. It poses a particular dilemma for attorneys who are also officers or directors, given their professional responsibility to respect client confidences.

6.   Controlling Person Liability.   With respect to all violations of the Securities Act—not just Section 11—there is a separate source of potential liability for certain persons. Section 15 imposes joint and several liability upon any person who controls a primary violator "unless the controlling person had no knowledge of or reasonable ground to believe in the existence of the facts by reason of which the liability of the controlled person is alleged to exist." The most obvious category of controlling person is the dominant shareholder, who in turn may be an individual, a group of individuals, or, in the parent-subsidiary context, another company. Issues involving control person status often cannot be resolved on the pleadings. *See, e.g., Plumbers' Union Local No. 12 Pension Fund v. Nomura Asset Acceptance Corp.*, 632 F.3d 762, 776 (1st Cir. 2011) ("Given the 'highly factual nature' of the control person inquiry, resolving that issue on a motion to dismiss is often inappropriate."). Controlling person liability will be explored in greater detail, along with the analogous provision under the Securities Exchange Act, in Chapter 14.

7.   Whose Material Misrepresentation Is It?   In order to prevail under Section 11, the plaintiff must establish the materiality of the misstatement or omission. In this regard, consider *J&R Marketing, SEP v. General Motors Corp.*, 549 F.3d 384 (6th Cir. 2008), where the court rejected the argument that by disclosing in the registration statement the credit rating assigned the issuer by independent rating agencies, the issuer of the bonds (GMAC) was warranting that the ratings were an accurate indication of the risk of default:

> GMAC's disclosure of its credit rating was merely a true statement of historical fact. Credit ratings are unique. Investors consider credit rating agencies' opinions important, and investors want to know those opinions, regardless of whether the company agrees or disagrees with the agencies' opinions. . . . The investors do not allege that GMAC lied to or misled the credit rating agencies, and there is no allegation in the complaint that would support such an assertion. The opinions, then, were arrived at through the agencies' usual methods, and all information they requested from GMAC to formulate their opinion was provided. Their opinions, therefore, were accurate according to the agencies' methods for determining risk of default. Because investors assigned independent meaning to the credit rating assigned by the agencies, they would not assume, absent any language to the contrary, that GMAC was in any way warranting the accuracy of the rating.

Id. at 393. Using similar reasoning, the court rejected the argument that in setting an interest rate on the bonds GMAC was warranting that the rate was appropriate or fair in light of the risk of default.

Also consider *In re Stac Electronic Securities Litigation*, 89 F.3d 1399 (9th Cir. 1996), where the company's prospectus included the usual generic warnings about the possibility of competitive products but failed to disclose its knowledge that Microsoft intended to introduce competitive software in its next version of DOS. In concluding the prospectus disclosures were adequate, the court emphasized the speculative nature of the threat of competition from Microsoft:

We agree with Stac that another company's plans cannot be known with certainty. Even assuming . . . that Microsoft had informed Stac that it planned to introduce data compression software, Stac could not have known whether or not Microsoft would truly do so. As Stac points out, the contingency of the event is underscored by the fact that a competitive product was liable to violate Stacker's patent. . . . Also, the market knew of the potential for Microsoft's inclusion of data compression technology.

Id. at 1407. *Compare In re Snap Inc. Sec. Litig.*, 2018 WL 2972528 (C.D. Cal. 2018) (refusing to dismiss claims that Snap misstated the threat to its product line from a new Instagram platform).

PROBLEMS

9-1.   Beta Corporation, a small software firm, recently made its IPO. At the time the registration statement was being prepared, a number of the company's sales staff had been hearing rumors from a variety of customers regarding the plans of one of the major software companies to launch a new product that would be comparable to Beta's most innovative and profitable offering. One had written a memo to the vice president for marketing, passing this information along. The vice president took no action other than to ask that he be kept posted in the event that any hard information came along. No other Beta officials were informed.

The registration statement highlighted various factors that made it able to withstand competition from others in Beta's particular software niche, with the usual disclaimer that there was no guarantee that competitive conditions would permit this niche to continue indefinitely. No mention was made of any more concrete market risks. A few months after the offering, Microsoft indeed came out with the competitive product, and a short time later Beta was on the verge of insolvency.

A Section 11 suit has been brought for failure to disclose the information in question, naming Beta and all the usual defendants. In discovery, the memo to the vice president was obtained. In deposition, the vice president testified that he had withheld the information from others because he did not want to throw a monkey wrench into the financing effort, especially since the information was "only in the form of rumors." Investigation and discovery by the plaintiffs have also established that when the registration statement was prepared, there was no publicly available information about the bigger company's plans, and the few investment analysts who followed Beta were recommending purchases at the time of the offering. On the other hand, there is some indication that a few analysts who specialize in technology stocks were aware of the new product, and information about the plans had indeed spread to its sales staff, who in a number of instances had asked retailers and others to hold off making major purchases of Beta's product.

How likely is it that, among the defendants, the following would be held liable: (a) the vice president; (b) Beta's CEO; (c) the managing underwriter; or (d) a software industry magazine publisher who sits on Beta's board?

9-2. Recall from Chapter 4 that Spotify engaged in a "direct listing" on the New York Stock Exchange to become a public company without directly raising any capital. At the time of its listing, it had a valuation around $26 billion. Many see direct listings as likely to become a common route to public status, and some worry that the rapid opening of a trading market for the shares of a heretofore large private company raises concerns about investor protection. Spotify employed three investment banks (including Goldman Sachs and J.P. Morgan) as "financial advisors" to assist with this listing, which had the purpose and effect of, among other things, proving liquidity to existing Spotify shareholders. Spotify did file an F-1'33 Act registration statement to enable existing shareholders who did not otherwise qualify for an exemption under Rule 144 to resell immediately. The F-1 stated that the advisors were not acting as underwriters but would provide "advice and assistance to [Spotify] with respect to [Spotify]'s (i) defining of objectives with respect to the Registration and Listing, (ii) drafting of the Form F-1 and (iii) drafting of public communications and investor presentations in connection with the Registration and Listing." At the behest of the NYSE and the SEC, one of the advisors (J.P. Morgan) was also retained to provide assistance to the Exchange's designated marketmaker as to pricing the shares when trading commenced. Based on what you studied in Chapter 6, are the financial advisors truly safe from being characterized as underwriters in a Section 11 suit brought by investors? Would it matter that some $35 million of the $46 million of costs incurred by Spotify were paid as fees to the advisers? *See* Horton, Spotify's Direct Listing: Is it a Recipe for Gatekeeper Failure?, 72 SMU L. Rev. 177 (2019); Nickerson, Comment: The Underlying Underwriter: An Analysis of the Spotify Direct Listing, 86 U. Chi. L. Rev. 985 (2019). If there is no underwriter with Section 11 exposure, does this suggest a danger to investors from direct listings?

b.   Shelf Registrations and Other Seasoned Offerings

The due diligence obligations of the underwriters in WorldCom's bond issuances totaling nearly $17 billion in 2000 and 2001 were at issue in what many believe to be the most important Section 11 case since *BarChris*. The lead underwriters were Salomon Smith Barney (now Citigroup Global Markets) and J.P. Morgan Securities.

It was undisputed that WorldCom executives manipulated the company's public filings, which were incorporated by reference into the registration statements. The underwriters argued that they were entitled to rely *without further investigation* on WorldCom's financial statements audited by Arthur Andersen as well as "comfort letters" from the auditor for the interim unaudited financial statements of the company. Plaintiffs, on the other hand, pointed to the poor documentation of any underwriter diligence efforts and the fact that several of the underwriters had downgraded their internal credit ratings of WorldCom at about the time of the offerings. They also pointed to several "red flags" that should have put the underwriters on notice of the need for further inquiries. For example, WorldCom's ratio of expenses to revenues (43 percent) reported in the company's SEC filings was significantly lower than that of its major competitors, AT&T (46.8 percent) and Sprint (53.2 percent). The underwriters countered that this data already was publicly available information and was insufficient as a matter of law to put them on notice of any accounting irregularities, and that the nature of the transaction—a shelf takedown of investment-grade debt securities issued by a world-class issuer—was such that underwriter investigation into WorldCom's accounting was neither practicable nor called for by industry practices.

In 2004, Citigroup settled claims against it for $2.65 billion. The following opinion addresses the summary judgment motions of the remaining underwriters.

In re WorldCom, Inc. Securities Litigation
346 F. Supp. 2d 628 (S.D.N.Y. 2004)

DENISE COTE, District Judge:

[B]eginning in the late 1960s, the SEC embarked on a "program to integrate the disclosure requirements of the Securities Act and the Securities Exchange Act of 1934." . . . The chief purpose of the integrated disclosure system was to furnish investors with "meaningful, nonduplicative information both periodically and when securities distributions are made to the public," while decreasing "costs of compliance for public companies." . . .

The push to incorporate by reference was motivated by the growing recognition that "for companies in the top tier, there is a steady stream of high quality corporate information continually furnished to the market and broadly digested, synthesized and disseminated." . . .

Short-form registration was accompanied by related changes in shelf registration, the process by which securities are registered to be offered or sold on a delayed or continuous basis. The purpose of shelf registration is to allow a single registration statement to be filed for a series of offerings. . . .

Together, the mechanism of incorporation by reference and the expansion of shelf registration significantly reduced the time and expense necessary to prepare public offerings, thus enabling more "rapid access to today's capital markets." SEC Rel. 6335, 1981 WL 31062, at 4. As the SEC recognized, these changes affected the time in which underwriters could perform their investigations of an issuer. Underwriters had weeks to perform due diligence for traditional registration statements. By contrast, under a short-form registration regime, "preparation time is reduced sharply" thanks to the ability to incorporate by reference prior disclosures. Id. at 5.

These two innovations triggered concern among underwriters. Members of the financial community worried about their ability "to undertake a reasonable investigation with respect to the adequacy of the information incorporated by reference from periodic reports filed under the Exchange Act into the short form registration statements utilized in an integrated disclosure system." Id. at 1. . . .

Because an underwriter could select among competing underwriters when offering securities through a shelf registration, some questioned whether an underwriter could "afford to devote the time and expense necessary to conduct a due diligence review before knowing whether it will handle an offering and that there may not be sufficient time to do so once it is selected." SEC Rel. 6499, 1983 WL 408321, at 5. Others doubted whether they would have the chance "to apply their independent scrutiny and judgment to documents prepared by registrants many months before an offering." Id.

Because of concerns like those described here, the SEC introduced Rule 176 in 1981 "to make explicit what circumstances may bear upon the determination of what constitutes a reasonable investigation and reasonable ground for belief as these terms are used in Section 11(b)." SEC Rel. 6335. . . .

Although "no court has ever been called upon to interpret Rule 176," the SEC's own commentary on the rule makes clear that Rule 176 did not alter the fundamental nature of underwriters' due diligence obligations. [Donald C.] Langevoort, Deconstructing Section 11: [Public Offering Liability in a Continuous Disclosure Environment, 63 Law & Contemp. Probs. 45, 65 (2000)]; Task Force Report, 48 Bus. Law. at 1210. . . . As recently as December 1998, the SEC recalled that it "expressly rejected the consideration of competitive timing and pressures when evaluating the reasonableness of an underwriter's investigation." 63 Fed. Reg. at 67231.

The SEC's intent to maintain high standards for underwriter due diligence is confirmed by its many discussions of appropriate due diligence techniques in the integrated disclosure system. In proposing Rule 176, the SEC acknowledged that different investigatory methods would be needed "in view of the compressed preparation time and the volatile nature of the capital markets." SEC Rel. 6335. Nonetheless, it emphasized that such techniques must be "equally thorough." Id. Among the strategies recommended by the SEC were the development of a "reservoir of knowledge about the companies that may select the underwriter to distribute their securities registered on short form registration statements" through a "careful review of [periodic Exchange Act] filings on an ongoing basis," consultation of analysts' reports, and active participation in the issuer's investor relations program, especially analysts and brokers meetings. Id.

At the time the SEC finalized the shelf registration rule two years later, it again recognized that "the techniques of conducting due diligence investigations of registrants qualified to use short form registration . . . would differ from due diligence investigations under other circumstances." SEC Rel. 6499. Nonetheless, it stressed the use of "anticipatory and continuous due diligence programs" to augment underwriters' fulfillment of their due diligence obligations. Id. Among other practices, the SEC approvingly noted the increased designation of one law firm to act as underwriters' counsel, which "facilitates continuous due diligence by ensuring ongoing access to the registrant on the underwriters' behalf"; the holding of "Exchange Act report 'drafting sessions,'" which allow underwriters "to participate in the drafting and review of periodic disclosure documents before they are filed"; and "periodic due diligence sessions," such as meetings between prospective underwriters, their counsel, and management shortly after the release of quarterly earnings. Id. . . .

It must be noted that academics and practitioners alike have asserted that the current regime for underwriter liability under Section 11 no longer makes sense. Professor Coffee, for one, has observed that "it is not clear that the underwriter today still performs the classic gatekeeping function. . . . Many argue that serious due diligence efforts are simply not feasible within the time constraints of shelf registration. Given these constraints, they claim that the solution lies in downsizing the threat under section 11." John C. Coffee, Jr., Brave New World?: The Impact(s) of the Internet on Modern Securities Regulation, 52 Bus. Law. 1195, 1211 (1997). Another professor has remarked that "there is a strong practical case to be made for absolving underwriters of all inquiry obligations short of recklessness. . . . As underwriter involvement diminishes in significance relative to the deal as a whole, it becomes that much more problematic to apply a negligence-based standard in the first place." Langevoort, 63 Law & Contemp. Probs. at 65. A third asserts that in today's capital markets, "it is reasonable to question whether the underwriter's 'due diligence' role is justified at all. . . . For shelf registrations, disinterested advance due diligence is the exception not the rule." Frank Partnoy, Barbarians at the Gatekeepers?: A Proposal for a Modified Strict Liability Regime, 79 Wash. U. L.Q. 491, 522 (2001) (citation omitted) ("Barbarians at the Gatekeepers").

In a related vein, a Task Force of experienced counsel to underwriters concludes that the "'integrated disclosure system' and the expansion of shelf registration statements have called into question whether underwriters any longer 'sponsor' an issue in a meaningful way, as opposed to delivering advice and distribution services." Task Force Report, 48 Bus. Law. at 1239. . . .

Thus, academics and practitioners have called for a reexamination of underwriters' liability under Sections 11 and 12(a)(2) on the grounds that "Congress's assumptions in 1933 and 1934 about registrants working with individual underwriters in a relatively leisurely atmosphere are at odds with today's competition by multiple underwriters for high-speed transactions." Id. Implicit in these calls for a legislative change is the recognition that current law continues to place a burden upon an underwriter to conduct a reasonable investigation of non-expertised statements in a registration statement, including an issuer's interim financial statements. . . .

[T]he Lead Plaintiff has shown that there are questions of fact . . . as to whether the Underwriter Defendants conducted a reasonable investigation in either 2000 or 2001. It points to what it contends is evidence of the limited number of conversations with the issuer or its auditor, the cursory nature of the inquiries, the failure to go behind any of the almost formulaic answers given to the questions, and the failure to inquire into issues of particular prominence in the Underwriter Defendants' own internal evaluations of the financial condition of the issuer or in the financial press. . . . Given the enormity of these two bond offerings, and the general deterioration in WorldCom's financial situation, at least at the time of the 2001 Offering, they argue that a particularly probing inquiry by a prudent underwriter was required. These issues of fact require a jury trial.

Focusing mainly on the red flags that are questions of fact and may have put the underwriters on notice of the need for further inquiries, the court rejected the underwriters' motions for summary judgment. Following the opinion, the remaining underwriters settled the claims on terms less favorable than the earlier Citigroup settlement. The underwriter settlements totaled approximately $6 billion. This was in addition to substantial settlements with Arthur Andersen ($65 million) and WorldCom directors ($61 million). The settlement involving directors is especially noteworthy because it includes $25 million in required personal payments, with only the balance covered by insurance.

NOTES AND QUESTIONS

1.   Sliding Scales and the WorldCom Directors.   Consider the precarious position of Bert C. Roberts, a former MCI executive who served as chairman of the WorldCom board following the company's acquisition of MCI. Arguing that he was entitled to rely on the integrity of the company's officers and auditor, Roberts requested summary judgment on the Section 11 claims against him. The court denied Roberts' motion. *See In re WorldCom, Inc. Securities Litigation,* 2005 U.S. Dist. LEXIS 4193 (S.D.N.Y. 2005). It reasoned that whether red flags should have alerted someone as highly experienced in the telecommunications industry as Roberts to the disclosure problems is an "exquisitely fact intensive inquiry into all the circumstances" and, therefore, cannot be disposed of through summary judgment. Whether Roberts should be treated as an inside or an outside director under a sliding-scale approach to diligence was among the facts requiring further development. This proved to be the last gasp for Roberts. Immediately after the decision, he agreed to settle the case for $4.5 million *from his own pocket.* As noted above, the director settlements totaled $61 million ($25 million to be paid personally and $36 million to be paid by insurers).

In Section 11 litigation, outside directors gain one form of protection not available to other defendants: Under subsection (f)(2), their liability is based on an assessment of proportionate fault. Proportionate liability is considered further in Chapter 13.

2.   Diligence in Context.   In the traditional form of underwriting, it makes some sense to think of the underwriter as a "gatekeeper" to the capital marketplace and thus properly chargeable with assuring the accuracy of the issuer's offering materials. *E.g.,* Kraakman, Corporate Liability Strategies and the Costs of Legal Controls, 93 Yale L.J. 857, 890-891 (1984). But what if the mechanics of public distributions change such that complete due diligence, even by the most responsible underwriter, is impracticable?

The problem arises most clearly in shelf registration takedowns and other transactions that occur quickly. Large capitalization issuers can readily have an effective registration statement on file, and wait for market windows to open that make selling desirable. When that happens, they contact underwriters to solicit bids, and expect that the sales will occur almost immediately. The prospectus supplement that completes the registration statement need not be filed with the SEC until two days after the takedown, so that the sales do not even have to await the completion of the required filings. How is an underwriter supposed to do "due diligence" in such a short time?

As Professor Merritt Fox has observed, *WorldCom* illustrates that the standard of liability for underwriters remains fixed even though their role has shifted from being a force to promote disclosure to being merely insurers for disclosure failures. Noting that shelf registration leaves underwriters without any realistic opportunity to discharge their statutory responsibilities, Professor Fox favors replacing the existing scheme of underwriter liability with a system in which an "external certifier" (an investment bank) would function to force disclosures both in public offerings and in annual filings. *See* Fox, Civil Liability and Mandatory Disclosure, 109 Colum. L. Rev. 237 (2009). *See also* Sjostrom, The Due Diligence Defense Under Section 11 of the Securities Act of 1933, 44 Brandeis L.J. 549 (2006) (discussing sliding-scale due diligence defenses generally and noting diligence in a shelf registered offering is necessarily more limited). Prior to *WorldCom*, underwriters were often willing to proceed with minimal inquiry, assuming (or perhaps hoping) that a court would—perhaps by reference to Rule 176—hold that the level of diligence is simply what is practicable given the nature of the issuer and the speed of the transaction. For example, Rule 176(g) states the type of underwriting that is relevant to determining the level of investigation, and paragraph (h) provides that the level of culpability should be sensitive to whether the fact misrepresented appeared in a document incorporated by reference and whether the particular party had any responsibility for the fact or preparing the document so incorporated. Those hopes were dashed by the court, though a careful reading of the case suggests that the outcome probably turned more on the red flags that may have been ignored than concern about the quality of the diligence in and of itself. In response to *WorldCom*, the investment banking community urged the SEC to expand the protections of Rule 176 as part of the 2005 securities offering reforms, but the Commission explicitly chose not to do so.

> **3.   *Post-Effective Liability Under Section 11.*** Section 11 speaks of imposing liability for material misstatements or omissions in a registration statement as of the effective date. This obviously creates a problem with respect to shelf registrations, where much may happen between the effective date and the date sales are made. A number of SEC rules seek to address the issue and expand the scope of liability. First, Item 512 of Regulation S-K has long required an undertaking from the issuer that any post-effective amendment and any subsequently filed 10-K are deemed the filing of a new registration statement, thus resetting the effective date for purposes of Section 11. Second, as part of the 2005 offering reforms, the Commission made clear in Rule 430B that in connection with a shelf takedown, the filing of a prospectus supplement resets the effective date for liability purposes to the earlier of the date of its first use or of the first sale for purposes of assessing issuer or underwriter liability. *See NCUAB v. UBS Securities Inc.*, 2017 WL 235013 (D. Kan. 2017). Other Section 11 defendants, such as officers, directors, and experts, are not subject to that effective date extension except when the filing is pursuant to Section 10(a)(3) or reflects a "fundamental" change with respect to the issuer or the offering. As a result, these defendants may sometimes escape the liability imposed on the issuer and the underwriters. Does this make sense? Before reading too much into this escape route, consider *Federal Housing Finance Agency v. HSBC North American Holdings Inc.*, 987 F. Supp. 2d 369 (S.D.N.Y. 2013), where the court dealt with this issue in the context of a securitization transaction. The initial registration statement and base prospectus was to be filled in via prospectus supplement with all the relevant details about the creditworthiness of the borrowers and the quality of the collateral underlying the certificates at the time of takedown. As a result, the misrepresentations about which purchasers complained were only in these later-filed prospectus supplements. The court rejected the officer and director

defendants' motion to dismiss, because the change from the skeletal base prospectus to the detailed prospectus supplement was patently fundamental.

PROBLEM

9-3. Eli Pilly & Co. is a well-known seasoned issuer with an effective shelf registration statement. It is current in its Exchange Act filings. On May 1, the company initiated a takedown of preferred stock, which was quickly sold through a number of underwriters. A prospectus supplement was filed within two days to reflect the terms of the transaction and other distribution-related disclosures.

In late April, Pilly's vice president for research learned of problems with a highly touted drug under development in the company's labs. This information was not communicated to the company's CEO or CFO, and neither the prospectus supplement nor any other filing mentioned the adverse development. For purposes of Section 11 liability, did Pilly's registration statement contain a misstatement as of the effective date? As to which potential parties to the lawsuit?

3. Opinions and Half-Truths

In considering whether a statement by the board of directors that $54 per share in a proposed merger was a "fair" and "high" price could be a material *fact*, the Supreme Court in *Virginia Bankshares, Inc. v. Sandberg*, 501 U.S. 1083 (1991), held such a statement of opinion could be a fact for purposes of a Section 14 claim when there was objective evidence before the speaker that was inconsistent with the opinion expressed. The Supreme Court revisited opinion statements in *Omnicare, Inc. v. Laborers Dist. Council Constr. Indus. Pension Fund*, 135 S. Ct. 1318 (2015), in the context of the absolute liability standard imposed on issuers by Section 11. Purchasers of Omnicare's registered securities sued the company following the stock's dramatic price decline in the wake of a government suit claiming that Omnicare obtained business by paying kickbacks to various health care providers in violation of the law. Omnicare's registration statement stated:

> We believe our contract arrangements with other healthcare providers, our pharmaceutical suppliers and our pharmacy practices are in compliance with applicable federal and state laws.
>
> We believe that our contracts with pharmaceutical manufacturers are legally and economically valid arrangements that bring value to the healthcare system and the patients that we serve.

Omnicare carefully notes that Section 11(a) reaches not just "an untrue statement of a material fact" but also applies when there is a failure "to state a material fact . . . necessary to make the statements therein not misleading." The latter is generally understood to reach so-called half-truths. Here, Omnicare did not make "an untrue statement of material fact" as the plaintiff did not allege Omnicare officers acted fraudulently or recklessly (although the plaintiff did allege Omnicare's directors and officers "possessed reasonable grounds" for believing the professed opinions were truthful and complete). Of greater significance, examined more fully in Chapter 12, is *Omnicare*'s holding with respect to examining opinion statements under the half-truth doctrine:

> [A]n investor cannot state a claim by alleging only that an opinion was wrong; the complaint must as well call into question the issuer's basis for offering the opinion. And to do so, the investor cannot just say that the issuer failed to reveal its basis. Section 11's omissions clause, after all, is not a general disclosure requirement; it affords a cause of action only when an issuer's failure to include a material fact has rendered a published statement misleading. . . . To be specific: The investor must identify particular (and material) facts going to the basis for the issuer's opinion—facts about the inquiry the issuer did or did not conduct or the knowledge it did or did not have—whose omission makes the opinion statement at issue misleading to a reasonable person reading the statement fairly and in context.

In remanding the case, the Supreme Court observed that the district court should determine whether the plaintiffs adequately alleged that Omnicare omitted warnings it had received from counsel that a particular contract carried a heightened risk of violating the anti-kickback laws and, if they so alleged, whether that omitted fact would have been material to reasonable investors so as to render the claims of legal compliance materially misleading. Query: If an issuer's general counsel states that it believes that a certain important business arrangement is lawful, what due diligence steps would be appropriate if the issuer were making a registered public offering?

4.   Damages

Akerman v. Oryx Communications Inc.
810 F.2d 336 (2d Cir. 1987)

MESKILL, J. This case arises out of a June 30, 1981, initial public offering of securities by Oryx, a company planning to enter the business of manufacturing and marketing abroad video cassettes and video discs of feature films for home entertainment. Oryx filed a registration statement and an accompanying prospectus dated June 30, 1981 . . . for a firm commitment offering of 700,000 units. Each unit sold for $4.75 and consisted of one share of common stock and one warrant to purchase an additional share of stock for $5.75 at a later date.

The prospectus contained an erroneous pro forma unaudited financial statement relating to the eight month period ending March 31, 1981. It reported net sales of $931,301, net income of $211,815, and earnings of seven cents per share. Oryx, however, had incorrectly posted a substantial transaction by its subsidiary to March instead of April when Oryx actually received the subject sale's revenues. The prospectus, therefore, overstated earnings for the eight month period. Net sales in that period actually totaled $766,301, net income $94,529, and earnings per share three cents.

Oryx's price had declined to four dollars per unit by October 12, 1981, the day before Oryx revealed the prospectus misstatement to the SEC. The unit price had further declined to $3.25 by November 9, 1981, the day before

Price dropping

Oryx disclosed the misstatement to the public. After public disclosure, the price of Oryx rose and reached $3.50 by November 25, 1981, the day this suit commenced.

Section 11(a) of the 1933 Act imposes civil liability on the signatories of a registration statement if the registration statement contains a material untruth or omission of which a "person acquiring [the registered] security" had no knowledge at the time of the purchase. Plaintiffs in the Akermans' situation, if successful, would be entitled to recover the difference between the original purchase price and the value of the stock at the time of suit. A defendant may, under section 11(e), reduce his liability by proving that the depreciation in value resulted from factors other than the material misstatement in the registration statement. A defendant's burden in attempting to reduce his liability has been characterized as the burden of "negative causation." *Beecher v. Able*, 435 F. Supp. 397, 409 (S.D.N.Y. 1975).

The district court determined that plaintiffs established a prima facie case under section 11(a) by demonstrating that the prospectus error was material "as a theoretical matter." The court, however, granted defendants' motion for summary judgment on damages under section 11(e), stating: "[Defendants] have carried their heavy burden of proving that the [Oryx stock price] decline was caused by factors other than the matters misstated in the registration statement." The precise issue on appeal, therefore, is whether defendants carried their burden of negative causation under section 11(e).

Defendants' heavy burden reflects Congress' desire to allocate the risk of uncertainty to the defendants in these cases. . . . The misstatement resulted from an innocent bookkeeping error whereby Oryx misposted a sale by its subsidiary to March instead of April. Oryx received the sale's proceeds less than one month after the reported date. The prospectus, moreover, expressly stated that Oryx "expect[ed] that [the subsidiary's] sales will decline." . . .

Thus, although the misstatement may have been "theoretically material," *Akerman*, 609 F. Supp. at 366, when it is considered in the context of the prospectus' pessimistic forecast of the performance of Oryx's subsidiary, the misstatement was not likely to cause a stock price decline. . . .

Indeed, the public not only did not react adversely to disclosure of the misstatement, Oryx's price actually *rose* somewhat after public disclosure of the error.

The applicable section 11(e) formula for calculating damages is "the difference between the amount paid for the security (not exceeding the price at which the security was offered to the public) and . . . the value thereof as of the time such suit was brought." The relevant events and stock prices are:

Date	Event	Oryx Stock Price
June 30, 1981	Initial public offering	$4.75
October 15, 1981	Disclosure of error to SEC	$4.00
November 10, 1981	Disclosure of error to public	$3.25
November 25, 1981	Date of suit	$3.50

The price decline before disclosure may not be charged to defendants. At first blush, damages would appear to be zero because there was no depreciation in Oryx's value between the time of public disclosure and the time of suit.

The Akermans contended at trial, however, that the relevant disclosure date was the date of disclosure to the SEC and not to the public. Under plaintiffs' theory, damages would equal the price decline subsequent to October 15, 1981, which amounted to fifty cents per share. . . . The district court invited statistical studies from both sides to clarify the causation issue. Defendants produced a statistical analysis of the stocks of the one hundred companies that went public contemporaneously with Oryx. The study tracked the stocks' performances for the period between June 30, 1981 (initial public offering date) and November 25, 1981 (date of suit). The study indicated that Oryx performed at the exact statistical median of these stocks and that several issues suffered equal or greater losses than did Oryx during this period. Defendants produced an additional study which indicated that Oryx stock "behaved over the entire period . . . consistent[ly] with its own inherent variation." Id.

Plaintiffs offered the following rebuttal evidence. During the period between SEC disclosure and public disclosure, Oryx stock decreased nineteen percent while the over-the-counter (OTC) composite index rose five percent (the first study). During this period, therefore, the OTC composite index outperformed Oryx by twenty-four percentage points. Plaintiffs also produced a study indicating that for the time period between SEC disclosure and one week after public disclosure, eighty-two of the one hundred new issues analyzed in the defendants' study outperformed Oryx's stock.

Plaintiffs' first study compared Oryx's performance to the performance of the OTC index in order to rebut a comparison offered by defendants to prove that Oryx's price decline resulted not from the misstatement but rather from an overall market decline. As previously stated, defendants' comparison indicated that the OTC index generally declined for the period between Oryx's offering date and the date of suit. The parties' conflicting comparisons, however, lack credibility because they fail to reflect any of the countless variables that might affect the stock price performance of a single company. . . . Statistical analyses must control for relevant variables to permit reliable inferences. . . .

The studies comparing Oryx's performance to the other one hundred companies that went public in May and June of 1981 are similarly flawed. The studies do not evaluate the performance of Oryx stock in relation to the stock of companies possessing any characteristic in common with Oryx, e.g., product, technology, profitability, assets or countless other variables which influence stock prices, except the contemporaneous initial offering dates.

Perhaps more important, the Akermans' study of the one hundred new issues focuses on a time frame which controverts one of their own theories explaining the public's failure to react adversely to disclosure. The Akermans argue that the thin market in Oryx stock prevented immediate public reaction to disclosure of the prospectus error. . . . Their study, however, measures Oryx's performance from SEC disclosure to *one week* after public disclosure. A thin market, according to the Akermans' own explanation, would not reflect the impact of bad news in such a short time period (one week). This internal inconsistency seriously undercuts the probative value of the Akermans' study. . . .

Defendants met their burden, as set forth in section 11(e), by establishing that the misstatement was barely material and that the public failed to react adversely to its disclosure. With the case in this posture, the plaintiffs had to come forward with "specific facts showing that there is a genuine issue for trial." . . . Despite extensive discovery, plaintiffs completely failed to produce any evidence, other than unreliable and sometimes inconsistent statistical studies and theories, suggesting that Oryx's price decline actually resulted from the misstatement. . . .

Summary judgment was properly granted.

NOTES AND QUESTIONS

1. **The Measure of Damages.** As *Akerman* indicates, Section 11 begins by creating a presumption in favor of a rescissionary measure of damages, based upon the difference between the amount paid for the security—so long as that does not exceed the offering price—and (a) its value at the time of the suit, (b) the consideration received on resale if the security was sold before the suit, or (c) the consideration received if the security was sold after suit, but before judgment, *if* that would produce a lesser measure than that stated in (a).

Note the use of the term *value*, rather than *market price*, in the principal formulation. This allows a party to argue that the market price at the time the suit was filed was improperly inflated or deflated in order to claim a larger recovery or mitigate damages, as the case may be. On the whole, however, courts are reluctant to disregard or even discount market price in the value calculation under Section 11(e). Consider the comments of the Second Circuit:

> [T]he value of a security may not be equivalent to its market price. Congress' use of the term "value," as distinguished from the terms "amount paid" and "price" indicates that, under certain circumstances, the market price may not adequately reflect the security's value. *See Beecher v. Able*, 435 F. Supp. 397, 404-05 (S.D.N.Y. 1977) (adjusting the market price to account for panic selling in the market that was unrelated to the misrepresentations in the registration statements). . . . However, instances where the market price of a security will be different from its value are "unusual and rare" situations. . . . Indeed, in a market economy, when market value is available and reliable, "market value will always be the primary gauge of an enterprise's worth." . . . Moreover, even where market price is not completely reliable, it serves as a good starting point in determining value. . . . In this case, market price appears to be the most reliable gauge of the Debentures' true value and, at the very least, an excellent starting point. . . .

McMahan & Co. v. Wherehouse Entertainment, 65 F.3d 1044, 1048-1049 (2d Cir. 1995).

The value versus market price issue has risen in a number of cases involving fixed income securities sold in registered offerings where investors were warned that resales would be difficult because of illiquid secondary markets. For the most part, courts have rejected defendants' arguments that because plaintiffs were adequately warned of the risks, damages should not be based on the depressed prices of weak and illiquid secondary markets. *See, e.g., Neca-Ibew Health & Welfare Fund v. Goldman Sachs & Co.*, 693 F.3d 143 (2d Cir. 2012) ("[U]nder §11, the key is not, as the district court concluded and as defendants contend, market price; the key is value."); *Genesee County Employees' Retirement System v. Thornburg Mortgage Securities Trust 2006-3*, 825 F. Supp. 2d 1082, 1150 (D.N.M. 2011) ("Section 11 prescribes a particular measure of damages, and [neither] the plaintiff nor the defendant can take advantage of another measure of damages to increase or reduce recovery.").

 2.   Negative Causation.   The proviso in subsection (e) with regard to damages resulting from factors unrelated to the misstatement effects an important qualification to rescissory recovery. In theory at least, it turns the measure into something closer to the standard "out of pocket" measure under the common law of fraud, which seeks to assess the difference between the consideration paid and the value of the commodity at the time of delivery. Under Rule 10b-5, as we shall see, the same concept is invoked under the rubric of "loss causation," albeit with the burden of showing a positive causal relationship assigned to the plaintiff instead of the defendant.

As in *Akerman*, the proviso can operate to temper the harshness of Section 11 substantially. A registration statement can have a number of misstatements in it, but there will be no liability if counsel for the defendants can show that the factors omitted or inaccurately stated had no bearing on some or all of the subsequent decline in the market price of the securities. The practical question, however, is how the absence of a causal relationship can be established in court. *Akerman* gives some insight into a successful defense, analyzing the stock's performance in the period after the information in question does become public. *See also In re Barclay Bank PLC Sec. Litig.*, 756 Fed. App'x 41 (2d Cir. 2018). No doubt, the lack of a perceptible and atypical negative impact resulting from the disclosure would seem to suggest a lack of causation. But was the court too quick to assume that the date of public disclosure was the appropriate one for purposes of this analysis? In *Levine v. AtriCure, Inc.*, 508 F. Supp. 2d 268, 273 n.5 (S.D.N.Y. 2007), the court expressed concern with "the possibility that declines in stock price prior to broad public disclosure may be reflective of leaking of relevant information into the marketplace." You will look into this problem in more depth in Chapter 13.

 3.   Joint and Several Liability.   For most Section 11 defendants, there is joint and several liability. Any one defendant is subject to the burden of the entire measure of damages, with a subsequent right of contribution against any codefendants (an issue that will be discussed infra). Absent some special compensation from the issuer, however, no underwriter may be liable for damages in excess of the total price at which the securities underwritten by it and distributed to the public were offered to the public. This modification—together with a shortened statute of limitations and the introduction of the "negative causation" defense with respect to measurement of damages—was part of the 1934 amendments to Section 11, a political victory for Wall Street.

 4.   Indemnification and Contribution.   The severity of the measure of damages under Section 11 that can be imposed upon a wide variety of defendants—who will have varying degrees of responsibility for the fraud—raises natural questions about loss shifting and spreading among defendants once liability is established. We have already noted the SEC's position on indemnification of officers and directors in public offerings. The handful of courts that have considered indemnification issues under the federal securities laws have provided ample support for the Commission's view—if not a broader reach to the policy—at least as it relates to liability under statutory provisions like Section 11 that are avowedly deterrent in nature. *See Globus v. Law Research Services Inc.*, 418 F.2d 1276 (2d Cir. 1969). In terms of policy, is there a compelling reason why the issuer and its shareholders should not be able to "purchase" (through an indemnification agreement) a less expensive—if less protective—form of underwriting so long as this is fully disclosed to prospective investors? Or is this an option Congress plainly foreclosed by the way it drafted the '33 Act?

Contribution—*spreading* the loss among defendants—is another matter, for it is expressly authorized by Section 11(f) "as in cases of contract." What does the reference to "contract" mean? So far as can be determined, this language was taken from a British statute that presumably was enacted to overcome the reluctance of courts to order contribution in tort cases. More difficult is the question of how shares should be allocated. The two most commonly invoked approaches are the *comparative fault* and the *per capita* standards. As their names imply, the former directs the court to inquire among the defendants regarding relative blameworthiness, while the latter simply divides responsibility equally among all the defendants. What are the relative merits of these approaches? What about an approach that modifies the per capita approach to treat as a single entity a group of defendants, for example, all the directors or all the underwriters? *See* Scott, Resurrecting Indemnification: Contribution Clauses in Underwriting Agreements, 61 N.Y.U. L. Rev. 223, 262-265 (1986).

Section 21D(f) of the '34 Act, added by the Private Securities Litigation Reform Act of 1995, addresses certain contribution issues affecting *outside directors* in Section 11 actions. Most importantly, a comparative fault standard is adopted for contribution claims by outside directors. In addition, outside directors who settle private actions prior to final verdicts are discharged from all claims for contribution brought by other parties (but also are not entitled to contribution from other parties).

PROBLEMS

9-4. Petrochemical Corporation was held liable in a Section 11 action for overstating its income for the fiscal year immediately preceding its IPO, wherein shares were sold to the public at $10. Six months after the offering, when the stock was trading at $7, the company corrected this misstatement in a press release carefully timed to coincide with an announcement of a major new government contract. There was little price movement other than that associated with normal market movements for over-the-counter stocks generally during the time period. Assuming the materiality of the initial misrepresentation, how would damages be measured?

9-5. AtriCure, Inc., a manufacturer of surgical devices sold to clinics and hospitals, had an IPO in August. The Cleveland Clinic is one of AtriCure's largest customers. In December, the Wall Street Journal published a story focusing on potential conflicts of interest between the Cleveland Clinic and its patients arising because the clinic is an investor in AtriCure and because several of its physicians are paid consultants for AtriCure. Two months later, AtriCure announced results for the year ending December 31 and indicated its business was experiencing a "negative impact" because of the conflicts disclosures. Immediately following this disclosure, the stock price dropped sharply. AtriCure's registration statement did not disclose the Cleveland Clinic's conflicts or their potential impact on the company's performance. Levine purchased shares in the August IPO. Three weeks before the Journal's December story, Levine sold his shares for a loss. Does he have standing to be a class representative in a Section 11 claim against AtriCure and its underwriters? *See Levine v. AtriCure, Inc.,* 508 F. Supp. 2d 268, 273 n.5 (S.D.N.Y. 2007).

B. Section 12(a)(1)

Pinter v. Dahl
486 U.S. 622 (1988)

BLACKMUN, J. . . . [This] controversy arises out of the sale prior to 1982 of unregistered securities (fractional undivided interests in oil and gas leases) by petitioner Billy J. "B.J." Pinter to respondents Maurice Dahl and Dahl's friends, family, and business associates. Pinter is an oil and gas producer in Texas and Oklahoma, and a registered securities dealer in Texas. Dahl is a California real estate broker and investor, who, at the time of his dealings with Pinter, was a veteran of two unsuccessful oil and gas ventures. In pursuit of further investment opportunities, Dahl employed an oilfield expert to locate and acquire oil and gas leases. This expert introduced Dahl to Pinter. Dahl advanced $20,000 to Pinter to acquire leases, with the understanding that they would be held in the name of Pinter's Black Gold Oil Company and that Dahl would have a right of first refusal to drill certain wells on the leasehold properties. Pinter located leases in Oklahoma, and Dahl toured the properties, often without Pinter, in order to talk to others and "get a feel for the properties." Upon examining the geology, drilling logs, and production history assembled by Pinter, Dahl concluded, in the words of the District Court, that "there was no way to lose."

After investing approximately $310,000 in the properties, Dahl told the other respondents about the venture. Except for Dahl and respondent Grantham, none of the respondents spoke to or met Pinter or toured the properties. Because of Dahl's involvement in the venture, each of the other respondents decided to invest about $7,500.

Dahl assisted his fellow investors in completing the subscription agreement form prepared by Pinter. Each letter-contract signed by the purchaser stated that the participating interests were being sold without the benefit of registration under the Securities Act, in reliance on Securities and Exchange Commission (SEC or Commission) Rule 146 [the precursor to Rule 506(b)]. In fact, the oil and gas interests involved in this suit were never registered with the Commission. Respondents' investment checks were made payable to Black Gold Oil Company. Dahl received no commission from Pinter in connection with the other respondents' purchases.

When the venture failed and their interests proved to be worthless, respondents brought suit against Pinter in the United States District Court for the Northern District of Texas, seeking rescission under §12[a](1) of the Securities Act, for the unlawful sale of unregistered securities.

In a counterclaim, Pinter alleged that Dahl, by means of fraudulent misrepresentations and concealment of facts, induced Pinter to sell and deliver the securities. Pinter averred that Dahl falsely assured Pinter that he would provide other qualified, sophisticated, and knowledgeable investors with all the information necessary for evaluation of the investment. Dahl allegedly agreed to raise the funds for the venture from those investors, with the understanding that Pinter would simply be the "operator" of the wells. . . .

[The Court thereupon indicated that an issue before it was whether Dahl was a seller of the securities, for, if so, he would be liable in contribution to Pinter.] In determining whether Dahl may be deemed a "seller" for purposes of §12[a](1), such that he may be held liable for the sale of unregistered securities to the other investor-respondents, we look first at the language of §12[a](1). That statute provides, in pertinent part: "Any person who . . . offers or sells a security" in violation of the registration requirement of the Securities Act "shall be liable to the person purchasing such security from him." This provision defines the class of defendants who may be subject to liability as those who offer or sell unregistered securities. But the Securities Act nowhere delineates who may be regarded as a statutory seller, and the sparse legislative history sheds no light on the issue. The courts, on their part, have not defined the term uniformly.

At the very least, however, the language of §12[a](1) contemplates a buyer-seller relationship not unlike traditional contractual privity. Thus, it is settled that §12[a](1) imposes liability on the owner who passed title, or other interest in the security, to the buyer for value. Dahl, of course, was not a seller in this conventional sense, and therefore may be held liable only if §12[a](1) liability extends to persons other than the person who passes title.

A

In common parlance, a person may offer or sell property without necessarily being the person who transfers title to, or other interest in, that property. We need not rely entirely on ordinary understanding of the statutory language, however, for the Securities Act defines the operative terms of §12[a](1). Section 2[a](3) defines "sale" or "sell" to include "every contract of sale or disposition of a security or interest in a security, for value," and the terms "offer to sell," "offer for sale," or "offer" to include "every attempt or offer to dispose of, or solicitation of an offer to buy, a security or interest in a security, for value." Under these definitions, the range of persons potentially liable under §12[a](1) is not limited to persons who pass title. The inclusion of the phrase "solicitation of an offer to buy" within the definition of "offer" brings an individual who engages in solicitation, an activity not inherently confined to the actual owner, within the scope of §12. . . .

An interpretation of statutory seller that includes brokers and others who solicit offers to purchase securities furthers the purposes of the Securities

Act—to promote full and fair disclosure of information to the public in the sales of securities. In order to effectuate Congress' intent that §12[a](1) civil liability be in terrorem, . . . the risk of its invocation should be felt by solicitors of purchases. The solicitation of a buyer is perhaps the most critical stage of the selling transaction. It is the first stage of a traditional securities sale to involve the buyer, and it is directed at producing the sale. In addition, brokers and other solicitors are well positioned to control the flow of information to a potential purchaser, and, in fact, such persons are the participants in the selling transaction who most often disseminate material information to investors. Thus, solicitation is the stage at which an investor is most likely to be injured, that is, by being persuaded to purchase securities without full and fair information. Given Congress' overriding goal of preventing this injury, we may infer that Congress intended solicitation to fall under the mantle of §12[a](1).

Although we conclude that Congress intended §12[a](1) liability to extend to those who solicit securities purchases, we share the Court of Appeals' conclusion that Congress did not intend to impose rescission based on strict liability on a person who urges the purchase but whose motivation is solely to benefit the buyer. When a person who urges another to make a securities purchase acts merely to assist the buyer, not only is it uncommon to say that the buyer "purchased" from him, but it is also strained to describe the giving of gratuitous advice, even strongly or enthusiastically, as "soliciting." Section 2[a](3) defines an offer as a "solicitation of an offer to buy . . . for value." The person who gratuitously urges another to make a particular investment decision is not, in any meaningful sense, requesting value in exchange for his suggestion or seeking the value the titleholder will obtain in exchange for the ultimate sale. The language and purpose of §12[a](1) suggest that liability extends only to the person who successfully solicits the purchase, motivated at least in part by a desire to serve his own financial interests or those of the securities owner. If he had such a motivation, it is fair to say that the buyer "purchased" the security from him and to align him with the owner in a rescission action. . . .

C

We are unable to determine whether Dahl may be held liable as a statutory seller under §12[a](1). The District Court explicitly found that "Dahl solicited each of the other plaintiffs (save perhaps Grantham) in connection with the offer, purchase, and receipt of their oil and gas interests." We cannot conclude that this finding was clearly erroneous. It is not clear, however, that Dahl had the kind of interest in the sales that make him liable as a statutory seller. We do know that he received no commission from Pinter in connection with the other sales, but this is not conclusive. Typically, a person who solicits the purchase will have sought or received a personal financial benefit from the sale, such as where he "anticipat[es] a share of the profits," *Lawler v. Gilliam*, 569 F.2d, at 1288, or receives a brokerage commission, *Cady v. Murphy*, 113 F.2d, at 990. But a person who solicits the buyer's purchase in order to serve the financial interests of the owner may properly be liable under §12[a](1) without showing that he expects to participate in the benefits the owner enjoys.

The Court of Appeals apparently concluded that Dahl was motivated entirely by a gratuitous desire to share an attractive investment opportunity with his friends and associates. *See* 787 F.2d, at 991. This conclusion, in our view, was premature. The District Court made no findings that focused on whether Dahl urged the other purchases in order to further some financial interest of his own or of Pinter. Accordingly, further findings are necessary to assess Dahl's liability. . . .

The judgment of the Court of Appeals is vacated and the case is remanded for further proceedings consistent with this opinion.

NOTES AND QUESTIONS

1.   The Scope of Section 12(a)(1).   Perhaps the most important thing about Section 12(a)(1) is what the plaintiff is *not* required to show in order to gain rescission. There is no state of mind element: This is strict liability. Nor is there any requirement that the plaintiff establish injury. All that is left to plaintiff to show is that (a) there was a violation of Section 5, (b) the facilities of interstate commerce were involved in the offer or sale to the plaintiff, (c) the plaintiff has made adequate tender of the security if it is still owned, and (d) the action has been brought within the time stated in the statute of limitations found in Section 13. Even more than Section 11, this provision is designed to *deter* violations; it is not compensatory in nature.

Literally, Section 12(a)(1) liability is triggered by any offer or sale in violation of Section 5. And the courts have given full effect to this construction. As a result, an illegal offer creates a right of rescission, even though the subsequent sale is lawful—for example, a written offer during the waiting period prior to the customer's order, even though the sale itself occurred only after delivery of the final prospectus. In *Diskin v. Lomasney & Co.*, 452 F.2d 871, 876 (2d Cir. 1971), the court stated that, harshness notwithstanding, Congress had made plain "that an offeror of a security who had failed to follow one of the allowed paths could not achieve absolution simply by returning to the road of virtue before receiving payment." Based on similar reasoning regarding Congress' remedial intent, should liability attach to unlawful deliveries in violation of Section 5, even though the language of Section 12(a)(1) refers expressly only to unlawful offers and sales?

2.   The Remedy.   Once the right to rescission is established, the only remaining step is exchanging the security, if it is still owned, for the consideration paid in the original transaction plus interest. If the plaintiff has disposed of the security, rescissory damages are granted—that is, the difference between the price paid and the amount received in the subsequent sale. We will discuss the possibility that this amount may be offset by income received by the plaintiff on the security before the suit was brought in connection with our consideration of Section 12(a)(2), infra.

3.   Responsibility Under State Law.   State blue sky laws also impose responsibility for selling unregistered securities, and without *Pinter*'s baggage. For example, *Lean v. Reed*, 876 N.E.2d 1104 (Ind. 2007), held liable directors of the issuer of unregistered shares when there was no available exemption. Lean was a director of a shell corporation that issued unregistered shares to Reed and others to acquire their Internet service company. The value of the shares collapsed and Reed sued. The court applied the well-recognized reasonable care defense, concluding that the defendant-director was liable because he either knew or in the exercise of reasonable care could have known that the transaction involved the unlawful issuance of unregistered securities. Some courts apply a stricter defense, imposing liability unless the defendant can prove that even in the exercise of reasonable care he would not have discovered that the securities should have been registered. *See, e.g., Robertson v. White*, 635 F. Supp. 851 (W.D. Ark. 1986) (applying Arkansas law).

PROBLEM

9-6. Duff & Phelps Credit Rating Company published positive comments on the securities of the Saintine Exploration Corporation. After reading the comments, Wilson learned Saintine was planning to have a private placement of common stock in the near future. He approached the CEO of Saintine for more information. The CEO asked the company's outside counsel, Ruffa & Hanover, to send offering materials for the private placement to Wilson. The materials fully disclosed the offering was on an "all-or-nothing" basis and that $5,000 of the proceeds would be used to pay Ruffa & Hanover for its work on the offering. The materials were accompanied by a cover letter on Ruffa & Hanover stationery stating that the materials were being transmitted at the request of Saintine.

Wilson purchased the securities. He now wishes to rescind on the grounds that the offering did not qualify as a private placement under Section 4(a)(2). Assuming Wilson is correct that the private placement exemption was not available, does he have a Section 12(a)(1) claim against Ruffa & Hanover? *See Wilson v. Saintine Exploration & Drilling Corp.*, 872 F.2d 1124 (2d Cir. 1989) (involving a Section 12(a)(2) claim). Against Duff & Phelps? *See Shain v. Duff & Phelps Credit Rating Co.*, 915 F. Supp. 575 (S.D.N.Y. 1996).

C. Section 12(a)(2)

Section 12(a)(2) extends the rescissionary remedy of Section 12(a)(1) to situations where a person offers or sells a security by the use of an instrumentality of interstate commerce by means of a false or misleading prospectus or oral communication. A defense based on lack of culpability is provided, requiring the defendant to show that he did not know, and in the exercise of reasonable care could not have known, of the falsity or omission.

1. By Means of a "Prospectus or Oral Communication"

For many years, courts and (most) commentators assumed that Section 12(a)(2) applies to issuer transactions, whether public or private and whether registered or exempt, as well as resales of securities by persons other than issuers. In 1991, the Third Circuit in *Ballay v. Legg Mason Wood Walker, Inc.*, 925 F.2d 682 (3d Cir. 1991), rejected this expansive view and, focusing on the section's use of the term *prospectus*, concluded that Section 12(a)(2) applies only to public offerings by issuers. Declining to follow *Ballay*, the Seventh Circuit in *Pacific Dunlop Holdings, Inc. v. Allen & Co., Inc.*, 993 F.2d 578 (7th Cir. 1993), concluded that Section 12(a)(2) applies to secondary market transactions, as well as initial offerings, and applied the section to a privately negotiated stock purchase agreement. In the case that follows, the Supreme Court resolves this conflict in a way that raises additional issues concerning the scope of Section 12.

Gustafson v. Alloyd Co.
513 U.S. 561 (1995)

Justice KENNEDY delivered the opinion of the Court.

Under Section 12[a](2) of the Securities Act of 1933 buyers have an express cause of action for rescission against sellers who make material misstatements or omissions "by means of a prospectus." The question presented is whether this right of rescission extends to a private, secondary transaction, on the theory that recitations in the purchase agreement are part of a "prospectus."

I

[Petitioners Gustafson, McLean, and Butler (collectively Gustafson) were the sole shareholders of Alloyd, Inc. (Alloyd). In 1989, Gustafson decided to sell Alloyd and engaged KPMG Peat Marwick to find a buyer. In response to information provided by KPMG, Wind Point Partners, L.P., agreed late in 1989 to buy the stock of Alloyd through Alloyd Holdings, Inc., a corporation formed by Wind Point to accomplish the purchase. The contract called for a purchase price of $18.8 million plus an additional amount of approximately $2.1 million (subject to adjustment based on post-closing financial information) reflecting the change in Alloyd's net worth since the end of the last fiscal year. After the sale was completed, the year-end audit of Alloyd's 1989 earnings revealed that the actual earnings were lower than the estimates used by the parties in negotiating the purchase price. Under the agreement, the buyers had a right to adjust the purchase price and recover $815,000 from the sellers. Rather than pursuing this agreed-upon remedy, the buyers argued that the contract of sale was a "prospectus" under Section 12[a](2) and sought rescission of the contract.]

Relying on the decision of the Court of Appeals for the Third Circuit in *Ballay v. Legg Mason Wood Walker, Inc.*, 925 F.2d 682 (1991), the District Court granted Gustafson's motion for summary judgment, holding "that section 12[a](2) claims can only arise out of the initial stock offerings." App. 20. Although the sellers were the controlling shareholders of the original company, the District Court concluded that the private sale agreement "cannot be compared to an initial offering" because "the purchasers in this case had direct access to financial and other company documents, and had the opportunity to inspect the seller's property."

On review, the Court of Appeals for the Seventh Circuit vacated the District Court's judgment and remanded for further consideration in light of that court's intervening decision in *Pacific Dunlop Holdings Inc. v. Allen & Co. Inc.*, 993 F.2d 578 (1993).

II

. . . As this case reaches us, we must assume that the stock purchase agreement contained material misstatements of fact made by the sellers and that Gustafson would not sustain its burden of proving due care. On these assumptions, Alloyd would have a right to obtain rescission if those misstatements were made "by means of a prospectus or oral communication." The parties (and the courts of appeals) agree that the phrase "oral communication" is restricted to oral communications that relate to a prospectus. *See Pacific Dunlop*, supra, 993 F.2d at 588; *Ballay*, supra, at 688. The determinative question, then, is whether the contract between Alloyd and Gustafson is a "prospectus" as the term is used in the 1933 Act.

Alloyd argues that "prospectus" is defined in a broad manner, broad enough to encompass the contract between the parties. This argument is echoed by the dissents. . . . Gustafson, by contrast, maintains that prospectus in the 1933 Act means a communication soliciting the public to purchase securities from the issuer.

Three sections of the 1933 Act are critical in resolving the definitional question on which the case turns: §2[a](10), which defines a prospectus; §10, which sets forth the information that must be contained in a prospectus; and §12, which imposes liability based on misstatements in a prospectus. In seeking to interpret the term "prospectus," we adopt the premise that the term should be construed, if possible, to give it a consistent meaning throughout the Act. That principle follows from our duty to construe statutes, not isolated provisions.

A

We begin with §10. It provides, in relevant part:

Except to the extent otherwise permitted or required pursuant to this subsection or subsections (c), (d), or (e) of this section—

(1) a prospectus relating to a security other than a security issued by a foreign government or political subdivision thereof, shall contain the information contained in the registration statement. . . .
(2) a prospectus relating to a security issued by a foreign government or political subdivision thereof shall contain the information contained in the registration statement. . . .

Section 10 does not provide that some prospectuses must contain the information contained in the registration statement. Save for the explicit and well-defined exemptions for securities listed under §3 (exempting certain classes of securities from the coverage of the Act), its mandate is unqualified: "[A] prospectus . . . shall contain the information contained in the registration statement."

Although §10 does not define what a prospectus is, it does instruct us what a prospectus cannot be if the Act is to be interpreted as a symmetrical and coherent regulatory scheme, one in which the operative words have a consistent meaning throughout. There is no dispute that the contract in this case was not required to contain the information contained in a registration statement and that no statutory exemption was required to take the document out of §10's coverage. It follows that the contract is not a prospectus under §10. That does not mean that a document ceases to be a prospectus whenever it omits a required piece of information. It does mean that a document is not a prospectus within the meaning of that section if, absent an exemption, it need not comply with §10's requirements in the first place.

An examination of §10 reveals that, whatever else "prospectus" may mean, the term is confined to a document that, absent an overriding exemption, must include the "information contained in the registration statement." By and large, only public offerings by an issuer of a security, or by controlling shareholders of an issuer, require the preparation and filing of registration statements. It follows, we conclude, that a prospectus under §10 is confined to documents related to public offerings by an issuer or its controlling shareholders.

This much (the meaning of prospectus in §10) seems not to be in dispute. Where the courts are in disagreement is with the implications of this proposition for the entirety of the Act, and for §12 in particular. . . .

The conclusion that prospectus has the same meaning, and refers to the same types of communications (public offers by an issuer or its controlling shareholders), in both §§10 and 12 is reinforced by an examination of the structure of the 1933 Act. Sections 4 and 5 of the Act together require a seller to file a registration statement and to issue a prospectus for certain defined types of sales (public offerings by an issuer, through an underwriter). Sections 7 and 10 of the Act set forth the information required in the registration statement and the prospectus. Section 11 provides for liability on account of false registration statements; §12[a](2) for liability based on misstatements in prospectuses. Following the most natural and symmetrical reading, just as the liability imposed by §11 flows from the requirements imposed by §§5 and 7 providing for the filing and content of registration statements, the liability imposed by §12[a](2), cannot attach unless there is an obligation to distribute the prospectus in the first place (or unless there is an exemption).

The primary innovation of the 1933 Act was the creation of federal duties—for the most part, registration and disclosure obligations—in connection with public offerings. . . . We are reluctant to conclude that §12[a](2) creates vast additional liabilities that are quite independent of the new substantive obligations the Act imposes. It is more reasonable to interpret the liability provisions of the 1933 Act as designed for the primary purpose of providing remedies for violations of the obligations it had created. Indeed, §§11 and 12[a](1)—the statutory neighbors of §12[a](2)—afford remedies for violations of those obligations.

On the other hand, accepting Alloyd's argument that any written offer is a prospectus under §12 would require us to hold that the word "prospectus" in §12 refers to a broader set of communications than the same term in §10.

The Court of Appeals was candid in embracing that conclusion: "The 1933 Act contemplates many definitions of a prospectus. Section 2[a](10) gives a single, broad definition; section 10(a) involves an isolated, distinct document—a prospectus within a prospectus; section 10(d) gives the Commission authority to classify many." *Pacific Dunlop Holdings Inc. v. Allen & Co.*, 993 F.2d at 584. The dissents take a similar tack. In the name of a plain meaning approach to statutory interpretation, the dissents discover in the Act two different species of prospectuses: formal (also called §10) prospectuses, subject to both §§10 and 12, and informal prospectuses, subject only to §12 but not to §10. Nowhere in the statute, however, do the terms "formal prospectus" or "informal prospectus" appear. Instead, the Act uses one term—"prospectus"—throughout. In disagreement with the Court of Appeals and the dissenting opinions, we cannot accept the conclusion that this single operative word means one thing in one section of the Act and something quite different in another. The dissenting opinions' resort to terms not found in the Act belies the claim of fidelity to the text of the statute.

Alloyd, as well as Justice Thomas in his dissent, respond that if Congress had intended §12[a](2) to govern only initial public offerings, it would have been simple for Congress to have referred to the §4 exemptions in §12[a](2). The argument gets the presumption backwards. Had Congress meant the term "prospectus" in §12[a](2) to have a different meaning than the same term in §10, that is when one would have expected Congress to have been explicit. Congressional silence cuts against, not in favor of, Alloyd's argument. The burden should be on the proponents of the view that the term "prospectus" means one thing in §12 and another in §10 to adduce strong textual support for that conclusion. And Alloyd adduces none.

B

Alloyd's contrary argument rests to a significant extent on §2[a](10), or, to be more precise, on one word of that section. Section 2[a](10) provides that "the term 'prospectus' means any prospectus, notice, circular, advertisement, letter, or communication, written or by radio or television, which offers any security for sale or confirms the sale of any security." Concentrating on the word "communication," Alloyd argues that any written communication that offers a security for sale is a "prospectus." Inserting its definition into §12[a](2), Alloyd insists that a material misstatement in any communication offering a security for sale gives rise to an action for rescission, without proof of fraud by the seller or reliance by the purchaser. In Alloyd's view, §2[a](10) gives the term "prospectus" a capacious definition that, although incompatible with §10, nevertheless governs in §12.

The flaw in Alloyd's argument, echoed in the dissenting opinions, is its reliance on one word of the definitional section in isolation. To be sure, §2[a](10) defines a prospectus as, inter alia, a "communication, written or by radio or television, which offers any security for sale or confirms the sale of any security." The word "communication," however, on which Alloyd's entire argument rests, is but one word in a list, a word Alloyd reads altogether out of context. . . .

There is a better reading. From the terms "prospectus, notice, circular, advertisement, or letter," it is apparent that the list refers to documents of wide dissemination. In a similar manner, the list includes communications "by radio or television," but not face-to-face or telephonic conversations. Inclusion of the term "communication" in that list suggests that it too refers to a public communication. . . .

D

It is understandable that Congress would provide buyers with a right to rescind, without proof of fraud or reliance, as to misstatements contained in a document prepared with care, following well established procedures relating to investigations with due diligence and in the context of a public offering by an issuer or its controlling shareholders. It is not plausible to infer that Congress created this extensive liability for every casual communication between buyer and seller in the secondary market. It is often difficult, if not altogether impractical, for those engaged in casual communications not to omit some fact that would, if included, qualify the accuracy of a statement. Under Alloyd's view any casual communication between buyer and seller in the aftermarket could give rise to an action for rescission, with no evidence of fraud on the part of the seller or reliance on the part of the buyer. In many instances buyers in practical effect would have an option to rescind, impairing the stability of past transactions where neither fraud nor detrimental reliance on misstatements or omissions occurred. We find no basis for interpreting the statute to reach so far. . . .

III

In sum, the word "prospectus" is a term of art referring to a document that describes a public offering of securities by an issuer or controlling shareholder. The contract of sale, and its recitations, were not held out to the public and were not a prospectus as the term is used in the 1933 Act.

The judgment of the Court of Appeals is reversed, and the case is remanded for further proceedings consistent with this opinion.

Justice THOMAS, with whom Justice SCALIA, Justice GINSBURG, and Justice BREYER join, dissenting.

From the majority's opinion, one would not realize that §12[a](2) was involved in this case until one had read more than halfway through. In contrast to the majority's approach of interpreting the statute, I believe the proper method is to begin with the provision actually involved in this case, §12[a](2), and then turn to the 1933 Act's definitional section, §2[a](10), before consulting the structure of the Act as a whole. Because the result of this textual analysis shows that §12[a](2) applies to secondary or private sales of a security as well as to initial public offerings, I dissent.

. . . There is no reason to seek the meaning of "prospectus" outside of the 1933 Act, because Congress has supplied just such a definition in §2[a](10). That definition is extraordinarily broad:

When used in this subchapter, unless the context otherwise requires—

(10) The term "prospectus" means any prospectus, notice, circular, advertisement, letter, or communication, written or by radio or television, which offers any security for sale or confirms the sale of any security.

For me, the breadth of these terms forecloses the majority's position that "prospectus" applies only in the context of initial distributions of securities. . . . We should use §2[a](10) to define "prospectus" for the 1933 Act, rather than, as the majority does, use the 1933 Act to define "prospectus" for §2[a](10). . . .

Justice GINSBURG, with whom Justice BREYER joins, dissenting.

[T]he Court maintains that a communication qualifies as a prospectus only if made during a public offering.[1] Communications during either secondary trading or a private placement are not "prospectuses," the Court declares, and thus are not covered by §12[a](2). . . .

To construe a legislatively defined term, courts usually start with the defining section. Section 2[a](10) defines prospectus capaciously as "any prospectus, notice, circular, advertisement, letter, or communication, written or by radio or television, which offers any security for sale or confirms the sale of any security." The items listed in the defining provision, notably "letters" and "communications," are common in private and secondary sales, as well as in public offerings. The §2[a](10) definition thus does not confine the §12[a](2) term "prospectus" to public offerings.

The Court bypasses §2[a](10), and the solid support it gives the Court of Appeals' disposition. Instead of beginning at the beginning, by first attending to the definition section, the Court starts with §10, a substantive provision. The Court correctly observes that the term "prospectus" has a circumscribed meaning in that context. A prospectus within the contemplation of §10 is a formal document, typically a document composing part of a registration statement; a §10 prospectus, all agree, appears only in public offerings. The Court then proceeds backward; it reads into the literally and logically prior definition section, §2[a](10), the meaning "prospectus" has in §10.

To justify its backward reading—proceeding from §10 to §2[a](10) and not the other way round—the Court states that it "cannot accept the conclusion that [the operative word prospectus] means one thing in one section of the Act and something quite different in another." . . .

In light of the text, drafting history, and longstanding scholarly and judicial understanding of §12[a](2), I conclude that §12[a](2) applies to a private resale of securities. If adjustment is in order, as the Court's opinion powerfully suggests it is, Congress is equipped to undertake the alteration. Accordingly, I dissent from the Court's opinion and judgment.

---

1. I understand the Court's definition of a public offering to encompass both transactions that must be registered under §5, and transactions that would have been registered had the securities involved not qualified for exemption under §3.

Gustafson leaves open the important question of what is a "public offering" for purposes of Section 12(a)(2) liability. The following case addresses this issue and also reminds us that even in the post-*Gustafson* era plaintiffs may be able to keep their Section 12(a)(2) claims alive (at least for a time) by making the "public offering" issue a fact-intensive inquiry that survives motions on the pleadings.

Hyer v. Malouf
Fed. Sec. L. Rep. (CCH) ¶94,857 (D. Utah 2008)

TENA CAMPBELL, Chief Judge.

[P]laintiffs allege Defendant Matt Malouf solicited funds from Plaintiffs for investment in three real estate development projects: (1) River Ridge—a condominium development near Banner-Elk, North Carolina; (2) West Indies Village—a condominium development in Pensacola, Florida; and (3) Isle de Mer—a condominium development also in Pensacola, Florida. Plaintiffs allege that these solicitations were accomplished through both oral and written communications. According to Plaintiffs, Defendants primarily used documents called "Project Offerings"—one for each of the three developments—to outline the merits of the investments.

Plaintiffs initially invested approximately $2.2 million in the development projects by purchasing ownership interests (the "Ownership Interests") in the companies developing them. . . .

Plaintiffs allege that the Ownership Interests were never conveyed, that the development projects were never constructed and that the proceeds from their investments were distributed to other investors. In the Amended Complaint, Plaintiffs outline a number of untrue statements and omissions allegedly made by Mr. Malouf in the course of soliciting the investment funds from Plaintiffs. . . .

Plaintiffs allege that the [Defendants] violated §12(a)(2) of the Securities Act of 1933 by making false statements and material omissions of fact in prospectuses and in oral communications in connection with Plaintiffs' purchase of the Ownership Interests. . . . Defendants argue that the Amended Complaint fails to state a claim for relief under §12(a)(2) because it does not allege a public offering.

Section 12(a)(2) provides a cause of action to a purchaser of a security against one who offers or sells a security "by means of a prospectus or oral communication" that includes an untrue statement or omission of material fact. In *Gustafson v. Alloyd Company, Inc.*, the Supreme Court held that the phrase "by means of a prospectus" limits the reach of §12(a)(2) to public offerings. Specifically, the Court held that the term "prospectus," as found in §§10 and 12 of the 1933 Act, "is confined to a document that, absent an overriding exemption, must include the 'information contained in the registration statement.'" . . .

Whether an offering is public or private "turn[s] on whether the particular class of persons affected needs the protection of the 1933 Act. An offering to those who are shown to be able to fend for themselves is a transaction 'not involving any public offering.'"[12] The following factors are considered in

---

12.   *SEC v. Murphy*, 626 F.2d 633, 644 (10th Cir. 1980) (quoting *SEC v. Ralston Purina Co.*, 346 U.S. 119, 125, 73 S. Ct. 981, 97 L. Ed. 1494 (1953)).

making this determination: "(1) the number of offerees; (2) the sophistication of the offerees; (3) the size and manner of the offering; and (4) the relationship of the offerees to the issuer."[13] Notably, "[a] court may only conclude that the investors do not need the protection of the [1933 Act] if *all* the offerees have relationships with the issuer affording them access to or disclosure of the sort of information about the issuer that registration reveals."[14]

Plaintiffs allege that Mr. Malouf offered the alleged securities through the Project Offerings, which, according to Plaintiffs, constitute "written prospectuses." Plaintiffs further allege that the offers were "made in connection with a public offering of securities," and were made "to the general public." Most important, Plaintiffs list twenty-one individuals and entities "known to Plaintiffs who received and/or accepted the offer (or a substantially similar offer)." As noted above, the public offering analysis is fact-intensive and requires extensive inquiry regarding each of the investors to whom the securities were offered or sold and their relationship with the offeror. Discovery is necessary to determine whether each of these offerees had access to the type of information in a registration statement [sufficient to negate the need for the protection of the 1933 Act].

Accordingly, the court finds that Plaintiffs have stated a claim for relief under §12(a)(2) that is plausible on its face and denies the Motion to Dismiss Claims 3 and 11. . . .

NOTES AND QUESTIONS

1. "Public Offerings" and Section 12(a)(2). Under *Hyer*'s reasoning, which, if any, of the following offerings may give rise to a Section 12(a)(2) claim after *Gustafson?*

- an offering of short-term notes (commercial paper) exempt under Section 3(a)(3)
- an offering to accredited investors under Rule 506(b) or (c)
- a private placement under Section 4(a)(2)
- an intrastate offering exempt under Section 3(a)(11) or Rule 147/147A
- an unregistered offshore offering within the Regulation S safe harbor

With respect to 144A offerings (which you studied in Chapter 6), *see In re American Realty Cap. Partners Inc. Litig.*, 2016 WL 11110435 (S.D.N.Y. 2016) (no 12(a)(2) liability even if the securities would later, after conversion, become freely tradable).

As you studied in Chapter 5, the JOBS Act added to the '33 Act a new Section 3(b)(2), which authorizes the SEC to develop a small issue exemption for offerings up to $50 million, substantially modifying the old version of Reg A. The section provides that the Section 12(a)(2) liability provision applies "to

---

13. Id. at 644-45 (citations omitted); *see also Kunz v. SEC*, 64 Fed. Appx. 659, 667 (10th Cir. 2003) (applying factors outlined in *Murphy*) (unpublished decision).

14. *Murphy*, 626 F.2d at 647 (emphasis added).

any person offering or selling" securities under the exemption. Does this post-*Gustafson* legislative development affect your views of the extent to which, if at all, Section 12(a)(2) applies to offerings that are neither registered nor made under the new Section 3(b)(2) exemption? Recall also that the JOBS Act created a new crowdfunding exemption and provides that purchasers of securities offered under the exemption may bring an action to recover the consideration paid (or damages if the securities are no longer owned). The legislation establishes liability through a new Section 4A(c) of the '33 Act, which provides for application of Section 12(b) (loss causation) and Section 13 (limitations period) to crowdfunding offerings "as if the liability were created under Section 12(a)(2)." Although Section 4A(c) authorizes an action against the issuer, for this purpose it defines issuer expansively to include "any person who is a director or partner of the issuer, and the principal executive officer or officers, principal financial officer, and controller or principal accounting officer of the issuer (and any person occupying a similar status or performing a similar function) that offers or sells a security in a transaction exempted by the provisions of section 4(6), and any person who offers or sells the security in such offering." Why the differences between these two new liability provisions?

2.   Gustafson *and Aftermarket Transactions.* A number of post-*Gustafson* decisions have concluded that only *original* purchasers in the registered public offering may assert Section 12(a)(2) claims, thus eliminating the possibility (albeit remote) that purchasers in the secondary market could bring such claims if they are able to trace their shares to the original offering. *See, e.g., Rogers v. Sterling Foster & Co.,* 222 F. Supp. 2d 216 (E.D.N.Y. 2002). Recall from the earlier discussion that plaintiffs who purchase in the aftermarket may bring Section 11 claims if they are able to trace their shares to the public offering to which the registration statement pertains. Relying on the different wording of Sections 11 and 12(a)(2), courts have drawn a distinction between the two sections as to aftermarket purchasers and concluded that the reasoning of *Gustafson* does not extend to Section 11. *See, e.g., Hertzberg v. Dignity Partners, Inc.,* supra.

3.   *Oral Communications.* Section 12(a)(2) speaks of a false or misleading prospectus or oral communication. *Gustafson* noted with approval circuit court decisions in agreement that the phrase "oral communication" is restricted to communications that relate to a prospectus. *Dietrich v. Bauer,* Fed. Sec. L. Rep. (CCH) ¶99,411 (S.D.N.Y. 1996), elaborated on the reasons for a restrictive definition of oral communications:

> The reasons for limiting actionable oral communications to those that relate to a prospectus are several. First, the 1933 Act was primarily intended to mandate registration and disclosure of certain information with regard to initial public offerings. . . . If oral communications are covered under the 1933 Act, they are only covered to the extent necessary to effectuate the purpose of the Act. Holding actionable oral communications made by brokers and other individuals unconnected with the initial offering, in the secondary market, is not necessary to effectuate the purpose of the 1933 Act.
>
> Second, canons of statutory construction support the finding that the terms "oral communication" and "prospectus" in [Section 12(a)(2)] be read as related terms. *Gustafson,* 115 S. Ct. at 1069 (the doctrine of noscitur a sociis provides that a

word is known by the company it keeps). The fact that the words "oral communication" in Section 12(a)(2) are directly preceded by the word "prospectus" indicates that the statute should be read so that the word "prospectus" limits the words "oral communication," giving one common reading to the statute rather than multiple antithetical meanings. . . .

Third, the absence in Section 12(a)(2) of the requirement that one prove reliance or fraud can only be explained by the meticulous care with which public offering documents are drafted and the extensive distribution of those documents. *Pollack v. Laidlaw Holdings, Inc.*, Fed. Sec. L. Rep. (CCH) ¶98,741 (S.D.N.Y. 1995). Holding actionable oral representations not made in connection with these documents creates liability for buyers and sellers in the secondary market where there are different standards governing disclosure. It is not plausible to infer that Congress created this extensive liability for every casual communication between buyer and seller in the secondary market. *Gustafson*, 115 S. Ct. at 1071.

How persuasive is this reasoning?

4. Free Writings and Section 12(a)(2). The practical effect of *Gustafson* has been to make Section 12(a)(2) mainly a supplement to Section 11 in policing the accuracy of disclosure in registered public offerings. As was discussed in Chapter 4, the securities offering reforms adopted by the Commission in 2005 permit the use of a free writing prospectus in the public offering of securities. Recall that a free writing prospectus does not become part of the registration statement unless the issuer either files it as part of the registration statement or includes it in a filing that is incorporated by reference into the registration statement. Although a free writing prospectus that is not part of the registration statement is beyond the reach of Section 11, the SEC has emphasized that "any person using the free writing prospectus would be subject to liability for prospectuses under [Section 12(a)(2)] and liability under the antifraud provisions of the federal securities laws." Securities Act Release No. 33-8591 (2005).

Along this line, Rule 433(a) provides that a free writing prospectus "will be deemed to be public, without regard to its method of use or distribution, because it is related to the public offering of securities that are the subject of a filed registration statement." Note that after *Gustafson* the characterization of the communication as "public" is necessary to bring it within the scope of Section 12(a)(2). All of this means that the 2005 reforms liberalizing communications associated with a registered offering will increase the importance of Section 12(a)(2) as a liability provision applicable to public offerings of securities, at least when free writings are used as part of the offerings. *See generally* Thel, Free Writing, 33 J. Corp. L. 941 (2008) (critical of extending Section 12(a)(2) liability to the free writing prospectus).

Against the backdrop of the Commission's intention to subject a free writing prospectus to Section 12(a)(2), consider the effect of the JOBS Act amendment of Section 2(a)(3) to liberalize certain communications concerning emerging growth companies. Specifically, the amendment provides that for purposes of Section 2(a)(10) (defining a prospectus) and Section 5(c), the publication by a broker or dealer (including an underwriter) of a research report concerning an emerging growth company will *not* be deemed an offer to sell a security. The amended section defines "research report" very broadly to cover a written, electronic, or oral communication that includes information, opinions, or recommendations with respect to securities of an issuer or an analysis of a security or an issuer. Does this mean that Section 12(a)(2) has no applicability to a broker's misleading free writing prospectus relating to an emerging growth company, or does *Gustafson*'s reliance on Section 10 rather than Section 2(a)(10) suggest that Section 12(a)(2) will apply to the communication?

5. "Seller" Issues Under Section 12(a)(2). Almost all courts that have decided the issue since *Pinter v. Dahl*, supra, have construed "seller" identically under Sections 12(a)(1) and 12(a)(2). *E.g.*, *Ackerman v. Schwartz*, 947 F.2d 841 (7th Cir. 1991) (concluding that attorney who provided tax opinion was not a seller under Section 12(a)(2)). This has particular implications in terms of who is a proper defendant under Section 12(a)(2). As the Supreme Court said in a footnote in *Pinter*, "§12(1) imposes liability on only the buyer's immediate seller; remote purchasers are precluded from bringing actions against remote sellers. Thus, a buyer cannot recover against his seller's seller." 486 U.S. at 644 n.21.

A particularly intriguing issue under Section 12(a)(2) thus has to do with the issuer's status in a public offering. When the shares are sold through a firm commitment underwriting, is the issuer a seller if it participated in preparing the misleading prospectus? Circuits have been split on the seller status of issuers in firm commitment underwritings. *See, e.g.*, *Abell v. Potomac Insurance Co.*, 858 F.2d 1104, 1114 n.8 (5th Cir. 1988), *cert. denied*, 492 U.S. 918 (1989) (concluding issuers may be sellers and analogizing the situation to an automobile dealer that creates a distribution chain and engages in intensive marketing to convince the public to buy the product); *Shaw v. Digital Equipment Corp.*, 82 F.3d 1194, 1215 (1st Cir. 1996) (rejecting the issuer's status as a seller in a firm commitment underwriting "[b]ecause the issuer in a firm commitment underwriting does not pass title to the securities [and is] no more than a 'seller's seller'").

Noting the "unwarranted uncertainty" as to issuer liability in firm commitment underwritings, the Commission as part of its 2005 offering reforms adopted Rule 159A. The Rule is aimed only at liability to purchasers in the initial distribution of securities as to securities offered by means of particular communications. For purposes of Section 12(a)(2) only, it makes the issuer a seller of securities sold to a person as part of an initial distribution if the securities are offered or sold by means of a statutory prospectus. As to sales made by means of free writing prospectus, the issuer has the status of a seller only if the communication "is prepared by or on behalf of the issuer or used or referred to by the issuer." Notes to the Rule make clear that a communication is made on behalf of the issuer if it is authorized or approved by an agent or representative of the issuer.

It remains to be seen whether Rule 159A will be followed by most courts. For example, in *Mass. Mut. Life Ins. Co. v. Residential Funding Co., LLC*, 843 F. Supp. 2d 191 (D. Mass. 2012), the court suggested the rule is contrary to *Pinter*, adding "numerous other courts that have considered this question—including courts in this circuit—have applied the Supreme Court's decision in *Pinter* to find that an issuer is not a statutory seller, without even mentioning Rule 159A." For a decision, discussed below, deferring to the SEC's approach as a reasonable resolution to the ambiguity as to the meaning of seller in the context of asset-backed securities transactions, *see FHFA v. Nomura Holding Inc.*, 873 F.3d 85 (2d Cir. 2017).

6. *The Breadth of Required Disclosures: How Much Information?* A fundamental question under Section 12(a)(2) and Section 17(a)(2) (discussed infra) is whether the sections mandate the disclosure of *all* material information. In adopting the 2005 offering reforms, the Commission concluded that they do not.

> [The sections] do not require that oral statements or the prospectus or other communications contain all information called for under our line-item disclosure rules or otherwise contain all material information. Rather, under these provisions the determination of liability is based on whether the communication includes a material misstatement or fails to include material information that is necessary to make the communication . . . not misleading.

Securities Act Release No. 33-8591 (2005). This appropriately focuses the inquiry under the two sections on the quality rather than the comprehensiveness of the disclosures.

7. *Post Investment-Decision Information.* Added as part of the 2005 offering reforms, Rule 159 makes clear that in evaluating the quality of disclosures, information conveyed to the investor after a contract of sale has been formed will not be considered. Significantly, the Rule is limited to liability under Section 12(a)(2) and Section 17(a)(2) and addresses post-sale information contained in a final prospectus supplement. For example, in a shelf registered offering the issuer may file a final prospectus not later than the second day after a takedown, which means an investor may make an investment decision without the benefit of information yet to be disclosed. In such a case, information new to the final prospectus will not be considered as conveyed to the investor for purposes of liability under Sections 12(a)(2) and 17.

The purpose of Rule 159 is to assure that purchasers who may have been misled by information provided to them at the time of sale do not lose their right to recover under Section 12(a)(2) because of truthful disclosures coming after the sale date. In *FHFA v. Nomura Holding Inc.*, 873 F.3d 85 (2d Cir. 2017), the court addressed whether purchasers can be misled by material misstatements in filings made after the commitment to purchase. The case involved prospectus supplements filed by the seller after shelf takedowns of mortgage-backed securities that misstated the quality of the underlying mortgage loans. Treating shelf takedowns as "a fluid process" wherein the more skeletal information in free writing prospectuses, used as the main sales tool, are then filled out by the prospectus supplement, the court took note of industry practice allowing purchasers to walk away from a purchase if information in the later-filed prospectus supplement was troubling. Under those circumstances, the misstated information remained material to the investment decision notwithstanding the timing. Besides this important timing question, *Nomura* also addressed numerous other issues as to the requirements for recovery under Section 12(a)(2), including the definition of "seller" in asset-backed securities distributions, the statute of limitations, loss causation, and the right to a jury trial. On the latter, the court said that Section 12(a)(2) (in contrast to Section 11) offers rescission as a remedy, and thus is an equitable claim not subject to the constitutional right to a jury. Query: In a case like this, which side is more likely to benefit from a bench trial as opposed to a jury trial?

PROBLEMS

9-7.   With the assistance of a broker-dealer firm, Apex Partners made an offering of investment limited partnership interests under Rule 505 of Regulation D. Most of the 40 purchasers were institutions; however, there were three wealthy individuals who counted as accredited investors even though they lacked investment sophistication. There were also two nonaccredited investors who were included in the deal as a personal favor to one of the promoters. Apex prepared an offering circular that contained numerous misrepresentations, given to all the offerees. In addition, certain oral misrepresentations were made by the brokers in soliciting each of the offerees. Allegations of culpability are based on negligence. Can any or all of the purchasers sue under Section 12(a)(2)?

9-8.   Portco recently completed a public offering of common stock. The offering was structured as a firm commitment undertaking with 15 underwriters participating in the syndicate. A number of negative developments subsequent to the offering have raised serious doubts about the adequacy of disclosures in the registration statement. For purposes of claims under Section 12(a)(2), is Portco a proper defendant? What about the officers and directors who signed the registration statement? *See In re Metropolitan Sec. Litig.*, 532 F. Supp. 2d 1260 (E.D. Wash. 2007). And the underwriters?

9-9.   An underwriter associated with Alpha's public offering prepares and distributes a free writing prospectus in the form of a brochure. Although Alpha's registration statement is accurate, the brochure is materially misleading in a number of respects. May Section 12(a)(2) be a basis for underwriter liability? Does it make a difference if Alpha is an emerging growth company?

9-10.   *Section 12(a)(1) Revisited.* Ecto Inc. sold unregistered common shares at $15 per share to 45 purchasers in violation of Section 5. Alice, two months after purchasing 1,000 of the shares from Ecto, sold those shares to Bob at $10. The value of the shares declined further to $7. What are Bob's rights under Section 12(a)(1)? Does Alice have any rights?

9-11.   *Section 12(a)(2) Compared.* Assume that in the foregoing problem the shares were registered, but the prospectus was materially misleading. Alice purchased the Ecto shares at $15 without reading the prospectus, although she did show it to Bob, who read it. Soon after, Alice sold her shares to Bob at $10. Ecto shares plummeted to $7 when the misleading aspects of the brochure were revealed. Is Ecto liable to Alice? Bob? What result if Ecto is insolvent and the facts reveal that its outside law firm prepared the misleading brochure?

2.   Liability Defense

Section 12(a)(2) includes a defense for those who can sustain the burden of proving that they did not know "and in the exercise of reasonable care could not have known" of the untruth or omission in the prospectus. To what extent does this defense assume the sort of due diligence inquiries required by Section

11? A leading, and controversial, Seventh Circuit decision concluded that a reasonable investigation is required for an underwriter defendant to avail itself of the defense under Section 12(a)(2). In *Sanders v. John Nuveen & Co.*, 619 F.2d 1222 (7th Cir. 1980), *cert. denied*, 450 U.S. 1005 (1981), 42 purchasers of unsecured promissory notes sued the underwriter, Nuveen, and its controlling persons because the certified financial statements overstated receivables and omitted certain indebtedness. Although only a handful of the purchasers ever received the misleading offering materials, the court concluded that the issuance was "by means of" misleading disclosure documents without regard to whether plaintiffs actually relied on the misrepresentations or omissions.[1] On Nuveen's reasonable care defense, the court reasoned:

> It is not at all clear that Congress intended to impose a higher standard of care under §11 than under §12[a](2). The difference in language appeared in the House bill and was retained in the Act as agreed to by the Joint Conference Committee and as passed by both Houses. The Conference Committee report, in its discussion of the standard of liability imposed for a misleading registration statement, describes the standard adopted not as one of "reasonable investigation," but one of "reasonable care." More specifically, Congress does not appear to have intended that a different standard apply to underwriters. Thus, the House Report draws no distinction between an underwriter's burden in the case of misleading statements in a prospectus, for which it can be liable only under §12[a](2), and its §11 duty to conduct a "reasonable investigation." The difference in language can be explained not as an attempt to impose different duties of care under §§11 and 12, but by the fact that §12[a](2) imposes the duty on all sellers of securities, while §11 imposes liability only on specified groups of persons having such a close relationship with the registration statement that the 1933 Act, before it was amended the following year, treated them as fiduciaries. *See* Securities Act of 1933 §11(c); Securities Exchange Act of 1934 §206(c). Thus the general duty of reasonable care, the specific requirements of which are determined by the circumstances of the case, was to be applied in §11 only to persons who had a stronger connection with a registration statement than a seller necessarily has to a prospectus, so a more stringent articulation of the standard was appropriate.
>
> In the circumstances of this case, the reasonable care standard required [a reasonable investigation.] Since what constitutes reasonable care under §12[a](2) depends upon the circumstances, we, of course, do not intimate that the duty of a seller under §12[a](2) is always the same as that of an underwriter in a registration offering under §11. . . .

Id. at 1228.

Dissenting from the Supreme Court's denial of certiorari in *Sanders*, Justice Powell argued that the Seventh Circuit had improperly inflated the notion of due care:

> The Court of Appeals' opinion may be read as holding that petitioner's duty of "reasonable care" under §12[a](2) required it independently to *investigate* the accuracy and completeness of the certified financial statements. It was customary, however—and in my view entirely reasonable—for petitioner to rely on these statements as accurately

---

1. Note that this was not a registered offering. After *Gustafson*, it is unlikely plaintiffs would have been able to maintain an action under Section 12(a)(2).

reflecting W & H's financial condition. Even under §11 of the Act, an underwriter is explicitly absolved from the duty to investigate with respect to "any part of the registration statement purporting to be made on the authority of an expert" such as a certified accountant if "he had no reasonable ground to believe, and did not believe," that the information therein was misleading. . . . This provision is in the Act because, almost by definition, it *is* reasonable to rely on financial statements certified by public accountants. Yet, in this case, the Court of Appeals nevertheless seems to have imposed the higher duty prescribed by §11 to investigate, but denied petitioner the right to rely on "the authority of an expert" that is also provided by §11. . . . Dealers may believe that they must undertake extensive independent investigations rather than rely on the accuracy of the certified financial statements. If this is so, the efficiency of the short-term financial markets will be impaired.

450 U.S. 1005, 1009-1011 (1981).

More recent cases seem to recognize that the 12(a)(2) standard may well be slightly less demanding than Section 11, but that the distinction between the two is not great. For a thorough discussion, granting summary judgment to plaintiffs on the issue of reasonable care in a mortgage-backed securities case noted earlier, *see FHFA v. Nomura Holding Inc.*, 873 F.3d 85 (2d Cir. 2017).

This seems to be the SEC's position as well. In *Sanders*, the SEC had filed an amicus brief arguing that Section 12(a)(2) does not require the same level of diligence that is imposed under Section 11. It reasoned, "Since Congress has determined that registration is not necessary in certain defined situations, we believe that it would undermine the Congressional intent—that issuers and other persons should be relieved of registration—if the same degree of investigation were to be required to avoid potential liability whether or not a registration statement is required." Although the Seventh Circuit rejected this argument, the Commission took the occasion of the adoption of the 2005 offering reforms to reiterate its position and to emphasize that context is relevant in measuring the adequacy of care taken:

> We believe . . . as we have stated previously, that the standard of care under Section 12(a)(2) is less demanding than that prescribed by Section 11 or, put another way, that Section 11 requires a more diligent investigation than Section 12(a)(2). Moreover, we believe that any practices or factors that would be considered favorably under Section 11, including pursuant to Rule 176, also would be considered as favorably under the reasonable care standard of Section 12(a)(2).

Securities Act Release No. 33-8591 (2005). The comment concerning Rule 176, which as noted earlier introduces the sliding-scale approach to due diligence, is interesting inasmuch as the Rule by its terms applies only to Section 11 offerings and the Commission in its 2005 statement noted without explanation that it was declining to adopt modifications of Rule 176 "at this time."

NOTES AND QUESTIONS

1. ***Reliance and Causation.*** A showing of reliance on the falsity or omission is not part of plaintiff's case under Section 12(a)(2). What about causation? The courts have indicated that some minimal showing that the prospectus or oral

communication—as opposed to the misstatement or omission itself—played a role in the purchase.

2.   Rescission and Damages.   As observed with respect to Section 12(a)(1), the rescission remedy is generally a simple one—the plaintiff gets his money back. As part of the Private Securities Litigation Reform Act of 1995, however, Congress amended Section 12 by adding subsection (b), providing for a loss causation defense in a Section 12(a)(2) action similar to that found in Section 11: Defendants are not liable for any portion of the rescissionary measure of damages that represents a decline in the value of the security unrelated to the subject of the misrepresentation or omission. *See Miller v. Thane Int'l,* 615 F.3d 1095 (9th Cir. 2010) (discussing loss causation under Section 12(a)(2) and concluding stock prices may be used as a benchmark for losses even in an inefficient market).

An interesting question concerning damages arises when the plaintiff has pocketed benefits prior to rescission. Interest or dividends paid are expressly deducted from the recovery. On the other hand, in *Randall v. Loftsgaarden,* 478 U.S. 647, 660 (1986), the Supreme Court held that Section 12(a)(2) "does not authorize an offset of tax benefits received by a defrauded investor against the investor's rescissionary recovery, either as 'income received' or as a return of 'consideration' and that this is so whether or not the security in question is classified as a tax shelter." In this one sense, at least, Section 12(a)(2) may put the plaintiff in a better position than he or she would have been but for the fraud. The Court justified this by reference to the deterrent, rather than simply compensatory, objective underlying the statutory provision.

3.   Cross-Liability and the Free Writing Prospectus.   Besides dealing with issuer liability issues under Section 12(a)(2), Rule 159A addresses the liability of an underwriter when a free writing prospectus has been prepared and used by another underwriter in a registered offering. An underwriter who does not prepare or use a free writing prospectus will not be considered to have offered securities by means of the free writing, which effectively limits the underwriter's liability for defects in a free writing prospectus not prepared or used by the underwriter.

D.   Section 17(a)

Aaron v. Securities and Exchange Commission
446 U.S. 680 (1980)

STEWART, J. . . . The language of §17(a) strongly suggests that Congress contemplated a scienter requirement under §17(a)(1), but not under §17(a)(2) or §17(a)(3). The language of §17(a)(1), which makes it unlawful "to employ any device, scheme, or artifice to defraud," plainly evinces an intent on the part of Congress to proscribe only knowing or intentional misconduct. Even if it be assumed that the term "defraud" is ambiguous, given its varied meanings at law and in equity, the terms "device," "scheme," and "artifice" all connote knowing or intentional practices. Indeed, the term "device," which also appears in §10(b) figured prominently in the Court's conclusion in [*Ernst & Ernst v. Hochfelder*] that the plain meaning of §10(b) embraces a scienter requirement. Id. at 199.

By contrast, the language of §17(a)(2), which prohibits any person from obtaining money or property "by means of any untrue statement of a material fact or any omission to state a material fact," is devoid of any suggestion whatsoever of a scienter requirement. As a well-known commentator has noted, "[t]here is nothing on the face of Clause (2) itself which smacks of scienter or intent to defraud." 3 L. Loss, Securities Regulation 1442 (2d ed. 1961). In fact, this Court in *Hochfelder* pointed out that the similar language of Rule 10b-5(b) "could be read as proscribing . . . any type of material misstatement or omission . . . that has the effect of defrauding investors, whether the wrongdoing was intentional or not." 425 U.S., at 212.

Finally, the language of §17(a)(3), under which it is unlawful for any person "to engage in any transaction, practice, or course of business which *operates* or *would operate* as a fraud or deceit," (emphasis added) quite plainly focuses upon the *effect* of particular conduct on members of the investing public, rather than upon the culpability of the person responsible. This reading follows directly from *Capital Gains*, which attributed to a similarly worded provision in §206(2) of the Investment Advisers Act of 1940 a meaning that does not require a "showing [of] deliberate dishonesty as a condition precedent to protecting investors." 375 U.S., at 200.

It is our view, in sum, that the language of §17(a) requires scienter under §17(a)(1), but not under §17(a)(2) or §17(a)(3). Although the parties have urged the Court to adopt a uniform culpability requirement for the three subparagraphs of §17(a), the language of the section is simply not amenable to such an interpretation. . . . Indeed, since Congress drafted §17(a) in such a manner as to compel the conclusion that scienter is required under one subparagraph but not under the other two, it would take a very clear expression in the legislative history of congressional intent to the contrary to justify the conclusion that the statute does not mean what it so plainly seems to say. . . .

NOTES AND QUESTIONS

1. The Scope of Section 17(a). Prior to the late 1970s, Section 17(a) had become something of a deadweight, for it was generally assumed that Rule 10b-5—which drew its substance directly from the language of Section 17(a), but extended its scope to fraudulent purchases as well as sales—served the needs of the SEC and private parties as well as anything. In those cases where Section 17(a) was at issue, courts usually construed it as in *pari materia* with Rule 10b-5 and thus to no substantially greater advantage. In this sense, the flourishing of the law under Rule 10b-5 may effectively have stunted the growth of its progenitor.

Once the period of retrenchment under Rule 10b-5 began, a desire to revisit Section 17(a) and test the *pari materia* assumption was kindled. After all, while Section 17(a) and Rule 10b-5 were virtually identical, the same could not be said for Section 10(b), and it was the language of that provision, with its emphasis on deception and manipulation, that was the ostensible justification for so much of the Supreme Court's pruning efforts. *Aaron* then gave effect to the statutory differences. Needless to say, the SEC's enforcement actions today invoke Section 17(a) to the greatest extent possible, especially when state of mind is likely to be at issue.

The scope of Section 17(a) is broad. In light of the history of Rule 10b-5—premised on the assumption that a broader rule was necessary in order to reach fraudulent purchases in addition to sales—it must be assumed that its scope is limited to fraud by sellers. Literally, of course, this is not inevitable. Every purchase involves a sale, and the statute only requires fraud "in the offer or sale" of a security.

More importantly, the Supreme Court has held that Section 17(a) is *not* limited to fraud in the process of a distribution of securities, even though that is the general thrust of the Securities Act. In *United States v. Naftalin*, 441 U.S. 768 (1979), the Court ruled that it covered a case where a customer defrauded his broker through a scheme of short-selling with respect to a general trading account. After reviewing the section's legislative history, it found sufficient indication that Congress meant to ensure a sense of honesty and fair dealing "in every facet" of the securities business and thus rejected the idea that such cases should be left to redress under the Securities Exchange Act.

Another possible distinction between Section 10(b) and Section 17(a) concerns whether liability attaches only when the defendant actually makes an untrue statement of a material fact or omits a material fact. As will be discussed in Chapter 14, liability under Section 10(b) normally requires a misleading statement or omission "made" by the defendant. As you will see in Chapter 13, the Supreme Court has indicated that the SEC may bring a "scheme"-based claim under Section 17(a)(1) or (3) against someone who intentionally passes on false information to another, regardless of whether that person actually "made" that misstatement. *See Lorenzo v. SEC*, 139 S. Ct. 1094 (2019).

2.   *Negligence May Be Costly.* The broad reach of Sections 17(a)(2) and 17(a)(3) to include claims based on negligence is all the more important because of the significant penalties (including disgorgement and civil monetary relief) that may accompany a finding of liability. For example, in 2011, J.P. Morgan Securities, LLC paid $153.6 million to settle SEC charges under Section 17 that it had misled investors purchasing securities tied to the U.S. housing market. *See* SEC Litigation Release No. 22008 (June 21, 2011).

3.   *Private Rights of Action.* Section 17(a) confers no express private right of action, and contemporary jurisprudence frowns on implication in the absence of direct congressional intent. Notwithstanding some earlier doubt on the question, it seems clear today that only government enforcers can bring suit directly under this provision. *E.g., In re Washington Public Power Supply System Securities Litig.*, 823 F.2d 1349 (9th Cir. 1987). In the chapters that follow, you will see a number of instances where courts either accept or reject implied right under various statutory provisions and SEC rules for which there is no express statutory remedy. All this difficulty stems from a period of time—roughly from the 1950s until the mid-1970s—when federal courts implied rights fairly freely to further the purposes of the securities laws. *See J.I. Case Co. v. Borak*, 377 U.S.

426 (1964) (implied right of action for proxy fraud). That came to a halt as
the Supreme Court took a conservative turn, so that the issue today is entirely
a matter of whether Congress intended to confer a right of action. Importantly,
however, the Court left in place those implied rights of action that were clearly
recognized during that judicially more activist time period, in particular Rule
10b-5, most of the language of which was borrowed from Section 17(a).

‖10‖

Financial Innovation: Trading Markets, Derivatives, and Securitization

A. *Technology and the Transformation of Securities Markets*

‖ **SEC Concept Release on Equity Market Structure**
Securities Exchange Act Release No. 61358 (Jan. 14, 2010)

Trading equities today is no longer as straightforward as sending an order to the floor of a single exchange on which the stock is listed. . . . [T]he current market structure can be described as dispersed and complex: (1) trading volume is dispersed among many highly automated trading centers that compete for order flow in the same stocks; and (2) trading centers offer a wide range of services that are designed to attract different types of market participants with varying trading needs.

The primary driver and enabler of this transformation of equity trading has been the continual evolution of technologies for generating, routing, and executing orders. These technologies have dramatically improved the speed, capacity, and sophistication of the trading functions that are available to market participants.

. . .

A. TRADING CENTERS

A good place to start in describing the current market structure is by identifying the major types of trading centers and giving a sense of their current share of trading volume in NMS stocks.[1] Figure 6 below provides this information . . . [updated since the SEC release with data provided by Healthy Markets Association to report relative trading volumes during June 2019]:

---

1.   [NMS refers to "national market system" and NMS stocks are those that are listed on a national exchange, thus excluding shares traded on markets such as the OTCBB and Pink Sheets, discussed later.—Eds.]

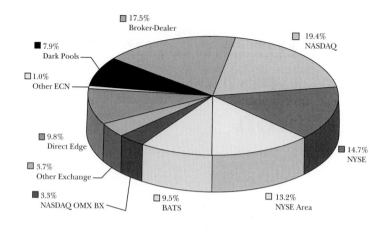

Figure 6   Trading Centers and Estimated % of Share Volume in NMS Stocks September 2009

Registered exchanges:

NASDAQ	19.4%
NYSE	14.7%
NYSE Arca	13.2%
BATS	9.5%
NASDAQ OMX BX	3.3%
Other	3.7%
Total Exchange	63.8%

ECNs:

2 Direct Edge	9.8%
3 Others	1.0%
Total ECN	10.8%
Total Displayed Trading Center	74.6%

Dark Pools:

Approximately 32	7.9%

Broker-Dealer Internalization:

More than 200	17.5%
Total Undisplayed Trading Center	25.4%

. . .

1. REGISTERED EXCHANGES

. . .

The registered exchanges all have adopted highly automated trading systems that can offer extremely high-speed, or "low-latency," order responses and executions. Published average response times at some exchanges, for example, have been reduced to less than 1 millisecond. Many exchanges offer individual data feeds that deliver information concerning their orders and trades directly to customers. To further reduce latency in transmitting market data and order messages, many exchanges also offer co-location services that enable exchange customers to place their servers in close proximity to the exchange's matching engine. . . .

2.   ECNS

. . . Almost all ECN volume is executed by two ECNs operated by Direct Edge . . . ECNs are regulated as alternative trading systems ("ATSs"). . . .

3.   DARK POOLS

Dark pools are ATSs that, in contrast to ECNs, do not provide their best-priced orders for inclusion in the consolidated quotation data. In general, dark pools offer trading services to institutional investors and others that seek to execute large trading interest in a manner that will minimize the movement of prices against the trading interest and thereby reduce trading costs. . . . ATSs, both dark pools and ECNs, fall within the statutory definition of an exchange, but are exempted if they . . . register . . . as broker-dealers with the Commission, which entails becoming a member of the Financial Industry Regulatory Authority ("FINRA") and fully complying with the broker-dealer regulatory regime. Unlike a registered exchange, an ATS is not required to file proposed rule changes with the Commission or otherwise publicly disclose its trading services and fees. ATSs also do not have any self-regulatory responsibilities, such as market surveillance.

4.   BROKER-DEALER INTERNALIZATION

The other type of undisplayed trading center is a non-ATS broker-dealer that internally executes trades, whether as agent or principal. Notably, many broker-dealers may submit orders to exchanges or ECNs, which then are included in the consolidated quotation data. The internalized executions of broker-dealers, however, primarily reflect liquidity that is not included in the consolidated quotation data. Broker-dealer internalization accordingly should be classified as undisplayed liquidity. . . .

Broker-dealers that internalize executions generally fall into two categories— OTC market makers and block positioners. . . . "Block size" is . . . an order of at least 10,000 shares or for a quantity of stock having a market value of at least $200,000. A block positioner generally means any broker-dealer in the business of executing, as principal or agent, block size trades for its customers. To facilitate trades, block positioners often commit their own capital to trade as principal with at least some part of the customer's block order.

Broker-dealers that act as OTC market makers and block positioners con-duct their business primarily by directly negotiating with customers or with other broker-dealers representing customer orders. OTC market makers, for example, appear to handle a very large percentage of marketable (immediately executable) order flow of individual investors that is routed by retail brokerage firms. A review of the order routing disclosures . . . of eight broker-dealers with significant retail customer accounts reveals that nearly 100% of their customer market orders are routed to OTC market makers. The review also indicates that most of these retail brokers either receive payment for order flow in connection with the routing of orders or are affiliated with an OTC market maker that executes the orders. The . . . payment for order flow generally is 0.1 cent per share or less.

B.   LINKAGES

Given the dispersal of liquidity across a large number of trading centers of different types, an important question is whether trading centers are sufficiently linked together in a unified national market system.

Stoll, Electronic Trading in Stock Markets
20 J. Econ. Persp. 153, 169-173 (2006)

Electronic trading is having a major effect on the structure of securities markets, that is, on the number and types of exchanges and how they interact. While important forces are leading to consolidation of markets, many observers believe stock trading is excessively fragmented.

Two economic forces tend to lead to the consolidation of trading in a single market—economies of scale in processing orders and network externalities—but the centralizing tendency can be offset if communication across markets is easy and if orders can readily be routed from one market to another. Economies of scale exist on the production side because the average cost of handling an order declines with the number of orders. . . .

Network externalities arise on the demand side because trades are easier to accomplish if others are trading at the same location. A centralized market maximizes the possibility of interaction with other traders—hence, traders want to trade where others are trading. . . .

The natural monopoly of an exchange is threatened by advanced communication. . . . Thus, with improved communication, the forces to fragment trading are stronger today and the forces of consolidation are weaker. . . .

Regulation has affected the balance between consolidation and fragmentation of markets. The Securities Acts Amendments of 1975 authorized the Securities and Exchange Commission to facilitate a national market system (NMS) with fair competition among brokers, dealers and markets, the availability to all of information on transactions prices and dealer quotes, the linking of markets and the ability to execute orders in the best market. Some interpreted the 1975 amendments as calling for the Securities and Exchange Commission to develop a single integrated national market system in which all orders would be routed to a national consolidated limit order book (CLOB). The Securities and Exchange Commission has vacillated over the years in the degree of force-fulness with which it has pursued a national market system. . . .

Recently the Securities and Exchange Commission approved . . . a series of rules to link markets while at the same time allowing for independent development by each market. On April 6, 2005, the Securities and Exchange Commission, under its authority (Section 11A of the Securities Exchange Act of 1934) to facilitate the establishment of a national market system, approved a controversial rule [Rule 611 of Reg NMS]—the order protection rule (also known as the order trade-through rule) that requires a market receiving an order to send the order to any other market that has better posted prices if those prices are automated and immediately accessible. . . . Put differently, the rule prohibits an incoming market order from ignoring (trading through) a better quote in market A to trade with a poorer quote in market B. . . .

The rule is controversial for several reasons. Opponents argue the rule interferes with the right of customers (through their brokers) to send orders to any market and improperly injects the government into everyday business decisions. They argue that customers should have the right to base order rout-ing on factors other than price, such as reliability, speed and creditworthiness. Consumers are not required to buy their TVs where the price is lowest, so inves-tors should not be required to buy their stocks where the price is lowest.

Supporters of the rule argue that price priority is central to a well-functioning market—the rule is only doing what brokers, acting in their cus-tomers' best interests, should do. . . .

The casual observer of the heated debate that has surrounded the order protection rule may well wonder what the fuss is all about. After all, we are just talking about pennies. But for the exchanges, it may be a matter of business survival. Pennies matter, but more important, the rule requires the linkage of markets, which threatens established markets and benefits new markets. The battle appears to be over pennies, but in fact, it is over the ability of markets to separate themselves from the pack. The linkage required by the Securities and Exchange Commission links trading centers directly. Each trading center, such as an electronic communication network, would be linked to every other trading center, such as the NYSE, and would be required to send orders to the competing market if that market had better quotes. A direct linkage tends to limit competition among markets because it forces markets to integrate their operations; in fact, it requires an exchange to send orders to a competi-tor. (It is like asking Wal-Mart and Target to cooperate by sending each other customers). . . .

Stock markets are central to modern capitalist economies. The prices formed on them provide signals about the economic viability of firms and facil-itate the proper allocation of resources among firms. Markets provide liquidity to investors that wish to save or consume. Electronic trading has improved the efficiency of stock markets and hence has reduced the cost of providing liquidity and has increased the accuracy of price signals. Electronic trading benefits investors in increasing the speed and lowering the cost of trading while at the same time creating a complete audit trail that facilitates monitor-ing brokers. . . .

NOTES AND QUESTIONS

1. The Rise of Global For-Profit Exchanges. Traditionally, stock exchanges around the world were organized as member owned and generally were not for-profit corporations. Since 2000, most of the major stock exchanges around the world, including both the NYSE and Nasdaq, have demutualized and are now themselves publicly traded, for-profit companies. *See* Gadinis & Jackson, Markets as Regulators: A Survey, 80 S. Cal. L. Rev. 1239 (2007); Karmel, Turning Seats into Shares: Causes and Implications of Demutualization of Stock and Futures Exchanges, 53 Hastings L.J. 367 (2002). Indeed, the NYSE is but a part, albeit a significant part, of the much larger, publicly owned International Exchange that also operates other electronic trading markets and clearing houses around the world. Not to be left out of the international action, Nasdaq today is wholly owned by Nasdaq, Inc., which operates several European exchanges in the Baltic and Nordic regions in addition to exchange activities in Boston and Philadelphia as well as extensive clearing activities.

2. Proprietary Data Feeds. Rule 603 of Reg NMS requires exchanges to transmit certain information regarding trades to a central network where the information is consolidated and distributed. This embodies real-time trading information, such as national best bid and offer for particular stocks. The data once aggregated is distributed to subscribers at rates overseen by the SEC. However, exchanges can privately sell more granular information, so-called proprietary information, such as every bid and order for a given stock on the exchange; proprietary information generally reaches subscribers faster than the mandated Rule 603 information since that information does not go through a process of aggregating the data. High frequency traders are major consumers of the proprietary information. *See City of Providence, R.I. v. BATS Global Mkts., Inc.,* 878 F.3d 36 (2d Cir. 2017) (exchanges are not immune to suits alleging they purposely design types of trading orders and data feeds so as to attract high frequency traders and stimulate trading on the exchanges).

3. The Maker-Taker Model, or How Do Exchanges Make Money? As seen in the preceding excerpt, Reg NMS's trade through requirement rests on there being an existing quote that a prospective trader can pursue to complete a customer's trade. With multiple markets in which a security can trade (e.g., a trade can now be executed on the NYSE even though its issuer is not formally listed there), a broker wishing to place a quote for the purchase (bid) or sale (ask) of a stock has a good deal of choice. That choice is likely impacted by the prevalent practice among exchanges of "payment for order flow" whereby the market center pays an inducement (typically $0.002 per share) to the broker placing the quote as an inducement for creating liquidity through the order. The broker placing the quote is the "maker"; the payment is made to the maker when the trade is executed against its resting order by its "taker" (who typically is charged $0.003 per share). The difference between the maker and taker payment is retained by the exchange. Exchanges in this way are thus remitting to makers a healthy portion of the trading fees brokers incur when trades are executed through the exchange's facilities, but in doing so they create a public good, price discovery:

> National securities exchanges play a critical role in the public price discovery process, as market participants generally look to prices displayed on the lit markets in making their trading and investment decisions. Venues that do not display their trading interest publicly, such as "dark pool" ATSs as well as wholesale broker-dealers that internalize customer order flow, depend on the public exchanges for the reference prices at which they execute trades. The displayed prices generated by exchanges therefore create a positive external reference and help assure the efficient functioning of our capital markets.

SEC Division of Trading and Markets Memorandum to SEC Market Structure Advisory Comm. 11 (Oct. 20, 2015).

Consider the following as you ponder why exchanges engage in this form of price competition:

> [W]e document that trading fees across major exchanges are economically very small. . . . [U]sing a variety of data sources to cut through this complexity, we compute that the average fee for regular-hours trading, across the three largest stock exchange families, is around $0.0001 per share per side—or about 0.0001% per side for a $100 stock. This implies that across approximately 1 trillion shares traded during regular hours each year, exchanges earn approximately $200 million in trading fees. To put this in perspective, StubHub, the largest secondary market venue for concert and sports tickets, has revenues exceeding $1 billion; that is, StubHub's revenue is over five times that for all U.S. regular-hours equities trading, despite the secondary market for event tickets being a tiny fraction of the secondary market for U.S. equities. Last, we document that exchanges earn significant revenues from the sale of co-location services and proprietary data feeds. For the BATS exchange family, for which the data is the cleanest, revenue from co-location and data is about 69% of total revenue. In aggregate across the three major exchange families (BATS, Nasdaq, NYSE), we document significant growth in ESST fees during the Reg NMS era (post 2007), with 2018 speed technology revenues estimated to be on the order of $1 billion.

Budish, Lee & Shim, Will the Market Fix the Market? A Theory of Stock Exchange Competition and Innovation, Becker Friedman Institute for Economics at Chicago Working Paper, 4 (May 2019), available at *https://ssrn/com/abstract=3391461*.

In late 2018, the SEC adopted a two-year pilot program where groups of stocks would be subject to differing amounts or no amount of maker fees; the program was soon suspended in the face of legal challenges from the major exchanges.

4. High Frequency Trading and Co-Location. As the excerpts above make clear, the trading of securities relies almost entirely on electronic execution of trades in one of any number of competing market centers. This has produced considerable benefits in terms of speed of execution, price competition, and innovation. But it has its costs as well. There are many different market centers, and the resulting "fragmentation" necessarily means that not all buy and sell orders will interact so as to create the best price at any given time. Consider that Reg NMS is premised in part on the belief that technology might overcome such fragmentation by virtually, simultaneously, and instantly placing all the markets on the screen together. But this assumes everyone's server is the same distance from the trading venue or the information feed that prompts a particular trade. However, even at the speed of light, distance matters and when the volume of shares traded is considered this difference matters a lot. Thus, many hedge funds and others using high frequency trading strategies seek to "co-locate" their computers at the exchanges and ATSs in order to minimize network latencies. Co-location actually provides a time advantage on two fronts: the information feeds from the exchange regarding price and volume of trades and execution of orders in response to the information feed. *See In re Barclays Liquidity Cross & High Frequency Trading Litig.*, 2019 U.S. Dist. LEXIS 89337 (S.D.N.Y. May 28, 2019) (denying motion to dismiss suits by pension funds against seven exchanges alleging they had engaged in manipulation by designing orders that enabled hedge funds to better exploit their co-location privilege at the expense of pension funds' trades); *In the Matter of NYSE, LLC*, Exchange Act Release No. 72065 (May 1, 2014) (sanction imposed for failure to monitor co-location granted trader who engaged in acts that were inconsistent with maintaining fair market).

Institutions have responded to concerns regarding co-location arrangements and their fears that high frequency traders will adversely impact their trades by trading through dark pools and other trading mediums. With respect to the latter strategy, consider the business model developed by the IEX stock trading platform, celebrated in Michael Lewis' book, Flash Boys. IEX has attracted a rapidly growing market share by purposely slowing down trades (installing an electronic "speed bump") so as to reduce that market's attractiveness to high frequency traders. In 2016, IEX was granted exchange status by the SEC. *See generally* Hu, Efficient Markets and the Law: A Predictable Past and an Uncertain Future, 4 Ann. Rev. Fin. Econ. 179, 183 (2012) ("The events of May 6, 2010 [generally known as the "Flash Crash" discussed below], are illustrative of the possibility of extremely sharp non-fundamentally driven price discontinuities associated with the modern structure of equity markets."). *See generally* Fox, Glosten & Rauterberg, The New Stock Market: Sense and Nonsense, 65 Duke L.J. 191 (2015) (closely examining multiple problems that surround contemporary trading markets and offering reforms to trading mechanisms).

5. Institutional Trades.   Suppose you are an institutional investor wanting to buy or sell a very large block of stock of a particular issuer. What would constitute best execution for your order? Were you simply to route the full order to an exchange or trading system, you could easily be "front-run." In other words, because such a large order will likely take time to execute, and might have a sizable impact on price, someone aware of your intentions could step in front of the order and profit at your expense. As a result, institutional investors often seek as much anonymity as possible, arranging private transactions or "slicing and dicing" their orders to conceal the size. Or they seek out trading sites that allow them to hide their interest. While all this seems to run counter to the full transparency sought by the national market system, such freedom is necessary to accommodate the special difficulties of block orders. Otherwise, institutions will go elsewhere for their trading. As a result of the demand for anonymity, so-called dark pools of capital have proliferated—private trading locations that can legitimately hide orders from public exposure. Because trading in dark pools is "off the market," the trade does not reveal price quotations, so the trade does not itself impact the security's price. Nonetheless, dark pools have proven to be a solution only for handling small trades; large trades are commonly handled by breaking down the transaction into smaller increments that are handled over time, albeit making the trade riskier due to uncertainties that accompany the inherent delay. Thus, the quest for anonymity has its downside. For a discussion of this challenge and how it is dealt with both in the United States and in Europe, *see* Gadinis, Market Structure for Institutional Investors: Comparing the E.U. and U.S. Regimes, 3 Va. L. & Bus. Rev. 311 (2008).

6. *Technology Can and Does Crash.* High-volume electronic trading in such a complex, interconnected setting means that technology failures are inevitable and potentially damaging. For example, in the highly publicized IPO by Facebook, the first day trading on Nasdaq was plagued by technological failures that meant that many orders were not executed promptly or at all. This risk of systems failure is substantially increased by the growth of high frequency trading activity—computer generated orders that seek to exploit small differences in available prices within or among trading centers—that make up a large portion of today's trading volume. Fears about high frequency trading were exacerbated on May 6, 2010, with the so-called Flash Crash—a sudden and inexplicable drop (in some cases to near zero) in the market prices of certain securities. During the space of four minutes, major equity indices plummeted 5-6 percent, which then led to some individual securities trading wildly, e.g., 3M shares fell from $82 to $68. The Flash Crash was apparently triggered by algorithmic trading programs. Responding to these events, the SEC adopted Regulation Systems Compliance and Integrity, Exchange Act Release No. 73639 (Nov. 14, 2014), which requires exchanges to take a variety of steps to assure they have adequate capacity, integrity, resilience, and security; the focus of these requirements is to push exchanges and clearing agencies to adopt rules to implement the regulation's objectives.

7. *Electronic Markets for Less Widely Traded Stocks.* Decades ago, securities of issuers not large enough to warrant a listing on an exchange were traded over-the-counter through the distribution of the "pink sheets"—printed lists of daily quotes from various securities dealers. The Nasdaq system arose initially just as a way to automate these quotes, but as we have seen, Nasdaq is today itself an exchange on which a wide variety of issuers' securities are traded, subject to demanding listing standards. Unlisted securities trade in a number of markets today, all of which are electronic. The OTC Bulletin Board, operated by FINRA, emerged as a trading site for smaller issuers, but since 1999 the OTCBB has been limited to reporting companies under the '34 Act, which made it less attractive to issuers unwilling to take on those responsibilities. *See* Bushee & Leuz, Economic Consequences of SEC Disclosure Regulation: Evidence from the OTC Bulletin Board, 39 J. Acct. & Econ. 233, 238 (2005). The major platforms for electronic "pink sheet" trading today are operated by OTC Market Groups, where almost 10,000 issuers trade on a world-wide basis. Because they focus on smaller, more thinly traded stocks that may or may not be registered with the SEC, these sites have a variety of investor protection features, including vivid caveat emptor warnings (e.g., a skull and crossbones symbol) with respect to issuers about which concerns have arisen. Finally, as noted in Chapter 6, electronic trading platforms such as SharesPost and SecondMarket have emerged to facilitate trading in shares of private companies so as to avoid resale problems under Section 5 of the '33 Act and registration under the '34 Act.

8. Consolidated Audit Trail. To better enable it to provide regulatory oversight of trading markets, the SEC adopted Exchange Act Rule 613 mandating the SROs create a comprehensive consolidated audit trail that allows regulators to efficiently and accurately track all activities in national market securities throughout U.S. markets. The system captures a complete record of all transactions relating to an order, from origination to execution or cancellation. The information is required to be transmitted to a central depository by 8:00 A.M. Eastern Time on the day following the trading date. Thereafter the information is accessible by regulators.

9. Bond Markets. In contrast to the securities markets, bond markets are almost totally dealer markets. Bond dealers are linked by computers, and most of the liquidity of bond markets has historically been provided by a few of the trading desks of large investment banking firms. In 2011, trading in corporate bonds was in excess of $8 trillion. However, depending on the scope of banking regulation introduced by the Dodd-Frank legislation intended to reduce the proprietary trading activities of banks, past may well not be prologue. From a different perspective, bonds remain the instrument of choice for corporate issuers; in 2018, the total amount of corporate bonds issued was $1.6 trillion, whereas corporate equity underwritings totaled $223.5 billion of which $46 billion were IPOs. *See* SIFMA 2018 Fact Book 22. Finally, bond markets are almost exclusively an institutional medium, i.e., retail investors compose a very small percentage of bond trading.

B. *Derivatives and Synthetic Investments*

1. Why Derivatives?

Derivative securities are financial instruments that *derive* value from other assets to which their values are linked. The standard derivative contract *derives* its value from the underlying item (called the reference item). The reference item may be a particular stock, a stock index, a debt instrument, a foreign currency, interest rates, commodities such as oil or corn, or foreign exchange rates. While derivatives use in financial, credit, and capital markets is relatively recent, derivatives have been used for centuries in connection with agriculture and other commodities.

The wide prevalence of derivatives can be attributed to addressing risk; derivatives, because their value is dependent on the underlying (reference) item, create exposure to risk that the underlying item will change in value.

Through derivatives, parties can isolate, even customize, risk exposure and the potential for financial reward. Broadly, derivatives may appeal to investors for four fundamental reasons: dealing, hedging, speculating, and arbitraging.

Derivatives dealers are typically banks or financial institutions who engage in derivative transactions as intermediaries, expecting to profit from transaction fees carried out on behalf of others. Sometimes the financial institution provides its expertise to develop and customize a particular derivative product to address the needs of the investor. For example, hedging involves protecting against a potential loss on an investment by entering into a distinct contract that is designed to result in a profit from the same conditions that would cause a loss in the reference item. Derivatives are a useful tool to hedge risk because of the ability to customize the risk related to the reference item and transfer that risk to another via the derivative contract. Another use of derivatives is to speculate about future price movements. Speculation has no well-understood definition but involves the practice of rapid trading in derivatives for profit; speculators use derivatives to profit by increasing their exposure to risk instead of reducing it. To be sure, the line between hedging and speculating is not always a clear one. Finally, arbitrage occurs when a trader purchases an asset at a lower price in one market and sells the same asset at a higher price in another. Such arbitrage opportunities depend on market inefficiencies in the sense that each market reflects a different price for the same asset. By purchasing in one market and selling in another, the arbitrageur's trading brings the two markets closer together.

2. Basic Forms of Derivatives

a. Options

An *option* on stock is one type of derivative security. The simplest type of option is the *call option*, which gives the holder the right to purchase a fixed number of shares at a specified price for a defined period of time. (In contrast, a *put option* is the right to sell to another at a fixed price.) Options may be traded on the organized securities exchanges. They also may be created by contract and not traded on an exchange, in which case they are often called *over-the-counter options*. Although the term *option* appears in the statutory definitions of a security, the nuanced ways in which this derivative is now used raise difficult questions, discussed below, concerning application of the securities acts.

b. Futures

Another type of derivative is the futures contract. In contrast with options, *futures* are contracts that call for future delivery of some commodity at a fixed price and date. Because options provide the holder the right, but not the obligation, to buy or sell the underlying item, options have the benefit over futures of limited downside risk. Thus, if Investor purchased a future to acquire 10,000 shares of IBM at $45 at some future date, the investor incurs a loss of $50,000 when the future is closed if on that date IBM trades at $40. If instead Investor had the option to purchase 10,000 IBM shares at $45 and the shares never rise above $40, the investor will simply not exercise the option, hence losing only the price paid for the option. Futures exchanges have long existed to allow for both hedging and speculation in standardized contracts for agricultural commodities. In the 1970s, however, the commodities exchanges (e.g., the Chicago Mercantile Exchange) expanded into financial futures, allowing participants to protect against and bet on market price movements of currency and "baskets" of securities. Today, for instance, one can buy or sell index futures (e.g., one based on the Standard & Poor's 500), that is, buy or sell the value of that index for "delivery" at some future date. In contrast to most agricultural commodities futures, settlements of financial futures are settled in cash, rather than actual delivery of the underlying securities. This provides a useful tool for financial managers, especially those who want the returns associated with securities, but worry about the volatility of their portfolios. Futures make up the majority of the commodity trading, but the growth in financial futures, such as futures for equities or indexes of equities, has expanded greatly.

c. *Swaps*

Another type of derivative is a *swap*, which is a negotiated arrangement between two parties in which each promises to make a payment to the other, with the payments occurring at different times and determined under different formulas. The swap market is a vast, multi-trillion-dollar market that historically has been largely unregulated and dominated by corporations and financial institutions. Credit default swaps, discussed below, were at the heart of the liquidity crisis that roiled the financial markets in 2008 and led to the demise of a number of financial institutions due to their exposure to swaps.

The following description of one type of swap, the interest rate swap, offers a good illustration of how swaps may be structured.

> A swap is a contract between two parties, referred to as counterparties, to exchange a series of cash flows over time. A swap agreement specifies the currencies to be exchanged, rate of interest applicable, payment timetable, and ancillary issues bearing on the relationship between the counterparties. Swap payments are calculated on the basis of hypothetical quantities of the underlying asset referred to as "notionals." In most swaps other than currency swaps, the notional amount does not trade hands and is not at risk.
>
> Swaps are customized contracts and they are not traded on exchanges. The primary dealers in swaps are commercial banks. . . .
>
> The simplest interest rate swap, termed a *plain vanilla* swap, is a fixed-for-floating interest rate swap. In such a swap, one counterparty agrees to make fixed-rate payments to the other counterparty, who agrees to make floating payments in return. . . . In practice, rather than each counterparty paying its respective payment, only the differential between the counterparties' payments changes hands. That is, if the fixed-rate payment due is, say, $600,000 and the floating-rate payment $500,000, the fixed-rate payer pays $100,000 to the floating-rate payer.

Romano, A Thumbnail Sketch of Derivative Securities and Their Regulation, 55 Md. L. Rev. 1, 46-47 (1996).

As seen from the above description, swaps are essentially bilateral contracts in which the parties agree to exchange (swap) cash flows. The two cash flows are frequently referred to as the legs and the settlement between the parties is a netting of the two legs. Interest rate swaps dominate the OTC derivatives market. Interest rate swaps are contracts where the countervailing parties exchange periodic payments based on an interest rate. Thus, for example, in a simple interest rate swap, one party exchanges a fixed leg for a floating leg. For example, counterparty *A* promises to pay counterparty *B* a fixed interest payment on a set (notional) amount and in return counterparty *B* promises to pay counterparty *A* a floating interest payment on the same notional amount. The floating rate is identified in the contract and generally is the LIBOR rate. When the contract date arrives, the parties exchange the net difference in payments. Thus, if the floating rate goes up, *B* will owe *A*; whereas, if it goes down, *A* will owe *B*. Thus, interest rate swaps allow parties to synthetically switch debt with a floating interest rate to one with a fixed rate, and they also allow investors to bet on interest rates rising or falling.

A total return swap (TRS) is similar to an interest rate swap. With a TRS, the counterparties are each contracting around periodic cash flows, but unlike the standard swap where the legs are based on interest rates, with the TRS one leg or both legs will be based on changes in the value of a reference asset. For example, assume that counterparty *A* owns a bond issued by Company. Counterparty *A* could swap the bond with counterparty *B* in return for payments that counterparty *B* will make to *A* based on an interest rate (this could be fixed or floating) times the notional amount of the bond. Counterparty *A* will further agree to pay counterparty *B* an amount equal to the periodic payments paid on the bond as well as any changes in the value of the bond. As a result of this TRS, any decline in value of the bond reduces the sum that counterparty *A* is required to pay counterparty *B*. But, if the bond increases in value, counterparty *A*'s payments to counterparty *B* will increase. The consequence of the TRS is that it transfers from counterparty *A* both the credit risk (i.e., the risk that Company will default) and market risk (changing interest rates due to macroeconomic effects). That is, in the preceding example, counterparty *B* has the credit and market risk.

> Total return swaps are increasingly used as synthetic repo instruments, most commonly by investors who wish to purchase the credit exposure of an asset without purchasing the asset itself. This is similar to what happened when interest rate swaps were introduced, enabling banks and other financial institutions to trade interest rate risk without borrowing or lending cash funds. Banks usually enter into synthetic repos to remove assets from their balance sheets temporarily. The reason may be that they are due to be analyzed by credit-rating agencies, or their annual external audit is imminent, or they are in danger of breaching capital limits between quarterly return periods.

M. Choudhry, Fixed-Income Securities and Derivatives: Analysis and Valuation 207 (2010).

Credit default swaps (CDS) play an important risk-management role. In a CDS, the protection seller agrees to pay the protection buyer a set amount if a "credit event" occurs. For this protection, the protection buyer pays the protection seller a periodic fee. For example, if Bank *A* loans $50 million to Company, then Bank *A* has the risk that Company will default and be unable to repay the $50 million. To address this risk, Bank *A* can be a protection buyer by entering into a CDS with a protection seller, Bank *B*. The two banks will agree on an appropriate fee for the protection in the event Company (referred to as the "reference entity") defaults. Notice that as a result of the CDS, Bank *B* essentially assumes an insurance role, for which it is paid a premium. It is not uncommon that CDS agreements cover a bundle of reference entities. Indeed, CDS indices have developed with financial products, usually in the form of options, based on the indices so that these products are a popular means to gain exposure to and to hedge credit risks. Financial institutions dominate the CDS market. For discussions of credit default swaps, *see* Kim, From Vanilla Swaps to Exotic Credit Derivatives: How to Approach the Interpretation of Credit Events, 13 Fordham J. Corp. & Fin. L. 705 (2008).

The risks associated with the exposure of large financial firms to their obligations as counterparties under credit default swaps largely were ignored until made apparent with the liquidity crisis that destabilized the financial markets in 2008. The credit default swap is effective only if there is confidence in the ability of the counterparty to meet its obligations. When that confidence erodes, for good reason or for no reason at all, a firm with substantial counterparty obligations under credit default swaps may face severe stresses and even challenges to its survival.

Consider, for example, the position of American International Group, Inc. (AIG). Prior to Fall 2008, it was one of the world's largest and most highly regarded insurers and an active participant in the CDS market. Having underestimated its exposure on the $440 billion in credit swaps on which it was a counterparty, AIG found itself unable to meet demands against its capital as losses in its investment portfolio mounted, prompting demands that it post additional collateral that it did not have. AIG was saved from a sudden collapse into bankruptcy only by a U.S. government intervention in the form of a loan of $85 billion and an effective federal takeover of the company. AIG's survival through federal intervention contrasts with both the forced sale of Bear Stearns to J.P. Morgan Chase & Co. earlier in 2008 (under pressure from the Federal Reserve) and the subsequent fall of Lehman Brothers into bankruptcy.

The CDS market developed free of regulation and without transparency. The events of 2008, however, transformed the once-obscure CDS into a major focus of public attention. Responding to the turmoil, the SEC Chairman in testimony to the Senate Banking Committee described the CDS market as a "regulatory hole" that is ripe for manipulation. The congressional response in Dodd-Frank was to provide a regulatory framework by defining "security-based swaps" to include CDSs and thereby bring the instruments under the SEC's jurisdiction. The legislation also requires establishment of a clearing mechanism for CDSs, requires registration of swap dealers and major swap participants, and limits government bailouts of swap entities. *See* Bloink, Does the Dodd-Frank Wall Street Reform Act Rein in Credit Default Swaps? An EU Comparative Analysis, 89 Neb. L. Rev. 587 (2010).

3.   Clearing

Clearing agents have a central role in regulating risk in derivatives whether they be in the form of swaps or options or futures. Clearing agents limit the risk that the counterparty will default. Under such a clearing mechanism, a central organization, the clearing house, becomes a counterparty to each of the contract's participants. In this way, each of the original parties is exposed to the risk that the clearing organization will default, not the risk that the other counterparty will default. Clearing houses manage their own risks by requiring the parties to post collateral as margin and they "net" out some of their risks by entering into offsetting transactions and limiting their exposure to individual parties. Clearing houses thus become a central system for collecting information on derivatives trading. *See* Craig Pirrong, The Economics of Central Clearing: Theory and Practice (ISDA Discussion Paper May 2011).

The Dodd-Frank Wall Street Reform and Consumer Protection Act makes it unlawful to enter into a swap contract unless that contract is submitted to a clearing organization or is exempt. The exemption extends to users who are not financial entities, use swaps to hedge commercial risk, and who notify the Commodity Futures Trading Commission (CFTC) or SEC of how it will meet its financial obligations flowing from the swap. Thus, the focus of mandating clearing is on financial institutions. The Dodd-Frank Act also mandates that other *standardized* derivatives must occur through clearing agents.

The explosion in trading of derivatives instruments are a testament not to just the demand for managing and engaging risk, but also the creativeness of lawyers and market professionals. While we may well celebrate the ingenuity behind the ever-expanding range of financial products, they do pose a downside risk in that they compete with capital markets and thereby drain liquidity from equity markets. *See* Gilson & Whitehead, Deconstructing Equity: Public Ownership, Agency Costs, and Complete Capital Markets, 108 Colum. L. Rev. 231 (2008).

4.   The Regulation of Derivatives

In the United States, derivatives are not regulated in the same way as securities. This reflects the fact that for much of the last century derivatives focused almost exclusively on futures and forward contracts involving agriculture and commodities. *See* Romano, The Political Dynamics of Derivative Securities Regulation, 14 Yale J. Reg. 279 (1997). As derivatives moved from the agrarian plains to Wall Street, pressures for regulation mounted as derivatives increasingly became investor focused. The modern regulation of derivatives did not occur until 1974 with the creation of the CFTC. The CFTC is overseen by five commissioners appointed by the President who serve staggered five-year terms. Like the SEC, one of the commissioners serves as chair. In 2000, Congress passed the Commodity Futures Modernization Act to promote innovation in futures and derivatives. The promotion of innovation came largely in the form of a hands-off approach to a wide range of derivative products. Indeed, derivatives regulation can best be described as being principles, rather than rules, based and historically the CFTC has *not* had as strong an enforcement record as the SEC. Whereas much of the securities laws is focused on disclosures aimed at investors, disclosure is not at the heart of the CFTC's regulatory mandate. As will be seen, the focus of regulatory initiatives by the CFTC is instead on requirements for, and manners of operation engaged in by, various market professionals—intermediaries—that operate in derivative markets. Thus, exchanges, clearing agents and broker-dealers are the targets of the CFTC's regulatory provisions.

In the wake of the 2008 financial crisis, Congress enacted Dodd-Frank, which in multiple ways authorizes the CFTC and SEC to take steps to limit systemic risk that derivatives can cause the financial system. The Act dramatically changes the regulatory landscape for derivatives, particularly over-the-counter derivatives and certain types of swaps.

Title VII of Dodd-Frank mandates the CFTC and SEC regulate "swaps" and "security-based swaps." A transaction involving either a swap or a security-based swap, as a result of post Dodd-Frank rules, is subject to clearing, trading, and reporting requirements. The Act does offer certain exemptions based on the nature of the parties themselves as well as the purpose of the trade. An additional consideration is the so-called Volcker Rule that requires that systemically significant financial institutions transfer their swap trading to a separately capitalized affiliate (this does not apply, however, if the CDS is centrally cleared).

a.   Swaps and Security-Based Swaps Defined

A major impetus of Dodd-Frank is expanded regulation of certain derivatives by the SEC and CFTC, and most particularly swaps. Prior to Dodd-Frank, most derivatives were regulated by the CFTC. The major exceptions to this statement were that the SEC had jurisdiction over options on securities and shared jurisdiction with the CFTC over any "basket" of securities that is not broadly based (a term discussed later). Dodd-Frank now provides that security-based swaps will be regulated by the SEC, that regulation will be shared by the SEC and CFTC when a swap involves a security and some other form of asset, and that all other swaps are regulated by the CFTC.

As is true with so much of financial regulation, the linchpin for regulating swaps is to be found in the definitions. Under the definitions adopted jointly by the CFTC and SEC (*see* Securities Act Release No. 9338 (July 18, 2012)), the term *swap* typically includes a derivative product referencing instruments (other than a single security, a single loan, or narrowly based index), such as those linked to interest rates, commodities prices, or foreign exchange rates. The CFTC generally has jurisdiction over swaps, although the SEC has some antifraud authority with respect to swaps. *See* Section 3(a)(68) of the Exchange Act (defining security-based swaps) and Section 3(a)(69) (defining swaps). *See also* Securities Act Rule 194 (adopting Exchange Act definitions of swap and security-based swap) and Exchange Act Rule 3a69-1 (same).

The term *security-based swap* refers to a derivative (such as a CDS) that references a single security, a single loan, or a narrowly based *security* index. The SEC has jurisdiction over security-based swaps.

The definition of a "narrowly based securities index" is multi-factored, and has some complexities; generally such an index is one that is made up of less than ten component securities, an index where one component security comprises more than 30 percent of the total index, or the five highest-weighted component securities comprise more than 60 percent of the index's total weighting. *See* Exchange Act Rules 3a68-1b.

Dodd-Frank provides a few important exclusions from the otherwise broad definitions for swaps and security-based swaps. First, excluded from the swap and security-based swap definitions are options, certificates of deposit, and indexes of securities that are subject to the '33 Act or the '34 Act. Second, swaps do not include a sale of a nonfinancial commodity, e.g., corn or copper, for deferred shipment or delivery, provided the transaction is to be physically settled (i.e., the classic forward contract). Similarly excluded are contracts that involve the sale (contingent or otherwise) of a security for which physical delivery will occur in the future. And, third, the Secretary of Treasury has the authority to exempt foreign exchange swaps, which make up a significant portion of the swap market.

b.   *Overview of Regulation of Swap Transactions and Their Participants*

The significance of the definitions for swap and security-based swap is that they lead to regulation of transactions and their participants in such products. Dodd-Frank amends the CFTA and Exchange Act to include definitions for "swap dealers" and "major swap participants" who are required to register with the CFTC; security-based swap dealers and major security-based swap participants must register with the SEC. Each of the agencies has adopted rules pursuant to Dodd-Frank to implement these requirements. *See* CFTC Rule 1.3 (ggg); SEC Exchange Act Rule 3a67. Those who are subject to the definition must clear swaps through a clearing agent or execute the trade through an exchange, as well satisfy certain capital, margin, reporting, and business conduct requirements with respect to their swap and security-based swap transactions.

In broad overview, a swap dealer/security-based swap dealer is one who (1) holds himself out as a dealer in swaps/security-based swaps, (2) makes a market in swaps/security-based swaps, (3) regularly in the ordinary course of business enters into swaps/security-based swaps with counterparties, or (4) engages in activities such that it is known in the trade as a dealer or market maker in swaps/security-based swaps. Importantly, the *de minimis* exception excludes dealers whose dealings do not exceed $8 billion; consequently there are less than 200 potential swap dealers in the mega-trillion-dollar swap market. A major swap participant and major security-based swap participant is one who (1) maintains a substantial position in swaps (substantial position is variously defined in the rule but the core definition is met if the entity's exposure exceeds $1 billion for any swap category); (2) has an outstanding swap position that creates a substantial counterparty exposure (the basic trigger for meeting the "substantial" test is when the average daily uncollateralized exposure is $5 billion or more); *or* (3) is a financial entity that is highly leveraged relative to its capital and that is subject to federally imposed banking requirements. The rules contain some technical safe harbors with a common theme that the amount and nature of the exposure pose limited threats to the financial system. An important exemption is the so-called end-user exception, which eases the burden of businesses using swaps to reduce or manage risk related to their commercial activities. An example of the end-user exception would be airlines that trade futures as a hedge against rising fuel prices. Even with such an exception, Dodd-Frank imposes reporting requirements for all swaps. Swap trading information is required to be reported to a registered swap data repository, the CFTC, or the SEC.

In 2016, the SEC adopted business conduct rules for swap dealers. The rules, among numerous other demands, require swap dealers to verify that counterparties are eligible contract participants, that any recommendation is suitable for the client, and that there is disclosure to the counterparty of material information bearing on the swap, such as risks, incentives, and conflicts of interest the dealer has. Exchange Act Release No. 77617 (Apr. 13, 2016).

Swap markets are truly international, with dealers regularly engaged in cross-border transactions. In 2016, applying a territorial approach, the SEC addressed the ticklish question of Dodd-Frank's reach to non-U.S. firms. The rule is deeply complicated, but its thrust requires non-U.S. firms that arrange, negotiate, or execute security-based swaps using personnel located in the United States to include such security-based swaps in the calculation of whether they have exceeded the *de minimis* level, referenced above; if they do exceed that level, they must register with the SEC. Arranging and negotiating at least includes interactions with counterparties and their agents; executing refers to engagement that causes one to become bound with a particular transaction. Why would the rule be written so that when a trader in Deutsche Bank's New York office arranges with HSBC London's office a swap focused on Siemens, the transaction would be included in assessing Deutsche Bank's calculations per the *de minimis* standard?

5. The Volcker Rule

The 2008 financial crisis was fueled significantly by commercial banks directing significant sums of cash into speculative trading in a variety of financial products for their own accounts. Indeed, many believe the seeds of the financial crisis were sown in 1999 with the Graham-Leach-Bliley Act's repeal of the Glass-Steagall Act, which was enacted in the Great Depression and mandated a separation among commercial banking, investment banking, and insurance. With the disappearance of Glass-Steagall, universal banking arose, whereby multiple financial activities were conducted within a single financial institution. Post 1999, banks increased in size, and an even more rapid increase occurred with respect to their deep engagement in speculative trading for their own accounts. Thus, concerns arose that financial institutions that held deposits of their banking customers placed those deposits at risk. The Volcker Rule, believed by many to be not only the most complex but also the most contentious of the many provisions of Dodd-Frank, was enacted to address concerns flowing from banks engaged in proprietary trading.

The Volcker Rule consists of two broad prohibitions, each of which applies only to "banking entities."

1. A banking entity may not sponsor or acquire an interest in a "covered fund."
2. A banking entity may not engage in "proprietary trading."

In broad overview, a banking entity is an insured depository institution, and the definition extends to any company that controls an insured depository institution or is itself an affiliate of either an insured depository institution or its control person.

Scope. The meaning of "covered fund" begins with the Investment Company Act of 1940. A covered fund is an entity that otherwise falls within that Act as an investment company, but is exempt under either Section 3(c)(1) (i.e., the number of investors in the fund do not exceed 100) or Section 3(c) (7) (all fund investors are "qualified purchasers"). Correlatively, a fund that registers as an investment company under the Investment Company Act is exempt from the Volcker Rule. As defined, any transaction in which a banking entity is involved that is using a privately offered entity that itself is relying on an Investment Company Act exemption will be a covered fund; this means the Volcker Rule reaches those funds commonly known as hedge funds and private equity funds. Also included are "foreign funds," a designation that refers to an entity organized outside the United States that offers interests in the United States in reliance on either Section 3(c)(1) or (3)(c)(7); the scope of foreign bank is broader in the case of a U.S. organized or located banking entity, as there is no requirement that interests be offered to investors in the United States, or of any reliance on either of the two Investment Company Act exemptions. A final component of a covered fund is a commodity pool, which depends on the definitions of commodity pool and commodity pool operator rules of the Commodity Futures Trading Commission.

As stated earlier, the first Volcker Rule prohibition is that of "sponsoring" a covered fund. Sponsorship is broadly defined and includes controlling the covered fund (e.g., selecting or having influence over a majority of its directors, trustees, or managers); being its general partner, manager, or trustee; or even sharing its name (or some variant) with the fund for marketing purposes. One is not a sponsor, however, by providing investment advisory services to the covered fund.

The Volcker Rule also prohibits a banking entity from having an "ownership interest" in a covered fund. Such an interest extends beyond a typical proprietary interest such as a partnership and includes "other similar interests" such as the right to participate in the selection of the fund manager; the right to share in the fund's income (however, the "carried interest" that fund advisers receive as compensation for profitable performance does not itself constitute an ownership interest); or the right to a residual interest in fund assets upon the fund's liquidation, or to obtain a return based on fund performance.

Exclusions.   There is, however, subject to numerous qualifications, a *de minimis* exception that allows a banking entity to have an ownership interest in a covered fund of not more than 3 percent of the total ownership interest in a single fund. An important exception to being a covered fund exists in the case of asset-backed securities; the Volcker Rule allows banking entities to sponsor or acquire an ownership interest in a covered fund that holds asset-backed securities comprised of loans, leases, receivables, and certain high-quality, highly liquid short-term investments. This exception thus allows banking entities to securitize their commercial and residential loans through CLOs and CDOs, respectively. A word of caution with this exception, and more broadly to the broad overview of a regulation that extends hundreds of pages in length: The exception established for CLOs and CDOs is very intricate and detailed, reflecting that under Dodd-Frank and even its final regulations, the various administrative agencies enjoy a significant amount of discretion as to the meaning of their intricate exceptions.

As seen, the Volcker Rule prohibits banking entities from acting as a principal in any transaction to purchase or sell any security, derivative, or future, or option on any security, derivative, or future for the purpose of short-term resale. The rule sets forth metrics that if complied with provide a rebuttable presumption that a transaction constitutes prohibited proprietary trading. Major exceptions to the bar of proprietary trading are market making, trading in U.S. government obligations, underwriting, hedging, and trading on behalf of customers. But each has its own technical qualifications.

To qualify for the market making exception the entity must hold itself out as willing to buy and sell positions in the particularly covered security, derivative, or future; that positions taken are not to exceed the near-term demands of customers or counterparties; and that the revenue the banking entity derives is primarily from commissions, including gains from bid/ask spreads. Most importantly, reliance on this exemption calls for active compliance efforts on the part of the bank.

Another important exemption is hedging transactions. To qualify for this exemption, the trade must hedge an existing position or positions, including a portfolio. To be a hedge, the trade must be reasonably correlated to the risk intended to be hedged and subject to regular compliance review to assure written policies with respect to hedging are satisfied.

Monitoring.   The Volcker Rule imposes monthly reporting of certain metrics to regulators with respect to market making, hedging, underwriting, and trading in U.S. government securities. As we have seen, the Volcker Rule imposes on banking entities substantial new obligations with respect to maintaining active compliance obligations, including independent testing of compliance.

C.   Structured Financial Products

Structured financial products and derivative contracts share common features. Each is complex and often non-standard. And, the value of each depends on the value of an underlying asset. On the other hand, derivatives are contracts that are separate from the underlying item whereas structured financial products are interests in a securitized item.

1.   An Overview of Securitization

Securitization is the transfer of illiquid debt into tradable securities. This process can take many forms. Any number of assets can be securitized. Most commonly, securitization involves home mortgages, car loans, credit card obligations, student loans, and even leases. Nearly any group of assets that yield a predictable cash stream can be securitized. To be sure, any third-party obligation to pay money poses risks of payment delay or payment default. Bundled together, such risks become a statistic around which investor assessment can occur.

The process of securitization begins with the *originator* gathering the assets to be securitized with the goal to create a portfolio of receivables that will be diversified enough to protect investors against some defaulting obligors on the debts being bundled together. The originator transfers the receivables to a separate entity known as a special purpose vehicle (SPV)—this entity is sometimes also referred to as a special purpose entity or special purpose corporation. Although organized by the originator, the SPV is a separate legal entity. The SPV pays for the assets transferred to it by issuing its own notes to investors whose return depends on the aggregate cash flow generated by the receivables held by the SPV. These notes are generally referred to as asset-backed securities—the reference is due to the notes being backed by the cash flow from the receivables transferred into the SPV. Real estate–related asset-backed securities are known as "mortgage-backed securities" or MBS. Because the SPV is legally isolated from the originator—it is a distinct legal entity—the risks involved with the SPV are limited to the assets securitized. It is the risks of those receivables and not the risks of the originator's business that are of interest to investors in the securities issued by the SPV. For example, a bank may bundle hundreds, even thousands, of 30-year mortgages and upon their transfer through an intermediary ("sponsor" or "aggregator") to an SPV receive cash the SPV derives by selling interests in itself. The bank can then use the cash received to lend to other customers, thus generating income through origination fees. Without securitization, the bank would face the likelihood of holding the mortgages until maturity, 30 years in the example, with only the cash received from periodic mortgage payments to relend. The process of securitization allows the lender, e.g., a bank, to transform future payments into instant cash. Securitization thus greatly liberates the bank and facilitates the extension of credit. Because there are non-trivial administrative costs related to the SPV operation, e.g., the collection of the cash flow from the receivables, distribution of the cash flow to the various holders of the SPV notes, and record keeping for both receipts and distributions, it is customary for the total assets for SPVs to be $100 million or more, i.e., economies of scale are not just important, but essential.

The SPV may issue "pass through" securities where investors take the risks and receive the benefits based on their share of the entire SPV. This would mean that all investors in the SPV hold the same type of security and therefore enjoy the same rights, privileges, and preferences of ownership. In contrast, the SPV issues multiple classes of security, with at least one senior class of debt being rated investment grade and one or more junior classes of debt. In addition, the SPV may issue equity. See Figure 10-1 below. The debt takes the form of notes. Each class of security is referred to as a tranche; the most senior tranche enjoying the most security, for example a prior right to payment of cash flows over the most junior tranche. Colloquially, the relative priorities to payment enjoyed among the tranches is referred to as the "waterfall," referring to those higher up in the priority chain enjoying the right to "draw" from the flow of cash before what is left drips down to lower tranches. The lowest tranche hopes there are a few drips remaining from the waterfall. The originator frequently is the holder of the lowest tranche. Note also that the originator is most frequently the underwriter for the note offering. The expression "collateralized debt obligation" (CDO) generally refers to ABSs with multiple tranches.

The sponsor/aggregator may resort to multiple devices to reduce the overall risk of the portfolio. The first line of defense is having multiple obligors on the receivables that are bundled together. Such bundling diversifies credit risk across the multiple obligors. However, as the 2008 financial crisis illustrated, if the economy as a whole, and the housing market in particular, sinks into the abyss, the risk is systemic with the result of greatly reducing the value of *all* receivables in the SPV. The originator may also seek some form of credit enhancer such as letters of credit from banks, surety bonds issued by so-called monoline insurance companies, and even a credit default swap on the portfolio. For example, many financial institutions face restrictions on the quality of assets they can invest; credit ratings, if high enough, enable the financial institution to invest in the securitized assets. Figure 10-1 illustrates the components of a securitized offering with four distinct tranches.

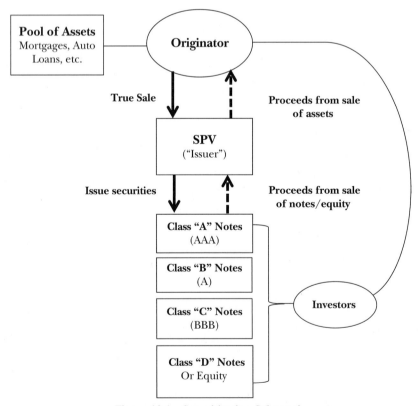

Figure 10-1   Securitization Schematic

2.   Public Offerings of Securitized Products: Residential Mortgage-Backed Securities

In the three years preceding the financial crisis, $3 trillion worth of private-labeled securitization securities (PLS) backed by residential mortgages were publicly sold (about 8 percent being purchased by Federal National Mortgage Association (Fannie Mae) and Federal Home Loan Mortgage Corporation (Freddie Mac)). The following decision arose from complaints that the offering materials used to sell PLS to both entities were misleading so that their sellers were liable under Section 12(a)(2) of the Securities Act. As you read the following excerpt that describes the steps involved in underwriting the public offering of residential mortgage asset-backed securities (RMBS), consider the disclosure requirements for such offerings that are summarized in the note that follows.

Federal Housing Finance Agency for Federal National Mortgage Ass'n v. Nomura Holding America, Inc.
873 F.3d 85 (2d Cir. 2017)

A.   The PLS Securitization Process

1.   Originating a Mortgage Loan Using Underwriting Guidelines

The first step in the PLS process was the issuance of residential mortgage loans. Mortgage loans were issued to borrowers by entities known as originators. Originators issued loans according to their loan underwriting guidelines, which listed the criteria used to approve a loan. . . . These guidelines helped each originator assess the borrower's ability to repay the loan and the value of the collateral. . . .

Following the underwriting guidelines, originators required each prospective borrower to complete a loan application, usually on the Uniform Residential Loan Application (the "URLA"). The URLA required borrowers to disclose, under penalty of civil liability or criminal prosecution, their income, employment, housing history, assets, liabilities, intended occupancy status for the property, and the sources of the funds they intended to use in paying the costs of closing the loan. Originators used this information to determine objective factors relevant to the borrower's credit risk, such as a credit score according to the Fair Isaac Corporation's model (a "FICO score"), credit history, and debt-to-income ratio. Once each borrower submitted the URLA, the originator kept it and other related documentation in the borrower's loan file.

The underwriting guidelines required originators to assess the reasonableness of the borrower's assertions on the URLA. This was easiest when borrowers supported their URLA applications with corroborating documentation. Some applications required verification of both the borrower's assets and income, while some required verification only of the borrower's assets. Other borrowers submitted stated-income-stated-assets ("SISA") applications, which did not require verification of income or assets, or no-income-no-assets ("NINA") applications, which were complete without the borrower even stating his or her income or assets. SISA and NINA applications were more difficult to assess, but not categorically ineligible to receive loans.

The underwriting guidelines generally permitted originators to accept SISA and NINA applications and to make other exceptions to the underwriting criteria if there were compensating factors that indicated the borrower's ability and willingness to repay the loan. The guidelines set forth the specific conditions under which exceptions would be permitted. Originators were required to mark the borrower's loan file whenever an exception to the underwriting criteria had been granted and to explain the basis for that decision.

After forming an opinion about a borrower's creditworthiness based on the URLA and related documentation, originators assigned the transaction a credit risk designation, which affected the interest rate for the loan. When an applicant had good credit, the transaction was labeled "prime." When an applicant had materially impaired credit, the transaction was labeled "subprime." And when an applicant's credit fell between good and materially impaired, the transaction was labeled "Alt-A." . . .

Once they had assessed the borrower's credit, originators balanced that assessment against the value of the collateral (*i.e.*, the present market value of the residence the borrower wanted to purchase or refinance), as determined by an appraiser, to measure the overall credit risk of the loan. Originators compared the amount of the loan against the value of the collateral to develop a loan-to-value ratio, a key indicator of credit risk. It was common in the RMBS industry to use a loan-to-value ratio of 80% as a benchmark. Relative to loans at that ratio, a loan worth between 80% and 90% of the collateral value was 1.5 times more likely to default and a loan worth between 95% and 100% of the collateral value was 4.5 times more likely to default. . . .

If the originator was comfortable with the overall credit risk after reviewing the buyer's creditworthiness, the value of the collateral, and the loan-to-value ratio, the loan would be approved.

The underwriting guidelines and loan files were crucial throughout and beyond the origination process. Supervisors employed by the originators could check loan files against the underwriting guidelines to ensure that loan issuance decisions met important criteria. . . . After the loan issued, originators used the information in the loan file to describe the loan characteristics for financial institutions interested in purchasing it.

2.   CREATING A PLS

The next step in the PLS process was the aggregation and securitization of the residential mortgage loans into an RMBS. Originators compiled their issued loans into "trade pools" and then solicited bids from PLS "sponsors" or "aggregators" to purchase them. The originators provided prospective bidders with a "loan tape" for each pool—"a spreadsheet that provided data about the characteristics of each loan in the trade pool" including "loan type (fixed or adjustable rate), . . . original and unpaid principal balance, amortization term, borrower's FICO score, the mortgaged property's purchase price and/or appraised value, occupancy status, documentation type and any prepayment penalty-related information." . . .

The sponsor that prevailed in the bidding process was given access to a limited number of loan files to conduct a due diligence review of the originators' underwriting and valuation processes before final settlement. The sponsor was entitled prior to closing to remove from the trade pool any loans that did not meet its purchasing requirements, such as those below a minimum FICO score or exceeding a maximum debt-to-income ratio. Upon closing, the prevailing sponsor acquired title to the loans in the trade pools and gained access to the complete set of loan files. The prevailing sponsor was also given a copy of the underwriting guidelines the originators used to issue the loans.

The sponsor then sold the loans to a "depositor," a special purpose vehicle created solely to facilitate PLS transactions. The true sale from sponsor to depositor was intended to protect the future PLS certificate-holders' interests in the loans in the event that the sponsor declared bankruptcy. It was common in the RMBS industry for the depositor and sponsor entities to act at the direction of the same corporate parent.

The depositor then grouped the loans into supporting loan groups ("SLGs") and transferred each group of loans to a trust. In exchange, the trust issued the depositor certificates that represented the right to receive principal and interest payments from the SLGs. The trustee managed the loans for the benefit of the certificate holders, often hiring a mortgage loan servicing vendor to manage the loans on a day-to-day basis. The depositor then sold most of the certificates to a lead underwriter, who would shepherd them to the public securities markets; a few certificates remained under the ownership of the depositor. It was also common in the industry for the lead underwriter to be controlled by the same corporate parent that controlled the sponsor and depositor.

3. PREPARING A PLS FOR PUBLIC SALE

The final steps in the PLS process were the preparation and sale to the public of the certificates. The lead underwriter, sponsor, and depositor (collectively, "PLS sellers") worked together to structure the securitization, to solicit credit ratings for the certificates principally from three major credit-rating agencies, Moody's Investors Service, Inc. ("Moody's"), Standard & Poor's ("S & P"), and Fitch Ratings ("Fitch") (collectively, the "Credit-Rating Agencies" or "Rating Agencies"), and to draft and confirm the accuracy of the offering documents. Once those tasks were completed, the lead underwriter would market the certificates to potential buyers.

The PLS sellers structured securitizations with two credit enhancements that distributed the risk of the loans unequally among the certificate holders. The first was subordination. The PLS certificates were organized into tranches, ranked by seniority. Each SLG supported one or more tranches of certificates and distributed payments in a "waterfall" arrangement. This arrangement guaranteed senior certificate-holders first claim to all principal and interest payments. Once all the senior certificate-holders were satisfied, the SLGs' payments spilled over to junior certificate-holders, who would receive the remaining balance of the payments.

The second of these credit enhancements was overcollateralization. The total outstanding balance of all of the mortgage loans supporting an entire PLS often exceeded the outstanding balance of the loans supporting the publicly available PLS certificates. As a result, some loans in the PLS were tethered to certificates owned by the depositor or sponsor and were not available for public purchase. These non-public loans served as a loss-saving measure by making payments to the public certificate-holders (in order of seniority) in the event that the loans supporting their public certificates defaulted.

After structuring the PLS, the PLS sellers would solicit a credit rating for each tranche. . . .

The Rating Agencies' review included examining draft offering documents for representations that the supporting loans were originated in accordance with originators' underwriting criteria. . . .

The PLS sellers explained these credit enhancements, credit ratings, and other important features of the PLS to the public primarily in three offering documents—a shelf registration, a free writing prospectus, and a prospectus supplement. The shelf registration was a pre-approved registration statement filed with the Securities and Exchange Commission (the "SEC") that contained generally applicable information about PLS. *See* 17 C.F.R. §§230.409, 230.415. The shelf registration enabled the lead PLS underwriter to make written offers to potential buyers using a free writing prospectus. *See* id. §230.433(b)(1). The free writing prospectus broadly described the characteristics of the certificate and the supporting SLGs. If an offeree was interested after reading the description, it could commit to purchasing the certificate. Title in the certificate and payment were exchanged within approximately a month of that commitment. The PLS sellers sent the buyer a prospectus supplement and filed the same with the SEC near the date of that exchange.

The prospectus supplement contained the most detailed disclosures of any of the offering documents. This document provided specific information regarding the certificate, the SLGs, and the credit quality of the underlying loans. It warranted the accuracy of its representations regarding loan characteristics. And, crucially, it affirmed that the loans in the SLGs were originated in accordance with the applicable underwriting guidelines. As the District Court noted, "whether loans were actually underwritten in compliance with guidelines was extremely significant to investors." . . . The prospectus supplement ordinarily disclosed that some number of loans in the SLG may deviate substantially from, or violate, the applicable underwriting guidelines.

NOTES AND QUESTIONS

1. Regulation AB. Regulation AB provides a comprehensive regime for the registration, disclosure, reporting, and communications with respect to public offerings of asset-backed securities. Responding to multiple issues that contributed to the collapse of the market for asset-backed securities in 2008 and the ensuing financial crisis, the SEC in 2014 substantially revised Regulation AB. SEC Securities Act Release No. 9638 (August 2014). The new rules apply to public offerings of ABS backed by residential mortgages, commercial mortgages, auto loans and leases, and debt securities. The new rules do not apply to exempt offerings, such as those carried out pursuant to Rule 144A, discussed in Chapter 6. New Regulation AB requires issuers to provide an expanded amount of standardized asset-level data to be provided in both prospectuses and periodic reports. These disclosures occur pursuant to Forms SF-1 and SF-3 (something of a parallel to Forms S-1 and S-3). Most ABS public offerings are shelf offerings and prior to the 2014 revision they occurred on Form S-3, which was available provided the ABS was rated "investment grade." The new rule abandons ratings as the gateway for ABS shelf offerings and limits ABS shelf offerings to Form SF-3. It creates conditions for eligibility to use Form SF-3:

—The issuer's CEO must certify that the CEO is familiar with certain factors about the offering and ABS, such as the prospectus, assets involved, structure of the offering, and material transaction documents, as well as state that the CEO has a reasonable basis to conclude the securitization is structured to produce cash flows in amounts sufficient to service scheduled payments;

—The transaction must provide for the appointment of an "asset representations reviewer" who will conduct a review of compliance representations and any warranties made with respect to the pool of assets; and

—The transaction documents must include a dispute resolution mechanism as well as a mechanism to accommodate requests by investors to communicate with other investors.

An important feature of new Regulation AB is the introduction of "speed bumps" in the offering process. For example, a preliminary prospectus must be filed with the SEC at least three business days prior to the first sale of any security in the offering; the SEC otherwise does not require such a filing prior to sales from the shelf. The intent of this change is to provide investors with additional time to assess the assets underlying the offering. And, any material change to the preliminary prospectus must be reflected in that prospectus 48 hours prior to the first sale.

Regulation AB now requires extensive data (asset-level "data points") regarding the underlying assets so that investors can assess the credit quality of the assets. These disclosures are to be made in a machine-readable format (e.g., XML) so that the information can be downloaded for analysis. Among the required asset-level data points to be provided are information bearing on the payment stream of underlying assets, such as contractual terms, payment schedule, interest rate calculations, and whether payments are scheduled to change over time; collateral supporting asset; geography of debtor and collateral; valuation of collateral; loan-to-value ratios; loss mitigation arrangements; and the extent of verification of debtors' income and employment status. Aside from enhanced disclosure focused on the underlying assets, Regulation AB requires extensive disclosure of those involved in the offering and their various undertakings, such as any power to modify the composition of the underlying assets or any agreement to repurchase underlying assets, as well as how similar pools (called "static pools") of assets by the ABS' sponsors have performed.

2.   Some Common Exemptions.   Registration can be avoided, of course, if the offering qualifies for one of the exemptions discussed earlier in Chapter 5. Because institutional investors and hedge funds make up a large part of the ABS market, it is not difficult to locate the offering safely within the private placement/Rule 506 exemption. Moreover, since these investors are most definitely QIBs, syndication of the ABS offering via Rule 144A using PORTAL is also available.

3.   Risk Retention.   A controversial provision Section 15G of the Exchange Act that requires securitizers/originators of asset-backed securities to retain at least 5 percent of the credit risk of the assets transferred, sold, or conveyed. The percentage can be less than 5 percent if underwriting due diligence meets high underwriting standards specific to the class of securitized assets. The risk retained is not allowed to be hedged. *See* Credit Risk Retention, Exchange Act Release No. 73407 (Oct. 22, 2014) (adopting risk retention rules with exemption where collateral is qualified residential mortgages and allowing risk 5 percent requirement to be met by placing that amount with one who can recover from securitizer/originator for losses suffered).

4.   Alchemy or Illusion.   Notice how the multiple tranches of securities issued by the SPV also affect risk. In the example in Figure 10-1, the Class A notes enjoy a higher rating not because they are labeled Class A but because of the priority to payment they enjoy over the lower three tranches. That is, their position on the waterfall makes it more likely the holders of Class A notes will be paid. The securitization example in Figure 10-1 reflects the range of ratings with AAA being investment grade. But, the cardinal rule of finance, "high risk, high return" suggests why investors may be attracted to the BBB-rated security in the example. Nonetheless, a lot can go wrong in a dynamic economy so investors may avoid the temptations of higher returns provided by lower rated securities. The following describes Wall Street's solution to marketing the lower rated tranches.

> Wall Street came up with a solution: in the words of one banker, they "created the investor." That is, they built new securities that would buy the tranches that had become harder to sell. Bankers would take those low investment-grade tranches, largely rated BBB or A, from many mortgage-backed securities and repackage them into the new securities—CDOs. Approximately 80% of these CDO tranches would be rated Triple-A despite the fact that they generally comprised the lower-rated tranches of mortgage-backed securities. CDO securities would be sold with their own waterfalls, with the risk-averse investors, again, paid first and the risk-seeking investors paid last. As they did in the case of mortgage-backed securities, the rating agencies gave their highest, triple-A, ratings to the securities at the top. . . .
>
> The securities firms argued—and the rating agencies agreed—that if they pooled many BBB rated mortgage-backed securities, they would create additional diversification benefits. The rating agencies believed that those diversification benefits were significant—that if one security went bad, the second had only a very small chance of going bad at the same time. And as long as losses were limited, only those investors at the bottom would lose money. They would absorb the blow, and the other investors would continue to get paid.
>
> Relying on that logic, the CDO machine gobbled up the BBB and other lower-rated tranches of mortgage-backed securities, growing from a bit player to a multi-hundred billion-dollar industry. Between 2003 and 2007, as house prices rose 27% nationally and $4 trillion in mortgage-backed securities were created, Wall Street issued nearly $700 billion in CDOs that included mortgage-backed securities as

collateral. With ready buyers for their own product, mortgage securitizers continued to demand loans for their pools, and hundreds of billions of dollars flooded the mortgage world. In effect, the CDO became the engine that powered the mortgage supply chain.

But when the housing market went south, the models on which CDOs were based proved tragically wrong. The mortgage-backed securities turned out to be highly correlated—meaning they performed similarly. Across the country, in regions where subprime and Alt-A mortgages were heavily concentrated, borrowers would default in large numbers. This was not how it was supposed to work. Losses in one region were supposed to be offset by successful loans in another region. In the end, CDOs turned out to be some of the most ill-fated assets in the financial crisis.

The Financial Crisis Inquiry Commission, The Financial Crisis Inquiry Report 127-129 (2011).

    5. *Beyond Disclosure?* As a final observation to the material in this chapter, recall that when the architecture of the securities laws was created, securities were predominantly stocks and bonds. These instruments remain important, but financial innovation has spawned a range of highly complex financial products each of which falls easily into the definition of a security. We might ponder whether their complexity calls for an approach other than the historical disclosure-oriented approach in light of the fact that many financial products pose complexities that are difficult to communicate and understand. *See generally* Hu, Too Complex to Depict? Innovation, "Pure Information," and the SEC Disclosure Paradigm, 90 Tex. L. Rev. 1601 (2012).

||11||
Financial Reporting: Mechanisms, Duties, and Culture

Earlier chapters examined the disclosure requirements of the Securities Act for issuer transactions. There we found that disclosure is triggered by the public offering of securities and that many exemptions from registration with the SEC are themselves conditioned on certain disclosures being made. Since raising capital by issuing securities is a very significant event in any firm's life, the disclosure compelled by the Securities Act can be seen as being *episodic*. In this chapter, we closely examine the *periodic* disclosure requirements of the Exchange Act, most notably the obligation of certain public companies to file quarterly and annual reports with the SEC. Materiality plays a central role in this area; a full inquiry into the scope and meaning of materiality follows in Chapter 12. The focus in this chapter is on important disclosure mechanisms provided by the Exchange Act and regulatory steps designed to enhance the quality of mandated disclosures.

We begin this examination by learning a bit about the origins of financial information and the important contributions of generally accepted accounting principles (GAAP) as well as the independent auditors in facilitating ownership by outside investors. As we will see, investors depend on the independent auditors to attest that the financial statements have been prepared in accordance with GAAP. There is an even more fundamental requirement of financial reporting—that the reports are accurate and honest. Central to this expectation is the requirement that public companies maintain reliable and trustworthy accounting records; as will be seen, this is an objective of the books and records requirements of the Foreign Corrupt Practices Act. But mere satisfaction of the technical metrics of GAAP or other disclosure rules is not the sole objective. An overarching disclosure requirement is that the information the firm releases to the public do more than comply technically with applicable reporting metrics; the report must also "fairly present" its financial position and operations. The meaning of this requirement is examined in the materials that follow. In response to the parade of financial and accounting scandals that have rocked financial markets in the earliest years of this century, multiple steps have been taken recently by the Congress, the SEC, and the exchanges to strengthen corporate governance for public companies with an emphasis on preventing financial frauds by strengthening the financial reporting process. Among the developments examined here are developments for the audit committee, officer certifications of reports filed with the SEC, and the treatment of *pro forma* financial reports.

As will be seen, a key component of disclosures mandated by the SEC is the Management Discussion and Analysis (MD&A) portion of a firm's registration statement and its periodic reports that are filed with it. The MD&A calls for narrative explanations of the financial statements for the purpose of increasing the transparency of a company's financial performance and providing overall better disclosure to investors. The precise demands of the MD&A are examined below. Later chapters examine the duty to disclose that arises under the antifraud provisions, where we find there are disclosure obligations that arise independently of the periodic disclosure requirements.

A.   *The Disclosure Requirements of Public Companies*

1.   The Origins and Metrics for Financial Information

Investors and shareholders are each interested in how a company is performing financially. They extrapolate from this information judgments regarding the company's future prospects. Their judgments regarding the firm's future are central to the investors' decision whether to purchase or sell a company's securities and whether to reward or terminate managers, each decision depending on just how positive or negative the information is regarding the company's prospects. Much of the information related to a company's financial position and performance, as well as its future prospects, is accounting-based information. Accounting is commonly referred to as the "language of business" because it is a highly refined system for measuring such items as the firm's assets, liabilities, revenues, expenses, and the equity held by the firm's owners. As is true with any language, expressions such as "asset" or "liability" have commonly understood meanings. The metrics that define such accounting-based expressions are collectively referred to as generally accepted accounting principles, or more commonly, GAAP.

Financial information is not relevant solely for outsiders, such as investors or shareholders. The firm's managers depend on financial information produced by the firm's accounting systems to guide them in their stewardship. Knowledge of rising expenses related to the manufacture of one product or increasing sales for another have significance because these are items whose meaning is found in GAAP. That is, whether a particular business transaction gives rise to an expense, or a sale, or neither, is determined according to a complex body of rules and customs that collectively form GAAP.

Although the Commission has the authority to prescribe accounting principles that will apply to financial information filed with it, the Commission with rare exception defers to the private sector's formulation of GAAP. The supreme authority over accounting standards in the private sector is the Financial Accounting Standards Board (FASB). Where there is not an express statement or interpretation issued by the FASB, then GAAP is also established by pronouncements of the American Institute of Certified Public Accountants, the accounting industry's trade group, as well as conventions and practices commonly followed by companies. Prior to 2002, the FASB was funded largely by donations from the major accounting firms; this financial dependence on the munificence of the large accounting firms unfortunately provided the accounting firms' audit clients some leverage over the content of GAAP because the clients sometimes prevailed upon their auditors to lobby the FASB for favorable accounting metrics. Now, as a result of the Sarbanes-Oxley Act of 2002, the FASB is funded from fees that reporting companies and registered investment companies pay in connection with their registration with the SEC.

The company's financial statements report on the firm's financial position and its recent performance. Financial statements also serve as a report card of the firm's managers. This poses a special problem for financial reporting because the officers of the firm in the first instance have operational control of the company's books and records. Because it is natural for any officer to desire a report that magnifies the officer's successes and minimizes any failings, there is an ever-present concern that the firm's financial statements may reflect the influence of the firm's managers over the content of the financial statements. The first line of defense to this abuse is that the accounting metrics used in preparing the financial statements are objective, not subjective, principles and rules, thereby reducing the opportunity for manipulation of the financial statements by the managers. Thus, a critical feature of GAAP is a body of principles, rules, and conventions that are to be adhered to in preparing financial statements.

However, the mere existence of a "rule book" does not mean that managers will adhere to the rules. Their temptation to distort the financial statements continues, so that some further assurance that the rules are being adhered to is necessary. Thus, the second line of defense is the role of the outside auditor (a/k/a the certified public accountant). The SEC requires that financial statements filed with it be certified by an independent auditor; the auditor's certification attests that the auditor has reviewed the financial statements according to generally accepted auditing standards (GAAS) to assure that the financial statements conform to GAAP. The audit procedures that make up GAAS historically were established by a body within the American Institute of Certified Public Accountants (AICPA), the national professional organization of CPAs. The Sarbanes-Oxley Act firmly placed GAAS under the control of the Public Company Accounting Oversight Board (PCAOB), a nonprofit corporation funded by fees paid by reporting companies.

Accounting information is by no means the only information that is relevant to investors and shareholders. A mineral discovery, the award of a patent, and the expropriation of the firm's assets by a hostile nation are each financially significant events that arise *outside* the firm's accounting information system. Thus, as you review the types of disclosure that are mandated by the SEC in its Regulation S-K, you should observe that the mandated disclosures are a rich blend of accounting-based information and non-accounting information. The SEC does not enjoy a monopoly on disclosure of information for public companies. There are a variety of other sources and mediums that provide significant information about issuers before that information may become embodied in a filing with the SEC. First, the firm may choose to voluntarily disclose information that is not required to be disclosed by the SEC or the firm may disclose the information earlier than is required by the SEC's requirements. Second, there are a variety of sources separate from the company who customarily provide important information regarding an individual firm. Examples of such independent sources are rating agencies, such as Standard & Poor's, financial analysts, and the press. Indeed, there is a good deal of information about a company or its products that is publicly available in sources other than documents filed with the SEC so that information filed with the SEC is typically just part of a rich tapestry of information that surrounds public companies.

2.   The Exchange Act's Periodic Reporting Obligations

As originally formulated, the Exchange Act's regulations proceeded on three distinct but interconnected initiatives. One was to control the trading practices of brokers, dealers, investors, and the exchanges themselves to prevent manipulation and undue speculation. Efforts in these areas are examined in Chapter 18, where we will see one underlying theme of the Exchange Act was creating a mechanism for self-regulation by brokers and the exchanges, but it was to be self-regulation under the watchful eye of the SEC. The second was to regulate certain aspects of the behavior of issuers and their managers whose stock was traded on the exchanges. The latter regulation took the form of heightening disclosures for proxy solicitations and insider trading by certain high-level individuals. The final initiative of the Exchange Act was in Section 13, which provides mechanisms for mandatory disclosure requirements for certain publicly traded issuers. The quest for this disclosure was driven not solely by a desire to make available to investors trading in securities information of a quantity and quality approaching that made available for public offerings of securities pursuant to the Securities Act of 1933. Mandated periodic disclosure was also driven by the belief that enhanced disclosures by public companies would allow sound investing to triumph over manipulation and speculation. Initially, Section 13 applied only to securities listed on national exchanges; however, in light of the significant growth in investor interest in smaller companies, in 1964 the reach of Section 13 was expanded to certain securities traded in the over-the-counter markets. For the classic analysis of the events leading to this landmark regulatory step, *see* Cohen, "Truth in Securities" Revisited, 79 Harv. L. Rev. 1340 (1966).

a.   Domestic Issuers

By and large the reporting processes ushered in by the securities laws are either episodic or periodic, and only in special situations can they be seen as even approaching being continuous. Chapter 4 examined the extensive disclosure mechanisms—a registration statement and accompanying prospectus—that are triggered when the issuer undertakes a public offering of securities. A public offering by any company is episodic and hence the accompanying disclosures are themselves episodic. In contrast, the core reports called for by Section 13—the annual Form 10-K and the quarterly Form 10-Q—are periodic since their filing is triggered by the passage of the requisite number of full moons, not by some seismic corporate event. Like the disclosures in a registration statement under the '33 Act, the "line items" that must be disclosed in an issuer's 10-K and 10-Q are set forth in Regulation S-K. In 2016, the SEC amended its rules to allow (but do not require) issuers to include within Form 10-K a summary of the form's information. Exchange Act Release No. 77969 (June 1, 2016).

As part of its reform of the public offering process that was discussed in Chapter 4, the SEC embraced two important changes for the periodic reporting system. First, reporting issuers must set forth on their annual and quarterly filings risk disclosures similar to those required in '33 Act registration statements; the disclosures include updating any material changes to previously disclosed risks as well as identifying any new risks. Second, to encourage a registrant's responsiveness to SEC comments on Exchange Act reports, the registrant must now disclose in its annual report any written staff comment the issuer believes is material that was issued more than 180 days before the end of the fiscal year covered by the annual report that remains unresolved when the annual report is filed.

Form 8-K is a current report whose filing is triggered by certain significant, if not extraordinary, events. Formerly, the 8-K was triggered by a handful of special events, such as a change of control, changing auditors, or a director's resignation. In most instances, the filing must occur within four business days of the event that triggers the obligations; for a few items the time period is even shorter. *See* McMullin, Miller & Twedt, Increased Mandated Disclosure Frequency and Price Formation: Evidence from the 8-K Expansion Regulation, 24 Rev. Acct. Studies 1 (2019) (2004 expanded 8-K disclosures had significant positive effect on stock prices). However, Cohen, Jackson & Mitts, The 8-K Trading Gap, Working Paper (August 2016), in reviewing over 15,000 8-K filings that were accompanied by management trades during the four days preceding the filing of the 8-K found that such trades on average yielded a material abnormal return.

After the financial and accounting scandals of 2001-2002, the triggering events have been greatly expanded. For example, Item 5.05 calls for disclosure of amendments or waivers to the issuer's code of ethics and Items 1.01 and 1.02 of Form 8-K require disclosure of the company entering into or terminating a material agreement outside the ordinary course of its business. And, addressing the potential for selective disclosures of financial information, Item 2.02 now requires any reporting company to file an 8-K after announcing financial information for a completed fiscal period; the filing is to include the text of such announcement. A variety of corporate governance matters trigger a filing, such as an amendment to the articles of incorporation or bylaws. *See* Item 5.03. Among the corporate events that must be disclosed is the issuance of stock without regulation, e.g., a private offering. *See* Item 3.02. The breadth of Form 8-K is documented by there being about 4,000 filings *each month*. As for the legal compulsion to disclose events or transactions not falling within the items covered by Form 8-K, disclosure will either wait for the filing of the upcoming 10-Q or 10-K, or could arise earlier as a result of a duty premised upon the antifraud provision, Rule 10b-5, as discussed in Chapters 13 and 14.

Section 13's reporting obligation is triggered if the issuer meets one of the following tests.

Exchange-Traded Companies. Section 12(a) makes it unlawful for any broker, dealer, or exchange member to effect transactions on a national securities exchange in securities (other than exempt securities) that are not registered. Subsection (b) then provides a mechanism by which issuers can register their securities with the exchanges (and, indirectly, with the SEC). The registration form (Form 10) is in essence a portrait of the management and financial condition of the issuer, today part of the integrated disclosure system.

Over-the-Counter Stocks. Section 12(g) sets forth the requirements for over-the-counter companies. Issuers must register a class of equity securities with the SEC if, on the last day of their fiscal year, that class is held by 2,000 or more *record holders* and the issuer has more than $10 million in assets. The JOBS Act of 2012 raised the record holders requirement to 2,000 and potentially complicated the life of the issuer (and the SEC) by (1) eliminating from the count shares held by persons who acquired them pursuant to an employee compensation plan, e.g., Rule 701 discussed in Chapter 5, and (2) eliminating from the count those who acquired securities through the crowdfunding exemption in Section 4(a)(6), but (3) imposing Section 12(g) if the issuer's shares are held by 500 or more unaccredited investors. With respect to the latter, Rule 12g-1 incorporates Rule 501(a)'s definition of accredited investor, which includes a "reasonable belief" standard; however, it does not provide a safe harbor or guidance regarding how issuers are to make the accreditation determination. *See* SEC, Changes to Exchange Act Registration Requirements, Securities Act Release No. 10075 (May 3, 2016).

Foremost among the compliance questions under Section 12(g) that faces issuers is determining just how many record holders an issuer has. Most investors own their securities as beneficial owners through their broker. This is commonly referred to as holding the shares in "street name" where the broker's identity is known to the securities depository. In the United States, the Depository Trust Company (DTC) holds, in the name of its nominee, Cede & Co., the vast majority of U.S. equity securities for brokers, banks, and other market intermediaries. The SEC's long-held position is that Cede & Co. is not considered a single holder; the SEC's position is that each broker, bank, etc. that has an account with DTC is considered the record holder, albeit that person is not the beneficial owner of the shares if held in street name by the broker, banks, etc. For example, Merrill Lynch would count as a single holder, even though its holdings are on behalf of thousands of individual investors. As a consequence, a majority of investors owning securities in widely traded companies are not individually reflected on the issuers' records and are not counted under the current construction of "held of record." In light of this approach to the owner of record requirement, how diligent does the issuer have to be to discover whether there are 500 or more nonaccredited investors in it?

Note the emphasis on the last day of the issuer's fiscal year: The practical effect is that issuers may meet the test for publicly held corporation at various times during the year and yet avoid the duty to register so long as one or the other of the tests is not met on that all-important day. This naturally invites some form of last-minute manipulation to escape registration (e.g., issuer repurchases, accounting write-downs). While bona fide transactions are not made unlawful simply because they have the effect of allowing the *issuer* to avoid registration, the SEC has adopted a series of definitional rules to deal with sham transactions. For example, Rule 12g5-1(b)(3), which states that, if the issuer knows or has reason to know that a manner of holding securities of record has been used primarily to circumvent the registration requirement, the beneficial owners of such securities shall be deemed the record owners. A different approach is taken, however, when shareholders, *without the issuer's involvement*, form a trust, deposit arrangement, etc. for holding shares. In such cases, the SEC per Rule 12g5-1(b)(1) "looks through" the holder of record of such trust or agreement. For similar reasons, *class* of stock is defined broadly in the statute in terms of securities with "substantially similar character" and with holders who have "substantially similar rights and privileges," thus precluding the artificial division of securities into separate classes (Section 12(g)(5)).

In Report on Authority to Enforce Exchange Act Rule 12g5-1 and Subsection (b)(3) (Oct. 15, 2012), the SEC staff observes that only about 13 percent of non-listed firms (less than 400 companies) have 2,000 or more record holders. However, most non-listed firms that were reporting companies when the JOBS Act provisions went into effect continue to be reporting companies because their record holders have not fallen below 300, the level discussed below, to cease being a reporting company. Is raising the record holder level a good development for the country or, for that matter, issuers that fall outside the reporting requirements? Consider that in 1964, when the reporting requirements were expanded to include larger over-the-counter stocks, this was found to reduce volatility and generated abnormal positive returns for those companies; each of these findings is consistent with enhanced stock price accuracy. Ferrell, Mandatory Disclosure and Stock Returns: Evidence from the Over the Counter Market, 36 J. Leg. Stud. 213 (2007). *See also* Macey, O'Hara & Pompilio, Down and Out in the Stock Market: The Law and Economics of the Delisting Process, 51 J.L. & Econ. 683 (2008) (spreads tripled and volatility doubled for firms migrating from NYSE to pink sheet market). Many financial institutions believe their fiduciary obligations prevent them from investing in non-reporting companies, even though the company is publicly traded. A further consideration is the decline in record holders in recent years. "Among all stocks tracked by S&P Dow Jones Indices, shareholders of record have shrunk to a median of 352 today from 1,626 two decades ago." Zweig, Disappearing from View: America's Shareholders, Wall St. J., June 11, 2016, at B-7.

The registration obligation triggered by Section 12(g) terminates, subject to SEC review for accuracy, 90 days after the issuer files a certification that the number of shareholders of record of such class is fewer than 300 persons or that there are fewer than 500 record holders of its stock and its total assets have not exceeded $10 million on the last day of each of the three most recent fiscal years. Section 12(g)(4) and Rule 12g-4. As we have seen, the JOBS Act did not tinker with the asset requirement, but it did dramatically change the record holder requirement for being subject to Section 12(g). Should the SEC increase the level of holders from the current 300 holders of record that remove the reporting obligations of Section 12(g)? In this regard, consider that the JOBS Act provides that if the issuer is a bank or a bank holding company, it may exit from Section 12(g) if its holders drop below 1,200. More generally, note that by conditioning deregistration on a much lower number of holders than is the number that triggers the initial registration requirement, the SEC effectively makes exiting from the periodic reporting system difficult for issuers. Why does it do this? *See* Rock, Securities Regulations as a Lobster Trap: A Credible Commitment Theory of Mandatory Disclosure, 23 Cardozo L. Rev. 675 (2002).

Section 15(d).　　Section 15(d), in place since 1936, requires an issuer that files a registration statement under the '33 Act in connection with a public distribution to file periodic reports thereafter under the scheme set forth in Section 13 of the '34 Act. In other words, such issuers become subject to the periodic disclosure obligations of publicly held companies, but not (as do Section 12 registrants) to the other post-registration provisions. This reporting duty ceases if at the beginning of any fiscal year, other than the one in which the registration statement became effective, the securities of each class to which the registration statement related came to be held of record by fewer than 300 persons.

PROBLEMS

11-1.　BioCare, Inc. is a private company with most of its shares owned by its employees, angel investors, and two different venture capital firms. Recently, it filed a registration statement with the SEC anticipating going public if market conditions remained strong. There has been a good deal in the press about BioCare. And, there have even been reports of investors doggedly pursuing existing employees and angel investors, seeking to acquire their shares. Believing it saw an opportunity to profit from investor interest in BioCare, Stremple Investment Services proposes to offer to its vast stable of very wealthy clients interests in a trust that would acquire BioCare shares from certain current BioCare shareholders. Stremple believes there are at least a couple of thousand of its customers who would likely purchase interests in the trust. After Stremple's plan was leaked to the press, BioCare's general counsel consults you regarding whether Stremple's plan poses any problems for BioCare. Does it? Consider Rule 12g5-1(a)(2) & (b)(3).

11-2.　Rumcola Corporation, with some $10 million in assets, is a registered company under Section 12(g). It has 347 shareholders of record. To avoid the costs of being a publicly held company, Rumcola began a program to buy out 100 of those shareholders. The largest shareholders (members of the founding family) object to this step, since they see the periodic reports as their only source of reliable information about Rumcola. They have proposed to create a series of approximately 100 trusts with portions of their shares. The company, in turn, has indicated that it will not recognize these trusts and will proceed with the deregistration process. What resolution on the merits? *See* Rule 12g5-1(b)(1) & (3).

b.　Foreign Issuers

Probably the most interesting policy choice in the area of registration and reporting has to do with foreign issuers, for this raises many of the same questions that were identified in connection with the registration of foreign offerings under the '33 Act. As the regulatory scheme has evolved, exchange-traded foreign issuers must conform to U.S. registration and disclosure requirements (albeit in altered form, as discussed below). The theory behind the choice not to exempt these foreign issuers is that they have voluntarily sought access to the

American securities markets, and thus it is hardly unfair to ask them to provide disclosure to investors that is at least somewhat comparable to what U.S.-based issuers must provide. Foreign issuers also gain an exemption from the regulation that would otherwise flow from registration: Rule 3a12-3(b) grants most foreign companies the freedom from the strictures of the proxy rules of Section 14 and the insider trading provisions of Section 16.

Important relief to foreign issuers who are *not* listed on a U.S. exchange is provided by Rule 12g3-2. Even though not listed on a U.S. exchange, foreign issuers can be subject to Section 12(g) because statutorily the shareholder and assets threshold standards of Section 12(g)(1) apply presumptively to *any* issuer "which is engaged in interstate commerce, or in a business affecting interstate commerce, or whose securities are traded by use of the mails or any means or instrumentality of interstate commerce." A first component of Rule 12g3-2(a) exempts the foreign issuer that has fewer than 300 holders who are U.S. residents. If the number of U.S. resident holders is 300 or greater, Rule 12g3-2(b) provides a different approach. Under Rule 12g3-2(b), a non-listed foreign issuer is exempt from further reporting requirements provided it publishes (in English) on the company's web site or similar media periodic reports they are required to file in their home country and if 55 percent or more of its worldwide trading volume during the preceding 12-month period occurred outside the United States.

Issuers that are not exempt by one of the provisions in Rule 12g3-2 (e.g., those listed on the exchanges) must annually file Form 20-F, which is the basic registration and periodic reporting form for foreign issuers brought into the '34 Act system by Section 12 or 15(d). As discussed in Chapter 4, the SEC has allowed issuers with foreign listings to use the somewhat less rigorous disclosure standards for nonfinancial items formulated by the International Organization of Securities Commissions (IOSCO); this accommodation was made in anticipation that someday there would be a regime of international portability for issuers seeking multiple sites for the trading of their securities. *See* International Disclosure Standards, Securities Act Release No. 7745 (Sept. 28, 1999). Even though foreign issuers are not required to file quarterly reports, those not excused from filing Form 20-F are required to file on Form 6-K information released to investors that is mandated by their home country or primary stock exchange. As you can imagine, Form 6-Ks cover a wide range of information and in a good many instances are analogous to information in Forms 10-Q and 8-K. *See* Boone et al., The Ongoing SEC Disclosures by Foreign Firms, Working Paper (July 1, 2019), available at *https:// papers.ssrn.com/sol3/papers.cfm?abstract_id=2626969.*

One of the principal means used by investors to hold foreign equities is the American depository receipt (ADR). An ADR represents an ownership interest in a specified number of securities that have been deposited with a depository, such as a U.S. bank or trust company. In exchange for the deposited securities, the depository issues the negotiable ADRs. There are several advantages to this procedure. One is the ability of the investors as a group to obtain favorable exchange rates on dividends paid on the deposited shares, with distributions then made in American dollars, rather than the foreign currency. Second, the depository facilitates the sometimes difficult process of directing communications from the issuer to the American investors. Moreover, in many foreign markets, such as London, non-domestic purchasers must incur burdensome custodial fees for shares that are purchased directly. Though the ADR depository charges a fee, it is usually much lower than the fees otherwise incurred. *See generally* Velli, American Depository Receipts: An Overview, 17 Fordham Int'l L.J. S38 (1994).

ADRs present disclosure issues under both the '33 and the '34 Acts. Under the Securities Act, the ADRs and the deposited securities are considered separate securities, so that for each there must be registration or an exemption. Thus, if a broker creates ADRs for Barclay shares purchased on the London Stock Exchange for the purpose of satisfying a customer's order, the deposited shares are exempt, and the registration of the ADRs is satisfied by the limited disclosure demanded by Form F-6. (However, if ADRs are used by the issuer to raise capital in the United States, it must comply with the more extensive disclosure pursuant to Form F-1 or F-3.) The Exchange Act's periodic reporting requirements apply to ADRs that are listed on a national securities exchange. Hence, on Form 20-F, the foreign issuer whose financial reports are not in conformance with IFRS as adopted by the IASB must, among other things, reconcile its financial statements to U.S. GAAP. Rule 12g3-2(b) is available to issuers whose ADRs are otherwise traded in the over-the-counter market so that its periodic disclosure demands can be satisfied by its placing on the web English versions of its home country filings.

c. *Compelling Honesty in Mandated Reports Through Private Actions*

Somewhat parallel to Congress' approach under the Securities Act, where it sought to assure full disclosure in registration statements via the private action created in Section 11, Congress explicitly provided a private right of action in Section 18 for persons harmed as a result of misleading filings required by the Exchange Act. Section 18 of the Securities Exchange Act imposes liability upon any person who makes or causes to be made a false or misleading statement in a required filing under the Act and permits recovery of damages by any person "who, in reliance upon such statement, shall have purchased or sold a security at a price which was affected by such statement" unless "the person sued shall prove that he acted in good faith and had no knowledge that such statement was false or misleading." Unfortunately for potential plaintiffs, the elements of a cause of action under Section 18 are exceedingly difficult to meet. First, there is the double reliance requirement: The plaintiff must actually have relied on the particular misstatement (i.e., must establish, apparently, that she read the document, *see Gould v. Winstar Comm., Inc.*, 686 F.3d 108 (2d Cir. 2012)), and the misstatement must have affected the market price of the security. Since documents themselves are rarely read by the typical investor, that by itself is a substantial hurdle to recovery. Second, there is the good-faith defense. And beyond this, there are procedural rules—for example, allowing the court to require plaintiff to post bond and to impose costs (including attorneys' fees) against an unsuccessful plaintiff—that can operate harshly. Nonetheless, financial institutions sometimes individually pursue suits under Section 18 instead of filing an antifraud claim under Rule 10b-5 so as to avoid the higher pleading standard, discussed in Chapter 13 for suits under the antifraud provision. Nonetheless, courts have been willing to permit "evasion of Section 18's double reliance requirement by allowing suits under Rule 10b-5 for false filings." *E.g.*, *Wachovia Bank & Trust Co. v. National Student Marketing Corp.*, 650 F.2d 342 (D.C. Cir. 1980), *cert. denied*, 452 U.S. 954 (1981); *Ross v. A.H. Robins Co.*, 607 F.2d 545 (2d Cir. 1979). At the same time, courts have tended not to imply an action for injured investors directly under Section 13(a), so as to allow them to avoid altogether the restrictions of either Rule 10b-5 or Section 18. *See In re Penn Central Securities Litigation*, 494 F.2d 528 (3d Cir. 1974). Nor have they implied actions for investors allegedly injured by violations of the accounting provisions of the Foreign Corrupt Practices Act. *See Lewis v. Sporck*, 612 F. Supp. 1316 (N.D. Cal. 1985).

B. The "Fairly Presents" Requirement

The opinion letter of the firm's auditor attests that the audit has been conducted pursuant to generally accepted auditing standards and as a result of such review the auditor has concluded that the financial statements have been prepared according to generally accepted accounting standards and "fairly presents" the firm's financial position and performance. As is seen in material later in this chapter, the CEO and CFO are now required on each quarterly and annual report filed with the SEC to certify, among other items, that they believe the financial statements fairly present the firm's financial position. The meaning and dominance of the fairly presents requirement is illustrated in the following case.

United States v. Simon
425 F.2d 796 (2d Cir. 1969), *cert. denied*, **397 U.S. 1006 (1970)**

FRIENDLY, Circuit Judge:

Defendant Carl Simon was a senior partner, Robert Kaiser a junior partner, and Melvin Fishman a senior associate in the internationally known accounting firm of Lybrand, Ross Bros. & Montgomery. They stand convicted after trial by Judge Mansfield and a jury in the District Court for the Southern District of New York under three counts of an indictment charging them with drawing up and certifying a false or misleading financial statement of Continental Vending Machine Corporation (hereafter Continental) for the year ending September 30, 1962. . . .

I.

[The trial hinged on transactions between Continental and its affiliate, Valley Commercial Corporation (Valley). Both corporations were controlled by Harold Roth. The jury found that money lent by Continental to Valley was thereafter advanced by Valley to Roth to finance his numerous stock market transactions. At the end of 1962, the amount of these loans, noted as the "Valley Receivable" on Continental's books, amounted to $3.5 million. Valley was owed the same amount by Roth. In the course of their review of Continental's financial statements, the outside auditors had discovered that Roth was not in a position to repay the loans made by Valley to him and, hence, that Valley was unable to pay the amount it owed to Continental. The auditors even demanded that Roth transfer collateral to an independent trustee for the purpose of securing the debt to Valley and Valley's obligation to Continental. Roth responded to the auditor's demands by transferring approximately $3 million in securities to a trustee; however, 80 percent of the collateral was Continental stock and $1 million of this amount was subject to prior liens of third parties. Even though the accountants were aware of the composition of the collateral and the prior liens, Continental's audited statements made no mention of these facts or that the Valley Receivable represented amounts ultimately loaned to the firm's controlling stockholder. Furthermore, even though the amount of the Valley Receivable increased by $400,000 in the time between the close of Continental's 1962 fiscal year and the date the auditors certified the financial statements, the auditors did not disclose this material change.

The auditors certified Continental's financial statements on February 15, 1963. The statements reported a disappointing year for Continental—an operating loss of $867,000 compared to profits of $1,249,000 the year before. Also, if the Valley Receivable was not included among Continental's current assets its current assets would have been less than its current liabilities. The financial statements reported the Valley Receivable at $3.5 million and disclosed the following regarding the Valley Receivable:]

NOTES TO CONSOLIDATED FINANCIAL STATEMENTS

2. The amount receivable from Valley Commercial Corp. (an affiliated company of which Mr. Harold Roth is an officer, director and stockholder) bears interest at 12% a year. Such amount . . . is secured by the assignment to the Company of Valley's equity in certain marketable securities. As of February 15, 1963, the amount of such equity at current market quotations exceeded the net amount receivable.

The Case against the defendants can be best encapsulated by comparing what Note 2 stated and what the Government claims it would have stated if the defendants had included what they knew.

2. The amount receivable from Valley Commercial Corp. (an affiliated company of which Mr. Harold Roth is an officer, director and stockholder), which bears interest at 12% a year, was uncollectible at September 30, 1962, since Valley had loaned approximately the same amount to Mr. Roth who was unable to pay. Since that date Mr. Roth and others have pledged as security for the repayment of his obligation to Valley and its obligation to Continental (now $3,900,000) . . . securities which, as of February 15, 1963, had a market value of $2,978,000. Approximately 80% of such securities are stock or convertible debentures of the Company.

Striking as the difference is, the latter version does not reflect the Government's further contention that in fact the market value of the pledged securities on February 15, 1963, was $1,978,000 rather than $2,978,000 due to liens of . . . [third parties]. . . .

III.

The defendants called eight expert independent accountants, an impressive array of leaders of the profession. They testified generally that, except for the error with respect to netting, the treatment of the Valley receivable in Note 2 was in no way inconsistent with generally accepted accounting principles or generally accepted auditing standards, since it made all the informative disclosures reasonably necessary for fair presentation of the financial position of Continental as of the close of the 1962 fiscal year. Specifically, they testified that neither generally accepted accounting principles nor generally accepted auditing standards required disclosure of the makeup of the collateral or of the increase of the receivable after the closing date of the balance sheet, although three of the eight stated that in light of hindsight they would have preferred that the make-up of the collateral be disclosed. The witnesses likewise testified that disclosure of the Roth borrowings from Valley was not required, and seven of the eight were of the opinion that such disclosure would be inappropriate. The principal reason given for this last view was that the balance sheet was concerned solely with presenting the financial position of the company under audit; since the Valley receivable was adequately secured in the opinion of the auditors and was broken out and shown separately as a loan to an affiliate with the nature of the affiliation disclosed, this was all that the auditors were required to do. To go further and reveal what Valley had done with the money would be to put into the balance sheet things that did not properly belong there; moreover, it would create a precedent which would imply that it was the duty of an auditor to investigate each loan to an affiliate to determine whether the money had found its way into the pockets of an officer of the company under audit, an investigation that would ordinarily be unduly wasteful of time and money. With due respect to the Government's accounting witnesses, an SEC staff accountant, and, in rebuttal, its chief accountant, who took a contrary view, we are bound to say that they hardly compared with defendants' witnesses in aggregate auditing experience or professional eminence.

Defendants asked for two instructions which, in substance, would have told the jury that a defendant could be found guilty only if, according to generally accepted accounting principles, the financial statements as a whole did not fairly present the financial condition of Continental at September 30, 1962, and then only if his departure from accepted standards was due to willful disregard of those standards with knowledge of the falsity of the statements and an intent to deceive. The judge declined to give these instructions. Dealing with the subject in the course of his charge, he said that the "critical test" was whether the financial statements as a whole "fairly presented the financial position of Continental as of September 30, 1962, and whether it accurately reported the operations for fiscal 1962." If they did not, the basic issue became whether defendants acted in good faith. Proof of compliance with generally accepted standards was "evidence which may be very persuasive but not necessarily conclusive that he acted in good faith, and that the facts as certified were not materially false or misleading." "The weight and credibility to be extended by you to such proof, and its persuasiveness, must depend, among other things, on how authoritative you find the precedents and the teachings relied upon by the parties to be, the extent to which they contemplate, deal with, and apply to the type of circumstances found by you to have existed here, and the weight you give to expert opinion evidence offered by the parties. Those may depend on the credibility extended by you to expert witnesses, the definiteness with which they testified, the reasons given for their opinions, and all the other facts affecting credibility. . . ."

Defendants contend that the charge and refusal to charge constituted error. We think the judge was right in refusing to make the accountants' testimony so nearly a complete defense. The critical test according to the charge was the same as that which the accountants testified was critical. We do not think the jury was also required to accept the accountants' evaluation whether a given fact was material to overall fair presentation, at least not when the accountants' testimony was not based on specific rules or prohibitions to which they could point, but only on the need for the auditor to make an honest judgment and their conclusion that nothing in the financial statements themselves negated the conclusion that an honest judgment had been made. Such evidence may be highly persuasive, but it is not conclusive, and so the trial judge correctly charged. . . .

Finding that the evidence was sufficient for submission to the jury and that no legal errors were committed, we must let the verdict stand.

Affirmed.

NOTES AND QUESTIONS

1. GAAP in the Criminal Case.   *Simon* was invoked in the criminal case arising from the collapse of WorldCom, whose CEO, Bernard Ebbers, ultimately received a 25-year sentence for his role in the largest accounting fraud to date. *United States v. Ebbers,* 458 F.3d 110 (2d Cir. 2006). Ebbers repeatedly instructed his CFO and other accounting personnel that WorldCom "had to make its numbers," referring to meeting analysts' expectations regarding the company's revenue and earnings growth. To achieve these results, the court found that Ebbers and his staff creatively employed accounting steps to inflate revenues and conceal costs. For example, to boost revenues for a quarter, they included in revenues estimated "underutilization penalties" for certain customers, even though they did not expect these sums would be collectible. The bulk of the financial manipulation was their systematic recording of billions of dollars of operating costs as assets rather than expenses. In appealing his conviction, Ebbers argued that the government should have been required to prove that these actions violated GAAP. Invoking *Simon,* the court disagreed:

> In a real sense, by alleging and proving that the financial statements were misleading, the government did, in fact, allege and prove violations of GAAP. According to the AICPA's Codification of Statements in Accounting Standards, AU §312.04, "financial statements are materially misstated when they contain misstatements whose effect, individually or in the aggregate, is important enough to cause them not to be fairly, in all material respects, in compliance with GAAP." Thus, GAAP itself recognizes that technical compliance with particular GAAP rules may lead to misleading financial statements, and imposes an overall requirement that the statements as a whole accurately reflect the financial status of the company.

To be sure . . . differences of opinion as to GAAP's requirements may be relevant to the defendant's intent where financial statements are prepared in a good
faith attempt to comply with GAAP. The rules are no shield, however, in a case
such as the present one, where evidence showed that the accounting methods
known to be misleading—although perhaps at times fortuitously in compliance
with GAAP rules—were used for the express purpose of intentionally misstating
WorldCom's financial condition and artificially inflating its stock price.

Id. at 126.

2. The Expanded Auditor Report.   The PCAOB has expanded the content
of the auditor's report that accompanies certified financial statements. Financial
statement users, such as investors and creditors, have long sought more disclosure from the auditors regarding the judgments, estimates, and assumptions
that underlie so much of a firm's financial reports. The expanded disclosure
requirements call for the auditor's report to set forth *critical* audit matters the
auditor discussed with the audit committee that relate to accounts or disclosures that are material to the financial statements. The new requirements, however, extend beyond such critical matters; they include highlighting financial
reporting matters that are especially challenging or subjective, or that involve
complex auditor judgment. Swept within the latter area are those matters that
the auditor is now required to communicate to the audit committee, such as
any significant reporting risks the auditor had identified, significant unusual
transactions, and any significant matter that arose in the auditor's evaluation
of relationships and transactions with related parties. The final standard also
includes a new required statement in the auditor's report disclosing the year in
which the audit firm began serving consecutively as the company's auditor. This
new reporting model becomes effective for audit reports prepared for large
accelerated filers after June 30, 2019; all other filers become subject to the new
standard for audited reports prepared after December 15, 2020.

C. Internal Controls

1. The Meaning and Mandate for Internal Controls

Beyond the threat of enforcement action, there is a specific requirement in
Section 13 that is clearly designed to increase the accuracy of corporate disclosure. It grew out of the discovery in the 1970s that many well-known
corporations—Gulf Oil Corporation and Lockheed Corporation being two notorious examples—had off-books "slush funds" (generally unknown to the board
of directors and occasionally even to senior management) for improper political
contributions or foreign or domestic bribery—this history is further developed
in Chapter 12. Congress responded to the scandal by enacting the Foreign
Corrupt Practices Act of 1978 (FCPA) to proscribe certain forms of bribery and
to set forth certain requirements regarding the quality and content of a public
firm's books and records as set forth in Section 13(b)(2) of the Exchange Act.

Section 13(b)(2) requires registered or reporting companies to (1) make and keep books and records that, in reasonable detail, accurately and fairly reflect the transactions and dispositions of assets of the issuer; and (2) have in place a system of internal accounting controls sufficient to provide reasonable assurances that (a) transactions are executed only in accordance with management's authorization, (b) transactions are recorded so as to permit proper accounting and maintain accountability for assets, (c) access to assets is only in accordance with management's authorization, and (d) recorded accountability for assets is compared with existing assets at reasonable intervals, and corrective action taken if appropriate. The phrases "reasonable detail" and "reasonable assurances" mean "such level of detail and degree of assurance as would satisfy prudent officials in the conduct of their own affairs" (Section 13(b)(7)). To the extent that an absence of adequate books and records or system of accounting controls renders the company's financial statements materially incomplete or misleading, this requirement serves little additional purpose: Such inaccuracy is itself unlawful. The power of this provision, signaled by its legislative history, lies primarily in its use in cases where the deficiency is immaterial in a quantitative sense, but raises questions about the character, competence, or integrity of management—situations where (as we will see in Chapter 12) the law governing the primary disclosure duty is quite fuzzy. Is there a disconnect within the FCPA by its housing Section 13(b)(2), which relates rationally to the disclosure objective of the securities laws, while also proscribing in Section 30A of the Securities Exchange Act corrupt payments to foreign officials if made to gain business?

Securities and Exchange Commission v. World-Wide Coin Investments Ltd.
567 F. Supp. 724 (N.D. Ga. 1983)

VINING, J. This is a securities fraud action in which the Securities and Exchange Commission (SEC) seeks a permanent injunction against World-Wide Coin Investments, Ltd. (World-Wide) and the individual defendants as well as an order for a full accounting and disclosure of wrongfully received benefits. In an order entered March 29, 1983, this court directed the clerk to enter judgment for the SEC on all counts of the complaint and further directed defendants Hale and Seibert to (1) retain an independent auditor to perform a full accounting of World-Wide of all receipts and disbursements of cash and all purchases and sales and other acquisitions and dispositions of inventory and assets since July 1, 1979, and (2) return whatever shares of World-Wide stock they might hold to World-Wide. Finally, the court ordered World-Wide to make a full disclosure to its present shareholders with respect to all material information relating to its operations since July 1, 1979. . . .

FACTUAL BACKGROUND

World-Wide Coin Investments, Ltd., is a Delaware corporation with its principal offices in Atlanta, Georgia, and is engaged primarily in the wholesale and retail sale of rare coins, precious metals, gold and silver coins, bullion, and, until 1979, in the retail sale of camera equipment. Its operations also include the sale of Coca-Cola collector items and certain commemorative items. . . .

World-Wide's common stock is registered with the SEC pursuant to the Securities Exchange Act of 1934, 15 U.S.C. §781(b), and until late 1981 was listed on the Boston Stock Exchange. Prior to July 1979, the company's assets totaled over $2,000,000, and it had over 40 employees. In August 1981, the time of the filing of this lawsuit, the company's assets amounted to less than $500,000, and it had only three employees. . . .

C. PROBLEMS WITH INTERNAL CONTROLS AND ACCOUNTING PROCEDURES

On November 5, 1979, Kanes, Benator, as World-Wide's independent auditor, warned . . .World-Wide that a good and sound internal accounting control system was necessary to ensure the safeguarding of assets against losses from unauthorized use of dispositions and of financial records for preparing financial statements and maintaining accountability for assets. Although the company was notified of the importance of a good system of internal controls, this warning was ignored, and any control system that had existed at World-Wide ceased to exist. The problems that occurred at the company with respect to internal controls and accounting procedures can be divided into three areas: (1) inventory problems, (2) problems with separation of duties and the lack of documentation of transactions, and (3) problems with the books, records, and accounting procedures of the company.

(1) Inventory Problems

The safeguarding of World-Wide's physical inventory was one of its most severe problems; there was considerable testimony at trial to the effect that the company's vault, where most of the rare coins were kept, was unguarded and left open all day to all employees. Furthermore, no one employee was responsible for the issuance of coins from the vault, according to the accounts from May, Zima, who performed the 1980 audit. Scrap silver and bags of silver coins were left unattended in the hallways and in several cluttered, unlocked rooms at World-Wide's offices. During the trial, Hale admitted that he was worried about thefts due both to faulty record-keeping and the system of safeguarding the assets. . . .

(2) Separation of Duties

The lack of qualified personnel working in World-Wide's offices and the company's policy of allowing one individual to accomplish numerous transactions was another primary reason for May, Zima's disclaimed opinion, and was a major concern of Kanes, Benator in its letter of November 5, 1979. This court has previously noted the lack of supervision over the accounting department, managed by Patricia Allen, and her lack of expertise in the area. World-Wide maintains no separation of duties in the area of purchase and sales transactions, and valuation procedures for ending inventory. For instance, a single salesperson can do all the following tasks without supervision or review by another employee or officer: appraise a particular coin offered for purchase by a customer, purchase that coin with a check that the salesperson alone has drawn, count that same coin into inventory, value the coin for inventory purposes, and sell the coin to another purchaser. . . .

(3) *Books and Records*

The lack of qualified accounting personnel not only created problems with World-Wide's inventory but also resulted in completely inaccurate and incomplete books and records. World-Wide [has] failed to make and keep books, records, and accounts which accurately and clearly reflect the transactions and dispositions of World-Wide's assets. As discussed previously, World-Wide employees have not been required to write purchase orders or any source document relating to the purchase and sale of coins and bullion, rendering it impossible to arrive at an accurate count or valuation of the inventory. . . .

APPLICATION OF LAW

I. FOREIGN CORRUPT PRACTICES ACT

. . . The accounting provisions of the FCPA will undoubtedly affect the governance and accountability mechanisms of most major and minor corporations, the work of their independent auditors, and the role of the Securities and Exchange Commission. The maintenance of financial records and internal accounting controls are major every-day activities of every registered and/or reporting company. The FCPA also has important implications for the SEC, since the incorporation of the accounting provisions into the federal securities laws confers on the SEC new rulemaking and enforcement authority over the control and record-keeping mechanisms of its registrants. The FCPA reflects a congressional determination that the scope of the federal securities laws and the SEC's authority should be expanded beyond the traditional ambit of disclosure requirements. The consequence of adding these substantive requirements governing accounting control to the federal securities laws will significantly augment the degree of federal involvement in the internal management of public corporations. . . .

The "books and records" provision, contained in section 13(b)(2)(A) of the FCPA has three basic objectives: (1) books and records should reflect transactions in conformity with accepted methods of reporting economic events, (2) misrepresentation, concealment, falsification, circumvention, and other deliberate acts resulting in inaccurate financial books and records are unlawful, and (3) transactions should be properly reflected on books and records in such a manner as to permit the preparation of financial statements in conformity with GAAP and other criteria applicable to such statements.

Congress' use of the term "records" suggests that virtually any tangible embodiment of information made or kept by an issuer is within the scope of section 13(b)(2)(A) of the FCPA, such as tape recordings, computer printouts, and similar representations. As indicated above, the purpose of this provision is to strengthen the accuracy of records and the reliability of audits.

During congressional consideration of the accounting provisions, there were numerous objections to the requirement that records be "accurate," which noted, for example, that inventories are typically valued on either the assumption that costs are recognized on a first-in, first-out basis or a last-in, first-out basis. Both of these theories, if correctly and honestly applied, produce "accurate" records, even though each may yield considerably different results in terms of the monetary value of inventories. Several objecting groups recommended that the accuracy requirement be subject to a materiality test so that inaccuracies involving small dollar amounts would not be actionable. This view is not accepted, but Congress did make it clear that:

> The term "accurately" in the bill does not mean exact precision as measured by some abstract principle. Rather, it means that an issuer's records should reflect transactions in conformity with accepted methods of recording economic events.

The only express congressional requirement for accuracy is the phrase "in reasonable detail." Although section 13(b)(2) expects management to see that the corporation's recordkeeping system is adequate and effectively implemented, how the issuer goes about this task is up to management; the FCPA provides no guidance, and this court cannot issue any kind of advisory opinion.

Just as the degree of error is not relevant to an issuer's responsibility for any inaccuracies, the motivations of those who erred are not relevant. There are no words in section 13(b)(2)(A) indicating that Congress intended to impose a scienter requirement, although there is some support among officials at the Securities and Exchange Commission for the addition of a scienter requirement and a form of materiality standard to the FCPA. . . . The concept that the books and records provision of the Act embodies a scienter requirement would be inconsistent with the language of section 13(b)(2)(A), which contains no words indicating that Congress intended to impose such a requirement. Furthermore, either inadvertent or intentional errors could cause the misapplication or unauthorized use of corporate assets that Congress seeks to prevent. Also, a scienter requirement is inappropriate because the difficulty of proving intent would render enforcement extremely difficult. As a practical matter, the standard of accuracy in records will vary with the nature of the transaction involved.

The second branch of the accounting provisions—the requirement that issuers maintain a system of internal accounting controls—appears in section 13(b)(2)(B). Like the recordkeeping provisions of the Act, the internal controls provision is not limited to material transactions or to those above a specific dollar amount. . . .

The main problem with the internal accounting controls provision of the FCPA is that there are no specific standards by which to evaluate the sufficiency of controls; any evaluation is inevitably a highly subjective process in which knowledgeable individuals can arrive at totally different conclusions. Any ruling by a court with respect to the applicability of both the accounting provisions and the internal accounting control provisions should be strictly limited to the facts of each case. . . .

The definition of accounting controls does comprehend reasonable, but not absolute, assurances that the objectives expressed in it will be accomplished by the system. The concept of "reasonable assurances" contained in section 13(b)(2)(B) recognizes that the costs of internal controls should not exceed the benefits expected to be derived. It does not appear that either the SEC or Congress, which adopted the SEC's recommendations, intended that the statute should require that each affected issuer install a fail-safe accounting control system at all costs. It appears that Congress was fully cognizant of the cost-effective considerations which confront companies as they consider the institution of accounting controls and of the subjective elements which may lead reasonable individuals to arrive at different conclusions. Congress has demanded only that judgment be exercised in applying the standard of reasonableness. The size of the business, diversity of operations, degree of centralization of financial and operating management, amount of contact by top management with day-to-day operations, and numerous other circumstances are factors which management must consider in establishing and maintaining an internal accounting controls system. However, an issuer would probably not be successful in arguing a cost-benefit defense in circumstances where the management, despite warnings by its auditors or significant weaknesses of its accounting control system, had decided, after a cost benefit analysis, not to strengthen them, and then the internal accounting controls proved to be so inadequate that the company was virtually destroyed. It is also true that the internal accounting controls provisions contemplate the financial principle of proportionality—what is material to a small company is not necessarily material to a large company.

. . . World-Wide's defense appears to be that such a small operation should not be required to maintain an elaborate and sophisticated internal control system, since the costs of implementing and maintaining it would financially destroy the company. It is true that a cost/benefit analysis is particularly relevant here, but it remains undisputed that it was the lack of any control over the inventory and inadequate accounting procedures that primarily contributed to World-Wide's demise. No organization, no matter how small, should ignore the provisions of the FCPA completely, as World-Wide did. Furthermore, common sense dictates the need for such internal controls and procedures in a business with an inventory as liquid as coins, metals, and bullion.

The evidence in this case reveals that World-Wide . . . violated the provisions of section 13(b)(2) of the FCPA. . . .

NOTES AND QUESTIONS

1. Interpreting the Accounting Provisions.   How should Section 13(b)(2) be construed? By its terms, it seems to allow the Commission to base liability upon any false statement or omission in any corporate record, no matter whether it is trivial, immaterial, or inadvertent. And the internal controls provision appears to allow the Commission to second-guess the information flow processes of any publicly held corporation—the lifeblood of corporate management. The SEC in exercising its "prosecutorial discretion" considers a number of factors, such as the egregiousness of the violation, its magnitude, and whether the conduct is ongoing, as well as whether the respondent is a recidivist or the case provides the

SEC with an opportunity to address a widespread practice. Department of Justice & SEC, A Resource Guide to the U.S. Foreign Corrupt Practices Act 53 (2012).

   2.   *The Scope of the Act.* The books and records requirement extends to conduct and processes that can ultimately impact accounting records. For example, the SEC has cautioned registrants that internal control requirements include cybersecurity issues. Securities Exchange Act Release No. 84429 (Oct. 16, 2018). For other interesting applications, *see In the Matter of General Motors Co.,* Securities Exchange Act Release No. 79825 (Jan. 18, 2017) (Section 13(b)(2)(B) violated, resulting in $1 million fine because automaker's internal communications were so inadequate that 18 months elapsed between when engineers discovered the widespread defective ignition switch problem that ultimately required a massive recall and their informing accountants of the problem); *In the Matter of Ignacio Cueto Plaza,* Securities Exchange Act Release No. 77057 (Feb. 4, 2016) (CEO sanctioned under Section 13(b)(2) for authorizing payment to a "consultant" with no expectation services would be rendered and did so in connection with efforts to settle a labor dispute).
   Rules 13b2-1 and 13b2-2 impose upon persons in the corporate hierarchy an obligation to avoid falsification of corporate books and records and require officers and directors to provide accurate information to accountants in connection with preparation of financial statements and reports to the Commission. And in 1987, Congress expanded the reach of these provisions by adding in Section 13(b)(5) a prohibition against any person knowingly circumventing or knowingly failing to implement a system of internal controls or knowingly falsifying a book or record. Thus, liability exposure in a Section 13(b)(2) case is not limited to the registrant alone. (However, the 1987 revisions to the law did make clear in subsection (b)(4) that *criminal* liability cannot be imposed on anyone except in the case of a willful violation.)

2.   Reporting on Internal Controls: SOX 404

By far the most controversial provision of Sarbanes-Oxley is Section 404. Paragraph (a) of this provision requires a corporation's management to report annually on the effectiveness of the company's internal financial controls and paragraph (b) calls for the auditors to annually certify the accuracy of management's assessment. A companion provision, Section 302, requires the CEO and CFO to certify in each quarterly and annual report not only their assessment of internal controls but to make other representations, discussed later, regarding the financial statements.
   Section 404 has been both lauded as enormously effective in improving the integrity of financial reporting while being widely criticized as being too costly for the benefits it produces. The SEC's rules implementing Section 404 require that senior officers must include in their certification a representation that they have brought to the auditor's and the audit committee's attention "all significant deficiencies in the design and operation of internal controls which could adversely affect the registrant's ability to record, process, summarize and report financial data . . ." and that the auditors are to attest to and report on

management's assessment. *See* Exchange Act Rule 13a-14. In practice, in order to evaluate management's assessment, the auditors separately assess the company's internal controls and in doing so seek to determine not only the accuracy of management's assessment but to evaluate whether any deficiencies are so grave as to cause the auditors to qualify or even withhold their opinion regarding the financial statements themselves. The auditors can provide an "unqualified opinion" even when there is a "material weakness" in internal controls, provided the deficiency did not restrict the scope of the accountant's reliance on the financial records in carrying out the audit. An auditor issues a qualified opinion when the material weakness does impose such a "scope" limitation, but that limitation was not so severe as to justify either the accountant's withdrawal from the audit or an adverse opinion. And finally, the worst case scenario for the issuer is that the material weakness cannot be audited around so that the accountant renders an adverse opinion or withdraws from the audit engagement.

Some, but not all, of the burdens of Section 404(b) were addressed when the PCAOB adopted Auditing Standard No. 5, which is a principles-based approach to assessing internal controls. AS No. 5 calls on the auditor to assume a risk-oriented focus so that attention is to be directed to areas that pose the greatest reporting risks. Also, under AS No. 5, the auditor is to address only those deficiencies that pose a material weakness (defined to mean a deficiency so great that it would lead to a material misstatement in the firm's annual or interim financial statements). Therefore, the auditor is not to address in its assessment all internal control lapses. Even though the new auditing standard greatly reduced compliance costs for Section 404(b), it did not remove all concerns.

The auditor attestation requirement, Section 404(b) of the Sarbanes-Oxley Act, became a focus for complaints premised on the impact of regulation on small issuers and more generally the harmful effects of disclosure requirements on the competitiveness of U.S. capital markets. Data clearly supports the charge that compliance with this requirement imposes proportionately greater costs on smaller companies than larger companies. This finding reflects that disclosure requirements inherently entail a large fixed cost component and, particularly in the case of smaller companies, there at least existed in the early years of compliance with Section 404(b) much more deferred maintenance in the internal control system than for larger companies. As a consequence of these protests, both the Congress and the SEC have taken their own steps to remove smaller firms from Section 404(b):

1. In 2010, the Dodd-Frank Act added Section 404(b) to SOX to exempt registrants with a market float not exceeding $75 million (known as non-accelerated filers) from the requirement, thereby excluding about 60 percent of all reporting companies from the auditor attestation requirement.

2. The on-ramp provisions of the JOBS ACT of 2012 for emerging growth companies, discussed in Chapter 4, excused such companies from Section 404(b) during the shorter of their meeting the emerging growth company definition or five years of going public.

3. As seen earlier in this chapter, the JOBS Act amended Section 12(g), raised the number of holders of record to 2,000 and thereby reduced

the instances in which non-listed public companies will become subject to Section 404(b).

4. The SEC has proposed further excusing registrants whose revenues are less than $100 million. *See* Exchange Act Release No. 85814 (May 9, 2019).

PROBLEMS

11-3. The Stout Import Corporation (SIC), a large wine importer, recently filed with the SEC a Form 10-K that included a statement that, based on (1) its unusually large existing inventory of fine French vintages and (2) orders that it and other importers had received over the past six months, signaling a sharp increase in demand for such vintages, it expected earnings for the forthcoming three quarters to be substantially greater than those for the current one. After this filing, the price of SIC stock, a Nasdaq-traded security, rose by 12 percent.

Two months later, SIC officials discovered an ongoing scheme of employee theft and misappropriation of inventory in its major warehouse in New Jersey. The employees involved were at a rank no higher than midlevel managers. They facilitated their scheme through the creative piling of boxes in the warehouse and the use of false statements in the inventory control system. SIC had no security system for its warehouse.

As a result of this misbehavior, SIC's inventory of wine was substantially less than announced, and the expectation of an earnings increase is no longer realistic. As counsel for SIC, you are now in the process of preparing the disclosure of the bad news. As you are doing this, the company's president asks you (a) whether an 8-K is either required or needed at this point to correct the disclosure; and (b) in any event, what SIC's legal exposure, including any SEC action, is based on the misinformation in the filed 10-K. What would you advise her? Would you need to ask some questions to have enough facts to give a useful answer? What are they?

11-4. Syntec Co. has just disclosed that for several years it had consistently overstated its revenues. In addressing questions raised by its prior misstatements and the ongoing SEC investigation, Syntec has retained you to prepare a report evaluating its existing disclosure controls and procedures. Syntec's CFO has told you that its past disclosure problems were caused solely by a rogue manager in its Southeast Asia regional office and that the manager has been removed. The CFO also relates that she has reviewed the company's internal control procedures for recording sales and found they were solid. That investigation revealed that the recent reporting difficulties were the result of the rogue manager fabricating invoices with the assistance of several family members who posed as customers. In preparing a report on the company's internal disclosure controls and procedures that will be included in its 10-K, do you need to independently verify the representations made by the CFO? Assume the assignment was somewhat different, namely that Syntec was considering acquiring another company and has asked you to perform a "due diligence" review of the other company's reporting system. How would this investigation differ from that called for in the annual report on the company's internal disclosure system?

D. Strengthening the Integrity of the Financial Reporting Process: The Marriage of the SEC and Governance

1. Audit Committees

Audit committees are made up of the company's directors and have as their central function oversight of the company's audit and financial reporting practices. The New York Stock Exchange and Nasdaq have long required that listed companies have audit committees. The audit committee was of central focus with the reforms introduced by the Sarbanes-Oxley Act, which amended Exchange Act Section 10A so that now each listed company (foreign as well as domestic) must have an audit committee comprised exclusively of "independent" directors. Among the criteria for being independent is that the director cannot receive any compensation from the issuer other than her director's fees. Significantly, amended Section 10A anchors the auditor's relationship with the audit committee—not the senior executive officers—by requiring that the "audit committee . . . shall be directly responsible for the appointment, compensation, and oversight of" the auditor's work in certifying the issuer's financial statements.

The SEC rules mandate a dialogue between the auditor and the audit committee on important matters related to the quality of the audited financial reports. *See* Rule 2-07 of Regulation S-X. Included within this dialogue is the need for the auditor to report to the audit committee prior to any filing of the audited financial statements with the SEC (1) all "critical accounting policies and practices" used in the reports, (2) the accounting treatment preferred by the auditor, and (3) "material written communications between" the audit firm and the issuer's management.

In addition to calling on the audit committee to superintend the engagement with the outside auditors, the Act provides a list of other tasks for audit committees. The audit committee must establish procedures for receiving and addressing complaints received by the issuer regarding its accounting, internal controls, or auditing matters, including anonymous reports (i.e., whistleblowing) from employees regarding such matters. Audit committee members are expressly empowered with authority to obtain funding to permit it to engage independent counsel or advisers as needed to discharge the committee's responsibilities.

Steps by Sarbanes-Oxley and the exchanges to strengthen audit committees for listed companies were influenced by a 1999 study of companies charged by the SEC with financial fraud from 1987-1997. Among the study's findings were that 25 percent of the surveyed companies did not have an audit committee, that of those that did have an audit committee nearly one-third of the committee members' independence was compromised by close relationship with, or actual participation in, the firm's management, and that 65 percent of the committee members lacked accounting or financial expertise. *See* Mark S. Beasley et al., Fraudulent Financial Reporting 1987-1997, An Analysis of U.S. Companies (COSO 2000).

Item 407(d)(5) of SEC Regulation S-K requires registrants to disclose whether their audit committee includes a "financial expert" and, if not, why such a person is not a member of their audit committee; Item 407(d)(5), Instruction (ii), sets forth the criteria to be considered a financial expert. Listing requirements for the NYSE, Nasdaq, and AMEX require that each audit committee member be financially literate and that the audit committee have a written charter. Because Sarbanes-Oxley's audit committee requirements do not distinguish between domestic and foreign companies, their governance requirements have significant extraterritorial effects. Consider how a German company, with a two-tier board, can comply with the SEC's audit committee requirements. In the German two-tier system, the *Vorstand* is comprised exclusively of managers and the *Aufsichtsrat* (the supervisory board, so called because it appoints who will sit on the *Vorstand*) is divided between labor and those with commercial and financial relationships with the company. Under German law, the audit committee of the *Aufsichtsrat* must include employee representatives who by definition are not "independent directors" under Sarbanes-Oxley. The SEC's rules have generally been responsive to the different governance structures of foreign issuers. For example, it permits non-executive employees to sit on the audit committee of foreign issuers.

PROBLEM

11-5. Grace is a new member of Xytec's board of directors and was recently placed on Xytec's audit committee. The two other members of the audit committee have been Xytec directors for 13 and 16 years, respectively. A few days before her first audit committee meeting, she received an agenda for the meeting and supporting materials. Included was a long memo prepared by the former associate chief financial officer, Sharon, who listed a series of transactions that she claimed were falsely reported among sales and included in reporting Xytec's net income; the document contained some supporting materials indicating that the challenged transactions were substantively little more than creative accounting on the part of Xytec's CEO and CFO. After reading these materials, Grace called the audit committee chair to express her concern. The chair reported that he had been aware of the allegations for several weeks, he had asked Xytec's outside law firm to investigate the matter, the law firm had interviewed the CEO and CFO, and on the basis of its review the law firm reported that Sharon had been recently terminated and appeared to be a disgruntled former employee. Grace relates all this to you and asks your advice regarding what her obligations are at this point.

2. Buttressing the Auditor's Independence

The financial and accounting scandals that preceded the enactment of Sarbanes-Oxley were some of the darkest moments in the history of public accounting profession.

> The prime suspect for the accounting profession's recent sorrowful performance as a gatekeeper against financial frauds is the rising importance of non-audit services in the overall operations of the major accounting firms. In 1976, audit fees constituted seventy percent of accounting firm revenues; by 1998 audit fees had fallen to thirty-one percent of their revenues. These changes occurred because nonaudit revenues were increasing three times faster than were revenues from audit services. There are multiple reasons why the accounting firms placed such an emphasis on growing their nonaudit services revenues. An unwitting accomplice in this effort was the effort of many audit committees to gauge their success by reducing the auditor's fees rather than, for example, enhancing the quality of the audit. The pressure on audit fees also gave rise to a need for accounting firms to distinguish themselves from their competitors by offering a wider range of services. There was, of course, the quest to share the good life enjoyed by the well-compensated investment bankers and others with whom the accountants frequently interacted. Much of the revenue growth for nonaudit services was based solely on client demand; clients, believing, that their auditors knew the clients' businesses better than anyone else, concluded that there would be economies of scale by retaining the auditors for a range of consulting services rather than selecting a provider that was unfamiliar with the clients' businesses and support systems. A further concern was the intense competition among accounting firms to recruit talent to the quiet life of the auditor. Consider that the number of accounting majors declined twenty-five percent between 1995 and 2000, matching a near identical decline in the number of individuals sitting for the national CPA exam. To attract talented auditors, the accounting firms had to offer a broader professional profile than being solely an auditor. This strategy also complemented the reality that auditing work had become more complex and technical by the 1990s so that audit teams needed to include technical non-accounting experts who would have been underemployed absent consulting opportunities.

Cox, Reforming the Culture of Financial Reporting: The PCAOB and the Metrics for Accounting Measurements, 81 Wash. U. L.Q. 301 (2003).

In response to the common practice of auditors to provide substantial non-audit services to their audit clients (e.g., Arthur Anderson received $25 million in audit fees and $27 million in non-audit revenues from Enron), Section 10A(g) of the Exchange Act, Sarbanes-Oxley amends Section 10A of the Exchange Act to bar auditors from providing certain non-audit services to their audit clients. *See, e.g., In the Matter of KPMG, LLP,* Exchange Act Release No. 71389 (Jan. 24, 2014) ($8.2 million fine for providing variety of services including bookkeeping and payroll services to audit client). Moreover, for services of the type not barred expressly by the Act (or pursuant to rulemaking authority enjoyed by both the SEC and the PCAOB), Section 10A requires that all services provided to the issuer by the auditor must be approved in advance by the audit committee (there is a narrowly provided *de minimis* exemption to pre-approval in the case of services not exceeding 5 percent of the total amounts paid the non-auditor). After Sarbanes-Oxley, the SEC tightened its earlier restrictions in Rule 2-01(c)(4) of Regulation S-X regarding the types of non-audit services auditors may perform for their audit clients. The over-arching principles underlying its proscription of certain types of non-audit services are that an auditor cannot

(1) audit his or her own work, (2) perform management functions, or (3) act as an advocate for the client. The issuer, whether foreign or domestic, must annually disclose the amount of audit and non-audit fees paid to its accountants. Despite these restrictions, since 2012 non-audit revenues of the Big Four firms grew 44 percent, compared to a modest 3 percent increase in audit revenues; now more than half of their revenues are from non-audit services. Rapoport, Consulting Now King at Big Four Auditors, Wall St. J., Apr. 9, 2018, at B-1.

Section 10A(l) bars an accounting firm from auditing the books of any firm whose chief executive officer or chief financial or accounting officer in the past year was an employee of the accounting firm. Sarbanes-Oxley, however, stopped short of requiring that public companies switch accounting *firms* at regular intervals (e.g., every seven years). Instead, Section 10A(g) requires that the lead audit partner for a client be rotated every five years. Pursuant to Sarbanes-Oxley, Regulation S-X Rule 2-01(c)(2) limits the ability of an issuer's former auditors to become employees of the issuer. Finally, in an express response to protect the auditor from the overzealous management, Exchange Act Rule 13b2-2(b)(2) broadly prohibits directors or officers from taking any action to fraudulently influence, coerce, manipulate, or mislead the issuer's auditor for the purpose of causing the issuer's financial statements to be materially misleading.

PROBLEM

11-6.   At a meeting of General Materials Co.'s audit committee, the outside accountant discloses that over the past several years it has provided extensive tax advice to General Materials' CEO. When asked about the nature and extent of the tax advice, the accountant reveals that the CEO had paid it nearly $400,000 in each of the last three years for various "financial products" the accounting firm sold the CEO to shelter from taxation gains the CEO obtained by exercising stock options and for its services in preparing the CEO's tax return. Robert is a member of the audit committee and seeks your advice regarding whether the accountant's relationship to the CEO should affect any matter before the audit committee.

3.   Executive Certifications and Directors' Signature Requirement

Exchange Act Rules 13a-14 and 15d-14 require the CEO and the CFO to certify on each quarterly and annual report filed with the SEC that (1) the officer has reviewed the report; (2) to the certifying officer's knowledge the report "does not contain any untrue statement of material fact"; (3) to the certifying officer's knowledge "the report fairly presents in all material respects the financial condition and results of operations of the issuer"; (4) the certifying officer is responsible for maintaining the firm's internal controls and, among other representations, has within the past 90 days evaluated their effectiveness; and (5) the officer has brought to the audit committee's attention any "significant deficiencies" in the internal controls as well as "any fraud, whether or not material, that involves management or other employees who have a significant role in the registrant's internal controls." *See* Item 601(31) of Regulation S-K.

The SEC seeks to involve the company's directors in at least reviewing the company's 10-K by requiring that it be signed by at least a majority of the directors. *See* General Instruction D(2)(a) for Form 10-K. The signature requirement is not a hollow ritual. In *AUSA Life Ins. Co. v. Dwyer*, 928 F.2d 1239 (S.D.N.Y. 1996), directors who signed the 10-K with knowledge it was false were held to violate the antifraud provision. *See also Howard v. Everex*, 228 F.3d 1057 (9th Cir. 2000) ("Key corporate officers should not be allowed to make important false statements knowingly . . . yet . . . shield themselves from liability to investors simply by failing to be involved in the preparation of those statements."). *But see Central Laborers' Pension Fund v. Integrated Elec. Serv., Inc.*, 497 F.3d 546 (5th Cir. 2007) (SOX executive certification alone does not indicate scienter).

4.   Reconstructing History with *Pro Forma* Financial Statements

The financial statements required to be filed with the SEC are prepared according to generally accepted accounting principles (GAAP). The conventions that underlie GAAP are by and large conservative: Gains are not recognized until realized and probable declines in assets are generally recorded as current period expenses. Neither of these conventions sits well with managers whose natural tendency is to provide as good a report of their stewardship as is possible. They prefer to recognize gains before they are realized and to ignore declines in asset values. Over the years, managers who were not content with weak reports of their firm's performance *à la* GAAP have placed in their SEC filings, including '33 Act registration statements, *pro forma* financial statements that do not purport to conform to GAAP but instead recast the firm's performance through the more optimistic eyes of managers. Thus, when net income per GAAP is, for example, depressed by rising fuel costs for the company's fleet of trucks, management may present in the *pro forma* financial statements of the company's net income as if fuel costs had not risen. Similarly, if GAAP required gains from the sale of a division to be recorded as an *extraordinary* item so that it did not contribute to net income from *ordinary* operations, a *pro forma* presentation would sweep that transaction into the calculus of ordinary income. Legendary investor Warren Buffet, expressing his own cynicism of managers' use of *pro forma* financials, quipped that on his recent round of golf he shot a *pro forma* 72 after restructuring 18 of his missed putts. As directed by the Sarbanes-Oxley Act Section 401(b), the SEC adopted Regulation G, requiring that reporting companies when issuing non-GAAP information (such as the common practice of setting forth "EBITDA" = earnings before interest, taxes, depreciation, and amortization) to compare that presentation to the most comparable financial measure calculated according to GAAP and to reconcile the difference between the non-GAAP and GAAP measurements. The collateral disclosures required by Regulation G have not dampened the practice of reporting non-GAAP performance figures; 97 percent of S&P 500 companies use at least one non-GAAP metric in SEC filings and when doing so for earnings per share the non-GAAP figure is on average 30 percent higher than GAAP EPS. Katz, SEC Scrutiny of Non-GAAP Financial Measures, Harv. L. S. Forum on Corp. Gov. & Fin. Reg. (Feb. 7, 2019).

PROBLEM

11-7.   Annually Advertising Age magazine asks all advertising agencies to provide a summary of their "ad revenue" for the calendar year. Advertising Age defines ad revenue much more broadly than it is defined under GAAP, because the magazine includes amounts that will be earned in future fiscal years whereas GAAP reports revenues only for advertising performed in the current fiscal year. Bogden Reed and Associates is a large advertising agency and is listed on the NYSE. What concerns should it have in responding to the data requested by Advertising Age?

E.   The Management Discussion and Analysis Section of SEC Filings: Is Past Prologue?

The Management Discussion and Analysis (MD&A) portion of SEC filing is set forth in Item 303 of Regulation S-K and calls on management to provide narrative explanations of the financial statements for the purpose of increasing the transparency of a company's financial performance and providing overall better disclosure to investors. Most significantly, the MD&A calls for a disclosure of trends and risks that have shaped the past and are *reasonably likely* to have an impact on the future long-term or short-term liquidity, and capital resources as well as discussing the performance of different segments of the firm's business and its critical accounting policies. With respect to the latter, the Commission asks registrants to provide a penetrating analysis of the most difficult and judgmental accounting estimates, the most important and pervasive accounting policies, and to provide analysis of how the bottom line is sensitive to these estimates and judgments. *See* Summary of Division of Corporation Finance of Significant Issues Addressed in the Review of the Periodic Reports of Fortune 500 Companies (Feb. 27, 2003) (finding too many companies in their MD&A merely recite financial statement information). Merger negotiations, however, need not be disclosed in the MD&A if the company believes the disclosure could jeopardize completion of the acquisition.

1.   The Scope of Item 303 Disclosure Obligation

▍▍ **Panther Partners Inc. v. Ikanos Communications, Inc.**
▍▍ **681 F.3d 114 (2d Cir. 2012)**

BARRINGTON D. PARKER . . .
Panther alleges that Ikanos and various of its officers, directors, and underwriters violated §§11, 12(a)(2), and 15 of the Securities Act by failing to disclose known defects in the Company's VDSL (very-high-bit-rate digital subscriber line) Version Four chips. Ikanos is a publicly-traded company that develops and markets programmable semiconductors. . . . Ikanos's customers are primarily

large original equipment manufacturers ("OEMs") in the communications industry that incorporate Ikanos's products into their products, which are then sold to telecommunications carriers. . . .

In 2005, Ikanos sold its VDSL Version Four chips to Sumitomo Electric and NEC, its two largest customers and the source of 72% of its 2005 revenues. Sumitomo Electric and NEC then incorporated the chips into products that were in turn sold to NTT and installed in NTT's network.

Ikanos learned in January 2006 that there were quality issues with the chips. In particular, the chips had developed a problem called "Kirkendahl voiding," traceable to a third party assembling company in China to which Ikanos had switched the majority of its assembly work during the third and fourth quarters of fiscal year 2005. In the weeks leading up to the Secondary Offering, the defect issues became more pronounced as Ikanos received an increasing number of complaints from Sumitomo Electric and NEC. The thrust of the complaints was that the chips that had been installed in the NTT network were defective and were causing the network to fail, and that end-users who had subscribed to NTT's television, Internet and telephone services were losing signals and access to their subscribed services. . . . Panther alleges that Ikanos's Board of Directors met and discussed the defect issue at the time it arose, and Company representatives regularly traveled to Japan to meet with Sumitomo and NEC representatives to evaluate the problem and to discuss possible solutions.

Panther goes on to allege that Ikanos did not disclose the magnitude of the defect issue in either the Registration Statement or the Prospectus for the Secondary Offering. . . .

Some 5.75 million shares of Ikanos stock were sold in the Secondary Offering at $20.75 per share, raising more than $120 million. The individual defendants sold stock valued at $7.3 million.

Ikanos ultimately determined that the chips had an "extremely high" failure rate of 25-30%. . . . In June 2006, three months after the Secondary Offering, the Company reached an agreement with Sumitomo Electric and NEC to replace at Ikanos's expense all of the units sold—not just the units containing observably defective chips. . . .

In July 2006, the Company reported a net loss of $2.2 million for the second quarter, causing the price of its shares to drop over 25% from $13.85 to $10.24. . . . [The] plaintiff filed its initial complaint, alleging, among other things, that in contravention of *Item 303* of SEC Regulation S-K, defendants failed to disclose the "known . . . uncertainty" that the VDSL Version Four chips were defective and were causing system failures where they were deployed. . . .

The district court dismissed . . . for failure to state a claim, concluding that "[n]o plausibly pleaded fact suggests that Ikanos knew or should have known of the scope or magnitude of the defect problem at the time of the Secondary Offering." . . .

DISCUSSION

. . .

One of the potential bases for liability under §§11 and 12(a)(2) is an omission in contravention of an affirmative legal disclosure obligation. Id. In this case, Item 303 of SEC Regulation S-K provides the basis for Ikanos's alleged disclosure obligation. The Regulation, as we have seen, requires registrants to "[d]escribe any known trends or uncertainties . . . that the registrant reasonably expects will have a material . . . unfavorable impact on . . . revenues or income from continuing operations." Instruction 3 to paragraph 303(a) provides that "[t]he discussion and analysis shall focus specifically on material events and uncertainties known to management that would cause reported financial information not to be necessarily indicative of future operating results or of future financial condition." 17 C.F.R. §229.303(a) instruction 3. According to the SEC's interpretive release regarding Item 303, the Regulation imposes a disclosure duty "where a trend, demand, commitment, event or uncertainty is both [1] presently known to management and [2] reasonably likely to have material effects on the registrant's financial condition or results of operations." Management's Discussion and Analysis of Financial Condition and Results of Operations, Securities Act Release No. 6835, Exchange Act Release No. 26,831, Investment Company Act Release No. 16,961, 43 SEC Docket 1330, 1989 SEC LEXIS 1011 (May 18, 1989). We believe that, viewed in the context of Item 303's disclosure obligations, the defect rate, in a vacuum, is not what is at issue. Rather, it is the manner in which uncertainty surrounding that defect rate, generated by an increasing flow of highly negative information from key customers, might reasonably be expected to have a material impact on future revenues.

   Litwin v. Blackstone Group, L.P., [634 F.3d 706 (2d Cir. 2011)] . . . is instructive on this point. There, investors sued Blackstone, an asset management company, under §§11 and 12(a)(2) for omitting from a registration statement and prospectus information regarding negative trends in the real estate market. Blackstone's real estate investments accounted for approximately 22.6% of its assets under management. Reversing the district court's dismissal of the complaint, we held that plaintiffs adequately alleged that Blackstone was required by Item 303 to disclose the trend, "already known and existing at the time of the IPO," because it "was reasonably likely to have a material impact on Blackstone's financial condition." 634 F.3d at 716. In so holding, we emphasized that

> the key information that plaintiffs assert should have been disclosed is whether, and to what extent, the particular known trend, event, or uncertainty might have been reasonably expected to materially affect Blackstone's investments. . . . Again, the focus of plaintiffs' claims is the required disclosures under Item 303—plaintiffs are not seeking the disclosure of the. . . downward trend in the real estate market. . . . Rather, plaintiffs claim that Blackstone was required to disclose the manner in which th[at] then-known trend[], event[], or uncertainly[] might reasonably be expected to materially impact Blackstone's future revenues.

Id. at 718-19.
   We hold that the . . . [complaint] plausibly alleges that the defect issue, and its potential impact on Ikanos's business, constituted a known trend or uncertainty that Ikanos reasonably expected would have a material unfavorable impact on revenues or income from continuing operations. . . . [The complaint] alleges that, before the Secondary Offering, Ikanos was receiving an increasing number of calls from Sumitomo Electric and NEC alerting Ikanos to the fact that its chips were defective and were causing network failures. The . . . [complaint]

also alleges that the "defect issues," which were becoming "more pronounced," were a "substantial problem for [Ikanos] to resolve"—so much so that members of Ikanos's Board of Directors were discussing the issue, and representatives from the Company were flying to Japan to meet with Sumitomo Electric and NEC. . . . However, the . . . [complaint] adds the critical allegations (1) that these customers accounted for 72% of Ikanos's revenues in 2005 and (2) that Ikanos knew at the time it was receiving an increasing number of calls from these customers that it would be unable to determine which chip sets contained defective chips. The . . . [complaint] then articulates the plausible inference to be drawn from these facts: that Ikanos "knew that . . . the chips that it had sold to . . . its largest customers and the largest source of its revenues[] were defective, . . . and that it [may] therefore have to accept returns of *all* of the chips that it had sold to these two important customers." Id. at 52 (emphasis added).

We have little difficulty concluding that Panther has adequately alleged that the disclosures concerning a problem of this magnitude were inadequate and failed to comply with Item 303. . . .

NOTES AND QUESTIONS

1. Even National Elections Have Disclosure Implications Under MD&A.   In *In the Matter of Caterpillar, Inc.,* Exchange Act Release No. 30532 (Mar. 31, 1992), the Commission, in reaching a settlement, underscored the importance it places on the MD&A portions of the continuous reporting requirements. In its 10-K report for 1989, Caterpillar did not disclose that 23 percent of its net profits of $497 million was derived from its Brazilian subsidiary (CBSA). CBSA results were not separately reported, but were included on Caterpillar's consolidated income statement (CBSA accounted for only 5 percent of the parent company's revenues, and GAAP does not require reporting as a separate segment until the subsidiary's revenues constitute at least 10 percent of all reported revenue). CBSA's operating profits were in line with those it had earned in prior years, but in 1989, hyperinflation in Brazil caused a number of non-operating items—currency translation gains, export subsidies, interest income, and Brazilian tax loss carryforwards—to contribute substantially to CBSA's profits.

Two weeks before filing its 10-Q report for the first quarter of 1990, Caterpillar's board of directors was informed that CBSA's impact on 1990 operations would be significant and that the situation in Brazil was volatile. But because the political and economic conditions in Brazil were unstable, it was not possible to predict the full impact of these conditions on CBSA and Caterpillar. The difficulty in forecasting CBSA's impact was largely due to uncertainty regarding what economic reforms would be introduced by the new Brazilian government. Caterpillar's first 1990 10-Q, however, did not disclose management's concern for CBSA's likely impact on the parent's 1990 operations. In June 1990, after the policies of the new Brazilian government became known, Caterpillar's management concluded that CBSA would suffer substantial losses for 1990. Soon thereafter, Caterpillar announced that 1990 results would be substantially lower than previously projected and that "more than half of the decrease in forecasted 1990 profit is due to a dramatic decline in results for [CBSA]." The company's stock price fell 9⅝ points within a day of the announcement.

The Commission found that in view of the magnitude of CBSA's contribution to Caterpillar's overall earnings, disclosure of the extent of that contribution was necessary under Item 303(a)(3)(i). Moreover, the Commission believed Caterpillar should have discussed the various factors that contributed to CBSA's profits in 1989. The Commission also found that both the 1989 10-K and the 1990 10-Q were deficient in failing to disclose the known uncertainties at CBSA, the possibility of Caterpillar having lower profits in 1990 because of the risks facing CBSA, and the overall failure to reasonably quantify the impact of these risks. In this respect, the Commission emphasized Item 303(a)(3)(ii), which requires the registrant to disclose "any known trends or uncertainties that have had or that the registrant reasonably expects will have a material favorable or unfavorable impact on net sales or revenues or income from continuing operations." *See also* Instruction 3 to Item 303.

2. *More on Private Suits.* Courts are divided on whether in private suits under Rule 10b-5 Item 303 provides the basis for a duty to disclose a pessimistic internal forecast so that a private recovery can occur under Rule 10b-5. *In re Verifone Securities Litigation*, 11 F.3d 865 (9th Cir. 1993) dismissed a Rule 10b-5 suit by investors who purchased a company's stock in reliance on the company's prospectus, which was filled with favorable financial information on the company's operations to date, but did not include various adverse facts and trends known to management and its underwriters that indicated that Verifone's future prospects were not as bright as its past performance. The court's majority reasoned that no misrepresentation occurs by the failure to include such a forecast so long as Verifone had not "withheld data or existing facts from which forecasts are typically derived." Id. at 869. *See also Oran v. Stafford*, 226 F.3d 275, 287 (3d Cir. 2000) (violation of Item 303 does not give rise to independent cause of action or a duty enforceable under Rule 10b-5).

In contrast to *Verifone* and *Oran*, *Stratte-McClure v. Morgan Stanley*, 776 F.3d 94 (2d Cir. 2015), held that the failure to satisfy the duty imposed by Item 303 can support a claim of a material omission in a private suit under Rule 10b-5. The Second Circuit reasoned, in part, that the failure to comply with Item 303 leads the reasonable investor to conclude there is no known trend or uncertainty that management reasonably expects will have a material impact. Recently, the Ninth Circuit in *Cohen v. NVIDIA*, 768 F.3d 1046 (9th Cir. 2014), reaffirmed its earlier position in *Verifone*. The Supreme Court granted certiorari to review whether Item 303 violations should give rise to Rule 10b-5 liability, but dropped the case after the parties agreed to a settlement. *See generally* Turk & Woody, The *Leidos* Mixup: The Misunderstood Duty to Disclose in Securities Law, 75 Wash. & Lee L. Rev. 957 (2018). Outside of Rule 10b-5 actions, circuits have agreed that obligations imposed by Item 303 can give rise to liability under Sections 11 and 12(a)(2). *See, e.g., Silverstrand Inv. v. AMAG Pharmaceuticals, Inc.*, 707 F.3d 95 (1st Cir. 2013); *Steckman v. Hart Brewing Co.*, 143 F.3d 1293 (9th Cir. 1998). *But see J&R Marketing v. General Motors Corp.*, 549 F.3d 384 (6th Cir. 2008) (Section 11 does not alter the knowledge requirement of Item 303, so a company that is negligent in failing to discover what it could have learned, but nonetheless disclosed the underlying conditions, did not violate the disclosure duty of Item 303).

PROBLEM

11-8. Cool Cola is a worldwide bottler of soft drinks. In recent years its sales growth has led the industry. During the past two years, Cool Cola has boosted its sales and income through its "gallon-pushing" marketing practice, whereby it provides low-interest loans to independent bottlers for the purpose of inducing them to acquire large inventories of cola syrup, thereby boosting Cool Cola's sales and income. Now, nearly two years into gallon pushing, Cool Cola asks you whether Item 303 requires disclosure of its gallon pushing practice. Should it matter in answering this question that bottlers are beginning to complain of difficulty finding space to store additional quantities of syrup? *See In the Matter of Coca-Cola Co.*, Exchange Act Release No. 51565 (Apr. 18, 2005).

2. Enron's Contribution to the MD&A and Other Disclosures

In the fall of 2001, the financial world was shocked when Enron Corporation filed for bankruptcy. Enron was the seventh largest American company and just a few months earlier it was the darling of the investment community. Enron's collapse occurred because of contingent liabilities that were triggered by the rapid decline in the value of its shares. Much of these liabilities were with so-called special purpose entities that Enron had created to exploit accounting standards that permitted liabilities to be moved off its books and onto the books of the special purpose entity, provided that entity was independent. Enron did not disclose that some of the special purpose entities were created and controlled by some of its senior officers.

   As partial response to the disclosure gaps highlighted by Enron, SOX added Section 13(j) to the Exchange Act thereby causing the SEC to expand Item 303 of Regulation S-K to require much more detailed presentation of "off-balance sheet arrangements" within the MD&A portions of the registrant's SEC filings. *See* Securities Act Release No. 8182 (Jan. 28, 2003). Item 303 now provides a fairly expansive definition of off-balance sheet arrangements so that they include a wide range of transactions that pose potential contingent claims upon the registrant. For such arrangements, Item 303(a)(4) enumerates disclosures that must be made for off-balance sheet items that either have or are reasonably likely to have a current or future effect on the registrant's financial condition, revenues, expenses, or liquidity that is material to investors. The first step of this determination is for management to determine whether a known trend, demand, commitment, event, or uncertainty is reasonably likely to occur. If management concludes that it is not reasonably likely to occur, no disclosure is required. However, if management cannot make this determination, disclosure is required unless management determines that a material effect on the registrant's financial condition, revenues, etc., is not reasonably likely to occur. Among the enumerated categories of information that must be disclosed regarding an off-balance sheet arrangement that has or is reasonably likely to have a current or future effect on the registrant's financial condition, revenues, etc., are the arrangement's nature and purpose and importance to the firm's liquidity, insights into the arrangement's overall magnitude, and the possibility of the arrangement being terminated or reduced.

Also in response to the various causes for Enron's collapse and its extensive use of mechanisms to conceal its liabilities, the SEC expanded the range of items to include among the events to be disclosed promptly on Form 8-K: (1) the making or terminating of a material agreement that is not part of the ordinary course of business; (2) the creation of, or default upon, a material financial obligation; (3) credit rating changes; and (4) asset impairment that leads to a material deduction to the financial statements.

As for the self-dealing features of Enron's special purpose entities, the SEC offered the following disclosure guidance:

> Disclosures about Effects of Transactions with Related and Certain Other Parties. . .
>
> [W]here related party transactions are material, MD&A should include discussion of those transactions to the extent necessary for an understanding of the company's current and prospective financial position and operating results. . . .
>
> Registrants should consider whether investors would better understand financial statements in many circumstances if MD&A included descriptions of all material transactions involving related persons or entities, with clear discussion of arrangements that may involve transactions terms or other aspects that differ from those which would likely be negotiated with clearly independent parties. . . .
>
> Registrants should also consider the need for disclosure about parties that fall outside the definition of "related parties," but with whom the registrant or its related parties have a relationship that enables the parties to negotiate terms of material transactions that may not be available from other, more clearly independent, parties on an arm's length basis. For example, an entity may be established and operated by individuals that were former senior management of, or have some other current or former relationship with, a registrant. . . .

Securities Act Release No. 8056 (Jan. 22, 2002). Under what provision of Item 303 of Regulation S-K would the related party disclosures most likely fall?

3.   The SEC, MD&A, and the Environment

The National Environmental Policy Act of 1969 (NEPA) mandates, among other things, that every federal agency "to the fullest extent possible" interpret and administer federal laws "in accordance with the policies set forth" in NEPA.[1] Reflecting NEPA, the SEC requires registrants to disclose *pending* governmental proceedings, whether judicial or administrative, that involve material amounts and relate to the environment to be disclosed. In contrast, pending nonenvironmental proceedings, even though material, need not be disclosed if they are "ordinary routine litigation incidental to the business." In addition to the generic standard of materiality, an item is deemed material if it exceeds 10 percent of current assets or $100,000. *See* Instruction 5 to Item 103 of Regulation S-K. The SEC rules also require disclosure of the cost to comply with environmental requirements that is expected to be incurred in the current year and the succeeding year, as well as any subsequent year. Note that the SEC's disclosure focus is the financial impact on the issuer of environmental requirements

---

1.   Pub. L. No. 91-190, 83 Stat. 852 (1970), *codified at* 42 U.S.C. ¶¶4321-4347.

and not the consequences of the issuer's operations on the environment. This reflects the SEC's view that its goal with respect to environmental disclosures is to aid investors and not to serve broader social objectives that might be included within NEPA; that is, the Commission does not believe that NEPA alters the historical objective of the federal securities laws of providing economically relevant information to investors. Securities Act Release No. 5627 (Oct. 14, 1975).

Obviously, to conclude that the reasonable investor is an economically driven person does not dispose neatly of the materiality of environmental, safety, or the range of other social disclosures that can be made. Moreover, heightened concerns today regarding climate change are linked as well to sustainability disclosures, a topic examined in the next chapter, where we consider whether such contemporary concerns can be expected to impact disclosures bearing on a range of environmentally linked items.

The following release amplifies the disclosure obligations of registrants in the MD&A portion of their filings, where in Item 303 of Regulation S-K registrants are required to disclose forward-looking information regarding known trends or any known demands, commitments, events, or uncertainties that are likely to have a material effect on net income, capital expenditures, or liquidity.

Prospective Information, Financial Reporting Release No. 36
Securities and Exchange Commission (May 24, 1989)

Where a trend, demand, commitment, event or uncertainty is known, management must make two assessments:

(1) Is the known trend, demand, commitment, event or uncertainty likely to come to fruition? If management determines that it is not reasonably likely to occur, no disclosure is required.

(2) If management cannot make that determination, it must evaluate objectively the consequences of the known trend, demand, commitment, event or uncertainty, on the assumption that it will come to fruition. Disclosure is then required unless management determines that a material effect on the registrant's financial condition or results of operations is not reasonably likely to occur.

Each final determination resulting from the assessments made by management must be objectively reasonable, viewed as of the time the determination is made.

Application of these principles may be illustrated using a common disclosure issue that was considered in the review of a number of Project registrants: designation as a potentially responsible party ("PRP") by the Environmental Protection Agency (the "EPA") under the Comprehensive Environmental Response, Compensation, and Liability Act of 1980 ("Superfund").

Facts: A registrant has been correctly designated a PRP by the EPA with respect to cleanup of hazardous waste at three sites. No statutory defenses are available. The registrant is in the process of preliminary investigations of the sites to determine the nature of its potential liability and the amount of remedial costs necessary to clean up the sites. Other PRPs also have been designated, but the ability to obtain contribution is unclear, as is the extent of insurance coverage, if any. Management is unable to determine that a material effect on future financial condition or results of operations is not reasonably likely to occur.

Based upon the facts of this hypothetical case, MD&A disclosure of the effects of the PRP status, quantified to the extent reasonably practicable, would be required. For MD&A purposes, aggregate potential cleanup costs must be considered in light of the joint and several liability to which a PRP is subject. Facts regarding whether insurance coverage may be contested, and whether and to what extent potential sources of contribution or indemnification constitute reliable sources of recovery may be factored into the determination of whether a material future effect is not reasonably likely to occur.

PROBLEM

11-9.   For years, U.S. Chemical Company has been disposing of its waste chemicals by paying a reliable waste management firm, Puralator Company, to properly store or neutralize the chemicals. About a year ago, U.S. Chemical learned that Puralator had been cited by both state and federal governmental agencies for reckless storage of waste chemicals, and this caused U.S. Chemical and many other chemical companies to cease doing business with Puralator. Last week, three events occurred that bear on U.S. Chemical's being required to pay a significant portion of the costs to clean up the storage site used by Puralator.

    a. Puralator denies that it has failed to properly dispose of any of U.S. Chemical's waste.

    b. The local appellate court has recently held that state environmental laws require companies to dispose of their toxic wastes through waste management firms and these companies are liable if the waste management firms default in their state-imposed duty to operate an environmentally sound waste disposal site.

    c. U.S. Chemical's insurance carrier has announced that its future position is that it is not responsible for waste cleanup costs under the general liability policy carried by U.S. Chemical. However, U.S. Chemical believes there is an even chance that a court would hold that the insurance carrier's interpretation is inconsistent with the express terms of its policy, so that the insurer is bound for any cleanup costs.

U.S. Chemical estimates that its liability with respect to Puralator could exceed $5 million. How much of this information must be disclosed in its upcoming 10-K?

‖12‖
Inquiries into the Materiality of Information

Materiality is a controlling concept when there are allegations of fraud. While the fraud provisions of the federal securities laws do not impose a duty to disclose information simply because it is material, they do require affirmative disclosure of material information in certain circumstances. And they bar both material misstatements and half-truths whenever information is given to investors.

Materiality determinations also have an important role in defining the content of state and federal mandatory disclosure requirements. The content and format of disclosures made in filings with the SEC are governed by the specific instructions for each form or by Regulations S-X and S-K.[1]

Most of this line-item disclosure is absolute in the sense that the elicited information must be disclosed and its disclosure is not dependent upon a separate determination by the registrant or the Commission of the information's probable impact upon investors or stockholders. Such line-item disclosure reflects the Commission's determination of information that on average will be considered useful, if not important, to investors and shareholders. In this way, there is some amount of information in the public domain regarding all public companies in a format that permits ready comparison among them.

At some points in the disclosure instructions, however, specific information is required to be disclosed only if it involves a *material* development or qualification. Moreover, Rule 408 requires that in addition to the information compelled to be disclosed under the Commission's line-item requirements, registrants must include in their '33 Act registration statement "such further *material* information . . . as may be necessary to make the required statement, in light of the circumstances . . . not misleading." A similar requirement applies to all '34 Act filings through the operation of Rule 12b-20.

Because the materiality concept is such a workhorse in securities regulation, learning to apply it is probably the most valuable skill a securities lawyer can acquire. As you consider the materials in this chapter, think about whether the sole issue is—or should be—determining what information investors want

---

1. The SEC rules defer to generally accepted accounting principles (GAAP) for normative standards used in the preparation of financial statements included in SEC filings.

or need. Or are other social policies relevant to determining what must be disclosed or what need not be disclosed?

A.   *Materiality Orthodoxy*

Determining what is material is a normative judgment having the same level of precision as determining what the reasonable person would do under the circumstances. In litigation, a fact's materiality is a mixed question of law and fact, so that it arises in pretrial motions as well as at trial. Outside of litigation, considering whether an item is material and thus must be disclosed is frequently an ulcerating experience.

In *Mills v. Electric Auto-Lite Co.*, 396 U.S. 375 (1970), the Supreme Court muddied the waters considerably when in the same paragraph it stated that materiality entails a finding that the information "*might* have been considered important by a reasonable" investor and then it observed that the test required "a significant *propensity* to affect" investors. The Court appeared to embrace two standards for judging materiality, one that tended toward the information's probable influence on investors and the other toward its possible effect. The full impact of the distinction between these standards is illustrated in *TSC Industries, Inc. v. Northway, Inc.*, 426 U.S. 438 (1976), *rev'g* 512 F.2d 324 (1975), involving an allegedly misleading proxy statement circulated in connection with TSC Industries' merger into National Industries. The Seventh Circuit, applying the "might" standard, held that certain omissions were material as a matter of law and granted Northway summary judgment on this issue. The Supreme Court reversed the grant of summary judgment, holding that under its standard of materiality, none of the alleged omissions was materially misleading as a matter of law:

> An omitted fact is material if there is a substantial likelihood that a reasonable shareholder would consider it important in deciding how to vote. This standard is fully consistent with *Mills'* general description of materiality as a requirement that "the defect have a significant propensity to affect the voting process." It does not require proof of a substantial likelihood that disclosure of the omitted fact would have caused the reasonable investor to change his vote. What the standard does contemplate is a showing of a substantial likelihood that, under all the circumstances, the omitted fact would have assumed actual significance in the deliberations of the reasonable shareholder. Put another way, there must be a substantial likelihood that the disclosure of the omitted fact would have been viewed by the reasonable investor as having significantly altered the "total mix" of information made available.

Id. at 449. Virtually all cases involving materiality determinations under the federal securities laws proceed after repeating the Supreme Court's formula as stated in *TSC Industries.*

NOTES AND QUESTIONS

1. The Properties of the Reasonable Investor. Who is the reasonable investor or reasonable shareholder? Consider the following:

> Speculators and chartists of Wall and Bay Streets are also "reasonable" investors entitled to the same legal protection afforded conservative traders. Thus, material facts include not only information disclosing the earnings and distributions of a company but also those facts which affect the probable future of the company and those which affect the desire of investors to buy, sell or hold the company's securities.

SEC v. Texas Gulf Sulphur Co., 401 F.2d 833, 849 (2d Cir. 1968), *cert. denied*, 394 U.S. 976 (1969). How does the description of the "reasonable investor" compare to the "reasonable person" in tort law? *See* Rose, The "Reasonable Investor" of the Federal Securities Law: Insights from Tort Law's "Reasonable Person" and Suggested Reforms, 47 J. Corp. L. 77 (2017).

Is the materiality standard pernicious? Consider *Jones v. National Distillers & Chemical Corp.*, 484 F. Supp. 679 (S.D.N.Y. 1979), in which the court held that it could not rule as a matter of law that the failure of the proxy statement to disclose that a winery was switching from 64 oz., half-gallon containers to 51.4 oz., magnum-size containers for some of its wines was not a material omission in a proxy statement seeking shareholder approval of the merger of the winery into a large conglomerate. The defendant company argued that the omission of this fact was immaterial because the proxy statement accurately forecast overall net income and that forecast took into account the switch to magnums. Shortly after this ruling, the case was settled for $750,000. *Jones v. National Distillers & Chem. Corp.*, [1979-1980 Transfer Binder] Fed. Sec. L. Rep. (CCH) ¶97,288 (S.D.N.Y. 1980). If *Jones* had gone to trial, how would the materiality of this omission have been determined? Was the registration statement of a well-known golf club manufacturer's materially misleading by stating its clubs were sold exclusively through authorized dealers and pro shops when 2 percent of its sales were through a discount store? *See In re Adams Golf Inc. Securities Litigation*, 381 F.3d 267 (3d Cir. 2004). What if a CEO has represented he graduated from college, but had only attended the college for three years? *See Greenhouse v. MCG Capital Corp.*, 392 F.3d 650 (4th Cir. 2004).

2. Rules of Thumb. Some disclosure items, while large in the absolute, become immaterial relative to the size of the firm. *See Hutchinson v. Deutsche Bank Securities, Inc.*, 647 F.3d 479 (2d Cir. 2011) ($52 million impairment in value of mezzanine loans in bank's portfolio is unquestionably large, but was immaterial in light of overall $1.1 billion portfolio). A common belief, or rule of thumb, has been that a misstatement regarding a financial statement item of 5 percent or less is not material. In SEC's Staff Accounting Bulletin No. 99 (1999), the staff rejects this approach to materiality determinations as being too limited in its scope. The Bulletin reminds lawyers and accountants to assess an item in light of the total mix of information so that a change of less than 5 percent could be material if, for example, it masked a change in sales or earnings trend, changed a loss into income, or vice versa, hides a factor to meet analysts' expectations, concerns a segment of the issuer's business that has been identified as playing a significant role in operations, and the like. *See Litwin v. The Blackstone Group LP*, 634 F.3d 706 (2d Cir. 2011) (invoking SAB No. 99 to hold that decline of 3.6 percent of total firm assets in the private equity portion of the business was material where registration statement identified private equity as having a significant role in the firm's operations and the loss equaled 9.4 percent of that portion of the business).

3. Is There a Market Test for Materiality? Should the materiality of an omission or misstatement be determined by whether it had an effect on the security's price when the security is traded in an efficient market? *Compare In the Matter of Navigant Consulting Inc. Sec. Litig.*, 275 F.3d 616 (7th Cir. 2001) (dismissing for want of materiality where no market decline) *with No. 84 Employer-Teamster Joint Council Pension Trust Fund v. America West Holding Corp.*, 320 F.3d 920 (9th Cir. 2003) (market subject to distortions that can prevent immediate market reaction).

4. The Subjective Test of Materiality. When dealings are on a face-to-face basis, should the materiality of a representation be determined by whether it is important to the person to whom the representation was made? Such an approach would shift the materiality standard from an objective one to a subjective one. Consider *Thomas v. Duralite Co., Inc.*, 524 F.2d 577 (3d Cir. 1975), where among the omissions committed was the failure to disclose to the plaintiff that merger talks were then taking place. *Thomas* stated that an objective standard of materiality is necessary in situations involving "a large number of shareholders who may have had no direct or continuing contact with the corporation." Id. at 584. However, where the subject transaction involves a single seller and single buyer, each well known to the other, the court believed "the distinction between objective materiality and subjective reliance becomes obscured." Id. The court nonetheless affirmed the judgment of the lower court under the objective "reasonable person" standard. Id. at 585. *See also SEC v. Morgan Keegan & Co.*, 678 F.3d 1233 (11th Cir. 2012) (even though the false representation was made only to a handful of investors, materiality is to be adjudged by the hypothetical "objective" reasonable investor standard); Sachs, Materiality and Social Change: The Case for Replacing "the Reasonable Investor" with "the Least Sophisticated Investor" in Inefficient Markets, 81 Tul. L. Rev. 473 (2006) (questioning *TSC Ind.* reasoning that unsophisticated investors trading in inefficient markets can be duped by representations that would not be deemed important to reasonable investor).

Recall however that materiality is distinct from the issue of causation where inquiries are made into whether the plaintiff relied in fact on a material misstatement or omission. *See Glickenhaus & Co. v. Household Int'l Inc.*, 787 F.3d 408 (7th Cir. 2015) (defendant surveyed nearly 43,000 class members to ascertain whether each would still have purchased the defendant's stock if they knew the price had been inflated by the misrepresentation—only 11,000 completed the survey with only 133 stating they would still have purchased).

5.   *Buried Facts.*   A frequent bromide is that the federal securities laws require full and fair disclosure. While the fullness of disclosure can be evaluated in terms of what was said and what should have been said, the element of fairness involves the format in which that disclosure occurred. *See Virginia Bankshares, Inc. v. Sandberg,* 501 U.S. 1083, 1097 (1991) ("not every mixture with the true will neutralize the deceptive. If it would take a financial analyst to spot the tension between the one and the other, whatever is misleading will remain materially so, and liability should follow"). Fairness is the essence of the "buried facts" doctrine, which applies to render misleading a document in which all the substantive information has been set forth, but in such manner that the mosaic can only be assembled with great difficulty and only with advanced knowledge that the whole picture requires a great deal of assembly. For example, *Campbell v. Transgenomic, Inc.,* 916 F.3d 1121 (8th Cir. 2019), held that a trier of fact could reasonable conclude the proxy statement for the merger of two biotechnology firms was materially misleading by forecasting future revenues under headings "technology" and "services" without further identifying how each company contributed to the forecasted amount in each category; the company defended by arguing that a close reading of financial information at other locations of the proxy statement would have enabled investors to identify that the acquired company's projects were set forth in the "services" category.

The leading buried facts case is *Kohn v. American Metal Climax, Inc.,* 322 F. Supp. 1331 (E.D. Pa. 1970), *modified,* 458 F.2d 255 (3d Cir.), *cert. denied,* 409 U.S. 874 (1972). At page two of the firm's proxy statement there appeared in bold print the statement of an investment adviser that the transaction was a favorable one. At page 125 of the 200-page proxy statement, there appeared a cross-reference to an appendix bearing on many aspects of the transaction, including the adviser's fairness opinion. The appendix revealed that the adviser did not perform an independent evaluation of the firm's assets. The appendix also included an opinion of the federal district court wherein the directors' conflict of interest was discussed; the proxy statement did not otherwise disclose the directors' conflict of interest. Held: The facts were not adequately disclosed. *See also Kennedy v. Tallant,* 710 F.2d 711, 720 (11th Cir. 1983) (fair disclosure cannot be achieved through piecemeal release of facts); *Marksman Partners LP v. Chantal Pharmaceutical Corp.,* 927 F. Supp. 1297 (C.D. Cal. 1996) (financial statement's inclusion in sales of goods shipped on consignment not corrected by including among 22 exhibits a copy of the marketing agreement that revealed shipments were not sales but for consignment).

What if it takes some calculations to derive from the disclosed information the magnitude of the event? *In re Merck & Co. Sec. Litig.,* 432 F.3d 261 (3d Cir. 2005), arose when Merck disclosed in an SEC filing that it was incurring revenue recognition problems in connection with co-payments received by its prescription drug administrator subsidiary, Medco. It did not, however, disclose the magnitude of the problem, and its stock actually rose in the days following the announcement. Two months later the Wall Street Journal estimated the revenue problem would be about $4.6 billion, basing its estimate on a couple of simple mathematical calculations involving material disclosed in the SEC filing and the assumption that there was about a $10 co-payment per prescription. The news story sent Merck's shares into a tailspin. The court concluded that the SEC filing was not materially misleading since the magnitude of the problem could be deduced by a couple of mathematical calculations and an assumption. *See also Ash v. LFE Corp.*, 525 F.2d 215, 219 (3d Cir. 1975) ("those responsible for the preparation of proxy solicitations must assume that stockholders . . . [can] perform simple subtraction"); *Singh v. Schikan*, 106 F. Supp. 3d 439 (S.D.N.Y. 2015) (no room for buried facts complaint where registration statement presented a summary of several scientific studies bearing on risks incident to firm's drug that was being developed, but drew no conclusions from the reviewed studies).

6. Boilerplate in Risk Disclosures: Costs and Benefits.   Relying on natural language processing tools used in the social sciences, Professor McClane's study of 2,751 IPOs between 1996-2015 found the following with respect to the use of "boilerplate" disclosures:

> The results of the analysis shed light on boilerplate's potential value as well as its risks. A securities class action filed against Wayfair.com provides an illustration. The lawsuit alleged that when Wayfair, an online retailer specializing in home goods and furniture, went public, its prospectus misled investors by forgoing a specific disclosure in favor of a boilerplate risk factor about its competitors: "Our business is rapidly evolving and intensely competitive, and we have many competitors in different industries. Our competition includes: furniture stores, big box retailers, department stores, specialty retailers, and online home goods retailers and marketplaces. . . ."
>
> Absent from this disclosure was any mention of a specific competitor, Overstock.com, whose similar business model posed a serious competitive threat to Wayfair. When securities analysts finally noticed the omission several months later, Wayfair stock fell and the investors lost money. This risk factor was not the only generic disclosure Wayfair used: fifty percent of the risk factors in its IPO prospectus included language copied from other companies' recent deals, according to the measure used in this study. By comparison, the average amount of risk factor boilerplate across all prospectuses in the dataset is thirty-two percent.
>
> . . . [I]t is easy to see why efficiency might have prompted Wayfair's counsel—a busy, national law firm—to use ready-made language if experience told them that it was sufficient to convey the risk of competition to investors. On the other hand, one can imagine how a prospectus that is nearly eighty percent boilerplate might gloss over important issues faced by a relatively unknown company. The data shows that both views may have merit. . . .
>
> I find that more boilerplate is associated with lower legal costs, but find no evidence that it is associated with lower auditing fees or underwriting fees. Moreover, I find no significant association between boilerplate and faster deal-completion times, the average amount a prospectus is amended, or the scrutiny it receives from the SEC.
>
> . . . I also find . . . a 10% increase in boilerplate in certain important sections of a registration statement is associated with as much as a 5.1% to 6.2% increase in deal underpricing. . . . This translates, on average, to as much as $6 million that an issuer leaves on the table for each 10% increase in the use of boilerplate in its disclosure. Higher levels of boilerplate are also associated with higher risk of prospectus-related litigation: a 10% increase in the amount of boilerplate in some sections of the prospectus is associated with a 1.5% to 4% increase in the probability of being sued for securities fraud related to the offering. The analyses also show a relationship between boilerplate and three other indicia of information asymmetry: greater probability of pre-IPO price revision, wider first-day bid-ask trading spreads, and greater divergence of recommendations among analysts following the issuer.

McClane, Boilerplate and the Impact of Disclosure in Securities Disclosures, 72 Vand. L. Rev. 191, 196-198 (2019). *See In re Snap Sec. Litig.*, 2018 U.S. Dist.

LEXIS 97704 (C.D. Cal. June 7, 2018) (denying motion to dismiss of complaint alleging IPO's registration statement setting forth risk factors was boilerplate).

PROBLEM

12-1.   Bloomsters, Inc. is in the process of raising $5 million by selling its common shares to about 30 investors. The offering brochure circulated among interested investors accurately sets forth the steady but unspectacular growth in its business since its beginning three years earlier. The brochure includes a narrative of how Bloomsters began as a company that initially sought to develop, using state-of-the-art biotechnology, new hybrid roses that were resistant to diseases common to rose hybrids. The narrative then describes how, in the past two years, Bloomsters substantially reduced its research staff as more and more of its activities became focused on its retail and wholesale rose operations. A subsequent portion of the materials presented financial information that shows both a steady increase in revenues from sales of roses and a precipitous decline in funding for the research activities that were at the heart of the business when it was formed. Finally, near the end of the offering materials, under the heading "Our Directors and Their Vision," there is a succinct statement: "The board at its recent meeting voted to discontinue all research activities." The offering brochure states that the proceeds of the offering will be used to expand Bloomsters' distribution facilities to meet the increasing demand for its variety of nursery products.

Carl, who has a passion for roses, received a copy of the Bloomsters offering brochure. After studying the offering brochure, Carl called Bloomsters' president, Eloise. Because he had read about Bloomsters' efforts to develop a disease-resistant rose, Carl asked what was to become of that project. Eloise told Carl that Bloomsters would continue to pursue its research efforts for a disease-resistant rose, but that Bloomsters' principal focus would be wholesaling nursery stock. Eloise did not disclose that Bloomsters' board of directors had decided to terminate all research efforts. Carl purchased $10,000 of Bloomsters' common stock. Was a material misrepresentation made to Carl?

B.   Speculative Information and Materiality

Basic Inc. v. Levinson
485 U.S. 224 (1988)

BLACKMUN, J. This case requires us to apply the materiality requirement of §10(b) of the Securities Exchange Act of 1934, and Rule 10b-5, promulgated thereunder, in the context of preliminary corporate merger discussions. . . .

I

Prior to December 20, 1978, Basic Incorporated was a publicly traded company primarily engaged in the business of manufacturing chemical refractories for the steel industry. As early as 1965 or 1966, Combustion Engineering, Inc., a company producing mostly alumina-based refractories, expressed some interest in acquiring Basic, but was deterred from pursuing this inclination seriously because of antitrust concerns it then entertained. . . .

Beginning in September 1976, Combustion representatives had meetings and telephone conversations with Basic officers and directors, including petitioners here, concerning the possibility of a merger. During 1977 and 1978, Basic made three public statements denying that it was engaged in merger negotiations.[4] On December 18, 1978, Basic asked the New York Stock Exchange to suspend trading in its shares and issued a release stating that it had been "approached" by another company concerning a merger. On December 19, Basic's board endorsed Combustion's offer of $46 per share for its common stock, and on the following day publicly announced its approval of Combustion's tender offer for all outstanding shares.

Respondents are former Basic shareholders who sold their stock after Basic's first public statement of October 21, 1977, and before the suspension of trading in December 1978. Respondents brought a class action against Basic and its directors, asserting that the defendants issued three false or misleading public statements and thereby were in violation of §10(b) of the 1934 Act and of Rule 10b-5. Respondents alleged that they were injured by selling Basic shares at artificially depressed prices in a market affected by petitioners' misleading statements and in reliance thereon. . . .

The United States Court of Appeals for the Sixth Circuit . . . reversed the District Court's summary judgment, and remanded the case. 786 F.2d 741 (1986). . . .

In the Court of Appeals' view, Basic's statements that no negotiations were taking place, and that it knew of no corporate developments to account for the heavy trading activity, were misleading. With respect to materiality, the court rejected the argument that preliminary merger discussions are immaterial as a matter of law, and held that "once a statement is made denying the existence of any discussions, even discussions that might not have been material in absence of the denial are material because they make the statement made untrue." 786 F.2d, at 749. . . .

We granted certiorari to resolve the split . . . among the Courts of Appeals as to the standard of materiality applicable to preliminary merger discussions. . . .

---

4.   On October 21, 1977, after heavy trading and a new high in Basic stock, the following news item appeared in the Cleveland Plain Dealer:

> [Basic] President Max Muller said the company knew no reason for the stock's activity and that no negotiations were under way with any company for a merger. He said Flintkote recently denied Wall Street rumors that it would make a tender offer of $25 a share for control of the Cleveland-based maker of refractories for the steel industry.

On September 25, 1978, in reply to an inquiry from the New York Stock Exchange, Basic issued a release concerning increased activity in its stock and stated that "management is unaware of any present or pending company development that would result in the abnormally heavy trading activity and price fluctuation in company shares that have been experienced in the past few days."

On November 6, 1978, Basic issued to its shareholders a "Nine Months Report 1978." This Report stated: "With regard to the stock market activity in the Company's shares we remain unaware of any present or pending developments which would account for the high volume of trading and price fluctuations in recent months."

II

. . . The Court . . . explicitly has defined a standard of materiality under the securities laws, *see TSC Industries, Inc. v. Northway, Inc.*, 426 U.S. 438 (1976), concluding in the proxy-solicitation context that "[a]n omitted fact is material if there is a substantial likelihood that a reasonable shareholder would consider it important in deciding how to vote." Id., at 449. Acknowledging that certain information concerning corporate developments could well be of "dubious significance," id., at 448, the Court was careful not to set too low a standard of materiality; it was concerned that a minimal standard might bring an overabundance of information within its reach, and lead management "simply to bury the shareholders in an avalanche of trivial information—a result that is hardly conducive to informed decisionmaking." Id., at 448-449. It further explained that to fulfill the materiality requirement "there must be a substantial likelihood that the disclosure of the omitted fact would have been viewed by the reasonable investor as having significantly altered the 'total mix' of information made available." Id., at 449. We now expressly adopt the *TSC Industries* standard of materiality for the §10(b) and Rule 10b-5 context.

III

The application of this materiality standard to preliminary merger discussions is not self-evident. Where the impact of the corporate development on the target's fortune is certain and clear, the *TSC Industries* materiality definition admits straightforward application. Where, on the other hand, the event is contingent or speculative in nature, it is difficult to ascertain whether the "reasonable investor" would have considered the omitted information significant at the time. Merger negotiations, because of the ever-present possibility that the contemplated transaction will not be effectuated, fall into the latter category. . . .

C

Even before this Court's decision in *TSC Industries*, the Second Circuit had explained the role of the materiality requirement of Rule 10b-5, with respect to contingent or speculative information or events, in a manner that gave that term meaning that is independent of the other provisions of the Rule. Under such circumstances, materiality "will depend at any given time upon a balancing of both the indicated probability that the event will occur and the anticipated magnitude of the event in light of the totality of the company activity." *SEC v. Texas Gulf Sulphur Co.*, 401 F.2d, at 849. Interestingly, neither the Third Circuit decision adopting the agreement-in-principle test nor petitioners here take issue with this general standard. Rather, they suggest that with respect to preliminary merger discussions, there are good reasons to draw a line at agreement on price and structure.

In a subsequent decision, the late Judge Friendly, writing for a Second Circuit panel, applied the *Texas Gulf Sulphur* probability/magnitude approach in the specific context of preliminary merger negotiations. After acknowledging that materiality is something to be determined on the basis of the particular facts of each case, he stated:

> Since a merger in which it is bought out is the most important event that can occur in a small corporation's life, to wit, its death, we think that inside information, as regards a merger of this sort, can become material at an earlier stage than would be the case as regards lesser transactions—and this even though the mortality rate of mergers in such formative stages is doubtless high.

SEC v. Geon Industries, Inc., 531 F.2d 39, 47-48 (CA2 1976). We agree with that analysis.

Whether merger discussions in any particular case are material therefore depends on the facts. Generally, in order to assess the probability that the event will occur, a factfinder will need to look to indicia of interest in the transaction at the highest corporate levels. Without attempting to catalog all such possible factors, we note by way of example that board resolutions, instructions to investment bankers, and actual negotiations between principals or their intermediaries may serve as indicia of interest. To assess the magnitude of the transaction to the issuer of the securities allegedly manipulated, a factfinder will need to consider such facts as the size of the two corporate entities and of the potential premiums over market value. No particular event or factor short of closing the transaction need be either necessary or sufficient by itself to render merger discussions material.[17]

As we clarify today, materiality depends on the significance the reasonable investor would place on the withheld or misrepresented information.[18] The fact-specific inquiry we endorse here is consistent with the approach a number of courts have taken in assessing the materiality of merger negotiations. Because the standard of materiality we have adopted differs from that used by both courts below, we remand the case for reconsideration of the question whether a grant of summary judgment is appropriate on this record.

---

17.   To be actionable, of course, a statement must also be misleading. Silence, absent a duty to disclose, is not misleading under Rule 10b-5. "No comment" statements are generally the functional equivalent of silence. *See In re Carnation Co.,* supra. *See also* New York Stock Exchange Listed Company Manual §202.01. . . .

It has been suggested that given current market practices, a "no comment" statement is tantamount to an admission that merger discussions are underway. *See Flamm v. Eberstadt,* 814 F.2d, at 1178. That may well hold true to the extent that issuers adopt a policy of truthfully denying merger rumors when no discussions are underway, and of issuing "no comment" statements when they are in the midst of negotiations. There are, of course, other statement policies firms could adopt; we need not now advise issuers as to what kind of practice to follow within the range permitted by law. . . .

18.   We find no authority in the statute, the legislative history, or our previous decisions, for varying the standard of materiality depending on who brings the action or whether insiders are alleged to have profited. *See, e.g., Pavlidis v. New England Patriots Football Club, Inc.,* 737 F.2d 1227, 1231 (CA1 1984) ("A fact does not become more material to the shareholder's decision because it is withheld by an insider, or because the insider might profit by withholding it"). . . .

NOTES AND QUESTIONS

1.   Offering Securities in a Bad Quarter.   The registrant must include in its registration statement quarterly report information for any quarter concluded prior to 135 days before the registration statement became effective. What must the issuer disclose about its performance during the quarter in which the offering is occurring? In *Shaw v. Digital Equipment*, 82 F.3d 1194, 1210 (1st Cir. 1996), the registration statement became effective two weeks before the end of the quarter in progress; internal reports reported substantial declines in business for the quarter in progress. In refusing to dismiss the case, the court in *Shaw* considered both a probability of a losing quarter, noting the proximity of the quarter's close to the effective date of the registration statement, and emphasized that the information showed a substantial likelihood that the current quarter would be an "extreme departure" from the past. Shortly thereafter, the First Circuit dismissed a case where the offering was occurring during the seventh week of a disastrous quarter, viewing the interim information too speculative to merit disclosure. *Glassman v. Computervision Corp.*, 90 F.3d 617 (1st Cir. 1996). *See also In re Sourcefire, Inc. Sec. Litig.*, 2008 U.S. Dist. LEXIS 33448 (D. Md. Apr. 23, 2008); *In re Ulta Salon Cosmetics & Fragrances, Inc. Sec. Litig.*, 604 F. Supp. 2d 1188 (N.D. Ill. 2009). *But see* Gulati, When Corporate Managers Fear a Good Thing Is Coming to an End: The Case of Interim Nondisclosure, 44 UCLA L. Rev. 675, 685 (1999) (arguing the focus in such cases should not be the relative certainty of the information about the quarter in progress, but whether the surrounding circumstances suggest management is acting strategically to hide information that would be useful to investors).

Stadnick v. Lima, 861 F.3d 31 (2d Cir. 2017), consistent with Professor Gulati, *supra*, reasons that whether information in the most recent quarter is material is to be determined in light of the "total mix" of information available to investors. The plaintiffs complained because the issuer failed to include in its registration statement the third quarter report; the non-disclosed third quarter report, even though showing an overall increase in revenues and earnings, reported a decline in earnings allocable to equity holders due to a variety of charges. The third quarter ended a day before the registration statement became effective and SEC rules do not require quarterly accounting reports that are not at least older than 135 days before the registration statement's effective date. The registration statement made clear that because of the firm's unique business model and accounting methods, quarterly wide variations in income to equity holders was typical. Relying on these factors, the Second Circuit held that the omitted third quarter report did not change the total mix of information.

2.   Measuring Probabilities and the Timing of Events.   *Basic* makes it difficult for the defendant to win on a motion for summary judgment. On remand, the Sixth Circuit held "that the district court's grant of summary judgment was not appropriate given the test of materiality outlined by the Supreme Court. . . ." *Levinson v. Basic Inc.*, 871 F.2d 562 (6th Cir. 1989). In such cases, the defendant's motion for summary judgment has rarely been granted.

One may have a legitimate fear that *Basic*'s probability/magnitude standard in practice is informed by 20/20 hindsight. *See* Loewenstein, Thinking Fast and Slow About the Concept of Materiality, 71 SMU L. Rev. 853 (2018) (reviewing several behavioral biases that can cause probabilities to be exaggerated ex post to an uncertain event's occurrence). Courts rarely require disclosure of internal forecasts and estimates, reasoning such types of information are not material unless "it is substantially certain." *See McDonald v. Kinder-Morgan, Inc.*, 287 F.3d 992 (10th Cir. 2002) (accurate presentation of historical facts not rendered misleading by failure to disclose risk that future events may render the firm less profitable). But how is such certainty to be assessed? Do events after the questioned disclosure impact a court's assessment of certainty at the time the decision was made? In *Fire and Police Pension Ass'n of Colorado v. Abiomed, Inc.*, 778 F.3d 228 (1st Cir. 2015), the court dismissed a suit alleging a company when it touted the efficacy of its drug by pointing to rising sales failed to disclose those sales involved questionable off-label marketing of the drug; the court reasoned the company did disclose that the FDA had expressed interest in its marketing, but the court emphasized that the FDA never brought any action against the company. Would you expect the same conclusion—the omission was immaterial—if the government had imposed a substantial fine for the off-label practices?

And we must not forget that the magnitude of an outcome with low probability of occurrence can also dominate the materiality determination. Thus, in a pre-*Basic* decision applying the probability/magnitude test, Trans World Airlines (TWA) issued a prospectus that discussed at length TWA's relationship with its parent, Trans World Corporation (TWC), and warned there were "no assurance[s]" that the present relationship would continue between the two corporations. When the prospectus was issued, TWC's management had already heard from its investment banker, Goldman Sachs, that a possible future option (among six others) was to terminate TWA as a subsidiary. None of the seven options, however, were disclosed in TWA's prospectus. After the shares were sold through the prospectus, Goldman Sachs presented its report to TWC's board of directors and thereafter the board decided to terminate TWA as a subsidiary. The court held it was materially misleading for the prospectus not to disclose that termination of TWA was under some consideration; the court reached this conclusion based upon the overall impact that terminating TWA as a subsidiary would have on share value, even though there was only a slight probability of this occurring. *Kronfeld v. Trans World Airlines, Inc.*, 832 F.2d 726 (2d Cir. 1987).

3.   Probabilities and the Duty to Disclose.   Later materials in this book explore the instances in which there is a duty to disclose. "[A] corporation is not required to disclose a fact merely because a reasonable investor would very much like to know that fact. Rather, an omission is actionable under the securities laws only when the corporation is subject to a duty to disclose the omitted fact." *In re Time Warner Securities Litigation*, 9 F.3d 259, 266-267 (2d Cir. 1993). Assessing probabilities and magnitudes of the undisclosed event are a means of assessing whether information currently in the public domain needs to be corrected or updated. For example, in *Matrixx Initiatives, Inc. v. Siracusano*, 563 U.S. 27 (2011), the Supreme Court's materiality decision involved Matrixx, a pharmaceutical manufacturer, whose product, Zicam, accounted for 70 percent of its sales. In late 2003, it began receiving reports from three physicians that after using Zicam their patients (ten in total) suffered anosmia, the permanent loss of the sense of smell. During the period it was receiving the reports it issued a series of rosy forecasts, even increasing an earlier earnings prediction by 80 percent. The Supreme Court rejected the defense that under *Basic*'s probability-magnitude test such reports were not material unless supported by a study documenting their statistical significance:

> Matrixx's argument rests on the premise that statistical significance is the only reliable indication of causation. This premise is flawed: As the SEC points out, "medical researchers . . . consider multiple factors in assessing causation." . . .
>
> Not only does the FDA rely on a wide range of evidence of causation, it sometimes acts on the basis of evidence that suggests, but does not prove, causation. For example, the FDA requires manufacturers of over-the-counter drugs to revise their labeling "to include a warning as soon as there is reasonable evidence of an association of a serious hazard with a drug; a causal relationship need not have been proved." 21 CFR §201.80(e). More generally, the FDA may make regulatory decisions against drugs based on postmarketing evidence that gives rise to only a suspicion of causation. . . .
>
> Given that medical professionals and regulators act on the basis of evidence of causation that is not statistically significant, it stands to reason that in certain cases reasonable investors would as well. As Matrixx acknowledges, adverse event reports "appear in many forms, including direct complaints by users to manufacturers, reports by doctors about reported or observed patient reactions, more detailed case reports published by doctors in medical journals, or larger scale published clinical studies." Brief for Petitioners 17. As a result, assessing the materiality of adverse event reports is a "fact-specific" inquiry, . . . that requires consideration of the source, content, and context of the reports. This is not to say that statistical significance (or the lack thereof) is irrelevant—only that it is not dispositive of every case.
>
> Application of *Basic*'s "total mix" standard does not mean that pharmaceutical manufacturers must disclose all reports of adverse events. Adverse event reports are daily events in the pharmaceutical industry; in 2009, the FDA entered nearly 500,000 such reports into its reporting system, see FDA, Reports Received and Reports Entered in AERS by Year (as of Mar. 31, 2010). . . . The fact that a user of a drug has suffered an adverse event, standing alone, does not mean that the drug caused that event. . . . The question remains whether a *reasonable* investor would have viewed the nondisclosed information "as having *significantly* altered the 'total mix' of information made available." *Basic*, 485 U.S., at 232. . . . For the reasons just stated, the mere existence of reports of adverse events—which says nothing in and of itself about whether the drug is causing the adverse events—will not satisfy this standard. Something more is needed, but that something more is not limited to statistical significance. . . .
>
> Applying *Basic*'s "'total mix'" standard in this case, we conclude that respondents have adequately pleaded materiality. . . . Matrixx received information that plausibly indicated a reliable causal link between Zicam and anosmia. That information included reports from three medical professionals and researchers about more than 10 patients who had lost their sense of smell after using Zicam. . . . Matrixx had received additional reports of anosmia. (In addition, during the class period, nine plaintiffs commenced four product liability lawsuits against Matrixx alleging a causal link between Zicam use and anosmia.) Further, Matrixx knew that . . . [two researchers] had presented their findings about a causal link between Zicam and anosmia to a national medical conference devoted to treatment of diseases of the nose. Their presentation described a patient who experienced severe burning in his nose, followed immediately by a loss of smell, after using Zicam—suggesting a temporal relationship between Zicam use and anosmia.

Critically, both . . . [researchers] had also drawn Matrixx's attention to previous studies that had demonstrated a biological causal link between intranasal application of zinc and anosmia. . . .

The information provided to Matrixx by medical experts revealed a plausible causal relationship between Zicam Cold Remedy and anosmia. . . .

It is substantially likely that a reasonable investor would have viewed this information "as having significantly altered the 'total mix' of information made available." *Basic*, 485 U.S., at 232. . . . Matrixx told the market that revenues were going to rise 50 and then 80 percent. Assuming the complaint's allegations to be true, however, Matrixx had information indicating a significant risk to its leading revenue-generating product. Matrixx also stated that reports indicating that Zicam caused anosmia were "completely unfounded and misleading" and that "the safety and efficacy of zinc gluconate for the treatment of symptoms related to the common cold have been well established." . . .

Assuming the facts to be true, these were material facts "necessary in order to make the statements made, in the light of the circumstances under which they were made, not misleading." . . .

Id. at 40-47.

PROBLEM

12-2.   Alice is completing the 10-K for her client, Chromatic Enterprises, Inc. It will be late if not filed within the next week. Much of the work has been a "clip and paste" effort with material borrowed from recent Chromatic filings with the SEC. Past filings, for example, describe Chromatic's only plant (its most valuable asset) as being centrally located in downtown Pleasantville on a large parcel of property that Chromatic "owns in fee simple." This information is responsive to Item 102 of Regulation S-K, which requires "to the extent material" a brief statement of "the location and general character of registrant's principal properties. . . . If any such property is not held in fee or is held subject to an encumbrance that is material to the registrant, so state and describe briefly how held."

In preparing to contest a recent revaluation of the plant by the county assessor, Alice discovers that a surveying error was made when Chromatic built the plant almost 20 years ago because the western edge of Chromatic's plant encroaches by two feet on the property of its major competitor. In three more months, the 20-year period for adverse possession will have run and the strip of property encroached upon will belong to Chromatic. Chromatic's management is shocked by this news. Local law grants the owner of land encroached upon the option of demanding that it receive the fair value of the property or that the encroaching structure be promptly removed. To cure the encroachment would render Chromatic's plant inoperable for the better part of a year. Is disclosure of the encroachment compelled by Exchange Act Rule 12b-20?

C.   The "Total Mix" of Information and Market Efficiency

As noted in Chapter 3, it is commonly assumed that the securities markets are "informationally" efficient, at least with respect to widely followed issuers. That is to say, new information about the issuer is impounded in the stock price relatively promptly. This would seem to suggest that post-disclosure market price movements can serve as a useful proxy for materiality, on the assumption that those movements reflect a consensus of reasonable investors about the significance of the information. Indeed, many courts have used the presence of such price movements, at least where no other factors seem to account for a price change, as strong evidence favoring a determination of materiality. *See In re Burlington Coat Factory Sec. Litig.*, 114 F.3d 1410, 1417 (3d Cir. 1997). But what about the converse? Should the *absence* of price movement following disclosure of the information in question preclude a finding of materiality? *See, e.g., In the Matter of Navigant Consulting Inc. Securities Litigation*, 275 F.3d 616 (7th Cir. 2001). Would such an approach present a problem if the information was not somehow "leaked" prior to public disclosure, so that it was not already impounded at the time of disclosure?

The underlying insights regarding the efficiency of the marketplace extend beyond the problem of materiality alone. Issues such as reliance, causation, and the measure of damages are also influenced by the same sort of assumptions about market efficiency. The materiality of a statement or omission is also affected by one's assumptions regarding the efficiency of the market in which a company's securities are traded. Recall that in *TSC Industries, Inc. v. Northway, Inc.*, 426 U.S. 438, 449 (1976), the Supreme Court stated that a fact is material if there is "a substantial likelihood that the disclosure of the omitted fact would have been viewed by the reasonable investor as having significantly altered the 'total mix' of information made available." What is the "mix of information"? Should it include what is already part of the public domain?

1.   Truth on the Market

Wielgos v. Commonwealth Edison Co.
892 F.2d 509 (7th Cir. 1989)

EASTERBROOK, J. Registration Form S-3 under the Securities Act of 1933 is reserved for firms with a substantial following among analysts and professional investors. The Securities and Exchange Commission believes that markets correctly value the securities of well-followed firms, so that new sales may rely on information that has been digested and expressed in the security's price. Securities Act Release No. 6383, 47 Fed. Reg. 11380 (1982). Registration on Form S-3 principally entails incorporation by reference of the firm's other filings, such as its comprehensive annual Form 10-K and its quarterly supplements. Firms eligible to use Form S-3 also may register equity securities "for the shelf" under Rule 415(a)(1)(x). Shelf registration allows the firm to hold stock for deferred sale. Information in the registration statement will be dated by the time of sale, but again the SEC believes that the market price of large firms accurately reflects current information despite the gap between registration and selling dates. . . .

I

Commonwealth Edison Company, an electric utility in Illinois, is eligible to register its securities on Form S-3. In September 1983 the firm put three million shares of common stock on the shelf, using Rule 415. The succinct registration statement incorporated 176 pages of other filings, as Form S-3 permits. Commonwealth Edison sold the shares to the public on December 5, 1983, for the market price of $27.625. Stanley C. Wielgos bought 500 of these shares.

Commonwealth Edison operates several nuclear reactors, and at the time of the shelf registration it had five more under construction—LaSalle 2, Byron 1 and 2, and Braidwood 1 and 2. None could operate without a license, which the Nuclear Regulatory Commission does not issue unless satisfied that the reactor is safe. Problems at Three Mile Island and Chernobyl, coupled with increasing sophistication in reactor engineering and testing that has revealed shortcomings in old designs, have led the NRC to be more and more demanding in recent years, which postpones the operation of reactors under construction and increases their cost. Delay alone substantially increases cost, because utilities must pay for the capital they have used; re-inspections and additional work come on top of the expenses of delay. Like other firms' reactors, Commonwealth Edison's have been afflicted with delay and cost overruns—some attributable to the benefit of hindsight (leading to more demanding regulations), some to bureaucratic error and delay, and some to shortcomings by Commonwealth Edison and its contractors in finishing the work to meet regulatory requirements.

Of the five reactors under construction in December 1983, Byron 1 was the closest to receiving an operating license. An arm of the NRC, the Atomic Safety and Licensing Board, was considering Commonwealth Edison's request for a license. On January 13, 1984, the ASLB did something it had never done before (and has not done since): it denied the application outright, implying that Byron 1 must be dismantled. . . . The next market day Commonwealth Edison's stock dropped to $21.50, a loss to equity investors of about $1 billion—which reflected not only the write-off of Byron 1 (discounted by the probability that the NRC would affirm the ASLB's decision) but also the likely increase in the costs of completing the other four reactors. The NRC's Atomic Safety and Licensing Appeal Board reversed the ASLB in May 1984 . . . , and five months later the ASLB recommended that the NRC issue a license for Byron 1 . . . , which it did. Stock prices rebounded. Delay in starting Byron 1, plus the expense of reinspections during that period, cost Commonwealth Edison more than $200 million. The Illinois Commerce Commission allowed Commonwealth Edison to add the outlay to its rate base, but the Supreme Court of Illinois disagreed. . . . State officials later excluded the costs, and Commonwealth Edison is in the process of refunding about $200 million to its customers.

Between the ASLB's decision and its reversal, Wielgos filed this suit on behalf of all who purchased in the shelf offering, naming as defendants the issuer and its underwriters. The complaint demanded $6.125 per share, the amount equity securities declined between purchase and suit. . . .

III

. . . Wielgos contended that the issuer and its underwriters violated §11. . . .

A

Documents incorporated by reference into the registration statement esti-mated the total costs of building Byron and Braidwood and the years these reac-tors would begin making power. Commonwealth Edison gave 1984 as the service date for Byron 1, 1985 for Byron 2 and Braidwood 1, and 1986 for Braidwood 2. It estimated the total costs of the two Byron reactors at $3.34 billion and of the two Braidwood reactors at $3.1 billion. Each projection came with a caution such as this:

> [T]he Company has under construction the additional generating units set forth below, the completion and operation of which will be subject to various regulatory approvals. These approvals may be subject to delay because of the opposition of parties who have intervened or may intervene in proceedings with respect thereto, changes in regulatory requirements or changes in design and construction of these units.

Anyone who followed Commonwealth Edison's filings would have seen that each year the firm increased the estimated costs and delayed the estimated startup date of one or more reactors. No one had to read the fine print of a Form 10-K to recognize that higher costs and deferred completion are facts of life in the nuclear power industry; newspapers report this regularly, and the analysts who specialize in utility stocks know the story in detail.

Estimates incorporated into the September 1983 prospectus were calcu-lated in December 1982. Commonwealth Edison updates its projections on an annual cycle; by September the December 1982 figures were stale, and Commonwealth Edison said so. Its latest quarterly report, also incorporated by reference into the registration statement, said that

> [t]he Company is in the process of conducting its annual review of the status of its construction program. While that review has not been completed, it appears likely that at the conclusion of the review the Company will announce a delay of approx-imately three months in the service date and a resultant cost increase for its Byron Unit 1. Any change in the service dates of the remaining generating units under construction will not be ascertained until the completion of the review.

Review began early in September 1983; in late December 1983 (after the secu-rities had been sold) the Manager of Projects submitted his revised estimates to the firm's Expenditure Control Committee. On January 10 that Committee approved a projection increasing the costs of Byron 1 and 2 by $330 million. When the ASLB denied the application for a license at Byron 1, the firm imme-diately added another $100 million to the estimate, which it disclosed in a Form 8-K filed on January 17, 1984.

The statements incorporated into the prospectus were erroneous—not only in the sense that they turned out to be inaccurate but also in the sense that by early December 1983, when it sold the stock, Commonwealth Edison's inter-nal cost estimates exceeded those in the documents on file. A material error in a prospectus usually is enough for liability. . . .

Form S-3 and the shelf registration rules . . . [assume] that readers are sophisticated, can understand the limits of a projection—and that if any given reader does not appreciate its limits, the reactions of the many professional investors and analysts will lead to prices that reflect the limits of the information. . . .

Commonwealth Edison made a projection but did not disclose data, assumptions, or methods. The cautions accompanying the projection were so much boilerplate. No one could have deduced from the cloud of legalese how much uncertainty the firm perceived in its estimates, and the market would have discounted them accordingly. Especially because professional analysts knew—although perhaps Wielgos did not—that Commonwealth Edison's estimates were biased. Not wrong in the sense of inaccurate; biased in the sense of having a predictable kind of inaccuracy. Like clockwork, every January the firm increased its estimate of the cost of getting the Byron and Braidwood reactors into service. Some years the estimates went up more than others, but up they went. Lack of a normal distribution of errors could suggest the absence of a "reasonable basis" or even of "good faith." More likely, though, the pattern of errors allowed the market to infer two assumptions: that there would be no new regulations or unanticipated delays. Commonwealth Edison was estimating the costs it would experience *if nothing went wrong and nothing unexpected happened.* These were poor assumptions. Something always goes wrong, and in the nuclear power business the unexpected is the norm. Perhaps the firm had no way to estimate the timing and gravity of coming jolts, but if so that made the estimate less useful.

[P]rofessional investors and analysts surely deduced what was afoot. Once they did so, they supplied their own assumptions about the likelihood that the firm will encounter trouble or that the rules will change. . . . Just as a firm needn't disclose that 50% of all new products vanish from the market within a short time, so Commonwealth Edison needn't disclose the hazards of its business, hazards apparent to all serious observers and most casual ones. . . .

It was no secret that the estimate prepared in December 1982 was too low. The firm said so in September 1983. Proceedings in the ASLB, including the staff's demand for re-inspections of Byron 1's plumbing—costly to perform, costly because of delay—were public knowledge. The market price of the firm's stock, which Wielgos and his class paid in the shelf offering, reflected this information. Prompt incorporation of news into stock price is the foundation for the fraud-on-the-market doctrine and therefore supports a truth-on-the-market doctrine as well. *In re Apple Computer Securities Litigation,* 886 F.2d 1109 (9th Cir. 1989); *Flamm v. Eberstadt,* 814 F.2d 1169, 1179-1180 (7th Cir. 1987); *Rodman v. Grant Foundation,* 608 F.2d 64, 70 (2d Cir. 1979). Knowledge abroad in the market moderated, likely eliminated, the potential of a dated projection to mislead. It therefore cannot be the basis of liability. . . .

Affirmed.

NOTES AND QUESTIONS

1. "Truth on the Market."   The approach taken in *Wielgos* is now referred to as the "truth on the market" defense. For example, a registration statement was not misleading in failing to disclose that a star asset manager would soon be leaving the money management company when this information was reported in three newspapers and three other SEC filings. *Garber v. Legg Mason, Inc.*, 2009 U.S. App. LEXIS 21404 (2d Cir. 2009). Similarly, a company's statement on February 17, 1998, that "we're not a company that's for sale" was not misleading when it announced three weeks later it would be acquired by an earlier suitor who after February 17 raised its offering price. The earlier statement did not significantly alter the total mix of information available to the market, which included public awareness of the rapidly consolidating nature of the industry and an analyst's statement that the company's revenues would be enhanced by an acquisition. *Phillips v. LCI International, Inc.*, 190 F.3d 609 (4th Cir. 1999). Just what information is in the public domain such that the truth on the market defense should apply? This issue commonly arises by the defendant asserting its *own* disclosures had established truth on the market; in such cases, courts demand that the defendant must ensure the true information was "transmitted to the public with a degree of intensity and credibility sufficient to effectively counterbalance any misleading misimpression created." *Countrywide Fin. Corp. Sec. Litig.*, 588 F. Supp. 2d 1132, 1160 (C.D. Cal. 2008). *See also Maverick Fund, L.D. C. v. Converse Tech., Inc.*, 41, 55 (E.D.N.Y. 2011); *Sgalambo v. McKenzie*, 739 F. Supp. 2d 453, 480 (S.D.N.Y. 2010). Moreover, the defendant cannot invoke the truth on the market defense when it has warned investors not to rely on the media, *Fresno Cnty. Employees Ret. Ass'n v. ComScore, Inc.*, 268 F. Supp. 3d 526 (S.D.N.Y. 2017), or issues authoritative responses to media coverage that has questioned the company's representations. *See, e.g., eSpeed, Inc. Sec. Litig.*, 457 F. Supp. 2d 266, 288 (S.D.N.Y. 2006).

An interesting contrast between general expressions of optimism about a new product and statements about a product's performance is provided in *In re Apple Computer Securities Litigation*, 886 F.2d 1109 (9th Cir. 1989). The case concerned several announcements Apple Computer made about its new computer products Lisa and Twiggy, both of which ultimately were commercial failures because of design problems. Statements and announcements that waxed eloquent that the products "were going to be phenomenally successful" and would make Apple's prior growth "look small," the court believed, were offset by more sober reports prepared by outside analysts. On the other hand, statements about the efforts to verify the products' capabilities and reliability were uniquely within the knowledge of the products' manufacturer, so that, if misleading, they were not countered by information already in the public domain.

Consider for a moment how you reconcile that the value of Commonwealth Edison common shares declined $1 billion following denial of the license for Byron 1 and the court's conclusion in *Wielgos* that the truth was in the market. What truth was known to the market? *Compare City of Monroe Employee Retirement Sys. v. Bridgestone Group*, 399 F.3d 651 (6th Cir. 2005), where the court held that, in light of a one-third decline in the value of the common shares in the weeks following the tire manufacturer's recall of tires because of their defects, a jury could reasonably conclude that published concerns regarding the safety of the products and the likelihood of a recall were not reflected in the pricing of the company's shares. A final question is whether the truth in the market defense is appropriate in an SEC enforcement action. *Cf. SEC v. Bank of America*, 677 F. Supp. 2d 717 (S.D.N.Y. 2010) (denying defense because allegedly misleading proxy statement had advised shareholders to ignore media reports questioning representations made in the proxy statement).

   2. *Should the Context Matter?* Should the failure to disclose a material fact in a particular document be overcome by the investors' ability to access that fact in another document filed with the SEC? In *United Paperworkers International Union v. International Paper Co.*, 985 F.2d 1190 (2d Cir. 1993), a reporting company included in its proxy statement a shareholder proposal calling for the company to adopt the so-called Valdez Principles, which generally would require the company to reduce waste matter and provide for its safe treatment. The company's management opposed the proposal, stating in the proxy statement that the company already had addressed environmental matters "in an appropriate and timely manner" and was in the "forefront" in protecting the environment. The court held that management's representations were misleading because they failed to disclose that the company had been accused of numerous environmental offenses, had pleaded guilty to felonious violation of environmental laws, and had agreed to pay substantial fines in environmental proceedings. The company defended the proxy statement by arguing that the "total mix" of information before the shareholders included the firm's Form 10-K as well as several press reports that disclosed these facts. The court rejected the company's argument. It reasoned that all but one of the eight press reports appeared more than six months before the proxy statement was released and the 10-K report was neither circulated to the stockholders nor referred to in the proxy statement. Moreover, because of the artful manner in which the 10-K report was drafted, a shareholder could reasonably conclude that the environmental violations were minor and that the violations did not bespeak a lack of social responsibility. However, the court reasoned that the shareholders would have reviewed the revelations in the 10-K report differently had they been informed that *felonies* were charged against the company, that some of the violations involved falsification of environmental reports, and that the fine of $2.2 million was the second largest ever assessed for violation of the hazardous waste laws. To what extent should the context in which a materiality determination occurs guide the breadth of the court's consideration of just what constitutes the total mix of information? What result if an investor alleged she purchased International Paper shares after reading management's representations in the proxy statement? Contrast *United Paperworkers* with *Garber*, in Note 1, supra.

   What if a graphic illustration in the prospectus is misleading, but accurate information is disclosed in a table in another part of the prospectus? *See DeMaria v. Andersen*, 318 F.3d 170 (2d Cir. 2003) (holding in such a case that prospectus was not misleading). And, should information in an SEC filing made by the defendant issuer's business partner that describes their joint venture relieve the defendant of the necessity to disclose the same information? *See Ganino v. Citizens Utilities Co.*, 228 F.3d 154 (2d Cir. 2000).

   Related to whether the context in which the disclosure gap is alleged to have occurred, consider the connection between the "buried facts" doctrine discussed in the introductory section of the chapter and "truth on the market." Are they complementary or in tension with one another?

PROBLEMS

12-3. Kiwi, Inc. is a multinational pharmaceutical company whose shares are traded on the NYSE. In its most recent Form 10-K, it described vitamin markets, in which it derived a significant portion of its profits, as highly competitive. After reviewing this report, Bill purchased 1,000 Kiwi shares. A week before Bill's purchase, an antitrust class action was filed by a Chicago law firm against Kiwi and eight other pharmaceutical companies alleging they had engaged in a worldwide conspiracy to fix vitamin prices. Kiwi shares declined slightly the day the antitrust suit was filed. Nearly a year later, Kiwi settled the antitrust suit by paying a substantial sum of money; it also announced that it expects future profit margins will be significantly lower for its vitamin operations. Thereafter, Bill filed suit against Kiwi alleging fraud in its earlier Form 10-K. Should his case be dismissed on the basis of the "truth on the market" defense? *See Pinker v. Roche Holding Ltd.*, 292 F.3d 361 (3d Cir. 2002).

12-4. Andrew "Doc" Watson is a world-renowned serial entrepreneur; he has launched many successful publicly traded ventures. One of his ventures involving high quality electric automobiles has encountered a variety of problems preventing the company from producing cars at a sufficient volume to be profitable. Over the last many months Doc repeatedly tweeted that production would soon reach a level that would be profitable, but each such forecast was met by press reports of new production problems and failed production levels. This only seemed to provoke Doc to tweet more often and somewhat more optimistically. The firm's once high-flying share price has recently sagged, losing about 25 percent of its value. In his most recent tweet, Doc boldly announced that production difficulties have bottomed out, that the firm would achieve its earlier forecasted production level, and that he would soon announce an offer to take the company private, using funds provided by an oil-rich sheikdom. The announcement stemmed the near daily decline in the stock's price. Three days later, following an SEC investigation, the company announced there were no plans to go private as there was never any funding source for the transaction. Assuming private suits are brought for the above, what defenses based on materiality can Doc's lawyers be expected to raise?

2. "Puffery"

Has a company committed a material misrepresentation by asserting its employees are held to the highest ethical standards if the statement was made when its employees are engaged in a broad and systematic effort to facilitate tax fraud by its clients? *See City of Pontiac Policemen and Firemen's Ret. Sys. v. UBS, AG*, 752 F.3d 173 (2d Cir. 2014). How about a statement that diversification will "lead to continued prosperity," if that statement is made with knowledge that such a plan will result in reduced profits? *See Lasker v. New York State Electric & Gas Co.*, 85 F.3d 55 (2d Cir. 1996). Or, perhaps the most poignant in light of the last financial crisis, that the company's "risk management processes . . . are highly disciplined." *ECA v. J.P. Morgan Chase*, 553 F.3d 187, 196 (2d Cir. 2009). *See generally*

O'Hare, The Resurrection of the Dodo: The Unfortunate Reemergence of the Puffery Defense in Private Securities Fraud Actions, 59 Ohio St. L.J. 1697 (1998); Note, Securities Fraud or Mere Puffery: Refinement of the Corporate Puffery Defense, 51 Vand. L. Rev. 1049 (1998). Consider the above examples in light of the following.

Eisenstadt v. Centel Corp.
113 F.3d 738, 745-746 (7th Cir. 1997)

[Centel Corporation announced it had retained two investment banking firms to assist it in orchestrating its sale through a competitive auction. Following the announcement, the stock quickly rose to $48 per share (from $37). In the ensuing weeks, Centel and its investment bankers were repeatedly disappointed as one prospective bidder after another informed them they were not interested in purchasing Centel. Despite such private bad news, Centel publicly exuded an optimistic image through repeated press announcements that the auction process was going smoothly. Ultimately, Centel received only seven disappointingly low bids. It rejected all seven and negotiated its sale at $33.50 per share to a nonbidder. A class action was initiated on behalf of those who purchased in reliance upon its optimistic press announcements. The court dismissed the suit, reasoning as follows:]

We doubt that nonspecific representations that an auction process is going well or going smoothly could, in the circumstances of this case (the significance of this qualification will become clear shortly), influence a reasonable investor to pay more for a stock than he otherwise would. *Everybody* knows that someone trying to sell something is going to look and talk on the bright side. You don't sell a product by bad mouthing it. And everybody knows that auctions can be disappointing. It would be unreasonable for investors to attach significance to *general* expressions of satisfaction with the progress of the seller's efforts to sell, just as it would be unreasonable for them to infer from a potential bidder's apparent lack of enthusiasm that the bidder was uninterested rather than just was jockeying for a better price. The heart of a reasonable investor does not begin to flutter when a firm announces that some project or process is proceeding smoothly, and so the announcement will not drive up the price of the firm's shares to an unsustainable level.

. . . Suppose that on February 18 Centel's lawyers had told Centel that it couldn't legally sell any of its assets because they were encumbered and the lienors would not give their consent to a sale. In these circumstances to have announced that the auction process was going smoothly would have been materially deceptive. "Going smoothly" may mean nothing more than—going; but it means at least that; if the process had been stopped, a representation that it is continuing may well induce purchasers of the stock at a price that reflects the prospect that the process will continue to its end. . . .

Centel was not, by its talk of smooth sailing, covering up a disaster. . . . The auction process was not interrupted. The results were disappointing, but that is a frequent outcome of auctions. . . .

An utterly candid statement of the company's hopes and fears, with emphasis on the fears, might well have pushed the company's stock below $40, but perhaps only because, given the expectation of puffing, such a statement would be taken to indicate that the prospects for the auction were much grimmer than they were. Where puffing is the order of the day, literal truth can be profoundly misleading, as senders and recipients of letters of recommendation well know. Mere sales puffery is not actionable under Rule 10b-5. . . .

NOTE AND QUESTIONS

1. Is Puffery All Puff? Are you persuaded that "going smoothly" is not material to the investor considering the purchase of Centel? A simulated exercise that asked subjects to weigh the importance of statements the courts had held to be harmless puffery (including the earlier quoted statements in *Raab* and *Burlington Coat Factory*) found that, depending on the precise "puffery" statement, 33-84 percent of the subjects considered the particular statement significant in their evaluation of the investment choice. *See* Padfield, Is Puffery Material to Investors? Maybe We Should Ask Them, 10 U. Pa. J. Bus. & Emp. L. 339 (2008); *see also* Hoffman, The Best Puffery Article Ever, 91 Iowa L. Rev. 1395, 1434-1439 (2006) (reviewing literature showing consumers consistently view puffery statements as important in their choice). Is a statement material only if a majority of those sampled believed it was important? Should the percentage change depending on whether the question arises in ruling on pretrial motions or at trial?

3. Opinion Statements and Half-Truths

Is a statement of one's opinion about an event or transaction distinguishable from puffery? Do statements of opinion, such as that the shareholders are receiving a "high" price or that a transaction "is in the stockholders' best interest," relate to material *facts*, so that they fall within the standard strictures of the antifraud provisions? In *Virginia Bankshares, Inc. v. Sandberg*, 501 U.S. 1083 (1991), the Supreme Court provided a qualified yes to the last question without considering the first question. The facts arose from a going-private transaction in which the minority shareholders of First American Bank of Virginia (FABV) were offered $42 per share by the parent corporation. The FABV directors recommended that the stockholders approve the transaction, stating that $42 was a "high value" and a "fair price," even though the directors had received a report that valued the shares at $60 and they were aware that valuing FABV's real estate would, at current market prices, yield a value greater than $42 per share. The plaintiff alleged that the FABV directors acted under pressure from FABV's parent in the hopes of continuing their positions with FABV or one of the other companies controlled by the parent. The majority opinion observed that such opinion statements assume material significance to shareholders: "Shareholders know that directors usually have knowledge and expertness far exceeding the normal investor's resources, and the directors' perceived superiority is magnified even further by the common knowledge that state law customarily obliges them to exercise their judgment in the shareholders' interest." Id. at 1091. The majority, however, distinguished between objective and subjective falseness. An assertion of "fairness" could be false because the price was not fair or high. The statement could also be false because the directors making it did not believe the price was fair, even if objectively the price was high or even fair. The former is objective falseness and can be the basis of liability. The latter is subjective falseness and not the basis for liability because of its dependence on matters that are not objectively verifiable such that if suit could be based merely on subjective false-hood it would invite strike suits. Because there was objective evidence before the directors that was inconsistent with their professed opinions, the Court held that the plaintiff had pled more than a mere subjective disbelief or undisclosed motive.

As you read the next case, consider its impact on the approach to opinion statements that the Supreme Court earlier embraced in *Virginia Bankshares*.

Omnicare, Inc. v. Laborers Dist. Council Constr. Indus. Pension Fund
135 S. Ct. 1318 (2015)

Justice KAGAN delivered the opinion of the Court.

Before a company may sell securities in interstate commerce, it must file a registration statement with the Securities and Exchange Commission (SEC). If that document either "contain[s] an untrue statement of a material fact" or "omit[s] to state a material fact . . . necessary to make the statements therein not misleading," a purchaser of the stock may sue for damages. . . . This case requires us to decide how each of those phrases applies to statements of opinion.

I. . . .

Section 11 thus creates two ways to hold issuers liable for the contents of a registration statement—one focusing on what the statement says and the other on what it leaves out. Either way, the buyer need not prove (as he must to establish certain other securities offenses) that the defendant acted with any intent to deceive or defraud. *Herman & MacLean v. Huddleston*, 459 U.S. 375, 381-382 . . . (1983).

This case arises out of a registration statement that petitioner Omnicare filed in connection with a public offering of common stock. Omnicare is the nation's largest provider of pharmacy services for residents of nursing homes. Its registration statement contained . . . analysis of the effects of various federal and state laws on its business model, including its acceptance of rebates from pharmaceutical manufacturers. . . . Of significance here, two sentences in the registration statement expressed Omnicare's view of its compliance with legal requirements:

- "We believe our contract arrangements with other healthcare providers, our pharmaceutical suppliers and our pharmacy practices are in compliance with applicable federal and state laws." . . .
- "We believe that our contracts with pharmaceutical manufacturers are legally and economically valid arrangements that bring value to the healthcare system and the patients that we serve." . . .

Respondents here, pension funds that purchased Omnicare stock in the public offering (hereinafter Funds), brought suit alleging that the company's two opinion statements about legal compliance give rise to liability under §11. Citing lawsuits that the Federal Government later pressed against Omnicare, the Funds' complaint maintained that the company's receipt of payments from drug manufacturers violated anti-kickback laws. . . . Accordingly, the complaint asserted, Omnicare made "materially false" representations about legal compliance. . . . And so too, the complaint continued, the company "omitted to state [material] facts necessary" to make its representations not misleading. . . . The Funds claimed that none of Omnicare's officers and directors "possessed reasonable grounds" for thinking that the opinions offered were truthful and complete. . . . Indeed, the complaint noted that one of Omnicare's attorneys had warned that a particular contract "carrie[d] a heightened risk" of liability under anti-kickback laws. . . . At the same time, the Funds made clear that in light of §11's strict liability standard, they chose to "exclude and disclaim any allegation that could be construed as alleging fraud or intentional or reckless misconduct." . . .

The District Court granted Omnicare's motion to dismiss. . . . In the court's view, "statements regarding a company's belief as to its legal compliance are considered 'soft' information" and are actionable only if those who made them "knew [they] were untrue at the time." . . . The Court of Appeals for the Sixth Circuit reversed. . . . [T]he court held, the Funds had to allege only that the stated belief was "objectively false"; they did not need to contend that anyone at Omnicare "disbelieved [the opinion] at the time it was expressed." 719 F.3d, at 506 (quoting *Fait v. Regions Financial Corp.*, 655 F.3d 105, 110 (CA2 2011)).

We granted certiorari . . . to consider how §11 pertains to statements of opinion. We do so in two steps, corresponding to the two parts of §11 and the two theories in the Funds' complaint. We initially address the Funds' claim that Omnicare made "untrue statement[s] of . . . material fact" in offering its views on legal compliance. . . . We then take up the Funds' argument that Omnicare "omitted to state a material fact . . . necessary to make the statements [in its registration filing] not misleading." . . . Unlike both courts below, we see those allegations as presenting different issues. In resolving the first, we discuss when an opinion itself constitutes a factual misstatement. In analyzing the second, we address when an opinion may be rendered misleading by the omission of discrete factual representations. Because we find that the Court of Appeals applied the wrong standard, we vacate its decision.

II

The Sixth Circuit held, and the Funds now urge, that a statement of opinion that is ultimately found incorrect—even if believed at the time made—may count as an "untrue statement of a material fact." . . . As the Funds put the point, a statement of belief may make an implicit assertion about the belief's "subject matter": To say "we believe X is true" is often to indicate that "X is in fact true." . . . In just that way, the Funds conclude, an issuer's statement that "we believe we are following the law" conveys that "we in fact are following the law"—which is "materially false," no matter what the issuer thinks, if instead it is violating an anti-kickback statute. . . .

But that argument wrongly conflates facts and opinions. . . . Congress effectively incorporated just that distinction in §11's first part by exposing issuers to liability not for "untrue statement[s]" full stop (which would have included ones of opinion), but only for "untrue statement[s] of . . . *fact*." §77k(a) (emphasis added).

Consider that statutory phrase's application to two hypothetical statements, couched in ways the Funds claim are equivalent. A company's CEO states: "The TVs we manufacture have the highest resolution available on the market." Or, alternatively, the CEO transforms that factual statement into one of opinion: "I *believe*" (or "I think") "the TVs we manufacture have the highest resolution available on the market." The first version would be an untrue statement of fact if a competitor had introduced a higher resolution TV a month before—even assuming the CEO had not yet learned of the new product. The CEO's assertion, after all, is not mere puffery, but a determinate, verifiable statement about her company's TVs; and the CEO, however innocently, got the facts wrong. But in the same set of circumstances, the second version would remain true. Just as she said, the CEO really did believe, when she made the statement, that her company's TVs had the sharpest picture around. And although a plaintiff could later prove that opinion erroneous, the words "I believe" themselves admitted that possibility, thus precluding liability for an untrue statement of fact. That remains the case if the CEO's opinion, as here, concerned legal compliance. If, for example, she said, "I believe our marketing practices are lawful," and actually did think that, she could not be liable for a false statement of fact—even if she afterward discovered a longtime violation of law. Once again, the statement would have been true, because all she expressed was a view, not a certainty, about legal compliance.

That still leaves some room for §11's false-statement provision to apply to expressions of opinion. As even Omnicare acknowledges, every such statement explicitly affirms one fact: that the speaker actually holds the stated belief. . . . For that reason, the CEO's statement about product quality ("I believe our TVs have the highest resolution available on the market") would be an untrue statement of fact—namely, the fact of her own belief—if she knew that her company's TVs only placed second. And so too the statement about legal compliance ("I believe our marketing practices are lawful") would falsely describe her own state of mind if she thought her company was breaking the law. In such cases, §11's first part would subject the issuer to liability (assuming the misrepresentation were material). . . .

The two sentences to which the Funds object are pure statements of opinion: To simplify their content only a bit, Omnicare said in each that "we believe we are obeying the law." And the Funds do not contest that Omnicare's opinion was honestly held. Recall that their complaint explicitly "exclude[s] and disclaim[s]" any allegation sounding in fraud or deception. . . . What the Funds instead claim is that Omnicare's belief turned out to be wrong—that whatever the company thought, it was in fact violating anti-kickback laws. But that allegation alone will not give rise to liability under §11's first clause because, as we have shown, a sincere statement of pure opinion is not an "untrue statement of material fact," regardless whether an investor can ultimately prove the belief wrong. That clause, limited as it is to factual statements, does not allow investors to second-guess inherently subjective and uncertain assessments. In other words, the provision is not, as the Court of Appeals and the Funds would have it, an invitation to Monday morning quarterback an issuer's opinions.

III

A

That conclusion, however, does not end this case because the Funds also rely on §11's omissions provision, alleging that Omnicare "omitted to state facts necessary" to make its opinion on legal compliance "not misleading."[3] . . . We therefore must consider when, if ever, the omission of a fact can make a statement of opinion like Omnicare's, even if literally accurate, misleading to an ordinary investor.

Omnicare claims that is just not possible. On its view, no reasonable person, in any context, can understand a pure statement of opinion to convey anything more than the speaker's own mindset. . . .

That claim has more than a kernel of truth. A reasonable person understands, and takes into account, the difference we have discussed above between a statement of fact and one of opinion. . . . She recognizes the import of words like "I think" or "I believe," and grasps that they convey some lack of certainty as to the statement's content. . . . And that may be especially so when the phrases appear in a registration statement, which the reasonable investor expects has been carefully wordsmithed to comply with the law. When reading such a document, the investor thus distinguishes between the sentences "we believe X is true" and "X is true." And because she does so, the omission of a fact that merely rebuts the latter statement fails to render the former misleading. In other words, a statement of opinion is not misleading just because external facts show the opinion to be incorrect. Reasonable investors do not understand such statements as guarantees, and §11's omissions clause therefore does not treat them that way.

---

3. Section 11's omissions clause also applies when an issuer fails to make mandated disclosures—those "required to be stated"—in a registration statement. §77k(a). But the Funds do not object to Omnicare's filing on that score.

But Omnicare takes its point too far, because a reasonable investor may, depending on the circumstances, understand an opinion statement to convey facts about how the speaker has formed the opinion—or, otherwise put, about the speaker's basis for holding that view. And if the real facts are otherwise, but not provided, the opinion statement will mislead its audience. Consider an unadorned statement of opinion about legal compliance: "We believe our conduct is lawful." If the issuer makes that statement without having consulted a lawyer, it could be misleadingly incomplete. In the context of the securities market, an investor, though recognizing that legal opinions can prove wrong in the end, still likely expects such an assertion to rest on some meaningful legal inquiry—rather than, say, on mere intuition, however sincere. Similarly, if the issuer made the statement in the face of its lawyers' contrary advice, or with knowledge that the Federal Government was taking the opposite view, the investor again has cause to complain: He expects not just that the issuer believes the opinion (however irrationally), but that it fairly aligns with the information in the issuer's possession at the time.[6] Thus, if a registration statement omits material facts about the issuer's inquiry into or knowledge concerning a statement of opinion, and if those facts conflict with what a reasonable investor would take from the statement itself, then §11's omissions clause creates liability.

An opinion statement, however, is not necessarily misleading when an issuer knows, but fails to disclose, some fact cutting the other way. Reasonable investors understand that opinions sometimes rest on a weighing of competing facts; indeed, the presence of such facts is one reason why an issuer may frame a statement as an opinion, thus conveying uncertainty. . . . Suppose, for example, that in stating an opinion about legal compliance, the issuer did not disclose that a single junior attorney expressed doubts about a practice's legality, when six of his more senior colleagues gave a stamp of approval. That omission would not make the statement of opinion misleading, even if the minority position ultimately proved correct: A reasonable investor does not expect that *every* fact known to an issuer supports its opinion statement.[8]

Moreover, whether an omission makes an expression of opinion misleading always depends on context. Registration statements as a class are formal documents, filed with the SEC as a legal prerequisite for selling securities to the public. Investors do not, and are right not to, expect opinions contained

---

6. The hypothetical used earlier could demonstrate the same points. Suppose the CEO, in claiming that her company's TV had the highest resolution available on the market, had failed to review any of her competitors' product specifications. Or suppose she had recently received information from industry analysts indicating that a new product had surpassed her company's on this metric. The CEO may still honestly believe in her TV's superiority. But under §11's omissions provision, that subjective belief, in the absence of the expected inquiry or in the face of known contradictory evidence, would not insulate her from liability.

8. We note, too, that a reasonable investor generally considers the specificity of an opinion statement in making inferences about its basis. Compare two new statements from our ever-voluble CEO. In the first, she says: "I believe we have 1.3 million TVs in our warehouse." In the second, she says: "I believe we have enough supply on hand to meet demand." All else equal, a reasonable person would think that a more detailed investigation lay behind the former statement.

in those statements to reflect baseless, off-the-cuff judgments, of the kind that an individual might communicate in daily life. At the same time, an investor reads each statement within such a document, whether of fact or of opinion, in light of all its surrounding text, including hedges, disclaimers, and apparently conflicting information. . . . So an omission that renders misleading a statement of opinion when viewed in a vacuum may not do so once that statement is considered, as is appropriate, in a broader frame. The reasonable investor understands a statement of opinion in its full context, and §11 creates liability only for the omission of material facts that cannot be squared with such a fair reading. . . .

According to Omnicare, any inquiry into the issuer's basis for holding an opinion is "hopelessly amorphous," threatening "unpredictable" and possibly "massive" liability. . . .

Omnicare way overstates both the looseness of the inquiry Congress has mandated and the breadth of liability that approach threatens. As we have explained, an investor cannot state a claim by alleging only that an opinion was wrong; the complaint must as well call into question the issuer's basis for offering the opinion. . . . To be specific: The investor must identify particular (and material) facts going to the basis for the issuer's opinion—facts about the inquiry the issuer did or did not conduct or the knowledge it did or did not have—whose omission makes the opinion statement at issue misleading to a reasonable person reading the statement fairly and in context. . . . That is no small task for an investor.

. . . B

Our analysis on this score counsels in favor of sending the case back to the lower courts for decision. . . . In doing so, however, we reemphasize a few crucial points pertinent to the inquiry on remand. Initially, as we have said, the Funds cannot proceed without identifying one or more facts left out of Omnicare's registration statement. . . . At oral argument . . . the Funds highlighted . . . [a] more specific allegation in their complaint: that an attorney had warned Omnicare that a particular contract "carrie[d] a heightened risk" of legal exposure under anti-kickback laws. . . . On remand, the court must review the Funds' complaint to determine whether it adequately alleged that Omnicare had omitted that (purported) fact, or any other like it, from the registration statement. And if so, the court must determine whether the omitted fact would have been material to a reasonable investor—*i.e.*, whether "there is a substantial likelihood that a reasonable [investor] would consider it important." *TSC Industries*, 426 U.S., at 449. . . .

Assuming the Funds clear those hurdles, the court must ask whether the alleged omission rendered Omnicare's legal compliance opinions misleading in the way described earlier—*i.e.*, because the excluded fact shows that Omnicare lacked the basis for making those statements that a reasonable investor would expect. . . . Insofar as the omitted fact at issue is the attorney's warning, that inquiry entails consideration of such matters as the attorney's status and expertise and other legal information available to Omnicare at the time. . . . Further, the analysis of whether Omnicare's opinion is misleading must address the statement's context. . . . That means the court must take account of whatever facts Omnicare *did* provide about legal compliance, as well as any other hedges, disclaimers, or qualifications it included in its registration statement. The court should consider, for example, the information Omnicare offered that States had initiated enforcement actions against drug manufacturers for giving rebates to pharmacies, that the Federal Government had expressed concerns about the practice, and that the relevant laws "could be interpreted in the future in a manner" that would harm Omnicare's business. . . .

With these instructions and for the reasons stated, we vacate the judgment below and remand the case for further proceedings.

It is so ordered.

Justice SCALIA, concurring in part and concurring in the judgment. (Opinion omitted.)

Justice THOMAS, concurring in the judgment. (Opinion omitted.)

NOTES AND QUESTIONS

1. **Virginia Bankshares** *After* **Omnicare.** Does *Omnicare* apply only in Section 11 cases? Does *Omnicare* overrule the approach to opinion statements set forth in *Virginia Bankshares*? If both approaches coexist, which approach is more favorable to the plaintiff? Why?

2. *What Is an Opinion?* The protection afforded "opinion" statements by *Virginia Bankshares* and *Omnicare* requires the statement be an opinion. Just what is an "opinion" elicits a good deal of uncertainty across the cases. *See, e.g., Fait v. Regions Fin. Corp.,* 655 F.3d 105 (2d Cir. 2011) (alleged inadequacy of loan loss reserves not actionable since the estimate was an opinion statement and there were no alleged facts to support claim that management did not believe the reserve was correct); *United States v. Skilling,* 554 F.3d 529 (5th Cir. 2009) (CFO's claim that "Enron's businesses were uniquely strong franchises with sustainable high earnings power" was opinion statement for which jury could conclude there were facts known to CFO that were at odds with the statement); *City of Monroe Employee Retirement Sys. v. Bridgestone Corp.,* 399 F.3d 651 (6th Cir. 2005) (management's statement of confidence in tires the firm manufactured and touting the rigorous testing procedures were puffery; the statements however became actionable when management represented their confidence was supported by objective evidence when studies repeatedly showed that about 15 percent of the tires failed). And what about the firm's comments regarding litigation pending against it? Is this a statement of opinion? Typically, the suits are characterized in dismissive, negative terms. Is it harmless puffery if the firm's officers know otherwise? *See Rosenbaum Capital LLC v. Boston Commc'ns Group, Inc.,* 445 F. Supp. 2d 170 (D. Mass. 2006) (statement that firm did not infringe on patent and had a meritorious defense, and that the third party held an invalid patent, not harmless puffery in light of judicial finding after statements made that found willful infringement). To what extent would *Omnicare* change the result in any of these cases?

PROBLEMS

12-5.   Assurance Inc. provides credit guarantees for asset-backed securities (ABS) made up of short-term consumer loans that are originated by community banks in North Dakota. The securities are sold to various financial institutions. The credit guaranty that Assurance provides greatly enhances the underwriters' ability to privately place the securities. Each such placement carries with it Assurance's statement that it "maintains a rigorous and consistent process for credit risk management." This representation is repeated regularly in its SEC filings, which, as a listed company, Assurance is required to file. Assurance has been sued by multiple financial institutions seeking to recover on its guaranty of several tranches of consumer loans that have become virtually worthless. The high default rate reflects the consequences of the long-term decline in oil prices that has caused serious increases in unemployment in the once booming Bakken Field in North Dakota. Because of the lawsuits, Assurance's stock has fallen precipitously. As a result of a whistleblower's disclosures, there have been press stories that Assurance's credit risk practices entailed only an annual review (conducted each May) of the condition of the national economy and various national statistics bearing on consumer credit risk. Based on this information, Assurance annually established minimum standards required in the upcoming year that loans must meet to be included within any ABS it would guaranty. Between the last May review and the suits filed by the institutions, Assurance has filed two 10-Qs with the SEC. Investors who purchased Assurance shares after these quarterly reports have consulted you as to whether they have a viable cause of action against Assurance. *See In re Wilmington Trust Sec. Litig.*, 29 F. Supp. 2d 432 (D. Del. 2014).

12-6.   The private placement memorandum Odyssey, Ltd. used in raising funds from a network of angel investors touted the prospects of its intellectual property that it listed on its balance sheet at $15 million, observing that "management believes the processes we have developed are significant advancements in the field and we will soon seek patents and copyrights for the protection of these cornerstones of our product lines." Six weeks after the private placement, Odyssey announced that much of its intellectual property infringed on the patents and copyrights held by an industry leader, Iliad, Inc. To avoid expensive protracted litigation, Odyssey announced it would license the needed technology from Iliad and that it was "writing down" its intellectual property rights to $500,000. Odyssey's general counsel, Sally, is quoted in the press: "When I first heard from Iliad slightly over two months ago (two weeks before the private placement), I did not then fully appreciate the magnitude of its allegations; we were caught off guard and instantly began an internal evaluation of the magnitude of any infringement on Iliad's rights." How strong a claim of misrepresentation do the angel investors have? *See Ford v. Voxx Int'l Corp.*, 2016 U.S. Dist. LEXIS 95956 (July 22, 2016).

D.   *Forward-Looking Information*

Soft information describes events or activities that will occur, if at all, at some future date. Soft information by definition is inherently uncertain, so that there is every reason to believe its materiality should be assessed by the probability/ magnitude standard applied in *Basic*. The Supreme Court, however, expressed no opinion whether the probability/magnitude test should be applied across the board in assessing the materiality of all uncertain events. In considering the scope of the probability/magnitude test, and particularly its application to soft information, the qualities of soft information should be contrasted with so-called historical information: reports on events that have occurred. For example, all accounting-based information in financial statements is essentially historical, reporting on such items as the sales, expenses, and income produced from operations for a period, as well as the assets, liabilities, and equity of the firm as of a specific date in the past. Except for the section for the Management Discussion and Analysis of Financial Condition and Results of Operations, Regulation S-K bears upon events and activities that have transpired within the firm, not those that are likely to occur.

Soft information is important largely because the past is not always prologue in the world of business and finance. That is, historical information, while an accepted basis for extrapolating what is likely to occur in the future, is not nearly as predictive as managers' forecasts. For much of its existence the SEC would not allow registrants to include soft information in their SEC filings because the SEC believed the information was too subjective and inherently unreliable and would be misused by unsophisticated investors. No position has earned the SEC more criticism than its stationing itself between those issuers that wished to disclose their managers' forecasts of future operations and the investment community's insatiable appetite for management forecasts, appraisals, and the like. In 1973,[2] the SEC announced that it had determined to change its policies with respect to soft information, and, in 1978, it assumed its current position, in which it encourages registrants to include projections in SEC filings.[3]

Also important is the SEC's development of Item 303, the Management Discussion and Analysis section of Regulation S-K, examined in the preceding chapter. Item 303 directly requests management to assess the past performance of the business and, importantly, to provide its view of what operations, trends, and forces will affect future operations. At several key points, Item 303 imposes upon management a duty to disclose trends that are likely to affect the firm's financial performance, liquidity, or capital resources as well as the effects of inflation on operations. Even though disclosures such as these necessarily involve a good many subjective judgments, predictive information and speculation, not only are registrants now encouraged to include such information in their SEC filings, but also in discrete areas such information is actually solicited by Regulation S-K. The full significance of this change in SEC disclosure practices is not so much that it has forced disclosures on unwilling registrants, but that it has removed the SEC opposition from the path of those who wish to include *optimistic* forward-looking information in their filings.

---

2. Disclosure of Projections of Future Economic Performance, Securities Act Release No. 5362 (1973).

3. Guides for Disclosure of Projections for Future Economic Performance, Securities Act Release No. 5992 (1978).

But what of the fact that the distinguishing characteristic of projections and appraisals is that they are seldom accurate? Should the policy choices surrounding soft information be determined on the basis of the relative accuracy of predictions and appraisals? The question posed by soft information is whether resources are better allocated among competing investment opportunities by encouraging the flow of soft information if that additional information is not accurate. To resolve this question upon the slender basis that forecasts or appraisals are untrustworthy overlooks some important considerations. First, it is naive to assume investors accept soft information uncritically. They may, and most likely do, adjust forecasts and appraisals to their own estimates of the possible outcomes. Second, some assumption must be made of the variance between the forecast or appraisal figure and the amount achieved that investors consider material. If the deviance is insignificant in light of the amount that investors have already discounted the forecast or appraisal by the time it was issued, it is difficult to conclude that investors or markets are disserved by the release of soft information. Even if the argument is based upon accuracy, it appears that we are better off by encouraging management to proffer forecasts. Managers are not the only ones that issue forecasts: Security analysts more frequently make published forecasts than do managers, and their forecasts are less accurate than those of managers. *See* Hutton, Lee & Shu, Do Managers Always Know Better? An Examination of the Relative Accuracy of Management and Analyst Forecasts, 50 J. Acct. Res. 1217 (2012).

Finally, since a forecast, prediction, and appraisal each speak of the future, and hence can be expected to deviate from what actually does occur, how do we determine if the forward-looking statement is materially inaccurate when it is made? Does a mere difference between the forecasted or appraised amount and the level ultimately realized mean that the forecast or appraisal is the basis for liability under the securities laws? In *Moss v. Healthcare Compare Corp.*, 75 F.3d 276 (7th Cir. 1996), the company expressed comfort with analysts' forecasts of earnings of $1.20 to $1.25 per share. Two months later the price of the shares lost one-third of their value when the company stated that analysts' estimates of $1.10 per share were too high. In dismissing the suit that was filed within 24 hours after the pessimistic announcement, the court provides the following insight to when a forecast is misleading:

> [C]ases involving forward-looking statements are unique. . . . [P]redictions of future performance are inevitably inaccurate because things almost never go exactly as planned. . . . [P]laintiffs must allege "specific facts which illustrate that the company's predictions lacked a reasonable basis. . . . Projections which turn out to be inaccurate are not fraudulent simply because subsequent events reveal that a different projection would have been more reasonable."

For example, the requisite scienter was found for management's rosy forecast that was made when the executives were aware that some divisions of the company were wilting, e.g., its important driveshaft division was experiencing losses of about 50 percent and its supply cost for steel was rising 75-120 percent. *Frank v. Dana Corp.*, 646 F.3d 954 (6th Cir. 2011).

As we will see in the material that follows, the first line of defense for a "missed" forecast under the case law as well as the statutory safe harbor for forward-looking statements is not the reasonableness of its preparer's efforts but whether the forecast was accompanied by meaningful cautionary language.

1.   The "Bespeaks Caution" Doctrine

▌▌ **Kaufman v. Trump's Castle Funding**
7 F.3d 357 (3d Cir. 1993)

BECKER, C.J. . . .

I.   FACTS AND PROCEDURAL HISTORY

In November, 1988 the Trump defendants offered to the public $675 million in first mortgage investment bonds (the "bonds") with Merrill Lynch acting as the sole underwriter. The interest rate on the bonds was 14%, a high rate in comparison to the 9% yield offered on quality corporate bonds at the time. The Trump defendants issued the bonds to raise capital to: (1) purchase the Taj Mahal, a partially-completed casino/hotel located on the boardwalk, from Resorts International, Inc. (which had already invested substantial amounts in its construction); (2) complete construction of the Taj Mahal; and (3) open the Taj Mahal for business.

As is well-known, the Taj Mahal was widely touted as Atlantic City's largest and most lavish casino resort. When ultimately opened in April, 1990, it was at least twice the size of any other casino in Atlantic City. It consisted of a 42-story hotel tower that contained approximately 1,250 guest rooms and an adjacent low-rise building encompassing roughly 155,000 square feet of meeting, ballroom and convention space, a 120,000 square foot casino, and numerous restaurants, lounges, and stores. The entire structure occupied approximately seventeen acres of land.

The prospectus accompanying the bonds estimated the completion cost of the Taj Mahal, including the payment of interest on the bonds for the first fifteen months of operation, at $805 million. It explained that, to obtain that amount, the Trump defendants were relying on the $675 million in bond proceeds, a $75 million capital contribution by Donald Trump, investment income derived from those sums, a contingent additional loan of $25 million from the Trump Line of Credit, and loans from other sources.

Plaintiffs [investors who purchased the bonds] ground their lawsuits in the text of the prospectus. Their strongest attack focuses on the "Management Discussion and Analysis" ("MD&A") section of the prospectus, which stated: "The Partnership believes that funds generated from the operation of the Taj Mahal will be sufficient to cover all of its debt service (interest and principal)." . . . The plaintiffs' primary contention is that this statement was materially misleading because the defendants possessed neither a genuine nor a reasonable belief in its truth. . . .

After learning that the Trump defendants planned to file Chapter 11 bankruptcy proceedings and establish a reorganization plan, various bondholders filed separate complaints. . . . The complaints each alleged that the prospectus accompanying the issuance of the bonds contained material misrepresentations and material omissions in violation of the 1933 and 1934 Acts. . . . [The district court dismissed the complaint for failure to state a claim and the plaintiffs appealed.] . . .

B. THE TEXT OF THE PROSPECTUS . . .

The statement the plaintiffs assail as misleading is contained in the MD&A section of the prospectus, which follows the sizable "Special Considerations" section, a section notable for its extensive and detailed disclaimers and cautionary statements. More precisely, the prospectus explained that, because of its status as a new venture of unprecedented size and scale, a variety of risks inhered in the Taj Mahal which could affect the Partnership's ability to repay the bondholders. For example, it stated:

> The casino business in Atlantic City, New Jersey has a seasonal nature of which summer is the peak season. . . . Since the third interest payment date on the Bonds [which constitutes the first interest payment not paid out of the initial financing] occurs before the summer season, the Partnership will not have the benefit of receiving peak season cash flow prior to the third interest payment date, which could adversely affect its ability to pay interest on the Bonds.
>
> . . . The Taj Mahal has not been completed and, accordingly, has no operating history. The Partnership, therefore, has no history of earnings and its operations will be subject to all of the risks inherent in the establishment of a new business enterprise. Accordingly, the ability of the Partnership to service its debt to [Taj Mahal Funding Inc., which issued the bonds], is completely dependent upon the success of that operation and such success will depend upon financial, business, competitive, regulatory, and other factors affecting the Taj Mahal and the casino industry in general, as well as prevailing economic conditions. . . .
>
> The Taj Mahal will be the largest casino/hotel complex in Atlantic City, with approximately twice the room capacity and casino space of many of the existing casino/hotels in Atlantic City. [No] other casino/hotel operator has had experience operating a complex the size of the Taj Mahal in Atlantic City. Consequently, no assurance can be given that, once opened, the Taj Mahal will be profitable or that it will generate cash flow sufficient to provide for the payment of the debt service. . . .

Prospectus at 8.

The prospectus went on to relate, as part of its "Security for the Bonds" subsection, the potential effect of the Partnership's default on its mortgage payments. For example, this subsection unreservedly explained that if a default occurred prior to completion of the Taj Mahal, "there would not be sufficient proceeds [from a foreclosure sale of the Taj Mahal] to pay the principal of, and accrued interest on, the Bonds." Prospectus at 9.

The "Special Considerations" section also detailed the high level of competition for customers the completed Taj Mahal would face once opened to the public:

> Competition in the Atlantic City casino/hotel market is intense. At present, there are twelve casino/hotels in Atlantic City. . . . Some Atlantic City casino/hotels recently have completed renovations or are in the process of expanding and improving their facilities. . . . *The Partnership believes* that, based upon historical trends, *casino win per square foot of casino space will decline in 1990* as a result of a projected increase in casino floor space, including the opening of the Taj Mahal.

Prospectus at 14 (emphasis added). In a section following the MD&A section, the prospectus reiterated its reference to the intense competition in the Atlantic City casino industry:

> Growth in Atlantic City casino win is expected to be restrained until further improvements to the City's transportation system and infrastructure are undertaken and completed and the number of noncasino hotel rooms and existing convention space are increased. No assurance can be given with respect to either the future growth of the Atlantic City gaming market or the ability of the Taj Mahal to attract a representative share of that market.

Prospectus at 33. The prospectus additionally reported that there were risks of delay in the construction of the Taj Mahal and a risk that the casino might not receive the numerous essential licenses and permits from the state regulatory authorities. . . .

[W]e must consider an alleged misrepresentation within the context in which the speaker communicated it. Here the context clearly and precisely relayed to the bondholders the substantial uncertainties inherent in the completion and operation of the Taj Mahal. The prospectus contained both general warnings that the Partnership could not assure the repayment of the bonds as well as specific discussions detailing a variety of risk factors that rendered the completion and profitable operation of the Taj Mahal highly uncertain. Within this broad context the statement at issue was, at worst, harmless.

C.   THE BESPEAKS CAUTION DOCTRINE

The district court applied what has come to be known as the "bespeaks caution" doctrine. In so doing it followed the lead of a number of courts of appeals which have dismissed securities fraud claims under Rule 12(b)(6) because cautionary language in the offering document negated the materiality of an alleged misrepresentation or omission. . . . We are persuaded by the ratio decidendi of these cases and will apply bespeaks caution to the facts before us.

The application of bespeaks caution depends on the specific text of the offering document or other communication at issue. . . . Nevertheless, we can state as a general matter that, when an offering document's forecasts, opinions or projections are accompanied by meaningful cautionary statements, the forward-looking statements will not form the basis for a securities fraud claim if those statements did not affect the "total mix" of information the document provided investors. In other words, cautionary language, if sufficient, renders the alleged omissions or misrepresentations immaterial as a matter of law.

. . . Of course, a vague or blanket (boilerplate) disclaimer which merely warns the reader that the investment has risks will ordinarily be inadequate to prevent misinformation. To suffice, the cautionary statements must be substantive and tailored to the specific future projections, estimates or opinions in the prospectus which the plaintiffs challenge.

Because of the abundant and meaningful cautionary language contained in the prospectus, we hold that the plaintiffs have failed to state an actionable claim regarding the statement that the Partnership believed it could repay the bonds. We can say that the prospectus here truly bespeaks caution because, not only does the prospectus generally convey the riskiness of the investment, but its warnings and cautionary language directly address the substance of the statement the plaintiffs challenge. That is to say, the cautionary statements were tailored precisely to address the uncertainty concerning the Partnership's prospective ability to repay the bondholders. . . .

D.   CONCLUSION

[W]e think it clear that the accompanying warnings and cautionary language served to negate any potentially misleading effect that the prospectus' statement about the Partnership's belief in its ability to repay the bonds would have on a reasonable investor. . . . Given this context, we believe that no reasonable jury could conclude that the subject projection materially influenced a reasonable investor. . . .

For the foregoing reasons we will affirm the orders of the district court dismissing the plaintiffs' complaints under Rule 12(b)(6). . . .

NOTES AND QUESTIONS

1.   The Meaning of "Meaningful Cautionary" Language.   Both the "bespeaks caution" doctrine and the statutory safe harbor for forward-looking statements, discussed in the next section of this chapter, place importance upon the forward-looking statement being accompanied by meaningful cautionary language. Whether cautionary warnings meet this test turns on the unique facts of the case. Thus, in response to a claim that Gateway's earnings forecast was not reasonably based because it underestimated certain production problems it might incur, the court dismissed the suit on the basis of the accompanying risk warnings that "the Company has experienced, and may continue to experience, problems with respect to the size of its work force and production facilities and the adequacy of its management information systems and inventory controls." *Parnes v. Gateway 2000, Inc.,* 122 F.3d 539 (3d Cir. 1997). And, allegedly false predictions about the company's capability to provide technical consulting services were not misleading when accompanied by a warning that there was a limited pool of qualified information technology professionals and that the company's success depended upon its ability to attract such professionals. *See Steinberg v. PRT Group, Inc.,* 88 F. Supp. 2d 294 (S.D.N.Y. 2000). In contrast, *Gray v. First Winthrop Corp.,* 82 F.3d 877 (9th Cir. 1996), held that a statement that a real estate project was "subject to the risk inherent in the ownership of real estate," and was accompanied also by disclosure of prior periods of business downturn for real estate, did not protect the statement that this project would be fully leased notwithstanding a market slowdown. In *Semerenko v. Cendant Corp.,* 223 F.3d 165 (3d Cir. 2000), on April 15, 1998, the company disclosed it had discovered certain accounting irregularities that it stated were confined to a single business unit that accounted for less than one-third of its business and forecasted a downward adjustment in quarterly earnings of $0.11 to $0.13 per share because of the irregularities. The statement was accompanied by a general warning regarding the vagaries of the company's business that made forecasting difficult and noted that its forecast was subject to "known and unknown risks and uncertainties including, but not limited to, the outcome of the Audit Committee's investigation." Three months later, the company announced the irregularities were much larger and more widespread than previously announced. The court held the earlier warning was mere boilerplate, lacked substance, and was not sufficiently tailored to satisfy the bespeaks caution doctrine. *See generally* Ripken, Predictions, Projections, and Precautions: Conveying Cautionary Warnings in Corporate Forward-Looking Statements, 2005 Ill. L. Rev. 929 (behavioral literature calls for crisp statements of not just the possibility but the probability events will occur that change the forecasted result and, to overcome the framing bias, the most effective warnings are those that list first the most significant risks, with lesser risks appearing later).

2.   Puffery Revisited.   Earlier in this chapter we found that vague, generally worded statements of optimism can be deemed immaterial because they are understood as mere puffery. The Fourth Circuit sometimes determines whether a forward-looking statement is harmless by a test similar to that employed in deciding whether a statement constitutes puffery; it holds that before a forward-looking statement is material it must rise to the level of a guarantee. *See Hillson Partners Ltd. Partnership v. Adage, Inc.,* 42 F.3d 204, 216 (4th Cir. 1994) (finding immaterial a statement of "looking for 1992 sales of about $100 million and 1993 sales of $110 million" as not "rising to the level of a guarantee"); *Raab v. General Physics Corp.,* 4 F.3d 286, 289-290 (4th Cir. 1993) (same). This "guaranty standard" from time to time is invoked in other circuits as well. *See Lasker v. New York State Electric & Gas Corp.,* 85 F.3d 55 (2d Cir. 1996). *See also Krim v. BancTexas Group, Inc.,* 989 F.2d 1435, 1446 (5th Cir. 1993). What role should the relative certainty of a forward-looking statement play in determining if the statement is material?

3.   Trump and the Investment Analyst.   One of the most publicized instances of a research analyst being pressured to serve a company's financial needs arose in connection with the financing of the Taj Mahal Casino. Marvin Roffman, a research analyst with a regional brokerage firm, published a highly critical assessment of the Taj Mahal's financial position when the bonds in the principal case were being offered for sale. Trump pressured the brokerage firm to retract the analyst's report and ultimately even secured a public apology from Roffman. However, Roffman retracted the apology the day after it was made, for which he was summarily fired. *See* A. Gart, Regulation, Deregulation, Reregulation: The Future of the Banking, Insurance, and Securities Industries 269 (1994). Roffman prevailed in his defamation suit against his employer and also obtained a handsome out-of-court settlement from Trump.

2.   Statutory Safe Harbor for Forward-Looking Statements

The Private Securities Litigation Reform Act of 1995 (PSLRA) adds Section 27A to the Securities Act and a parallel provision in Section 21E to the Exchange

Act, which provide a statutory safe harbor for certain forward-looking state-ments made by companies that are subject to the Exchange Act's continuous reporting provisions. The legislation was prompted by fears that private suits too frequently were brought against innocent corporations and their repre-sentatives for forward-looking statements regarding their performance or products. Congress was persuaded that corporations were reluctant to make forward-looking statements out of fear that any inaccuracy in their projections would trigger the filing of a securities class action lawsuit. Concern for liability for forward-looking statements was argued to cause corporate disclosures to be less helpful than if the regulatory climate were more hospitable to announce-ments such as forecasts, appraisals, and business plans. In the words of former SEC Commissioner Beese, "legions of lawyers scrub required filings to ensure that disclosures are as Milquetoast as possible, so as to provide no grist for the litigation mill."

The safe harbors' subsection (c)(1) shields persons specified in the provi-sion from liability in *private* actions for forward-looking statements under one of two alternative safe harbors. The first safe harbor (in addition to shielding any immaterial forward-looking statement) reaches a forward-looking state-ment that "is accompanied by meaningful cautionary statements identifying the important factors that could cause actual results to differ materially from those in the forward-looking statement." Alternatively, the safe harbor is available if the plaintiff fails to prove that the forward-looking statement "was made with actual knowledge" it was misleading. Because the absence of actual knowledge is a separate basis for the safe harbor's availability, the specter arises that pri-vate parties will be unable to recover from even a knowingly false forecast if that forecast is accompanied by "meaningful cautionary" language. The Reform Act's Conference Committee Report provides the following gloss to the scope of "meaningful cautionary language":

> The cautionary statements must convey substantive information about factors that realistically could cause results to differ materially from those projected in the forward-looking statement, such as, for example, information about the issuer's business. . . .
>
> "Important" factors means the stated factors identified in the cautionary state-ment must be relevant to the projection and must be of a nature that the factor or factors could actually affect whether the forward-looking statement is realized.
>
> The Conference Committee expects that the cautionary statements identify important factors that could cause results to differ materially—but not all factors. Failure to include the particular factor that ultimately causes the forward-looking statement not to come true will not mean that the statement is not protected by the safe harbor. The Conference Committee specifies that the cautionary state-ments identify "important" factors to provide guidance to issuers and not to pro-vide an opportunity for plaintiff counsel to conduct discovery on what factors were known to the issuer at the time the forward-looking statement was made. . . .
>
> Courts may continue to find a forward-looking statement immate-rial. . . . [Hence,] the Conference Committee includes language in the safe harbor that no liability attaches to forward-looking statements that are "immaterial." . . .
>
> Forward-looking statements will have safe harbor protection if they are accompanied by a meaningful cautionary statement. A cautionary statement that misstates historical facts is not covered by the safe harbor. It is not sufficient,

however, in a civil action to allege merely that a cautionary statement misstates historical facts. The plaintiff must plead with particularity all facts giving rise to a strong inference of a material misstatement in the cautionary statement to survive a motion to dismiss.

H.R. Conf. Rep. No. 369, 104th Cong., 2d Sess. 11 (1995). The statutory safe harbor also extends to oral forward-looking statements. When relying on the "meaningful cautionary" prong, there is a further requirement that the oral statement identify where the listener can find the qualifying "meaningful cautionary" information.

In addition to being restricted to reporting companies, the safe harbor is not available to forward-looking statements made in connection with certain types of transactions, such as initial public offerings, tender offers, and going-private transactions. Does it make sense to exclude these transactions? Issuers and persons acting on behalf of issuers, as well as underwriters who obtained their information from issuers, can invoke the safe harbor. Transactions and parties not covered by the Reform Act's safe harbor may still seek protection under SEC Rule 175 and the judicially created "bespeaks caution" doctrine. Further teeth are added to the safe harbor in subsection (f), staying discovery during the pendency of any motion to dismiss the complaint based upon the application of the safe harbor.

Asher v. Baxter International, Inc.
377 F.3d 727 (7th Cir. 2004)

EASTERBROOK, Circuit Judge. Baxter International, a manufacturer of medical products, released its second-quarter financial results for 2002 on July 18 of that year. Sales and profits did not match analysts' expectations. Shares swiftly fell from $43 to $32. This litigation followed; plaintiffs contend that the $43 price was the result of materially misleading projections on November 5, 2001, projections that Baxter reiterated until the bad news came out on July 18, 2002. Plaintiffs want to represent a class of all investors who purchased during that time either in the open market or by exchanging their shares of Fusion Medical Technologies. (Baxter acquired Fusion in a stock-for-stock transaction; plaintiffs think that Baxter juiced up the market price so that it could secure Fusion in exchange for fewer of its own shares.) . . . [T]he district court dismissed the complaint for failure to state a claim on which relief may be granted. 2003 U.S. Dist. LEXIS 12905 (N.D. Ill. July 17, 2003). . . . [I]t held, Baxter's forecasts come within the safe harbor created by the Private Securities Litigation Reform Act of 1995. . . .

Baxter's projection, repeated many times (sometimes in documents filed with the SEC, sometimes in press releases, sometimes in executives' oral statements), was that during 2002 the business would yield revenue growth in the "low teens" compared with the prior year, earnings-per-share growth in the "mid teens," and "operational cash flow of at least $500 million." . . .

According to the complaint, Baxter's projections were materially false because: (1) its Renal Division had not met its internal budgets in years; . . . (3) Baxter closed plants in Ronneby, Sweden, and Miami Lakes, Florida, that had been its principal source of low-cost dialysis products; . . . (5) sales of that division's IGIV immunoglobulin products had fallen short of internal predictions; and (6) in March 2002 the Bio-Science Division had experienced a sterility failure in the manufacture of a major product, resulting in the destruction of multiple lots and a loss exceeding $10 million. The district court assumed, as shall we, that failure to disclose these facts would create problems but for the statutory safe harbor. . . .

The statutory safe harbor forecloses liability if a forward-looking statement "is accompanied by meaningful cautionary statements identifying important factors that could cause actual results to differ materially from those in the forward-looking statement" [§27A(c)(1)(A)(i)]. . . . The fundamental problem is that the statutory requirement of "meaningful cautionary statements" is not itself meaningful. What must the firm say? Unless it is possible to give a concrete and reliable answer, the harbor is not "safe"; yet a word such as "meaningful" resists a concrete rendition and thus makes administration of the safe harbor difficult if not impossible. It rules out a caution such as: "This is a forward-looking statement: caveat emptor." . . . A safe harbor matters only when the firm's disclosures (including the accompanying cautionary statements) are false or misleadingly incomplete; yet whenever that condition is satisfied, one can complain that the cautionary statement must have been inadequate. The safe harbor loses its function. Yet it would be unsound to read the statute so that the safe harbor never works; then one might as well treat . . . [it] as defunct.

Baxter provided a number of cautionary statements throughout the class period. This one, from its 2001 Form 10-K filing—a document to which many of the firm's press releases and other statements referred—is the best illustration:

> Statements throughout this report that are not historical facts are forward-looking statements. These statements are based on the company's current expectations and involve numerous risks and uncertainties. . . .
>
> Many factors could affect the company's actual results, causing results to differ materially, from those expressed in any such forward-looking statements. These factors include, but are not limited to, interest rates; technological advances in the medical field; economic conditions; demand and market acceptance risks for new and existing products, technologies and health care services; the impact of competitive products and pricing; manufacturing capacity; new plant startups; global regulatory, trade and tax policies; regulatory, legal or other developments relating to the company's Series A, AF, and AX dialyzers; continued price competition; product development risks, including technological difficulties; ability to enforce patents; actions of regulatory bodies and other government authorities; reimbursement policies of government agencies; commercialization factors; results of product testing; and other factors described elsewhere in this report or in the company's other filings with the Securities and Exchange Commission. . . .
>
> The company believes that its expectations with respect to forward-looking statements are based upon reasonable assumptions within the bounds of its knowledge of its business operations, but there can be no assurance that the actual results or performance of the company will conform to any future results or performance expressed or implied by such forward-looking statements.

The district court concluded that these are "meaningful cautionary statements identifying important factors that could cause actual results to differ materially from those in the forward-looking statement." They deal with Baxter's business specifically, mentioning risks and product lines. Plaintiffs offer two responses. First they contend that the cautionary statements did not cover any of the six matters that (in plaintiffs' view) Baxter had withheld. That can't be dispositive; otherwise the statute would demand prescience. As long as the firm reveals the principal risks, the fact that some other event caused problems cannot be dispositive. Indeed, an unexpected turn of events cannot demonstrate a securities problem at all, as there cannot be "fraud by hindsight." *Denny v. Barber*, 576 F.2d 465, 470 (2d Cir. 1978). . . . The other response is that the cautionary statement did not follow the firm's fortunes: plants closed but the cautionary statement remained the same; sterilization failures occurred but the cautionary statement remained the same; and bad news that (plaintiffs contend) Baxter well knew in November 2001 did not cast even a shadow in the cautionary statement.

Before considering whether plaintiffs' objections defeat the safe harbor, we ask whether the cautionary statements have any bearing on Baxter's potential liability for statements in its press releases, and those its managers made orally. The press releases referred to, but did not repeat verbatim, the cautionary statements in the Form 10-K and other documents filed with the Securities and Exchange Commission. The oral statements did not do even that much. Plaintiffs say that this is fatal, because §[27A](c)(1)(A)(i) provides a safe harbor only if a written statement is "accompanied by" the meaningful caution; a statement published elsewhere differs from one that accompanies the press release. As for the oral statements: §[27A](c)(2)(A)(ii), a special rule for oral statements, provides a safe harbor only if the statement includes "that the actual results could differ materially from those projected in the forward-looking statement" and in addition:

   (i)   the oral forward-looking statement is accompanied by an oral statement that additional information concerning factors that could cause actual results to differ materially from those in the forward-looking statement is contained in a readily available written document, or portion thereof;
  (ii)   the accompanying oral statement referred to in clause (i) identifies the document, or portion thereof, that contains the additional information about those factors relating to the forward-looking statement; and
 (iii)   the information contained in that written document is a cautionary statement that satisfies the standard established in paragraph

. . . [§27A](c)(2)(B). When speaking with analysts Baxter's executives did not provide them with all of this information, such as directions to look in the 10-K report for the full cautionary statement. It follows, plaintiffs maintain, that this suit must proceed with respect to the press releases and oral statements even if the cautionary language filed with the SEC in registration statements and other documents meets the statutory standard.

If this were a traditional securities suit—if, in other words, an investor claimed to have read or heard the statement and, not having access to the truth, relied to his detriment on the falsehood—then plaintiffs' argument would be correct. But this is not a traditional securities claim. It is a fraud-on-the-market claim. None of the plaintiffs asserts that he read any of Baxter's press releases or listened to an executive's oral statement. Instead the theory is that other people (professional traders, mutual fund managers, securities analysts) did the reading, and that they made trades or recommendations that influenced the price. In an efficient capital market, all information known to the public affects the price and thus affects every investor. *Basic Inc. v. Levinson*, 485 U.S. 224 . . . (1988), holds that reliance on the accuracy of the price can substitute for reliance on the accuracy of particular written or oral statements, when the statements affect the price—as they do for large and well-followed firms such as Baxter, for which there is a liquid public market. This works only to the extent that markets efficiently reflect (and thus convey to investors the economic equivalent of) all public information. . . .

An investor who invokes the fraud-on-the-market theory must acknowledge that all public information is reflected in the price, just as the Supreme Court said in *Basic. See* 485 U.S. at 246. . . . Thus . . . if a cautionary statement has been widely disseminated, that news too affects the price just as if that statement had been handed to each investor. If the executives' oral statements came to plaintiffs through professional traders (or analysts) and hence the price, then the cautions reached plaintiffs via the same route; market professionals are savvy enough to discount projections appropriately. Then §[27A](c)(2)(B) has been satisfied for the oral statements (and so too §[27A](c)(1)(A)(i) for the press releases). And if the cautions did not affect the price, then the market must be inefficient and the suit fails for that reason. So we take the claim as the pleadings framed it: the market for Baxter's stock is efficient, which means that Baxter's cautionary language must be treated as if attached to every one of its oral and written statements. That leaves the question whether these statements satisfy the statutory requirement that they adequately "identify[] important factors that could cause actual results to differ materially from those in the forward-looking statement."

The parties agree on two propositions, each with support in decisions of other circuits. First, "boilerplate" warnings won't do; cautions must be tailored to the risks that accompany the particular projections. Second, the cautions need not identify what actually goes wrong and causes the projections to be inaccurate; prevision is not required. *See Halperin v. EBanker USA.com, Inc.*, 295 F.3d 352, 359 (2d Cir. 2002). . . .

Plaintiffs say that Baxter's cautions were boilerplate, but they aren't. Statements along the lines of "all businesses are risky" or "the future lies ahead" come to nothing other than caveat emptor (which isn't enough); these statements, by contrast, at least included Baxter-specific information and highlighted some parts of the business that might cause problems. . . .

What investors would like to have is a full disclosure of the assumptions and calculations behind the projections; then they could apply their own discount factors. . . . [T]his is not a sensible requirement. Many of the assumptions and calculations would be more useful to a firm's rivals than to its investors. Suppose, for example, that Baxter had revealed its sterility failure in the BioSciences Division, the steps it had taken to restore production, and the costs and prospects of each. Rivals could have used that information to avoid costs and hazards that had befallen Baxter, or to find solutions more quickly, and as Baxter could not have charged the rivals for this information they would have been able to undercut Baxter's price in future transactions. Baxter's shareholders would have been worse off. . . .

The PSLRA does not require the most helpful caution; it is enough to "identify[] important factors that could cause actual results to differ materially from those in the forward-looking statement." This means that it is enough to point to the principal contingencies that could cause actual results to depart from the projection. The statute calls for issuers to reveal the "important factors" but not to attach probabilities to each potential bad outcome, or to reveal in detail what could go wrong; as we have said, that level of detail might hurt investors (by helping rivals) even as it improved the accuracy of stock prices. . . .

Yet Baxter's chosen language may fall short. There is no reason to think—at least, no reason that a court can accept at the pleading stage, before plaintiffs have access to discovery—that the items mentioned in Baxter's cautionary language were those that at the time were the (or any of the) "important" sources of variance. The problem is not that what actually happened went unmentioned; issuers need not anticipate all sources of deviations from expectations. Rather, the problem is that there is no reason (on this record) to conclude that Baxter mentioned those sources of variance that (at the time of the projection) were the principal or important risks. For all we can tell, the major risks Baxter objectively faced when it made its forecasts were exactly those that, according to the complaint, came to pass, yet the cautionary statement mentioned none of them. Moreover, the cautionary language remained fixed even as the risks changed. When the sterility failure occurred in spring 2002, Baxter left both its forecasts and cautions as is. When Baxter closed the plants that (according to the complaint) were its least-cost sources of production, the forecasts and cautions continued without amendment. This raises the possibility—no greater confidence is possible before discovery—that Baxter omitted important variables from the cautionary language and so made projections more certain than its internal estimates at the time warranted. Thus this complaint could not be dismissed under the safe harbor, though we cannot exclude the possibility that if after discovery Baxter establishes that the cautions did reveal what were, ex ante, the major risks, the safe harbor may yet carry the day.

Baxter urges us to affirm the judgment immediately, contending that the full truth had reached the market despite any shortcomings in its cautionary statements. If this is so, however, it is hard to understand the sharp drop in the price of its stock. A "truth-on-the-market" defense is available in principle, . . . but not at the pleading stage. Likewise one must consider the possibility that investors looked at all of the projections as fluff and responded only to the hard numbers; on this view it was a reduction in Baxter's growth rate, not the embarrassment of a projection, that caused the price decline in July 2002; again it is too early in the litigation to reach such a conclusion. . . .

Nor has the time arrived to evaluate Baxter's contention that its projections panned out, so there was no material error. Baxter insists that all of the projections dealt with the entire calendar year 2002, and that by year-end performance was up to snuff—close enough to the projections that any difference was immaterial. Once again, it is inappropriate to entertain such an argument at the pleading stage. The district court will need to determine whether all of the forward-looking statements referenced calendar 2002 as a whole, rather than anticipated improvements quarter-by-quarter over the preceding year. . . . Reversed and remanded.

NOTES AND QUESTIONS

1.   The Meaning of "Forward-Looking Statement."   The threshold requirement for the statutory safe harbor's application is that the challenged statement must be a "forward-looking statement." Exchange Act Section 21E(i) and
Securities Act 27A(i) define *forward-looking statements* so they at least include
the classic announcements of "projections," "plans," and statements "of future
economic performance." Many statements fall fairly easily within the definition,
such as a prediction of future earnings. However, close questions frequently
arise. For example, is it a forward-looking statement when an airline announces
that the recent settlement with the FAA over certain safety violations "will not
have a material adverse effect on the Company's operations or financial affairs"
and that the airline does not anticipate any major increase in costs going forward as a result of the settlement? *See, e.g., No. 84 Employer-Teamster Joint Council
Pension Trust Fund v. America West Holdings*, 320 F.3d 920 (9th Cir. 2003). *See
also P. Stolz Family Partnership v. Daum*, 355 F.3d 92 (2d Cir. 2004) (statement
there is no plan to undertake a public offering is a statement of present fact);
Ehlert v. Singer, 245 F.3d 1313 (11th Cir. 2001) ("The company's future success
will depend . . . [on enhancing] its current products." . . . "Company is devoting significant resources to the development of enhancements to its existing
products" deemed a forward-looking statement); *Graham v. Taylor Capital Group*,
135 F. Supp. 2d 480 (D. Del. 2001) (estimated reserve for uncollectible loans is
statement of current financial condition and not a forward-looking statement).
Historical facts are usually beyond the protection of either the bespeaks caution
doctrine or statutory safe harbor. *See, e.g., Livid Holdings Ltd. v. Salomon Smith
Barney Inc.*, 403 F.3d 1050 (9th Cir. 2005). However, what if historical facts are
intertwined with forward-looking statements? Most circuits hold the defendant
cannot transform a non-forward-looking statement into a forward-looking statement by interconnecting the former with the latter. *See, e.g., City of Miami v.
Quality Systems, Inc.*, 865 F.3d 1130 (9th Cir. 2017); *Makor Issues & Rights, Ltd. v.
Tellabs Inc. (Tellabs II)*, 513 F.3d 702 (7th Cir. 2008). Consider in this regard the
reasoning of *Tellabs II*:

> [A] mixed present/future statement is not entitled to the safe harbor with respect
> to the part of the statement that refers to the present. When Tellabs told the world
> that sales of its 5500 system were "still going strong," it was saying both that the
> current sales were strong and that they would continue to be so, at least for a time,
> since the statement would be misleading if Tellabs knew that its sales were about to
> collapse. The element of prediction in saying that the sales are "still going strong"
> does not entitle Tellabs to a safe harbor with regard to the statement's representa-
> tion concerning current sales.

Id. at 705. *But see Harris v. IVAX Corp.*, 182 F.3d 799 (11th Cir. 1999) (the plaintiff
unsuccessfully argued a half-truth had been committed when the defendant's
forecast depended on six factors, some of which were historical and others that
were forward-looking statements; the court held that the six factors were so integrated that all should be treated as forward-looking statements such that they
were protected by meaningful cautionary language).

2. Can Fibbers Provide Meaningful Cautionary Language? Should the defendant be protected by meaningful cautionary language if the defendant issues a forward-looking statement the defendant knows is false? When this issue arises within the statutory safe harbor, the circuits are split in their approaches. A majority hold that the meaningful cautionary language defense is available even though the defendant knows the forward-looking statement is misleading. *See In re Cutera Sec. Litig.*, 610 F.3d 1103, 1112-1113 (9th Cir. 2010); *Edward J. Goodman Life Income Trust v. Jabil Circuit, Inc.*, 594 F.3d 783 (11th Cir. 2009); *Miller v. Champion Enters., Inc.*, 346 F.3d 660, 672 (6th Cir. 2003); *Helwig v. Vencor, Inc.*, 251 F.3d 540, 554 (6th Cir. 2001), *overruled in part on other grounds, Konkol v. Diebold, Inc.*, 590 F.3d 390, 396 (6th Cir. 2009). Consider the reasoning representative of the minority that hold knowledge of the forward statement's preparer is linked to determining whether the cautionary language was indeed meaningful.

> The safe harbor protects forward-looking statements that are "accompanied by meaningful cautionary statements identifying important factors that could cause actual results to differ materially from those in the forward-looking statement." . . .
>
>   While the Conference Committee expected that "cautionary statements identify important factors that could cause results to differ materially," it did not expect them to identify all factors. . . . The Conference Committee explicitly advised that its requirement that the cautionary statement identify important facts is not intended to provide "an opportunity for plaintiff counsel to conduct discovery on what factors were known to the issuer" at the time the statement was made. . . . It stressed that "[c]ourts should not examine the state of mind of the person making the statement." . . .
>
>   We find Congress's directions difficult to apply in this case. On the one hand, the Conference Report makes quite plain that it does not want courts to inquire into a defendant's state of mind, i.e., a defendant's knowledge of the risks at the time he made the statements. At the same time, however, the Conference Report requires cautionary statements to convey substantive information about factors that realistically could cause results to differ materially from projections. In order to assess whether an issuer has identified the factors that realistically could cause results to differ, we must have some reference by which to judge what the realistic factors were at the time the statement was made. We think that the most sensible reference is the major factors that the defendants faced at the time the statement was made. But this requires an inquiry into what the defendants knew because in order to determine what risks the defendants faced, we must ask of what risks were they aware.
>
>   Congress may wish to give further direction on how to resolve this tension, and in particular, the reference point by which we should judge whether an issuer has identified the factors that realistically could cause results to differ from projections. May an issuer be protected by the meaningful cautionary language prong of the safe harbor even where his cautionary statement omitted a major risk that he knew about at the time he made the statement? In this case, however, we need not decide that thorny issue because we conclude that at any rate the cautionary statement the defendants point to here was vague.

Slayton v. American Express Co., 604 F.3d 758, 770 (2d Cir. 2010). *See also Arkansas Pub. Emp. Ret. System v. Harman Int'l Indus., Inc.*, 791 F.3d 90 (D.C. Cir. 2015) (holding that cautionary language that misleads as to *facts* known to exist cannot provide a defense that the forward-looking statement was accompanied by *meaningful* cautionary language); *Lormand v. U.S. Wired, Inc.*, 565 F.3d 228 (5th Cir. 2009). *Slayton* also holds that the plaintiff not only has the burden under the statutory safe harbor to establish that the forward-looking statement was known to be misleading, but also to survive a motion to dismiss the plaintiff must satisfy the heightened pleading requirement by alleging with particularity facts that establish a strong inference of such knowledge.

Outside the statutory safe harbor, cases fairly consistently reject the "meaningful cautionary language" defense when the defendant knows the forecast is unreliable. *See, e.g., Huddleston v. Herman & MacLean*, 640 F.2d 534, 544 (5th Cir. 1981), *rev'd in part on other grounds*, 459 U.S. 375 (1983) ("To warn that the untoward may occur when the event is contingent is prudent; to caution that it is only possible for the unfavorable events to happen when they have already occurred is deceit."); *Kline v. First Western Government Securities Inc.*, 24 F.3d 480 (3d Cir. 1994) (disclaimer in a legal opinion that attorney cannot predict the IRS's treatment of transaction if facts are other than those set forth in the offering materials does not protect the attorney who knows the facts vary materially from those set forth in the offering materials); *Franklin High Yield v. County of Martin Minnesota*, 152 F.3d 736 (8th Cir. 1998) (statement of uncertainties whether to resort to municipality's taxing authority to satisfy payments required by municipal bond were misleading when officials for the bond's issuer did not intend to use the taxing authority to meet the payments called for in the bonds).

What explains the difference on this point between the result reached by most circuit courts interpreting the statutory safe harbor and the judicial construction of bespeaks caution? *Compare* Horwich, Cleaning the Murky Safe Harbor for Forward-Looking Statements: An Inquiry into Whether Actual Knowledge of Falsity Precludes the Meaningful Cautionary Statement Defense, 35 J. Corp. L. 519 (2010) (the cautionary language renders the false statement immaterial) *with* Beck, The Substantive Limits of Liability for Inaccurate Predictions, 44 Am. Bus. L.J. 161 (2007) (ultimate question for Congress was not materiality but falsity, so that presence of cautionary language allows investors to assess reliability of statement regardless of intent behind those making the statement). More generally, does meaningful cautionary language address instead the reasonableness of the investor's asserted reliance on the forward-looking statement? *See* Langevoort, Disclosures That "Bespeak Caution," 49 Bus. Law. 481, 487 (1994).

3. Assumptions. Disclosure of the assumptions underlying a forward-looking statement can itself prevent the statement from being misleading. *See, e.g., Connett v. Justus Enterprises of Kansas, Inc.*, 68 F.3d 382 (10th Cir. 1995) (statement that assets had appraised value of $11 million "in continued use" was not misleading when business failed and assets sold for $1.5 million because appraisal was based on assumption of assets' use in ongoing business, which implies a lower value if business failed). Assumptions, however, generally do not rise to the level of themselves being meaningful cautionary language. Thus, a forecast accompanied by management's view of how various commercial activities are interconnected and will diminish the company's operating losses does not warn investors of the risk those events will in fact occur. *See In re NationsMart Securities Litigation*, 130 F.3d 309 (8th Cir. 1997).

The statutory safe harbor, by including the underlying assumptions within the definition of forward-looking statement, extends its protective shield to assumptions. But what is the effect of disclosing an assumption known to be false? *Cf. Jakobe v. Rawlings Sporting Goods Co.*, 943 F. Supp. 1143, 1159 (E.D. Mo. 1994) (forecast of profits for baseball sales that was expressly premised on order level being equal to prior year was misleading when managers knew orders were trailing a year earlier due to Major League players' strike). And, what should be the effect under the statutory safe harbor of not disclosing a key assumption that underlies the forecasted item?

A leading pre-PSLRA case held that failure to disclose key assumptions was itself materially misleading. *See Beecher v. Able*, 374 F. Supp. 341 (S.D.N.Y. 1976) (forecast by Douglas Aircraft Company that it would break even based on undisclosed assumption that materials and labor shortages related to the Vietnam War would abate; however, the shortages persisted and the company instead reported a $52 million loss). Should meaningful cautionary language protect the company in this situation?

4. The Impact of the PSLRA on Forecasting. Law frequently not only matters, but matters a lot. This seems to be the case for the PSLRA's impact on the willingness of companies to engage in forecasting. In the year following the PSLRA's enactment, there was a significant increase in the number of firms proffering financial forecasts, with the greatest increases among riskier firms. *See* Johnson, Kasznik & Nelson, The Impact of Securities Litigation Reform on the Disclosure of Forward-Looking Information by High Technology Firms, 39 J. Acct. Res. 297 (2001). Interestingly, Johnson et al. do not find a significant increase in specific forecasts (such as point or bounded range); increases were general, qualitative forecasts of good news for the long-term or short-term forecasts of bad news. A substantial number of the forecasting firms in the post-PSLRA period had not released forecasts in the pre-PSLRA era. Finally, the authors found no evidence of a general decline in the accuracy of forecasts in the post-PSLRA era from what was observed for pre-PSLRA forecasts.

PROBLEMS

12-7. GoPro, Inc.'s CEO, in a quarterly meeting with analysts, stated that "the company is on track to meet our previous forecast of earning $3.45 this fiscal year." Is this a forward-looking statement? *See Institutional Investors Group v. Ayaya*, 564 F.3d 242 (3d Cir. 2009); *Bielousov v. GoPro, Inc.*, 2017 U.S. Dist. LEXIS 117223 (N.D. Cal. July 26, 2017).

12-8. BanCorp, a publicly traded bank with most of its operations in the Southeast, includes on its balance sheet a good many mortgage loans made to residential and commercial customers. The financial statements used in connection with its recent public offering reflected the following among its assets:

Mortgage Loans	$550,000,000
Estimated Allowance for Uncollectible	$25,000.000
Net Mortgage Loans	$525,000,000

Most of BanCorp's lending was in an area widely understood to be hard pressed by the collapse of land values and suffering from a general downturn in the local economy. Among the risk warnings in its registration statement was the following: "Consistent with generally accepted accounting principles, our financial statements are based on numerous estimates, judgments and assumptions, each of which can be affected by changing events specific to the company or exogenous to the firm so as to affect substantially reported figures." Three weeks after completing the public offering, under pressure from banking regulators, BanCorp increased the allowance for uncollectible mortgages to $250,000,000. Assume that any number above $75 million is material to the financial position and performance of BanCorp. In light of the materials covered thus far in this chapter, assess the defenses BanCorp might invoke if sued for overstating the amount of its assets? *See Stratte-McClure v. Morgan Stanley*, 784 F. Supp. 2d 373 (S.D.N.Y. 2011); *In re MoneyGram Int'l Inc. Sec. Litig.*, 626 F. Supp. 2d 947 (D. Minn. 2009).

E.   *The SEC and Corporate Governance*

1.   Integrity and Incentives of Managers

In the Matter of Franchard Corp.
42 S.E.C. 163 (1964)

CARY, Chairman. These are consolidated proceedings pursuant to Sections 8(c) and 8(d) of the Securities Act of 1933 ("Securities Act") to determine whether a stop order should issue suspending the effectiveness of three registration statements filed by Franchard Corporation, formerly Glickman Corporation ("registrant"). . . . These proceedings raise important issues as to the disclosures to be required in a registration statement concerning (1) the use of substantial amounts of a company's funds for the personal benefit of its controlling person on whose business reputation public offerings of its securities were largely predicated; (2) the pledge by a dominant stockholder of his control stock; (3) the adequacy of performance of a board of directors. . . . In essence, we are concerned here with the role that can and should be performed by the disclosure requirements of the Securities Act in assisting investors to evaluate management. . . .

I.   FACTS

A.   BACKGROUND

Louis J. Glickman ("Glickman") has for many years been a large-scale real estate developer, operator and investor. From 1954 to 1960, he acquired control of real estate in this country and in Canada by means of "syndication" arrangements. These arrangements involved the acquisition by Glickman, through purchase, contract or option, of an interest in real estate; the organization of a legal entity, usually a limited partnership but in some instances a corporation, in which Glickman retained a controlling position, and in which interests were sold to the public for cash; and the acquisition by this entity of the property interest in question. Glickman conducted some of these syndication activities and certain other phases of his real estate business through a number of wholly owned corporations, the most important of which was Glickman Corporation of Nevada, now known as Venada Corporation ("Venada").

In May of 1960, Glickman caused registrant to be formed in order to group under one entity most of the publicly owned corporations and limited partnerships under his control. Registrant was to operate on a so-called "cash flow" basis, i.e., the amount available for distribution to its stockholders was to be gauged by the excess of cash receipts over cash disbursements. . . . Registrant's stock was divided into two classes, Class A common and Class B common, with the B stockholders given the right to elect 2/3 of registrant's directors. . . . Glickman established control of registrant by acquiring 450,000 of its 660,000 authorized B shares for $1 per share. He exercised a dominant role in the management of registrant's affairs as president at the time of its formation and later as its first chairman of the board.

The first of the three registration statements here involved ("1960 filing") became effective on October 12, 1960. . . .

The second of the three registration statements ("first 1961 filing") became effective on October 2, 1961. . . . The third registration statement ("second 1961 filing") became effective on December 1, 1961. . . .

B.   GLICKMAN'S WITHDRAWALS AND PLEDGES

. . . On October 14, 1960—two days after the effective date of registrant's 1960 filing—Glickman began secretly to transfer funds from the registrant to Venada, his wholly owned corporation. Within 2 months the aggregate amount of these transfers amounted to $296,329. By October 2, 1961, the effective date of registrant's first 1961 filing, Glickman had made 45 withdrawals which amounted in the aggregate to $2,372,511. Neither the 1961 prospectuses nor any of the effective amendments to the 1960 filing referred to these transactions.

All of registrant's prospectuses stated that Glickman owned most of its B as well as a substantial block of its A stock. On the effective date of the 1960 filing Glickman's shares were unencumbered. In the following month, however, he began to pledge his shares to finance his personal real estate ventures. By August 31, 1961, all of Glickman's B and much of his A stock had been pledged to banks, finance companies, and private individuals. On the effective dates of the two 1961 filings the loans secured by these pledges aggregated about $4,250,000. The effective interest rates on these loans ran as high as 24 percent annually. Glickman retained the right to vote the pledged shares in the absence of a default on the loans. The two 1961 filings made no mention of Glickman's pledges or the loans they secured.

C.   ACTION OF THE BOARD OF DIRECTORS

In May 1962, the accountants who had audited the financial statements in registrant's 1960 and 1961 filings informed its directors that Glickman had from time to time diverted funds from the registrant's treasury to Venada. The directors then met with Glickman, who assured them that the withdrawals had been without wrongful intent and would not recur. Glickman agreed to repay all of the then known unauthorized withdrawals with interest at the rate of 6 percent. Registrant's directors soon discovered that Glickman had made other withdrawals, and they retained former United States District Court Judge Simon H. Rifkind to determine Glickman's liability to registrant. . . .

In a report submitted on August 20, 1962, Judge Rifkind found that Glickman had on many occasions withdrawn substantial sums from registrant; . . . that registrant's inadequate administrative procedures had to some extent facilitated Glickman's wrongdoing; and that all of the withdrawals had been made good with 6 percent interest. Judge Rifkind also found that 6 percent was an inadequate interest rate because Glickman and Venada had been borrowing at appreciably higher interest rates from commercial finance companies and others. . . .[10]

On November 30, 1962, registrant's directors learned that Glickman had continued to make unauthorized withdrawals after he had promised to desist from so doing and after the issuance of the Rifkind report, that Glickman and his wife had pledged all of their shares of the registrant's stock, and that Glickman and Venada were in financial straits. Glickman . . . thereupon resigned from all of [his] posts with the registrant, and Glickman sold all his B stock and some of his Class A stock to a small group of investors. Monthly cash distributions to A stockholders, which registrant had made every month since its inception, were discontinued in January 1963, and registrant changed its name from Glickman Corporation to Franchard Corporation.

II.   ALLEGED DEFICIENCIES—ACTIVITIES OF MANAGEMENT

A.   GLICKMAN'S WITHDRAWALS OF REGISTRANT'S FUNDS AND PLEDGES OF HIS SHARES

Of cardinal importance in any business is the quality of its management. Disclosures relevant to an evaluation of management are particularly pertinent where, as in this case, securities are sold largely on the personal reputation of a company's controlling person. The disclosures in these respects were materially deficient. The 1960 prospectus failed to reveal that Glickman

---

10.   In February 1963, Glickman and Venada filed petitions in the United States District Court for the Southern District of New York alleging that they were unable to meet their debts as they matured and seeking arrangements with their creditors pursuant to Chapter XI of the Bankruptcy Act. . . .

intended to use substantial amounts of registrant's funds for the benefit of Venada, and the 1961 prospectuses made no reference to Glickman's continual diversion of substantial sums from the registrant. Glickman's pledges were not discussed in either the effective amendments to the 1960 filings or in the two 1961 filings.

. . . How do you tell a "good" business manager from a "bad" one in a piece of paper? Managerial talent consists of personal attributes, essentially subjective in nature, that frequently defy meaningful analysis through the impersonal medium of a prospectus. Direct statements of opinion as to management's ability, which are not susceptible to objective verification, may well create an unwarranted appearance of reliability if placed in a prospectus. The integrity of management—its willingness to place its duty to public shareholders over personal interest—is an equally elusive factor for the application of disclosure standards. . . .[18]

Glickman's withdrawals were material transactions between registrant and its management, and the registration forms on which registrant's filings were made called for their disclosure. Registrant's argument that the withdrawals were not material because Glickman's undisclosed indebtedness to registrant never exceeded 1.5 percent of the gross book value of registrant's assets not only minimizes the substantial amounts of the withdrawals in relation to the stockholders' equity and the company's cash flow, but ignores the significance to prospective investors of information concerning Glickman's managerial ability and personal integrity. Registrant as such had no operating history. It concedes that the initial public offering in 1960 was made primarily, if not solely, on Glickman's name and reputation as a successful real estate investor and operator, and it is equally clear that the 1961 offerings were also predicated on his reputation. All of the prospectuses spoke of Glickman's many years of experience "in the creation and development of real estate investment opportunities" as "an investor in real property for his own account." The prospectuses also made it clear that Glickman would dominate and control registrant's operations, and prospective investors in registrant's securities were, in effect, being offered an opportunity to "buy" Glickman management of real estate investments.

A description of Glickman's activities was important on several grounds. First, publication of the facts pertaining to Glickman's withdrawals of substantial funds and of his pledges of his control stock would have clearly indicated his strained financial position and his urgent need for cash in his personal real estate ventures. In the context here, these facts were as material to an evaluation of Glickman's business ability as financial statements of an established company would be to an evaluation of its management's past performance.

Second, disclosure of Glickman's continual diversion of registrant's funds to the use of Venada, his wholly owned corporation, was also germane to an evaluation of the integrity of his management. This quality is always a material factor. . . . Even aside from the issues relating to Glickman's character, publication

---

18. In *The Richmond Corporation*, 41 S.E.C. 398, 401-2 (1968), we found a registration statement materially deficient in failing to disclose that certain officers and directors intended to engage in personal business ventures that would compete with registrant's business operations.

of the fact that he was diverting funds to Venada to bolster that company's weak financial condition was important in evaluating registrant's own operations.

Third, Glickman's need for cash as indicated by withdrawals from registrant and his substantial borrowings and pledges of registrant's shares gave him a powerful and direct motive to cause registrant to pursue policies which would permit high distribution rates and maintain a high price for registrant's A shares. . . . Investors were entitled to be apprised of these facts and such potential conflicts of interest.

Finally, the possibility of a change of control was also important to prospective investors. As we have noted, registrant's public offerings were largely predicated on Glickman's reputation as a successful real estate investor and operator. Disclosure of Glickman's secured loans, the relatively high interest rates that they bore, the secondary sources from which many of the loans were obtained, and the conditions under which lenders could declare defaults would have alerted investors to the possibility of a change in the control and management of registrant and apprised them of the possible nature of any such change.

With respect to disclosure of pledged shares, registrant is not aided by pointing out that our registration forms under the Securities Act and the reports required under the Securities Exchange Act do not call for disclosure of encumbrances on a controlling stockholder's shares, and that proposals to require such disclosures in reports filed with us under the Securities Exchange Act have not been adopted. The fact that such disclosures are not required of all issuers and their controlling persons in all cases does not negate their materiality in specific cases. The registration forms promulgated by us are guides intended to assist registrants in discharging their statutory duty of full disclosure. They are not and cannot possibly be exhaustive enumerations of each and every item material to investors in the particular circumstances relevant to a specific offering. The kaleidoscopic variety of economic life precludes any attempt at such an enumeration. The preparation of a registration statement is not satisfied, as registrant's position suggests, by a mechanical process of responding narrowly to the specific items of the applicable registration form. On the contrary, Rule 408 under the Securities Act makes clear to prospective registrants that: "In addition to the information expressly required to be included in a registration statement, there shall be added such further material information, if any, as may be necessary to make the required statements in the light of the circumstances under which they were made, not misleading."

B. ACTIVITIES OF REGISTRANT'S DIRECTORS

Another issue raised in these proceedings concerns the disclosure to be required in a prospectus regarding the adequacy of performance of managerial functions by registrant's board of directors. The Division urges that the prospectuses, by identifying the members of the board of directors, impliedly represented that they would provide oversight and direction to registrant's officers. . . .

It was obvious . . . that Glickman would exercise the dominant role in managing registrant's operations and the prospectuses contained no affirmative representations concerning the participation of the directors in registrant's affairs. Moreover, the board met regularly and received information as to registrant's affairs from Glickman and in connection with the preparation of registrant's registration statements, post-effective amendments, and periodic reports filed with us. It is clear we are not presented with a picture of total abdication of directorial responsibilities. Thus, the question posed by the Division must be whether the prospectuses were deficient in not disclosing that the directors, in overseeing the operations of the company, failed to exercise the degree of diligence which the Division believes was required of them under the circumstances in the context of the day-to-day operations of the company. We find no deficiencies in this area.

This is an issue raising fundamental considerations as to the functions of the disclosure requirements of the Securities Act. The civil liability provisions of Section 11 do establish for directors a standard of due diligence in the preparation of a registration statement—a Federal rule of directors' responsibility with respect to the completeness and accuracy of the document used in the public distribution of securities. The Act does not purport, however, to define Federal standards of directors' responsibility in the ordinary operations of business enterprises and nowhere empowers us to formulate administratively such regulatory standards. The diligence required of registrant's directors in overseeing its affairs is to be evaluated in the light of the standards established by State statutory and common law.

In our view, the application of these standards on a routine basis in the processing of registration statements would be basically incompatible with the philosophy and administration of the disclosure requirements of the Securities Act. Outright fraud or reckless indifference by directors might be readily identifiable and universally condemned. But activity short of that, which may give rise to legal restraints and liabilities, invokes significant uncertainty. . . . To generally require information in Securities Act prospectuses as to whether directors have performed their duties in accordance with the standards of responsibility required of them under State law would stretch disclosure beyond the limitations contemplated by the statutory scheme and necessitated by considerations of administrative practicality. . . . [T]he disclosures sought here by the staff would require evaluation of the entire conduct of a board of directors in the context of the whole business operations of a company in the light of diverse and uncertain standards. In our view, this is a function which the disclosure requirements of the Securities Act cannot effectively discharge. It would either result in self-serving generalities of little value to investors or grave uncertainties both on the part of those who must enforce and those who must comply with that Act.

V.   CONCLUSIONS

The deficiencies we have found in registrant's effective filings are serious. . . . Omissions of so material a character would normally require the issuance of a stop order.

Here, however, several factors taken together . . . [—the company's cooperation, the removal of Glickman, and new management's substantial investment in the firm—] lead us to conclude that the distribution of copies of this opinion to all of registrant's past and present stockholders, as registrant has proposed, will give adequate public notice of the deficiencies in registrant's effective filings, and that neither the public interest nor the protection of investors requires the issuance of a stop order. . . .

NOTES AND QUESTIONS

1.   Line-Item Disclosure Requirements and Management Integrity.   Subpart 400 of Regulation S-K requires disclosure of information that bears on the incentives, integrity, and commitment of the registrant's management. In addition to extensive background information for each director, executive officer, and others expected to make a significant contribution to the firm,[4] Item 401(f) calls for disclosure of certain types of adjudications within the past ten years that are material to an evaluation of the ability or integrity of any director, person nominated to become a director, or executive officer. A broad range of adjudications are singled out including insolvency proceedings, criminal proceedings (including a pending criminal proceeding), adjudications by a court, the SEC, or the CFTC that federal or state securities laws or the commodity laws were violated, or the person was subject to a judicial or administrative order (not subsequently reversed or vacated) relating to an alleged violation of securities, commodities or other identified financial regulatory provisions.

In a provision addressing concerns similar to those raised by the staff in *In re Franchard Corp.*, Item 403(c) of Regulation S-K requires disclosure of "any arrangements, known to the registrant, including any pledge . . . the operation of which may at a subsequent date result in a change in control of the registrant."

Certain conflict-of-interest transactions ("related party transactions") are required to be disclosed under Item 404. Disclosure is required if the transaction exceeds $120,000 and is between the registrant (or any of its subsidiaries) and its director, its executive officer, a director nominee, an owner of more than 5 percent of any class of the registrant's stock, or an immediate family member of any of the above. *See Beaver Cnty. Emp. Ret. Fund v. The Shop Holdings, Inc.*, 94 F. Supp. 3d 1035 (D. Minn. 2015) (Item 404 violated by failing to disclose CEO's brother was intermediary in most of the firm's transactions). Registrants must also describe their policies, procedures, and standards to be applied when there is a related-party transaction.

Special disclosures are also required of any transactions between the registrant and its promoters that have occurred or will occur (and if the promoter acquired any assets two years prior to their transfer to the registrant, the promoter's cost to acquire the assets must be disclosed). Details of any loans by the

---

4.   *See* Regulation S-K, Item 401(e). The breadth of Item 401(e) may come at the expense of specificity, as is reflected in *SEC v. Carriba Air, Inc.*, 681 F.2d 1318 (11th Cir. 1981), where the registration statement was held to be materially defective for failing to disclose that an airline's promoters and executive officers had over the past ten years been deeply involved in several unsuccessful commuter airline ventures. Indeed, the current venture involved the same routes as were flown by a now-bankrupt company in which most of the current promoters were involved.

registrant must be disclosed when made to its executive officers, directors and director nominees, as well as to members of their immediate families or firms in which such persons have specified interests. Information is also required on transactions between the registrant and another business entity to which its director or director nominee is related.[5] This requirement applies specifically to dealings between the registrant and a law firm or investment banking firm of which a director or director nominee of the registrant is a member.[6] Companies that qualify as "smaller reporting companies," as defined in Item 10(f) of Regulation S-K (roughly having a market float less than $75 million) are relieved of many of Item 404's disclosures.

   2. Pending Litigation.   Item 103 of Regulation S-K calls for disclosure of litigation that involves the issuer; the disclosures the issuer must make regarding its litigation are broader than disclosures it must make regarding litigation involving its officers, directors, promoters, and controlling stockholder. As seen in Note 1, the disclosure for officers, directors, promoters, and control persons is triggered by civil and administrative actions of the type therein specified, and disclosure arises only if the matter has been *adjudicated.* With the exception of a pending criminal proceeding, Item 401(f) does not expressly require *pending* claims involving officers, directors, promoters, or controlling stockholders to be disclosed. In contrast, Item 103 requires a brief description of "any material *pending* legal proceedings, other than ordinary routine litigation incidental to the business. . . ."

   Whether pending litigation against executive officers, directors, nominees to the board, promoters, and the like must be disclosed is not guided by the specific disclosure instructions of Regulation S-K, but is determined by whether the pending suit bears on management's stewardship of the firm or its overall integrity. For example, in *United States v. Peterson,* 101 F.3d 375 (5th Cir. 1996), the general partner negotiated the sale of a limited partner's interest without disclosing to the buyer that another limited partner was suing the general partner for various acts of mismanagement and self-dealing. The Fifth Circuit held that the failure to disclose the pending suit was a material omission. *See also United States v. Yeaman,* 194 F.3d 442 (3d Cir. 1999) (officer and director under a duty to disclose an SEC investigation of a separate company with which he was affiliated); *Zell v. Intercapital Income Securities, Inc.,* 675 F.2d 1041 (9th Cir. 1982) (investment company's proxy statement seeking shareholder approval of the management contract with its adviser was materially misleading in failing to disclose the actions pending against that adviser under state and federal securities laws). What are a reporting company's disclosure obligations when its president stands accused of murdering his wife? *See* Bigness, Crime Charges of Executives Test Companies, Wall St. J., Apr. 1, 1996, at B-1; *SEC v. Electronics Warehouse, Inc.,* 689 F. Supp. 53 (D. Conn. 1988), *aff'd,* 891 F.2d 459 (2d Cir. 1989) (important to disclose pending criminal action against company's president even though there is a genuine belief the indictment will be dismissed).

---

   5. Id., Item 404(b)(1), (2).
   6. Id., Item 404(b)(3), (4).

Consider the Second Circuit's treatment of pending allegations of fraud and breach of trust by a director nominee's own sister in *GAF Corp. v. Heyman*, 724 F.2d 727 (2d Cir. 1983). As a consequence of a bitter proxy contest, GAF stockholders voted decisively to replace incumbent directors with the insurgent slate headed by Samuel Heyman. The deposed incumbents complained that Heyman's proxy statement failed to disclose that Heyman was the target of a suit by his sister in Connecticut state court arising from his alleged breach of fiduciary duty in managing the family trust. The Second Circuit recognized that Regulation S-K contains the SEC's "expert view of the types of legal proceedings that are most likely to be matters of concern to shareholders in a proxy contest." Id. at 739.

> In our view, the regulation's [Item 401(f)] emphasis on orders, judgments, decrees and findings in civil proceedings, in stark contrast to its express coverage of all pending criminal proceedings, strongly suggests that regardless of how serious they may appear on their face, unadjudicated allegations in a pending civil action against a director-nominee should not automatically be deemed material. In a society as litigious as ours, where plaintiffs are permitted great latitude in their pleadings, a reasonable shareholder would not place much stock in the bald, untested allegations in a civil complaint not involving the subject corporation without first examining, among other relevant factors, the relationship between the parties, the nature of the allegations, the circumstances out of which they arose, and the extent to which the action has been pursued.

Id. at 739-740. Applying this test, the Second Circuit determined that the nondisclosure of the Connecticut action was not a material omission. Also, the *GAF* court evidently found the seriousness of the Connecticut allegations to be offset by the fact that the plaintiff in that suit supported Heyman in his effort to win a seat on GAF's board.

Just how much must be disclosed about such pending suits? The courts generally hold the disclosure is adequate if the "basic facts" surrounding the suit are disclosed. Moreover, there is no need for the registrant to characterize its conduct as illegal, criminal, fraudulent, improper, and so forth. The courts and the SEC rationalize the disclosure of basic facts and not characterizations or conclusions as providing all the information for investors to apply their expertise to make informed judgments of the litigation's outcome and impact on the firm. It is not necessary to predict the outcome of the suit. Furthermore, it is generally not inappropriate for the disclosure to offer such general assertions as the "suit is without merit," "the issuer is confident in its defense," or the action "will not materially affect operations." On the other hand, caution is advised, for statements that *unduly* minimize the likelihood of the suit's success or magnitude can themselves be materially misleading. *Kreidler v. Sambo's Restaurants, Inc.*, [1981-1982 Transfer Binder] Fed. Sec. L. Rep. (CCH) ¶98,312 (S.D.N.Y. 1981).

Finally, Item 401(f) makes no reference to enforcement actions that have been *settled*. For the view that such actions need not be disclosed in a proxy statement seeking the reelection of directors on whose watch the violations giving rise to the settlement occurred, *see In re Browning-Ferris Industries Shareholder Litigation*, 830 F. Supp. 361 (D. Tex. 1993). Does the failure of the SEC's guidelines to address settlements encourage corner cutting? Consider the case of a public company that announced the arrival of a new CEO, touting his 32 years at a major accounting firm, but failed to disclose that a month earlier the new hire had, in response to charges by state board of accounting that alleged he had engaged in "unprofessional conduct" in supervising the audit of a failed bank, entered into a settlement barring his work on audits of public companies for seven years. *See* Zuckerman, Action Performance Kept Mum on Executive's Background, Wall St. J., Apr. 21, 2004, at C-1.

3. Disclosure of Executive Compensation.   Item 402 of Regulation S-K calls for extensive disclosures bearing on overall executive compensation. With the increasing national attention executive compensation has attracted, the disclosure requirements of Item 402 have expanded.

In broad overview, the rules for disclosing executive compensation involve five primary components:

1. a "Compensation Discussion and Analysis" (CD&A) section to SEC filings as well as a Compensation Committee Report;
2. detailed disclosure of compensation for "named executive officers" (NEOs) for the last fiscal year and the two preceding fiscal years;
3. extensive disclosure of grants, holdings, and realization of equity-related interests (e.g., stock options, stock appreciation rights) to NEOs;
4. retirement plans, deferred compensation, and other post-employment payments and benefits for NEOs; and
5. director compensation.

The CD&A is a central component of the new disclosure requirements. The rules for this component of SEC filings is principles-based, meaning that Item 402 broadly calls for registrants to set forth in a comprehensive way the material factors underlying the company's executive compensation policies and practices (instead of setting forth narrow categories of information that is to be provided). Areas of policy to be addressed include the following: what are the objectives of the company's compensation program, what is sought to be rewarded by the compensation, what are the elements of the executive's compensation, how did the company determine the amount for each such element, and how does each element fit with the company's overall compensation objectives. The CD&A is also part of the CEO's and CFO's certification requirements. The expanded disclosure requirements call for discussion of whether the company's compensation policies and practices are reasonably likely to have a material adverse impact on the company (for example, by encouraging excessive risk taking by subordinates).

The Compensation Committee Report must address two items: first, whether the committee has reviewed and discussed the CD&A and, second, based on any review and discussion, whether the committee has recommended to the board that the CD&A be included in the company's SEC filing. What disclosure objective appears to be served by the Compensation Committee Report?

NEOs include the firm's principal executive officer (e.g., CEO) and principal financial officer (e.g., CFO) plus the other three most highly compensated officers (provided the person's compensation exceeds $100,000).

Executive compensation for NEOs is to be disclosed in a tabular format with the following set forth in separate columns: salary; bonus; dollar value of stock awards; dollar value of option awards; non-equity incentive plan compensation earned during the year; annual change in actuarial value of accumulated pension benefits; aggregate amount of all other compensation, including perquisites; and total compensation.

4.   *Median Pay Disclosures.* In response to a Dodd-Frank mandate, the SEC promulgated Item 402(u) to Regulation S-K requiring disclosure of median annual total compensation of all employees (excluding the CEO), the annual total compensation of the CEO, and the ratio of these two amounts. SEC, Pay Ratio Disclosure, Securities Act Release No. 9877 (Aug. 5, 2015). Emerging growth companies, smaller reporting companies, registered investment companies, and foreign private companies are exempt from the requirement.

The manner for determining the many factors that define who is an employee and how to calculate "median employee's" compensation are quite technical. Essentially, employees included in the calculation are all employees of the reporting company (as well as its subsidiaries that, under accounting rules, are consolidated with the parent for financial reporting). The calculation includes both full-time and part-time employees, seasonal and non-seasonal workers, and those inside and outside the United States (there is a *de minimis* exemption for foreign employees who collectively account for 5 percent or less of all employees).

The regulations allow the "median employee" to be determined every three years, unless there has been a significant change in the company's employee population. While companies have flexibility in the way they determine the median employee, such as using statistical sampling, companies must disclose the methodology used to identify their median employee. Once the median employee is identified, the registrant must then calculate the median employee's compensation and briefly disclose the methodology by which total compensation was estimated. *See* Bank & Georgiev, Securities Disclosure as Soundbite: The Case of CEO Pay Ratios, 60 B.C. L.J. 1123 (2019) (even though providing political salience to public discourse on income and wealth inequality, the disclosures, due to problems of accuracy and interpretation, have low informational value).

5.   *Failing the Duty of Good Faith.* In *Maldonado v. Flynn*, 597 F.2d 789 (2d Cir. 1979), a proxy statement was materially misleading in failing to disclose that directors seeking reelection had approved interest-free loans to six optionees to enable them to exercise their stock options and had accelerated the exercise date of their options to allow the optionees to exercise their rights prior to a foreseen rise in the market price due to the issuer's secret plans to make an above-market issuer tender offer. The Second Circuit concluded that the reasonable shareholder would have considered this information important in deciding how to vote for the directors.

> Since self-dealing presents opportunities for abuse of a corporate position of trust, the circumstances surrounding corporate transactions in which directors have a personal interest are directly relevant to a determination of whether they are qualified to exercise stewardship of the company.

Id. at 796. What if the directors are not themselves engaged in self-dealing? Today, most forms of loans to officers and directors of reporting companies are prohibited by Exchange Act Section 13(k).

In *Berkman v. Rust Craft Greeting Cards, Inc.*, 454 F. Supp. 787 (S.D.N.Y. 1978), the company was the subject of a friendly takeover, and its directors obtained an appraisal opinion from an investment banking firm. Some members of the board of directors were aware that the investment banking firm was not independent because it owned 5 percent of the company's stock. Nevertheless, they did not disclose this to their colleagues. At a later board meeting at which the reelection slate was being considered, some directors moved that those directors who knew of the investment banker's conflict of interest should not be renominated. *Berkman* held it was a material omission for the proxy statement to fail to disclose the defendant directors' nondisclosure to their colleagues of the investment banking firm's conflict of interest.

6.   *The Purpose or Effect of an Event.*   Frequently, proxy statements are challenged because they fail to affirmatively state the purpose or effect of a transaction. For example, in *Lewis v. Chrysler Corp.*, 949 F.2d 644 (3d Cir. 1991), management was not required to disclose a possible entrenchment motive for amending the terms of the company's poison pill when the changes to be made were themselves fully disclosed. *See also Ieradi v. Mylan Laboratories, Inc.*, 230 F.3d 594 (3d Cir. 2000) (10-Q that discloses that FTC is investigating firm for anticompetitive activities is not misleading by omitting that firm acquired suppliers for the purpose of dominating its product market); *Kowal v. MCI Communications Corp.*, 16 F.3d 1271, 1274 (D.C. Cir. 1994) ("pejorative adjective [that business was deteriorating] will not alter the total mix of information"); *Biesenbach v. Guenther*, 588 F.2d 400 (3d Cir. 1978) (details of loans to officers were fully disclosed and there is no further need to disclose that their effect is to benefit officers). The reasoning in such cases is that it is not a material omission if the omitted information can logically be inferred from the information that is disclosed. *See Heliotrope General Inc. v. Ford Motor Co.*, 189 F.3d 971 (9th Cir. 1999) (market is aware of tax benefits of operating through controlled subsidiaries so no need to disclose that subsidiary was created for tax purposes).

PROBLEM

12-9.   An interesting report in the press raises an intriguing disclosure question. Stephen L. Lane, chief executive of Emerson Radio Corporation, a large publicly traded corporation, sued his wife for mismanaging his account while she was a broker with Drexel Burnham Lambert. Mr. Lane complained that unsuitable stocks and options were purchased for his account at the suggestion of his broker-wife over a three-year period during which Mr. Lane alleged he was unable to monitor his personal finances due to his having undergone surgery twice for brain tumors and once for a spinal tumor. During that same period, no public disclosure of Mr. Lane's medical problems was made by Emerson or anyone else. Mr. Lane did manage to participate in several meetings with investment analysts in that three-year period. N.Y. Times, Sept. 13, 1990, at A1.

Assuming that Mr. Lane was indeed unable to monitor his own affairs and assuming further that during the period of Mr. Lane's illness Emerson sold securities pursuant to a registration statement that did not disclose Mr. Lane's problems, did the registration statement omit a material fact? *See* Horwich, The Securities Regulation Disclosure Rules of the Road Regarding Executive Illness, 46 Sec. Reg. L.J. 1 (2018).

2.   Materiality Links to Corporate Governance

Many provisions of Regulation S-K focus on a variety of contemporary features of what is believed to be good corporate governance. For example, Item 407 contains various disclosure requirements related to director independence and corporate governance. Item 407 requires companies to disclose whether (and why) each director and director nominee is independent and whether any audit, nominating, or compensation committee member is not independent pursuant to any applicable listing standard (or a chosen standard if listing does not apply). Companies that have adopted definitions of independence for directors must either set forth the definitions or disclose if they appear on its web site. Specific disclosure is required of the compensation committee's governance structure, such as its processes and procedures for reaching compensation decisions, including the involvement of executive officers and compensation consultants in setting compensation. Disclosures of whether and why a member of the audit committee can be considered a financial expert are also covered by Item 407. Consider the relevance of Item 407(b)'s requirement of disclosure of any director who has attended fewer than 75 percent of committee meetings.

Item 406 of Regulation S-K requires each reporting company (domestic and foreign) to disclose whether it has a code of ethics (a/k/a code of conduct) that covers the principal executive officer, financial officer, and accountant, as well as its controller. If it has no such code, it must explain why it has not adopted one. Item 406 defines a code of ethics as written standards "reasonably designed to deter wrongdoing and to promote: (1) [h]onest and ethical conduct, including ethical handling of actual or apparent conflicts of interest; . . . (2) [f]ull, fair, accurate, timely, and understandable disclosure in reports and documents . . . [filed with SEC as well as for other public disclosures]; (3) [c]ompliance with applicable governmental laws . . . ; (4) [t]he prompt internal reporting of violations of the code to an appropriate person or persons identified in the code; and (5) [a]ccountability for adherence to the code." The SEC rules require that the code be filed annually as an exhibit to the issuer's annual report. *See In re Ramp Corp. Sec. Litig.*, [2006 Transfer Binder] Fed. Sec. L. Rep. (CCH) ¶93,914 (S.D.N.Y. 2006) (CEO violates annual certification of truthfulness of reports by failing to disclose his receipt of gifts from vendors without disclosing them to the board as required by code of ethics that was appended to Form 10-K). The listing requirements of both the NYSE and Nasdaq require companies to have a code of ethics.

Any waiver of a provision of an existing code of ethics must be reported per Item 505(b) of Form 8-K. *See* Mori, A Proposal to Revise the SEC Instructions for Reporting Waivers of Corporate Codes of Ethics for Conflicts of Interest, 24 Yale J. Reg. 293 (2007) (observing that many companies avoid waivers to their code by artfully drafting their code to provide that pre-approval of a conflict of interest results in the transaction falling outside the definition of a conflict of interest).

The failure of a company to follow the procedures set forth in its code of conduct can be penalized under Exchange Act Section 13(b)(2), discussed earlier in Chapter 11. For example, United Airlines was sanctioned for failing to follow its code's procedures when its chairman caused the airline to maintain an unprofitable route between Newark, where he worked, and his vacation home in South Carolina. The code prescribed steps to be taken whenever a conflict of interest transaction occurred, and the company failed to follow its own procedures in accommodating its chairman's wish for quick access to the beach. *In the Matter of United Continental Holdings, Inc.*, Exchange Act Release No. 79454 (Dec. 2016).

A related question posed by codes of conduct is whether a violation can give rise to a misrepresentation of compliance. In 2006, a major scandal arose at Hewlett-Packard Company (HP) that ultimately led to criminal charges against its board chair and general counsel. Mark Hurd, although CEO during the time, not only was not implicated in these events but won national attention for the high level of integrity he demonstrated in guiding HP through the crisis. He gained further national stature by championing the promotion of ethical behavior within the company and causing the firm to adopt a sweeping standards of business conduct code (SBC). The investor community was therefore shocked in 2010 to learn not only that Hurd was the object of a sexual harassment claim by Jodie Fisher, but that he had falsified expense reimbursement forms to cover up his ongoing meetings with Fisher, and that he was deceitful during HP's internal inquiry into the matter. Hurd was sacked and the investor community punished HP, as its stock lost about $10 billion in market value.

The ensuing securities fraud suit alleged HP had committed both material misstatements and omissions through its repeated references to the SBC and representations in the SBC, such as its statement "we maintain accurate business records" and "create business records that accurately reflect the truth of the underlying transaction or event." The SBC also set forth various protocols such as how to report misconduct, and embraced qualities such as treating others with respect and not tolerating harassment. The suit emphasized that the SBC was couched in affirmative statements made in the present tense. The Ninth Circuit held the SBC was aspirational, stating no more than that business ethics were important to HP. *Retail, Wholesale and Department Store Local 338 Retirement Fund v. Hewlett Packard Co.*, 845 F.3d 1268 (9th Cir. 2017). It concluded that HP did not make a statement that was objectively verifiable, and therefore did not commit fraud. The panel reasoned that to reach a different conclusion "could turn all corporate wrongdoing into securities fraud." Moreover, the court reasoned that since Item 406(a) of Regulation S-K requires firms with codes of conduct to disclose their codes, the act of disclosing the SBC, coupled with its aspirational quality, did not alter the total mix of information. Hence, it held the SBC was not material. Even though the plaintiff emphasized how Hurd's conduct was inconsistent in many ways with the SBC, the court concluded that the SBC could not fairly be understood to mean that there would be no violations of the SBC by its officers. *See also Singh v. CIGNA Corp.*, 918 F.3d 57 (2d Cir. 2019) (statements about the firm's "policies and procedures" and "significant compliance resources" were too tentative and generic to be relied upon by investors regarding regulatory compliance and, hence, are inactionable puffery). *But see Retail Wholesale & Department Store Union Local 338 Ret. Fund v. SAIC*, 818 F.3d 85, 98 (2d Cir. 2016) ("Some statements, in context, may amount to more than 'puffery' and may in some circumstances violate the securities laws: for example, a company's specific statements that emphasize its reputation for integrity or ethical conduct as central to its financial condition or that are clearly designed to distinguish the company from other specified companies in the same industry."). How should we consider such "don't worry" reassurances that are accompanied by evidence of ongoing misconduct? Is this an area where scienter should play a pivotal role? *See generally* Langevoort, Disasters and Disclosures: Securities Fraud Liability in the Face of Corporate Catastrophe, 107 Geo. L.J. 967 (2019).

NOTES AND QUESTIONS

1. Polemics of the Boardroom. Just what must be disclosed about divisions of opinion regarding a matter to be submitted to the stockholders for approval or when a course for future action is set forth in materials seeking to raise funds to carry out a business plan? Must the corporation disclose that the CEO opposes the business plan set forth in the company registration statement, *see Cooperman v. Individual Inc.*, 171 F.3d 43 (1st Cir. 1999), or a merger being submitted for shareholder approval? *See Lane v. Page*, [2008 Transfer Binder] Fed. Sec. L. Rep. (CCH) ¶94,852 (D.N.M. 2008). Must it disclose that its largest shareholder is opposed to the reorganization that is being submitted to the stockholders for approval? *See Fry v. UAL Corp.*, 84 F.3d 936 (7th Cir. 1996).

2. Who's Independent? A cornerstone of corporate governance is the role that outside directors play in reviewing transactions that pose a conflict of interest, such as a contract between the corporation and its officer. Sometimes bond covenants call for certain transactions to be approved by a majority of the board of independent directors. For example, in *McMahan & Co. v. Wherehouse Entertainment, Inc.*, 900 F.2d 576 (2d Cir. 1990), the corporation issued bonds whose covenants provided that if the company was acquired in a debt-financed acquisition the bonds must be redeemed at their face amount, unless the acquisition was approved by the "independent" directors. A few months after the bonds were issued, the board of directors approved the sale of the company to the company's officers, who planned to borrow substantial sums to carry out the transaction. Do you agree with the court that the outside directors' consistent support for several years of positions advocated by management was a material omission for failure to disclose when the bonds were issued? *Compare Wherehouse with Migdal v. Rowe Price Fleming Int'l Inc.*, 248 F.3d 321 (4th Cir. 2001), which reasoned there was no material omission in a matter turning on the provision of the Investment Company Act requiring that not less than 40 percent of the directors of mutual funds be independent. T. Rowe Price's annual proxy seeking election of directors to its many funds was unsuccessfully challenged on the ground that it failed to identify that directors labeled independent served on as many as 38 multiple T. Rowe Price boards and received directors' fees totaling $81,000 from such compound service.

3.   Risk Management.   Post financial crisis, an important focus is how the company addresses the management of risk. Companies face a variety of risks, including credit, liquidity, and operational risks. In adopting Item 305 of Regulation S-K, the SEC identified risk oversight as a key competence of the board and that disclosure of the board's engagement with the oversight of the risk management process will provide useful information to investors regarding how the company perceives the role of the board and the relationship between the board and senior management in managing the material risks the company faces. Securities Act Release No. 9089 (Dec. 16, 2009).

Cybersecurity risks are very much a contemporary concern. Hence, in 2018 the Commission provided interpretative guidance calling for registrants when making filings with the SEC to set forth material cybersecurity risks; the agency also encouraged firms to adopt comprehensive policies and procedures related to cybersecurity and to assess their compliance and disclosure of the risks regularly. Securities Act Release No. 10459 (Feb. 21, 2018). *See also Iowa Public Employees Ret. Sys. v. MF Global, Ltd.*, 620 F.3d 137 (2d Cir. 2010) (statement regarding a firm's risk management system is a statement of present condition and not a forward-looking statement); *In the Matter of Altaba, Inc. (Yahoo)*, Securities Act Release No. 10485 (Apr. 24, 2018) (company sanctioned $35 million for failing to make timely disclosure of cybersecurity breach).

4.   Materiality of Managerial Philosophy.   Materiality has rarely been established when related to information that reflects management's antisocial or ethical attitudes. In a leading case, the district court held that a textile company's proxy statement seeking the election of directors was not materially misleading for failing to disclose that *all* its nominees knowingly and willfully acted in concert to thwart the labor laws. *Amalgamated Clothing & Textile Workers v. J.P. Stevens & Co.*, 475 F. Supp. 328 (S.D.N.Y. 1979), *vacated as moot per curiam*, 638 F.2d 7 (2d Cir. 1980). *See also Oklahoma Firefighters Pension & Ret. Sys. v. Capell Educ. Co.*, 2012 U.S. Dist. LEXIS 76011 (D. Minn. June 1, 2012) (when reporting that improved performance was because of strong demand for the firm's educational product, it was not a material omission to not disclose that the for-profit college was aggressively promoting product to students without regard to their welfare, their ability to complete post-secondary education, or their understanding of the costs they would incur). How do you distinguish *In re Gilead Sciences Sec. Litig.*, 536 F.3d 1049 (9th Cir. 2008), holding that defendant engaged in material misrepresentation when it touted that strong consumer demand for its product contributed to profits and did not disclose that the demand was fueled by the firm's unlawful marketing practices?

PROBLEMS

12-10.   Actonomics, Inc. is listed on the NYSE and has a code of conduct that among other features requires that "any transaction must be approved by the company's Audit Committee if the transaction involves an amount in excess of $10,000 between the company and a senior officer, or between the company and an entity in which its senior officer has a financial interest, is a director, or is an officer." Willis is Actonomics' CEO, a devoted alumnus of prestigious Ivy University, and a member of that institution's board of trustees. To make it more likely that he will be selected to be the next chair of Ivy's board of trustees, he persuades Actonomics' board of directors to approve a $5 million donation to establish the Willis Student Center at Ivy University. Are there reasonable arguments for concluding this transaction is not material?

12-11.   Badger, Inc. circulated a proxy statement among its shareholders seeking their approval of Badger's acquisition by ComTech Company. The proxy statement disclosed that the board of directors approved the merger at its most recent meeting and that the board recommends shareholder approval because it believes the acquisition by ComTech is in the best interests of the shareholders. The proxy statement did not reveal the following: that ComTech had balked at retaining Badger's CEO, Bridgette, in a senior management position following the acquisition; that part of the attraction of the stock-for-stock acquisition by ComTech was that Badger's board believed ComTech's management team was superior to Badger's; that Bridgette as a director voted against the acquisition; and that recently Bridgette had, without the support of the board of directors, engaged Dynaco in exploratory merger discussions about its possibly acquiring Badger. Is the proxy statement materially misleading?

3.   Materiality of Social Matters

The Dodd-Frank Act mandates that the SEC impose a range of disclosure requirements focused on the manner in which the firm conducts its business. For example, in response to Dodd-Frank the SEC has entered the following areas for reporting companies: disclosing whether certain minerals used in the business originated in the Democratic Republic of the Congo (or adjoining countries defined as DRC countries)—*see* Item 104 of Regulation S-K; requiring operators of coal and other mines to disclose in '34 Act reports specified information about mine and health safety—*see* former Item 106 of Regulation S-K requiring firms engaged in resource extraction to disclose any payments made to a foreign government for the purpose of commercial development of oil, gas, or minerals (invalidated in 2017 by action pursuant to the Congressional Review Act)—*see* Item 105 of Regulation S-K; and disclosing annually the ratio of CEO's total compensation to the median compensation of all firm employees—*see* Dodd-Frank Section 953(b). Are these disclosures linked to the historical goal of enabling investors to assess the economic risks and returns posed by a firm? To the extent they are not, what are the benefits and risks of such a regulatory pivot? *Compare* Williams, The Securities and Exchange Commission and Corporate Social Responsibility, 112 Harv. L. Rev. 1197, 1296 (1999) ("If it is true that managers 'manage what they measure,' then measuring social and environmental effects in a consistent, comparable way could act as an impetus for management to reduce those impacts that shareholders could interpret as negative.") *with* Langevoort, Commentary: Stakeholder Values, Disclosure, and Materiality, 48 Cath. U. L. Rev. 93 (1998) ("My sense is that one dominating reason for the success of the SEC is the focus that comes from a clearly defined mission—the protection of investors against overreaching by promoters, managers and the like. . . . The introduction of the protection of potentially conflicting non-investor interests as a regulatory objective is contrary to this focus, and would threaten a coherence that has long existed at the agency.")

What if the disclosures that are compelled cast the registrant as being of a particular ideological bent? The SEC's conflict mineral rules were so viewed because they required registrants who could not, after a penetrating inquiry, conclude that their products were free of minerals from the Democratic Republic of Congo to disclose that they could not state that their products were free of conflict minerals. The D.C. Circuit held this violated the registrants' First Amendment rights because the SEC failed to adequately identify an underlying governmental interest, so the rule could not be understood to alleviate the harm asserted to be remediated. *National Ass'n of Mfrs. v. SEC*, 800 F.3d 518 (D.C. Cir. 2015). In an earlier decision, the D.C. Circuit observed:

> [I]t is far from clear that the description at issue—whether a product is "conflict free"—is factual and non-ideological. Products and minerals do not fight conflicts. The label "conflict free" is a metaphor that conveys moral responsibility for the Congo war. It requires an issuer to tell consumers that its products are ethically tainted, even if they only indirectly finance armed groups. An issuer, including an issuer who condemns the atrocities of the Congo war in the strongest terms, may disagree with that assessment of its moral responsibility. By compelling an issuer to confess blood on its hands, the statute interferes with that exercise of the freedom of speech under the First Amendment.

National Ass'n of Mfrs. v. SEC, 748 F.3d 359 (D.C. Cir. 2014).

Despite the D.C. Circuit's holding, reporting companies continue to be subject to extensive disclosure requirements including disclosing their due diligence processes and procedures to determine whether their products contain conflict minerals.

4.   Disclosure Bearing on Sustainability

**❙❙ SEC Concept Release, Business and Financial Disclosure
Required by Regulation S-K, 205-210**
Securities Act Release No. 10064 (Apr. 22, 2016)

F.   DISCLOSURE OF INFORMATION RELATING TO PUBLIC POLICY AND SUSTAINABILITY MATTERS

In recent years, Congress has mandated new disclosure requirements that address specific public policy concerns. For example, . . . Dodd-Frank Act mandated that the Commission adopt rules regarding registrants' use of "conflict minerals" originating in specified countries, and . . . directed the Commission to adopt rules regarding the disclosure of payments made by resource extraction issuers to foreign governments or the federal government for the purpose of the commercial development of oil, natural gas, or minerals. In addition, . . . Dodd-Frank Act requires certain registrants to disclose information about health and safety violations at mining-related facilities. Some investors and interest groups also have expressed a desire for greater disclosure of a variety of public policy and sustainability matters, stating that these matters are of increasing significance to voting and investment decisions. For example, some have urged the Commission to adopt disclosure requirements on political spending. The Commission, however, has determined in the past that disclosure relating to environmental and other matters of social concern should not be required of all registrants unless appropriate to further a specific congressional mandate or unless, under the particular facts and circumstances, such matters are material. We are interested in receiving feedback on the importance of sustainability and public policy matters to informed investment and voting decisions. In particular, we seek feedback on which, if any, sustainability and public policy disclosures are important to an understanding of a registrant's business and financial condition and whether there are other considerations that make these disclosures important to investment and voting decisions. We also seek feedback on the potential challenges and costs associated with compiling and disclosing this information.

In 1975, the Commission considered a variety of "environmental and social" disclosure matters, as well as its own authority and responsibilities to require disclosure under the federal securities laws. Following extensive proceedings on these topics, the Commission concluded that it generally is not authorized to consider the promotion of goals unrelated to the objectives of the federal securities laws when promulgating disclosure requirements. . . . However, the Commission has recognized that the task of identifying what information is material to an investment and voting decision is a continuing one in the field of securities regulation. The role of sustainability and public policy information in investors' voting and investment decisions may be evolving as some investors are increasingly engaging on certain ESG matters.

According to one study, investors are more likely to engage registrants on sustainability issues than on financial results or transactions and corporate strategy. One observer expressed the view that ESG is not only a public policy issue but also a financial issue, noting a positive correlation between a "strong ESG record" and excellence in operations and management. Moreover, this observer specifically noted that regulatory risks posed by climate change are investment issues. Recent studies have also found that asset managers increasingly incorporate or have committed to incorporating ESG considerations into their financial analyses.

In seeking public input on sustainability and public policy disclosures, we recognize that some registrants historically have not considered this information material. Some observers continue to share this view and have expressed concern that sustainability or policy-driven disclosure requirements do not always result in disclosure that a reasonable investor would consider material. Some have expressed concerns that policy-driven disclosure requirements represent a shift away from the Commission's mission to protect investors, maintain fair, orderly, and efficient markets, and facilitate capital formation, and that such requirements could risk burdening both registrants and investors with costly disclosure that is not material to any investment or voting decision. Similarly, concerns have been expressed that adopting sustainability or policy-driven disclosure requirements may have the goal of altering corporate behavior, rather than producing information that is important to voting and investment decisions. Additionally, one observer has noted numerous attempts to use the Commission's regulatory apparatus to address societal issues. As the costs of compiling and disclosing information about sustainability and public policy issues are borne by the registrant, and ultimately its shareholders, as is all disclosure, we are seeking input on whether these disclosures are important to investors' voting and investment decisions.

Request for Comment:

Are there specific sustainability or public policy issues [that] are important to informed voting and investment decisions? If so, what are they? If we were to adopt specific disclosure requirements involving sustainability or public policy issues, how could our rules elicit meaningful disclosure on such issues? How could we create a disclosure framework that would be flexible enough to address such issues as they evolve over time? . . . Would line-item requirements for disclosure about sustainability or public policy issues cause registrants to disclose information that is not material to investors? Would these disclosures obscure information that is important to an understanding of a registrant's business and financial condition? . . . Some registrants already provide information about ESG matters in sustainability or corporate social responsibility reports or on their websites. . . . Why do some registrants choose to provide sustainability information outside of their Commission filings? Is the information provided on company websites sufficient to address investor needs? What are the advantages and disadvantages of registrants providing such disclosure on their websites? How important to investors is integrated reporting, as opposed to separate financial and sustainability reporting? If we permitted registrants to use information on their websites to satisfy any ESG disclosure requirement, how would this affect the comparability and consistency of the disclosure? . . .

NOTES AND QUESTIONS

1. The SEC and Global Warming.   Responding to rising concern among institutional investors regarding the impacts of climate change, the SEC provided interpretative guidance as to how registrants should apply existing disclosure rules with respect to the risks they face due to climate change. Among the areas the SEC identified that could trigger disclosure requirements are (1) the impact of climate change legislation and regulation on the firm's business; (2) the impact of international climate change accords on the firm; (3) the indirect consequences of business and regulation trends in response to climate change (e.g., consumer preference shift to more carbon-neutral products); and

(4) physical risks posed by changing weather patterns. Each of these is subject to the materiality standard. Commission Guidance Regarding Disclosure Related to Climate Change, Securities Act Release No. 9106 (Feb. 2, 2010). The SEC's 2010 guidance did not abate investor complaints that substantial unevenness existed across public companies in their disclosure practices related to climate change as well as their disclosures on a broader range of sustainability issues, such as resource scarcity, corporate social responsibility, and good corporate citizenship. In response, the SEC incorporated these concerns into its potentially sweeping reconsideration of the scope of disclosure required by Regulation S-K in the Concept Release excerpted above. For an evaluation of the steps thus far taken by former chairs and directors of the SEC, *see* Higgins, Beller, White & Schapiro, The SEC and Improving Sustainability Reporting, 29 J. Applied Fin. 22 (2017) (initial guidance focuses on material events to the company from which much can be learned as to what the next steps may best be).

2.   An Interim Report Card on ESG.   Consider the following regarding the observed benefits of ESG matters:

Recent investment industry analyses are confirming the financial materiality of much ESG information. For instance, a June, 2017, Bank of America Merrill Lynch study highlighted by the Sustainability Accounting Standards Board found sustainability factors to be "strong indicators of future volatility, earnings risk, price declines, and bankruptcies." Also in June of 2017, Allianz Global Investors produced a research report with similar findings, concluding that the heightened transparency of ESG disclosure lowered companies' cost of capital by reducing the "investment risk premium" that sophisticated investors would require. In September of 2017, Nordea Equity Research published an analytic research report concluding that there is "solid evidence that ESG matters, both for operational and share price performance." Goldman Sachs concluded in April of 2018 that "integrating ESG factors allows for greater insight into intangible factors such as culture, operational excellence and risk that can improve investment outcomes."

These industry studies are consistent with, and indeed rely upon, a number of influential academic studies that have analyzed the over 2,000 research studies also showing the economic materiality of ESG information. Two such studies are of particular note. Deutsch Asset & Wealth Management . . . analyzed 2,250 individual studies of the relationship between ESG data and corporate financial performance. From this analysis, the researchers concluded that improvements in ESG performance generally lead to improvements in financial performance. A comprehensive review published in 2015 of empirical studies found that 90% of studies show that sound sustainability standards lower firms' cost of capital; 80% of studies show that companies' stock price performance is positively influenced by good sustainability practices; and 88% of studies show that better E, S, or G practices result in better operational performance. . . .

The Commission has often developed new disclosure requirements in response to increased investor interest in emerging systemic environmental or social risks, such as its 2011 guidance on disclosure of risks related to cybersecurity. We thus conclude that the SEC properly recognizes that there can be material information which is not yet required to be reflected in financial statements but which may be decision-relevant to investors. As stated by Alan Beller, former Director of the Division of Corporation Finance, "[i]n today's rapidly changing business landscape, investors often look beyond financial statement to understand how companies create long-term value. Financial reporting today has not kept pace with both company managers and investors' interest in broader categories of information that are also material to operations and financial performance." The touchstone is the "reasonable investor," and what information the reasonable investor relies upon in voting, investing, and engagement with portfolio companies.

Williams & Fisch, Petition to the SEC for Rulemaking on Environmental, Social and Governance (Oct. 1, 2018). Is the more challenging issue for the SEC moving forward not whether there will be ESG disclosures but how the disclosures can be meaningfully comparable?

    3.   *Round Peg in a Square Hole?*   Consider whether there is a mismatch between contemporary justifications for sustainability disclosures and what may be the real concern that underlies such disclosures:

> . . . [A]ttention to sustainability may serve as a useful proxy for good corporate governance. Businesses that address social and environmental risks may exhibit greater discipline and commitment to long-term planning than peers. Investors may therefore seek out sustainability information as part of a holistic evaluation of management quality.
>
>   But the elephant in the room is that this is not the only reason why investors—and the public—urge greater transparency around sustainability. Much of the movement is not predicated on the idea that sustainable companies produce greater returns but is instead predicated on the idea that investors may *care about things other than* financial returns. . . .
>
>   Institutional investors caught . . . [in a legal regime that mandates they maximize return while minimizing risk] are subject to conflicting demands: the general public—and many of their clients—may insist that they use their power as investors to press for improved attention to sustainability issues regardless of their effects on fund returns. But if these institutions admit that their concerns extend beyond the financial, they risk running afoul of their legal obligations. . . . With shareholder involvement in corporate governance still contested and fragile, any open admission by large investors that they are advocating for non-wealth maximizing action would only hand managers additional leverage in the fight to persuade state and federal regulators to minimize shareholder power.

Lipton, Mixed Company: The Audience for Sustainability Disclosures, 107 Geo. L.J. Online 81 (2018).

    4.   *The Environmental Impact of Disclosure.*   Do enhanced environmental disclosure requirements ultimately redound to the benefit of the environment? Consider the following:

> Increased disclosure by registrants should provide the least-cost source of information on environmental liabilities, reducing the environmental information asymmetry between registrants and the financial markets. Investors will then be better able to incorporate environmental compliance cost information into securities prices. As prices adjust, each firm's cost of capital changes—it should rise for firms with substantial environmental liabilities as investors bid down [their] stock price to reflect future environmental expenditures, and it should fall as investors bid up

the prices of non-polluting firms. Managers tend to minimize their cost of capital and should be expected to reduce environmental liabilities and uncertainties. In the past, any environmental discount to stock prices probably affected entire industry groups that the financial markets suspected were facing uncertain future cleanup and abatement costs. However, as more firm-specific information becomes reliably available, the price impact should shift to only those individual firm stock prices and be based on their disclosures. Individual firms may experience stock price increases if they were previously lumped together in an industry suspected to have environmental problems. Firm-specific disclosures should have the benefit of rewarding companies with a responsible environmental record, while steering investment away from companies with looming environmental problems.

Bagby, Murray & Andrews, How Green Was My Balance Sheet? Corporate Liability and Environmental Disclosure, 14 Va. Envtl. L.J. 225, 338-339 (1995). What impact will disclosure of significant environmental liabilities have on management's relationship to the firm's stockholders, products, and cost of credit?

PROBLEM

12-12.   For many years, global energy companies have lawfully made contributions to support conservative, moderate, and liberal politicians in many countries that are the major markets for their products. Because the amounts are typically less than 1 percent of a company's global revenues, they never separately report on the contributions or how they are divided among the many politicians they supported or for that matter in what countries the payments are made. Recently, however, there is an increasing trend among a sizable number of politicians not to accept contributions from energy companies, largely in response to their concern that fossil fuels are impacting climate change around the globe. What issues would you raise in preparing a comment in response to an SEC proposal to require disclosure of such payments?

F.   The Materiality of Being a "Bad" Citizen: Violations of State or Federal Law

The foregoing materials addressed management integrity in settings involving alleged conflicts of interest and disclosures related to the firms' governance. Should the notion be extended further to illegal activity that is not self-serving, but rather undertaken in the best interest of the company? One of the most interesting chapters in the SEC's history began with the serendipitous discovery by the Watergate special prosecutor that several corporations and their officers used corporate funds for illegal domestic political contributions. Extensive investigations by the SEC revealed widespread practices among public companies involving illegal campaign contributions, bribery, and questionable foreign payments. Some 450 American companies ultimately disclosed they had engaged in questionable and illegal payments. The basis for the SEC enforcement actions on these varied fronts was the materiality of such payments and practices.

To understand the materiality of illegal activity, consider *Roeder v. Alpha Industries, Inc.*, 814 F.2d 22 (1st Cir. 1987). The corporation authorized a bribe to Raytheon's contract officer to secure his assistance in winning for the corporation a valuable subcontracting award. This occurred just before the plaintiff purchased some shares of the company on the market. When the bribery was ultimately disclosed, the company's stock plummeted in value because the illegal payment carried serious sanctions, such as the company being barred from future government contract work. The First Circuit, even though holding that information about the bribe was material, nevertheless held there was no duty to disclose it. *See also Villella v. Chemical Mining Co. of Chile, Inc.*, 2017 U.S. LEXIS 45501 (S.D.N.Y. 2017) (even though bribes to government officials represented less than 0.5 percent of annual earnings they were material due to the likely reputational hit the firm would suffer upon disclosure).

Roeder illustrates the wide array of issues posed by management's nondisclosure of its violation of federal or state laws. First, there is the question of whether the nondisclosed information is material. For example, would the bribe in *Roeder* have been material in the absence of any government sanctions? Does the amount of the bribe payment determine its materiality, or is materiality to be determined in some other context? If the materiality of the bribe is conceded, what is the basis for the firm's duty to disclose that it has engaged in bribery? In this regard, consider that *Roeder* held there was no duty to disclose the bribe to investors purchasing the company's shares in the market. Would the First Circuit require disclosure in the company's 10-K? How about on Form S-1? Would it require disclosure in its proxy statement seeking the reelection of the directors who authorized the bribe? What about the reelection of directors who, while not aware of the bribe, ignored obvious warning signs that important contracts were being obtained by bribing contract officers?

Securities and Exchange Commission v. Jos. Schlitz Brewing Co.
452 F. Supp. 824 (E.D. Wis. 1978)

GORDON, J.

I.   INTRODUCTION

. . . This is an action brought by the Securities and Exchange Commission (Commission) against the Jos. Schlitz Brewing Company (Schlitz) . . . to restrain and enjoin Schlitz from engaging in practices alleged to violate the federal securities laws. Schlitz is a Wisconsin corporation engaged in the business of selling beer and malt beverages whose securities are registered with the Commission and are publicly traded.

The complaint sets forth three causes of action. The first cause of action alleges violations of section 17(a) of the Securities Act of 1933, and section[s] 10(b)[, 13(a) & 14(a)] of the Securities Exchange Act of 1934 and Rule 10b-5. Schlitz is alleged to have failed to disclose a nationwide scheme to induce retailers of beer and malt beverages to purchase Schlitz' products by making payments or furnishing things of value of at least $3 million in violation of federal, state and local liquor laws. It is also charged that the defendant failed to disclose its alleged participation in violations of Spanish tax and exchange laws in connection with transactions with certain Spanish corporations described as affiliates. Schlitz allegedly falsified its books and records with respect to these payments and transactions. By failing to disclose these matters, Schlitz' financial statements, registration statements, periodic reports and proxy solicitation materials filed with the Commission are said to be materially false and misleading. Schlitz is also charged with aiding and abetting violations of sections 17(a) and 10(b) by the public companies which allegedly received unlawful inducement payments. . . .

II.   SUBJECT MATTER JURISDICTION

Schlitz [in its present motion to dismiss] contends that the Commission lacks the jurisdiction to bring this action because the acts and practices upon which the action is predicated fall outside its regulatory jurisdiction which is limited to "acts or practices which constitute or will constitute a violation" of the federal securities laws. The inducement payments which Schlitz is alleged to have made to its customers may violate the Federal Alcohol Administration Act, 27 U.S.C. §201 et seq., the enforcement of which rests exclusively with the secretary of the treasury, through the bureau of alcohol, tobacco and firearms and the attorney general. On March 15, 1978, a federal grand jury sitting in the eastern district of Wisconsin returned an indictment charging Schlitz with, inter alia, conspiracy and substantive violations of the Federal Alcohol Administration Act. Accordingly, Schlitz contends that this action is an impermissible encroachment on and a duplication of the functions assigned by statute to the bureau of alcohol, tobacco and firearms and the attorney general.

I am unable to accept the defendant's characterization of this action as one to enforce the Federal Alcohol Administration Act. The Commission seeks by this action to enforce the disclosure requirements of the federal securities laws for the protection of shareholders and the investing public generally, a function clearly within the Commission's regulatory authority. Moreover, it is well established that more than one governmental agency may investigate the same conduct simultaneously and bring simultaneous civil and criminal actions based on such conduct so long as the respective remedies are not mutually exclusive and there is an otherwise rational basis for their individual proceedings. Since the basis for this action by the Commission is the alleged failure of Schlitz to disclose its potentially criminal marketing practices in its filings with the Commission, mailings to shareholders and press releases, I believe that the Commission has a rational basis for instituting this enforcement proceeding.

Attempting to demonstrate that the Commission is acting beyond its jurisdiction, Schlitz emphasizes that no statute, rule or regulation specifically requires that a corporation report its involvement in marketing or business practices that may at some future time be adjudicated to be illegal. The Commission argues in response that the reporting of such information is mandated by the philosophy of full disclosure upon which the federal securities laws are predicated.

The parties are essentially in agreement that whether Schlitz' potentially illegal activities must be disclosed depends upon whether such matter is material information. This inquiry . . . depends upon whether there is a substantial likelihood that a reasonable person would attach importance to these matters in making investment decisions regarding Schlitz securities. *TSC Industries, Inc. v. Northway, Inc.*, 426 U.S. 438 (1976).

The Commission suggests several reasons why the information concerning Schlitz' allegedly improper activities is material. First, the Commission argues that this information has a direct bearing on the integrity of management. In *Securities and Exchange Commission v. Kalvex, Inc.*, 425 F. Supp. 310, 315 (S.D.N.Y. 1975), and *Cooke v. Teleprompter Corp.*, 334 F. Supp. 467 (S.D.N.Y. 1971), courts found that information of improprieties committed by corporate directors might be material to investor decisions concerning who should control the corporation. Without disputing that such information might be material to investors, Schlitz contends that the integrity of management is not at issue in this case because the complaint makes no reference to individual directors.

I am not persuaded that the omission of allegations implicating individual directors is significant. Paragraph 9(e) of the complaint alleges that Schlitz' marketing practices continued even after Schlitz was warned by the bureau of alcohol, tobacco, and firearms that such marketing practices must be terminated. I believe that the question of the integrity of management gives materiality to the matters the Commission claims should have been disclosed. . . .

The Commission also contends that the allegedly improper transactions were material from an economic standpoint. Schlitz disagrees, emphasizing that when measured against Schlitz' 1976 net sales of approximately $1 billion the alleged $3 million in payments to retailers and others would amount to only .3% of its net sales for that year.

The Commission's position is that the relatively small amount of the payments involved alone is not dispositive. In its report on questionable and illegal corporate payments and practices submitted to the Senate Housing & Urban Affairs Committee, May 12, 1976, the Commission stated, at pp. 29-30:

> Under most circumstances, the amount of the payment is not dispositive of the materiality issue unless, of course, the payment is significant by itself. Where the size of the payment does not otherwise require disclosure, the materiality of such payments would depend on the relative economic implications of the payment to the company as a whole or to a significant line of the company's business. Thus, for example, a questionable or illegal payment that seems relatively small in relation to corporate revenues, income or assets may assume much greater importance when one assesses the amount of business that may be dependent on or affected by it.

In addition, the Commission suggests that its discovery may reveal that the amount of payments involved was much greater than $3 million. These arguments amply demonstrate the potential materiality of the information in question.

The Commission also stresses that the allegedly illegal practices engaged in by Schlitz and its customers posed a substantial threat to their licenses to sell beer—licenses upon which many of the operations of Schlitz and its customers depend.

The parties have different views as to whether Schlitz' efforts to disclose the risk of license suspension or revocation were timely or adequate, and I am unable to resolve this dispute on the present motion. However, I am unconvinced by Schlitz' argument that the risk of license suspension was not material as a matter of law because of the infrequency of past criminal prosecutions against brewers or wholesalers for violations of the Federal Alcohol Administration Act; the complaint alleges that Schlitz was given a warning in 1973 that such practices must cease.

Schlitz also argues that some of the allegedly unlawful transactions are immaterial because the applicable statute of limitations bars a criminal prosecution for such transactions. However, even if a criminal prosecution for certain of the transactions is now barred, a matter disputed by the Commission, this does not establish the immateriality of these activities insofar as a civil action to enforce securities laws is concerned. . . .

NOTES AND QUESTIONS

1. *The Duty to Disclose Bribery.* Is *Jos. Schlitz* inconsistent with the reasoning invoked in *Roeder*? Both actions were brought under the antifraud provisions of the Exchange Act, and both cases held the bribe payment was material. In addition, *Jos. Schlitz* held that the company violated Sections 13(a) and 14(a) of the Exchange Act by failing to disclose the bribe in its annual and quarterly reports filed with the Commission as well as in its proxy statement. In their suits arising from management's failure to disclose its bribe of public officials or others, private litigants' victories have been narrow ones. *Roeder* typifies the result reached in suits brought by investors who seek to recover the decline in their share values due to management's nondisclosure of bribery.

Shareholders have had modest success by alleging the proxy statement circulated in connection with the directors' reelection was materially deficient in failing to disclose their approval or acquiescence in a prior or ongoing bribery scheme. The relief in such suits, however, is limited to compelling a new election of the directors to occur with appropriate disclosures of their involvement with the bribery. Courts have overwhelmingly denied any monetary recovery in such proxy-based suits for past bribery amounts. In denying such recovery, the courts have reasoned that, since the proxy solicitation sought not the stockholders' approval of the bribes, but only the election of the directors, no causal relationship exists between the defective proxy statement and the payment of the bribes. In sum, if bribes are material, it is because they bear upon the integrity and stewardship of the director nominees.

Is bribery alone a sufficient basis to implicate the directors' integrity in a civil action? In *Gaines v. Haughton*, 645 F.2d 761 (9th Cir. 1981), *cert. denied*, 454 U.S. 1145 (1982), the shareholders alleged that the failure to disclose massive foreign bribes by the company in its proxy statement seeking the directors' reelection violated Section 14(a) of the Exchange Act. In dismissing the action, the court reasoned:

We draw a sharp distinction . . . between allegations of director misconduct involving breach of trust or self-dealing—the nondisclosure of which is presumptively material—and allegations of simple breach of fiduciary duty/waste of corporate assets—the nondisclosure of which is never material for §14(a) purposes. . . .

Many corporate actions taken by directors in the interest of the corporation might offend and engender controversy among some stockholders. Investors share the same diversity of social and political views that characterizes the polity as a whole. The tenor of a company's labor relations policies, economic decisions to relocate or close established industrial plants, commercial dealings with foreign countries which are disdained in certain circles, decisions to develop (or not to develop) particular natural resources or forms of energy technology, and the promulgation of corporate personnel policies that reject (or embrace) the principle of affirmative action, are just a few of [the] business judgments, soundly entrusted to the broad discretion of the directors which may nonetheless cause shareholder dissent and provoke claims of "wasteful," "unethical," or even "immoral" business dealings. Should corporate directors have a duty under §14(a) to disclose all such corporate decisions in proxy solicitations for their reelection? We decline to extend the duty to disclose under §14(a) to these situations. While we neither condone nor condemn these similar types of corporate conduct (including the now-illegal practice of questionable foreign payments), we believe that aggrieved shareholders have sufficient recourse to state law claims against the responsible directors and, if all else fails, can sell or trade their stock in the offending corporation in favor of an enterprise more compatible with their own personal goals and values.

Id. at 778. *See Weisberg v. Coastal States Gas Corp.*, 609 F.2d 650 (2d Cir. 1979), *cert. denied*, 445 U.S. 951 (1980) (dismissal of action reversed to allow plaintiff to undertake discovery where plaintiff alleged directors had concealed bribery as well as received kickbacks); *Shields v. Erikson*, [1989-1990 Transfer Binder] Fed. Sec. L. Rep. (CCH) ¶94,723 (N.D. Ill. 1989) (relying on *Gaines* and *Weisberg* to conclude that a proxy statement was materially misleading in failing to disclose that the board of directors received gifts that were illegally charged to the U.S. government). An alternative approach toward kickbacks is to view them as self-dealing contracts that are required to be disclosed under the specific disclosure requirements of Regulation S-K for self-dealing transactions. *See United States v. Fields*, 592 F.2d 638 (2d Cir. 1978), *cert. denied*, 442 U.S. 917 (1979).

   2. SEC Bases for Concluding Bribery Is Material.   An illuminating discussion of bribery and questionable payment practices by American corporations appears in SEC, Report of the Securities and Exchange Commission on Questionable Payments and Practices, submitted to the Senate Banking, Housing and Urban Affairs Committee, 94th Cong., 2d Sess. (May 12, 1976). In addition to the two theories advanced in *Jos. Schlitz* for the materiality of its bribes, the SEC in its early involvement in the post-Watergate bribery cases also argued that bribes of any amount are material per se because of their illegality. The SEC soon distanced itself from this position and came to view the illegality of the bribe as only a "particularly important factor" in the materiality equation. Id. at 24. A far sounder basis for the Commission's concern with bribery is the effect it frequently has upon the reliability of the firm's accounting system and records. The SEC investigation of questionable payment practices revealed a pattern among bribing firms. Corporate books and records were customarily falsified to facilitate the surreptitious accumulations of funds from which payments would be made. Vast sums of cash were accumulated in a manner that kept them completely outside the firm's accounting system. These practices themselves cast doubt on the integrity and reliability of the firm's accounting records and their resulting reports and ultimately led to Congress enacting in 1977 the Foreign Corrupt Practices Act (FCPA), which added Section 30A to the Exchange Act to prohibit reporting companies from bribing any "foreign official" and also added Section 13(b)(2), requiring reporting companies to maintain records that "accurately and fairly reflect" transactions and to "devise and maintain a system of internal accounting controls sufficient to provide reasonable assurance that" transactions are executed in compliance with management's authorization. The FCPA's books and records provisions are examined in Chapter 11. Finally, the SEC has easily sustained its cases against brokers who obtain underwriting business with municipal governments without disclosing kickbacks the broker will make to the city treasurer. *See Santos v. Securities and Exchange Comm'n*, 355 F. Supp. 2d 917 (N.D. Ill. 2003).

3.   ***Must Directors Announce, "I'm a Crook"?***   In *United States v. Mathews*, 787 F.2d 38 (2d Cir. 1986), the government argued that Mathews had violated the securities laws by failing to disclose in a proxy statement accompanying his election to the board of directors that he was a member of the bribery conspiracy. The Second Circuit found no merit in the government's argument that Mathews, in effect, should have publicly pronounced himself guilty of the uncharged crime in 1981, three years before his indictment on that charge. The court noted that Item 401(f) did not require Mathews to make the disclosure in question. Id. at 43-44.

> [S]o long as uncharged criminal conduct is not required to be disclosed by any rule lawfully promulgated by the SEC, nondisclosure of such conduct cannot be the basis of a criminal prosecution. Our unwillingness to permit section 14(a) to be used as expansively as the Government has done here rests not only on the history of the Commission's approach to the problem of qualitative disclosures and the case law that has developed on this subject, but on the obvious due process implications that would arise from permitting a conviction to stand in the absence of clearer notice as to what disclosures are required in this uncertain area.

Id. at 49. Is the result in *Mathews* consistent with *Franchard* or merely explained by its being a criminal prosecution? *See also City of Pontiac Policemen and Firemen's Ret. Sys. v. UBS AG*, 752 F.3d 173 (2d Cir. 2014) (firm, when announcing it was under investigation, did not have to disclose it was actively involved in criminal misconduct). Would Mathews have to disclose when he seeks reelection that he was the object of a grand jury investigation involving an alleged earlier bribery of corporate officials? What if the earlier bribery activities had involved kickbacks of minor sums to Mathews?

4.   ***"We're Clean" Statements.***   Frequently, a company's failure to comply with the law becomes material in considering the company's claims that it is the model corporate citizen. For example, BP's Annual Report stated: "Management

believes that the Group's activities are in compliance in all material respects with applicable environmental laws and regulations." This was deemed false because when the company made the statement it was actively discussing with various environmental agencies corrective steps it should take to mitigate further damage to the environment. *Reese v. Malone*, 747 F.3d 557 (9th Cir. 2014). *Public Pension Fund Group v. KV Pharmaceutical Co.*, 679 F.3d 972 (8th Cir. 2012) (substantial likelihood reasonable investor would consider it important that company had received not just an FDA warning but one that posed serious consequence before company stated it was in compliance with FDA regulations).

PROBLEMS

12-13. The CEO of a publicly owned national bank had over some period of time caused an excessive amount of bank money to be funneled to a series of related real estate development projects being promoted by an old college friend. Ultimately, these projects failed, and the bank is now in serious trouble. Among other things, such loans violated a provision of the federal banking laws that precludes committing too much of the bank's assets to a single borrower. The federal banking authorities are now seeking the CEO's removal from office on grounds that he willfully endangered the safety and soundness of the bank. That matter is currently in litigation.

Was the nondisclosure of such malfeasance at the time *material?* To whom? Under what circumstances? Must the ongoing action by the federal banking authorities be disclosed?

12-14. In response to numerous press reports that heart stints manufactured by Science Devices Inc. were unreliable, Science Devices issued a press release stating the devices were reliable and quoted from a study that supported the belief that problems were due to physicians installing the stints incorrectly. This caused the price of Science Devices shares to recover the losses suffered by the earlier press reports. The press release did not disclose, however, that under pressure from the FDA, and its own product quality staff, Science Devices was addressing a design problem that sometimes caused stints to misperform. Has Science Devices engaged in a material misrepresentation? *See Mississippi Public Employees Ret. Sys. v. Boston Scientific Corp.*, 523 F.3d 75 (1st Cir. 2008).

‖13‖
Fraud in Connection with the Purchase or Sale of a Security

Section 10(b) of the Securities Exchange Act prohibits the use of "any manipulative or deceptive device or contrivance in contravention of such rules and regulations as the Commission may prescribe" in connection with securities trading (regardless of whether the issuer is publicly held). In 1942, the Commission exercised that authority to promulgate Rule 10b-5, which has become the principal tool for promoting the informational integrity of securities transactions. The Rule bars any use of an instrumentality of interstate commerce:

(a) To employ any device, scheme, or artifice to defraud,
(b) To make any untrue statement of a material fact or to omit to state a material fact necessary in order to make the statements made, in the light of the circumstances under which they were made, not misleading, or
(c) To engage in any act, practice, or course of business which operates or would operate as a fraud or deceit upon any person, in connection with the purchase or sale of any security.

A number of observations are worth making about Rule 10b-5 at the outset. First, its language is taken verbatim from Section 17(a) of the Securities Act, mainly substituting the words "in connection with the purchase or sale of a security" for "in the offer or sale of any securities" for purposes of defining its scope. This tracking of language is completely understandable, since Rule 10b-5's original purpose was simply to supplement the Commission's enforcement capacity under Section 17(a) by extending antifraud protection to sellers of securities as well as purchasers—its attention having been drawn to a matter in which a corporate official in Boston was buying up shares of his company's stock while at the same time making pessimistic public statements about his company. *See* Remarks of Milton Freeman, Colloquium Foreword—Happy Birthday Rule 10b-5, 61 Fordham L. Rev. S1 (1993).

Second, as we shall see, courts interpreting the Rule have drawn heavily from the underlying statute and its sparse official history, while at various times both broadening and restricting its scope. Today, Rule 10b-5 proscribes all fraud that touches on the purchase or sale of a security—reaching misbehavior running from the smallest closely held corporation to the largest "blue-chip" issuers, so long as the misconduct is intentional and truly deceptive in nature. It is enforceable both publicly and through an implied private right of action.

A study of the legislative history of Section 10(b) by Professor Steve Thel suggests that the Rule's current function may be far different from what the drafters really had in mind. Thel, The Original Conception of Section 10(b) of the Securities Exchange Act, 42 Stan. L. Rev. 385 (1990). According to Professor Thel, Section 10(b) was meant largely to give the newly created SEC the ability to reach novel forms of speculative or manipulative behavior that might be practiced with respect to exchange-traded securities. A different portion of the Exchange Act, Section 9, was intended to prohibit traditional forms of manipulation and provide injured investors with a private remedy when it occurred, while Section 10 was to give the Commission broader authority to protect marketplace integrity in the abstract by prohibiting conduct that might simply have a distortive effect. Section 10(b)'s reference to "deceptive" conduct, on which—we shall see—so much subsequent history has rested, may largely have been an afterthought, designed if anything to enlarge, rather than restrict, the scope of the section. From this perspective, contrary to the Supreme Court's teachings, neither a strict deception nor a scienter requirement is implicit in the statute. (Nor, on the other hand, is a private right of action.) But that is all water over the dam. By virtue of decades of judicial interpretation and occasional congressional action, the Rule stands as the centerpiece antifraud provision under the federal securities laws.

This chapter focuses on the elements of a cause of action under Rule 10b-5, with particular attention to private rights of action. It begins by looking at some of the key elements of a cause of action—the "in connection with" requirement, standing to sue, the scienter standard, and the circumstances under which nondisclosure (as opposed to an affirmative misrepresentation) is fraudulent. Then, it turns to questions relating to investor injuries: reliance, causation, and choice of remedies. It ends with a brief look at the law of manipulation. The two chapters that follow then expand more broadly on securities regulation's effort to combat fraud. Chapter 14 explores more broadly some private litigation and governmental enforcement issues. Chapter 15 looks at a specific form of securities fraud addressed largely under Rule 10b-5: insider trading.

A.   Fraud "in Connection with" the Purchase or Sale of a Security

A close look at Rule 10b-5 shows that to establish a prima facie case of securities fraud, the plaintiff—whether the SEC or investors in a private lawsuit—must at the very least establish two things. First, there must be fraud, whether in the form of an affirmative misrepresentation, actionable omission, or some sort of "device, scheme or artifice to defraud." Later on, we will look at various ways of satisfying this requirement, especially when the alleged misconduct is in the form of silence or concealment, rather than an abject lie.

Second, that fraud must be "in connection with" the purchase or sale of a security. Does this mean that the wrongdoer must have been a purchaser or seller? Courts have said no; instead, the typical focus of the "in connection with" requirement is the link between defendants' fraud and purchases or sales of securities by the victims. The most commonly cited case along these lines is *SEC v. Texas Gulf Sulphur Co.*, 401 F.2d 833 (2d Cir. 1968) (en banc), *cert. denied*, 394 U.S. 976 (1969), where the court found the requirement satisfied by a showing that the false corporate publicity was disseminated "in a manner reasonably calculated to influence the investing public." This implies that the person who commits the fraud deceives—and thus conceivably bears liability to—the entire marketplace of traders. Indeed, that quickly proved to be the case under the so-called fraud-on-the-market theory of liability. This theory was at work in *Basic Inc. v. Levinson*, 485 U.S. 224 (1988), a case we studied in Chapter 12 and one that we will revisit later in this chapter.

As far as the "in connection with" standard is concerned, it is not necessary to show that the purpose of the misleading statement was to influence investors—only that a material misstatement was disseminated in a medium on which investors rely. *See Semerenko v. Cendant Corp.*, 216 F.3d 315 (3d Cir. 2000) (shareholders of target company may bring Section 10(b) claims against potential acquirer for misrepresenting its own financial condition, which allegedly inflated target's stock price). Thus, the recipient of the information need not be a person to whom it was specifically directed. *See In re Carter-Wallace Sec. Litig.*, 150 F.3d 153 (2d Cir. 1998) (shareholders may bring Section 10(b) claim regarding allegedly false medical advertisement).

While the standard way of looking at the requirement is to focus on the *victims'* purchases or sales, it is not necessarily the only one. Much of the open-endedness in this area grows out of the Supreme Court's decision in *Superintendent of Insurance v. Bankers Life & Casualty Co.*, 404 U.S. 6 (1971), the last of the Court's expansive securities law decisions before the period of retrenchment that soon followed. There the principal defendant, Begole, caused the initiation of a complex series of securities transactions in order to misappropriate proceeds from the company (Manhattan), which he ended up controlling. The Court's opinion does not indicate clearly the specific fraud involved; it simply assumes that "the Manhattan board was deceived into authorizing [the] sale by the misrepresentation that the proceeds would be exchanged for a certificate of deposit of equal value." Id. at 8 n.1. Justice Douglas rejected an allegation that the fraud need go to any stock market-based transaction, finding in the totality of the circumstances sufficient evidence of a fraudulent scheme within the scope of Section 10(b). The Court stated that it was enough that the fraud (presumably the misappropriation itself) simply "touch" the sale of securities in order for the Rule to become applicable. *See generally* Cox, Fraud Is in the Eye of the Beholder: Rule 10b-5's Application to Corporate Mismanagement, 47 N.Y.U. L. Rev. 674 (1972).

In other words, there are numerous possible ways of establishing "in connection with." In *SEC v. Pirate Capital LLC*, 580 F.3d 233, 244 (4th Cir. 2009), the Fourth Circuit summarized the prevailing approach this way:

We find direction in several factors that other courts have considered relevant when determining whether the "in connection with" requirement has been satisfied in a particular case. These factors include, but are not limited to: (1) whether a securities sale was necessary to the completion of the fraudulent scheme, (2) whether the parties' relationship was such that it would necessarily involve trading in securities, (3) whether the defendant intended to induce a securities transaction, and (4) whether material misrepresentations were "disseminated to the public in a medium upon which a reasonable investor would rely," [quoting *Semerenko*, supra]. Importantly, these factors are not mandatory requirements that a fraud must satisfy in order to meet §10(b)'s "in connection with" requirement. They exist merely to guide the inquiry, and we do not presume to exclude other factors that could help distinguish between fraud in the securities industry and common law fraud that happens to involve securities.

The one organizing principle seems to be that the fraud must relate to investment activity of the sort Congress was seeking to protect via the securities laws. In other words, the investment aspect must be "essential" to the wrongful scheme, rather than an "incidental" element, *e.g., Taylor v. First Union Corp.*, 857 F.2d 240, 245 (4th Cir. 1988); *Chemical Bank v. Arthur Andersen & Co.*, 726 F.2d 930 (2d Cir.), *cert. denied*, 469 U.S. 884 (1984) (stock pledged as collateral for fraudulently obtained bank loan is not fraud "in connection with" a security transaction).

PROBLEM

13-1.   Purchasers of stock in JDS Uniphase Corp. brought suit against Nortel Networks Inc. for false statements relating to Nortel's projected revenue and earnings growth. Nortel was JDS' largest customer, and so, according to plaintiffs, Nortel's lies also artificially boosted the price of JDS stock because they suggested an increase in forthcoming orders. There was evidence that when Nortel later lowered its estimates, the stock prices of both Nortel and JDS fell. Would this be "in connection with" the purchase or sale of a security? Which security? *See Ontario Public Service Employees Union Pension Trust Fund v. Nortel Networks Inc.*, 369 F.3d 27 (2d Cir. 2004).

B.   Private Rights of Action Under Rule 10b-5

1.   Creation and Controversy

Within a decade after its adoption, courts began implying a private right of action under Rule 10b-5. *See Kardon v. National Gypsum Co.*, 73 F. Supp. 798 (E.D. Pa. 1947). Today, the existence of an implied private right of action under Rule 10b-5 is well established, if by nothing more than passage of time and congressional acquiescence. *See Herman & MacLean v. Huddleston*, 459 U.S. 375, 380 (1983).

The early enthusiasm for the implied right came from the natural inclination to compensate investors harmed by lies and deception. Over time, however, questions have grown about the efficacy of broad private rights of action. *Texas Gulf Sulphur* abandoned the notion that fraudsters must communicate directly with their victims to violate Section 10(b), and instead embraced the idea that publicly disseminated false statements run afoul of the statute. As a result, issuers and others associated with false corporate publicity can potentially be liable to extraordinarily large numbers of investors, creating the possibility of "draconian" liability in class actions seemingly disproportionate to the underlying misconduct (consider *Basic Inc. v. Levinson* from Chapter 12, where potentially large liability exposure was premised upon an apparently well-meaning lie protecting the confidentiality of merger negotiations). To many, fear of private liability under Rule 10b-5 has led to excessive precaution costs and chilled legitimate corporate activity (e.g., voluntary disclosure). *See* Kasznick & Lev, To Warn or Not to Warn? Management Disclosures in the Face of an Earnings Surprise, 70 Acct. Rev. 115 (1995); Mahoney, Precaution Costs and the Law of Fraud in Impersonal Markets, 78 Va. L. Rev. 623 (1992). But the fear is even greater than one of alleged "fraud by hindsight." Once such large sums of money were at stake, the stage was set for plaintiffs' attorneys to use the threat of liability as a vehicle to pressure corporations into settling, even though the merits of their claims might be quite speculative. To counter this pressure, some — including a former SEC Commissioner — wanted the SEC itself to cut back on the private liability consequences of Rule 10b-5. *See* Grundfest, Why Disimply?, 108 Harv. L. Rev. 727 (1995). Consider the following, from the legislative history leading up to the adoption of the Private Securities Litigation Reform Act of 1995.

H.R. Rep. No. 104-50
Committee on Commerce (Feb. 24, 1995)

A SUMMARY OF A TYPICAL CASE

A typical case involves a stock, usually of a high-growth, high-tech company, that has performed well for many quarters, but ultimately misses analysts' expectations:

Whenever there is any sudden change in stock price, there is, by definition some surprise (e.g., a disappointing earnings announcement or an adverse product development). Securities class action lawyers can then file a complaint (frequently many are filed immediately after any sudden price drop) claiming that some group of defendants "knew or should have known" about the negative information and disclosed it earlier.

Officers, directors, accountants, and consultants are also named as defendants. Damages sought by plaintiffs — on behalf of anyone who bought the company's stock prior to the earnings announcement — amount to hundreds of millions of dollars. The plaintiffs who bring the suit typically hold only a handful of shares in the company. They almost certainly have filed such cases before, usually working with the same law firm. Known as "professional plaintiffs," they sue companies many times throughout the year, and receive bonuses above what they recover in the settlement. The driving force behind many of these suits are not angry investors, but entrepreneurial trial lawyers who use the "professional plaintiff."

Using professional plaintiffs, law firms often file complaints within days of a substantial movement in stock price. The leading plaintiffs' law firm reported that 69 percent of the cases it filed over a three year period were filed within 10 days of the event or disclosure that gave rise to the allegations of fraud. Firms are able to do this by keeping a stable of professional plaintiffs who hold a few shares in a broad range of companies. As William Lerach, whose firm filed 229 different suits over forty-four months—one every 4.2 business days—told Forbes magazine: "I have the greatest practice of law in the world. I have no clients." . . .

One recent case is illustrative of the current state of affairs. On April 2, 1993, Philip Morris announced that it would reduce the average price of its cigarettes, and therefore, that it expected earnings in the future to decline. Less than five hours later, the first of several lawsuits were filed on behalf of a plaintiff who had bought 60 shares during the alleged class period. Four more lawsuits were filed the same day. And on the next day, five additional lawsuits were filed. Two of the complaints contained identical allegations "that the defendants . . . engaged in conduct to create and prolong the illusion of Philip Morris' success in the toy industry." Apparently, these complaints are lodged in some computer bank of fraud complaints, available for quick access but without much regard to accuracy.

In the typical case, after some legal skirmishing, the court refuses to dismiss the complaints and discovery begins. With relatively little specific evidence other than a drop in stock price, the plaintiffs have succeeded in filing a lawsuit, triggering the costly discovery process, and imposing massive costs on the defendant who possesses the bulk of the relevant information. As Dennis W. Bakke, President and Chief Executive Officer of the AES Corporation, testified:

> After the motion to dismiss was decided, the financial blood letting began in earnest with the onset of the discovery process as the rest of the suit proceeded. Discovery is an extremely broad and a formidable weapon in the hands of skilled plaintiffs' attorneys. Our business is enormously paper intensive. Therefore, we were immediately served with document production requests that resulted in us reviewing enormous numbers of boxes of paper. Depositions for a significant amount of our staff at our plant, plus a number of executive officers, were served. Worse yet, we were not the only people served with intrusive discovery requests. Plaintiffs served notice of depositions, and incredibly broad requests for document production, on at least four of our potential customers, various suppliers, certain of our lenders, and our largest construction contractor. I cannot begin to describe the disruption to important business relationships that this caused. . . .

As the costs of discovery rise, the pressure to settle becomes enormous. Many cases settle before the completion of discovery. Others will go as far as a summary judgment motion and if that is unsuccessful, settle immediately with defendants paying a substantial sum. The plaintiffs' lawyers take one-third of the settlement, and the rest is distributed to the members of the class, resulting in pennies of return for each individual plaintiff. There is no adjudication of the merits of the case. James Kimsey, Chairman of America Online Inc., testified: "Even when a company committed no fraud, indeed no negligence, there is still the remote possibility of huge jury verdicts, not to mention the costs of litigation. In the face of such exposure, defendant companies inevitably settle these suits rather than go to trial."

Throughout the process, it is clear that the plaintiff class has difficulty in exercising any meaningful direction over the case brought on its behalf. Class counsel may also have incentives that differ from those of the underlying class members. Because class counsels' fees and expenses sometimes amount to one-third or more of recovery, class counsel frequently has a significantly greater interest in the litigation than any individual member of the class.

Furthermore, class counsel usually advances the costs of the litigation, which means that counsel may have a greater incentive than the members of the class to accept a settlement that provides a significant fee and eliminates any risk of failure to recoup funds already invested in the case. Even if a substantially higher recovery might be obtained through litigation, the return on counsel's investment might be lower than that provided by the settlement, especially if lost opportunity costs are taken into account.

As a practical matter, members of the class who object must opt out of the class, obtain separate counsel, and oppose a settlement that is supported both by class counsel and the corporate defendant. The expense and difficulty of this process makes it unusable for most plaintiffs, although in light of plaintiff attorney conflicts of interest, this effort may be worthwhile. The Corporations Commissioner of the State of California submitted a statement to the Subcommittee outlining his experience in connection with a class action brought by the leading plaintiffs' law firm:

> In the VMS Realty Partnership case, limited partnerships interests were sold to thousands of unsuitable investors, often on the basis of materially misleading statements. A class action suit based upon these abuses was brought by Milberg, Weiss, Bershad, Hynes & Lerach, the nation's largest class action law firm. Despite the strong evidence of securities law violations, this case was settled for less than 8 cents on the dollar. While this may have represented a significant recovery for the lawyers, it woefully undervalued the investors' claims. Investors who opted out of the class action settlement and are now participating in the independent arbitration process are frequently receiving 100% of their losses. In addition, these investors haven't had to share their recovery with a lawyer "representing their interest."

Finally, although class actions require judicial approval, courts have a natural incentive to clear complicated cases from their dockets and have been known to adopt the premise that a bad settlement is almost always better than a good trial. . . .

Concerns such as those expressed in the House Report had affected the courts long before the adoption of the PSLRA in 1995. A variety of judicial decisions restricting the scope of Rule 10b-5—including a line of Supreme Court decisions dating back to *Blue Chip Stamps v. Manor Drug Stores*, 421 U.S. 723 (1975), have been justified at least in part by the fear of meritless securities litigation. The enactment of the Private Securities Litigation Reform Act of 1995 (PSLRA) was the most significant and dramatic acceptance of the view that the litigation system had become dysfunctional and might be costing investors more than any benefits it delivered. Rule 10b-5 was its primary target. Some of Congress' reforms (e.g., the safe harbor for forward-looking information) were covered in Chapter 12. Many others will be treated in this chapter and the one that follows.

Precisely how real the concern was about meritless litigation is an open question, of course. Managers, accountants, and securities professionals had ample reason to overstate the concern and gain excessive protection from the courts and Congress. To be sure, the data on the costs of litigation was not conclusive. *See* Seligman, The Merits Do Matter, 107 Harv. L. Rev. 438 (1994). And even if there was a good deal of speculative litigation, what of the need to compensate investors in good cases and — just as important, if not more — the compelling need to deter fraud effectively? By all accounts, the SEC does not have the resources to police the securities markets comprehensively; private rights of action have long been seen as a necessary adjunct to the public enforcement effort. Too harsh a pruning of private litigation under Rule 10b-5 threatens to tip the balance in favor of encouraging an excessive level of fraud and deception, harming the basic integrity of the American capital markets. For reviews of the empirical evidence on the efficacy of securities class actions and the extent to which the PSLRA has achieved its stated goals, *see* Cox & Thomas, Mapping the American Shareholder Litigation Experience: A Survey of Empirical Studies of the Enforcement of the U.S. Securities Laws, 6 Eur. Comp. & Fin. L. Rev. 164 (2009); Perino, Did the Private Securities Litigation Reform Act Work?, 2003 U. Ill. L. Rev. 913.

2. Standing to Sue

Blue Chip Stamps v. Manor Drug Stores
421 U.S. 723 (1975)

[In 1963, the federal government charged that a number of retailers had violated the antitrust laws by coordinating activities through a corporation known as Blue Chip Stamps. To settle the charges, the defendants agreed to create a new version of Blue Chip Stamps, and offer to sell shares to retailers injured by the original scheme. The new stock was registered and offered to the injured retailers, though not all chose to participate. Later, offerees who declined to purchase shares in the new company charged that the offering documents were unduly pessimistic about its prospects, so that victims of the original scheme would fail to claim the redress to which they were legally entitled.]

Justice REHNQUIST delivered the opinion of the Court.

The only portion of the litigation thus initiated which is before us is whether respondent may base its action on Rule 10b-5 of the Securities and Exchange Commission without having either bought or sold the securities described in the allegedly misleading prospectus. . . .

[V]irtually all lower federal courts facing the issue in the hundreds of reported cases presenting this question over the past quarter century have reaffirmed . . . that the plaintiff class for purposes of § 10(b) and Rule 10b-5 private damage actions is limited to purchasers and sellers of securities. . . .

When we deal with private actions under Rule 10b-5, we deal with a judicial oak which has grown from little more than a legislative acorn. . . . It is therefore proper that we consider . . . what may be described as policy considerations when we come to flesh out the portions of the law with respect to which neither the congressional enactment nor the administrative regulations offer conclusive guidance. . . .

There has been widespread recognition that litigation under Rule 10b-5 presents a danger of vexatiousness different in degree and in kind from that which accompanies litigation in general. . . . These concerns have two largely separate grounds.

The first of these concerns is that . . . even a complaint which by objective standards may have very little chance of success at trial has a settlement value to the plaintiff out of any proportion to its prospect of success at trial so long as he may prevent the suit from being resolved against him by dismissal or summary judgment. The very pendency of the lawsuit may frustrate or delay normal business activity of the defendant which is totally unrelated to the lawsuit. . . .

The second ground for fear of vexatious litigation is based on the concern that, [if liability is not limited to purchasers and sellers, it] would throw open to the trier of fact many rather hazy issues of historical fact the proof of which depended almost entirely on oral testimony. . . .

In today's universe of transactions governed by the 1934 Act, privity of dealing or even personal contact between potential defendant and potential plaintiff is the exception and not the rule. The stock of issuers is listed on financial exchanges utilized by tens of millions of investors, and corporate representations reach a potential audience, encompassing not only the diligent few who peruse filed corporate reports or the sizable number of subscribers to financial journals, but the readership of the Nation's daily newspapers. Obviously neither the fact that issuers or other potential defendants under Rule 10b-5 reach a large number of potential investors, or the fact that they are required by law to make their disclosures conform to certain standards, should in any way absolve them from liability for misconduct which is proscribed by Rule 10b-5.

But . . . [t]he manner in which the defendant's violation caused the plaintiff to fail to act could be as a result of the reading of a prospectus, as respondent claims here, but it could just as easily come as a result of a claimed reading of information contained in the financial pages of a local newspaper. Plaintiff's proof would not be that he purchased or sold stock, a fact which would be capable of documentary verification in most situations, but instead that he decided not to purchase or sell stock. Plaintiff's entire testimony could be dependent upon uncorroborated oral evidence of many of the crucial elements of his claim, and still be sufficient to go to the jury. . . . [A purchaser and seller rule] limits the class of plaintiffs to those who have at least dealt in the security to which the prospectus, representation, or omission relates. And their dealing in the security, whether by way of purchase or sale, will generally be an objectively demonstrable fact in an area of the law otherwise very much dependent upon oral testimony. [Otherwise] bystanders to the securities marketing process could await developments on the sidelines without risk, claiming that inaccuracies in disclosure caused nonselling in a falling market and that unduly pessimistic predictions by the issuer followed by a rising market caused them to allow retrospectively golden opportunities to pass. . . .

The actual holding of *Blue Chip Stamps*—that standing to sue in private actions under Rule 10b-5 is limited to actual purchasers or sellers of securities (though not necessarily to those in privity with the defendant) — reaffirmed the well-known *Birnbaum* rule (a reference to *Birnbaum v. Newport Steel Corp.*, 193 F.2d 461 (2d Cir.), *cert. denied*, 343 U.S. 956 (1952)). However, its application in this particular case was contestable, given that the consent decree that occasioned the offering in the first place specified precisely who was entitled to buy, in what amounts, and at what prices, thus eliminating some of the "hazy issues of historical fact" that the Court feared. The animating factor behind the decision, then — as reflected in Justice Rehnquist's tone and style of reasoning — appears to have been the assumption that Rule 10b-5 had become a dangerous weapon in the hand of strike-suit plaintiffs and for that reason alone deserved curtailment. In dissent, Justices Blackmun, Douglas, and Brennan charged the Court with a "preternatural solicitousness for corporate well-being and a seeming callousness toward the investing public." Id. at 762.

Rhetoric aside, the extent of the Court's holding should be clear: Even in the case where fraudulent inducement of a person's "no sale" or "no purchase" decision can be established beyond any doubt — that is, where the bona fides of a "frustrated seller's" suit is unquestioned — there is still no standing to sue. *See, e.g., Gurley v. Documation Inc.*, 674 F.2d 253, 256-257 (4th Cir. 1982). Is this throwing the baby out with the bath water?

As commonly understood prior to the Supreme Court's ruling, the *Birnbaum* rule was filled with judicially recognized exceptions, and the logical question after *Blue Chip Stamps* has been the extent to which these various exceptions survive the Court's holding. For example, what of the plaintiff who complains that he was fraudulently induced to delay a planned transaction? *See Gurley*, supra (delayed sale exception does not survive *Blue Chip Stamps*).

NOTES AND QUESTIONS

1. Equitable Relief.   Given the reasoning behind *Blue Chip Stamps*, should the purchaser-seller rule be applied when the plaintiff seeks only equitable relief? The leading pre-*Blue Chip Stamps* case recognizing this exception was *Mutual Shares Corp. v. Genesco*, 384 F.2d 540 (2d Cir. 1967), where current shareholders of a corporation were granted standing to seek an injunction against management, which was alleged to have kept dividends to a minimum in fraudulent fashion in order to induce existing minority shareholders to sell their stock at depressed prices. Subsequently, a number of courts have "assumed" that this sort of reasoning still applies, at least with respect to the right sort of case. *See Tully v. Mott Supermarkets Inc.*, 540 F.2d 187 (3d Cir. 1976); *Warner Communications Inc. v. Murdoch*, 581 F. Supp. 1482, 1494 (D. Del. 1984). *But see Cowin v. Bresler*, 741 F.2d 410 (D.C. Cir. 1984).

2. Employee Benefit Plans.   Should employees who receive employer stock (or options) as part of the retirement portion of their compensation package have standing to sue the company for problems that were undisclosed at the time they received the stock? In a well-known case, *International Brotherhood of Teamsters v. Daniel*, 439 U.S. 551 (1979), the Supreme Court held that interests in pension plans that are noncontributory and involuntary (i.e., employees have no choice but to participate in the plan) are not securities, because — per the

Howey test, discussed in Chapter 2—labor is not an "investment of money." The *Daniel* decision has since been extended to awards of stock options to employees, on the theory that while options are "securities," their award as part of a broad, company-wide plan does not count as a "sale" for the purposes of a private lawsuit. *See Fraser v. Fiduciary Trust Co. Int'l*, 417 F. Supp. 2d 310, 318 (S.D.N.Y. 2006). Individually negotiated compensation packages that include an options component, however, may be treated as securities sales. Securities Act Release No. 6188 (Feb. 1, 1980); *see also In re Cendant Corp. Sec. Litig.*, 76 F. Supp. 2d 539, 543-546 (D.N.J. 1999). For a criticism of this line of case law, *see* Bodie, Aligning Incentives with Equity: Employee Stock Options and Rule 10b-5, 88 Iowa L. Rev. 539 (2003). Note, however, that at least some employee benefit plans are regulated by ERISA, which permits claims for breach of fiduciary duty by plan administrators, including nondisclosure. Thus, many securities class actions have a companion ERISA claim on behalf of company employees, which can be awkward because the PSLRA does not apply to ERISA claims. *See Rogers v. Baxter Int'l Inc.*, 521 F.3d 702, 704 (7th Cir. 2008).

PROBLEM

13-2. Cary Pierpoint was a large shareholder of the Molybdenum Corporation of America (MCA). Desiring to liquidate his investment, he entered into an arrangement with Boister Partners Inc. to sell his block of securities for a combination of cash and promissory notes, subject to a 30-day "cooling-off" clause giving Pierpoint the opportunity to back out if "facts or conditions arose that, in the judgment of [Pierpoint], made performance impracticable." Upon learning of the deal, the officials of MCA were troubled: They knew of the Boister group and its reputation as takeover artists. At a meeting with Pierpoint, MCA officials gave him false information regarding Boister's willingness and ability to pay its debts. As a result, Pierpoint invoked the cooling-off clause and refused to perform. Upon subsequently learning of the fraudulent statements, Pierpoint brought suit against MCA and its officials, claiming a violation of Rule 10b-5. Does Pierpoint have standing to sue?

C. Scienter: Hochfelder *and Beyond*

1. Defining Scienter

In one of its first major "retrenchment" decisions dealing with Rule 10b-5 in the mid-1970s, the Supreme Court held in *Ernst & Ernst v. Hochfelder*, 425 U.S. 185 (1976), that private actions under Rule 10b-5 must show that the defendant acted with scienter in order to succeed. *Hochfelder* involved the fraudulent mismanagement of the First Securities Company by its principal executive, Nay, who misappropriated customer funds in so-called escrow accounts that he had helped establish. By the time of the lawsuit, Nay had committed suicide and First Securities was bankrupt. In search of compensation, plaintiffs brought suit against the accounting firm of Ernst & Ernst, charging it with aiding and abetting Nay's fraud by failing to utilize appropriate audit procedures that, among other things, would have uncovered Nay's "mail rule" barring any other firm employees from opening mail addressed to him. Plaintiffs argued that had Ernst & Ernst exposed the mail rule as an irregular procedure preventing an effective audit, the resulting investigation would have revealed the fraudulent scheme. In this sense, plaintiffs' argument was based simply upon Ernst & Ernst's lack of diligence—a negligence claim.

In rejecting plaintiffs' argument, the Court derived a "scienter" requirement largely from the language of Section 10(b), which gives the Commission rulemaking authority to proscribe manipulative or deceptive devices or contrivances—all words that connote some form of deliberate scheme. "When a statute speaks so specifically in terms of manipulation and deception, and of implementing devices and contrivances—the commonly understood terminology of intentional wrongdoing—and when its history reflects no more expansive intent, we are quite unwilling to extend the scope of the statute to negligent conduct." Id. at 214. The Court contrasted Section 10(b)'s language with those statutory provisions (such as Section 11 of the '33 Act) that specifically impose liability for negligent conduct, and reasoned that to permit Section 10(b) claims to be grounded in negligence would obliterate the distinction between the different types of liability, thus "nullify[ing] the effectiveness of the carefully drawn procedural restrictions" placed on the express private rights of action contained in the '33 Act. Id. at 210. Subsequently, *Hochfelder* was extended to actions brought by the SEC in *SEC v. Aaron*, 446 U.S. 680 (1980).

Unfortunately, while *Hochfelder* rejected negligence as sufficient to trigger Section 10(b) liability, the Court provided little clarity as to what, precisely, it meant by *scienter*. In a footnote, the Court described *scienter* as referring to "a mental state embracing intent to deceive, manipulate or defraud"; elsewhere, it spoke of action "other than in good faith." *Hochfelder*, 425 U.S. at 193 n.12. But what does this mean? *See* Cox, *Ernst & Ernst v. Hochfelder:* A Critique and Evaluation, 28 Hastings L.J. 569 (1977).

The question mainly arises in private litigation, because the SEC can avoid showing scienter entirely by bringing a case under Section 17(a) of the '33 Act (discussed supra in Chapter 9). Two questions about the scienter requirement are particularly important. First, what sort of intent must the defendant harbor? Must the defendant have intended to harm victims of the fraud, or merely to mislead them? Though the latter is the dominant view, there is some authority for the former. *Compare Basic Inc. v. Levinson*, 485 U.S. 224, 239 n.17 (1988) (good-faith lie intended to protect company's interests is still prohibited by Section 10(b)); *Nakkhumpun v. Taylor*, 782 F.3d 1142 (10th Cir. 2015) ("scienter does not require the defendants to act with the primary purpose of deceiving shareholders. Scienter would also exist if [the defendant misled shareholders] out of an effort to fulfill his fiduciary duties"); *United States v. Simon*, 425 F.2d 796 (2d Cir. 1969) (affirming criminal conviction for conspiracy to violate the Exchange Act; government's burden "was not to show that defendants were wicked men with designs on anyone's purse, which they obviously were not, but rather that they had certified a statement knowing it to be false") *with ECA & Local 134 IBEW Joint Pension Trust of Chi. v. JP Morgan Chase Co.*, 553 F.3d 187 (2d Cir. 2009) (JP Morgan lacked scienter when falsifying its own financial statements to disguise loans to Enron as trades; "Plaintiffs have argued that JPMC concealed its transactions with Enron in return for excessive fees. . . . It seems implausible to have both an intent to earn excessive fees for the corporation and also an intent to defraud Plaintiffs by losing vast sums of money.").

The second interpretative issue, the subject of a good bit more litigation, is the question of the level of purposefulness required to trigger liability. Must the defendant have intended to bring about a particular result, or is it sufficient if the defendant either knew the result would follow or was recklessly indifferent to the possibility? Although the Supreme Court left this question open in *Hochfelder*, the overwhelming weight of authority among the courts of appeals has been that knowledge is sufficient, as is some high degree of recklessness. *See AUSA Life Insurance Co. v. Ernst & Young*, 206 F.3d 202 (2d Cir. 2000) (reversing district court because it "inappropriately [made] the scienter issue one of 'what did the defendant want to happen,' as opposed to 'what could the defendant reasonably foresee as a potential result of his action'"); *SEC v. Falstaff Brewing Co.*, 629 F.2d 62, 76 (D.C. Cir. 1980) (enough that the defendant appreciated the misleading nature and consequences of his words or actions); *Masel v. Villarreal*, 924 F.3d 734 (5th Cir. 2019) (scienter includes "severe recklessness" . . . defined as an extreme departure from the standards of ordinary care" such that the "danger of misleading buyers or sellers . . . is either known to the defendant or is so obvious that the defendant must have been aware of it"). For a discussion of lingering indeterminacies in how the standard is interpreted, *see* Buell, What Is Securities Fraud?, 61 Duke L.J. 511 (2011).

One final question that often arises in this area has to do with "ignorance of the law." Not surprisingly, it is no excuse. But what if the defendant was advised by counsel that his action was lawful? Does that negate *Hochfelder*'s bad faith standard? In *Pittsburgh Terminal Corp. v. Baltimore & Ohio Railroad*, 680 F.2d 933, 942 (3d Cir. 1982), *cert. denied*, 459 U.S. 1056 (1983), the court distinguished two situations:

> Advice of counsel may bear upon scienter in some cases; where, for example, directors rely upon counsel to conduct an investigation of the truth of information to be released; or where counsel mistakenly but in good faith represent that some information is either immaterial or clear. In such instances the defendants may not have an appreciation of the consequences of their conduct. But where, as here, they know the materiality of the concealed information and intend the consequences of concealment, advice of counsel that they will not incur liability cannot be recognized as a defense.

But see Hawes & Sherrard, Reliance on Advice of Counsel in Corporate and Securities Cases, 62 Va. L. Rev. 1 (1976).

PROBLEM

13-3.   Advanced Technologies Inc. (ATI) was a fast-growing firm in terms of both its internal revenue growth and its repeated acquisitions of other companies that were financed with ATI stock. In October 2005, it was notified by the SEC that an investigation was underway, looking into various accounting practices regarding the way the company was recognizing revenue. A week later, ATI was about to issue its first-quarter revenue and earnings results, which were coming in just above Wall Street analyst estimates. ATI was also nearing completion of a major acquisition of a would-be competitor, a deal considered very significant to the company's long-term strategy. At a high-level meeting to discuss the substance of the revenue and earnings release, ATI's CEO, Sarah Ferguson, asked whether disclosure of anything related to the SEC investigation was necessary, pointing out that if the accounting wasn't right, ATI was "in serious muck." The company's general counsel and CFO said they had been discussing the matter and had "gotten comfortable" with not disclosing anything. The outside auditor, they said, agreed, and they were confident that ATI's accounting would be vindicated. Hence, Ferguson signed off on the release.

A year later, under pressure from the SEC, ATI restated its financials for the period in question, and is now enmeshed in litigation on a variety of fronts. Assuming that ATI's accounting was false and misleading at the time, did Ferguson violate Rule 10b-5? What about ATI itself?

2.   Pleading Scienter

Once we have settled on a specific state of mind that will trigger Section 10(b) liability, a separate but related issue concerns how the existence or absence of that state of mind will be established in court. Direct insight into a defendant's true mental state is, of course, impossible; therefore, indirect evidence must be presented. Problems of this sort are common to any action that contains a state-of-mind requirement, but Section 10(b) presents particular challenges because in 1995, Congress imposed a special, heightened pleading requirement for private complaints alleging Section 10(b) violations.

Tellabs, Inc. v. Makor Issues & Rights, Ltd.
551 U.S. 308 (2007)

Justice GINSBURG delivered the opinion of the Court.
This Court has long recognized that meritorious private actions to enforce federal antifraud securities laws are an essential supplement to criminal prosecutions and civil enforcement actions brought, respectively, by the Department of Justice and the Securities and Exchange Commission (SEC). Private securities fraud actions, however, if not adequately contained, can be employed abusively to impose substantial costs on companies and individuals whose conduct conforms to the law. As a check against abusive litigation by private parties, Congress enacted the Private Securities Litigation Reform Act of 1995 (PSLRA).

Exacting pleading requirements are among the control measures Congress included in the PSLRA. . . . As set out in §21D(b)(2) of the PSLRA, plaintiffs must "state with particularity facts giving rise to a strong inference that the defendant acted with the required state of mind."

Congress left the key term "strong inference" undefined, and Courts of Appeals have divided on its meaning. In the case before us, the Court of Appeals for the Seventh Circuit held that the "strong inference" standard would be met if the complaint "allege[d] facts from which, if true, a reasonable person could infer that the defendant acted with the required intent." That formulation, we conclude, does not capture the stricter demand Congress sought to convey in §21D(b)(2). . . .

I

Petitioner Tellabs, Inc., manufactures specialized equipment used in fiber optic networks. During the time period relevant to this case, petitioner Richard Notebaert was Tellabs' chief executive officer and president. Respondents (Shareholders) are persons who purchased Tellabs stock between December 11, 2000, and June 19, 2001. They accuse Tellabs and Notebaert (as well as several other Tellabs executives) of engaging in a scheme to deceive the investing public about the true value of Tellabs' stock.

Beginning on December 11, 2000, the Shareholders allege, Notebaert (and by imputation Tellabs) "falsely reassured public investors, in a series of statements . . . that Tellabs was continuing to enjoy strong demand for its products and earning record revenues," when, in fact, Notebaert knew the opposite was true. . . . Based on Notebaert's sunny assessments, the Shareholders contend, market analysts recommended that investors buy Tellabs' stock.

The first public glimmer that business was not so healthy came in March 2001 when Tellabs modestly reduced its first quarter sales projections. In the next months, Tellabs made progressively more cautious statements about its projected sales. On June 19, 2001, the last day of the class period, Tellabs disclosed that demand for [its flagship product] had significantly dropped. Simultaneously, the company substantially lowered its revenue projections for the second quarter of 2001. The next day, the price of Tellabs stock, which had reached a high of $67 during the period, plunged to a low of $15.87. . . .

II

In an ordinary civil action, the Federal Rules of Civil Procedure require only "a short and plain statement of the claim showing that the pleader is entitled to relief." [Rule 8(a)(2).] . . . Prior to the enactment of the PSLRA, the sufficiency of a complaint for securities fraud was governed not by Rule 8, but by the heightened pleading standard set forth in Rule 9(b). Rule 9(b) applies to "all averments of fraud or mistake"; it requires that "the circumstances constituting fraud . . . be stated with particularity" but provides that "[m]alice, intent, knowledge, and other condition of mind of a person, may be averred generally."

Courts of Appeals diverged on the character of the Rule 9(b) inquiry in §10(b) cases. . . . Setting a uniform pleading standard for §10(b) actions was among Congress' objectives when it enacted the PSLRA. . . . But "Congress did not . . . throw much light on what facts . . . suffice to create [a strong] inference," or on what "degree of imagination courts can use in divining whether" the requisite inference exists. . . . Our task is to prescribe a workable construction of the "strong inference" standard, a reading geared to the PSLRA's twin goals: to curb frivolous, lawyer-driven litigation, while preserving investors' ability to recover on meritorious claims.

III

A

We establish the following prescriptions: *First*, faced with a Rule 12(b)(6) motion to dismiss a §10(b) action, courts must, as with any motion to dismiss for failure to plead a claim on which relief can be granted, accept all factual allegations in the complaint as true. . . .

Second, courts must consider the complaint in its entirety, as well as other sources courts ordinarily examine when ruling on Rule 12(b)(6) motions to dismiss, in particular, documents incorporated into the complaint by reference, and matters of which a court may take judicial notice. The inquiry, as several Courts of Appeals have recognized, is whether *all* of the facts alleged, taken collectively, give rise to a strong inference of scienter, not whether any individual allegation, scrutinized in isolation, meets that standard.

Third, in determining whether the pleaded facts give rise to a "strong" inference of scienter, the court must take into account plausible opposing inferences. The Seventh Circuit expressly declined to engage in such a comparative inquiry. A complaint could survive, that court said, as long as it "alleges facts from which, if true, a reasonable person could infer that the defendant acted with the required intent"; in other words, only "[i]f a reasonable person could not draw such an inference from the alleged facts" would the defendant prevail on a motion to dismiss. But in §21D(b)(2), Congress did not merely require plaintiffs to "provide a factual basis for [their] scienter allegations," *i.e.*, to allege facts from which an inference of scienter rationally *could* be drawn. Instead, Congress required plaintiffs to plead with particularity facts that give rise to a "strong"—*i.e.*, a powerful or cogent—inference.

The strength of an inference cannot be decided in a vacuum. The inquiry is inherently comparative: How likely is it that one conclusion, as compared to others, follows from the underlying facts? To determine whether the plaintiff has alleged facts that give rise to the requisite "strong inference" of scienter, a court must consider plausible nonculpable explanations for the defendant's conduct, as well as inferences favoring the plaintiff. The inference that the defendant acted with scienter need not be irrefutable, *i.e.*, of the "smoking-gun" genre, or even the "most plausible of competing inferences." Recall in this regard that §21D(b)'s pleading requirements are but one constraint among many the PSLRA installed to screen out frivolous suits, while allowing meritorious actions to move forward. Yet the inference of scienter must be more than merely "reasonable" or "permissible"—it must be cogent and compelling, thus strong in light of other explanations. A complaint will survive, we hold, only if a reasonable person would deem the inference of scienter cogent and at least as compelling as any opposing inference one could draw from the facts alleged.

B

Tellabs contends that when competing inferences are considered, Notebaert's evident lack of pecuniary motive will be dispositive. The Shareholders, Tellabs stresses, did not allege that Notebaert sold any shares during the class period. While it is true that motive can be a relevant consideration, and personal financial gain may weigh heavily in favor of a scienter inference, we agree with the Seventh Circuit that the absence of a motive alle-gation is not fatal. As earlier stated, allegations must be considered collectively; the significance that can be ascribed to an allegation of motive, or lack thereof, depends on the entirety of the complaint. . . .

The judgment of the Court of Appeals is vacated, and the case is remanded for further proceedings consistent with this opinion.

Justice SCALIA, concurring in the judgment.

I fail to see how an inference that is merely "at least as compelling as any opposing inference," can conceivably be called what the statute here at issue requires: a "strong inference." If a jade falcon were stolen from a room to which only A and B had access, could it *possibly* be said there was a "strong inference" that B was the thief? I think not, and I therefore think that the Court's test must fail. In my view, the test should be whether the inference of scienter (if any) is *more plausible* than the inference of innocence.

With the above exceptions, I am generally in agreement with the Court's analysis, and so concur in its judgment.

Justice STEVENS, dissenting.

The basic purpose of the heightened pleading requirement in the context of securities fraud litigation is to protect defendants from the costs of discovery and trial in unmeritorious cases. Because of its intrusive nature, discovery may also invade the privacy interests of the defendants and their executives. Like cit-izens suspected of having engaged in criminal activity, those defendants should not be required to produce their private effects unless there is probable cause to believe them guilty of misconduct. Admittedly, the probable-cause standard is not capable of precise measurement, but it is a concept that is familiar to judges. As a matter of normal English usage, its meaning is roughly the same as "strong inference." Moreover, it is most unlikely that Congress intended us to adopt a standard that makes it more difficult to commence a civil case than a criminal case.

If, using that same methodology, we assume (as we must) the truth of the detailed factual allegations attributed to 27 different confidential informants described in the complaint, and view those allegations collectively, I think it clear that they establish probable cause to believe that Tellabs' chief executive officer "acted with the required intent," as the Seventh Circuit held.

Makor Issues & Rights, Ltd. v. Tellabs Inc.
513 F.3d 702 (7th Cir. 2008)

POSNER, Circuit Judge. The [Supreme] Court [has] remanded the case to us with directions to consider whether the plaintiffs' allegations of securi-ties fraud in violation of section 10(b) of the Securities Exchange Act of 1934 and SEC Rule 10b-5 create the "strong inference" of scienter, as defined by the Supreme Court. . . .

There are two competing inferences (always assuming of course that the plaintiffs are able to prove the allegations of the complaint). One is that the company knew (or was reckless in failing to realize, but we shall not have to discuss that possibility separately) that the statements were false, and material to investors. The other is that although the statements were false and material, their falsity was the result of innocent, or at worst careless, mistakes at the executive level. Suppose a clerical worker in the company's finance department accidentally overstated the company's earnings and the erroneous figure got reported in good faith up the line to Notebaert or other senior management, who then included the figure in their public announcements. Even if senior management had been careless in failing to detect the error, there would be no corporate scienter. . . . To establish corporate liability for a violation of Rule 10b-5 requires "look[ing] to the state of mind of the individual corporate official or officials who make or issue the statement (or order or approve it or its making or issuance, or who furnish information or language for inclusion therein, or the like) rather than generally to the collective knowledge of all the corporation's officers and employees acquired in the course of their employment." *Southland Securities Corp. v. INSpire Ins. Solutions, Inc.*, 365 F.3d 353, 366 (5th Cir. 2004) (footnote omitted). A corporation is liable for statements by employees who have apparent authority to make them. . . .

The critical question, therefore, is how likely it is that the allegedly false statements that we quoted earlier in this opinion were the result of merely careless mistakes at the management level based on false information fed it from below, rather than of an intent to deceive or a reckless indifference to whether the statements were misleading. It is exceedingly unlikely. The 5500 and the 6500 were Tellabs's most important products. The 5500 was described by the company as its "flagship" product and the 6500 was the 5500's heralded successor. They were to Tellabs as Windows XP and Vista are to Microsoft. That no member of the company's senior management who was involved in authorizing or making public statements about the demand for the 5500 and 6500 knew that they were false is very hard to credit, and no plausible story has yet been told by the defendants that might dispel our incredulity. . . .

[D]efendants argue that they could have had no motive to paint the prospects for the 5500 and 6500 systems in rosy hues because within months they acknowledged their mistakes and disclosed the true situation of the two products, and because there is no indication that Notebaert or anyone else who may have been in on the fraud profited from it financially. The argument confuses expected with realized benefits. Notebaert may have thought that there was a chance that the situation regarding the two key products would right itself. If so, the benefits of concealment might exceed the costs. Investors do not like to think they're riding a roller coaster. Prompt disclosure of the truth would have caused Tellabs's stock price to plummet, as it did when the truth came out a couple of months later. Suppose the situation had corrected itself. Still, investors would have discovered that the stock was more volatile than they thought, and risk-averse investors (who predominate) do not like volatility and so, unless it can be diversified away, demand compensation in the form of a lower price; consequently the stock might not recover to its previous level. The fact that a gamble — concealing bad news in the hope that it will be overtaken by good news — fails is not inconsistent with its having been a considered, though because of the risk a reckless, gamble. See *First Commodity Corp. of Boston v. CFTC*, 676 F.2d 1, 7-9 (1st Cir. 1982). It is like embezzling in the hope that winning at the track will enable the embezzled funds to be replaced before they are discovered to be missing.

So the inference of corporate scienter is not only as likely as its opposite, but more likely. And is it cogent? Well, if there are only two possible inferences, and one is *much* more likely than the other, it must be cogent. . . . Because the alternative hypotheses—either a cascade of innocent mistakes, or acts of subordinate employees, either or both resulting in a series of false statements—are far less likely than the hypothesis of scienter at the corporate level at which the statements were approved, the latter hypothesis must be considered cogent.

And at the top of the corporate pyramid sat Notebaert, the CEO. The 5500 and the 6500 were his company's key products. Almost all the false statements that we quoted emanated directly from him. Is it conceivable that he was unaware of the problems of his company's two major products and merely repeating lies fed to him by other executives of the company? It is conceivable, yes, but it is exceedingly unlikely.

The defendants complain, finally, about the complaint's dependence on "confidential sources." The 26 "confidential sources" referred to in the complaint are important sources for the allegations not only of falsity but also of scienter. Because the Reform Act requires detailed fact pleading of falsity, materiality, and scienter, the plaintiff's lawyers in securities-fraud litigation have to conduct elaborate pre-complaint investigations—and without the aid of discovery, which cannot be conducted until the complaint is filed. Unable to compel testimony from employees of the prospective defendant, the lawyers worry that they won't be able to get to first base without assuring confidentiality to the employees whom they interview, even though it is unlawful for an employer to retaliate against an employee who blows the whistle on a securities fraud, and even though, since informants have no evidentiary privilege, their identity will be revealed in pretrial discovery, though of course a suit might never be brought or if brought might be settled before any discovery was conducted. . . .

The confidential sources listed in the complaint in this case . . . are numerous and consist of persons who from the description of their jobs were in a position to know at first hand the facts to which they are prepared to testify. . . . It would be better were the informants named in the complaint, because it would be easier to determine whether they had been in a good position to know the facts that the complaint says they learned. But the absence of proper names does not invalidate the drawing of a strong inference from informants' assertions.

We conclude that the plaintiffs have succeeded, with regard to the statements identified in our previous opinion as having been adequately alleged to be false and material, in pleading scienter in conformity with the requirements of the Private Securities Litigation Reform Act. We therefore adhere to our decision to reverse the judgment of the district court dismissing the suit.

NOTES AND QUESTIONS

1. Policy. While the courts have been fairly faithful to Congress' desire to cut back on securities fraud actions by being more demanding at the pleading stage, there have been occasional notes of frustration. Consider the following:

Remember when we were One L's? How the civil procedure professors extolled the virtues of notice pleading? . . . This case writes a sad (and over-long) epitaph to that era. Who could have expected that, in little over half a century, society would become so chary of dealing with cases on the merits that the law, like some ancient amphibian, would begin to slip back into the primeval ooze of common law forms of pleading?

In re Number Nine Visual Technology Corp. Sec. Litig., 51 F. Supp. 2d 1, 4 (D. Mass. 1999) (Young, J.). Does *Tellabs* strike a healthy balance?

   2.   What Kinds of Facts?   The Second Circuit in *Novak v. Kasaks,* 216 F.3d 300 (2d Cir. 2000), said that a strong inference may arise when the complaint sufficiently alleges

> that the defendants (1) benefited in a concrete and personal way from the purported fraud; (2) engaged in deliberately illegal behavior; (3) knew facts or had access to information suggesting that their public statements were not accurate; or (4) failed to check information that they had a duty to monitor.

The court in *Novak* upheld a complaint against the Ann Taylor stores chain for misrepresenting its inventory condition. Given what the court saw as strong circumstantial evidence (the company's subsequent large inventory write-down), it refused to insist that the plaintiff name in the complaint its confidential sources for the details of the scienter allegations.
   Can the plaintiffs put forward motive in order to demonstrate a strong inference of scienter? *Tellabs* says that motive is relevant, but not dispositive. One kind of motivation that courts have credited is unusual insider trading activity shortly after the alleged fraud. *See, e.g., No. 84 Employer-Teamster Fund v. American West,* 320 F.3d 920, 939 (9th Cir. 2003). On the other hand, courts have cautioned that in light of typical executive compensation arrangements, merely saying that the officers were motivated to lie to maximize compensation or keep their jobs is not enough.

   3.   Fraud by Hindsight.   One of the more often quoted phrases when courts dismiss plaintiffs' complaints alleging securities fraud is that it is impermissible to plead "fraud by hindsight." Consider the following:

> The story of this complaint is familiar in securities litigation. At one time the firm bathes itself in a favorable light. Later the firm discloses that things are less rosy. The plaintiff contends that the difference is attributable to fraud. "Must be" is the critical phrase, for the complaint offers no information other than the differences between the two statements of the firm's condition. Because only a fraction of financial deteriorations reflect fraud, plaintiffs may not proffer the differential financial statements and rest. . . . There is no "fraud by hindsight," in Judge Friendly's felicitous phrase, *Denny v. Barber,* 576 F.2d 465, 470 (2d Cir. 1978), and hindsight is all the DiLeos offer.

DiLeo v. Ernst & Young, 901 F.2d 624 (7th Cir. 1990) (Easterbrook, J.) While that may be so, requiring contemporaneous evidence of intent poses difficult problems of inference. *DiLeo* involved an action against an accounting firm and its partners for participating in false financial reporting. With no smoking gun evidence of complicity, plaintiffs argued motive and opportunity—that accounting firms gain from acquiescing in client misreporting. Judge Easterbrook rejected this inference, noting that

> [a]n accountant's greatest asset is its reputation for honesty, followed closely by its reputation for careful work. Fees for two years' audits could not approach the losses [the auditor] would suffer from a perception that it would muffle a client's fraud. And although the interests of [the audit firm's] partners and associates who worked on the audits may have diverged from the firm's . . . covering up fraud and imposing large damages on the partnership will bring a halt to the most promising career. . . . It would have been irrational for any of them to have joined cause with [the client].

Id. at 629. After Enron and the other financial scandals, which offered ample evidence of auditor acquiescence in financial misreporting—hindsight evidence, to be sure—is Judge Easterbrook's inference about likely auditor behavior convincing? If not, what is a better inference?

   4.   *Corporate Scienter.*   As Judge Posner makes clear in *Tellabs*, assessing corporate scienter—as opposed to the scienter of any given individual—is central to most fraud claims, in terms of both pleading and proof. Does the plaintiff have to show that the corporate executives who made or authorized the misstatement acted with scienter in order for the corporation to act with scienter? If not, whose scienter will be attributed to the corporation? The Sixth Circuit has extended the zone of attribution to include the knowledge of any agent "who authorized, requested, commanded, furnished information for, prepared (including suggesting or contributing language for inclusion therein or omission therefrom), reviewed, or approved the statement in which the misrepresentation was made." To that, it added "any high managerial agent or member of the board of directors who ratified, recklessly disregarded or tolerated the misrepresentation after its utterance or issuance." *In re Omnicare Inc.*, 769 F.3d 455, 477 (6th Cir. 2014).

PROBLEM

13-4.   Horizon Shipping Lines pleaded guilty to a price-fixing arrangement by which it illegally increased profits from shipments between the United States and Puerto Rico, which made up roughly one-third of the company's line of business. Thereafter, investors brought a securities class action against Horizon, alleging that the company's filings and publicity had falsely attributed its financial success to efficiencies and other legitimate competitive advantages. Without the aid of discovery, plaintiffs have no direct evidence of senior manager complicity in the conspiracy, and the company has filed a motion to dismiss for failure to meet the pleading requirement in Section 21D(b). In addition to the guilty plea, plaintiffs' complaint points out that (1) the company completed a registered public offering, with extensive due diligence, during the period of the alleged fraud; (2) the CFO during the time period resigned suddenly just before the Justice Department announced its investigation of the company, forfeiting a very large amount of accrued pension benefits as a result; (3) the company reported increasing profits during the time in question even in the face of a shrinking customer base and decline in the number of shipments; and (4) the sentencing memorandum in the antitrust case credited one of the conspirators, a mid-level manager, with providing "helpful information" about senior management's involvement in the violation, without any further elaboration. Would this be enough for the case to go forward under the heightened pleading standard? *See City of Roseville Emp. Ret. System v. Horizon Lines, Inc.*, 442 Fed. App'x 672 (3d Cir. 2011).

D.　The Affirmative Duty to Disclose

Rule 10b-5(b) proscribes false statements of material fact, and the omission of information necessary to make surrounding statements not misleading. While an outright lie easily falls within the language of the Rule, many cases are not so simple, raising the question of when a defendant's failure to speak can trigger liability.

Gallagher v. Abbott Laboratories, Inc.
269 F.3d 806 (7th Cir. 2001)

EASTERBROOK, Circuit Judge.

Year after year the Food and Drug Administration inspected the Diagnostic Division of Abbott Laboratories, found deficiencies in manufacturing quality control, and issued warnings. The Division made efforts to do better, never to the FDA's satisfaction, but until 1999 the FDA was willing to accept Abbott's promises and remedial steps. On March 17, 1999, the FDA sent Abbott another letter demanding compliance with all regulatory requirements and threatening severe consequences. This could have been read as more saber rattling—Bloomberg News revealed the letter to the financial world in June, and Abbott's stock price did not even quiver—but later developments show that it was more ominous. By September 1999 the FDA was insisting on substantial penalties plus changes in Abbott's methods of doing business. On September 29, 1999, after the markets had closed, Abbott issued a press release describing the FDA's position, asserting that Abbott was in "substantial" compliance with federal regulations, and revealing that the parties were engaged in settlement talks. Abbott's stock fell more than 6%, from $40 to $37.50, the next business day. On November 2, 1999, Abbott and the FDA resolved their differences, and a court entered a consent decree requiring Abbott to remove 125 diagnostic products from the market until it had improved its quality control and to pay a $100 million civil fine. Abbott took an accounting charge of $168 million to cover the fine and worthless inventory. The next business day Abbott's stock slumped $3.50, which together with the earlier drop implied that shareholders saw the episode as costing Abbott (in cash plus future compliance costs and lost sales) more than $5 billion. . . .

Plaintiffs in these class actions under §10(b) of the Securities Exchange Act of 1934, and the SEC's Rule 10b-5, contend that Abbott committed fraud by deferring public revelation. . . .

Much of plaintiffs' argument reads as if firms have an absolute duty to disclose all information material to stock prices as soon as news comes into their possession. Yet that is not the way the securities laws work. We do not have a system of continuous disclosure. Instead firms are entitled to keep silent (about good news as well as bad news) unless positive law creates a duty to disclose. *See, e.g., Basic, Inc. v. Levinson*, 485 U.S. 224, 239 n.17 (1988). . . . Until the Securities Act of 1933 there was no federal regulation of corporate disclosure. The 1933 Act requires firms to reveal information only when they issue securities, and the duty is owed only to persons who buy from the issuer or an underwriter distributing on its behalf; every other transaction is exempt under §4. (No member of either class contends that he purchased securities from Abbott, or an underwriter on Abbott's behalf, between March 17 and November 2.) Section 13 of the Securities Exchange Act of 1934 adds that the SEC may require issuers to file annual and other *periodic* reports—with the emphasis on periodic rather than continuous. Section 13 and the implementing regulations contemplate that these reports will be snapshots of the corporation's status on or near the filing date, with updates due not when something "material" happens, but on the next prescribed filing date.

Regulations implementing §13 require a comprehensive annual filing, the Form 10-K report, and less extensive quarterly supplements on Form 10-Q. The supplements need not bring up to date everything contained in the annual 10-K report; counsel for the plaintiff classes conceded at oral argument that nothing in Regulation S-K (the SEC's list of required disclosures) requires either an updating of Form 10-K reports more often than annually, or a disclosure in a quarterly Form 10-Q report of information about the firm's regulatory problems. The regulations that provide for disclosures on Form 10-Q tell us *which* items in the annual report must be updated (a subset of the full list), and how often (quarterly).

Many proposals have been made to do things differently—to junk this combination of sale-based disclosure with periodic follow-up and replace it with a system under which *issuers* rather than *securities* are registered and disclosure must be continuous. E.g., American Law Institute, Federal Securities Code xxvii-xxviii, §602 & commentary (1978); Securities and Exchange Commission, Report of the Advisory Committee on the Capital Formation and Regulatory Process 9-14, 36-38 (1996). . . . Whatever may be said for and against these proposals, they must be understood as projects for legislation (and to a limited extent for the use of the SEC's rulemaking powers); judges have no authority to scoop the political branches and adopt continuous disclosure under the banner of Rule 10b-5. *Especially* not under that banner, for Rule 10b-5 condemns only fraud, and a corporation does not commit fraud by standing on its rights under a periodic-disclosure system. . . .

Trying to locate some statement that was either false or materially misleading because it did not mention the FDA's position, plaintiffs pointed in the district court to several reports filed or statements made by Abbott before November 2, 1999. All but two of these have fallen by the wayside on appeal. What remain are Abbott's Form 10-K annual report for 1998 filed in March 1999 and an oral statement that Miles White, Abbott's CEO, made at the annual shareholders' meeting the next month.

Plaintiffs rely principally on Item 303(a)(3)(ii) of Regulation S-K, which provides that registration statements and annual 10-K reports must reveal

> any known trends or uncertainties that have had or that the registrant reasonably expects will have a material favorable or unfavorable impact on net sales or revenues or income from continuing operations.

The FDA's letter, and its negotiating demands, are within this description, according to the plaintiff classes. We shall assume that this is so. . . . But there is a fundamental problem: The 10-K report was filed on March 9, 1999, and the FDA's letter is dated March 17, eight days later. Unless Abbott had a time machine, it could not have described on March 9 a letter that had yet to be written.

Attempting to surmount this temporal problem, plaintiffs insist that Abbott had a "duty to correct" the 10-K report. Yet a statement may be "corrected" only if it was incorrect when made, and nothing said as of March 9 was incorrect. In order to maintain the difference between periodic-disclosure and continuous-disclosure systems, it is essential to draw a sharp line between duties to correct and duties to update. We drew just this line in *Stransky* [*v. Cummins Engine Co.*, 51 F.3d 1329 (7th Cir. 1995)] and adhere to it now. If, for example, the 10-K report had said that Abbott's net income for 1998 was $500 million, and the actual income was $400 million, Abbott would have had to fix the error. But if the 10-K report had projected a net income of $125 million for the first quarter of 1999, and accountants determined in May that the actual profit was only $100 million, there would have been nothing to correct; a projection is not rendered false when the world turns out otherwise. *See Wielgos v. Commonwealth Edison Co.*, 892 F.2d 509 (7th Cir. 1989). Amending the 10-K report to show the results for 1999 as they came in—or to supply a running narrative of the dispute between Abbott and the FDA—would *update* the report, not *correct* it to show Abbott's actual condition as of March 9.

Updating documents has its place in securities law. A registration statement and prospectus for a new issue of securities must be accurate when it is used to sell stock, and not just when it is filed. Section 12(a)(2) of the '33 Act; Regulation S-K, Item 512(a). Material changes in a company's position thus must be reflected in a registration statement promptly. But this does not imply changes in a 10-K annual report, even when that report is used (as it can be with securities registered on Form S-3, or for a shelf offering under Rule 415) as the principal disclosure document. Instead of changing the 10-K report weekly or monthly, the issuer must file and distribute an addendum to that document bringing matters up to date. *See* Form S-3, Item 11. Anyway, as we've already mentioned, Abbott did not sell any stock to the class members during the period from March 17 to November 2, 1999.

As for White's statements at the annual meeting: he said very little that was concrete (as opposed to puffery), and everything concrete was true. White said, for example:

> The outcome [of our efforts] has been growth more than five times faster than the diagnostics market. We expect this trend to continue for the foreseeable future, due to the unprecedented state of our new product cycle. By supplementing our internal investment with opportunistic technology acquisitions, Abbott's diagnostics pipeline is fuller than ever before.

The statement about past performance was accurate, and the plaintiffs have not given us any reason to doubt that White honestly believed that similar growth would continue, or that White honestly believed "Abbott's diagnostics pipeline [to be] fuller than ever before." Even with the benefit of hindsight these statements cannot be gainsaid. Here is where Rule 9(b) pinches: Plaintiffs have done nothing to meet the requirements for pleading fraud with respect to the annual meeting, even if it were possible (which we doubt) to treat as "fraud" the predictive components in White's boosterism.

NOTES AND QUESTIONS

1. Possession. Today, all courts agree that the mere possession of material nonpublic information by an issuer does not by itself give rise to a duty of disclosure. *See, e.g., Backman v. Polaroid Corp.,* 910 F.2d 10 (1st Cir. 1990) (en banc). As a result, corporate silence even with respect to highly material information may not be actionable. *See, e.g., Hill v. Gozani,* 651 F.3d 151 (1st Cir. 2011) (unsustainable marketing practices). This is true even if the marketplace is filled with misimpressions or rumors, so long as they are not attributable to the issuer. *See State Teachers Retirement Bd. v. Fluor Corp.,* 654 F.2d 843, 850 (2d Cir. 1981).

2. Half-Truths. Recall the duty to speak *completely* when voluntary statements are made (i.e., to avoid half-truths). (This was the subject, as you will recall, of the Supreme Court's *Omnicare* decision, studied in Chapter 12, the reasoning of which has been extended to cases under Rule 10b-5 as well. *E.g., Tongue v. Sanofi,* 816 F.3d 199 (2d Cir. 2016).) For example, it would be a fraud to disclose the contents of an FDA warning letter detailing regulatory problems with one product while omitting those portions of the letter objecting to an associated product that was marketed in conjunction with the first. *See In re Atossa Genetics Inc. Sec. Litig.,* 868 F.3d 784, 797 (9th Cir. 2017). Also fraudulent would be for a government contractor to tout its backlog of orders yet to be filled without revealing that there were "stop work" orders on some of them, which raises the risk that they may never be completed. *Berson v. Applied Signal Technology Inc.,* 527 F.3d 982 (9th Cir. 2008). While this doctrine does not prohibit total silence, it does say that, if the issuer thereafter comments on a matter related to the issue it wants to keep quiet, it runs the risk of liability for not saying enough to avoid misleading the public. This issue is always highly fact intensive and always bound up with questions of materiality. Would it be a half-truth for a company to announce a merger with one entity while engaging in confidential discussions regarding an alternative transaction that would preclude the merger? *See Employees' Ret. Sys. of Rhode Island v. Williams Companies*, 889 F.3d 1153 (10th Cir. 2018). *See generally* Langevoort, Half-Truths: Protecting Mistaken Inferences by Investors and Others, 52 Stan. L. Rev. 87 (1999).

3. ***Duty to Update.***   Although *Gallagher* rejects such an approach, other courts have indicated that, when an issuer makes a statement that is true when released, it assumes a duty to revise or update that statement to reflect subsequent events so long as the original statement remains "alive"—that is, it is still being relied on in the marketplace. *See Khoja v. Orexigen Therapeutics, Inc.,* 899 F.3d 988, 1015, 1017 (9th Cir. 2018) (having previously disclosed positive interim results from an ongoing drug trial, company was required to disclose subsequently obtained data that diminished their significance); *Finnerty v. Stiefel Laboratories, Inc.,* 756 F.3d 1310 (11th Cir. 2014) (plausible failure to update when company had repeatedly indicated its commitment to remaining private and family-owned but secretly began exploring a possible sale). The underlying theory is that the earlier statement is a continuing representation by its maker. *See In re Burlington Coat Factory Securities Litigation*, 114 F.3d 1410, 1432 (3d Cir. 1997). Courts that accept the duty to update often draw distinctions between forward-looking statements of important company policy (like plans to maintain a specific debt-to-equity ratio, *see Weiner v. Quaker Oats Co.,* 129 F.3d 310 (3d Cir. 1997)) and more ordinary business matters. Thus, for example, the Second Circuit refused to impose a duty to update with respect to a sudden change in a company's cigarette pricing strategy. *San Leandro Emergency Medical Group v. Philip Morris Cos.,* 75 F.3d 801 (2d Cir. 1996). Many lawyers today advise clients explicitly to disclaim the duty to update whenever making a forward-looking statement, on the assumption that investors cannot be misled by the failure to update when apprised that there will be no updating.

4. ***Duty to Correct.***   What if a company makes a statement that is false at the time, but the company has no scienter? Later, the truth is discovered. Is there an immediate duty to correct? The answer here, as *Gallagher* acknowledges, seems to be a clear-cut yes. *See In re Healthcare Compare Corp. Securities Litigation*, 75 F.3d 276 (7th Cir. 1996) (distinguishing between the duty to correct and the duty to update, and holding that a company would have a duty to correct upon discovering information regarding declining patient enrollments that was in existence when the misstatement was made but not at that time known to management).

A harder issue here tends to go to the question of when the issuer is responsible for correcting erroneous statements by third parties—such as investment analysts—that are floating around in the marketplace. In *Elkind v. Liggett & Myers Inc.,* 635 F.2d 156 (2d Cir. 1980), the court dealt with a claim by plaintiffs that Liggett & Myers (L&M) had a duty to correct overly optimistic projections and forecasts made by certain analysts. Under the facts presented, it held that the company had no such duty, since these forecasts were solely the product of persons unrelated to L&M: The company had not "placed its imprimatur, expressly or impliedly, on the analysts' projections." Id. at 163. The court suggested, however, that had L&M so involved itself with the analysts' published reports that such reports had the express or implied endorsement of the company, a duty to correct might have been triggered. Since then, many cases have imposed liability where issuers have become overly entangled with analyst reports—for example, where they edit some portions of the report but leave other statements (e.g., an overly optimistic estimate) uncorrected. *See In the Matter of Presstek Inc.*, Exchange Act Release No. 39472, Dec. 22, 1997; *In re Cypress Semiconductor Securities Litigation*, 891 F. Supp. 1369 (N.D. Cal. 1995), *aff'd sub nom. Eisenstadt v. Allen*, 113 F.3d 1240 (9th Cir. 1997). Note that while the cases on this subject often use the "duty to correct" language, what really is going on here is a determination that the company is liable for disseminating false information through the third party. If so, the issue blends into the vexing problem of separating out "primary" and "secondary" liability, to be treated in the next section. Note also that many cases charging issuers with liability for false statements by analysts and other third parties utilize a somewhat different approach, claiming that the company "adopted" the misleading third-party report after it was published. Id. This might occur, for example, if the company distributes copies of the report, or creates a hyperlink connection to the report on its own web site. On this latter issue, *see* Commission Guidance on the Use of Company Websites, Release No. 34-58288, Aug. 7, 2008. Should a company be liable if it creates a hyperlink to a favorable but erroneous report by a brokerage firm if at the same time it places a blanket warning on the site saying that it is not responsible for the content or accuracy of third-party statements?

5. *Fiduciary Duties.*   To this list of possible exceptions to the privilege not to disclose, one would also have to add the situation where there is some preexisting, fiduciary-like duty to disclose. *See SEC v. Zandford*, 535 U.S. 813 (2002) ("any distinction between omissions and misrepresentations is illusory in the context of a broker who has a fiduciary duty to her clients"); *SEC v. Cochran*, 214 F.3d 1261 (10th Cir. 2000) (officer in municipal bond firm may have a duty to disclose bid rigging to firm's government agency clients). This duty is the basis for much of the law of insider trading, which is explored thoroughly in Chapter 15.

One place where the fiduciary disclosure obligation has particular bite is in the closely held corporation context, where courts often treat shareholders as if they were mutual partners and hence fiduciaries of each other. On this basis, for example, the court in *Jordan v. Duff & Phelps*, 815 F.2d 429 (7th Cir. 1987), *cert. denied*, 485 U.S. 901 (1988), held that Duff & Phelps had a duty to disclose a deal under negotiation that would raise the book value of the company's stock in the near future to an employee-shareholder who had decided to resign and would therefore be obligated by contract to sell his stock back to the company. In dissent, Judge Posner disagreed, saying "[t]he agreement entitled Duff & Phelps to terminate Jordan as shareholder, subject only to a duty to buy back his shares at book value. The arrangement that resulted (call it 'shareholder at will') is incompatible with an inference that Duff & Phelps undertook to keep him abreast of developments affecting the value of the firm. . . ."

One should also take note of a handful of other cases that suggest the possibility of a disclosure duty when the facts and circumstances give investors reason to rely upon a particular person as a source of complete and accurate information. *See Arthur Young & Co. v. Reves*, 937 F.2d 1310, 1329-1331 (8th Cir. 1991) (imposing such a duty of disclosure upon an accounting firm assisting an agricultural cooperative in raising funds from its members). In *Jensen v. Kimble*, 1 F.3d 1073 (10th Cir. 1993), on the other hand, the court held that, even if a relationship of trust and confidence was found, there was no violation of Rule 10b-5 when a promoter negotiating a merger bought shares in one of the companies from a sophisticated investor, telling him that this sale was necessary to make the transaction happen, while (allegedly) possessing undisclosed material information. Recovery was denied because the promoter had specifically refused to share the details of the deal during the conversation and had said, "Look, Dave, I'm basically looking at this deal. You don't know it, but you want this deal to go down. . . . You have done things with me, and have I ever screwed you?" Assuming that the nondisclosed information was indeed material, would you have dismissed the case?

6.   *The Lawyer's Dilemma.*   Given the exceptions just detailed, the lingering question is whether as a practical matter they threaten to swallow up the rule. *See* Langevoort & Gulati, The Muddled Duty to Disclose Under Rule 10b-5, 57 Vand. L. Rev. 1639 (2004). When asked by a client whether immediate disclosure is required (as in the problem below), are you likely to have time to investigate thoroughly whether the conditions for the exceptions are present? And even if no immediate duty exists, what about the problem noted above—especially severe for highly visible, widely followed companies—of avoiding half-truths in any future contacts with the press or analysts if the negative information is withheld? Many experienced practitioners advise clients that, unless business circumstances indicate a compelling short-term need for confidentiality, they should behave as if the federal securities laws imposed an affirmative disclosure obligation. Keep in mind, moreover, the temporary nature of this legal issue. Even if Rule 10b-5 imposes no duty at all, it will not be long before the issuer with something to hide must file its next 10-K or 10-Q. And the scope of the 8-K "current" filing obligation is gradually expanding (though, at least for some matters, the mere failure to file a required 8-K cannot itself form the basis of Rule 10b-5 liability. *See* Exchange Act Rules 13a-11 and 15d-11).

7.   *Listing Standards.*   Quite apart from the duty to disclose under the securities laws, issuers may face an affirmative disclosure obligation from another source: the listing standards of the various stock exchanges. The New York Stock Exchange, for instance, states that a listed company "is expected to release quickly to the public any news or information which might reasonably be expected to materially affect the market for securities." New York Stock Exchange Listed Company Manual §202.05. At the same time, the NYSE permits the issuer to "weigh" the possibility that legitimate corporate goals may be endangered against "the fairness to both present and potential shareholders who at any given moment may be considering buying or selling the company's stock" in deciding when to disclose. NYSE Listed Company Manual §202.06(A).

A practical question, moreover, is what will happen if these standards are violated—delisting is unlikely except in the most rare and extreme case, and most courts are unwilling to allow investors to sue issuers for nondisclosure based on violation of the exchange listing requirements. *See, e.g., State Teachers Retirement Bd. v. Fluor Corp.*, 654 F.2d at 851-853.

PROBLEMS

13-5. You are counsel to a large, publicly held pharmaceutical company whose research and development people have been working for the past few years on a new drug that hopefully would significantly reduce the incidence of heart disease among the elderly. A year ago, a breakthrough was announced, and a number of patents were obtained, generating a good bit of excitement in both the medical and the investment communities. The company has been on a number of "top ten" buy-recommendation lists from some well-known market analysts.

Yesterday, the senior vice president for research informed the CEO that a serious side effect had been discovered by some of the company's researchers and extensive preliminary testing had indicated no immediately obvious way of overcoming the problem. It is her opinion that, while work would proceed on the drug, the prospect of it ever successfully being marketed was now less than 50 percent.

    a. Would Rule 10b-5 require prompt public disclosure of this news? (You may assume your client has no desire whatsoever to make such disclosure, hoping that subsequent testing will show the problem to be less serious than it now appears to be.) What, if any, additional facts would you need to answer the question?

    b. Suppose the company receives a phone call from a journalist who is about to publish a story for a financial publication about companies that are on track to make big breakthroughs in the coming year. She asks how the work on the drug is going and expresses concern that the company has not made any recent announcements regarding progress on the drug. How would you advise the company to respond?

13-6. In early February, Time Warner announced that it would pursue strategic alliances with other firms to reduce its substantial debt. However, by mid-March Time Warner's management quietly began exploring a stock offering as an alternative mechanism for raising the needed capital. Even though management was aware that a stock offering would substantially dilute the interest of the present stockholders with the consequential effect of adversely impacting the market price of the Time Warner shares, the company did not disclose that it was considering this option. On May 1st, Time Warner announced it would undertake a large public offering of common shares; the disclosure caused a substantial decline in its stock price. An investor class action ensued, alleging the company failed to alert investors that it was considering a dilutive public offering of shares. How would you advise the court on a pending motion to dismiss the suit? *See In re Time Warner Securities Litigation*, 9 F.3d 259, 266-267 (2d Cir. 1993).

E.　*Who Is Liable?*

One of the most challenging questions in securities litigation is who is a proper defendant when fraud is alleged. Rule 10b-5 refers to persons who "engage" in a fraudulent practice, "make" a misrepresentation or actionable omission, or "employ" a device, artifice, or scheme to defraud. Beyond this, the Exchange Act (like the Securities Act) extends liability to a person who controls a violator, with certain affirmative defenses. Controlling person liability will be covered in Chapter 14, infra.

　　Until 1994, the scope of primary liability was not often litigated because courts uniformly held that "aiding and abetting" a securities fraud was sufficient to create joint and several liability. Intentionally providing substantial assistance to a fraud would thus trigger liability. So it became common to name as defendants a wide variety of secondary participants supposedly involved in planning or executing the fraud—bankers, accountants, lawyers, and the like. Then, however, the Supreme Court held in *Central Bank of Denver v. First Interstate Bank*, 511 U.S. 164 (1994), that nothing in the language or structure of Section 10(b) indicated any congressional intent to extend the reach of the prohibition beyond the confines of primary liability. The key to the Court's analysis was that

> [i]t is inconsistent with settled methodology in §10(b) cases to extend liability beyond the scope of conduct prohibited by the statutory text. . . . As in earlier cases considering conduct prohibited by §10(b), we again conclude that the statute prohibits only the making of a material misstatement (or omission) or the commission of a manipulative act. *See Santa Fe Industries*, 430 U.S. [462,] 473 [(1977)] ("language of §10(b) gives no indication that Congress meant to prohibit any conduct not involving manipulation or deception"). . . . The proscription does not include giving aid to a person who commits a manipulative or deceptive act. We cannot amend the statute to create liability for acts that are not themselves manipulative or deceptive within the meaning of the statute. . . .

The absence of §10(b) aiding and abetting liability does not mean that secondary actors in the securities markets are always free from liability under the securities acts. Any person or entity, including a lawyer, accountant, or bank, who employs a manipulative device or makes a material misstatement (or omission) on which a purchaser or seller of securities relies may be liable as a primary violator under 10b-5, assuming all of the requirements for primary liability under Rule 10b-5 are met. In any complex securities fraud, moreover, there are likely to be multiple violators. . . .

As you will study in Chapter 14, Congress soon thereafter restored aiding and abetting liability for SEC enforcement, but not in private rights of action. From that point on, then, the question of what constitutes primary liability became crucial, at least in private litigation.

Janus Capital Group Inc. v. First Derivative Traders
564 U.S. 135 (2011)

Justice THOMAS delivered the opinion of the Court.

This case requires us to determine whether Janus Capital Management LLC (JCM), a mutual fund investment adviser, can be held liable in a private action under Securities and Exchange Commission (SEC) Rule 10b-5 for false statements included in its client mutual funds' prospectuses. Rule 10b-5 prohibits "mak[ing] any untrue statement of a material fact" in connection with the purchase or sale of securities. We conclude that JCM cannot be held liable because it did not make the statements in the prospectuses.

I

Janus Capital Group, Inc. (JCG), is a publicly traded company that created the Janus family of mutual funds. These mutual funds are organized in a Massachusetts business trust, the Janus Investment Fund. Janus Investment Fund retained JCG's wholly owned subsidiary, JCM, to be its investment adviser and administrator. JCG and JCM are the petitioners here.

Although JCG created Janus Investment Fund, Janus Investment Fund is a separate legal entity owned entirely by mutual fund investors. Janus Investment Fund has no assets apart from those owned by the investors. JCM provides Janus Investment Fund with investment advisory services, which include "the management and administrative services necessary for the operation of [Janus] Fun[d]," but the two entities maintain legal independence. At all times relevant to this case, all of the officers of Janus Investment Fund were also officers of JCM, but only one member of Janus Investment Fund's board of trustees was associated with JCM. This is more independence than is required: By statute, up to 60 percent of the board of a mutual fund may be composed of "interested persons."

As the securities laws require, Janus Investment Fund issued prospectuses describing the investment strategy and operations of its mutual funds to investors. The prospectuses for several funds represented that the funds were not suitable for market timing [i.e., the practice of rapidly trading mutual fund shares to take advantage of slight mismatches between the prices of those shares and the value of assets held by the fund] and can be read to suggest that JCM would implement policies to curb the practice. . . . Although market timing is legal, it harms other investors in the mutual fund.

In September 2003, the Attorney General of the State of New York filed a complaint against JCG and JCM alleging that JCG entered into secret arrangements to permit market timing in several funds run by JCM. After the complaint's allegations became public, investors withdrew significant amounts of money from the Janus Investment Fund mutual funds. Because Janus Investment Fund compensated JCM based on the total value of the funds and JCM's management fees comprised a significant percentage of JCG's income, Janus Investment Fund's loss of value affected JCG's value as well. JCG's stock price fell nearly 25 percent, from $17.68 on September 2 to $13.50 on September 26.

Respondent First Derivative Traders (First Derivative) represents a class of plaintiffs who owned JCG stock as of September 3, 2003. Its complaint asserts claims against JCG and JCM for violations of Rule 10b-5 and §10(b) of the Securities Exchange Act of 1934. First Derivative alleges that JCG and JCM "caused mutual fund prospectuses to be issued for Janus mutual funds and made them available to the investing public, which created the misleading impression that [JCG and JCM] would implement measures to curb market timing in the Janus [mutual funds]." "Had the truth been known, Janus [mutual funds] would have been less attractive to investors, and consequently, [JCG] would have realized lower revenues, so [JCG's] stock would have traded at lower prices."

II

We granted certiorari to address whether JCM can be held liable in a private action under Rule 10b-5 for false statements included in Janus Investment Fund's prospectuses. Under Rule 10b-5, it is unlawful for "any person, directly or indirectly, . . . [t]o make any untrue statement of a material fact" in connection with the purchase or sale of securities. To be liable, therefore, JCM must have "made" the material misstatements in the prospectuses. We hold that it did not. . . .

One "makes" a statement by stating it. When "make" is paired with a noun expressing the action of a verb, the resulting phrase is "approximately equivalent in sense" to that verb. 6 Oxford English Dictionary 66 (def. 59) (1933) (hereinafter OED); accord, Webster's New International Dictionary 1485 (def. 43) (2d ed. 1934) ("*Make* followed by a noun with the indefinite article is often nearly equivalent to the verb intransitive corresponding to that noun"). For instance, "to make a proclamation" is the approximate equivalent of "to proclaim," and "to make a promise" approximates "to promise." See 6 OED 66 (def. 59). The phrase at issue in Rule 10b-5, "[t]o make any . . . statement," is thus the approximate equivalent of "to state."

For purposes of Rule 10b-5, the maker of a statement is the person or entity with ultimate authority over the statement, including its content and whether and how to communicate it. Without control, a person or entity can merely suggest what to say, not "make" a statement in its own right. One who prepares or publishes a statement on behalf of another is not its maker. And in the ordinary case, attribution within a statement or implicit from surrounding circumstances is strong evidence that a statement was made by—and only by—the party to whom it is attributed. This rule might best be exemplified by the relationship between a speechwriter and a speaker. Even when a speechwriter drafts a speech, the content is entirely within the control of the person who delivers it. And it is the speaker who takes credit—or blame—for what is ultimately said.

This rule follows from *Central Bank of Denver, N.A. v. First Interstate Bank of Denver, N. A.*, 511 U.S. 164 (1994), in which we held that Rule 10b-5's private right of action does not include suits against aiders and abettors. Such suits—against entities that contribute "substantial assistance" to the making of a statement but do not actually make it—may be brought by the SEC, but not by private parties. A broader reading of "make," including persons or entities without ultimate control over the content of a statement, would substantially undermine *Central Bank*. If persons or entities without control over the content of a statement could be considered primary violators who "made" the statement, then aiders and abettors would be almost nonexistent. . . .

Our holding also accords with the narrow scope that we must give the implied private right of action. Although the existence of the private right is now settled, we will not expand liability beyond the person or entity that ultimately has authority over a false statement.

B

Under this rule, JCM did not "make" any of the statements in the Janus Investment Fund prospectuses; Janus Investment Fund did. Only Janus Investment Fund—not JCM—bears the statutory obligation to file the prospectuses with the SEC. The SEC has recorded that Janus Investment Fund filed the prospectuses. There is no allegation that JCM in fact filed the prospectuses and falsely attributed them to Janus Investment Fund. Nor did anything on the face of the prospectuses indicate that any statements therein came from JCM rather than Janus Investment Fund—a legally independent entity with its own board of trustees.

First Derivative suggests that both JCM and Janus Investment Fund might have "made" the misleading statements within the meaning of Rule 10b-5 because JCM was significantly involved in preparing the prospectuses. But this assistance, subject to the ultimate control of Janus Investment Fund, does not mean that JCM "made" any statements in the prospectuses. Although JCM, like a speechwriter, may have assisted Janus Investment Fund with crafting what Janus Investment Fund said in the prospectuses, JCM itself did not "make" those statements for purposes of Rule 10b-5.[12] . . .

Justice BREYER, with whom Justice GINSBURG, Justice SOTOMAYOR, and Justice KAGAN join, dissenting.

. . . [W]here can the majority find legal support for the rule that it enunciates? The English language does not impose upon the word "make" boundaries of the kind the majority finds determinative. Every day, hosts of corporate officials make statements with content that more senior officials or the board of directors have "ultimate authority" to control. So do cabinet officials make statements about

---

12. That JCM provided access to Janus Investment Fund's prospectuses on its Web site is also not a basis for liability. Merely hosting a document on a Web site does not indicate that the hosting entity adopts the document as its own statement or exercises control over its content.

matters that the Constitution places within the ultimate authority of the President. So do thousands, perhaps millions, of other employees make statements that, as to content, form, or timing, are subject to the control of another. . . .

The possibility of guilty management and innocent board is the 13th stroke of the new rule's clock. What is to happen when guilty management writes a prospectus (for the board) containing materially false statements and fools both board and public into believing they are true? Apparently under the majority's rule, in such circumstances *no one* could be found to have "ma[d]e" a materially false statement—even though under the common law the managers would likely have been guilty or liable (in analogous circumstances) for doing so as *principals* (and not as aiders and abettors). . . .

In my view, . . . [t]he specific relationships alleged among Janus Management, the Janus Fund, and the prospectus statements warrant the conclusion that Janus Management did "make" those statements. . . . The complaint states that "Janus Management, as investment advisor to the funds, is responsible for the day-to-day management of its investment portfolio and other business affairs of the funds. Janus Management furnishes advice and recommendations concerning the funds' investments, as well as administrative, compliance and accounting services for the funds." Each of the Fund's 17 officers was a vice president of Janus Management. The Fund has "no assets separate and apart from those they hold for shareholders." *In re Mutual Funds Inv. Litigation*, 384 F. Supp. 2d 845, 853, n. 3 (D. Md. 2005). Janus Management disseminated the fund prospectuses through its parent company's Web site. Janus Management employees drafted and reviewed the Fund prospectuses, including language about "market timing." And Janus Management may well have kept the trustees in the dark about the true "market timing" facts.

Given these circumstances, as long as some managers, sometimes, can be held to have "ma[d]e" a materially false statement, Janus Management can be held to have done so on the facts alleged here. The relationship between Janus Management and the Fund could hardly have been closer. Janus Management's involvement in preparing and writing the relevant statements could hardly have been greater. And there is a serious suggestion that the board itself knew little or nothing about the falsity of what was said. Unless we adopt a formal rule (as the majority here has done) that would arbitrarily exclude from the scope of the word "make" those who manage a firm—even when those managers perpetrate a fraud through an unknowing intermediary—the management company at issue here falls within that scope. We should hold the allegations in the complaint in this respect legally sufficient.

With respect, I dissent.

Justice Breyer's dissent notwithstanding, lower courts did not interpret *Janus* so strictly as to preclude liability for a corporate officer who issues false statements without board authorization. *See, e.g., In re Merck & Co., Sec., Derivative & "ERISA" Litig.*, 2011 U.S. Dist. LEXIS 87578 (D.N.J. Aug. 8, 2011). Moreover, despite *Janus'* admonition that a statement is "made by—and only by—the party to whom it is attributed," courts have been willing to infer (at least for pleading purposes) that statements can be "made" by multiple persons, even without explicit attribution. *See, e.g., Rabkin v. Lion Biotechnologies, Inc.*, 2018 U.S. Dist. LEXIS 25326 (N.D. Cal. Feb. 15, 2018); *City of Pontiac Gen. Employees' Retirement Sys. v. Lockheed Martin Corp.*, 875 F. Supp. 2d 359 (S.D.N.Y. 2012).

Nonetheless, *Janus* posed a different sort of interpretative problem, in that it focused exclusively on Rule 10b-5(b), which prohibits only "mak[ing]" a misstatement. Rules 10b-5(a) and (c) are drafted much more broadly, to prohibit "device[s]," "scheme[s]," "act[s]," and "practice[s]" to defraud. Thus, after *Janus*, there was some confusion as to whether forms of deceptive conduct that did not involve making a misstatement could nonetheless run afoul of those alternative subsections (thus rendering *Janus* itself trivial), or whether instead *Janus* should be interpreted to mean that conduct such as drafting false statements for another's use is outside the scope of the Rule entirely (a curious result, given Section 10(b)'s broad prohibition on "manipulative or deceptive device[s]"). That question was answered—somewhat—a few years later.

Lorenzo v. Securities and Exchange Commission
139 S. Ct. 1094 (2019)

[Francis Lorenzo was the director of investment banking at a broker-dealer firm. At the direction of his boss, the firm's owner, he knowingly sent e-mails to two clients that falsely described an upcoming debenture offering. The owner provided the text of the e-mails, and Lorenzo captioned each e-mail by stating that they were sent at the owner's request. Lorenzo signed each e-mail with his own name and contact information, and a note to "[p]lease call with any questions." After the SEC found that Lorenzo had violated both Rule 10b-5 and Section 17(a) of the '33 Act, Lorenzo appealed to the D.C. Circuit. The panel agreed that under *Janus*, Lorenzo had not "made" the statements in the e-mails due to the owner's authority over them, but held that his conduct nonetheless violated the other subsections of Rule 10b-5, as well as Section 17(a)(1).]

Justice BREYER delivered the opinion of the Court.

We granted review to resolve disagreement about whether someone who is not a "maker" of a misstatement under *Janus* can nevertheless be found to have violated the other subsections of Rule 10b-5 and related provisions of the securities laws, when the only conduct involved concerns a misstatement.

Section 10(b) makes it unlawful to "use or employ . . . any manipulative or deceptive device or contrivance" in contravention of Commission rules and regulations. By its authority under that section, the Commission promulgated Rule 10b-5. [Section] 17(a)(1) . . . makes it unlawful to "employ any device, scheme, or artifice to defraud." . . .

It would seem obvious that the words in these provisions are, as ordinarily used, sufficiently broad to include within their scope the dissemination of false or misleading information with the intent to defraud. By sending e-mails he understood to contain material untruths, Lorenzo "employ[ed]" a "device," "scheme," and "artifice to defraud" within the meaning of subsection (a) of the Rule, §10(b), and §17(a)(1). By the same conduct, he "engage[d] in a[n] act, practice, or course of business" that "operate[d] . . . as a fraud or deceit" under subsection (c) of the Rule. Recall that Lorenzo does not challenge the appeals court's scienter finding, so we take for granted that he sent the emails with "intent to deceive, manipulate, or defraud" the recipients. Under the circumstances, it is difficult to see how his actions could escape the reach of those provisions. . . .

These provisions capture a wide range of conduct. Applying them may present difficult problems of scope in borderline cases. Purpose, precedent, and circumstance could lead to narrowing their reach in other contexts. But we see nothing borderline about this case, where the relevant conduct . . . consists of disseminating false or misleading information to prospective investors with the intent to defraud. And while one can readily imagine other actors tangentially involved in dissemination—say, a mailroom clerk—for whom liability would typically be inappropriate, the petitioner in this case sent false statements directly to investors, invited them to follow up with questions, and did so in his capacity as vice president of an investment banking company. . . .

Lorenzo argues that, despite the natural meaning of these provisions, they should not reach his conduct. This is so, he says, because the only way to be liable for false statements is through those provisions that refer *specifically* to false statements. Other provisions, he says, concern "scheme liability claims" and are violated only when conduct other than misstatements is involved. Thus, only those who "make" untrue statements under subsection (b) can violate Rule 10b-5 in connection with statements. . . . Holding to the contrary, he and the dissent insist, would render subsection (b) of Rule 10b-5 "superfluous."

The premise of this argument is that each of these provisions should be read as governing different, mutually exclusive, spheres of conduct. But this Court and the Commission have long recognized considerable overlap among the subsections of the Rule and related provisions of the securities laws. . . . The idea that each subsection of Rule 10b-5 governs a separate type of conduct is also difficult to reconcile with the language of subsections (a) and (c). It should go without saying that at least some conduct amounts to "employ[ing]" a "device, scheme, or artifice to defraud" under subsection (a) as well as "engag[ing] in a[n] act . . . which operates . . . as a fraud" under subsection (c). . . .

Lorenzo's view that subsection (b), the making-false-statements provision, *exclusively* regulates conduct involving false or misleading statements would mean those who disseminate false statements with the intent to cheat investors might escape liability under the Rule altogether. But using false representations to induce the purchase of securities would seem a paradigmatic example of securities fraud. We do not know why Congress or the Commission would have wanted to disarm enforcement in this way. . . .

Lorenzo and the dissent make a few other important arguments. They contend that applying subsections (a) or (c) of Rule 10b-5 to conduct like his would render our decision in *Janus* . . . "a dead letter." But we do not see how that is so. In *Janus*, we considered the language in subsection (b), which prohibits the "mak[ing]" of "any untrue statement of a material fact." . . . We said nothing about the Rule's application to the dissemination of false or misleading information. And we can assume that *Janus* would remain relevant (and preclude liability) where an individual neither *makes* nor *disseminates* false information—provided, of course, that the individual is not involved in some other form of fraud.

. . . Lorenzo claims that imposing primary liability upon his conduct would erase or at least weaken what is otherwise a clear distinction between primary and secondary (*i.e.*, aiding and abetting) liability. He emphasizes that, under today's holding, a disseminator might be a primary offender with respect to subsection (a) of Rule 10b-5 (by employing a "scheme" to "defraud") and also secondarily liable as an aider and abettor with respect to subsection (b) (by providing substantial assistance to one who "makes" a false statement). . . .

We do not believe, however, that our decision creates a serious anomaly. . . . The holding of *Central Bank*, we have said, suggests the need for a "clean line" between conduct that constitutes a primary violation of Rule 10b-5 and conduct that amounts to a secondary violation. . . . The line we adopt today is just as administrable: Those who disseminate false statements with intent to defraud are primarily liable under Rules 10b-5(a) and (c), §10(b), and §17(a)(1), even if they are secondarily liable under Rule 10b-5(b). . . .

Justice THOMAS, with whom Justice GORSUCH joins, dissenting.

Even though Lorenzo undisputedly did not "make" the false statements at issue in this case under Rule 10b-5(b), the Court follows the SEC in holding him primarily liable for those statements under other provisions of the securities laws. . . . The majority's interpretation of these provisions cannot be reconciled with their text or our precedents. . . .

We can quickly dispose of Rule 10b-5(a) and §17(a)(1). The act of knowingly disseminating a false statement at the behest of its maker, without more, does not amount to "employ[ing] any device, scheme, or artifice to defraud" within the meaning of those provisions. As the contemporaneous dictionary definitions cited by the majority make clear, each of these words requires some form of planning, designing, devising, or strategizing. . . . Here, it is undisputed that Lorenzo did not engage in any conduct involving planning, scheming, designing, or strategizing, as Rule 10b-5(a) and §17(a)(1) require for a primary violation. He sent two e-mails drafted by a superior, to recipients specified by the superior, pursuant to instructions given by the superior, without collaborating on the substance of the e-mails or otherwise playing an independent role in perpetrating a fraud. That Lorenzo knew the messages contained falsities does not change the essentially administrative nature of his conduct here; he might have *assisted* in a scheme, but he did not himself plan, scheme, design, or strategize. . . .

The remaining provision, Rule 10b-5(c), seems broader at first blush. But the scope of this conduct-based provision—and, for that matter, Rule 10b-5(a) and §17(a)(1)—must be understood in light of its codification alongside a prohibition specifically addressing primary liability for false statements . . . and therefore cannot be construed to encompass primary liability solely for false statements. This view is consistent with our previous recognition that "each subparagraph of §17(a) 'proscribes a distinct category of misconduct'" and "'is meant to cover *additional* kinds of illegalities.'" *Aaron* [*v. SEC*, 446 U.S. 680,] 697 [(1980)]. . . .

[T]his approach does not . . . prevent the securities laws from mutually reinforcing one another or overlapping to some extent. It simply contemplates giving full effect to the specific prohibitions on false statements in Rule 10b-5(b) and §17(a)(2) instead of rendering them superfluous. . . .

[T]he majority fails to maintain a clear line between primary and secondary liability in fraudulent-misstatement cases. . . . If Lorenzo's conduct here qualifies for primary liability under §10(b) and Rule 10b-5(a) or (c), then virtually any person who assists with the making of a fraudulent misstatement will be primarily liable and thereby subject not only to SEC enforcement, but private lawsuits. . . .

The Court attempts to cabin the implications of its holding by highlighting several facts that supposedly would distinguish this case from a case involving a secretary or other person "tangentially involved in disseminat[ing]" fraudulent misstatements. None of these distinctions withstands scrutiny. The fact that Lorenzo "sent false statements directly to investors" in e-mails that "invited [investors] to follow up with questions," puts him in precisely the same position as a secretary asked to send an identical message from her e-mail account. And under the unduly capacious interpretation that the majority gives to the securities laws, I do not see why it would matter whether the sender is the "vice president of an investment banking company" or a secretary,—if the sender knowingly sent false statements, the sender apparently would be primarily liable. To be sure, I agree with the majority that liability would be "inappropriate" for a secretary put in a situation similar to Lorenzo's. Ibid. But I can discern no legal principle in the majority opinion that would preclude the secretary from being pursued for primary violations of the securities laws. . . .

NOTES AND QUESTIONS

1. *Is* Janus *a "Dead Letter"?*   The majority and dissent jousted over whether *Lorenzo*'s reading of the securities laws renders *Janus* a nullity. Do you think it does? How would the *Janus* defendants' conduct stack up if analyzed under the *Lorenzo* majority's standards? Under the dissent's?

As you ponder the continuing significance of *Janus*, be sure to consider how *Janus* interacts with the element of *reliance*—necessary for Section 10(b) actions brought by private plaintiffs, though not those brought by the government—and how reliance was interpreted in *Stoneridge Inv. Partners LLC v. Scientific-Atlanta Inc.*, 552 U.S. 148 (2008), discussed in the next section.

2. *Section 17(a).*   The SEC charged Lorenzo with violations of both Rule 10b-5 and Section 17(a)(1) of the '33 Act. Because Section 17(a)(1), like 10b-5(a), prohibits the use of "any device, scheme, or artifice to defraud," the Supreme Court did not separately interpret that statute. But even before *Lorenzo*, the SEC was able to avoid the impact of *Janus* by relying on Section 17(a)(2), which prohibits "any person . . . to obtain money or property by means of" false statements in connection with securities transactions, rather than by focusing on those who "make" a statement as used in Rule 10b-5(b). *See SEC v. Big Apple Consulting USA,*

783 F.3d 786 (11th Cir. 2015) (agreeing that *Janus* does not apply to Section 17(a)).

   3.   Section 20(b).   In a footnote in *Janus*, the Court stated that it would not address whether "Congress created liability for entities that act through innocent intermediaries" via Section 20(b) of the '34 Act. Section 20(b) provides that "[i]t shall be unlawful for any person, directly or indirectly, to do any act which would be unlawful for such person to do under the provisions of this title or any rule or regulation thereunder through or by means of any other person." Would that provision have helped plaintiffs?

PROBLEMS

13-7.   Octagon Corp. filed a Form 10-Q that contained false financial information regarding recent sales activity. Plaintiffs have brought a class action against the company and its senior officials charging a violation of Rule 10b-5(b) as to both the false financials and a misleading discussion in the Management Discussion and Analysis portion of the filing. The complaint claims that the wrongdoing was the fault of an overly aggressive Vice President for Marketing and his team, and that both the CEO and the CFO either knew of, or recklessly disregarded, the fraud. Assuming a sufficient showing of scienter as to each, could plaintiffs' lawsuit proceed against any of these individual defendants? Recall the materials in Chapter 11 about public company filings.

[handwritten margin note: Entity itself is liable → ultimate authority is the board under Janus]

13-8.   MGIC had a 50 percent ownership interest in C-BASS, a company heavily involved in securitizations of subprime mortgages, which were under a great deal of stress as the global financial crisis deepened in 2007. Because the earnings from C-BASS were material to MGIC's financial performance, MGIC invited two senior executives of C-BASS to take part in a conference call with investment analysts discussing MGIC's most recent financial results. According to plaintiffs, some of what the C-BASS executives said on the call to assure investors that problems were manageable was deliberately false. Would MGIC be liable? What if plaintiffs say that the MGIC executives also involved in the call either knew or recklessly disregarded this falsity but said nothing to correct the misimpressions? *See Fulton County Emp. Ret. System v. MGIC Investment Co.*, 675 F.3d 1047 (7th Cir. 2012).

13-9.   GT Advanced Technologies (GTAT) issued a series of press releases that, according to plaintiffs, falsely described its technological capabilities. GTAT's general counsel filed the press releases with the SEC on Form 8-K and signed the 8-K filings, but was otherwise uninvolved in drafting the releases themselves, all of which contained quotes attributed to other GTAT officers. Assuming the general counsel was aware that the press releases were false, did the general counsel violate Rule 10b-5? *See Levy v. Gutierrez*, 2017 U.S. Dist. LEXIS 68016 (D.N.H. May 4, 2017).

F.   *Reliance*

1.   Face-to-Face Transactions

‖ **Affiliated Ute Citizens v. United States**
‖ 406 U.S. 128 (1972)

BLACKMUN, J. [Gale and Haslem, and the bank that employed them, acted as agents for members of a tribe of Native Americans to assist them in selling their shares in a corporation (UDC) that had been formed to hold tribal assets.]

We conclude . . . that the Court of Appeals erred when it held that there was no violation of [Rule 10b-5] unless the record disclosed evidence of reliance on material fact misrepresentations by Gale and Haslem. We do not read Rule 10b-5 so restrictively. To be sure, the second subparagraph of the rule specifies the making of an untrue statement of a material fact and the omission to state a material fact. The first and third subparagraphs are not so restricted. These defendants' activities, outlined above, disclose, within the very language of one or the other of those subparagraphs, a "course of business" or a "device, scheme, or artifice" that operated as a fraud upon the Indian sellers. This is so because the defendants devised a plan and induced the mixed-blood holders of UDC stock to dispose of their shares without disclosing to them material facts [e.g., that higher prices were available in the real estate market] that reasonably could have been expected to influence their decisions to sell. The individual defendants, in a distinct sense, were market makers, not only for their personal purchases constituting 8⅓% of the sales, but for the other sales their activities produced. This being so, they possessed the affirmative duty under the Rule to disclose this fact to the mixed-blood sellers. *See Chasins v. Smith, Barney & Co.*, 438 F.2d 1167 (CA2 1970). It is no answer to urge that, as to some of the petitioners, these defendants may have made no positive representation or recommendation. The defendants may not stand mute while they facilitate the mixed-bloods' sales to those seeking to profit in the non-Indian market the defendants had developed and encouraged and with which they were fully familiar. The sellers had the right to know that the defendants were in a position to gain financially from their sales and that their shares were selling for a higher price in that market.

Under the circumstances of this case, involving primarily a failure to disclose, positive proof of reliance is not a prerequisite to recovery. All that is necessary is that the facts withheld be material in the sense that a reasonable investor might have considered them important in the making of this decision. This obligation to disclose and this withholding of a material fact establish the requisite element of causation in fact. . . .

NOTES AND QUESTIONS

1.   Reliance.   One of the most challenging doctrinal puzzles of private litigation under Rule 10b-5 is the relationship between the reliance and causation requirements. Though reliance is not a required element for government enforcement actions, courts have long said that reliance is an essential element of a private plaintiff's claim (presumably drawing on Rule 10b-5's common law antecedents). *See List v. Fashion Park Inc.*, 340 F.2d 457 (2d Cir. 1965), *cert. denied*, 382 U.S. 811 (1966). However, they have also tended to be very forgiving in applying the "requirement." But as *Affiliated Ute* shows, presumptions often are invoked to aid the plaintiff's case. In many ways, the *Affiliated Ute* presumption seems to be based on the notion that it is really causation that is the important element of the plaintiff's case. Reliance is simply the means by which causation is typically established, but other means may be substituted in the appropriate case. *See also Flamm v. Eberstadt*, 814 F.2d 1169, 1173 (7th Cir. 1986), *cert. denied*, 484 U.S. 833 (1987) ("'reliance' means only materiality and causation 'in conjunction,'" and reliance is no longer "an element independent of causation and materiality in a case under Rule 10b-5"). To this end, some courts refer to reliance as "transaction causation." *See, e.g., Schlick v. Penn-Dixie Cement Corp.*, 507 F.2d 374, 380-381 (2d Cir. 1974).

Is there anything left with respect to an independent reliance requirement? It is probably only a question of semantics. Certainly, in a case involving none of the special factors identified in *Affiliated Ute*—such as an arm's-length transaction involving an affirmative misrepresentation—the plaintiff will at least have to show enough familiarity with the document or other communication that contained the alleged falsity to negate the possibility that the transaction would have gone forward on identical terms even had there been full disclosure. The interesting questions arise in cases where some, but not all, of these factors are present.

> **2.   *Applying the Presumption.***   There is substantial authority for holding that the *Affiliated Ute* presumption is limited to cases involving omissions due to the unique difficulties of proof in that context. Thus, a number of courts have suggested that the plaintiff's burden of proving reliance remains even in a "half-truth" sort of omission case—that is, one where something was left out of a particular document or communication, rather than a case of complete silence. *E.g., Abell v. Potomac Insurance Co.*, 858 F.2d 1104 (5th Cir. 1988), *cert. denied*, 492 U.S. 918 (1989). There is authority for dispensing with proof of reliance where the allegation is of a broad scheme to defraud, rather than a specific misrepresentation or omission. *See Competitive Assocs. Inc. v. Laventhal, Krekstein, Horwath & Horwath*, 516 F.2d 811 (2d Cir. 1975) (allegedly corrupt falsifications of accounting materials as part of scheme to defraud). As you are about to see, a separate and very powerful presumption of reliance can be invoked for certain kinds of misrepresentations.

2.   Open Market Frauds: The Fraud-on-the-Market Theory

Recall *Basic Inc. v. Levinson*, 485 U.S. 224 (1988), from Chapter 12. Besides its holding on materiality, the Court also addressed reliance in the context of class actions under Rule 10b-5, and established a rebuttable presumption of reliance (much like *Affiliated Ute*) when plaintiffs claim that the market price of a company's stock was distorted by fraud and the stock was traded in an efficient marketplace. This holding was crucial to the emergence of "fraud on the market" litigation, and the precursor to all the political controversy and resulting reform efforts considered earlier in this chapter.

Halliburton Co. v. Erica P. John Fund, Inc.
573 U.S. 258 (2014)

ROBERTS, C.J.

I

Respondent Erica P. John Fund, Inc. (EPJ Fund), is the lead plaintiff in a putative class action against Halliburton and one of its executives (collectively Halliburton) alleging violations of section 10(b) of the Securities Exchange Act of 1934 . . . and Securities and Exchange Commission Rule 10b-5. . . . According to EPJ Fund, between June 3, 1999, and December 7, 2001, Halliburton made a series of misrepresentations regarding its potential liability in asbestos litigation, its expected revenue from certain construction contracts, and the anticipated benefits of its merger with another company—all in an attempt to inflate the price of its stock. . . .

II

. . .

A

The reliance element ensures that there is a proper connection between a defendant's misrepresentation and a plaintiff's injury. The traditional (and most direct) way a plaintiff can demonstrate reliance is by showing that he was aware of a company's statement and engaged in a relevant transaction—*e.g.,* purchasing common stock—based on that specific misrepresentation.

In *Basic* [*Inc. v. Levinson,* 485 U.S. 224 (1988)], however, we recognized that requiring such direct proof of reliance "would place an unnecessarily unrealistic evidentiary burden on the Rule 10b-5 plaintiff who has traded on an impersonal market." 485 U.S., at 245. That is because, even assuming an investor could prove that he was aware of the misrepresentation, he would still have to "show a speculative state of facts, *i.e.,* how he would have acted . . . if the misrepresentation had not been made." *Ibid.*

We also noted that "[r]equiring proof of individualized reliance" from every securities fraud plaintiff "effectively would . . . prevent[] [plaintiffs] from proceeding with a class action" in Rule 10b-5 suits. If every plaintiff had to prove direct reliance on the defendant's misrepresentation, "individual issues then would . . . overwhelm[] the common ones," making certification under Rule 23(b)(3) inappropriate.

To address these concerns, *Basic* held that securities fraud plaintiffs can in certain circumstances satisfy the reliance element of a Rule 10b-5 action by invoking a rebuttable presumption of reliance, rather than proving direct reliance on a misrepresentation. The Court based that presumption on what is known as the "fraud-on-the-market" theory, which holds that "the market price of shares traded on well-developed markets reflects all publicly available information, and, hence, any material misrepresentations." *Id.*, at 246. The Court also noted that, rather than scrutinize every piece of public information about a company for himself, the typical "investor who buys or sells stock at the price set by the market does so in reliance on the integrity of that price"—the belief that it reflects all public, material information. *Id.*, at 247. As a result, whenever the investor buys or sells stock at the market price, his "reliance on any public material misrepresentations . . . may be presumed for purposes of a Rule 10b-5 action." *Ibid.*

Based on this theory, a plaintiff must make the following showings to demonstrate that the presumption of reliance applies in a given case: (1) that the alleged misrepresentations were publicly known, (2) that they were material, (3) that the stock traded in an efficient market, and (4) that the plaintiff traded the stock between the time the misrepresentations were made and when the truth was revealed.

At the same time, *Basic* emphasized that the presumption of reliance was rebuttable rather than conclusive. Specifically, "[a]ny showing that severs the link between the alleged misrepresentation and either the price received (or paid) by the plaintiff, or his decision to trade at a fair market price, will be sufficient to rebut the presumption of reliance." 485 U.S., at 248. So for example, if a defendant could show that the alleged misrepresentation did not, for whatever reason, actually affect the market price, or that a plaintiff would have bought or sold the stock even had he been aware that the stock's price was tainted by fraud, then the presumption of reliance would not apply. *Id.*, at 248-249. In either of those cases, a plaintiff would have to prove that he directly relied on the defendant's misrepresentation in buying or selling the stock.

B

. . .

2

Halliburton's primary argument for overruling *Basic* is that the decision rested on two premises that can no longer withstand scrutiny. The first premise concerns what is known as the "efficient capital markets hypothesis." *Basic* stated that "the market price of shares traded on well-developed markets reflects all publicly available information, and, hence, any material misrepresentations." *Id.*, at 246. From that statement, Halliburton concludes that the *Basic* Court espoused "a robust view of market efficiency" that is no longer tenable, for "'overwhelming empirical evidence' now 'suggests that capital markets are not fundamentally efficient.'" Brief for Petitioners 14-16 (quoting Lev & de Villiers, Stock Price Crashes and 10b-5 Damages: A Legal, Economic, and Policy Analysis, 47 Stan. L. Rev 7, 20 (1994)). To support this contention, Halliburton cites studies purporting to show that "public information is often not incorporated immediately (much less rationally) into market prices." . . .

Halliburton does not, of course, maintain that capital markets are *always* inefficient. Rather, in its view, *Basic*'s fundamental error was to ignore the fact that "'efficiency is not a binary, yes or no question.'" Brief for Petitioners 20 (quoting Langevoort, *Basic* at Twenty: Rethinking Fraud on the Market, 2009 Wis. L. Rev. 151, 167)). The markets for some securities are more efficient than the markets for others, and even a single market can process different kinds of information more or less efficiently, depending on how widely the information is disseminated and how easily it is understood. . . . Yet *Basic*, Halliburton asserts, glossed over these nuances, assuming a false dichotomy that renders the presumption of reliance both underinclusive and overinclusive: A misrepresentation can distort a stock's market price even in a generally inefficient market, and a misrepresentation can leave a stock's market price unaffected even in a generally efficient one. . . .

Halliburton's criticisms fail to take *Basic* on its own terms. . . . To recognize the presumption of reliance, the Court explained, was not "conclusively to adopt any particular theory of how quickly and completely publicly available information is reflected in market price." *Id.*, at 248, n. 28. The Court instead based the presumption on the fairly modest premise that "market professionals generally consider most publicly announced material statements about companies, thereby affecting stock market prices." *Id.*, at 247, n. 24. *Basic*'s presumption of reliance thus does not rest on a "binary" view of market efficiency. Indeed, in making the presumption rebuttable, *Basic* recognized that market efficiency is a matter of degree and accordingly made it a matter of proof.

The academic debates discussed by Halliburton have not refuted the modest premise underlying the presumption of reliance. Even the foremost critics of the efficient-capital-markets hypothesis acknowledge that public information generally affects stock prices. . . . Debates about the precise *degree* to which stock prices accurately reflect public information are thus largely beside the point. . . . Halliburton has not identified the kind of fundamental shift in economic theory that could justify overruling a precedent on the ground that it misunderstood, or has since been overtaken by, economic realities. . . .

Halliburton also contests a second premise underlying the *Basic* presumption: the notion that investors "invest 'in reliance on the integrity of [the market] price.'" . . . Halliburton identifies a number of classes of investors for whom "price integrity" is supposedly "marginal or irrelevant." . . . The primary example is the value investor, who believes that certain stocks are undervalued or overvalued and attempts to "beat the market" by buying the undervalued stocks and selling the overvalued ones. . . . If many investors "are indifferent to prices," Halliburton contends, then courts should not presume that investors rely on the integrity of those prices and any misrepresentations incorporated into them. . . .

But *Basic* never denied the existence of such investors. . . . *Basic* concluded only that it is reasonable to presume that *most* investors—knowing that they have little hope of outperforming the market in the long run based solely on their analysis of publicly available information—will rely on the security's market price as an unbiased assessment of the security's value in light of all public information.

In any event, there is no reason to suppose that even Halliburton's main counterexample—the value investor—is as indifferent to the integrity of market prices as Halliburton suggests. Such an investor implicitly relies on the fact that a stock's market price will eventually reflect material information—how else could the market correction on which his profit depends occur? To be sure, the value investor does not believe that the market price accurately reflects public information *at the time he transacts.* But to indirectly rely on a misstatement in the sense relevant for the *Basic* presumption, he need only trade stock based on the belief that the market price will incorporate public information within a reasonable period. The value investor also presumably tries to estimate *how* undervalued or overvalued a particular stock is, and such estimates can be skewed by a market price tainted by fraud. . . .

C . . .

Finally, Halliburton and its *amici* contend that, by facilitating securities class actions, the *Basic* presumption produces a number of serious and harmful consequences. Such class actions, they say, allow plaintiffs to extort large settlements from defendants for meritless claims; punish innocent shareholders, who end up having to pay settlements and judgments; impose excessive costs on businesses; and consume a disproportionately large share of judicial resources. . . .

These concerns are more appropriately addressed to Congress, which has in fact responded, to some extent, to many of the issues raised by Halliburton and its *amici.* Congress has, for example, enacted the Private Securities Litigation Reform Act of 1995 (PSLRA), which sought to combat perceived abuses in securities litigation. . . .

III

. . . Halliburton contends that defendants should at least be allowed to defeat the presumption at the class certification stage through evidence that the misrepresentation did not in fact affect the stock price. We agree. . . .

There is no dispute that defendants may introduce such evidence at the merits stage to rebut the *Basic* presumption. *Basic* itself made clear that the presumption was just that, and could be rebutted by appropriate evidence, including evidence that the asserted misrepresentation (or its correction) did not affect the market price of the defendant's stock.

Nor is there any dispute that defendants may introduce price impact evidence at the class certification stage, so long as it is for the purpose of countering a plaintiff's showing of market efficiency, rather than directly rebutting the presumption. . . .

After all, plaintiffs themselves can and do introduce evidence of the *existence* of price impact in connection with "event studies"—regression analyses that seek to show that the market price of the defendant's stock tends to respond to pertinent publicly reported events. In this case, for example, EPJ Fund submitted an event study of various episodes that might have been expected to affect the price of Halliburton's stock, in order to demonstrate that the market for that stock takes account of material, public information about the company. The episodes examined by EPJ Fund's event study included one of the alleged misrepresentations that form the basis of the Fund's suit. . . .

Defendants—like plaintiffs—may accordingly submit price impact evidence prior to class certification. . . .

Suppose a defendant at the certification stage submits an event study looking at the impact on the price of its stock from six discrete events, in an effort to refute the plaintiffs' claim of general market efficiency. All agree the defendant may do this. Suppose one of the six events is the specific misrepresentation asserted by the plaintiffs. All agree that this too is perfectly acceptable. Now suppose the district court determines that, despite the defendant's study, the plaintiff has carried its burden to prove market efficiency, but that the evidence shows no price impact with respect to the specific misrepresentation challenged in the suit. The evidence at the certification stage thus shows an efficient market, on which the alleged misrepresentation had no price impact. And yet under EPJ Fund's view, the plaintiffs' action should be certified and proceed as a class action (with all that entails), even though the fraud-on-the-market theory does not apply and common reliance thus cannot be presumed.

Such a result is inconsistent with *Basic*'s own logic. Under *Basic*'s fraud-on-the-market theory, market efficiency and the other prerequisites for invoking the presumption constitute an indirect way of showing price impact. As explained, it is appropriate to allow plaintiffs to rely on this indirect proxy for price impact, rather than requiring them to prove price impact directly, given *Basic*'s rationales for recognizing a presumption of reliance in the first place.

But an indirect proxy should not preclude direct evidence when such evidence is available. As we explained in *Basic*, "[a]ny showing that severs the link between the alleged misrepresentation and . . . the price received (or paid) by the plaintiff . . . will be sufficient to rebut the presumption of reliance" because "the basis for finding that the fraud had been transmitted through market price would be gone." 485 U.S., at 248. And without the presumption of reliance, a Rule 10b-5 suit cannot proceed as a class action: Each plaintiff would have to prove reliance individually, so common issues would not "predominate" over individual ones, as required by Rule 23(b)(3). Id., at 242. Price impact is thus an essential precondition for any Rule 10b-5 class action. While *Basic* allows plaintiffs to establish that precondition indirectly, it does not require courts to ignore a defendant's direct, more salient evidence showing that the alleged misrepresentation did not actually affect the stock's market price and, consequently, that the *Basic* presumption does not apply. . . .

Our choice in this case, then, is not between allowing price impact evidence at the class certification stage or relegating it to the merits. Evidence of price impact will be before the court at the certification stage in any event. The choice, rather, is between limiting the price impact inquiry before class certification to indirect evidence, or allowing consideration of direct evidence as well. As explained, we see no reason to artificially limit the inquiry at the certification stage to indirect evidence of price impact. Defendants may seek to defeat the

Basic presumption at that stage through direct as well as indirect price impact evidence. . . .

Because the courts below denied Halliburton that opportunity, we vacate the judgment of the Court of Appeals for the Fifth Circuit and remand the case for further proceedings consistent with this opinion.

It is so ordered.

Justice THOMAS, with whom Justice SCALIA and Justice ALITO join, concurring in the judgment.

Today we are asked to determine whether *Basic* was correctly decided. The Court suggests that it was, and that *stare decisis* demands that we preserve it. I disagree. Logic, economic realities, and our subsequent jurisprudence have undermined the foundations of the *Basic* presumption, and *stare decisis* cannot prop up the facade that remains. *Basic* should be overruled.

1

The Court's first assumption was that "most publicly available information"—including public misstatements—"is reflected in [the] market price" of a security. *Id.*, at 247. The Court grounded that assumption in "empirical studies" testing a then-nascent economic theory known as the efficient capital markets hypothesis. *Id.*, at 246-247. . . . This view of market efficiency has since lost its luster. See, *e.g.*, Langevoort, *Basic* at Twenty: Rethinking Fraud on the Market, 2009 Wis. L. Rev. 151, 175 ("Doubts about the strength and pervasiveness of market efficiency are much greater today than they were in the mid-1980s"). As it turns out, even "well-developed" markets (like the New York Stock Exchange) do not uniformly incorporate information into market prices with high speed. "[F]riction in accessing public information" and the presence of "processing costs" means that "not all public information will be impounded in a security's price with the same alacrity, or perhaps with any quickness at all." Cox, Understanding Causation in Private Securities Lawsuits: Building on *Amgen*, 66 Vand. L. Rev. 1719, 1732 (2013). For example, information that is easily digestible (merger announcements or stock splits) or especially prominent (Wall Street Journal articles) may be incorporated quickly, while information that is broadly applicable or technical (Securities and Exchange Commission filings) may be incorporated slowly or even ignored. . . .

Further, and more importantly, "overwhelming empirical evidence" now suggests that even when markets do incorporate public information, they often fail to do so accurately. Lev and de Villiers, Stock Price Crashes and 10b-5 Damages: A Legal, Economic and Policy Analysis, 47 Stan. L. Rev. 7, 20-21 (1994). "Scores" of "efficiency-defying anomalies"—such as market swings in the absence of new information and prolonged deviations from underlying asset values—make market efficiency "more contestable than ever." Such anomalies make it difficult to tell whether, at any given moment, a stock's price accurately reflects its value as indicated by all publicly available information. In sum, economists now understand that the price impact *Basic* assumed would happen reflexively is actually far from certain even in "well-developed" markets.

Thus, *Basic*'s claim that "common sense and probability" support a presumption of reliance rests on shaky footing.

2

The *Basic* Court also grounded the presumption of reliance in a second assumption: that "[a]n investor who buys or sells stock at the price set by the market does so in reliance on the integrity of that price." 485 U.S., at 247. In other words, the Court assumed that investors transact based on the belief that the market price accurately reflects the underlying "'value'" of the security. . . .

It cannot be seriously disputed that a great many investors do *not* buy or sell stock based on a belief that the stock's price accurately reflects its value. Many investors in fact trade for the opposite reason — that is, because they think the market has under- or overvalued the stock, and they believe they can profit from that mispricing. *Id.*, at 256 (opinion of White, J.). . . . Other investors trade for reasons entirely unrelated to price — for instance, to address changing liquidity needs, tax concerns, or portfolio balancing requirements. . . . These investment decisions — made with indifference to price and thus without regard for price "integrity" — are at odds with *Basic*'s understanding of what motivates investment decisions. In short, *Basic*'s assumption that all investors rely in common on "price integrity" is simply wrong. . . .

The majority also suggests that "there is no reason to suppose" that investors who buy stock they believe to be undervalued are "indifferent to the integrity of market prices.". . . Whether the majority's unsupported claims about the thought processes of hypothetical investors are accurate or not, they are surely beside the point. Whatever else an investor believes about the market, he simply does not "rely on the integrity of the market price" if he does not believe that the market price accurately reflects public information *at the time he transacts*. That is, an investor cannot claim that a public misstatement induced his transaction by distorting the market price if he did not buy at that price while believing that it accurately incorporated that public information. For that sort of investor, *Basic*'s critical fiction falls apart.

NOTES AND QUESTIONS

1.   Class Certification and Market Efficiency.   What factual findings does the trial judge have to make to justify class certification? Putting aside questions about the lead plaintiffs (typicality of their claims, adequacy of representation, etc.), *Halliburton* explained that the plaintiffs are entitled to a presumption of reliance — which will then establish commonality among class members — if they establish the three prerequisites for that presumption. The most important of these is that the securities in question were traded in an "efficient market." Typically, market efficiency has been assessed by reference to the so-called *Cammer* factors. *See Cammer v. Bloom*, 711 F. Supp. 1264 (D.N.J. 1989) (five-factor test: extent of weekly volume, how many stock analysts follow the company, number of market-makers and arbitrageurs, status as an S-3 issuer, data showing close connections between release of information and prompt changes in stock price). Prior to *Halliburton*, courts could be quite strict about the application of these factors, requiring a close relationship between the release of news and its impoundment in price. *See In re Polymedica Sec. Litig.*, 432 F.3d 1 (1st Cir. 2005) (courts must determine if the "market price responds so quickly to new information that ordinary investors cannot make trading profits on the basis of such information"). After *Halliburton*, however, the Supreme Court's admonition that the presumption of reliance rests on only the "modest premise . . . that public information generally affects stock prices" has apparently caused some courts to soften their approach. *See, e.g., Waggoner v. Barclays PLC*, 875 F.3d 79, 97 (2d Cir. 2017) ("the burden required to establish market efficiency 'is not an onerous one'" (quoting *In re Petrobras Securities Litig.*, 862 F.3d 250, 278 (2d Cir. 2017))); *see also In re Groupon Inc. Sec. Litig.*, 2015 U.S. Dist. LEXIS 27334 (N.D. Ill. Mar. 5, 2015) (plaintiffs' expert "correctly analyzed 'market efficiency' from the perspective of whether unexpected information quickly affected Groupon stock prices—not whether the price of Groupon stock accurately reflected *all* information").

2. *Price Impact and the Role of Event Studies.* The *Halliburton* Court described the role of "event studies" in class certification. An event study is a statistical method for determining whether some corporate event, such as an announcement of earnings, is associated with a change in the price of a company's securities. In a securities class action, event studies play multiple roles. First, the plaintiffs may use them to establish the fifth *Cammer* factor, namely, the general association between news and changes in the relevant security's price, thereby contributing to a finding that the security traded in an efficient market. Second, defendants may use them to try to prove that a particular alleged false statement *did not* in fact affect the price of the security, thereby rebutting the presumption of price impact, and thus reliance. Third, both plaintiffs and defendants may use them to assess the damages associated with a particular false statement once the truth finally emerges.

As originally developed by financial economists, event studies observed phenomena shared by a portfolio of companies, such as earnings increases announced by multiple firms. Event studies in securities litigation, however, almost always involve only a single firm as they seek to isolate and measure price moves of a particular (defendant) firm involved in the litigation. Importing a methodology long used by economists for studies of phenomena shared by multiple firms into a single-firm context raises profound methodological concerns, namely in terms of the model's predictive power. *See, e.g.,* Heaton & Brav, Event Studies in Securities Litigation: Low Power, Confounding Effects, and Bias, 93 Wash. U. L. Rev. 583 (2015).

This concern is beginning to be reflected in court decisions. In *Waggoner v. Barclays PLC*, 875 F.3d 79 (2d Cir. 2017), the Second Circuit held that when other factors support a finding that a particular security traded in an efficient market, plaintiffs need not introduce an event study demonstrating a cause-and-effect relationship between company-specific news and movements in its securities' prices. In so doing, the court relied on its earlier holding in *In re Petrobras Securities Litig.*, 862 F.3d 250 (2d Cir. 2017), where Judge Garaufis noted that "event studies offer the seductive promise of hard numbers and dispassionate truth, but methodological constraints limit their utility in the context of single-firm analyses."

3.   *Rebutting the Presumption.* *Halliburton* expected that defendants would rebut the presumption of reliance by proving a particular false statement did not impact prices (likely by way of an event study). *Halliburton* additionally held that issues going to the merits of the class action—common to all class members—are not generally appropriate for consideration at the class certification stage. In *Amgen Inc. v. Connecticut Retirement Plans*, 568 U.S. 455 (2013), a divided Supreme Court ruled that materiality (including whether there was price distortion from the fraud) is a merits issue, rejecting the argument that it is unfair to defendants to defer such a crucial determination to the trial stage given the settlement pressures that grow stronger as soon as a class is certified. In this light, *Halliburton*'s willingness to allow the defendant to introduce evidence of *lack* of price impact to defeat class certification may seem puzzling. The Second Circuit has made clear that once plaintiffs establish the prerequisites for a presumption of price impact, defendants then must prove by a preponderance of evidence that their alleged misstatements did *not* impact prices, *see Waggoner v. Barclays PLC*, 875 F.3d 79 (2d Cir. 2017), but beyond that, courts have struggled to identify what kind of evidence, precisely, speaks to that fact, without running afoul of *Amgen* and *Halliburton*. A particularly vexing challenge is posed when plaintiffs allege—as is common—that defendants' fraud did not push stock prices up, but instead simply *maintained* prices at a level when the truth would have caused a decline. What is a court to draw from an event study purporting to show the absence of any price movement in a case like that? For a good discussion, *see* Fox, *Halliburton II:* It All Depends on What Defendants Need to Show to Establish No Impact on Price, 70 Bus. Law. 437 (2015). These same types of questions also plague merits issues like loss causation and measurement of damages, considered infra.

4.   *Reliance and Secondary Liability.* In *Stoneridge Inv. Partners LLC v. Scientific-Atlanta Inc.*, 552 U.S. 148 (2008), the Supreme Court held that the reliance requirement is not satisfied in a fraud-on-the-market case when the nexus between any false statements and plaintiffs' trading is "too attenuated" or "too remote." Plaintiffs claimed that Charter Communications falsely reported its earnings and revenues, and that two vendors with whom Charter did a great deal of business—Scientific-Atlanta and Motorola—enabled this fraud by providing Charter's management with invoices and other documents that misrepresented and concealed the substance of their business dealings. These fabrications were, in turn, utilized by Charter's accountants and auditors in preparing Charter's financials. To the Court, that was too much distance for a plausible case of plaintiffs' reliance on the vendors' misconduct. In supporting this conclusion, the Court noted that the two vendors were engaged in simple commercial transactions, not investment-related activity, and nothing that they did made it "necessary or inevitable" that Charter would transmit the false financial information to investors.

One question going forward is how *Stoneridge*, *Janus*, and *Lorenzo* will interact. *Janus*, elaborating on its narrow definition of what it means to "make" a statement, held that if an actor does not have "ultimate authority" over a statement, it is not "necessary or inevitable" under *Stoneridge* that the actor's falsehoods will be included in the statement. *Lorenzo* clarified that forms of deceptive conduct beyond "making" a misstatement violate Rule 10b-5, but private plaintiffs may still be unable to recover unless they can demonstrate their reliance on that conduct specifically, or its "necessary" consequences. That said, *Stoneridge* is not insurmountable; prior to *Lorenzo*, the Eighth Circuit held in *West Virginia Pipe Trades Health & Welfare Fund v. Medtronic, Inc.*, 845 F.3d 384 (8th Cir. 2016) that a pharmaceutical company violated Rules 10b-5(a) and (c) by concealing payments to physicians involved in clinical studies to establish the safety and efficacy of its new drug. The plaintiffs alleged that the payments caused doctors to overstate the drug's benefits, and understate the drug's risks, in medical journals. The Eighth Circuit pointed out that Medtronic's CEO touted the company's strong clinical trials, and reasoned that

> Medtronic's deceptive conduct directly caused the production of the information on which the market relied. Unlike the suppliers' conduct in *Stoneridge*, Medtronic's purported conduct would not merely assist or enable the physician-authors to deceive the market. Rather, Medtronic's alleged conduct would deceive the market with the assistance of the physician-authors. A company cannot instruct individuals to take a certain action, pay to induce them to do it, and then claim any causal connection is too remote when they follow through. In this way, Medtronic's alleged manipulative conduct directly caused the biased clinical trial results that the market relied upon. This alleged causal connection is sufficient to support a finding of reliance. Thus, *Stoneridge*'s concern about resurrecting private aiding and abetting claims does not arise here.

PROBLEMS

13-10.   Mary Fletcher is a reasonably sophisticated investor who actively trades her portfolio valued at over $250,000. In May, she bought stock in ZCorp, a manufacturer of electronic auto parts. ZCorp was a small, but promising, company, actively traded in the over-the-counter market and included in Nasdaq. Her purchase came after she had determined, based upon conversations with people in the auto repair business, that electronic auto replacement parts were likely to become a hot item. She obtained a copy of the company's annual report and, after looking at its highlights and comparing the share price to those of others in the market, concluded that the market seemed to be "undervaluing" the company.

A year later, ZCorp filed for protection from creditors, and its shares are worth little. The reason for bankruptcy seems to have been a combination of the fact that the major auto manufacturers have begun to come out with their own replacement parts for electronic devices in their cars and inadequate cash flow, given the debt incurred in the course of its expansion. Fletcher has brought a class action against the company and its principal executives, charging that the 2002 annual report overstated the company's earnings by some 6 percent because faulty accounting procedures were used.

Assuming the court were to find a violation of Rule 10b-5, what impediments might exist to Fletcher's recovery? What result if Fletcher selected investments solely by throwing darts at the financial pages of the local newspaper? What result if Fletcher knew that the 2002 annual report was misleading, but on the basis of her analysis of other information believed ZCorp was a good buy?

13-11.   Executives at Best Buy Inc. issued a press release early in the morning of September 14, predicting a significant increase in earnings per share for the forthcoming quarter. Later that same day, the executives elaborated on the estimates and offered more factual detail in a conference call with analysts. Immediately after the press release, the stock price rose 7.5 percent in response to the optimism. There was no perceptible additional movement after the mid-day conference call. Best Buy did not meet those estimates over the following quarter, and there was a 14 percent price decline in December when actual results were announced. Plaintiffs claimed that the projection was fraudulent.

The district court ruled that the safe harbor for forward-looking information protected the press release from being fraudulent, because there was meaningful cautionary language. On the other hand, the safe harbor did not protect the statements made in the conference call. In such a case, can defendants seek to defeat class certification simply by showing the absence of any abnormal market price movement in response to the conference call? What if plaintiffs respond by saying that the conference call statements did have an impact, but that it occurred slowly over the next few weeks, not right away? *See IBEW Local 98 Pension Fund v. Best Buy Inc.*, 818 F.3d 775 (8th Cir. 2016).

13-12.   Consider the facts of *Janus*, where the adviser and sponsor for a group of mutual funds allegedly drafted false prospectuses on the funds' behalf, which ultimately affected the market price of the sponsor's stock. If, as *Janus* held, the adviser and sponsor did not "make" the false statements—and if, hypothetically, their conduct was nonetheless deemed to violate Rule 10b-5(a) and (c) under *Lorenzo*—would plaintiffs be able to establish the element of reliance? *Cf. In re Mutual Funds Inv. Litig.*, 566 F.3d 111 (4th Cir. 2009).

13-13.   Consider the facts of *Lorenzo*, where the director of investment banking at a broker-dealer firm circulated a false e-mail to clients but specified that it was sent at the behest of the firm's owner. If the clients had brought a lawsuit under Rule 10b-5, would they be able to satisfy the element of reliance? Recall that the majority and the dissent sparred over whether the majority's interpretation would preclude liability for a secretary or a mail-room clerk who (knowingly) disseminated the same e-mail. If those were the facts, would it change your analysis? *Cf. Thomas H. Lee Equity Fund V, L.P. v. Mayer Brown, Rowe & Maw LLP*, 612 F. Supp. 2d 267 (S.D.N.Y. 2009).

3.   Fraud on the Market: Some Variations

Suppose an investor purchases newly issued securities that do not trade in anything like the "well-developed markets" envisioned by *Halliburton*. The investor does not read the offering documents and therefore cannot prove reliance in the traditional sense, but claims that the offering was so deficient that *but for the fraud*, the securities would never have issued. This may be, for example, because the offering itself is unlawful (perhaps the issuer had no legal authority to sell the securities), or because the issuer was so financially unstable that no underwriter would have participated in the distribution had the truth been disclosed. May the element of reliance be satisfied?

For a time, the answer appeared to be yes. In *Shores v. Sklar*, 647 F.2d 462 (5th Cir. 1981) (en banc), *cert. denied*, 459 U.S. 1102 (1982), the Fifth Circuit endorsed what came to be known as the fraud-created-the-market theory, holding that investors may rely on the "integrity of the offerings of the securities market." The theory enjoyed some brief success, *see Kirkpatrick v. J.C. Bradford & Co.*, 827 F.2d 718 (11th Cir. 1987); *T.J. Rainey & Sons v. Fort Cobb Irrigation Fuel Authority*, 717 F.2d 1330 (10th Cir. 1983), but eventually, even those courts that accepted it began to sharply circumscribe the conditions under which it could be used, especially when the fraud went only to the *value* of the security rather than its legality, *Ross v. Bank South, N.A.*, 885 F.2d 723 (11th Cir. 1989) (en banc), *cert. denied*, 495 U.S. 905 (1990).

In *Malack v. BDO Seidman LLP*, 617 F.3d 743 (3d Cir. 2010), the Third Circuit strongly rejected the fraud-created-the-market theory because "[t]he security's promoter and other entities involved in the issuance, such as the underwriter, the auditor, and legal counsel—the very entities often charged with fraud—cannot be reasonably relied upon to prevent fraud." *See also Ross*, supra (Tjoflat, J., concurring); *Eckstein v. Balcor Film Investors*, 8 F.3d 1121 (7th Cir. 1993), *cert. denied*, 510 U.S. 1073 (1994). In light of what you learned about the role of underwriters in distributing a newly issued security, do you agree with this reasoning? For a call for the fraud-created-the-market theory's resurrection, *see* Kaufman & Wunderlich, Fraud Created the Market, 63 Ala. L. Rev. 275 (2012).

4. The Reasonableness of the Reliance: Due Care

Should a plaintiff be asked to demonstrate either the reasonableness of the reliance or due care? To some extent, the notion of materiality recognizes that certain statements are so inherently unreliable that liability should not follow. *See Thompson v. Smith Barney Harris Upham & Co.*, 709 F.2d 1413 (11th Cir. 1983). But what about misstatements whose falsity, though not patently obvious, either should have put the plaintiff on notice of the possibility of fraud or could have been discovered in the exercise of due care? In the early case law on this subject, courts tended to place a burden on the plaintiff of affirmatively showing the reasonableness of his reliance, particularly in cases premised on the defendant's negligence. *E.g., Herpich v. Wallace*, 430 F.2d 792 (5th Cir. 1970). This reflected the common law notion that recovery in a fraud case is limited to those who establish a right to rely on defendant's representations. *See* Sachs, The Relevance of Tort Law Doctrines to Rule 10b-5: Should Careless Plaintiffs Be Denied Recovery?, 71 Cornell L. Rev. 96 (1985).

Since then, courts have concluded that because Rule 10b-5 is limited to intentional wrongs, the defense of lack of due care by the plaintiff is limited to situations where the plaintiff acted at least recklessly in allowing the harm to occur. *See Teamsters Local 282 Pension Fund v. Angelos*, 762 F.2d 522 (7th Cir. 1985) (investors in a private placement have no affirmative duty to investigate representations made by sellers). But while there is substantial agreement that simple contributory negligence will not bar a plaintiff's claim, there is no accord over the standards for making the determination of whether the plaintiff has acted in a fashion that is sufficiently more than negligent to bar her recovery.

Some courts in fact articulate an approach that remains surprisingly close to a reasonableness standard. *E.g., Davidson v. Wilson*, 973 F.2d 1391 (8th Cir. 1992); *Sharp v. Coopers & Lybrand*, 649 F.2d 175, 194 (3d Cir. 1981), *cert. denied*, 455 U.S. 938 (1982). As to what factors ought be considered in determining justifiable reliance, the First Circuit has endorsed an inquiry that takes into account:

> (1) [t]he sophistication and expertise of the plaintiff in financial and securities matters; (2) the existence of long standing business or personal relationships; (3) access to the relevant information; (4) the existence of a fiduciary relationship; (5) concealment of the fraud; (6) the opportunity to detect the fraud; (7) whether the plaintiff initiated the stock transaction or sought to expedite the transaction; and (8) the generality or specificity of the misrepresentations.

Kennedy v. Josephthal & Co., 814 F.2d 798, 804 (1st Cir. 1987).

One of the most common uses of the "unjustifiable reliance" defense is where plaintiff alleges some form of fraud and defendant shows that had plaintiff taken the time to read a prospectus or other offering document carefully, the truth would have been discovered. If indeed, as many people suspect, most investors do not read such documents, is it fair to call such failure reckless? This issue is revisited in Chapter 18's treatment of fraud by broker-dealers. A similar issue is posed by cases where the defendants misrepresent the truth but the final transactional documents also contain a "no reliance" clause. Is reliance unreasonable per se? This issue is complicated by the fact that Section 29(a) of the '34 Act bars waivers of claims. As a result, courts have reached mixed conclusions on this issue, *compare AES Corp. v. Dow Chemical Co.*, 325 F.3d 174 (3d Cir. 2003) (permitting fraud claim to go forward) *with Cornielsen v. Infinium Capital Management, LLC*, 916 F.3d 589 (7th Cir. 2019) ("non-reliance clauses in written stock-purchase agreements preclude any possibility of damages under the federal securities laws for prior oral statements"), and may simply treat the clause as one factor in the analysis, *O'Connor v. Cory*, 2018 U.S. Dist. LEXIS 180227 (N.D. Tex. Oct. 19, 2018).

PROBLEM

13-14. Royal American Managers Inc. (RAM) was interested in purchasing a controlling interest in an insurance corporation. It negotiated with IRC Holding Corp., a New York-based insurance company, and offered a favorable price. One question that came up in the negotiations was whether a transfer of a controlling interest would require the approval of the New York State Insurance Department (NYSID). An attorney/director associated with IRC—said to be an expert in insurance law—opined that, although a transfer of a 50 percent interest would, any figure below that would not require the Department's approval. Hence, the parties agreed upon the sale of a 49 percent interest, and the transaction was consummated. Subsequently, the NYSID commenced an investigation and has threatened an enforcement proceeding against RAM, citing legal authority for the view that the sale of any controlling interest requires approval. RAM has sued IRC and the attorney/director under Rule 10b-5. Assuming scienter on the part of the defendants, should RAM's failure to do any independent legal research bar its claim? *See Royal American Managers Inc. v. IRC Holding Corp.,* 885 F.2d 1011 (2d Cir. 1989).

G.   *Loss Causation and Damages*

Section 28(a) of the '34 Act provides that no person who brings suit under the Act may recover "a total amount in excess of his actual damages on account of the act complained of." Assuming this provision is meant to apply to implied as well as express actions, its only clear message is that punitive damages may not be awarded based upon federal securities law violations (although they may be in pendent state claims). *E.g., Grogan v. Garner,* 806 F.2d 829 (8th Cir. 1986). This limitation aside, how literally are we to take Section 28(a)'s direction to measure damages with a view solely toward compensation? Many of the cases suggest some discomfort with a purely compensatory approach, presumably on the assumption such a measure (especially given the difficulty of detection) systematically under-deters fraudulent misconduct and/or sometimes improperly permits a wrongdoer to keep some portion of his ill-gotten gains.

1.   Face-to-Face Transactions

Fraud in face-to-face transactions often has a "zero sum" character. Plaintiff's loss is defendant's gain, at least as measured as of the time of the fraud. Most of the interesting problems in this area therefore boil down to the question of who will capture the unanticipated gains or suffer the unexpected losses arising from post-transaction events.

AUSA Life Insurance Co. v. Ernst & Young
206 F.3d 202 (2d Cir. 2000)

OAKES, Senior Circuit Judge:
. . . [A]ppellants are insurance companies that invested in the securities of JWP, Inc., a company which ultimately went belly-up, causing the appellants to lose most of their investments. The appellee is the accounting firm that served as the independent auditor for JWP from 1985 through 1992, the period during which the appellants invested in JWP and the period during which the allegedly fraudulent activity was occurring. . . . The appellants made their initial purchases of JWP's notes in November of 1988. Through March 1992, they purchased additional JWP notes, the investments totaling $149 million. . . .

In purchasing the notes, appellants relied on JWP's past financial statements, including annual reports certified by E&Y. These financial statements were required, under the Note Agreements, to be kept in accordance with generally accepted accounting principles ("GAAP"). Also, at the time of each annual audit by E&Y, E&Y was required under the Note Agreements to furnish to JWP a letter for JWP to transmit to noteholders, referred to as a "no-default certificate" or a "negative assurance letter," which stated that E&Y had audited JWP's financial statements and that JWP was in compliance with the financial covenants in the Note Agreements.

In this instance and consistently, E&Y's statements about JWP's financial health were less than accurate and were not always in accordance with GAAP or GAAS ("generally accepted auditing standards"). However, E&Y did not fail to notice that often JWP's financial representations about itself were not in accordance with GAAP; rather, E&Y consistently noticed, protested, and then acquiesced in these misrepresentations.

E&Y's failure lay in the seeming spinelessness of John LaBarca [the partner in charge of the JWP audit] and the other E&Y accountants in their dealings with JWP, and particularly with its CEO, Ernest Grendi. . . . Grendi almost invariably succeeded in either persuading or bullying them to agree that JWP's books required no adjustment. Part of the problem was undoubtedly the close personal relationship between Grendi and LaBarca. Grendi had been a partner of LaBarca in E&Y's predecessor firm and they continued to be good friends, regularly jogging together in preparation for the New York City Marathon. *AUSA* [*Life Ins. Co. v. Ernst & Young*], 991 F. Supp. [234], 248 [(S.D.N.Y. 1997)]. "It became a well-worn inside joke to refer to the lax accounting standards at JWP as 'EGAAP,' an acronym for Ernest Grendi's Accepted Accounting Practices." Id. at 253.

JWP rapidly expanded between 1984 and 1992 with many aggressive acquisitions. The expansion was mainly financed by private placements of debt securities, which put JWP in an increasingly leveraged position. JWP's final, fatal acquisition was that of Businessland, Inc., in 1991. . . .

JWP was able to continue paying the interest due on its notes through 1992, and JWP made partial payments through April 1993. However, JWP ultimately defaulted [largely as a result of the Businessland failure] and was placed in involuntary bankruptcy in December 1993. . . . At the end of the day, appellants sustained at least a loss of approximately $100 million in lost principal and unpaid interest. . . . [Appellants then brought suit against E&Y. After a lengthy bench trial, the district court dismissed the case for failure to prove "loss causation."]

B. CAUSATION

[W]e part company with the district court on its determination that it was "unforeseeable post-audit developments [that] caused JWP's insolvency and default even if its financial condition had been fully as healthy as was represented in those reports."

Causation in this context has two elements: transaction causation and loss causation. *See Schlick v. Penn-Dixie Cement Corp.*, 507 F.2d 374, 380-381 (2d Cir. 1974). Loss causation is causation in the traditional "proximate cause" sense—the allegedly unlawful conduct caused the economic harm. *See* id. at 380. Transaction causation means that "the violations in question caused the appellant to engage in the transaction in question." *See* id. at 380. Transaction causation has been analogized to reliance. *See Currie v. Cayman Resources Corp.*, 835 F.2d 780, 785 (11th Cir. 1988). . . .

2. LOSS CAUSATION

Addressing loss causation is [the] more difficult endeavor. How far back should the line be drawn in the causal chain, before which, "because of convenience, of public policy, of a rough sense of justice," proximate cause cannot be found? *Palsgraf v. Long Island R. Co.*, 248 N.Y. 339, 352, 162 N.E. 99, 103 (1928). In the vernacular, where does the buck stop? . . .

We have consistently said that "loss causation in effect requires that the damage complained of be one of the foreseeable consequences of the misrepresentation." *Manufacturers Hanover [Trust v. Drysdale Secs. Corp.*, 801 F.2d 13], 21 [(2d Cir. 1986)]. . . . The foreseeability query is whether E&Y could have reasonably foreseen that their certification of false financial information could lead to the demise of JWP, by enabling JWP to make an acquisition that otherwise would have been subjected to higher scrutiny, which led to harm to the investors. Given that the district court did not make factual findings as to foreseeability specifically, we remand for more factual findings. In accordance with the factual findings, the court is then instructed to reconsider proximate cause in the context of its factual determinations on foreseeability. . . .

JACOBS, Circuit Judge, concurring:
Judge Oakes believes that the district court's discussion of loss causation fails to decide whether JWP would have been able to purchase Businessland absent E&Y's misstatements. I think that is the wrong question. It has been found—and all opinions on appeal agree—that JWP's acquisition of Businessland was a calamity that overwhelmed all other financial circumstances and brought about JWP's bankruptcy. Therefore, I think that the loss causation inquiry should be: Was it foreseeable that E&Y's misstatement of accounts would cause the plaintiffs to suffer losses caused by the disastrous Businessland acquisition? In my view, the question is sufficiently answered by the district court's findings that the plaintiffs' chief investment concern was JWP's actual cash flow (which was perfectly adequate to fund plaintiffs' bonds and was unaffected by the misrepresentations) and that the disastrous nature of the Businessland investment was unforeseeable. *See AUSA Life Ins. Co.*, 991 F. Supp. at 239, 250. [Notwithstanding this belief, Judge Jacobs concurred in the remand in order to allow for a disposition of the appeal, rather than a three-way deadlock among the panel.]

Whether or not the acquisition was a foreseeable consequence of the misrepresentations cannot matter unless the misrepresentations are shown to have caused the resulting collapse. Even if one assumes (a stretch) that E&Y's misrepresentations allowed JWP to buy Businessland, E&Y's misrepresentations were not the reason for the resulting company's failure: JWP's ruin is easily attributable to business factors that were more potent than E&Y's misrepresentations, and were unrelated to them. The dispositive question is whether the JWP/Businessland combination would have collapsed even if JWP's books were accurately stated. . . .

The misrepresentations in JWP's books (concerning treatment of acquisition costs, small tool inventories, net operating losses, and software costs) were not the proximate cause—i.e., the loss causation—for the plaintiffs' loss. Those misrepresentations affected JWP's apparent cash flow, but they had no effect on JWP's actual cash flow. This is a critical distinction. While JWP's equity investors were rightfully concerned with the discrepancies in the company's books (because such variances would have affected the company's stock price), JWP's debt holders—the plaintiffs—would not necessarily have had cause for alarm. The primary concern of a debt holder is actual cash flow, the ability of the debt issuer to pay interest and principal as required. Indeed, even after JWP's annual reports were restated, the company continued to meet its interest payment schedule. . . .

WINTER, Chief Judge, dissenting:

I would ask the following question: Would a reasonable investor—knowing in 1990 (i) that a firm's financial statements have deliberately and systematically misstated its condition over at least a two-year period, (ii) that the firm's auditor has supinely acquiesced in those statements, and (iii) that the auditor had also issued fraudulent no-fault letters on outstanding notes—reasonably apprehend a new and significant danger that business decisions involving volatile risks might be made and that one such decision might lead to financial collapse without the investor having a timely opportunity to make an informed decision as to the exercise of contractual rights that might cap its losses? I would answer the question in the affirmative.

The core of my disagreement with my colleagues goes to the scope of the matters on which appellants were misled by what the district court aptly described as E&Y's "lap dog" approach to the auditing of JWP and to the preparation of the no-fault letters. To be sure, appellants were misled as to JWP's financial condition. But they were also misled as to two other matters: (i) the quality of the firm's management and auditor and (ii) the firm's current incentives with regard to risk aversion.

First, the various financial statements and no-default letters misstated the firm's financial condition and compliance with the terms of the notes, not only for the current year but also for prior years. By 1990, therefore, when the first purchase of notes at issue occurred, what was concealed was not simply the true financial condition of JWP but also the critical facts of (at least) two years of false financial statements and no-default letters. If aware of those facts, a reasonable lender would have inferred that JWP had a management quite willing to lie systematically to investors and an auditor willing to certify the lies. A reasonable lender would then have discounted JWP's creditworthiness not only because of its less favorable financial condition but also, far more devastatingly, because of the questionable quality of its management and auditor. Reasonable investors surely view firms with an untrustworthy management and auditor far more negatively than they view financially identical firms with honest management and a watch-dog auditor. Moreover, a reasonable lender informed of the truth would also have known that outstanding notes held by the investor were actually in default. Such defaults would have prompted serious consideration of the exercise of contractual remedies. Indeed, had the defaults been known, the Businessland acquisition could not have occurred without either a cure by JWP detailing the years of fraud or a waiver by appellants.

Second, the concealed information about JWP's management and E&Y's performance as an auditor would have alerted a reasonable lender to JWP's incentives to make risky decisions such as the Businessland acquisition. When the management of a firm and its auditor knowingly issue a series of certified annual financial statements that depict a financial condition more favorable than the truth, a dilemma is created. Both know that the truth will ultimately emerge. All things being equal, the value of the firm's outstanding securities will then decline, and fresh capital will be more costly or simply unavailable without installing a new management and auditor. Only a deal so profitable as to improve the firm's financial condition sufficiently to offset both the financial implications of the false statements and the decline in confidence in management will preserve the firm's standing in capital markets. The "huge-deal" solution to the firm's dilemma, however, puts lenders at risk. Unknown to them, the firm is far less risk averse than would be expected from the publicly available financial statements, and the chances of a default resulting from a deal with high volatility risk—like the Businessland acquisition—are much greater. . . .

Loss causation in the context of federal securities law thus requires consideration of the significance to a reasonable investor of the truth compared to the content of the misrepresentations or omissions. If the significance of the truth is such as to cause a reasonable investor to consider seriously a zone of risk that would be perceived as remote or highly unlikely by one believing the fraud, and the loss ultimately suffered is within that zone, then a misrepresentation or omission as to that information may be deemed a foreseeable or proximate cause of the loss. . . .

Finance is about risk probabilities—i.e., risk allocation, diversification, and minimization. Every lender, when deciding whether and on what terms to make a loan, must evaluate the probability of default. . . . When appellants invested in JWP, they bargained for a certain risk profile that governed the decision to lend and matters such as maturity and interest rate. They also bargained for E&Y to monitor JWP's compliance with GAAP and for contractual rights, including acceleration, that might cap their losses should JWP default. E&Y's conduct deprived them of all these bargains and subjected them to concealed risks that resulted in losses.

NOTES AND QUESTIONS

1. Loss Causation.   Long considered by most courts an element of the plaintiff's case under Rule 10b-5, this requirement was codified by Congress in the PSLRA (Section 21D(b)(4)). The concept was described by Judge Posner in *Bastian v. Petren Research Co.*, 892 F.2d 680, 685 (7th Cir. 1990):

Loss causation is an exotic name . . . for the standard rule of tort law that the plaintiff must allege and prove that, but for the defendant's wrongdoing, the plaintiff would not have incurred the harm of which he complains. Like a stock market crash, the collapse of oil prices in the early 1980's reverberated throughout the economy. Since the United States is a net importer of oil, the reverberations were for the most part good ones. But there were some losers. No social purpose would be served by encouraging everyone who suffers an investment loss because of an unanticipated change in market conditions to pick through offering memoranda with a fine-tooth comb in the hope of uncovering a misrepresentation. Defrauders are a bad lot and should be punished, but Rule 10b-5 does not make them insurers against national economic calamities. If the defendants' oil and gas ventures failed not because of the personal shortcomings that the defendants concealed but because of industry-wide phenomena that destroyed all or most such ventures, then the plaintiffs, given their demonstrated desire to invest in such ventures, lost nothing by reason of the defendant's fraud and have no claim to damages.

Cases arising out of the global financial crisis pose hard loss causation issues because of the overwhelming severity of the impact of the crisis on all financial institutions. For recent cases taking a fairly pro-plaintiff approach in the aftermath of the crisis, *see Financial Guarantee Insurance Co. v. Putnam Advisory Co.*, 783 F.3d 395 (2d Cir. 2015), and *Loreley Financing (Jersey) v. Wells Fargo Securities LLC*, 797 F.3d 160 (2d Cir. 2015) (Calabresi, J.), both of which stressed that knotty factual questions about causation in face-to-face fraud cases should be reserved for trial, not in attacking the pleadings.

    2. Out-of-Pocket Versus Rescission. In measuring damages (assuming loss causation), courts are open to any appropriate compensatory measurement of damages in light of the type of fraud established. One common standard used in Rule 10b-5 cases is the tort-based out-of-pocket measure, which awards (to a plaintiff buyer) the difference between the amount paid for the security and its actual value as of the time of the transaction. If (as most courts say) compensation is deemed the primary objective of a damage award under the '34 Act, this measure provides the most precise fit. Therein lies its popularity.

    Out-of-pocket damages, however, are difficult to determine, since courts must calculate the hypothetical value of the security had there been full disclosure as of the transaction date. When applied strictly, the out-of-pocket measure ignores post-transaction events, such as a bankruptcy that renders the security valueless) except to the extent these later events shed light on the true value of the security as of the transaction's date. Many courts, therefore, modified the strict approach by making the measure turn on the difference between the transaction price and the price when the truth was discovered, which turns into something closer to a rescissionary measure of damages. In face to face settings, a fair number of courts do allow a plaintiff either to elect a rescissionary remedy—return of either the purchase price or the security—or to seek a rescissionary measure of damages (i.e., if the securities that were fraudulently acquired have already been sold, the difference between the purchase price and the value of the securities upon disposition). Note, by the way, that in an appropriate case Section 29(b) of the '34 Act provides a mechanism by which to seek avoidance of a transaction made in violation of any provision of the Act. We explore this separate statutory standard in Chapter 14. With respect to the rescissionary measure, the Supreme Court in *Randall v. Loftsgaarden*, 478 U.S. 647 (1986), reserved the question of whether a rescission-based remedy is appropriate under Rule 10b-5. But assuming arguendo that it was (since defendants did not specifically challenge its application), the Court ruled that there should be no offset from the recovery for tax benefits the plaintiff had gained from the transaction they were seeking to unwind. Nothing in Section 28(a)'s reference to "actual damages," it reasoned, limits the plaintiff's recovery to "net economic harm." In justifying this conclusion, the Court emphasized the role of deterrence of misconduct in the formulation of a remedy under Section 10(b), finding such an objective implicit in Congress' reasons for enacting the '34 Act.

This rationale, of course, seems to support an affirmative answer to the threshold question formally reserved by the Court, for the rescissionary remedy is useful not only because it provides simplicity, but also because it will often operate to deprive the defendant of a windfall in a way that the out-of-pocket measure will not.

3. Restitution. For many of the same reasons articulated in the rescission cases, some courts have been willing to introduce explicit restitutionary elements into the damage calculation so as to deprive the defendant of any windfall that might have been gained as a result of the breach. In *Janigan v. Taylor*, 344 F.2d 781 (1st Cir. 1965), *cert. denied*, 382 U.S. 879 (1966), for example, the plaintiffs had sold their stock to the defendant, the issuer's president, for $40,000. Soon thereafter, the defendant resold the stock for some $700,000. The court granted a restitutionary recovery, stating that "[i]t is more appropriate to give the defrauded party the benefit even of windfalls than to let the fraudulent party keep them." Id. at 786. Support for this approach, too, can be found in the Supreme Court's decision in *Randall*, which cites and quotes *Janigan* with approval. For a useful synthesis of the cases where courts have favored rescissionary or restitutionary remedies, urging a more explicit recognition that damages measures ought and do operate consciously as a means of preventing unjust enrichment, *see* Thompson, The Measure of Recovery Under Rule 10b-5: A Restitution Alternative to Tort Damages, 37 Vand. L. Rev. 349 (1984).

PROBLEM

13-15. Two brothers founded a small, closely held corporation. The first brother was conservative by nature and resisted expansion and growth. The second was entrepreneurial, a risk-taker. By use of an elaborate fraudulent scheme, the second brother caused the first to sell him his shares in the corporation. Two years later, after the business had grown substantially, the second brother sold it to a conglomerate for, on a per share basis, some five times what he had paid his brother for it. Upon uncovering the fraud, the first brother brings suit under Rule 10b-5 and establishes liability. How should damages be measured? See *Rochez Bros. Inc. v. Rhodes*, 491 F.2d 402, 412 (3d Cir. 1973).

2. Open Market Transactions

The issue of loss causation becomes even more problematic in fraud-on-the-market cases. Assuming that plaintiffs are seeking out-of-pocket damages, what is the necessary showing? In *Dura Pharmaceuticals Inc. v. Broudo*, 544 U.S. 336 (2005), the Supreme Court ruled that it was not enough for the plaintiffs to prove that the stock price was artificially inflated by the fraud. There must be a showing of proximate cause between an actionable misrepresentation or omission and the economic harm suffered by the plaintiff class. Otherwise, the Court said, issuers and other defendants would become insurers for declines in market value having nothing to do with the fraud. And plaintiffs might be able to recover even though they had sold their stock before the truth was revealed. Having said all this, the Court offered little guidance as to how a requirement of loss causation should be applied in open market cases, either at pleading or trial.

In re Vivendi, S.A. Securities Litigation
838 F.3d 223 (2d Cir. 2016)

[Vivendi Universal was a French utilities company that rapidly transformed itself into a media conglomerate through a rapid series of debt-fueled acquisitions. As a result, Vivendi's debt load ballooned from €3 billion in early 2000 to over €21 billion in 2002. Though Vivendi internally recognized that it might not have sufficient liquidity to make the necessary payments, Vivendi publicly expressed confidence that its high cash flows were sufficient to meet its obligations. Eventually, Vivendi undertook a series of measures to quickly raise the necessary cash, including rapid sales of peripheral assets. Its stock price fell as market analysts speculated that Vivendi was facing a cash shortfall, and ratings agencies downgraded its debt. Ultimately, Vivendi admitted its liquidity problems and announced additional sales of €5 billion worth of assets, sending its stock price tumbling even further.]

LIVINGSTON, Circuit Judge.

. . .

As Plaintiffs defined it at trial, liquidity is "the ease or difficulty with which a company can timely meet its financial obligations and fund its operations." Liquidity *risk*, then, is simply a financial-accounting term for the concept of being "debt rich and cash poor." . . . The jury found that knowledge of Vivendi's true liquidity risk at any given time would have been material to a reasonable investor and that the fifty-seven statements were individually false or misleading with respect to this risk. . . .

Given that Vivendi was in a phase of intense buying, moreover, any investor attuned to Vivendi's pattern of behavior would be keen to know whether and how Vivendi was making sufficient profits to translate into cash flow that would cover all of Vivendi's sundry debt obligations. We find the evidence introduced at trial sufficient to support the jury's conclusion that a reasonable investor could find Vivendi's statements . . . misleading for omission to disclose Vivendi's liquidity risk. . . .

"Loss causation 'is the causal link between the alleged misconduct and the economic harm ultimately suffered by the plaintiff.'" *Lentell v. Merrill Lynch & Co.*, 396 F.3d 161, 172 (2d Cir. 2005) (quoting *Emergent Capital Inv. Mgmt., LLC v. Stonepath Grp., Inc.*, 343 F.3d 189, 197 (2d Cir. 2003)). In some respects, loss causation resembles the tort-law concept of proximate cause, which generally requires that a plaintiff's injury be the foreseeable consequence of the defendant's conduct. But this traditional foreseeability test is "imperfect" in the §10(b) context, for "it cannot ordinarily be said" that the alleged misstatements themselves, "as opposed to the underlying circumstance that is concealed or misstated" "cause[]" investors' loss. *See Lentell*, 396 F.3d at 173. We thus clarified in *Lentell* that to establish loss causation, a plaintiff must show that "the loss [was a] foreseeable" result of the defendant's conduct (*i.e.*, the fraud), "*and* that the loss [was] caused by the materialization of the . . . risk" concealed by the defendant's alleged fraud. *Id.*

Put more simply, proof of loss causation requires demonstrating that the *subject* of the fraudulent statement or omission was the cause of the actual loss suffered. If the relationship between the plaintiff's investment loss and the information misstated or concealed by the defendant is sufficiently direct, loss causation is established. But if the connection is attenuated, or if the plaintiff fails to demonstrate a causal connection between the content of the alleged misstatements or omissions and the harm actually suffered, a fraud claim will not lie.

. . . Vivendi contends that the loss that Plaintiffs sought to establish here was not a materialization of the risk concealed by Vivendi's alleged misstatements. According to Vivendi, the risk that it allegedly concealed (*i.e.*, the risk of a liquidity crisis) must have materialized into a more significant problem (*i.e.*, an actual liquidity crisis) in order for Plaintiffs to show that Vivendi's alleged fraud caused them loss. Since it is undisputed that Vivendi's liquidity risk "never materialized" into "an objective event such as bankruptcy, default, or insolvency," Vivendi asserts that Plaintiffs cannot establish loss causation. We disagree.

Vivendi fails to appreciate that to show loss causation, it is enough that the loss caused by the alleged fraud results from the "relevant truth . . . leak[ing] out." *Dura Pharm., Inc. v. Broudo*, 544 U.S. 336, 342 (2005). Although we have previously stated that a plaintiff can establish loss causation either by showing a "materialization of risk" or by identifying a "corrective disclosure" that reveals the truth behind the alleged fraud, our past holdings do not suggest that "corrective disclosure" and "materialization of risk" create fundamentally different pathways for proving loss causation. . . . "[T]o establish loss causation, [plaintiffs must show that a] . . . misstatement or omission concealed *something* from the market that, *when disclosed*, negatively affected the value of the security." [*Lentell*, 396 F.3d at 173.] Whether the truth comes out by way of a corrective disclosure describing the precise fraud inherent in the alleged misstatements, or through events constructively disclosing the fraud, does not alter the basic loss-causation calculus. . . .

Vivendi's conception of loss causation would have the effect of insulating companies from securities-fraud liability whenever the thing concealed in a material misstatement never ripens from a mere risk to an out-and-out disaster—unless a specific corrective disclosure issues.

A simple hypothetical helps bring into stark relief why Vivendi cannot be right that the Plaintiffs, short of pointing to explicit corrective disclosures, had to point to an event, such as a bankruptcy, to demonstrate loss causation in this case. Suppose that a company knows that it faces tremendous risk of bankruptcy, yet fraudulently informs the market that there is no risk of bankruptcy. Soon, the risk becomes too great to ignore, and a series of events indicating that the company is on the verge of bankruptcy takes place: a major bank backs out of a potential loan agreement with the company; a large deal with another firm falls through after the other firm does due diligence into the company; the company rapidly sells off an abnormally large amount of its assets in an effort to raise capital; and so on. The company's stock price sinks, indeed becomes all but valueless.

The company in this hypothetical lied about its *risk* of bankruptcy—a lie that was separate and distinct from any lie about whether the company actually filed for bankruptcy—and events revealing the truth about the company's *risk* of bankruptcy caused investors to lose money. Yet, Vivendi would have us believe that, absent a specific corrective disclosure, the actual filing of bankruptcy is the *necessary* "materialization of risk" that must occur in order for the company to have caused investors any loss under §10(b). But whether the company caused loss to investors under §10(b) does not turn on whether the company actually files Chapter 11 at some point or manages to steer clear of bankruptcy at the last minute. . . .

Here, although no specific corrective disclosure ever exposed the precise extent of Vivendi's alleged fraud, Plaintiffs' theory of loss causation nevertheless rested on the revelation of the truth. According to Plaintiffs, Vivendi's alleged misstatements concealed its liquidity risk, and a series of events in the first half of 2002 made the truth about that liquidity risk come to light. . . . [T]hose events took place on nine days, when the following news reached the market: (1) January 7, 2002 news that Vivendi sold 55 million of its treasury shares; (2) May 3, 2002 news that Moody's downgraded Vivendi's long-term senior debt to a notch above junk status; (3) June 21, 2002 news that Vivendi sold a stake in its subsidiary Vivendi Environnement, despite earlier statements that it would wait to sell; (4) June 24, 2002 news just three days later that Vivendi sold an even larger stake in Vivendi Environnement; (5) July 2, 2002 news that Moody's downgraded Vivendi's long-term senior debt to junk status, followed by S&P's downgrade of Vivendi's short-term senior debt; (6) July 3, 2002 news that Vivendi acknowledged its short-term liquidity problems and its €1.8 billion in obligations that were due that very month; (7) July 10, 2002 news that rating agencies cautioned that further downgrades were possible, and that French authorities had raided Vivendi's Paris headquarters to investigate possible securities fraud; (8) July 15, 2002 news that a member of Vivendi's board of directors was urging Vivendi quickly to sell Canal+, which was not generating earnings as expected; and (9) August 14, 2002 news that Vivendi planned to sell €10 billion in assets over the following two years, €5 billion of which it hoped to sell within just nine months.

There was ample evidence to support the jury's finding of a "sufficiently direct" "relationship between the . . . loss [that Plaintiffs suffered on these nine days] and the information misstated or concealed by [Vivendi]." . . .

The *Vivendi* case distinguishes between two common theories of loss causation: materialization of the risk and corrective disclosure. The "materialization of the risk" theory is rooted in the notion that securities fraud subjects investors to risks of which they were unaware and did not accept, and investors deserve compensation when those risks materialize in a manner that results in an economic loss. Thus, in *Vivendi*, plaintiffs argued that the company concealed its "liquidity risk," namely, the danger that it did not have sufficient cash flow to pay its debt. One mechanism by which such a risk might materialize would be if the company filed for bankruptcy or defaulted on its debt—something that, in the *Vivendi* case, never occurred. "Corrective disclosure" theory, by contrast, refers to the losses that occur when the market becomes aware of the lie itself, or the underlying fraudulent practices that had previously been concealed. The clearest example might be a company that issues a formal restatement of its financial information, thereby explicitly admitting to the falsity of the earlier-issued reports (although not all corrective disclosure cases are quite as stark).

That said, as illustrated in *Vivendi,* the alternatives might be described as existing on a continuum rather than representing distinct poles. When risks materialize, they may (or may not) raise suspicion of an underlying fraud; disclosure of the underlying fraud may represent one mechanism by which a foreseeable risk materializes. For this reason, the Ninth Circuit recently explained, "Because loss causation is simply a variant of proximate cause, the ultimate issue is whether the defendant's misstatement, as opposed to some other fact, foreseeably caused the plaintiff's loss. . . . Revelation of fraud in the marketplace is simply one of the 'infinite variety' of causation theories a plaintiff might allege to satisfy proximate cause." *Mineworkers' Pension Scheme v. First Solar Inc.,* 881 F.3d 750 (9th Cir. 2018). In truth, although most circuits have recognized some version of "materialization of the risk" as a means by which false statements may cause recoverable injuries to investors, courts can vary widely in the precise relationship they require between the underlying fraud and the market revelation that precipitates the claimed losses.

Can you imagine scenarios where plaintiffs would be able to satisfy a materialization of the risk standard without demonstrating the existence of any corrective disclosure alerting the market to the presence of an earlier lie?

NOTES AND QUESTIONS

1. Opportunism in Corrective Disclosures.   Courts that accept "materialization of the risk" as an alternative mechanism for proving loss causation often highlight that to do otherwise risks allowing defendants to escape liability merely by manipulating their public admissions. *See, e.g., OPERS v. Federal Home Loan Mortgage Corp.,* 830 F.3d 376 (6th Cir. 2016) ("We are mindful of the dangerous incentive that is created when the success of any loss causation argument is made contingent upon a defendant's acknowledgement that it misled investors."). That danger persists regardless of the definition of loss causation. What happens, for example, when lots of material information is released into the market about the issuer, both at the time of the alleged fraud and at the time of the truthful revelations, so that disentangling the marketplace impact of the truthful from the fraudulent becomes nearly impossible? As you have seen, some courts insist that plaintiff's claim fails unless it can show by solid empirical evidence exactly what the impact of the lie was on the market price. Does this create an opportunity for issuers to avoid liability by making sure that when disclosure is made, it is bundled so that it becomes impossible to separate out the value associated with the correction? *See* Spindler, Why Shareholders Want Their CEOs to Lie More After *Dura Pharmaceuticals,* 95 Geo. L.J. 653 (2007). One study conducted after *Dura* found that firms that bundled corrective disclosures with unrelated news were not only less likely to become the targets of litigation, but also had claims against them dismissed at higher rates, and settled for lower amounts. *See* Bliss, Partnoy & Furchtgott, Information Bundling and Securities Litigation, 65 J. Acct. & Econ. 61 (2018).

   2.   *Measuring Damages.* Does *Dura* guide the courts in measuring damages for open market securities fraud? At one time, the near-universal approach was the out-of-pocket measure, which assesses the difference between the price paid by the plaintiff and a hypothetical value that represents what the stock would have traded at absent the fraud. By definition, this ignores all post-transaction changes in price and is thus sensitive to the loss causation problem. For instance, does *Dura* permit recovery for defrauded buyers if the price is above the purchase price at the time of the lawsuit? *See In re CIGNA Corp. Sec. Litig.*, 459 F. Supp. 2d 338 (E.D. Pa. 2006); Burch, Reassessing Damages in Securities Fraud Class Actions, 66 Md. L. Rev. 348 (2007); Fisch, Cause for Concern: Causation and Federal Securities Fraud, 94 Iowa L. Rev. 811 (2009). In *Acticon AG v. China North East Petroleum Holdings Ltd.*, 692 F.3d 34 (2d Cir. 2012), the court said that the fact that the stock price rebounds shortly after the drop associated with revelation of the fraud does not defeat a claim of loss causation.

   3.   *Proof.* How, as a practical matter, would you go about proving loss? The most sophisticated approaches use modern finance theory either to create a hypothetical index that seeks to estimate what the returns on the security in question would have been absent the fraud or (more commonly) to create an "event study" that assumes intrinsic and actual values are identical except on days when fraud-related data is disseminated. In either case, "[t]he basic notion is to disentangle the effects of types of information on stock prices—information that is specific to the firm under question (e.g., dividend announcement) and information that is likely to affect stock prices marketwide (e.g., change in interest rates)"—and then measure the abnormal returns caused by the specific misinformation. Mitchell & Netter, The Role of Financial Economics in Securities Fraud Cases: Applications at the Securities & Exchange Commission, 49 Bus. Law. 545, 556-557 (1994); *see also* Cornell & Morgan, Using Finance Theory to Measure Damages in Fraud on the Market Cases, 37 UCLA L. Rev. 883 (1990). This can be a miserably difficult task, of course, especially when the truth leaked out slowly into the market or various pieces of accurate firm-specific information were disclosed at the same time as the correction of the misinformation. For doubts that event study tools are up to the task assigned, *see* Brav & Heaton, Event Studies in Securities Class Actions: Low Power, Confounding Effects and Bias, 93 Wash. U. L. Rev. 583 (2015).

   There are also likely to be disagreements regarding entitlements to damages among investors who traded during the class period. Active traders may well have bought *and* sold during the class period without being harmed. These traders must be separated out. *See Wool v. Tandem Computers Inc.*, 818 F.2d 1433 (9th Cir. 1987); Barclay & Torchio, A Comparison of Trading Models Used for Calculating Aggregate Damages in Securities Litigation, 64 Law & Contemp. Probs. 105 (2001-2002). Determining who is entitled to damages will be time-consuming, and information about such specific trading activity will not be available early in the proceedings, making settlement negotiations difficult. Because of these practical difficulties, financial economists retained to make these calculations on behalf of plaintiffs and defendants will often differ wildly in their estimates. In the Apple Computer securities litigation, for example, the two sides came out $120 million apart, even though they used essentially the same methodology. *See* Alexander, The Value of Bad News in Securities Class Actions, 41 UCLA L. Rev. 1421, 1424-1426 (1994) (discussing all the foregoing problems). Various other difficulties may also plague the event study process. Once fraud is exposed, for instance, the market will react by factoring in the anticipated litigation costs attendant to the fraud, as well as loss of credibility on the part of issuer management. Should this "collateral damage" be included within the out-of-pocket measure? *See, e.g.*, Ferrell & Saha, The Loss Causation Requirement for Rule 10b-5 Causes of Action: The Implication of *Dura Pharmaceuticals v. Broudo*, 63 Bus. Law. 163 (2007).

PROBLEM

13-16.   Allegiance Corp. was a fast-growing telecommunications company. One way it signaled its growth was by disclosing the number of new "line installations" for customers. Toward the end of its fiscal year, Allegiance revealed publicly that its previous estimates of line installations had been significantly overstated. In the same press release, it also indicated that the forthcoming year would bring a substantial reduction in revenue and earnings growth compared to prior estimates. Immediately afterward, the price of Allegiance stock dropped by some 30 percent. What difficulties would plaintiffs face in showing loss causation?

13-17.   AGC announced that it had procured a lucrative contract that was expected to generate hundreds of millions of dollars in revenues. Over the next two years, AGC's reported revenues remained at the level they had always been, and AGC made no further mention of the contract. During the same period, its stock price gradually declined. Plaintiffs now claim that AGC never had the contract in the first place. What facts might plaintiffs have to prove in order to establish loss causation?

3.   Proportionate Liability

One of the most noteworthy reforms of the PSLRA is Section 21D(g), which substitutes a system of proportionate liability for joint and several liability in cases under the '34 Act for defendants who did not act knowingly when they committed the violation. Congress' intent was largely to aid "secondary" defendants, particularly accountants, in cases where recklessness is the basis for culpability. *See* Palmrose, The Joint & Several v. Proportionate Liability Debate: An Empirical Investigation of Audit-Related Litigation, 1 Stan. J.L. Bus. & Fin. 53 (1995); Mednick & Peck, Proportionality: A Much Needed Solution to the Accountants' Legal Liability Crisis, 28 Val. U. L. Rev. 867 (1994). To this end, reckless defendants are entitled to have the fact-finder assess their relative percentage of fault, and are liable only for that portion of the damages. The provision can thus have a powerful effect on how much money is ultimately awarded to plaintiffs. When one or more of the defendants are bankrupt or otherwise judgment-proof—as will often be the case in securities class actions—it may leave plaintiffs undercompensated. Undercompensation will also occur to the extent that the statutory standard is read to permit the judge or jury to apportion shares of responsibility to parties who are not liable to the plaintiffs at all (e.g., because they lacked scienter).

Sensing that all this might be a political concern, proponents did add a provision, which they advertised as giving full protection to the "small investor" (*see* 141 Cong. Rec. S17934 (Dec. 5, 1995) (remarks of Sen. D'Amato)), that forces reckless violators to fund full recovery by investors whose net worth is less than $200,000 and who lost more than 10 percent of their net worth as a result of the violation. But how many such investors are ever in a position to lose that large a percentage of their wealth in a single transaction?

Read Section 21D(g) carefully before answering the following problem.

PROBLEM

13-18. Blancor Inc., a small corporation, was driven to bankruptcy by the misfeasance of two senior executive officers who concealed their wrongdoing through false financial statements. Both individuals have pled guilty to criminal charges and have few or no assets remaining. Their story was that they were pressured into the embezzlement to pay off gambling debts to some organized criminals. The Alpha Pension Trust purchased $7 million of high-yield bonds issued by Blancor in a nonpublic offering in which Blancor was assisted by a regional investment banking firm, Triangle Capital Corporation. The financial statements were audited and certified by an accounting firm, Mulch & Gump. Alpha's internal investment regulations bar speculative investments, but this restriction was ignored by Alpha's investment manager, Kate Singer, who made the decision to buy the bonds under heavy pressure to improve the performance of the portfolio. Alpha brought suit against Mulch & Gump and the two audit partners who did the Blancor work, as well as Triangle, charging all of them with violating Rule 10b-5.

In the ensuing trial, the jury found the accountants liable, based on recklessness. Triangle was found not liable because it lacked scienter. You are the trial judge. Instruct the jury with respect to how, and upon whom, to apportion liability.

4.   Securities Litigation Reform

Based on what you have learned in this chapter about fraud-on-the-market class actions, do you think they are warranted on either compensatory or deterrence grounds? This question has generated substantial debate. For instance, is it possible that even after *Dura*, loss-based measures may tend to overpenalize securities law violations? In a classic article, Easterbrook and Fischel say yes. *See* Easterbrook & Fischel, Optimal Damages in Securities Cases, 52 U. Chi. L. Rev. 611 (1985). In an open market case—for example, overly optimistic publicity by the issuer, with no insider trading—for every disadvantaged investor (the buyer) there is another (the innocent seller) who receives a windfall. Therefore, the *net* economic loss to marketplace traders is something close to zero. If the law is meant merely to deter wrongdoing, damages should equal only the costs of detection and prosecution and any external harms of the misconduct, adjusted upward to reflect the possibility of nondetection. This figure is unlikely to approach the aggregate gross out-of-pocket harm to every disadvantaged buyer. Moreover, this is precisely the area where we should worry most about the chilling effect of the damage rule on socially useful behavior. Once again, there is concern that issuers will fail to release information (e.g., forecasts or projections) when they are under no affirmative obligation to do so, for fear of liability. This would operate to the disadvantage of marketplace traders—a social cost attributable to the possibility of large damage awards under Rule 10b-5.

Nor should we be concerned about undercompensating investors on the losing side of a trade. These investors are likely to be diversified and, over time, the fortuitous gains and losses from marketplace misinformation will tend—albeit incompletely—to cancel each other out, rendering a case-by-case damages remedy unnecessary. *See* Thakor, The Economic Reality of Securities Litigation (Navigant Consulting, 2005) (large institutional investors frequently have net gains notwithstanding large losses). Investors may also be "compensated" for the risk of fraud ex ante, in that the efficient market hypothesis suggests that any residual risk of fraud will be reflected in lower securities prices to begin with. Finally, to the extent that shareholders of the issuer fund most or all of the settlements and judgments in fraud-on-the-market-type cases, either through payments made directly by the issuer or through director and officer insurance policies, investors as a group are essentially creating a very expensive—and perhaps inefficient—scheme of self-insurance. As an investor ex ante, would you opt for a system that provided compensation for open market fraud out of corporate funds where some 20-30 percent of any recovery went to the plaintiffs' attorneys and at least an equal amount would have to be paid to the defense attorneys, also out of corporate funds, with each transfer of funds? This so-called circularity argument has gained many adherents. For a criticism of the argument, *see* Spindler, We Have a Consensus on Fraud on the Market—And It's Wrong, 7 Harv. Bus. L. Rev. 67 (2017).

On the other hand, we must acknowledge that at least some victims of securities fraud do have a strong case for compensation, and that private securities litigation may play a useful deterrent and symbolic role in combating securities fraud. *See* Cox, Making Securities Class Actions Virtuous, 39 Ariz. L. Rev. 497 (1997). In terms of deterrence, is there a meaningful figure that approximates the net social loss, adjusted for the risk of nondetection? Easterbrook and Fischel suggest that the "best rule might be a mechanical one—say, one percent of the gross movement in the price of the firm's stock attributable to the wrong." 52 U. Chi. L. Rev. at 642 n.44. Would damage limitations such as this leave in place sufficient incentives for plaintiffs' lawyers to bring these complex cases?

This debate has led to numerous reform recommendations. For a sampling of the literature, *see* Bratton & Wachter, The Political Economy of Fraud on the Market, 160 U. Pa. L. Rev. 69 (2011) (abolish fraud on the market but increase SEC enforcement budget); Rose, Reforming Securities Litigation Reform: A Proposal for Restructuring the Relationship Between Public and Private Enforcement of Rule 10b-5, 108 Colum. L. Rev. 1301 (2008) (giving SEC greater control over private lawsuits); Langevoort, On Leaving Corporate

Executives "Naked, Homeless and Without Wheels": Corporate Fraud, Equitable Remedies and the Debate over Entity Versus Individual Liability, 42 Wake Forest L. Rev. 627 (2007) (greater emphasis on recovery from individual wrongdoers); Alexander, Rethinking Damages in Securities Class Actions, 48 Stan. L. Rev. 501 (1996) (damage limitations); Mahoney, Precaution Costs and the Law of Fraud on Impersonal Markets, 78 Va. L. Rev. 623 (1992) (eliminate fraud-on-the-market presumption entirely); Arlen & Carney, Vicarious Liability for Fraud on Securities Markets: Theories and Evidence, 1992 U. Ill. L. Rev. 691 (shift liability away from issuers). Some have suggested that litigation be curtailed and some form of investor insurance put in its place. *See* Davis Evans, The Investor Compensation Fund, 33 J. Corp. L. 223 (2007); Cunningham, Choosing Gatekeepers: The Financial Statement Insurance Alternative to Auditor Liability, 52 UCLA L. Rev. 413 (2004).

H.   Federalism and Rule 10b-5: The Problem of Corporate Mismanagement

Especially in the aftermath of Enron and the related financial scandals and Congress' adoption of the Sarbanes-Oxley Act, the question of how far securities regulation reaches to cover breaches of fiduciary duty by corporate management is an important one. As shown in Chapter 12, breaches of duty are often material. Does that mean that their concealment violates Rule 10b-5?

Certainly, a corporation can be defrauded by one of its own officers or employees, for example, if he misrepresents to senior officials the value of certain property or services given in exchange for company stock. Indeed, this is the category into which the *Bankers Life* case falls. In such a case, there is some company official acting on behalf of the corporation who is in fact deceived in the course of authorizing the transaction. Thus, the party injured—the company that purchased or sold the securities—is properly deemed defrauded and has a right to sue.

But what if those who are in a position to authorize the transaction are themselves the wrongdoers? In perhaps the most fundamental of the Supreme Court's retrenchment decisions under Rule 10b-5, *Santa Fe Industries v. Green*, 430 U.S. 462 (1977), the Court distinguished between the spheres of federal securities regulation, which deals with deception practiced on investors, and state corporation law, which deals with the fiduciary responsibility of corporate officials. The case before the Court was one in which the minority shareholders of Kirby Lumber Corporation objected to a freeze-out short-form merger effected by Kirby's parent corporation, Santa Fe, charging both gross undervaluation of the company's stock and lack of justifiable business purpose. In a controversial decision, the Second Circuit invoked the common law notion of constructive (or equitable) fraud to hold that an allegation of breach of fiduciary duty—unfair price and lack of proper business purpose—was sufficient to state a claim. *Green v. Santa Fe Industries*, 533 F.2d 1283 (2d Cir. 1976).

The Supreme Court reversed. Relying both on evidence of legislative intent and federalism concerns that would arise were such a distinction not to be respected, the Court held that plaintiffs did not state a claim under Section 10(b) simply by attacking the fairness of a freeze-out short-form merger. Deception, not simply unfairness or breach of fiduciary duty, must be present, and the complaint had not alleged any misinformation. In the first portions of the opinion, the Court justified this result by noting that the term *manipulative or deceptive devices or contrivances* appears to refer to conduct that is actively fraudulent, and the legislative history does not give sufficient indication that any broader reading is warranted.

However, in Part IV of the opinion (which two members of the majority refused to join), the Court turned to more overarching justifications for its conclusion. First, it emphasized that full and fair disclosure is the fundamental purpose of the '34 Act; once such disclosure has occurred, "the fairness of the terms of the transaction is at most a tangential concern of the statute." 430 U.S. at 478. Then, it observed that the sort of breach of duty at issue was historically the sort of issue traditionally relegated to state law:

> The reasoning behind a holding that the complaint in this case alleged fraud under Rule 10b-5 could not be easily contained. It is difficult to imagine how a court could distinguish, for purposes of Rule 10b-5 fraud, between a majority stockholder's use of a short-form merger to eliminate the minority at an unfair price and the use of some other device, such as a long-form merger, tender offer, or liquidation, to achieve the same result; or indeed how a court could distinguish the alleged abuses in these going private transactions from other types of fiduciary self-dealing involving transactions in securities. The result would be to bring within the Rule a wide variety of corporate conduct traditionally left to state regulation. In addition to posing a "danger of vexatious litigation" which could result from a widely expanded class of plaintiffs under Rule 10b-5 . . . this extension of the federal securities laws would over-lap and quite possibly interfere with state corporate law. . . . Absent a clear indication of congressional intent, we are reluctant to federalize the substantial portion of the law of corporations that deals with transactions in securities, particularly where established state policies of corporate regulation would be overridden.

Id. at 478-479. After the Sarbanes-Oxley Act of 2002, is this posture of deference to state law with respect to corporate governance so clearly warranted?

The analysis in *Santa Fe* is much more illuminating about the approach it rejects than what it would instead consider the better approach to be. What constitutes deception? Understood broadly, some form of deception is present in virtually all fiduciary misconduct. Very few breaches of duty are committed openly; instead, they tend to be concealed, actively or simply by distance, from those who would be harmed. Is an allegation of this sort of deception enough to state a claim under Rule 10b-5?

By and large, the answer has been yes, and, hence *Santa Fe* has been of somewhat limited significance as a check on the expansiveness of Rule 10b-5. In *Goldberg v. Meridor*, 567 F.2d 209 (2d Cir. 1977), *cert. denied*, 434 U.S. 1069 (1978), the court found a violation of Rule 10b-5 in a derivative action charging a company's board of directors with issuing stock to acquire the assets and liabilities of an affiliated corporation for inadequate consideration. Because no shareholder action was required to approve the transaction, the victim of the fraud was said to be the corporation itself as the seller of the securities. The knowledge of the inadequacy was not attributed to the board because of the conflicting interests of the board members. In essence, then, the fraud was really on the minority shareholders, who were lulled by the misleading disclosure of the inadequate consideration into forgoing some state law remedy to block the transaction. The court squared its decision with *Santa Fe* by pointing to this latter form of deception. Quite a number of circuits have joined in this sort of reasoning in related sorts of mismanagement cases. *E.g., Estate of Soler v. Rodriguez*, 63 F.3d 45 (1st Cir. 1995) (holding that the shareholders need not even know that the challenged transaction occurred); *Wright v. Heizer Corp.*, 560 F.2d 236 (7th Cir. 1977), *cert. denied*, 434 U.S. 1066 (1978).

While *Santa Fe* dealt with the hard case of fraud "on" the issuer, the Court's rhetoric has affected a broader range of disputes under Rule 10b-5. Many open market claims allege that the company concealed various forms of mismanagement, such as a failure to comply with regulatory requirements or a willingness to engage in high-risk business practices. So long as plaintiffs can identify a deceptive statement, the case falls within the Rule, even when, boiled down to its essentials, it might more properly be characterized as alleging breaches of fiduciary duty. In this manner, as with the cases discussed in Chapter 12, the federal securities laws function to police the quality of corporate governance. For discussions of these issues, *see* Thompson & Sale, Securities Fraud as Corporate Governance: Reflections Upon Federalism, 56 Vand. L. Rev. 859 (2003); Langevoort, Seeking Sunlight in *Santa Fe*'s Shadow: The SEC's Pursuit of Managerial Accountability, 79 Wash. U. L.Q. 449 (2001).

PROBLEM

13-19. Zeta Corporation announced the acquisition of Parkersburg Mining in a transaction that did not require the approval of Zeta's shareholders. The announcement was enthusiastic in its description of the benefits that the deal would bring, noting that Parkersburg had been chosen after an exhaustive search for a partner that would provide the right strategic and financial fit. Later, however, the acquisition proved disastrous: Environmental and legal problems caused Zeta to spend nearly a billion dollars, substantially reducing Zeta's profitability. Shareholders who purchased Zeta stock after the announcement have now brought suit charging that Zeta's board and senior managers were reckless in hurrying the acquisition without adequate due diligence, which would have uncovered the risks. Does this state an appropriate 10b-5 claim?

I. *Manipulation*

The legislative history of the '34 Act makes clear that it was driven by congressional dissatisfaction with two characteristics that had seemed to dominate stock exchange trading: speculation and manipulation. For this reason, the Act's substantive anti-manipulation provisions might well be seen as a linchpin of Congress' reform program.

Two of the prohibitions of Section 9(a) illustrate the specific types of practices that were seen as offensive. Subsection (1) prohibits "wash sales" and matched orders: in essence, transactions where the same person (or an affiliate) is for all practical purposes both purchaser and seller. A wash sale has thus only the appearance of a bona fide transaction. Its function should be obvious: A group of investors (often referred to in the legislative history as pool operators) would engage in a series of wash sales at successively higher prices, hoping to lure other investors into purchases by the illusion that the stock price was on a steady upward trend. If successful, members of the pool would dump their holdings of the stock at the high price and then watch the price fall. (Allegedly, these pools included high-level insiders of the issuer. And quite often, the pool's interest in the supply of securities subject to the wash sales would be in the form of options, and the subsequent fall in value would be exploited by short sales—explaining why the regulation of these practices is found in the middle of the Act's anti-manipulation provisions.) For a revisionist account of this history, *see* Mahoney, The Stock Pools and the Securities Exchange Act, 51 J. Fin. Econ. 343 (1999).

Subsection (4) prohibits brokers, dealers, and others who are offering or selling a security from making statements that they know or should know to be false or misleading "for the purpose of inducing the purchase or sale of such security." This practice of spreading misinformation or rumors regarding a security that the person was trying to unload—or paying someone else to "tout" that stock—had as its objective to stoke investor enthusiasm, thereby driving the price upward. Pool operators, not surprisingly, often employed wash sales, falsely optimistic statements, and touting simultaneously.

The common characteristic of these two classic forms of manipulation is behavior that has the effect of artificially distorting the market price of the stock in question, typically by appeals to the speculative impulses of other investors. This is premised on the assumption that market prices and evidence of trading behavior are themselves bits of material information that investors use to make purchase or sale decisions. All this is captured in what may be the "catchall" prohibition of Section 9(a)(2), which makes it unlawful to "effect, alone or with one or more other persons, a series of transactions in any [exchange traded] security . . . creating actual or apparent active trading in such security or raising or depressing the price of such security, for the purpose of inducing the purchase or sale of such security by others." Congress' serious concern with such practices was made clear by its decision to create an express private right of action in Section 9(e), which authorizes any person who purchased a security at a price that was affected by conduct that was in violation of Section 9(a) to sue any person who "willfully" participated in that violation.

This fairly specific statutory scheme is supplemented by Section 10(b), which gives the SEC rulemaking authority to prescribe (assuming the proper nexus with interstate commerce) any manipulative or deceptive device or contrivance in connection with the purchase or sale of any security, whether or not traded on an exchange. As we have seen, courts today assume Section 10(b) gives the Commission the authority to bar only those practices that are both intentional and deceptive. *See Santa Fe Indus. v. Green*, 430 U.S. 462 (1977); *Ernst & Ernst v. Hochfelder*, 425 U.S. 185 (1976); *cf. Schreiber v. Burlington Northern Inc.*,

472 U.S. 1 (1985) (comparable authority with regard to manipulation under Section 14(e), part of the Williams Act).

This legal conclusion, however, is by no means obvious, at least as applied to manipulative conduct. As to intent, note first that Congress throughout Section 9 repeatedly introduced intent-based locutions when it wished to do so; it did not in Section 10(b). Second, note that one of the basic substantive prohibitions, Section 9(a)(4), expressly bars the spreading of misinformation where the person "knew or had reasonable ground to believe" that the information was false or misleading—a negligence standard. As to deception, note that Section 9(a)(2) refers to "actual or apparent active trading" in its prohibition and that Section 10(b) follows not only Section 9(a), but also grants of plenary authority to the Commission to regulate both options trading (Sections 9(b)-(d)) and short selling (Section 10(a)), neither of which is necessarily characterized by any element of deception. By both reference to this sort of structural analysis and a detailed exploration of the legislative history of Section 10(b), Professor Steve Thel has concluded that Section 10(b) was intended to give the SEC plenary rulemaking authority over any act or practice involving speculative activity or otherwise distorting stock prices as fair indicators of investment value, without regard to either intent or a necessary element of deception. *See* Thel, Regulation of Manipulation Under Section 10(b): Securities Prices and the Text of the Securities Exchange Act of 1934, 1988 Colum. Bus. L. Rev. 359 (1988).

1.   Defining Manipulation

United States v. Mulheren
938 F.2d 364 (2d Cir. 1991)

McLAUGHLIN, Circuit Judge: In the late 1980's a wide prosecutorial net was cast upon Wall Street. Along with the usual flotsam and jetsam, the government's catch included some of Wall Street's biggest, brightest, and now infamous—Ivan Boesky, Dennis Levine, Michael Milken, Robert Freeman, Martin Siegel, Boyd L. Jeffries, and Paul A. Bilzerian—each of whom either pleaded guilty to or was convicted of crimes involving illicit trading scandals. Also caught in the government's net was defendant-appellant John A. Mulheren, Jr., the chief trader at and general partner of Jamie Securities Co. ("Jamie"), a registered broker-dealer. . . .

This appeal thus focuses solely on the convictions concerning Mulheren's alleged manipulation of G & W [Gulf & Western] common stock. The government sought to prove that on October 17, 1985, Mulheren purchased 75,000 shares of G & W common stock with the purpose and intent of driving the price of that stock to $45 per share. This, the government claimed, was a favor to Boesky, who wanted to sell his enormous block of G & W common stock back to the company at that price. Mulheren assails the convictions on several grounds. . . .

BACKGROUND

In 1985, at the suggestion of his longtime friend, Carl Icahn, a prominent arbitrageur and corporate raider, Ivan Boesky directed his companies to buy

G & W stock, a security that both Icahn and Boesky believed to be "significantly undervalued." Between April and October 1985, Boesky's companies accumulated 3.4 million shares representing approximately 4.9 percent of the outstanding G & W shares. According to Boesky, Icahn also had a "position of magnitude."

On September 5, 1985, Boesky and Icahn met with Martin Davis, the chairman of G & W. At the meeting, Boesky expressed his interest in taking control of G & W through a leveraged buyout or, failing that, by increasing his position in G & W stock and securing seats on the G & W board of directors. Boesky told Davis that he held 4.9 percent of G & W's outstanding shares. Davis said he was not interested in Boesky's proposal, and he remained adamant in subsequent telephone calls and at a later meeting on October 1, 1985.

At the October 1, 1985 meeting, which Icahn also attended, Boesky added a new string to his bow: if Davis continued to reject Boesky's attempts at control, then G & W should buyout his position at $45 per share. At that time, G & W was, indeed, reducing the number of its outstanding shares through a repurchase program, but, the stock was trading below $45 per share. Davis stated that, although he would consider buying Boesky's shares, he could not immediately agree to a price. Icahn, for his part, indicated that he was not yet sure whether he would sell his G & W stock.

During—and for sometime before—these negotiations, Mulheren and Boesky also maintained a relationship of confidence and trust. The two had often shared market information and given each other trading tips. At some point during the April-October period when Boesky was acquiring G & W stock, Mulheren asked Boesky what he thought of G & W and whether Icahn held a position in the stock. Boesky responded that he "thought well" of G & W stock and that he thought Icahn did indeed own G & W stock. Although Boesky told Mulheren that G & W stock was "a good purchase and worth owning," Boesky never told Mulheren about his meetings or telephone conversations with Davis because he considered the matter "very confidential." Speculation in the press, however, was abound. Reports in the August 19, 1985 issue of Business Week and the September 27, 1985 issue of the Wall Street Journal indicated that Boesky and Icahn each owned close to five percent of G & W and discussed the likelihood of a take-over of the company. Mulheren, however, testifying in his own behalf, denied reading these reports and denied knowing whether Boesky and Icahn held positions in G & W. . . .

Sometime after the close of the market on October 16, 1985, Boesky called Davis, offering to sell his block of shares back to G & W at $45 per share. NYSE trading had closed that day at $44¾ per share, although at one point during that day it had reached $45. Davis told Boesky that the company would buy his shares back, but only at the "last sale"—the price at which the stock traded on the NYSE at the time of the sale—and that Boesky should have his Goldman, Sachs representative contact Kidder Peabody & Co. to arrange the transaction.

After this conversation with Davis, but before 11:00 A.M. on October 17, 1985, Boesky called Mulheren. According to Boesky's testimony, the following, critical exchange took place:

Boesky: Mr. Mulheren asked me if I liked the stock on that particular day, and I said yes, I still liked it. At the time it was trading at 44¾. I said I liked it; however, I would not pay more than 45 for it and it would be great if it traded at 45. The design for the comment—

Defense Counsel Mr. Puccio: Objection to the "design of the comment." I would ask only for the conversation.

A.U.S.A. Gilbert: What if anything did he say to you?

Boesky: I understand.

Shortly after 11:00 A.M. on October 17, 1985, Jamie (Mulheren's company) placed an order with Oliver Ihasz, a floor broker, to purchase 50,000 shares of G & W at the market price. Trading in G & W had been sluggish that morning (only 32,200 shares had traded between 9:30 A.M. and 11:03 A.M.), and the market price was holding steady at $44¾, the price at which it had closed the day before. At 11:04 A.M., Ihasz purchased 16,100 shares at $44¾ per share. Unable to fill the entire 50,000 share order at $44¾, Ihasz purchased the remaining 33,900 shares between 11:05 A.M. and 11:08 A.M. at $44⅞ per share.

At 11:09 A.M., Ihasz received another order from Jamie; this time, to purchase 25,000 shares of G & W for no more than $45 per share. After attempting to execute the trade at $44⅞, Ihasz executed the additional 25,000 share purchase at $45 per share at 11:10 A.M. In sum, between 11:04 A.M. and 11:10 A.M., Jamie purchased a total of 75,000 shares of G & W common stock, causing the price at which it traded per share to rise from $44¾ to $45. At 11:17 A.M., Boesky and Icahn sold their G & W stock — 6,715,700 shares between them — back to the company at $45 per share. Trading in G & W closed on the NYSE on October 17, 1985 at $43⅝ per share. At the end of the day, Jamie's trading in G & W common stock at Mulheren's direction had caused it to lose $64,406.

Discussion . . .

The government's theory of prosecution in this case is straightforward. In its view, when an investor, who is neither a fiduciary nor an insider, engages in securities transactions in the open market with the sole intent to affect the price of the security, the transaction is manipulative and violates Rule 10b-5. Unlawful manipulation occurs, the argument goes, even though the investor has not acted for the "purpose of inducing the purchase or sale of such security by others," an element the government would have had to prove had it chosen to proceed under the manipulation statute, §9(a)(2). Mulheren was not charged with violating §9(a)(2). When the transaction is effected for an investment purpose, the theory continues, there is no manipulation, even if an increase or diminution in price was a foreseeable consequence of the investment.

Although we have misgivings about the government's view of the law, we will assume, without deciding on this appeal, that an investor may lawfully be convicted under Rule 10b-5 where the purpose of his transaction is solely to affect the price of a security. The issue then becomes one of Mulheren's subjective intent. . . .

Assuming that Mulheren knew that Boesky held a substantial position in G & W stock, the government nevertheless failed to prove that Mulheren agreed to and then purchased the 75,000 shares for the sole purpose of raising the price at which G & W common stock traded.

The strongest evidence supporting an inference that Mulheren harbored a manipulative intent, is the telephone conversation between Boesky and

Mulheren that occurred either late in the day on October 16 or before 11:00 A.M. on October 17, 1985. In discussing the virtues of G & W stock, Boesky told Mulheren that he "would not pay more than 45 for it and it would be great if it traded at 45." To this Mulheren replied "I understand." The meaning of this cryptic conversation is, at best, ambiguous, and we reject the government's contention that this conversation "clearly conveyed Boesky's request that the price of the stock be pushed up to $45 . . . [and Mulheren's] agreement to help." Boesky never testified (again, he was not asked) what he meant by his words.

We acknowledge that, construed as an innocent tip—i.e., G & W would be a "great" buy at a price of $45 or below—the conversation appears contradictory. It seems inconsistent for Boesky to advise, on one hand, that he would not pay more than $45, yet on the other to exclaim that it would be a bargain ("great") at $45. The conversation does not make any more sense, however, if construed as a request for illicit manipulation. That Boesky put a limit on the price he would pay for the stock ("I would not pay more than 45 for it") seems inconsistent with a request to drive up the price of the stock. If a conspiracy to manipulate for his own selfish benefit had been Boesky's intent, and if Davis were poised to repurchase the shares at the "last sale," Boesky would obviously have preferred to see Mulheren drive the trading in G & W stock to a price above $45. In this regard, it is noteworthy that there was no evidence whatever that Mulheren knew of Boesky's demand to get $45 per share from G & W. Moreover, during the four to six weeks preceding this conversation, Mulheren repeatedly asked Boesky what he thought of G & W—evincing Mulheren's predisposition (and Boesky's knowledge thereof) to invest in the company. In fact, Mulheren took a position in G & W when he shorted a broker 25,000 shares of G & W after the market closed on October 16.

Clearly, this case would be much less troubling had Boesky said "I want you to bring it up to 45" or, perhaps, even, "I'd like to see it trading at 45." But to hang a conviction on the threadbare phrase "it would be great if it traded at 45," particularly when the government does not suggest that the words were some sort of sinister code, defies reason and a sense of fair play. Any doubt about this is dispelled by the remaining evidence at trial.

First, and perhaps most telling, is that Jamie lost over $64,000 on Mulheren's October 17th transactions. This is hardly the result a market manipulator seeks to achieve. One of the hallmarks of manipulation is some profit or personal gain inuring to the alleged manipulator.

Second, the unrebutted trial testimony of the G & W specialist demonstrated that if raising the price of G & W to $45 per share was Mulheren's sole intent, Mulheren purchased significantly more shares (and put Jamie in a position of greater risk) than necessary to achieve the result. The G & W specialist testified that at the time Jamie placed its second order, 5,000 shares would "definitely" have raised the trading price from $44 to $45 per share. Yet, Jamie bought 25,000 shares.

Although there was no evidence that Mulheren received a quid pro quo from Boesky for buying G & W stock, the government, nevertheless, claims that Mulheren had a "strong pecuniary interest" in accommodating Boesky in order to maintain the close and mutually profitable relationship they enjoyed. With this argument the government is hoist with its own petard. Precisely because of this past profitable relationship, the more reasonable conclusion is that

Mulheren understood Boesky's comment as another tip—this time to buy G & W stock. Indeed, there was no evidence that Boesky had ever asked Mulheren to rig the price of a stock in the past. . . .

We acknowledge that this case treads dangerously close to the line between legitimate inference and impermissible speculation. We are persuaded, however, that to come to the conclusion it did, "the jury must have engaged in false surmise and rank speculation." . . .

NOTES AND QUESTIONS

1. Regulating Manipulation. Does the court's approach to the question of subjective intent create an insuperable obstacle to proving unlawful manipulation? Or is this decision largely a product of the criminal nature of the proceeding? Professors Fischel and Ross have argued that the attempt to regulate manipulation (apart from forms that are clearly deceptive) is inevitably unnecessary and inefficient. They claim that, in efficient markets at least, trading itself will rarely move prices in such a way as to permit the hoped for profit: Manipulative trading therefore is largely self-deterring. In any event, it is nearly impossible to define with precision, meaning that the law will adopt standards that emphasize "bad intent"—with all the difficulties of enforcement and lack of predictability that emphasis on subjective intent always brings. Fischel & Ross, Should the Law Prohibit "Manipulation" in Financial Markets?, 105 Harv. L. Rev. 503 (1991). Their thesis is challenged by Professor Thel, who argues that manipulation has a substantial capacity to succeed, making *Mulheren* the inspiration for an article entitled "$850,000 in Six Minutes: The Mechanics of Securities Manipulation," 79 Cornell L. Rev. 219 (1994).

2. Deception. As noted above, the Supreme Court has imposed a deception requirement in Rule 10b-5 cases generally. As a result, bona fide trading activity would seem not to be manipulative, whatever its purpose. But there is much disagreement in the courts about what factors suffice when the traders' motivation is suspect. For example, what about deliberately trading at the close of the market, because that becomes the day-end reported price? *See Koch v. SEC,* 793 F.3d 147 (D.C. Cir. 2015) (liability for "marking the close"). For a case applying the *Janus Capital* "maker" analysis to market manipulation, *see Fezzani v. Bear Stearns & Co. Inc.,* 716 F.3d 18 (2d Cir. 2013).

3. Manipulation by Trading Platforms. The Exchange Act's drafters may have been concerned about particular types of market manipulation, such as orders placed for the purpose of affecting stock prices and "wash" sales among compatriots, but new technologies have also birthed new ways to manipulate stock prices. In *City of Providence, Rhode Island v. Bats Global Markets, Inc.,* 878 F.3d 36 (2017), the Second Circuit held that plaintiff stock traders had successfully alleged that certain national securities exchanges had engaged in market manipulation by granting high frequency traders (HFTs) special data access and the ability to place complex orders that remained hidden from other traders. According to the court, allegations that these special privileges "created a false appearance of market liquidity" and deprived plaintiffs of "best available prices" were sufficient to show that the exchanges' behavior "artificially affected market activity" in violation of Rule 10b-5, even without any claim that the exchanges themselves engaged in manipulative trading. In so doing, the court rejected any argument that the exchanges merely "aided and abetted" the HFTs' fraud, reasoning that by selling special services to HFTs and misleading others about those services, the exchanges "created a fraudulent scheme . . . that catered to the HFT firms at the expense of individual and institutional traders."

4. Internet Fraud and Manipulation. The SEC has become concerned about the Internet as a vehicle for "pump and dump" and "short and distort" schemes, whereby a commenter—often using an Internet pseudonym—proffers "analysis" of a small or mid-cap company and urges readers to buy/sell, profiting from the resulting price movements. As the problem below shows, however, these schemes pose difficult conceptual issues. Much of what gets posted on these sites sounds like puffery at most. Do other investors really rely on this? *See* Langevoort, Taming the Animal Spirits of the Stock Markets: A Behavioral Approach to Securities Regulation, 97 Nw. U. L. Rev. 135, 158-159 (2002) ("Studies of online investors have shown some lack of insight, but hardly extreme foolishness. . . . The SEC's theory of causation remains dubious if all we can do is point to bounded rationality."). One study of these schemes concludes that pseudonymous commenters lose influence if the market movements occasioned by their articles quickly reverse themselves; however, they respond by abandoning the tainted identities and adopting new ones. *See* Mitts, Short and Distort, Colum. Law & Econ. Working Paper (Jan. 10, 2019), https://papers .ssrn.com/sol3/papers.cfm?abstract_id=3198384. For a statement of the SEC's views, *see* Walker & Levine, You've Got Jail: Current Trends in Internet Securities Fraud, 38 Am. Crim. L. Rev. 405 (2001); Starr & Herman, The Same Old Wine in a Brand New Bottle: Applying Traditional Market Manipulation Principles to Internet Stock Scams, 29 Sec. Reg. L.J. 236 (2001).

PROBLEM

13-20. In late 2000, the SEC brought a celebrated enforcement action against Jonathan Lebed, a New Jersey teenager. *See* Lewis, Jonathan Lebed's Extracurricular Activities, N.Y. Times Mag., Feb. 25, 2001, at 26. Jonathan would buy stock in small, thinly traded technology companies and then make numerous postings on a variety of investment chat room sites. The postings would say such things as "this is the next stock to gain 1,000 percent" or "this is the most undervalued stock ever." Sometimes he would predict a 50 percent gain in a day or two. According to the SEC, trading volume increased after these postings so that the price would go up, after which Lebed would sell. Ultimately, Lebed made more than half a million dollars. Is this fraud? Manipulation?

2. Issuer Repurchases

Investors are not the only ones tempted to manipulate stock prices. Issuers and their associates also have a motive to move their stock price up or down (usually up). This problem arises, for example, in the public offering context, where there is an obvious temptation for those associated with an offering to create the impression that it is a "hot" issue. This was considered in Chapter 4, where we saw the regulatory response in the form of Regulation M.

Another setting where this concern emerges is in a program of open market repurchases by the issuer. A buying program can have an upward influence on price, and an artificially high price might deter or defeat a hostile takeover and certainly will enhance the value of the company's executive compensation package to the extent that some compensation comes in the form of stock or options. In contrast, an artificially low price may be useful to company insiders who are planning to take the company private in a management buyout or freeze-out transaction. Given these temptations, it should hardly be surprising that there is a substantial body of law relating to issuer manipulation. We defer until Chapter 17 the study of the anti-manipulation rules that relate specifically to defensive tactics in connection with a takeover. For now, we concentrate on issuer repurchases generally. Imagine an issuer secretly goes into the market with a large-scale buying program, whether to simply repurchase stock or to fund a pension or employee stock ownership plan, that has the effect of increasing the market price of the stock. Assume further it could not be established that the issuer is in possession of material nonpublic information (since varying this assumption would create a significant insider trading problem). Could this properly be characterized as a violation of Section 9(a) or Rule 10b-5? Why or why not? If there is a problem, does it have to do conceptually with the possibility of inside information (putting aside the proof of possession or misuse)? Or is it simply the market impact? If the latter, why would any restriction relate to the issuer, as opposed to any person who is buying in sufficient volume? Or is the concern primarily that company insiders are often strongly tempted to use company money to inflate stock prices in some self-serving fashion? In any event, would some or all of these concerns be avoided simply by making the issuer disclose the existence of its repurchase plans? For a discussion, *see* Fried, Insider Trading via the Corporation, 164 U. Pa. L. Rev. 801 (2014).

During the 1960s and 1970s, the SEC took a series of enforcement actions against issuers in connection with such repurchase programs. For instance, an action against Georgia-Pacific Corporation (GP) claimed that repurchases were undertaken in a manner that would and did cause its common stock "to rise in order that GP's obligation to issue additional shares of its common stock in return for the interest in other corporations would be avoided or reduced." In particular, at least with respect to one company that GP was seeking to acquire, the company's purchases of some 22,900 of its shares were allegedly timed in such a way that the last sale price of the day—that reported in the financial media—would not drop below the level necessary to avoid triggering those obligations. *SEC v. Georgia Pacific Corp.*, [1964-1966] Fed. Sec. L. Rep. (CCH) ¶91,680 (S.D.N.Y. 1966) (consent).

The difficulties in discerning purpose are such that many issuers saw this type of enforcement action as a threat to their own repurchase programs. After nearly a decade of debate over the proper course, and finally recognizing that the resulting uncertainty might well chill otherwise legitimate repurchase activity, the Commission adopted Rule 10b-18 in 1982. Rule 10b-18 is in the nature of a safe harbor, rather than a prohibition, albeit a safe harbor that is not available in circumstances when certain alternative regulatory schemes (e.g., for issuer repurchases in connection with either a hostile or a self-tender offer) are operative. It provides that an issuer will not be deemed to have violated Section 9(a)(2) or Rule 10b-5 by repurchasing its own securities on the open market if (with certain technical exceptions) (a) the issuer uses only one broker or dealer on any given day; (b) its purchases would not be the opening transaction of the trading day or occur less than half an hour before its close (ten minutes before for large-cap issuers); (c) its purchases are made at prices that do not exceed the highest independent bid or last independent transaction, whichever is higher; and (d) except for certain block transactions, its purchases do not exceed a specified volume level (e.g., 25 percent of the average trading volume for that security over the preceding four calendar weeks). These standards are designed to encourage something of a "dribble-in" process—the converse of the "dribble-out" contemplated for affiliate transactions by Rule 144 under the '33 Act—so that the upward influence of the purchases on the prevailing market price will be minimized. By its terms, Rule 10b-18 states that noncompliance with the safe harbor does not raise a presumption of a violation of Section 9 or Rule 10b-5. For an empirical study of compliance with the safe harbor provisions—indicating that while most issuers stay within its boundaries, noncompliance is reasonably frequent, especially when the issuer's stock price has recently declined—*see* Cook et al., An Analysis of SEC Guidelines for Executing Open Market Repurchases, 76 J. Bus. 289 (2003). What about an issuer that announces a repurchase plan but fails to follow through on it? *See* Fried, supra.

3. Short Selling

Short selling is the process whereby a person commits to an order to sell securities when she does not own any such securities. In order to perform, the seller borrows (hypothecates) the securities, from her broker or another broker, and has them delivered to the clearing agency. After that, if the market price indeed declines, the person can buy the same securities at the lower price, "return" the securities to the broker, and pocket the difference:

> Preparation for a short sale begins with a request that the arbitrageur's broker find a lender for the shares that are to be sold. The universe for potential lenders includes the broker itself if it has an inventory of the desired stock, or institutional investors, including pension funds, insurance companies, and index funds, all of whom have long-term strategies that are unlikely to be negatively affected by liquidity constraints resulting from securities lending. The arbitrageur transfers collateral to the lender in the amount of 102% of the value of the borrowed securities, typically in cash. The lender then pays interest to the arbitrageur on the cash collateral, termed the rebate rate, and has the right to call the loan at any time. If the loan is called at a time when the shares have risen in value, the arbitrageur will be forced to close her position at a loss unless another lender is found. . . . In general, the lending market available to short sellers for large issuer securities is broad and deep. Large cap stocks are generally easy and cheap to borrow, with the great majority requiring loan fees of less than 1% per year. In contrast, borrowing smaller cap stocks with little institutional ownership may be difficult and expensive. As many as 16% of the stocks in the Center for Research in Security Prices file

may be impossible to borrow. . . . Recent theoretical and empirical work suggests that it is more costly to borrow a stock the greater the divergence of opinion in the security's value. The logic reflects the fact that those who do not lend the security forego the price they would have received for its loan. Thus, those holding a stock must value it more highly than those who lend it by an amount in excess of the loan fee. The greater the divergence of opinion concerning the stock's value, the higher the loan fees, yielding the perverse result that the transaction costs of arbitrage increase in precisely the circumstance when the activity is most important.

Gilson & Kraakman, The Mechanisms of Market Efficiency Twenty Years Later: The Hindsight Bias, 28 J. Corp. L. 715, 728-729 (2003).

Short selling is of concern in securities regulation for a variety of reasons. *See* Worley, The Regulation of Short Sales: The Long and Short of It, 55 Brook. L. Rev. 1255 (1990). Perhaps the most familiar concern is the temptation that short positions create to try to *cause* a price drop. Thus, there has been a good bit of attention to the problem of "bear raids," where persons take a short position in a particular stock and then plant stories in the press and spread rumors that lead to the desired price decline. This leads to concern about market volatility. In a rapidly declining market, the temptation to sell short is very strong, and widespread short selling could exacerbate the decline.

The courts have held fairly consistently that even the most aggressive short selling is not manipulative. *E.g., ATSI Communications Inc., v. The Shaar Fund, Ltd.*, 493 F.3d 87, 101 (2d Cir. 2007). On the other hand, short selling that is part of a broader deceptive scheme does violate Rule 10b-5. *E.g., United States v. Russo*, 74 F.3d 1383 (2d Cir. 1996). Besides the direct prohibition against fraud and manipulation, there is substantial regulation of the short selling process, designed to counter its manipulative and destabilizing potential. For some time, the key feature of regulation has been the so-called uptick rule, which prohibited short sales in situations where the last sale price was lower than the immediately previous one. The purpose was to bar short selling in a falling market. This and other restrictions on short selling were controversial; critics argued that it chills the ability of short sellers to act on negative information, thereby undermining market efficiency. Gilson and Kraakman, supra, point out that legal restrictions on short-selling are not the only limitation—self-imposed restrictions on short selling by mutual funds and other institutional investors contribute to the lack of robust down-side pressure on stock prices.

Responding to evidence that short-sale restrictions have at least some dampening effect on market efficiency, the SEC modernized its short selling rules in 2004 through the new "Reg SHO," and in mid-2007, abolished the uptick rule. The SEC's new-found affection for short selling quickly waned, however, with the onset of the credit crisis and meltdown in the financial services industry that began later that same year. As stock prices fell rapidly, especially for banks and securities firms, there was renewed fear of bear raids and threats to the safety and soundness of these firms from downward pressure on their stock prices—threats apparently realized with the collapse of Bear Stearns and Lehman Brothers in 2008. Initially, the SEC's attention was focused on "naked" short selling, a practice of selling short without borrowing the shares for delivery. This has long been treated as at least potentially fraudulent vis-à-vis the seller's broker (*see United States v. Naftalin*, 441 U.S. 768 (1979)), but it can also exacerbate the downward pressure on the stock price because the amount of short selling can increase dramatically when there is no effort to locate securities currently available for borrowing. In the worst case, the seller may have no intent ever to deliver—the aim of the naked short sales is simply to drive the price down temporarily as the bogus sales are reported upon execution. To combat this, the SEC imposed a specific prohibition against manipulative naked shorting and strengthened brokers' obligation to locate securities to cover their customers' short sales and to close out positions where there is persistent failure to deliver. More extraordinary intervention occurred when the SEC temporarily banned short selling activity entirely with respect to specified issuers related to the financial services industry, just before the U.S. government intervened with a massive bailout program for that industry. Thereafter, the SEC debated whether to reinstate the up-tick rule but settled for a middle ground approach with a short sale-related "circuit breaker" designed to halt trading in the event of sharp sudden declines in the price of a particular stock.

‖14‖
The Enforcement of the Securities Laws

This chapter takes a close look at the various approaches to enforcing the securities laws: private actions, SEC enforcement proceedings, and criminal prosecutions. In earlier chapters we examined the substantive elements that give rise to a violation of a statute or regulation. Here we probe the special considerations that arise in the private and public prosecutions that can flow from a violation. This chapter also focuses on the legal and professional responsibilities of lawyers with respect to their client's securities violations.

A. *More on the Private Enforcement of the Securities Laws*

Private remedies are an indispensable component of the overall design of the securities laws. Not only do the various private remedies provide relief to those harmed by a securities law violation, but, more importantly, the existence of a private remedy is a powerful incentive for individuals and companies to comply with the securities laws. The latter is especially significant in light of the Commission's limited resources for oversight and enforcement.

Nevertheless, we should not lose sight of the fact that onerous disclosure obligations and their accompanying liability are like the rain—they fall on the good and the bad alike. The fear of liability is felt not solely by sharp operators, but also by those engaged in legitimate enterprises. Thus, the true task of private remedies, if they are to be socially optimal, is to minimally impose liability on those who are responsible for the loss. Responsibility is a theme that runs through the materials in the first section of this chapter. In deciding responsibility, more is involved than bland inquiries into whether the plaintiff would have suffered the loss "but for" the defendant's behavior. In the many areas examined below, the courts make hard, perhaps even tragic, choices based on their belief of the appropriate duty each party assumes in the transaction. As you examine the many doctrines that follow, consider the relative costs and benefits of the courts' decisions on the parties.

Congress' awareness of the importance of strong private remedies is most evident in the '33 Act. For example, Section 11 provides a private action designed to assure that filed registration statements are accurate, and Section 12(a)(1) exposes sellers to liability regardless of whether they acted innocently in selling securities that should have been registered. The same Congress lost some of its steel when it provided weaker express causes of action for selective '34 Act violations and later, when it addressed the problem of express remedies, was even more oblique in its passage of the Investment Company Act and Investment Advisers Act. This lack of expression, however, has been filled by the courts' recognizing that private rights of action exist by implication for the most important regulatory provisions. The Supreme Court has employed various bases to imply private actions under selected provisions of the securities laws. *See, e.g., J.I. Case Co. v. Borak*, 377 U.S. 426 (1964) (implied cause of action for Section 14(a) of the Exchange Act); *Herman & MacLean v. Huddleston*, 459 U.S. 375 (1983) (existence of implied cause of action under Section 10(b) and Rule 10b-5 "is simply beyond peradventure"). However, in doing so the Court emphasized that the overriding concern was whether implication was consistent with Congress' intent and particularly the broad remedial purposes to be served by each of the federal securities acts.

The materials before and after this chapter examine more closely specific remedies, express and implied, for securities law violations. Overall, their message is the same: Private causes of action supplement the Commission's enforcement efforts and thus assure greater compliance with the securities laws. The materials in this section provide a broader examination of this theme—they consider how developments and doctrines that cut across private and SEC enforcement further the securities laws' goals. We examine the doctrines and arguments that impose responsibility on individuals and entities other than the primary violator. Among the approaches examined below are the scope of aiding and abetting, control person liability, principles of agency law, and standards of conspiracy law. Reaching collateral participants, such as directors, accountants, attorneys, and dominant stockholders, is of interest not only because they provide a deep pocket, but also because by expanding the range of responsible parties there are more individuals who have a stake in compliance with the securities laws, particularly honest dealings on their own part. On this point, consider the questions asked in connection with the court's review of the settlement in one of the largest fraud cases arising from the thrift crisis in the 1980s:

> Where were these professionals when these clearly improper actions were being consummated? Why didn't any of them speak up or disassociate themselves from the transaction? Where also were the outside accountants and attorneys when these transactions were effectuated? What is difficult to understand is that with all the professional talent involved (both accounting and legal), why at least one professional would not have blown the whistle to stop the over-reaching that took place in this case.

Lincoln Sav. & Loan Ass'n v. Wall, 743 F. Supp. 901, 920 (D.D.C. 1990) (Sporkin, J.). The chapter also examines the right to rescind transactions in violation of the securities laws, contribution rights among wrongdoers, possible equitable defenses, and the statute of limitations for private actions.

1. Champion of the Little Guy: The Class Action

A significant portion of the private litigation under the securities laws occurs through the class action procedures of Federal Rule of Civil Procedure 23. Recall that the class representative must establish among other things that (1) common questions of law or fact predominate in the claims raised by the various class members (the commonality requirement) and (2) the claim of the class representative is sufficiently typical of those of the class generally to conclude that she is an appropriate representative (the typicality requirement). Once the suit is certified as a class action, notice is given to all potential class members of the action so they can opt out of the class action and thus avoid the res judicata effects of that action on their rights. Characteristic of so many of the suits under Rule 10b-5 for false corporate announcements by a publicly traded company is that most purchasers or sellers have relatively small amounts at stake. When there are numerous investors who have suffered a common misrepresentation, the class action device is often the only economically viable means of achieving the compensatory and deterrent goals underlying the private action. But in light of the fact that few, if any, members of the class have a significant stake in the litigation's outcome, the class action device raises concerns about abuses of the device as well as abuses of the class by either the representative of the class or the class action's lawyer. *See, e.g.,* Coffee, Understanding the Plaintiffs' Attorney: The Implications of Economic Theory for Private Enforcement Through Class and Derivative Actions, 86 Colum. L. Rev. 669 (1986). Therefore, reform efforts in this area have focused on mechanisms believed to reduce the incidence of harmful "strike suits."

2. Securities Actions After the Private Securities Litigation Reform Act of 1995

Through the early years of the 1990s, securities class actions were very much on the mind of Congress as hearings were held to consider the impact of securities class action suits. The hearings before the Senate and House amassed a good deal of evidence focused on the costs and benefits of securities class actions. The rallying point for those seeking wholesale reform of the securities class action was the broad concern that the number of securities class actions filed annually was growing at an increasing rate and that a significant portion of the suits were settled for under $2 million, suggesting they were the classic form of "strike suit." The testimony provided to Congress reflected that settlements rarely yield even half of what is in dispute and that the plaintiff's lawyers are paid "off the top," thereby causing some disquiet not simply over whether the suits' merits matter, but also whether generally the merits matter enough.[1] Though the congressional hearings did not

---

1. A synthesis of the empirical data presented before the Congress appears in Private Securities Litigation, Staff Report, Senate Subcommittee on Securities of the Comm. on Banking, Housing and Urban Affairs, 98th Cong., 2d Sess. 108 (May 17, 1994). A close analysis of this data appears in Seligman, The Merits Do Matter, 108 Harv. L. Rev. 438 (1994).

amass evidence that there was an epidemic of securities class action litigation or that there were widespread abuses of private securities class actions, the hearings did serve as a vehicle for accountants, underwriters, and executives of high-tech companies to voice their collective concern that securities law class actions needed reforming. Their efforts produced the Private Securities Litigation Reform Act of 1995. The PSLRA's provisions dealing with class action procedures are set forth in Section 27 of the Securities Act, with identical provisions added to the Exchange Act in its Section 21D. The centerpiece of the PSLRA's procedural changes is the appointment of a "lead plaintiff." Fearing that diligence in evaluating and drafting complaints often suffered because class action counsel is customarily chosen on a first-to-file basis, the PSLRA in Section 27(a)(3) of the Securities Act and Section 21D(a)(3) of the Exchange Act set forth procedures by which the court is to appoint from the members of the class a lead plaintiff; the PSLRA provides a rebuttable presumption that the member of the purported class with the largest financial stake in the relief sought is the "most adequate plaintiff." The new procedures require that notice be given to all members of the purported class action so they may request to be the lead plaintiff. Among the tasks of the lead plaintiff is to select and retain counsel to represent the class. An obvious object of the lead plaintiff provision is to harness the institutional investor's self-interest to guide the direction of the class action. Just as institutions are "heavy hitters" in securities markets, they also garner a substantial portion of the funds recovered in class action settlements. One study found that the 50 largest claimants in 82 class actions had an average allowed loss of $597,000 and the 50 claimants accounted for an average of 57.5 percent of all allowed losses, with the average of the largest and the second largest claimants accounting for 13.1 percent and 6.7 percent, respectively, of the total recognized losses of a subset of 20 class actions within their sample. Weiss & Beckerman, Let the Money Do the Monitoring: How Institutional Investors Can Reduce Agency Costs in Securities Class Actions, 104 Yale L.J. 2053, 2089-2090 (1995).

In thinking about the relationship of lead plaintiff and its counsel, consider the double-whammy effects of the PSLRA barring discovery until after the defendant's motion to dismiss[2] and, as discussed in Chapter 13, the PSLRA raising the pleading standard to require for fraud claims each defendant's knowledge to be plead with such particularity as to raise a "strong inference" the defendant has committed a violation. *See* Exchange Act Section 21D(b)(1)(2). What impact are these twin obstacles to the suit going forward likely to have on the willingness of a financial institution to serve as a lead plaintiff? A further consideration is what type of financial institution is most likely to take on the role of a lead plaintiff. A bank? Private pension fund? Mutual fund?

---

2. Section 27(b)(1) of the Securities Act and Section 21D(b)(3)(B) of the Exchange Act. The courts infrequently invoke an exception if "undue prejudice" would otherwise occur. *See, e.g., In re Royal Ahold Nv. Sec. and ERISA Litig.*, 220 F.R.D. 246 (D. Md. 2004).

NOTES AND QUESTIONS

1.   Hiring and Paying Class Counsel.   The PSLRA empowers the lead plaintiff to "select and retain" counsel to represent the class. In an early case, the Third Circuit held the district court erred in selecting counsel via competitive bidding among law firms and thereby disregarding the lead plaintiff's choice of counsel as well as the terms of the retainer (which incidentally was substantially below all competitive bids) it had negotiated with its chosen counsel. *In re Cendant Corp. Sec. Litig.*, 264 F.3d 201 (3d Cir. 2001). Why not select counsel via an auction presided over by the court whereby bids from competing law firms would determine who would represent the lead plaintiff? *See generally* Fisch, Lawyers on the Auction Block: Evaluating the Selection of Class Counsel by Auction, 102 Colum. L. Rev. 650 (2002). Would the process be improved if as part of the process for selecting the lead plaintiff the court gave more consideration to the existence and content of an ex ante fee agreement with proposed class counsel? *See also Herrott v. Cavanaugh*, 306 F.3d 726 (9th Cir. 2002) (reversing district court's selection of lead plaintiff with a $59,000 loss who had negotiated a fee arrangement one-half the percentage rate of five businessmen with losses of $3.3 million; the Ninth Circuit reasoned that size of loss, not attorneys' fees, guides the selection of the lead plaintiff).

A comprehensive study found that there was competition to be the lead plaintiff in 71 percent of the cases studied; only 11 percent of the time was an ex ante fee agreement discussed by the court in making the lead plaintiff appointment; fees tend to be lower in federal courts that see a high volume of securities class actions; fees are lower (as a percentage of the settlement) when there was an ex ante fee agreement between the lead plaintiff and class counsel; and public pension funds are more likely to negotiate ex ante fee agreements with counsel (27 percent of the time for public pension funds versus 13 percent for other types of lead plaintiff). Baker, Perino & Silver, Is the Price Right? An Empirical Study of Fee Setting in Securities Class Actions, 115 Colum. L. Rev. 1371 (2015).

2.   Aggregation.   Should the court be persuaded that the most adequate plaintiff is a group of 137 individual investors who collectively have lost more money than a pension fund that is also seeking to be appointed? *Compare Yousefi v. Lockheed Martin Corp.*, 70 F. Supp. 2d 1061 (C.D. Cal. 1999) (aggregation of 137 individual investors denied) *with Netsky v. Capstead Mortgage Corp.*, 2000 U.S. Dist. LEXIS 9941 (N.D. Tex. 2000) (group of 1,155 investors aggregated and represented by panel of six of them, one of whom accounted for $1.26 million of the group's total losses). *See generally* Heck, Comment, Conflict and Aggregation: Appointing Institutional Investors as Sole Lead Plaintiffs Under the PSLRA, 66 U. Chi. L. Rev. 1199 (1999).

3.   The Motives and Moves of the Institutional Investor.   As set forth in the Weiss and Beckerman study discussed earlier, institutions typically have significant claims in most securities class actions. Certainly this is to be expected in those suits involving larger issuers that meet the liquidity concerns most institutional investors have. But do you expect all institutions—banks, insurers, mutual funds, pension funds, and endowments—have the same willingness to serve as a lead plaintiff? Also, just what reward does an institution gain by serving as a lead plaintiff, particularly if we recognize that its decision and ongoing participation as a lead plaintiff is not costless to it. On the association between institutions and settlement amounts, *see* Cox, Thomas & Kiku, Does the Plaintiff Matter? An Empirical Analysis of Lead Plaintiffs in Securities Class Actions, 106 Colum. L. Rev. 1587 (2006) (while provable losses are positively related to settlement amount, the presence of an institutional lead plaintiff substantially increases the settlement amount).

Not totally divorced from these questions is the insight from a study of settled securities class actions that nearly two-thirds of the institutions that had provable claims failed to submit their claims when the suits were settled. *See* Cox & Thomas, Letting Billions Slip Through Your Fingers: Empirical Evidence and Legal Implications of the Failure of Financial Institutions to Participate in Securities Class Action Settlements, 58 Stan. L. Rev. 411 (2005); Cox & Thomas, Leaving Money on the Table: Do Institutional Investors Fail to File Claims in Securities Class Actions?, 80 Wash. U. L.Q. 855 (2002).

4. Congress Addresses the Strike Suit.   The PSLRA introduces a number of changes that respond directly to Congress' concern about the number of securities class actions that are strike suits. It limits the number of class actions for which any person can serve as a lead plaintiff to five securities class actions during any three-year period, caps attorneys' fees at a reasonable percentage of the amount of any damages, expands the disclosure to class members that must accompany any settlement submitted to the court for approval, and mandates that the class action court provide a finding respecting each party's and attorney's compliance with Rule 11(b) of the Federal Rules of Civil Procedure. It should be added that Rule 11(b)'s sanction for failing to make reasonable inquiry that a complaint, responsive pleading, or motion is well founded in law or fact has rarely been invoked in securities litigation. In a leading Rule 11 securities fraud case, the attorneys were sanctioned because they did not separately investigate the allegations of the earlier-filed complaint, but merely filed a so-called copycat complaint that repeated the allegations of an earlier action, *Garr v. U.S. Healthcare, Inc.*, 28 F.3d 1333 (3d Cir. 1994). *See also Gurary v. Nu-Tech Bio Med, Inc.*, 303 F.3d 212 (2d Cir. 2002) (awarding fees because the few claims that were not frivolous were not sufficient to prevent the suit on the whole from lacking merit, and recoverable fees included the costs incurred to pursue the sanction). For characteristics of low-settlement suits, *see* Cox, Thomas & Bai, There Are Plaintiffs and . . . There Are Plaintiffs: An Empirical Analysis of Securities Class Action Settlements, 61 Vand. L. Rev. 355, 380-384 (2008) (settlements under $2 million settle more quickly, involve smaller firms, have shorter class periods, and have lower provable losses than larger settlement cases).

5. Private Ordering and Securities Litigation.   The Delaware courts have provided strong support for corporations to embrace private ordering as a way of addressing shareholder litigation. *See ATP Tour, Inc. v. Deutscher Tennis Bund*, 91 A.3d 554 (Del. 2014) (upholding bylaw that shifted the defense's litigation costs to the plaintiff when the suit was not "substantially successful"); *Boilermakers Local 154 Ret. Fund v. Chevron Corp.*, 73 A.3d 934 (Del. Ch. 2013) (upholding board-adopted forum selection bylaw for shareholder suits). Such developments at the state level have hastened a movement among public companies through bylaw provisions that alter the rules that normally apply to shareholder suits to address fears of securities fraud suits. Private ordering initiatives cover a range of matters such as discarding the "American Rule" whereby litigants are responsible for their own litigation costs and adopting fee shifting whereby an "unsuccessful" plaintiff must reimburse the corporation's litigation expenses, restricting use of the class action by shareholders, requiring shareholders to post security for the corporation's litigation expenses, and calling for arbitration of all shareholder disputes.

In 2012, the registration statement of Carlyle Group L.P. caused a good deal of discussion because it disclosed that its limited partnership agreement included a mandatory arbitration provision that would cover shareholder suits, including any suit under Section 11 for any misrepresentation in the then pending registration statement; Carlyle ultimately removed the arbitration provision when the SEC indicated the provision might prevent the staff from agreeing to acceleration of the registration statement's effectiveness. The SEC's reticence was based on the anti-waiver provisions set forth in Section 14 of the Securities Act and Section 29(a) of the Exchange Act that broadly prohibit agreements "to waive compliance with any provision" of the securities laws. A related development is the SEC agreeing with a company's exclusion from its proxy statement of a shareholder proposal that would require securities claims be arbitrated. Johnson & Johnson SEC No-Action Letter (Feb. 11, 2019) (relying on submission by the attorney general of the company's domicile that the state would likely follow *Sciabacucchi v. Salzberg*, 2018 Del. Ch. LEXIS 578 (Dec. 19, 2018), holding that state corporate law authorizes charter or bylaw provisions to regulate only those matters and relationships internal to the corporation). Does the PSLRA's comprehensive treatment of class actions specifically, and securities fraud generally, raise additional legal issues to such private ordering, namely federal preemption of state law authorizing incursions into the prosecution of securities law claims, and particularly those brought as a class action? *See* Lipton, Manufactured Consent: The Problem of Arbitration Clauses in Corporate Charters and Bylaws, 104 Geo. L.J. 583 (2016); Sjostrom, The Intersection of Fee-Shifting Bylaws and Securities Fraud Litigation, 93 Wash. U. L. Rev. 379 (2015).

As discussed later in Chapters 18 and 20, the Supreme Court, reflecting the effect of the Federal Arbitration Act, has, in limited instances, upheld such agreements, e.g., between a broker and her customer. *See, e.g., Shearson/American Express, Inc. v. McMahon*, 482 U.S. 220, 226-230 (1987). Is there a stronger argument for violation of the anti-waiver provision in the case of class actions than in individual actions?

6.   Why Private Suits?   While securities class actions are accepted by the courts, they have not been universally acclaimed by academics. Some would replace private suits entirely. *See, e.g.,* Bratton & Wachter, The Political Economy of Fraud on the Market, 160 U. Pa. L. Rev. 69 (2011) (arguing that SEC enforcement is more efficient than private suits); Grundfest, Why Disimply?, 108 Harv. L. Rev. 727 (1995) (private litigation currently negatively impacts capital formation and SEC can better reform contours of private suit through its rulemaking than can Congress or courts). An intermediate approach is to interject the SEC into an oversight role for private suits so that the agency's approval would be a precondition to the suit proceeding. Rose, Reforming Securities Litigation: Restructuring the Relationship Between Public and Private Enforcement of Rule 10b-5, 108 Colum. L. Rev. 1301 (2008). In contrast, Professor Park extolls the virtue of the present system, reasoning there are benefits of melding SEC enforcement with politically and socially inspired enforcement by state attorney generals and entrepreneurial class action lawyers. Park, Rules, Principles, and the Competition to Enforce the Securities Laws, 100 Cal. L. Rev. 115 (2012). The question of the relative efficacy of private vs. SEC enforcement is empirically testable. *See, e.g.,* Choi & Pritchard, SEC Investigations and Securities Class Actions: An Empirical Comparison, 13 J. Empirical L. Studies 27 (2016) (using various market-based measures, the authors conclude that class action attorneys target disclosure violations more precisely than the SEC and they produce more resignations of senior officers likely connected to the violation than do SEC-initiated suits that are not accompanied by any private action).

3. Closing the Bypass: The Securities Litigation Uniform Standards Act

The PSLRA was just the first shoe to fall on the plaintiff counsel's aggressive pursuit of class actions. In the year following the passage of the PSLRA, there was a noticeable increase in the number of securities class action suits filed in state courts. Congress, thus fearing that its 1995 reform efforts were being circumvented by the class action lawyers' flight to the state courts, returned to the subject of securities class actions. In 1998, the Securities Litigation Uniform Standards Act (SLUSA) was enacted and thereby amended Section 28(f) of the Securities Exchange Act to confer on the federal courts the exclusive jurisdiction over most securities class actions. SLUSA reflects Congress' belief that an unintended consequence of the PSLRA was that the plaintiff's bar frequently avoided substantive and procedural standards imposed by the PSLRA to address abuses of the securities class action by filing their suits in state courts. *See* Painter, Responding to a False Alarm: Federal Preemption of State Securities Fraud Causes of Action, 84 Cornell L. Rev. 1 (1998). To counter such a migration to state courts, SLUSA preempts state court jurisdiction for class action suits involving "covered securities," a term defined in Section 18(b) of the Securities Act that includes NYSE well as Nasdaq/ National Market System securities and securities issued by a registered investment company. *Class actions* are defined as suits that seek relief on behalf of 50 or more persons. SLUSA excludes several types of suits from its otherwise broad preemptive effects. The most notable of its exclusions is the so-called Delaware carve-out that preserves the state court's jurisdiction to hear certain state law fiduciary claims focused on misrepresentations by the firm's officers, directors, or control persons; such suits primarily arise in connection with statements involving tender offers, mergers, and other acquisitions. By permitting such suits to continue to be brought in state court, SLUSA preserves a rich and quickly developing body of state fiduciary duty law. *See generally*

Hamermesh, Calling Off the Lynch Mob: The Corporate Director's Fiduciary Disclosure Duty, 49 Vand. L. Rev. 1087 (1996).

There is a good deal of uncertainty regarding SLUSA's scope. Much of this uncertainty focuses on Section 28(f)'s language "party *alleging* . . . [a misrepresentation or deceptive device] *in connection with* the purchase or sale of a covered security." *Chadbourne & Parke LLP v. Troice*, 134 S. Ct. 1058 (2014), held that "in connection with" requires the "fraudulent representation" to be one that "is material to the decision by one or more individuals (other than the fraudster) to buy or sell a covered security." Applying this test, the Court held that SLUSA did not bar investors suing the issuer of certificates of deposit (a non-covered security) where the issuer falsely represented it could pay above-market rates of interest because it invested in "highly marketable securities" (which clearly referred to securities that were "covered securities"). In fact, the bank was engaged in a Ponzi scheme that ultimately collapsed. A different issue arose in another case spawned by another Ponzi scheme. In *Criterium Capital Funds B.V. v. Tremont (Berm.) Ltd.*, 784 F.3d 128 (2d Cir. 2015), a class action was brought against an investment adviser who functioned as a "feeder fund" to the infamous Bernard Madoff. When Madoff's Ponzi scheme unraveled, the investors lost nearly all their initial investment, about $1.8 billion. The Second Circuit held it was error for SLUSA to have been applied solely because the complaint alleged that Madoff had engaged in misstatements in connection with the purchase and sale of securities. Instead, the Second Circuit reasoned "SLUSA's preclusion applies when the state law claim is predicated on conduct *of the defendant* specified in SLUSA's operative provisions, which reference the anti-falsity provisions of the 1933 and 1934 Acts." Id. at 149 (emphasis original). Applying this rule, the Second Circuit held that the investors' claims that were premised on the adviser's failure to monitor the portfolio and contract claims related to the adviser's oversight; hence they were not, therefore, subject to SLUSA; however, state law claims alleging the adviser negligently and knowingly committed false representation were subject to SLUSA. *But see Brown v. Calamos*, 664 F.3d 123 (7th Cir. 2011) (SLUSA applied on reasoning that nondisclosure underlies any claim of a breach of fiduciary duty).

Recall that Section 22(a) provides for concurrent state and federal jurisdiction in '33 Act suits. A unanimous Supreme Court held in *Cyan, Inc. v. Beaver Cnty. Employees Ret. Fund*, 138 S. Ct. 1061 (2018), that SLUSA does not apply to '33 Act suits, so they can be brought in state courts and are not removable to federal court. A separate question is whether the Class Action Fairness Act compels '33 Act–based class actions to be in the federal courts when joined with state law claims that are removable under CAFA. *Compare Katz v. Gerardi*, 552 F.3d 558 (7th Cir. 2008) (CAFA applies) *with Luther v. Countrywide Home Loans Servicing LP*, 533 F.3d 1031 (9th Cir. 2008) (CAFA does not apply). *See* Klausner, Hegland, LeVine & Leonard, State Section 11 Litigation in the Post-*Cyan* Environment, Stanford Working Paper 2019 (consistent with more permissive state procedural rules on matters such as pleading and availability of discovery, *Cyan* is associated with increase in Section 11 cases being filed in state courts, dismissal rates in state courts are significantly below those in federal courts, and settlements occur in about 80 percent of all the state filings even if the parallel federal case has been dismissed).

PROBLEMS

14-1.   Shortly after announcing it had "turned the corner" and expected to break even in the upcoming fiscal period, Exacto Inc. filed for bankruptcy. Bob filed a class action against Exacto's officers who prepared the misleading announcement. The action was filed in state court on behalf of hundreds of investors, each of whom is prepared to establish that he or she would have sold their Exacto shares but for Exacto's false announcement. Is this suit within SLUSA? *See Merrill Lynch, Pierce, Fenner & Smith, Inc. v. Dabit,* 547 U.S. 71 (2006).

14-2. WhaleCo shareholders narrowly approved its acquisition of Minnow, Ltd., with only 50.21 percent of the shareholders voting in favor. The proxy statement made certain material disclosures about each company, but stated that neither company would further update any of the disclosures made in the proxy statement. The proxy statement went to great lengths in describing the risks for the disclosures that were made as well as the risks of there being no updating of the disclosures that were made even if there was intervening material information. Four months after the acquisition was completed, WhaleCo disclosed that a number of financial and operating problems existed in the former Minnow operations. WhaleCo's stock plummeted. A shareholder class action was filed in state court alleging the directors had breached their fiduciary duty by failing to disclose a range of adverse information the directors learned of in the intervening period between the circulation of the proxy and the merger's disclosure. The lawyers for the directors relying on SLUSA have moved for the suit's removal to federal court. How should the court rule? *See Paradise Wire & Cable Defined Pension Plan v. Weil,* 918 F.3d 312 (4th Cir. 2019).

14-3.   Beta Inc. engaged Silver Baggs, an investment bank, to assist it in finding a firm to acquire Beta. Ultimately, with the assistance of Silver Baggs, Beta merged with Alpha Inc. Pursuant to the merger one share of Alpha was exchanged for each Beta share. A short time after the merger, Alpha announced a significant earnings restatement. Thereupon Alpha shares lost sixty percent of their value. Alice, on behalf of the former Beta shareholders, initiated in state court a class action against Silver Baggs, alleging Silver Baggs acted in a grossly negligent manner in carrying out due diligence of Alpha at the request of Beta. Alice alleges that because of Silver Baggs' negligence the Beta shareholders incurred substantial losses. Alpha has filed a petition under SLUSA to remove the case to federal court. Should the petition be granted? *See Madden v. Cowen & Co.,* 576 F.3d 957 (9th Cir. 2009).

B.   *Secondary Liability Under the Securities Laws*

Who bears responsibility for a securities law violation? This is an easy question when there is but a single actor in the transaction, as when an individual sells her securities to another by means of a false representation. But seldom do securities violations occur in such a simple setting. Generally, the violation is committed by an employee, officer, or partner of a firm whose actions are assisted in many ways by the efforts of others. For example, in the case of the fraudulent sale of securities on behalf of Enterprise, the misrepresentations frequently appear in an offering brochure prepared by Enterprise's outside law firm. That brochure contains financial information reviewed by its independent public accountants, and the overall distribution is overseen by a broker-dealer. Which of these parties, if any, should share in the responsibility for any misrepresentations that appear in the offering brochure that they reviewed? And while it may be an easy matter to conclude in the abstract that Enterprise is financially responsible for misrepresentations made in its offering brochure, how is this result achieved under the federal securities laws? Remember, the company acts only through individuals. Should responsibility extend through Enterprise to reach those who control Enterprise's overall activities—for example, its directors and senior executive officers? Should responsibility be extended even farther down into the organization to reach the immediate supervisor of the person who prepared the misleading brochure? Should Enterprise be vicariously liable?

In addressing the question of who should share responsibility for a securities violation, analytically it is helpful to distinguish between so-called primary and secondary violators. A *primary violator* commits the act proscribed by the statute or rule; a *secondary violator* either assists or supports the primary violator or is liable because of a relationship with the violator. Because some courts impose liability on secondary parties solely because of their relationship with the violator, for example, under the doctrine of respondeat superior, it is something of a misnomer in these cases to refer to them as secondary *violators*. Whatever the basis of expanding the scope of liability, whether due to the secondary party's assistance or its relationship with the primary violator, one cannot ignore the fact that overall the consequences have both a compensatory and a deterrent effect. The compensatory nature reflects the natural tendency of the private plaintiff to seek the "deep pocket" because the most culpable participant to a securities violation frequently has fled the country, is bankrupt, or has too few assets to fully compensate the plaintiff. Hence, lawyers, accountants, and banks, to mention just a few, are pursued by the injured investor on the theory that they were sufficiently involved with key aspects of the transaction giving rise to the violation that they are financially responsible for the plaintiff's losses. And, of course, by expanding the universe of those responsible for compliance with the securities laws, many who are only collaterally involved in transactions are conscripted to ensure no securities law violations occur in connection with those transactions. Importantly in this regard, certain professionals—attorneys, accountants, and underwriters come quickly to mind—serve important policing functions as a consequence of the potential liability they may have under the securities laws. Indeed, they are frequently cast in the role of gatekeepers, but with little debate over why this should be so, other than the broad incantations that investor protection and the objectives of the securities laws depend heavily on their commitment as professionals to ensuring their clients' compliance. While certainly this is the case, we may question why this need be so. Are the sanctions against primary violators too weak to deter their wrongdoing? Is the chance for their apprehension and successful prosecution too slight to deter their violations? In the overall enforcement arena, is the public conscription of the private gatekeeper the most efficient enforcement mechanism? *See generally* Kraakman, Gatekeepers: The Anatomy of a Third-Party Enforcement Strategy, 2

J.L. Econ. & Org. 53 (1986). Aiding and abetting as well as control person liability, discussed below, are mechanisms for expanding the scope of responsibility for compliance with the securities laws.

1.   Aiding and Abetting

For three decades, accountants, lawyers, underwriters, banks, and others were routinely held liable under Section 10(b) and Rule 10b-5 of the Exchange Act on the ground they had aided and abetted their client's violation. Each of the circuits held that aiding and abetting was itself a violation of the antifraud provision. In light of the universal acceptance of aiding and abetting liability, the litigation bar was shocked when *Central Bank of Denver v. First Interstate Bank of Denver*, 511 U.S. 164 (1994), held that aiding and abetting liability was not within the reach of Section 10(b) and Rule 10b-5. As seen in Chapter 13, *Central Bank* held that the antifraud provision "prohibits only the making of a material misstatement (or omission) or the commission of a manipulative act." *Janus Capital Group, Inc. v. First Derivative Traders*, 565 U.S. 135, 142, (2011), narrowed *Central Bank*, holding primary participant liability reached those with "ultimate authority over the statement including its content and whether and how to communicate it." Congress responded to *Central Bank* by expressly authorizing SEC enforcement actions for aiding and abetting in Section 20(e) to the Exchange Act.

> ## Securities and Exchange Commission v. Apuzzo
> ### 689 F.3d 204 (2d Cir. 2012)

Judges: Before: WINTER, RAGGI, Circuit Judges, and RAKOFF, District Judge.*

RAKOFF, *District Judge.*

The Securities and Exchange Commission ("SEC") alleges that defendant Joseph Apuzzo aided and abetted securities laws violations through his role in a fraudulent accounting scheme. In order for a defendant to be liable as an aider and abettor in a civil enforcement action, the SEC must prove: "(1) the existence of a securities law violation by the primary (as opposed to the aiding and abetting) party; (2) 'knowledge' of this violation on the part of the aider and abettor; and (3) 'substantial assistance' by the aider and abettor in the achievement of the primary violation.". . . . After Apuzzo moved to dismiss the Complaint, the district court, Thompson, J., granted Apuzzo's motion to dismiss. Although the district court found that the Complaint plausibly alleged that Apuzzo had actual knowledge of the primary violation, it concluded that the Complaint did not adequately allege "substantial assistance." Specifically, the district court held that the "substantial assistance" component required that the aider and abettor proximately cause the harm on which the primary violation was predicated, and that the Complaint did not plausibly allege such proximate causation. . . .

---

*   [Sitting by designation.—EDS.]

FACTUAL ALLEGATIONS . . .

The Terex Corporation ("Terex") manufactures equipment primarily for use in the construction, infrastructure, and surface to mining industries. Apuzzo was the Chief Financial Officer of Terex. . . . United Rentals, Inc. ("URI") is one of the largest equipment rental companies in the world. Michael J. Nolan was URI's Chief Financial Officer. . . .

URI and Nolan, with Apuzzo's assistance, carried out two fraudulent "sale-leaseback" transactions. These transactions were designed to allow URI to "recognize revenue prematurely and to inflate the profit generated from URI's sales." . . .

Briefly stated, the scheme worked as follows: URI sold used equipment to General Electric Credit Corporation ("GECC"), a financing corporation, and leased the equipment back for a short period. . . . [GECC was willing to undertake the purchase because Terex guaranteed 96 percent of the equipment's value at the end of the short lease period; GECC was thereby assured it had very little risk related to resale of the equipment at the end of each lease. However, to obtain Terex's participation, URI secretly agreed to indemnify Terex for any loss it may suffer on its guaranty to GECC. As an inducement to Terex to participate in the transactions, URI agreed to make substantial equipment purchases from Terex that would improve Terex's year-end sales. Since through the indemnification agreement URI essentially retained the "risks and rewards of ownership" of the equipment, the indemnification agreement violated Generally Accepted Accounting Principles (GAAP) for the recognition of any revenue by URI. Under GAAP a sale requires an arm's-length transaction, which minimally means a transaction where the risks and rewards have been transferred to another.]

Apuzzo knew that if the full extent of the three party transactions was transparent, URI would not be able to claim the increased revenue. Apuzzo therefore executed various agreements that disguised URI's continuing risks and financial obligations, and he also approved inflated invoices from Terex that were designed to conceal URI's indemnification payments to Terex.[1] . . .

DISCUSSION

Section 20(e) of the Securities Exchange Act of 1934[, 15 U.S.C. §78t(e),] allows the SEC, but not private litigants, to bring civil actions against aiders and abettors of securities fraud. . . . The SEC may bring such an action against "any person that knowingly provides substantial assistance" to a primary violator of the securities laws.[6] Specifically, as noted above, the SEC must prove: (1) the existence of a securities law violation by the primary (as opposed to the aiding

---

[1]. The Complaint alleges that Apuzzo approved inflated invoices relevant to the first transaction. . . . With respect to the second transaction, . . . the Complaint alleges that Apuzzo knew about the inflated invoices, and that he was in charge of the transaction, but it does not specifically allege that he approved those invoices.

[6]. The Dodd-Frank Act of 2010 amended Section 20(e) to add the words "or recklessly" after "knowingly." . . . This amendment does not apply in this case.

and abetting) party; (2) knowledge of this violation on the part of the aider and abettor; and (3) "substantial assistance" by the aider and abettor in the achievement of the primary violation. *DiBella*, 587 F.3d at 566. Apuzzo conceded below that the SEC had adequately pleaded the existence of a primary violation, and he does not contest on appeal the district court's finding that the SEC adequately pleaded his actual knowledge of the fraud. Therefore, the only disputed question on appeal is whether the facts alleged plausibly plead that Apuzzo substantially assisted the primary violator in committing the fraud.

In assessing this issue, we draw guidance from the well-developed law of aiding and abetting liability in criminal cases; for if the conduct of an aider and abettor is sufficient to impose criminal liability, *a fortiori* it is sufficient to impose civil liability in a government enforcement action. Nearly seventy-five years ago, Judge Learned Hand famously stated that in order for a criminal defendant to be liable as an aider and abettor, the Government—in addition to proving that the primary violation occurred and that the defendant had knowledge of it (the equivalent of the first two elements of *DiBella*)—must also prove "that he in some sort associate[d] himself with the venture, that [the defendant] participate[d] in it as in something that he wishe[d] to bring about, [and] that he [sought] by his action to make it succeed." *United States v. Peoni*, 100 F.2d 401, 402 (2d Cir. 1938). The Supreme Court later adopted Judge Hand's formulation. *Nye & Nissen v. United States*, 336 U.S. 613, 619 . . . (1949). In fact, as the Seventh Circuit has recognized, Judge Hand's standard is "[t]he classic formula for aider and abettor liability." *United States v. Irwin*, 149 F.3d 565, 569 (7th Cir. 1998). Judge Hand's standard has thus survived the test of time, is clear, concise, and workable, and governs the determination of aider and abettor liability in securities fraud cases.

. . . Apuzzo argues that substantial assistance should, instead, be defined as proximate cause, his argument ignores the difference between an SEC enforcement action and a private suit for damages. "Proximate cause" is the language of private tort actions; it derives from the need of a private plaintiff, seeking compensation, to show that his injury was proximately caused by the defendants' actions. . . .

We now clarify that, in enforcement actions brought under 15 U.S.C. §78t(e), the SEC is not required to plead or prove that an aider and abettor proximately caused the primary securities law violation. In fact, the statute under which the SEC here proceeds, 15 U.S.C. §78t(e), was passed in the wake of *Central Bank* precisely to allow the SEC to pursue aiders and abettors who, under the reasoning of *Central Bank*, were not the [sic] themselves involved in the making of the false statements that proximately caused the plaintiffs' injuries. *See Stoneridge Inv. Partners, LLC v. Scientific-Atlanta*, 552 U.S. 148, 158, . . . (2008). This statutory mandate would be undercut if proximate causation were required for aider and abettor liability in SEC enforcement actions.

Indeed, because only the SEC may bring aiding and abetting claims for securities law violations, many if not most aiders and abettors would escape all liability if such a proximate cause requirement were imposed, since, almost by definition, the activities of an aider and abettor are rarely the direct cause of the injury brought about by the fraud, however much they may contribute to the success of the scheme. We therefore welcome the opportunity to clarify that the appropriate standard for determining the substantial assistance component of aider and abettor liability in an SEC civil enforcement action is the Judge Hand standard set forth above.[11]

Applying the test we have laid out above, it is clear that the Complaint plausibly alleges that Apuzzo provided substantial assistance to the primary violator in carrying out the fraud, and therefore we must reverse the district court. Apuzzo associated himself with the venture, participated in it as something that he wished to bring about, and sought by his action to make it succeed. Specifically, Apuzzo agreed to participate in the Terex I & Terex II transactions;[12] negotiated the details of those transactions, through which he extracted certain agreements from URI in exchange for Terex's participation; approved and signed separate agreements with GECC and URI, which he knew were designed to hide URI's continuing risks and financial obligations relating to the sale-leaseback transactions in furtherance of the fraud; and approved or knew about the issuance of Terex's inflated invoices, which he also knew were designed to further the fraud.

Apuzzo argues that his participation in the transactions alone is insufficient to demonstrate substantial assistance because, he contends, "there is simply no allegation in the Complaint that these transactions were unusual." Appellee's Br. at 30. This, however, is doubly erroneous, both because Apuzzo's substantial assistance extended beyond his agreement to participate in the transactions and because the well-pleaded allegations of the Complaint aver that these transactions were hardly ordinary transactions. Thus, for example, the Complaint alleges that the agreements detailed in the Complaint "were *designed* to hide URI's continuing risks and financial obligations" Compl. ¶2 (emphasis added), and that "Apuzzo *knew* . . . that the three-party transaction was *designed* to inflate the gain that URI would recognize from the sale-leaseback transaction by *disguising* the indemnification payment to Terex," Compl. ¶45. (emphases added). At this stage, we must view the SEC's plausible allegations as true.

Moreover, when evaluating whether Apuzzo rendered substantial assistance, we must consider his high degree of actual knowledge of the primary violation (the second component of aiding and abetting). As we have repeatedly held, the three components of the aiding and abetting test "cannot be considered in isolation from one another." *DiBella*, 587 F.3d at 566 (quoting *Cornfeld*, 619 F.2d at 922). Where, as here, the SEC plausibly alleges a high degree of

---

11. This is not to suggest that evidence of proximate cause may not be relevant to identifying when an aider and abettor has provided substantial assistance to a primary violator. One who proximately causes a primary violation with actual knowledge of the primary violation will inherently meet the test we have set forth above. Therefore, the SEC *may* prove substantial assistance by demonstrating that the aider and abettor was a proximate cause of the violation. Our recognition of "proximate cause" as a factor relevant to identifying substantial assistance, however, does not establish proximate cause as a distinct element of an aiding and abetting claim.

12. Although Apuzzo took on more of a supervisory role for . . . [the second transaction] and was less involved in some of the day to day communication with URI, his actions were more than sufficient to meet the substantial assistance standard set forth above. He retained ultimate control over the transaction, negotiated its key terms with Nolan and URI, approved the agreements with URI and GECC, and knew about the issuance of inflated invoices.

actual knowledge, this lessens the burden it must meet in alleging substantial assistance.

Apuzzo argues that while a high degree of substantial assistance lowers the SEC's burden to prove scienter, the converse is not true. A close look at our case law, however, reveals that Apuzzo is incorrect. In *DiBella*, when discussing the knowledge factor of the aiding and abetting test, we stated that "'there may be a nexus between the degree of knowledge and the requirement that the alleged aider and abettor render substantial assistance.'" *Id.* at 566 (quoting *Cornfeld*, 619 F.2d at 922) (brackets omitted). And, in *Cornfeld*, we explained that we "must consider" the issue of substantial assistance in light of the allegations that the defendants "actually knew" of the fraud. 619 F.2d at 925. Therefore, a high degree of knowledge may lessen the SEC's burden in proving substantial assistance, just as a high degree of substantial assistance may lessen the SEC's burden in proving *scienter*.

It is particularly appropriate to consider the degree of scienter in evaluating substantial assistance in light of the test for substantial assistance that we have laid out above. When determining whether a defendant sought by his actions to make the primary violation succeed, if a jury were convinced that the defendant had a high degree of actual knowledge about the steps he was taking and the role those steps played in the primary violation, they would be well justified in concluding that the defendant's actions, which perhaps could be viewed innocently in some contexts, were taken with the goal of helping the fraud succeed.

As quoted above, the district court found that the Complaint here alleges, in detail, a very high degree of knowledge of the fraud on Apuzzo's part. Considered in light of those allegations, the allegations of substantial assistance can no longer be viewed, as Apuzzo argues, as "business as usual," but rather as an effort to purposely assist the fraud and help make it succeed. . . .

CONCLUSION

In sum, applying the standard we have set forth for evaluating substantial assistance, we conclude that the Complaint should not have been dismissed because it adequately alleged that Apuzzo aided and abetted the primary violator in carrying out his fraudulent scheme. We therefore reverse the district court's Opinion and remand for further proceedings consistent with this opinion.

NOTES AND QUESTIONS

1. The Dilemma of Prosecutorial Theory. The PSLRA's express authority for the SEC to prosecute aiders and abettors indirectly poses problems for private litigants. A fear of the plaintiff's bar is that, while private litigants seek to establish a broad definition of primary participant liability, the SEC's efforts will perpetuate the ambiguity between primary participant and aiding and abetting standards. As a result, plaintiffs would be confronted by precedents created in SEC enforcement actions that mischaracterize primary participants as aiders and abettors, so that defendants such as accountants and attorneys could successfully argue, on the basis of SEC enforcement actions, that their conduct constituted aiding and abetting and as such is not the basis for private liability.

   2.   *The Accountant's Duty to Blow the Whistle.*   The PSLRA adds Section 10A to the Exchange Act, imposing affirmative duties on public accountants when they become aware of an "illegal act" by their audit client. When the auditor discovers an illegal act, it has an obligation to determine whether that act will have a material impact on the company's financial statements. If such an impact is likely, the auditor not only must bring the matter to the attention of the appropriate level of management, but also must bring it to the attention of the client's audit committee or board of directors. Thereafter, if the corporation has not taken appropriate remedial steps, the auditor has a duty under Section 10A(b)(3) that ultimately leads to notice being given to the SEC of the facts surrounding the discovered illegal act. *See SEC v. Solucorp Ind. Ltd.,* 197 F. Supp. 2d 4 (S.D.N.Y. 2002) (accountant who knew that certain financial entries were inappropriate but took no further action likely to be found to have violated Section 10A). Assume the auditor, upon visiting a client's industrial site to verify the existence of inventory, discovers that the client is discharging pollutants into the environment. Does this trigger an obligation under Section 10A? Should the auditor's failure to fulfill its duties under Exchange Act Section 10A be the basis of liability to investors who would not have purchased a corporation's shares had they been aware of the ongoing illegal act? Does Section 10A strengthen or weaken the hand of the auditor when dealing with its client?

PROBLEM

14-4.   Redrill, Ltd. is raising funds to support its efforts to extract oil from oil shale. The offering materials circulated among investors touts its state-of-the-art technology, which it claims will enable the company to efficiently turn the vast oil shale deposits in the western United States into a source of petroleum equal to that of Saudi Arabia. Included in the offering materials are financial statements that have been certified by the accountant, Wallace. In carrying out her audit of Redrill, Wallace learns that Redrill's promoters have served serious prison sentences for various financial frauds and that the technology touted in the offering materials is completely bogus. In spite of this knowledge, Wallace certified the financial statements. Wallace's motive in not withdrawing from the audit was that she was negotiating to sell her practice to a major accounting firm and believed having Redrill among her clients would cause a higher price to be paid for her practice. Evaluate the strength of an SEC enforcement action under Rule 10b-5 against Wallace. *See Roberts v. Peat, Marwick, Mitchell & Co.,* 857 F.2d 646 (9th Cir. 1989).

2.   Control Person and Respondeat Superior Liability

Section 15 of the Securities Act and Section 20(a) of the Exchange Act hold control persons liable to the same extent as the person they control. Congress included the control person provision in the Securities Act to curb the possibility of corporations using nominal or "dummy" directors who, at the command of those controlling them, would sign registration statements so that the control person could avoid liability under Section 11. Congress provided no definition of *control*, stating simply that control could arise through "stock ownership, agency, or otherwise" or through "an agreement or understanding." The passage of one year did not improve the image of nominal directors or dummies generally, so that a control provision was included in the Exchange Act reaching "every person who, directly or indirectly, controls" any person who violates a statute or rule of the Act.

An important clause in each control provision is the affirmative defense it provides. Under Section 15 of the Securities Act, the control person avoids liability if it is established that "the controlling person had no knowledge of or reasonable grounds to believe in the existence of the facts" upon which the liability of the control person is alleged to exist. The defense clause's language in Section 15 mirrors that found in the affirmative defenses provided in Sections 11 and 12(a)(2) of the Act, so that Section 15 liability is consistent with that which the '33 Act imposes on primary violators, save for liability under Section 12(a)(1). Somewhat mysteriously, the affirmative defense provided in Exchange Act Section 20(a) is more generally expressed: Liability arises under Section 20(a) "unless the controlling person acted in good faith and did not directly or indirectly induce the act or acts constituting the violation or cause of action." The legislative history of the provision does not explain why the '34 Act's control provision did not track the language of its sister provision. One possible explanation is that because Section 20(a) has potential application when any statute or rule of the Exchange Act is violated, Congress may well have chosen the more ambiguous "good faith" standard, rather than parroting the language used in its sister provision in the Securities Act. Regrettably, the legislative history sheds little light on the congressional intent surrounding Section 20(a). A further distinction between the two provisions is that Section 20(a) conditions the defense on proof the control person did not "induce the act" constituting a violation, whereas Section 15 of the Securities Act does not contain this provision. Even though there has been a good deal of litigation under Section 20(a), the meaning of *control* and the contours of its affirmative defense remain very unclear.

Donohoe v. Consolidated Operating & Production Corp.
30 F.3d 907 (7th Cir. 1994)

CUDAHY, Circuit Judge. We address here the one remaining issue in this complex securities fraud suit arising out of an ill-fated oil-drilling project. The plaintiffs' claim, in a nutshell, is that the defendants fraudulently lured them into investing in a project to drill oil wells on land in which the defendants fully knew there wasn't any oil to be found. Terrence Donohoe and 53 other aggrieved investors brought suit against Consolidated Operating & Production Corporation (COPCO) and its principals and shareholders: Jack Nortman, Morando Berrettini, Dennis Bridges and two companies that Bridges owned and operated (Ona Drilling Corporation and Onshore Rig Corporation). Bridges, it now appears, defrauded everyone. But he entered bankruptcy and the default judgments against his two companies (that never responded to the complaint) are likely of little value. That left Nortman, Berrettini and COPCO as the remaining defendants.

The amended complaint offered various theories of liability, primarily violation of the anti-fraud and registration requirements of the federal securities laws, together with RICO and state law theories. Finding that there was no evidence of either recklessness or intent to defraud (bad faith), the district court granted summary judgment in favor of the defendants on most of the claims. . . .

The plaintiffs appealed. While we otherwise affirmed the district court's entry of summary judgment, we observed that the court, in a lengthy and otherwise carefully detailed opinion, failed to address the argument that Nortman and Berrettini may have "controlled" Bridges, and thus be liable for his malfeasance under a "control person" theory. We therefore remanded the matter to the district court for its consideration of this question. 982 F.2d at 1137. . . .

[The opinion that follows considers the district court's decision granting the defendant's motion for summary judgment based on its finding that Nortman and Berrettini had met the good-faith defense for control persons under the securities laws. In reaching this issue, the court was satisfied that the issue of control person liability on the part of Nortman and Berrettini was sufficiently pled with allegations that they controlled COPCO, even though there was no specific pleading that Nortman and Berrettini controlled Bridges. The court reasoned that under liberal notice pleading standards the complaint sufficiently put Nortman and Berrettini on notice of the claim they controlled Bridges.]

II

Given our assumption that such a claim is adequately alleged, the question is whether the defendants are entitled to summary judgment on the claim that they "controlled" Bridges and are thus liable for his fraud. Section 20(a) of the 1934 Act . . . and Section 15 of the 1933 Act . . . both set out "control person" liability—providing a vehicle to hold one defendant vicariously liable for the securities violations committed by another.

As we recognized in considering the first appeal in this case, our opinion in *Harrison v. Dean Witter Reynolds Inc.*, 974 F.2d 873, 880-81 (7th Cir. 1992), *cert. denied,* . . . 113 S. Ct. 2994 (1993), sets out a two-prong test for determining control person liability. 982 F.2d at 1138. First, the "control person" needs to have actually exercised general control over the operations of the wrongdoer, and second, the control person must have had the power or ability—even if not exercised—to control the specific transaction or activity that is alleged to give rise to liability. It was in this case clear enough that because Bridges used COPCO as a vehicle to perpetrate fraud, and because Nortman and Berrettini between them had majority control and played an active role in the day to day operations of the business, that they could be seen as "controlling." *Bridges*, 982 F.2d at 1138-39.

We further recognized, however, that good faith is a defense to control person liability. . . . But unlike the plaintiffs' other claims in which the defendant's bad faith was an element of the offense, because good faith was an affirmative defense to control person liability, the burden of proving good faith was on the defendants. Hence, while we had otherwise concluded that the plaintiffs had not brought forward sufficient evidence of the defendants' bad faith for their claims to go forward, we sent the case back to the district court to decide whether the plaintiffs' evidence of . . . [the defendants'] good faith entitled . . . [the defendants] to summary judgment on the "control person" theory.

Control person liability is most frequently encountered when a defendant seeks to hold a brokerage house liable for the securities violations committed by its employees. In that context, as the district court observed on remand, good faith is typically determined by examining whether the control person set up and enforced with reasonable diligence sufficient systems of internal supervision and control designed to detect securities violations.

But this type of analysis was obviously designed for, and cannot sensibly be applied outside of, the respondeat superior context. Thus, in other contexts the Fifth Circuit has employed a more flexible approach, asking simply whether the control person has taken reasonable measures, in light of the situation, to prevent the securities violation. "The test of whether the controlling person has done enough to prevent the violation depends on what he could have done under the circumstances." *G.A. Thompson & Co. v. Partridge*, 636 F.2d 945, 959 (5th Cir. 1981).

The Supreme Court has also suggested, though this is not a factor that—until recently—our cases have emphasized much, that the good faith defense exculpates defendants whose behavior is merely negligent. *See Ernst & Ernst v. Hochfelder*, 425 U.S. 185, 209 n.28, 96 S. Ct. 1375, 1389 n.28, 47 L. Ed. 2d 668 (1976). "The controlling person must also act recklessly; negligence alone is insufficient." *Monieson v. Commodities Futures Trading Commission*, 996 F.2d 852, 860 (7th Cir. 1993). It therefore seems to us that our task is to examine what the defendants could have done under the circumstances to prevent the violation, and then ask whether the defendants—aware that they could take such measures—decided not to. This is just to say that we are to determine whether there is a genuine issue of fact regarding the defendants' recklessness. We agree with the district court that the defendants have shown that there is not.

As the district court noted in originally concluding that the defendants lacked bad faith, . . . the defendants conducted an extensive check into Bridges' background, set up an escrow system to check the disbursement of money into Ona's bank account and regularly checked up on Bridges' work. Even so, the defendants, who themselves controlled the administrative and financial aspects of COPCO's business, were required to rely heavily on Bridges' superior technical expertise. And there is no suggestion in the record that the defendants had any reason to believe that the sources to whom they looked in evaluating Bridges would prove unreliable. And perhaps most importantly, the defendants invested a large amount of their own energies and funds (more than $100,000) in this project, making it fairly clear that their actions taken with respect to the undertaking were in good faith, as that term is commonly understood.

We therefore agree with the district court that the defendants were entitled to summary judgment on the arguable claim that they "controlled" Bridges since their good faith represents an affirmative defense to control person liability. Hence, since we would in any event affirm the entry of summary judgment, we have no need to examine further whether this claim was—in fact—sufficiently alleged in the complaint to justify our remand. The judgment of the district court is accordingly

Affirmed.

NOTES AND QUESTIONS

1. Who Is a Controlling Person? Should the test of control depend upon one's status, for example, chairman of the board, or should the test inquire into certain functional considerations to determine either control in fact or the potential to control the primary participant? Consider the following approach:

> Although section 20(a) clearly requires a showing that the alleged controlling persons have the power to control or influence the controlled person, it is silent as to the necessary scope of such power: is the potential for control over all phases of Tandem's business necessary, is the potential for control over Tandem's securities issues sufficient, or is the potential for control over Tandem's particular transactions giving rise to the securities violation sufficient? Section 20(a) is equally silent on the *degree* of control that the alleged controlling persons must possess over the securities violator: for example, is section 20(a) aimed only at high level corporate executives who actually formulate and carry out the securities violations; is section 20(a) aimed also at outside directors, as opposed to inside directors, who are basically inactive in corporate matters but who supervise the activity of the corporate officers; or is section 20(a) aimed also at minority shareholders who only possess limited and indirect power to influence management and policies of the securities violators?

Wool v. Tandem Computers, Inc., 818 F.2d 1433, 1441 n.9 (9th Cir. 1987) (emphasis in original).

Most circuits apply a two-prong test that was first developed by the Eighth Circuit to determine if a defendant is a controlling person.

> In *Metge v. Baehler,* [762 F.2d 621, 630-631 (8th Cir. 1985),] . . . the plaintiff sought to hold liable, as a controlling person, a lending institution that had lent funds to the corporation that committed the violation. The court held that the plaintiff must prove that the defendant lender, as a controlling person, had "actually participated in (i.e., exercised control over) the operations of the corporation in general." In addition, it was necessary to "prove that the defendant possessed the power to control the specific transaction or activity upon which the primary violation is predicated, but he need not prove that this power was exercised."
>
> . . . Thus, a plaintiff should show the controlling person's real control over the violator. This may be shown from the relationship in general, as in showing that the primary violator was an employee of the defendant corporation. The plaintiff then should show that the scope of control included the conduct that was the basis of the primary violation, as in showing that the employee's particular violative conduct was within the scope of the corporation's control. The plaintiff need not show however, that the control was exercised to cause the violation.

Kuehnle, Secondary Liability Under the Federal Securities Laws—Aiding and Abetting, Conspiracy, Controlling Person, and Agency: Common-Law Principles and the Statutory Scheme, 14 J. Corp. L. 313, 359-360 (1988).

In some areas, control is easily established by one's status. Employers are clearly controlling persons with respect to employee misconduct occurring within the scope of employment. Promoters are control persons as to their fellow promoters. *G.A. Thompson & Co. v. Partridge*, 636 F.2d 945 (5th Cir. 1981). Senior *officers* are also held to be control persons. *In re Stocker Yale Sec. Litig.*, 453 F. Supp. 2d 345 (D.N.H. 2006). But in the vast majority of the cases determining controlling person status is a highly fact specific inquiry so that, for example, merely occupying the position of chairman of the board is not itself determinative; there must be further evidence the position conferred authority over the company's operations. *In re Allstate Life Ins. Litig.*, 2013 U.S. Dist. LEXIS 29046 (Mar. 1, 2013). This evidence was found in *In re China Education Alliance Inc. Sec. Litig.*, 2012 U.S. Dist. LEXIS 49055 (C.D. Cal. Apr. 6, 2012), where the defendant was viewed by other members of the audit committee as having the most experience, was brought on the committee for that reason, and signed communications on behalf of audit committee. Similarly, in *Domarko v. Hemodynamics, Inc.*, 848 F. Supp. 1335 (W.D. Mich. 1993), while outside directors were held not to be control persons, the director, who also served as general counsel, reviewed most corporate announcements, and drafted a communication that contained many misrepresentations, was a control person). *Heck v. Triche*, 775 F.3d 265 (5th Cir. 2014), held the outside CPA on whom the CEO depended to draft several misleading documents was a control person. Substantial stock ownership, however, often is not definitive of whether a stockholder is a control person. *Compare Flag Telecom Holding Ltd. Securities Litigation*, 352 F. Supp. 2d 429 (S.D.N.Y. 2005) (largest stockholder who appointed three of nine members of the board was not a control person) *with No. 84 Employer-Teamster Joint Council Pension Trust Fund v. Amer. West Holding Corp.*, 320 F.3d 920 (9th Cir. 2003) (two companies that held 57.4 percent of voting stock and placed their officers on the violator's board were control persons).

Outside the corporate setting, *compare Buhler v. Audio Leasing Corp.*, 807 F.2d 833 (9th Cir. 1987) (brokerage firm that licensed salespersons across the country to sell securities for it was not deemed a control person as to sales they made of tax shelters that were not authorized by the brokerage firm) *with Martin v. Shearson Lehman Hutton, Inc.*, 986 F.2d 242 (8th Cir. 1993) (brokerage house deemed a control person because it had indirect means to discipline broker who made initial solicitation of defrauded investors while in employ of the brokerage house, even though fraudulent transaction was not routed through the employing brokerage house). Banks sometimes have been the target of potential control person liability, but have rarely been held liable. *See, e.g., Paracor Fin., Inc. v. General Capital Corp.*, 79 F.3d 878 (9th Cir. 1996) (Section 20(a) liability does not exist where there is no evidence that lender exercised influence on a daily basis). And the good news for attorneys and accountants is that they are not control persons solely because of their ability to persuade and counsel the primary violator. *See Barker v. Henderson, Franklin, Starnes & Holt*, 797 F.2d 490 (7th Cir. 1986). *But see Burket v. Hyman Lippit P.C.*, 560 F. Supp. 2d 571 (E.D. Mich. 2008) (attorney who drafted subscription agreements that lured customers to his client's scam and boasted he controlled his client was unable to have suit dismissed on motion for summary judgment).

2. Culpable Participation. What is the purpose of the controlling person provision? Is it intended to reach those whose involvement through control is on such a scale that they are "culpable participants," or is it intended to impose liability upon those who, because of the control they hold over the primary violator, could have prevented harm to the plaintiff, but instead were passive? A minority of the circuits take the position that Congress intended to impose liability only upon those who qualify as a control person *and* are in some meaningful sense culpable participants in the acts perpetrated by the controlled persons.

In those circuits that adhere to the "culpable participant" standard, the control person himself must either be an actor in the violation or intend his passivity to further the violation. *See, e.g., Sharp v. Coopers & Lybrand,* 649 F.2d 175, 185 (3d Cir. 1981) ("To impose secondary liability on a controlling person for inaction, the plaintiff must prove the inaction 'was deliberate and done intentionally to further the fraud.'"); *Boguslavaky v. Kaplan,* 159 F.3d 715, 720 (2d Cir. 1998) (requiring proof "that the control person was in some meaningful sense a culpable participant" in the violation); *Belmont v. MB Inv. Partners, Inc.,* 708 F.3d 470 (3d Cir. 2013) (more fault is required than reckless inaction in overseeing compliance system).

One has to compare the tests applied in those circuits requiring culpable participation with the language of the control person provisions where, for example, in Section 20(a) the question of the control person's involvement arises as a defense and the focus is on whether the control person acted with "good faith" and "did not directly or indirectly induce the act . . . constituting the violation." Courts not employing the culpable participation standard instead, after finding the defendant meets the standard of being a control person, emphasize that good faith and lack of participation are affirmative defenses. *See, e.g., Arthur Children's Trust v. Keim,* 994 F.2d 1390 (9th Cir. 1993). Notable circuits that have rejected the culpable participation standard are the Fifth Circuit (*G.A. Thompson & Co. v. Partridge,* 636 F.2d 945, 958 (5th Cir. 1981)); Sixth Circuit (*Herm v. Stafford,* 663 F.2d 669, 684 (6th Cir. 1981)); Seventh Circuit (*Harrison v. Dean Witter,* 974 F.2d 873, 880-881 (7th Cir. 1992)); Eighth Circuit (*Metge v. Baehler,* 762 F.2d 621 (8th Cir. 1985)); and Ninth Circuit (*Hollinger v. Titan Capital Corp.,* 914 F.2d 1564 (9th Cir. 1990) (en banc)).

3. The Expansive Meaning of "Good Faith." Generally, the good-faith defense requires proof the control person did not act recklessly. *See Dellastatious v. Williams,* 243 F.3d 191 (4th Cir. 2001). Are there instances when "good faith" or perhaps even the meaning of recklessness can be interpreted to require a reasonable system of supervision and internal controls by a control person? In *Kersh v. General Council of Assemblies of God,* 804 F.2d 546 (9th Cir. 1986), the court suggested such an extension should be judged by the following factors:

> a) whether the controlling person derives direct financial gain from the activity of the controlled person, b) the extent to which the controlled person is tempted to act unlawfully because of the controlling person's policies (e.g., compensation system), c) the extent to which statutory or regulatory law or the defendant's own

policies require supervision, d) the relationship between the *plaintiff* and the controlling person, and e) the demonstration of some public policy need to impose such a requirement.

Id. at 550 (emphasis in original). Using the above standards, *Kersh* held that a national church organization did not have a duty to maintain a system of supervision for the fundraising activities of a local church. In contrast, courts consistently read the good faith standard to require brokerage firms to maintain reasonably designed legal compliance systems. What if the firm has such a system but fails to enforce it? In *Henricksen v. Henricksen*, 640 F.2d 880 (7th Cir. 1981), Smith Barney was unsuccessful in establishing its good faith where the evidence was that it failed to consistently apply its procedures in the case of the plaintiff's account. Wendee placed her recently received inheritance in several discretionary accounts that were managed by her husband, George, a Smith Barney broker. Soon thereafter Wendee and George separated (she was upset with him because he hung out with a crowd that engaged in drinking and gambling); Wendee however had not lost total faith in George—she left her account under George's control. Her faith was misplaced. George commenced to trade excessively on behalf of Wendee's account, garnering for himself $21,000 in commissions in eight months. He also embezzled substantial sums. To conceal his misdeeds, George switched the mailing address for her account to his office and extracted the fund from her account by issuing checks to himself. The court found that Smith Barney had violated its internal rule barring a Smith Barney office from being the address for any customer account and violated its rule that forbids customer checks being issued to a broker. Smith Barney also had an internal rule that required supervisors to periodically review trading practices in discretionary accounts; the court faulted Smith Barney for not diligently inquiring into the volume of trading George carried out in Wendee's account.

    4. Respondeat Superior and Other Vicarious Liability Theories. By and large, most circuits to date view the control person provisions as designed to expand liability, not to limit it, so that there is no frustration of legislative intent if respondeat superior liability is imposed even beyond the scope of the control person provisions. *See, e.g., Hollinger v. Titan Capital Corp.*, 914 F.2d 1564 (9th Cir. 1990) (en banc).

    The Third Circuit embraces a "middle ground" by permitting respondeat superior liability only in the context of cases involving employers with a "high" duty to supervise their employees based on some compelling public interest. Examples of such employers include broker-dealers, accounting firms, and the like. For "typical" employers, the Third Circuit limits vicarious liability to Section 20(a). *See Sharp v. Coopers & Lybrand*, 649 F.2d 175 (3d Cir. 1981), *cert. denied*, 455 U.S. 938 (1982).

    Most courts invoke the traditional "master-servant" approach of respondeat superior liability under which the employer (or other principal) is vicariously liable so long as the employee's or agent's violation was committed within the scope of employment. These cases emphasize that the employee must act within the scope of his actual authority. A finding that the employee acted within the scope of employment requires a showing that the violation was actuated, at least in part, by a desire to serve or benefit the employer. *See, e.g., Pugh v. Tribune Co.*,

521 F.3d 686 (7th Cir. 2008) (parent company not liable under agency principles for inflated revenue figures supplied by officers of subsidiary where officers' wrongful acts were intended to serve their interest and not the parent's interests). Once the action is established to fall within the scope of employment, issues of good faith or noninducement by the employer become completely irrelevant. *See Marbury Management Inc. v. Kohn*, 629 F.2d 705 (2d Cir. 1980), *cert. denied*, 449 U.S. 1011 (1981).

On the other hand, the First Circuit, though otherwise siding with the majority, has expressed a preference for an "apparent authority" approach under which the employer is liable for the fraud of an employee to the extent that the employer put the employee in a position to commit the fraud by cloaking her with the appearance of authority, even if the wrongdoing employee is in this instance acting in an entirely self-serving fashion and thus otherwise outside the scope of actual authority. *See In re Atlantic Financial Management, Inc.*, 784 F.2d 29 (1st Cir. 1986), *cert. denied*, 481 U.S. 1072 (1987). Under this approach, respondeat superior liability did not exist when the broker did not expressly or impliedly represent he was an agent of the brokerage house and when the transaction was not carried out through the brokerage house or was not the type the broker is authorized to undertake. *See Bates v. Shearson Lehman Bros., Inc.*, 42 F.3d 79 (1st Cir. 1994).

Worth emphasizing is that even under the more restrictive view of the Third Circuit, corporate liability is automatic if the false or misleading statements or omissions are properly chargeable to the firm directly, rather than to the natural persons who actually speak the words. In other words, when a high-level executive speaks at a press conference, we would naturally say that he is speaking "for" the corporation, not in an individual capacity. In this situation, the liability of the corporation is primary, not vicarious.

Is respondeat superior liability inconsistent with the reasoning the Supreme Court employed in *Central Bank of Denver*, where the Court held there was no implied cause of action for aiding and abetting liability? *See generally* Prentice, Conceiving the Inconceivable and Judicially Implementing the Preposterous: The Premature Demise of Respondeat Superior Liability Under Section 10(b), 58 Ohio St. L.J. 1325 (1997).

PROBLEMS

14-5. Fred Merritt is the vice president (finance) of Beta Industries, Inc. A few weeks ago, he received a fairly routine phone call from a business reporter seeking to clarify some earnings projections that the company had recently released. Having heard his superiors recently lamenting the doldrums in which Beta's stock price was languishing, he embellished his comments, going so far (off the record) as to hint at some exciting developments "just around the corner" from the company's labs. In fact, although the company had some promising projects under development, this was misleading. The business magazine mentioned Beta favorably in its "Company Watch" column the next week, and its stock price has jumped a bit. Merritt reports directly to Alexine, Beta's CEO, who has instructed Merritt not only to be accessible to financial reporters, but also to think of some ways to improve the price of Beta shares. Beta's web site, under the "Employee Relations" window, sets forth a variety of company policies, one being that employees must provide to the general counsel a summary of any communications that an employee has with the media. Fred did not submit a summary of his conversation with the reporter, and it appears that Beta had no procedures for reviewing press reports to monitor employee communications with the press.

What is the company's liability exposure, assuming that the false statement by Merritt violates the antifraud provision? Is Alexine liable?

14-6. Alpha Inc. owns 100 percent of several newspaper and magazine publishing companies, one of which is PressDay, the leading daily newspaper on Long Island. Alpha's most recent annual report announced increases in revenues and income for all its companies and specifically reported that PressDay "continues to enjoy increasing subscribers and revenues in one of the most highly competitive markets in America." Unbeknownst to Alpha's management, Raymond, the president of PressDay, had for several years inflated the number of PressDay's subscribers, along with its revenues and income, so as to increase his annual bonus. The inflated figures were included in Alpha's annual financial statements reporting results consolidated from all its operations. Ultimately, Raymond revealed his years of deceit. Alpha promptly disclosed that prior reported revenues and income had been materially overstated "due to employee fraud," and the value of Alpha shares immediately plummeted. What are the issues involved with holding Alpha liable as a primary participant? As a control person? Liable under agency doctrines of respondeat superior or apparent authority? *See Pugh v. Tribune Co.*, 521 F.3d 686 (7th Cir. 2008).

C.   *Rescission and Restitution of Contracts in Violation of the Securities Laws*

Berckeley Inv. Group, Ltd. v. Colkitt
455 F.3d 195 (3d Cir. 2006)

FISHER, Circuit Judge. . . .

I.   BACKGROUND

Douglas Colkitt, M.D., is the Chairman of the Board and principal shareholder of National Medical Financial Services Corporation ("NMFS"), a corporation whose shares were traded on the NASDAQ stock exchange. [In 1996, seeking capital for an unrelated business venture, Colkitt entered into an arrangement with Berckeley Investment Group, Ltd., a Bahamian corporation, under which Berckeley purchased NMFS debentures for $2 million. The debentures granted Berkeley the option to convert the debentures into unregistered NMFS shares at a 17 percent discount of the then-prevailing market price. Berckeley was permitted by the agreement to convert one-half of the principal amount 100 days after closing of the agreement and remaining principal amount

120 days after the closing date. The transaction was structured to qualify under Regulation S and Berckeley warranted that any subsequent offers and resales of the debentures or shares would comply with Regulation S. Indeed, their agreement expressly provided that Berckeley would "not resell the Debentures or the Shares to U.S. Persons . . . until after the forty (40) days period commencing on the date of completion of the offering." In 1996, Regulation S then had a 40-day restricted period for resales; the restricted period was increased to one year in 1997. Berckeley represented in the agreement that it understood Colkitt was relying on the accuracy of its representations regarding compliance with federal securities law requirements. Berckeley, pursuant to the terms of the agreement, subsequently gave notice of its intent to convert the debentures and receive NMFS shares. Colkitt allowed Berckeley to convert some of the debentures so that Berckeley received 18,320 shares, but refused to allow any further conversion. This litigation ensued.]

B.   SECTION 29(B) OF THE SECURITIES ACT OF 1934

Colkitt contends that he is entitled to rescind the Agreement under Section 29(b) of the Securities Exchange Act of 1934 (the "Exchange Act"). . . .

Section 29(b) itself does not define a substantive violation of the securities laws; rather, it is the vehicle through which private parties may rescind contracts that were made or performed in violation of other substantive provisions. . . . Although the word "void" is contained in the statute, the Supreme Court has read Section 29(b) to be "merely voidable at the option of the innocent party." *Mills v. Elec. Auto-Lite Co.*, 396 U.S. 375, 387-88 (1970).

In order to void the Agreement under Section 29(b), Colkitt must establish that: (1) the contract involved a prohibited transaction; (2) he is in contractual privity with Berckeley; and (3) Colkitt is in the class of persons that the securities acts were designed to protect. *Regional Properties, Inc. v. Financial and Real Estate Consulting Co.*, 678 F.2d 552, 559 (5th Cir. 1982). . . . Colkitt must demonstrate a direct relationship between the violation at issue and the performance of the contract; i.e., the violation must be "inseparable from the performance of the contract" rather than "collateral or tangential to the contract." *GFL Advantage Fund, Ltd.*, 272 F.3d at 201.

In this case, Colkitt asserts that the Agreement was made "in violation of" Section 10(b) and Rule 10b-5 of the Exchange Act, and that the "performance" of the contract violated Section 10(b), Rule 10b-5, and Section 5 of the Securities Act of 1933 (the "Securities Act") because Berckeley perpetuated securities fraud in violation of the statutes. We consider each of these arguments below.

1.   *Colkitt Cannot Advance a Section 29(b) Rescission Claim Pursuant to Section 5 of the 1933 Securities Act*

Colkitt asserts that he is entitled to rescind the Agreement under Section 29(b) . . . based upon a violation of Section 5 of the Securities Act.

We recently addressed the scope of Section 29(b) regarding downstream securities transactions in *GFL Advantage Fund, Ltd. v. Colkitt*, 272 F.3d 189 (3d Cir. 2001). In that case, we considered a virtually identical financing transaction that Colkitt entered into with GFL. Colkitt argued that he was entitled to rescind the agreement between the parties because subsequent short sales made by GFL following the agreement violated Section 10(b). . . . We addressed first whether Colkitt could even maintain a Section 29(b) rescission claim based upon the subsequent short sales. Surveying the applicable case law on the subject, we took a narrow view of the phrases "made in violation of" and "the performance of which involves the violation of" contained in Section 29(b). The test, as we applied it in *GFL Advantage Fund*, is whether the securities violations are inseparable from the underlying agreement between the parties. *Id.* at 201. If an agreement cannot be performed without violating the securities laws, that agreement is subject to rescission under Section 29(b). *Id.* at 202. Thus, we held that:

> Despite the theory of Colkitt's case, however, GFL's short sales are completely independent of the parties' respective obligations under the terms of the notes— namely, GFL's obligation to lend Colkitt a total of $13,000,000, and Colkitt's obligation to repay the loans at GFL's option with shares of National Medical and EquiMed stock. In the end, GFL's alleged unlawful activity (*i.e.*, its short sales) is too attenuated from the parties' valid, lawful contracts (*i.e.*, the National Medical and EquiMed notes) or GFL's performance thereunder. Therefore, we conclude that the notes were neither made nor performed in violation of any federal securities laws as is required for rescission under Section 29(b).

Id.

Two cases we discussed in *GFL Advantage Fund* and relied upon by Colkitt in the instant appeal confirm that Colkitt's Section 5 claim cannot proceed under Section 29(b). In *Grove v. First National Bank of Herminie*, 489 F.2d 512 (3d Cir. 1974), a debtor obtained a series of loans from a bank to purchase registered securities. Regulation U, promulgated under the Exchange Act, provided that such loans were limited to set percentages of the value of the stock to be purchased. The bank, however, failed to inform Grove of the Regulation U margin requirements and loaned him the money. We held that Section 29(b) precluded the bank from recovering a loan deficiency because the loans were made in direct violation of Regulation U. Similarly, in *Regional Properties, Inc. v. Financial and Real Estate Consulting Co.*, a securities broker entered into an agreement with the principals of several limited partnerships to market the limited partnerships for a fee. 678 F.2d 552 (5th Cir. 1982). It turned out that the broker, a former New York lawyer who had been disbarred, failed to register as a broker dealer as required by Section 15(a)(1) of the Exchange Act. The Fifth Circuit determined that the broker's performance of the agreement was a prohibited transaction under Section 29(b) because the agreement, although lawful on its face, could not have been performed by the unregistered broker without violating the securities laws.

As we explained in *GFL Advantage Fund*, the key in both of those cases was that neither agreement could be performed without violating the securities laws. 272 F.3d at 202. In contrast, in *GFL Advantage Fund* the downstream short sales were neither connected to nor "inseparable" from the agreement between the parties. Thus, we determined that the transactions at issue in that case could not support a claim under Section 29(b), regardless of whether they violated Section 10(b). *Id.*

In this case, although the Agreement contains references to Section 5 that allegedly induced Colkitt to enter into the Agreement, Berckeley's downstream sales were tangential to the parties' basic obligations under the Agreement: Berckeley's obligation to loan Colkitt $2,000,000 and Colkitt's obligation to provide Berckeley with convertible debentures.[1] At the time the parties entered into the Agreement, the Agreement could be performed without violating provisions of the securities laws. *Id.* . . .

For these reasons, we will uphold the District Court's decision to grant summary judgment in favor of Berckeley as to Colkitt's Section 29(b) claim premised on a violation of Section 5 of the Securities Act.

2.   *The District Court Erred in Dismissing Colkitt's Section 29(b) Claim Premised on a Violation of Section 10(b)*

Section 10(b) of the Exchange Act, 15 U.S.C. §78j(b), makes it unlawful for any person to employ "manipulative or deceptive" conduct "in connection with the purchase or sale of any security." . . .

As a private party, Colkitt must establish each of the following elements to prove that Berckeley violated Section 10(b) and Rule 10b-5: (1) Berckeley made a misstatement of material fact, (2) with scienter, (3) in connection with the purchase or sale of a security, (4) upon which Colkitt reasonably relied, and (5) that Colkitt's reliance was the proximate cause of his injury. . . . In the Section 29(b) context, a plaintiff seeking rescission does not have to establish reliance and causation. . . .

Colkitt's case does not present the "typical" fact pattern seen in securities violations brought under Section 10(b). . . . In this case, Colkitt's theory of liability is not based upon an alleged material misrepresentation relating to the value of NMFS stock, but rather a misrepresentation regarding Berckeley's intent to comply downstream with the registration requirements contained in the Securities Act. Colkitt's argument in favor of establishing Berckeley's liability proceeds as follows: . . .

- Berckeley represented in . . . the Agreement that all subsequent sales of converted shares would be made in accordance with the registration requirements of the Securities Act of 1933.
- Berckeley's later-acknowledged sale of 18,320 unregistered NMFS shares violated Section 5 and, therefore, the Agreement because the shares were not registered and Berckeley was an "underwriter" not entitled to an exemption under Section 4(1). Because Berckeley was not exempt under Section 4(1), it knowingly engaged in a scheme and artifice to defraud *at the time it entered into the agreement.* . . .

---

1.   The distinction between this claim and the Section 29(b) claim premised on a violation of Section 10(b) is readily apparent. The Section 10(b) claim alleges that Berckeley made material misrepresentations that induced Colkitt to enter into the Agreement. If Colkitt is able to prove that claim, then the Agreement was "made in violation of" Section 10(b). The misrepresentations that induced Colkitt to enter into the Agreement would be "inseparable from the underlying agreement between the parties." *GFL Advantage Fund,* 272 F.3d at 202.

There is no dispute between the parties that the Agreement was made "in connection" with the purchase or sale of a security. . . .

a.   Material Issues of Fact Exist Regarding Berckeley's Intent to Resell Unregistered Shares and Its Status as an Underwriter . . .

Colkitt bases his Section 10(b) claim on the argument that Berckeley intentionally misrepresented in . . . the Agreement that all subsequent sales of converted shares would be made in accordance with the registration requirements of the Securities Act of 1933. . . . Colkitt's theory breaks down into two discrete subissues as to which he must point to a dispute of material fact: (1) that there is evidence in the record that Berckeley intended at the time the Agreement was executed to sell shares back into the United States without registering them, and (2) Berckeley was aware at the time of the Agreement that it would be reselling the shares as an "underwriter," i.e., the company knew that it was not entitled to an exemption from the registration requirement under Section 4(1) of the Securities Act of 1933.

(1)   There is sufficient evidence that Berckeley intended to resell NMSF shares back into the United States without registering them. . . .

[The court reviewed several affidavits from Berckeley's investment adviser and directors, each clearly reflecting the intent to resell the NMSF shares pursuant to an exemption.]

In addition to these affidavits, Berckeley made two binding judicial admissions in its complaint and in its brief on appeal. Berckeley stated unequivocally in its complaint that "[i]t was always Berckeley's intent to exercise its conversion rights as to all of the debentures as quickly as possible, selling the National Medical stock in the market as quickly as reasonably possible, and thereby maximizing its return." Furthermore, Berckeley stated in its brief on appeal to us that its "intention was . . . to convert the Debentures into shares of National Medical stock after a period of 100-120 days and then proceed slowly to sell the stock in a reasonable manner as an investment objective." . . .

The deal provided Berckeley with the unilateral option to convert one-half of the debentures into NMFS shares 100 days from closing and the remaining debentures 120 days from closing. In addition, the Agreement provided that any unredeemed debentures would be automatically converted into NMFS shares within one year. Thus, in all likelihood Berckeley knew that it would be holding a large number of unregistered shares within one year of the Agreement. These timetables built into the Agreement are even more important when we consider that, for all practical purposes, Berckeley could only receive the maximum return on its investment (the 17% premium it received from Colkitt as part of the deal) if it resold the unregistered NMFS shares back into the United States. The affidavits and the admissions referenced above confirm that it was Berckeley's intent from the outset to resell at least a portion of the unregistered NMFS shares "as quickly as reasonably possible . . . thereby maximizing its return." As discussed more fully below, Berckeley has not shown that there was any real marketplace for the unregistered NMFS shares other than in the United States, thus adding to the inference at this stage of the litigation that Berckeley intended to resell unregistered shares back into the United States.

For these reasons, we find that there is sufficient evidence at this stage of the proceedings to create a material issue of fact that Berckeley intended, at the time of the Agreement, to resell the converted shares back into the United States following the Restricted Period set forth in the Agreement.

> (2) Material issues of fact exist as to whether Berckeley was aware it was not entitled to an exemption under Section 4(1). . . .

Section 4(1) exempts from the registration requirements under Section 5 "transactions by any person other than issuer, underwriter, or dealer." 15 U.S.C. §77d(1). At issue here is whether Berckeley was an "underwriter.". . . Because the burden of proving entitlement to the exemption rests with Berckeley, it can establish that it is entitled to the exemption if it proves that: (1) the acquisition of the unregistered shares through conversion was not made "with a view to" distribution; or (2) the sale of the 18,320 shares was not made in connection with a "distribution." *See Ackerberg v. Johnson*, 892 F.2d 1328, 1336 (8th Cir. 1989). . . .

Berckeley's quick turnaround sale of the converted shares at least creates an issue of fact as to whether Berckeley acquired the shares with a "view to distribution" under the statutory exemption as well. *See Gilligan, Will & Co. v. Securities and Exchange Comm'n*, 267 F.2d 461, 467-68 (2d Cir. 1959) (finding that ten-month holding period was sufficient to support SEC finding that security holder bought shares "with a view to distribution").

Berckeley, however, can still demonstrate that it did not act as an "underwriter" if the sale of the 18,320 shares was not made in connection with a "distribution." . . .

We agree with the rationale of those courts and similarly hold that the term "distribution" in §2(a)(11) is synonymous with "public offering."

In the landmark decision of *SEC v. Ralston Purina*, the United States Supreme Court explained that whether an issuance of stock is a "public offering" turns on the need of the offerees for the protections of the securities laws. . . .

On the basis of the record we have before us, Berckeley has not adduced any evidence to meet its burden that it is entitled to an exemption under §4(1). The record is clear that Berckeley intended to resell a quantity of the shares within two years. As stated in Berckeley's complaint, "[i]t was always Berckeley's intent to exercise its conversion rights as to all of the debentures as quickly as possible, selling the National Medical stock in the market as quickly as possible." Berckeley has not advanced any evidence that there was any "market" for NMFS shares outside the United States, particularly considering that Berckeley placed the 18,320 shares for sale with a United States broker. Inferring from these facts that the only market for NMFS shares was in the United States, Berckeley did not bring forward any evidence that the NMFS shares would be sold *solely* to sophisticated investors who do not need the protections of the registration requirements of the securities laws. To the contrary, placing the 18,320 shares with a broker suggests that those shares would be sold to the highest bidder without regard to the bidder's level of investing acumen. . . . For these reasons, we find that Berckeley failed to meet its burden to show it was entitled to an exemption under Section 4(1).

Accordingly, we conclude that the record contains sufficient evidence that Berckeley made a misrepresentation of material fact regarding its intent to resell and its status as an underwriter in a resale.

b.   Material Issues of Fact Exist Regarding Whether Berckeley Was Reckless in Its Belief That It Would Be Entitled to the Section 4(1) Exemption

. . . In order to defeat summary judgment, Colkitt must point to evidence in the record creating an issue of fact regarding whether Berckeley was reckless in its belief that it would be entitled to an exemption under Section 4(1) of the Securities Act of 1933. . . .

Regulation S was enacted in 1990 to provide generally that an offer or sale of a security that occurs outside the United States is not subject to the registration requirements under Section 5 of the Securities Act. . . . Regulation S contains two non-exclusive safe harbor provisions, Rule 903 and Rule 904. . . . Both safe-harbor rules contain a 40-day "distribution compliance period" under which resales of unregistered shares may not be made in any event. *See id.* The SEC interpretive release issued in connection with Regulation S explained that Regulation S did not alter the availability of the Section 4(1) exemption for the resale of securities. Notice of Adoption of Rule 144, SEC. Release No. 5223, 55 Fed. Reg. 18319 (January 11, 1972). The interpretive release further stated that Regulation S did not apply to "any transaction or series of transactions that, although in technical compliance with the rules, is part of a plan or scheme to evade the registration provisions of the Securities Act." . . .

In June 1995, in response to "a number of problematic practices [that] . . . developed involving unregistered sales of equity securities of domestic reporting companies purportedly in reliance upon Regulation S," the SEC published an interpretive release entitled "Problematic Practices Under Regulation S." *See* Problematic Practices Under Regulation S, SEC Release No. 33-7190, 60 Fed. Reg. 35663 (July 10, 1995). That publication stated that the safe harbors under Rules 903 and 904 were not available "for a transaction or series of transactions that, although in technical compliance with the regulation, is part of a plan or scheme to evade the registration requirements of the Securities Act." *Id.* The publication was concerned primarily with so-called "parking transactions," under which domestic issuers or distributors sold securities to offshore shell entities to hold for the forty-day restricted period, after which such securities were sold back into the United States. In the end, proceeds from the sales would make their way, directly or indirectly, back to the domestic issuer or distributor. *Id.* at 35664. The SEC made clear in the release that the forty-day restricted period could not be used for this purpose, i.e., to "wash off" resale restrictions such as the 2-year holding requirement under Rule 144, [which applied until shortened in 2007]. The release concluded by stating that "any distributions by a statutory 'underwriter' must be registered pursuant to Section 5" unless subject to a statutory exemption. *Id.*

The net effect of all of these Rules and interpretive releases is to create an issue of fact as to whether it would have been reckless for Berckeley to rely *solely* on the forty-day restricted period to foreclose any possibility that it was an "underwriter" at the time it entered into the Agreement with Colkitt. . . .

Based upon all the information available to Berckeley at the time it entered into the Agreement, we conclude that there is an issue of fact as to whether Berckeley was reckless in its belief that the resale of securities back into the United States would not violate Section 5 of the Securities Act. This issue must be resolved by the trier of fact, which may or may not accept Berckeley's explanation that the law was so unclear at the time to dispel Colkitt's contention that it acted with scienter. Accordingly, we will reverse the District Court's grant of summary judgment on Colkitt's Section 29(b) claim premised on a violation of Section 10(b) and remand the case for a trial on the merits. . . .

NOTES AND QUESTIONS

1.   The Pervasiveness of the Remedy.   Section 215 of the Investment Advisers Act of 1940 replicates Section 29(b) of the Exchange Act in pronouncing "void" "every contract" in violation of any provision, rule, or regulation of the Act. The Supreme Court in *Mills v. Electric Auto-Lite Co.*, 396 U.S. 375 (1970), held that statutory language rendering contracts "void" did not create an automatic power to avoid the contract and embraced instead the position long followed in the lower courts that have read Section 29(b) "as rendering the contract merely voidable at the option of the innocent party. This interpretation is eminently sensible. The interests of the victims are sufficiently protected by giving him the right to rescind." Id. at 388. To this end, consider the language in Section 47(b)(1) of the Investment Company Act, which provides that a contract made in violation of any provision, rule, or regulation of the Act "is unenforceable by either party . . . unless a court finds that under the circumstances enforcement would produce a more equitable result than nonenforcement and would not be inconsistent with the purpose of this title."

2.   Is the Avoidance Remedy Limited to Investors?   When a court is considering whether to grant relief under a provision such as Section 29(b) of the Exchange Act, should it consider whether the individual plaintiff is within the class of individuals protected by the provision or regulation the defendant violated? For example, Section 15(a)(1) of the Exchange Act provides a mechanism for the Commission to exercise control over broker-dealers because once a broker is registered, the broker must also be a member of the self-regulatory organization (i.e., FINRA) that has not only established rules of practice for the protection of investors, but also mechanisms to discipline those who violate the rules. Also, under Section 15(c), the Commission can discipline registered broker-dealers who violate the securities laws. At the same time, it should be apparent that each provision, rule, and regulation seeks to improve or protect the quality of American securities markets generally, which in turn redounds to the benefit of the nation as a whole. Thus, we can say everyone is in some oblique way an independent beneficiary of each and every provision of the securities laws. *See generally* Note, A Structural Analysis of Section 29(b) of the Securities Exchange Act, 56 U. Chi. L. Rev. 865 (1989). Furthermore, can a provision such as Section 29(b) be used to avoid technical requirements that may otherwise apply to the plaintiff's suit if she sues under an applicable express or implied cause of action?

For example, suits for damages under Rule 10b-5 require that the plaintiff be an actual purchaser or seller of securities. Can this requirement be avoided by the plaintiff's suing under Section 29(b) by alleging the defendant committed a misrepresentation in a securities transaction with another person?

PROBLEM

14-7. Chilcutt, Smith & Company is a registered broker-dealer that specializes in managing investment accounts for wealthy investors. During the past two years, it has produced superior returns when managing its clients' portfolios. A year ago, Alice opened a discretionary trading account with Chilcutt, transferring $250,000 in cash, which Chilcutt then invested in various growth securities. Shortly after Alice opened her account, Chilcutt lost its golden touch for the investment choices made, and its clients' accounts consistently underperformed the market. Chilcutt concealed this poor performance from everyone, it continued to promote itself as a superior "stock picker," and new accounts continued to be opened with it. Chilcutt, in a Ponzi-like scheme, used some of the money received from new accounts opened with it to pay to its older clients the extraordinary gains and income it falsely represented it had earned for their accounts. For example, Alice's most recent account statement represented that her account balance was $300,000; in fact, the balance was $210,000, as poor investment choices by Chilcutt had lost $40,000 of her account, and the gains falsely reported in her account represented money from new accounts that had been fraudulently transferred to her account. Can Alice rescind her account with Chilcutt under Section 29(b)? *Cf. Abrahamson v. Fleschner,* 568 F.2d 862 (2d Cir. 1977), *cert. denied,* 436 U.S. 905 (1978). What result if Chilcutt is not registered?

D.   *Responsibility and Its Costs*

1.   **Equitable Bars to the Plaintiff's Recovery**

Defendants are not the only ones who must shoulder responsibility under the securities laws. At discrete junctions of the express and implied rights of action, the plaintiff is barred from recovering due to his own faults. For example, as we have seen in other chapters, questions arise not just as to whether the plaintiff relied upon a misrepresentation, but also as to whether his reliance was justified or reasonable under the circumstances. Under Sections 11(a) and 12(a)(2) of the '33 Act, the plaintiff is barred if he knew of "the untruth or omission," and the so-called due diligence requirement has developed under Rule 10b-5, which bars recovery by a plaintiff who was reckless in failing to discover the true facts. And, below we see that a plaintiff may be barred from recovering equitable relief by the defense of laches where the plaintiff's delay in prosecuting his action was prejudicial to the defendant. The materials in this section introduce several other affirmative defenses that bar recovery because of actions or even inaction on the plaintiff's part. The defenses discussed here are estoppel, waiver, and *in pari delicto*. These equitable defenses have been established through litigation under the implied causes of action, although some could possibly arise when suit is based upon one of the express causes of action. *See generally* Bell, How to Bar an Innocent Investor—The Validity of Common Law Defenses to Private Actions Under the Securities Exchange Act of 1934, 23 U. Fla. L. Rev. 1 (1970); Note, Applicability of Waiver, Estoppel, and Laches Defenses to Private Suits Under the Securities Act and the SEC Rule 10b-5: Deterrence and Equity in Balance, 73 Yale L.J. 1477 (1964).

Estoppel.   Estoppel has much the same tone to it that the defense of laches has, except that estoppel is available to bar the plaintiff's recovery of damages; laches applies only to actions seeking equitable relief. In sum, the plaintiff is estopped to recover in the following circumstances:

> Four elements must be present to establish the defense of estoppel: (1) The party to be estopped must know the facts; (2) he must intend that his conduct shall be acted on or must so act that the party asserting the estoppel has a right to believe it is so intended; (3) the latter must be ignorant of the true facts; and (4) he must rely on the former's conduct to his injury.

Hecht v. Harris, Upham & Co., 430 F.2d 1202, 1208 (9th Cir. 1970). In *Hecht*, a brokerage house's customer was barred by estoppel from complaining that the brokerage house's employee recommended unsuitable securities because the customer had over several years discussed the broker's handling of her account almost on a daily basis and had failed to object. Attempts to obtain rescission in that case were barred by the defense of laches. Because scienter is a requirement in most actions under the antifraud provision, the opportunities for the defendant to meet the third element above are most likely to occur where the plaintiff seeks to hold the defendant liable vicariously, as was the situation in *Hecht*. Perhaps *Hecht* should be understood for what it held and not what it said: It denied the vicarious liability of the rogue broker's employer. Is it appropriate in such a setting to deny recovery if the plaintiff's acquiescence prolonged the period, and hence frequency, of the broker's misconduct? *See Tranchina v. Howard*, 1997 WL 472664 (E.D. La. 1997) (jury to decide whether brokerage house is shielded from liability due to customer's failure to ask and thus receive confirmation slips that if reviewed would reveal the broker's fraudulent transactions).

Waiver.   Waiver generally refers to "the voluntary or intentional relinquishment of a known right." *Royal Air Properties, Inc. v. Smith*, 333 F.2d 568, 571 (9th Cir. 1964). Waiver is a particularly technical question because not only does it raise close factual issues as to whether the plaintiff was sufficiently aware of all the facts to have actual knowledge—a requirement for any waiver—but also there is the problem whether waivers, even if knowingly made, are so inconsistent with the securities laws as to be void. The latter issue arises from provisions such as Section 14 of the '33 Act, which provides "any condition, stipulation or provision binding any person acquiring any security to waive compliance with any provision of this title or the rules and regulations . . . shall be void."

Similarly, Section 29(a) of the '34 Act renders void "any condition, stipulation, or provision binding any person to waive compliance with" the provisions or regulations of the Act. As we will see in Chapter 18, the Supreme Court, relying on the policy embodied in the National Arbitration Act, has held that neither of these provisions voids agreements under which the investor agrees to arbitrate any future claims he has under the securities laws. In contrast, a provision imposing additional steps the investor must undertake before bringing suit for a violation is void. *See McMahan & Co. v. Wherehouse Enter., Inc.*, 65 F.3d 1044 (2d Cir. 1995). Waiver clauses extend beyond mere agreements to arbitrate and invariably raise questions whether investors fully appreciate the possible downside of such clauses. *See* Prentice, Contract-Based Defenses in Securities Fraud Litigation: A Behavioral Analysis, 2003 U. Ill. L. Rev. 337.

When entering into a contract, can a party waive any possible disclosure violation by consenting to a contract that includes a statement that "all material facts pertinent to the purchase of the securities have been disclosed" or that "any facts not disclosed are agreed not to have been material"? *See AES Corp. v. Dow Chemical Co.*, 325 F.3d 174 (3d Cir. 2003) (non-reliance clause is one of the circumstances to be considered in determining whether alleged reliance by plaintiff was reasonable but would violate Section 29(b) to accord clause automatic power to dismiss the suit); *Rissman v. Rissman*, 213 F.3d 381 (7th Cir. 2000) (such an agreement between sophisticated parties precludes reliance on oral misrepresentations); *Cornielsen v. Infinium Capital Mgmt., LLC*, 916 F.3d 589 (7th Cir. 2019) (applying *Rissman* to employees without evaluating their degree of sophistication); *Emergent Capital Management LLC v. Stonepath Group, Inc.*, 343 F.3d 189 (2d Cir. 2003) ("integration clause" that stated the negotiated agreement embodied the full and final expression of the agreement barred a sophisticated purchaser from arguing there were other representations made that were false). *See* Miller, Rule 10b-5 and Business Combination Transactions, 21 U. Pa. J. Bus. L. 533 (2019) (non-reliance provision is necessary and economically efficient in complex securities transactions that regularly involve extended negotiations and successive representations by numerous individuals).

Courts distinguish between waivers of matured claims and waivers that would permit violations to continue. *See Pasternak v. Shrader*, 863 F.3d 162, 172 (2d Cir. 2017) (waiver ineffective if focus is to waive future compliance with the securities laws as opposed to settling claims arising from a past violation); *Pearlstein v. Scudder & German*, 429 F.2d 1136 (2d Cir. 1970) (striking down a stipulation between a broker and his customer whereby the customer waived any right to sue the broker for damages under the securities laws due to the broker extending more credit to the customer than permitted by the margin requirements).

In Pari Delicto.   Literally, *in pari delicto* means "of equal fault" and when successfully invoked bars the plaintiff's recovery at law because the court concludes that the plaintiff and the defendant had the mutual intent to violate the securities laws. In considering whether the plaintiff should be so barred, the courts consider the comparative fault of the plaintiff and the defendant, barring suit only when the plaintiff's culpability, particularly knowledge, rises to a level equal to that of the defendant. Thus, in *Bateman Eichler, Hill Richards, Inc. v. Berner*, 472 U.S. 299 (1985), a broker was sued by his customer who claimed the broker falsely represented that his recommendation to purchase a stock was based on "inside information." The broker's *in pari delicto* defense was unsuccessful because the Court did not believe the customer's culpability was equal to that of the broker. For an application of *in pari delicto* to bar a recovery, *see In re Dublin Securities, Inc. v. Hurd*, 133 F.3d 377, 380 (6th Cir. 1997) (receiver for defunct brokerage firm could not recover from lawyers who assisted brokerage firm's managers to carry out several fraudulent offerings, even though attorneys knew the offerings were fraudulent). Since the defense arises only in private actions, should special consideration be given to the relative harm that each party's conduct poses to the public? *See Fogarty v. Security Trust Co.*, 532 F.2d 1029, 1033 (5th Cir. 1976). On this point, consider the language of the Supreme Court in *Bateman Eichler*, that it was appropriate to bar a suit, provided "preclusion of suit would not significantly interfere with the effective enforcement of the securities laws and protection of the investing public." 472 U.S. at 311. When the plaintiff seeks equitable relief, the defense of unclean hands bars the action where the plaintiff's conduct not only is reprehensible (although that need not include a violation of the securities laws), but also is closely related to the subject matter of the suit against the defendant.

An interesting application of the *in pari delicto* doctrine arises when the company seeks to recover from its auditor for the auditing firm's collusion with the company's managers in releasing false financial reports. Most courts apply the doctrine to bar such suits. *See, e.g., Cenco, Inc. v. Seidman & Seidman*, 686 F.2d 449 (7th Cir. 1982); *Alleghany Health v. PriceWaterhouseCoopers, LLP*, 989 A.2d 313 (Pa. 2010). *Contra NCP Litig. Trust v. KPMG LLP*, 901 A.2d 871 (N.J. 2006). Does the doctrine's application in this context make sense in light of the role auditors assume with respect to the financial reporting process?

2. Indemnity and Contribution

Indemnification involves shifting the burden of paying the damage award from one person who has paid the judgment to another; on the other hand, contribution refers to the right of a joint tortfeasor to obtain an equitable sharing of the damage award among those liable for the violation. Indemnification need not delay us long, for with rare exception indemnification is not permitted in securities law cases. In the leading case, *Globus v. Law Research Service, Inc.* (*Globus I*), 418 F.2d 1276 (2d Cir. 1969), *cert. denied*, 397 U.S. 913 (1970), the Second Circuit denied indemnification to the underwriters involved in a distribution under Regulation A where the underwriters were alleged to have had actual knowledge of the fraud and the defrauded investors were suing under the antifraud provisions of the '33 and '34 Acts. Although Section 11 of the Securities Act was not at issue, the court referred to it for the purposes of discussion:

> Civil liability under section 11 and similar provisions was designed not so much to compensate the defrauded purchaser as to promote enforcement of the Act and to deter negligence by providing a penalty for those who fail in their duties. . . . [T]he "in terrorem effect" of civil liability might well be thwarted if underwriters were free to pass their liability on to the issuer. Underwriters who knew that they could be indemnified simply by showing that the issuer was "more liable" than they

> (a process not too difficult when the issuer is inevitably closer to the facts) would
> have a tendency to be lax in their independent investigations.

Id. at 1288.

Following the lead of *Globus I,* indemnification is always denied to those who have violated the securities laws. *See, e.g., Eichenholtz v. Brennan,* 52 F.3d 478 (3d Cir. 1995); *King v. Gibbs,* 876 F.2d 1275 (7th Cir. 1989); *In re Livent Securities Litigation,* 193 F. Supp. 2d 750 (S.D.N.Y. 2002); *Gould v. American-Hawaiian Steamship Co.,* 387 F. Supp. 163 (D. Del. 1974), *vacated and remanded on other grounds,* 535 F.2d 761 (3d Cir. 1976) (negligent party not entitled to indemnification from party who acted with knowledge of fraudulent scheme). An even more sweeping approach was taken in *King,* supra, where the court did not base its decision on the ground that indemnification was against public policy, but rather found that there was no implied cause of action for indemnification.

But what should be the result if the person seeking indemnification is only vicariously liable? For example, in earlier materials, we found that most of the circuits hold the employer vicariously responsible for the securities violations the employee commits in the scope of employment. Some courts have permitted indemnification of those whose liability is only vicarious. *See, e.g., Johnson Controls, Inc. v. Rowland Tompkins Corp.,* 585 F. Supp. 969 (S.D.N.Y. 1984); *Maryville Academy v. Loeb Rhoades & Co.,* 530 F. Supp. 1061 (N.D. Ill. 1981).

Furthermore, recall from Chapter 4 the indirect indemnification that occurs between the underwriters and the issuer and its lawyers and accountants through assignment of areas of responsibility in review of the registration statement. The overall objective of such delegations among the parties to the agreement is to provide the underwriter with a cause of action against the issuer, its accountants, or its lawyers if a misrepresentation occurs in that portion of the registration statement for which the issuer, accountant, or lawyer assumed primary responsibility. Thus, this device seeks to achieve the same result condemned in *Globus I.* Are such arrangements contrary to sound public policy?

Contribution—seeking through court order to force other wrongdoers to *share* in any award where there is joint and several liability—is something of a mixed question under the securities laws. Three of the seven express liability provisions of the '33 and '34 Acts (Section 11(f) of the '33 Act and Sections 9(e) and 18(b) of the '34 Act) provide for contribution. In *Musick, Peeler & Garret v. Employers Insurance of Wausau,* 508 U.S. 286 (1993), the Supreme Court held there is an implied right to contribution under Section 10(b). Though contribution does not have the same effect of undercutting the statutory standards of conduct prescribed by the federal securities laws as indemnification, is this solely a question of scale, so that we should be concerned that contribution among securities law violators is socially harmful? Contribution is granted under the securities laws, even to those who intentionally violated the securities laws. Should plaintiffs be neutral to the question of whether and on what basis contribution exists among co-violators? Is contribution consistent with the deterrent objectives of the federal securities laws? Keeping in mind the deterrent objectives, how should the various defendants' relative shares of the burden be allocated? Should those defendants that have previously reached a settlement of the case with the plaintiff be liable in contribution to the nonsettling defendants?

Securities law cases are by and large complex; they usually involve multiple defendants, and over the course of the litigation, many of the defendants will choose to enter into a settlement with the plaintiff. In negotiating such a settlement, the parties—the plaintiff, as well as the settling defendants—need to know how that settlement will affect the rights and duties of the nonsettling defendants, particularly whether the nonsettling defendants' rights to obtain contribution from the settling defendants will be affected and whether the amount of the settlement will reduce any judgment the plaintiff later is able to obtain against the nonsettling defendants. In these considerations, there should be a healthy respect for the fact that allowing the nonsettling defendants wide contribution rights against the settling defendants necessarily dampens the willingness of defendants generally to consider settlement prior to trial. By way of an illustration of many of these questions, consider how the rules of contribution could have played a role in the events leading up to *Smith v. Mulvaney*, 827 F.2d 558 (9th Cir. 1987). After settling with many of the defendants for $722,000, the plaintiff offered to settle the case against Mrs. Smith for $150,000. Mrs. Smith rejected the settlement and proceeded to trial; the court awarded the plaintiff $5.1 million. Who should bear the risk of Mrs. Smith seeking her day in court? *See generally* Nichols, Symmetry and Consistency and the Plaintiff's Risk: Partial Settlement and the Right of Contribution in Federal Securities Actions, 19 Del. J. Corp. L. 1 (1994).

The PSLRA adds Section 21D(f)(8) to the Exchange Act, requiring that certain types of contribution claims be "determined based upon the percentage of responsibility of the claimant and of each person against whom a claim for contribution is made." This provision essentially embraces a proportionate fault standard for contribution claims and applies only to claims for contribution arising because of the claimant's liability under some provision of the Exchange Act or under Section 11 of the Securities Act as an *outside* director. The provision does not cover contribution claims based upon some other provision of the securities laws, such as an officer's or underwriter's liability under Section 11 or a seller's liability under Section 12(a)(2) of the Securities Act, although one can expect its influence in those actions as well.

The PSLRA's full effects on contribution appear in the competing situations of defendants who have settled with the plaintiff versus those who go to trial and lose, such as Mrs. Smith, supra. Should the nonsettling defendant who suffers a big judgment (e.g., Mrs. Smith) be able to ask the earlier-settling defendant to contribute toward the big jury award? The process adopted by the PSLRA is essentially that followed in *Franklin v. Kaypro Corp.*, 884 F.2d 1222 (9th Cir. 1989), *cert. denied*, 498 U.S. 890 (1990). *Kaypro* identifies three goals that should be satisfied in resolving the question of the impact of partial settlement: the statutory goal of punishing each wrongdoer, the equitable goal of limiting liability to relative culpability, and the policy goal of encouraging settlement.

> [The approach envisioned by the court] contemplates a partial settlement approved by the district court under Rule 23. Nonsettling defendants are then barred from further rights of contribution from the settling defendants. At trial, the jury is asked not only to determine the total dollar damage amount, but also the percentage of culpability of each of the nonsettling defendants as well as that of the settling defendants. Nonsettling defendants as a whole will then be required

> to pay the percentage of the total amount for which they are responsible. The non-settling defendants will be jointly and severally liable for that percentage, and will continue to have rights of contribution against one another.

Id. at 1231. This is the approach embraced in Exchange Act Section 21D(f)(8) for all contribution claims arising under the Exchange Act and for those brought by outside directors held liable under Section 11 of the Securities Act.[3] Under the Reform Act, is the interest of the nonsettling defendants adequately protected by the hearing envisioned for the partial pretrial settlement? Is the *Kaypro* formula equally suited to nonclass actions where such partial settlements do not require court approval? Does *Kaypro* encourage or discourage settlement? *See generally* Kornhauser & Revesz, Settlements Under Joint and Several Liability, 68 N.Y.U. L. Rev. 427 (1993).

In court-approved settlements, the PSLRA directs the court to enter an order discharging the settling party from all claims for contribution from other parties. *See* Section 21D(f)(7)(A). Does such an order also bar state law claims against the settling defendant that are based on tort or contract claim? For example, consider that after Cendant and its auditor agreed to settle a securities class action by paying $3.2 billion to investors, Cendant initiated a common law fraud, negligence, and breach of contract action against the settling auditor, alleging it had failed to discover by the exercise of reasonable care that the managers of the company acquired by Cendant had carried out a massive scheme of financial deception. *In re Cendant*, 139 F. Supp. 2d 585, 596 (D.N.J. 2001) (claims were not barred). Is it inconsistent with the policy of the bar order to permit such a suit to continue? Is this consistent with the PSLRA? Does it undercut the compensatory or deterrence objectives of private actions? *See In re HealthSouth Corp. Sec. Litig.*, 572 F.3d 854 (11th Cir. 2009) (bar order against nonsettling CEO extinguished his contractual right to indemnification against employer); *In re Heritage Bond Litig.*, 546 F.3d 667 (9th Cir. 2008) (PSLRA bar orders extend only to claims arising from defendant's liability to the plaintiff and do not bar claims that arise from a separate duty the defendant may have breached to one of his co-defendants); Kaplan, The Scope of Bar Orders in Federal Securities Fraud Settlements, 52 Duke L.J. 211 (2002).

PROBLEM

14-8.   EarthCom was the darling of the investment community and has grown rapidly in recent years. A couple of years ago it announced that much of its rising profits were fabricated by creative accounting engaged in by its senior officers and occurred under the slumbering eyes of its board of directors. Among the various ensuing class actions was a suit under Section 11 of the Securities Act against EarthCom's ten underwriters and six outside directors. The underwriters

---

3. Setoff rights become more complicated under *Mary Carter Agreements*, whereby the settlement is not a specific sum, but a formula that includes consideration of the amount of any recovery the plaintiff later obtains from nonsettling defendants. *See, e.g., Robertson v. White*, 81 F.3d 752 (8th Cir. 1996). *See generally* Bernstein & Klerman, An Economic Analysis of Mary Carter Settlement Agreements, 83 Geo. L.J. 2215 (1995).

had equal allotments of $100 million of securities covered by the registration statement and the securities are now worthless. It is acknowledged that the registration statement was materially misleading and all agree that the division of responsibility is roughly 60 percent for the senior officers, 20 percent by the outside auditor, and 10 percent each for the underwriters as a group and the outside directors as a group. The court is now asked to approve a settlement by all but one of the underwriters. The settling nine underwriters agree to contribute collectively $4 million towards settlement, provided the court enters an order barring a contribution claim being brought against them by the non-settling underwriter. The directors collectively will contribute $2 million. The plaintiffs have also requested an order that the "impact of any settlement with any other defendant will be to reduce such other defendant's liability by the amount of said settlement or settlements." What arguments can the nonsettling underwriter make in opposition to the proposed settlement? *See Worldcom, Inc. Securities Litigation*, [Current] Fed. Sec. L. Rep. (CCH) ¶93,129 (S.D.N.Y. 2005).

E.   *Statutes of Limitations*

For each of the express liability provisions of the securities laws, Congress specified an applicable statute of limitations. *See, e.g.*, Section 13 of the '33 Act and Sections 9(e) and 18(c) of the '34 Act. Not surprisingly, no express limitations period is specified for the various implied causes of action, so the courts have had to imply one, lest there be no limitation whatsoever on such actions. *Lampf, Pleva, Lipkind, Prupis & Petigrow v. Gilbertson*, 501 U.S. 350 (1991), held that the limitations period for causes of action under Rule 10b-5 is that provided by Section 9(f) of the Exchange Act for express causes of action (i.e., one year of discovery of facts constituting the violation and no more than three years of the plaintiff's purchase or sale). The Court reasoned that the clearest guidance of probable congressional intent is the limitations period specified for express causes of action in the same Act that is the origin of the implied cause of action.

The Sarbanes-Oxley Act amended Section 1658 of U.S. Code Title 28 to provide that any "claim of fraud, deceit, manipulation, or contrivance in contravention of a regulatory requirement concerning securities" must be brought not later than the earlier of "2 years after discovery of the facts constituting the violation" or "5 years after such violation." Section 1658 posed its own uncertainties, chief of which are (1) just what constitutes "discovery" so that the two-year period commences and (2) must the action be dismissed if not commenced within five years of the violation regardless of whether discovery of the violation was possible?

In *Merck & Co. v. Reynolds*, 559 U.S. 633 (2010), the Supreme Court rejected a broad "inquiry notice" standard for the commencement of the statute of limitations under Section 1658(b), holding that

> . . . the limitations period in §1658(b)(1) begins to run once the plaintiff did discover or a reasonably diligent plaintiff would have "discover[ed] the facts

constituting the violation"—whichever comes first. In determining the time at which "discovery" of those "facts" occurred, terms such as "inquiry notice" and "storm warnings" may be useful to the extent that they identify a time when the facts would have prompted a reasonably diligent plaintiff to begin investigating. But the limitations period does not begin to run until the plaintiff thereafter discovers or a reasonably diligent plaintiff would have discovered "the facts constituting the violation," including scienter—irrespective of whether the actual plaintiff undertook a reasonably diligent investigation.

The *Merck* litigation alleged that the pharmaceutical company knowingly misrepresented the risk of heart attacks accompanying use of Merck's pain-killing drug Vioxx, which, once acknowledged, led to serious economic losses and declines in the price of Merck's common stock. Because the suit was filed November 6, 2003, the question was whether the plaintiffs had (or should have) discovered before November 6, 2001 "facts constituting a violation." If so, their suit was barred by the two-year limitation period that commences "2 years after discovery." The Court believed the following did *not* commence the two-year limitation period: A March 2000 study revealed that approximately 4 of every 1,000 study participants who took Vioxx suffered heart attacks; Merck's press releases in response to the March 2000 study provided a hypothesis that would explain why Vioxx was not the cause of the increase in heart attack risk; the study and Merck's response were widely reported by journalists and in the financial press; in May 2001 a product class action lawsuit was filed against Merck alleging that, based on the earlier study reports, Vioxx increased the risk of heart attacks; in August 2001 the Journal of the American Medical Association warned that available data raised a "cautionary flag" regarding Vioxx and strongly called for a study to assess the product's cardiovascular risk; in September 2001 the FDA sent a warning letter to Merck that its marketing of Vioxx was false in failing to provide a balanced view of the product's cardiovascular risks; and in October 2001 the FDA ordered Merck to send healthcare providers a corrective letter to Merck's earlier promotional efforts in which Merck provided a one-sided explanation for the increased cardiovascular risk associated with use of Vioxx. *See also City of Pontiac Gen'l Employees Ret. Sys. v. MBIA*, 637 F.3d 169, 175 (2d Cir. 2011) ("a fact is discovered . . . [when] a reasonably diligent plaintiff would have sufficient information about that fact to adequately plead it in a complaint . . . with sufficient detail and particularity to survive a . . . motion to dismiss").

Resolving whether claims can be brought more than five years after the violation depends on whether Section 1658 is deemed a statute of limitations or a statute of repose. If the former, doctrines such as the "discovery rule" and "equitable tolling" exist. *Merck* illustrates the discovery rule. Equitable tolling bars the defendant who actively conceals his misconduct from taking refuge in a statute of limitations. This requires fraudulent concealment above and beyond the violation itself. In contrast, if a statute of repose, the statute bars a suit after the passage of the specified period of time. *See, e.g., McCann v. Hy-Vee Inc.*, 663 F.3d 926 (7th Cir. 2011) (five-year period is a statute of repose).

PROBLEM

14-9.   Throughout 2011, 2012, and 2013, Life Systems, Inc. reported double-digit increases in earnings in each of its periodic filings with the SEC. In each of the three calendar year annual reports Life Systems' outside auditors reported there were significant weaknesses in Life Systems' internal controls and each of the audit opinions stated the internal control weaknesses were "unremediated." Nonetheless, the auditors provided an unqualified opinion to the financial statements. As a result of a whistleblower's disclosures, in July 2013 the SEC launched an investigation of Life Systems; soon thereafter Life Systems announced it would restate earnings for each of the three prior years and that it was terminating its CEO and CFO because of "a lack of confidence in their stewardship of the firm." In early August 2013 a securities fraud class action was filed against Life Systems and its auditors seeking damages on behalf of investors who had purchased Life System shares between March 2011, the release date of the admittedly misleading 2011 quarterly report, and August 2013. How should the district court respond to a motion to bar claims by investors who purchased before August 2011? *See L.C. Capital Partners v. Frontier Ins. Group*, 318 F.3d 1148 (2d Cir. 2003); *Young v. Lepone*, 305 F.3d 1 (1st Cir. 2002).

F.   *Enforcement Actions by the SEC*

1.   Investigations

a.   *The Investigatory Process*

Each of the acts administered and enforced by the SEC empowers the Commission to investigate whether violations have occurred, are occurring, or are likely to occur. For example, Section 21(a) of the Exchange Act provides that the Commission may, "in its discretion, make such investigations as it deems necessary to determine whether any person has violated, is violating, or is about to violate any provision of" the Act or its rules or regulations. The Commission's Rules of Practice govern the conduct of such investigations. 17 C.F.R. §§201.1 et seq. There are many possible causes for the staff to launch an investigation: Its review of filings with the Commission may suggest a disclosure violation has occurred; the staff, as well as self-regulatory organizations, periodically inspects broker-dealers, investment advisers, and investment companies, and such inspections may raise the staff's eyebrows and prompt a further investigation of some matter; news stories, complaints, and tips from whistleblowers are significant in prompting SEC investigations.

The initial investigation by the staff, referred to as an *informal* or *preliminary investigation,* simply entails asking questions of parties involved, without issuing subpoenas or seeking to compel testimony. A preliminary investigation is nonpublic unless the Commission orders that it be public, a step it rarely has taken. The preliminary investigation's success heavily depends upon the voluntary cooperation of the company and individuals that are the object of the investigation. Consider the conflicting tugs on their counsel during the informal investigation:

> Counsel's principal responsibility in the preliminary investigation is to assess tactical considerations for responding to an informal inquiry. Counsel must balance the corporation's interests. On one hand, there is great incentive to provide the information necessary to allay the staff's suspicions of violation without graduating to a formal investigation. Counsel also may be able to quickly eliminate areas of concern and focus the staff's attention on relevant information. On the other hand, counsel may wish to prevent a wholesale disclosure of broadly identified corporate information, and may be forced to make a more limited presentation of information.

Ferrara & Nerkle, Overview of an SEC Enforcement Action, 8 Corp. L. Rev. 306, 307-308 (1985). If the staff's concerns are not satisfied by the information available to it through its informal investigation, it can seek to advance matters to a formal investigation by persuading a senior officer in the Division of Enforcement to go to the full Commission for approval of a formal order of investigation. The grant of a formal order reflects the Commission's view that there is reason to believe a violation has occurred, is occurring, or is about to occur.

Once the formal order is granted, the staff has the power to issue subpoenas nationwide against any person or records significant to the investigation. If a person refuses to comply with the subpoena, the SEC staff must apply to the federal district court to enforce the subpoena. An SEC subpoena can be judicially enforced against recalcitrant parties without the staff having to prove probable cause that the securities laws have been violated. *See SEC v. Brigadoon Scotch Distributing Co.*, 480 F.2d 1047 (2d Cir. 1973), *cert. denied*, 415 U.S. 915 (1974). Subpoenas are not enforced, however, if the investigation is not for a proper purpose, the information sought is not relevant to that purpose, the SEC already possesses the information it seeks, or the administrative procedures for issuing the subpoena have not been followed. *See SEC v. Blackfoot Bituminous, Inc.*, 622 F.2d 512, 514 (1980). The ability of the investigation's target to mount challenges to an SEC subpoena is greatly compromised by the Supreme Court's holding that the target of an SEC investigation is not entitled to prior notice when a subpoena is directed toward a third party. *SEC v. Jerry O'Brien, Inc.*, 467 U.S. 735 (1984). By and large, the Commission's power to investigate suspected cases of securities law violations is unrestricted.

The courts have held with some consistency that, so long as the staff is acting in good faith, its discretion to determine who will be required to testify before it or what documentary information will have to be produced will not be second-guessed. To be sure, constitutional protections apply to SEC investigations. Thus, for example, the Fourth Amendment's guarantee against unreasonable searches and seizures has been interpreted to limit the Commission's ability to make unreasonably burdensome investigatory demands, and the Fifth Amendment's privilege against self-incrimination applies to SEC investigations and proceedings, although that privilege can be raised only by individuals and sole proprietorships and not by corporations and partnerships. (On this point, consider *Braswell v. United States*, 487 U.S. 99 (1988), where the court held that an officer must produce corporate records, even though those records will incriminate the officer.)

Later materials in this chapter explore the various criminal sanctions that are available for willful violations of the securities laws. It is not unusual for the SEC investigation to occur simultaneously with a criminal grand jury investigation being conducted by the Department of Justice. Also, the fruits of the SEC's investigatory efforts can constitutionally be shared with the Department of Justice provided there is no deceit or trickery on the part of the SEC that suggests its investigation was a ruse to gather evidence to support a subsequent criminal prosecution. *See United States v. Stringer*, 535 F.3d 929 (9th Cir. 2008).

b.   *Responding to the Investigation: White Papers and Wells Notices*

As seen, approval by the full Commission raises the profile of the enforcement matter. Before securing this approval, it is within the discretion of the staff member whether to provide the prospective defendant with a summary of the evidence and legal theories the staff will rely upon in prosecuting the action if commencement of the enforcement action is approved. This is known as a *Wells notice* (so named because the Commission formally instituted the practice in its Securities Act Release No. 5310 in response to the Advisory Committee on Enforcement Policies, called the Wells Committee, after its chairman); the notice identifies the specific provisions violated and generally provides some factual support for the staff's belief that the violation has occurred. The defendant is thereby provided with an opportunity to submit a written statement, referred to as a *Wells submission*. The Dodd-Frank Act added Section 4E to the Exchange Act, requiring the SEC staff within 180 days of issuing a Wells notice either to file an action or to notify the Director of Enforcement that an enforcement action will not be pursued (one 180-day extension is permitted). However, the 180-day requirement appears not to create any rights in an enforcement target.

Even though there is no *formal* opportunity to address factual or legal issues raised in the investigation before a Wells notice is received, the practice has developed whereby counsel frequently present "white papers" that set forth the respondent's views bearing on key factual and legal issues; the goals that can be pursued in such a white paper include possibly avoiding the matter reaching the formal investigation level and the likely attendant adverse publicity, getting a better understanding of the staff's theories, and simply providing the respondent's views of the facts and law. Many of these points are resurrected by the respondent in its submission to a Wells notice.

The preparation of a white paper and a Wells submission is an important, but delicate, undertaking. On the one hand, the opportunity to make a case against the institution of an enforcement proceeding may be valuable, especially for one whose participation is peripheral to the investigation's principal focus. On the other hand, they entail cost, may deflect or weaken the cooperative spirit the SEC expects from respondents, and may provide admissions that the staff or third parties (other government agencies or private litigants) may later invoke against the respondent. *See, e.g., In re Steinhardt Partners, L.P.,* 9 F.3d 230 (2d Cir. 1993). On the other hand, to hold back information may also erode the overall effectiveness of the submission.

The SEC is not without limits in using its enforcement powers to establish regulatory policy. Of significance in this regard are cases where SEC enforcement actions have been dismissed on the ground the defendant lacked adequate notice of what act the SEC regarded as a violation by the defendant. Thus in *Upton v. SEC,* 75 F.3d 92 (2d Cir. 1996), the court dismissed the SEC's prosecution of a broker for failing to *continuously* segregate and compute the amount of funds held on behalf of the broker's customers. The SEC's rule mandated *weekly* segregation and computations so that the broker could reasonably argue that it had complied with the requirement by each seventh day segregating the customer's funds and tallying their sum. *Upton* also relied on evidence that industry practice was contrary to the SEC's interpretation of the rule.

There is a wide range of options available to the Commission when it believes some form of action is necessary. The least severe is for the staff to issue a cautionary letter advising the subjects of the investigation that their practices or conduct raises serious questions under the securities laws or constitutes a minor offense. The cautionary letter is not publicly available and is infrequently used.

The Commission sometimes believes it is desirable to give wider publicity to what its investigation has unearthed, even though no further action is to be taken against the investigation's subjects, by publishing a Report of Investigation, which is authorized by Section 21(a) of the Exchange Act. Because the report issued under Section 21(a) generally has some unfavorable observations about the investigated company or individual, emerging from a Commission investigation with a Section 21(a) report is less than a clear victory for the investigation's target. As we will see later, the Commission has sometimes expanded the overall mission of the report, so that it frequently embodies formal undertakings akin to those in consent decrees.

When the subjects are members of an SRO, such as an exchange or FINRA, the Commission may forward the information it has gathered to the appropriate SRO, if the information suggests that the SRO's rules have been violated, so that the SRO can take appropriate disciplinary action. Occasionally, the Commission provides information to state or federal regulatory bodies whose rules or regulations it believes the subjects have violated.

Options that are more adversarial in nature are separately examined in the following materials. These options include administrative disciplinary proceedings, administrative cease-and-desist orders, and injunctive actions in the federal courts as well as fines and disgorgement orders in appropriate cases. Once there is the hint of wrongdoing, the defensive strategy the respondent decides to pursue is inevitably guided by the healthy awareness that a government enforcement action customarily has a significant negative effect on the price of its shares. *See generally,* Solomon & Soltes, Is "Not Guilty" the Same as "Innocent"? Evidence from SEC Financial Fraud Investigations, Working Paper (June 12, 2019), available at *https://ssrn.com/abstract=3402780;* Karpoff, Lee & Martin, The Cost to Firms of Cooking the Books, 43 J. Fin. & Quant. Analysis 581 (2008). But why take such risks? *See* Amiram, Huang & Rajgopal, Does Financial Reporting Misconduct Pay Off Even When Discovered?, 2019 Working Paper, available at *https://ssrn.com/abstract=3353823* (nearly one-third of the perpetrators of discovered serious financial reporting misconduct experience an overall net benefit).

NOTES AND QUESTIONS

1. Whistleblowers. A significant source of information about potential violations flows from the Dodd-Frank Act's addition of Section 21F of the Exchange Act directing the Commission to pay a reward (10 to 30 percent) to whistleblowers who provide "original information" that "led to the successful enforcement" action recovering monetary sanctions in excess of $1 million or more. Regulation 21F sets forth procedures for such tips to be provided to the SEC and submission of claims of a reward as well as the criteria for establishing the amount of a reward. Since the program's inception in 2011, the SEC has recovered $1.7 billion in sanctions (including $901 million in disgorgements) based on meritorious whistleblower claims and awarded $326 million to 59 whistleblowers; in fiscal 2018 the SEC received 5,800 tips and awarded $168 million directed to 13 individuals. SEC Annual Report on Dodd-Frank Whistleblower Program (2018).

To accommodate concerns that the SEC whistleblower provision not preempt internal compliance provisions that companies maintain, whistleblowers remain eligible for a reward, even though they first reported their knowledge pursuant to an entity's compliance system, provided the whistleblower report to the SEC occurs within 120 days of such an internal report. *See* Implementation of the Whistleblower Provisions of Section 21F of the Securities Exchange Act, Exchange Act Release No. 64545 (May 25, 2011). Does the whistleblower provision nonetheless compete with internal compliance efforts that seek employee cooperation in identifying possible misconduct? Will an unintended consequence of garnering an SEC bounty be removing this source of information frequently resorted to by class action lawyers with the consequential effect that we might see a rise in SEC enforcement suits accompanied by a decline in private securities class actions? *See* Rose, Better Bounty Hunting: How the SEC's New Whistleblower Program Changes the Securities Fraud Class Action Debate, 108 Nw. U. L. Rev. 1235 (2014). For evidence that the whistleblower program has improved accounting quality and reduced audit fees, *see* Berger & Lee, Do Corporate Whistleblower Laws Deter Accounting Fraud?, Working Paper (March 2019).

Section 21F(h)(1) prohibits employers from retaliating against individuals when they engage in whistleblowing activities. *Lawson v. FMR LLC*, 571 U.S. 429 (2014), held that anti-retaliation claims are not limited to employees of publicly traded companies, but also extend to employees of contractors to public companies who report problems with the public company client. However, the whistleblowing and termination must be linked to a misconduct involving the securities laws. *See, e.g., Verfuerth v. Orion Energy Sys., Inc.*, 879 F.3d 798 (7th Cir. 2018) (anti-retaliation provision not triggered when the whistleblower's complaint related only to overbilling customers, mishandling of IP disputes, and handling of conflicts of interest). The provision is enforceable by the Commission; whistleblowers have a private cause of action as well. However, in *Digital Realty Trust, Inc. v. Somer*, 138 S. Ct. 767 (2018), the Justices unanimously limited retaliation protection to employees who report to the SEC. Some companies have tried to discourage whistleblowing through employee confidentiality agreements. *See In the Matter of KBR Inc.*, Exchange Act Release No. 74619 (Apr. 1, 2015) (settling enforcement action where the SEC took the position that confidentiality agreement that company imposed on employees that barred employees from discussing company matters with outside parties was a violation of Rule 21F-17(a) proscription that "no person may take any action to impede an individual communicating directly with the Commission staff about a possible securities law violation").

2. *Obstruction of Justice and SEC Investigations.* A development arising from Enron of far-reaching significance was the indictment and conviction of Big Five accounting firm Arthur Andersen for obstruction of justice. After learning in late August 2001 that its client, Enron, was the focus of an SEC investigation, Arthur Andersen assembled a "crisis response" team that included its in-house counsel, Temple. Thereafter Temple at several points circulated to Arthur Andersen staff, including members of the crisis response team and the Enron auditors, pointed reminders of the necessity to comply with the firm's "document retention" policy. This policy clearly stated that due to litigation concerns the firm's records pertaining to an audit client should be reviewed regularly to assure the records contain only such information that is necessary to support the audit work that was performed. Throughout the month of October 2001, in response to Temple's notice, Arthur Andersen's staff shredded documents related to its Enron audit. For example, the facts revealed that on October 26th, four days before the SEC announced its formal investigation of Enron and then requested it produce all accounting documents, the audit partner in charge of the Enron audit was seen shredding a document labeled "smoking gun." As a consequence of its destruction of documents relevant to an ongoing SEC investigation, Arthur Andersen was convicted under 18 U.S.C. §1512(b)(2)(A), one of the many federal obstruction of justice provisions. This provision makes it a crime when one "knowingly . . . corruptly persuades another . . . with intent to cause or induce any person to . . . withhold . . . a record, document, or other object, from an official proceeding." The provision is somewhat unique in the obstruction of justice arsenal because it focuses on obstruction prior to a hearing or trial. Once Arthur Andersen was convicted, per SEC rules it could no longer be an auditor of public companies. It therefore quickly closed its doors so that no longer was there a Big Five, but instead, merely the Final Four. It was small consolation that the Supreme Court ultimately reversed Arthur Andersen's conviction, holding that the "corruptly persuade" language in the statute called for the jury instruction that emphasized "dishonesty"; the instruction that was given permitted conviction upon a finding that Arthur Andersen acted with the intent to "impede" an investigation. *See Arthur Andersen LLP v. United States*, 544 U.S. 696 (2005).

Would the jury's instruction be correct today under 18 U.S.C. §1519, which is part of the Sarbanes-Oxley Act of 2002 and proscribes one who "knowingly alters, destroys . . . any record . . . with intent to impede, obstruct, or influence the investigation . . . of any matter within the jurisdiction of any department or agency . . ."? *See Yates v. United States*, 135 S. Ct. 1074 (2015) ("record" refers only to documents that record or preserve information and not to contraband garnered through the violation). Sarbanes-Oxley also mandates that auditors retain for five years the audit and review working papers for their reporting company clients. 18 U.S.C. §1520(a)(1). Destruction of evidence aside, those questioned in the course of an investigation should bear in mind the consequences of being less than honest with investigators. *See United States v. Stewart*, 362 F. Supp. 2d 854 (S.D.N.Y. 2004) (media personality Martha Stewart was convicted for obstruction of justice in connection with an investigation on whether she traded on inside information by making false statements to investigators to conceal her knowledge that the CEO of ImClone, a close friend, was dumping his shares in the firm just before public announcement that the FDA had rejected the firm's application for approval of its cancer-fighting drug).

PROBLEMS

14-10.   Merko, Inc. is a reporting company. Over the past year it and several of its officers have received a succession of Wells notices. During this period, Merko filed two 10-Qs and most recently its 10-K for the past fiscal year with no mention of the Wells notices. Three weeks after filing the 10-K, Merko finally disclosed it had received over the past many months Wells notices related to "an ongoing investigation of its reporting practices." Merko stock declined 3.2 percent following the disclosure. Has Merko violated its disclosure obligations under Item 103 of Regulation S-K? *See In re Lions Gate Entertainment Corp. Sec. Litig.*, 2016 U.S. Dist. LEXIS 7721 (Jan. 22, 2016).

14-11.   BuyArama, Ltd. recently completed its acquisition of SaleCo. The market greeted the acquisition favorably—BuyArama's shares rose more than 20 percent as a result of the acquisition. Cheryl, an accountant on the staff of SaleCo, was frustrated that her superiors had ignored her repeated efforts to provide disclosure of several significant SaleCo contingent liabilities in the proxy statement used in obtaining shareholder approval of the stock-for-stock acquisition. Just before the completion of the acquisition, Cheryl spoke with an SEC staff person about her concerns. He made some very preliminary inquiries but decided there was not enough to justify further inquiry into the matter. A week following the acquisition's closing, the Wall Street Journal reported several issues related to SaleCo's financial reporting in the months leading up to the acquisition, including several undisclosed significant contingent liabilities. The story prompted a formal SEC investigation that ultimately yielded a $50 million civil penalty. Is Cheryl an eligible whistleblower? *See* Exchange Act Rule 21F-4(b)(c). What, if anything, should the whistleblower receive? *See* Exchange Act Rule 21F-6.

2.   Sanctioning in SEC Enforcement Proceedings

a.   *The Administrative Enforcement Proceeding*

The federal securities laws empower the Commission to adjudicate a wide range of matters through administrative proceedings. The authority most frequently invoked is the Commission's power to issue cease-and-desist orders. *See, e.g.*, Securities Act Section 8A and Exchange Act Section 21C. The Commission also has disciplinary authority that it can exercise through an administrative proceeding over various market professionals, for example, brokers and investment advisers, which are examined later in Chapters 18 and 19. Many other provisions are sprinkled throughout the securities laws empowering the Commission administratively to sanction those who violate the statute or its rules.

The procedural requirements for Commission administrative proceedings are set forth in its Rules of Practice. The initial pleading is the Order Instituting Proceedings issued by the Commission, which sets forth, among other matters, a simple statement of the alleged violation and the matters of law and fact to be considered and determined. Answers to the Order are required to be filed, generally within 20 days after the respondent has been served with the notice. The resulting hearing is presided over by an independent administrative law judge, who has the power to issue subpoenas on behalf of any party to the proceeding. Rule 230 of the Rules of Practice requires the Division of Enforcement to make available to the respondent certain categories of documents, but the staff may withhold documents on the ground of privilege, work product, or a need to protect the confidentiality of sources. The respondent therefore cannot expect to gain access to all the evidence the staff has gathered in its investigation, much of it through ex parte depositions. The Federal Rules of Evidence do not apply, so that the major constraint on the evidence produced is the administrative law judge's power to "exclude all irrelevant, immaterial or unduly repetitious" evidence as well as evidence the judge believes to be "unreliable." Rule of Practice 320. A common feature of most of the provisions under which the Commission derives its authority to discipline certain persons is that any resulting sanction must be "in the public interest."

The Supreme Court, relying on Section 7 of the Administrative Procedure Act, in *Steadman v. SEC*, 450 U.S. 91 (1981), held that the Commission's staff in administrative proceedings has the burden of proving a violation by a preponderance of the evidence. The administrative law judge's findings and conclusions are set forth in his written opinion and can be appealed to the commissioners by any party to the proceeding by filing a petition to review. The commissioners' review is assisted by briefs from the parties, and if the commissioners so decide, oral arguments are permitted. The respondent can appeal final orders of the Commission to the U.S. Court of Appeals for the circuit in which the respondent resides or has its principal place of business or the District of Columbia. An SEC order is upheld unless the court finds it is not supported by substantial evidence.

After Dodd-Frank authorized the SEC to impose fines in administrative proceedings against non-regulated entities and following several high-profile enforcement setbacks in the federal courts, the SEC began to bring more cases before administrative law judges. This shift in its caseload exacerbated existing fears that the SEC enjoyed something of a home court advantage when proceeding in house. *See* Zaring, Enforcement Discretion at the SEC, 94 Tex. L. Rev. 102 (2016). *Compare* Choi & Pritchard, The SEC's Shift to Administrative Proceedings: An Empirical Assessment, 34 Yale J. Reg. 1 (2017) (finding support for the view that the SEC resorts to administrative proceedings for cases that are weaker and/or of lower enforcement priority) *with* Velikonja & Grundfest, Amicus Brief in *Lucia v. SEC*, available at *https://ssrn.com/abstract=3140931*

(collecting data supporting view SEC neither sends weaker cases to administrative law judges nor does better in that forum).

b.   The Panoply of SEC Enforcement Sanctions

Prior to 1990, the Commission had a more limited range of administrative enforcement options than it does today. As seen in Chapter 4, under the Securities Act the Commission can use its refusal order and stop order powers of Section 8 to address defects in a filed registration statement. With respect to disclosure violations under the Exchange Act, the Commission's administrative sanction arose under Section 15(c)(4), which reaches "any person subject to the provisions of section 12, 13, 14, or subsection (d) of section 15" of the '34 Act who "has failed to comply with any such provision, rule or regulation in any material respect."

The Securities Enforcement Remedies and Penny Stock Reform Act of 1990 expanded significantly the array of sanctions available to the SEC for securities law violations. The legislation was prompted by a call from public and private quarters to add to the Commission's enforcement arsenal sanctions that would both enhance the deterrent effects of its sanctions and provide greater flexibility in addressing violations and violators. With the enactment of the Securities Enforcement Remedies and Penny Stock Reform Act of 1990, the various securities acts were amended to authorize civil penalties, administrative cease-and-desist orders, and bars to individuals serving as officers and directors of reporting companies. The clear objective of the legislation was to provide the SEC a panoply of sanctions so that the agency could better fit the sanction to the offense. In Chapter 18, we examine how this legislation expands the SEC's regulatory powers to deal with penny stock frauds. The material here describes how the sanctions available to the agency have been significantly expanded by the Act. As you review the following summary of these new expanded powers, consider whether over time they will substantially supplant the traditional enforcement mechanisms examined in the preceding sections of this chapter.

By far the most significant augmentation of the SEC's enforcement arsenal is the cease-and-desist order.

> In general, a cease-and-desist order is an administrative remedy that directs a person to refrain from engaging in conduct or a practice which violates the laws. The Committee believes the power to impose a cease-and-desist order will enhance the SEC's ability to flexibly tailor remedies to the facts and circumstances of a particular case. . . .
>
> A violation of a cease-and-desist order may be punishable by a court-imposed civil penalty in addition to a mandatory injunction directing compliance with the order. . . .
>
> The legislation authorizes the SEC to issue a temporary cease-and-desist order against broker-dealers, investment advisers, investment companies, and other regulated entities and persons associated with them if it has determined that a respondent is engaging or about to engage in a violation that is likely to result in significant dissipation of assets, conversion of property, or significant harm to investors, or that is otherwise likely to result in substantial harm to the public interest before the completion of a permanent cease-and-desist proceeding. . . .

In view of the potential significant consequences of a cease-and-desist order, the SEC, as a general matter, will be required to provide prior notice to the respondent before the temporary cease-and-desist order becomes effective, to enable the respondent to show cause why such an order should not be issued. However, the Committee recognizes that there are instances where prior notice is inappropriate. Therefore, if the SEC determines that giving notice is impracticable or contrary to the public interest, a temporary cease-and-desist order would become effective upon service. The Committee believes that prior notice would be contrary to the public interest when, for example, it is reasonably likely to result in a respondent's flight from prosecution, destruction of or tampering with evidence, transfer of assets or records, improper conversion of assets, impeding the SEC's ability to identify or trace the source or disposition of funds, or further harm to investors. . . .

The SEC may seek enforcement of both temporary and permanent cease-and-desist orders in Federal district court. In addition to seeking a court order directing compliance, the SEC may request, and the court may impose, a civil money penalty for each violation as provided for in this bill.

The Securities Law Enforcement Remedies Act of 1990, Report of the Committee on Banking, Housing and Urban Affairs, S. Rep. No. 5-23, 101st Cong., 2d Sess. (June 26, 1990).

KPMG, LLP v. SEC
289 F.3d 109 (D.C. Cir. 2002)

[In January 1995, as part of an effort to separate its consulting functions from its auditing practice, KPMG entered into a series of arrangements with KPMG BayMark, LLC, whereby KPMG licensed Baymark to use "KPMG" as part of its name and KPMG loaned $100,000 to each of Baymark's four founding principals as their equity contributions. In return, 5 percent of Baymark's net income was to be paid to KPMG. Representatives of KPMG met with the SEC's Chief Accountant to discuss the arrangements and the Chief Accountant cautioned KPMG not to provide any audit services to Baymark clients. Notwithstanding this warning, Leonard Sturm, the KPMG engagement partner for the audit client, PORTA, introduced PORTA to Baymark, who was then retained to provide consulting services to PORTA. The Baymark-PORTA relationship was further cemented by PORTA hiring one of Baymark's founding principals, Edward Olson, to be its chief operating officer. Compensation for this arrangement included a "success fee" to Baymark based on many accounting factors including a percentage of PORTA's profits. Several conversations occurred within the KPMG hierarchy, including with Conway, the head of KPMG's Department of Professional Practice, over whether the PORTA-Baymark relationship violated the SEC's independence requirements that apply to auditors. This led to meetings between Conway and the SEC Chief Accountant in late 1995, who indicated that to resolve the independence matter (1) Baymark must cease using the initials KPMG, (2) repay the $400,000 loans, and (3) eliminate the licensing fee arrangement between KPMG and Baymark. The SEC was not informed by Conway of any of the details of the arrangement between PORTA and Baymark, such as the "success fee" arrangement. KPMG's senior manager, Chris Trattou, misrepresented to Sturm that the SEC was aware of the PORTA situation so that KPMG's audit of PORTA could continue. Even though KPMG did not follow the steps recommended by the Chief Accountant, it proceeded to certify PORTA's 1995 financial statements. The SEC staff thereafter concluded that KPMG was not independent and informed KPMG that it considered PORTA's 1995 annual report unaudited.

The SEC initiated a cease-and-desist proceeding against KPMG and ultimately the Commission concluded that KPMG had violated Rule 2-02(b)(1) regarding its independence and that PORTA violated Section 13(a)'s requirement that reporting companies file financial reports certified by independent public accountants. In reaching its conclusion, the Commission found that each of the impairments—the debtor/creditor relationship and contingency fee arrangement—considered on its own compromised KPMG's independence and each was sufficient to support a finding of a violation of Section 13(a) and a violation of Rule 2-02(b)(1). It further found that KPMG had engaged in negligent conduct that was the cause of a primary violation and that KPMG had acted negligently in determining it was independent. As a result, the Commission issued a cease-and-desist order against KPMG.]

C.

KPMG . . . challenges the propriety of a negligence standard under Section 21C. . . .

[T]he Commission was virtually compelled by Congress' choice of language in enacting Section 21C to interpret the phrase "an act or omission the person knew or should have known would contribute to such violation" as setting a negligence standard . . . the plain language of Section 21C invokes, as the Commission stated, "classic negligence language." . . .

III. . . .

The Commission's cease-and-desist order required that KPMG cease and desist from committing present or future violations of Rule 2-02(b) of Regulation S-X, or being the cause of any present or future violation of Section 13(a) of the Exchange Act or Rule 13a-1 thereunder due to an act or omission that KPMG knows or should know will contribute to such violation, by having any transactions, interests or relationships that would impair its independence under Rule 2-01 of Regulation S-X or under GAAS. . . .

A. . . .

KPMG's challenge to the cease-and-desist order on vagueness grounds is . . . without merit. KPMG contends that because GAAS standards are "vague and open-ended" the Commission could not properly enjoin compliance with broad prohibitions that require subjective interpretation and complex judgments over which reasonable professionals may disagree. This court has observed, in light of the severity of monetary penalties under antitrust laws, that cease-and-desist orders should be "sufficiently clear and precise to avoid raising serious questions as to their meaning and application." *Joseph A. Kaplan*, 347 F.2d at 790. . . . KPMG nevertheless fails to show that such serious questions will necessarily arise to its detriment.

Section 21C allows for the order to enjoin the "causing [of] such violation and any future violation of the same provision, rule, or regulation." That is all the order did; it ordered KPMG to "cease and desist from committing any violation or future violation of Rule 2-02(b) of Regulation S-X, or from being a cause of any violation or future violation of Section 13(a) of the Securities Exchange Act of 1934 or Rule 13a-1 thereunder." The order merely tracks the statutory language and inserts the relevant provisions. Further, although GAAS may be a complex scheme and reasonable professionals may differ as to its application to discrete sets of facts, it is not a set of indefinite and open-ended standards subject to the whims of the Commission. Rather, as with most provisions of the law, there are broad areas of clarity and instances closer to the line where there will be some doubt. . . . The rule . . . includes examples of when independence will be found lacking, and while non-exclusive, the examples nonetheless inform the general standard. Although absolute precision is impossible, even with an objective standard, . . . KPMG fails to show that it will have "difficulty applying the Commission's order to the vast majority of their contemplated future [actions]." *Colgate-Palmolive*, 380 U.S. at 394. But, as KPMG is aware, if a situation arises where KPMG is "sincerely unable to determine whether a proposed course of action would violate the present order, [KPMG] can . . . oblige the Commission to give . . . definitive advice as to whether [the] proposed action if pursued, would constitute compliance with the order." Id. . . .

B.

More problematic, however, is KPMG's contention that in entering the cease-and-desist order, the Commission created an improper presumption that a past violation is sufficient evidence of "some risk" of future violation, and applied it in an arbitrary and capricious manner whereby it is, "in essence, irrebutable," ignoring KPMG's evidence of serious remediation and the ALJ's finding there was no future threat of harm. In seeking reconsideration by the Commission, KPMG argued that the Commission had failed to comply with the standard that it had established for issuance of a cease-and-desist order—namely some likelihood of future violation based on proof of some continuing or threatened conduct by KPMG creating an increased likelihood of future violations—and that there was no such evidence. The plain language of Section 21C, as well as the legislative history, *see* S. Rep. No. 101-337, at 18; H.R. Rep. No. 101-616, at 24, undermine KPMG's contention that the Commission erred in proceeding on the basis of a lower risk of future violation than is required for an injunction. However, the precise manner in which the standard is met is unclear from the Commission's analysis on reconsideration.

In its original opinion, the Commission had stated that a single violation sufficed to show the necessary likelihood. *See* id. at 54. On reconsideration, the Commission explained that, consistent with the history leading up to the enactment of Section 21C, it had applied a standard for showing a risk of future violations that was significantly less than that required for an injunction. . . . To the Commission, "although 'some risk' of future violations is necessary, it need not be very great to warrant issuing a cease-and-desist order and that in the ordinary case and absent evidence to the contrary, a finding of past violation raises a sufficient risk of future violation." Id. Disclaiming that issuance of a cease-and-desist order is "automatic" on a finding of past violation, the Commission stated that "along with the risk of future violations, we will continue to consider our traditional factors in determining whether a cease-and-desist order is an appropriate sanction based on the entire record." Id.

. . . The risk of future violations arises here, the Commission explained, "from the manifestly inadequate level of scrutiny given to independence issues and [KPMG's] consistent failure to recognize the seriousness of this misconduct." Id. The Commission then noted that the loan to Olson, an officer of a registrant, was, in the words of a witness, "an absolute blatant out-and-out violation" of GAAS. Id. More specifically, the Commission stated:

> . . . We . . . determined that the violations flowed from the negligent failures of the head of [KPMG]'s DPP [Conway] and the audit partner [Sturm] to inform themselves about facts material to specific issues about independence attending [KPMG]'s audit engagement—when both had questions or concerns about the propriety of the audit and had ready access to relevant information. *These findings, as well as others* detailed in our opinion, are based on the record as a whole and *are more than adequate to support our conclusion* that there was not just "some" risk but a "serious" risk of future violation, which, *together* with the traditional sanctioning factors we considered, fully warranted the cease-and-desist relief we issued. (Emphasis added)

Id. at 11.

. . .

The Commission stated in its original order that either the outstanding loan or the "success" fee/royalty arrangement, standing alone, compromised KPMG's independence and that "each of the violations we have found today independently calls for cease-and-desist relief.". . . On reconsideration, the Commission continued to find multiple violations of sufficient seriousness to warrant cease-and-desist relief under either a "some-risk-of-future-violation" standard or a "serious-risk-of-future-violation" standard. Reconsideration Order at 11. . . . [The Commission found conduct it] characterized as "an absolute blatant out-and-out violation" of GAAS in the form of the loan to Olson. Order at 30; Reconsideration Order at 11. Similarly, removing the alleged negligence of Sturm, who was perhaps the only "careful guy" involved in the "strategic alliance" between KPMG and BayMark, still leaves, at the very least, "the negligence of the head of [KPMG's] Department of Professional Practice," Conway, who, according to the Commission, rendered a "manifestly inadequate level of scrutiny . . . to independence issues" when scrutiny was most needed. . . . Under these circumstances, and consistent with remanding only when we conclude "that there is a significant chance that but for [an] error the agency might have reached a different result," . . . we conclude that "it would be meaningless to remand." *NLRB v. Wyman-Gordon*, 394 U.S. 759, 766 n.6 . . . (1969).

IV. . . .

We affirm the Commission's determination that negligence is an appropriate basis for violations underlying a Section 21C cease-and-desist order, and reject KPMG's contentions that the order is overbroad and vague. . . . Finally, we conclude that a remand to allow the Commission to clarify whether simply one or a combination of two or more of the violations it found suffice to meet its standard for finding a risk of future violation to enter a cease-and-desist order is unwarranted in light of the Commission's alterative findings of violations in its original order. We therefore deny KPMG's petition for review.

NOTES AND QUESTIONS

1. Likelihood of Future Misbehavior.   *KPMG* leaves open what facts support a finding that there is likely a threat of future misconduct so that a cease-and-desist order is justified. On this question, consider *WHX Corp. v. SEC*, 362 F.3d 854 (D.C. Cir. 2004), where the court reversed the SEC's imposition of such an order. WHX, a takeover bidder, first sought a no-action letter approving, under the Williams Act takeover provisions, the way it planned to structure its bid. The SEC's staff responded that it did not grant no-action letters on such matters. WHX interpreted this as the staff was not persuaded by WHX's reasons for believing its proposed structure complied with the law. WHX proceeded with its bid, believing the staff was wrong, and that, if an enforcement action was brought, WHX could successfully persuade the commissioners via its Wells submission. This strategy did not work: The Commission approved an injunctive action whereupon WHX changed the structure of its bid and no injunctive action occurred. A year passed and the SEC initiated a cease-and-desist proceeding against WHX based on purchases WHX had made before it revised its bid. The SEC argued that such an order was justified by WHX's past violation, that it was a frequent takeover bidder, and that its prior violation was a serious one. The D.C. Circuit reversed the SEC's issuance of a cease-and-desist order, reasoning in part that the order could not be justified on the basis that merely being "in the business" is not determinative of a future violation and that the facts did not support the belief WHX was acting in bad faith but rather in a desire to contest the staff's view. On this point, the court explained that "finding a violation 'serious' or 'willful' simply because of a failure to comply immediately with the staff's interpretation effectively punishes parties who make Wells submissions that are ultimately unsuccessful." Id. at 860-861.

2. Civil Money Penalties and Disgorgement.   The SEC's authority to obtain civil money penalties in an administrative proceeding is contained in Section 21B of the Exchange Act. Section 20(d) of the Securities Act or Section 21(d)(3) of the Exchange Act authorize courts to impose civil penalties and disgorgement orders against those who violate the provisions or regulations under those Acts. Three tiers of penalties are authorized, with penalties beginning at $5,000 per violation for the most minor offenses and the largest possible penalty ($100,000 for a natural person and $500,000 for other violators) for fraudulent and deceitful conduct that results in a substantial loss to others. Courts can substitute a penalty equal to the gross amount the defendant gained through the violation when such amount is greater than the statutorily prescribed amount.

Pursuant to the "fair fund" provision of Section 308 of the Sarbanes-Oxley Act, the SEC can designate that any fine it recovers in an enforcement action or the settlement of an enforcement action can be added to and become a part of a disgorgement fund for the benefit of any investors harmed by the defendant's violation. A detailed analysis of 243 fair funds created between 2002 and 2013 that aggregated $14.46 billion found that in more than half the cases investors "did not receive compensation in parallel securities litigation, either because no private action was filed or because the litigation became victim to one of the PSLRA screens. As a result, in a majority of fair fund cases, the fair fund is the only source of investor compensation." Velinkonja, Public Compensation for Private Harm: Evidence from the SEC's Fair Fund Distributions, 67 Stan. L. Rev. 331, 371 (2015).

3. *Officer and Director Bars.* Section 20(e) to the Securities Act and Section 21(d)(2) to the Exchange Act authorize the courts in SEC enforcement actions to bar or suspend a defendant from serving as an officer or a director of a reporting company upon finding that the defendant has violated the antifraud provision of either the Securities Act or the Exchange Act and defendant's "unfitness" to so serve. Under an earlier formulation of the court's authority to impose such a bar only when there was "substantial unfitness," the Second Circuit in *SEC v. Patel*, 61 F.2d 137 (2d Cir. 1995), refused to bar a defendant from serving as a corporate officer where there was no record developed of securities violations other than the defendant's single violation of the insider trading laws. The court reasoned that, before a person can be barred from corporate office, there must be a basis for a finding that the defendant's violation is likely to recur. In a rebuke to *Patel*, Sarbanes-Oxley loosened the criteria by conditioning the bar on evidence of "unfitness" not "substantial unfitness." Nonetheless, courts have refused to impose the bar when the underlying violation is not egregious and there appears to be little likelihood that the misconduct would be repeated. *See, e.g., SEC v. Brown*, 878 F. Supp. 109 (D.D.C. 2012). Egregious misconduct was found and a permanent bar (as well as a substantial fine) was issued against Joseph Apuzzo, the aider and abettor discussed in section B supra. *SEC v. Apuzzo*, 2016 U.S. Dist. LEXIS 58977 (D. Conn. 2016). Moreover, the legislation empowers the SEC in a cease-and-desist proceeding to impose a bar when the defendant has violated the antifraud provisions. *See* Section 21C(f) of the Exchange Act and Section 8A(f) of the Securities Act. *See generally* Barnard, SEC Disbarment of Officers and Directors After Sarbanes-Oxley, 59 Bus. Law. 391 (2004).

4. *Clawbacks in the Wake of an Earnings Restatement.* Earnings restatement refers to a company announcing that the financial reports of earlier years were in error. Commonly, the error is that the earlier year's financial statements overstated the company's revenue and net income. Such restatements occur generally because in the earlier (restated) year the company misapplied generally accepted accounting principles when reporting the firm's performance.

Sarbanes-Oxley was enacted one month after WorldCom's announcement and most attribute its restatement as providing the political momentum for the Act's passage. Section 304 of the Act provides that, when an issuer makes an earnings restatement as a result of earlier "misconduct" with respect to any financial reporting requirement, the CEO and CFO of the issuer must disgorge to the issuer any bonus or other incentive compensation received from the issuer during the 12-month period following the first public release of the financial reports that were later restated. The SEC has consistently and successfully maintained the position that Section 304 clawbacks do not require establishing that the corporate executive himself was responsible or otherwise implicated in wrongdoing related to the restatement. *See, e.g., SEC v. Jenkins*, 835 F.3d 1100 (9th Cir. 2016); courts have consistently held there is no implied private action to enforce Section 304 so that the SEC enjoys exclusive authority to seek relief under the provision. *See, e.g., In re Digimarc Corp. Derivative Litig.*, 594 F.3d 1223 (9th Cir. 2008).

Dodd-Frank calls on the SEC to issue rules to prohibit listing a company on any exchange that does not have a policy, and disclose its policy, to recover any incentive-based compensation for executive officers during the three-year period prior to an accounting restatement resulting from material noncompliance of the issuer with reporting requirements.

5.   *Trading Suspensions.* Under Section 12(j) of the Exchange Act, the Commission may suspend trading of a security. Most actions under the provision are for delinquent filings of Exchange Act periodic filings. The SEC also has the authority under paragraph (k) to summarily suspend trading in a security, whether or not registered, for a period not exceeding ten days if in the Commission's opinion "the public interest and the protection of investors so require." In *SEC v. Sloan*, 436 U.S. 103 (1978), the Supreme Court held that the SEC cannot issue a series of ten-day suspensions without according the company notice and a hearing on the cause for the suspensions. In *Sloan*, the Commission issued a continuous series of ten-day suspensions over a 13-month period for Canadian Javelin, Inc., because the firm had allegedly issued misleading press releases concerning certain of its business activities. The Court reasoned, in part, that the power to suspend is an awesome power and should not be exercised for longer than ten days without a clear mandate from Congress to do so, which it believed was not suggested by the language of Section 12(k). The Commission can prevent trading in a security indirectly under Section 12(j) by revoking the registration of a security under the Exchange Act; however, this requires it to issue an order after notice and a hearing resulting in a finding that such revocation is necessary or appropriate for the protection of investors. What is the downside of suspending trading in a firm's shares?

6.   *Section 21(a) Reports.* Section 21(a) of the Exchange Act authorizes the Commission, in connection with its power to investigate violations, "to publish information concerning any such violation." Periodically, the Commission relies on this provision to announce the commencement of an enforcement action as the result of its investigation, or to remind the public or securities market professionals of their obligations under the securities laws, or to call for new legislation to deal with an emerging problem. The Commission sometimes uses Section

21(a) to achieve results akin to those obtained in administrative or injunctive proceedings, relying on Section 21(a)'s language that the Commission "may require or permit any person to file with it a statement in writing . . . as to all the facts and circumstances concerning the matter to be investigated." The probable intent of this language is to provide an opportunity for the object of the investigation to give her version of the facts. However, Section 21(a) reports can embody confessions or undertakings to reform or change practices by the target of the investigation. In a sense, the Section 21(a) reports bear a strong resemblance to what one finds in a consent decree with the agency.

The SEC from time to time uses Section 21(a) reports to state its position on practices it believes inappropriate, but not quite rising to the level of a violation. In this regard, consider its Report of Investigation in the Matter of the Cooper Companies, [1994-1995 Transfer Binder] Fed. Sec. L. Rep. (CCH) ¶85,472 (1994), wherein the Commission chastised the board of directors of Cooper Companies for failing to act decisively once it learned that Gary Singer, a member of its senior management, had concealed fraudulent self-dealing transactions that not only caused the corporation to suffer losses in excess of $500,000, but also caused its reports filed with the SEC to be misleading in failing to disclose these self-dealing transactions. Though the board was informed by both SEC and Department of Justice investigators that they believed Singer's misconduct was part of a fraudulent scheme practiced on Cooper, as well as investors generally, the board remained passive. Singer's brother filled the void and drafted a press release denying on behalf of the company any wrongdoing or knowledge of any wrongdoing. The report concludes: "Cooper's Board failed to satisfy its obligations when confronted with serious indications of management fraud. . . . The board failed to take immediate and effective action to protect the interests of the company's investors." Was this report a valid exercise of SEC enforcement power?

7.   *The SEC's Authority to Impose Control Person Responsibility.*   The Dodd-Frank Act added "including the Commission . . ." to Section 20(a) to make it clear that the SEC can proceed against control persons with enforcement actions in the federal court.

8.   *Limitation on SEC Enforcement Actions?*   The omnibus limitation provision that applies to federal enforcement actions is 28 U.S.C. §2462 (1988). It provides that "civil fines, penalties, and forfeiture, pecuniary or otherwise, shall not be entertained unless commenced within five years from the date when the claim first accrued." *Kokesh v. SEC*, 137 S. Ct. 1635 (2017), held that disgorgement is a penalty, so that the five-year period barred the SEC from recovering ill-gotten gains the defendant derived more than five years before the enforcement action commenced. The limitations period is not stayed because the SEC could not through reasonable diligence have discovered the violation. *Gabelli v. SEC*, 568 U.S. 442 (2013). Does an order barring an individual from the securities industry fall within the omnibus provision? What if the order broadly requires the defendant to "obey the law" when engaged in future securities transactions? *See SEC v. Collyard*, 861 F.3d 760, 764 (8th Cir. 2017) (Section 2562 does not apply); *SEC v. Gentile*, 2017 U.S. Dist. LEXIS 204883 (D.N.J. 2017) (applying Section 2562).

3.　Injunctions

Each of the federal securities laws empowers the Commission to enforce violations of the statutes and their supporting rules and regulations by initiating an action in federal district court. For example, Exchange Act Section 21(d) empowers the Commission to sue in the federal district court to seek a permanent or temporary injunction "whenever it shall appear to the Commission that any person is engaged or about to engage in acts or practices constituting a violation of any provision" of rules or regulations of the '34 Act or the rules of one of the SROs. Similar authorization is provided in Section 20(b) of the Securities Act, Section 42(d) of the Investment Company Act, and Section 209 of the Investment Advisers Act.

Upon a proper showing of the facts supporting the staff's belief that the defendant has committed a securities violation, the courts generally grant a temporary restraining order (TRO) against the defendant; a TRO is nonetheless temporary and subject to a hearing within ten days on whether to substitute a preliminary injunction. Not infrequently, the SEC obtains the TRO on an ex parte basis. Other preliminary remedies related to protecting investors, or more particularly the fruits of the defendant's ill-gotten gains, are orders to make a full accounting and sometimes the appointment of receivers to collect and preserve funds. *See generally* Edmundson & Kirkpatrick, Defending Against SEC Emergency Enforcement Actions, 30 Sec. Reg. L.J. 200 (2002).

It is well established that an agency cannot obtain injunctive relief on a bare showing that a violation has been committed. *See generally Aaron v. SEC*, 446 U.S. 680 (1980) (concurring opinion of Chief Justice Burger). In the abstract, an injunction is remedial and prophylactic in nature in that its overall purpose is to protect investors or the market's integrity against future harm; the action is not punitive in nature. On the question of whether an injunction is an appropriate remedy, consider the cautionary words of Judge Friendly:

> It is fair to say that the current judicial attitude toward the issuance of injunctions on the basis of past violations at the SEC's request has become more circumspect than in earlier days. Experience has shown that an injunction, while not always a "drastic remedy" . . . often is much more than . . . [a] "mild prophylactic." . . . In some cases the collateral consequences of an injunction can be very grave. . . . The Securities Act and the Securities Exchange Act speak, after all, of enjoining "any person [who] is engaged or about to engage in any acts or practices" which constitute or will constitute a violation. . . . Except for the case where the SEC steps in to prevent an ongoing violation, this language seems to require a finding of "likelihood" or "propensity" to engage in future violations. . . . Our recent decisions have emphasized, perhaps more than older ones, the need for the SEC to go beyond the mere facts of past violations and demonstrate a realistic likelihood of recurrence.

SEC v. Commonwealth Chemical Securities Inc., 574 F.2d 90, 99-100 (2d Cir. 1978).

Commonwealth Chemical was a classic penny stock fraud scheme in which the promoters first raised funds from investors through a registered blind pool investment. That offering was on an "all or nothing" basis and was closed only with a purchase by the promoter's bookkeeper, Mrs. Sharpe, who purported to purchase 1,000 shares for her mother and soon after the offering closed sold the shares at a small profit, which she kept. The promoters then proceeded to engage in massive market purchases of the stock, which drove its price upward. Most of those purchases occurred through accounts and mutual funds controlled by the promoters. The Second Circuit affirmed the trial court's injunction against the promoters, but held that no injunction should be issued against Mrs. Sharpe or the promoter's wife, Marlane Kleinman, who on two occasions purchased shares (100 and 500 shares, respectively), under the name of Maria Klein, under circumstances that appeared clearly part of the promoters' manipulative scheme. The district court had reasoned that the SEC had met its burden because it believed there was "no reason to believe that, should a similar opportunity arise in the future, [Mrs. Kleinman and Mrs. Sharpe] . . . would shy away" from participating in another fraudulent scheme. Even though the Second Circuit believed this finding was insufficient to justify an injunction against Mrs. Kleinman and Mrs. Sharp, it upheld the district court's order that the profits each had made on their shares had to be disgorged.

NOTES AND QUESTIONS

1. Ancillary Relief. As it did in *Commonwealth Chemical*, the Commission frequently obtains relief in addition to enjoining the defendant from further violations of the securities laws. Such ancillary relief is tailored to rectify past violations, to require the defendant to bring itself into compliance, to preserve the status quo pending a final adjudication of the Commission's enforcement claims, or to prevent recidivism on the part of the defendant. In this area, the Commission, with the courts' support, has been very creative, if not a bit assertive, in crafting remedies collateral to an injunction such that the most significant relief in many cases is not the injunction, but the ancillary relief ordered by the court.

Another device the SEC sometimes employs is obtaining the appointment of a special counsel whose task it is to carry out an investigation into prior conduct by the corporation or its management. The SEC has also obtained the appointment of independent directors to a company. *See generally* Wallace & Dryden, Use of Independent Consultants as a Remedy in Security Enforcement Actions, 42 BNA Sec. Reg. & L. Rep. 750 (Apr. 19, 2010).

2. Disgorgement: The Remedy's Existence and the Amount to Be Disgorged. Prior to *SEC v. Kokesch*, 137 S. Ct. 1635 (2017), there was little doubt that disgorgement was among the panoply of ancillary remedies available to the SEC. However, *Kokesh*, in holding that disgorgement is a penalty subject to a five-year limitation period, somewhat gratuitously observed that the court was not deciding whether disgorgement was a permissible remedy. Id. at 1642 n.3. And during the oral argument, five Justices raised questions whether disgorgement could be imposed. *See* Nagy, The Statutory Authority for Court-Ordered Disgorgement in SEC Enforcement Actions, 71 SMU L. Rev. 895 (2018).

A leading pre-*Kokesch* case for applying the disgorgement remedy is *SEC v. First City Financial Corp.*, 890 F.2d 1215 (D.C. Cir. 1989). On March 25, 1986, First City announced that it owned between 8 and 9 percent of Ashland Oil stock and that it intended to make a tender offer at $60 per share. The price rose dramatically, and Ashland's board of directors scurried for advice on what to do about the unwanted suitor. A few days later, it was announced that Ashland had purchased all the Ashland shares owned by First City, yielding an overall profit to First City in the amount of $15.4 million. An SEC investigation revealed that First City should have made its takeover filing under Section 13(d)(1) on March 14 and that First City had purchased 890,000 Ashland shares between that date and March 25, when it finally did make the required disclosures. In upholding the district court's order requiring First City to disgorge $2.7 million, the profits realized on the 890,000 shares it had acquired in violation of Section 13(d)(1), the D.C. Circuit reasoned:

> Since disgorgement primarily serves to prevent unjust enrichment, the court may exercise its equitable power only over property causally related to the wrongdoing. The remedy may well be a key to the SEC's efforts to deter others from violating the securities laws, but disgorgement may not be used punitively. . . . [First City sought at the trial to mitigate its liability by introducing evidence to support its argument that the post-March 25 price increase was due to events unrelated to its own activities and that therefore the disgorgement ordered was excessive and thus punitive.]
>
> If exact information were obtainable at negligible cost, we would not hesitate to impose upon the government a strict burden to produce that data to measure the precise amount of the ill-gotten gains. Unfortunately, we encounter imprecision and imperfect information. . . .
>
> Accordingly, disgorgement need only be a reasonable approximation of profits causally connected to the violation.
>
> Although the SEC bears the ultimate burden of persuasion . . . we believe the government's showing of appellants' actual profits on the tainted transactions at least presumptively satisfied that burden. Appellants, to whom the burden of going forward shifted, were then obliged clearly to demonstrate that the disgorgement figure was not a reasonable approximation.

Id. at 1231. *See also SEC v. Merchant Capital LLC*, 2012 U.S. App. LEXIS 16359 (11th Cir. Aug. 7, 2012) (disgorgement based on salaries received by defendants who were the principals of a finance company during period of their violating the registration and antifraud provisions). Should the disgorged sums be turned over to Ashland, its stockholders, or the U.S. Treasury? *See SEC v. Drexel Burnham Lambert, Inc.*, 956 F. Supp. 503 (S.D.N.Y. 1997).

3.   Collateral Estoppel.   In *Parklane Hosiery Co. v. Shore*, 439 U.S. 322 (1979), the Supreme Court upheld the offensive use of collateral estoppel in private litigation under the securities laws, even though the plaintiff was not a party to the earlier litigation. The plaintiff brought a class action against Parklane Hosiery Company alleging material misrepresentations had been committed in proxy statements in connection with a going-private transaction. Before the trial of the private suit, the Commission had sought injunctive relief against the defendants based upon the same misleading proxy statements. The district court held the proxy statements were materially misleading, but denied the Commission the requested injunction because it found it unlikely the defendant would engage in further violations. The private plaintiff's request for partial summary judgment on the issues determined in the Commission's action was upheld by the Supreme Court, which reasoned that the defendants had "received a full and fair opportunity to litigate their claims in the SEC action." Id. at 332-333. *Parklane Hosiery* is not without its qualifications. The Supreme Court limited the offensive use of collateral estoppel to instances where the plaintiff could not easily have joined the prior action and where the defendant has had a full and fair opportunity in the prior action to litigate. These, however, are not substantial qualifications when the prior litigation is an SEC enforcement action, for private litigants cannot join SEC enforcement actions, *see, e.g.,* Section 21(g) of the Exchange Act, and given the extreme consequences that accompany SEC enforcement actions, it is not reasonable to expect defendants will offer a less than vigorous defense. Should private plaintiffs also be able to make use of administrative adjudications by the Commission? Overall, courts have given preclusive effect to agency adjudications where it is shown the defendant has been accorded an opportunity to fairly and fully litigate the issue. What impact do you believe *Parklane Hosiery* has on the course of Commission enforcement proceedings? *SEC v. Chapman,* 826 F. Supp. 2d 847 (D. Md. 2011) (CEO collaterally estopped from disputing elements established in prior criminal trial). A related consideration is the risk that a defendant's admission made in settling a government action can be invoked against the defendant in a private suit. *But see Renzer v. Hypo-Verinsbank AG,* 630 F.3d 873 (9th Cir. 2010) (admission in deferred prosecution agreement only proved the defendant had defrauded the United States but did not establish harm to the plaintiff).

4.   *Removing or Modifying the Scarlet "I."* How long must one be the subject of an injunction? Most courts continue to follow Cardozo's guidance in *United States v. Swift,* 286 U.S. 106 (1932), that only an *unforeseen and significant* change in circumstances can justify vacation or dissolution of an injunction. *See, e.g., SEC v. Coldicutt,* 258 F.3d 939 (9th Cir. 2001).

5.   *Injunctions and the Foreign Offender.* Is an injunction an effective enforcement weapon against a foreign defendant? A court that has jurisdiction over the defendant can require the defendant to repatriate assets upon a showing that funds have been moved offshore. *See, e.g., SEC v. Dunlap,* 253 F.3d 768, 771 (4th Cir. 2001). Courts even order defendants to perform acts overseas, such as disgorging their illegal gains. *See, e.g., SEC v. Banner Fund Int'l,* 211 F.3d 602 (D.C. Cir. 2000).

6.   *Asset Freezes and Other "Emergency" Enforcement Powers.* The Commission's power to obtain a court order freezing assets is set forth in Exchange Act Section 21C(c)(3), which now authorizes freezes of "extraordinary payments" by an issuer to a controlling person, officer, director, or employee. Such a freeze is authorized for an initial temporary 45 days whenever there is a "lawful investigation" into possible securities law violations with the potential for extension throughout any ensuing enforcement proceeding. *See SEC v. Gemstar-TV Guide Int'l, Inc.,* 401 F.3d 1031 (9th Cir. 2005) (upholding freeze order covering severance payments by issuer alleged to have inflated reports of earnings which payments were to senior officers that were six times greater than their base salaries).

PROBLEM

14-12. Reprise of Problem 12-4. Andrew "Doc" Watson is a world-renowned serial entrepreneur behind many successful publicly traded ventures. One of his ventures involves high quality electric automobiles, but the company has been plagued by a variety of problems so that it has been unable to produce cars at a sufficient volume to be profitable. Doc is a billionaire, holds a controlling block in the company, and is both flamboyant and irrepressible. Executives, including general counsels, are hired by and depart regularly from the firm in the wake of his dominance.

Over the last many months Doc repeatedly tweeted that production would soon reach a level that would be profitable, but each such forecast was met by press reports of new production problems and failed production levels. In his most recent tweet, Doc boldly asserted that he would soon announce an offer to take the company private, using funds provided by an oil-rich sheikdom. The announcement sparked a 10 percent rise in the stock's price. Three days later, following an SEC investigation, the company announced there were no plans to go private as there was never any funding source for the transaction. The SEC has filed an enforcement action against the company and Doc in the federal district court. The firm and Doc are eager to settle the matter. What relief should the SEC seek through the settlement? Would it be appropriate in settlement to enjoin Doc from engaging in any dissemination, by any form of media, of potentially material information without clearing the matter with the company's disclosure committee?

4. Discretion in SEC Enforcement

a. Whether to Charge, Who to Charge, and Waivers

Report of Investigation Pursuant to Section 21(a) of the Securities Exchange Act of 1934 and Commission Statement on the Relationship of Cooperation to Agency Enforcement Decisions
Securities Exchange Act of 1934 Release No. 44969 (Oct. 23, 2001)

Today, we commence and settle a cease-and-desist proceeding against Gisela de Leon-Meredith, former controller of . . . [Seaboard Corporation's] subsidiary. Our order finds that Meredith caused the parent company's books and records to be inaccurate and its periodic reports misstated, and then covered up those facts.

We are not taking action against the parent company, given the nature of the conduct and the company's responses. Within a week of learning about the apparent misconduct, the company's internal auditors had conducted a preliminary review and had advised company management who, in turn, advised the Board's audit committee, that Meredith had caused the company's books and records to be inaccurate and its financial reports to be misstated. The full Board was advised and authorized the company to hire an outside law firm to conduct a thorough inquiry. Four days later, Meredith was dismissed, as were two other employees who, in the company's view, had inadequately supervised Meredith; a day later, the company disclosed publicly and to us that its financial statements would be restated. The price of the company's shares did not decline after the announcement or after the restatement was published. The company pledged and gave complete cooperation to our staff. It provided the staff with all information relevant to the underlying violations. Among other things, the company produced the details of its internal investigation, including notes and transcripts of interviews of Meredith and others; and it did not invoke the attorney-client privilege, work product protection or other privileges or protections with respect to any facts uncovered in the investigation.

The company also strengthened its financial reporting processes to address Meredith's conduct—developing a detailed closing process for the subsidiary's accounting personnel, consolidating subsidiary accounting functions under a parent company CPA, hiring three new CPAs for the accounting department responsible for preparing the subsidiary's financial statements, redesigning the subsidiary's minimum annual audit requirements, and requiring the parent company's controller to interview and approve all senior accounting personnel in its subsidiaries' reporting processes.

Our willingness to credit such behavior in deciding whether and how to take enforcement action benefits investors as well as our enforcement program. . . .

In brief form, we set forth below some of the criteria we will consider in determining whether, and how much, to credit self-policing, self-reporting, remediation and cooperation—from the extraordinary step of taking no enforcement action to bringing reduced charges, seeking lighter sanctions, or including mitigating language in documents we use to announce and resolve enforcement actions.

1. What is the nature of the misconduct involved? Did it result from inadvertence, honest mistake, simple negligence, reckless or deliberate indifference to indicia of wrongful conduct, willful misconduct or unadorned venality? Were the company's auditors misled?

2. How did the misconduct arise? Is it the result of pressure placed on employees to achieve specific results, or a tone of lawlessness set by those in control of the company? What compliance procedures were in place to prevent the misconduct now uncovered? Why did those procedures fail to stop or inhibit the wrongful conduct?

3. Where in the organization did the misconduct occur? How high up in the chain of command was knowledge of, or participation in, the misconduct? Did senior personnel participate in, or turn a blind eye toward, obvious indicia of misconduct? How systemic was the behavior? Is it symptomatic of the way the entity does business, or was it isolated?

4. How long did the misconduct last? Was it a one-quarter, or one-time, event, or did it last several years? In the case of a public company, did the misconduct occur before the company went public? Did it facilitate the company's ability to go public?

5. How much harm has the misconduct inflicted upon investors and other corporate constituencies? Did the share price of the company's stock drop significantly upon its discovery and disclosure?

6. How was the misconduct detected and who uncovered it?

7. How long after discovery of the misconduct did it take to implement an effective response?

8. What steps did the company take upon learning of the misconduct? Did the company immediately stop the misconduct? Are persons responsible for any misconduct still with the company? If so, are they still in the same positions? Did the company promptly, completely and effectively disclose the existence of the misconduct to the public, to regulators and to self-regulators? Did the company cooperate completely with appropriate regulatory and law enforcement bodies? Did the company identify what additional related misconduct is likely to have occurred? Did the company take steps to identify the extent of damage to investors and other corporate constituencies? Did the company appropriately recompense those adversely affected by the conduct?

9. What processes did the company follow to resolve many of these issues and ferret out necessary information? Were the Audit Committee and the Board of Directors fully informed? If so, when?

10. Did the company commit to learn the truth, fully and expeditiously? Did it do a thorough review of the nature, extent, origins and consequences of the conduct and related behavior? Did management, the Board or committees consisting solely of outside directors oversee the review? Did company employees or outside persons perform the review? If outside persons, had they done other work for the company? Where the review was conducted by outside counsel, had management previously engaged such counsel? Were scope limitations placed on the review? If so, what were they?

11. Did the company promptly make available to our staff the results of its review and provide sufficient documentation reflecting its response to the situation? Did the company identify possible violative conduct and evidence with sufficient precision to facilitate prompt enforcement actions against those who violated the law? Did the company produce a thorough and probing written report detailing the findings of its review? Did the company voluntarily disclose information our staff did not directly request and otherwise might not have uncovered? Did the company ask its employees to cooperate with our staff and make all reasonable efforts to secure such cooperation?

12. What assurances are there that the conduct is unlikely to recur? Did the company adopt and ensure enforcement of new and more effective internal controls and procedures designed to prevent a recurrence of the misconduct? Did the company provide our staff with sufficient information for it to evaluate the company's measures to correct the situation and ensure that the conduct does not recur?

13. Is the company the same company in which the misconduct occurred, or has it changed through a merger or bankruptcy reorganization?*

NOTES AND QUESTIONS

1.   Who Benefits by Cooperation.   A study of 1,249 earnings restatements from 1997 through 2005 reports that launching an internal investigation by registrants reduced their fines but not the penalty imposed on individuals within the firm. Regulatory sanctions and penalties are reduced further for both registrants and individuals who make more timely corrective disclosures than those that do not. Files, SEC Enforcement: Does Forthright Disclosure and Cooperation Really Matter, 53 J. Acct. & Econ. 353 (2011).

2.   When Is It Appropriate to Fine the Entity?   The Commission has set forth considerations it will use in determining whether to impose financial penalties on an entity whose agents had engaged in a securities violation in the scope of performing their employment. *See* Statement of the SEC Concerning Financial Penalties, Press Release 2006-4 (Jan. 4, 2006). The Commission's formulation grapples with two competing fears: that sanctions imposed on the entity may adversely impact its innocent shareholder-owners and that failure to sanction the entity may erode the deterrent effect of the enforcement action or permit ill-gotten gains to be retained.

It identified two principal considerations in sanctioning a corporation:

1. the presence or absence of a direct benefit to the corporation as a result of the violation; and
2. the degree to which the penalty will recompense or further harm the injured shareholders.

In addition to these two principal considerations, the Commission stated that the following additional factors are in appropriate cases to be considered:

1. the need to deter the particular offense;
2. the extent of the injury to innocent parties;
3. whether complicity in the violation is widespread throughout the corporation;
4. the level of intent on the part of the perpetrators;
5. the degree of difficulty in detecting the type of offense;
6. the presence or lack of remedial steps by the corporation; and
7. the extent of cooperation with the Commission and other law enforcement agencies.

The Release does not, however, identify factors that will be considered in setting a fine, should an entity fine be justified under the above factors.

---

*   [The SEC Enforcement Manual ¶6.2 expressly adopts the *Seaboard* criteria and in ¶6.1 adopts parallel considerations addressing enforcement heuristics for individuals. *http://www.sec.gov/divisions/enforce/enforcementmanual.pdf. See also* Policy Statement Concerning Cooperation by Individuals in Its Investigations and Related Enforcement Actions, Securities Exchange Act Release No. 61340 (Jan. 13, 2010).—Eds.]

3.   Validity of "Obey the Law" Orders.   The typical SEC injunction orders the defendant to do what it is already required to do, namely "obey the law." That is, the order does not proscribe the conduct that was the focus of the enforcement action but is instead focused on securing broad compliance with the securities laws generally. Future transgressions of the securities laws would thus be a violation of the order and can give rise to an action for contempt. The constitutionality of obey the law orders was questioned in *SEC v. Smyth*, 420 F.3d 1225 (11th Cir. 2005) (reasoning the defendant is deprived of due process by permitting the government to initiate a contempt proceeding in the jurisdiction issuing the initial order for a securities violation committed in another jurisdiction). Such a broad order was even held to violate FRCP 65(d), which requires that injunctions describe "in reasonable detail . . . the act or acts sought to be restrained." *See SEC v. Washington Inv. Network*, 475 F.3d 392 (D.C. Cir. 2007).

4.   Deferred Prosecution and Non-prosecution Agreements.   Until 2010, respondents in SEC enforcement investigations had but two options to resolve an adverse investigation other than litigation—consenting to an administrative order or consenting to an injunctive action in federal court. Now added to these options are deferred prosecution agreements (DPA) and non-prosecution agreements (NPA). Each is a written agreement approved by the Commission, and each calls for the respondent, in exchange for the SEC forgoing the enforcement action, to cooperate, to undertake compliance with specified undertakings, to waive the statute of limitations, and even to pay penalties and disgorgement. There are two principal distinctions between the two types of agreement. First, the NPA does not contemplate it will be made public, whereas the DPA will be made public unless the Commission directs otherwise. Second, the DPA may require the respondent to agree to or not dispute facts the SEC "could assert" in a later enforcement action, whereas the SEC Enforcement Manual makes no reference to a NPA, including any factual statements regarding the respondent's conduct. Both the DPA and NPA are carrots that are awarded to respondents who proffer what the staff believes is "substantial assistance" to the investigation. Among the attractions of a DPA or NPA are that neither triggers the disclosure obligations of Item 401(f) of Regulation S-K of judicial or administrative orders the registrant has been subject to in the last ten years and neither triggers certain "bad actor" disqualifiers that appear in many SEC rules. Periodic reports customarily generated in connection with deferred prosecutions (either by the government or an independent monitor) are not public records; hence, they cannot be accessed by third parties. *SEC v. Am. Int'l Group*, 712 F.3d 1 (D.C. Cir. 2013). In recent years, there has been substantial criticism of such arrangements, in part because of the secrecy surrounding periodic monitoring reports. *See, e.g.,* Brandon L. Garrett, Too Big to Jail: How Prosecutors Compromise with Corporations (2014).

5.   Collateral Consequences of an SEC Order and Court Injunction and Their Waiver.   What is the practical impact of an SEC order or injunction? Obviously, there is the embarrassment that comes from the public determination of fault. And there is the threat of contempt if violations continue. Minimally, the Commission's rules require disclosure of such orders in all documents required to be filed with the Commission—for example, a registration statement under the '33 Act and periodic reports filed under the '34 Act. The specific format and details of the disclosures are set forth in Item 401(f) of Regulation S-K.

More significantly, however, are the multiple "bad actor" provisions that disqualify individuals and entities from taking advantage of exemptions and other regulatory dispensations if they have been the subject of an administrative or court order arising in connection with a securities violation. Illustrative of bad actor provisions are Rule 262 of Regulation A and Rules 505(b)(iii) and 506(d) of Regulation D. Furthermore, the multiple benefits enjoyed by well-known seasoned issuers, studied in Chapter 4, are not available to an issuer whose earlier misconduct has given rise to an order, so it is deemed an "ineligible issuer" as defined in Rule 405. Finally, anyone subject to a temporary or permanent injunction arising from his activities as a market professional (e.g., broker, dealer, underwriter, investment adviser) is automatically barred by Section 9 of the Investment Company Act from any employment or advisory relationship with an investment company. Hence, we should appreciate Judge Friendly's observation, quoted earlier in *Commonwealth Chemical*, that the collateral consequences of an enforcement order can be very grave.

Because bad actor and ineligible issuer provisions can add immensely to the consequences of an individual or firm violating the securities laws, respondents frequently request the SEC to exercise its authority to grant a waiver of such disqualification by showing "good cause." In considering whether good cause exists for a waiver, the Division of Corporate Finance considers the following: the nature of the violation, who was responsible for the misconduct, duration of the misconduct, remedial action taken by the party, and likely impact if a waiver request is denied. *See, e.g.,* Credit Suisse AG, SEC No-Action Letter, [2014 Transfer Binder] Fed. Sec. L. Rep. (CCH) ¶77,704 (May 19, 2014) (having settled charges that it facilitated tax fraud that thereby triggered various bad actor disqualifiers, SEC granted waiver with respect to about 40 entities controlled by Credit Suisse on the justification the entities had not themselves engaged in the unlawful practice); *Raymond James Financial Inc.*, [2011 Transfer Binder] Fed. Sec. L. Rep. (CCH) ¶76,743 (July 1, 2011) (relief granted to preserve respondent's status under Rule 405 as a WKSI).

Professor Urska Velikonja reports that of the 201 waivers that were granted from July 2003 through 2014, 82 percent were to large financial firms (92 percent if we add large nonfinancial firms), and two-thirds of the waiver grants were in connection with violations involving multiple enforcement actions; waivers rarely occur in matters involving accounting fraud. Velikonja, Waiving Disqualification: When Do Securities Violators Receive a Reprieve?, 103 Cal. L. Rev. 1081 (2015).

PROBLEMS

14-13.   You are the outside counsel for Seltex, Inc., a rapidly growing software company that is listed on Nasdaq. Seltex's products depend heavily on the creativity and fame of its founder, Sels, a famous and brilliant software engineer.

Indeed, Sels is widely recognized as one of the five most significant individuals in the field. He is Seltex's CEO. Seltex's board chair just called you to report that Seltex's comptroller has discovered that apparently a series of bogus invoices were prepared on the authority of Sels and the firm's CFO. The overall effect of the invoices was to inflate revenues by a material amount for the most recent financial quarter. The board chair seeks your advice on how to proceed. How helpful is the preceding SEC's "Seaboard Release" in formulating your response?

14-14.   After a lengthy SEC investigation, Brobade Inc. recently proposed a settlement with the SEC agreeing to restate its reported earnings for the past five years. The restatement reflects widespread backdating of stock options by a committee of executives who repeatedly approved option grant dates that were much earlier than the dates options were in fact awarded. The dates selected yielded prices that were materially lower than the price of its shares on the actual grant date. The effect of this difference was that upon the grant of an option the recipient experienced an immediate financial benefit because the option when granted was "in the money."

Anticipating shareholder litigation and hoping to preserve the attorney-client privilege for the nondisclosed portions of the report, Brobade refused to share with the SEC the results of an internal investigation that had been carried out by an outside law firm that had no historical relationship with the company. The company did disclose to the SEC excerpts from the report showing that about 75 percent of the backdated options went to senior management. Brobade explained that the backdating practices were widespread in the industry and that it engaged in the practice so as to recruit and retain high-quality personnel. A schedule from the report that was released to the SEC showed that about 60 percent of the individuals who received backdated options were employees who prior to the grant had been with the company less than three months.

The SEC enforcement staff recommends that no settlement be approved unless Brobade agrees to pay a substantial financial penalty. The matter is now before the Commissioners. On these facts, is a penalty appropriate under the SEC's 2006 guidelines? What additional facts would you wish to know in making this decision?

b.   Settlements

Most SEC enforcement proceedings (over 90 percent) are settled, not litigated. Indeed, most staff enforcement recommendations to the Commission are accompanied by offers of settlement by one or more subjects. The reasons for this high rate of settlement vary. From the subject's perspective, litigation itself (even if ultimately successful on the merits) will be expensive and provoke unwanted publicity. Unsuccessful defense, on the other hand, may result not only in the defendant's being immediately sanctioned, but also in its being collaterally estopped from relitigating questions of violation in a subsequent private action (see section F.3, supra), whereas settlement has no such collateral effect. From the staff's perspective, there is the severe problem of limited resources—the trial staff is too small to handle more than a fraction of the cases being investigated. Thus, it is often possible to arrive at a settlement whereby the defendant consents to an injunction or other relief without either admitting or denying the underlying violation, allowing the staff to claim a victory without subjecting the defendant to a more demanding sanction and the adverse publicity that frequently accompanies litigation. *See* Winship & Robbennott, An Empirical Study of Admissions in SEC Settlements, 60 Ariz. L. Rev. 1 (2018) (finding admission of violating the securities laws occurs in about 3 percent of SEC settlements). Conclusions of law and fact that are negotiated by the parties in reaching a settlement are set forth in settlement releases issued by the SEC; these releases are frequently relied on in later SEC enforcement actions as a type of precedent. Thus, settlements create a body of securities law principles that have not been tested through formal rulemaking or litigation proceedings.

It should also be noted that a clause standard to SEC settlements requires an undertaking on the part of the defendant not to make any public statement denying any allegation in the SEC's complaint or creating the impression the complaint was without factual basis. This stipulation can raise problems for market professionals. In any later administrative action, such as to revoke the license of that market professional, the earlier settlement is treated by the Commission as barring the defendant in the earlier action from denying the factual allegations in the injunctive complaint. *See In the Matter of Marshall E. Melton, Inv. Adv.* Release No. 2151 (July 25, 2003). Moreover, if the complaint in the settled action involved fraud, this is deemed to create a presumption that revocation or suspension of the respondent's license is in the public interest.

SEC v. Citigroup Global Mkts.
752 F.3d 285 (2d Cir. 2014)

POOLER, Circuit Judge:

. . .

BACKGROUND

I. COMPLAINT AND PROPOSED CONSENT JUDGMENT

In October 2011, the S.E.C. filed a complaint against Citigroup, alleging that Citigroup negligently misrepresented its role and economic interest in structuring and marketing a billion-dollar fund, known as the Class V Funding III ("the Fund"), and violated Sections 17(a)(2) and (3) of the Securities Act of 1933 (the "Act"). The complaint alleges that Citigroup "exercised significant influence" over the selection of $500 million worth of the Fund's assets, which were primarily collateralized by subprime securities tied to the already faltering U.S. housing market. Citigroup told Fund investors that the Fund's investment portfolio was chosen by an independent investment advisor, but, the S.E.C. alleged, Citigroup itself selected a substantial amount of negatively projected mortgage-backed assets in which Citigroup had taken a short position.

By assuming a short position, Citigroup realized profits of roughly $160 million from the poor performance of its chosen assets, while Fund investors suffered millions of dollars in losses.

Shortly after filing of the complaint, the S.E.C. filed a proposed consent judgment. In the proposed consent judgment, Citigroup agreed to: (1) a permanent injunction barring Citigroup from violating Act Sections 17(a)(2) and (3); (2) disgorgement of $160 million, which the S.E.C. asserted were Citigroup's net profits gained as a result of the conduct alleged in the complaint; (3) prejudgment interest in the amount of $30 million; and (4) a civil penalty of $95 million. Citigroup also agreed not to seek an offset against any compensatory damages awarded in any related investor action. Citigroup consented to make internal changes, for a period of three years, to prevent similar acts from happening in the future. Absent from the consent decree was any admission of guilt or liability. . . .

II.   PROCEEDINGS BEFORE THE DISTRICT COURT

The district court scheduled a hearing in the matter, and presented the S.E.C. and Citigroup with a list of questions to answer. The questions included:

- Why should the Court impose a judgment in a case in which the S.E.C. alleges a serious securities fraud but the defendant neither admits nor denies wrongdoing?
- Given the S.E.C.'s statutory mandate to ensure transparency in the financial marketplace, is there an overriding public interest in determining whether the S.E.C.'s charges are true? Is the interest even stronger when there is no parallel criminal case?
- How was the amount of the proposed judgment determined? In particular, what calculations went into the determination of the $95 million penalty? Why, for example, is the penalty in this case less than one-fifth of the $535 million penalty assessed in *S.E.C. v. Goldman Sachs & Co.* . . .? What reason is there to believe this proposed penalty will have a meaningful deterrent effect?
- The proposed judgment imposes injunctive relief against future violations. What does the S.E.C. do to maintain compliance? How many contempt proceedings against large financial entities has the S.E.C. brought in the past decade as a result of violations of prior consent judgments?
- Why is the penalty in this case to be paid in large part by Citigroup and its shareholders rather than by the "culpable individual offenders acting for the corporation?" [] If the S.E.C. was for the most part unable to identify such alleged offenders, why was this?
- How can a securities fraud of this nature and magnitude be the result simply of negligence? . . .

[After a hearing and a] few weeks later, the district court issued a written opinion declining to approve the consent judgment. . . . The district court stated that before a court may employ its injunctive and contempt powers in support of an administrative settlement, it is required, even after giving substantial deference to the views of the administrative agency, to be satisfied that it is not being used as a tool to enforce an agreement that is unfair, unreasonable, inadequate, or in contravention of the public interest.

. . . It found that the proposed consent decree

is neither fair, nor reasonable, nor adequate, nor in the public interest . . . because it does not provide the Court with a sufficient evidentiary basis to know whether the requested relief is justified under any of these standards. Purely private parties can settle a case without ever agreeing on the facts, for all that is required is that a plaintiff dismiss his complaint. But when a public agency asks a court to become its partner in enforcement by imposing wide-ranging injunctive remedies on a defendant, enforced by the formidable judicial power of contempt, the court, and the public, need some knowledge of what the underlying facts are: for otherwise, the court becomes a mere handmaiden to a settlement privately negotiated on the basis of unknown facts, while the public is deprived of ever knowing the truth in a matter of obvious public importance.

. . .

Thus, the district court concluded:

An application of judicial power that does not rest on facts is worse than mindless, it is inherently dangerous. The injunctive power of the judiciary is not a free-roving remedy to be invoked at the whim of a regulatory agency, even with the consent of the regulated. If its deployment does not rest on facts—cold, hard, solid facts, established either by admissions or by trials—it serves no lawful or moral purpose and is simply an engine of oppression.

. . .

The district court refused to approve the consent judgment . . . [and set a trial date].

We review the district court's denial of a settlement agreement under an abuse of discretion standard. . . .

III.   THE SCOPE OF DEFERENCE

. . . Our Court recognizes a "strong federal policy favoring the approval and enforcement of consent decrees." *Wang*, 944 F.2d at 85. "To be sure, when the district judge is presented with a proposed consent judgment, he is not merely a 'rubber stamp.'" *S.E.C. v. Levine*, 881 F.2d 1165, 1181 (2d Cir. 1989). The district court here found it was "required, even after giving substantial deference to the views of the administrative agency, to be satisfied that it is not being used as a tool to enforce an agreement that is unfair, unreasonable, inadequate, or in contravention of the public interest." *Citigroup I*, 827 F. Supp. 2d at 332. Other district courts in our Circuit view "[t]he role of the Court in reviewing and approving proposed consent judgments in S.E.C. enforcement actions [as] 'restricted to assessing whether the settlement is fair, reasonable and adequate within the

limitations Congress has imposed on the S.E.C. to recover investor losses.'"
S.E.C. v. CR Intrinsic Investors, LLC, 939 F. Supp. 2d 431, 434 (S.D.N.Y. 2013). . . .

The "fair, reasonable, adequate and in the public interest" standard
invoked by the district court finds its origins in a variety of cases. . . . The Ninth
Circuit—in circumstances similar to those presented here, a proposed consent
decree aimed at settling an S.E.C. enforcement action—noted that "[u]nless a
consent decree is unfair, inadequate, or unreasonable, it ought to be approved."
S.E.C. v. Randolph, 736 F.2d 525, 529 (9th Cir. 1984).

Today we clarify that the proper standard for reviewing a proposed consent judgment involving an enforcement agency requires that the district court
determine whether the proposed consent decree is fair and reasonable, with
the additional requirement that the "public interest would not be disserved,"
eBay, Inc. v. MercExchange, 547 U.S. 388, 391 . . . (2006), in the event that the consent decree includes injunctive relief. Absent a substantial basis in the record
for concluding that the proposed consent decree does not meet these requirements, the district court is required to enter the order.

We omit "adequacy" from the standard. Scrutinizing a proposed consent
decree for "adequacy" appears borrowed from the review applied to class action
settlements, and strikes us as particularly inapt in the context of a proposed
S.E.C. consent decree. *See* Fed. R. Civ. P. 23(e)(2) ("If the proposal would bind the
class members, the court may approve it only after a hearing and on a finding that
it is fair, reasonable, and adequate."). The adequacy requirement makes perfect
sense in the context of a class action settlement—a class action settlement typically precludes future claims, and a court is rightly concerned that the settlement
achieved be adequate. By the same token, a consent decree does not pose the
same concerns regarding adequacy—if there are potential plaintiffs with a private
right of action, those plaintiffs are free to bring their own actions. If there is no
private right of action, then the S.E.C. is the entity charged with representing the
victims, and is politically liable if it fails to adequately perform its duties.

A court evaluating a proposed S.E.C. consent decree for fairness and reasonableness should, at a minimum, assess (1) the basic legality of the decree; . . .
(2) whether the terms of the decree, including its enforcement mechanism, are
clear; . . . (3) whether the consent decree reflects a resolution of the actual claims
in the complaint; and (4) whether the consent decree is tainted by improper
collusion or corruption of some kind. . . . The primary focus of the inquiry . . .
should be on ensuring the consent decree is procedurally proper, using objective
measures similar to the factors set out above, taking care not to infringe on the
S.E.C.'s discretionary authority to settle on a particular set of terms.

It is an abuse of discretion to require, as the district court did here, that the
S.E.C. establish the "truth" of the allegations against a settling party as a condition
for approving the consent decrees. *Citigroup I*, 827 F. Supp. 2d at 332-33. Trials
are primarily about the truth. Consent decrees are primarily about pragmatism.
"[C]onsent decrees are normally compromises in which the parties give up something they might have won in litigation and waive their rights to litigation." *United
States v. ITT Continental Baking Co.*, 420 U.S. 223, 235 . . . (1975). Thus, a consent
decree "must be construed as . . . written, and not as it might have been written
had the plaintiff established his factual claims and legal theories in litigation."
United States v. Armour & Co., 402 U.S. 673 . . . (1971). Consent decrees provide
parties with a means to manage risk. "The numerous factors that affect a litigant's
decision whether to compromise a case or litigate it to the end include the value
of the particular proposed compromise, the perceived likelihood of obtaining a

still better settlement, the prospects of coming out better, or worse, after a full trial, and the resources that would need to be expended in the attempt." *Citigroup III*, 673 F.3d at 164; *see also Randolph*, 736 F.2d at 529 ("Compromise is the essence of settlement. Even if the Commission's case against [defendants] is strong, proceeding to trial would still be costly. The S.E.C.'s resources are limited, and that is why it often uses consent decrees as a means of enforcement . . ."). These assessments are uniquely for the litigants to make. It is not within the district court's purview to demand "cold, hard, solid facts, established either by admissions or by trials," *Citigroup I*, 827 F. Supp. 2d at 335, as to the truth of the allegations in the complaint as a condition for approving a consent decree.

. . .

As noted earlier, when a proposed consent decree contains injunctive relief, a district court must also consider the public interest in deciding whether to grant the injunction. . . .

The job of determining whether the proposed S.E.C. consent decree best serves the public interest, however, rests squarely with the S.E.C., and its decision merits significant deference:

> [F]ederal judges—who have no constituency—have a duty to respect legitimate policy choices made by those who do. The responsibilities for assessing the wisdom of such policy choices and resolving the struggle between competing views of the public interest are not judicial ones: "Our Constitution vests such responsibilities in the public branches."

Chevron, U.S.A., Inc. v. Natural Res. Def. Council, Inc., 467 U.S. 837, 866 (1984) (quoting *TVA v. Hill*, 437 U.S. 153 . . . (1978)). . . .

. . . [T]he district court made no findings that the injunctive relief proposed in the consent decree would disserve the public interest, in part because it defined the public interest as "an overriding interest in knowing the truth." *Id.* at 335. The district court's failure to make the proper inquiry constitutes legal error. On remand, the district court should consider whether the public interest would be disserved by entry of the consent decree. For example, a consent decree may disserve the public interest if it barred private litigants from pursuing their own claims independent of the relief obtained under the consent decree. What the district court may not do is find the public interest disserved based on its disagreement with the S.E.C.'s decisions on discretionary matters of policy, such as deciding to settle without requiring an admission of liability.

To the extent the district court withheld approval of the consent decree on the ground that it believed the S.E.C. failed to bring the proper charges against Citigroup, that constituted an abuse of discretion. . . . The exclusive right to choose which charges to levy against a defendant rests with the S.E.C. *See, e.g., United States v. Microsoft Corp.*, 56 F.3d 1448, 1459 . . . (D.C. Cir. 1995). . . . Nor can the district court reject a consent decree on the ground that it fails to provide collateral estoppel assistance to private litigants—that simply is not the job of the courts.

Finally, we note that to the extent that the S.E.C. does not wish to engage with the courts, it is free to eschew the involvement of the courts and employ its own arsenal of remedies instead. *See, e.g.*, Exchange Act §21C(a). . . . Admittedly, these remedies may not be on par with the relief afforded by a so-ordered consent decree and federal court injunctions. But if the S.E.C. prefers to call upon the power of the courts in ordering a consent decree and issuing an injunction, then the S.E.C. must be willing to assure the court that the settlement proposed is fair and reasonable. . . . For the courts to simply accept a proposed S.E.C. consent decree without any review would be a dereliction of the court's duty to ensure the orders it enters are proper.

CONCLUSION

For the reasons given above, we vacate the November 28, 2011 order of the district court and remand this case for further proceedings in accordance with this opinion. . . .

LOHIER, Circuit Judge, concurring:
I would be inclined to reverse on the factual record before us and direct the District Court to enter the consent decree. It does not appear that any additional facts are needed to determine that the proposed decree is "fair and reasonable" and does not disserve the public interest. . . .

———————————

For a critical analysis of *Citigroup, see* Edwards, Of Truth, Pragmatism, and Sour Grapes: The Second Circuit's Decision in *SEC v. Citigroup Global Markets,* 65 Duke L.J. 1241 (2016).

PROBLEM

14-15.   Through false claims about her firm's technology and business performance in connection with its "portable blood analyzer," Elizabeth Holmes over the years was able to raise more than $700 million from investors for her private company, Theranos, Inc. She touted the analyzer's supposed ability from a few drops of blood to quickly and cheaply provide blood tests commonly prescribed by doctors. Holmes held a controlling block of the company's stock, chaired its board, and was CEO. Its board included a former U.S. Secretary of State, and its investors were financial institutions as well as several very wealthy individuals (including the U.S. Secretary of Education, who invested more than $100 million in Theranos). Assume Holmes has indicated a willingness to settle with the SEC. What would you require to be in the settlement with her? *See https://www .sec.gov/news/press-release/2018-41.*

G.   *The SEC's Power to Discipline Professionals*

A potent and highly controversial enforcement weapon appears in Rule 102(e) of the Commission's Rules of Practice, which provides that the Commission "may deny, temporarily or permanently, the privilege of appearing or practicing before it in any way to any person who is found by the Commission" after notice and hearing:

(i)   not to possess the requisite qualifications to represent others, or

(ii) to be lacking in character or integrity or to have engaged in unethical or improper professional conduct, or

(iii) to have willfully violated, or willfully aided and abetted the violation of any provision of the Federal securities laws . . . or the rules and regulations thereunder.

Subparagraph (f) of the Rule provides a nonexclusive definition of *practice*, so that it includes not only transacting business with the Commission but also, more significantly, preparing "any statement, opinion, or other paper by any attorney, accountant, engineer, or other professional or expert" that is included in any document filed with the Commission. As such, not only is this disciplinary proceeding directed at those whose behavior has corrupted the Commission's administrative proceedings—for example, by giving false testimony or concealing evidence—but also, and more importantly, Rule 102(e) reaches the activities of professionals who in the course of rendering a professional service well beyond the Commission's hearing rooms have acted in a dishonest, incompetent, unethical, or unprofessional manner. It also reaches those inside the firm filing reports with the SEC. *See In the Matter of Aichun Li*, Exchange Act Release No. 69945 (July 8, 2013) (CFO barred for two years for ignoring red flags that if pursued would reveal related party transactions that were required to be disclosed in SEC filings overseen by the CFO). As interpreted by the Commission, there is little that a securities lawyer does that does not qualify as practice before the Commission.

The Commission is further empowered under Rule 102(e)(3) to *temporarily* suspend without a hearing any person from practicing before the Commission if the person has been permanently enjoined in a Commission action from violating the securities laws or has been found by a court in a Commission action or in a Commission administrative proceeding to have violated or aided and abetted the violation of the securities laws. The suspension under this provision becomes permanent if the person so suspended does not within 30 days petition the Commission for a hearing to consider lifting the suspension. In such a proceeding, the petitioner has the burden of proof.

The sanction provided in Rule 102(e) is a temporary or permanent bar of the respondent from "practicing" before the Commission; again, the scope of the expression "practice" is such that a bar can and has operated to prevent individuals and entire firms from engaging in any work related to a document to be filed with the Commission. For example, the Commission earlier temporarily barred national accounting firms from assuming Securities Act responsibilities for any new clients even though the audit transgressions it found related only to a small percentage of the total audits undertaken by the firm. *See, e.g.*, Peat Marwick Mitchell & Co., Accounting Series Release No. 173 (1975). In imposing the disciplinary sanction under Rule 102(e), the Commission is not required to prove a reasonable likelihood of any further violations as is required in judicial injunctive actions. *See, e.g., SEC v. Geotek*,

426 F. Supp. 715 (N.D. Cal. 1976), *aff'd sub nom. SEC v. Arthur Young & Co.*, 590 F.2d 785 (9th Cir. 1979). The length of the bar is guided roughly by how egregious the professional's offense was, so that willful participation in the client's fraudulent scheme has resulted in a lifetime ban from practicing before the Commission, *see, e.g., In re James McGovern*, Exchange Act Release No. 24379 (Feb. 22, 1988), whereas less culpable involvement has resulted in bars of five years or less, *see, e.g., McCurdy v. SEC*, 396 F.3d 1258 (D.C. Cir. 2005).

Settlement orders under Rule 102(e) as a matter of course are far more encompassing than barring the professional from practicing before the Commission. For example, in *In re Edward M. Grushko*, Exchange Act Release No. 33625 (1994), the attorney agreed to take 30 hours of continuing legal education courses during each of the five years of his suspension.

Consider the possible interpretations the Commission can give to "improper professional conduct." For example, does an accountant's single departure from either GAAP or generally accepted auditing standards fall within Rule 102(e)'s proscription? In response to an unqualified rebuke in *Checkosky v. SEC*, 139 F.3d 221 (D.C. Cir. 1998), that Rule 102(e) was too vague with respect to its "improper professional conduct" standard, the Commission amended its disciplinary rule. Securities Act Release No. 7593 (Oct. 19, 1998). The amendment adds the following:

> 102(e)(1) . . . (iv) With respect to persons licensed to practice as accountants, "improper professional conduct" . . . means:
>> (A) Intentional or knowing conduct, including reckless conduct, that results in a violation of applicable professional standards; or
>> (B) Either of the following two types of negligent conduct:
>>> (1) A single instance of highly unreasonable conduct that results in a violation of applicable professional standards in circumstances in which an accountant knows, or should know, that heightened scrutiny is warranted.
>>> (2) Repeated instances of unreasonable conduct, each resulting in a violation of applicable professional standards, that indicate a lack of competence to practice before the Commission.

To what extent does the above amendment address *Checkosky's* condemnation that Rule 102(e)(1)(ii) "yields no clear and coherent standard for violations"? *See Dearlove v. SEC*, 573 F.3d 801 (D.C. Cir. 2009) (102(e)(1)(iv)(B)(2) does not require SEC to establish a standard of care separate from Generally Accepted Auditing Standards).

The disciplinary authority the Commission enjoys under Rule 102(e) is now expressly authorized in Section 4C of the Exchange Act via Section 602 of the Sarbanes-Oxley Act. Why does the Commission need the authority to discipline professionals who practice before it? What does this authority add to the other enforcement powers the Commission can wield against professionals? In exercising this authority, should it exhibit a lighter hand for attorneys than for accountants? Sarbanes-Oxley, in addition to legitimizing the power the SEC had long exercised under Rule 102(e), poses some important questions. Recall that one of the central provisions of Sarbanes-Oxley was the creation of the Public Company Accounting Oversight Board (PCAOB), which has authority to discipline accountants. How and when should the SEC wield its Rule 102(e) disciplinary powers when Congress has created the PCAOB with the specific task of overseeing auditors of public companies? A further question regards how active the Commission will be in disciplining attorneys under Rule 102(e). *See, e.g., In the Matter of Nancy R. Heinen,* Exchange Act Release No. 58553 (Sept. 16, 2008) (three-year suspension of attorney because of her participation in backdating executive stock options).

The SEC, of course, has other enforcement mechanisms available to it that in appropriate cases will cause it to proceed against an attorney who has violated or contributed to another's violation of the securities laws. *See In re Weiss v. SEC,* 468 F.3d 849 (D.C. Cir. 2006) (sustaining cease-and-desist order against an experienced bond attorney for violating Securities Act Sections 17(a)(2) and (3) through conduct that "was at least negligent" by providing an unqualified legal opinion erroneously concluding that interest to be paid in connection with municipal bond to be sold to the public would be exempt from taxation). Whereas before Sarbanes-Oxley, the Commission followed a practice of not instituting a Rule 102(e) proceeding against an attorney unless there had been a prior determination that the lawyer had engaged in unethical or illegal conduct, that practice is no longer followed. *See Altman v. SEC,* 666 F.3d 1322 (2d Cir. 2011) (upholding permanent bar under Rule 102(e) against an attorney who knowingly violated three New York disciplinary rules of conduct).

PROBLEMS

14-16. An SEC investigation has revealed that Alpha Numeric's most recent Form 10-K overstates its revenues and income for the year. This occurred because several large shipments of goods to wholesalers were recorded as sales when in fact they were instead consignments. In the case of a consignment, revenues are reported only when the consigned goods are sold by the wholesaler to a third party. The evidence also reveals that on three occasions Alpha Numeric's outside auditor opined that the shipments were sales and thus could be reported as revenues for the fiscal period. The evidence also suggests that a closer reading of the underlying documents for the shipments would have readily revealed the shipments were not sales but goods on consignment. How strong a case does the SEC have against the accountants under Rule 102(e)? For a cease-and-desist order under Section 21C of the Exchange Act? *See In re Steinberg,* SEC Admin. Proc. File 3-9608 (May 22, 1998).

14-17. Good, Rep and Howe (GR&H) is a general commercial law firm with eleven partners and eight associates. The firm operates in a highly departmental fashion. For several years, GR&H has served as primary counsel to American Financial Bank, representing more than one-half of GR&H's yearly revenues. As a result of a recent review of American Financial's Form 10-K by the SEC, it was learned that the 10-K did not disclose that a substantial loan by American Financial to its dominant stockholder, Charles, had been forgiven by American Financial's board of directors. The 10-K continued to represent that the loan was outstanding and collectible. Further investigation by the SEC convinced its staff that (i) Denise, the GR&H partner who drafted the 10-K for American Financial, was not aware that the board had forgiven the loan to Charles; (ii) Ed, another GR&H partner, attended the American Financial board meeting when the loan was forgiven and advised the board about its actions; (iii) a GR&H senior associate, Frieda, on instructions from Ed, drafted the documents to release Charles from his obligation on the note; and (iv) GR&H had no procedures for, as part of its preparing SEC filings, collecting from its partners and associates information about the firm's representation of its clients that might bear on the disclosures that are to be made. Has there been a violation of the standards set forth in Rule 102(e)? Which standard? By whom? *See In re Keating,* Muething & Klekamp, Exchange Act Release No. 15982 (July 2, 1979).

H.   The Duties of the Securities Lawyer

There are many reasons why one chooses to become a lawyer: The work is steady, generally prestigious, and sometimes lucrative. The profession's many possible undertakings enlist a wide array of talents and skills, so that the profession appeals equally to the philosophical as well as the more technically inclined. Moreover, the profession is pluralistic, enjoying a rich diversity in the educational, economic, and social backgrounds of its members. Although the legal profession is neither monolithic nor homogeneous, it is a profession. But what does it mean to affirm the status of law practice as a profession? Some would take a cynical view and argue "profession" is nothing more than a label designed to restrict competition and thereby preserve the monopoly of those fortunate enough to have entered the trade. Others take a loftier view and emphasize that the responsibilities assumed by those who enter the legal profession and the importance of those responsibilities distinguish it from purely commercial endeavors. *See, e.g.,* R. Pound, The Lawyer from Antiquity to Modern Times 7 (1953) (an organized profession is not "the same sort of thing as a retail grocers' association"); Painter, The Moral Interdependence of Corporate Lawyers and Their Clients, 67 S. Cal. L. Rev. 507 (1994) (attorneys are not independent of the transactions for which professional services are provided, and their obligations extend to those harmed by such transactions). Whatever the merits of the debate between cynics and idealists, most who consider the matter agree that membership in the legal profession *should* carry with it significant responsibilities that may conflict with a lawyer's self-interest. These responsibilities include, at a minimum, duties to clients (e.g., confidentiality of communications, vigorous advocacy), duties to courts (e.g., the notion of the lawyer as an officer of the court), and duties to the public generally (e.g., the obligation to work to improve the administration of justice).

The profession's baseline standards are delineated in codes of professional responsibility developed by the American Bar Association (ABA) and adopted by state bar associations and supreme courts. The first such code was promulgated in 1908 as the Canons of Professional Ethics. The Model Code of Professional Responsibility followed the Canons in 1969. While the Model Code was uniformly adopted by the states, the ABA's most recent effort in this area, the 1983 Model Rules of Professional Conduct, has not produced a uniform set of principles across the states; in fact, the states have departed significantly from the Model Rules when enacting their own codes of professional responsibility. In the end, the codes developed by the legal profession for the regulation of its members are a mixed bag of lofty ideals and, more importantly, pragmatic compromises often shaped by the lawyers' commercial interests. *See, e.g.*, Zacharias, Reconciling Professionalism and Client Interests, 36 Wm. & Mary L. Rev. 1303 (1995); Riger, The Model Rules and Corporate Practice—New Ethics for a Competitive Era, 17 Conn. L. Rev. 729 (1985); Gillers, What We Talked About When We Talked About Ethics: A Critical View of the Model Rules, 46 Ohio St. L.J. 243 (1985). Whatever their substantive merits, however, the bar's ethics codes have traditionally been viewed as the primary resource for defining the professional responsibility of attorneys.

When lawyers represent clients in securities matters, the primacy of the legal profession's ethics codes (and in particular their emphasis on duties to clients) may clash with notions of public responsibility derived from the federal securities laws. Consider that SEC Chair Clayton repeatedly admonished attorneys assisting businesses with initial coin offerings, discussed in Chapter 2, who provided assurances to their clients that the tokens were not securities when they in fact had many similarities with securities. *See* Clayton, Opening Remarks at the Securities Regulation Institute (Jan. 22, 2018), available at *www.SEC.gov/news/speech/speechclayton*. Were those lawyers "the cause" of their client's violations in such instances?

The materials in this section focus on the duties of the securities lawyer that may arise from the aiding and abetting standards, the Commission's power to discipline attorneys through Rule 102(e), and the SEC's new standards of Professional Conduct for Attorneys. As will be seen, these duties are broader than those found in the ethics codes and raise a significant policy question: To what extent does the securities lawyer have both a *public* duty to assure compliance with the securities laws and a *private* duty to advance the interests of the client?

1. A Historic Step Toward Socializing the Securities Lawyer

Securities and Exchange Commission v. National Student Marketing Corp.
457 F. Supp. 682 (D.D.C. 1978)

PARKER, J. This opinion covers the final act in a civil proceeding brought by the Securities and Exchange Commission (Commission or SEC) seeking injunctive sanctions against numerous defendants as a result of their participation in alleged securities laws violations relating to the National Student Marketing Corporation (NSMC) securities fraud scheme. The original defendants included the corporation and certain of its officers and directors; the accounting firm of Peat, Marwick, Mitchell & Co. (Peat Marwick) and two of its partners; several officers and directors of Interstate National Corporation (Interstate); the law firm of White & Case and one of its partners; and the law firm of Lord, Bissell & Brook (LBB) and two of its partners. The majority of these defendants are not now before the Court. . . . NSMC and other principal defendants consented to the entry of final judgments of permanent injunction or otherwise reached a resolution of the charges against them. The only defendants remaining are Lord, Bissell & Brook; its two partners, Max E. Meyer and Louis F. Schauer; and Cameron Brown, a former president and director of Interstate, and presently a director of and consultant to NSMC.

The focal point of the Commission's charges against these defendants is the corporate merger of Interstate with NSMC on October 31, 1969. . . .

I.   BACKGROUND

A.   THE COMPANIES

National Student Marketing Corporation was incorporated in the District of Columbia in 1966. The company enjoyed early prosperity; it grew rapidly and experienced a steady increase in assets, sales and earnings. Its common stock, which was registered with the SEC and traded on the over-the-counter market, rose from an initial public offering of $6 per share in the spring of 1968 to a high of $144 per share in mid-December 1969. The financial community held the company and its potential in high regard, and in anticipation of continued high market performance, it was seen as a good "buy" prospect. Its management was considered aggressive, imaginative and capable; if there was a question of its integrity and honesty, it did not surface in the public arena until a later period. During this period, White & Case served as its outside legal counsel, with Marion J. Epley, III, as the partner immediately in charge of the firm's representation. Peat Marwick served as its outside accountant.

Interstate National Corporation, a Nevada corporation, was an insurance holding company. Its principal assets were several wholly-owned subsidiary insurance companies. The company's common stock was traded on the over-the-counter market and owned by approximately 1200 shareholders. Cameron Brown was president, chief executive officer, principal shareholder and a director of the company. . . . Max E. Meyer, a director and shareholder, was a partner in the Chicago law firm of Lord, Bissell & Brook, which had long represented Interstate and served as its outside legal counsel in all matters relating to the merger of the corporation with NSMC. Meyer, a personal friend and legal advisor to Cameron Brown, served as the contact partner for the Interstate account and was otherwise in overall charge of his firm's representation. Another partner of the firm, Louis F. Schauer, was also involved in the merger transaction due to his experience in corporate and securities law. Peat Marwick served as Interstate's outside accountant during the period in question.

B.   THE MERGER NEGOTIATIONS

National Student Marketing Corporation developed a reputation for having a unique and successful marketing network for selling its own and other products to college and high school students. Commencing in 1969, it undertook a highly active program to acquire companies specializing in selling goods and services to students. It was in this connection that NSMC first approached representatives of Interstate.

Initially, NSMC discussed the possibility of acquiring an Interstate subsidiary that specialized in selling insurance to students. After Interstate indicated an unwillingness to dispose of a single subsidiary, NSMC expressed interest in acquiring its entire insurance holding company operation. Cortes W. Randell, NSMC's president and chief executive officer, proposed a merger of the two corporations, offering one share of NSMC stock for every two shares of Interstate stock.

On June 10, 1969, NSMC representatives, including Randell and James F. Joy, a senior vice president and finance committee member, were invited before the Interstate directors to make a presentation concerning the proposed merger. The directors were provided with NSMC's 1968 annual report and its financial report for the first half of 1969. Randell discussed the company's acquisition program, reviewed several pending corporate acquisition commitments, and made certain earnings predictions for the fiscal year ending August 31, 1969. He also increased the earlier offer to two shares of NSMC common for every three shares of Interstate common. . . . Very few questions were asked by Randell or Joy about the business and financial affairs of Interstate, an aspect of the meeting which surprised several of Interstate's representatives. . . .

. . . [T]he transaction represented approximately a 100 percent premium for the Interstate shares based on their market value at the time. . . . The Merger Agreement set forth fully the terms and conditions of the understanding between the two corporations. . . .

The Agreement also provided several conditions precedent to the obligations of the two corporations to consummate the merger. One required the receipt by NSMC of an opinion letter from Interstate's counsel LBB to the effect, inter alia, that Interstate had taken all actions and procedures required of it by law and that all transactions in connection with the merger had been duly and validly taken, to the best knowledge of counsel, in full compliance with applicable law; a similar opinion letter was required to be delivered from NSMC's counsel to Interstate. Another condition was the receipt by each company of a "comfort letter" from the other's independent public accountants. Each letter was required to state: (1) that the accountants had no reason to believe that the unaudited interim financial statements for the company in question were not prepared in accordance with accounting principles and practices consistent with those used in the previous year-end audited financials; (2) that they had no reason to believe that any material adjustments in those financials were required in order fairly to present the results of operations of the company; and (3) that the company had experienced no material adverse change in its financial position or results of operations from the period covered by its interim financial statement up to five business days prior to the effective date of the merger. Although setting forth these specific conditions to consummation of the merger, the final paragraph of the Agreement also provided that:

> Anything herein to the contrary notwithstanding and notwithstanding any stockholder vote of approval of this Agreement and the merger provided herein, this Agreement may be terminated and abandoned by mutual consent of the Boards

of Directors of NSMC and Interstate at any time prior to the Effective Date and the Board of Directors of any party may waive any of the conditions to the obligations of such party under this Agreement.

. . . Both NSMC and Interstate utilized proxy statements and notices of special stockholder meetings to secure shareholder approval of the proposed merger. Interstate's materials included a copy of the Merger Agreement and NSMC's Proxy Statement; the latter contained NSMC's financial statements for the fiscal year ended August 31, 1968, and the nine-month interim financial statement for the period ending May 31, 1969. . . . The boards of both companies recommended approval of the merger and at special shareholder meetings that approval was secured by large majorities.

In mid-October, Peat Marwick began drafting the comfort letter concerning NSMC's unaudited interim financials for the nine-month period ended May 31, 1969. As issued by NSMC, those financials had reflected a profit of approximately $700,000.

Soon after beginning work on the comfort letter, Peat Marwick representatives determined that certain adjustments were required with respect to the interim financials. Specifically, the accountants proposed that a $500,000 adjustment to deferred costs, a $300,000 write-off of unbilled receivables, and an $84,000 adjustment to paid-in capital be made retroactive to May 31 and be reflected in the comfort letter delivered to Interstate. Such adjustments would have caused NSMC to show a loss for the nine-month period ended May 31, 1969, and the company as it existed on May 31 would have broken even for fiscal 1969. Although Peat Marwick discussed the proposed adjustments with representatives of NSMC, neither the accountants nor NSMC informed Interstate of the adjustments prior to the closing. A draft of the comfort letter, with the adjustments, was completed on October 30 and on the next day, the morning of the closing, it was discussed among senior partners of Peat Marwick.

C. THE CLOSING AND RECEIPT OF THE COMFORT LETTER

The closing meeting for the merger was scheduled at 2 P.M. on Friday, October 31, at the New York offices of White & Case. Brown, Meyer and Schauer were present in addition to Interstate directors Bach, Allison and Tate. The representatives of NSMC included Randell, Joy, John G. Davies, their attorney Epley and other White & Case associates.

Although Schauer had had an opportunity to review most of the merger documents at White & Case on the previous day, the comfort letter had not been delivered. When he arrived at White & Case on the morning of the merger, the letter was still not available, but he was informed by a representative of the firm that it was expected to arrive at any moment.

The meeting proceeded. When the letter had not arrived by approximately 2:15 P.M., Epley telephoned Peat Marwick's Washington office to inquire about it. Anthony M. Natelli, the partner in charge, thereupon dictated to Epley's secretary a letter which provided in part:

[N]othing has come to our attention which caused us to believe that:

1. The National Student Marketing Corporation's unaudited consoli-
    dated financial statements as of and for the nine months ended May
    31, 1969:

    a. Were not prepared in accordance with accounting principles and
        practices consistent in all material respects with those followed in the
        preparation of the audited consolidated financial statements which
        are covered by our report dated November 14, 1968;

    b. Would require any material adjustments for a fair and reasonable
        presentation of the information shown except with respect to
        consolidated financial statements of National Student Marketing
        Corporation and consolidated subsidiaries as they existed at May 31,
        1969 and for the nine months then ended, our examination in con-
        nection with the year ended August 31, 1969, which is still in process,
        disclosed the following significant adjustments which in our opinion
        should be reflected retroactive to May 31, 1969:

        1. In adjusting the amortization of deferred costs at May 31, 1969,
            to eliminate therefrom all costs for programs substantially com-
            pleted or which commenced 12 months or more prior, an adjust-
            ment of $500,000 was required. Upon analysis of the retroactive
            effect of this adjustment, it appears that the entire amount could
            be determined applicable to the period prior to May 31, 1969.

        2. In August 1969 management wrote off receivables in amounts of
            $300,000. It appears that the uncollectibility of these receivables
            could have been determined at May 31, 1969 and such charge off
            should have been reflected as of that date.

        3. Acquisition costs in the amount of $84,000 for proposed acquisi-
            tions which the Company decided not to pursue were transferred
            from additional paid-in capital to general and administrative
            expenses. In our opinion, these should have been so transferred
            as of May 31, 1969. . . .

Epley delivered one copy of the typed letter to the conference room where the
closing was taking place. Epley then returned to his office.

Schauer was the first to read the unsigned letter. He then handed it to
Cameron Brown, advising him to read it. Although there is some dispute as to
which of the Interstate representatives actually read the letter, at least Brown
and Meyer did so after Schauer. They asked Randell and Joy a number of questions relating to the nature and effect of the adjustments. The NSMC officers
gave assurances that the adjustments would have no significant effect on the
predicted year-end earnings of NSMC and that a substantial portion of the
$500,000 adjustments to deferred costs would be recovered. Moreover, they
indicated that NSMC's year-end audit for fiscal 1969 had been completed by
Peat Marwick, would be published in a couple of weeks, and would demonstrate that NSMC itself had made each of the adjustments for its fourth quarter.
The comfort letter, they explained, simply determined that those adjustments
should be reflected in the third quarter ended May 31, 1969, rather than
the final quarter of NSMC's fiscal year. Randell and Joy indicated that while
NSMC disagreed with what they felt was a tightening up of its accounting practices, everything requested by Peat Marwick to "clean up" its books had been
undertaken.

At the conclusion of this discussion, certain of the Interstate representatives, including at least Brown, Schauer and Meyer, conferred privately to consider their alternatives in light of the apparent nonconformity of the comfort letter with the requirements of the Merger Agreement. Although they considered the letter a serious matter and the adjustments as significant and important, they were nonetheless under some pressure to determine a course of action promptly since there was a 4 P.M. filing deadline if the closing were to be consummated as scheduled on October 31. Among the alternatives considered were: (1) delaying or postponing the closing, either to secure more information or to resolicit the shareholders with corrected financials; (2) closing the merger; or (3) calling it off completely.

The consensus of the directors was that there was no need to delay the closing. The comfort letter contained all relevant information and in light of the explanations given by Randell and Joy, they already had sufficient information upon which to make a decision. Any delay for the purpose of resoliciting the shareholders was considered impractical because it would require the use of year-end figures instead of the stale nine-month interim financials. Such a requirement would make it impossible to resolicit shareholder approval before the merger upset date of November 28, 1969, and would cause either the complete abandonment of the merger or its renegotiation on terms possibly far less favorable to Interstate. The directors also recognized that delay or abandonment of the merger would result in a decline in the stock of both companies, thereby harming the shareholders and possibly subjecting the directors to lawsuits based on their failure to close the merger. The Interstate representatives decided to proceed with the closing. They did, however, solicit and receive further assurances from the NSMC representatives that the stated adjustments were the only ones to be made to the company's financial statements and that 1969 earnings would be as predicted. When asked by Brown whether the closing could proceed on the basis of an unsigned comfort letter, Meyer responded that if a White & Case partner assured them that this was in fact the comfort letter and that a signed copy would be forthcoming from Peat Marwick, they could close. Epley gave this assurance. Meyer then announced that Interstate was prepared to proceed, the closing was consummated, and a previously arranged telephone call was made which resulted in the filing of the Articles of Merger at the Office of the Recorder of Deeds of the District of Columbia. Large packets of merger documents, including the required counsel opinion letters, were exchanged. The closing was solemnized with a toast of warm champagne.

Unknown to the Interstate group, several telephone conversations relating to the substance of the comfort letter occurred on the afternoon of the closing between Peat Marwick representatives and Epley. The accountants were concerned with the propriety of proceeding with the closing in light of the adjustments to NSMC's nine-month financials. One such conversation occurred after Epley delivered the unsigned letter to the Interstate participants but before the merger had been consummated. At that time Epley was told that an additional paragraph would be added in order to characterize the adjustments. The paragraph recited that with the noted adjustments properly made, NSMC's unaudited consolidated statement for the nine-month period would not reflect a profit as had been indicated but rather a net loss, and the consolidated operations of NSMC as they existed on May 31, 1969, would show a breakeven as to net earnings for the year ended August 31, 1969. Epley had the additional paragraph typed out, but failed to inform or disclose this change to Interstate. In a second conversation, after the closing was completed and the Interstate representatives had departed, Epley was informed of still another proposed addition, namely, a paragraph urging resolicitation of both companies' shareholders and disclosure of NSMC's corrected nine-month financials prior to closing. To this, he responded that the deal was closed and the letter was not needed. Peat Marwick nonetheless advised Epley that the letter would be delivered and that its counsel was considering whether further action should be taken by the firm.

The final written draft of the comfort letter arrived at White & Case late that afternoon. . . .

The signed letter was virtually identical to the unsigned version delivered at the closing, except for the addition of the following two paragraphs:

> Your attention is called, however, to the fact that if the aforementioned adjustments had been made at May 31, 1969 the unaudited consolidated statement of earnings of National Student Marketing Corporation would have shown a net loss of approximately $80,000. It is presently estimated that the consolidated operations of the company as it existed at May 31, 1969 will be approximately a breakeven as to net earnings for the year ended August 31, 1969.
>
> In view of the above mentioned facts, we believe the companies should consider submitting corrected interim unaudited financial information to the shareholders prior to proceeding with the closing.

The only other change was the reduction in the write-off to receivables from $300,000 to $200,000, making a total negative adjustment to NSMC's nine-month financials in the amount of $784,000. . . .

Over the next several days the Interstate directors continued their discussion of the matter, consulting frequently with their counsel, Meyer and Schauer. As they viewed it, the available options were to attempt to undo the merger, either permanently or until the shareholders could be resolicited, or to leave things as they were. The attorneys indicated that rescission would be impractical, if not impossible, since Interstate no longer existed and NSMC had indicated that it would oppose any effort to undo the merger. Meanwhile, the market value of NSMC stock continued to increase, and the directors noted that any action on their part to undo the merger would most likely adversely affect its price. By the end of the week, the decision was made to abstain from any action. Thereafter, Brown issued a memorandum to all Interstate employees announcing completion of the merger. No effort was ever made by any of the defendants to disclose the contents of the comfort letter to the former shareholders of Interstate, the SEC or to the public in general. . . .

E.   SUBSEQUENT EVENTS

Following the acquisition of Interstate and several other companies NSMC stock rose steadily in price, reaching a peak in mid-December. However, in early 1970, after several newspaper and magazine articles appeared questioning NSMC's financial health, the value of the stock decreased drastically. Several private lawsuits were filed and the SEC initiated a wide-ranging investigation which led to the filing of this action.

II.   THE PRESENT ACTION

. . . Numerous charges, all of which appear to allege secondary liability, are leveled against the attorney defendants. Schauer is charged with "participating in the merger between Interstate and NSMC," apparently referring to his failure to interfere with the closing of the merger after receipt of the comfort letter. Such inaction, when alleged to facilitate a transaction, falls under the rubric of aiding and abetting. *See Kerbs v. Fall River Industries, Inc.*, 502 F.2d 731, 739-40 (10th Cir. 1974). Both Schauer and Meyer are charged with issuing false opinions in connection with the merger . . . and with acquiescence in the merger after learning the contents of the signed comfort letter. The Commission contends that the attorneys should have refused to issue the opinion in view of the adjustments revealed by the unsigned comfort letter, and after receipt of the signed version, they should have withdrawn their opinion with regard to the merger and demanded resolicitation of the Interstate shareholders. If the Interstate directors refused, the attorneys should have withdrawn from the representation and informed the shareholders or the Commission. . . . And finally, LBB is charged with vicarious liability for the actions of Meyer and Schauer with respect to the attorneys' activities on behalf of the firm.

Since any liability of the alleged aiders and abettors depends upon a finding of a primary violation of the antifraud provisions, the Court will first address the issues relating to the Commission's charges against the principals. . . .

[The court considered the case against Brown and Meyer, finding the merger of Interstate into NSMC was a sale of a security that did not occur until the merger was in fact consummated after the issuance of the opinion letters and that the failure to disclose the changes in NSMC's nine-month financial report was a material misrepresentation in connection with that sale. The court further found Brown and Meyer acted with scienter, relying in large measure upon their intention to reap a large profit through reselling the substantial amount of NSMC stock they received in the exchange. Accordingly, the court found Brown and Meyer violated the antifraud provisions of Sections 10(b) and 17(a) through their participation in the closing of the Interstate/NSMC merger without first disclosing the material information contained in the unsigned comfort letter.]

IV.   Aiding and Abetting

The Court must now turn to the Commission's charges that the defendants aided and abetted these two violations of the antifraud provisions. The violations themselves establish the first element of aiding and abetting liability, namely that another person has committed a securities law violation. . . . The remaining elements, though not set forth with any uniformity, are essentially that the alleged aider and abettor had a "general awareness that his role was part of an overall activity that is improper, and [that he] knowingly and substantially assisted the violation." *SEC v. Coffey*, supra. . . .

The Commission's allegations of aiding and abetting by the defendants, specified . . . (1) the failure of the attorney defendants to take any action to interfere in the consummation of the merger; (2) the issuance by the attorneys of an opinion with respect to the merger; (3) the attorneys' subsequent failure to withdraw that opinion and inform the Interstate shareholders or the SEC of the inaccuracy of the nine-month financials. . . . The Court concurs with regard to the attorneys' failure to interfere with the closing, but must conclude that the remaining actions or inaction alleged to constitute aiding and abetting did not substantially facilitate . . . the merger. . . .

As noted, the first element of aiding and abetting liability has been established by the finding that Brown and Meyer committed primary violations of the securities laws. Support for the second element, that the defendants were generally aware of the fraudulent activity, is provided by the previous discussion concerning scienter. With the exception of LBB, which is charged with vicarious liability, each of the defendants was actually present at the closing of the merger when the comfort letter was delivered and the adjustments to the nine-month financials were revealed. Each was present at the Interstate caucus and the subsequent questioning of the NSMC representatives; each knew of the importance attributed to the adjustments by those present. They knew that the Interstate shareholders and the investing public were unaware of the adjustments and the inaccuracy of the financials. Despite the obvious materiality of the information, each knew that it had not been disclosed prior to the merger and stock sale transactions. . . .

The final requirement for aiding and abetting liability is that the conduct provide knowing, substantial assistance to the violation. . . . The major problem arising with regard to the Commission's contention that the attorneys failed to interfere in the closing of the merger is whether inaction or silence constitutes substantial assistance. While there is no definitive answer to this question, courts have been willing to consider inaction as a form of substantial assistance when the accused aider and abettor had a duty to disclose. . . .

Upon receipt of the unsigned comfort letter, it became clear that the merger had been approved by the Interstate shareholders on the basis of materially misleading information. In view of the obvious materiality of the information, especially to attorneys learned in securities law, the attorneys' responsibilities to their corporate client required them to take steps to ensure that the information would be disclosed to the shareholders. However, it is unnecessary to determine the precise extent of their obligations here, since it is undisputed that they took no steps whatsoever to delay the closing pending disclosure to and resolicitation of the Interstate shareholders. But, at the very least, they were required to speak out at the closing concerning the obvious materiality of the information and the concomitant requirement that the merger not be closed until the adjustments were disclosed and approval of the merger was again obtained from the Interstate shareholders. Their silence was not only a breach of this duty to speak, but in addition lent the appearance of legitimacy to the closing, *see Kerbs v. Fall River Industries, Inc.*, supra. The combination of these factors clearly provided substantial assistance to the closing of the merger.

. . . Courts will not lightly overrule an attorney's determination of materiality and the need for disclosure. However, where, as here, the significance of the information clearly removes any doubt concerning the materiality of the information, attorneys cannot rest on asserted "business judgments" as justification for their failure to make a legal decision pursuant to their fiduciary responsibilities to client shareholders.

The Commission also asserts that the attorneys substantially assisted the merger violation through the issuance of an opinion that was false and misleading due to its omission of the receipt of the comfort letter and of the completion of the merger on the basis of the false and misleading nine-month financials. . . .

Contrary to the implication made by the SEC, the opinion issued by the attorneys at the closing did not play a large part in the consummation of the merger. Instead, it was simply one of many conditions to the obligation of NSMC to complete the merger. It addressed a number of corporate formalities required of Interstate by the Merger Agreement, only a few of which could possibly involve compliance with the antifraud provisions of the securities laws. Moreover, the opinion was explicitly for the benefit of NSMC, which was already well aware of the adjustments contained in the comfort letter. Thus, this is not a case where an opinion of counsel addresses a specific issue and is undeniably relied on in completing the transaction. *Compare SEC v. Coven*, 581 F.2d 1020, at 1028; *SEC v. Spectrum, Ltd.*, 489 F.2d 535 (2d Cir. 1973). Under these circumstances, it is unreasonable to suggest that the opinion provided substantial assistance to the merger.

The SEC's contention with regard to counsel's alleged acquiescence in the merger transaction raises significant questions concerning the responsibility of counsel. The basis for the charge appears to be counsel's failure, after the merger, to withdraw their opinion, to demand resolicitation of the shareholders, to advise their clients concerning rights of rescission of the merger, and ultimately, to inform the Interstate shareholders or the SEC of the completion of the merger based on materially false and misleading financial statements. The defendants counter with the argument that their actions following the merger are not subject to the coverage of the securities laws. . . .

Meyer, Schauer and Lord, Bissell & Brook are, in essence, here charged with failing to take any action to "undo" the merger. The Court has already concluded that counsel had a duty to the Interstate shareholders to delay the closing of the merger pending disclosure and resolicitation with corrected financials, and that the breach of that duty constituted a violation of the antifraud provisions through aiding and abetting the merger transaction. The Commission's charge, however, concerns the period following that transaction. Even if the attorneys' fiduciary responsibilities to the Interstate shareholders continued beyond the merger, the breach of such a duty would not have the requisite relationship to a securities transaction, since the merger had already been completed. It is equally obvious that such subsequent action or inaction by the attorneys could not substantially assist the merger. . . .

Thus, the Court finds that the attorney defendants aided and abetted the violation of §10(b), Rule 10b-5, and §17(a) through their participation in the closing of the merger.

V. Appropriateness of Injunctive Relief

Although the Commission has proved past violations by the defendants, that does not end the Court's inquiry. . . . The crucial question, though, remains not whether a violation has occurred, but whether there exists a reasonable likelihood of future illegal conduct by the defendant, "something more than the mere possibility which serves to keep the case alive." *United States v. W.T. Grant Co.*, supra. Thus, the SEC must "go beyond the mere facts of past violations and demonstrate a realistic likelihood of recurrence." *SEC v. Commonwealth Chemical Securities, Inc.*, 574 F.2d 90, 100 (2d Cir. 1978). . . .

The Commission has not demonstrated that the defendants engaged in the type of repeated and persistent misconduct which usually justifies the issuance of injunctive relief. Instead, it has shown violations which principally occurred within a period of a few hours at the closing of the merger in 1969. . . . Thus, the violations proved by the SEC appear to be part of an isolated incident, unlikely to recur and insufficient to warrant an injunction. . . .

After considering the "totality of circumstances" presented here, the Court concludes that the Securities and Exchange Commission has not fulfilled its statutory obligation to make a "proper showing" that injunctive relief is necessary to prevent further violations by these defendants. Accordingly, judgment will be entered for the defendants and the complaint will be dismissed.

NOTES AND QUESTIONS

1. The Clarity of 20/20 Hindsight.   It is, of course, always useful to gauge the reasonableness and propriety of one's actions by the circumstances that existed when one acted or failed to act. Consider what would have been the position of Interstate's lawyers had they withheld their opinion and thereby forced Interstate to resolicit the stockholders' approval of the merger. Heroes they certainly would have been if, as actually did occur, the price of NSMC's shares declined, for the lawyers would then have protected the stockholders from entering into a bad deal. But what if NSMC shares increased in value, so that if the merger were to occur, it would be at an exchange less favorable to the Interstate stockholders than they were provided under the original terms? The lawyers would no longer be heroes, and their actions would appear to have been unjustified, especially since, under this scenario, NSMC's stock price did not go down, suggesting the questioned representations were not material, at least not to the market. In this light, consider further whether the court didn't really choose a middle ground, stopping short of requiring the attorneys to withdraw their opinion. Whose call should it be on whether the information is material? Does the lawyer only have a duty to raise the possibility of a material misrepresentation, or does he have to meet his client with a firmer resolve?

Consider for a moment just what *National Student Marketing* requires of the lawyer. Suppose Lord, Bissell & Brook had withdrawn its opinion. Can its lawyers stick around and otherwise help with the closing? Also, if the opinion had been withdrawn, what would NSMC have done? Note in this regard that the opinions could be waived.

Consider also the role played here by the accountants. Were they out of line in recommending resubmission to the shareholders? And of all the parties at the closing, can it be said that Marion Epley probably was in the best position to stop the transaction from going forward?

2. And What of Mr. Epley?   The SEC cast a broad net in the NSMC litigation. Epley and his firm, White & Case, were among the defendants it charged with participating in the securities laws violations. Before trial, however, a settlement was reached. Without admitting the allegations in the complaint, Epley agreed not to practice securities laws for 180 days, and the firm agreed to develop internal procedures concerning its securities practice. A premise (untested because of the settlement) underlying the SEC's case against Epley and his firm was that counsel for NSMC owed a duty to Interstate's shareholders and that that duty was breached when they failed to take steps to block the merger. What is the basis for asserting a lawyer's duty to another party when that party is represented by competent counsel and full disclosure of material adverse facts has been made to representatives of the party? What would shareholders of Interstate expect and want of Epley and White & Case?

Consider for a moment lessons concerning the practice of law that can be drawn from this case. Epley knew in advance of the closing that there would be problems with the comfort letter NSMC was required to provide, yet he failed to advise the Interstate lawyers of this fact. One might read into his conduct a very aggressive, tough approach to the practice of law and a tactical decision to withhold information until the last possible moment to pressure Interstate to make a hurried decision. Although admittedly not genteel, is such a tactic inappropriate for a lawyer? And what might counsel for Interstate have done to avoid surprises of this nature at the closing?

3. "Dirty" Pooling.   Why was NSMC in such a hurry to close its merger with Interstate on October 31? The answer to this lies in the effects of "pooling of interest" accounting on NSMC's earnings per share. Without the merger, NSMC would end the year with little earnings to report. On the other hand, with the merger completed before midnight October 31, NSMC was able to report as earnings for the year the combined amounts of itself and Interstate. This reporting technique, commonly known as the pooling of interest method of accounting, was an important consideration for the Interstate acquisition. Thus, upon the merger being closed, the greater earnings of Interstate could be combined with NSMC's loss so that an overall rise in earnings from the prior year would be reported by NSMC. Without the merger, its earnings would have dropped below the level reported in the prior year. Would an efficient market be taken in by this? Was Interstate aware of NSMC's motives for rushing the closing? "Pooling of interest" accounting is no longer acceptable under GAAP.

4. The Attorney as Aider and Abettor.   An interesting application of the aiding and abetting standard to an attorney is *SEC v. Fehn*, 97 F.3d 1276 (9th Cir. 1996), *cert. denied,* 522 U.S. 813 (1997). Fehn, an attorney, was retained by CTI Technical, Inc., when the SEC commenced its investigation of CTI's IPO. Fehn learned that CTI had not filed the Form 10-Q quarterly reports, as required by Section 15(d) of the Exchange Act, after making its IPO. Fehn also was aware that CTI had failed to disclose in its registration statement that Edwin "Bud" Wheeler was the company's promoter and controlled its nominal directors. Fehn advised Wheeler that CTI was required to file the quarterly Form 10-Q and discussed with him the need to disclose Wheeler's role in the corporation. Wheeler flatly refused to make the disclosure; Fehn later testified that he told Wheeler it was his professional opinion that such disclosures were unnecessary and that it would likely compromise Wheeler's ability to assert his Fifth Amendment privilege if CTI made full disclosure of Wheeler's status. An employee of CTI prepared a draft Form 10-Q that stated Wheeler had just recently been appointed CEO and president. It did not disclose that he promoted, incorporated, and controlled CTI. Fehn reviewed and edited the draft Form 10-Q but did not alter its disclosure misrepresenting Wheeler's status.

The court held that CTI's quarterly report violated Rule 10b-5, not only because it misrepresented Wheeler's position but also because it failed to disclose CTI's contingent liability to purchasers in the IPO who could recover because the registration statement was materially misleading in failing to disclose Wheeler's relationship to CTI. The Ninth Circuit held that Fehn's review and editing of the Form 10-Q constituted substantial assistance in CTI's securities violations. The Ninth Circuit rejected Fehn's argument that he had exercised "good faith and reasonable efforts" to obtain compliance with the securities laws; the court reasoned instead that the defense was not available since the SEC's disclosure requirements clearly required disclosure of the items Fehn concurred could be either omitted or misrepresented.

It is worth noting the following policy consideration the court invoked to support upholding a permanent injunction against Fehn:

> We observe, furthermore, that effective regulation of the issuance and trading of securities depends, fundamentally, on securities lawyers such as Fehn properly advising their clients of the disclosure requirements and other relevant provisions of the securities regulations. Securities regulation in this country is premised on open disclosure, and it is therefore incumbent upon practitioners like Fehn to be highly familiar with the disclosure requirements and to insist that their clients comply with them.

Id. at 1294.

What would result if Fehn were a labor lawyer who had been retained by CTI because of a formal investigation by the Equal Employment Opportunity Commission for alleged discriminatory promotion practices? Assume in that position that he approved and edited a Form 10-Q that did not disclose (nor did its earlier registration statement) that CTI had unlawfully discriminated against women and minorities such that it potentially was liable for substantial damages its discriminatory practices had caused present and former employees. Would the result be the same?

PROBLEM

14-18.   For the past year, Arnold and Phylis Smith have been renovating a historic hotel in downtown Atlanta, seeking to convert the property into elegant apartments. The project has been plagued by many problems, and most of the contractors have not been paid for their work. Arnold engaged Suzanne Jones, a real estate lawyer, to negotiate with the various contractors. Jones' main task has been to seek the contractors' agreement that they would not file any construction liens for nonpayment. To raise more capital, Arnold and Phylis transferred their equity in the hotel property to a new partnership and began work toward raising $5 million through the sale of limited partnership interests in a private placement.

The private offering circular was prepared by a prominent securities lawyer, A. Bove Raproach, who was unaware of the financial problems the Smiths were having with the project. Financial statements prepared by a local C.P.A., Claude Duboise, were included in the offering circular. Pursuant to standard practice, Duboise mailed a letter to all lawyers who had represented the Smiths during the past year, asking whether they were aware of any outstanding claims against the Smiths or the property being developed. In responding to Duboise's letter, Jones stated she was not aware of any outstanding claims against either the Smiths or the property. Jones therefore did not disclose that more than $3 million in overdue payments was owed by the Smiths to various contractors. Also, the offering circular did not disclose that $22,000 of its proceeds would be paid to Jones in satisfaction of the Smiths' overdue account for professional services. The offering circular stated that all proceeds would "be applied to complete the construction that remains on the property."

Interested investors were solicited with the misleading offering brochure. The offering was on an "all or nothing" basis, so that any funds raised were first placed in escrow and would revert to the investors unless a total of $5 million was raised. After three weeks of hard selling efforts, the $5 million goal was reached, and a date was set for closing the escrow and issuing the limited partnership interests to the 32 investors. Just prior to the closing, Raproach discovered, quite by accident, that substantial sums were owed to the project's contractors that were not disclosed in the offering circular. Raproach nevertheless presided over the formalities of the closing without disclosing this information to anyone.

The partnership failed two months after the offering was completed. The disappointed investors learned for the first time that over $3 million of the proceeds were paid to contractors in satisfaction of their overdue claims. Are Raproach and Jones aiders and abettors? Who are the primary participants in the disclosure violation?

2.   The SEC's Rules of Professional Conduct for Attorneys

As the financial and accounting scandals of 2001-2002 unfolded, it became apparent that attorneys advising their client-firms on transactions too frequently knew more about the officers' misconduct than they disclosed to the client-firm's directors. Therefore, it did not come as a total surprise that Sarbanes-Oxley's Section 307 directed the SEC to adopt "standards of professional conduct for attorneys appearing and practicing before the Commission." In response, the SEC adopted Part 205 of the Commission Rules of Practice. The operative provision of the new Standard of Professional Conduct is 205.3(b):

> (b) Duty to report evidence of a material violation. (1) If an attorney, appearing and practicing before the Commission in the representation of an issuer, becomes aware of evidence of a material violation by the issuer or by any officer, director, employee, or agent of the issuer, the attorney shall report such evidence to the issuer's chief legal officer (or the equivalent thereof) or to both the issuer's chief legal officer and its chief executive officer (or the equivalent thereof) [or to a qualified legal compliance committee] forthwith. . . .

A material violation is defined in Part 205.2(i) as a material breach of an applicable federal or state securities law, a material breach of fiduciary duty, "or similar violation of any . . . federal or state law." The attorney's "report" of evidence of a violation there upon triggers the obligation of the chief legal officer to undertake an inquiry to determine if a material violation has occurred, is occurring, or is about to occur. Alternatively, the chief legal officer can refer the attorney's report to a "qualified legal compliance committee," the composition and operation of which is set forth in great detail in Part 205. The attorney must also raise her concerns with the audit committee or the full board of directors (when there is no committee made up exclusively of independent directors), unless the attorney "believes that the chief legal officer or chief executive officer of the issuer . . . has provided an appropriate response within a reasonable time." Part 205.3(b)(3). When the company has a qualified legal compliance committee, the attorney, instead of lodging her report with the chief legal officer, may report the evidence of a violation to the committee. When this latter course is taken, the attorney has no further obligations under the rule.

The following excerpt from the adopting release provides a more detailed description of the scope and operation of Part 205. Notwithstanding the imprimatur of Sarbanes-Oxley, the SEC steps in adopting attorney responsibility requirements incurred significant pressure from the ABA in particular, and lawyers generally, not to disturb classic formulations of attorney-client relationships. Indeed, the SEC's consideration of Part 205 was one of its most controversial actions. The greatest sensitivities surround the question of whether it is appropriate for the SEC to develop standards for when the attorney must not only withdraw from representing a client but also that there should be some disclosure to the SEC of the attorney's resignation, i.e., "noisy withdrawal." As will be seen in the following release, the SEC initially delayed and has never returned to noisy withdrawal, so its overall approach remains "up the ladder" reporting responsibilities of attorneys who practice before the Commission.

Implementation of Standards of Professional Conduct for Attorneys
Securities Act Release No. 8185 (Jan. 29, 2003)

Section 307 of the Sarbanes-Oxley Act of 2002 requires the Commission to prescribe minimum standards of professional conduct for attorneys appearing and practicing before the Commission in any way in the representation of issuers. The standards must include a rule requiring an attorney to report evidence of a material violation of securities laws or breach of fiduciary duty or similar violation by the issuer up-the-ladder within the company to the chief legal counsel or the chief executive officer of the company (or the equivalent thereof); and, if they do not respond appropriately to the evidence, requiring the attorney to report the evidence to the audit committee, another committee of independent directors, or the full board of directors. Proposed Part 205 responds to this directive. . . . We are still considering the "noisy withdrawal" provisions of our original proposal. . . .

II.   Section-by-Section Discussion of the Final Rule

section 205.1 purpose and scope . . .

The language which we adopt today clarifies that this part does not pre-empt ethical rules in United States jurisdictions that establish more rigorous obligations than imposed by this part. At the same time, the Commission reaffirms that its rules shall prevail over any conflicting or inconsistent laws of a state or other United States jurisdiction in which an attorney is admitted or practices.

section 205.2 definitions

For purposes of this part, the following definitions apply:
   (a) Appearing and practicing before the Commission:
      (1) Means:
         (i) Transacting any business with the Commission, including communications in any form;
         (ii) Representing an issuer in a Commission administrative proceeding or in connection with any Commission investigation, inquiry, information request, or subpoena;
         (iii) Providing advice in respect of the United States securities laws or the Commission's rules or regulations thereunder regarding any document that the attorney has notice will be filed with or submitted to, or incorporated into any document that will be filed with or submitted to, the Commission, including the provision of such advice in the context of preparing, or participating in the preparation of, any such document; or
         (iv) Advising an issuer as to whether information or a statement, opinion, or other writing is required under the United States securities laws or the Commission's rules or regulations thereunder to be filed with or submitted to, or incorporated into any document that will be filed with or submitted to, the Commission; but
      (2) Does not include an attorney who:
         (i) Conducts the activities in paragraphs (a)(1)(i) through (a)(1)(iv) of this section other than in the context of providing legal services to an issuer with whom the attorney has an attorney-client relationship; or
         (ii) Is a non-appearing foreign attorney. . . .

Attorneys who advise that, under the federal securities laws, a particular document need not be incorporated into a filing, registration statement or other submission to the Commission will be covered by the revised definition. In addition, an attorney must have notice that a document he or she is preparing or assisting in preparing will be submitted to the Commission to be deemed to be "appearing and practicing" under the revised definition. The definition in the final rule thereby also clarifies that an attorney's preparation of a document (such as a contract) which he or she never intended or had notice would be submitted to the Commission, or incorporated into a document submitted to the Commission, but which subsequently is submitted to the Commission as an exhibit to or in connection with a filing, does not constitute "appearing and practicing" before the Commission. . . .

This portion of the definition will also have the effect of excluding from coverage attorneys at public broker-dealers and other issuers who are licensed to practice law and who may transact business with the Commission, but who are not in the legal department and do not provide legal services within the context of an attorney-client relationship. Non-appearing foreign attorneys, as defined below, also are not covered by this definition.

205.2(b) . . . provides:

(b) Appropriate response means a response to an attorney regarding reported evidence of a material violation as a result of which the attorney reasonably believes:

(1) That no material violation, as defined in paragraph (i) of this section, has occurred, is ongoing, or is about to occur;

(2) That the issuer has, as necessary, adopted appropriate remedial measures, including appropriate steps or sanctions to stop any material violations that are ongoing, to prevent any material violation that has yet to occur, and to remedy or otherwise appropriately address any material violation that has already occurred and to minimize the likelihood of its recurrence; or

(3) That the issuer, with the consent of the issuer's board of directors, a committee thereof to whom a report could be made pursuant to §205.3(b)(3), or a qualified legal compliance committee, has retained or directed an attorney to review the reported evidence of a material violation and either:

(i) Has substantially implemented any remedial recommendations made by such attorney after a reasonable investigation and evaluation of the reported evidence; or

(ii) Has been advised that such attorney may, consistent with his or her professional obligations, assert a colorable defense on behalf of the issuer (or the issuer's officer, director, employee, or agent, as the case may be) in any investigation or judicial or administrative proceeding relating to the reported evidence of a material violation.

The definition of "appropriate response" emphasizes that an attorney's evaluation of, and the appropriateness of an issuer's response to, evidence of material violations will be measured against a reasonableness standard. The Commission's intent is to permit attorneys to exercise their judgment as to whether a response to a report is appropriate, so long as their determination of what is an "appropriate response" is reasonable. . . .

The standard set forth in the final version of Section 205.2(b) requires the attorney to "reasonably believe" either that there is no material violation or that the issuer has taken proper remedial steps. The term "reasonably believes" is defined in Section 205.2(m). In providing that the attorney's belief that a response was appropriate be reasonable, the Commission is allowing the attorney to take into account, and the Commission to weigh, all attendant circumstances . . . [including] the amount and weight of the evidence of a material violation, the severity of the apparent material violation and the scope of the investigation into the report. . . .

The Commission believes that the revisions to this subparagraph make clear that the issuer must adopt appropriate remedial measures or sanctions to prevent future violations, redress past violations, and stop ongoing violations and consider the feasibility of restitution. . . .

Subparagraph (b)(3) permits an issuer to assert as an appropriate response that it has directed its attorney, whether employed or retained by it, to undertake an internal review of reported evidence of a material violation and has substantially implemented the recommendations made by an attorney after reasonable investigation and evaluation of the reported evidence. However, the attorney retained or directed to conduct the evaluation must have been retained or directed with the consent of the issuer's board of directors, a committee thereof to whom a report could be made pursuant to 205.3(b)(3), or a qualified legal compliance committee. . . .

205.2(e) provides:

(e) Evidence of a material violation means credible evidence, based upon which it would be unreasonable, under the circumstances, for a prudent and competent attorney not to conclude that it is reasonably likely that a material violation has occurred, is ongoing, or is about to occur. . . .

Evidence of a material violation must first be credible evidence. An attorney is obligated to report when, based upon that credible evidence, "it would be unreasonable, under the circumstances, for a prudent and competent attorney not to conclude that it is reasonably likely that a material violation has occurred, is ongoing, or is about to occur." This formulation, while intended to adopt an objective standard, also recognizes that there is a range of conduct in which an attorney may engage without being unreasonable. The "circumstances" are the circumstances at the time the attorney decides whether he or she is obligated to report the information. These circumstances may include, among others, the attorney's professional skills, background and experience, the time constraints under which the attorney is acting, the attorney's previous experience and familiarity with the client, and the availability of other lawyers with whom the lawyer may consult. . . . [A]n attorney is not required (or expected) to report "gossip, hearsay, [or] innuendo." Nor is the rule's reporting obligation triggered by "a combination of circumstances from which the attorney, in retrospect, should have drawn an inference," as one commenter feared.

On the other hand, the rule's definition of "evidence of a material violation" makes clear that the initial duty to report up-the-ladder is not triggered only when the attorney "knows" that a material violation has occurred or when the attorney "conclude[s] there has been a violation, and no reasonable fact finder could conclude otherwise." That threshold for initial reporting within the issuer is too high. Under the Commission's rule, evidence of a material violation must be reported in all circumstances in which it would be unreasonable for a prudent and competent attorney not to conclude that it is "reasonably likely" that a material violation has occurred, is ongoing, or is about to occur. To be "reasonably likely" a material violation must be more than a mere possibility, but it need not be "more likely than not." If a material violation is reasonably likely, an attorney must report evidence of this violation. The term "reasonably likely" qualifies each of the three instances when a report must be made. Thus, a report is required when it is reasonably likely a violation has occurred, when it is reasonably likely a violation is ongoing or when reasonably likely a violation is about to occur. . . .

205.2(i) provides:
(i) Material violation means a material violation of an applicable United States federal or state securities law, a material breach of fiduciary duty arising under United States federal or state law, or a similar material violation of any United States federal or state law. . . .

205.2(j) . . .
(j) Non-appearing foreign attorney . . . The final rule provides that a "non-appearing foreign attorney" does not "appear and practice before the Commission" for purposes of the rule. . . .

Foreign attorneys who provide legal advice regarding United States securities law, other than in consultation with United States counsel, are subject to the rule if they conduct activities that constitute appearing and practicing before the Commission. For example, an attorney licensed in Canada who independently advises an issuer regarding the application of Commission regulations to a periodic filing with the Commission is subject to the rule. Non-United States attorneys who do not hold themselves out as practicing United States law, but who engage in activities that constitute appearing and practicing before the Commission, are subject to the rule unless they appear and practice before the Commission only incidentally to a foreign law practice or in consultation with United States counsel. . . .

Foreign lawyers who are concerned that they may not have the expertise to identify material violations of United States law may avoid being subject to the rule by declining to advise their clients on United States law or by seeking the assistance of United States counsel when undertaking any activity that could constitute appearing and practicing before the Commission. Mere preparation of a document that may be included as an exhibit to a filing with the Commission does not constitute "appearing and practicing before the Commission" under the final rule, unless the attorney has notice that the document will be filed with or submitted to the Commission and he or she provides advice on United States securities law in preparing the document.

. . . Non-United States attorneys who believe that the requirements of the rule conflict with law or professional standards in their home jurisdiction may avoid being subject to the rule by consulting with United States counsel whenever they engage in any activity that constitutes appearing and practicing before the Commission. In addition, as discussed in Section 205.6(d) below, the Commission is also adopting a provision to protect a lawyer practicing outside the United States in circumstances where foreign law prohibits compliance with the Commission's rule. . . .

205.2(n) provides:
(n) Report means to make known to directly, either in person, by telephone, by e-mail, electronically, or in writing.

The definition for this term has not been changed from the one included in the proposed rule.

SECTION 205.3 ISSUER AS CLIENT

205.3 (a) provides:
 (a) Representing an Issuer. . . .

This section makes explicit that the client of an attorney representing an issuer before the Commission is the issuer as an entity and not the issuer's individual officers or employees that the attorney regularly interacts with and advises on the issuer's behalf. . . .

SECTION 205.4 RESPONSIBILITIES OF SUPERVISORY ATTORNEYS

(a) An attorney supervising or directing another attorney who is appearing and practicing before the Commission in the representation of an issuer is a supervisory attorney. An issuer's chief legal officer (or the equivalent thereof) is a supervisory attorney under this section.

(b) A supervisory attorney shall make reasonable efforts to ensure that a subordinate attorney, as defined in §205.5(a), that he or she supervises or directs conforms to this part. To the extent a subordinate attorney appears and practices before the Commission in the representation of an issuer, that subordinate attorney's supervisory attorneys also appear and practice before the Commission.

(c) A supervisory attorney is responsible for complying with the reporting requirements in §205.3 when a subordinate attorney has reported to the supervisory attorney evidence of a material violation. . . .

SECTION 205.5 RESPONSIBILITIES OF A SUBORDINATE ATTORNEY

(a) An attorney who appears and practices before the Commission in the representation of an issuer on a matter under the supervision or direction of another attorney (other than under the direct supervision or direction of the issuer's chief legal officer (or the equivalent thereof)) is a subordinate attorney.

(b) A subordinate attorney shall comply with this part notwithstanding that the subordinate attorney acted at the direction of or under the supervision of another person. . . .

(c) A subordinate attorney [fulfills his/her obligation by reporting to his/her supervising attorney evidence of a material violation the] subordinate attorney became aware of in appearing and practicing before the Commission.

This section confirms that a subordinate attorney is responsible for complying with the rule. We do not believe that a subordinate attorney should be exempted from the application of the rule merely because he or she operates under the supervision or at the direction of another person. . . . Indeed, because subordinate attorneys frequently perform a significant amount of work on behalf of issuers, we believe that subordinate attorneys are at least as likely (indeed, potentially more likely) to learn about evidence of material violations as supervisory attorneys.

SECTION 205.6 SANCTIONS AND DISCIPLINE . . .

(c) An attorney who complies in good faith with the provisions of this part shall not be subject to discipline or otherwise liable under inconsistent standards imposed by any state or other United States jurisdiction where the attorney is admitted or practices.

(d) An attorney practicing outside the United States shall not be required to comply with the requirements of this part to the extent that such compliance is prohibited by applicable foreign law. . . .

SECTION 205.7 NO PRIVATE RIGHT OF ACTION

(a) Nothing in this part is intended to, or does, create a private right of action against any attorney, law firm, or issuer based upon compliance or noncompliance with its provisions.

(b) Authority to enforce compliance with this part is vested exclusively in the Commission.

NOTES AND QUESTIONS

1. The Commission's Earlier Approach. Until the adoption of Part 205, the template for what the Commission held should be the securities lawyer's professional obligations was *In re Carter and Johnson*, Securities and Exchange Commission (Feb. 28, 1981). The SEC commenced a disciplinary proceeding under then Rule 2(e)—now Rule 102(e)—against two attorneys, Carter and Johnson, alleging they had engaged in "unethical or improper professional conduct." The attorneys were aware that their client, National Telephone Co., had not disclosed in its SEC reports provisions in a loan agreement that if triggered would require it to wind up its affairs. They urged the CEO, Hart, to disclose the loan covenant and Hart flatly stated he did not want the loan covenant disclosed. National's affairs deteriorated and the wind-up covenant was ultimately triggered. However, Hart refused to disclose the covenant and approved the release of a very buoyant annual report to the company's stockholders.

> The Commission is of the view that a lawyer engages in "unethical or improper professional conduct" under the following circumstances: When a lawyer with significant responsibilities in the effectuation of a company's compliance with the disclosure requirements of the federal securities laws becomes aware that his client is engaged in a substantial and continuing failure to satisfy those disclosure requirements, his continued participation violates professional standards unless he takes prompt steps to end the client's noncompliance. The Commission has determined that this interpretation will be applicable only to conduct occurring after the date of this opinion.
>
> We do not imply that a lawyer is obliged, at the risk of being held to have violated Rule 2(e), to seek to correct every isolated disclosure action or inaction which he believes to be at variance with applicable disclosure standards, although there may be isolated disclosure failures that are so serious that their correction becomes a matter of primary professional concern. It is also clear,

however, that a lawyer is not privileged to unthinkingly permit himself to be co-opted into an ongoing fraud and cast as a dupe or a shield for a wrongdoing client.

Initially, counseling accurate disclosure is sufficient, even if his advice is not accepted. But there comes a point at which a reasonable lawyer must conclude that his advice is not being followed, or even sought in good faith, and that his client is involved in a continuing course of violating the securities laws. At this critical juncture, the lawyer must take further, more affirmative steps in order to avoid the inference that he has been co-opted, willingly or unwillingly, into the scheme of nondisclosure.

The lawyer is in the best position to choose his next step. Resignation is one option, although we recognize that other considerations, including the protection of the client against foreseeable prejudice, must be taken into account in the case of withdrawal. A direct approach to the board of directors or one or more individual directors or officers may be appropriate; or he may choose to try to enlist the aid of other members of the firm's management. What is required, in short, is some prompt action that leads to the conclusion that the lawyer is engaged in efforts to correct the underlying problem, rather than having capitulated to the desires of a strong-willed, but misguided client.

Some have argued that resignation is the only permissible course when a client chooses not to comply with disclosure advice. We do not agree. Premature resignation serves neither the end of an effective lawyer-client relationship nor, in most cases, the effective administration of the securities laws. The lawyer's continued interaction with his client will ordinarily hold the greatest promise of corrective action. So long as a lawyer is acting in good faith and exerting reasonable efforts to prevent violations of the law by his client, his professional obligations have been met. In general, the best result is that which promotes the continued, strong-minded and independent participation by the lawyer.

We recognize, however, that the "best result" is not always obtainable, and that there may occur situations where the lawyer must conclude that the misconduct is so extreme or irretrievable, or the involvement of his client's management and board of directors in the misconduct is so thoroughgoing and pervasive that any action short of resignation would be futile. We would anticipate that cases where a lawyer has no choice but to resign would be rare and of an egregious nature.

Because the above standard had not been announced before the proceeding against Carter and Johnson, the Commission did not apply this standard to them and effectively dismissed the matter.

2. Comparison to the Model Rules. Compare the requirements of Part 205.3(b) with ABA Model Rule 1.13(b) (amended in August 2003), which provides:

If a lawyer for an organization knows that an officer, employee or other person associated with the organization is engaged in action, intends to act or refuses to act in a matter related to the representation that is a violation of a legal obligation to the organization, or a violation of law that reasonably might be imputed to the organization, *then* the lawyer shall proceed as is reasonably necessary in the best interest of the organization.

Are the demands of Model Rule 1.13(b) equal to those of Part 205.3(b)? Rule 1.13(b) further provides:

> Unless the lawyer reasonably believes that it is not necessary in the best interests of the organization to do so, the lawyer shall refer the matter to higher authority in the organization, including, if warranted by the circumstances, to the highest authority that can act on behalf of the organization. . . .

Paragraph (c) of Rule 1.13 provides that when the highest authority:

> fails to address in a timely and appropriate manner an action or a refusal to act, that is clearly a violation of law and . . . the lawyer reasonably believes that the violation is reasonably certain to result in substantial injury to the organization, then the lawyer may reveal information relating to the representation whether or not Rule 1.6 permits such disclosure, but only if and to the extent the lawyer reasonably believes necessary to prevent substantial injury to the organization.

Paragraph (c) does not apply to information the lawyer acquires in the defense of the organization or one of its personnel or acquired pursuant to an investigation of a violation for the organization.

For an excellent discussion of issues left open by Part 205, *see* Cramton, Cohen & Koniak, Legal and Ethical Duties of Lawyers After Sarbanes-Oxley, 49 Vill. L. Rev. 725 (2004). On the implications of companies employing qualified legal compliance committees, *see* The Qualified Legal Compliance Committee: Using the Attorney Conduct Rules to Restructure the Board of Directors, 53 Duke L.J. 517 (2003).

3. Whistleblowing. Should lawyers and accountants reveal their clients' wrongdoing—and to whom they should reveal their clients' misbehavior? As stated in National Student Marketing, the SEC's complaint caused quite a stir when it charged: "As part of the fraudulent scheme [the law firms and the partners identified in the case] . . . failed to insist that . . . shareholders be resolicited, and failing that, to . . . notify the plaintiff Commission concerning the misleading nature of the nine month financial statements." *SEC v. National Student Marketing Corp.*, [1971-1972 Transfer Binder] Fed. Sec. L. Rep. (CCH) ¶93,360 (D.D.C., filed Feb. 3, 1972). For a restrictive view of the lawyer's obligation, consider *Barker v. Henderson, Franklin, Starnes & Holt*, 797 F.2d 490, 497 (7th Cir. 1986) ("Neither lawyers nor accountants are required to tattle on their clients in the absence of some duty to disclose. To the contrary, attorneys have privileges not to disclose.").

Debate over the proper professional role of the attorney takes two forms. One focuses on the duty *to the client*: To what extent should serving the client corporation involve disclosure to the shareholders, the true owners of the enterprise? Would it be reasonable to expect attorneys to cause such disclosure, given that the decisions regarding their retention and payment for services are completely in the hands of management? *See* Slovak, The Ethics of Corporate Lawyers: A Sociological Approach, 1981 Am. B. Found. Res. J. 753. Would such disclosure provide meaningful protection? Perhaps one useful way to think about this issue, borrowing from the law and economics literature on agency costs, is to imagine the hypothetical bargain that would be reached between shareholders and management on this question. If you were a shareholder, would you insist that the corporation's lawyer have either a right or a duty to "blow the whistle"? What differences in this obligation to go up the ladder do you see between the Model Rules and Part 205? Which do you believe is most likely supported by the above hypothetical bargain approach?

The second area of debate over the attorney's duty is the so-called duty to warn, a matter dealt with in Model Rule 1.6. That is, to what extent must an attorney disclose otherwise confidential information to a third party to prevent harm to that person? Until the August 2003 amendments to Model Rule 1.6(b), the ABA's approach had little application to the securities laws because it stated the lawyer may reveal confidential information only "to the extent necessary . . . to prevent the client from committing a criminal act that the lawyer believes is likely to result in imminent death or substantial bodily harm." Now Rule 1.6 permits (but does not require) the attorney to disclose such information:

> (2) to prevent the client from committing a crime or fraud that is reasonably certain to result in substantial injury to the financial interests or property of another and in furtherance of which the client has used or is using the lawyer's services;
> (3) to prevent, mitigate or rectify substantial injury to the financial interests or property of another that is reasonably certain to result or has resulted from the client's commission of a crime or fraud in furtherance of which the client has used the lawyer's services.

In some respects, the ABA amendments closed the barn door after the horse departed. By the time the ABA acted, 42 state disciplinary rules permitted attorneys to disclose client information to prevent a client's fraud and 19 states permitted disclosure to rectify a substantial loss from the client's crime or fraud. *See also* A.L.I. Restatement (Third) of the Law Governing Lawyers §67 (2000) (lawyer may disclose when she believes it reasonably necessary to prevent fraud client intends to commit from causing substantial financial loss to third party).

4. Noisy Withdrawal. When should an attorney resign, rather than continue representation of a recalcitrant client? *In re Carter and Johnson* seems not to encourage this step. Model Rule 1.16(a)(1) provides that an attorney must resign if "the representation will result in violation of the rules of professional conduct or other law." Thus, there is no discretion with respect to the resignation question if continued representation would constitute aiding and abetting of the client's fraud or otherwise involve counseling or assisting that fraud. Rule 1.16(b) then states that the attorney may resign if such withdrawal "can be accomplished without material adverse effect on the interests of the client," or if "the client persists in a course of action involving the lawyer's services that the lawyer reasonably believes is criminal or fraudulent," or if "a client insists upon pursuing an objective that the lawyer considers repugnant or imprudent." What does Part 205 say about this? Assuming the resignation is permissible (or even required), how "public" should the resignation be? Can it be such that it creates suspicion regarding the client's activities? Or would this in itself be a breach of the duty of confidentiality? In this regard, the Official Comment to Rule 1.2 states that "[i]n some cases, withdrawal alone might be insufficient. It may be necessary for the lawyer to give notice of the fact of withdrawal and to disaffirm any opinion, document, affirmation, or the like." The following ethics opinion addresses the courses of action available to the lawyer who has just discovered that her work product has assisted her client in the commission of a fraud.

> First, the lawyer must withdraw from any representation of the client that, directly or indirectly, would have the effect of assisting the client's continuing or intended future fraud. Second, the lawyer may withdraw from all representation of the client, and must withdraw from all representation if the fact of such representation is likely to be known to and relied upon by third persons to whom the continuing fraud is directed, and the representation is therefore likely to assist in the fraud. Third, the lawyer may disavow any of her work product to prevent its use in the client's continuing or intended future fraud, even though this may have the collateral effect of disclosing inferentially client confidences obtained during the representation. . . . Fourth and finally, if the fraud is completed, and the lawyer does not know or reasonably believe that the client intends to continue the fraud or commit a future fraud by use of the lawyer's services or work product, the lawyer may withdraw from representation of the client but may not disavow any work product.

ABA Comm. on Ethics and Professional Responsibility, Formal Op. 366 (1992) (Withdrawal When a Lawyer's Services Will Otherwise Be Used to Perpetrate a Fraud).

PROBLEMS

14-19. Hillary is outside counsel to Whammo Enterprises. Lately she has been advising Whammo's general counsel, Ed, with respect to the private placement of $7 million shares pursuant to Rule 506(b). Hillary and Ed have had serious disagreements regarding whether two of the individuals expected to purchase a substantial amount of the shares are accredited purchasers. This turns out to be important, because if they are not, Whammo will not be able to raise the targeted level of $7 million by selling, as Rule 506(b) requires, to no more than 35 nonaccredited purchasers. In their last conversation, Ed told Hillary that her "work on the 506 transaction was concluded. We can take it from here." What responsibility does Hillary have under Part 205? How would this matter be decided under Model Rule 1.13?

14-20. Wilma is a real estate lawyer and has been engaged in a significant transaction for World Realty, Inc., in which a major World Realty property, GreenFields, will be leased to Shop Co. After drafting the lease contract, but before its execution with Shop Co., Wilma learned that World Realty does not hold clear title to GreenFields. Wilma brought this to the immediate attention of World Realty's general counsel. She then learned that World Realty is undertaking a public offering of its securities, that the lease of GreenFields is described prominently in the registration statement without disclosing the ongoing title problems, and that the lease with Shop Co. will be included among the exhibits to the registration statement. What responsibility does Wilma have under Part 205?

14-21.   Partial Reprise of Problem 14-11. BuyArama, Ltd. recently completed its acquisition of SaleCo. The market greeted the acquisition favorably— BuyArama's shares rose more than 20 percent as result of the acquisition. Cheryl, a member of the general counsel's staff of SaleCo, was frustrated that the senior SaleCo officers had ignored her repeated advice that the financial statements needed to disclose several significant SaleCo contingent liabilities; the financial statements were used by both companies in seeking shareholder approval of the stock-for-stock merger. Just before the completion of the acquisition, Cheryl spoke with an SEC staff person about her concerns. He made some very preliminary inquiries but decided there was not enough to justify further inquiry into the matter. A week following the acquisition's closing, the Wall Street Journal reported several issues related to SaleCo's financial reporting in the months leading up to the acquisition, the most serious being several undisclosed contingent liabilities. The story prompted a formal SEC investigation that ultimately yields a $50 million civil penalty. Has Cheryl acted in accordance with her obligations under Part 205 as well as her ethical obligations as an attorney? Is she available to receive an award as a whistleblower? *See* Exchange Act Rule 21F-4(b)(c).

14-22.   Jack, a newly minted partner with a major law firm, has been working for weeks on the public offering of preferred shares by the firm's client, Quincy Products, Inc. The securities will be registered on Form S-3, incorporating by reference Quincy's annual Form 10-K filed with the SEC two months earlier. Three weeks after the 10-K was filed, the SEC raised many questions regarding the disclosure of several significant items in the filed 10-K. Jack believes the SEC's position is correct and that Quincy's filed Form 10-K is materially misleading. For the last several days, Jack has worked with senior Quincy officials preparing a corrected Form 10-K. Last night, Jack ran into his law school classmate Jill at a party. In chatting, Jill, who works for a rival firm, observed that she, too, had done some work for Quincy, stating that she had just closed a private placement of Quincy common shares. Jack delicately inquired, "Was disclosure a problem in the transaction?" To this, Jill casually observed, "Disclosure was easy. We simply used Quincy's filed Form 10-K in the private placement memorandum." Jack, hearing that Jill had used the uncorrected Form 10-K, dropped the conversation, said he had a headache, and left the party early. What implications does Quincy's private placement have for Jack in preparing the public offering for Quincy? What should Jack do?

14-23.   Assume the same facts as in Problem 14-22, except that neither Jack nor Jill discussed Quincy at the party. Instead of going to the party, Jill stayed at her office late that evening to catch up with work that got pushed aside in the rush to complete Quincy's private placement, which closed earlier that day. While at work, Quincy's CFO, Melody, phoned to disclose the problems Quincy was having with the SEC with its most recent Form 10-K. Melody explained that Jack's firm had been working on the problem and that Melody did not want to burden Jill with the SEC problem because she thought everything would work itself out. But, as Melody explained, the firm was about to file a corrected Form 10-K that would be significantly different from the one included in the private placement brochure. Jill was speechless. What obligation does Jill have to the investors who purchased in the private placement? To Jack? To the SEC?

I.   *The Criminal Provisions of the Federal Securities Laws*

> The regulatory and penal provisions of this statute [the Securities Exchange Act] thus stand side by side in strange communion like the recruits of modern economic theory shouldering the veterans of medieval criminal law. By legislative fiat and with presidential blessings, they have set out to make the world safe for investments, to conquer dishonest security practices, and to chaperon the relations between Wall Street and the innocent public.
>
> *Herlands, Criminal Law Aspects of the Securities Exchange Act of 1934,*
> *21 Va. L. Rev. 139, 139 (1934)*

As the above quotation demonstrates, the regulatory provisions are so inter-related with the criminal provisions of the federal securities laws that the former are today increasingly enforced through a criminal proceeding, thus raising important questions about whether this is a proper use of the criminal justice system. As will be seen, the criminal sanctions available are severe, and there can be little doubt their use or even threatened use is a potent deterrent. For such a sanction, the government has several statutory provisions to consider. In addition to the criminal provisions within most of the federal securities laws, the government may be able in a particular case to prosecute the defendant for mail or wire fraud or under the Racketeering Influenced and Corrupt Organizations Act. The materials in this section provide an overview of each of these criminal provisions.

Federal criminal prosecutions are handled by the Department of Justice, generally through the local U.S. Attorney's Office. For simplicity, references throughout this section will be only to the Department of Justice. Frequently, the Department's interest is piqued by a referral from the Commission that includes information the enforcement staff has gathered in its investigation. Such referral does not always end the Commission's interest, as frequently the defendant faces parallel enforcement proceedings—civil proceedings by the Commission and criminal proceedings by the Department of Justice. Also, it is common for a member of the Commission to be assigned to work with the Department of Justice in preparing the case for trial. Rarely, however, do SEC attorneys get a special appointment that will enable them at the trial to examine witnesses or otherwise participate as an attorney of record.

The decision to make a referral to the Department of Justice involves Commission personnel at all levels, from the field investigator to the director of enforcement. Any delineation of the type of cases most likely to be referred is impressionistic at best, but the factors likely to cause a referral include whether the defendant is someone who is associated with organized crime or otherwise has a reputation as a chronic offender of the laws, whether the particular offense is of the type that is becoming increasingly a threat to investors, whether the conduct is especially egregious, and whether in connection with the violation the defendant attempted to corrupt a member of the staff. Both the SEC and the Department of Justice can proceed separately against the same defendant without placing her in double jeopardy, provided the sanction the SEC seeks is not seen as advancing the traditional goals of punishment—that is, retribution and deterrence. *See Hudson v. United States*, 522 U.S. 93 (1997).

Not only do regulatory and penal provisions coexist within the federal securities laws, but also increasingly the former depends on the latter for their enforcement. With the exception of the Investment Advisers Act, each of the federal securities laws deals with the criminal aspects of securities violations through three provisions: first, by making it a crime for any person to "willfully" violate any statutory provision as well as any rule or regulation promulgated thereunder; second, by making it a crime to willfully (and in the case of the Exchange Act, willfully and knowingly) make a false statement in a filing submitted to the SEC; and third, by establishing maximum penalties that can be imposed upon conviction. The criminal provisions for the '33 Act that appear in Section 24 and those for the '34 Act that appear in Section 32 parallel this scheme and also contain an important contrasting difference. Both the '33 and '34 Acts subject willful violations of their provisions and accompanying rules and regulations to possible criminal sanctions; however, willful misrepresentations in Commission filings under the '34 Act are sanctioned only if made "willfully and knowingly," whereas false filings pursuant to the '33 Act are sanctioned if willfully made. *See* Beveridge, Is *Mens Rea* Required for a Criminal Violation of the Federal Securities Laws?, 52 Bus. Law. 35 (1996) (review of legislative history strongly suggests "and knowingly" language was added to clarify that "willful" meant "knowingly").

The distinction between *willfully* and *knowingly* is vague, but important to the defendant wishing to avoid a criminal sanction. As the Supreme Court has observed in a non-securities law case, "Willful . . . is a word of many meanings, its construction often being influenced by its context." *Screws v. United States*, 325 U.S. 91, 101 (1945). In the civil context, willfulness generally encompasses knowing and reckless violation of a standard, *Safeco Ins. Co. of Am. v. Burr*, 551 U.S. 47, 55 (2007). In the criminal context, willful conduct exists where there is a general awareness of the wrongfulness of the conduct. *See United States v. Kaiser*, 609 F.3d 556 (2d Cir. 2010). In *United States v. Crosby*, 294 F.2d 928 (2d Cir. 1961), *cert. denied*, 368 U.S. 984 (1962), the defendant broker-dealers successfully established they did not act willfully when participating in the sale of unregistered stock; they relied in good faith upon their attorney's opinion that they were not underwriters and hence were exempt from Section 5. On the other hand, knowledge requires proof of more consciousness of guilt on the defendant's part, although this can include the defendant deliberately closing his eyes to what he had every reason to believe were the facts. *See United States v. Schlei, B.J.*, 122 F.3d 944 (11th Cir. 1997).

There is some room within the criminal proceeding for the defendant to plead ignorance of the regulation and rule allegedly violated. Such a defense is appropriate not only because of the sheer number of rules and regulations that exist, but also because of the reality that their demands are sometimes comprehensible only to one experienced in the fine art of interpreting the securities laws. While ignorance is not always bliss under the securities laws, Section 32 of the Exchange Act does provide that "no person shall be subject to imprisonment under this section for the violation of any rule or regulation if he proves that he had no knowledge of such rule or regulation." The protection provided by this provision arises defensively, i.e., the defendant despite having plead guilty to, for example, violating Rule 10b-5, can avoid imprisonment by establishing by a *preponderance* of the evidence his lack of knowledge of a SEC rule or regulation that proscribed the conduct to which he plead guilty. *See United States v. Behrens*, 713 F.3d 926 (8th Cir. 2013); *United States v. Reyes*, 577 F.3d 1069 (9th Cir. 2009). *But see United States v. Lilley*, 291 F. Supp. 989, 993 (S.D. Tex. 1968) ("proof of an ignorance of the substance of the rule, proof that they did not know that their conduct was contrary to law" would suffice; thus, because the defendants had admitted they had engaged in fraud, the essence of the Rule's proscription, the court sentenced the defendants to prison).

It is easy to understand why fraudulent practices are criminalized under the securities laws. Fraud in other settings, whether it be the sale of the Brooklyn Bridge or unimproved desert real estate, is also criminally proscribed. It can thus be seen that the securities laws specifically proscribe behavior that is common to criminal violations and for which there is usually a tangible victim. But what of conduct that is not inherently fraudulent and for which there is no clear victim? As you are now painfully aware, the sweep of the securities laws is broad, including many directives that serve only a regulatory function. The securities acts' criminal provisions, however, do not distinguish between offenses that are inherently fraudulent and those that are merely regulatory. Moreover, the victim of a securities law violation is frequently only the ethereal notion of investor or public confidence or corporate suffrage. To be sure, these are important concerns, but the absence of a tangible victim of the violation should introduce some caution into the decision to prosecute that violation criminally, rather than civilly. The next case illustrates such a use of the criminal prosecution and also sheds light on the meaning and distinction between willfulness and knowledge.

United States v. Dixon
536 F.2d 1388 (2d Cir. 1976)

[Lloyd Dixon, Jr., was the president of AVM Corporation, a company subject to the Exchange Act's reporting requirements. Dixon was prosecuted because AVM's proxy statement and annual report on Form 10-K failed to disclose loans to him by AVM. The disclosure requirements of that time required registrants to disclose on their proxy statements an officer's indebtedness to the issuer if it exceeded $10,000. Similar disclosure was required on the registrant's Form 10-K if the officer's loan exceeded $20,000. Through most of 1970, Dixon's indebtedness to AVM was in excess of $65,000. However, just before the close of AVM's fiscal year, Dixon instructed AVM's secretary, Lewis, to switch $9,000 of the debt to Dixon's father's account and $5,000 of the debt was reduced when Lewis borrowed money from the company and used the loan to reduce Dixon's account by $5,000. Finally, Dixon paid $30,000 of the debt with a recently obtained bank loan. As a result, Dixon's debt to AVM on December 31, 1970, was $19,100.

Then, in February 1971, Dixon took out a new loan with AVM, which he used to retire the bank loan and settle Lewis's account with AVM. AVM's filings were made by its general counsel, Entwisle, who was never informed by Dixon of his indebtedness to the company.

Counts II and VI of the indictment against Dixon were for "willfully" violating the disclosure requirements of the proxy rules and reporting requirements, respectively, by failing to disclose his indebtedness to AVM. Dixon offered a technical justification for his nondisclosure, asserting that he thought the "SEC rules" provided for a $20,000 exemption (both for the proxy statement and Form 10-K) determined on the basis of the *year-end* indebtedness. The Commission's rules, however, required disclosure if the loan balance *at any time* during the year exceeded the prescribed amount. Ultimately, the amount of the loans was disclosed in a company press release and on Form 8-K when Lewis began reviewing AVM's books shortly after he learned that Dixon was under investigation by the grand jury for possible bribery of municipal officials.

The jury found Dixon guilty, and the judge sentenced him to one year's imprisonment on each count (with the sentences to run concurrently) and a $10,000 fine for each count.]

FRIENDLY, J. . . . The failure to include a statement of Dixon's indebtedness in the proxy statement and a Schedule II in the 10-K report were clear violations of . . . the language of the first clause of §32(a). The principal questions before us are whether Dixon was shown to have had the state of mind required for a conviction and whether the jury was properly charged.

In *United States v. Peltz*, 433 F.2d 48, 54-55 (2d Cir. 1970), *cert. denied*, 401 U.S. 955 (1971), we pointed out that in regard to violations of the statute or applicable rules or regulations, §32(a) requires only willfulness; that the "willfully and knowingly" language occurs only in the second clause of §32(a) relating to false or misleading statements in various papers required to be filed; that the final proviso that "no person shall be subject to imprisonment under this section for the violation of any rule or regulation if he proves that he had no knowledge of such rule or regulation" shows that "A person can willfully violate an SEC rule even if he does not know of its existence"; and that whatever may be true in other contexts,[5] "willfully" thus has a more restricted meaning in §32(a). However, since the term must have some meaning, we held, as the late Judge Herlands wrote in the very year the statute was passed and long before his appointment to the federal bench, the prosecution need only establish "a realization on the defendant's part that he was doing a wrongful act," Criminal Law Aspects of the Securities Exchange Act of 1934, 21 U. Va. L. Rev. 139, 144-49 (1934); it is necessary, we added, only that the act be "wrongful under the securities laws and that the knowingly wrongful act involve a significant risk of effecting the violation that has occurred."

---

5. As the Supreme Court has pointed out, "'[W]illful' is a word 'of many meanings, its construction often being influenced by its context.'" *Screws v. United States*, 325 U.S. 91, 101 (1945), quoting *Spies v. United States*, 317 U.S. 492, 497 (1943). The Model Penal Code would have requirements of "willfulness" satisfied by proof that the person had acted "knowingly." ALI Proposed Official Draft §2.02 (1962).

While evidence was scarcely needed to show that the chief officer of a corporation required to file 10-K reports and issue proxy statements knew that the content of these was prescribed by statute or rule, the testimony of Lewis and Entwisle sufficed to meet any burden the Government had on that score. Indeed, Dixon does not deny his knowledge that there were SEC rules requiring the reporting of loans to officers, of which there clearly was sufficient evidence; his contention is that he was incorrectly informed of their content. As the sentencing minutes show, Chief Judge Curtin believed Dixon knew that the exemptive provisions of those rules were not satisfied by a sufficiently low balance at year-end, however high the figure had previously been. Dixon contends the evidence of the latter was not sufficient to convince a reasonable juror beyond a reasonable doubt, *United States v. Taylor*, 464 F.2d 240 (2d Cir. 1972). Both the factual issue and the question of the effect of a decision on it favorable to Dixon may be close ones, but we need not resolve them. We do not have here the case of a defendant manifesting an honest belief that he was complying with the law. Dixon did a "wrongful act," in the sense of our decision in *Peltz*, when he caused the corporate books to show, as of December 31, 1970, debts of his father and of Lewis which in fact were his own. True, Dixon may have thought his year-end thimblerig would provide escape from a rule different from the one that existed. But such acts are wrongful "under the Securities Acts" if they lead, as here, to the very violations that would have been prevented if the defendant had acted with the aim of scrupulously obeying the rules (which would have necessarily involved correctly ascertaining them) rather than of avoiding them. Such an intention to deceive is enough to meet the modest requirements of the first clause of §32(a) when violations occur. . . .

PROBLEM

14-24. Elaine Howard, a noted actress, was retained by Alpha Investments Corporation of Los Angeles to narrate and appear in a promotional video to help sell some real estate limited partnership interests sponsored by Alpha. The Alpha video was very slick and attracted a good deal of interest after being shown to various investment clubs and at some continuing education seminars to doctors and lawyers. Unfortunately, it was riddled with fraud as to the intended use of the proceeds. The partnership interests are being offered pursuant to Regulation A.

Howard's involvement was limited to a single day's work, but during her negotiations with Alpha and the course of that day, she became increasingly concerned about the character and integrity of the promoters. At one point, she questioned one of the promoters how a specific parcel of land that Howard knew was within the city's designated green belt could possibly be the subject of the limited partnership offering. She received a disturbingly evasive answer. Howard asked pointedly whether the partnership interests were registered "with the authorities." Her inquiry was more or less informed by a former marriage to a Wall Street securities lawyer. To this inquiry, Archie Muldoon, one of the promoters remarked, "The deal was just too solid to require its approval by the feds." And later a technician whispered to her at one point that the principal promoter had once done "some jail time." Nonetheless, she raised no objections and did her work as directed.

Would a criminal prosecution of Howard under the securities laws be successful?

NOTES AND QUESTIONS

1.   Old Wine in New Bottle?   Section 807 of the Sarbanes-Oxley Act added 18 U.S.C. §1348 to the prosecutor's arsenal, proscribing "securities fraud" to reach anyone who "knowingly executes, or attempts to execute, a scheme or artifice to defraud any person in connection with any security" of a reporting company or "to obtain, by means of false or fraudulent . . . representations . . . any money . . . in connection with the purchase or sale of any security" of a reporting company. The legislative history reflects that Congress felt prosecutors were hobbled by existing fraud provisions by, for example, the necessity of proving the willful violation of complex technical securities provisions as well as satisfying a technical requirement of establishing the use of the mails, the use of an instrumentality of interstate commerce, or the actual purchase or sale of a security. Hence, the new securities fraud provision is believed to provide needed enforcement flexibility. Are these complaints of the existing securities law criminal provisions well taken? *See generally* Note, A New Arrow in the Quiver of Federal Securities Fraud Prosecutors: Section 807 of the Sarbanes-Oxley Act of 2002 (18 U.S.C. §1348), 81 Wash. U. L.Q. 801 (2003).

2.   Is Moral Culpability a Necessary Condition for Criminality?   Why are willful offenses of any rule or regulation of the securities laws subject to criminal prosecution? What is gained by so sanctioning regulatory violations? Why wasn't an SEC civil enforcement action sufficient protection of the public interest in Dixon? Did Mr. Dixon's offense merit not only a criminal sanction, but also imprisonment? One of the most dramatic events of the 1980s was the criminalization of the securities laws. Many of the offenses prosecuted criminally involved insider trading, but the prosecutions that riveted public attention were those involving Messrs. Ivan Boesky and Michael Milken, each a major figure in investment banking, who were criminally prosecuted and incurred significant criminal sanctions as a result of their plea bargains. The larger portion of their offenses was not insider trading, but various disclosure violations they engaged in to conceal their significant ownership interest in certain takeover stocks. Sometimes, their lack of candor for such ownership also concealed a violation of the Commission's net capital rule. As we will see in Chapter 18, the net capital rule is the most complex of the Commission's regulatory provisions. Overall, the net capital rule is designed to preserve broker-dealers' solvency and to protect their customers. Is this the type of conduct that merits criminal prosecution? Compare these questions to the following views on whether economic-regulatory violations should be criminal offenses.

Typically the conduct prohibited by economic regulatory laws is not immediately distinguishable from modes of business behavior that are not only socially acceptable, but affirmatively desirable in an economy founded upon an ideology (not denied by the regulatory regime itself) of free enterprise and the profit motive. Distinctions there are, of course, between salutary entrepreneurial practices and those which threaten the values of the very regime of economic freedom. And it is possible to reason convincingly that the harms done to the economic order by violations of many of these regulatory laws are of a magnitude that dwarf in significance the lower-class property offenses. But the point is that these perceptions require distinguishing and reasoning processes that are not the normal governors of the passion of moral disapproval. . . .

The consequences of the absence of sustained public moral resentment for the effective use of the criminal sanction may be briefly stated. The central distinguishing aspect of the criminal sanction appears to be the stigmatization of the morally culpable. . . . Without moral culpability there is in a democratic community an explicable and justifiable reluctance to affix the stigma of blame. This perhaps is the basic explanation, rather than the selfish machinations of business interests, for the reluctance of administrators and prosecutors to invoke the criminal sanction, the reluctance of jurors to find guilt and the reluctance of judges to impose strong penalties. And beyond its effect on enforcement, the absence of moral opprobrium interferes in another more subtle way with achieving compliance. Fear of being caught and punished does not exhaust the deterrent mechanism of the criminal law. It is supplemented by the personal disinclination to act in violation of the law's commands, apart from immediate fear of being punished. One would suppose that especially in the case of those who normally regard themselves as respectable, proper and law-abiding the appeal to act in accordance with conscience is relatively great. But where the violation is not generally regarded as ethically reprehensible, either by the community at large or by the class of businessmen itself, the private appeal to conscience is at its minimum and being convicted and fined may have little more impact than a bad selling season.

Kadish, Some Observations on the Use of Criminal Sanctions in Enforcing Economic Regulations, 30 U. Chi. L. Rev. 423, 436-437 (1963). *See also* H.L. Packer, The Limits of the Criminal Sanction 359 (1968) (arguing that "moral outrage" is a necessary, but not a sufficient condition for criminal liability).

What factors other than moral culpability should enter into the decision to initiate a criminal prosecution? For example, should the prosecutor be more willing to prosecute criminally in instances where those harmed by the violation lack an effective private remedy? *See generally* Coffee, Does "Unlawful" Mean "Criminal"? Reflections on the Disappearing Tort/Crime Distinction in American Law, 71 B.U. L. Rev. 193 (1991). And, should the substantive elements of a regulation be interpreted differently depending on whether the enforcement is in the civil or criminal arena? *See* Sachs, Harmonizing Civil and Criminal Enforcement of Federal Regulatory Statutes: The Case of the Securities Exchange Act of 1934, 2001 U. Ill. L. Rev. 1025.

15

The Regulation of Insider Trading

A. Introduction

From the earliest congressional hearings leading to the adoption of the federal securities laws to the present, *insider trading*—for our purposes, a term of art referring generally to any unlawful trading by persons possessing material non-public information, whether or not the trader is truly a corporate "insider"—has been a subject of both fascination and concern. Reasonable or not, a fear that the average investor would respond to the belief that systematic trading advantages accrue to those "in the know" (corporate executives, their families, and friends) by withdrawing from the securities marketplace has echoed repeatedly. Also, the attack against insider trading, a campaign for fair play in the stock markets, has had enduring political appeal. In some sense, it is a "brand" symbol for American-style securities regulation. *See* Langevoort, Rereading *Cady, Roberts:* The Ideology and Practice of Insider Trading Regulation, 99 Colum. L. Rev. 1319 (1999).

As anyone in a course on securities regulation is probably already well aware, Congress has never defined with any degree of precision the nature of the insider trading prohibition. Originally, the Securities Exchange Act of 1934 sought to deal with the problem only by forcing full disclosure by issuers via the continuing reporting obligation (reducing somewhat the opportunity to exploit an informational advantage) and by creating in Section 16 a scheme for the reporting of securities transactions by *certain* insiders and a bar (enforceable only privately) against short-swing trading by such insiders. Plainly, however, those specific mechanisms do not even purport to reach the full range of perceived trading abuses.

As concern about insider trading grew in the years after 1934, the search began for other means for reaching these abuses. The natural candidate was Rule 10b-5, and that general antifraud prohibition has since become the most important regulatory tool. Building on the common law of fraud, which had in many cases declared fraudulent the exploitation of inside information by corporate insiders in face-to-face transactions, the doctrinal structure of Rule 10b-5 was enlarged to cover open-market insider trading in two landmark cases: the SEC's decision in *Cady, Roberts & Co.*, 40 S.E.C. 907 (1961), and the Second Circuit endorsement in *SEC v. Texas Gulf Sulphur Co.*, 401 F.2d 833 (2d Cir. 1968) (en banc), *cert. denied*, 394 U.S. 976 (1969). Both decisions premised the necessary finding of fraud on the unfairness of allowing insiders to profit from their special access to sensitive information—an unfairness, according to the court in *Texas Gulf Sulphur*, that frustrates "the justifiable expectation of the securities marketplace that all investors trading on impersonal exchanges have relatively equal access to material information." *Id.* at 848.

But herein lies a problem. The elements of a Rule 10b-5 case (e.g., deception, reliance, scienter) are reasonably well suited to instances of false publicity and similar frauds, whether involving affirmative misrepresentations or half-truths. They fit awkwardly, however, when applied to conduct the existence of which is hidden from public view, not meant (or even having the capacity) to mislead. In what sense is open-market insider trading *deceptive*, as opposed to unfair? Had the insider simply abstained from trading, as was his or her principal obligation, those on the other side of the transaction presumably would have traded anyway. Much of the conceptual difficulty in the law of insider trading is the product of a misfit between the broad fairness-based aim of the prohibition and the narrower statutory mechanism that must be used to combat it.

The economics of insider trading regulation are uncertain. Some economics-oriented legal scholars remain convinced that insider trading regulation is both unnecessary and counterproductive in that it frustrates prompt price adjustment to new private information. Others justify restriction on a diverse set of grounds: the reduction of informational asymmetry as a means of lowering market transaction costs, the elimination of disincentives to prompt public disclosure of information by management, and—perhaps most commonly—the desire to protect confidential information as a form of corporate property. Naturally, one's answer to why insider trading should be regulated determines both who should regulate (federal, state, or private arrangements) and how regulation should be designed.

The stress on "equal access" that is such a big part of insider trading law easily extends to a range of issues in today's high-tech trading environment. Does high-speed algorithmic trading make a mockery of "equal access"? Is it wrong for an exchange to sell data feeds to investors who pay premium prices for quicker access (or are allowed to co-locate their computers slightly nearer the source of the feed)? For a brokerage firm to sell (or give away) advance notice of its analysts' recommendation changes to preferred clients? The New York State Attorney General's Office has raised concerns about a variety of "preferred access" practices, terming these issues "Insider Trading 2.0." For a good discussion of the economics behind these and many other contemporary legal issues, *see* Fox, Glosten & Rauterberg, Informed Trading and Its Regulation, 43 J. Corp. L. 817 (2018).

B.   The Source of a Duty to Abstain or Disclose

|| **Chiarella v. United States**
445 U.S. 222 (1980)

POWELL, J. The question in this case is whether a person who learns from the confidential documents of one corporation that it is planning an attempt to secure control of a second corporation violates §10(b) of the Securities Exchange Act of 1934 if he fails to disclose the impending takeover before trading in the target company's securities.

I

Petitioner is a printer by trade. In 1975 and 1976, he worked as a "markup man" in the New York composing room of Pandick Press, a financial printer. Among documents that petitioner handled were five announcements of corporate takeover bids. When these documents were delivered to the printer, the identities of the acquiring and target corporations were concealed by blank spaces or false names. The true names were sent to the printer on the night of the final printing.

The petitioner, however, was able to deduce the names of the target companies before the final printing from other information contained in the documents. Without disclosing his knowledge, petitioner purchased stock in the target companies and sold the shares immediately after the takeover attempts were made public. By this method, petitioner realized a gain of slightly more than $30,000 in the course of 14 months. . . .

II

. . . [A]dministrative and judicial interpretations have established that silence in connection with the purchase or sale of securities may operate as a fraud actionable under §10(b) despite the absence of statutory language or legislative history specifically addressing the legality of nondisclosure. But such liability is premised upon a duty to disclose arising from a relationship of trust and confidence between parties to a transaction. Application of a duty to disclose prior to trading guarantees that corporate insiders, who have an obligation to place the shareholder's welfare before their own, will not benefit personally through fraudulent use of material, nonpublic information. . . .

III

. . . [N]ot every instance of financial unfairness constitutes fraudulent activity under §10(b). *See Santa Fe Industries, Inc. v. Green*, 430 U.S. 462, 474-477

(1977). . . . [T]he element required to make silence fraudulent—a duty to disclose—is absent in this case. No duty could arise from petitioner's relationship with the sellers of the target company's securities, for petitioner had no prior dealings with them. He was not their agent, he was not a fiduciary, he was not a person in whom the sellers had placed their trust and confidence. He was, in fact, a complete stranger who dealt with the sellers only through impersonal market transactions.

We cannot affirm petitioner's conviction without recognizing a general duty between all participants in market transactions to forgo actions based on material, nonpublic information. Formulation of such a broad duty, which departs radically from the established doctrine that duty arises from a specific relationship between two parties, should not be undertaken absent some explicit evidence of congressional intent.

As we have seen, no such evidence emerges from the language or legislative history of §10(b). Moreover, neither the Congress nor the Commission ever has adopted a parity-of-information rule. Instead the problems caused by misuse of market information have been addressed by detailed and sophisticated regulation that recognizes when use of market information may not harm operation of the securities markets. For example, the Williams Act limits but does not completely prohibit a tender offeror's purchases of target corporation stock before public announcement of the offer. Congress' careful action in this and other areas contrasts, and is in some tension, with the broad rule of liability we are asked to adopt in this case.

Indeed, the theory upon which the petitioner was convicted is at odds with the Commission's view of §10(b) as applied to activity that has the same effect on sellers as the petitioner's purchases. "Warehousing" takes place when a corporation gives advance notice of its intention to launch a tender offer to institutional investors who then are able to purchase stock in the target company before the tender offer is made public and the price of shares rises. In this case, as in warehousing, a buyer of securities purchases stock in a target corporation on the basis of market information which is unknown to the seller. In both of these situations, the seller's behavior presumably would be altered if he had the nonpublic information. Significantly, however, the Commission has acted to bar warehousing under its authority to regulate tender offers after recognizing that action under §10(b) would rest on a "somewhat different theory" than that previously used to regulate insider trading as fraudulent activity.

We see no basis for applying such a new and different theory of liability in this case. As we have emphasized before, the 1934 Act cannot be read "'more broadly than its language and the statutory scheme reasonably permit.'" *Touche Ross & Co. v. Redington*, 442 U.S. 560, 578 (1979), quoting *SEC v. Sloan*, 436 U.S. 103 (1978). Section 10(b) is aptly described as a catchall provision, but what it catches must be fraud. When an allegation of fraud is based upon nondisclosure, there can be no fraud absent a duty to speak. We hold that a duty to disclose under §10(b) does not arise from the mere possession of nonpublic market information. The contrary result is without support in the legislative history of §10(b) and would be inconsistent with the careful plan that Congress has enacted for regulation of the securities markets. *Cf. Santa Fe Industries, Inc. v. Green*, 430 U.S. at 479. . . .

[Having decided that Chiarella had not breached any disclosure duty to marketplace traders, the Court turned to an alternative theory presented by the government, that a fraud occurred as a result of Chiarella's misappropriation of confidential information from his employer. The Court did not consider the merits of this argument, finding that the jury had not been charged properly with respect to a violation on this theory. We consider the post-*Chiarella* evolution of this theory infra.

Justices Stevens and Brennan concurred, and Chief Justice Burger and Justices Blackmun and Marshall dissented. The Stevens and Burger opinions raised the possibility that, at least in a case properly pleaded, some version of the misappropriation theory could form the basis for liability for trading even absent a fiduciary relationship between the trader and others in the marketplace.]

BLACKMUN, J. (dissenting). . . . I, of course, agree with the Court that a relationship of trust can establish a duty to disclose under §10(b) and Rule 10b-5. But I do not agree that a failure to disclose violates the Rule only when the responsibilities of a relationship of that kind have been breached. As applied to this case, the Court's approach unduly minimizes the importance of petitioner's access to confidential information that the honest investor no matter how diligently he tried, could not legally obtain. In doing so, it further advances an interpretation of §10(b) and Rule 10b-5 that stops short of their full implications. Although the Court draws support for its position from certain precedent, I find its decision neither fully consistent with developments in the common law of fraud, nor fully in step with administrative and judicial application of Rule 10b-5 to "insider" trading.

The common law of actionable misrepresentation long has treated the possession of "special facts" as a key ingredient in the duty to disclose. *See Strong v. Repide*, 213 U.S. 419, 431-433 (1909). . . . Traditionally, this factor has been prominent in cases involving confidential or fiduciary relations, where one party's inferiority of knowledge and dependence upon fair treatment is a matter of legal definition, as well as in cases where one party is on notice that the other is "acting under a mistaken belief with respect to a material fact." *Frigitemp Corp. v. Financial Dynamics Fund, Inc.*, 524 F.2d 275, 283 (CA2 1975); *see also* Restatement of Torts §551 (1938). Even at common law, however, there has been a trend away from strict adherence to the harsh maxim caveat emptor and toward a more flexible, less formalistic understanding of the duty to disclose. *See, e.g.*, Keeton, Fraud—Concealment and Non-Disclosure, 15 Texas L. Rev. 1, 31 (1936). Steps have been taken toward application of the "special facts" doctrine in a broader array of contexts where one party's superior knowledge of essential facts renders a transaction without disclosure inherently unfair. . . .

By its narrow construction of §10(b) and Rule 10b-5, the Court places the federal securities laws in the rearguard of this movement, a position opposite to the expectations of Congress at the time the securities laws were enacted. . . . I cannot agree that the statute and Rule are so limited. . . .

NOTES AND QUESTIONS

1. A Critique. The negative implication of *Chiarella* seems clear: A person does owe an affirmative duty of disclosure to marketplace traders if she stands in a direct or indirect fiduciary relationship with them. From what source does Justice Powell purport to derive this rule? Language or legislative history? The common law? If the latter, does the Court's suggestion (later made explicit in *Dirks v. SEC*, 463 U.S. 646 (1983), discussed infra) that caveat emptor necessarily prevails absent a fiduciary relationship accurately describe the common law as it stood when Rule 10b-5 was adopted? As it stands today? *See* Restatement (Second) of Torts §551 (1976); *Ollerman v. O'Rourke Co.*, 288 N.W.2d 95 (Wis. 1980) (basic standards of honesty and fair play as giving rise to a duty to disclose). If not, why did the Court choose to draw this line? What purpose is its fiduciary nexus test really designed to serve? Is the Court's own test a meaningful one when applied to situations where an insider *sells* stock? How do we establish a fiduciary relationship for the benefit of investors—theretofore strangers to the company—purchasing its stock? *See Chiarella*, 445 U.S. at 227 n.8 (citing *Gratz v. Claughton*, 187 F.2d 46, 49 (2d Cir. 1951) ("[I]t would be a sorry distinction to allow [an insider] to use the advantage of his position to induce the buyer into the position of a beneficiary although he was forbidden to do so once the buyer had become one.")). What about the situation where an insider uses inside information to *forgo* a purchase or sale that had been contemplated or planned? *See* Fried, Insider Abstention, 113 Yale L.J. 455 (2004).

2. Who Is an Insider? *Chiarella* makes fairly clear that the category of insiders owing fiduciary duties to corporate shareholders includes all officers and directors of the issuer. Does it extend also to all corporate employees? The prevailing view seems to be yes. Why? Should the prohibition also extend to the issuer itself (e.g., when it engages in a program of open market repurchases of its shares)? Again, the prevailing view suggests so. *See Shaw v. Digital Equipment Corp.*, 82 F.3d 1194, 1203-1204 (1st Cir. 1996) (dicta). But is it really accurate to say that the issuer itself stands in a fiduciary relationship to its shareholders?

3. Material Nonpublic Information. Most courts have used the same definition of materiality used in the securities laws generally—the "reasonable shareholder"/"total mix" test stated in *TSC Corp. v. Northway*—for insider trading purposes. *E.g., SEC v. Bausch & Lomb Inc.*, 565 F.2d 8, 18 (2d Cir. 1977). Thus, the same judgmental problems about ripeness and soft information occur here as well. In the *Texas Gulf Sulphur* case, noted earlier, the court concluded that the existence of a core drilling sample, indicating the strong possibility—though not certainty—of a rich mineral discovery, was material information, invoking a test that asks the fact-finder to balance the likelihood that a significant event will occur against its magnitude if it should occur. In many cases (especially with respect to relatively inactive investors), the fact of the defendant's own trading is considered probative of materiality.

On the meaning of *nonpublic*, the significant question is whether an insider must wait until the information is reasonably accessible to all investors (e.g., reported in the newspapers or on some widely disseminated web site). Or is it enough that the company has simply released it to (or that it was otherwise through previous leaks in the hands of) a substantial number of investors, on the assumption that that is all it takes to have an immediate market impact (and thus the loss of the "unfair" trading opportunity for the insider)? A "public access" approach is suggested in *Faberge Inc.*, 45 S.E.C. 249, 256 (1973), where the Commission indicated that information must be disclosed "in a manner calculated to reach the securities marketplace in general through recognized channels of distribution, and public investors must be afforded a reasonable waiting period to react to the information." *See also Texas Gulf Sulphur*, supra, where the court stated that the defendant in question "should have waited until the news could reasonably have been expected to appear over the media of widest circulation, the Dow Jones broad tape, rather than hastening to insure an advantage to himself and his broker son-in-law." 401 F.2d at 854. Does this mean he could have traded instantly upon the news' appearance on the tape (i.e., with phone in hand, watching the tape)? In contrast to this notion of general access, the court in *United States v. Libera*, 989 F.2d 596, 601 (2d Cir. 1993), suggested that the better approach is simply to ask whether the information has yet been fully impounded in market price, on the assumption that if it has—whether the general public has access or not—the opportunity for wrongful profit has disappeared. Which approach would you favor? One issue that often arises is where public media is speculating about the information (e.g., an imminent takeover). Can insiders use that as a justification for trading? Courts here have insisted that there be true informational parity: It is not enough if the public *thinks* a merger is likely, when the insider *knows* that it is a sure thing. *See SEC v. Mayhew*, 121 F.3d 44 (2d Cir. 1997).

4. Types of Securities. *Chiarella* makes clear the duty of insiders to abstain or disclose with respect to common stock, since there the existence of a fiduciary duty to the shareholder is well established. But what of insider trading in options? Prior to 1984, a number of courts found no duty of disclosure owing to options traders, since they are not necessarily shareholders and thus not the intended beneficiary of any recognized fiduciary duty owed by corporate insiders. *See Leventhall v. General Dynamics Corp.*, 704 F.2d 407 (8th Cir.), *cert. denied*, 464 U.S. 806 (1983). However, in the Insider Trading Sanctions Act of 1984, Congress closed this potential loophole by adding Section 20(d) of the Securities Exchange Act, making it unlawful to trade in any derivative instruments while in possession of material nonpublic information whenever trading in the underlying security would be prohibited. But this deals only with securities-based derivative instruments. *See* Yadav, Insider Trading in Derivative Instruments, 103 Geo. L.J. 381 (2015). What about insider trading in bonds or debentures? Are debt holders the beneficiaries of a relationship of trust or confidence with corporate insiders? *See* Pitt & Groskaufmanis, A Tale of Two Instruments: Insider Trading in Non-Equity Securities, 49 Bus. Law. 187 (1993).

5. Scienter. What is the necessary state of mind for an insider trading violation? Is it necessary that the insider actually be seeking to profit from the information in question (i.e., to trade "on the basis of" the information)? Or is it enough to show that the insider possessed the information and was aware that the information was nonpublic? For some time, the SEC expressed a strong preference for the "possession" test, and received some judicial support for this view. *See United States v. Teicher*, 987 F.2d 112 (2d Cir. 1993). But a challenge then emerged. In *SEC v. Adler*, 137 F.3d 1325 (11th Cir. 1998), an insider twice allegedly sold stock while in possession of bad news about his company's financial condition. He argued with respect to one of the sales that he had already made plans to sell the stock, in part because he needed money to purchase an 18-wheel truck for his son. Citing a variety of sources (including dicta from *Chiarella*), the court held that there is no violation of Rule 10b-5 unless there is a causal connection between the receipt of the information and the trading. However, it determined that upon a showing of possession by the SEC, a strong inference arises of causation, so that it becomes the defendant's burden to show that there was no causation. Applying this standard, the court reversed the district court's grant of summary judgment for the defendant, finding it a triable issue of fact as to whether the defendant had successfully rebutted the presumption of misuse. In response to Adler and similar holdings (*e.g., United States v. Smith*, 155 F.3d 1051 (9th Cir. 1998) (criminal proceeding)), the SEC then adopted Rule 10b5-1. Selective Disclosure and Insider Trading, Securities Act Release No. 7881 (Aug. 15, 2000). It defines trading "on the basis of" inside information simply in terms of whether the trader was "aware" of the information at the time of the trade. However, the Rule provides an affirmative defense if the trader can show that the trade was executed pursuant to a binding contract, specific instruction, or written trading plan that was entered into before the trader became aware of the information.

This latter defense has led to the widespread adoption of "Rule 10b5-1 plans," designed to enable insiders to engage in regularly scheduled transactions (usually sales of stock) without having to worry about later-acquired confidential information. Under the Rule, such plans must (1) specify the amount of securities to be traded and the price and date of the transaction; (2) include a written formula for determining amount, price, and date; or (3) not permit the insider to exercise any subsequent influence over how, when, or whether to effect the purchase or sales, so long as the broker or other who is granted that discretion is not aware of any material nonpublic information when making those decisions. For interesting discussions, *see* Horwich, The Origin, Application, Validity and Potential Misuse of Rule 10b5-1, 62 Bus. Law. 913 (2007); Henderson, Insider Trading and CEO Pay, 64 Vand. L. Rev. 505 (2011) (10b5-1 plans can be part of a "bargain" between the board and the issuer's executives about potential trading profits). One study showed that 10b5-1 plans outperformed the market by 3.6 percent over a six-month period after initiation, leading to the suspicion that they are indeed strategic. *See* Jagolinzer, SEC Rule 10b5-1 and Insiders' Strategic Trade, 55 Mgmt. Sci. 224 (2009).

The scienter issue becomes particularly vexing where a large financial institution is the purchaser of shares. Suppose one department of the firm has insider status (e.g., as a result of an investment banking relationship) and learns material nonpublic information. A different department trades for the firm's own account without actually knowing the information. Should the firm's imputed knowledge, together with its trading, be enough to establish a violation of Rule 10b-5?

C. *"Outsider" Trading: Corporate Connections*

After *Chiarella*, it is clear that true insiders—corporate officers and directors, at the very least—are subject to the "abstain or disclose" rule. What about persons who have some other form of contractual association with the issuer—for instance, the company's outside attorneys or accountants? On this latter point, the Supreme Court construing *Chiarella* in the *Dirks* case, infra, stated:

> Under certain circumstances, such as where corporate information is revealed legitimately to an underwriter, accountant, lawyer or consultant working for the corporation, these outsiders may become fiduciaries of the shareholders. The basis for recognizing this fiduciary duty is not simply that such persons acquired nonpublic corporate information, but rather that they have entered into a special confidential relationship in the conduct of the business of the enterprise and are given access to the information solely for corporate purposes. . . . For such a relationship to be imposed, however, the corporation must expect the outsider to keep the undisclosed nonpublic information confidential, and the relationship must at least imply such a duty.

463 U.S. at 655 n.14.

PROBLEM

15-1. Loss, Banker & Biddle is a large law firm that often does legal work for emerging high-tech companies. You are the senior securities partner at the firm, designated as the person to advise firm partners and employees regarding personal trading activities.

    a. John Bugle, another senior partner, owns a substantial number of Wizardry Graphics Inc. shares, which he acquired when he helped the company go public a few years ago. Wizardry continues to be a client of Loss, Banker & Biddle. During the past year, Bugle and his investment adviser have begun a plan of selling some of the Wizardry shares on a regular basis to generate additional income. On May 15, one of the litigation partners of the firm mentioned to Bugle that a competitor had privately threatened to file a $100 million lawsuit charging Wizardry with copyright violations and unfair competition. The firm hopes to be able to head off the suit, which it views as having relatively little merit, on a confidential basis. Meritorious or not, if the suit becomes public, it could damage Wizardry's reputation. Bugle's broker has instructions to sell a significant block of stock next week. What would you advise Bugle as to his legal obligations?

    b. Suppose instead that Bugle had given his broker instructions to sell at a time when he possessed no material nonpublic information. Yesterday, he learned information relating to litigation involving Wizardry that, when made public, is likely to increase the company's share price. Can Bugle call his broker and tell her to put off the planned sales for this month?

D. *The Misappropriation Theory*

Recall that Vincent Chiarella used confidential information—the identity of firms soon to be takeover targets—that he acquired as an employee of Pandick Press to purchase target shares. Drawing on experience in the criminal law of mail and wire fraud, where secret breaches of trust have long been treated as fraudulent, the government in *Chiarella* argued on appeal that two alternative bases for liability existed. Chiarella's conviction should be affirmed, it said, because (1) the fact that Chiarella had misappropriated the information in question from his employer (the printing firm) and his employer's client (the takeover bidder) itself gave rise to a duty of disclosure to marketplace traders, and (2) the misappropriation operated as a fraud on his employer and his employer's client "in connection with the purchase or sale of a security." A majority of the Court, however, found that the jury was not properly instructed on either of these two "misappropriation" theories and thus refused to consider their validity under Rule 10b-5 generally. In his dissent, Chief Justice Burger disagreed, arguing that the former theory (misappropriation as giving rise to a duty of disclosure to other traders) was an appropriate basis for liability. And in his concurring opinion, Justice Stevens, though agreeing that the latter theory (the so-called fraud-on-the-source theory) was not properly presented in this particular case, discussed it in somewhat approving terms.

Not surprisingly, the SEC (and government prosecutors in criminal cases) quickly began to utilize the "fraud on the source" (i.e., Justice Stevens') misappropriation theory in subsequent enforcement actions where neither Rule 14e-3 nor the newly restricted "abstain or disclose" theory would otherwise create liability. From this grew an alternative insider trading theory.

United States v. O'Hagan
521 U.S. 642 (1997)

GINSBURG, J. . . .

I

Respondent James Herman O'Hagan was a partner in the law firm of Dorsey & Whitney in Minneapolis, Minnesota. In July 1988, Grand Metropolitan PLC (Grand Met), a company based in London, England, retained Dorsey & Whitney as local counsel to represent Grand Met regarding a potential tender offer for the common stock of the Pillsbury Company, headquartered in Minneapolis. Both Grand Met and Dorsey & Whitney took precautions to protect the confidentiality of Grand Met's tender offer plans. O'Hagan did no work on the Grand Met representation. Dorsey & Whitney withdrew from representing Grand Met on September 9, 1988. Less than a month later, on October 4, 1988, Grand Met publicly announced its tender offer for Pillsbury stock.

On August 18, 1988, while Dorsey & Whitney was still representing Grand Met, O'Hagan began purchasing call options for Pillsbury stock. Each option gave him the right to purchase 100 shares of Pillsbury stock by a specified date in September 1988. Later in August and in September, O'Hagan made additional purchases of Pillsbury call options. By the end of September, he owned 2,500 unexpired Pillsbury options, apparently more than any other individual investor. O'Hagan also purchased, in September 1988, some 5,000 shares of Pillsbury common stock, at a price just under $39 per share. When Grand Met announced its tender offer in October, the price of Pillsbury stock rose to nearly $60 per share. O'Hagan then sold his Pillsbury call options and common stock, making a profit of more than $4.3 million.

The Securities and Exchange Commission initiated an investigation into O'Hagan's transactions, culminating in a 57-count indictment. The indictment alleged that O'Hagan defrauded his law firm and its client, Grand Met, by using for his own trading purposes material, nonpublic information regarding Grand Met's planned tender offer. According to the indictment, O'Hagan used the profits he gained through this trading to conceal his previous embezzlement and conversion of unrelated client trust funds. . . . A jury convicted O'Hagan on all 57 counts, and he was sentenced to a 41-month term of imprisonment.

A divided panel of the Court of Appeals for the Eighth Circuit reversed all of O'Hagan's convictions. 92 F.3d 612 (1996). Liability under Section 10(b) and Rule 10b-5, the Eighth Circuit held, may not be grounded on the "misappropriation theory" of securities fraud on which the prosecution relied. Id. at 622. . . .

Decisions of the Courts of Appeals are in conflict on the propriety of the misappropriation theory under Section 10(b) and Rule 10b-5. . . . We granted certiorari, and now reverse the Eighth Circuit's judgment.

II

We address first the Court of Appeals' reversal of O'Hagan's convictions under Section 10(b) and Rule 10b-5. Following the Fourth Circuit's lead, *see United States v. Bryan*, 58 F.3d 933, 943-959 (1995), the Eighth Circuit rejected the misappropriation theory as a basis for Section 10(b) liability. We hold, in accord with several other Courts of Appeals, that criminal liability under Section 10(b) may be predicated on the misappropriation theory.[4] . . .

---

4. Twice before we have been presented with the question whether criminal liability for violation of Section 10(b) may be based on a misappropriation theory. In *Chiarella v. United States*, 445 U.S. 222 (1980), the jury had received no misappropriation theory instructions, so we declined to address the question. In *Carpenter v. United States*, 484 U.S. 19 (1987), the Court divided evenly on whether, under the circumstances of that case, convictions resting on the misappropriation theory should be affirmed. *See* Aldave, The Misappropriation Theory: *Carpenter* and Its Aftermath, 49 Ohio St. L.J. 373, 375 (1988) (observing that "*Carpenter* was, by any reckoning, an unusual case," for the information there misappropriated belonged not to a company preparing to engage in securities transactions, e.g., a bidder in a corporate acquisition, but to The Wall Street Journal).

A

The "misappropriation theory" holds that a person commits fraud "in connection with" a securities transaction, and thereby violates Section 10(b) and Rule 10b-5, when he misappropriates confidential information for securities trading purposes, in breach of a duty owed to the source of the information. Under this theory, a fiduciary's undisclosed, self-serving use of a principal's information to purchase or sell securities, in breach of a duty of loyalty and confidentiality, defrauds the principal of the exclusive use of that information. In lieu of premising liability on a fiduciary relationship between company insider and purchaser or seller of the company's stock, the misappropriation theory premises liability on a fiduciary-turned-trader's deception of those who entrusted him with access to confidential information. . . . The misappropriation theory is thus designed to "protect the integrity of the securities markets against abuses by 'outsiders' to a corporation who have access to confidential information that will affect the corporation's security price when revealed, but who owe no fiduciary or other duty to that corporation's shareholders" [quoting *Dirks v. SEC*, 463 U.S. 646, 655 (1983)].

In this case, the indictment alleged that O'Hagan, in breach of a duty of trust and confidence he owed to his law firm, Dorsey & Whitney, and to its client, Grand Met, traded on the basis of nonpublic information regarding Grand Met's planned tender offer for Pillsbury common stock. This conduct, the Government charged, constituted a fraudulent device in connection with the purchase and sale of securities.

B

We agree with the Government that misappropriation, as just defined, satisfies Section 10(b)'s requirement that chargeable conduct involve a "deceptive device or contrivance" used "in connection with" the purchase or sale of securities. We observe, first, that misappropriators, as the Government describes them, deal in deception. A fiduciary who "[pretends] loyalty to the principal while secretly converting the principal's information for personal gain," Brief for United States 17, "dupes" or defrauds the principal. . . .

Deception through nondisclosure is central to the theory of liability for which the Government seeks recognition. As counsel for the Government stated in explanation of the theory at oral argument: "To satisfy the common law rule that a trustee may not use the property that [has] been entrusted [to] him, there would have to be consent. To satisfy the requirement of the Securities Act that there be no deception, there would only have to be disclosure."

The misappropriation theory advanced by the Government is consistent with *Santa Fe Industries, Inc. v. Green*, 430 U.S. 462 (1977), a decision underscoring that Section 10(b) is not an all-purpose breach of fiduciary duty ban; rather, it trains on conduct involving manipulation or deception. In contrast to the Government's allegations in this case, in *Santa Fe Industries*, all pertinent facts were disclosed by the persons charged with violating Section 10(b) and Rule 10b-5; therefore, there was no deception through nondisclosure to which liability under those provisions could attach. Similarly, full disclosure forecloses liability under the misappropriation theory: Because the deception essential to the misappropriation theory involves feigning fidelity to the source of information, if the fiduciary discloses to the source that he plans to trade on the nonpublic information, there is no "deceptive device" and thus no Section 10(b) violation—although the fiduciary-turned-trader may remain liable under state law for breach of a duty of loyalty.

We turn next to the Section 10(b) requirement that the misappropriator's deceptive use of information be "in connection with the purchase or sale of [a] security." This element is satisfied because the fiduciary's fraud is consummated, not when the fiduciary gains the confidential information, but when, without disclosure to his principal, he uses the information to purchase or sell securities. The securities transaction and the breach of duty thus coincide. This is so even though the person or entity defrauded is not the other party to the trade, but is, instead, the source of the nonpublic information. A misappropriator who trades on the basis of material, nonpublic information, in short, gains his advantageous market position through deception; he deceives the source of the information and simultaneously harms members of the investing public.

The misappropriation theory targets information of a sort that misappropriators ordinarily capitalize upon to gain no-risk profits through the purchase or sale of securities. Should a misappropriator put such information to other use, the statute's prohibition would not be implicated. The theory does not catch all conceivable forms of fraud involving confidential information; rather, it catches fraudulent means of capitalizing on such information through securities transactions. . . . [At this point, the Court dealt with the concern expressed in the dissent of Justice Thomas, infra, that misappropriation is not securities fraud because the misappropriation of information does not necessarily result in securities trading. The majority responded that it was enough that such misappropriation "ordinarily" results in a securities trade.]

The misappropriation theory comports with Section 10(b)'s language, which requires deception "in connection with the purchase or sale of any security," not deception of an identifiable purchaser or seller. The theory is also well-tuned to an animating purpose of the Exchange Act: to insure honest securities markets and thereby promote investor confidence. *See* 45 Fed. Reg. 60412 (1980) (trading on misappropriated information "undermines the integrity of, and investor confidence in, the securities markets"). Although informational disparity is inevitable in the securities markets, investors likely would hesitate to venture their capital in a market where trading based on misappropriated nonpublic information is unchecked by law. An investor's informational disadvantage vis-à-vis a misappropriator with material, nonpublic information stems from contrivance, not luck; it is a disadvantage that cannot be overcome with research or skill. *See* Brudney, Insiders, Outsiders, and Informational Advantages Under the Federal Securities Laws, 93 Harv. L. Rev. 322, 356 (1979) ("If the market is thought to be systematically populated with . . . transactors [trading on the basis of misappropriated information] some investors will refrain from dealing altogether, and others will incur costs to avoid dealing with such transactors or corruptly to overcome their unerodable informational advantages."). . . .

In sum, considering the inhibiting impact on market participation of trading on misappropriated information, and the congressional purposes underlying Section 10(b), it makes scant sense to hold a lawyer like O'Hagan a Section

10(b) violator if he works for a law firm representing the target of a tender offer, but not if he works for a law firm representing the bidder. The text of the statute requires no such result.[9] The misappropriation at issue here was properly made the subject of a Section 10(b) charge because it meets the statutory requirement that there be "deceptive" conduct "in connection with" securities transactions. . . . [The Court then went on to show that its previous decisions did not compel a rejection of the misappropriation theory. Having found the theory consistent with text, policy, and precedent, it remanded to the lower court for further proceedings on O'Hagan's other defenses to liability.]

[The concurring and dissenting opinion of Justice SCALIA is omitted.]

Justice THOMAS, with whom Chief Justice REHNQUIST joins, concurring in the judgment in part and dissenting in part.

. . . Central to the majority's holding is the need to interpret Section 10(b)'s requirement that a deceptive device be "used or employed, in connection with the purchase or sale of any security." Because the Commission's misappropriation theory fails to provide a coherent and consistent interpretation of this essential requirement for liability under Section 10(b), I dissent.

I

I do not take issue with the majority's determination that the undisclosed misappropriation of confidential information by a fiduciary can constitute a "deceptive device" within the meaning of Section 10(b). . . . Unlike the majority, however, I cannot accept the Commission's interpretation of when a deceptive device is "used . . . in connection with" a securities transaction. Although the Commission and the majority at points seem to suggest that any relation to a securities transaction satisfies the "in connection with" requirement of Section 10(b), both ultimately reject such an overly expansive construction and require a more integral connection between the fraud and the securities transaction. The majority states, for example, that the misappropriation theory applies to undisclosed misappropriation of confidential information "for securities trading purposes," thus seeming to require a particular intent by the misappropriator in order to satisfy the "in connection with" language. The Commission goes further, and argues that the misappropriation theory satisfies the "in connection with" requirement because it "depends on an inherent connection between the deceptive conduct and the purchase or sale of a security." . . .

---

9. As noted earlier, however, the textual requirement of deception precludes Section 10(b) liability when a person trading on the basis of nonpublic information has disclosed his trading plans to, or obtained authorization from, the principal—even though such conduct may affect the securities markets in the same manner as the conduct reached by the misappropriation theory. Contrary to the dissent's suggestion, the fact that Section 10(b) is only a partial antidote to the problems it was designed to alleviate does not call into question its prohibition of conduct that falls within its textual proscription. Moreover, once a disloyal agent discloses his imminent breach of duty, his principal may seek appropriate equitable relief under state law. Furthermore, in the context of a tender offer, the principal who authorizes an agent's trading on confidential information may, in the Commission's view, incur liability for an Exchange Act violation under Rule 14e-3(a).

The Commission's construction of the relevant language in Section 10(b), and the incoherence of that construction, become evident as the majority attempts to describe why the fraudulent theft of information falls under the Commission's misappropriation theory, but the fraudulent theft of money does not. The majority correctly notes that confidential information "qualifies as property to which the company has a right of exclusive use." It then observes that the "undisclosed misappropriation of such information, in violation of a fiduciary duty . . . constitutes fraud akin to embezzlement—the fraudulent appropriation to one's own use of the money or goods entrusted to one's care by another." So far the majority's analogy to embezzlement is well taken, and adequately demonstrates that undisclosed misappropriation can be a fraud on the source of the information. . . . What the embezzlement analogy does not do, however, is explain how the relevant fraud is "used or employed, in connection with" a securities transaction. And when the majority seeks to distinguish the embezzlement of funds from the embezzlement of information, it becomes clear that neither the Commission nor the majority has a coherent theory regarding Section 10(b)'s "in connection with" requirement. . . .

It seems obvious that the undisclosed misappropriation of confidential information is not necessarily consummated by a securities transaction. In this case, for example, upon learning of Grand Met's confidential takeover plans, O'Hagan could have done any number of things with the information: He could have sold it to a newspaper for publication, he could have given or sold the information to Pillsbury itself, or he could even have kept the information and used it solely for his personal amusement, perhaps in a fantasy stock trading game. . . .

In upholding respondent's convictions under the new and improved misappropriation theory, the majority also points to various policy considerations underlying the securities laws, such as maintaining fair and honest markets, promoting investor confidence, and protecting the integrity of the securities markets. But the repeated reliance on such broad-sweeping legislative purposes reaches too far and is misleading in the context of the misappropriation theory. It reaches too far in that, regardless of the overarching purpose of the securities laws, it is not illegal to run afoul of the "purpose" of a statute, only its letter. The majority's approach is misleading in this case because it glosses over the fact that the supposed threat to fair and honest markets, investor confidence, and market integrity comes not from the supposed fraud in this case, but from the mere fact that the information used by O'Hagan was nonpublic.

NOTES AND QUESTIONS

1.   Some Other Uses of the Misappropriation Theory.   As with *O'Hagan*, most misappropriation cases have involved partners or employees associated with acquiring companies, investment banking firms, law firms, or financial printers who profited from information relating to merger and acquisition activity. *E.g., SEC v. Materia*, 745 F.2d 197 (2d Cir. 1984); *United States v. Newman*, 664 F.2d 12 (2d Cir. 1981), *cert. denied*, 464 U.S. 837 (1984). But the theory has been used in cases well beyond these fairly conventional forms of misuse of business information. For example, in the well-known case of *United States v. Carpenter*, 791

F.2d 1024 (2d Cir. 1986), a journalist for the Wall Street Journal, Foster Winans, traded with advance knowledge of stocks that would receive favorable mention in the widely read "Heard on the Street" column. Certiorari was granted in *Carpenter*, but the Court split 4-4 on the misappropriation theory's validity as applied to the case. For an interesting discussion of how close the Court came to rejecting the theory at that point, *see* Pritchard, *United States v. O'Hagan:* Agency Law and Justice Powell's Legacy for the Law of Insider Trading, 78 B.U. L. Rev. 13 (1998). What about a case where a psychiatrist trades after learning some information in a counseling session? *See United States v. Willis*, 778 F. Supp. 205 (S.D.N.Y. 1992).

In another unconventional case, the Second Circuit held in *United States v. Chestman*, 947 F.2d 551 (2d Cir. 1991) (en banc), *cert. denied*, 503 U.S. 1004 (1992), that a husband-wife relationship was not fiduciary per se so as to give rise to a duty to respect confidential information. The court said:

> A fiduciary relationship involves discretionary authority and dependency: One person depends on another—the fiduciary—to serve his interests. In relying on a fiduciary to act for his benefit, the beneficiary of the relation may entrust the fiduciary with custody over property of one sort or another. Because the fiduciary obtains access to this property to serve the ends of the fiduciary relationship, he becomes duty bound not to appropriate the property for his own use. . . . These characteristics represent the measure of the paradigmatic fiduciary relationship. A similar relationship of trust and confidence consequently must share these qualities.

Id. at 569. Though determining that not all spousal relationships meet this standard, the court did leave open the possibility that a fiduciary relationship could be found to exist between spouses or other family members in specific cases. How might this be established as an evidentiary matter? *See United States v. Reed*, 601 F. Supp. 685 (S.D.N.Y. 1985).

Responding to the uncertainty created in these kinds of settings, the SEC has adopted Rule 10b5-2, which states that a duty of trust and confidence exists for purposes of the misappropriation theory whenever (1) a person agrees to maintain information in confidence; (2) persons sharing information have a history, pattern, or practice of sharing confidences such that the recipient knows or should know that there is an expectation of confidentiality; or (3) information is shared by a person with his or her parent, spouse, child or sibling, unless the recipient can show that there was no reasonable expectation of confidentiality within the particular family relationship. For a discussion of how this pushes the fiduciary principle to (and maybe beyond) its outer limits, *see* Nagy, Insider Trading and the Gradual Demise of Fiduciary Principles, 94 Iowa L. Rev. 1315 (2009). Subsection (1) was at issue in the SEC's case against entrepreneur Mark Cuban, which involved the factually contested issue of whether he agreed to maintain the confidentiality of the issuer's plans to engage in a PIPE transaction, which management shared with him even though they suspected that he would not be pleased by what he learned. Is promising to keep something confidential the same as agreeing not to profit from it? *See SEC v. Cuban*, 620 F.3d 551 (5th Cir. 2010). After being tried, Cuban was found not liable.

2.   The Potential in the Theory.   Applying the misappropriation theory in its broad form, are there any cases of "classic" insider trading—as defined by *Chiarella* and *Dirks*—that are not also misappropriations? If not, is the misappropriation theory really "the" law of insider trading? *See* Gubler, A Unified Theory of Insider Trading, 105 Geo. L.J. 1225 (2017), calling for the abandonment of the classical theory in favor of misappropriation.

3.   The Limits of the Theory.   *O'Hagan* makes clear that misappropriation is present only when there is a secretive breach of an expectation of loyalty. This means two things. First, employers and other sources can presumably authorize insider trading if they so desire. Is this sensible policy, given the basic purpose(s) of the insider trading prohibition? Consider the testimony of one of your authors on versions of a bill, noted above, that would effectively have codified the misappropriation theory as the basic prohibition against insider trading:

> Each bill's findings emphasize that wrongful trading interdicts the "fairness, efficiency and integrity" of capital markets. However, the bills' definition of wrongfulness rests on purely private considerations such as theft, bribery or a breach of fiduciary duty. Therefore, the wrongfulness of the defendant's act is determined not by a perceived harm to investors or to markets, but to the party from whom the information was obtained by "theft," etc. Without more, therefore, the bills fail to answer the prevalent question: why and how does the unauthorized use of another's information justify regulation through the federal securities laws? Moreover, there is a grave danger that such a privatized view of insider trading will ultimately cause our present concern for preserving the integrity of fair and efficient capital markets to be subordinated to the vagaries of private arrangements between the defendant and his employer. Just as the successful prosecution of Mr. Winans should not have been scuttled if his employer, Dow Jones & Co., had licensed him to trade on the advance knowledge of companies touted in his column, the proscription of trading which poses a threat to the fairness and efficiency of capital markets should not be subordinated to private arrangements between an employer and his employees.

Testimony of Professor James Cox, Hearings on S.1380 Before the Subcommittee on Securities of the Senate Comm. on Banking, Housing and Urban Affairs, 100th Cong., 1st Sess. 80-81 (Dec. 15, 1987). Second, note the obvious: If the trader *tells* the source in advance of his intent to trade, there can be no secretive breach. *See* Painter, Krawiec & Williams, Don't Ask, Just Tell: Insider Trading After *United States v. O'Hagan*, 84 Va. L. Rev. 153 (1997).

This limitation was tested in *SEC v. Rocklage*, 470 F.3d 1 (1st Cir. 2006). The wife of a company insider learned bad news about the company from her husband and then conveyed the information—with a "wink and a nod"—to her brother. But she did this only after telling her husband what she was going to do. He strongly urged her not to, but she did anyway. The court acknowledged that under the dicta in *O'Hagan*, these facts alone would render the misappropriation theory inapplicable. However, the court took note of the SEC's claim that because the wife had a preexisting understanding with her brother that she would tip him off if she learned negative information from her husband, the deceptive scheme arose before her receipt of the information and her brother's trading. In other words, according to the court, her deception in concealing this scheme enabled her to obtain the information in the first place, and that was sufficient to constitute securities fraud.

**4. *Insider Trading Without a Fiduciary Breach.* In *SEC v. Dorozhko*, 574 F.3d 42 (2d Cir. 2009), the court was faced with allegations of trading based on information gained by hacking into a computer system. Presumably, a hacker is not a fiduciary, so the court had to address whether breach of fiduciary duty as per *Chiarella* and *O'Hagan* was essential to insider trading liability. It said no, because deception is the key to liability under Rule 10b-5 and secretive breach of fiduciary duty is only a way of satisfying the deception requirement. Here, the SEC alleged that tricking the host system into "believing" that access was authorized was a form of active deception, making resort to fiduciary principles unnecessary. The court remanded for further proceedings, saying that "depending on how the hacker gained access, it seems to us entirely possible that computer hacking could be, by definition, a 'deceptive device or contrivance.' . . ."

**5. *Insider Trading in the Government.* In the STOCK Act of 2012, Congress made clear that the insider trading prohibition applies to members of Congress and their staff (as well as other federal governmental officials). New Section 21A(g) of the '34 Act provides that members and staff owe "a duty arising from a relationship of trust and confidence to the Congress, the United States Government, and the citizens of the United States with respect to material, nonpublic information derived from such person's position as a Member of Congress or employee of Congress or gained from the performance of such person's official responsibilities." The legislation leaves the standards as to materiality, non-publicness, etc., as generally understood in insider trading law. There are many interesting questions that could arise as a result. Suppose a member of Congress met with lobbyists opposed to certain proposed legislation and reported, privately, that he had made great progress in stopping that legislation from going forward. Could the lobbyists sell short the shares of companies that would benefit were the legislation to pass as publicly expected? Although there has not yet been a contemporary insider trading case involving congressional activity, there have been numerous actions against other government officials, both federal and state. *E.g., United States v. Royer*, 549 F.3d 886 (2d Cir. 2008) (tips from FBI official about ongoing investigations, used by short seller).

PROBLEMS

15-2. Majorica Inc. is a small, financially troubled publicly traded company. In recent weeks, it has been contemplating a PIPE financing deal (see Chapter 6, *supra*), whereby it would issue deeply discounted shares to one or more hedge funds in a private placement, and then register those securities with the SEC for resale by the hedge funds into the public markets. So far, this has been kept entirely confidential, and Majorica believes that were this news to get out, it would drive down the price of its stock even further. Pursuant to this plan, it contacted Alpha Dog, a hedge fund known to be interested in PIPE financing deals. Alpha Dog was indeed interested and, after a week of negotiations, agreed to take part in the deal. In the meantime, Alpha Dog sold short a large number of Majorica shares. Does this violate Rule 10b-5?

15-3. Susan Tandy, the CEO of ChiOmicron Inc., was hosting a family reunion picnic at her home. Fred Brown, who was married to one of Susan's cousins, was at the picnic, and at one point when everyone was particularly busy outside, asked where the nearest bathroom was in the house. He went in, and after leaving the bathroom, went quietly into Susan's office, which was unlocked. Fred read some materials and looked at her e-mails on the computer—and discovered a draft press release, sent for Susan's final approval, announcing far greater earnings and revenues than expected. Fred later called his broker and bought ChiOmicron stock and options. Did he violate Rule 10b-5? What additional facts might either strengthen or weaken the SEC's case against him?

E. Tippers and Tippees

1. Tipper/Tippee Liability Defined

Chiarella indicates, by negative implication at least, that the key to establishing a violation of the "abstain or disclose" rule is to find a fiduciary nexus between the trader and the marketplace. This can be done quite readily when the trader in fact works for the issuer and was entrusted with confidential information. But what if an insider does not trade, but instead "tips" someone else (e.g., a friend or relative) who then trades? Of what use is the fiduciary principle here? And does this idea also apply with respect to the misappropriation theory articulated in *O'Hagan*?

Dirks v. Securities and Exchange Commission
463 U.S. 646 (1983)

POWELL, J. Petitioner Raymond Dirks received material nonpublic information from "insiders" of a corporation with which he had no connection. He disclosed this information to investors who relied on it in trading in the shares of the corporation. The question is whether Dirks violated the antifraud provisions of the federal securities laws by this disclosure.

I

In 1973, Dirks was an officer of a New York broker-dealer firm who specialized in providing investment analysis of insurance company securities to institutional investors. On March 6, Dirks received information from Ronald Secrist, a former officer of Equity Funding of America. Secrist alleged that the assets of Equity Funding, a diversified corporation primarily engaged in selling life insurance and mutual funds, were vastly overstated as the result of fraudulent corporate practices. Secrist also stated that various regulatory agencies had failed to act on similar charges made by Equity Funding employees. He urged Dirks to verify the fraud and disclose it publicly.

Dirks decided to investigate the allegations. He visited Equity Funding's headquarters in Los Angeles and interviewed several officers and employees of the corporation. The senior management denied any wrongdoing, but certain corporation employees corroborated the charges of fraud. Neither Dirks nor his firm owned or traded any Equity Funding stock, but throughout his investigation he openly discussed the information he had obtained with a number of clients and investors. Some of these persons sold their holdings of Equity Funding securities, including five investment advisers who liquidated holdings of more than $16 million.

While Dirks was in Los Angeles, he was in touch regularly with William Blundell, the Wall Street Journal's Los Angeles bureau chief. Dirks urged Blundell to write a story on the fraud allegations. Blundell did not believe, however, that such a massive fraud could go undetected and declined to write the story. He feared that publishing such damaging hearsay might be libelous.

During the 2-week period in which Dirks pursued his investigation and spread word of Secrist's charges, the price of Equity Funding stock fell from $26 per share to less than $15 per share. This led the New York Stock Exchange to halt trading on March 27. Shortly thereafter California insurance authorities impounded Equity Funding's records and uncovered evidence of the fraud. Only then did the Securities and Exchange Commission (SEC) file a complaint against Equity Funding and only then, on April 2, did the Wall Street Journal publish a front-page story based largely on information assembled by Dirks. Equity Funding immediately went into receivership.

The SEC began an investigation into Dirks' role in the exposure of the fraud. After a hearing by an Administrative Law Judge, the SEC found that Dirks had aided and abetted violations of §17(a) of the Securities Act of 1933, §10(b) of the Securities Exchange Act of 1934, and SEC Rule 10b-5, by repeating the allegations of fraud to members of the investment community who later sold their Equity Funding stock. The SEC concluded: "Where 'tippees'—regardless of their motivation or occupation—come into possession of material 'corporate information that they know is confidential and know or should know came from a corporate insider,' they must either publicly disclose that information or refrain from trading." 21 S.E.C. Docket 1401, 1407 (1981) (footnote omitted) (quoting *Chiarella v. United States*, 445 U.S. 222, 230 n.12 (1980)). Recognizing, however, that Dirks "played an important role in bringing [Equity Funding's] massive fraud to light," 21 S.E.C. Docket, at 1412, the SEC only censured him. . . .

III

We were explicit in *Chiarella* in saying that there can be no duty to disclose where the person who has traded on inside information "was not [the corporation's] agent, . . . was not a fiduciary, [or] was not a person in whom the sellers [of the securities] had placed their trust and confidence." 445 U.S., at 232. Not to require such a fiduciary relationship, we recognized, would "depar[t] radically from the established doctrine that duty arises from a specific relationship between two parties" and would amount to "recognizing a general duty between all participants in market transactions to forgo actions based on material, nonpublic information." Id., at 232, 233. . . .

Imposing a duty to disclose or abstain solely because a person knowingly receives material nonpublic information from an insider and trades on it could have an inhibiting influence on the role of market analysts, which the SEC itself recognizes is necessary to the preservation of a healthy market. It is commonplace for analysts to "ferret out and analyze information," 21 S.E.C. Docket, at 1406, and this often is done by meeting with and questioning corporate officers and others who are insiders. And information that the analysts obtain normally may be the basis for judgments as to the market worth of a corporation's securities. The analyst's judgment in this respect is made available in market letters or otherwise to clients of the firm. It is the nature of this type of information, and indeed of the markets themselves, that such information cannot be made simultaneously available to all of the corporation's stockholders or the public generally. . . .

The conclusion that recipients of inside information do not invariably acquire a duty to disclose or abstain does not mean that such tippees always are free to trade on the information. The need for a ban on some tippee trading is clear. Not only are insiders forbidden by their fiduciary relationship from personally using undisclosed corporate information to their advantage, but they also may not give such information to an outsider for the same improper purpose of exploiting the information for their personal gain. See 15 U.S.C. §78t(b) (making it unlawful to do indirectly "by means of any other person" any act made unlawful by the federal securities laws). Similarly, the transactions of those who knowingly participate with the fiduciary in such a breach are "as forbidden" as transactions "on behalf of the trustee himself." Mosser v. Darrow, 341 U.S. 267, 272 (1951). As the Court explained in Mosser, a contrary rule "would open up opportunities for devious dealings in the name of others that the trustee could not conduct on his own." 341 U.S., at 271. Thus, the tippee's duty to disclose or abstain is derivative from that of the insider's duty. . . . As we noted in Chiarella, "[t]he tippee's obligation has been viewed as arising from his role as a participant after the fact in the insider's breach of a fiduciary duty." [445 U.S.] at 230, n.12.

Thus, some tippees must assume an insider's duty to the shareholders not because they receive inside information, but rather because it has been made available to them improperly. And for Rule 10b-5 purposes, the insider's disclosure is improper only where it would violate his Cady, Roberts duty. Thus, a tippee assumes a fiduciary duty to the shareholders of a corporation not to trade on material nonpublic information only when the insider has breached his fiduciary duty to the shareholders by disclosing the information to the tippee and the tippee knows or should know that there has been a breach. . . . Whether disclosure is a breach of duty therefore depends in large part on the purpose of the disclosure. This standard was identified by the SEC itself in Cady, Roberts: a purpose of the securities laws was to eliminate "use of inside information for personal advantage." 40 S.E.C., at 912, n.15. Thus, the test is whether the insider personally will benefit, directly or indirectly, from his disclosure. Absent some personal gain, there has been no breach of duty to stockholders. And absent a breach by the insider, there is no derivative breach. /. . In determining whether the insider's purpose in making a particular disclosure is fraudulent, the SEC and the courts are not required to read the parties' minds. Scienter in some cases is relevant in determining whether the tipper has violated his *Cady, Roberts* duty. But to determine whether the disclosure itself "deceive[s], manipulate[s], or defraud[s]" shareholders, *Aaron v. SEC*, 446 U.S. 680, 686 (1980), the initial inquiry is whether there has been a breach of duty by the insider. This requires courts to focus on objective criteria, i.e., whether the insider receives a direct or indirect personal benefit from the disclosure, such as a pecuniary gain or a reputational benefit that will translate into future earnings. There are objective facts and circumstances that often justify such an inference. For example, there may be a relationship between the insider and the recipient that suggests a quid pro quo from the latter, or an intention to benefit the particular recipient. The elements of fiduciary duty and exploitation of nonpublic information also exist when an insider makes a gift of confidential information to a trading relative or friend. The tip and trade resemble trading by the insider himself followed by a gift of the profits to the recipient.

Determining whether an insider personally benefits from a particular disclosure, a question of fact, will not always be easy for courts. But it is essential, we think, to have a guiding principle for those whose daily activities must be limited and instructed by the SEC's inside-trading rules, and we believe that there must be a breach of the insider's fiduciary duty before the tippee inherits the duty to disclose or abstain. In contrast, the rule adopted by the SEC in this case would have no limiting principle.

IV

Under the inside-trading and tipping rules set forth above, we find that there was no actionable violation by Dirks. It is undisputed that Dirks himself was a stranger to Equity Funding, with no preexisting fiduciary duty to its shareholders. He took no action, directly or indirectly, that induced the shareholders or officers of Equity Funding to repose trust or confidence in him. There was no expectation by Dirks's sources that he would keep their information in confidence. Nor did Dirks misappropriate or illegally obtain the information about Equity Funding. Unless the insiders breached their *Cady, Roberts* duty to shareholders in disclosing the nonpublic information to Dirks, he breached no duty when he passed it on to investors as well as to the Wall Street Journal.

It is clear that neither Secrist nor the other Equity Funding employees violated their *Cady, Roberts* duty to the corporation's shareholders by providing information to Dirks. The tippers received no monetary or personal benefit for revealing Equity Funding's secrets, nor was their purpose to make a gift of valuable information to Dirks. As the facts of this case clearly indicate, the tippers were motivated by a desire to expose the fraud. In the absence of a breach of duty to shareholders by the insiders, there was no derivative breach by Dirks. Dirks therefore could not have been "a participant after the fact in [an] insider's breach of a fiduciary duty." *Chiarella*, 445 U.S., at 230, n.12.

V

We conclude that Dirks, in the circumstances of this case, had no duty to abstain from use of the inside information that he obtained. The judgment of the Court of Appeals therefore is

Reversed.

Justice BLACKMUN, with whom Justice BRENNAN and Justice MARSHALL join, dissenting.

The Court today takes still another step to limit the protections provided investors by §10(b) of the Securities Exchange Act of 1934. *See Chiarella v. United States*, 445 U.S. 222, 246 (1980) (dissenting opinion). The device employed in this case engrafts a special motivational requirement on the fiduciary duty doctrine. This innovation excuses a knowing and intentional violation of an insider's duty to shareholders if the insider does not act from a motive of personal gain. Even on the extraordinary facts of this case, such an innovation is not justified. . . .

In my view, Secrist violated his duty to Equity Funding shareholders by transmitting material nonpublic information to Dirks with the intention that Dirks would cause his clients to trade on that information. Dirks, therefore, was under a duty to make the information publicly available or to refrain from actions that he knew would lead to trading. Because Dirks caused his clients to trade, he violated §10(b) and Rule 10b-5. Any other result is a disservice to this country's attempt to provide fair and efficient capital markets. I dissent.

Salman v. United States
137 S. Ct. 420 (2016)

Justice ALITO delivered the opinion of the Court.

Maher Kara was an investment banker in Citigroup's healthcare investment banking group. He dealt with highly confidential information about mergers and acquisitions involving Citigroup's clients. Maher enjoyed a close relationship with his older brother, Mounir Kara (known as Michael). After Maher started at Citigroup, he began discussing aspects of his job with Michael. At first he relied on Michael's chemistry background to help him grasp scientific concepts relevant to his new job. Then, while their father was battling cancer, the brothers discussed companies that dealt with innovative cancer treatment and pain management techniques. Michael began to trade on the information Maher shared with him. At first, Maher was unaware of his brother's trading activity, but eventually he began to suspect that it was taking place.

Ultimately, Maher began to assist Michael's trading by sharing inside information with his brother about pending mergers and acquisitions. Maher sometimes used code words to communicate corporate information to his brother. Other times, he shared inside information about deals he was not working on in order to avoid detection. . . . Without his younger brother's knowledge, Michael fed the information to others—including [Bassam] Salman, Michael's friend and Maher's brother-in-law. By the time the authorities caught on, Salman had made over $1.5 million in profits that he split with another relative who executed trades via a brokerage account on Salman's behalf.

Salman was indicted on one count of conspiracy to commit securities fraud, see 18 U.S.C. §371, and four counts of securities fraud, see 15 U.S.C. §§78j(b) . . . [and] 17 CFR §240.10b-5. Facing charges of their own, both Maher and Michael pleaded guilty and testified at Salman's trial. . . .

After a jury trial in the Northern District of California, Salman was convicted on all counts. He was sentenced to 36 months of imprisonment, three years of supervised release, and over $730,000 in restitution. . . . Salman appealed to the Ninth Circuit. While his appeal was pending, the Second Circuit issued its opinion in *United States v. Newman*, 773 F.3d 438 (2014), cert. denied, 136 S. Ct. 242 (2015). There, the Second Circuit reversed the convictions of two portfolio managers who traded on inside information. The *Newman* defendants were "several steps removed from the corporate insiders" and the court found that "there was no evidence that either was aware of the source of the inside information." 773 F.3d, at 443. The court acknowledged that *Dirks* and Second Circuit case law allow a factfinder to infer a personal benefit to the tipper from a gift of confidential information to a trading relative or friend. 773 F.3d, at 452. But the court concluded that, "[t]o the extent" *Dirks* permits "such an inference," the inference "is impermissible in the absence of proof of a meaningfully close personal relationship that generates an exchange that is objective, consequential, and represents at least a potential gain of a pecuniary or similarly valuable nature." 773 F.3d, at 452. . . . [In affirming Salman's conviction, the Ninth Circuit rejected *Newman*'s interpretation of *Dirks*.]

Our discussion of gift giving [in *Dirks*] resolves this case. Maher, the tipper, provided inside information to a close relative, his brother Michael. *Dirks* makes clear that a tipper breaches a fiduciary duty by making a gift of confidential information to "a trading relative," and that rule is sufficient to resolve the case at hand. As Salman's counsel acknowledged at oral argument, Maher would have breached his duty had he personally traded on the information here himself then given the proceeds as a gift to his brother. Tr. of Oral Arg. 3-4. It is obvious that Maher would personally benefit in that situation. But Maher effectively achieved the same result by disclosing the information to Michael, and allowing him to trade on it. *Dirks* appropriately prohibits that approach, as well. . . . *Dirks* specifies that when a tipper gives inside information to "a trading relative or friend," the jury can infer that the tipper meant to provide the equivalent of a cash gift. In such situations, the tipper benefits personally because giving a gift of trading information is the same thing as trading by the tipper followed by a gift of the proceeds. Here, by disclosing confidential information as a gift to his brother with the expectation that he would trade on it, Maher breached his duty of trust and confidence to Citigroup and its clients—a duty Salman acquired, and breached himself, by trading on the information with full knowledge that it had been improperly disclosed.

To the extent the Second Circuit held that the tipper must also receive something of a "pecuniary or similarly valuable nature" in exchange for a gift to family or friends, *Newman*, 773 F.3d, at 452, we agree with the Ninth Circuit that this requirement is inconsistent with *Dirks*. . . . Salman's jury was properly instructed that a personal benefit includes "the benefit one would obtain from simply making a gift of confidential information to a trading relative." . . . As the Court of Appeals noted, "the Government presented direct evidence that the disclosure was intended as a gift of market-sensitive information." 792 F.3d, at 1094. And, as Salman conceded below, this evidence is sufficient to sustain his conviction under our reading of *Dirks*. . . . Accordingly, the Ninth Circuit's judgment is affirmed.

NOTES AND QUESTIONS

1. Critique. Why did the Supreme Court introduce the "personal bene-fit" test for tipper/tippee liability? In light of the types of personal benefit iden-tified by the Court that might create liability, is there really much predictability added to the law in this area? Note that for some time, lower courts were unclear on whether *Dirks* set the standard for tipper-tippee liability in misappropriation cases as well as under the classical theory. *Salman* and other recent cases now seem in agreement that the standard is the same for both.

2. The Nature of a "Tip." It seems fairly clear from *Dirks* that a commu-nication by an insider must be both self-serving and meant to facilitate trading by the recipient of the information. As a result, conversations among insiders that are overheard by some third party who then trades cannot be deemed tips. *See SEC v. Switzer*, 590 F. Supp. 756 (W.D. Okla. 1984). There, the court found that University of Oklahoma football coach Barry Switzer traded in a company's stock after overhearing a company insider mention a planned liq-uidation of the company to his wife while both they and Switzer were in the stands at a track meet. Since, in the court's view, this was not meant as a tip and did not involve a breach of fiduciary duty by the insider, there could be no liability under Rule 10b-5. The court rejected the SEC's version of the facts, which emphasized that the insider was a major Oklahoma football booster, had spoken to Switzer about other matters four or five times during the track meet, and had recently gotten Switzer as a favor to upgrade his seating arrangements for Oklahoma football games. Does *Dirks* require that there be tipper liability for there to be tippee liability? In *United States v. Evans*, 486 F.3d 315, 323 (7th Cir. 2007), the court said no: "It is not essential that the tipper know that his disclosure was improper. Where the tippee has a relationship with the insider and the tippee knows the breach to be improper, the tippee may be liable for trading on the ill-gotten information." Persuaded? Can there be such a thing as a "reckless" tip? *See SEC v. Obus*, 693 F.3d 276 (2d Cir. 2012) (yes). How does this square with *Dirks*?

3. Retrenchment? In *Salman*, the Supreme Court clearly rejects *Newman*'s gloss about a gift benefit under *Dirks* being objective, consequential, and of a pecuniary-like nature. But there was a further gloss about the family or friend-ship relationship being "meaningfully close," which the Court didn't address because of the palpable closeness within the Kara family. Subsequently, the Second Circuit held that *Dirks* proscribes any conveyance of material nonpublic information that is intended as a gift, without the need to show a close rela-tionship between tipper and tippee. *United States v. Martoma*, 894 F.3d 64 (2d Cir. 2018). For a discussion of this issue, *see* Heminway, Tipper/Tippee Insider

Trading as Unlawful Deceptive Conduct: Insider Gifts of Material Nonpublic Information to Strangers, 56 Wash. U. J.L. & Pol'y 66 (2018).

As the Supreme Court explicitly acknowledged, *Salman* also did not address the separate holding in *Newman* that, at least in the context of a criminal case, prosecutors must show that the tippee (no matter how far along in the chain of tips) *knew* of the existence and nature of the benefit to the tipper. Does this insulate market insiders who avoid asking questions about where a seemingly valuable tip was coming from? Can knowledge be inferred from "conscious avoidance" of the source? Left open is whether these strictures apply at all in a civil case brought by the SEC.

4. ***The Investment Analyst and Selective Disclosure.***   The *Dirks* Court takes pains to credit investment analysts—persons whose business it is to gather and analyze information relating to specific securities, whether on behalf of institutional investors or research departments of broker-dealers—with an important function. That function, which inevitably involves a constant informal communication process between the issuer and competing individual analysts, has indeed been recognized as an important contribution to marketplace efficiency. *E.g.*, Fischel, Insider Trading and Investment Analysts: An Economic Analysis of Dirks v. SEC, 13 Hofstra L. Rev. 127 (1984). Does the Court effectively create a safe harbor for good-faith analyst activity? Does it go too far in this direction? Consider both Problem 15-5 and the subsection that follows, and *see* Langevoort, Investment Analysts and the Law of Insider Trading, 76 Va. L. Rev. 1023 (1990).

PROBLEMS

15-4.   You are a new associate at a large Atlanta law firm, assigned to a number of sensitive mergers and acquisitions projects. During a visit home one weekend—in an effort to impress your parents with your newfound responsibilities—you carry on at length about a yet unannounced merger, mentioning (for effect) the names of the well-known companies involved. The next day, your father buys stock in one of the companies and later sells it at a considerable profit. Has your father violated Rule 10b-5? Did you? Under what theory? Would it matter if your father bought stock in a company that was not a client of the firm? If you were found reckless in how you behaved?

15-5. Maria is an ambitious junior investment banker working on a couple of major deals. She eventually hopes to get into the hedge fund business and dreams of creating her own firm. Brazenly, she sees a big name hedge fund manager at a party, walks up to him, and puts in his pocket a note with a tip about one of her deals, with a "you're welcome," her name, and e-mail address. Has Maria violated Rule 10b? What about the recipient, assuming that he trades?

15-6.   Fred Perkins is an assistant to the vice president of finance of Alco Pharmaceuticals, Inc. He is visited one day by Rachel Smith, a well-known investment analyst, who begins probing for information about the company's earnings prospects for the coming quarters. Perkins has heard his superiors speak well of Smith, crediting her with enhancing the company's reputation with investors by favorable recommendations in the past. Figuring that such past favors deserve reward, Perkins releases to Smith the company's highly confidential earnings forecast. Recognizing this to be material nonpublic information, Smith trades both for her own account and for those of her clients. Has either Perkins or Smith violated Rule 10b-5? Would your answer change if the information was less clearly material—for example, that a new product was coming out that some company officials thought would help recapture a lost market share?

2.   Selective Disclosure: Regulation FD

❚❚ **Securities Act Release No. 33-7881**
Securities and Exchange Commission (Aug. 15, 2000)

[W]e have become increasingly concerned about the selective disclosure of material information by issuers. As reflected in recent publicized reports, many issuers are disclosing important nonpublic information, such as advance warnings of earnings results, to securities analysts or selected institutional investors or both, before making full disclosure of the same information to the general public. Where this has happened, those who were privy to the information beforehand were able to make a profit or avoid a loss at the expense of those kept in the dark.

We believe that the practice of selective disclosure leads to a loss of investor confidence in the integrity of our capital markets. Investors who see a security's price change dramatically and only later are given access to the information responsible for that move rightly question whether they are on a level playing field with market insiders.

Issuer selective disclosure bears a close resemblance in this regard to ordinary "tipping" and insider trading. In both cases, a privileged few gain an informational edge—and the ability to use that edge to profit—from their superior access to corporate insiders, rather than from their skill, acumen, or diligence. Likewise, selective disclosure has an adverse impact on market integrity that is similar to the adverse impact from illegal insider trading: investors lose confidence in the fairness of the markets when they know that other participants may exploit "unerodable informational advantages" derived not from hard work or insights, but from their access to corporate insiders. The economic effects of the two practices are essentially the same. Yet, as a result of judicial interpretations, tipping and insider trading can be severely punished under the antifraud provisions of the federal securities laws, whereas the status of issuer selective disclosure has been considerably less clear.

Regulation FD is also designed to address another threat to the integrity of our markets: the potential for corporate management to treat material information as a commodity to be used to gain or maintain favor with particular analysts or investors. As noted in the Proposing Release, in the absence of a prohibition on selective disclosure, analysts may feel pressured to report favorably about a company or otherwise slant their analysis in order to have continued access to selectively disclosed information. We are concerned, in this regard, with reports that analysts who publish negative views of an issuer are sometimes excluded by that issuer from calls and meetings to which other analysts are invited.

Finally . . . technological developments have made it much easier for issuers to disseminate information broadly. Whereas issuers once may have had to rely on analysts to serve as information intermediaries, issuers now can use a variety of methods to communicate directly with the market. In addition to press releases, these methods include, among others, Internet webcasting and teleconferencing. Accordingly, technological limitations no longer provide an excuse for abiding the threats to market integrity that selective disclosure represents.

To address the problem of selective disclosure, we proposed Regulation FD. It targets the practice by establishing new requirements for full and fair disclosure by public companies.

1.   BREADTH OF COMMENT ON THE PROPOSAL

The Proposing Release prompted an outpouring of public comment—nearly 6,000 comment letters. The vast majority of these commenters consisted of individual investors, who urged—almost uniformly—that we adopt Regulation FD. Individual investors expressed frustration with the practice of selective disclosure, believing that it places them at a severe disadvantage in the market. Several cited personal experiences in which they believed they had been disadvantaged by the practice. Many felt that selective disclosure was indistinguishable from insider trading in its effect on the market and investors, and expressed surprise that existing law did not already prohibit this practice. . . .

3.   EFFECT OF REGULATION FD ON ISSUER COMMUNICATIONS

One frequently expressed concern was that Regulation FD would not lead to broader dissemination of information, but would in fact have a "chilling effect" on the disclosure of information by issuers. In the view of these commenters, issuers would find it so difficult to determine when a disclosure of information would be "material" (and therefore subject to the regulation) that, rather than face potential liability and other consequences of violating Regulation FD, they would cease informal communications with the outside world altogether. Some of these commenters therefore recommended that the Commission not adopt any mandatory rule prohibiting selective disclosure, like Regulation FD, but instead pursue voluntary means of addressing the problem, such as interpretive guidance, or the promotion of a "blue ribbon" panel to develop best practices for issuer disclosure. Other commenters recommended various ways that Regulation FD could be made narrower or more well-defined, in order to ameliorate some of the concerns about chilling. Other commenters, however, took issue with the supposition that issuer disclosures would be chilled. As some commenters stated, the marketplace simply would not allow issuers to cease communications with analysts and security holders.

We have considered these views carefully. . . . [W]e are mindful of the concerns about chilling issuer disclosure; we agree that the market is best served by more, not less, disclosure of information by issuers. Because any potential "chill" is most likely to arise—if at all—from the fear of legal liability, we included in proposed Regulation FD significant safeguards against inappropriate liability. Most notably, we stated that the regulation would not provide a basis for private liability, and provided that in Commission enforcement actions under Regulation FD we would need to prove knowing or reckless conduct.

4. REVISIONS TO NARROW THE SCOPE OF REGULATION FD

Nevertheless, to provide even greater protection against the possibility of inappropriate liability, and to guard further against the likelihood of any chilling effect resulting from the regulation, we have modified Regulation FD in several respects.

First, we have narrowed the scope of the regulation so that it does not apply to all communications with persons outside the issuer. The regulation will apply only to communications to securities market professionals and to any holder of the issuer's securities under circumstances in which it is reasonably foreseeable that the security holder will trade on the basis of the information.

Second, we have narrowed the types of issuer personnel covered by the regulation to senior officials and those persons who regularly communicate with securities market professionals or with security holders. The effect of these first two changes is that Regulation FD will not apply to a variety of legitimate, ordinary-course business communications or to disclosures to the media.

Third, to remove any doubt that private liability will not result from a Regulation FD violation, we have revised Regulation FD to make absolutely clear that it does not establish a duty for purposes of Rule 10b-5 under the Securities Exchange Act of 1934 ("Exchange Act"). The regulation now includes an express provision in the text stating that a failure to make a disclosure required solely by Regulation FD will not result in a violation of Rule 10b-5.

Fourth, we have made clear that where the regulation speaks of "knowing or reckless" conduct, liability will arise only when an issuer's personnel knows or is reckless in not knowing that the information selectively disclosed is both material and nonpublic. This will provide additional assurance that issuers will not be second-guessed on close materiality judgments. Neither will we, nor could we, bring enforcement actions under Regulation FD for mistaken materiality determinations that were not reckless.

Fifth, we have expressly provided that a violation of Regulation FD will not lead to an issuer's loss of eligibility to use short-form registration for a securities offering or affect security holders' ability to resell under Rule 144 under the Securities Act of 1933 ("Securities Act"). This change eliminates additional consequences of a Regulation FD violation that issuers and other commenters considered too onerous.

We have made two other significant changes to the scope of Regulation FD, which, while not specifically addressed to concerns about chilling disclosure, narrow its scope. In response to concerns about the interplay of Regulation FD with the Securities Act disclosure regime, we have expressly excluded from the scope of the regulation communications made in connection with most securities offerings registered under the Securities Act. We believe that the Securities Act already accomplishes most of the policy goals of Regulation FD for purposes of registered offerings, and we will consider this topic in the context of a broader Securities Act rulemaking. Also, we have eliminated foreign governments and foreign private issuers from the coverage of the regulation.

With these changes, we believe Regulation FD strikes an appropriate balance. It establishes a clear rule prohibiting unfair selective disclosure and encourages broad public disclosure. Yet it should not impede ordinary-course business communications or expose issuers to liability for non-intentional selective disclosure unless the issuer fails to make public disclosure after it learns of it. Regulation FD, therefore, should promote full and fair disclosure of information by issuers and enhance the fairness and efficiency of our markets.

NOTES AND QUESTIONS

1. *Policy.* Does Regulation FD strike an appropriate balance between investor protection and market efficiency? Some of the commentary on Regulation FD has been critical, pointing to the illusory nature of seeking to "even the playing field" for the average investor when compared to the potential costs in terms of loss of the use of private communications as a means of getting difficult-to-understand information out to the markets and the need (especially among smaller firms) to use selective disclosure as a way of encouraging analysts to initiate and maintain coverage. *See, e.g.,* Epstein, Returning to Common Law Principles of Insider Trading After *United States v. Newman,* 125 Yale L.J. 1482 (2016). Some empirical evidence on Regulation FD indicates that it has led to a higher cost of capital, at least for smaller issuers who otherwise lack non-private channels for communicating firm-specific information. *See* Gomes et al., SEC Regulation Fair Disclosure, Information and the Cost of Capital, 13 J. Corp. Fin. 300 (2007). Other studies have suggested that there is now more disagreement among analysts and that the accuracy of analyst forecasts has decreased on average. *E.g.,* Bailey et al., Regulation Fair Disclosure and Earnings Information: Market, Analyst and Corporate Responses, 58 J. Fin. 2487 (2003). If so, is that good or bad?

2. *"Public."* Once information is publicly available, there are no restrictions on its transmission to favored parties. This places a great deal of stress on what constitutes adequate "publicity." When Regulation FD was adopted, the SEC indicated that merely posting information on the company's web site was not sufficient (though voluntarily filing with the SEC on an 8-K was). In an interpretive release issued in 2008 (see Commission Guidance on the Use of Company Web Sites, Release No. 33-58288 (Aug. 1, 2008)), the Commission softened this stance, suggesting that web site publicity might be adequate, but only if it had become a "recognized channel of distribution" and there has been a reasonable waiting period for the market to react to the information. This was further expanded in a Report of Investigation involving Netflix Inc., addressing the use of a Facebook post by its CEO to reveal purportedly material information. The SEC said that social media could constitute public dissemination, but only if the market was made aware of particular uses (like the CEO's Facebook page) that would commonly contain public dissemination of information. The Commission expressed doubts about the particular Facebook post but it took

no enforcement action in light of uncertainty about social media as a disclosure tool. *In re Netflix and Hastings,* Securities Act Release No. 69279 (Apr. 2, 2013). Are there First Amendment issues here?

3.   Exemptions.   As noted in the adopting release, there are two large carve-outs from the application of Regulation FD. One is for communications made in connection with registered public offerings. The effect here is to permit limited access "road shows" in which otherwise confidential information is discussed. The Commission's justification for this is that '33 Act registration assures the disclosure of all material nonpublic information in the prospectus once the selling begins, so that it is not necessary to limit private communications beforehand. Do you agree? Should the same logic be extended to private placements? (Pursuant to the 2005 securities offering reforms discussed in Chapter 4, this exemption was revised to make clear the kinds of communications that are permitted and the kinds that are not.) The other major exemption is for foreign issuers, who need not comply with Reg FD. What could justify such disparate treatment of U.S. and foreign companies? *See* Fox, Reg FD and Foreign Issuers: Globalization's Strains and Opportunities, 41 Va. J. Int'l L. 653 (2001). There had also been an exception for disclosures to credit rating agencies, but this was eliminated at the direction of Congress in the Dodd-Frank Act.

4.   Enforcement.   In its first enforcement cases under Regulation FD, the SEC adhered closely to the spirit of the regulation, going after companies that used private channels of communication to reach out to analysts who didn't seem to get what the company was trying to say in its public announcements. In a "21(a) Report" involving Motorola Inc., Exchange Act Release No. 46898 (Nov. 25, 2002), the SEC described a situation where company officials had publicly stated that sales for the quarter in question would be "significantly" lower. Analysts reacted by reducing their earnings estimates, but in the company's view, insufficiently. Hence, company officials called key analysts to explain that the use of the term significant means a drop of at least 25 percent. The Commission found this to be a violation of Regulation FD, making the following observation:

> When communicating with securities industry professionals, issuers may not use "code" words to selectively disclose information that they could not selectively disclose expressly. Issuers may not evade the public disclosure requirements of Reg FD by using "code" words or "winks and nods" to convey material nonpublic information during private conversations. What is particularly troubling about this case is that Motorola communicated to the public using general terms such as "significant" and then engaged in private discussions with analysts to provide a more detailed quantitative definition of the code word "significant."

5.   Analyst Conflicts.   As noted in the adopting release, one concern about selective disclosure is that it might lead analysts to be excessively kind to the company in their recommendations in order to maintain access to private information. Subsequent to the adoption of Regulation FD, a stronger reason to doubt the objectivity of analyst recommendations became clear in the course of investigations into whether multi-service financial firms were pressuring their own analysts into unduly favorable research to enhance the firms' ability to gain investment banking business from the companies being covered. This issue—and the resulting regulatory and enforcement responses—was raised in Chapter 4 and is discussed again in Chapter 18, dealing with the responsibilities of broker-dealer firms.

PROBLEMS

15-7. Soconics Corp., which is publicly traded, hit a rough period in revenue growth in the fourth quarter due to a number of factors, including the loss of a major customer. Its public disclosures have fully reflected this, cautiously expressing the hope that new contracts under negotiation would soon make up for the losses and permit the company to regain its momentum. In the last week or so, Soconics has all but finalized two of the biggest new sales that it was hoping for, and optimism is growing internally. This evening, the Soconics CFO will have a dinner meeting with portfolio managers from one of its largest institutional shareholders. He expects to be asked how the company is doing in its negotiations. What if he tells them about the sales? What if instead he says that he's not in a position to give any details but that the company is "very, very pleased" with what is happening? What if he says that it would be premature to comment on the status of the negotiations, but mentions the names of the two major potential customers—and analysts use this lead to contact those companies and confirm the status of the deals? *See SEC v. Siebel Systems*, 384 F. Supp. 2d 694 (S.D.N.Y. 2005) (dismissing complaint because what was privately disclosed was not sufficiently at odds with the public disclosures).

15-8. As counsel for a publicly traded company, you have been asked to help with compliance with Regulation FD. The company is about to release an earnings forecast that will surprise the market. As a result, many phone calls from analysts and investors are likely, which will seek further details (some of which relate to matters not yet fully disclosed by the company). What procedure would you recommend for dealing with these contacts? Would it be acceptable to tell those who call that there will be a conference call later in the week to which all interested parties can listen? What about a web cast of the conference call?

F. Rule 14e-3

By the time that *Chiarella* was decided, the SEC had determined that trading in connection with knowledge of impending tender offers was one of the most prevalent and profitable forms of insider trading. Thus, the Supreme Court's decision was a substantial blow to the Commission's enforcement program. In response, the Commission quickly adopted Rule 14e-3, which makes conduct of the sort in which Chiarella engaged a violation of the Williams Act.

Rule 14e-3 operates in a reasonably straightforward fashion. First, once a substantial step toward the commencement of a tender offer has been taken, it bars any person (other than the bidder) from acquiring any securities while in possession of material information that he knows or has reason to know: (a) is nonpublic; and (b) was acquired from the bidder, the target, or any person associated with either one of these. In this regard, two points are noteworthy. First, there is no reference to any breach of fiduciary duty. Second, the state of mind emphasizes the "reason to know" locution. Rule 14e-3 also contains an anti-tipping provision—barring the communication of material nonpublic information concerning a tender offer to persons where it is reasonably foreseeable that such communication is likely to result in unlawful trading. On the meaning of a "substantial step," *see SEC v. Mayhew*, 123 F.3d 44 (2d Cir. 1997) (test satisfied where bidder had retained a consulting firm, signed a confidentiality agreement, and was having ongoing meetings with target officials).

Given the extent to which the SEC has sought to avoid the impact of *Chiarella* through this non-10(b) rule, the obvious question is whether it exceeded its statutory authority in so doing. In adopting the Rule, the SEC pointed to bits of legislative history in the Williams Act to support the view that fraud (at least for insider trading purposes) could be understood differently under Section 14(e) as compared to Section 10(b). In *O'Hagan*, in addition to affirming the use of the misappropriation theory, the Supreme Court upheld the validity of Rule 14e-3, finding it a proper exercise of the authority to define "and prescribe means reasonably designed to prevent" tender offer fraud. The Court said:

> The United States emphasizes that Rule 14e-3(a) reaches trading in which "a breach of duty is likely but difficult to prove." "Particularly in the context of a tender offer," as the Tenth Circuit recognized, "there is a fairly wide circle of people with confidential information," [*SEC v. Peters*, 978 F.2d 1162, 1167 (10th Cir. 1992)], notably, the attorneys, investment bankers, and accountants involved in structuring the transaction. The availability of that information may lead to abuse, for "even a hint of an upcoming tender offer may send the price of the target company's stock soaring." *SEC v. Materia*, 745 F.2d 197, 199 (2d Cir. 1984). Individuals entrusted with nonpublic information, particularly if they have no long-term loyalty to the issuer, may find the temptation to trade on that information hard to resist in view of "the very large short-term profits potentially available [to them]." *Peters*, 978 F.2d at 1167.
>
> "It may be possible to prove circumstantially that a person [traded on the basis of material, nonpublic information], but almost impossible to prove that the trader obtained such information in breach of a fiduciary duty owed either by the trader or by the ultimate insider source of the information." Ibid. The example of a "tippee" who trades on information received from an insider illustrates the problem. Under Rule 10b-5, "a tippee assumes a fiduciary duty to the shareholders of a corporation not to trade on material nonpublic information only when the insider has breached his fiduciary duty to the shareholders by disclosing the information to the tippee and the tippee knows or should know that there has been a breach." *Dirks*, 463 U.S. at 660. To show that a tippee who traded on nonpublic information about a tender offer had breached a fiduciary duty would require proof not only that the insider source breached a fiduciary duty, but that the tippee knew or should have known of that breach. "Yet, in most cases, the only parties to the [information transfer] will be the insider and the alleged tippee." *Peters*, 978 F.2d at 1167.

In sum, it is a fair assumption that trading on the basis of material, nonpublic information will often involve a breach of a duty of confidentiality to the bidder or target company or their representatives. The SEC, cognizant of the proof problem that could enable sophisticated traders to escape responsibility, placed in Rule 14e-3(a) a "disclose or abstain from trading" command that does not require specific proof of a breach of fiduciary duty. . . . Therefore, insofar as it serves to prevent the type of misappropriation charged against O'Hagan, Rule 14e-3(a) is a proper exercise of the Commission's prophylactic power under Section 14(e). . . .

521 U.S. at 674-676. This disposition, however, led the Court in footnote 17 to suggest limits on the use of the Rule:

We leave for another day, when the issue requires decision, the legitimacy of Rule 14e-3(a) as applied to "warehousing," which the Government describes as "the practice by which bidders leak advance information of a tender offer to allies and encourage them to purchase the target company's stock before the bid is announced." As we observed in *Chiarella*, one of the Commission's purposes in proposing Rule 14e-3(a) was "to bar warehousing under its authority to regulate tender offers." 445 U.S. at 234. The Government acknowledges that trading authorized by a principal breaches no fiduciary duty. The instant case, however, does not involve trading authorized by a principal; therefore, we need not here decide whether the Commission's proscription of warehousing falls within its Section 14(e) authority to define or prevent fraud.

PROBLEM

15-9. While in the secret planning stage for a corporate takeover of Beta Pharmaceuticals, Alpha Corporation entered into a formal arrangement with a hedge fund pursuant to which the hedge fund would acquire Beta stock (and derivatives on such stock), which could be expected to increase in value if and when the bid was publicly announced. The hedge fund agreed that it would use its power to support the acquisition, and if it succeeded, transfer the securities to Alpha. Would this violate Rule 14e-3? Would it make a difference if they described themselves as partners or co-bidders in the acquisition? *See Allergan Inc. v. Valeant Pharmaceuticals Int'l Inc.*, 2014 WL 5604539 (C.D. Cal. 2014) (finding that the plaintiffs "raised serious questions" that the conduct there would violate the Rule).

G. Enforcement of the Insider Trading Prohibition

Until 1984, the SEC was effectively limited in the remedies it could pursue in insider trading cases. It could, of course, seek an injunction against the defendants as well as an order of disgorgement of profits. Beyond that, the only option was to refer the matter to the Justice Department for possible criminal prosecution, a decision wholly out of the Commission's hands.

Sensing that this did not create a sufficient level of deterrence, Congress in 1984 added a new section to the Securities Exchange Act, giving the Commission the authority to seek a civil penalty of up to three times the amount of profits made or losses avoided by any person who violates Rule 10b-5 or 14e-3 by trading or tipping. This penalty is in addition to any disgorgement or criminal fine that might be ordered. This penalty mechanism is exclusive for insider trading cases; the SEC cannot resort to the more general civil penalty authority for securities law violations that you studied in Chapter 14 in order to seek more than three times profit. *See SEC v. Rosenthal,* 650 F.3d 156 (2d Cir. 2011).

In 1988, Congress once again visited the remedial question and in the Insider Trading and Securities Fraud Enforcement Act revised what is now Section 21A of the Securities Exchange Act in a number of discrete respects, while seeking to preserve its basic structure. Most importantly, Congress established a scheme of liability for those who "control" others found liable for insider trading or tipping. Section 21A(a)(3) provides that controlling persons shall *independently* be liable for a civil penalty of the greater of $1 million (now adjusted upward to account for inflation) or treble the profits made or losses avoided by the controlled person. Where liability is based upon tipping by the controlled person, the profits portion of the cap is based upon trading by direct tippees, not remote ones—a provision, by the way, that obviously reflects the belief on the part of the drafters that remote tippee trading, in general, is otherwise covered by Rule 10b-5 (recall the debate on this supra). Liability is limited, however, to situations where either (1) the controlling person "knew or recklessly disregarded the fact that such controlled person was likely to engage in the act or acts constituting the violation and failed to take appropriate steps to prevent such act or acts before they occurred"; or (2) if the controlling person was a registered brokerage firm or investment adviser—and thus independently required under other provisions of the 1988 legislation to adopt policies and procedures to discourage employee insider trading—the firm knowingly or recklessly failed to establish, maintain, or enforce such procedures and such failure substantially contributed to or permitted the occurrence of the violation.

This sort of legislation—which also authorized heavier criminal penalties for violators—reflects a strong desire to deter insider trading. But deterrence will occur only to the extent that persons who engage in unlawful trading have reason to believe that they will be caught and prosecuted. *See generally* Seyhun, The Effectiveness of Insider Trading Sanctions, 35 J.L. & Econ. 149 (1992) (expressing skepticism about the value of increased sanctions standing alone). With trading on the exchanges done anonymously, and false names and dummy and foreign bank accounts readily available, how likely is detection? Unfortunately, there is much evidence that insider trading is fairly widespread notwithstanding the strong prohibition. Many studies document significant price movements before major corporate events such as mergers, issuer repurchases, and earnings releases. *E.g.,* Ke et al., What Insiders Know About Future Earnings and How They Use It: Evidence of Insider Trades, 35 J. Acct. & Econ. 315 (2003). While there might be some innocent explanations, the literature cautions that unlawful trading may still be pervasive.

The SEC's principal method of detection is to work backward from circumstantial evidence. Stock exchanges, for example, have online surveillance
systems designed to alert officials when trading in a company's stock moves
outside of predetermined parameters (i.e., behaves oddly in comparison to the
rest of the market). Upon such an event, company officials can be contacted
to see if there is any legitimate explanation. If not (or if shortly thereafter
there is a major announcement by the company or a bidder that suggests that
the strange pattern of trading was in anticipation thereof), an investigation
will probably begin. All brokerage firms are obligated to keep records of precisely who traded at any given time and turn them over to the exchanges in
computer-readable form. With this, the identities of traders can be obtained.
At this point, a process of computer analysis begins, designed to spot any "clus-
ters" of trading—for example, was there an unusual volume attributable to
a particular geographic location or emanating from a particular brokerage
office? Assisting in this function are increasingly sophisticated computer algo-
rithms that search for suspicious patterns, permitting cross-checking on such
matters as social affiliations and even school ties. Once suspicious evidence
begins to turn up, the exchange will probably refer the matter to the SEC for
a more formal investigation. The SEC can seek to subpoena phone records
and take depositions—occasionally promising immunity to certain persons in
order to break walls of silence—in order to focus in on the source of the information. Once a source is identified, it is not that much more difficult to obtain
the identities of all persons who both traded in the stock and had some contact
with that source. In the end, then, even "small fry" trading can be detected.

What about the role of private rights of action? In the 1970s, there was some
reason to believe that an insider would be liable to all persons who traded
during the period of time between the breach and the subsequent disclosure
of the information in question, liability that could truly be draconian if each
of those traders was awarded the difference between the trading price and
the value of the shares had disclosure been made at the time of the breach.
See Shapiro v. Merrill Lynch, Pierce, Fenner & Smith, 495 F.2d 228 (2d Cir. 1974).
Subsequent case law, however, narrowed this exposure considerably. The 1988
legislation codifies the narrower approach in Section 20A, establishing a private right of action for contemporaneous traders to sue insiders, tippers, and
tippees, regardless of what theory is used to impose liability, thus implicitly
overruling *Moss v. Morgan Stanley Inc.*, 719 F.2d 5 (2d Cir. 1983) (denying standing to marketplace traders under the misappropriation theory). But recovery
is limited to the amount of the trading profits and then further reduced to the
extent that the SEC has already obtained disgorgement of those profits. What
does this do to the economic viability of such an action? To the deterrence
effect? The language and legislative history of the 1988 law make clear that
codification of this private right of action is not meant to preclude suits by
other persons who can demonstrate injury as a result of insider trading. Does
this mean that a bidding company might be able to sue an insider or tippee
for damages if it could show that as a result of the trading, it had to pay more
to make the acquisition or lost the deal? What legal and practical problems
do you foresee in proving such allegations? *See Litton Industries v. Lehman Bros.
Kuhn Loeb Inc.*, 967 F.2d 742 (2d Cir. 1992).

PROBLEM

15-10. Seeking Alpha LLC is a very large hedge fund run by a celebrated trader and investor, Alphonse Smith. Recently, a trader at Seeking Alpha—Ian Rambo—was arrested for insider trading, based on evidence that he used contacts associated with a variety of pharmaceutical companies to gain inside information about pending drug trials. Smith is famous for his hands-on relationships with his traders and analysts, and for his system of rewarding superior performance lavishly, and being merciless with laggards. Seeking Alpha has a formal insider trading compliance policy that warns employees to avoid situations where insider trading issues might arise, and to seek advice should they find themselves in gray areas. There is random monitoring of e-mail traffic and phone conversations by compliance officers, but most traders and analysts have their own smart phones that are not readily subject to surveillance. What is the risk that Smith would personally be liable if it were determined that Rambo had broken the law? If you were an SEC enforcement attorney, what would you be looking for to build a case against Smith?

H. *Insider Trading and Section 16*

As the foregoing materials have indicated, the reach of the antifraud provisions of the Securities Exchange Act was not extended to open-market insider trading until the 1960s. Prior to that, the only federal response to concern about insider trading was Section 16. There Congress sought to regulate the problem prophylactically, primarily by depriving high-level insiders of any profits made as a result of short-swing trading. The orthodox explanation for this is that, while Congress considered insider trading abusive, it did not think that direct regulation was practicable. Now that more and more emphasis is being placed on encouraging insider ownership of securities in order to align the incentives of managers and shareholders in corporate governance, the question of the efficacy of this sort of regulation is increasingly controversial. *See* Fox, Insider Trading Deterrence Versus Managerial Incentives: A Unified Theory of Section 16(b), 92 Mich. L. Rev. 2088 (1994). For interesting (and unconventional) explorations of what Congress was really trying to get at, *see* Okamoto, Rereading Section 16(b) of the Securities Exchange Act, 27 Ga. L. Rev. 183 (1992); Thel, The Genius of Section 16: Regulating the Management of Publicly Held Corporations, 42 Hastings L.J. 393 (1991).

Most of what follows focuses on Section 16(b). But we ought to first pay some attention to Section 16(a). That provision is a reporting obligation, imposed on officers, directors, and 10 percent shareholders, to file with the SEC forms that indicate holdings in the issuer's stock upon achieving insider status (Form 3). Thereafter, most purchases or sales by the insider have to be reported by the end of the second business day following the transaction on Form 4. *See* Rule 16a-3(g). This "real time" reporting of insider transactions is a product of the Sarbanes-Oxley Act of 2002, stemming from concern that many insiders bailed out of company stock in advance of discovery that the company had not been honest in its financial reporting, without the public being aware of those trades until much later. These reports are now made available electronically through the EDGAR system, and on the issuer's web site, if it has one. *See* Rule 16a-3(k). An annual filing (Form 5) is permitted to report certain other ownership changes—largely transactions exempt from the operation of Section 16(b) and certain "small acquisitions"—although even here the Sarbanes-Oxley Act narrowed the category of transactions subject to delayed disclosure.

These filings serve a dual purpose. No doubt the intended one is to discourage high-level insider trading by assuring its publicity and to assist in the enforcement of Section 16(b). But there is also a substantial private demand for Form 4 filings because many investors believe that tracking trading by insiders—even where there is no illegality—is a useful way of assessing the prospects of a company. Indeed, major financial newspapers report regularly on significant insider transactions, utilizing these filings. In 1991, the SEC imposed greater obligations upon issuers to assure compliance with Section 16(a) by requiring mandatory reporting on such compliance in proxy statements and 10-Ks. Would it make better sense to require disclosure by insiders before they trade, rather than two days afterwards? For a proposal that would make such pre-trading disclosure the primary weapon against trading by the full range of corporate insiders, *see* Fried, Reducing the Profitability of Insider Trading Through Pretrading Disclosure, 71 S. Cal. L. Rev. 303 (1998).

1.   The Scope of Section 16(b)

Huppe v. WPCS Int'l Inc.
670 F.3d 214 (2d Cir. 2012)

PARKER, J.:

Section 16(b) of the Securities Exchange Act of 1934 imposes strict liability on insiders whose purchases and sales of securities result in "short-swing profits." Insiders include directors, officers, and "beneficial owners" of more than 10% of a company's registered securities—namely, persons who exercise voting or investment control over, and hold a pecuniary interest in, more than 10% of a company's registered securities.

This appeal concerns whether a beneficial owner's acquisition of securities directly from an issuer—at the issuer's request and with the board's approval—should be exempt from the definition of a "purchase" under Section 16(b), on the theory that such a transaction lacks the "potential for speculative abuse" that Section 16(b) was designed to curb. *See Kern Cnty. Land Co. v. Occidental Petroleum Corp.*, 411 U.S. 582, 599 (1973). We hold that such transactions are covered by Section 16(b). We further hold that the Defendants–Appellants, who are limited partnerships, are beneficial owners for the purposes of Section 16(b) liability, notwithstanding their delegation of voting and investment control over their securities portfolios to their general partners' agents. Accordingly, we affirm the judgment of the district court.

Background

Defendants–Appellants, Special Situations Fund III QP, L.P. ("QP") and Special Situations Private Equity Fund, L.P. ("PE") (together, the "Funds") are Delaware limited partnerships. The Funds invest in publicly traded companies through so-called "PIPE" (private investment in public equity) transactions—privately negotiated acquisitions of positions in publicly traded companies. At all relevant times, each fund owned over 10% of the shares of nominal Defendant WPCS International Incorporated ("WPCS"), a wireless infrastructure engineering and special communications systems company whose shares trade on the NASDAQ.

The Funds' limited partnership agreements provide that "the management, operation and control of the business of the Fund shall be vested completely and exclusively in [a] General Partner" who "shall have the right, power and authority, on behalf of the Fund and in its name, to exercise all rights, powers and authority of a general partner under the laws of Delaware." The partnership agreements further empower each general partner to invest or reinvest the limited partnership's assets, and to appoint agents to perform the general partner's duties. PE's general partner is a limited liability company of which Austin W. Marxe and David M. Greenhouse are members. QP's general partner is a limited partnership of which Marxe and Greenhouse are limited partners. Through these arrangements, Marxe and Greenhouse hold the exclusive power to make all investment and voting decisions on behalf of the general partners and, in turn, on behalf of the Funds.

Beginning in December 2005 and continuing until the end of January 2006, the Funds sold WPCS shares in their portfolios on the open market at prices between $9.183 and $12.62 per share. These sales constituted the first leg of the trades for which the Funds now face disgorgement liability under Section 16(b).

In March 2006, WPCS announced that a change in applicable accounting rules required it to restate certain financial statements. WPCS's share price fell precipitously on the announcement, compromising WPCS's plans for a secondary public offering intended to raise capital for a critical strategic acquisition. At that point, WPCS approached Marxe and Greenhouse to gauge their interest in a PIPE transaction. (Marxe and Greenhouse had already closed one PIPE transaction with WPCS in November 2004 for $5 million.) They responded favorably and, on April 11, 2006, the Funds, together with other funds managed by Marxe and Greenhouse, bought 876,931 additional shares directly from WPCS at $7.00 per share—a discount of approximately 7% from the market price. WPCS's board of directors approved the transaction. WPCS used the new capital to make the acquisition, and the company's share price began to improve.

Plaintiff–Appellee Maureen A. Huppe, a WPCS shareholder, subsequently filed this derivative action alleging that the Funds, as ten percent holders, were liable to WPCS under Section 16(b) for their short swing profits—namely, the difference between the prices at which the Funds sold WPCS shares from December 2005 to January 2006, and the lower prices of the April purchases. Matching these sales and purchases, Huppe sought disgorgement of approximately $486,000. . . .

DISCUSSION

The Funds argue that the district court erred in its determinations that the 2006 PIPE transaction was a non-exempt purchase of WPCS shares and that the Funds were "beneficial owners" under Section 16(b). Section 16(b) provides that officers, directors, and principal shareholders of a company are liable for profits realized from the purchase and sale (or sale and purchase) of its shares within a six-month period. The section was designed to prevent these insiders from engaging in speculative transactions on the basis of information not available to others. The 1934 Act defines "purchases" and "sales" broadly. As we have observed, it is "quite apparent" that Section 16(b) may be applied not only to routine cash purchases and sales, but also to acquisitions and dispositions of equity securities in transactions such as conversions, options, stock warrants, and reclassifications. *See Blau v. Lamb*, 363 F.2d 507, 516 (2d Cir. 1966). The Funds' acquisition of stock from WPCS in April 2006 clearly falls within the literal terms of Section 16(b). . . .

Nevertheless, the Funds argue that we should exempt the April transaction from Section 16(b)'s coverage because it was the product of direct negotiations between WPCS and the Funds and approved by WPCS's board of directors. Thus, they argue, even if one assumes the Funds had access to inside information about WPCS, it was impossible for the Funds to gain any speculative advantage from such information because WPCS and its board—which approved the transaction—had access to the same information.

Section 16(b) has been described as a "blunt instrument," *Magma Power Co. v. Dow Chem. Co.*, 136 F.3d 316, 321 (2d Cir. 1998), "a flat rule taking the profits out of a class of transactions in which the possibility of abuse was believed to be intolerably great," *Reliance Elec. Co. v. Emerson Elec. Co.*, 404 U.S. 418, 422, 92 S. Ct. 596, 30 L. Ed. 2d 575 (1972). Significantly, no showing of actual misuse of inside information or of unlawful intent is necessary to compel disgorgement. In limited circumstances, we scrutinize "borderline" or "unorthodox" transactions "pragmatic[ally]" to determine whether they serve as a "vehicle for the evil which Congress sought to prevent—the realization of short-swing profits based upon access to inside information." *Kern Cnty.*, supra. However, "[t]his Circuit has suggested that . . . an [1] involuntary transaction by an insider [2] having no access to inside information . . . are prerequisites to use of the *Kern County* analysis." Moreover, we have been clear that Section 16(b) should be applied without further inquiry if there is "at least the possibility" of speculative abuse of inside information.

The 2006 PIPE transaction was not a "borderline" transaction within the meaning of *Kern County* because the Funds gave WPCS a wholly volitional capital infusion and had access to inside information. Indeed, the SEC has taken the position that ten percent holders "can be presumed to have access to inside information because they can influence or control the issuer as a result of their equity ownership." Ownership Reports and Trading by Officers, Directors and Principal Stockholders, Exchange Act Release No. 34-28869, 56 Fed. Reg. 7242, 7244 (Feb. 21, 1991). Nothing about the 2006 PIPE transaction foreclosed the Funds' potential influence over WPCS. . . .

Section 16(b) provides that it shall not "be construed to cover . . . any transaction . . . which the Commission by rules and regulations may exempt as not comprehended within the purpose of [Section 16(b)]." 15 U.S.C. §78p(b). Exercising its broad authority under the statute, the SEC promulgated Rule 16b-3(d), which exempts from Section 16(b)'s coverage directors' and officers' board-approved acquisition of securities directly from issuers. Relying on this exemption, the Funds argue that, even though they are not directors or officers, their acquisition of stock directly from WPCS via the 2006 PIPE transaction was similarly "not comprehended within the purpose" of Section 16(b). . . .

Because the Funds are neither directors by deputization, nor officers or directors, Rule 16b-3(d) does not apply. Significantly, the SEC has expressly declined to include ten percent holders within Rule 16b-3(d)'s exemption because, unlike officers and directors, they do not necessarily owe fiduciary duties to a corporation. *See* Ownership Reports and Trading by Officers, Directors and Principal Security Holders, Exchange Act Release No. 34-37260, 61 Fed. Reg. 30376, 30378 n. 42 (June 14, 1996) (1996 Adopting Release) ("Such duties, which act as an independent constraint on self-dealing, may not extend to ten percent holders. The lack of other constraints argues against making new Rule 16b-3 available to ten percent holders.").

Moreover, our finding . . . that the transactions covered by Rule 16b-3 (d) were properly exempted from Section 16(b) *by the SEC*—which has broad exemptive authority under the statute not shared by the courts—does not mean those transactions lack any risk of speculative abuse, such as the possible exploitation of information asymmetry. Similarly, the fact that issuers and insiders will share access to the same "inside" information in most issuer-insider transactions does not mean that *every* issuer-insider transaction is invulnerable to information asymmetry. . . . Faced with the "possibility" that such transactions may be "susceptible to abuse of inside information," and no statutory exemption for beneficial owners, our inquiry ends. Therefore, since their purchases are not exempt from the statute's coverage, if the Funds are beneficial owners, they are liable for short-swing profits.

NOTES AND QUESTIONS

1. Officers and Directors. The tension between the realistic and the mechanical approaches to statutory construction surfaces in the definitions of both officer and director. Should any person with the title "vice president" be considered an officer, even if she is in fact a relatively mid-level manager? What of a person with power, but without the title? *See* Rule 16a-1(f) (defining officer). As to directors, does putting a director on the board to represent the interests of another make the other a "director," too? *See Feder v. Martin Marietta Corp.*, 406 F.2d 260 (2d Cir. 1969).

It is clear from the statute that a person need not be an officer or a director at the time of both the purchase and the sale. The SEC has provided in Rule 16a-2(a), however, that transactions occurring within six months *prior* to the person achieving such status are exempt from Section 16(b). Why not *after* as well?

2.   Ten Percent Shareholders.   Contrasting with the treatment of officers and directors, Section 16(b) explicitly states that liability will not arise with respect to any matched purchase and sale "where such [10 percent] beneficial owner was not such *both* at the time of the purchase and sale, or the sale and purchase, of the security involved" (emphasis added). The Supreme Court has construed this to mean that (1) the transaction that makes a person a 10 percent share-holder is not a purchase for purposes of the section (hence those securities are free from taint), *see Foremost McKesson Inc. v. Provident Securities Co.,* 423 U.S. 232 (1976); and (2) the transaction that brings him below that level is a Section 16(b) sale, but any subsequent bona fide sales (even if only a day later) are not covered, *see Reliance Electric Co. v. Emerson Electric Co.,* 404 U.S. 418 (1972).

With respect to 10 percent shareholders, perhaps the most often litigated question is what constitutes beneficial ownership. For instance, is a wife the beneficial owner of the securities of her estranged husband? Is a father the beneficial owner of the securities owned by a college-age son? As *Huppe* points out, for purposes of determining whether a person is a 10 percent holder, the test here is one of the power to vote or dispose of the securities in question. Rule 16a-1(a)(1). That contrasts with an entirely different definition of benefi-cial ownership in Rule 16a-1(a)(2), which addresses whether a purchase or sale nominally by some third party should be attributed to an insider. This second definition turns on whether the insider has a direct or indirect pecuniary inter-est in the transaction. Why should the definition of 10 percent ownership be different from that for determining whether to attribute a third-party purchase or sale to an insider?

3.   Securities Covered.   One of the most important concepts under Section 16(b) is that of fungibility: There is no requirement that the insider has bought and sold the same share of stock. Economic equivalence is the test. Thus, for example, the purchase of a convertible debenture can be matched with the sale of common stock, whether or not there was conversion. *See Gund v. First Florida Banks Inc.,* 726 F.2d 682 (11th Cir. 1984). This approach raises very difficult problems with respect to options and other "derivative" securities. In 1991, the SEC decided to rationalize the law in this area, making clear that for purposes of short-swing liability, the acquisition or disposition of the derivative security is the operative event. Exercise or conversion is not important. *See* Rules 16a-1(c), 16a-4. One consequence of this rule change was that executives holding large numbers of stock options given to them by the company became free to exer-cise those options and sell immediately—enabling them to quickly take advan-tage of market movements (or market distortions). For a critique, *see* Okamoto, Oversimplification and the SEC's Treatment of Derivative Securities Trading by Corporate Insiders, 1993 Wis. L. Rev. 1287.

4.   Timing.   Precisely how long is six months? Assume the shares were pur-chased on September 30. Precisely what is the first day on which such shares could be sold? Is it March 30? Is it 180 days from September 30? Is it the last day of March, since September 30 was the last day of September? *See Jammies Int'l Inc. v. Nowinski,* 700 F. Supp. 189 (S.D.N.Y. 1988). Consider carefully the effects of short months and leap years in making up your mind.

5. Unorthodox Transactions. Ever since the Supreme Court announced its *Kern County* pragmatic approach, the lower courts have had trouble applying it. Three factors in particular have received disparate judicial treatment. One is whether the challenged sale is volitional. Some courts have suggested that to qualify as unorthodox the transaction in question must be involuntary, while others have indicated a more flexible approach; *see, e.g., Pay Less Drug Stores v. Jewel Cos.*, 579 F. Supp. 1396 (N.D. Cal. 1984). Courts also vary in their approach to the possibility of speculative abuse—is the question one of actual access to information, or is the only issue whether the defendant's status was of the sort that would normally create such access? *Compare Gold v. Sloan*, 486 F.2d 340 (4th Cir. 1973) (access in fact) *with Kay v. Scientex Corp.*, 719 F.2d 1009 (9th Cir. 1983) (status inquiry only). Is it possible to formulate a rational policy regarding unorthodox transactions?

6. Enforcement. Section 16(b) is curious in many respects. One is that it cannot be enforced publicly. The only mechanism for short-swing profit recovery is a suit by the issuer or a shareholder suing on its behalf. For this reason, perhaps, courts have been quite willing to read the statute in a way that facilitates both the willingness to bring suit and the deterrence against insiders. *See Smolowe v. Delendo Corp.*, 136 F.2d 231 (2d Cir. 1943). In this regard, courts measure profits according to the "lowest in, highest out" approach in cases where there are multiple purchases and sales to be matched. Id. The lowest purchase price is matched with the highest sale price, then the second lowest and highest, and so on until there are no more profits to be found. Any remaining purchases or sales that net out to a loss are disregarded. Under this approach, an insider can be liable for large amounts of profits, even where he lost money on his purchase and sale activity in the aggregate. *See Gratz v. Claughton*, 187 F.2d 46, 52-53 (2d Cir. 1951), *cert. denied*, 341 U.S. 920 (1952) (recovery of some $300,000, even though insider lost over $400,000 on the trading). Should recovery under Section 16(b) be limited if the SEC has already obtained disgorgement of insider trading profits? *See National Westminster Bancorp v. Leone*, 703 F. Supp. 1132 (D.N.J. 1988). On the statute of limitations for Section 16(b) actions, the Supreme Court has ruled that the statute of limitations begins to run regardless of whether the insider disclosed the trading as required via a Form 4. *Credit Suisse Securities LLC v. Simmonds*, 566 U.S. 221 (2012). It divided equally on the question of whether the doctrine of equitable tolling applies so that the time does not begin to run until the trading could have been discovered.

PROBLEMS

15-11. James McLaughlin owns 9 percent of the outstanding common shares of Raybell Corp., a company he founded and then sold a few years ago. He is separated from his wife, but is required pursuant to the separation agreement to provide such funds as are necessary to the "educational well-being" of their teenage children. Also as part of the separation, his children received shares equal to 1.5 percent of the company in a trust, which will be the primary resource for their college expenses. McLaughlin's former wife was named as trustee. The separation is relatively amicable, and McLaughlin's wife—an English professor with little interest in business matters—typically consults him regarding matters relating to the Raybell stock. On May 1, McLaughlin was invited to rejoin the Raybell board of directors, from which he had resigned when he sold most of his interest. That same day, he bought 500 shares of Raybell convertible preferred stock. On July 1, McLaughlin formally became a director. On July 15, his wife sold 600 shares of Raybell common for the trust, and McLaughlin sold 100 shares of common stock. Any Section 16(b) problems? What are McLaughlin's beneficial ownership interests here?

15-12.   Balkan Corp. acquired some 22.4 percent of Ferris Metals Corp. (FMC), at prices ranging from $22 to $27 per share, and threatened a takeover. Soon thereafter, FMC offered to buy back Balkan's stock at $35 per share, with a standstill agreement, and Balkan agreed in principle. But Section 16(b) was a problem. At the crucial point in the negotiations, 40 percent of Balkan's stock had been acquired more than six months previously and the other 60 percent only within the last few months. The parties thereupon agreed to artificially adjust the price upward so that when Balkan "conceded" its liability under Section 16(b)—and returned to FMC that portion of its profits attributable to the shares that were acquired within the six-month period—it just happened to be left with a sum of money equal to $35 per share for all its shares. Could there be any recovery under Section 16(b) by a disgruntled shareholder? *See Sterman v. Ferro Corp.*, 785 F.2d 162 (6th Cir. 1986).

2.   Executive Compensation

Of all the practical problems under Section 16(b), none has been more complicated than dealing with the acquisition of securities by insiders pursuant to executive compensation programs. Were the section to be applied strictly, executives who regularly receive some form of stock or stock equivalents as part of a compensation package would find themselves constantly concerned with potential liability whenever they sought to sell any of their holdings.

Recognizing that some forms of compensation programs are such that the opportunity for speculative abuse is remote, the SEC adopted Rule 16b-3. In 1996, as *Huppe* notes, the Commission dramatically expanded the scope of the exemption so as to eliminate much of the coverage of Section 16(b), and simplify significantly the reporting obligations as well, with respect to transactions between the issuer (or its employee benefit plan) and its officers and directors. Exchange Act Release No. 37260 (May 31, 1996). This is based on the idea that transactions with the issuer do not involve the same kind of abuses as open-market transactions. Tax-conditioned plans receive almost full exemption; other acquisitions from the issuer are exempt if (a) the transaction is approved by the board of directors or a committee of at least two nonemployee directors; (b) it is approved by shareholders; or (c) the security is held for six months. What is the purpose of the "corporate governance" conditions in (a) and (b)? What harm comes when transactions are with the company rather than with members of the investing public?

3.   Pension Blackout Periods

Quite distinct from Section 16(b) but having to do with insider trades connected with employee benefit plans, the Sarbanes-Oxley Act of 2002 bars executive officers and directors of public companies from trading in issuer securities at the same time that the issuer has imposed a "blackout period" barring rank and file employees from buying or selling issuer stock in individually directed accounts in the company's pension or employee benefit plans. This was a specific response to the Enron scandal: Enron executives reportedly sold substantial amounts of stock at a time, not much before bankruptcy, when Enron prohibited its employees from selling company stock in their individual pension fund accounts. This provision creates a 16(b)-like cause of action whereby the issuer, or a shareholder suing on its behalf, can recapture the executive's or director's profits. Issuers must give notice to their executives and directors so that they know when this obligation is triggered.

4.   Is There a Need for Reform?

From American Bar Association's Committee on the Federal Regulation of Securities, Report of the Task Force on Regulation of Insider Trading—Part II: Reform of Section 16, 42 Bus. Law. 1087 (1987):

> In recent years, a number of commentators have suggested that section 16(b) causes more harm than good and that it should be repealed. It has been argued that section 16(b) is ineffectual in preventing insider trading and does not even address all of the ways in which insider trades can be perpetrated, while it imposes punitive liability on the innocent, the naive, and the unaware corporate officers who unwittingly sell in violation of, for example, the labyrinthine restrictions of rule 16b-3. These commentators raise the question: Given the development of the insider trading doctrine under rule 10b-5, the substantial limitations of section 16(b) in preventing insider trading, and the hardships that it imposes, is the statute needed?
>
> The task force believes that it is. Section 16(b) has a different legislative focus than the prohibition of trading on inside information. Indeed, it is the only provision of the 1934 Act that specifically regulates insider trading. It is aimed at three specific types of insider trading abuses, only one of which involves abuse of inside information.
>
> First, section 16(b) was intended to remove the temptation for corporation executives to profit from short-term stock price fluctuations at the expense of the long-term financial health of their companies. It prevents insiders from being obsessed with trading in their companies' securities to the detriment of their managerial and fiduciary responsibilities. In this regard, based on the testimony of insider abuses presented at the hearings, it was Congress's judgment that short-swing trading by corporate executives is not good for their companies or the American capital markets.
>
> Second, the section was intended to penalize the unfair use of inside information by insiders. This includes both trading on inside information in violation of rule 10b-5 and the use of "softer" information of the type that insiders often have but that members of the investing public do not: the ability to make better informed guesses as to the success of new products, the likely results of negotiations, and the

real risks of contingencies and other uncertainties, the underlying facts of which have been publicly disclosed.

Third, section 16(b) was designed to eliminate the temptation for insiders to manipulate corporate events so as to maximize their own short-term trading profits. Before the enactment of section 16(b), insiders had been able to make quick profits from short-term price swings by such practices as the announcement of generous (but imprudent) dividend programs followed by post-insider trading dividend reductions. Thus, the section provides a minimum standard of fiduciary conduct for corporate insiders.

NOTES AND QUESTIONS

1. ***Repeal?***   For a view taking issue with the Task Force's conclusion that Section 16(b) serves a salutary purpose, *see* O'Connor, Toward a More Efficient Deterrence of Insider Trading: The Repeal of Section 16(b), 58 Fordham L. Rev. 309 (1989). For a more equivocal view, *see* Fox, Insider Trading Deterrence Versus Managerial Incentives: A Unified Theory of Section 16(b), 92 Mich. L. Rev. 2088 (1994). In its rulemaking proposal leading to the 1996 revisions, the SEC asked for comment on the issue of repeal, but ultimately chose simplification instead. What would you do?

2. ***Short Sales.***   It is worthy of note that Section 16 also contains a prohibition (except as where permitted by SEC rule) against officers, directors, and 10 percent shareholders of the issuer selling stock short—that is, selling stock that they do not own. Similarly, "sales against the box"—certain sales involving delayed delivery—are regulated. Do you understand why?

I.   *Insider Trading Abroad*

The United States is by no means the only nation to seek to limit insider trading. Legislation has been in place for many years in France and Great Britain, and now most other capital marketplace countries have joined the "crusade." The most dramatic step in this direction was the adoption by the European Union of a Directive that compelled each member country to have in place a statutory scheme for the regulation of insider trading satisfying certain minimum standards by mid-1992. That Directive was superseded by the EU's Market Abuse Directive in 2002, which has since been revised on specific issues but retains its basic structure. In many ways, the current EU law governing insider trading is broader and more comprehensive than that found in the United States, and is closely tied to an issuer's affirmative disclosure obligation. *See* Greene & Schmid, Duty-Free Insider Trading?, 2013 Colum. Bus. L. Rev. 369. For instance, the definition of insider extends well beyond officers and directors of the issuer to include those who have inside information by virtue of access derived from their "employment profession or duties," or through criminal activity, or through any other means where the person "knows or could reasonably be expected to know" that he had inside information. Insider trading regulation is common outside Europe as well: More than 100 countries now have insider trading prohibitions. *See* Bhattacharaya & Daouk, The World Price of Insider Trading, 57 J. Fin. 75 (2002).

‖16‖
Shareholder Voting

Like insider trading, the regulation of the shareholder voting process is a subject that was undoubtedly given substantial emphasis in your Corporations course. Indeed, since voting rights are so fundamental to the process of corporate governance, there are few areas of securities regulation where both the interplay and the tension between federal securities law and state corporation law are as vivid. In this chapter, we try to place this regulatory scheme in the broader fabric of securities regulation generally.

To do that, a brief review of some "corporate law" issues may be useful. The starting point for any discussion is the fact that in large, publicly held corporations, management has rarely been opposed when it seeks shareholder approval of an election of directors or an extraordinary corporate transaction, much less defeated. Why? One explanation is that for most companies, most of the time, shareholders are satisfied (or at least not dissatisfied) with the management of the company. Other forces—the capital and labor markets, for instance, and the market for corporate control—may operate in such a way to cause management to behave in a manner fairly attentive to shareholder interests. The truly dissatisfied shareholders will simply sell their shares. But surely there are situations where this is not so. Even then, however, successful proxy fights have been relatively rare. Again, why? The answer appears to be a matter of simple economics. The *average* shareholder—especially the individual with a small sum invested in the corporation—will gain only a relatively small amount from any action that improves the governance of the corporation. For most shareholders, the time, effort, and expense of communicating and coordinating with other shareholders to plan a common course of action far outweigh the expected personal gain from such collective action. The rational response, then, is often apathy: failure to take interest in and become informed about the matter at hand.

The rapid institutionalization of stock ownership, however, implies a reduction of the collective action problem and thus an enhancement of the efficacy of shareholder voting. If a small number of large institutions have large financial stakes in the company and can vote a significant portion of its stock, they may well have both the incentive and the ability to coordinate and influence management, using their voting power as the ultimate (perhaps unneeded) threat. And indeed there is rapidly increasing concentration of voting rights in the hands of the largest institutional investors, especially those who manage index funds. *See, e.g.*, Bebchuk & Hirst, The Specter of the Giant Three, 99 B.U. L. Rev. 721 (2019). Activist hedge funds have emerged that seek to leverage this institutional power. *See, e.g.*, Gilson & Gordon, The Agency Costs of Agency Capitalism: Activist Investors and the Revaluation of Governance Rights, 113 Colum. L. Rev. 863 (2013). In turn, concern about rising shareholder activism and power has led some prominent corporations (e.g., Facebook) to adopt dual-class voting structures at the time of their IPOs that assure that effective voting control remains in the hands of the company's founders and their allies. As you will see, SEC proxy regulation operates in the shadow of these big controversies. This chapter begins with a look at how the proxy rules operate with respect to routine matters—the election of directors, shareholder proposals, and the like. It then moves on to the triggering definitional term with respect to proxy regulation: the "solicitation." Here, we see a clear-cut intersection between matters of proxy disclosure and issues of corporate governance and shareholder activism. Next, we explore the problem of proxy fraud. In the course of all this, we consider two controversial issues. One is the extent of the SEC's authority to intervene on substantive issues of corporate governance, including shareholder access to the corporate proxy machinery. The other involves a kind of transaction that often involves a shareholder vote—the "going private" proposal, wherein a company or its affiliates seeks to acquire most or all the shares held by the public shareholders, so that it ceases to be a publicly held corporation.

A.   The Election of Directors and Other Routine Matters

1.   Mandatory Disclosure

When the management of a publicly held company seeks proxies for approval of actions under circumstances where no organized opposition is expected—the annual election of directors being the most common example—it probably sees the process as little more than a chore or, at best, an opportunity for improved public and shareholder relations. Here the operation of the federal regulatory scheme is fairly simple.

With some important exceptions that will be considered later, Rule 14a-3 requires anyone seeking proxies, before or concurrent with the making of any "solicitation" of shareholders, to furnish them with a *proxy statement* (Schedule 14A). *Solicitation* is defined broadly, as we shall see, to include virtually any communication that is reasonably calculated to result in the procurement of a proxy (Rule 14a-1(l)). The proxy statement contains the information material to the decision at hand—information about the directors to be elected, the transaction to be approved, etc.—with many of the required items and instructions drawn from Regulation S-K. For elections of directors, management solicitations must disclose information relating to the composition and operation of the existing board—for example, how often it met; whether it has audit, nominating, and compensation committees; and whether any directors attended less than 75 percent of full board or committee meetings held—as well as information relating to the compensation and business transactions or relationships with the issuer of individual nominees. As you have gleaned from previous chapters, the corporate governance reforms introduced by both the Sarbanes-Oxley Act of 2002 and the Dodd-Frank Act of 2010 include many disclosures that find their way into the proxy statement. The proxy statement must be written in clear and readable terms (Rule 14a-5).

Under Rule 14a-6, "preliminary" copies of the proxy statement must be filed with the SEC at least ten calendar days prior to the date they are to be sent out *unless* the shareholders meeting relates only to routine matters (e.g., the election of directors, ratification of accountants, and/or shareholder proposals included under Rule 14a-8 (discussed infra)) and the company is not commenting in the material on any opposing solicitation. For most annual meetings, this exception from the filing requirement will apply. Whether or not filing in preliminary form is necessary, definitive copies of all forms of soliciting materials must be filed with the SEC, generally on the first day used.

In addition, management solicitations relating to a meeting at which directors are to be elected must be accompanied or preceded by an annual report to security holders (ARS). *See* Rule 14a-3(b). The ARS is a portrait of the financial condition of the *company*, with most of its line items and instructions also drawn from Regulation S-K. The logic of the annual report requirement is twofold: First, in electing directors, shareholders should be given an accurate picture of the corporation so that they can properly evaluate the fitness of incumbent management to continue their stewardship; and second, simply in terms of their interest as investors (without regard to suffrage), shareholders deserve information at least once a year relating to the value of the company. In this latter sense, the ARS plays a role in securities regulation beyond the limited focus of Section 14(a) by itself. Copies of the ARS must be filed with the SEC no later than the date the report is sent out or preliminary proxy material is filed with the SEC, although as a formal matter (e.g., for purposes of liability under Section 18, the false filings private right of action), this annual report is not itself deemed a "filing" with the Commission.[1] The requirement that the ARS accompany or precede the proxy materials is not satisfied when the method of mailing the former (e.g., fourth-class mail) indicates that it will arrive after the latter. *Ash v. GAF Corp.*, 723 F.2d 1090 (3d Cir. 1983).

Beyond providing shareholders with two disclosure documents, issuers soliciting proxies must adhere to the Commission's Rule 14a-4 on the proxy form. Among other things, the proxy form itself must indicate who is doing the soliciting, provide clearly for a date of execution, and indicate each matter or group of matters intended to be acted upon at the meeting in question. Proxies

---

1. Since the content of the annual report is integrated with that of Form 10-K, it is likely that any misstatement or omission will also show up in a filing. Hence, the exclusion of the ARS from the definition of a filing is not all that important. Rule 14a-3(c) further provides that the ARS is not subject "to this regulation otherwise than as provided in this Rule." This language has led one court to conclude that misstatements in the ARS cannot be the basis for antifraud liability under Rule 14a-9, considered infra. *See Dillon v. Berg*, 326 F. Supp. 1214 (D. Del.), *aff'd per curiam*, 453 F.2d 876 (3d Cir. 1971).

may not be solicited that confer authority to vote at more than one annual meeting.

On issues other than election of directors, the form must give the shareholder the right to vote to approve, disapprove, or abstain on each particular issue—improper "bundling" of separate matters is prohibited. Why? *See* Cox et al., Quieting the Shareholders' Voice: Empirical Evidence of Pervasive Bundling in Proxy Solicitations, 89 S. Cal. L. Rev. 1175 (2016). In *Greenlight Capital, L.P. v. Apple, Inc.*, 2013 WL 646547 (S.D.N.Y. Feb. 22, 2013), the court enjoined Apple from combining various charter amendments into a single shareholder proposal. The proposals would have (a) eliminated language relating to directors' terms in office in order to facilitate majority voting; (b) eliminated blank check preferred stock authority; and (c) established a par value for Apple stock. In a subsequent Compliance and Disclosure Interpretation, the SEC staff clarified its position that bundling of otherwise material voting matters was appropriate only where they were "inextricably intertwined." Question 101.01, Jan. 24, 2014. With respect to election of directors, there must be some mechanism by which shareholders can withhold their vote on a particular nominee. Proxies may confer discretionary authority on the holder to vote only in limited circumstances (e.g., on matters "which the persons making the solicitation do not know, a reasonable time before the solicitation, are to be presented at the meeting, if a specific statement to that effect is made in the proxy statement or form of proxy"). *See United Mine Workers v. Pittston Co.*, [1989-1990 Transfer Binder] Fed. Sec. L. Rep. (CCH) ¶94,946 (D.D.C. 1989) (discretionary authority not available when management had notice of union proposal before the last solicitation that it made). Finally, the form of proxy must provide that, except in certain unusual circumstances, the shares will in fact be voted as the shareholder directs. Proxy forms are filed with the SEC at the same time as the proxy statement.

Mailing hard copies of proxy statements, ballots, and annual reports is quite expensive. Following on state law changes that permit proxy voting by electronic means, the SEC has taken a number of steps to facilitate Internet availability and electronic delivery of these documents. In Rule 14a-16, adopted in 2007 and amended in 2010, the Commission requires an issuer to post materials on its web site and then notify shareholders of their availability there. That satisfies the delivery requirement, so long as the form of notice provides a mechanism by which shareholders can request that the materials be sent to them, unless the issuer chooses to send the materials along with the notice (the "full set delivery" option).

2.   Proposals, Recommendations, and Elections

The assumption underlying regulation of the uncontested election is that management has set the agenda for the annual meeting. The mandated disclosure relates to its proposals. You will recall, however, that in one respect federal securities regulation gives corporate shareholders the power to force management to include referendum items in the issuer's proxy materials. Rule 14a-8 is structured in such a way that proposals by qualified shareholders—that is, shareholders who have been such for at least one year and who own at least 1 percent of the outstanding voting shares of the issuer or issuer stock having a market value of at least $2,000—must be included by the issuer, along with a 500-word supporting statement by the proponent, unless a specific ground for exclusion exists. If management wishes to exclude a proposal, it must notify the SEC, which then reviews the decision through its no-action process. Courts have implied rights of action against the issuer on behalf of shareholders who object to an exclusion. *See Roosevelt v. E.I. DuPont de Nemours & Co.*, 958 F.2d 416 (D.C. Cir. 1992).

The SEC has been accused of inconsistency and unjustified shifts in its views on various controversial matters. *E.g.*, Palmiter, The Shareholder Proposal Rule: A Failed Experiment in Merit Regulation, 45 Ala. L. Rev. 879 (1994). This concern was very visible in litigation following the SEC's position on proposals related to employment practices involving equal rights issues. For some time, these were treated like any other social issue, and thus routinely nonexcludable if (as usual) they involved highly political matters. In 1992, in a highly visible about-face stemming from a gay-rights campaign directed at the allegedly discriminatory practices of a restaurant chain, the SEC began to allow the exclusion of employment-related proposals notwithstanding their social import. Cracker Barrel Old Country Stores, Inc., SEC No-Action Letter (available Oct. 13, 1992). A district court then set aside the determination that such proposals were excludable as unjustified without formal rulemaking, *New York City Employees' Retirement System v. SEC*, [1994 Transfer Binder] Fed. Sec. L. Rep. (CCH) ¶98,052 (S.D.N.Y. 1994), but this was reversed as a matter of administrative law, on grounds that the no-action letter was purely interpretive and thus nonreviewable. *New York City Employees' Retirement System v. SEC*, 45 F.3d 7 (2d Cir. 1995). In Exchange Act Release No. 40018 (May 21, 1998), the Commission reversed its position yet again, essentially returning the law to its original state, so that employment-related proposals are analyzed on a case-by-case basis for their social significance.

For some time, as in the Cracker Barrel example, Rule 14a-8 was used most visibly by shareholders who wished to put forth a question of social or political importance regarding company policies. This is an issue that you no doubt studied in your Corporations course. The standards were muddied in *Trinity Church Wall Street v. Wal-Mart Stores, Inc.*, 792 F.3d 323 (3d Cir. 2015), where the court ruled that Wal-Mart could exclude a shareholder proposal asking the board of directors to amend the Governance Committee charter to provide for oversight and reporting of policies and standards for determining whether Wal-Mart should sell dangerous or offensive products. Though not singled out in the proposal, the shareholders' immediate concern was with Wal-Mart's sale of high capacity firearms like the Bushmaster AR-15. The proponents believed this raised an issue of social, moral, and political importance, and so was not excludable under the "ordinary business" exemption. The court disagreed, holding that although such significance might take the proposal out of ordinary business if it is sufficiently "transcendent," the company can nonetheless exclude by demonstrating that the issue is nonetheless so deeply enmeshed in basic business decisionmaking that it improperly treads on a core management responsibility, like creating an optimal product mix in the face of shifting consumer demand. Query: Would the proponents have been better off limiting their proposal to high-powered weapons? Although the SEC staff had indicated that Wal-Mart could exclude this particular proposal, it later expressed disagreement with the

Third Circuit's holding. *See* Staff Legal Bulletin 14H, Oct. 22, 2015. Over the next few years, the staff added more guidance on the effort to separate bona fide social policy proposals from impermissible attempts at micromanagement. *See* Staff Legal Bulletins 14I and 14J, Nov. 1, 2017 and Oct. 23, 2018. But the criticism from both sides of the debate has not ceased, and there is continuous pressure on the SEC to engage in comprehensive reform.

There is also heavy use of Rule 14a-8 regarding matters of corporate governance. *See* Rose, Shareholder Proposals in the Market for Corporate Influence, 66 Fla. L. Rev. 2179 (2014). These often receive high levels of shareholder support. Depending upon the factual context, management may sometimes argue that a particular governance proposal is "not a proper subject for action by security holders" (exclusion 1) or, in a rare case, that its effectuation would be a violation of law (exclusion 2). One major issue here is the extent to which shareholder proposals can go beyond simply recommending a matter to creating a binding effect by styling it as a by-law amendment. *See CA, Inc. v. AFSCME Employees Pension Plan*, 953 A.2d 227 (Del. 2008) (rejecting particular by-law proposal dealing with reimbursement of election expenses because it unduly interfered with board fiduciary responsibilities, though perhaps leaving room for similar by-laws that are restyled to give directors a "fiduciary out"). In a special procedure utilized in the *CA* case, supra, Delaware permits its supreme court to hear and decide questions of law certified to it by the SEC. Does this suggest a growing sense of shared responsibility between federal and state law on access to the corporate ballot? For an argument that the increasing frequency of negotiated settlements of such corporate governance proposals prior to a shareholder vote is problematic for lack of oversight, *see* Haan, Shareholder Proposal Settlements and the Private Ordering of Public Elections, 126 Yale L.J. 262 (2017).

For most of its history, Rule 14a-8 did not apply to matters relating to elections of directors. Those wishing to nominate their own candidates had to do their own solicitations, even if they were not seeking to take control. Beginning in the early 2000s, the SEC began to consider changing this policy, generating a great deal of political controversy, including about whether the Commission even had the authority to wade so deeply into substantive corporate governance. In the Dodd-Frank Act of 2010, Congress made clear that it did, and the Commission adopted Rule 14a-11 shortly thereafter to provide that shareholders holding 3 percent or more of the voting stock of an issuer had a right to put forward a limited number of nominations of their own candidates in the company's proxy soliciting materials, so long as they were not seeking to shift control of the company (i.e., they were seeking only minority representation on the board). That rule was immediately challenged as invalid.

Business Roundtable v. SEC
647 F.3d 1144 (D.C. Cir. 2011)

GINSBURG, Circuit Judge.

The Business Roundtable and the Chamber of Commerce of the United States, each of which has corporate members that issue publicly traded securities, petition for review of Exchange Act Rule 14a-11. The rule requires public companies to provide shareholders with information about, and their ability to vote for, shareholder-nominated candidates for the board of directors. The petitioners argue the Securities and Exchange Commission promulgated the rule in violation of the Administrative Procedure Act because, among other reasons, the Commission failed adequately to consider the rule's effect upon efficiency, competition, and capital formation, as required by Section 3(f) of the Exchange Act and Section 2(c) of the Investment Company Act of 1940. . . . For these reasons and more, we grant the petition for review and vacate the rule.

I.   BACKGROUND

. . . Rule 14a-11 provides shareholders an alternative path for nominating and electing directors. Concerned the current process impedes the expression of shareholders' right under state corporation laws to nominate and elect directors, the Commission proposed the rule, and adopted it with the goal of ensuring "the proxy process functions, as nearly as possible, as a replacement for an actual in-person meeting of shareholders."

The Commission concluded that Rule 14a-11 could create "potential benefits of improved board and company performance and shareholder value" sufficient to "justify [its] potential costs." The agency rejected proposals to let each company's board or a majority of its shareholders decide whether to incorporate Rule 14a-11 in its bylaws, saying that "exclusive reliance on private ordering under State law would not be as effective and efficient" in facilitating shareholders' right to nominate and elect directors. . . . The two Commissioners voting against the rule faulted the Commission on both theoretical and empirical grounds. . . .

II.   ANALYSIS

Under the APA, we will set aside agency action that is "arbitrary, capricious, an abuse of discretion, or otherwise not in accordance with law." We must assure ourselves the agency has "examine[d] the relevant data and articulate[d] a satisfactory explanation for its action including a rational connection between the facts found and the choices made." *Motor Vehicle Mfrs. Ass'n of U.S., Inc. v. State Farm Mut. Auto. Ins. Co.*, 463 U.S. 29, 43 (1983). The Commission also has a "statutory obligation to determine as best it can the economic implications of the rule." *Chamber of Commerce v. SEC*, 412 F.3d 133, 143 (D.C. Cir. 2005).

Indeed, the Commission has a unique obligation to consider the effect of a new rule upon "efficiency, competition, and capital formation," and its failure to "apprise itself—and hence the public and the Congress—of the economic consequences of a proposed regulation" makes promulgation of the rule arbitrary and capricious and not in accordance with law.

The petitioners argue the Commission acted arbitrarily and capriciously here because it neglected its statutory responsibility to determine the likely economic consequences of Rule 14a-11 and to connect those consequences to efficiency, competition, and capital formation. . . .

We agree with the petitioners and hold the Commission acted arbitrarily and capriciously for having failed once again—as it did most recently in *American Equity Investment Life Insurance Company v. SEC*, 613 F.3d 166, 167-68 (D.C. Cir. 2010), and before that in *Chamber of Commerce*, 412 F.3d at 136—adequately to assess the economic effects of a new rule. Here the Commission inconsistently and opportunistically framed the costs and benefits of the rule; failed adequately to quantify the certain costs or to explain why those costs could not be quantified; neglected to support its predictive judgments; contradicted itself; and failed to respond to substantial problems raised by commenters. . . . Because we conclude the Commission failed to justify Rule 14a-11, we need not address the petitioners' additional argument the Commission arbitrarily rejected proposed alternatives that would have allowed shareholders of each company to decide for that company whether to adopt a mechanism for shareholders' nominees to get access to proxy materials.

A.   CONSIDERATION OF ECONOMIC CONSEQUENCES

In the Adopting Release, the Commission predicted Rule 14a-11 would lead to "[d]irect cost savings" for shareholders in part due to "reduced printing and postage costs" and reduced expenditures for advertising compared to those of a "traditional" proxy contest. The Commission also identified some intangible, or at least less readily quantifiable, benefits, principally that the rule "will mitigate collective action and free-rider concerns," which can discourage a shareholder from exercising his right to nominate a director in a traditional proxy contest, and "has the potential of creating the benefit of improved board performance and enhanced shareholder value." The Commission anticipated the rule would also impose costs upon companies and shareholders related to "the preparation of required disclosure, printing and mailing . . ., and [to] additional solicitations," and could have "adverse effects on company and board performance," for example, by distracting management. The Commission nonetheless concluded the rule would promote the "efficiency of the economy on the whole," and the benefits of the rule would "justify the costs" of the rule.

The petitioners contend the Commission neglected both to quantify the costs companies would incur opposing shareholder nominees and to substantiate the rule's predicted benefits. They also argue the Commission failed to consider the consequences of union and state pension funds using the rule and failed properly to evaluate the frequency with which shareholders would initiate election contests.

1. *Consideration of Costs and Benefits*

In the Adopting Release, the Commission recognized "company boards may be motivated by the issues at stake to expend significant resources to challenge shareholder director nominees." Nonetheless, the Commission believed a company's solicitation and campaign costs "may be limited by two factors": first, "to the extent that the directors' fiduciary duties prevent them from using corporate funds to resist shareholder director nominations for no good-faith corporate purpose," they may decide "simply [to] include the shareholder director nominees . . . in the company's proxy materials"; and second, the "requisite ownership threshold and holding period" would "limit the number of shareholder director nominations that a board may receive, consider, and possibly contest."

The petitioners object that the Commission failed to appreciate the intensity with which issuers would oppose nominees and arbitrarily dismissed the probability that directors would conclude their fiduciary duties required them to support their own nominees. The petitioners also argue it was arbitrary for the Commission not to estimate the costs of solicitation and campaigning that companies would incur to oppose candidates nominated by shareholders, which costs commenters expected to be quite large. The Chamber of Commerce submitted a comment predicting boards would incur substantial expenditures opposing shareholder nominees through "significant media and public relations efforts, advertising . . ., mass mailings, and other communication efforts, as well as the hiring of outside advisors and the expenditure of significant time and effort by the company's employees." It pointed out that in recent proxy contests at larger companies costs "ranged from $14 million to $4 million" and at smaller companies "from $3 million to $800,000." In its brief the Commission maintains it did consider the commenters' estimates of the costs, but reasonably explained why those costs "may prove less than these estimates."

We agree with the petitioners that the Commission's prediction directors might choose not to oppose shareholder nominees had no basis beyond mere speculation. . . .

The petitioners also maintain, and we agree, the Commission relied upon insufficient empirical data when it concluded that Rule 14a-11 will improve board performance and increase shareholder value by facilitating the election of dissident shareholder nominees. The Commission acknowledged the numerous studies submitted by commenters that reached the opposite result. One commenter, for example, submitted an empirical study showing that "when dissident directors win board seats, those firms underperform peers by 19 to 40% over the two years following the proxy contest." Elaine Buckberg, NERA Econ. Consulting, & Jonathan Macey, Yale Law School, Report on Effects of Proposed SEC Rule 14a-11 on Efficiency, Competitiveness and Capital Formation 9 (2009). The Commission completely discounted those studies "because of questions raised by subsequent studies, limitations acknowledged by the studies' authors, or [its] own concerns about the studies' methodology or scope."

The Commission instead relied exclusively and heavily upon two relatively unpersuasive studies, one concerning the effect of "hybrid boards" (which include some dissident directors) and the other concerning the effect of proxy contests in general, upon shareholder value . . . citing Chris Cernich et al., IRRC Inst. for Corporate Responsibility, Effectiveness of Hybrid Boards (May 2009) and J. Harold Mulherin & Annette B. Poulsen, *Proxy Contests & Corporate Change: Implications for Shareholder Wealth*, 47 J. Fin. Econ. 279 (1998)). Indeed, the Commission "recognize[d] the limitations of the Cernich (2009) study," and noted "its long-term findings on shareholder value creation are difficult to interpret." In view of the admittedly (and at best) "mixed" empirical evidence, we think the Commission has not sufficiently supported its conclusion that increasing the potential for election of directors nominated by shareholders will result in improved board and company performance and shareholder value. . . .

2. Shareholders with Special Interests

The petitioners next argue the Commission acted arbitrarily and capriciously by "entirely fail[ing] to consider an important aspect of the problem," *Motor Vehicle Mfrs. Ass'n,* 463 U.S. at 43, to wit, how union and state pension funds might use Rule 14a-11. Commenters expressed concern that these employee benefit funds would impose costs upon companies by using Rule 14a-11 as leverage to gain concessions, such as additional benefits for unionized employees, unrelated to shareholder value. The Commission insists it did consider this problem, albeit not *in haec verba,* along the way to its conclusion that "the totality of the evidence and economic theory" both indicate the rule "has the potential of creating the benefit of improved board performance and enhanced shareholder value." Specifically, the Commission recognized "companies could be negatively affected if shareholders use the new rules to promote their narrow interests at the expense of other shareholders," but reasoned these potential costs "may be limited" because the ownership and holding requirements would "allow the use of the rule by only holders who demonstrated a significant, long-term commitment to the company," and who would therefore be less likely to act in a way that would diminish shareholder value. The Commission also noted costs may be limited because other shareholders may be alerted, through the disclosure requirements, "to the narrow interests of the nominating shareholder." . . .

Notwithstanding the ownership and holding requirements, there is good reason to believe institutional investors with special interests will be able to use the rule and, as more than one commenter noted, "public and union pension funds" are the institutional investors "most likely to make use of proxy access." Nonetheless, the Commission failed to respond to comments arguing that investors with a special interest, such as unions and state and local governments whose interests in jobs may well be greater than their interest in share value, can be expected to pursue self-interested objectives rather than the goal of maximizing shareholder value, and will likely cause companies to incur costs even when their nominee is unlikely to be elected. By ducking serious evaluation of the costs that could be imposed upon companies from use of the rule by shareholders representing special interests, particularly union and government pension funds, we think the Commission acted arbitrarily.

[The court also found fault with the SEC's estimate of the likely frequency of contested elections, and its analysis of the issues relating to proxy access in mutual fund elections. It thus vacated the rule.]

NOTES AND QUESTIONS

1. The SEC, Corporate Governance, and the D.C. Circuit. What does the court's opinion say about how agencies like the SEC are to assess costs and benefits? *See* Cox & Baucom, The Emperor Has No Clothes: Confronting the D.C. Circuit's Usurpation of SEC Rulemaking Authority, 90 Tex. L. Rev. 1811 (2012). Unmentioned in the D.C. Circuit's opinion was language in the Dodd-Frank Act explicitly recognizing the SEC's authority to adopt a proxy access rule, in light of claims that venturing this far into corporate governance was beyond the scope of Section 14(a). Should this be relevant? This was by no means the first time that the D.C. Circuit had frustrated the SEC's effort to become more active on the corporate governance front. In *Business Roundtable v. SEC*, 905 F.2d 406 (D.C. Cir. 1990), the court invalidated the SEC's effort to mandate—through stock exchange listing requirements—a prohibition on dual class capitalizations that effectively disenfranchised public shareholders, finding that neither Section 14(a) nor its authority over the stock exchanges authorized a rule that mandated one share, one vote. This particular setback for the SEC was not all that concerning, however, because the exchanges soon thereafter chose "voluntarily" to adopt anti-disenfranchisement listing standards, which continue to operate. *See* Bainbridge, The Short Life and Resurrection of SEC Rule 19c-4, 15 J. Corp. L. 721 (1990).

2. Rule 14a-8 and Elections. As part of the same proxy access rulemaking addressed by the D.C. Circuit in *Business Roundtable*, the SEC also amended Rule 14a-8 to make clear that the elections exclusion is limited to proposals directed at particular nominees, either to support or oppose their candidacies. The consequence is that a proposal to amend the company's by-laws to create some form of access to the company's ballot would not be excludable. This change was not challenged. More recently, the SEC has discussed the possibility of a universal ballot, which would not address the nomination process but would provide that all qualified nominees be on the ballot circulated by the issuer.

3. Say on Pay and Other Voting Rights. The Dodd-Frank Act directly created additional shareholder voting rights. New Section 14A of the '34 Act, as implemented in Rule 14a-21, requires every public company to hold nonbinding "say on pay" votes to approve the compensation of certain executives. Shareholders will also vote on the frequency of such approvals, whether every year or every two or three. In addition, in any shareholder vote to approve a merger or acquisition transaction, shareholders must be permitted to vote—again, on a nonbinding basis—on any golden parachute compensation arrangement. *See* Fisch et al., Is Say on Pay All About Pay? The Impact of Firm Performance, 8 Harv. Bus. L. Rev. 101 (2018). Institutional investment managers subject to Section 13(f) of the '34 Act must disclose no less than annually how they voted on any say on pay or golden parachute arrangements. As a result of the JOBS Act of 2012, say on pay and say on golden parachute voting rights will not apply to "emerging growth companies."

4. Conflicting Proposals. One tactic that some companies had used to exclude corporate governance–related proposals was to offer their own proposal on the same subject. That triggered Rule 14a-8(i)(9), authorizing exclusions for conflicting shareholder and management proposals. This became controversial in late 2014 when Whole Foods sought to counter a proxy access proposal with one of their own, even though it appeared that no existing shareholder could possibly satisfy the conditions set forth by the company, which limited access to holders for the previous 5 years of 9 percent or more of the company's stock (in contrast to the proponents' 3 percent threshold). In Staff Legal Bulletin 14H, Oct. 22, 2015, the staff revised its interpretation so that exclusion is permissible only where no reasonable shareholder would logically vote in favor of both.

PROBLEM

16-1. A large activist shareholder of Capital One Financial Corp. has made a proposal for the forthcoming annual meeting asking that the board amend the by-laws to allow holders of 10 percent or more of the company's voting stock to call a special meeting. In response, the board has scheduled a vote at the same meeting ratifying the current by-law, which limits the shareholder power to call such a meeting to 25 percent of the vote. Is this excludable under 14a-8(i)(9)? Should it be? Assuming exclusion is permissible, are there disclosures associated with the board's ratification proposal that would make this more fair? *See* Capital One Fin. Corp., SEC No-Action Letter (Feb. 21, 2018).

B.   *The Reach of the Proxy Rules*

The idea of a "shareholder vote" is deceptively simple. As you will remember from Corporations, there must be a record date set for a shareholder meeting to determine who is entitled to vote (i.e., those shareholders of record as of that chosen point in time). In an era of rapid share turnover, this by itself compromises the vote as an expression of the preferences of the real parties in interest. More broadly, one might ask what the sense is in shareholder voting in the first place if so many record-date voters have no long-term interest in the performance of the issuer but are instead just trying to take advantage of short-term price movements.

To be sure, there are plenty of longer-term voters, both retail and institutional. Recall the massive growth in index investing described in Chapter 3, where so much investor money goes into funds that engage in no active research but instead just hold positions that conform to broad market indices. It is important to understand that for most institutional holdings, like mutual funds and pension funds, the portfolio manager votes the shares—not the beneficiaries. Guidance from both the SEC and the Department of Labor (which oversees pension plans under ERISA) makes clear that portfolio managers have a fiduciary responsibility to vote diligently in the best interest of their beneficiaries. That is quite a challenge for institutions that may have many different portfolios holding many different securities, and it has spawned an industry of proxy advisory firms that assist institutions in exercising those fiduciary duties. Institutional Investor Services and Glass Lewis dominate the market. This has itself become controversial, with anguished claims by corporate managers that these large proxy advisers face conflicts of interest and often have no rigorous basis for the advice they give—yet they have the power to affect corporate elections with their recommendations. The SEC has been urged to regulate, and the issue has now become a global one. *See* Balp, Regulating Proxy Advisors Through Transparency: Pros and Cons of the EU Approach, 14 Eur. Co. & Fin. L. Rev. 1 (2017) (comparing reform proposals in the United States and the EU). We will come back to this shortly.

There are numerous "plumbing" issues in proxy voting that may affect elections. Take the common practice of stock lending, whereby a brokerage firm "lends" the shares of a customer (without the customer's knowledge) to another firm or customer who wants to sell short. As a result, those particular shares are transferred to another owner, who as a result gains the right to vote. But the original customer has not sold any shares, and will expect to vote as well. Unless votes are carefully scrutinized, there may be systematic "overvoting" in elections. *See* Kahan & Rock, The Hanging Chads of Shareholder Voting, 96 Geo. L.J. 1227 (2008).

Many of these plumbing issues affect retail shareholders in particular. First, what should be done in situations where the shareholder of record is not the beneficial owner of the security? This problem arises primarily in two contexts: so-called street name holdings by broker-dealers, where the customer directs that the broker be the record holder as a matter of convenience (or for margin purposes), and fiduciary or nominee accounts created by financial institutions or partnerships thereof, usually for the benefit of their customers.

On the assumption that the beneficial owner normally deserves the disclosure mandated by the proxy rules, Section 14(b) allows the Commission to adopt rules designed to facilitate the dissemination to beneficial owners of proxy forms and disclosure documents. Pursuant to this authority, Rules 14a-13, 14b-1, and 14b-2, taken together, impose on issuers the obligation to seek to communicate with their beneficial owners. The issuer may request from its record holders a list of beneficial owners who do not object to being identified for the issuer (so-called NOBOs, for non-objecting beneficial owners) and thereafter send all proxy materials to these shareholders directly. With respect to beneficial owners whose names are not discovered under this identification procedure, a pass-through system is established, with the issuer forced to pay the expenses associated with such indirect communication. Record holders in turn are required to cooperate with the issuer in this process. In 1985, Congress enacted the Shareholders Communications Act specifically bringing banks—who theretofore had been notorious in failing to communicate with beneficial owners to seek voting instructions—into this system. If the beneficial owner does not express any interest or direct the record holder how to vote, should the broker be able to vote the shares as it wishes? This is an important question with respect to the ability of the company to get a quorum of shareholders for its meetings. For some time, stock exchange rules permitted brokers to vote shares held for customers' accounts on "routine" matters. But these rules were changed. For example, the New York Stock Exchange prohibits broker voting on elections of directors, even if uncontested, or on compensation matters.

It seems generally agreed today that the technology exists to redo the proxy plumbing and resolve many of these problems. Blockchain technology seems promising. *See* Geis, Traceable Shares and Corporate Law, 113 Nw. U. L. Rev. 227 (2018). But this is a daunting task with potentially profound consequences in corporate governance. As to retail investors in particular, are there ways to encourage greater voting participation? Efforts to encourage online voting have not made a positive difference. Are there other possibilities that are worth the effort? For a good discussion, *see* Fisch, Standing Voting Instructions: Empowering the Excluded Retail Investor, 102 Minn. L. Rev. 11 (2017).

A different scope question under the federal proxy rules arises when a company chooses *not* to solicit proxies in connection with a meeting or makes only a partial solicitation. This could be the case when there is a controlling shareholder, such that other shareholders' votes are inconsequential. If the sole purpose of the proxy rules were to promote informed voting choices by shareholders, regulatory intervention would be called for only to the extent necessary to protect the decisions of those whose votes are in fact solicited. But this is not the regulatory approach. To the contrary, Section 14(c) requires registrants that do not solicit proxies from all shareholders to send both an "information statement," containing information that is essentially the same as that which would be required in the proxy statement, and, in connection with an annual meeting for the election of directors, an annual report to shareholders. What use is a shareholder supposed to make of this material? Perhaps more vividly than anywhere else, this Rule demonstrates the regulatory view underlying proxy regulation generally that there is a value to the *process* of disclosure, stemming from the discipline that it imposes, that goes beyond the specific use to which shareholders actually put the material.

C.   *"Solicitations"*

In routine meetings, the term *solicitation* rarely takes on much practical importance. On the other hand, when a matter is controversial, or when there is an organized opposition or insurgency, it is crucial. Rule 14a-1(l) sets the basic framework: The term includes *both* the actual request for a proxy from a shareholder and any "other communication to security holders under circumstances reasonably calculated to result in the procurement, withholding or revocation of a proxy."

To understand the interpretation of the term *solicitation*, it is important to recognize a strong conceptual similarity between the system for regulating proxies and the system for regulating public distributions of securities under the Securities Act. Both seek to have a mandatory disclosure document (with SEC review) make its way into the hands of investors before they purchase shares or vote, as the case may be. And as a result, both assume some sort of a "quiet" period prior to the availability of the disclosure. Thus, it should come as no surprise that the definitions of "solicitation" in the proxy setting and "offer" in the distribution setting are similar. As discussed below, both have been construed to cover communications that are designed to "condition the minds" of investors, even if no formal action is requested. Even in the absence of any opposition to management, the broad definition of solicitation is at least a potential restraint on management's ability to communicate with shareholders in advance of the actual solicitation of written proxies. To date, the Commission and the courts have taken a view similar to that in the Securities Act area: So long as these communications are in the normal course of business and do not unduly "hype" the company or its management, they are unlikely to be treated as solicitations. *See Smallwood v. Pearl Brewing Co.*, 489 F.2d 579 (5th Cir. 1974), *cert. denied*, 419 U.S. 873 (1975); Exchange Act Release No. 5276 (1956).

But it is when there is opposition to management that the breadth of the definition has its most potent effect. Advertisements, speeches, broadcasts, mailings, and personal phone calls can all be subtle (or not so subtle) media for influencing how shareholders feel about management and the company, which will affect the likelihood of whether they will grant a proxy to one side or the other if asked. *E.g., Long Island Lighting Co. v. Barbash*, 779 F.2d 793 (2d Cir. 1985) (accepting the possibility that a newspaper ad attacking a company's nuclear energy policy may be a solicitation). But is it necessarily in the public interest to subject all such forms of speech to the risk and expense involved in complying with the requirements of Regulation 14A?

This was a question the SEC first addressed in 1992 as it considered complaints by institutional investors that the proxy rules were thwarting the growth of shareholder activism. Securities Exchange Act Release No. 31226 (Oct. 16, 1992). Believing that such activism was on balance a positive influence for shareholder protection, the Commission determined to take away the "chill" that comes from the definition of solicitation as it relates to communications among investors. It did so mainly through three rule changes:

(1) Rule 14a-2(b) was amended to create an exemption from the proxy statement delivery and disclosure requirements (but not the antifraud rule) for communications with shareholders, where the person soliciting is not seeking proxy authority and does not have a substantial interest in the matter subject to a vote or is otherwise ineligible for the exemption. Public notice of written soliciting activity is, however, required by beneficial owners of more than $5 million of the registrant's securities through publication, broadcast, or submission to the Commission of the written soliciting materials. Would this exception be available if an institutional investor opposes management's solicitation and sends to each recipient a blank duplicate copy of management's proxy card? On grounds that the most likely purpose of the blank card was to encourage shareholders to revoke votes previously cast in management's favor, the Second Circuit in *MONY Group v. Highfields Capital*, 368 F.3d 138 (2d Cir. 2004), said no.

(2) The definition of *solicitation*, Rule 14a-1(l)(2)(iv), was amended to specify that a shareholder can publicly announce how it intends to vote and provide the reasons for that decision without having to comply with any of the proxy rules.

(3) Rule 14a-3 was amended to add a new paragraph (f), exempting solicitations conveyed by public broadcast or speech or publication from the proxy statement delivery requirements, provided a definitive proxy statement is on file with the Commission. Unlike the first two reforms, this rule change was available to management as well as shareholders.

In 1999, the SEC returned to the regulation of proxy solicitations in connection with its "Reg M-A" rule revisions. Securities Act Release No. 7760 (Oct. 22, 1999). As you will recall from Chapter 7, Reg M-A is designed to bring regulatory parity to the process by which mergers and acquisitions occur, regardless of whether cash or stock is used as consideration or whether the transaction involves shareholder voting or instead is conducted via a tender offer. The underlying idea is that preliminary communications with investors regarding the trans-action should largely be free from regulatory restraint—a philosophy that the Commission extended to the entire public offering context in 2005. To accomplish this in the proxy setting, the SEC revised Rule 14a-12 to permit communications with shareholders that do not actually request a proxy without any obligation to file or deliver a proxy statement. Written soliciting material must, however, be filed with the SEC as of the date of first use, and must include certain disclosures about the participants in the solicitation and a legend advising recipients to read the proxy statement before actually voting. In revising Rule 14a-12, the Commission made clear that it is not simply applicable to merger and acquisition transactions. Thus, parties—both management and outsiders—are much more free than before in all settings to communicate (even to "condition the minds" of shareholders) without preparing or distributing a proxy statement. Consider, for example, the extent to which Rule 14a-12 essentially supersedes much of what the SEC did in 1992. Keep this in mind as you answer the problem below.

Proxy solicitations are likely simpler and less costly as a result of the SEC's shift to Internet-based delivery of required disclosures in Rule 14a-16, described earlier. The Rule provides that those opposing incumbent management are free to solicit fewer than all of the company's shareholders if they wish—in other words, they can do a targeted rather than a broad-based solicitation.

NOTES AND QUESTIONS

1. Solicitations.   Even though the 1992 and 1999 reforms made significant changes in the overall structure of Regulation 14A by providing a number of exemptions from the proxy filing and delivery requirements, the basic definition of *solicitation* has remained unchanged (except for the exclusion of voting intentions). The primary effect of this is to leave applicable the prohibition against proxy fraud (Rule 14a-9), discussed in the next section.

A deeper sense of the scope of the definition can be found in two classic Second Circuit cases: *SEC v. Okin*, 132 F.2d 784 (2d Cir. 1943) (requests to other shareholders to join in demand for shareholder list is a solicitation) and *Studebaker Corp. v. Gittin*, 360 F.2d 692 (2d Cir. 1966) (same, even without formal requests for authorization). *See also Canadian Javelin Ltd. v. Brooks*, 462 F. Supp. 190 (S.D.N.Y. 1978) (letter to shareholders urging support of Protective Committee efforts). In contrast, consider *Brown v. Chicago, Rock Island & Peoria Railroad*, 328 F.2d 122 (7th Cir. 1964), where the court determined that the management of the Union Pacific Railroad, which had agreed to merge with the Rock Island line, did not engage in a solicitation in publishing an ad in the news-paper expressing opposition to an attempt by another railroad, Northwestern, to gain control of Rock Island. The court so ruled even though the shareholders of Rock Island would have to vote no on the merger with Union Pacific in order for Northwestern's bid to succeed. Do you agree? Should it be significant that the ad appeared before the shareholders' meeting was scheduled?

2. The First Amendment.   Obviously, there is a tension between much of securities regulation, which seeks to limit the freedom of communication with the public about business and financial matters, and the First Amendment. So far, the courts have not been willing to question proxy regulation on constitutional grounds, even when there is a substantial political component to the solicitation. *E.g., Long Island Lighting Co. v. Barbash,* 779 F.2d 793 (2d Cir. 1985), noted supra. The constitutional issue will be explored more explicitly in another intriguing setting, the regulation of investment advisers, in Chapter 19.

3. *Shareholder Lists.* A successful proxy fight requires knowledge of who the electorate is, and as you may recall, state corporation law has often been notoriously ineffective in allowing dissidents to obtain that list. Rule 14a-7 gives some relief, forcing issuers to choose between (1) giving the shareholder the list or (2) undertaking promptly (or at least no later than the time of its own solicitation) to mail the solicitation materials for the insurgent, at the insurgent's expense. *See Haas v. Weiboldt Stores Inc.,* 725 F.2d 71 (7th Cir. 1984) (implying a private right of action). For the issuer, which option would normally be preferable? Note that the 1992 amendments to Regulation 14A eliminated management's discretion here with respect to going-private transactions and limited partnership roll-ups.

4. *Proxy Advisory Firms.* As noted earlier in the chapter, there is immense controversy over the supposedly large influence that proxy advisory firms like Institutional Shareholder Services have on proxy votes of all sorts. Is a recommendation to vote one way or another by an advisory firm a solicitation that triggers filing and disclosure obligations? Currently, firms can take advantage of a carve-out for proxy voting advice in Rule 14a-2(b)(3). As noted earlier, the SEC is under considerable pressure to reconsider and increase the regulation of proxy advisers. The leading advisory firm, ISS, has registered as an investment adviser (a category you will study in Chapter 19), which subjects them to some regulatory oversight and makes them a fiduciary vis-à-vis their many clients.

5. *Electronic Forums.* The SEC encourages companies and others to create Internet-based shareholder forums so that shareholders can communicate with each other and with management about company performance. To this end, Rule 14a-17 provides liability protection to the sponsors of such sites for statements made by participants in the forums. And Rule 14a-2(b)(6) provides an exemption from the filing and disclosure provisions of Regulation 14A for statements made on such forums that might otherwise be deemed solicitations, so long as the person making the statement does not actually furnish or request a form of proxy. This protection applies only to statements made more than 60 days prior to the shareholder meeting date.

PROBLEM

16-2. The former CEO of a company wrote the following letter to company shareholders:

Dear Shareholder,

My name is Richard M. Osborne, former Chairman and CEO of Gas Natural Inc. After saving the company from near bankruptcy, I was tossed out because the attorney of our Derivative Lawsuit told our board members it would be the easiest way to settle. Mark Kratz, Gas Natural's current Securities Attorney who represented me personally for 35 years and Mike Victor, Chairman of the Compensation Committee, promised me three years severance for wrongful discharge. They later reneged on this promise. Lawsuits are in process for the $750,000 owed to me in earn-outs. I am also owed a minimum of $5,250,000 for pipelines they have been using illegally.

The company is now being run by accountants. It is a disaster and employee morale is at an all time low. Those in charge believe they can make a difference by pushing buttons. At the June 25th board meeting, cash flow was a cause for concern. I suggested we take the Directors Fees from $5,000 to $2,000 to help in this matter. The directors instead chose to milk the company and instead of giving the money to the share holders [sic] by granting themselves each 4,000 shares, the equivalent of $44,000 per director. Another example of their antics, during the only meeting I ever missed due to a surgery in 2013, the remaining board members raised the Directors Fees from $2,000 to $4,000.

I am asking for your help in running these greedy individuals out of our company. You will receive additional letters from me in the future. If you have your own concerns or complaints, please address them to me in writing to my office or directly. . . .

Would this be a proxy solicitation? An exempt solicitation? *See Gas Natural Inc. v. Osborne*, 624 Fed. App'x 944 (6th Cir. 2015).

D.   Proxy Fraud

The filing and disclosure requirements under the proxy rules are all subject to one overriding prohibition, the source of virtually all litigation in this area. Rule 14a-9 makes it unlawful to make any false or misleading statement in connection with any solicitation covered by the rules, whether the misstatement is in the proxy statement or any other written or oral communication. More specifically—and without regard to whether the election is contested or not—the Rule makes unlawful any solicitation made by means of any written or oral form of communication that, at the time and under the circumstances of its making, "is false and misleading with respect to any material fact, or which omits to state any material fact necessary in order to make the statements therein not false or misleading, or necessary to correct any statement in any earlier communication with respect to the solicitation of a proxy for the same meeting or subject matter which has become false or misleading." Rule 14a-9 goes on to give examples of statements that may be misleading under the Rule, including "predictions as to future market values" and "material which . . . impugns character, integrity or personal reputation . . . without factual foundation."

To what extent is Rule 14a-9 the conceptual equivalent for proxy solicitations of Rule 10b-5 for purchases and sales? Some overlap is clear. Both are enforceable through implied rights of action by private plaintiffs, as well as the SEC. *See J.I. Case Co. v. Borak*, 377 U.S. 426 (1964), the first of the Supreme Court's expansive implied private rights cases under the federal securities laws, which emphasized the salutary role of private plaintiffs as "private attorneys general" in enforcing the federal statutory scheme. Rule 14a-9 and Rule 10b-5 also use a common definition of *materiality*. *See TSC Industries v. Northway, Inc.*, 426 U.S. 438 (1976). But are there differences in purpose that make the analogy inapt under other circumstances?

Virginia Bankshares, Inc. v. Sandberg
501 U.S. 1083 (1991)

[Eighty-five percent of the shares of First American Bank of Virginia (FABI) were held by Virginia Bankshares (VBI), so that when VBI initiated a freeze-out merger, the minority shareholders had insufficient votes to block the merger. Even though minority shareholders lacked the power to disapprove the transaction, the directors nonetheless solicited the proxies of the minority shareholders. The first part of Justice Souter's opinion, dealing with the actionability of the fairness opinion that was part of the proxy materials, was discussed in Chapter 12.

The Court then turned to the element of causation. Plaintiffs made two causation arguments. One, that the fraud caused the minority shareholders to lose their remedy under state law, was rejected on grounds that they had not demonstrated any such loss: The minority vote did not operate to immunize the transaction from attack, and plaintiffs had made no claim that the false statements misled the shareholders "into entertaining a false belief that they had no chance to upset the merger until the time for bringing suit had run out." As to the other argument:]

[Respondents] argue . . . that a link existed and was essential simply because VBI and FABI would have been unwilling to proceed with the merger without the approval manifested by the minority shareholders' proxies, which would not have been obtained without the solicitation's express misstatements and misleading omissions. On this reasoning, the causal connection would depend on a desire to avoid bad shareholder or public relations, and the essential character of the causal link would stem not from the enforceable terms of the parties' corporate relationship, but from one party's apprehension of the ill will of the other. . . .

Blue Chip Stamps [*v. Manor Drug Stores*, 421 U.S. 723 (1975),] set an example worth recalling as a preface to specific policy analysis of the consequences of recognizing respondents' first theory, that a desire to avoid minority shareholders' ill will should suffice to justify recognizing the requisite causality of a proxy statement needed to garner that minority support. It will be recalled that in *Blue Chip Stamps* we raised concerns about the practical consequences of allowing recovery, under §10(b) of the Act and Rule 10b-5, on evidence of what a merely hypothetical buyer or seller might have done on a set of facts that never occurred, and foresaw that any such expanded liability would turn on "hazy" issues inviting self-serving testimony, strike suits, and protracted discovery, with little chance of reasonable resolution by pretrial process. Id., at 742-743. These were good reasons to deny recognition to such claims in the absence of any apparent contrary congressional intent.

The same threats of speculative claims and procedural intractability are inherent in respondents' theory of causation linked through the directors' desire for a cosmetic vote. Causation would turn on inferences about what the corporate directors would have thought and done without the minority shareholder approval unneeded to authorize action. A subsequently dissatisfied minority shareholder would have virtual license to allege that managerial timidity would have doomed corporate action but for the ostensible approval induced by a misleading statement, and opposing claims of hypothetical diffidence and hypothetical boldness on the part of directors would probably provide enough depositions in the usual case to preclude any judicial resolution short of the credibility judgments that can only come after trial. Reliable evidence would seldom exist. Directors would understand the prudence of making a few statements about plans to proceed even without minority endorsement, and discovery would be a quest for recollections of oral conversations at odds with the official pronouncements, in hopes of finding support for ex post facto guesses about how much heat the directors would have stood in the absence of minority approval. The issues would be hazy, their litigation protracted, and their resolution unreliable. Given a choice, we would reject any theory of causation that raised such prospects, and we reject this one.[12]

Justice KENNEDY, with whom Justice MARSHALL, Justice BLACKMUN, and Justice STEVENS join, concurring in part and dissenting in part. . . . There is no authority whatsoever for limiting §14(a) to protecting those minority shareholders whose numerical strength could permit them to vote down a proposal. One of Section 14(a)'s "chief purposes is 'the protection of investors.'" *J.I. Case Co. v. Borak*, 377 U.S., at 432. Those who lack the strength to vote down a proposal have all the more need of disclosure. The voting process involves not only casting ballots but also the formulation and withdrawal of proposals, the minority's right to block a vote through court action or the threat of adverse consequences, or the negotiation of an increase in price. The proxy rules support this deliberative process. These practicalities can result in causation sufficient to support recovery.

The facts in the case before us prove this point. Sandberg argues that had all the material facts been disclosed, FABI or the Bank likely would have withdrawn or revised the merger proposal. The evidence in the record, and more that might be available upon remand, meets any reasonable requirement of specific and nonspeculative proof.

FABI wanted a "friendly transaction" with a price viewed as "so high that any reasonable shareholder will accept it." App. 99. Management expressed concern that the transaction result in "no loss of support for the bank out in the

---

12.   In parting company from us on this point, Justice Kennedy emphasizes that respondents in this particular case substantiated a plausible claim that petitioners would not have proceeded without minority approval. FABI's attempted freeze-out merger of a Maryland subsidiary had failed a year before the events in question when the subsidiary's directors rejected the proposal because of inadequate share price, and there was evidence of FABI's desire to avoid any renewal of adverse comment. The issue before us, however, is whether to recognize a theory of causation generally, and our decision against doing so rests on our apprehension that the ensuing litigation would be exemplified by cases far less tractable than this. Respondents' burden to justify recognition of causation beyond the scope of *Mills* must be addressed not by emphasizing the instant case but by confronting the risk inherent in the cases that would be expected to be characteristic if the causal theory were adopted.

community, which was important." Id., at 109. Although FABI had the votes to push through any proposal, it wanted a favorable response from the minority shareholders. Id., at 192. Because of the "human element involved in a transaction of this nature," FABI attempted to "show those minority shareholders that [it was] being fair." Id., at 347. . . .

NOTES AND QUESTIONS

1. Scienter. Most courts have held that plaintiffs do not have to show scienter to state a claim under Rule 14a-9. Instead, negligence suffices, or perhaps there is no state of mind requirement at all. *See, e.g., Beck v. Dobrowski,* 559 F.3d 680 (7th Cir. 2009); *Gould v. American-Hawaiian Steamship Co.,* 535 F.2d 761 (3d Cir. 1976). But there is some disagreement. In *Adams v. Standard Knitting Mills, Inc.,* 623 F.2d 422 (6th Cir. 1980), *cert. denied,* 449 U.S. 1067 (1981), the court held that scienter was the proper standard to apply in a case against the issuer's accountants because of their indirect responsibility for the alleged misstatements. The Eighth Circuit has agreed, but determined that negligence is the appropriate standard for cases against corporate officers. *SEC v. Das,* 723 F.3d 923 (8th Cir. 2013). In addition, as under Section 11, under the '33 Act (discussed in Chapter 9), if plaintiffs' complaint alleging a false or misleading proxy solicitation "sounds in fraud," it might be held to a heightened pleading standard.

2. Standing, Reliance, and Causation. Courts generally allow a shareholder who is not misled by the fraud to bring suit under Section 14(a), on the assumption that, if enough other shareholders were misled and thus approved the challenged transaction, all shareholders are harmed. *E.g., Stahl v. Gibraltar Fin. Corp.,* 967 F.2d 335 (9th Cir. 1992); *Cowin v. Bresler,* 741 F.2d 410, 427 (D.C. Cir. 1984).

This leads to the questions of reliance and causation. Along with *Virginia Bankshares,* the seminal case here is *Mills v. Electric Auto-Lite Co.,* 396 U.S. 375 (1970). In *Mills,* the Supreme Court held that a shareholder who can demonstrate that a misstatement or omission in a proxy statement was material is entitled to a presumption of reliance. It is not necessary to demonstrate that votes were actually influenced by the misstatement or omission. This holding under Rule 14a-9 was a progenitor of the similar presumptions that are now commonly invoked under Rule 10b-5, as we saw in Chapter 13. On the other hand, courts have also emphasized that plaintiffs seeking damages in private actions under Rule 14a-9 must still make at least a threshold showing of loss causation in order for recovery to be granted. Thus, shareholders could not seek to recover damages based on the failure of those standing for election to the company's board to disclose a pattern of illicit payments, since the alleged injury (the unlawful payments) occurred before the violation and hence could not have been caused by it. Even if the injury follows, courts insist on a fairly direct relationship between the fraud and the ensuing harm. In *General Electric Co. v. Cathcart,* 980 F.2d 927 (3d Cir. 1992), the court dismissed an action seeking monetary losses from alleged managerial misconduct that purportedly occurred because of the lax supervision of the board of directors. Since the shareholders did not approve the transactions complained of—but merely elected the directors—the link between the election and the monetary harm was too remote. Does this mean that the fraudulent election of directors can never lead to monetary damages? *Compare In re Wells Fargo & Co.*, 282 F. Supp. 3d 1974 (N.D. Cal. 2017) (finding sufficient causal link between election of directors and approval of compensation and the continuation of illegal retail selling practices at the bank).

Virginia Bankshares sets forth the rule on causation in freeze-out situations, but leaves open whether, on a proper showing, minority shareholders might succeed by showing that they were deceived into forgoing some state law remedy, such as appraisal or an injunction. To date, courts have been receptive to such claims. *See Wilson v. Great American Industries Inc.*, 979 F.2d 924 (2d Cir. 1992); *Howing Co. v. Nationwide Corp.*, 972 F.2d 700 (6th Cir. 1992), *cert. denied*, 507 U.S. 1004 (1993). What kind of showing should be necessary? That the state law claim was lost completely? That had the truth been told, there would have been a greater likelihood of success on the merits or a better opportunity for an adequate remedy?

3. Remedies.   According to the Supreme Court in *Mills*, there is substantial judicial discretion with respect to relief once a showing of proxy fraud is made. Under some circumstances, a new solicitation or election can be ordered, and this no doubt is the preferred remedy. But what if the passage of time has made the undoing of an election—particularly with respect to something like approval of a complicated corporate merger—impracticable? In the *Mills* case itself, which involved an alleged failure to disclose adequately in a subsidiary's proxy materials soliciting approval of a merger with the parent the fact that the parent controlled the subsidiary's board of directors, the Court left open the possibility of monetary damages as an appropriate remedy. On remand in *Mills*, the Seventh Circuit determined that, while damages were in theory the appropriate remedy in a case such as this, the shareholders had in fact suffered no damages: Notwithstanding the material misstatement in the proxy materials, the resulting merger was on fair terms. As evidence, it determined that minority shareholders had received more than a 10 percent increase in the value of their shares as a result of the merger, a fair distribution of the gains that the transaction produced. *Mills v. Electric Auto-Lite Co.*, 552 F.2d 1239 (7th Cir. 1977), *cert. denied*, 434 U.S. 922 (1978). In other words, after 14 years of litigation over the existence of a violation of Rule 14a-9, the Court finally determined that the impropriety had been harmless. *See* Dennis, Materiality and the Efficient Capital Market Model: A Recipe for the Total Mix, 25 Wm. & Mary L. Rev. 373, 389-392 (1984); Lorne, A Reappraisal of Fair Shares in Controlled Mergers, 126 U. Pa. L. Rev. 956 (1978). For a discussion of how damages should be measured in a case involving proxy fraud, *see Wilson v. Great American Industries Inc.*, 855 F.2d 987 (2d Cir. 1988). There the court held that the measure of damages for shareholders who were deceived into approving an ill-advised merger could be based on what the court described as a "benefit of the bargain" approach, giving them the equivalent of what they would have been able to obtain had full disclosure been made.

4. Settlements.   In Delaware corporate law, it had become common for suits to be filed claiming false or misleading disclosures in M&A transactions, and then settled simply for revised disclosures of arguably marginal value, plus sizable attorneys' fees. Seeing this practice as abusive, Delaware courts put a stop to this by refusing to approve settlements in the absence of palpable materiality. *See* Cain et al., The Shifting Tides of Merger Litigation, 71 Vand. L. Rev. 603 (2018). Plaintiffs then started bringing their cases outside Delaware, particularly in federal court by pleading violations of Rule 14a-9. Should federal courts follow Delaware's lead? *See In re Walgreen Co. Stockholder Litig.*, 832 F.3d 718 (7th Cir. 2016) (Posner, J.: yes).

5. *Going Private.* The Supreme Court's decisions in *Mills* and *Virginia Bankshares* involved merger transactions where the acquiring party was a controlling shareholder of the subsidiary. They thus present significant conflicts of interest, and in Delaware particularly, fairly searching judicial review of the fairness of the deal, with particular stress on the controller's candor in presenting the transaction for shareholder approval. That is in addition to the requirements of federal proxy regulation when the subsidiary is a public company and shareholders have a meaningful vote. But there is more. In going-private transactions where a conflict is present, the SEC's Rule 13e-3 operates to require a heightened level of disclosure as to the fairness of the transaction in a Schedule 13E-3, including a statement as to "whether the subject company or affiliate filing the statement reasonably believes that the Rule 13e-3 transaction is fair or unfair to unaffiliated security holders," with particularized reasons why. By making the controller address fairness specifically, the Rule blurs the line between fraud and fiduciary—it is very hard to fulfill this disclosure obligation honestly if a transaction is in fact not objectively fair to shareholders. *See In re Meyers Parking Systems,* Exchange Act Release No. 26069 (1988). Perhaps because of the evolution of state corporation law in this area, there is relatively little litigation today in federal court, even though there is judicial support for an implied private right of action. *See Howing v. Nationwide Corp.,* 826 F.2d 1470 (6th Cir. 1986). Still, the expansive disclosures triggered by Rule 13e-3 are often noted by state courts reviewing freeze-out mergers, and play a role in the "cooperative federalism" at work here. Note that the category of transactions triggering Rule 13e-3 includes leveraged buy-outs commonly associated with private equity deals, where the acquirer is not at the time of the transaction a controlling shareholder but affiliates with incumbent managers to take the company private.

PROBLEM

16-3. Municipal Savings Bank (MSB) and Fidelity Bancorporation (FB) were in merger negotiations, which ultimately led to an agreement submitted to MSB's shareholders for their approval. During the negotiations, MSB was approached by another bank stating that it was willing to make a higher bid, subject to being given the ability to do a limited due diligence investigation into MSB's financial condition. MSB management rejected the overture and denied the other bank the same access to information that it was already affording to FB. Unwilling to make a hostile bid, the third party departed.

In seeking shareholder approval of the MSB-FB merger, the proxy materials stated that "a third party had approached MSB with respect to the possibility of making an offer but had withdrawn prior to making one." After shareholders approved the merger, some shareholders brought suit claiming that the proxy statement was misleading for failing to disclose the circumstances of the third party's potentially more lucrative bid and the reasons for the withdrawal. Plaintiffs alleged that MSB's management was opposed to the third party's bid because FB was offering lucrative employment, consulting and severance payments, while the third party had made it clear that it would not do so. Does this state a cause of action under Rule 14a-9? What about the argument that causation is lacking because shareholders would surely have voted in favor of the FB merger anyway—because MSB's management was opposed to the third party's bid it could never have been a viable option for shareholder consideration, so that the only rational choice was to vote for the only value-enhancing deal management was willing to offer? *See Minzer v. Keegan,* 218 F.3d 144 (2d Cir. 2000).

||17||
Corporate Takeovers

A. *Introduction: The Policy Dilemma*

Few subjects have so captured the imagination of the investing public as corporate takeovers. The possibility of a bidder suddenly appearing and offering a premium over the prevailing market price—perhaps to be followed by a bidding war that drives the premium itself to a level that may match or exceed the original per share price—contributes significantly to shareholder wealth. Even when bids are defeated, as by the intervention of a "white knight" or a defensive restructuring of the business by incumbent management, target shareholders often gain. And add the disciplinary effect on management, since poor performance might cause the market price of the company's shares to drop and make a takeover bid more likely.

   Given that investors perceive them so favorably, why should corporate takeovers be a concern of federal securities regulation? One response is that some bids—especially those offering target shareholders something other than cash for their shares—may be fraudulent or manipulative. And when new securities are being offered, the traditional justifications for mandatory disclosure under the '33 Act come into play. Other bids may contain some element of coercion. While all these are genuine concerns, overall the premiums paid in takeovers result in most investors being substantial "net gainers" from the takeover phenomenon, and there is ample empirical support for this view. In a now-classic study, Jarrell & Bradley, The Economic Effects of Federal and State Regulation of Cash Tender Offers, 23 J.L. & Econ. 371 (1980), the authors reported that the overall effect of increasing amounts of takeover regulation is a substantial increase in the premiums paid in connection with successful takeovers. In this sense, the effect of regulation is to force bidders who choose to go ahead with their bids to share with target shareholders a significant portion of the expected gains from the acquisition. While at first glance this sounds good from the investor's perspective, is it? What about the bids that never occur at all because of the regulatory costs and risks?

The dynamics of corporate takeovers have shifted since their emergence in the 1950s and 1960s. Though hostile bids are not uncommon, state law developments—both statutory and judicial—have given incumbent management a wide variety of tools to employ to resist hostile bids. *See* Coates, Measuring the Domain of the Mediating Hierarchy: How Contestable Are U.S. Public Corporations?, 24 J. Corp. L. 837 (1999). Bids are now more likely to be sufficiently compelling that they give target management, increasingly more likely to be represented by its independent directors, less justification to resist without risking the wrath of either its large shareholders or the state courts. To a large extent, therefore, state corporation law and changing norms of corporate governance have eclipsed federal tender offer regulation in determining the outcome of hostile bids. *See* Davidoff, The SEC and the Failure of Federal Takeover Regulation, 34 Fla. St. L. Rev. 211 (2007).

This chapter begins with a provision of the Williams Act that goes beyond the tender offer context: Section 13(d)'s disclosure of beneficial ownership requirements. It then moves on to tender offer regulation, covering issues relating to disclosure, conduct, and the prohibition against fraud as well as the definition of the term *tender offer*. It ends with a look at some ways in which the Williams Act governs defensive tactics by incumbent management and the problem of tender offer–related manipulation.

B.   The Early Warning System: Section 13(d)

The starting point for the regulation of corporate takeovers—though by no means tied to their existence—is Section 13(d) of the Securities Exchange Act, part of the Williams Act amendments enacted by Congress in 1968. Section 13(d) requires a filing by any person who becomes the beneficial owner of more than 5 percent of a class of equity securities registered pursuant to Section 12 or of certain other issuers (i.e., publicly held companies). The filing is the Schedule 13D, which is transmitted to the SEC, the relevant stock exchanges, and the issuer of the securities in question. Similar in many ways to the disclosure in a contested proxy fight, the Schedule 13D must disclose such matters as the background and identity of the acquirer, the source of funding, the number of shares owned, any contracts or arrangements with respect to such shares, and the purpose of the acquisition, including any plans or proposals regarding possible exercise of control over the issuer. In other words, if the person contemplates doing a tender offer to take control of the company, that must be disclosed in advance.

There are a variety of exemptions from the filing requirement under Section 13(d)(6) and Rule 13d-1, most of which relate to acquisitions where alternative regulatory schemes under the securities laws will apply. The most important exemption not falling into this "alternative regulation" category is that provided for so-called creeping acquisitions—situations where the acquisition in question, together with all others made by the same person during the preceding 12 months, does not exceed 2 percent of the class. There is also a separate, more relaxed, regulatory regime—Schedule 13G—for acquirers who do not intend to exercise control over the issuer, discussed below.

The Schedule 13D must be filed within ten days of passing the 5 percent threshold. Thereafter, amendments must be filed promptly whenever any "material" changes occur with respect to the original disclosures. According to Rule 13d-2, an acquisition or disposition of 1 percent or more of the class of securities in question is presumptively material; acquisitions or dispositions of less than that amount may or may not be material, depending upon the circumstances.

What purpose is Section 13(d) designed to serve? It seems to be some sort of "early warning system." But for whom? What are such persons supposed to do with this information? The ostensible statutory purpose is to notify shareholders of the target company of a potential shift in control. Presumably, a shareholder so notified might delay a contemplated sale of stock of the issuer in hopes of getting the higher premium price. But one other beneficiary of the disclosure is quite clear. If it is not already aware of the bidder's activity, target management will take the early warning and begin defensive efforts in earnest.

This leads naturally to a more fundamental question about the impact—whether intended or simply foreseeable—of such a filing requirement on the market for control of publicly held corporations. While the precise effects are debatable, it seems clear that forcing a bidder to tip its hand with regard to a planned bid will (a) result in an immediate increase in the market price of the issuer's shares, (b) cause target management to adopt an immediate defensive posture, and (c) alert other potential bidders to the possibility that the company is "in play." In this sense, Section 13(d) increases both the cost and the risk, and thus lowers the bidder's expected return, associated with an acquisition affected by it. By hypothesis, fewer bids will occur under such regulation. *See* Jarrell & Bradley, The Economic Effects of Federal and State Regulations of Cash Tender Offers, 23 J.L. & Econ. 371 (1980). It is in this light that the desirability of the Rule—and the plausibility of its ostensibly investor-oriented justification—ought to be considered. This is precisely the framing for the current debate over whether Congress should shorten the time period for a 13(d) filing from ten days to two. The shorter filing period would give more information to the market, but perhaps at the price of discouraging activist shareholders from pursuing value-enhancing strategies. *See* Gilson & Gordon, The Agency Costs of Agency Capitalism: Activist Investors and the Revaluation of Governance Rights, 113 Colum. L. Rev. 863, 906 (2013).

One hint as to actual legislative purpose may come by considering the surprising breadth of Section 13(d). The most intriguing language in this regard is found in Section 13(d)(3), which states that "[w]hen two or more persons act as a partnership, limited partnership, or other group for the purpose of acquiring, *holding, or disposing* of securities of an issuer, such syndicate or group shall be deemed a 'person' for purposes of this subsection" (emphasis added). This provision was at issue in the following case.

Wellman v. Dickinson
682 F.2d 355 (2d Cir. 1982), *cert. denied*, 460 U.S. 1069 (1983)

MOORE, J. This appeal arises from seven separate actions brought against defendant-appellant, Fairleigh S. Dickinson, Jr., and eleven other defendants, for alleged violations of the federal securities laws. . . . These seven actions include an enforcement action brought by the Securities and Exchange Commission ("SEC"), a private action filed by Becton, Dickinson & Company ("Becton") and certain of its officers, and five class actions brought on behalf of certain Becton shareholders. All seven actions stem from the acquisition by Sun Company, Inc. of approximately 34% of the outstanding stock of Becton, a New Jersey corporation engaged in the manufacture of health care products and medical testing and research equipment. . . .

As Judge Carter observed: "The background and governing facts in this complex drama embrace personality conflicts, animosity, distrust, and corporate politics, as well as a display of ingenuity and sophistication by brokers, investment bankers and corporate counsel." *Wellman v. Dickinson*, 475 F. Supp. [787] at 797-98 [S.D.N.Y. 1979].

One of the principal personalities was Fairleigh S. Dickinson, Jr., the son of a founder of Becton and a major stockholder of the company. He individually held 802,138 shares of Becton stock (4.2% of the outstanding shares). In addition, Dickinson held 140,794 shares (.64%) as a co-trustee and at least 198,922 shares (1%) as a member of the Dickinson family.

Dickinson personally managed Becton for over twenty-five years. In 1974, Dickinson relinquished his management responsibilities and became Chairman of the Board. In late 1976, however, differences between the new management and Dickinson emerged. On April 20, 1977, after a bitter internal power struggle over the course of several months, the new management team prevailed, and the board of directors voted to remove Dickinson as its chairman.

The day following his removal as chairman, Dickinson met with representatives of Salomon Brothers ("Salomon"), a New York limited partnership engaged in the investment banking and brokerage business, to obtain advice on how to regain control of Becton. . . . These men discussed several possible strategies. Dickinson ultimately agreed to a plan to vote with outside directors as a means of bringing pressure on Becton's management and selling a block of the company's shares, including his own, to a corporation interested in taking over Becton. Dickinson hired Salomon to assist him in locating a corporation that would be interested in purchasing his substantial holdings in Becton and those of his friends as the springboard for a complete or partial takeover of the company. . . .

The presentations by Salomon and Eberstadt [another investment banking firm] to the corporations potentially interested in purchasing Becton stock were virtually identical. A representative from one of the two brokerage houses would inform the corporation that Salomon and Eberstadt were representing Dickinson. They would then describe Dickinson's animosity toward Becton's management and his desire to dispose of his stock in the company. They would also disclose that other stockholders shared Dickinson's ill feelings and were interested in selling their shares. . . . The labors of the two brokerage houses eventually bore fruit when Sun Company, Inc. ("Sun"), a Pennsylvania corporation whose principal business involves oil and gas, entered the picture. On November 28, 1977, Kenneth Lipper of Salomon approached Horace Kephart, a senior vice president of Sun in charge of the company's corporate development and diversification program, and suggested that Sun might want to consider Becton as a possible acquisition. Lipper informed Kephart that 15% of Becton's stock was available and that this initial block included 1,200,000 shares owned by Dickinson, 300-400,000 shares owned by Dunning, 400,000 shares owned by Lufkin, and 500,000 shares owned by the Chemical Fund, one of the Eberstadt-managed mutual funds. Lipper also advised Kephart that Sun would be able to acquire quickly an additional 10-20% of Becton stock. Kephart was aware of the rift between Dickinson and Becton's management and learned of Becton's public announcement in June of its desire to remain independent. . . .

DISCUSSION

Section 13(d) of the Securities Exchange Act of 1934 requires a group that has acquired, directly or indirectly, beneficial ownership of more than 5% of a class of a registered equity security, to file a statement with the SEC, disclosing, inter alia, the identity of its members and the purpose of its acquisition. The central question on appeal is whether the district court erred in finding that Dickinson joined a group holding beneficial ownership of approximately 13% of the outstanding shares of Becton, and in finding that the members of this group agreed to dispose of the Becton stock under their control but failed to disclose this fact pursuant to Section 13(d). A group, under Section 13(d)(3), is defined as an aggregation of persons or entities who "act . . . for the purpose of acquiring, holding or disposing of securities. . . ." The statute contains no requirement, however, that the members be committed to acquisition, holding, or disposition on any specific set of terms. Instead, the touchstone of a group within the meaning of Section 13(d) is that the members combined in furtherance of a common objective. *Bath Industries, Inc. v. Blot*, 427 F.2d 97, 111 (7th Cir. 1970). Of course, the concerted action of the group's members need not be expressly memorialized in writing. *Securities and Exchange Commission v. Savoy Indus., Inc.*, 587 F.2d 1149, 1163 (D.C. Cir. 1978), *cert. denied*, 440 U.S. 913 (1979).

Dickinson contends that plaintiffs have not demonstrated that he entered into a formal or informal agreement with any other person to dispose of his Becton stock, or that the purported members of the Section 13(d) group had beneficial ownership of sufficient Becton stock to form a Section 13(d) group with him. . . .

Ample evidence supports the district court's finding that Dickinson, Eberstadt, Eberstadt M & D, Lufkin, and Dunning "were all part of a group formed to dispose of their shares to aid a third party acquisition of a controlling interest in [Becton]." *Wellman v. Dickinson*, supra, 475 F. Supp. at 830. In reaching its conclusion that an express or implied understanding existed between the group members, the district court relied to a great extent on the representations made by Dickinson and his representatives from Salomon and Eberstadt to potential purchasers concerning the availability of the shares controlled by Dickinson, Dunning, Lufkin, Eberstadt, and Eberstadt M & D.

One vivid example of testimony concerning the assurances made by Dickinson's representatives to potential purchasers is that of William LaPorte, chairman of the board of directors of American Home Products Corporation, one of the companies approached with the Becton takeover proposal. LaPorte testified at trial that Kenneth Lipper of Salomon called to inform him that Dickinson was seeking a company interested in merging with Becton and that 16-17% of the outstanding shares were readily available for sale. Specifically, Lipper indicated, according to LaPorte, that Eberstadt controlled 500,000 shares of Becton and that the shares controlled by Dickinson and Dunning were available and would "go with [the] deal." . . .

Dickinson contends that the representations made by him and his representatives to potential purchasers are not probative of an understanding among the group members because the statements were simply "predictions" as to which Becton shareholders would sell. We reject Dickinson's claim and conclude that, in light of all the facts, the district court could reasonably infer from the evidence that assurances, not mere predictions, were made by the group. . . .

Dickinson, Dunning, Eberstadt, Eberstadt M & D and Lufkin were linked by a desire to profit from a shift in the corporate control of Becton. The evidence clearly supports the district court's finding that in an effort to achieve their common objective, Dickinson, Eberstadt, Dunning, Eberstadt M & D and Lufkin formed a group to dispose of the Becton shares under their control.

Dickinson also contends that the district court erred in finding that Eberstadt, Eberstadt M & D, Dunning and Lufkin held beneficial ownership of sufficient Becton stock to form a Section 13(d) group with him because they possessed "the *power to commit* [Becton] shares to the group purpose of effectuating a shift in corporate control." *Wellman v. Dickinson*, supra, 475 F. Supp. at 829 (emphasis supplied). Dickinson contends that control over present voting power should be the sole determinant of beneficial ownership and that the power to dispose of stock is not a relevant consideration.

We reject Dickinson's argument. Although voting control is alone sufficient to support a finding of beneficial ownership, it need not be the only indicium. *See* Rule 13d-3. A rule that beneficial ownership can be established only by proof of voting control would exclude from the coverage of Section 13(d) a range of conduct that Congress clearly intended should be covered. Section 13(d) was designed to alert investors in securities markets to potential changes in corporate control and to provide them with an opportunity to evaluate the effect of these potential changes. *GAF Corp. v. Milstein*, 453 F.2d 709, 717 (2d Cir. 1971), *cert. denied*, 406 U.S. 910 (1972). The power to dispose of a block of securities represents a means for effecting changes in corporate control in addition to the possession of voting control. Moreover, Congress intended beneficial ownership to mean more than voting control when it specifically included within the definition of "person[s]" subject to Section 13(d), a "group" acting in concert for the "purpose of . . . disposing of securities of an issuer." 15 U.S.C. §78m(d)(3) (1976). . . .

The evidence clearly supports the district court's findings that the members of the group possessed the power to commit sufficient shares of Becton stock to satisfy the 5% holding requirement of Section 13(d)....

VAN GRAAFEILAND, Circuit Judge, concurring in part and dissenting in part:

When reputable and honest businessmen, advised by able and ethical lawyers, are held to have violated a federal statute, the likelihood is that there is something faulty in the statute, the manner in which it is administered, or both. In this case, I believe that the fault lies with both. Under the Williams Act, Congress and the SEC have attempted to regulate both purchases and sales of stock with the same set of rules and with an inadequate definition of terms. The result has been less than admirable....

My own reading of the record does not satisfy me that Dickinson, Eberstadt, Dunning, and Lufkin had the powers of disposition over stock owned by others which the district court found to exist. For example, the district court's finding that Eberstadt had the power to make a "binding commitment" to sell the Fund shares is, in my opinion, clearly erroneous. That finding treats the Fund directors as automatons, which they were not, and disregards Eberstadt's specific disavowal of the power to assure a sale. In short, if Eberstadt had been sued because it found itself unable to carry out its "binding commitment," I would have been delighted to be the lawyer handling its defense....

With all due respect to my learned colleagues, I cannot join them in affirming a decision that unjustifiably has besmirched an honorable name. I would reverse the district court's holding that appellant Dickinson violated section 13(d) of the Securities Exchange Act....

NOTES AND QUESTIONS

1.   Intent.   Note that Item 4 of Schedule 13D distinguishes between disclosure of "purpose" and disclosure of "plans or proposals." What disclosure is appropriate in the event that a person or group is yet undecided on its plans—that is, is thinking about a takeover, but is not yet sure what it will do? Is an ambiguous statement that the acquisition is "for investment purposes" acceptable? In *K-N Energy Inc. v. Gulf Interstate Corp.*, 607 F. Supp. 756 (D. Colo. 1983), the court held that such a statement was false and misleading in light of the group's efforts in fact to influence the affairs of the subject company and suggested that disclosure of the options under consideration was required. In *Azurite v. Amster & Co.*, 52 F.3d 15 (2d Cir. 1995), on the other hand, the court refused to compel disclosure of tentative plans for a proxy contest (including consultations with counsel and other investors) that had not yet ripened into a "fixed" decision—even though the current Schedule 3D had indicated no purpose to affect control. The court rejected plaintiff's claim that the meaning of plans and intentions should be the same as assessing materiality, suggesting that there needs to be room for investors to rethink their ownership intentions without the chill of a strict updating obligation. Does this approach allow large shareholders to conceal too much of what Section 13(d) seems to insist on?

Challenges to the accuracy of statements of intent can be made circumstantially. In *Chevron Corp. v. Pennzoil Corp.*, 974 F.2d 1156 (9th Cir. 1992), the court allowed a case to proceed against Pennzoil, which stated in its Schedule 13D that its acquisition was for investment intent with no current plans for any control activity, based upon evidence that from a tax standpoint it would be highly advantageous (if not necessary) for it to seek a seat on Chevron's board and obtain some managerial influence.

2. Groups. Suppose a group is formed in such a manner that, in light of *Wellman*, it falls within the scope of Section 13(d) and the aggregate holdings of the individual group members exceed the 5 percent threshold. This raises the question of whether there is an immediate filing obligation or whether the group can instead wait until it makes its first acquisition or disposition of its shares. The answer is the former according to Rule 13d-5(b), which codifies an earlier judicial holding in *GAF Corp. v. Milstein*, 453 F.2d 709 (2d Cir. 1971), *cert. denied*, 406 U.S. 910 (1972). The court emphasized that the purpose of Section 13(d) is to alert investors to the presence of one or more shareholders with the power to influence control of the issuer, and this presence comes about upon formation of the group regardless of whether any shares are purchased or sold thereafter.

3. Beneficial Ownership. As to the meaning of *beneficial ownership*, whether for groups or otherwise, Rule 13d-3 emphasizes as the proper test for such ownership whether the person in question directly or indirectly has either voting power or investment power over the securities in question. *Voting power* includes "the power to vote or direct the voting" of the securities; *investment power* means the ability to dispose (or direct the disposition) of the security in question. The definition also encompasses situations where, through options or warrants, the person has a right to acquire securities of the issuer. Recall the use of this term under the short-swing insider trading restriction found in Section 16(b). As we saw in Chapter 15, there are two separate definitions of beneficial ownership. Section 13(d) uses the same one employed to determine whether a person owns 10 percent or more of the equity securities of the issuer, and cases under Section 16(b) often cite precedent under Section 13(d) (and vice versa). One implication of the emphasis on beneficial ownership is that persons who are legal owners, but lack the indicia of beneficial ownership (e.g., lawyers acting as trustees or nominees), need not file in their own right. *Calvary Holdings Inc. v. Chandler*, 948 F.2d 59 (1st Cir. 1991).

One practice in this area deserves mention. In the past, some persons have arranged to place "ownership" of stock formally in the hands of third parties (e.g., through a sale) in an effort to avoid passing the 5 percent threshold, when in fact they retain effective control over it. This is referred to as "parking" and—because of the expansive definitions of beneficial ownership and group— is typically unlawful. *See SEC v. First City Financial Corp.*, 890 F.2d 1215 (D.C. Cir. 1989). In *First City Financial*, the court found sufficient evidence of a "put and call" agreement between First City Financial (FCF) and a brokerage firm, pursuant to which the broker would purchase stock and hold it in its account subject to both the right of FCF to acquire it at a prearranged price and the option of the broker to require FCF to take it at that price. As both parties conceded, this plainly falls within the definition of beneficial ownership by FCF.

4. Remedies. Section 13(d) may be enforced by the SEC, of course, and for such actions, there is no scienter requirement. *See SEC v. Savoy Industries Inc.*, 587 F.2d 1149 (D.C. Cir. 1978). As to private rights of action, virtually all courts have permitted issuers to sue for equitable relief. *See Portsmouth Square Inc. v. Shareholders Protective Comm.*, 770 F.2d 866, 871 n.8 (9th Cir. 1985); *Florida Commercial Banks v. Culverhouse*, 772 F.2d 1513 (11th Cir. 1984) (corrective disclosure only). As discussed later in this chapter, however, the private right of action under the Williams Act generally may be subject to reconsideration. As to the proper remedy for a violation, courts have not considered damages to be an appropriate form of relief under Section 13(d), even in actions brought by subject company shareholders. *See Kammerman v. Steinberg*, 891 F.2d 424 (2d Cir. 1989).

Even serious equitable relief may be difficult to come by under certain circumstances. In *Rondeau v. Mosinee Paper Corp.*, 422 U.S. 49 (1975), the Supreme Court held, in the context of an inadvertent and quickly corrected violation of Section 13(d), that an injunction barring the voting of the defendant's shares for five years was impermissible, since the traditional standards governing such equitable relief—for example, irreparable harm if relief is not granted—had not been established. Following the lead of *Rondeau,* courts have been reluctant to order much beyond corrective disclosure in Section 13(d) cases, with perhaps a short "cooling-off" period for the market to internalize the information ordered to be disclosed. In *ICN Pharmaceuticals Inc. v. Khan*, 2 F.3d 484 (2d Cir. 1993), the court set aside an injunction permanently barring a person from engaging in any takeover-related activity, even though he was found to have omitted significant information in his disclosures and misused inside information in acquiring shares of the target. The emphasis instead was on corrective disclosure and appropriate relief for the insider trading and breach of fiduciary duty.

Probably the most extensive example of equitable relief for a Section 13(d) violation was that ordered in *SEC v. First City Financial Corp.*, 890 F.2d 1215 (D.C. Cir. 1989), the parking case noted earlier. There, the acquiror was forced to disgorge $2.7 million of the profits made when it later resold stock to the target in return for a standstill agreement. The figure was calculated by making the assumption that had the acquiror complied with the law, its purchases would have been in a market that "would have been affected by the disclosures that [the acquiror] had taken a greater than 5 percent stake in [the target] and would soon propose a tender offer." *Id.* at 1231. Thus, it had to give back the profits from the stock that was acquired more than ten days after the violation. In affirming the disgorgement order, the court of appeals emphasized the need to deter violations and therefore gave the SEC the benefit of the doubt with respect to the calculation of the appropriate sum. The ancillary relief issue is considered more fully in Chapter 14.

5. "Passive" Ownership Reports. One other statutory provision regarding ownership of publicly held corporations bears note. Section 13(g), adopted in 1977, requires a filing along the lines of the Schedule 13D by persons who are 5 percent beneficial owners, thus extending the disclosure scheme to persons who attained that level of ownership before the Williams Act was adopted or by means of a transaction exempted under Section 13(d) or its rules. The SEC has integrated the requirements of Sections 13(d) and (g) in order to make clear when a person falls within the more rigorous requirements of Section 13(d), rather than the more lenient ones imposed under the rules adopted pursuant to Section 13(g). Under Rule 13d-1(b), the most important category of persons entitled to use the simplified filing procedures is the "passive" investor who acquired the stock in the ordinary course of business and without any intent to change or influence the control of the issuer. For these investors, only annual filings are required (except upon passing a 10 percent ownership threshold or thereafter when such ownership increases or decreases by more than 5 percent), and the form is a substantially shortened version of the Schedule 13D. Importantly, however, if a person entitled to file on Schedule 13G changes her intentions, so that a "control purpose" comes into existence, she is precluded from acquiring any additional shares for ten days after filing Schedule 13D.

6. *Institutional Activism.*   To what extent can the aggressive activism that the SEC's proxy reforms tried to promote be thwarted by Section 13(d)? Note that the SEC's rule on group responsibilities, Rule 13d-5(b)(1), refers not only to groups formed to buy or sell securities of the issuer but also to "vote" those securities. *See* Black, Next Steps in Proxy Reform, 18 J. Corp. L. 1 (1992), suggesting that reform will not be complete until the full set of rules that chill institutional activism (including Sections 13(d) and 16(b)) are also addressed.

7. *Derivatives and "Morphable" Ownership.*   Section 13(d)'s definition of beneficial ownership is tied to the right to vote or dispose of the issuer's equity securities. Suppose that an activist hedge fund enters into a swap agreement with one or more counterparties (typically investment banks) pursuant to which the hedge fund is paid the cash value of any returns—dividends or capital appreciation—that would come from share ownership in the issuer net of payments the hedge fund agrees to make to induce the banks to take on such an obligation. Such an arrangement is referred to as a total return swap. The counterparties hedge their risk by acquiring securities of the issuer in an amount equal to their exposure. The hedge fund then begins a campaign to pressure the issuer to make changes to increase shareholder value. Would the hedge fund have to disclose its swap arrangement under Section 13(d)? Would it matter whether the counterparties are likely, though not required, to vote those shares in accord with the preferences of the hedge fund? On these kinds of issues generally, *see* Hu & Black, The New Vote Buying: Empty Voting and Hidden (Morphable) Ownership, 79 S. Cal. L. Rev. 811 (2006); Hu & Black, Equity and Debt Decoupling and Empty Voting II: Importance and Extensions, 156 U. Pa. L. Rev. 625 (2008). In *CSX Corp. v. Children's Investment Fund Management LLP*, 562 F. Supp. 2d 511 (S.D.N.Y. 2008), the district court held that the deliberate structuring of an economic interest in the issuer through a total return swap was an arrangement to prevent the vesting of beneficial ownership as part of a scheme to evade the reporting requirements of Section 13(d)—and hence a violation of Rule 13d-3(b), which prohibits such schemes. The court noted the specific efforts of the hedge fund to influence the voting position of the counterparties, as well as the likelihood that if the hedge fund chose to unwind the arrangement, as it could do at any time, the counterparties would immediately sell the underlying securities, thereby making it easy for the hedge fund to acquire the equivalent voting ownership if it

wished. On appeal, the Second Circuit found it unnecessary to address this issue, though it did remand on a separate legal question involving group status. *CSX Corp. v. Children's Investment Fund Management LLP*, 654 F.3d 276 (2d Cir. 2011). Judge Winter wrote a lengthy concurring opinion expressing strong disagreement with the district court's reasoning as to beneficial ownership and the swap transactions. In his view, a total return swap involves two counterparties dealing at arm's length; the fact that the "long" party may have an incentive to act consistently with the short party's interest does not make the short party an owner of the shares in any meaningful sense. Nor can structuring the transaction in such a way be "evasive." Judge Winter concluded that this is a policy issue for the SEC, something now made fairly clear by the Dodd-Frank Act. There, Congress added Section 13(o) to the '34 Act to provide that derivative arrangements such as these confer beneficial ownership only to the extent the SEC affirmatively provides by rule. The SEC responded by maintaining the highly uncertain status quo in this area.

PROBLEM

17-1.   You represent a client, Jana Williams, who owns 2.1 percent of the outstanding equity securities of Ajax Computers Inc., a Nasdaq-traded company. Williams is dissatisfied with current management and wishes to explore the possibility of a hostile takeover through her holding company. She has already retained an investment banker to do an analysis and strategy memo and had preliminary discussions regarding financing with a variety of sources. In discussions with you, she has indicated a real desire to do the deal "if it will work," but concedes that it may be just as likely that she will choose to sell out her block to the company at a handsome premium. Indeed, her opening gambit with the company may be to approach key members of the board and start demanding a shakeup in top management. For now, she wants to keep things quiet and buy some additional shares. However, she also wants to contact a number of other large Ajax investors to discuss whether they would be on her side in any fight. What advice would you give her as to whether and when a Schedule 13D would be required? How should she structure the discussions to minimize the likelihood of having to file, while still making them meaningful? Assuming, on the other hand, that a Schedule 13D must be filed in the near future, what would she have to disclose about her plans and intentions?

C.   *Tender Offer Regulation: Controlling the Bidder*

At the heart of the Williams Act are Sections 14(d) and (e), which set forth substantive "rules of the road," prohibit fraud, and give the SEC extensive rulemaking authority in connection with tender offers. To understand the Act fully, it is necessary to appreciate some of the most common distinctions and their significance for investors faced with a bid.

The Form of Consideration.   Bidders may offer target shareholders cash, securities, or some combination thereof for their shares; the new securities may be common stock, preferred stock, or debt securities. When securities are offered, the shareholder faces a new investment decision. As a result, exchange offers are governed by the Securities Act, and absent some exemption, the bidder is forced to go through the registration process and make the attendant prospectus disclosure with respect to the shares being offered. As discussed below, Regulation M-A makes this a simpler process, but the inevitable risks and expenses of registration remain.

When the form of consideration is all cash, the problems are somewhat simpler. At first glance, in fact, there may seem to be little need for regulation at all: The offered price is above the prevailing market price, and the shareholder can take it or leave it. But even here, there can be some uncertainty. Will (or can) the bidder actually pay for the tendered shares? Will some regulatory agency (e.g., the FCC in a broadcast takeover) intervene to bar the bid or force divestiture? Is the market value of target stock reflective of long-term value? Will some other bidder (or the target) enter the action and drive up the target price? Some shareholder deliberation is still warranted.

"Any and All" Versus Partial Tender Offers.   A bidder may indicate that it is willing to take any and all shares that are tendered—albeit almost inevitably subject to a condition that some minimum number of shares be tendered. Or it can say, for example, that its bid is only for 51 percent of the outstanding shares of the target. In that case, in the event of oversubscription (i.e., more than 51 percent of the shares are tendered), it indicates that it will return any excess shares to the shareholders. As we shall see, the Williams Act rules require proration in choosing which shares to accept and which to return.

Here the differential impact on the shareholder is clear. In the any and all bid, the shareholder knows that, if he tenders 100 shares and the bid is successful, the premium will be paid on all of those shares. In the partial bid, on the other hand, the shareholder who tenders 100 shares must realize that as many as 49 of those shares may be returned and no premium paid thereupon. Naturally, the "value" of the partial bid to the investor is lower than the any and all; in evaluating it, he must think in terms of a "blended" price made up of the post-bid value of shares taken down plus the expected market value of those that remain in the investor's portfolio. In other words, if a partial bid is successful, the tendering shareholder will probably remain an investor in a business controlled by the new owners, with a revised set of risks and expectations.

PROBLEM

17-2.   Before we turn to the specifics of the Williams Act disclosure, a more general inquiry may be appropriate. Consider the following settings.

   a.   Goldfinger Enterprises announces a bid to purchase 51 percent of Mediocre Ltd. at $20 cash per share, a premium of $7 above current market value. Goldfinger reveals that it has in a series of past acquisitions consistently had something of a "Midas touch," turning a number of low-performing enterprises into highly profitable ones by introducing the talents of a skilled management team. On average, firms acquired by Goldfinger have doubled their profitability one year after the acquisition and tripled them within two. If you were a Mediocre shareholder, would you tender? What more information, if any, would you want? Would it matter if Goldfinger had made an any and all offer?

b.   Josh Bumbles is a major player in the takeover world, although he lives with a checkered past. In five prior instances, he has bled the corporations that he has acquired by applying all available cash reserves to provide large salaries and perquisites for members of his family and to pay off the debt used to obtain control. Furthermore, there have been numerous derivative actions filed against him, involving allegations of both self-dealing and gross negligence. Bumbles has just announced a cash bid for 51 percent of Silverplate Company. As a Silverplate shareholder, would you accept? Is there any information that would be particularly important to you? What if Bumbles' offer is for any and all and the offering price is only a few dollars above the current market price?

1.   Disclosure by Bidders and the Antifraud Prohibition

The basic thrust of tender offer regulation under the Williams Act is full disclosure. Section 14(d)(1) makes it unlawful to make a tender offer for the equity securities of any publicly held company (as defined for registration purposes in Section 12, as well as certain other non-registrants), if upon consummation the bidder would own more than 5 percent of the class in question unless the bidder files and transmits to the target company a Schedule TO. Very much like the Schedule 13D, the line items of this form require the bidder to describe, among other things, its identity and background, its source of financing, the purpose of the bid, and any plans or proposals with respect to the target company. When must "material," financial statements of the bidder be disclosed? Under what circumstances would that be important to target shareholders? *See MAI Basic Four Inc. v. Prime Computer Inc.*, 871 F.2d 212 (1st Cir. 1989). After commencement of the bid, material changes in the prevailing terms and conditions, as well as an updating of the required disclosure, must be reported. Copies of other soliciting material must also be filed with the Commission. *See* Rule 14d-3(b).

Under the philosophy of Regulation M-A, which you studied in Chapters 7 and 16 with respect to negotiated acquisitions, acquiring companies are permitted to communicate with investors without fear of "gun jumping" restraints. Recall that Rule 165 under the '33 Act largely eliminates Section 5's gunjumping restraints when securities are offered as consideration in any kind of acquisition, subject only to a duty to file written soliciting material with the SEC upon use. The same structure was imported into the proxy rules, so that communications with investors regarding a negotiated deal can occur without the need to file and distribute a proxy statement, again so long as written soliciting materials are filed. To complete the consistency, the Williams Act rules were revised as well. The Williams Act filing obligation discussed above is triggered by the *commencement* of the bid, which is defined in Rule 14d-2(a) to be the date "when the bidder has first published, sent or given the means to tender to securities holders." The focus of this definition as revised by Regulation M-A is on the actual ability to tender, not "conditioning the minds" of target shareholders. Rule 14d-2(b) then makes clear that pre-commencement communications will not trigger the filing obligations so long as they do not provide any means to tender and all written communications are filed with the SEC (and delivered to the target) as of the date they are used.

Completing the disclosure package from the bidder's side, Rule 14d-9 requires any other person who solicits or makes recommendations to shareholders with respect to the tender offer to file a Schedule 14D-9, indicating her relationship to the bidder and disclosing certain conflict of interest information. Pursuant to Regulation M-A, this rule is structured to provide freedom of communication for the target similar to that given to the bidder.

These mandatory disclosures are supplemented by Section 14(e) of the Williams Act, which makes it unlawful to make any untrue statement of material fact, or to omit to state any material fact necessary to make statements made not misleading, or to otherwise engage in any fraudulent, deceptive, or manipulative acts or practices in connection with any tender offer—whether or not the bid is covered by Section 14(d). In addition, the SEC is given rulemaking authority to "define, and prescribe means reasonably designed to prevent," such acts or practices. You have already seen one of these rules in Chapter 15: the prohibition against insider trading using tender offer related information, Rule 14e-3. Also, keep in mind that Rule 10b-5 applies to tender offers, creating the potential for fraud on the market liability when misstatements are made—whether by the bidder, the target or anyone else—that "foreseeably" distort the price of the target's stock. *See Semerenko v. Cendant Corp.*, 216 F.3d 315 (3d Cir. 2000).

An open question is who, besides the SEC, can bring a case under Sections 14(d) or 14(e). Congress did not provide for any express private right of action, but remember that the Williams Act was enacted at a time when rights were implied rather freely. As you shall see shortly in the *Emulex* case, dealing with target company disclosures, this issue has recently come back into play, potentially for all of the Act. *Emulex* also addresses whether scienter is required under 14(e).

2. Substantive Regulation

Besides setting forth disclosure and antifraud rules with respect to tender offers, the Williams Act establishes some rudimentary substantive rules governing their conduct. While at first glance the rules may seem mundane, they do establish the framework that determines how quickly a bid can go forward and what the likelihood is that the bidder will face an auction situation—the issue that we considered conceptually at the outset of the chapter.

The statute itself sets forth a few of these rules. Most importantly, Section 14(d)(5) permits shareholders to withdraw shares tendered both during the first seven days of the bid and after 60 days from its commencement, and Section 14(d)(6) requires bidders to prorate in the event of oversubscription with respect to shares tendered during the first ten days of a partial bid. By and large, these provisions are designed to eliminate the pressure to tender quickly that would exist were a bidder permitted, in some form or another, to announce that it would deal with target shareholders on a first-come, first-served basis. Another rule has a more egalitarian thrust to it. Section 14(d)(7) requires that an increase in consideration announced by the bidder during the offer be paid to all persons whose shares are bought by the bidder, even if the purchase occurred before the announcement of the increase.

Beyond these specific requirements, the Williams Act also gives to the SEC substantial rulemaking authority. Section 14(d)(4) gives the Commission the power to regulate solicitations and recommendations regarding tender offers, and Section 14(e) allows it to define and prescribe means reasonably designed to prevent tender offer fraud—an amorphous grant by all accounts—even for tender offers directed at companies that are not publicly held. These specific grants of authority are supplemented by Section 23(a)(1), which gives the SEC the power to make "such rules and regulations as may be necessary or appropriate to implement the provisions of this title" as well as the Commission's broad exemptive authority.

a.   Duration

Rule 14e-1(a) requires that tender offers be held open for at least 20 business days (i.e., four weeks) from the date they are first published, and Rule 14e-1(b) requires that bids be held open an additional ten business days in the event that there is an increase or decrease in the consideration offered or the percentage of shares being sought. Subsection (c) provides that shares tendered must promptly be either paid for or returned upon the termination or withdrawal of a bid.

What is the purpose of the minimum duration period? Even before the Rule was adopted, the seven-day withdrawal right and ten-day proration rule effectively eliminated the "Saturday Night Special"—the tender offer that sought to pressure shareholders into "hasty and ill-informed" decisions by setting extremely short tender offer periods. What, then, do the additional days add in terms of investor protection? In what respect is it a means reasonably designed to prevent *fraud*? The answer, it would seem, is that the SEC views the 20-day period as necessary in order to get all material information relating to the bid out into the marketplace—something like the waiting period with respect to a public distribution.

The more intriguing question has to do with the regulatory costs associated with the Rule. No doubt any extended duration increases the riskiness of a bid, given the various things that may happen—for example, management's defensive efforts—to defeat it during this longer period of time. And there is the additional cost of carrying the financing for the extended period. Apparently recognizing this, the SEC stated in the release adopting the Rule that it had considered a 30-day minimum, but rejected it as "excessive." *See* Exchange Act Release No. 16384, [1979-1980 Transfer Binder] Fed. Sec. L. Rep. (CCH) ¶82,373 (Nov. 29, 1979).

Is there a subtext to Rule 14e-1? Probably its most benign effect from a shareholder perspective is to keep offers open long enough that competing bidders (whether associated with target management or not) will have the time to launch their own bids and thus perhaps create an auction for target company shares. Such auctions, when they occur, typically result in substantially higher premiums paid to target shareholders. *See* Bebchuk, The Case for Facilitating Tender Offers, 95 Harv. L. Rev. 1028 (1982); Schwartz, Search Theory and the Tender Offer Auction, 2 J.L. Econ. & Org. 229 (1986) (which is followed by a reply by Bebchuk, id. at 253). Once again, the underlying question is whether this benefit to investors is outweighed by the unquantifiable losses stemming from tender offers that never happen because of the perceived increased costs imposed by the regulation and the consequent lower expected value of any particular bid. Or are the risks minimal given that even failed bidders tend to sell the shares they have acquired to the victor at a tidy profit? Strangely, the SEC has never indicated that facilitating an auction was any part of its purpose in adopting Rule 14e-1.

b.   *Withdrawal and Proration*

As noted earlier, the Williams Act as originally enacted also provided two rules designed to avoid the stampede effect that might arise if a bidder were to make a partial bid on a first-come, first-served basis. Section 14(d)(5) states that shares tendered pursuant to a bid may be withdrawn by the shareholder at any time up to seven days from commencement or more than 60 days after commencement. And Section 14(d)(6) requires bidders to prorate among any shares tendered during the first ten days of the bid when less than all are to be taken down. In Rules 14d-7 and 14d-8, the SEC extended these statutory withdrawal and proration rights to apply throughout the duration of the bid. (Pursuant to Rule 14d-11, however, bidders can do a final "subsequent offering period" without withdrawal rights simply to obtain remaining shares after a successful tender offer.) Can it be argued that the SEC was overriding a well-thought-out congressional preference for shorter periods? Whatever your answer, it does seem that this change was necessary in order to make the 20-day minimum duration of Rule 14e-1 work as intended. In *Pryor v. United States Steel Corp.*, 794 F.2d 52 (2d Cir. 1986), the court held that the proration rule may be enforced via a private right of action on behalf of shareholders whose shares should have been afforded equal treatment, but were not.

c.   *The All-Holders/Best-Price Rule*

▌ **Epstein v. MCA Corp.**
▌ **50 F.3d 644 (9th Cir. 1995)**

[Matsushita Company acquired the large entertainment conglomerate MCA Inc. in a tender offer. Former MCA shareholders who tendered their shares brought suit, charging that Matsushita paid an MCA insider, Lew Wasserman, excessive compensation for their shares in violation of Rule 14d-10, the all-holders/best-price rule. After holding that an implied private right of action exists under the Rule, the court turned to whether it had been violated.]

Captioned the "Equal treatment of securities holders," Rule 14d-10 prohibits a bidder from making a tender offer that is not open to all shareholders or that is made to shareholders at varying prices. The gist of plaintiffs' claims is that Matsushita violated the antidiscrimination requirements of the Rule by paying Wasserman and Sheinberg premiums pursuant to the tender offer.

Negotiations between Matsushita and MCA began in August 1990, when a representative of Matsushita telephoned MCA's financial advisor to express interest in acquiring MCA. During the course of the talks, Matsushita stressed that it wanted Wasserman and Sheinberg to commit their shares to Matsushita in advance of the friendly takeover and to remain in MCA's employment for five years. On the morning of November 26, 1990, Matsushita and Wasserman entered into the Capital Contribution and Loan Agreement, pursuant to which Wasserman agreed to exchange his MCA shares for preferred stock in a subsidiary Matsushita would create called "MEA Holdings."

Performance of the Capital Contribution and Loan Agreement was conditioned on the tender offer in several respects. First, neither Matsushita nor Wasserman was obligated to perform the Agreement if any of the conditions of the tender offer were not satisfied. If, for example, Matsushita did not acquire 50% of MCA's common stock as a result of the tender offer, the Wasserman deal would be off. Second, the timing of performance was tied to the tender offer. The Wasserman exchange was scheduled to take place "immediately following the time at which shares of MCA Common Stock are accepted for payment pursuant to and in accordance with the terms of the offer. . . ." Third, the amount of cash Matsushita was required to contribute in order to fund MEA Holdings was dependent upon the tender price, with Matsushita agreeing to contribute to MEA Holdings 106% of the "highest price paid . . . for any shares of MCA Common Stock, pursuant to the [tender] offer. . . ."

Moments after signing the Capital Contribution and Loan agreement, Matsushita and MCA announced the $71 per share tender offer. Shareholders were given from the time of the announcement until 12:01 A.M. on December 29, 1990 to tender their shares. The owners of 91% of MCA's common stock did so, and at 12:05 A.M., Matsushita accepted all tendered shares for payment. At 1:25 A.M., Matsushita exchanged Wasserman's shares for MEA Holdings preferred stock pursuant to the Capital Contribution and Loan Agreement. MCA was merged into Matsushita as a wholly owned subsidiary on January 3, 1991.

Whether the Wasserman transaction violated Rule 14d-10 depends on whether Wasserman received greater consideration than other MCA shareholders "during such tender offer," Rule 14d-10(a)(2), or whether he received a type of consideration not offered to other MCA shareholders "in a tender offer." Rule 14d-10(c).

Matsushita argues that the Wasserman transaction falls outside the Rule's ambit because it closed *after* the tender offer period expired. The tender offer period, Matsushita contends, ended when it accepted the tendered MCA shares for payment—at 12:05 A.M. on December 29, 1990, one hour and 20 minutes before Wasserman's shares were exchanged. In Matsushita's view, liability under Rule 14d-10 boils down to a pure question of timing: the Rule is simply a "mechanical provision" concerned with "payments to shareholders of a target corporation only *during a specifically-defined tender offer period.*" Brief of Matsushita at 23 (emphasis in original). Outside that period, Matsushita insists, "Rule 14d-10 is without effect" because the Rule "is engaged (or not engaged) depending upon *when payment is made.*" Id. at 23, 35 (emphasis in original).

Although Matsushita argues that Rule 14d-10 is designed to operate only during a "specifically-defined tender offer period," neither the phrase "tender offer period" nor a specific time frame is to be found in the Rule's text. To be sure, section (a)(2) of the Rule prohibits paying one security holder more than another "during such tender offer." But the term "tender offer," as used in the federal securities laws, has never been interpreted to denote a rigid period of time. On the contrary, in order to prevent bidders from circumventing the Williams Act's requirements, Congress, the SEC, and the courts have steadfastly refused to give the term a fixed definition. Instead, we have held that "[t]o serve the purposes of the Williams Act, there is a need for flexibility in fashioning a definition of a tender offer." *SEC v. Carter Hawley Hale Stores, Inc.*, 760 F.2d 945, 950 (9th Cir. 1985). . . .

An inquiry more in keeping with the language and purposes of Rule 14d-10 focuses not on when Wasserman was paid, but on whether the Wasserman transaction was an integral part of Matsushita's tender offer. If it was, Matsushita violated Rule 14d-10 because it paid him, pursuant to the tender offer, different, and perhaps more valuable consideration than it offered to other shareholders.

Matsushita contends that the Wasserman transaction cannot be deemed a part of the tender offer because it was merely a private exchange of stock, structured to take place after the tender offer finished. But Matsushita's assumption that the Wasserman transaction was private, rather than a part of the tender offer, begs the question. In *Field v. Trump*, 850 F.2d at 944, the Second Circuit held that "[w]hether [an] acquisition of shares in a corporation is part of the tender offer for purposes of the Act cannot be determined by rubberstamping the label used by the acquiror." To hold otherwise, the court stated, would render "virtually all of the provisions of the Williams Act, including its filing and disclosure requirements," subject to evasion "simply by an offeror's announcement that offers to purchase . . . stock were private purchases." Id. Thus, the court observed that because the Williams Act and its implementing regulations do not define the term "tender offer," "[c]ourts faced with the question of whether purchases of a corporation's shares are privately negotiated or are part of a tender offer have applied a functional test that scrutinizes such purchases in the context of various salient characteristics of tender offers and the purposes of the Williams Act." Id. at 943-44.

Because the terms of the Wasserman Capital Contribution and Loan Agreement were in several material respects conditioned on the terms of the public tender offer, we can only conclude that the Wasserman transaction was an integral part of the offer and subject to Rule 14d-10's requirements. Two facts compel this conclusion: first, the redemption value of Wasserman's preferred stock incorporated the tender offer price by reference, and second, the Capital Contribution and Loan Agreement was conditioned on the tender offer's success. If the tender offer failed, Wasserman would have remained the owner of his MCA stock. This is precisely the arrangement Matsushita made with its shareholders through its public tender offer: if an insufficient number of shares were tendered, each shareholder too would have retained ownership of her

MCA stock. The deal Matsushita made with Wasserman thus differed from the tender offer in only one material respect—the type (and possibly the value) of consideration provided. Rule 14d-10(c)(1) forbids just such a transaction.

To be sure, the fact that a private purchase of stock and a public tender offer are both part of a single plan of acquisition does not, by itself, render the purchase a part of a tender offer for purposes of Rule 14d-10. Rule 14d-10 does not prohibit transactions entered into or effected before, or after, a tender offer—provided that all material terms of the transaction stand independent of the tender offer. Thus a bidder who purchases shares from a particular shareholder before a tender offer begins does not violate Rule 14d-10. *See, e.g., Kahn v. Virginia Retirement Systems*, 13 F.3d 110 (4th Cir. 1993) (bidder's unconditional private purchase of target's shares two days before tender offer was formally announced did not violate section 14(d)(7) and Rule 14d-10), *cert. denied*, 114 S. Ct. 1834 (1994).

If, in advance of the tender offer, Wasserman had become unconditionally obligated to exchange his MCA shares, the transaction would not have violated Rule 14d-10, even if Matsushita believed that acquiring Wasserman's shares was a first step in acquiring MCA. In such a case, both Wasserman and Matsushita would have assumed the burdens of their agreement despite the risk that an anticipated tender offer would fail, or command a different price. But such a course was not followed. Matsushita sought to acquire MCA *without* purchasing the holdings of individual shareholders block by block and accordingly subjecting itself to the risk that it would end up with a huge investment in MCA stock, but without control. The tender offer device is designed to avoid this risk, but only if holders of the same security are offered precisely the same consideration. . . .

[*Epstein* was later vacated by the Supreme Court on grounds that a state court-approved settlement of the dispute arising from the takeover barred further litigation of the securities law questions.]

NOTES AND QUESTIONS

1.   Construing the Rule.   Does *Epstein* make Rule 14d-10 too open-ended, without providing enough predictability? For criticism of the Ninth Circuit's decision along these lines, *see Lerro v. Quaker Oats Co.*, 84 F.3d 239 (7th Cir. 1996) (need for a "bright line" approach to permit transactions to proceed with reasonable certainty). In *In re Digital Island Securities Litigation*, 357 F.3d 322 (3d Cir. 2004), the Third Circuit agreed with *Lerro* that a brighter line than the one drawn in *Epstein* was needed, and that the mere fact that a purchase was conditional on the success of a tender offer should not be enough to make it "pursuant" to that tender offer. However, the court acknowledged that purchases that take place before or after the tender offer can sometimes be deliberate efforts to conceal side payments designed to induce shareholders (including shareholders who are also managers or directors) to favor the bid. In essence, the court said, this would be a form of fraud—that the purchase was intentionally structured to hide the inducement. If plaintiffs allege such deception, then the complaint must be tested under the heightened pleading standard of the PSLRA (i.e., there must be facts giving rise to a *strong inference* of scienter).

*2. **Authority.***   What rational purpose does Rule 14d-10 serve? In the proposing release, the SEC was fairly obscure about the need for the Rule, saying only that it reads the Williams Act as "containing an implicit requirement of equal treatment of security holders." Exchange Act Release No. 22198, [1984-1985 Transfer Binder] Fed. Sec. L. Rep. (CCH) ¶83,797 (July 1, 1985). Perhaps the best support for this egalitarian view is Section 14(d)(7), which requires the bidder to extend the benefit of a price increase during the bid to previously tendering shareholders. In any event, the authority to adopt the all-holders/best-price rule was explicitly upheld as consistent with the Williams Act in *Polaroid Corp. v. Disney*, 862 F.2d 987 (3d Cir. 1988). Interestingly, however, the court in *Polaroid* also ruled that the target corporation itself has no standing to claim a violation of the Rule on behalf of its shareholders, citing the conflict of interest between target and shareholders with respect to this aspect of the bid.

Authority aside, is there a good reason why the bidder should not be able to negotiate on varying terms with different types of shareholders? Rule 14d-10 was adopted shortly after the Delaware Supreme Court had held that an issuer could as a defensive mechanism in a takeover fight make a discriminatory self-tender—that is, one open to all of its shareholders except the hostile bidder. *Unocal Corp. v. Mesa Petroleum Corp.*, 493 A.2d 946 (Del. 1985). This decision was roundly criticized by many as unduly favoring target managements. The effect of Rule 14d-10 was to overrule *Unocal* as a matter of federal law, although this is not stated explicitly in the proposing release.

*3. **Executive Compensation.***   What if the bidder arranges to purchase the shares of a high-ranking insider of the target at the public tender offer price and also agrees to a particularly lucrative compensation or termination agreement with that insider? Could that be a disguised way of paying more for the insider's shares, in violation of Rule 14d-10? This issue generated a substantial amount of case law (*see, e.g., Gerber v. Computer Associates*, 303 F.3d 126 (2d Cir. 2002)) before the SEC revised the rule in 2006 to make clear that it does not apply to severance or compensation agreements. A safe harbor was created to give complete protection so long as the payments were approved by independent directors of either the bidder or the target company. The revision to the rule also clarified the SEC's position that only consideration paid to security holders for securities tendered into the bid will be evaluated in determining the highest consideration paid to other holders.

*4. **Rule 14e-5.***   Rule 14e-5 (which used to be Rule 10b-13) prohibits any person who makes a tender offer from purchasing or making any arrangement to purchase otherwise than pursuant to that offer during the duration of the bid. There are a number of technical exceptions, and the Commission may by order grant exemptions from the operation of the Rule. In contrast to Rule 14d-10, Rule 14e-5 is clear that it applies only once the tender offer has been publicly announced; in *Epstein*, the court rejected Matsushita's argument that the two Rules should be read *in pari materia.*

What is Rule 14e-5's purpose? One goal, reminiscent of Regulation M in the public offering context, is the prevention of manipulation. Secret open market purchases by the bidder may "distort" the market price, leading the investing public to believe that the market considers the bid more attractive than it really is. *See* Lowenfels, Rule 10b-13, Rule 10b-6 and Purchases of Target Company Securities During an Exchange Offer, 69 Colum. L. Rev. 1392 (1969). But it is probably also correct to say that the Rule is a natural analog to the best-price/all-holders rule, reinforcing the notion of equal treatment of target shareholders. *See, e.g., Beaumont v. American Can Co.*, 797 F.2d 79 (2d Cir. 1986) (suggesting that no private right of action would exist for nontendering shareholders, since they were not among the class to be protected by the Rule); *Warren v. Bokum Research Corp.*, 433 F. Supp. 1360 (D.N.M. 1977) (conferring a right of acting on tendering shareholders). As with the all-holders rule, courts have given Rule 14e-5 a reasonably expansive scope. *E.g., City Nat'l Bank v. American Commonwealth Fin. Corp.*, 801 F.2d 714 (4th Cir. 1986) (affirming the finding of a violation where the founding family's shares were delivered and paid for during the bid, even though the agreement to purchase occurred prior thereto).

5. Pre-Commencement Communications.   To avoid the market manipulation that would come from a false statement of intent or ability to launch a tender offer, Rule 14e-8 prohibits public announcements of bids without both bona fide intent and reasonable belief in its ability to complete the bid.

6. Short Tenders.   Another "egalitarian" rule is Rule 14e-4 (formerly 10b-4), which prohibits people from tendering more securities into a partial bid than they own. One reason for doing this is to avoid the risk of proration. As noted above, in a partial bid for 51 percent of the company's stock, an investor who owns and tenders 100 shares will possibly have only 51 of those purchased at the premium price. But if he tenders 198 shares—even though he owns only 100—there is a good chance that all or substantially all of those 100 will be taken. Rule 14e-4 prohibits the tendering of shares not owned. And as amended in 1984, it also bars tendering coupled with an immediate sale into the market or the purchase of a call option ("hedged" tendering) and tendering the same security to more than one bidder ("multiple" tendering). For a look at the operation of the short-tendering rule, *see Merrill Lynch, Pierce, Fenner & Smith v. Bobker*, 808 F.2d 930 (2d Cir. 1986). Why should short tendering be unlawful if the investor—typically an arbitrageur (i.e., a professional trader who buys or sells in anticipation of tender offer developments)—is willing to bear the attendant risk? At least in part, the answer may be that such strategies are often successful and thus result in unequal treatment between the professional and the average investor. On the other hand, does such a rule unduly burden beneficial arbitrage activity? *See* Exchange Act Release No. 20799, [1984 Transfer Binder] Fed. Sec. L. Rep. (CCH) ¶83,601 (Mar. 29, 1984). Dissenting from the extension of the Rule to hedged tendering in 1984, Commissioner Charles Cox argued that, if anything, such practices shift wealth from tendering shareholders to those shareholders who sell into the market (who benefit because of the increased demand for their stock), hardly a reason for burdening otherwise beneficial economic activity.

PROBLEM

17-3.   Acquiror Co. launched a tender offer for the shares of Target Co. at $24 per share. A handful of large institutional shareholders of Target then indicated their intent not to tender because the price was inadequate. Soon thereafter, Acquiror publicly announced an end to its bid. The next day it purchased those institutional shares in a private deal for $27 per share. The day after that, Acquiror announced that it was making a new tender offer, and was now willing to pay $25 for all remaining Target shares. Would this violate Rule 14d-10? *See Field v. Trump*, 850 F.2d 938 (2d Cir. 1988), *cert. denied*, 489 U.S. 1012 (1989).

3.   "Tender Offer"

As should be clear from the foregoing materials, most tender offers take on a very visible, identifiable form. There is pervasive, nationwide publicity by both bidder and target highlighting the specific choice or choices with which target shareholders are now faced. Regulations 14D and 14E are structured with this type of bid in mind. But rapid accumulations of the stock of a publicly held company—and thus shifts in control—can occur through more unconventional means as well, and since the passage of the Williams Act, the courts and the SEC have struggled with applying the rules to these sorts of acquisitions.

Two very different types of acquisitions pose problems along these lines. One is the "privately" negotiated acquisition, where the acquirer deals on some sort of individualized basis with a handful of large stockholders of the target in an effort to gain a controlling block. While Congress stated that Section 14(d) was not meant to reach a truly private transaction, additional factors may creep in that give the bid some flavor of a hostile takeover. In the best known case in this area, *Wellman v. Dickinson*, 475 F. Supp. 783 (S.D.N.Y. 1979), *aff'd*, 682 F.2d 355 (2d Cir. 1982), *cert. denied*, 460 U.S. 1099 (1983)—involving the Sun Oil/Becton Dickinson takeover studied earlier with regard to Section 13(d) in *Wellman*—the court found a tender offer within the meaning of the Williams Act in Sun's rapid acquisition of 34 percent of Becton Dickinson from the controlling group and through what the court saw as "high pressure" telephone solicitations to a relatively small number of institutional investors. The other setting is the open market purchase, where a company makes a public announcement that it will commence, for a limited period of time, a significant buying program for a stock. Does this create the kind of pressure situation that the Williams Act was designed to remove? In *SEC v. Carter Hawley Hale Stores Inc.*, 760 F.2d 945 (9th Cir. 1985), the court applied the following factors, taken from *Wellman*: "(1) active and widespread solicitation of public shareholders for the shares of an issuer; (2) solicitation made for a substantial percentage of the issuer's stock; (3) offer to purchase made at a premium over the prevailing market price; (4) terms of the offer are firm rather than negotiable; (5) offer contingent on the tender of a fixed number of shares, often subject to a fixed maximum number to be purchased; (6) offer open only for a limited period of time; (7) offeree subjected to pressure to sell his stock; [and (8)] public announcements of a purchasing program concerning the target company precede or accompany rapid accumulation of a large amount of target company's securities." The court determined that not enough of these factors were present to turn the open market purchase into a tender offer. For a more recent holding along similar lines involving private purchases, *see Corre Opportunities Fund v. Emmis Commc'ns Corp.*, 892 F. Supp. 3d 1076 (S.D. Ind. 2012).

PROBLEM

17-4.   On March 1, officials of the Rosecream Fragrance Corp. and their investment bankers embarked on an acquisition program designed to gain between 25 percent and 35 percent of the outstanding common shares of the Beta Beauty Corp. (BBC). Apart from some preliminary open market purchases (not exceeding Section 13(d)'s 5 percent threshold), the sole acquisition method was to place late-afternoon telephone calls to the 30 largest institutional investors of BBC, stating that the purchaser would be willing to pay a 20 percent premium over market price for any shares tendered to it by nine o'clock the next morning. The terms were nonnegotiable. Would such activity constitute a tender offer?

D.   *The Williams Act and the Global Tender Offer*

As with so many issues, the internationalization of the securities markets makes Williams Act compliance somewhat difficult. Other jurisdictions have quite different regulatory schemes, reflecting entirely different attitudes toward the takeover issue generally. *See, e.g.*, Armour & Skeel, Who Writes the Rules for Hostile Takeovers and Why? The Peculiar Divergence of U.S. and U.K. Takeover Regulation, 95 Geo. L.J. 1727 (2007). At the very least, simultaneous compliance is problematic when significant shareholdings are found both in the United States and abroad. Where there are relatively few American investors, one approach has been simply to exclude them from the bid. While this will work in principle, American courts have been careful to assure literal compliance with the terms of the exclusion. *See Consolidated Gold Fields PLC v. Minorca, S.A.*, 871 F.2d 252 (2d Cir. 1988) (the fact that tender offer materials were given to British nominees and would thus be passed on to American beneficial owners triggered U.S. jurisdiction, even though the bid was formally structured to exclude American investors). Is it the best policy to allow the strictures of the Williams Act to operate as an obstacle to American investor participation in foreign bids?

In 1999, the SEC codified in Rule 14d-1(b) its increasingly permissive approach toward tender offers for foreign companies with some U.S. shareholders in order to avoid prejudice against U.S. investors. To this end, it adopted exemptive provisions along two separate "tiers." Tier I deals with tender offers for foreign targets when U.S. shareholders own 10 percent or less of its shares. Here, there is an almost complete exemption from the Williams Act and related rules. Offers relying on the Tier I exemption must treat U.S. holders on terms at least as favorable as non-U.S. holders. Antifraud and anti-manipulation rules continue to apply. Tier II, in turn, deals with foreign targets when U.S. share-holders own between 10 and 40 percent of its shares. Here, the exemption is far more limited, largely to certain provisions that conflict with the regulatory regimes found elsewhere. In 2008, the SEC clarified and extended these exemptions in order to smooth out many of the difficulties that still challenged global tender offers. *See* Securities Act Release No. 8957 (Sept. 19, 2008). Consistent with the approach now being applied in other areas relating to foreign issuer disclosure, the Commission has made it easier to identify certain kinds of transactions eligible for the Tier I or Tier II exemption by comparing average daily U.S. trading volume to average worldwide trading volume for purposes of calculating the 10 percent or 40 percent cutoff instead of having to do a head count of U.S. beneficial owners, which turns out to be a very difficult task.

E. Tender Offer Defense: Controlling Target Management

1. Disclosure and Enforcement

The Williams Act is avowedly neutral as between the bidder and target management, purporting to leave the choice as to the future control of the company in the hands of the target's shareholders. To this end, a number of Williams Act provisions and rules apply specifically to target management. For example, under Rule 14d-5, management is forced to choose between giving the bidder a shareholder list or agreeing to mail its materials for it, just as it must do for insurgents under the proxy rules. Another form of control, noted earlier in its application to persons associated with bidders, is Rule 14d-9, which requires the filing and transmittal of a Schedule 14D-9 by any person—including the target company or its management—who makes a solicitation or recommendation to target shareholders regarding a tender offer once the bid has been commenced. Of particular note here is Item 7, which requires (by reference to Reg M-A) the subject company to disclose whether any negotiation is under way that relates to a possible defensive merger, acquisition, sale of assets, tender offer, or restructuring. The target's board, however, is privileged not to disclose the possible *terms* of the transactions or the *parties* involved in such negotiations if no agreement in principle has been reached and it believes that such disclosure would jeopardize the negotiations. In terms of controlling the defense, probably the most pointed form of regulation through disclosure is found in Section 14(e) and Rule 14e-2, which requires the target company to (a) take a public position on the tender offer—recommending its acceptance or rejection; (b) express no opinion one way or the other; or (c) state that it is unable to take any position at this time. In any event, the statement must include the reasons for the position taken or the inability to take a position.

When the Williams Act was enacted, hostile tender offers were the norm. As noted earlier, state law has shifted dramatically so that, today, bidders have to be more strategic. Often, the end game is to seek shareholder pressure to get the target board to recommend the bid, or at least not oppose it. The following case addresses Williams Act enforcement in this more contemporary context.

Varjabedian v. Emulex Corp.
888 F.3d 399 (9th Cir. 2018)

Plaintiff–Appellant Jerry Mutza ("Plaintiff") appeals the district court's dismissal of his putative securities class action complaint, brought on behalf of former Emulex Corporation shareholders. The district court dismissed Plaintiff's complaint because he failed to plead a strong inference of scienter for Defendants' alleged violations of Section 14(e) of the Securities Exchange Act of 1934 ("Exchange Act"). In so concluding, the district court followed out-of-circuit authorities holding that Section 14(e) claims require proof of scienter. The district court noted, however, that the Ninth Circuit had yet to decide whether Section 14(e) claims require plaintiffs to plead that defendants acted with scienter. We now hold that Section 14(e) of the Exchange Act requires a showing of negligence, not scienter. Accordingly, we reverse the dismissal of the complaint and remand the case to the district court for it to reconsider Defendants' motion to dismiss under a negligence standard.

I.   BACKGROUND

This case centers on the merger between Emulex Corp. ("Emulex") and Avago Technologies Wireless Manufacturing, Inc. ("Avago"). Emulex was a Delaware-incorporated technology company that sold storage adapters, network interface cards, and other products. On February 25, 2015, Emulex and Avago issued a joint press release announcing that they had entered into a merger agreement, with Avago offering to pay $8.00 for every share of outstanding Emulex stock. The $8.00 price reflected a premium of 26.4% on Emulex's stock price the day before the merger was announced.

Pursuant to the terms of the announced merger agreement, a subsidiary of Avago, Emerald Merger Sub, Inc. ("Merger Sub"), initiated a tender offer for Emulex's outstanding stock on April 7, 2015. . . . When a tender offer is made, the target company often issues a statement to its shareholders recommending that they either accept or reject the tender offer. Emulex decided to issue such a statement but, before doing so, hired Goldman Sachs to determine whether the proposed merger agreement would be fair to shareholders. Goldman Sachs determined that the agreement would be fair to shareholders and provided Emulex with financial analyses supporting Goldman Sachs's position. Based in part on Goldman Sachs's opinion, Emulex filed a 48-page Recommendation Statement with the Securities and Exchange Commission ("SEC") pursuant to Schedule 14D-9.

The Recommendation Statement supported the tender offer and recommended that shareholders tender their shares. It listed nine reasons for the recommendation: (1) the value shareholders would receive in the merger "was greater than could be reasonably expected" in the future if they continued to hold Emulex stock; (2) other available alternatives and transactions were less favorable; (3) Emulex shareholders would receive a premium on their stock; (4) Goldman Sachs found that the merger was fair; (5) the cash consideration shareholders would receive was certain; (6) the agreement provided that Emulex could back out if it received a better offer before closing; (7) the agreement permitted Emulex to modify its recommendation; (8) a termination fee built into the merger agreement would not preclude subsequent third-party offers for Emulex; and (9) closing conditions were appropriate. . . .

Goldman Sachs also produced a one-page chart titled "Selected Semiconductor Transactions," alternatively referred to as the "Premium Analysis." The Premium Analysis selected certain transactions in the industry that Goldman Sachs deemed most similar to the proposed merger between Avago and Emulex, and reviewed the respective premiums stockholders received in those transactions. Altogether, the Premium Analysis collected seventeen transactions involving a semiconductor company between 2010 and 2014. Emulex's 26.4% premium fell within the normal range of semiconductor merger premiums listed in the Premium Analysis, but it was below average. Goldman Sachs opined that the merger was fair despite a below-average premium, and Emulex elected not to summarize the one-page Premium Analysis in the Recommendation Statement. . . .

Not all the shareholders, however, were happy with the merger's terms. Some believed the $8.00-per-share price offered was inadequate given Emulex's significant growth leading up to the tender offer and the company's prospects for future growth. This class of shareholders, who claimed they were misled by Emulex, Avago, Merger Sub, and the Emulex Board of Directors (collectively, "Defendants") into believing that the merger was better than it actually was, brought a lawsuit against Defendants. The district court eventually named Mutza Lead Plaintiff. Plaintiff alleges that Defendants violated federal securities laws, specifically Section 14(e) of the Exchange Act, by failing to summarize the Premium Analysis in the Recommendation Statement, which would have disclosed that the 26.4% premium was below average compared to similar mergers. . . .

The district court dismissed the complaint with prejudice. . . . Because Plaintiff argues that Section 14(e) of the Exchange Act requires Plaintiff to show Defendants were negligent by not including the Premium Analysis in the Recommendation Statement—not that Defendants intentionally excluded the Premium Analysis to mislead shareholders—this case requires us to interpret Section 14(e).

III.   DISCUSSION

A.   SECTION 14(E) CLAIM

. . . Section 14(e) was not part of the original Exchange Act enacted in 1934. Rather, Congress added Section 14(e) as an amendment to the Securities Exchange Act as part of the Williams Act. The purpose of Section 14(e) is to regulate the conduct of a broad range of people who could influence the outcome of a tender offer. To that end, Section 14(e) "was expressly directed at the conduct of a broad range of persons, including those engaged in making or opposing tender offers or otherwise seeking to influence the decision of investors or the outcome of the tender offer." *Id.*

2. Whether Section 14(e) Requires Plaintiff to Show Defendants Knew Their Actions Were Wrong or Only That They Were Negligent

The main question here is whether Section 14(e) requires proof of scienter, as the district court held, or mere negligence. . . . A plain reading of Section 14(e) readily divides the section into two clauses, each proscribing different conduct:

> It shall be unlawful for any person [1] to make any untrue statement of a material fact or omit to state any material fact necessary in order to make the statements made, in the light of the circumstances under which they are made, not misleading, *or* [2] to engage in any fraudulent, deceptive, or manipulative acts or practices, in connection with any tender offer. . . .

The use of the word "or" separating the two clauses in Section 14(e) shows that there are two different offenses that the statute proscribes; to construe the statute otherwise would render it "hopelessly redundant" and would mean "one or the other phrase is surplusage." *Hart v. McLucas*, 535 F.2d 516, 519 (9th Cir. 1976).

In concluding that claims under Section 14(e) require allegations of scienter, the district court stated: "Considering the wealth of persuasive case law to the contrary, the Court concludes that the better view is that the similarities between Rule 10b-5 and §14(e) require a plaintiff bringing a cause of action under §14(e) to allege scienter." The district court relied on decisions from five other circuits holding that Section 14(e) claims require alleging scienter. However, we are persuaded that the rationale underpinning those decisions does not apply to Section 14(e) of the Exchange Act. At their core, the decisions from these five circuits rest on the shared text found in both Rule 10b-5 and Section 14(e). Yet important distinctions exist between Rule 10b-5 and Section 14(e)—distinctions that strongly militate against importing the scienter requirement from the context of Rule 10b-5 to Section 14(e).

The first of the other circuits' decisions came in 1973, a few years after Section 14(e) was enacted, when the Second Circuit held that Section 14(e) requires a showing of scienter: "[W]e shall follow the principles developed under Rule 10b-5 regarding the elements of [Section 14(e)] violations." *Chris-Craft Indus. Inc. v. Piper Aircraft Corp.*, 480 F.2d 341, 362 (2d Cir. 1973). . . . [However], in 1976, the Supreme Court in *Ernst & Ernst v. Hochfelder*, 425 U.S. 185, 193 (1976), held that claims under Section 10(b) of the Exchange Act and Rule 10b-5 must allege scienter. Importantly, as it relates to this case, the Supreme Court's reasoning in reaching that decision casts doubt on the rationale of *Chris-Craft*. . . . The Court in *Ernst & Ernst* began with the text of Rule 10b-5(b), which states: "It shall be unlawful . . . [t]o make any untrue statement of a material fact or omit to state any material fact. . . ." *Ernst & Ernst*, 425 U.S. at 195-96, 96 S. Ct. 1375. Addressing that phrase, the Court noted, "[v]iewed in isolation the language of [Rule 10b-5(b)] . . . could be read as proscribing, respectively, *any type* of material misstatement or omission . . . *whether the wrongdoing was intentional or not.*" *Ernst & Ernst*, 425 U.S. at 212, 96 S. Ct. 1375 (emphases added). In other words, the Court acknowledged that the wording of Rule 10b-5(b) could reasonably be read as imposing a scienter *or a negligence* standard. This means that Rule 10b-5(b)'s text, and by extension the identical phrasing in the first clause of Section 14(e), did not necessarily compel finding a scienter requirement.

The Court in *Ernst & Ernst* nevertheless went on to conclude that Rule 10b-5(b) requires a showing of scienter because of the relationship between Rule 10b-5 and its authorizing legislation, Section 10(b) of the Exchange Act. Significantly, the Court's conclusion that scienter is an element of Rule 10b-5(b) had nothing to do with the text of Rule 10b-5. As the Court explained:

> Rule 10b-5 was adopted pursuant to authority grand [*sic*] the [SEC] under §10(b). . . . [The scope of Rule 10b-5] cannot exceed the power granted the [SEC] by Congress under §10(b). . . . *[W]e think the [SEC's] original interpretation of Rule 10b-5 was compelled by the language and history of §10(b).* . . . When a statute speaks so specifically in terms of manipulation and deception, and of implementing devices and contrivances—the commonly understood terminology of intentional wrongdoing—and when its history reflects no more expansive intent, we are quite unwilling to extend the scope of the statute to negligent conduct.

Put simply, Rule 10b-5 requires a showing of scienter because it is a regulation promulgated under Section 10(b) of the Exchange Act, which allows the SEC to regulate *only* "manipulative or deceptive device[s]." This rationale regarding Rule 10b-5 does not apply to Section 14(e), which is a statute, not an SEC Rule. . . .

The conclusion that Section 14(e) requires a showing of negligence, as opposed to scienter, also finds some support in the legislative history and purpose of the Williams Act. The Senate Report that accompanied Section 14(e) states: "This provision would affirm the fact that persons engaged in making or opposing tender offers or otherwise seeking to influence the decision of investors or the outcome of the tender offer are under an obligation to make full disclosure of material information to those with whom they deal." S. Rep. No. 510, 90th Cong., 2d Sess. (1968). Moreover, the Supreme Court has noted, "[t]he purpose of the Williams Act is to insure that public shareholders who are confronted by a cash tender offer for their stock will not be required to respond without adequate information." *Rondeau v. Mosinee Paper Corp.*, 422 U.S. 49, 58 (1975). The legislative history suggests that the Williams Act places more emphasis on the quality of information shareholders receive in a tender offer than on the state of mind harbored by those issuing a tender offer. Such a purpose supports a negligence standard.

Ultimately, because the text of the first clause of Section 14(e) is devoid of any suggestion that scienter is required, we conclude that the first clause of Section 14(e) requires a showing of only negligence, not scienter.

IV.   CONCLUSION

We are aware that our holding today parts ways from our colleagues in five other circuits. However, for the reasons discussed above, we are persuaded that intervening guidance from the Supreme Court compels the conclusion that Section 14(e) of the Exchange Act imposes a negligence standard.

NOTES AND QUESTIONS

1. **Emulex** *in the Supreme Court.* The Supreme Court granted certiorari in *Emulex,* on the scienter question and—not an issue in the Ninth Circuit—whether there is an implied private right of action at all under Section 14(e). The court of appeals simply assumed, based on ample precedent, that there was one, although it rejected an implied right of action for another tender offer provision in the Williams Act (Section 14(d)(4)), which requires certain disclosures by any person, including the issuer, who makes a recommendation or solicitation with respect to the offer.

The case made its way to oral argument, and the Justices' questions indicated substantial disagreement about the standards for implication. This was especially challenging because the Court had decided two 14(e) cases on the merits—including *Piper v. Chris-Craft Indus. Inc.,* 430 U.S. 1 (1977) (denying the bidder standing to sue for damages on grounds that the shareholders are the intended beneficiaries of the Williams Act)—and lower courts had uniformly allowed bidders and targets to litigate 14(e) matters at least for the purpose of injunctive and other equitable relief. Indeed, SEC enforcement in the tender offer area is almost non-existent—lawsuits by the bidder, target, or both (or perhaps target shareholders) do nearly all the enforcement work. Shortly after oral argument, the Court surprisingly dismissed certiorari as improvidently granted, leaving a cloud not only over the scienter question but all the private rights of action that have been recognized under various provisions of the Williams Act.

2. ***Breaches of Fiduciary Duty.*** In *Schreiber v. Burlington Northern Inc.,* 472 U.S. 1 (1985), the Supreme Court held that claims of "manipulation" under Section 14(e) must be based on deception, not mere abuse of power or breach of fiduciary duty. How much room is there left to turn claims of improper defensive activity into nondisclosure allegations under Section 14(e) (or Rule 14e-2)? In *Field v. Trump,* 850 F.2d 938 (2d Cir. 1988), *cert. denied,* 489 U.S. 1012 (1989), the Second Circuit discussed the failure to disclose certain self-serving actions of management in, among other things, the tender offer documents of an affiliated bidder. Holding that allegations of simple mismanagement or failure to maximize shareholder value would not state a fraud claim, the court nonetheless left the door open a little bit for federalizing claims of improper defensive activity:

> [W]here the remedy of an injunction is needed (and is available under state law) to prevent irreparable injury to the company from willful misconduct of a self-serving nature, disclosure of facts necessary to make other statements not misleading is required where the misleading statements will lull shareholders into foregoing the injunctive remedy.

Id. at 948.

2.   Purchases by (or for) the Issuer of Its Own Securities

Back in the days of truly hostile takeover bids, a common response to an actual or threatened hostile tender offer is for either the issuer or some associated person (perhaps a "white knight," a controlling shareholder, or a captive pension fund) to begin purchasing issuer shares. One way is to launch a self-tender—entering into competition with the bidder, albeit with shareholder money. Another is to acquire shares on the market. An open-market purchase strategy has a number of potential goals from a defensive standpoint: (1) When the purchases are by an affiliate, they take away shares that otherwise might fall into the hands of the aggressor; (2) when they are by the issuer itself and the issuer has excess cash, they deplete some of that cash supply, and when the funds are borrowed, they may add a significant debt burden to the company's capital structure—either way making the issuer potentially less attractive as a takeover target; and (3) in any event, the purchases may drive up the price of the target shares and thus help defeat the bid. For an analysis, *compare* Bradley & Rosenzweig, Defensive Stock Repurchases, 99 Harv. L. Rev. 1378 (1986) *with* Gordon & Kornhauser, Takeover Defensive Tactics: A Comment on Two Models, 96 Yale L.J. 295 (1986).

No matter what type of repurchase is involved, a variety of provisions and rules under the Securities Exchange Act will come into play. Some are rules we have already considered. For example, issuer repurchases could be considered unlawful insider trading under Rule 10b-5 if there was undisclosed material information in the issuer's possession. If the repurchase program by the issuer (or an affiliate, as in certain leveraged buyout transactions) would result in the delisting of the issuer stock from a national securities exchange or loss of status as a publicly held company, Rule 13e-3, the Commission's going-private rule, will apply to compel detailed "fairness" disclosure, as we saw in Chapter 16.

Of all these regulatory concerns, fear of manipulation is surely high on the list, and there is a substantial body of case law in this area. The best known of the cases is *Crane Co. v. Westinghouse Air Brake Co.*, 419 F.2d 787 (2d Cir. 1969), *cert. denied*, 400 U.S. 822 (1970). In that case, American Standard and Westinghouse Air Brake had agreed to merge. Crane launched a takeover bid for Westinghouse Air Brake and tried to persuade its shareholders not to approve the merger. In response, American Standard began a large-scale program of buying Westinghouse Air Brake stock, coupled with large secret sales off the market. The result, according to the court, was a distortion in the market price, deceiving Westinghouse Air Brake shareholders into believing that there was an extraordinary demand for their stock and deterring them from tendering to Crane. This was found to violate both Section 9(a)(2) and Rule 10b-5. However, in *Crane Co. v. American Standard Inc.*, 603 F.2d 244 (2d Cir. 1979), the same court thereafter held, in light of the Supreme Court's *Piper* decision, that American Standard did not have standing to seek damages under Rule 10b-5 or Section 9(e).

Crane involved open market purchases of target shares by a "white knight" in the midst of a tender offer battle. What about purchases directly by the issuer? Here, Rule 13e-1 is explicit: When a person other than the issuer has commenced a tender offer for the shares of an issuer subject to Section 13(e) (i.e., a publicly held company), the issuer may not purchase any of its own securities during the period of the offer unless, prior to the purchases, it discloses basic factual information (e.g., the amount to be purchased, the market to be entered, the source of funds) in a filing with the Commission. This, however, is a far less intrusive regulation than that faced by the bidder with respect to an acquisition program outside the tender offer. Recall the discussion of Rule 14e-5, supra.

Issuer self-tenders need not be defensive, of course. They may simply be an alternative to open market repurchases. *See* Fried, Insider Signaling and Insider Trading with Repurchase Tender Offers, 67 U. Chi. L. Rev. 421 (2000) (raising concern that they may operate as a backdoor form of insider trading). Section 14(d)(8)(B) excludes issuer self-tenders from the scope of Section 14(d). But this is an illusory exclusion. Utilizing its rulemaking authority under Section 13(e) to regulate issuer repurchases generally, the SEC has adopted Rule 13e-4, which applies virtually all the rules that exist under Regulations 14D and 14E to issuer tender offers. As a result, for instance, issuers cannot do "discriminatory" self-tenders (i.e., self-tenders that exclude a competing bidder from participation—the issuer offers the premium to all its shareholders who wish to tender, but provides that no shares will be bought from the hostile bidder) because of the all-holders/best-price rule applied to issuers in Rule 13e-4(f)(8). In sum, there is now substantial parity in the regulation of issuer and third-party tender offers.

‖18‖
Regulation of Broker-Dealers

Earlier chapters explored the role of disclosure in promoting well-informed decisions by investors, in terms of both mandatory reporting and the prohibition against fraud. The focus of that discussion was largely on the issuer itself (or persons associated with the issuer, e.g., underwriters or accountants) as the primary source of information that investors consider significant. Realistically, however, most investors do not rely directly upon the companies in which they are interested to gain the knowledge needed to make their investment decisions. To be sure, the Internet has substantially enabled individual investors to gather data and make their own trading decisions—though whether they do so successfully is another question entirely. In any event, the quantity of information in the marketplace remains overwhelming for many investors. Sensing this, many individual investors look to others, particularly professionals in the securities business such as stockbrokers and investment advisers, for assistance and recommendations. In this way, it is fair to say that much disclosure is "filtered" before it reaches the typical investor.

Yet this filtering process is fraught with conflicts of interest. Those who advise investors might themselves have positions in securities that could be benefited by resulting purchases or sales. Or they could secretly be agents of issuers or their associated persons, hired to "tout" the securities in question. Or since in the stock brokerage industry compensation for both advice and execution often comes in the form of commissions and spreads on a per transaction basis, there may be an incentive to cause investors simply to buy or sell actively or pay too much. The regulation of broker-dealers occurs at a number of levels. There is direct regulation by the SEC, and state "blue sky" regulation of broker-dealers as well. But much of the day-to-day work of regulating the broker-dealer industry is done by FINRA, the industry's "self-regulator." FINRA has its own extensive body of rules as to broker conduct; an inspection, enforcement and disciplinary system; and conducts arbitration of broker-customer and broker-employee disputes.

A.   *Regulation of the Broker-Dealer Industry: Structure and Oversight*

1.   Entry

The starting point for broker-dealer regulation in the United States is the basic requirement of Section 15(a) of the '34 Act: No person may act as a broker or a dealer in securities unless registered with the SEC or expressly exempted from the registration requirement. *Broker* is defined in Section 3(a)(4) as a person "engaged in the business of effecting transactions in securities for the account of others," while *dealer* is defined in Section 3(a)(5) as a person engaged "in the business of buying and selling securities for his own account." It is important to emphasize at the outset that a large portion of securities firms act as both brokers and dealers (which itself, as we shall see, is a potential source of abuse); firms in the business are thus generally referred to as broker-dealers.

Obviously, particularly as to the definition of dealer, substantial stress is placed upon the phrase "in the business"; otherwise, many individuals and firms who do substantial investing would fall within the definition. In general, the requirement applies to those who engage in the covered activity *on a regular basis* and typically in a fairly public fashion, rather than on an isolated basis. *See SEC v. Ridenour,* 913 F.2d 515 (8th Cir. 1990).

Broker-dealer registration questions arise in many different contexts, for which securities lawyers must keep their eyes wide open. In many private placements, for example, issuers may use and compensate "finders" for helping them locate potential investors. Are finders broker-dealers? While merely making introductions is not enough to trigger registration, compensating them based on the success of the transactions (i.e., in the form of a commission) would push the finder into regulated territory. The policy seems to be that if someone is regularly in a position to play the role of securities salesman, and will profit when sales are made, registration is appropriate. *See SEC v. Collyard,* 861 F.3d 760 (8th Cir. 2017), where the court applied a multi-factor test asking whether there was "[1] regular participation in securities transactions, [2] employment with the issuer of the securities, [3] payment by commission as opposed to salary, [4] history of selling the securities of other issuers, [5] involvement in advice to investors [or] [6] active recruitment of investors," quoting *SEC v. George,* 426 F.3d 786, 797 (6th Cir. 2005). On the murkiness of this line, *see SEC v. Kramer,* 778 F. Supp. 2d 1320 (M.D. Fla. 2011) (insufficient transaction-based activity). Lawyers and accountants can easily find themselves in trouble as unregistered broker-dealers. *See, e.g., SEC v. Feng,* 2017 WL 6551107 (C.D. Cal. 2017) (immigration attorney steered clients seeking a green card by making qualified investments in the United States pursuant to the EB-5 visa program to certain private placement opportunities; attorney received substantial fees from promoters).

What about playing a role in facilitating mergers? Recall from the *Landreth Timber* case in Chapter 2 that a sale of a business to new owners that is structured as a stock purchase is a sale of securities, even if other ways of structuring the transaction might not be. In a no-action letter, the SEC staff allowed financial advisers to play a role "in connection with the transfer of ownership and control of a privately-held company through the purchase, sale, exchange, issuance, repurchase, or redemption of, or a business combination involving, securities or assets of the company, to a buyer that will actively operate the company or the business conducted with the assets of the company," without registration. This was subject to numerous restrictions, however (*see* M&A Broker No-Action Letter (available Jan. 31, 2014)), which makes this tricky for others who might try to rely on the guidance. See Problem 18-2, below. Note that Wall Street– style investment banking with respect to M&A activity is generally understood to be well within the purview of broker-dealer regulation. *See* Tuch, The Self Regulation of Investment Bankers, 83 Geo. Wash. L. Rev. 101 (2014). In an effort to provide some regulatory relief for firms engaged in limited M&A work, FINRA has created, with the SEC's blessing, a more lightly regulated category of "Capital Acquisition Broker."

Technology has also brought with it a host of interesting interpretive questions regarding broker-dealer status. As we saw in the previous section, a proliferation of electronic systems operate as alternatives to traditional exchanges as places for buy and sell orders to be matched. Many of these are treated as broker-dealers. But is *any* system or facility that helps investors trade subject to broker-dealer characterization?

As you saw in Chapter 5, the JOBS Act has encouraged the use of the Internet for capital raising, via the elimination of the ban on general solicitations in Rule 506(c) and crowdfunding. For crowdfunding, transactions must be through either a registered broker or a registered crowdfunding portal, which in turn must become a member of FINRA and be subject to its oversight. Entities that assist in the offer of sale of transactions exempt under Rule 506 are also exempt from broker-dealer registration, but only if they receive no compensation for so acting.

As we see in the next section, the SEC and the SROs (particularly FINRA) share responsibility for supervising the conduct of broker-dealers and persons associated with them. As to entry, the SEC is given the authority pursuant to Section 15(b)(1) to deny (or subsequently revoke) a registration based on evidence of misconduct or false statements to the Commission. In addition, Section 15(b)(7) gives the Commission the power to set standards of operational capacity, training, experience, competence, and other qualifications for registered broker-dealers and their associated persons. To this end, persons associated with broker-dealers—for example, the stockbrokers who deal directly with the firm's customers—must pass tests designed to ensure a basic level of expertise in the securities business, administered by the SROs.

PROBLEMS

18-1. John Phillips is a physician. He also fancies himself as quite an expert in medical technology stocks and has put together an extensive portfolio, concentrating on some 23 companies that he finds "particularly interesting." With some regularity, he has contacted the market makers for those stocks, indicating his interest in buying and/or selling at certain prices, and is considering creating his own web site on the Internet for this purpose. During the past year, he has bought and sold over $3 million of those stocks. Is he a "dealer"?

18-2. Whitestreet Capital Management is a private equity firm, which raises capital from investors to acquire companies and then later sell them off (hopefully at a large profit for the firm and its investors) via an IPO or acquisition. After a company went into its portfolio, Whitestreet would be actively involved in identifying potential buyers, negotiating and structuring transactions, arranging financing, and executing deals involving that company. Fees would be charged to the portfolio companies for this work. Would Whitestreet have to register as a broker-dealer? *See* Blackstreet Cap. Mgmt., Exchange Act Release No. 77959 (June 1, 2016).

2.   Supervising the Conduct of Broker-Dealers and Their Associated Persons

a.   *Self-Regulation*

No doubt the most visible aspect of broker-dealer regulation is the disciplinary process. So far as the statutory structure goes, the starting point for broker-dealer discipline is the set of rules that the various SROs have established—most importantly, the rules of conduct regulation designed to promote the "just and equitable principles of trade." In the following materials, we shall examine some of the specific SRO rules. It is important, however, to keep in mind that the conduct rules are really quite open-ended: FINRA's rules, for example, begin with the broad—and independently enforceable—command that members "observe high standards of commercial honor and just and equitable principles of trade" (Rule 2010). Most of what follows are simply elaborations on that principle. We have already seen some of these rules in operation—for example, the restrictions on excessive underwriter compensation and the rules relating to free riding and withholding in the public offering setting, discussed in Chapter 4.

While there has been some controversy about the legitimacy of giving such broad-based legal responsibility to what is essentially a private body, this aspect of the regulatory scheme has been upheld against the challenge that it operates as an unconstitutional delegation of administrative responsibility. *See First Jersey Securities Inc. v. Bergen*, 605 F.2d 690 (3d Cir. 1979), *cert. denied*, 444 U.S. 1074 (1980). The basic fairness of these disciplinary procedures, however, is a matter of statutory requirement: SRO disciplinary rules must provide a "fair procedure." *E.g.*, Section 15A(b)(8). At the same time, the level of judicial supervision tends to be fairly minimal. For example, in *Bergen*, supra, the respondent broker-dealer (First Jersey) complained that it was inherently unfair to subject it to a disciplinary hearing before a panel made up of its business competitors, thus violating due process. In response, the court said:

> [T]o uphold First Jersey's contention [of systemic bias] would destroy the valuable congressional scheme for self-regulation in the securities area and the destruction could very well extend to other areas employing intramural controls.

The Maloney Act expresses Congress' thoughtful view that self-regulation is the best "first line" defense against unethical or illegal securities practices. It allows the industry to set its own standards of proper conduct and permits their members to discipline themselves applying their own expertise and experience.

Although Congress preferred self-regulation by a private body over direct involvement of a governmental agency, it established safeguards to prevent abuse of the system. . . . For example, the NASD Code of Procedure . . . requires the disqualification of any panel member who may have a personal interest in the outcome of the case. Further insurance against abuse is provided by the supervisory role of the SEC. . . . We believe that the intrinsic benefits of a system of self-regulation, insulated with extensive procedural and substantive protections and subject to judicial review, render[] insignificant objections of bias to the system which inherently involves disciplining by potential competitors.

605 F.2d at 698-699. On the awkward status of self-regulatory law, *see* Henderson & Birdthistle, Becoming a Fifth Branch, 99 Cornell L. Rev. 101 (2013).

b. Direct SEC Supervision of Brokers and Dealers

The SROs do not have either exclusive or primary authority in the area of conduct regulation. To the contrary, the SEC is given independent power with respect to setting standards for both the conduct of broker-dealers and discipline. So far as rulemaking is concerned, an important source of authority is Section 10(b) of the '34 Act. As we shall see, a fair number of the 10b series of rules relate specifically to broker-dealer practices that may be characterized as deceptive or manipulative. And, of course, there is Rule 10b-5. This authority is supplemented by Section 15(c)(1) and (2), which gives the Commission a separate source of authority to deal with fraudulent, deceptive, or manipulative acts in the OTC market. There are also other grants of rulemaking power with respect to particular matters of concern, for example, the financial responsibility of broker-dealers' firms (Section 15(c)(3)). In the following sections of this chapter, we look at some of the 10b and 15c rules and their interplay with the SRO rules on the same subjects.

The Commission also has independent authority with respect to discipline. Pursuant to Section 15(b)(4) and (6), it has the authority to institute administrative proceedings in order to discipline broker-dealers and their associated persons (e.g., registered representatives and other employees). Essentially, such sanctions may be imposed in three types of circumstances: (1) if the Commission finds that the broker-dealer or associated person has committed a willful violation of the federal securities laws or the rules and regulations thereunder or "willfully aided, abetted, counseled, commanded, induced or procured" such a violation by any other person; (2) if it finds that such a person willfully made a false statement in any application for registration or report to the SEC; or (3) if it finds that such a person is subject to a "statutory disqualification"—for example, that he, she, or it has been convicted of a business-related crime within the past ten years or has elsewhere been enjoined from acting as a securities professional. Procedurally, the SEC need only find a violation by a preponderance of the evidence, even if the underlying misconduct is fraud. *See Steadman v. SEC*, 450 U.S. 91 (1981). The sanctions that may be imposed in an SEC proceeding include the suspension of registration, permanent or temporary bars from the industry, restrictions on activities, civil penalties, disgorgement, and censure. Broker-dealers and their associated persons can appeal the SEC's determination to a federal court of appeals. In addition to discipline for direct misconduct, Section 15(b)(4)(E) provides that broker-dealer firms and their associated persons may be disciplined simply for failing to supervise their employees with a view toward preventing such violations. As to this latter standard, the Commission has made clear in its enforcement actions that adequate supervision is not present simply by charging branch managers, for example, with responsibility for monitoring their employees. Adequate supervision is a firm-wide responsibility, often requiring a more formalized compliance program and comprehensive oversight by senior officials, as we will see in the following case.

In the Matter of John Gutfreund et al.
[1992 Transfer Binder] Fed. Sec. L. Rep. (CCH) ¶85,067 (Dec. 3, 1992)

[In 1991, senior officials of Salomon Brothers Inc., a large investment banking firm, learned that the head of their Government Trading desk, Paul Mozer, had submitted a false bid in the amount of $3.15 billion to the United States Treasury. Later, Mozer committed two other violations. The SEC took action against the senior officials for failing to supervise properly. In what may be the most interesting portion of the opinion, the Commission discussed the conduct of Salomon's chief *legal* officer:]

Donald Feuerstein, Salomon's chief legal officer, was informed of the submission of the false bid by Paul Mozer in late April of 1991, at the same time other senior executives of Salomon learned of that act. Feuerstein was present at the meetings in late April at which the supervisors named as respondents in this proceeding discussed the matter. In his capacity as a legal adviser, Feuerstein did advise Strauss and Gutfreund that the submission of the bid was a criminal act and should be reported to the government, and he urged them on several occasions to proceed with disclosure when he learned that the report had not been made. However, Feuerstein did not direct that an inquiry be undertaken, and he did not recommend that appropriate procedures, reasonably designed to prevent and detect future misconduct, be instituted, or that other limitations be placed on Mozer's activities. Feuerstein also did not inform the Compliance Department, for which he was responsible as Salomon's chief legal officer, of the false bid.

Unlike Gutfreund, Strauss and Meriwether, however, Feuerstein was not a direct supervisor of Mozer at the time he first learned of the false bid. Because we believe this is an appropriate opportunity to amplify our views on the supervisory responsibilities of legal and compliance officers in Feuerstein's position, we have not named him as a respondent in this proceeding. Instead, we are issuing this report of investigation concerning the responsibilities imposed by Section 15(b)(4)(E) of the Exchange Act under the circumstances of this case.

Employees of brokerage firms who have legal or compliance responsibilities do not become "supervisors" for purposes of Sections 15(b)(4)(E) and 15(b)(6) solely because they occupy those positions. Rather, determining if a particular person is a "supervisor" depends on whether, under the facts and circumstances of a particular case, that person has a requisite degree of responsibility, ability or authority to affect the conduct of the employee whose behavior is at issue. Thus, persons occupying positions in the legal or compliance departments of broker-dealers have been found by the Commission to be "supervisors" for purposes of Sections 15(b)(4)(E) and 15(b)(6) under certain circumstances.

In this case, serious misconduct involving a senior official of a brokerage firm was brought to the attention of the firm's chief legal officer. That individual was informed of the misconduct by other members of senior management in order to obtain his advice and guidance, and to involve him as part of management's collective response to the problem. Moreover, in other instances of misconduct, that individual had directed the firm's response and had made recommendations concerning appropriate disciplinary action, and management had relied on him to perform those tasks.

Given the role and influence within the firm of a person in a position such as Feuerstein's and the factual circumstances of this case, such a person shares in the responsibility to take appropriate action to respond to the misconduct. Under those circumstances, we believe that such a person becomes a "supervisor" for purposes of Sections 15(b)(4)(E) and 15(b)(6). As a result, that person is responsible, along with the other supervisors, for taking reasonable and appropriate action. It is not sufficient for one in such a position to be a mere bystander to the events that occurred.

Once a person in Feuerstein's position becomes involved in formulating management's response to the problem, he or she is obligated to take affirmative steps to ensure that appropriate action is taken to address the misconduct. For example, such a person could direct or monitor an investigation of the conduct at issue, make appropriate recommendations for limiting the activities of the employee or for the institution of appropriate procedures, reasonably designed to prevent and detect future misconduct, and verify that his or her recommendations, or acceptable alternatives, are implemented. If such a person takes appropriate steps but management fails to act and that person knows or has reason to know of that failure, he or she should consider what additional steps are appropriate to address the matter. These steps may include disclosure of the matter to the entity's board of directors, resignation from the firm, or disclosure to regulatory authorities.[26]

These responsibilities cannot be avoided simply because the person did not previously have direct supervisory responsibility for any of the activities of the employee. Once such a person has supervisory obligations by virtue of the circumstances of a particular situation, he must either discharge those responsibilities or know that others are taking appropriate action. . . .

---

26. Of course, in the case of an attorney, the applicable Code of Professional Responsibility and the Canons of Ethics may bear upon what course of conduct that individual may properly pursue.

NOTES AND QUESTIONS

1.   What Would You Do?   In light of *In the Matter of John Gutfreund*, suppose you were the general counsel of a large securities firm and you received an anonymous letter indicating that the firm's most productive broker was repeatedly engaging in illegal insider trading and that the CEO knew about it and was doing nothing. How would you proceed? On the regulatory problems associated with a strict duty to supervise for persons with compliance responsibilities, *see* Fanto, The Vanishing Supervisor, 41 J. Corp. L. 117 (2015). It is also worth noting that under FINRA Rule 4530(b), a member must promptly report to FINRA that it or any associated person has violated any securities or investment-related law, rule, or regulation. This is different from most other industries, where companies may be encouraged to self-report illegal behavior to regulators but are not required to do so.

2.   Compliance and Insider Trading.   The combination of the statutory duty to supervise and more detailed FINRA rules means that all broker-dealer firms must have extensive real-time compliance programs for surveillance and monitoring of potential misconduct. With respect to insider trading, compliance obligations are heightened even more explicitly, reflecting the many difficulties multi-service financial firms face. For example, suppose a large broker-dealer firm's corporate finance department (i.e., the group that specializes in advising corporate clients on financial matters) is retained by a particular corporate client and, in the course of that representation, the client conveys certain adverse information about its financial condition to the firm. Soon thereafter, some other department of the firm trades. Is there a violation of Rule 10b-5? By most accounts (and as reflected in Rules 10b5-1 and 14e-3), the question turns—unless there is affirmative evidence of actual leakage of the information to the department that traded—on whether the firm had implemented and enforced a reasonable system of internal controls to prevent the leakage of information from one department to another.

Even harder problems arise when that other department is in the business of making recommendations to customers about particular stocks. For instance, would the firm potentially be liable to customers if, at the same time, the research department was aggressively recommending the purchase of that company's stock? The answer may be yes, at least according to *Slade v. Shearson Hammill & Co.*, [1974 Transfer Binder] Fed. Sec. L. Rep. (CCH) ¶94,329 (S.D.N.Y. 1974), *aff'd on other grounds*, 577 F.2d 398 (2d Cir. 1974). But should this really be the case, even if persons in the research department did not actually know the information? *See Black v. Shearson Hammill & Co.*, 266 Cal. App. 2d 362, 72 Cal. Rptr. 157 (1968). Should it matter here whether reasonable internal controls were in place to prevent such interdepartmental leaks?

An awareness of both the intractability and the pervasiveness of some of these problems led Congress, in the Insider Trading and Securities Fraud Enforcement Act of 1988, to add Section 15(f) to the '34 Act, requiring broker-dealers to establish, maintain, and enforce written policies and procedures "reasonably designed to prevent misuse . . . of material nonpublic information" in violation of the federal securities laws. Failure to comply with this requirement may result in an administrative disciplinary proceeding or an injunctive action, and knowing or reckless failure to establish, enforce, or maintain such procedures, where such failure contributed substantially to or permitted the occurrence of an insider trading violation, may result in the imposition of a civil penalty. *See* Section 21A(b). The legislative history emphasizes the need not only to adopt meaningful procedures, but also to communicate them effectively to firm employees; it also makes clear that compliance must be monitored regularly and the system revised as circumstances evolve. *See generally* Tuch, Financial Conglomerates and Information Barriers, 39 J. Corp. L. 563 (2014).

PROBLEM

18-3. Melissa Wong is the Chief Compliance Officer of Foster Archibald Securities, a full-service brokerage firm. At the behest of the Head of Sales, Foster recently hired Tom Phillipi, a high-producing broker. Wong and her team had investigated Phillipi and were quite concerned with the fact that he had had numerous customer complaints at firms where he had previously worked, and his attitude and demeanor in interviews gave them pause about how he regards his obligations as a broker. They recommended that he not be hired, but the Head of Sales rejected their advice. She then brought the matter up with the firm's CEO, who said that this was the Sales Department's call. Since that time, they have kept a close eye on Phillipi, and found numerous disturbing incidents. They brought these to the attention of the Head of Sales, who said he would watch over him but pointed out that he had already become the region's number one seller. Eventually, FINRA discovered that Phillipi was systematically violating the law with respect to customer accounts—including unauthorized trading to pump up the distribution of unregistered securities—and Foster had to pay significant penalties and compensation as a result. Should Wong be sanctioned for failure to supervise?

B.   The Responsibilities of Brokers to Their Customers

1.   Acting in the Customer's Best Interest

a.   Best Execution

At the heart of the debate over the fragmentation of trading markets described in Chapter 10 is the issue of how investors can expect the orders to be executed "optimally" when there is more than one market. To understand the policy problems here, think of the investor who wants an order executed. If there is only one market, her order is routed there and she will get the price and speed of execution that that market offers. The virtue of a "centralized" system is that her order will come together with all others, so that the resulting market price will reflect the full range of supply and demand. The problem is that centralization implies monopolization, with the possible—and historically observable—abuses that such power invites. *See Gordon v. New York*

Stock Exchange, 422 U.S. 659 (1975). So why not have multiple markets that compete with each other, albeit in a setting where the markets are linked by a communications system so that brokers can search for the best trade for their customers?

While this sounds simple and appealing, many problems lurk. The starting point is the principle of agency law that says that a broker has a fiduciary-like duty to seek "best execution" for the customer. But what does this mean? Stated somewhat differently, if the customer and broker could costlessly contract to set forth the terms of their relationship, including precisely what the broker's obligation was with respect to pursuing the most favorable terms for each of the customer's future trades, just what would they require the broker to do if the security is traded in four or five different markets?

> Best execution refers to traders receiving the most favorable terms available for their trades. Despite the seeming simplicity of this concept, few issues in today's securities markets are more contentious than the debate surrounding best execution. Does clearing a trade in one market at the best available current quote constitute best execution if trades frequently clear between the quotes in another market? Does the mechanism that provides best execution change when trade size is considered? Can investment professionals comply with their legal best execution obligation if their trade price implicitly provides a rebate to the broker rather than a better price to the trader? . . .
>
> Unlike pornography, which while difficult to define is known when it is seen, best execution is easily defined but is often unrecognizable. This reflects the difficulty that the term "best execution" does not connote a single execution attribute, such as a price, but rather attaches to a vector of execution components. These certainly include the trade price, but they also involve the timing of trades, the trading mechanism used, the commission charged, and even the trading strategy employed. . . .
>
> In a single market setting with an easily discernible price, the "duty" of best execution is both obvious and direct. When markets compete in different ways with respect to different components of trade executions, it is no longer so clear what "best" execution is, let alone how or when it is attained. . . . Well-meaning attempts to mandate best execution as a consumer-protection device run counter to attempts to make markets less centralized and more competitive. . . .

Macey & O'Hara, The Law and Economics of Best Execution, 6 J. Fin. Intermediation 188 (1997).

Best execution for retail investors was addressed in *Newton v. Merrill, Lynch, Pierce, Fenner & Smith,* 135 F.3d 267 (3d Cir. 1998) (en banc). There, the Third Circuit considered the question of whether the defendant broker-dealers defrauded their customers during a 1992-1994 class period when they executed their orders at the readily available NBBO—the prevailing best published quote from among competing market makers—rather than engage in additional search efforts to find a better price, such as using the Instinet system. Plaintiffs argued that new technological developments had made such searches practicable, and that the duty of best execution is always an evolving one. Noting the SEC's recent revisions in this area, the court held that a reasonable trier of fact could infer that a deliberate and systematic failure to seek out a superior price could be a deceptive practice. It thus remanded for further proceedings on both the viability of the alternative search systems and whether the defendants acted with scienter.

Newton is interesting for its description of the broker's agency law based obligations to its customers. According to the court, "[s]ince it is understood by all that the client-principal seeks his own economic gain and the purpose of the agency is to help the client-principal achieve that objective, the broker-dealer, absent instruction to the contrary, is expected to use reasonable efforts to maximize the economic benefit to the client in the transaction." Id. at 270. That means "the best reasonably available price." Id. Though conceding that there is no bright-line definition of that term, the court concluded that it "is not so vague as to be without ascertainable content in the context of a particular trade or trades." Id. at 270-271. Hence, further factual inquiry with respect to plaintiffs' allegations was both necessary and appropriate. The SEC has attempted to shine some sunlight on the best execution issue, by requiring market centers to publish standardized monthly statistics on order execution quality, and by requiring broker-dealers to report both aggregate and individualized data as to which markets they are routing their orders. Disclosure of Order Execution and Routing Practices, Exchange Act Release No. 34-43590 (Nov. 17, 2000). These issues blend into the questions about market structure and high frequency trading discussed in Chapter 10. *See In the Matter of Citadel Securities LLC*, Admin. Proc. File 3-17772, Jan. 13, 2017 (misleading disclosure by wholesale broker about how it executes marketable orders routed to it by other broker-dealers).

b.   *Advice and Recommendations*

Broker-dealers profit by executing transactions for customers, whether as agent or principal. It is in their interest, therefore, to stimulate demand for securities so as to promote robust investor trading. Historically, they have sought to do so by offering investment advice and recommendations. Given the complexity of the world of investing, this can be a great service to customers, but also creates the temptation to make hard-core sales pitches. We have already seen FINRA rules that seek to restrain inequitable sales practices.

As will be studied further in Chapter 19, those who offer investment advice to the public but are not broker-dealers have long been treated as fiduciaries, subject to categorical obligations of loyalty, care, and utmost good faith over the course of that relationship. So shouldn't broker-dealers be treated the same, at least at the time they recommend a purchase or sale, since they are offering the same kind of advice? As a matter of common law, there is case law going both ways on whether and when brokers are fiduciaries, but by and large courts have not been willing to treat the broker-customer relationship as one of trust and confidence unless the broker actually "controls" the account. *See, e.g., Lefkowitz v. Smith Barney, Harris Upham & Co.*, 804 F.2d 154 (1st Cir. 1986); *De Kwiatkowski v. Bear Stearns & Co.*, 306 F.3d 1293 (2d Cir. 2002) (no fiduciary duties as to recommendations unless the facts clearly show that the broker had agreed to act as an adviser on the customer's behalf). The case law in this area is quite fact-specific.

In Section 913 of the Dodd-Frank Act of 2010, Congress empowered the SEC to resolve this tension under federal law and heighten broker-dealer responsibilities by adopting rules to harmonize investment adviser and broker-dealer duties. In studies both before and after this statutory directive, the evidence was considerable that customers and clients do not understand the distinction between advisers and brokers, or what legal difference it makes. They tend to trust their financial adviser, whatever his or her status. The natural response would be to make broker-dealers fiduciaries as well, since the only other form of unification would be to lower the standard for advisers. But in 2019, the SEC chose not to unify but rather to adopt a new regulatory regime, Rule 15*l*-1, as a stand-alone requirement that brokers and their associated persons act in the best interests of retail customers when making recommendations or giving advice.

Regulation Best Interest: The Broker-Dealer Standard of Conduct
Release 34-86031 (June 5, 2019)

Like many principal-agent relationships—including the investment adviser-client relationship—the relationship between a broker-dealer and a customer has inherent conflicts of interest, including those resulting from a transaction-based (e.g., commission) compensation structure and other broker-dealer compensation. These and other conflicts of interest may provide an incentive to a broker-dealer to seek to increase its own compensation or other financial interests at the expense of the customer to whom it is making investment recommendations.

Notwithstanding these inherent conflicts of interest in the broker-dealer-customer relationship, there is broad acknowledgment of the benefits of, and support for, the continuing existence of the broker-dealer business model, including a commission or other transaction-based compensation structure, as an option for retail customers seeking investment recommendations. For example, retail customers that intend to buy and hold a long-term investment may find that paying a one-time commission to a broker-dealer recommending such an investment is more cost effective than paying an ongoing advisory fee to an investment adviser merely to hold the same investment. Retail customers with limited investment assets may benefit from broker-dealer recommendations when they do not qualify for advisory accounts because they do not meet the account minimums often imposed by investment advisers. Other retail customers who hold a variety of investments, or prefer differing levels of services (e.g., both episodic recommendations from a broker-dealer and continuous advisory services including discretionary asset management from an investment adviser), may benefit from having access to both brokerage and advisory accounts. Nevertheless, concerns exist regarding (1) the potential harm to retail customers resulting from broker-dealer recommendations provided where conflicts of interest exist and (2) the insufficiency of existing broker-dealer regulatory requirements to address these conflicts when broker-dealers make recommendations to retail customers. More specifically, there are concerns that existing requirements do not require a broker-dealer's recommendations to be in the retail customer's best interest.

OVERVIEW OF REGULATION BEST INTEREST

The Commission has crafted Regulation Best Interest to draw on key principles underlying fiduciary obligations, including those that apply to investment advisers under the Advisers Act, while providing specific requirements to address certain aspects of the relationships between broker-dealers and their retail customers. Regulation Best Interest enhances the existing standard of conduct applicable to broker-dealers and their associated persons at the time they recommend to a retail customer a securities transaction or investment strategy involving securities. This includes recommendations of account types and rollovers or transfers of assets and also covers implicit hold recommendations resulting from agreed-upon account monitoring. When making a recommendation, a broker-dealer must act in the retail customer's best interest and cannot place its own interests ahead of the customer's interests (hereinafter, "General Obligation"). The General Obligation is satisfied only if the broker-dealer complies with four specified component obligations. The obligations are: (1) providing certain prescribed disclosure before or at the time of the recommendation, about the recommendation and the relationship between the retail customer and the broker-dealer ("Disclosure Obligation); (2) exercising reasonable diligence, care, and skill in making the recommendation ("Care Obligation"); (3) establishing, maintaining, and enforcing policies and procedures reasonably designed to address conflicts of interest ("Conflict of Interest Obligation"), and (4) establishing, maintaining, and enforcing policies and procedures reasonably designed to achieve compliance with Regulation Best Interest ("Compliance Obligation").

First, under the Disclosure Obligation, before or at the time of the recommendation, a broker-dealer must disclose, in writing, all material facts about the scope and terms of its relationship with the customer. This includes a disclosure that the firm or representative is acting in a broker-dealer capacity; the material fees and costs the customer will incur; and the type and scope of the services to be provided, including any material limitations on the recommendations that could be made to the retail customer. Moreover, the broker-dealer must disclose all material facts relating to conflicts of interest associated with the recommendation that might incline a broker-dealer to make a recommendation that is not disinterested, including, for example, conflicts associated with proprietary products, payments from third parties, and compensation arrangements.

Second, under the Care Obligation, a broker-dealer must exercise reasonable diligence, care, and skill when making a recommendation to a retail customer. The broker-dealer must understand potential risks, rewards, and costs associated with the recommendation. The broker-dealer must then consider those risks, rewards, and costs in light of the customer's investment profile and have a reasonable basis to believe that the recommendation is in the customer's best interest and does not place the broker-dealer's interest ahead of the retail customer's interest. A broker-dealer should consider reasonable alternatives, if any, offered by the broker-dealer in determining whether it has a reasonable basis for making the recommendation. Whether a broker-dealer has complied with the Care Obligation will be evaluated as of the time of the recommendation (and not in hindsight). When recommending a series of transactions, the broker-dealer must have a reasonable basis to believe that the transactions taken together are not excessive, even if each is in the customer's best interest when viewed in isolation.

Third, under the Conflict of Interest Obligation, a broker-dealer must establish, maintain, and enforce reasonably designed written policies and procedures addressing conflicts of interest associated with its recommendations to retail customers. These policies and procedures must be reasonably designed to identify all such conflicts and at a minimum disclose or eliminate them. Importantly, the policies and procedures must be reasonably designed to mitigate conflicts of interests that create an incentive for an associated person of the broker-dealer to place its interests or the interest of the firm ahead of the retail customer's interest. Moreover, when a broker-dealer places material limitations on recommendations that may be made to a retail customer (e.g., offering only proprietary or other limited range of products), the policies and procedures must be reasonably designed to disclose the limitations and associated conflicts and to prevent the limitations from causing the associated person or broker-dealer from placing the associated person's or broker-dealer's interests ahead of the customer's interest. Finally, the policies and procedures must be reasonably designed to identify and eliminate sales contests, sales quotas, bonuses, and non-cash compensation that are based on the sale of specific securities or specific types of securities within a limited period of time.

Fourth, under the Compliance Obligation, a broker-dealer must also establish, maintain, and enforce written policies and procedures reasonably designed to achieve compliance with Regulation Best Interest as a whole. Thus, a broker-dealer's policies and procedures must address not only conflicts of interest but also compliance with its Disclosure and Care Obligations under Regulation Best Interest.

NOTES AND QUESTIONS

1. *The Commission Business.* For much of the last century, commission rates for the execution of transactions by broker-dealers were fixed by stock exchange rules, preventing competition on price alone. In the 1970s, however, this practice was abolished, and the industry became much more competitive. Low-cost brokers like Charles Schwab emerged and thrived (online today), making it harder for full-service brokers to make money via commissions alone. Increasingly, then, full-service brokers had to stress their ability to deliver financial advice, and offered products and services that came with recurring fees to supplement their revenue streams. This shift made brokers seem more like investment advisers, which in turn gave rise to the move toward a fiduciary standard. *See* Laby, Reforming the Regulation of Broker-Dealers and Investment Advisers, 65 Bus. Law. 395 (2010); Langevoort, Brokers as Fiduciaries, 71 U. Pitt. L. Rev. 439 (2010). There are still brokerage firms, of course, that remain commission-driven, which demands savvy salesmanship and itself raises worrisome questions about opportunistic behavior. *See* Egan et al., The Market for Financial Adviser Misconduct, 127 J. Pol. Econ. 233 (2019) ("our findings are consistent with some firms specializing in misconduct and catering to unsophisticated consumers").

2. Investment Products and Best Interest. The old-fashioned securities business involved selling individual stocks and bonds to retail investors at a fixed commission or markup. The fears then were that brokers would be making inflated representations about returns, or hiding risks in what they were promoting, driven by some conflict of interest (e.g., payments by issuers or promoters, or their own inventories of the securities in question). Or maybe they were "churning" their customers, persuading them to buy and sell actively just to accelerate the stream of commissions they received. As we have seen, today retail investors are more likely to look for investment products than individual securities—mutual funds, exchange-traded funds, annuities of various sorts, securities-based insurance products, and the like. These tend to have complicated cost and fee structures that may be difficult for investors to understand, imposing costs not only at the time of transaction but on a recurring basis over the life of the investment. We will look more closely at these in the next chapter. Such products can have many advantages for investors—diversification, professional management, record-keeping, and the like—but also create the possibility of high cost structures not necessarily justified by better risk-adjusted returns. This is one reason that Regulation Best Interest makes cost such a crucial part of the Disclosure, Care, and Conflict of Interest obligations. Recall from Chapter 3 that in efficient capital markets, it is doubtful that many ordinary investors can beat the market, and thus should not pay financial professionals considerable sums of money to try. That is behind the rapid growth of index investing, which as you saw creates its own set of issues. But investors pay billions of dollars in fees and expenses for active management, at considerable cost. *See* Del Guerco & Reuter, Mutual Fund Performance and the Incentive to Generate Alpha, 69 J. Fin. 1673 (2014). Of course, not all markets are efficient, and profitable investment opportunities exist (e.g., startup financing). But recall from Chapter 5 how various securities law rules effectively exclude non-sophisticated, nonaccredited investors from certain kinds of securities. *See* Rodrigues, Securities Law's Dirty Little Secret, 81 Fordham L. Rev. 3389 (2013). And even when there is a way to invest in these darker spaces, imbalances in sophistication make it unlikely that such investors will usually be on the profitable side of the transaction. As you think about new Rule 15*l*-1, consider the challenge regulation faces to address all these issues, especially if there is no strong regulatory appetite for challenging the basic business model on which the securities industry is based.

3. Form CRS. As a mechanism to improve disclosure and promote comparisons among financial professionals, the SEC adopted Form CRS ("customer relationship summary") to summarize for clients and customers the nature of their relationship, information about costs and expenses, and material conflicts of interest, among other things. This is used to convey some of the disclosure required by Rule 15*l*-1 but does not by itself necessarily satisfy the Disclosure Obligation. If a customer reads it carefully enough, it should convey the consequences of choosing a broker rather than an investment adviser.

4. Blue Sky Law. State securities regulation has long involved licensing, oversight, and enforcement with respect to broker-dealers operating in their jurisdictions. And many state officials were in favor of a federal fiduciary rule for all broker-dealers. When the SEC made clear that it would adopt Regulation Best Interest instead, a number of states began rulemaking efforts to impose a fiduciary obligation on broker-dealers subject to their oversight. This would no doubt trigger lawsuits by the securities industry claiming that these efforts would frustrate the SEC's efforts to establish a uniform regulatory approach and thus be subject to federal preemption.

PROBLEMS

18-4.   Like many brokerage firms, Klingon has long used luxury trips as an inducement for individual brokers to sell investment products that are especially revenue-generating—those who perform the best are treated lavishly. Informally, Klingon also uses the system to identify underperforming brokers, who are given special guidance to help them improve but if improvement is not forthcoming, are terminated. Is this permissible under Regulation Best Interest?

18-5.   You are chief legal and compliance officer at a medium-sized brokerage firm that specializes in serving the needs of individual investors over the long term, including retirement planning. The firm offers a limited number of mutual fund "families" to its customers, each of which pays your firm a portion of the revenue it receives in commissions, fees, and expenses incurred by customers who purchase shares in these funds, a practice known as revenue-sharing. These mutual funds are diversified and perform comparably to their peers in terms of portfolio returns. But because of the fees and expenses, they underperform many other funds in terms of annual returns to investors. The managers at your firm claim that the higher than normal fees and expenses encourage individual brokers to spend more time with their clients and guide them through the anxieties of contemporary investing. What does Regulation Best Interest require of your firm?

2.   Sales Practices: Litigation and Enforcement

Regulation Best Interest is built on the base of broker-dealer regulation fashioned by the SEC, FINRA, and the courts over the last century. The Care Obligation, in particular, addresses familiar issues with more clarity and emphasis, perhaps, but not in completely novel ways. As you consider what follows in this section, ask yourself what, if anything, the new rule adds to the solution of old problems.

In adopting Regulation Best Interest, the SEC indicated that it was not its intent to create any private right of action under the new rule, or any increased liability for broker-dealers beyond existing law. So a customer alleging injury will have to make either a rescission claim under Section 29(b) of the Exchange Act (which you studied in Chapter 14) or some federal or state law claim independent of the violation of the rule. While there may be a number of possible litigation strategies along these lines (especially if the nature of the broker-customer relationship can conceivably be characterized as fiduciary under common law), the most potent weapon has been something called the "shingle" theory under the workhorse of federal securities regulation, Rule 10b-5. According to this theory, by the very step of going into the business, a broker-dealer impliedly represents that he will deal fairly with customers. The theory has its judicial origins in the case of *Charles Hughes & Co. v. SEC*, 139 F.2d 434 (2d Cir. 1943), *cert. denied*, 321 U.S. 786 (1944), holding that it was a fraud for a broker-dealer to solicit customer transactions at excessive markups—that is, prices unreasonably in excess of the prevailing market. Broadly construed, the magic of the shingle theory is not only that it creates a duty of fair dealing, but also that any breach of that duty can easily be deemed fraudulent, since it also constitutes a breach of the implied representation. A finding of fraud, of course, both permits the SEC to impose administrative sanctions on its own and gives rise to damage liability in a private action under Rule 10b-5. *See Grandon v. Merrill Lynch & Co.*, 147 F.3d 184 (2d Cir. 1998). Is the shingle theory really a fiction? Too much of a fiction in light of the Supreme Court's insistence on actual deception in order to impose liability under Rule 10b-5? *See* Karmel, Is the Shingle Theory Dead?, 52 Wash. & Lee L. Rev. 1271 (1995). The materials that follow draw heavily on the shingle theory, which will continue to be tested in private litigation and arbitration even after the new regulatory structure. There is also a long line of authority that when making recommendations, broker-dealers have a "trust-based" obligation to disclose all material information in their possession that would matter to the customer in deciding whether to follow the recommendation, even if the relationship is not strictly fiduciary. *See, e.g.*, *Harris v. SEC*, 712 Fed. App'x 46 (2d Cir. 2017). This includes conflict of interest disclosures of the sort now addressed in Regulation Best Interest, but also any unusual risks associated with the investment being recommended.

a. *"Know Your Security"*

Hanly v. Securities and Exchange Commission
415 F.2d 589 (2d Cir. 1969)

TIMBERS, J. Five securities salesmen petition to review an order of the Securities and Exchange Commission which barred them from further association with any broker or dealer. The Commission found that petitioners, in the offer and sale of the stock of U.S. Sonics Corporation (Sonics) between September 1962 and August 1963, willfully violated the antifraud provisions of Section 17(a) of the Securities Act of 1933, Sections 10(b) and 15(c)(1) of the Securities Exchange Act of 1934, and Rule 10b-5. Specifically, the Commission held that

> the fraud in this case consisted of the optimistic representations or the recommendations . . . without disclosure of known or reasonably ascertainable adverse information which rendered them materially misleading. . . . It is clear that a salesman must not merely avoid affirmative misstatements when he recommends the stock to a customer; he must also disclose material adverse facts of which he is or should be aware.

Petitioners individually argue that their violations of the federal securities laws were not willful but involved at most good faith optimistic predictions concerning a speculative security, and that the sanctions imposed by the Commission exceeded legally permissible limits. . . .

Gladstone (along with Paras) first heard of Sonics in September 1962 during a conversation with one Roach who had been a sales manager for his prior employer, Edwards and Hanly. Roach compared Sonics to Ilikon, whose stock he had previously recommended and which had been highly successful. Sonics was praised for its good management, large research and development expenses and, most important, its development of a ceramic filter. In January 1963 Roach told Gladstone of the possibility of a domestic license and furnished him with a copy of an allegedly confidential 14 page report which predicted a bright future for the company. In February Gladstone met with Eric Kolm, Sonics president, who confirmed most of the statements in the report. During the spring of 1963 Gladstone learned of the licensing and merger negotiations mentioned above.

Evidence of affirmative misrepresentations by Gladstone to his customers regarding Sonics stock included the following: Sonics was a winner and would make money. It had a fabulous potential and would double or triple. It would make Xerox look like a standstill and would revolutionize the space age industry. Gladstone himself had purchased the stock for his own account and he would be able to retire and get rich on it. It had possibilities of skyrocketing and would probably double in price within six months to a year. Although it had not earned money in the past, prospects were good for earnings of $1 in a year. Sonics had signed a contract with General Instrument. The stock would go from 6 to 12 in two weeks and to 15 in the near future. The 14 page report had been written by Value Line. The company was not going bankrupt. Its products were perfected and it was already earning $1 per share. It was about to have a breakthrough on a new product that was fantastic and would revolutionize automobile and home radios.

Brokers and salesmen are "under a duty to investigate, and their violation of that duty brings them within the term 'willful' in the Exchange Act." Thus, a salesman cannot deliberately ignore that which he has a duty to know and recklessly state facts about matters of which he is ignorant. He must analyze sales literature and must not blindly accept recommendations made therein. The fact that his customers may be sophisticated and knowledgeable does not warrant a less stringent standard. Even where the purchaser follows the market activity of the stock and does not rely upon the salesman's statements, remedial sanctions may be imposed since reliance is not an element of fraudulent misrepresentation in this context. . . .

In summary, the standards by which the actions of each petitioner must be judged are strict. He cannot recommend a security unless there is an adequate and reasonable basis for such recommendation. He must disclose facts which he knows and those which are reasonably ascertainable. By his recommendation he implies that a reasonable investigation has been made and that his recommendation rests on the conclusions based on such investigation. Where the salesman lacks essential information about a security, he should disclose this as well as the risks which arise from his lack of information.

A salesman may not rely blindly upon the issuer for information concerning a company, although the degree of independent investigation which must be made by a securities dealer will vary in each case. Securities issued by smaller companies of recent origin obviously require more thorough investigation.

NOTES AND QUESTIONS

1.   The Duty to Investigate.   Under Regulation Best Interest, the duty to investigate is part of the Care Obligation. As noted, however, for customer claims there must be some independent doctrine like the shingle theory under Rule 10b-5. How is it that the failure to investigate becomes a fraud? Does this comport with the scienter requirement under Rule 10b-5? *See McDonald v. Alan Bush Brokerage Co.*, 863 F.2d 809 (11th Cir. 1989) (Rule 10b-5 requires more than just an unreasonable recommendation: There must be an awareness of the lack of knowledge and the propensity of the recommendation to mislead). And how much investigation is called for? Is it the equivalent of due diligence in the underwriting context? A useful discussion of broker-dealer responsibilities in this area is *In re Merrill Lynch, Pierce, Fenner & Smith*, [1977-1978 Transfer Binder] Fed. Sec. L. Rep. (CCH) ¶81,365 (1977). There, the Commission indicated that the duty of investigation is stronger for new companies than for seasoned ones and that "blind reliance" on company management for information is not acceptable: "A recommendation by a broker-dealer is perceived by a customer as (and it in fact should be) the product of independent and objective analysis [that] can only be achieved when the scope of the investigation is extended beyond the company's management." The Commission also noted that the duty of investigation is a continuing one, with a special obligation to monitor management projections to see if they indeed pan out.

Whatever the extent of the duty in general, it is worth also noting the operation of Rule 15c2-11, studied in Chapter 7, which prohibits a broker-dealer from publishing a quotation for an OTC security unless the firm has created a file (and can make it available to customers) that includes certain basic information about the issuer's business and management and reports of its financial condition.

2.   Disclaimers.   Would it be acceptable for the broker to make a practice of recommending securities without investigation, subject to a disclaimer indicating such absence? What sort of disclaimer would be necessary? (To some extent, this shades into consideration of the anti-waiver provision of the Exchange Act, Section 29(a), discussed in Chapter 14 and considered further in connection with securities arbitration, infra.) In an old general counsel's opinion, the SEC staff took the position that hedge clauses by brokers—for example, stating that information has been obtained from certain sources and is believed to be reliable, but that reliability is not guaranteed—are not in violation of the anti-waiver clause so long as the statements made about source and belief are indeed true. Securities Act Release No. 3411 (1951). How far can this logic be extended? FINRA Rule 2111, which today expresses the "know your security" obligation, prohibits disclaimers. In adopting Regulation Best Interest, the SEC made clear that its requirements cannot be waived or disclaimed.

3.   Penny Stocks.   The market for low-priced securities, so-called penny or microcap stocks, is fertile ground for misrepresentations and omissions by brokers using boiler room tactics. Many of these calls are made from predetermined "scripts." *See SEC v. Hasho,* 784 F. Supp. 1059 (S.D.N.Y. 1992). This potential for telemarketing and online abuse has led to special regulation of sales practices in this area, to be considered in the next section.

4.   False Tips.   What if a stockbroker tells a customer that he has secret inside information that makes a particular purchase a route to risk-free profits? In fact, he has no inside information and is just pushing the stock. If the customer sues for fraud, can the broker defend by saying that insider trading is illegal, so that the customer is barred from recovery for attempting to engage in it? *See Bateman Eichler, Hill Richards, Inc. v. Berner,* 472 U.S. 299 (1985) (no, because the parties are not "in pari delicto").

PROBLEM

18-6.   John Frederick was discussing investment strategy with his new broker and indicated that he had an interest in computer stocks. The broker took from a drawer behind her desk a copy of an article entitled "Can Dallas Have Its Own IBM?," a glowing story about a local firm that appeared in a local business monthly. Her words to John were "Take a look at this—it seems really interesting." After reading the article, John bought 100 shares of the company's stock. Unfortunately, the article was grossly misleading, and a careful look at the company's filings with the SEC would have raised serious questions about the optimism. The broker, however, had not done any investigation to that end. Did the broker commit a fraud in violation of Rule 10b-5?

b.   Investment Analysts and Their Conflicts of Interest

Implicit in the "know your security" rule is the idea that customers are entitled to trust their brokers to make carefully researched, objective recommendations. *Hanly* and its progeny explore the first prong of that entitlement, the duty of due diligence. But what about the objectivity of the advice? Chapter 4 offered an introduction to this problem in the context of analyst recommendations in connection with public offerings. The problem—and the regulatory responses—reach much more broadly, however.

In the aftermath of Enron, public attention was directed to potentially pernicious aspects of "sell-side" investment analysis, triggered by the realization that just before the company's bankruptcy, most well-known analysts were still rating the company a "buy." (*Sell-side analysts* are those employed by brokerage firms to make recommendations to current and potential customers, while *buy-side analysts* are those employed by investors, such as mutual funds, on a proprietary basis.) In fact, among academics at least—and gradually within the SEC—concerns about the objectivity of analyst ratings had been growing for some time. *See, e.g.,* Michaely & Womack, Conflicts of Interest and the Credibility of Underwriter Analyst Recommendations, 12 Rev. Fin. Stud. 653

(1999). While the specific concerns were numerous, the main one was that investment banking departments were enlisting the firm's analysts in the effort to attract business from issuers, which is more likely if the analysts' projections and recommendations are pleasing to the issuer's management. The fear was that analysts' compensation would be tied, in large part, to fees generated by investment banking, rather than the quality of their research.

A prominent investigation into analyst conflicts was launched by the New York Attorney General, Eliot Spitzer, who claimed substantial evidence of abuse. Internal e-mails allegedly described issuers as "a piece of crap" or confessed that there was "nothing interesting about the company except banking fees" at a time when buy recommendations were outstanding and hence customers of the firm were encouraged to invest in them. The firm he first targeted, Merrill Lynch, settled by agreeing to certain internal reforms and payment of $100 million.

As noted in Chapter 4, the NYSE and the NASD also became involved, considering and then quickly adopting a number of rule changes. Besides a number of rules relating to research in connection with public offerings, the rules target some structural issues. For example, investment banking departments are prohibited from supervising or controlling analysts. The rules also called for more extensive disclosure of conflicts of interest and recommendation practices.

Congress was not satisfied with self-regulatory reform, and the Sarbanes-Oxley Act required further efforts at curbing conflicts of interest. This led the SROs to return for a second round of rules, which were implemented in July 2003. Exchange Act Release 34-48252, July 29, 2003. Among other things, the second set of rules: (1) prohibit analysts from issuing "booster shot" research that supplements or reiterates a buy recommendation around the expiration of a lock-up on insider selling as part of a public offering; (2) bar analyst participation in "pitch meetings" designed to solicit issuer business; (3) limit pre-publication review of reports by persons not directly responsible for research in the firm; and (4) bar retaliation against an analyst who issues a report adversely affecting the firm's investment banking relationships.

While the SROs were at work, the SEC also entered into the regulatory arena by adopting Regulation AC. That rule requires analysts to certify that their recommendations, including those made in public appearances, accurately reflect their personal views about the issuer, and to indicate whether their compensation was, is, or will be related to specific recommendations or views contained in their reports.

During this time, enforcement proceedings went forward as well, with New York extending the scope of its investigation to include conflicts at other firms. Fearing that the issue was going away from federal oversight, the SEC and the SROs intervened and sought, with the states, a "global settlement" in the area of analyst conflicts. Under the settlement, ten large investment banking firms agreed to sever the links between analysis and investment banking and to provide their customers, for five years, with research purchased from no less than three independent research firms. Most dramatically, the ten firms also agreed to penalties and restitution totaling $1.4 billion, at least some of which would be paid out through a fund for the benefit of aggrieved investors. *See* SEC Press Release: SEC, NY Attorney General, NASD, NASAA, NYSE and State Regulators Announce Historic Agreement to Reform Investment Practices (Dec. 20, 2002).

Although these initiatives are substantial, questions remain. Most pressing is do these reforms result in less "sell-side" research than before? Given that the research is largely made available for free, are there sufficient sources of income other than banking fees to justify the firms' investment in research? Would a drop-off in sell-side coverage be a bad thing? What would the effect be on market efficiency? *See* Fisch, Does Analyst Independence Sell Investors Short?, 55 UCLA L. Rev. 39 (2007). Recall from Chapter 4 that in the JOBS Act of 2012, Congress relaxed some (though by no means all) of the protections associated with analyst involvement in the initial public offerings of "emerging growth companies." There are also serious questions about whether the reforms were adequate to rein in analyst enthusiasm when their employers were keen to get a banking mandate. In a 2014 FINRA enforcement action charging a number of investment banks with failure to supervise, analysts were quoted as saying "I would crawl on broken glass . . . to get this deal" and "my whole life is about posturing for the Toys R Us IPO." FINRA News Release, Dec. 11, 2014. On the complicated ways analyst biases of various sorts play out, *see* Malmendier & Shanthikumar, Do Analysts Speak in Two Tongues?, 27 Rev. Fin. Stud. 1287 (2014).

PROBLEM

18-7. Mary Striker is a relatively new analyst at Milgrom Sedgwick & Co., a multiservice financial firm. She has prepared a draft report on an up-and-coming company in the industry she covers, making very bullish predictions about its likely revenue growth and market performance. At a meeting, her immediate supervisor was harshly critical, suggesting that she had "gone off the deep end" given the company's limited record of profitability. After much screaming and yelling about rookie analysts who always think they've found the next Microsoft, he insisted that she tone down the recommendation in more neutral terms. She complied, but was very upset because she was quite proud of the research and believes the company to be significantly undervalued. What are Mary's obligations under Regulation AC?

c. Suitability

i. The Basic Obligation

▌Brown v. E.F. Hutton Group Inc.
991 F.2d 1020 (2d Cir. 1993)

JACOBS, J. . . . Plaintiffs-appellants, are approximately 400 presumably unsophisticated, income-oriented investors in a limited partnership called the Hutton/Indian Wells 1983 Energy Income Fund, Ltd. (the "Partnership"). According to the Partnership's October 14, 1983 prospectus (the "Prospectus"), it was organized to acquire properties upon which existing oil and gas wells are located and to provide regular cash distributions to investors from sales of oil and gas produced from those properties.

After their investments allegedly became worthless, the plaintiffs-appellants (the "Limited Partners") brought suit in the United States District Court for the Southern District of New York against Hutton, the Indian Wells Production Company and related entities (collectively, the "defendants"). In their amended complaint, the Limited Partners assert two claims arising under §10(b) and two claims arising under state common law theories of fraud and breach of fiduciary duty. . . .

A. ALLEGATIONS IN THE AMENDED COMPLAINT

The district court, for purposes of Hutton's summary judgment motion and without objection from Hutton, accepted as true the following allegations from the amended complaint: (a) that each of the more than 400 Limited Partners was unsophisticated; (b) that each Limited Partner told a Hutton account executive that his or her investment objectives included some combination of income, capital appreciation, tax benefits and savings; and (c) that the Hutton account executives gave oral assurance to each Limited Partner that the Partnership had either no risk or low risk. Hutton's motion did, however, contest the Limited Partners' allegations that they made their purchases in justifiable reliance on the brokers' oral representations and that the Brochure and Prospectus were materially false and misleading.

B. THE OFFERING MATERIALS

As the Limited Partners contend, the Brochure depicts the Partnership's financial outlook in bright terms. In this regard, the Brochure distinguishes the Partnership from prototypically risky oil and gas investments by emphasizing that the purchase of "only producing oil and gas properties" eliminates exploration risk. The Brochure's disclosure concerning other risks is by reference to the Prospectus. The jacket of the Brochure contains the following caution:

> The use of this material is authorized only when preceded or accompanied by a prospectus for Hutton Indian Wells 1983 Energy Income Fund, Ltd. Prospective investors are encouraged to read the prospectus, including the section entitled "Risk Factors."

Although the Brochure again and again references the risk disclosure sections in the Prospectus, nowhere does the Brochure quote or otherwise recite the cautionary statements in the Prospectus.

After a review of the Brochure in its entirety there can be no doubt that it is a selling tool. In contrast, the Prospectus' disclosure of the Partnership's risks is thorough and materially complete, if not decidedly glum. The cover of the Prospectus warns that "[n]o person has been authorized to give any information or to make any representations, other than those contained in this prospectus, and if given or made, such information or representations must not be relied upon." The first page of the prospectus states:

THIS OFFERING INVOLVES CERTAIN RISKS
See "RISK FACTORS"

The "RISK FACTORS" section takes up roughly three single spaced pages.
It is prominently featured immediately after the opening "SUMMARY OF
OFFERING" section. The "RISK FACTORS" section states at the outset that
"[t]here can be no assurance that properties selected will produce oil or gas in
the quantities or at the cost anticipated, or that they will not cease producing
entirely." It ends by disclosing the Limited Partners' potential obligations in the
event the Partnership is "involuntarily liquidated because of insolvency." . . .

II.   §10(B) UNSUITABILITY CLAIM

In granting Hutton's motion for summary judgment on the Limited
Partners' §10(b) unsuitability claim, the district court concluded that "the offering materials are not misleading as a matter of law, or, to the same effect, that
plaintiffs' reliance on certain portions of the materials was not reasonable as a
matter of law." 735 F. Supp. at 1200. The district court also concluded that the
Limited Partners could not have reasonably relied on the alleged oral representations by Hutton account executives. Id. at 1202. Based on our review of the
facts and the law, we believe the district court reached the proper result.

This Court recognized the viability of a §10(b) unsuitability claim in *Clark
v. John Lamula Investors, Inc.*, 583 F.2d 594, 600-01 (2d Cir. 1978). A plaintiff
must prove (1) that the securities purchased were unsuited to the buyer's needs;
(2) that the defendant knew or reasonably believed the securities were unsuited
to the buyer's needs; (3) that the defendant recommended or purchased the
unsuitable securities for the buyer anyway; (4) that, with scienter, the defendant made material misrepresentations (or, owing a duty to the buyer, failed to
disclose material information) relating to the suitability of the securities; and
(5) that the buyer justifiably relied to its detriment on the defendant's fraudulent conduct. *See generally* id. at 600; *National Union Fire Insurance Co. v. Woodhead*,
917 F.2d 752, 757 (2d Cir. 1990). Scienter may be inferred by finding that the
defendant knew or reasonably believed that the securities were unsuited to
the investor's needs, misrepresented or failed to disclose the unsuitability of
the securities, and proceeded to recommend or purchase the securities anyway. A plaintiff's burden with respect to the reliance element of an unsuitability claim, as in other §10(b) and Rule 10b-5 actions, may vary depending on
whether the claim alleges fraudulent representations or fraudulent omissions.
See Burke v. Jacoby, 981 F.2d 1372, 1378-79 (2d Cir. 1992).

A.   DISCLOSURE OF SUITABILITY

The first count of the amended complaint generally asserts that Hutton's
account executives' oral recommendations of the Partnership as a low risk, conservative investment misled the Limited Partners into purchasing unsuitable
securities. The Limited Partners acknowledge that Hutton sent the Brochure
and Prospectus, and that they received those documents; they insist, however,

that the Brochure and Prospectus (a) fail to state expressly that the Partnership is unsuited to an investor who seeks an opportunity for "no risk," "low risk" or "conservative" capital appreciation, income or savings, and (b) understate, obscure or elide discussion of the real risks of the investment. We disagree.

We find that the Limited Partners' reliance on the oral statements presumptively made by Hutton as to the low risk, conservative character of the investment is not justified as a matter of law and that the alleged oral statements are contradicted by the offering materials sent to the Limited Partners. We find further that the information available to the Limited Partners about the suitability of their investments was materially complete and not misleading. . . .

Although for present purposes we presume that the Limited Partners are unsophisticated investors and that the brokers initiated the transactions, . . . other relevant factors preclude a conclusion that the alleged reliance could have been justifiable. Initially, we note that none of the Limited Partners allege the existence of a fiduciary relationship or of a longstanding business or personal relationship with Hutton or its brokers. The dominant considerations here, however, are that the Hutton brokers forwarded the offering materials to the Limited Partners; that the offering materials detailed the investment characteristics bearing upon suitability; that they did so in comprehensive and understandable language; and that the offering materials thereby contradicted the brokers' alleged general assurances. . . . No reasonable investor reviewing the disclosure documents could fail to appreciate that the Partnership could result in a total loss.

The disclosure of risks adequately informed the Limited Partners that the investment was not suitable for the purpose of generating low risk capital appreciation or income, and the disclosure of the investment's limited transferability and liquidity adequately informed the Limited Partners that the investment was not a suitable savings vehicle. Thus, the information made available to the Limited Partners accurately reflected the suitability of the investment (or lack thereof) for the individual investors; the Limited Partners' asserted reliance on the brokers' alleged oral statements, without further inquiry, was therefore reckless and unjustifiable.

We also find that the Brochure and Prospectus provided the Limited Partners with full and objective disclosure of non-misleading factual material. That is all they were entitled to receive. There is no requirement that written offering materials counteract the enticements of salesmen by anticipating each sales pitch and rebutting it explicitly. . . .

NOTES AND QUESTIONS

1. Suitability as a Rule of Law. The SROs for the brokerage industry have long had suitability rules as part of their authority to promote the just and equitable principles of the trade. *See* FINRA Rules 2090 ("know your customer") and 2111 ("suitability," which is described in terms of "reasonable basis suitability," "customer specific suitability" and "quantitative suitability"). Of these, the classic suitability obligation is the second, which requires that a broker, based on a particular customer's investment profile, has a reasonable basis to believe that the recommendation is suitable for that customer. This is now embedded in Regulation Best Interest under the Care Obligation. Under the suitability

doctrine as generally understood, the broker must attempt to obtain and analyze a broad array of customer-specific factors to support this determination.
Suitability issues often arise in broker-customer disputes. While most courts
say that there is no implied private right of action under SRO rules, the trend
toward mandatory arbitration of customer-broker disputes, discussed infra, gives
claimants wider latitude in styling their claims, and many invoke the suitability
standards one way or another. Arbitration will be discussed later in the chapter.

2. *What Renders an Investment Unsuitable?* Even though plaintiffs lost in
Brown, the basic authority of courts to grant recovery to customers whose brokers have made unsuitable recommendations is well established. In *Clark v. John
Lamula Investors, Inc.*, 583 F.2d 594 (2d Cir. 1978), an unsuitability claim was
upheld where a recent retiree had $100,000 to invest from a divorce settlement
and wanted a yield of $1,000 per month. The broker sold her (at a considerable
markup) convertible debentures that had the desired yield. She was not told,
however, of the risk associated with the debentures and contended that she
would not have bought them had she known of the risk necessary to obtain that
yield. What guides the matching of risk and return that is appropriate under
the suitability rule for the individual investor? Is it the client's age? *See Lefkowitz
v. Smith Barney, Harris Upham & Co.*, 804 F.2d 154 (1st Cir. 1986) (fact that plaintiff was aged and ill did not by itself dictate lower-risk securities). What about
the client's ability to understand the risks? *See Follansbee v. Davis, Skaggs & Co.*,
681 F.2d 673 (9th Cir. 1983) (college graduate who had taken graduate economics course and could understand financial statements denied recovery). In
the end, it may well turn upon just how extreme the facts are, including the relative dependence of the plaintiff on the income. In this regard, consider *Leone
v. Advest, Inc.*, 624 F. Supp. 297, 304 (S.D.N.Y. 1986), where the plaintiff, a 58-
year-old teletype operator, lived alone but supported her father in a senior citizens home. Wishing a secure flow of income, she committed her substantial nest
egg of $413,000 to her broker, who said she could become a millionaire within
five years and enjoy a tax-free income of $30,000 per year. The broker convinced
Ms. Leone to invest in commodities futures, options, and tax shelters. Hers was
not the promised land, however, for within five months the account had dwin-
dled to $240,000 and in two years to $60,000. On these facts, the court held
the plaintiff had stated a cause of action against the broker for recommending
unsuitable securities.

Other questions abound in this area as well. Is the riskiness of a single security the sole factor if the client has many other securities that are substantially
less risky? *See* Booth, The Suitability Rule, Investor Diversification and Using
Spread to Measure Risk, 54 Bus. Law. 1599 (1999). Should we be concerned
solely with the relative riskiness of the specific security in question or with the
trading strategy as a whole? If the client is truly unsophisticated, is the mere
disclosure of the risks of an aggressive trading strategy likely to be sufficient?

3. *The Duty to Read.* Is it fair to impose upon a customer, sophisticated
or not, a duty to read carefully the dense prospectuses relating to a security
that has been recommended as suitable by a broker whom the customer trusts?
After all, isn't the main reason customers rely upon (and are so willing to compensate) brokers and other sources of advice to avoid having to make their own

valuation and suitability determinations? The SEC has been far less enamored with the duty to read in customer-broker cases than the courts. *E.g., In re Foster*, 57 S.E.C. Docket 455 (1994) (expressly disagreeing with *Brown*). Indeed, it takes the position that disclosure of risk is irrelevant if the broker is recommending an unsuitable security. *E.g., In re Stein*, 79 S.E.C. Docket 1777 (Feb. 10, 2003). What does Regulation Best Interest say about practices like this? Note that the Care Obligation is distinct from the Disclosure Obligation, and the SEC has stressed that disclosure alone cannot justify a breach of the rule's duty of care. Assuming there is a duty to read in general, what would you do with a case where the broker tells the customer to disregard the disclosures as a mere formality or just so much "lawyers' talk"? *See Bruschi v. Brown*, 876 F.2d 1526, 1528 (11th Cir. 1989).

4.   The Limits of the Suitability Rule: The Aggressive Customer.   What should a broker do with regard to a customer—perhaps someone on a fixed income or of relatively little sophistication—who insists on engaging in risky, and clearly imprudent, transactions? Can the broker at that point recommend securities that satisfy the investor's desires? *See generally* Mundheim, Professional Responsibilities of Broker-Dealers: The Suitability Doctrine, 1965 Duke L.J. 445. For a case that addresses this question—and serves as a useful reminder that questions of broker-dealer obligations are a matter of state as well as federal law—*see Twomey v. Mitchum, Jones & Templeton Inc.*, 262 Cal. App. 2d 690, 69 Cal. Rptr. 222 (1968). Occasionally, the claim is made that even when making no recommendations at all, the broker has a duty to rescue a customer from buying unsuitable securities; this is sometimes referred to as the "economic suicide" doctrine. *See generally* Gedicks, Suitability Claims and Purchases of Unrecommended Securities: An Agency Theory of Broker-Dealer Liability, 37 Ariz. St. L.J. 535 (2005); Black & Gross, Economic Suicide: The Collision of Ethics and Risk in Securities Law, 64 U. Pitt. L. Rev. 483 (2003).

As a separate matter, should the broker be required to initiate an inquiry into the customer's financial resources and sophistication? Or can the broker base the recommendation upon such information as is volunteered by the customer or is otherwise readily apparent? FINRA's "know your customer" rule (Rule 2090) provides explicitly that the broker shall use "reasonable diligence, in regard to the opening and maintenance of every account, to know (and retain) the essential facts concerning every customer." For better or worse, application of the suitability rule must take account of the fact that many customers of broker-dealers are quite greedy, placing as much (if not more) pressure upon the broker to generate profits as the broker places upon the customer in order to generate commissions. Many suitability cases appear to arise only after particular investments have turned sour, leading a customer who heretofore was satisfied with a program of aggressive, risky investments to conclude that such investments were "overly risky" and hence unsuitable. In this light, many courts have shown caution in this area, demanding a fairly concrete showing that recommendations or transactions were contrary to either an expressed desire or a manifest need to avoid excessive risk. *See, e.g., Lefkowitz v. Smith Barney, Harris Upham & Co.*, 804 F.2d 154 (1st Cir. 1986).

5.   Online Brokerage Accounts.   There has been an explosive growth in the number of online brokers. Initially, Internet-based brokerage firms specialized in very low-cost execution, with no investment advice at all. But as competition has grown, many of these brokers have looked for ways to offer a more attractive package of services to customers—especially ways that might help them through the thicket of web-based investment information. *See* SEC Special Study—On-Line Brokerage: Keeping Apace of Cyberspace, [1999-2000 Transfer Binder] Fed. Sec. L. Rep. (CCH) ¶86,222 (Nov. 22, 1999). For example, firms might track previous inquiries and investment decisions to build a customer preference profile, and then "push" customized data onto the customer's screen so as to bring information about other attractive investment possibilities into view. Would this kind of marketing effort trigger an enforceable suitability obligation? What about brokers' use of "robo-adviser" tools? A FINRA Report on Digital Investment Advice, dated March 15, 2016, stressed that they "cannot rely on the tool as a substitute for the requisite knowledge about the securities or customer necessary to make a suitable recommendation."

6. *Penny Stocks and "Microcap" Fraud.*   One substantial problem area—the province of the classic boiler rooms—has been "cold call" telephone solicitations pushing the stocks of small issuers whose shares trade in very thin markets at low prices. These shares have historically been referred to as "penny stocks." Both the "know your security" and "know your customer" principles are addressed to this situation. But prompted by evidence of continuing abuses in this area and Congress' enactment of the Penny Stock Reform Act of 1990, the SEC has strengthened its regulation through the adoption of a special set of penny stock rules (Rule 15g-1 through 9). Some of these provisions are concerned primarily with disclosure: A customer in a penny stock transaction initiated by a brokerage firm that does a substantial amount of penny stock business (*penny stock* being defined in Rule 3a51-1 as stocks of smaller issuers trading at less than $5 per share, with numerous other restrictions and exclusions) must receive a form document warning investors about the generic risks and pitfalls of investing in penny stocks, and must receive information regarding both the price quotations and the compensation paid to the brokers at the time of the transaction. But there is also an affirmative suitability requirement that must be satisfied prior to executing the transaction. Most notable about the requirements—especially the basic selling rule, Rule 15g-9—is the way they seek to disrupt the high-pressure telephone sales tactics. A penny stock transaction with a new customer is unlawful unless the broker has previously approved the investor's account. Account approval in turn requires first that the investor provide the broker with *written* data regarding his or her financial situation and objectives and sign an account form. The broker must then return to the investor a *written* statement with additional disclosures. Even at this point, a transaction can be executed only upon *written* instructions from the customer. Is this formality necessary? Though few doubt that the penny stock market is full of abuses, there have been serious expressions of concern that these paperwork burdens—and the resulting chill on the salesperson's arts—will adversely affect the legitimate capital-raising efforts of small companies. For an exploration of the regulatory difficulties in this, *see* Goldstein et al., An Investment Masquerade: A Descriptive Overview of Penny Stock Fraud and the Federal Securities Laws, 47 Bus. Law. 773 (1992). In 2005, the SEC modernized the penny stock rules to deal with such innovations as e-mail, which

obviously provided a means to speed up what the Commission wanted to be a slowed-down process. The revised rules mandate a two-day cooling-off period, regardless of the method of communication used by the brokers. *See* Exchange Act Release No. 34-51983 (July 7, 2005).

PROBLEM

18-8. John Lee is an 84-year-old widower living on a combination of Social Security and the proceeds of a life insurance policy on his wife, who died a couple of years ago. He and his broker have to this point invested in conservative securities and bank certificates of deposit. Recently, John came to his broker and told him that he simply can't "make ends meet" on the income from his current investments. He brought clippings from magazines describing investment possibilities that offer much higher yields, and said that he needs at least 25 percent more income. He fears that without more money he will become a burden to his grown children, which he does not want. His broker explained that "with yield comes risk." If John persists, what should the broker do?

ii. Suitability, Risk Disclosure, and the Sophisticated Investor

As noted in earlier chapters, the recent meltdown of the credit markets was the product, initially at least, of troubles arising out of the widespread investment in securitized subprime mortgage loans. One of the important questions emerging from this is whether securities firms inappropriately sold CDOs and other complex instruments to institutional investors who were unaware of the risks embedded in them and who thought they were buying safe, investment-grade products. *See* Thompson, Market Makers and Vampire Squid: Regulating Securities Markets After the Financial Meltdown, 89 Wash. U. L. Rev. 323-376 (2011). Naturally, the meltdown triggered numerous lawsuits by institutional investors. What duties do securities salespeople owe to institutional customers? What hurdles stand in the way of recovery by the customers? Consider the following case and problem.

Banca Cremi, S.A. v. Alex. Brown & Sons, Inc.
132 F.3d 1017 (4th Cir. 1997)

[Banca Cremi, a Mexican bank with nearly $5 billion in assets, bought a number of collateralized mortgage obligations (CMOs) from the Baltimore-based investment banking firm of Alex. Brown & Co. CMOs are interests in pools of mortgage obligations. As commonly structured, the interests in a pool of mortgage obligations are divided into different *tranches*—classes that have different classes of risk and return. Banca Cremi had purchased both "inverse floaters" and "inverse interest-only strips," both of which were at the high end of the risk spectrum. Inverse floaters have a fixed principal amount and earn interest at a rate that moves inversely to a specified index rate. They earn high returns if rates decline or remain constant, but lose substantial value if interest rates increase. Inverse IO strips do not receive principal payments, but receive a rate of interest that also floats inversely to an index rate. At first, the bank played the CMO market aggressively, and made considerable profits. When interest rates went up unexpectedly in 1994, however, much of the CMO market collapsed and the bank lost around $21 million on an original purchase price of some $40 million. Banca Cremi sued Alex. Brown on a number of grounds related to fraud and suitability. In general, it alleged a series of misrepresentations and nondisclosures relating to the risks associated with the kinds of CMO interests it had purchased. In considering defendants' motion for summary judgment, the court acknowledged, citing the *Brown* case, that the crucial issue in litigation like this under Rule 10b-5 is whether the plaintiff had a right to rely, and agreed that the proper standard for barring plaintiff's claim is whether its failure of diligence amounted to recklessness. In discussing this issue, drawing from a list of factors as set forth in *Myers v. Finkle*, 950 F.2d 165 (4th Cir. 1991), Judge Magill said:]

The first *Myers* factor, the sophistication of the investor, has long been a critical element in determining whether an investor was entitled to §10(b) relief. *See Kohler v. Kohler Co.*, 319 F.2d 634, 642 (7th Cir. 1963) (considering an investor's "business acumen" and access to "extrinsic sources of sound business advice" to conclude there was no reliance, although the transaction might not have been fair if the investor "had been a novice"); *List v. Fashion Park, Inc.*, 340 F.2d 457, 463-64 (2d Cir. 1965) (no reliance where investor was "an experienced and successful investor in securities" who did not ask his broker for information regarding the claimed omission). A sophisticated investor requires less information to call a "[mis-]representation into question" than would an unsophisticated investor. *Angelos*, 762 F.2d at 530. Likewise, when material information is omitted, a sophisticated investor is more likely to "know[] enough so that the. . .omission still leaves him cognizant of the risk." Id.

When an investor is an individual, this Court looks to several factors to determine if the investor is sophisticated, including "wealth[,] . . . age, education, professional status, investment experience, and business background." *Myers*, 950 F.2d at 168. Some of these factors may not be perfectly suited for application to an institutional investor. *Cf.* C. Edward Fletcher, Sophisticated Investors Under the Federal Securities Laws, 1988 Duke L.J. 1081, 1149-53 (reviewing factors gauging sophistication of individual investors, and concluding that there should be a "conclusive presumption" that all institutional investors are sophisticated). However, the factors which are relevant to an institution strongly support the sophistication of the Bank. The Bank, with assets of $5 billion, is unquestionably wealthy. In addition, while the Bank's investment choices may have been unwise, its investment experience is extraordinary, and far surpasses most sophisticated individual investors. As a business entity, the Bank obviously has a business background, and its employees—hired for their business expertise—had extensive education and experience in economics and finance.

Despite its extensive investment experience and extraordinary resources, the Bank nevertheless contends that, while it may be sophisticated in certain types of investments, it was not sophisticated in CMO investments. *See, e.g., McAnally v. Gildersleeve*, 16 F.3d 1493, 1500 (8th Cir. 1994) (recognizing that an individual's sophistication in "stocks and bonds" did not necessarily suggest sophistication in commodities futures options); Order Approving NASD Suitability Interpretation, 61 Fed. Reg. 44,100, 44,112 (1996) (NASD Fair Practice Rules) (in approving NASD fair practice rules, SEC recognized that even a sophisticated institutional investor may not be capable of understanding a "particular investment risk"). The Bank argues that deposition testimony of its employees and an expert witness that the Bank was unsophisticated in CMO investments created a genuine issue of fact.

We reject this argument. The Bank's NNI unit, whose function was to invest Bank funds in dollar-denominated investments, employed three well-educated investment professionals to select a sound, but profitable, investment strategy. Mendez, Aguirre, and Buentello conducted a thorough, independent investigation of the benefits of risks of CMO investments by attending seminars, purchasing treatises on the subject, and developing a multi-step review process for each CMO investment. Rather than blindly relying on Epley and Alex. Brown, the record shows that the Bank rejected Epley's suggested investments far more often than it accepted them. Indeed, the Bank consulted with five other brokerage houses regarding CMO investments, and each of these brokerage houses gave the Bank detailed information describing the benefits and the risks of CMO investments. After a year of trading in CMOs, the Bank displayed a knowledge and an aggressiveness that belie its current claim that it did not understand CMO investments. *See J.A.* at 447-48 (indicating dramatic price changes over short time periods for many of the Bank's profitable CMO trades: FNMA 92 112 SC was sold after one day at a profit reflecting an annual increase of over 350 percent, FN 93-115 SB was sold after two weeks at a profit reflecting an annual increase of around 58 percent; FNMA 1992 162 SB was sold after two weeks at a profit reflecting an annual increase of around 38 percent); NASD Fair Practice Rules, 61 Fed. Reg. at 44,105 n.20 ("[An institution] who initially needed help understanding a potential investment may ultimately develop an understanding and make an independent investment decision."). Accordingly, we agree with the district court that the Bank was a "sophisticated investor" for the purposes of this case. *See Banca Cremi v. Alex. Brown*, 955 F. Supp. 499, 515 (D. Md. 1997). . . .

In this case the Bank had access to an extraordinary wealth of information regarding CMOs. With few exceptions, the depth and breadth of this information illustrated one overriding point: investments in CMOs, while potentially very profitable, were undoubtedly highly risky. As a sophisticated business entity handling five billion dollars of other people's money, the Bank had the advice of its own employees and a horde of the defendants' competitors. Nevertheless, the Bank invested in CMOs through arm's length dealings with the defendants. While the vast majority of these investments were profitable for the Bank, a half-dozen proved disastrously timed, and the Bank now alleges that its misfortune resulted from its justifiable naivete in listening to the defendants' purported lies. As in any "action [] for fraud, reliance on false statements must be accompanied by a right to rely." *Foremost Guar. Corp. v. Meritor Sav. Bank*, 910 F.2d 118, 125 (4th Cir. 1990). Here, the Bank lost its right to rely by its own recklessness. The Bank continued to purchase CMOs after it had sufficient information, given its sophistication, to be well apprised of the risks it would face were interest rates to rise. Given that the Bank was aware of the risks involved in investing in CMOs, the Bank was not justified in relying on Epley and Alex. Brown's alleged omissions and misstatements. Accordingly, we affirm the district court's grant of summary judgment against the Bank on this claim. . . .

NOTES AND QUESTIONS

1. *Suitability and the Institutional Investor.* Are there any circumstances where an institutional customer—presumably, with professional in-house staff—should be able to sue a broker for selling unsuitable securities? This issue has become a contentious one, particularly in suits arising from the sale of derivatives. Well before the most recent financial crisis, many large companies (e.g., Procter & Gamble, Gibson Greeting Cards) had lost millions of dollars on such transactions and contended that their sellers failed to warn them of the risky nature of what they were getting into. In a case arising from the sale of derivatives by Bankers Trust (BT) to Gibson Greeting Cards, a salesperson for BT was quoted as saying, "These guys [the financial people at Gibson] have done some pretty wild stuff. And you know, they probably do not understand it quite as well as they should. I think that they have a pretty good understanding of it, but not perfect. And that's like perfect for us." *In the Matter of BT Securities Corp.*, [1994-1995 Transfer Binder] Fed. Sec. L. Rep. (CCH) ¶85,477, at 86,114 (Dec. 22, 1994).

Not surprisingly, the global financial crisis led to many disputes between investment bankers and institutional customers about "toxic" complex financial products and derivatives. Perhaps responding to unfavorable cases like *Banca Cremi*, many of these cases have been brought in the New York state courts, where plaintiffs have had more success in overcoming reasonable reliance defenses. *See, e.g., ACA Fin. Guar. Corp. v. Goldman Sachs & Co.*, 25 N.Y.3d 1043 (2015).

These cases are complicated by the fact that derivatives, being customized synthetic instruments, have no readily ascertainable value; buyers are often forced to rely upon the extraordinarily complex mathematical models and data generated by the sellers. In many of these cases, moreover, sellers allegedly lied about the investments—if so, making it unnecessary to resort to a suitability analysis. Assuming no affirmative misrepresentations, however, are institutional buyers just trying to shift the blame for their own imprudence in going forward with a transaction they knew they did not understand, especially given sellers' obvious conflict of interest? On the other hand, are there situations where even professional investors may reasonably be led by experienced and reputable salespeople to trust in a recommendation for an investment whose risks they do not appreciate? Here, of course, we must consider the wide range in sophistication of agents for institutional investors. *See West Virginia v. Morgan Stanley & Co.*, 459 S.E.2d 906, 917-919 (W. Va. 1995), where Morgan Stanley was charged with unlawfully participating in a violation of a state statute barring speculative investments for public funds. The court observed that the state officials who enthusiastically purchased risky securities, though "professional" in one sense, "were not potential nominees for the Nobel Prize in Economics" and, "[l]ike so many enthusiastic and ambitious persons before them, tended to confuse profits in a bull market with intelligence." On this problem generally, *see* Poser, Liability of Broker-Dealers for Unsuitable Recommendations to Institutional Investors, 2001 BYU L. Rev. 1493; Langevoort, Selling Hope, Selling Risk: Some Lessons for Law from Behavioral Economics About Stockbrokers and Sophisticated Customers, 84 Cal. L. Rev. 627 (1996). Recall from Chapter 10 that the Dodd-Frank Act has led to the adoption of many new rules relating to the sale of both derivatives and securitized debt instruments, including a ban on securitization participants engaging in any transaction that would involve or result in any material conflict of interest with respect to any investor in a securitization transaction.

2. *FINRA Rules and Regulation Best Interest.* FINRA has made clear that the obligation to recommend only suitable investments extends to institutional customers unless the broker "has a reasonable basis to believe that the institutional customer is capable of evaluating investment risks independently, both in general and with respect to the particular transactions and investment strategies" involved, and "the institutional customer affirmatively indicates that it is exercising independent judgment in evaluating the . . . recommendations." *See* Rule 2111(b). By its terms, Regulation Best Interest applies only to recommendations to retail customers, and does not address sales practices with respect to institutional purchasers.

PROBLEM

18-9. The investment banking firm of Goodwin Smythe sold a complicated subprime mortgage-based derivative product to an institutional customer, a large European bank. In essence, this product would provide an attractive stream of income to the buyer so long as the hundred or so mortgages referenced in the contract performed in line with normal expectations; however, if there were significantly more defaults, the buyer would have to pay the counterparty a large sum of money. As such, the buyer was betting that the housing market would stay stable, while the counterparty was effectively "shorting" it. The buyer was told that the reference mortgages were selected by an independent management company that specialized in handling derivative products such as these. Would Goodwin be guilty of fraud for not disclosing to either the buyer or the management company that (a) it had structured this arrangement for the benefit of a particular counterparty, a large hedge fund that was extremely anxious to find a short position to bet against an imminent housing decline; (b) the hedge fund wanted certain mortgages included in the reference portfolio that it believed were particularly subject to default; and (c) the management company had acceded to Goodwin's request without knowing that the "short" counterparty was demanding their inclusion? If a lawsuit under Rule 10b-5 were brought against Goodwin by the buyer, what issues would likely be raised? Would it make any difference if there was evidence that Goodwin itself had recently positioned itself on the "short" side of the subprime housing market, whether in this or separate transactions?

3.   Churning and Other "Relational" Frauds

|| **Merrill Lynch, Pierce, Fenner & Smith v. Arceneaux**
767 F.2d 1498 (11th Cir. 1985)

FAY, J. Appellants challenge on appeal the jury verdict and certain rulings by the district court, 595 F. Supp. 171, in this "churning" suit, alleging violations of federal and state securities laws, breach of fiduciary duty and gross negligence. . . .

I.   FACTUAL BACKGROUND

On March 2, 1983, plaintiffs Phillip Arceneaux and his wife Barbara Arceneaux ("Arceneaux") filed this action in the United States District Court for the Middle District of Florida. Arceneaux alleged both federal and state claims arising from the handling of Arceneaux's securities accounts by defendants. Specifically, plaintiffs alleged that the defendants, Merrill Lynch, Pierce, Fenner & Smith, Inc. ("Merrill Lynch"), broker Don M. Ribaudo ("Ribaudo") and the Clearwater office manager, C. Richard Hill, engaged in excessive trading or "churning" in plaintiff's securities account. Plaintiffs sought both compensatory and punitive damages.

On May 2, 1984, the jury returned a verdict on all counts in favor of the plaintiffs. The jury awarded $46,675 in compensatory damages against Merrill Lynch, Ribaudo and Hill, $15,000 in punitive damages against Ribaudo, and $300,000 in punitive damages against Merrill Lynch. Defendants filed posttrial motions for judgment n.o.v., for a new trial or for remittitur, all of which were denied. . . .

In October of 1980, Arceneaux opened a securities account with the Clearwater office of Merrill Lynch, after attending an investment seminar hosted by defendant Ribaudo and Joseph Granville, a prominent investment analyst. Arceneaux graduated from Louisiana State University with a B.S. degree in Mechanical Engineering in 1954. Beginning in 1970, Arceneaux was employed by Walter Kidde & Co. as a regional sales manager. Prior to opening his account with the Clearwater office of Merrill Lynch, Arceneaux had had some investment experience. He opened his first account in Dallas with Merrill Lynch in 1977. After a few months, Arceneaux became interested in options trading and signed an options information sheet which indicated that his investment objective was "trading profits." After moving to Mobile, Alabama, he opened an options account also with Merrill Lynch. In 1980, Arceneaux moved to Clearwater and opened an account with William Provinse in the Merrill Lynch office there. After hearing broker Ribaudo at the investment seminar, Arceneaux decided to open a securities account with him also at Merrill Lynch.

When he opened his account with Ribaudo, Arceneaux signed an options information sheet, stating that his investment objective was trading profits. He also signed an options agreement which, by plaintiffs' own admission, clearly warned of the risks inherent in trading options. Arceneaux' recollection of the initial meeting between Ribaudo and himself presents a different picture as to how informed Arceneaux was as to the risks involved. Arceneaux testified that Ribaudo did not discuss any risks with plaintiffs and Arceneaux did not ask him any questions "from a risk standpoint."

The history of Arceneaux' investment account with Merrill Lynch reflects numerous purchases and sales and substantial reliance on Ribaudo's recommendations. In October, 1980, the first month of trading, Arceneaux' account sustained a loss of $2,281.00. In November, however, the account had made a profit of $24,000.00. A month later, the value of Arceneaux' holdings dropped from $77,000 to $44,000. Arceneaux continued to trade, but the value of his account continued to decline. By June 1, 1982, when Arceneaux closed his account, he was left with a net loss of $45,697.00. Ribaudo had earned $11,179.00 in commissions in the fifteen months that he managed Arceneaux' account.

Plaintiffs' expert, Mr. Landauer, testified that the average monthly equity in Arceneaux' account turned over eight times on an annualized basis and that the account was turned over ten times during the fifteen months. He also testified that the Arceneaux' financial status was not suitable for the option trading program that was undertaken. In addition, he testified that the velocity of the trading in Arceneaux' account made no sense and noted that "25 percent of the original starting capital ended up in commission to Mr. Ribaudo."

The defendants elicited testimony from Arceneaux that he was aware of the volume of trading in his account and had received confirmation slips. Arceneaux also testified that he was in frequent contact with Ribaudo. On cross examination, plaintiffs' expert testified that if a broker were trying to maximize his commissions, he would not allow numerous options to expire, as Ribaudo did. . . .

Appellants contend that the jury's verdict in favor of the plaintiffs was not supported by substantial evidence and was against the great weight of the evidence. We disagree. This was a classic jury case, where the jury was presented with two conflicting versions of the transactions between plaintiff and defendant, and was forced to choose between them. On review, "[w]e may only insure that there is sufficient evidence in the record to support the existence of each of the three requisite elements of a federal securities churning violation. . . ." *Miley v. Oppenheimer & Co.*, 637 F.2d 318, 325 (5th Cir. Unit A 1981).

"Churning occurs when a securities broker buys and sells securities for a customer's account, without regard to the customer's investment interests, for the purpose of generating commissions." *Thompson v. Smith Barney, Harris Upham & Co.*, 709 F.2d 1413, 1416 (11th Cir. 1983). The plaintiff must prove three elements in order to establish a cause of action for churning:

   (1) the trading in his account was excessive in light of his investment objectives;
   (2) the broker in question exercised control over the trading in the account; and
   (3) the broker acted with the intent to defraud or with willful and reckless disregard for the investor's interest.

Id. at 1416-417 (quoting *Miley*, 637 F.2d at 324).

Both Arceneaux and his expert Mr. Landauer presented sufficient evidence to support each of the three elements of plaintiffs' churning claim. There is no doubt that the evidence conflicted as to each of these elements; however, the jury chose to believe plaintiffs' version of the story. . . .

On the issue of excessive trading, appellants assert that trading in a securities account can not be excessive if it is consistent with the investor's investment objectives. *See Landry v. Hemphill, Noyes & Co.*, 473 F.2d 365 (1st Cir.), *cert. denied*, 414 U.S. 1002 (1973). Appellants point to the fact that Arceneaux had traded heavily in options in the past and was aware of the volume of trading in his account with Ribaudo. That may be, but plaintiffs' expert testified that the trading in the account was excessive, regardless of the investment objective, and the jury chose to believe him. We will not disturb that credibility choice. Moreover, plaintiffs' expert testified that plaintiffs' account had turned over eight times on an annualized basis. The courts which have addressed this issue have indicated that an annual turnover rate in excess of six reflects excessive trading. *See Mihara v. Dean Witter & Co.*, 619 F.2d 814, 821 (9th Cir. 1980); *Rush v. Oppenheimer & Co.*, 592 F. Supp. 1108, 1112 (S.D.N.Y.), *modified on other grounds*, 596 F. Supp. 1529 (S.D.N.Y. 1984). We believe that, at the very least, there was sufficient evidence for the jury to find excessive trading.

With regard to the second element of control, appellants focus on their contention that Arceneaux "was a well-educated and experienced options trader who had sufficient financial acumen to determine his own best interests." Appellants also note that Arceneaux was in frequent contact with his broker. Plaintiffs' expert, however, noted that "there was a wide departure from what Mr. Arceneaux was trading prior to meeting Mr. Ribaudo." Though Arceneaux apparently discussed his account frequently with Ribaudo, the jury could have concluded from Arceneaux' testimony that he was somewhat intimidated by his broker and reluctant to make suggestions or contradict any suggestions that Ribaudo made.

With regard to the third element of churning, scienter, appellants point to the fact that plaintiffs' expert stated on cross-examination that if a broker were trying to churn an account, he would not have allowed numerous options to expire. However, plaintiffs' expert also testified that the velocity of trading in plaintiffs' account made no sense, other than to generate commissions. The jury simply believed plaintiffs' expert's version of the reason why there was so much activity in plaintiffs' account. We conclude, therefore, that there was sufficient evidence for the jury to find the existence of all three elements of plaintiffs' churning claim. *See Miley*, 637 F.2d at 325. . . .

NOTES AND QUESTIONS

1. Churning and Control. The prohibition against churning arises under the Care Obligation of Regulation Best Interest, FINRA Rule 2111 (where it is expressed as a requirement of "quantitative suitability"), and judicial authority. The case law stresses control of the account. Is there adequate allegation of control if the customer retains formal decision-making authority, but in fact rather blindly follows all the broker's recommendations? *Arceneaux* seems to go in this direction, and other courts have said that a control finding can be based on little more. *E.g., Mihara v. Dean Witter & Co.*, 619 F.2d 814 (9th Cir. 1980). Others, however, have expressed concern that this may pose too easy a test for control, suggesting that the better inquiry is whether the customer "has sufficient intelligence and understanding to evaluate the broker's recommendations and to reject one when he thinks it unsuitable." *Follansbee v. Davis, Skaggs & Co.,* 681 F.2d 673, 677 (9th Cir. 1982). In this regard, how often the customer follows the advice would be relevant, but hardly dispositive.

2.   *Excessive Trading.*   How does one determine what is excessive? What does it mean to say, as in *Arceneaux,* that a "turnover" of six times in one year is generally regarded as excessive? The *turnover ratio* is probably the most commonly used statistical test in this area: It is the ratio of the total cost of purchases made for the account during a given period to the total amount invested in the account, thereby giving the fact-finder the ability to determine how many times in that period the securities in a customer's account have been replaced by new securities recommended by the broker. *See Costello v. Oppenheimer & Co.,* 711 F.2d 1361, 1369 & n.11 (7th Cir. 1983). A close look at the volume of commissions— as a percentage of the broker's income, or of the branch's, or in relation to comparable accounts handled by other brokers—is also typical. *E.g., Hecht v. Harris Upham & Co.,* 283 F. Supp. 414 (N.D. Cal. 1968), *aff'd in part,* 430 F.2d 1202 (9th Cir. 1970) (an account that represented less than 0.1 percent of all the office's business in terms of size generated 4.7 percent of that office's commissions). And patterns of "in and out" trading (i.e., purchases followed by almost immediate resales), "cross trading" (i.e., transfers among various customer accounts handled by the broker), and "switching" (i.e., making inconsistent recommendations to various customers—having one buy stock in a company and another sell it) can do in a broker who controls an account.

3.   *The Deception and "in Connection with" Requirement in Broker-Dealer Cases.*   Where a broker controls and misuses a customer's account (i.e., a discretionary trading account), what is the nature of the *deception* that creates liability under Rule 10b-5? In a number of cases—most notably in the churning context—courts have emphasized that the broker's improper trades are themselves fraudulent acts; no misleading recommendation to the customer need have been made. *E.g., Clark v. Kidder Peabody & Co.,* 636 F. Supp. 195, 198 (S.D.N.Y. 1986) (purchases of securities unsuitable for the discretionary account of a college sophomore violate Rule 10b-5 without proof that any misrepresentations were made).

In *SEC v. Zandford,* 535 U.S. 813 (2002), the Supreme Court addressed the applicability of Rule 10b-5 to a situation in which a stockbroker with discretionary authority over an account caused the sale of some of his customers' shares as part of a scheme to misappropriate the proceeds—in essence, a way of stealing the clients' money. In a heavily federalism-laden opinion, the Fourth Circuit had found this not to be "in connection with" the purchase or sale of a security, because the sale alone was not improper, only the subsequent taking of the money. Hence, it was not within the purview of the federal securities laws. *SEC v. Zandford,* 238 F.3d 559 (4th Cir. 2001). The Supreme Court reversed, however, emphasizing that when a "scheme to defraud" is involved, artificial separation into separate steps is inappropriate:

> The Woods were injured as investors through respondent's deceptions, which deprived them of any compensation for the sale of their valuable securities. They were duped into believing respondent would "conservatively invest" their assets in

the stock market and that any transactions made on their behalf would be for their benefit for the "'safety of principal and income.'" The fact that respondent misappropriated the proceeds of the sales provides persuasive evidence that he had violated §10(b) when he made the sales, but misappropriation is not an essential element of the offense. . . . It is enough that the scheme to defraud and the sale of securities coincide. . . .

Respondent was only able to carry out his fraudulent scheme without making an affirmative misrepresentation because the Woods had trusted him to make transactions in their best interest without prior approval. Under these circumstances, respondent's fraud represents an even greater threat to investor confidence in the securities industry. . . . Not only does such a fraud prevent investors from trusting that their brokers are executing transactions for their benefit, but it undermines the value of a discretionary account like that held by the Woods. The benefit of a discretionary account is that it enables individuals, like the Woods, who lack the time, capacity, or know-how to supervise investment decisions, to delegate authority to a broker who will make decisions in their best interests without prior approval. If such individuals cannot rely on a broker to exercise that discretion for their benefit, then the account loses its added value. Moreover, any distinction between omissions and misrepresentations is illusory in the context of a broker who has a fiduciary duty to her clients. See *Chiarella v. United States*, 445 U.S. 222, 230, 63 L. Ed. 2d 348, 100 S. Ct. 1108 (1980) (noting that "silence in connection with the purchase or sale of securities may operate as a fraud actionable under §10(b)" when there is "a duty to disclose arising from a relationship of trust and confidence between parties to a transaction"); *Affiliated Ute Citizens of Utah v. United States*, 406 U.S. at 153.

535 U.S. at 822-823.

PROBLEM

18-10. Fred Blackburn, a wealthy investor, had a discretionary trading account at the brokerage firm of Shaw Smith Sellers Inc., under the supervision of branch manager Sarah Smithson. The account was heavily invested in options and over time had lost money. On March 1, Blackburn instructed Smithson to cease trading in options for the account. Nonetheless, five days later, Smithson bought $3,000 worth of options with Blackburn's money. She says that she thought these particular options were "a sure thing" and she wanted to help Blackburn recoup some of his earlier losses. She had to "act quickly" to take advantage of a fast-moving market. Unfortunately, Smithson's judgment was wrong: The options trading lost money yet again. Has Smithson violated Rule 10b-5?

4. Price Protection: Markups and Other Matters

As noted earlier, the first use to which the shingle theory was put was to find a fraud when a broker-dealer sold stock to customers (as principal, i.e., in a dealer transaction) at excessive prices. The underlying theory is that the broker-dealer has an implied obligation to obtain the best possible price for its customer, and this duty is violated when the broker-dealer interposes itself between the customer and the best market. In *Charles Hughes & Co. v. SEC*, 139 F.2d 434 (2d Cir. 1943), *cert. denied*, 321 U.S. 786 (1944), noted earlier for its invention of the shingle theory, the prices charged ranged from 16 to 41 percent over current market value. For a long time, this prohibition has been expressed in a clear and often-enforced restriction on profit-seeking activity by broker-dealers codified in an FINRA rule of fair practice In its interpretations, the NASD stated early on that its business conduct committees should take note of a 1943 survey that indicated that some 71 percent of all transactions had markups of 5 percent or less; that has become known as the "5 percent rule." *See Handley Inv. Co. v. SEC*, 354 F.2d 64 (10th Cir. 1965). However, both the FINRA and the courts have made clear that it is not a hard-and-fast standard. There may be some circumstances (e.g., special costs) where a larger markup is appropriate. Conversely, markups below 5 percent can sometimes be unlawful, especially where the price of the security is high. *See Grandon v. Merrill Lynch & Co.*, 147 F.3d 184 (2d Cir. 1998) (noting that markups in the municipal bond markets are usually lower than for equities). Note that while Regulation Best Interest does not limit markups directly, it does make cost an important aspect of the Care Obligation.

The hardest cases in this area arise when, because of market domination or thinness, prevailing market price is difficult to assess. *See* Alstead, Dempsey & Co., 47 S.E.C. 1034 (1984). In *Application of Meyer Blinder*, [1992 Transfer Binder] Fed. Sec. L. Rep. (CCH) ¶85,038 (Aug. 26, 1992) (admin. proc.), the SEC stated that when there is a dominating market maker, the test is one of "contemporaneous cost," looking first at purchases from other dealers and then (if there are no interdealer transactions) to retail purchases, adjusted to reflect any markdowns. Both the courts and the SEC have been very skeptical of brokers' attempts to use prevailing quotations as the basis for markups. Id. Quotations merely propose transactions and may not be reliable indicators of prevailing market value, especially in thin markets. *See Orkin v. SEC*, 31 F.3d 1056 (11th Cir. 1994). In an amusing illustration of markup and broker-dealer regulation carried to something of an extreme, the SEC brought an action against a promoter who sold shares of Walt Disney Company common stock, suitable for framing, presumably as gifts to children. A settlement allowed the sales to continue, with restrictions to ensure that certificates were not being sold for investment purposes. *See* Harlan, A Goofy Ruling from the SEC Puts Disney Up Against the Wall, Wall St. J., Mar. 18, 1993, at C1.

The SEC has sought to supplement the direct approach with mandatory disclosure. Rule 10b-10 requires written confirmations of transactions that include disclosure of such matters as whether the broker was acting as principal or agent, whether it was acting as a market maker with respect to the securities, and—in principal transactions—specific information about the size of the markup or spread. In *Ettinger v. Merrill Lynch, Pierce, Fenner & Smith*, 835 F.2d 1031 (3d Cir. 1987), the court held that compliance with Rule 10b-10 is not a complete defense to a charge of fraud, however; there may be matters that the broker is obliged to disclose to the customer beyond that called for by the Rule. There the court found that the investor stated a claim against Merrill Lynch for failing to disclose an excessive markup in the zero-coupon bond called the Treasury investment growth receipt (TIGR), even though the SEC had not extended Rule 10b-10 to such transactions.

5.   Arbitration

The Privatization of Customer-Broker Disputes.   Until the mid-1980s, litigation between brokers and their customers was the commonplace mechanism for resolving their disputes. In light of a Supreme Court decision, *Wilko v. Swan,* 345 U.S. 427 (1953)—a matter brought under the Securities Act of 1933—it was generally assumed that contracts requiring arbitration of securities disputes were invalid because of the securities laws' bars against waivers of compliance with any provision of the statutes. In a series of decisions, however, the Supreme Court shifted ground and made clear that the federal policy favoring arbitration, embodied in the Federal Arbitration Act (FAA), extended to securities arbitration as well. The most important of these cases was *Shearson/American Express Inc. v. McMahon,* 482 U.S. 220 (1987), where the Court took note not only of the FAA, but also of increasing SEC supervision of the arbitration process as a basis for declaring the historic "mistrust" of securities arbitration to be anachronistic with respect to claims under the Exchange Act. *McMahon* was soon followed by a formal overruling of *Wilko. Rodriguez de Quijas v. Shearson/ American Express Inc.,* 490 U.S. 477 (1989).

Not surprisingly, *McMahon* pointed the way to substantial privatization of securities law disputes. Pre-dispute arbitration clauses quickly became the norm for accounts that involve borrowing on margin or options trading, and is a big reason why there have been many fewer judicial decisions addressing broker-dealer responsibilities than there had been up until the late 1980s. FINRA handles the vast majority of securities arbitrations. FINRA's arbitration process for three member panels requires at least two public arbitrators "independent" of the securities industry plus one industry member, with a recent option given to claimants to choose an all independent panel. This is in response to long-standing disagreement as to what independence means, particularly as applied to people such as lawyers who have (or had) clients in the industry. *See* Choi et al., The Influence of Arbitrator Background and Representation on Arbitration Outcomes, 9 Va. L. & Bus. Rev. 43 (2014).

An important and troubling spillover effect of mandatory arbitration is the relative disappearance of judicial precedent to help interpret and apply broker-dealer obligations. Note how much of the "authority" you read earlier in this chapter on issues like suitability and churning involves relatively old cases. For a discussion of many issues relating to mandatory arbitration, *see* Gross, The Historical Basis of Arbitration as an Investor Protection Mechanism, 2016 J. Disp. Resol. 171.

The Controversy over Mandatory Arbitration.   The primary benefit of arbitration to investors, supposedly, is that it is quicker and cheaper than a lawsuit. Precisely to what extent this is so is controversial: There is anecdotal evidence that high-stakes arbitration has come to resemble litigation in terms of motions practice, discovery disputes, and the like. Another benefit is that the kinds of arguments that might convince a panel to make an award may be broader (e.g., equitable considerations). Panels have considerable latitude in construing what the law is. This, plus the reasonably high rate of proceedings in which some award is given, has led some observers to believe that while mandatory arbitration is far from perfect, it still is preferable to litigation.

There are also many critics of the arbitration process who believe that investors are systematically disadvantaged by a regime operated under the auspices of a membership organization of the securities industry. In Section 921 of the Dodd-Frank Act, Congress responded to pressure from investor advocates and gave the SEC the authority to prohibit, condition, or restrict pre-dispute mandatory arbitration clauses as used in the securities industry. To date, it has not exercised that authority. For an assessment of the issue and criticism of the delay, *see* Barr, Mandatory Arbitration in Consumer Finance and Investor Contracts, 11 N.Y.U. J.L. & Bus. 793 (2015).

Do broker-dealer firms always want to arbitrate customer disputes? Interestingly, in arrangements with institutional customers and complex contractual terms, broker-dealers often seek a waiver of the right to arbitrate otherwise afforded by FINRA Rule 12200. Although it seems clear that customers can execute a waiver of that right, there is a notable split in the circuits about whether a forum selection clause (i.e., providing that a particular court will hear any case arising therefrom) by itself operates as a waiver. For a good discussion of the issue and the conflicting opinions, *see Reading Health Inc. v. Bear Stearns & Co.*, 900 F.3d 87 (3d Cir. 2018).

Overturning an Arbitral Award. An arbitral award does not necessarily end the dispute, because the award must be enforced. Under the FAA, there are grounds for non-enforcement, such as arbitrator partiality or bias, and it must be clear that the issue was in fact subject to arbitration as a matter of contract law. Until recently, it had been assumed by the courts that a separate ground for non-enforcement was when the arbitrators had acted in "manifest disregard of the law." Although that standard was very narrowly construed, it did operate as a check in extreme cases. For a rare application, *see Interactive Brokers LLC v. Saroop*, 279 F. Supp. 3d 699 (E.D. Va. 2018).

Punitive Damages. To what extent are arbitrators free to award punitive damages, and how often do they do so? *See* Choi, Punitive Damages in Securities Arbitration: An Empirical Study, 39 J. Leg. Stud. 497 (2010). Under the substantive law of New York, arbitrators lack such power. In *Mastrobuano v. Shearson Lehman Hutton Inc.*, 514 U.S. 52 (1995), the Supreme Court ruled that an award of $400,000 in addition to the $159,327 in compensatory damages was permissible in a dispute arising in Illinois between two customers and their broker, even though the contract stated that "it shall be governed by the laws of the State of New York." Treating the issue largely as one of contract interpretation—and invoking the maxim that an ambiguous contract should be construed against its drafter—the Court found insufficient evidence that the parties intended by that language to invoke New York's punitive damages rule. The Court also held that the New York rule would be preempted by the FAA were it sought to be imposed upon non-consenting parties. Does this mean that brokerage firms can now simply revise their forms to be more explicit? In *Mastrobuano*, the Court took note of (though it did not rely upon) NASD Rule of Fair Practice 21(f)(4), which states that for contracts entered into after September 1989, "[n]o agreement . . . shall include any condition which . . . limits the ability of a party to file any claim in arbitration or limits the ability of the arbitrators to make any award." Today, punitive damage awards in broker-customer arbitrations are not uncommon.

C. Substantive Regulation: Credit and Financial Soundness

1. Margin Requirements

Customer Protection.   Often, a customer may wish to purchase securities but does not have cash on hand or wishes to put his immediately available funds to other uses. It should come as no surprise that broker-dealers (and others) are generally quite willing to make loans for securities purchases to qualified investors.

Borrowing to invest (borrowing on "margin") is a direct form of leveraging: It increases the return on the initial investment if the investment is successful (i.e., if the income or price appreciation exceeds the debt plus the transactions costs), but it also increases the loss if the investment does not succeed. That is to say, both the level of risk and the expected return may be increased, perhaps substantially, by the borrowing. When broker-dealers encourage their customers to invest on margin—an appealing strategy to the customer anxious to make lots of money—we encounter the same potential suitability problems discussed above. Besides dealing with the problem as a suitability issue, courts have held that broker-dealers violate Rule 10b-5 directly by not providing their customers with all information necessary to evaluate the nature and risks of margin borrowing, whether in connection with a specific securities transaction, *see Arrington v. Merrill Lynch, Pierce, Fenner & Smith*, 651 F.2d 615 (9th Cir. 1981), or at the time the account is established, *see Angelastro v. Prudential Bache Securities Corp.*, 764 F.2d 939 (3d Cir. 1984). In the latter case, how is it that the "in connection with" requirement is properly satisfied? On the other hand, it has also been held that any compensable losses must flow from the risk improperly assumed, rather than the investor's own poor investment judgment with respect to the securities purchased. In other words, there must be loss causation. In *Bennett v. United States Trust Co.*, 770 F.2d 308 (2d Cir. 1985), *cert. denied*, 474 U.S. 1058 (1986), for example, the court held that no compensable damages occurred where plaintiffs came to U.S. Trust with the specific intent to buy certain public utility securities and were misinformed about the applicability of the margin rules with respect to such purchases. Even though "but for" causation might be present, the court found the relationship between the loss and the misrepresentation too tenuous to state a claim.

Rule 10b-5 is supplemented in this area by a more specific antifraud rule, Rule 10b-16, which operates as something of a "truth in lending" provision. That Rule requires broker-dealers to establish procedures by which customers are given full disclosure of the terms and conditions of a margin account as well as periodic statements regarding account status. It also precludes changes in the terms and conditions governing the margin account without giving the customer at least 30 days' written notice, except for changes required by law. At least to the extent that violations are made with scienter, a fair number of courts have implied rights of action for investors injured by violations of this Rule. *E.g., Angelastro*, supra; *Robertson v. Dean Witter Reynolds Inc.*, 749 F.2d 530 (9th Cir. 1984).

Restraints on Speculation.   There exists another sort of regulation governing margin lending, one going well beyond disclosure for the protection of borrowers. An important feature of the Securities Exchange Act of 1934 was the grant of authority in Section 7 to the Federal Reserve Board (Fed) to set limitations (subject to certain ceilings) on the amount of credit that may be extended for any securities purchase. The avowed purpose was to control speculation in securities trading. Since that time, the Fed has established a series of regulations for various classes of lenders, controlling both the sorts of securities that are available for margin lending and the amounts that can be loaned (e.g., Regulation T for broker-dealers, Regulation U for banks, Regulation G for other lenders).

While the Fed's rules do not require margin "maintenance," the rules of a number of the SROs (as well as the business practices of many broker-dealers) do. For instance, Rule 431 of the NYSE requires (with a few exceptions) that an account maintain an amount equal to 25 percent with respect to securities "long" in the account. Thus, a decline in the value of the securities purchased on margin may lead to a *margin call*—a demand for additional cash or securities. This possibility itself can have a serious impact on the customer, since a failure to meet the margin call will lead the broker-dealer to liquidate some of the account at a loss. It can also have a severe market impact: A decline in the stock market may cause extensive margin calls and hence substantial selling activity, thereby exacerbating the decline. Margin calls were one (of many) significant reasons for the collapse of both the equity and debt markets during the subprime crisis of 2007-2008. For an interesting insider trading case involving trading on the part of a Wall Street firm that was employed to conduct the orderly liquidation of securities in a Russian automotive company held as collateral in the face of numerous margin calls, *see Veleron Holdings B.V. v. Morgan Stanley,* 117 F. Supp. 3d 404 (S.D.N.Y. 2014) (denial of summary judgment), verdict for defendant sustained, 694 F.3d 858 (2d Cir. 2017).

Why did Congress enact the margin rules? While there is some indication that investor protection was a concern, the dominant reason was to curb the possibility of "speculative excess" of the sort that led to the stock market crash of October 1929. Whether or not these rules do indeed dampen speculation is open to question. In any event, acceptance of Congress' "macroeconomic" emphasis on controlling market risk has led many courts to refuse to imply private rights of action for customers "injured" by violations of the Fed's margin rules, e.g., *Bennett,* supra, a conclusion reinforced by the addition of Section 7(f) to the Exchange Act in 1970, which makes it unlawful for a person to borrow in violation of the margin rules. Is this fair? Should an unsophisticated customer be barred from complaining about a transaction that violates the margin rules where the borrowing was actively encouraged by the broker? Consider this question in light of the *Berner* case, supra, and *see Shearson Lehman Bros. v. M&L Investments,* 10 F.3d 1520 (10th Cir. 1993).

Like many highly technical rules, the margin requirements can have unexpected application. In the Enron scandal, for example, one commentator contends that the company was effectively lending its special purpose entities money to acquire Enron stock because of the way it structured its complex financing arrangements. This, he argues, was a violation of Regulation

G—and a good hook on which to catch the insiders, lawyers, and bankers who participated in the financing arrangements even if they were not actually aware of the regulatory requirements. *See* Widen, Enron at the Margin, 58 Bus. Law. 961 (2003).

2.   The Financial Soundness of Broker-Dealers

There is a substantial federal interest in the financial solvency of broker-dealer firms. Many customer/investors are creditors of such firms: They are beneficial owners of securities held in street name by the firms or have credit balances on account with them. And, of course, at any time brokerage firms have possession of a large amount of cash pending payment to their customers, for example, the proceeds of the sale of customers' securities. In this sense, an insolvency will be to the detriment of a fair number of investors. There is also the perception of substantial interdependence among securities firms. As in the banking industry, the failure of one can sometimes lead to a domino effect within the industry—as was amply demonstrated during the financial meltdown and credit crisis of 2007-2008. Not surprisingly, the SEC has been heavily involved in regulation designed to keep firms financially sound, in a manner resembling that for many other forms of financial intermediaries, like banks, pension funds, and insurance companies. *See* Clark, The Soundness of Financial Intermediaries, 86 Yale L.J. 1 (1976). Historically, there were four strategies for assuring the financial condition of broker-dealers.

First, broker-dealers must keep extensive records and file reports on their financial condition (*see* Section 17(a); Rule 17a-5). They are also subject to inspections to ensure compliance with the regulatory scheme (Section 17(b)). In addition, they must send certain information about their financial position to customers on a periodic basis. The reporting system is designed as an early-warning system for government regulators, although inspections serve the equally important purpose of monitoring broker-dealer compliance with conduct-type rules as well. And, of course, disclosure plays the same disciplinary role that it does in securities regulation generally: Forcing brokerage practices and conditions into the "sunlight" may lead to more prudent behavior within the industry. In 1990, Congress extended the reporting and record-keeping scheme to reach the activities of affiliates of broker-dealer firms (e.g., investment or merchant banking firms that are part of a holding company structure and thus closely connected to the broker-dealer).

The second strategy, authorized by Section 15(b)(7) of the '34 Act, has to do with capital adequacy:

> The primary purpose of the net capital rule (Securities Exchange Act Rule 15c3-1; 17 CFR §240.15c3-1) is to protect customers and creditors of registered broker-dealers from monetary losses and delays that can occur when a registered broker-dealer fails. The rule requires registered broker-dealers to maintain sufficient liquid assets to enable firms that fall below the minimum net capital requirements to liquidate in an orderly fashion without the need for a formal proceeding. In doing so, the rule enhances investor confidence in the financial integrity of securities firms. Similarly, the rule promotes transactions between broker-dealers,

lenders, and creditors, on one hand, and the counterpart broker-dealers on the other, because those entities are more likely to consider a broker-dealer credit-worthy if it must comply with a liquidity-based capital adequacy standard. . . .

Exchange Act Release No. 27249, [1989-1990 Transfer Binder] Fed. Sec. L. Rep. (CCH) ¶84,501 (Sept. 15, 1990). The SEC has made significant changes in the net capital standards in recent years, raising the base amounts and adjusting required capital depending upon the nature of the particular activities carried on by the broker-dealer. We shall return to this shortly, in the aftermath of the global financial crisis.

The third form of control has to do with segregation of customer funds. Funds or securities that are left by customers on account with the broker-dealers—but that remain the customers' property—must be carefully separated from the firm's own assets. *See* Rules 8c-1, 15c2-1. This addresses a problem that became particularly serious during the "back room" crises of the late 1960s and early 1970s, when the volume of customer business increased beyond the capacity of many brokers to handle it. Upon the insolvency of several firms, it was discovered that they had lost total control over assets in their possession, so that no one could identify who owned what of the remaining assets. The rules also operate to limit the hypothecation of customer securities—that is, the use of those securities by the broker as collateral in order to facilitate borrowing or making its own short sales.

Finally, as perhaps the most comforting means of protecting the customers of broker-dealers, Congress in 1970 established the Securities Investor Protection Corporation (SIPC) and required all registered brokers and dealers to become members. The SIPC operates for the brokerage industry in much the same way as the Federal Deposit Insurance Corporation does for the banking industry: It insures customers of member broker-dealers who have money or securities on account at a broker-dealer at the time of its failure up to certain limits and provides a mechanism for liquidating troubled firms in an orderly fashion. For a critique of this structure, *see* Joo, Who Watches the Watchers? The Securities Investor Protection Act, Investor Confidence and the Subsidization of Failure, 72 S. Cal. L. Rev. 1071 (1999).

3. Dodd-Frank and Systemic Risk

The global financial crisis that began in 2007-2008 was traumatic for securities regulation, just as it was for the world at large. You have seen throughout this book many changes in the law, mostly called for in the Dodd-Frank Act of 2010, that were stimulated by the meltdown: asset-backed securitization reform, profound changes in the regulation of derivatives, revisions in credit ratings, etc.

The meltdown had many antecedents. But at its core, it began with changes in the securities industry that had been occurring for quite a while. As you may know, in 1933 Congress enacted the Glass-Steagall Act, which purported to draw a strict line of separation between the securities industry and the business of commercial banking. Banking was highly regulated with a view toward safety and soundness, with deposit insurance as a principal strategy to keep the system safe from runs and panics. This "wall of separation" was motivated by a desire to insulate banking from the temptations, subtle and otherwise, of speculation in securities. But Glass-Steagall gradually broke under the economic artificiality of any distinction between securities and banking. For example, as noted in Chapter 8, commercial paper (very short-term corporate debt) has long been a securities product used by many issuers for day-to-day financial management. As that market grew, issuers found it and related money market instruments extremely attractive, relying more and more on that market for their debt needs. On the deposit side, the securities industry innovated with money market funds that had the liquidity of a bank deposit without banking regulation (or deposit insurance) to support it. What emerged came to be known as the "shadow banking system"—a wide array of ways in which the securities industry offered substitutes for bank products, at lower cost and with less regulatory burden. *See* Whitehead, Reframing Financial Regulation, 90 B.U. L. Rev. 1 (2010). Gradually, Glass-Steagall was weakened, and then repealed, enabling securities firms to be even more aggressive in debt product innovation. That, in turn, caused commercial banks to demand banking deregulation in order to allow them to compete on a more level playing field. Mergers of commercial and investment banks created massively large and powerful financial conglomerates, like Citigroup and JP Morgan Chase.

Subprime mortgage securitization was born in the midst of this struggle. Mortgage loan packaging has a long history, supported by governmentally sponsored entities like Fannie Mae and Freddie Mac. "Private label" securitization was invented by large securities firms to enter this market as competitors in the design and delivery of increasingly complex securities (or derivatives)— essentially selling instruments whose value was tied to the housing market, were highly rated by the credit rating agencies, and that paid a little more than Treasury bills, but by enough to be attractive to portfolio managers frustrated by the low interest rates of the early 2000s.

The effect of all this was a displacement of traditional banking regulation— demanding safety and soundness—by securities regulation, which was founded on the idea that risks are largely to be addressed through full disclosure, not merit regulation. But in the face of extraordinarily complex product innovation, was such heavy reliance on disclosure justified? *See* Hu, Too Complex to Depict? Innovation, "Pure Information" and the SEC Disclosure Paradigm, 90 Tex. L. Rev. 1601 (2012). Some of the issues raised by the sale of such products to otherwise sophisticated institutional investors were treated earlier in this chapter. More recently, there has been growing alarm about risk to the financial system from leveraged loans and collateralized loan obligations, as you may recall from Chapter 2.

The fall of securities firms like Lehman and Bear Stearns set off alarms. It became clear that securities firms were not simply middlemen, quickly offloading all the risk to others; they were instead holding on to a massive amount of increasingly risky securitized debt. And for some time they had become accustomed to financing themselves in the short-term collateralized debt market, so that their activities were highly leveraged across the board. Because their assets and liability mix was so opaque, the firms that failed made money providers nervous about other securities firms and the money providers pulled back, generating a crisis for all who had depended on those sources of funds. Forced to sell many kinds of assets to meet margin and capital adequacy demands into a market with few willing buyers, the prices—and "mark to market" values—of such assets went into free fall. Many more financial institutions became insolvent, and when deemed "too big to fail," had to be bailed out or acquired by a healthier financial institution, with long-term government support. *See* Mishkin, Over the Cliff: From the Subprime to the Global Financial Crisis, 25 J. Econ. Persp. 49 (Winter 2011). For example, the largest retail brokerage/investment banking firm, Merrill Lynch, became part of Bank of America.

The various Dodd-Frank reforms we have already examined are partial responses to all of this. You saw the so-called Volcker Rule in Chapter 10, and there are now also rules limiting broker-dealer contracts that might encourage too much risk taking, new approaches to risk capital, and the like. More generally, Dodd-Frank represents an acknowledgment of the obvious—that any large provider of financial services may be too big to fail, either by itself or because of its interconnectedness with other systemically significant institutions. That means that providers of funds will be less sensitive (maybe completely insensitive) to firm risk, so long as they believe that there will be a bailout in the event of trouble. Safety and soundness cannot simply be a "bank regulation" goal, unless banking is redefined so that it takes in the shadow banking system as well. For a time immediately after the crisis set in, many policy makers expressed the view that we could no longer have a separate SEC with jurisdiction over securities, CFTC with jurisdiction over commodities, banking regulators with jurisdiction over commercial banks and bank holding companies because all those product markets have blended into a single financial services marketplace. The effort to consolidate regulation failed for political reasons, leaving the SEC standing. Instead, Dodd-Frank demanded coordination, under the direction of a council of regulators (the Financial Stability Oversight Council, or FSOC) which has been a painstakingly difficult process. Even though many Dodd-Frank rulemaking mandates had deadlines, many of those were missed and remain unfulfilled coming up on a decade after the legislation. For some more recent perspectives on the aftermath of the financial crisis and the Dodd-Frank reform effects, *see* Judge, Investor Driven Financial Regulation, 8 Harv. Bus. L. Rev. 291 (2018), and Allen, The SEC as a Financial Stability Regulator, 43 J. Corp. L. 715 (2018).

||19||

Investment Advisers and Investment Companies

Chapter 18 emphasized that investors today seek out a great deal of investment advice and information before making their trading decisions. Brokerage firms are only one source of such advice. Investors also turn to a variety of other sources: professional investment counselors and financial planners, who do not execute securities transactions; newsletter writers; and a wide variety of sources in the public media and on the web (e.g., the Wall Street Journal, Barron's, Motley Fool, CNBC, Yahoo Finance). Alternatively (and increasingly often, as you by now know), investors buy shares in entities that turn around and invest in a portfolio of securities, passing on the dividends and capital gains to their shareholders after deducting a management fee for the advisory work. These investment companies are another means by which individual investors can try to take advantage of professional investment expertise.

Just as in the brokerage industry, however, all these practices raise substantial conflict of interest and other investor protection concerns. Recognizing this, Congress enacted two separate, but related, securities statutes in 1940: the Investment Advisers Act and the Investment Company Act. We discuss these important regulatory interventions in this chapter, as well as take a brief look at other purveyors of investment expertise: credit rating agencies, hedge funds, and other private funds.

The materials in this chapter raise issues of immense economic importance. Some way or another, extraordinary amounts of household money is under advice or management of some form or another, including much on which investors depend on for their retirements. The kinds of conflicts of interest described in the last chapter are present here, too, in ways both subtle and complex. A number of commentators believe this has become the most important subject area in securities regulation. *See* Zingales, The Future of Securities Regulation, 47 J. Acct. Res. 391 (2009); Krug, Downstream Securities Regulation, 94 B.U. L. Rev. 1589 (2014).

A.   *The Regulation of Investment Advisers*

Investment advisers are persons who are in the business of giving such advice, but who do not buy or sell securities or execute trades as part of that business. Investment adviser recommendations may come in a variety of forms, ranging from personalized consultations through advisory letters sent in identical form to thousands of subscribers. In the Investment Advisers Act of 1940, Congress imposed a broad and pervasive scheme of federal regulation on the activities of investment advisers generally, thus seeking to cover the advisory spectrum within a single regulatory scheme.

From a regulatory perspective, the business of investment advisers and broker-dealers may usefully be both compared and contrasted. As noted earlier, the most serious conflict of interest problem in terms of broker-dealer activity results from the fact that the compensation of broker-dealers was traditionally on a per transaction basis (the commission or the spread), creating an incentive to "sell" customers simply on the need to trade, sometimes contrary to the customers' best interests. Investment advisers, on the other hand, are usually not compensated in this way; many simply charge hourly fees, or a percentage of assets, or fees for subscriptions to their publications. The same conflict, then, is not always present. In recent years, the compensation of many full-service brokers has become more similar to that of advisers, raising questions about whether the regulatory distinctions still make sense. For example, many brokerage firms now charge fees based on percentage of assets (e.g., 1 percent) in so-called wrap accounts, in return for which the customer receives execution services, record-keeping, and advice.

The potential for abuses in the advisory industry are both obvious and subtle. For example, advisers who charge by the hour may secretly be compensated by issuers or hold positions in securities for their own accounts that might benefit from the increased investor interest that flows from a particular recommendation. Or they may simply be incompetent. Given this, there is a case to be made for some form of regulation, as a means of both protecting clients and supervising the flow of information into the marketplace generally.

1.   The Registration Requirement

The starting point for regulation under the Investment Advisers Act is registration. Unless exempt, it is unlawful under Section 203 of the Act for any person to act as an investment adviser unless registered with the SEC. *Investment adviser,* in turn, is defined in Section 202(11) to include any person

> who, for compensation, engages in the business of advising others, either directly or through publications or writings, as to the value of securities or as to the advisability of investing in, purchasing or selling securities, or who, for compensation and as part of a regular business, issues or promulgates analyses or reports concerning securities.

The statutory definition of investment adviser *excludes* (1) most banking activity; (2) lawyers or other professionals whose investment-related services are solely incidental to their practice; (3) broker-dealers whose advisory activities are solely incidental to the conduct of that business; (4) publishers of bona fide newspapers and other publications of general and regular circulation; and (5) certain persons whose advice relates solely to government securities. Among these, note the difficulty in drawing clean lines between the brokerage and advisory businesses. What about brokers who offer so-called wrap accounts, charging a fee to manage the customers' investments? The SEC's rulemaking effort to exclude these kinds of managed account arrangements from Investment Adviser Acts coverage was struck down in *Financial Planning Association v. SEC*, 482 F.3d 481 (D.C. Cir. 2007), leaving the distinction blurry. This eventually led to the provision in the Dodd-Frank Act directing the SEC to bring the responsibilities of both brokers and advisers closer to a fiduciary standard, as noted in Chapter 18, so that less stress would be put on this exemption. We will see how that played out shortly. In connection with that effort, the SEC issued an interpretative release giving guidance about the meaning of "solely incidental," in general taking the view that "a broker-dealer's provision of advice as to the value and characteristics of securities or as to the advisability of transacting in securities is consistent with the solely incidental prong if the advice is provided in connection with and is reasonably related to the broker-dealer's primary business of effecting securities transactions." Release IA-5249 (June 5, 2019). This is so without regard to the amount of advice offered, though not where the broker exercises investment discretion over the account. Many brokers are "dually registered" as advisers as well; which body of law applies to them is based on which hat they are wearing as to the particular advice in question.

There are many situations where a person may be deemed an investment adviser based on activities short of "hanging out a shingle" as a professional investment counselor. The best known case in this area is *Abrahamson v. Fleschner*, 568 F.2d 862 (2d Cir. 1977), *cert. denied*, 436 U.S. 913 (1978). There, the court held that a general partner in a limited partnership formed to invest in securities—whose compensation was based on the performance of the investments—had to register as an investment adviser. The court found two grounds for this ruling. First, the adviser was required to provide information to the limited partners with respect to the performance of the investments, enabling them to decide whether to withdraw their funds. Second, the court believed that, based on the legislative history of the Investment Advisers Act, managing a discretionary account by itself involves the giving of investment advice for compensation. The definition of investment advisers is broad enough that large numbers of persons are covered. The SEC has complained that it lacks the resources to police such an extensive industry, and in 1996, Congress enacted a division of responsibility that effectively concentrates SEC supervision on those advisers who are associated with mutual funds or who have more than $25 million under advisement. The others were left to the states. In the Dodd-Frank Act, Congress raised the threshold for SEC registration for most advisers to $100 million. Subject to a wide variety of exceptions, small advisers (those with less than $25 million under advisement) still register solely with one or more states, so long as they are subject to registration in at least one state. Mid-size advisers (between $25 million and $100 million) are solely state supervised as well, so long as they are subject to registration and examination in at least one state. In the aftermath of the budget crisis facing many states, their ability to regulate effectively in this area has been called into question. Note that although most substantive regulation under the Advisers Act is tied to registration with the SEC, the Act's antifraud provisions are not, and hence are applicable regardless of whether the adviser is large, mid-size, or small. And a failure to register when required makes any contracts entered into in connection with the advisory activities subject to rescission. *See In re Living Benefits Asset Management LLC,* 916 F.3d 528 (5th Cir. 2019), affirming liability based on failure to register by a consulting firm specializing in the purchase and sale of life settlements.

Another important reform made by Dodd-Frank was to subject hedge fund advisers, who theretofore had taken advantage of an exemption for advisers with fewer than 15 clients, to register, albeit with separate requirements for "private fund" activities. Hedge fund regulation will be treated later in this chapter.

2.   Substantive Regulation

Upon registration with the SEC, an investment adviser faces fairly comprehensive regulation, including extensive disclosure requirements via Form ADV. Most importantly, there is a disciplinary scheme very much like that for broker-dealers—that is, registration may be denied or subsequently suspended or revoked (temporarily or permanently) or the adviser fined if the Commission finds in the course of an administrative proceeding that the investment adviser has, inter alia, made any false statement to the Commission, has been enjoined by any court of competent jurisdiction from acting as a securities professional, or has willfully violated any provision of the federal securities laws. Along similar lines, persons associated with an investment adviser may be disciplined as well. It is worth noting, however, that this scheme of controlled entry does *not* give the Commission the power to set financial qualification or competence standards for investment advisers the way the Securities Exchange Act does with respect to broker-dealers. Is there any justification for this distinction?

Unless exempt from registration, investment advisers must keep records, file periodic reports with the Commission, and be subject to inspection (Section 204). Advisory firms, like broker-dealers, must also adopt written policies and procedures designed to prevent the misuse of material nonpublic information (Section 204A) and face the threat of civil penalties if they recklessly permit a violation by an employee.

Perhaps the most intriguing form of substantive restriction on investment adviser activity is found in Section 205(a)(1), which bars the use of advisory contracts that provide for compensation based upon the client's capital gains or capital appreciation. Statutory exceptions are provided for contracts that provide "for compensation based upon the total value of a fund averaged over a definite period," contracts with an investment company, and contracts (except for certain trust accounts) where the amount under investment exceeds $1 million. This prohibition on "contingent fees" historically was justified in light of allegations that many advisers had adopted "heads I win, tails you lose" compensation schemes that provided for high levels of compensation for good performance, with no offset for bad. But it goes beyond that, since by its terms it bars all contingent arrangements. This breadth has been defended by reference to a second objective: The provision is designed to bar compensation arrangements that create an undue incentive for the adviser to recommend risky transactions simply in order to increase its fees. *See* Release No. IA-721, 5 Fed. Sec. L. Rep. (CCH) ¶56,336 (May 23, 1980); Bieber & Price, Fulcrum Fees: Registered Funds' Alternative Fee Structures, 21 Inv. Law., no. 9 (Sept. 2014). But are these rationales persuasive? Shouldn't clients be able to choose compensation schemes that offer a reward for high performance? Is the effect of such a provision really to dampen competition within the advisory industry? In Rule 205-3, the Commission has used its exemptive power to limit the scope of this provision substantially, permitting contingent contracts between the adviser and a client with substantial net worth ($2 million, exclusive of primary residence), or assets under the adviser's management ($1 million).

Section 205(a)(2) restricts the assignability of advisory contracts without the consent of the advisees, thus recognizing and giving some protection to the fiduciary relationship that exists between the client and the particular adviser. To complete the set of substantive rules that are the heart of the Act, Section 206 authorizes the adoption of special antifraud rules governing the conduct of investment advisers, a topic to be discussed in the next subsection. Sections 205 and 206 apply whether or not the adviser is exempt from registration.

3. Conduct Regulation: Section 206

Securities and Exchange Commission v. Capital Gains Research Bureau Inc.
375 U.S. 180 (1963)

GOLDBERG, J. We are called upon in this case to decide whether under the Investment Advisers Act of 1940 the Securities and Exchange Commission may obtain an injunction compelling a registered investment adviser to disclose to his clients a practice of purchasing shares of a security for his own account shortly before recommending that security for long-term investment and then immediately selling the shares at a profit upon the rise in the market price following the recommendation. The answer to this question turns on whether the practice—known in the trade as "scalping"—"operates as a fraud or deceit upon any client or prospective client" within the meaning of the Act. We hold that it does and that the Commission may "enforce compliance" with the Act by obtaining an injunction requiring the adviser to make full disclosure of the practice to his clients.

. . . Respondents publish two investment advisory services, one of which—"A Capital Gains Report"—is the subject of this proceeding. The Report is mailed monthly to approximately 5,000 subscribers who each pay an annual subscription price of $18. It carries the following description:

An Investment Service devoted exclusively to (1) The protection of investment capital. (2) The realization of a steady and attractive income there-from. (3) The accumulation of CAPITAL GAINS thru the timely purchase of corporate equities that are proved to be undervalued.

Between March 15, 1960 and November 7, 1960, respondents, on six different occasions, purchased shares of a particular security shortly before recommending it in the Report for long-term investment. On each occasion, there was an increase in the market price and the volume of trading of the recommended security within a few days after the distribution of the Report. Immediately thereafter, respondents sold their shares of these securities at a profit. They did not disclose any aspect of these transactions to their clients or prospective clients.

On the basis of the above facts, the Commission requested a preliminary injunction as necessary to effectuate the purposes of the Investment Advisers Act of 1940. The injunction would have required respondents, in any future Report, to disclose the material facts concerning, inter alia, any purchase of recommended securities "within a very short period prior to the distribution of a recommendation . . .," and "[t]he intent to sell and the sale of said securities . . . within a very short period after distribution of said recommendation. . . ."

I

The Investment Advisers Act of 1940 was the last in a series of Acts designed to eliminate certain abuses in the securities industry, abuses which were found to have contributed to the stock market crash of 1929 and the depression of the 1930's. A fundamental purpose, common to these statutes, was to substitute a philosophy of full disclosure for the philosophy of caveat emptor and thus to achieve a high standard of business ethics in the securities industry. . . .

This concern was not limited to deliberate or conscious impediments to objectivity. Both the advisers and the Commission were well aware that whenever advice to a client might result in financial benefit to the adviser—other than the fee for his advice—"that advice to a client might in some way be tinged with that pecuniary interest [whether consciously or] subconsciously motivated." The report quoted one leading investment adviser who said that he "would put the emphasis . . . on subconscious" motivation in such situations. It quoted a member of the Commission staff who suggested that a significant part of the problem was not the existence of a "deliberate intent" to obtain a financial advantage, but rather the existence "subconsciously [of] a prejudice in favor of one's own financial interests." The report incorporated the Code of Ethics and Standards of Practice of one of the leading investment counsel associations, which contained the following canon:

> [An investment adviser] should continuously occupy an impartial and disinterested position, as free as humanly possible from the *subtle* influence of prejudice, *conscious or unconscious*; he should scrupulously avoid any affiliation, or any act, which subjects his position to challenge in this respect. (Emphasis added.) . . .

This study and report—authorized and directed by statute—culminated in the preparation and introduction by Senator Wagner of the bill which, with some changes, became the Investment Advisers Act of 1940. . . .

Although certain changes were made in the bill following the hearings, there is nothing to indicate an intent to alter the fundamental purposes of the legislation. The broad proscription against "any . . . practice . . . which operates . . . as a fraud or deceit upon any client or prospective client" remained in the bill from beginning to end. And the Committee Reports indicate a desire to preserve "the personalized character of the services of investment advisers," and to eliminate conflicts of interest between the investment adviser and the clients as safeguards both to "unsophisticated investors" and to "bona fide investment counsel." The Investment Advisers Act of 1940 thus reflects a congressional recognition "of the delicate fiduciary nature of an investment advisory relationship," as well as a congressional intent to eliminate, or at least to expose, all conflicts of interest which might incline an investment adviser—consciously or unconsciously—to render advice which was not disinterested. It would defeat the manifest purpose of the Investment Advisers Act of 1940 for us to hold, therefore, that Congress, in empowering the courts to enjoin any practice which operates "as a fraud or deceit," intended to require proof of intent to injure and actual injury to clients.

II

We turn now to a consideration of whether the specific conduct here in issue was the type which Congress intended to reach in the Investment Advisers Act of 1940. It is arguable—indeed it was argued by "some investment counsel representatives" who testified before the Commission—that any "trading by investment counselors for their own account in securities in which their clients were interested . . ." creates a potential conflict of interest which must be eliminated. We need not go that far in this case, since here the Commission seeks only disclosure of conflict of interests with significantly greater potential for abuse than in the situation described above. An adviser who, like respondents, secretly trades on the market effect of his own recommendation may be motivated—consciously or unconsciously—to recommend a given security not because of its potential for long-run price increase (which would profit the client), but because of its potential for short-run price increase in response to anticipated activity from the recommendation (which would profit the adviser). An investor seeking the advice of a registered investment adviser must, if the legislative purpose is to be served, be permitted to evaluate such overlapping motivations, through appropriate disclosure, in deciding whether an adviser is serving "two masters" or only one, "especially . . . if one of the masters happens to be economic self-interest." *United States v. Mississippi Valley Generating Co.*, 364 U.S. 520, 549. Accordingly we hold that the Investment Advisers Act of 1940 empowers the courts, upon a showing such as that made here, to require an adviser to make full and frank disclosure of his practice of trading on the effect of his recommendations.

III

Respondents argue, finally, that their advice was "honest" in the sense that they believed it was sound and did not offer it for the purpose of furthering personal pecuniary objectives. This, of course, is but another way of putting the rejected argument that the elements of technical common-law fraud—particularly intent—must be established before an injunction requiring a disclosure may be ordered. It is the practice itself, however, with its potential for abuse, which "operates as a fraud or deceit" within the meaning of the Act when relevant information is suppressed. The Investment Advisers Act of 1940 was "directed not only at dishonor, but also at conduct that tempts dishonor." *United States v. Mississippi Valley Generating Co.*, 364 U.S. 520, 549. Failure to disclose material facts must be deemed fraud or deceit within its intended meaning, for, as the experience of the 1920's and 1930's amply reveals, the darkness and ignorance of commercial secrecy are the conditions upon which predatory practices best thrive. To impose upon the Securities and Exchange Commission the burden of showing deliberate dishonesty as a condition precedent to protecting investors through the prophylaxis of disclosure would effectively nullify the protective purposes of the statute. Reading the Act in light of its background we find no such requirement commanded. Neither the Commission nor the courts should be required "to separate the mental urges," *Peterson v. Greenville*, 373 U.S. 244, 248, of an investment adviser, for "[t]he motives of man are too complex . . . to separate." *Mosser v. Darrow*, 341 U.S. 267, 271. The statute, in recognition of the adviser's fiduciary relationship to his clients, requires that his advice be disinterested. To insure this it empowers the courts to require disclosure of material facts. It misconceives the purpose of the statute to confine its application to "dishonest" as opposed to "honest" motives. As Dean Shulman said in discussing the nature of securities transactions, what is required is "a picture not simply of the show window, but of the entire store . . . not simply truth in the statements volunteered, but disclosure." The high standards of business morality exacted by our laws regulating the securities industry do not permit an investment adviser to trade on the market effect of his own recommendations without fully and fairly revealing his personal interests in these recommendations to his clients.

NOTES AND QUESTIONS

1. Investment Adviser as Fiduciary.   Is *Capital Gains* convincing in its reasoning that all advisers should be treated as fiduciaries? For an interesting discussion of the *Capital Gains* litigation, questioning whether it should be read to create the federal fiduciary obligation for which it is regularly cited, *see* Laby, *SEC v. Capital Gains Research Bureau* and the Investment Advisers Act of 1940, 91 B.U. L. Rev. 1051 (2011). In conjunction with the adoption of Regulation Best Interest for broker-dealers, the SEC issued an interpretative release on the role of "best interest" in the fiduciary obligations of investment advisers, making clear that what is expected of advisers and brokers is indeed very similar. Release IA-5248 (June 5, 2019). Of particular importance is whether disclosure and informed consent by the client will necessarily protect the adviser from liability for breach of fiduciary duty. On this, the Commission said:

> [A]n adviser must eliminate or at least expose through full and fair disclosure all conflicts of interest which might incline an investment adviser—consciously or unconsciously—to render advice which was not disinterested. We believe that while full and fair disclosure of all material facts relating to the advisory relationship or of conflicts of interest and a client's informed consent prevent the presence of those material facts or conflicts themselves from violating the adviser's fiduciary duty, such disclosure and consent do not themselves satisfy the adviser's duty to act in the client's best interest. . . . In some cases, conflicts may be of a nature and extent that it would be difficult to provide disclosure to clients that adequately conveys the material facts or the nature, magnitude, and potential effect of the conflict sufficient for a client to consent to or reject it. In other cases, disclosure may not be specific enough for a client to understand whether and how the conflict could affect the advice it receives. For retail clients in particular, it may be difficult to provide disclosure regarding complex or extensive conflicts that is sufficiently specific, but also understandable. In all of these cases where an investment adviser cannot fully and fairly disclose a conflict of interest to a client such that the client can provide informed consent, the adviser should either eliminate the conflict or adequately mitigate (i.e., modify practices to reduce) the conflict such that full and fair disclosure and informed consent are possible.

2.   Enforcement Proceedings Against Investment Advisers.   Capital Gains rejects the idea that fraud by investment advisers should depend upon a showing of motive or intent. In *SEC v. Steadman*, 967 F.2d 636 (D.C. Cir. 1992), the court indicated that scienter must be shown under Section 206(1), but not under subsection (2). Note that for a variety of administrative disciplinary sanctions and for material omissions from disclosure documents filed with the Commission, the violation must be "willful." You have seen this word used in many different places in the securities laws, with some disagreement as to its meaning. For purposes of liability for omissions in filings (Section 207), the D.C. Circuit insists that there be more culpability than mere negligence. *SEC v. Robare Group*, 922 F.3d 468 (D.C. Cir. 2019). With respect to Section 206(4), it is not necessary for the fraud to be on an existing, or even a prospective, client. *See United States v. Elliott*, 62 F.3d 1304 (11th Cir. 1995).

3.   Private Rights of Action.   Is the antifraud prohibition of Section 206 a good candidate for an implied private right of action for damages? In *Transamerica Mortgage Advisors Inc. v. Lewis*, 444 U.S. 11 (1979), the Supreme Court said no, stressing the absence of any affirmative statement of congressional intent in that direction. Is it any different in this regard from Section 10(b) of the '34 Act, however? The Court's ruling in *Transamerica* may not be of overly dramatic consequence, however, in the sense that investors aggrieved by fraudulent advisory conduct will still often be able to claim that such fraud was in connection with the purchase or sale of a security and hence (assuming scienter) a violation of Rule 10b-5. In *Laird v. Integrated Resources Co.*, 897 F.2d 826 (5th Cir. 1990), the court relied heavily on *Capital Gains* in holding that an adviser's fiduciary status gives rise under Rule 10b-5 to an affirmative duty of "utmost good faith" to disclose conflicts of interest (e.g., commissions it was being paid to promote a particular stock) to its advisees.

Moreover, the Supreme Court held in *Transamerica* that Section 215, a voidability provision similar to Section 29(b) under the '34 Act, does provide a basis for a private suit seeking the rescission of a contract made in violation of the Investment Advisers Act. The Court made clear that this right is limited to recovery of the consideration paid attendant to the tainted contract, not "compensation for any diminution in the value of the rescinding party's investment alleged to have resulted from the adviser's action or inaction." 444 U.S. at 24 n.14.

4. Advertising. Apart from its specific prohibitions, ranging from the general antifraud provision applied in *Capital Gains* to a specific bar against dealing in an undisclosed capacity with a client, Section 206 also gives the SEC wide-ranging rulemaking authority to prevent fraud by investment advisers. And the Commission has responded with rules in a number of areas, perhaps the most interesting of which is advertising. Rule 206(4)-1 prohibits any advertisement—a term broadly defined to include virtually any communication sent to more than one person that offers analyses, reports, information, graphs, charts, formulae, etc.—that, among other things, (1) refers to any kind of testimonial concerning the adviser's services, (2) refers to past successful recommendations without disclosing all recommendations during the previous year by such adviser, or (3) represents that any graph, chart, or formula can "in and of itself" be used to make investment decisions or that any such device will assist such decisionmaking unless there is prominent disclosure of "the limitations thereof and the difficulties with respect to its use." By and large, such cases as have made their way into the courts have endorsed the Commission's views. In *SEC v. C.R. Richmond & Co.*, 565 F.2d 1101 (9th Cir. 1977), for instance, the court upheld a sanction against an investment adviser who had written a book called The Money Machine, which was sold at his seminars. The book was deemed an advertisement and violated the advertising rule because it did not contain the proper disclaimers or a full statement of the "track record." Similarly, in *Marketlines Inc. v. SEC*, 384 F.2d 264, 266 (2d Cir. 1967), *cert. denied*, 390 U.S. 947 (1968), dealing with advertisements that described an investment service as "unique" and backed by the efforts of "financial scientists," the court held that the Commission had properly concluded that "the entire content and tone of the advertisements was designed to whet the appetite of the unsophisticated" and was thus unlawful. Is this an example of fiduciary ideology run amok? What, for example, is wrong with using celebrity or other testimonials in advertising?

5. The Madoff Scandal. In late 2008, the investing world was stunned by revelations that Bernard Madoff, owner of a large brokerage firm and a major figure in the trading world, had run a multi-billion dollar "Ponzi scheme," duping hundreds of wealthy, sometimes well-known, investors. Adding to the outrage was evidence that the SEC had received numerous tips about Madoff's activities and had several times begun investigations that would have exposed and shut down his advisory operations, but was never able to discover his fraud. A report by the SEC's own Inspector General describes and severely criticizes the staff's futile efforts. *See* Investigation of the Failure of the SEC to Uncover Bernard Madoff's Ponzi Scheme, Aug. 31, 2009 (available on the SEC's web site).

Madoff used a small handful of so-called feeder funds to channel investors' money to him, and did not register with the SEC as an investment adviser until fairly late, when the SEC changed the rules on the exemption for advisers with fewer than 15 clients. In light of this and other scandals, the Commission has taken another look at its Advisers Act rules to see if they could be improved so as to make schemes like Madoff's less likely. One change is the requirement that all registered advisers who maintain custody of client funds (1) undergo an annual surprise examination by an independent public accountant to verify those assets; (2) have the qualified custodian maintaining those funds and securities send account statements directly to the clients; and (3) where the funds and securities are not maintained by an independent qualified custodian, to obtain a report of the internal controls relating to custody from an independent public accountant. *See* Release IA-2968 (Dec. 30, 2009). *See SEC v. Nutmeg Group LLC*, 162 F. Supp. 3d 754 (N.D. Ill. 2016).

6. *Pay to Play.* Responding to another set of scandals involving investment advisers to governmental actors, the SEC adopted Rule 206(4)-5 to bar advisers from soliciting advisory business for two years after making any campaign contribution to an official connected to that work. Interested parties challenged the Rule under the First Amendment, but the case stumbled on procedural grounds. *New York State Republican Party v. SEC*, 799 F.3d 1126 (D.C. Cir. 2015). Later on, the D.C. Circuit upheld against a First Amendment and administrative law challenge a related FINRA rule designed to assure that advisers did not circumvent the ban by channeling payments through brokers acting as placement agents. *New York State Republican Party v. SEC*, 927 F.3d 499 (D.C. Cir. 2019).

4. Investment Advice, Investment Information, and the First Amendment

Lowe v. Securities and Exchange Commission
472 U.S. 181 (1985)

STEVENS, J. The question is whether petitioners may be permanently enjoined from publishing nonpersonalized investment advice and commentary in securities newsletters because they are not registered as investment advisers under §203(c) of the Investment Advisers Act of 1940 (Act), 54 Stat. 850, 15 U.S.C. §80b-3(c).

Christopher Lowe is the president and principal shareholder of Lowe Management Corporation. From 1974 until 1981, the corporation was registered as an investment adviser under the Act. During that period Lowe was convicted of misappropriating funds of an investment client, of engaging in business as an investment adviser without filing a registration application with New York's Department of Law, of tampering with evidence to cover up fraud of an investment client, and of stealing from a bank. Consequently, on May 11, 1981, the Securities and Exchange Commission (Commission), after a full hearing before an Administrative Law Judge, entered an order revoking the registration of the Lowe Management Corporation, and ordering Lowe not to associate thereafter with any investment adviser.

In fashioning its remedy, the Commission took into account the fact that petitioners "are now solely engaged in the business of publishing advisory publications." The Commission noted that unless the registration was revoked, petitioners would be "free to engage in all aspects of the advisory business" and that even their publishing activities afforded them "opportunities for dishonesty and self-dealing."

A little over a year later, the Commission commenced this action by filing a complaint in the United States District Court for the Eastern District of New York, alleging that Lowe, the Lowe Management Corporation, and two other corporations, were violating the Act, and that Lowe was violating the Commission's order. The principal charge in the complaint was that Lowe and the three corporations (petitioners) were publishing two investment newsletters and soliciting subscriptions for a stock-chart service. The complaint alleged that, through those publications, the petitioners were engaged in the business of advising others "as to the advisability of investing in, purchasing, or selling securities . . . and as a part of a regular business . . . issuing reports concerning securities." Because none of the petitioners was registered or exempt from registration under the Act, the use of the mails in connection with the advisory business allegedly violated §203(a) of the Act. The Commission prayed for a permanent injunction restraining the further distribution of petitioners' investment advisory publications; for a permanent injunction enforcing compliance with the order of May 11, 1981; and for other relief.

Although three publications are involved in this litigation, only one need be described. A typical issue of the Lowe Investment and Financial Letter contained general commentary about the securities and bullion markets, reviews of market indicators and investment strategies, and specific recommendations for buying, selling, or holding stocks and bullion. The newsletter advertised a "telephone hotline" over which subscribers could call to get current information. The number of subscribers to the newsletter ranged from 3,000 to 19,000. It was advertised as a semimonthly publication, but only eight issues were published in the 15 months after the entry of the 1981 order.

Subscribers who testified at the trial criticized the lack of regularity of publication, but no adverse evidence concerning the quality of the publications was offered. There was no evidence that Lowe's criminal convictions were related to the publications; no evidence that Lowe had engaged in any trading activity in any securities that were the subject of advice or comment in the publications; and no contention that any of the information published in the advisory services had been false or materially misleading. . . .

III

The basic definition of an "investment adviser" in the Act reads as follows:

"Investment adviser" means any person who, for compensation, engages in the business of advising others, either directly or through publications or writings, as to the value of securities or as to the advisability of investing in, purchasing, or selling securities, or who, for compensation and as part of a regular business, issues or promulgates analyses or reports concerning securities. . . .

Petitioners' newsletters are distributed "for compensation and as part of a regular business" and they contain "analyses or reports concerning securities." Thus, on its face, the basic definition applies to petitioners. The definition, however, is far from absolute. The Act excludes several categories of persons from its definition of an investment adviser, lists certain investment advisers who need not be registered, and also authorizes the Commission to exclude "such other person" as it may designate by rule or order.

One of the statutory exclusions is for "the publisher of any bona fide newspaper, news magazine or business or financial publication of general and regular circulation." Although neither the text of the Act nor its legislative history defines the precise scope of this exclusion, two points seem tolerably clear. Congress did not intend to exclude publications that are distributed by investment advisers as a normal part of the business of servicing their clients. The legislative history plainly demonstrates that Congress was primarily interested in regulating the business of rendering personalized investment advice, including publishing activities that are a normal incident thereto. On the other hand, Congress, plainly sensitive to First Amendment concerns, wanted to make clear that it did not seek to regulate the press through the licensing of nonpersonalized publishing activities. . . .

The exclusion itself uses extremely broad language that encompasses any newspaper, business publication, or financial publication provided that two conditions are met. The publication must be "bona fide," and it must be "of regular and general circulation." Neither of these conditions is defined, but the two qualifications precisely differentiate "hit and run tipsters" and "touts" from genuine publishers. Presumably a "bona fide" publication would be genuine in the sense that it would contain disinterested commentary and analysis as opposed to promotional material disseminated by a "tout." Moreover, publications with a "general and regular" circulation would not include "people who send out bulletins from time to time on the advisability of buying and selling stocks," *see* Hearings on H.R. 10065, at 87, or "hit and run tipsters." Ibid. Because the content of petitioners' newsletters was completely disinterested, and because they were offered to the general public on a regular schedule, they are described by the plain language of the exclusion. . . .

The language of the exclusion, read literally, seems to describe petitioners' newsletters. Petitioners are "publishers of any bona fide newspaper, news magazine or business or financial publication." The only modifier that might arguably disqualify the newsletters are the words "bona fide." Notably, however, those words describe the publication rather than the character of the publisher; hence Lowe's unsavory history does not prevent his newsletters from being "bona fide." In light of the legislative history, this phrase translates best to "genuine"; petitioners' publications meet this definition: they are published by those engaged solely in the publishing business and are not personal communications masquerading in the clothing of newspapers, news magazines, or financial publications. Moreover, there is no suggestion that they contained any false or misleading information, or that they were designed to tout any security in which petitioners had an interest. Further, petitioners' publications are "of general and regular circulation." Although the publications have not been "regular" in the sense of consistent circulation, the publications have been "regular" in the sense important to the securities market: there is no indication that they have been timed to specific market activity, or to events affecting or having the ability to affect the securities industry.

The dangers of fraud, deception, or overreaching that motivated the enactment of the statute are present in personalized communications but are not replicated in publications that are advertised and sold in an open market. To the extent that the chart service contains factual information about past transactions and market trends, and the newsletters contain commentary on general market conditions, there can be no doubt about the protected character of the communications, a matter that concerned Congress when the exclusion was drafted. The content of the publications and the audience to which they are directed in this case reveal the specific limits of the exclusion. As long as the communications between petitioners and their subscribers remain entirely impersonal and do not develop into the kind of fiduciary, person-to-person relationships that were discussed at length in the legislative history of the Act and that are characteristic of investment adviser-client relationships, we believe the publications are, at least presumptively, within the exclusion and thus not subject to registration under the Act.

We therefore conclude that petitioners' publications fall within the statutory exclusion for bona fide publications and that none of the petitioners is an "investment adviser" as defined in the Act. It follows that neither their unregistered status, nor the Commission order barring Lowe from associating with an investment adviser, provides a justification for restraining the future publication of their newsletters. It also follows that we need not specifically address the constitutional question we granted certiorari to decide.

The judgment of the Court of Appeals is reversed.

NOTES AND QUESTIONS

  1.   Newsletters and the Fiduciary Rhetoric.   What does *Lowe* do to *Capital Gains*? Was Capital Gains Research Bureau an investment adviser in the first place?

  2.   Freedom of Speech.   For further discussion on the First Amendment in the advisory context, upholding a broad scope to regulation, *see SEC v. Wall Street Publishing Institute*, 851 F.2d 365 (D.C. Cir. 1988), *cert. denied*, 489 U.S. 1066 (1989) ("Speech relating to the purchase and sale of securities, in our view, forms a distinct category of communications in which the government's power to regulate is at least as broad as with respect to the general rubric of commercial speech"). And the regulation of investment advisers is only one—albeit the most visible—of many areas where there is a tension between the values underlying securities regulation and the values underlying the First Amendment. Under the Securities Act, for example, a "quiet period" is imposed upon issuers and underwriters prior to filing a registration statement, barring many otherwise innocent forms of publicity. The content of the registration statement is carefully reviewed by a government agency, with changes often compelled; "free writing" and numerous other communications are limited while this review is ongoing. This is far from a free market of (economic) "ideas," but the assumption is that such regulation is permissible. *See Bulldog Investors v. Secretary of the Commonwealth*, 953 N.E.2d 691 (Mass. 2011) (rejecting First Amendment challenge to state blue sky restrictions on the Internet sale of unregistered securities). *But see* Heyman, The Quiet Period in a Noisy World: Rethinking Securities Regulation and Corporate Free Speech, 74 Ohio St. L.J. 189 (2013). While the First Amendment thus far has not constrained securities regulation to any great degree, the potential for constitutional challenges is thought to be growing.

3. Web Sites. Where do web sites containing investment advice fit into the Advisers Act scheme? Are they forms of protected speech akin to newsletters? *See* the problem that follows, as well as *SEC v. Park*, [2000 Transfer Binder] Fed. Sec. L. Rep. (CCH) ¶90,974 (N.D. Ill. 2000). What about "robo-adviser" software products? *See* Baker & Delleart, Regulating Robo-Advice Across the Financial Services Industry, 103 Iowa L. Rev. 713 (2018). The SEC made clear in its fiduciary duty interpretation that robo-advisory products must be fully compliant with all aspects of the Advisers Act, including fiduciary responsibilities.

PROBLEM

19-1. Adrian Boehm has established a web site for investors, aimed at day traders. Her "picks" are made throughout the trading day, and change rapidly. Occasionally, she invites an online chat with investors, answering their questions about her choices. For a fee, investors may subscribe to a special service pursuant to which they are given prompt e-mail alerts just before a new recommendation is posted, and gain access to "subscriber restricted" portions of the site with special selections. On the site's home page, Adrian indicates that she "may" own stock in some of the companies recommended. Using a variety of pseudonyms, Adrian and her associates began posting testimonials to her investment success on a large number of well-known bulletin boards and chat rooms. Shortly after she started doing this, her subscriber base grew considerably. Since then, she has made hundreds of thousands of dollars from a combination of subscriptions and profits from selling stocks from her portfolio shortly after a recommendation is made. Is Adrian an investment adviser? If so, has she violated any provisions of the Advisers Act? If not, has she nonetheless violated Rule 10b-5?

B.　*Credit Rating Agencies*

As noted in Chapter 4, credit rating agencies have long played an important role in both public and private debt financing, assigning creditworthiness ratings to new issuances and monitoring outstanding debt for changes in the risk of default. Moody's and Standard & Poor's dominated the industry, and—notwithstanding a broad claim of First Amendment protection for their work—became regulated as Nationally Recognized Statistical Rating Organizations, or NRSROs. *E.g.*, Hill, Regulating the Rating Agencies, 82 Wash. U. L.Q. 43 (2004). One conflict of interest was obvious: Issuers are the ones who select and pay for the credit ratings. As rating agencies extended their work to securitized debt products and derivatives based on them, questions intensified about how reliable these ratings were. With the sudden market crash in 2007, it seemed clear that the rating agencies had failed. In 2015, the Justice Department and the SEC settled crisis-related enforcement actions against S&P, with aggregate penalties of nearly a billion and a half dollars.

　　Dodd-Frank's reform takes three directions. The first is greater SEC oversight, including as to the procedures for assigning ratings that had previously been off limits to the Commission. The second direction relates to liability, including changes with respect to the '33 Act "expert" status. Separately, the Act creates a new private right of action provision with respect to an NRSRO for securities law violations based on the NRSRO's failure either to conduct a reasonable investigation of the rated security with respect to the factual elements it relied upon in its methodology for evaluating credit risk or to obtain reasonable verification of such factual elements from other sources it considered to be competent and that were independent of the issuer and underwriter.

　　Potentially, the most far-reaching changes made by the legislation come from its insistence that the SEC and other federal agencies begin the process of eliminating from various forms of regulation any reference to credit ratings that effectively confer a regulatory "privilege." Congress was concerned that these regulations—by insisting that certain investments have the desired investment-grade rating—effectively made the rating agencies insensitive to the quality of their ratings—all that was needed for them to make money was to confer the stamp of approval that allowed the sale of securities to occur. In early 2011, the SEC began the process of eliminating these references. In so doing, it expressed concern that taking away the references would leave institutional investors on their own in assessing the creditworthiness of the instruments in which they invest. However, it has made some progress in eliminating such privileges. *See, e.g.*, Securities Act Release No. 33-9245 (July 27, 2011) (removing references in Securities Act forms).

　　For a critical assessment of the reforms, *see* Partnoy, What's (Still) Wrong with Credit Ratings, 92 Wash. L. Rev. 1407 (2017) (criticizing SEC for "gutting" useful changes). A fairly pessimistic empirical study is Dimitrov et al., Impact of the Dodd-Frank Act on Credit Ratings, 115 J. Fin. Econ. 505 (2015).

C. *Mutual Funds and Other Investment Companies*

It has long been recognized that regulation is required to deal with the potential for abuse when persons manage large pools of other people's money. *See* Morley, The Separation of Funds and Managers: A Theory of Investment Fund Structure and Regulation, 123 Yale L.J. 1228 (2014). For the most part, however, the substantive task of regulating the activities of financial institutions (e.g., bank trust departments, pension funds, insurance companies) has not been made part of securities regulation. The exception is the investment company. Pursuant to the Investment Company Act of 1940 ('40 Act), investment companies are subject to an intense degree of federal oversight in their day-to-day governance and operations, even though they are also established (and thus also regulated) as business associations under state law.

Investment companies—especially in their most common form, the "mutual fund"—are immensely important in the world of investing. A mutual fund (or open-end investment company) allows investors to purchase and redeem fund shares on a daily basis at a price based on the net asset value of the fund at the end of the trading day. At the beginning of 2018, U.S.-based mutual funds held more than $22 *trillion* in assets, largely on behalf of over 100 million retail investors. *See* Investment Company Institute, 2018 Fact Book. The mutual fund adviser—usually, as we shall see, a separate entity from the fund itself—typically charges a management fee, based on assets under management. Note, by the way, that by its nature, a mutual fund is engaged in a continuous offering of its shares to the public, and thus constantly in registration under the '33 Act, thereby extending its regulatory responsibilities. This massive presence no doubt explains why Congress insisted that mutual funds operate relatively conservatively via risk-reducing devices like limitations on both leverage and incentive compensation for their advisers.

The materials that follow are not intended to be exhaustive of the subject of investment company regulation. The '40 Act is one of the most complicated and technical of all the securities statutes. Rather, we shall examine some of the more interesting aspects of regulation. The dominating issue in investment company regulation—as in so much of securities regulation generally—is how much to rely upon the discipline of the marketplace, aided by mandatory disclosure, to control the behavior of investment companies and how much substantive supplementation is needed. If there is one thing clear about the industry, it is competitive, and mutual funds, at least, must constantly search for new money. *See* Coates & Hubbard, Competition in the Mutual Fund Industry: Evidence and Implications for Policy, 33 J. Corp. L. 151 (2007). There are many and varied companies competing for investor funds, and new entrants appear constantly. The financial press regularly evaluates fund performance, and substantial evidence shows that investors as a group are sensitive (perhaps hypersensitive) to evidence of good performance. To a disproportionate degree, new money flowing into mutual funds goes to funds that recently have outperformed their competitors. *E.g.*, Gruber, Another Puzzle: The Growth of Actively Managed Mutual Funds, 51 J. Fin. 783 (1996). This might suggest that a disclosure regime should be sufficient, supplemented by the kinds of fiduciary duties of loyalty and care normally imposed upon managers—not a system of detailed and burdensome federal standards governing the structure and behavior of mutual funds and other investment companies. *See generally* W. Baumol et al., The Economics of Mutual Fund Markets: Competition Versus Regulation (1990). And indeed, full disclosure is at the heart of investment company regulation. The SEC has taken pains to make mutual fund disclosure "user friendly," by highlighting key information in summary form. Within this framework is emphasis on fund performance—including a management discussion and analysis and standardized performance data, with graphic comparison of the fund's performance to a broad-based securities market index—and fees and expenses. Funds are also required to disclose the identity of the individual person or persons primarily responsible for the day-to-day management of the fund's portfolio. And with increased attention to derivatives and other risky financial products, the SEC has also stepped up its requirement that funds effectively disclose the riskiness of their portfolios. But is disclosure likely to be enough? Before making any judgments, consider two things. One is the teachings of the efficient market hypothesis. Whatever the theoretical debate about market behavior, evidence is slim that investors benefit greatly from the research that portfolio managers do. While some studies show that funds do outperform market indices on average simply in terms of their stock-picking ability, this margin is largely offset by the fees they charge and the returns forgone when fund assets are kept in the form of cash or cash equivalents. *See* Wermers, Mutual Fund Performance: An Empirical Decomposition into Stock-Picking Talent, Style, Transactions Costs, and Expenses, 55 J. Fin. 1655 (2000). In terms of net performance, there is some evidence that actively managed mutual funds on average *underperform* the market. And the costs are often compounded by the taxes investors have to pay each year to reflect capital gains distributions generated by active trading. *See* Disclosure of Mutual Fund After-Tax Returns, Investment Company Act Release No. 24,339 (Mar. 15, 2000). Nor is there strong evidence that investors can anticipate a lengthy period of above-average returns simply by investing in "top ranked" funds (i.e., those that have performed well in the past), though there is some evidence of a "hot hand" phenomenon among funds. For good discussions of some of the imperfections in mutual fund investor behavior, *see* Frazzini & Lamont, Dumb Money: Mutual Fund Flows and the Cross Section of Stock Returns, 88 J. Fin. Econ. 299 (2008); Mahoney, Manager-Investor Conflicts in Mutual Funds, 18 J. Econ. Persp. 161 (2004). This makes those investors subject to influence via aggressive selling, which connects to the debates we have seen in this and the last chapter about "best interest" duties of brokers and advisers. The "broker channel" for promoting mutual funds is fraught with conflicts. *See* Bergstresser et al., Assessing the Costs and Benefits of Brokers in the Mutual Fund Industry, 22 Rev. Fin. Stud. 4129 (2009); Del Guerco & Reuter, Mutual Fund Performance and the Incentive to Generate Alpha, 69 J. Fin. 1673 (2014) (underperformance heavily concentrated in broker-sold funds). And efforts to improve retail investor decisionmaking via disclosure have not been particularly successful. For suggestions on how better to promote investor understanding, *see* Fisch & Wilkinson-Ryan, Why Do Retail Investors Make Costly Mistakes? An Experiment on Mutual Fund Choice, 162 U. Pa. L. Rev. 605 (2014); Cox & Payne, Mutual Fund Expense Disclosures: A Behavioral Perspective, 83 Wash. U. L.Q. 923 (2005).

Besides these issues of investor protection, we should take note of the immense power mutual funds hold based on their authority to vote the shares they own of companies in their portfolios. In contested battles, how the funds vote will have a significant effect on the outcome. However, for many years, how the funds exercised this power was a private matter. In early 2003, the SEC adopted new Rule 30b1-4, requiring mutual funds to disclose the policies and procedures used to determine how to vote proxies relating to their holdings and to file with the SEC and make available a record of their voting decisions. This was a very controversial change. Critics of the rule proposal charged that making public the voting decisions would open fund managers to increased pressures, both from issuer management and special interest groups, and thereby make them less effective at "behind the scenes" governance. In the end, the Commission decided that investors' right to know about the voting decisions of fund managers outweighed these risks and disclosure of how a fund voted would lead to an enhanced, rather than diminished, level of shareholder oversight. *See* Disclosure of Proxy Voting Policies and Proxy Voting Records by Registered Management Investment Companies, Release 33-8188 (Jan. 31, 2003). As noted in Chapter 16, the influence of proxy advisory firms on mutual fund voting decisions is a matter of considerable political controversy.

1. The Structure and Governance of a Mutual Fund

▌▌ **Investment Company Act Release No. 24,082**
Securities and Exchange Commission (Oct. 14, 1999)

Mutual funds are formed as corporations or business trusts under state law and, like other corporations and trusts, must be operated for the benefit of their shareholders. Mutual funds are unique, however, in that they are "organized and operated by people whose primary loyalty and pecuniary interest lie outside the enterprise" [citing Division of Investment Management, Protecting Investors: A Half Century of Investment Company Regulation 251 (1992)]. As described below, this "external management" of virtually all mutual funds presents inherent conflicts of interest and potential for abuses.

An investment adviser typically organizes a mutual fund and is responsible for its day-to-day operations. The adviser generally provides the seed money, officers, employees, and office space, and usually selects the initial board of directors. In many cases, the investment adviser sponsors several funds that share administrative and distribution systems as part of a "family of funds." As a result of this extensive involvement, and the general absence of shareholder activism, investment advisers typically dominate the funds they advise.

Investment advisers to mutual funds are generally organized as corporations, which have their own shareholders. These shareholders may have an interest in the mutual fund that is quite different from the interests of the fund's shareholders. For example, while fund shareholders ordinarily prefer lower fees (to achieve greater returns), shareholders of the fund's investment adviser might want to maximize profits through higher fees. And while fund shareholders might prefer that advisers use brokers that charge the lowest possible commissions, advisers might prefer to use brokers that are affiliates of the adviser. These types of conflicts (and others) resulted in the pervasive abuses that led Congress in 1940 to enact legislation regulating the activities of mutual funds.

The Investment Company Act establishes a comprehensive regulatory scheme designed to protect fund investors by addressing the conflicts of interest between funds and their investment advisers or other affiliated persons. The Act strictly regulates some of the most serious conflicts. For example, the Act prohibits certain transactions between a fund and its affiliates, including the investment adviser, unless approved by the Commission. The Act also relies on fund boards of directors to police conflicts of interest.

Under state law, directors are generally responsible for the oversight of all of the operations of a mutual fund. In addition, the Investment Company Act assigns many specific responsibilities to fund boards. For example, fund boards must evaluate and approve a fund's advisory contract and any assignment of the contract, and may unilaterally terminate the contract. Directors also approve the fund's principal underwriting contract, select the fund's independent accountant, and value certain securities held by the fund. In addition, under the Act and our rules, directors have responsibility for evaluating the reasonableness of advisory and distribution-related fees charged the fund and managing certain operational conflicts. Just recently, for example, we clarified that boards must assume oversight responsibility for personal securities transactions by employees of the fund and its adviser.

The Act requires that independent directors constitute at least 40 percent of a fund's board, and sets the standards for when a person will be disqualified from being an independent director (i.e., will be considered an "interested person" under the Act). These independent directors play an important role in representing and guarding the interests of investors. As has been stated many times, Congress intended these directors to be the "independent watchdogs" for investors and to "supply an independent check on management."

Many requirements of the Act and our rules that protect investors from conflicts of interest specifically rely on action by these independent directors. The Act, for example, requires independent directors to separately evaluate and approve the fund's contract with an investment adviser or principal underwriter. Our rules have permitted innovative types of funds, more efficient fund operations, and new distribution arrangements by exempting funds from prohibitions related to conflicts of interest. While these rules have provided important flexibility to allow mutual funds to meet the changing needs of investors, they also rely on approval, oversight, and monitoring by independent directors to protect investors.

As the materials on fiduciary responsibility that will follow shortly make clear, courts, too, have adopted a posture of deference to the decisions of the unaffiliated directors as a means of cleansing the self-dealing taint that would otherwise call into question transactions involving the fund and its adviser so long as the kind of disclosure called for in *Moses* occurs. In *Burks v. Lasker*, 441

U.S. 471 (1979), for instance, the Supreme Court ruled that the independent directors of any investment company could, consistent with federal law, terminate a shareholder's derivative suit in an appropriate case over the objections of the plaintiffs. After a lengthy exposition of the role of the disinterested director under the '40 Act, the Court concluded that Congress intended such directors to assume the position of independent "watchdogs" over the fund, adding that "it would have been paradoxical for Congress to have been willing to rely largely upon 'watchdogs' to protect shareholder interests and yet, where the 'watchdogs' have done precisely that, require that they be totally muzzled." Id. at 485.

How successful is this approach? Given what you recall from your Corporations course about corporate governance, do you agree that such deference is warranted? Especially if shareholders seem to have so little to do in practice with the selection of the outside directors, choosing instead to redeem their shares when dissatisfied with fund performance? A number of commentators have expressed doubts. *E.g.*, Brudney, The Independent Director—Heavenly City or Potemkin Village?, 95 Harv. L. Rev. 597, 617-619 (1982) (pointing out that few, if any, instances of investment adviser misconduct show that "independent" directors tried to do much to stop it). Worth noting, perhaps, is that most mutual funds that are formed as corporations are incorporated in Maryland, a state whose laws are particularly attractive to mutual fund sponsors. A number of commentators have called for the abolition of the traditional mutual fund structure—with all its corporate governance baggage—in favor of structures acknowledging that funds are products managed and sold by their sponsors (the management companies), for which other kinds of investor protection strategies are better suited. *See* Roiter, Disentangling Mutual Fund Governance from Corporate Governance, 6 Harv. Bus. L. Rev. 1 (2016); Morley & Curtis, Taking Exit Rights Seriously: Why Governance and Fee Litigation Doesn't Work in Mutual Funds, 120 Yale L.J. 84 (2010); Palmiter, The Mutual Fund Board: A Failed Experiment in Regulatory Outsourcing, 1 Brook. J. Corp. Fin. & Com. L. 165 (2006). Indeed, this is the approach followed in Europe.

PROBLEM

19-2.   Consider whether any of the following persons is a "disinterested" person with regard to a mutual fund for purposes of Section 10(a):

a.   the spouse of an attorney who acts as the principal outside counsel to the fund's adviser;
b.   the CEO of an industrial company if the fund owns 5.5 percent of the voting shares of that company;
c.   a person who is otherwise disinterested, but who also serves on the board of directors of a number of other funds in the same fund complex.

(*Note:* "Interested person" is defined in Section 2(a)(19) of the '40 Act. That subsection, in turn, makes reference to "affiliated person" as defined in Section 2(a)(3). Both require careful reading.)

2.   Sales and Redemptions of Mutual Fund Shares

a.   *Prices and Distribution Charges*

The system of pricing and distributing mutual fund shares is fixed firmly by a combination of statute and SEC rules. Within this framework, the most important regulatory requirement in practical terms is Rule 22c-1, which provides, with limited exceptions, that both sales and redemptions of fund shares must occur at the net asset value that is next computed after the receipt of the order or tender. In general, net asset value must be computed no less than once daily (Monday through Friday) at the time prescribed by the fund's board of directors.

The fund's pricing discretion, then, is effectively limited to issues relating to sales charges and expenses. Here, there are a number of variations. Some funds are classified as "load" funds and charge the investor a certain percentage of the purchase price of the security. This load is used to compensate those involved in the selling of the security: the underwriters, brokers, and dealers—who may or may not be affiliates of the sponsor. FINRA's Rules of Fair Practice limit the maximum sales charges that can be imposed upon mutual fund shares to 8.5 percent. Though once commonplace, load funds represent a smaller percentage of mutual funds sales today. Many load fees vary depending on how much is invested, with lower loads for higher amounts ("breakpoints"). An alternative to the front-end load is the so-called contingent deferred sales charge, pursuant to which the investor is charged a fee upon redemption. The fee typically varies over time, diminishing the longer the investor holds the mutual fund shares.

Funds that charge no sale or redemption fee are referred to as "no-load" funds. For the most part, this occurs when the fund itself or its affiliates undertake to internalize most or all of the advertising and marketing expenses associated with the sale of shares, seeking compensation for this elsewhere. One of the most notable recent developments in mutual fund marketing is the distribution of multiple classes of shares in the same fund, where the differences among classes relate largely to expense charges. Some shares might be no-load and sold via advertising to one market segment, while others with distribution charges would be sold by a brokerage sales force targeting different groups of investors. *See* SEC Staff Report, Protecting Investors: A Half Century of Investment Company Regulation 330-332 (1992). The SEC has become increasingly concerned that investors are not always well served by this complexity, with investors often pushed to purchase classes of shares with heavier (if perhaps hidden) fees or in amounts that fail to take advantage of attractive breakpoints. Mutual fund distributors may also waive fees for large sophisticated investors, making up lost revenue elsewhere.

The question of the financing of distribution expenses other than through front-end or deferred sales loads is an extremely controversial regulatory issue. Historically, the SEC had taken the position—with support from the legislative history of Section 12(b)—that distribution expenses, such as advertising, printing and mailing costs, and commissions and other compensation paid to sales personnel to promote sales of fund shares, should not be borne by the fund itself. The underlying rationale no doubt was concern about conflict of interest, since a principal beneficiary of increased sales of fund shares is the adviser, and, thus, a level of expenditures might be made that would be unjustified in terms of benefit to the fund's shareholders. In 1980, however, the Commission adopted Rule 12b-1, permitting in certain circumstances a distribution fee to be charged to the fund's shareholders as a group.

In terms of possible benefits to shareholders, it is possible that the increased sales generated by such marketing expenditures may create some efficiencies, such as lowering the per unit cost of research expenses charged to each shareholder or improving the liquidity position of the fund, so that management can concentrate on performance without having to worry excessively about an unexpectedly high level of redemptions. And for new funds, at least, the use of 12b-1 plans may obviate the need for front-end sales loads.

The difficult 12b-1 issue is whether the amounts paid out pursuant to such plans are likely to be fair or not in relation to potential benefits to fund investors, given the influence that advisers may have even over these disinterested directors. Some evidence calls into question whether increased expenditures on sales and marketing do produce compensating benefits for fund shareholders. *See* Malkiel, The Regulation of Mutual Funds: An Agenda for the Future, in Modernizing U.S. Securities Regulation 476 (K. Lehn & R. Kamphuis eds., 1993) ("What has been happening is that . . . new 12b-1 distribution charges have been imposed that greatly exceed any potential gain from the economies of scale that could come from an expanded asset base."). Recognizing some basis for concern, the SEC has heightened the disclosure requirements regarding all investor- and fund-borne charges, including advisory fees and 12b-1 charges, which must be presented in tabular form in the synopsis found at the beginning of the fund's prospectus. The presentation of performance data must reflect these recurring charges. As noted, this all connects to Regulation Best Interest for broker-dealers and the fiduciary duties of investment advisers, which highlights costs to investors as an important factor in what can be recommended. The SEC has brought numerous cases against both broker-dealers and investment advisers for putting clients and customers into mutual fund shares with 12b-1 fees when they were eligible for a class of shares without such trailing fees. *See In the Matter of PNC Investments*, Exchange Act Release 83004 (Apr. 6, 2018).

b. *Abusive Trading Practices*

The issue of fees and adviser compensation became a scandal in the summer of 2003 with the revelation of widespread late trading and market timing activity in mutual funds. Late trading involves submitting an order after the fund has priced its shares, usually at 4:00 P.M. Eastern Time, for execution at the 4:00 P.M. price. This is akin to insider trading because the transaction is executed after some significant announcement, made just after the markets' 4:00 P.M. close, that is likely to affect the fund's portfolio value. The fund violates Rule 22c-1 if it permits this. Evidence uncovered by New York Attorney General Eliot Spitzer and the SEC suggests that some funds allowed such late trading as part of a quid pro quo; big investors such as hedge funds would take large positions in the funds (thereby increasing the adviser's management fee) if they permitted late trading.

Market timing is a more difficult issue. Take, for example, an international fund that invests heavily in Asian securities. It is common that the fund will value its portfolio at 4:00 P.M. Eastern Time here as well. However, the Asian markets close much earlier, making it possible that the closing prices will be stale by the New York close because of news announced in the meantime. Empirical evidence had been mounting for some time that arbitrageurs seek to exploit the stale prices. *See, e.g.*, Zitzewitz, Who Cares About Shareholders? Arbitrage-Proofing Mutual Funds, 19 J.L. Econ. & Org. 245 (2003); Chalmers et al., On the Perils of Security Pricing by Financial Intermediaries: The Wildcard Option in Transacting Mutual Fund Shares, 56 J. Fin. 2209 (2001). Because the transactions are made before 4:00 P.M., there is no violation of Rule 22c-1. The strategy, however, is typically to sell the purchased fund shares quickly, perhaps in a matter of days. Most funds state in their prospectuses that they either "discourage" market timing by disallowing this activity or impose redemption fees. Evidence showed that funds would indeed discourage or penalize smaller traders who tried to engage in market timing, but permit such activity by large investors—who again may have committed to a quid pro quo in return for this privilege. In some instances, moreover, it turns out that executives at the advisory firm were themselves engaged in market timing, or investors in hedge funds were doing timing trades. For a discussion of the market impact of these scandals, *see* Choi & Kahan, The Market Penalty for the Mutual Fund Scandals, 87 B.U. L. Rev. 1021 (2007). Beside numerous federal and state enforcement actions, one response to the frequent trading problem was the SEC's adoption of Rule 22c-2, which requires fund boards to either charge a fee of up to 2 percent when an investor seeks to redeem shares within seven days of purchase or determine that such a policy is not necessary or appropriate for the fund. *See* Mutual Fund Redemption Fees, Investment Company Act Release No. 26782 (Mar. 11, 2005).

Recall from Chapter 13 the Supreme Court's decision in *Janus Capital*, which held that the advisory firm was not the "maker" of misstatements relating to market timing and late trading in the prospectuses filed by funds that they advised. Given what you have learned in this chapter, what is your reaction to the decision? *See* Birdthistle, The Supreme Court's Theory of the Fund, 37 J. Corp. L. 771 (2012).

PROBLEM

19-3. Ajax Diversified Funds is managed by Ajax Advisers, Inc. Evidence has shown that advisory personnel have permitted market timing trades in 35 or so instances at the behest of various large investors, allowing those investors to profit by millions of dollars because the price at 4:00 P.M., when the net asset value of funds shares was computed, was stale because of market developments around the world. In what way does this practice injure anyone? In what way is it unlawful? Would it matter if Ajax's fund prospectuses stated that the fund's policy was to discourage market timing?

c.   Money Market Funds

A money market mutual fund is a fund that invests mainly in short-term "safe obligations," operating as the functional equivalent of a bank deposit account—but without the FDIC insurance as protection. They have become popular with both retail and individual investors, with nearly $3 trillion in assets. Generally, the money market fund "commits" to maintain a net asset value of $1 per share, to preserve functional parity in liquidity with bank accounts. But what if—as happened at the onset of the global financial crisis—a fund's NAV goes below $1 because the fund's investments turn out to have been more risky than expected ("breaking the buck")? The absence of deposit insurance makes such funds susceptible to a run by nervous investors. In Rule 2a-7, the SEC required more transparency and restraint with respect to fund investment portfolios. But the fear of runs persists, and with it the likelihood that the government would have to intervene to stabilize the situation if a run threatened a very large, "systemically significant" fund. And if there is an implicit federal guarantee, money market funds gain a competitive advantage over banks, which fund their own insurance. The SEC acted in 2014 with a series of compromise measures, including a modified "floating" NAV. For a criticism, *see* Fisch, The Broken Buck Stops Here: Embracing Sponsor Support in Money Market Fund Reform, 93 N.C. L. Rev. 935 (2015).

3.   The Compensation of Investment Company Affiliates

Jones v. Harris Associates L.P.
559 U.S. 335 (2010)

Alito, J. We consider in this case what a mutual fund shareholder must prove in order to show that a mutual fund investment adviser breached the "fiduciary duty with respect to the receipt of compensation for services" that is imposed by §36(b) of the Investment Company Act of 1940, 15 U.S.C. §80a-35(b) (hereinafter §36(b)).

Petitioners are shareholders in three different mutual funds managed by respondent Harris Associates L.P., an investment adviser. Petitioners filed this action in the Northern District of Illinois pursuant to §36(b) seeking damages, an injunction, and rescission of advisory agreements between Harris Associates and the mutual funds. The complaint alleged that Harris Associates had violated §36(b) by charging fees that were "disproportionate to the services rendered" and "not within the range of what would have been negotiated at arm's length in light of all the surrounding circumstances."

The District Court granted summary judgment for Harris Associates. Applying the standard adopted in *Gartenberg v. Merrill Lynch Asset Management, Inc.*, 694 F.2d 923 (C.A.2 1982), the court concluded that petitioners had failed to raise a triable issue of fact as to "whether the fees charged . . . were so disproportionately large that they could not have been the result of arm's-length bargaining." The District Court assumed that it was relevant to compare the challenged fees with those that Harris Associates charged its other clients. But in light of those comparisons as well as comparisons with fees charged by other investment advisers to similar mutual funds, the Court held that it could not reasonably be found that the challenged fees were outside the range that could have been the product of arm's-length bargaining.

A panel of the Seventh Circuit affirmed based on different reasoning, explicitly "disapprov[ing] the *Gartenberg* approach." 527 F.3d 627, 632 (2008). Looking to trust law, the panel noted that, while a trustee "owes an obligation of candor in negotiation," a trustee, at the time of the creation of a trust, "may negotiate in his own interest and accept what the settlor or governance institution agrees to pay." Ibid. (citing Restatement (Second) of Trusts §242, and Comment *f*). The panel thus reasoned that "[a] fiduciary duty differs from rate regulation. A fiduciary must make full disclosure and play no tricks but is not subject to a cap on compensation." 527 F.3d, at 632. In the panel's view, the amount of an adviser's compensation would be relevant only if the compensation were "so unusual" as to give rise to an inference "that deceit must have occurred, or that the persons responsible for decision have abdicated." Ibid.

The panel argued that this understanding of §36(b) is consistent with the forces operating in the contemporary mutual fund market. Noting that "[t]oday thousands of mutual funds compete," the panel concluded that "sophisticated investors" shop for the funds that produce the best overall results, "mov[e] their money elsewhere" when fees are "excessive in relation to the results," and thus "create a competitive pressure" that generally keeps fees low. Id., at 633-634. The panel faulted *Gartenberg* on the ground that it "relies too little on markets." 527 F.3d, at 632. And the panel firmly rejected a comparison between the fees that Harris Associates charged to the funds and the fees that Harris Associates charged other types of clients, observing that "[d]ifferent clients call for different commitments of time" and that costs, such as research, that may benefit several categories of clients "make it hard to draw inferences from fee levels." Id., at 634.

The Seventh Circuit denied rehearing en banc by an equally divided vote. 537 F.3d 728 (2008). The dissent from the denial of rehearing argued that the panel's rejection of *Gartenberg* was based "mainly on an economic analysis that is ripe for reexamination." 537 F.3d, at 730 (opinion of Posner, J.). Among other things, the dissent expressed concern that Harris Associates charged "its captive funds more than twice what it charges independent funds," and the dissent questioned whether high adviser fees actually drive investors away. Id., at 731. . . .

Under the Act, scrutiny of investment adviser compensation by a fully informed mutual fund board is the "cornerstone of the . . . effort to control conflicts of interest within mutual funds." *Burks [v. Lasker]*, 441 U.S. [471] at 482 [(1979)]. . . . From this formulation, two inferences may be drawn. First, a measure of deference to a board's judgment may be appropriate in some instances. Second, the appropriate measure of deference varies depending on the circumstances.

Gartenberg heeds these precepts. *Gartenberg* advises that "the expertise of the independent trustees of a fund, whether they are fully informed about all facts bearing on the [investment adviser's] service and fee, and the extent of care and conscientiousness with which they perform their duties are important factors to be considered in deciding whether they and the [investment adviser] are guilty of a breach of fiduciary duty in violation of §36(b)." 694 F.2d, at 930.

While both parties in this case endorse the basic *Gartenberg* approach, they disagree on several important questions that warrant discussion.

The first concerns comparisons between the fees that an adviser charges a captive mutual fund and the fees that it charges its independent clients. As noted, the *Gartenberg* court rejected a comparison between the fees that the adviser in that case charged a money market fund and the fees that it charged a pension fund. 694 F.2d, at 930, n.3 (noting the [sic] "[t]he nature and extent of the services required by each type of fund differ sharply"). Petitioners contend that such a comparison is appropriate, but respondent disagrees. Since the Act requires consideration of all relevant factors, we do not think that there can be any categorical rule regarding the comparisons of the fees charged different types of clients. Instead, courts may give such comparisons the weight that they merit in light of the similarities and differences between the services that the clients in question require, but courts must be wary of inapt comparisons. As the panel below noted, there may be significant differences between the services provided by an investment adviser to a mutual fund and those it provides to a pension fund which are attributable to the greater frequency of shareholder redemptions in a mutual fund, the higher turnover of mutual fund assets, the more burdensome regulatory and legal obligations, and higher marketing costs. 527 F.3d, at 634 ("Different clients call for different commitments of time"). If the services rendered are sufficiently different that a comparison is not probative, then courts must reject such a comparison. Even if the services provided and fees charged to an independent fund are relevant, courts should be mindful that the Act does not necessarily ensure fee parity between mutual funds and institutional clients contrary to petitioners' contentions. See id., at 631. ("Plaintiffs maintain that a fiduciary may charge its controlled clients no more than its independent clients").

By the same token, courts should not rely too heavily on comparisons with fees charged to mutual funds by other advisers. These comparisons are problematic because these fees, like those challenged, may not be the product of negotiations conducted at arm's length. See 537 F.3d, at 731-732 (opinion dissenting from denial of rehearing en banc); *Gartenberg, supra,* at 929 ("Competition between money market funds for shareholder business does not support an inference that competition must therefore also exist between [investment advisers] for fund business. The former may be vigorous even though the latter is virtually non-existent").

Finally, a court's evaluation of an investment adviser's fiduciary duty must take into account both procedure and substance. Where a board's process for negotiating and reviewing investment-adviser compensation is robust, a reviewing court should afford commensurate deference to the outcome of the bargaining process. Thus, if the disinterested directors considered the relevant factors, their decision to approve a particular fee agreement is entitled to considerable weight, even if a court might weigh the factors differently. This is not to deny that a fee may be excessive even if it was negotiated by a board in possession of all relevant information, but such a determination must be based on evidence that the fee "is so disproportionately large that it bears no reasonable relationship to the services rendered and could not have been the product of arm's-length bargaining." *Gartenberg, supra,* at 928.

In contrast, where the board's process was deficient or the adviser withheld important information, the court must take a more rigorous look at the outcome. When an investment adviser fails to disclose material information to the board, greater scrutiny is justified because the withheld information might have hampered the board's ability to function as "an independent check upon the management." . . .

It is also important to note that the standard for fiduciary breach under §36(b) does not call for judicial second-guessing of informed board decisions. . . . In reviewing compensation under §36(b), the Act does not require courts to engage in a precise calculation of fees representative of arm's-length bargaining. See 527 F.3d, at 633 ("Judicial price-setting does not accompany fiduciary duties"). As recounted above, Congress rejected a "reasonableness" requirement that was criticized as charging the courts with rate-setting responsibilities. Congress' approach recognizes that courts are not well suited to make such precise calculations. *Gartenberg*'s "so disproportionately large" standard, 694 F.2d, at 928, reflects this congressional choice to "rely largely upon [independent director] 'watchdogs' to protect shareholders' interests."

By focusing almost entirely on the element of disclosure, the Seventh Circuit panel erred. See 527 F.3d, at 632 (An investment adviser "must make full disclosure and play no tricks but is not subject to a cap on compensation"). The *Gartenberg* standard, which the panel rejected, may lack sharp analytical clarity, but we believe that it accurately reflects the compromise that is embodied in §36(b), and it has provided a workable standard for nearly three decades. The debate between the Seventh Circuit panel and the dissent from the denial of rehearing regarding today's mutual fund market is a matter for Congress, not the courts.

For the foregoing reasons, the judgment of the Court of Appeals is vacated, and the case remanded for further proceedings consistent with this opinion.

NOTES AND QUESTIONS

1. Plaintiffs' Chance of Success. In light of *Jones*, what practical chance does the plaintiff class have of convincing a court that a fee is outside the zone of reasonableness in a situation where a fund is highly successful and continues to compete well in the market? While the test seems very defendant friendly, there is a steady stream of settlements, largely because of the fact-specific nature of the inquiry under *Jones*. For a critical assessment of the litigation environment, *see* Morley & Curtis, Taking Exit Rights Seriously: Why Governance and Fee Litigation Don't Work in Mutual Funds, 120 Yale. L.J. 84 (2011).

2. Some Procedural Rules. Section 36(b) is an interesting statutory provision procedurally. Does it establish what is essentially a derivative lawsuit? If so, should requirements like demand on directors be applicable? Although some courts said yes, the Supreme Court ruled in 1984 that congressional intent was to provide a direct cause of action for fund shareholders, albeit as a group, and that therefore no demand requirement should be imposed. *Daily Income Fund Inc. v. Fox*, 464 U.S. 523 (1984). Another rule worth noting is the short limitations period, closely bound up with its measure of damages; recovery is limited by the statute to compensation improperly paid to the defendant within one year before the plaintiff's suit was brought.

> **3.   *The Enigmatic Section 36(a).***   The litigation over advisory fees has mainly been under Section 36(b), because it creates an express private right of action to recover excessive compensation. But what of other breaches of duty? Section 36(a) grants the SEC the power to seek relief in situations where an investment company officer, director, adviser, depositor, advisory board member, or principal underwriter (except in the case of a closed-end company) has engaged or is about to engage in a "breach of fiduciary duty involving personal misconduct" with respect to that investment company. According to the legislative history, actual intent is unnecessary for there to be personal misconduct, and "[i]n appropriate cases, nonfeasance of duty or abdication of responsibility would constitute" a violation of Section 36(a). H.R. Rep. No. 1382, 91st Cong., 2d Sess. 37 (1970). For some time, courts had allowed shareholders to bring private actions under Section 36(a). However, in recent years, courts have reconsidered the implied rights issue and cut off investors' recourse. *See Bellikoff v. Eaton Vance*, 481 F.3d 110 (2d Cir. 2007). Hence, these other duties are largely left to the SEC to enforce.

PROBLEM

19-4.   You are an outside director of the Gladiator Fund, an aggressive mid-cap stock fund. Over the last few years, the fund's performance has been average for its peers, as have its expenses. On the agenda for the next board meeting is a proposal from the firm's long-standing adviser, GFM Inc., to increase the management fee by some 15 percent. As justification, GFM states a need to increase its salaries for portfolio managers and renovate its offices to make it more attractive to the best talent in the business. What issues would you raise, and what questions would you pose, at the meeting?

4.   Self-Dealing by Investment Company Affiliates

The delegation of the primary operating responsibilities for an investment company to a group of "outsiders" (i.e., the adviser, the primary underwriter, one or more broker-dealers) makes the potential for self-dealing transactions and other conflicts of interest a fairly serious one. This is compounded in many fund settings, where the adviser controls the entities charged with distribution and custodial responsibilities. Congress responded to this concern with one of the most complicated sets of provisions in the entire Investment Company Act framework, found primarily in Section 17.

The policing of conflict of interest transactions is divided into three major substantive parts in Section 17. The first regulates transactions involving the investment company as principal: An affiliated person (or an affiliate of an affiliate) may not sell any security or property to the investment company or a company controlled by the investment company (Section 17(a)(1)) or buy any security or property from the investment company or one it controls (Section

17(a)(2)). Section 17(a)(3) extends the prohibitory approach to loan transactions, with certain limited exceptions. Statutory exceptions from Section 17(a) exist with respect to transactions in securities sold by the affiliate as part of a general offering or in securities issued by the investment company. And, quite importantly, Section 17(c) states that notwithstanding Section 17(a), a person may in the ordinary course of business buy or sell merchandise or enter into a lease arrangement with any other person.

   Note that these are *absolute bars*, unlike the general approach to self-dealing transactions under state corporation law, which tends toward an ad hoc review of the substantive and/or procedural fairness of a challenged transaction. The prophylactic effect is ameliorated, however, by Section 17(b), which establishes a procedure by which the investment company may apply to the SEC for an exemption from the bar upon a showing that the proposed transaction is reasonable, that it is fair and does not involve any overreaching, and that it is consistent with both the investment policy of the petitioner and the general purposes of the '40 Act. In proceedings under Section 17(b), the Commission has emphasized that its duty is to assure fairness to all parties concerned in the proposed transaction by measuring the proposal against a hypothetical arm's-length bargain involving the same sort of property. And the burden of proof is on the petitioner. Section 17(a) deals with situations where the investment company and an affiliate are on opposite sides of a transaction, with the obvious potential for overreaching. In contrast, the other principal substantive self-dealing provision, Section 17(d), deals with situations where the investment company and the affiliate are "joint" participants in some transaction—that is, on the same side of the table. Here, the concern is to ensure an equitable distribution of benefits and burdens from the transaction. *See* Interpretive Matters Concerning Independent Directors of Investment Companies, Investment Company Act Release No. 24083 (Oct. 14, 1999). Section 17(d) is only an enabling provision, authorizing the SEC to adopt such rules as are appropriate to deal with this sort of conflict transaction. In Rule 17d-1, however, the Commission has imposed the same sort of pre-transaction review requirement that is found under Sections 17(a) and 17(b). Its authority to require pre-clearance of such transactions was upheld in *SEC v. Talley Industries Inc.*, 399 F.2d 396 (2d Cir. 1968), *cert. denied*, 393 U.S. 1015 (1969).

   Closely related to the foregoing conflict of interest rules is Section 17(e)(1), which prohibits any investment company affiliate (or affiliate of an affiliate) from accepting any compensation from a third party in connection with services as an agent in the purchase or sale of property to or for an investment company. This provision is the subject of frequent litigation. In *United States v. Ostrander*, 999 F.2d 27 (2d Cir. 1993), for example, the criminal conviction of a Fidelity portfolio manager was affirmed upon a showing that she purchased warrants in a leveraged buyout situation made available to her personally by Michael Milken of Drexel Burnham Lambert, which was underwriting the transaction, while at the same time causing Fidelity to purchase some $95 million worth of the LBO securities. These warrants were not available to the general public and ultimately netted her some $750,000 on a $13,200 investment. Finally, observe the presence of Section 17(j), which gives the SEC broad rulemaking authority both to proscribe fraudulent practices by persons affiliated with investment companies and to require codes of ethics by such companies. In Rule 17j-1, the

Commission used this authority to bar all forms of fraud on investment companies and require both the implementing of codes of ethics and the reporting of personal trading. One issue that has generated substantial controversy here is whether funds should go beyond simply requiring "access" persons to report their personal financial holdings and restrict their trading activities. *See* Rock, Foxes and Hen Houses? Personal Trading by Mutual Fund Managers, 73 Wash. U. L.Q. 1601 (1995). What are the likely costs and benefits of restricting the ability of analysts and portfolio managers to trade for their own accounts when they discover an attractive investment? For example, should fund managers be prohibited from engaging in short-term trading (e.g., purchases and sales within 60 days)? Prohibited from participating in initial public offerings? In 1999, the SEC amended Rule 17j-1 to increase the oversight role of independent directors over personal trading activities of investment company personnel (including portfolio managers), and to require prior approval of investments in initial public offerings and certain limited offerings. Personal Investment Activities of Investment Company Personnel, Investment Company Act Release No. 23958 (Aug. 20, 1999).

5. The Definitional Problem

As noted at the outset, there is a very complicated test for determining whether an entity is an investment company and hence subject to the complicated federal supervision detailed above. One reason is that there are two main threshold tests for making the determination of what is an investment company. While one of these, Section 3(a)(1)(A), is fairly commonsensical in its drafting, the other, Section 3(a)(1)(C), is simply an objective accounting-based test, drafted in such a way as presumptively to bring within its scope many institutions that would not normally be thought of at all as traditional investment companies. *See Securities and Exchange Commission v. Fifth Avenue Coach Lines Inc.*, 289 F. Supp. 3 (S.D.N.Y. 1968), *aff'd*, 435 F.2d 510 (2d Cir. 1970). Both Microsoft and Yahoo! have had to deal with the possibility that they were, at some point at least, investment companies because of numerous investments in other technology issuers. *See UFCW Local Pension Fund v. Mayer*, 895 F.3d 695 (9th Cir. 2018), dismissing a derivative suit challenging continued reliance by Yahoo! on an earlier SEC exemptive letter after its investments in Alibaba, holding that there is no implied private right of action for registration violations.

Section 3(a)(1)(C) deems a company to be an investment company if it is in the business of owning or holding "investment securities" having a value exceeding 40 percent of its total assets (exclusive of government securities or cash items). Investment securities are all securities except government securities, securities issued by employees' securities companies, and securities issued by majority-owned subsidiaries that are not themselves investment companies. *But see* Rule 3a-1, which provides that, notwithstanding the statistical test of Section 3(a)(1)(C), a company is *not* deemed an investment company if no more than 45 percent of its total assets (exclusive of government securities and cash items) consists of and no more than 45 percent of its total income is derived from— essentially—securities other than government securities and securities issued by affiliates of the issuer. The boom in stock market valuation in the 1990s has created many interesting problems relating to the investment company definition. Naturally, the statistical approach puts substantial stress on the definition of *security* in Section 2(a)(36), which reads much like its cousins in the other securities acts. But given the different purposes that the '40 Act serves, should the methodology of interpretation be the same? For instance, how should a certificate of deposit be treated, whether for purposes of the numerator (is it a security and thus included) or the denominator (is it a cash item and thus excluded)? *See* Bradford, Expanding the Investment Company Act: The SEC's Manipulation of the Definition of a Security, 60 Ohio St. L.J. 995 (1999).

The breadth of the definition of *investment company* is ameliorated to some extent by a long series of both statutory- and rule-based exemptions. Some are reasonably straightforward. Section 3(b)(1) excepts any issuer primarily engaged (by itself or through wholly owned subsidiaries) in a business *other* than that of investing, owning, holding, or trading in securities. In *SEC v. National Presto Industries Inc.*, 486 F.3d 305 (7th Cir. 2007), the court found this exemption applicable to a company that had divested itself of many of its tangible assets (so that most of its assets were indeed in the form of investments), but which nonetheless had significant operating income through the sale of products manufactured by subcontractors with which it had done business. Section 3(b)(2) then goes on to create a procedure whereby companies can seek a Commission order exempting them from the Act on grounds that their business (directly or through *majority-owned* subsidiaries) is primarily other than investment. In addition, Section 3(b)(3), as interpreted under Rule 3a-3, excepts any company that is wholly owned by another company that is not itself an investment company—in other words, an industrial company can have an investment subsidiary without that subsidiary being required to register.

PROBLEM

19-5. Hypotech Inc. is an "incubator" for Internet startup companies. It owns office space that it rents to startups, taking stock and options in these firms instead of cash. In addition, it provides consulting advice and administrative services to its affiliated "tenants." Does it risk being characterized as an investment company? *See* Lane & McPhee, Is It Time to Redefine "Investment Company" in the Age of the Internet?, 14 InSights, no. 5 (May 2000), at 2.

6. ETFs

A different type of investment company product has emerged and grown rapidly: the so-called exchange-traded fund (ETF). These are somewhat complicated structures whereby a sponsor creates an indexed fund stipulating that only "authorized providers" can transact in shares directly with the ETF. In turn, the APs create marketable shares that can be listed on an exchange and bought or sold by retail investors at any time during the trading day at a price that reflects the net asset value of the fund. This is an arbitrage mechanism, one that, in theory at least, will keep the trading price of the listed shares very close to net asset value. But on occasion the arbitrage has failed. What's the benefit from such complexity? One advantage is more favorable taxation. Another is that the prices will fluctuate over the course of the trading day, as opposed to the "hard close" of once-a-day pricing. Shares can also be sold short. For an influential analysis of ETFs with proposals for regulatory reform, *see* Hu & Morley, A Regulatory Framework for Exchange Traded Funds, 91 S. Cal. L. Rev. 839 (2018).

D. *Hedge Funds and Other Private Investment Vehicles*

Certain important investment vehicles mentioned throughout this book—hedge funds, private equity funds, and venture capital funds—would be registered investment companies but for specific exemptions from investment company status, two of which are of particular importance here. Section 3(c)(1) of the Investment Company Act exempts companies with 100 or fewer shareholders. Section 3(c)(7) exempts a company whose shareholders are "qualified purchasers" with high net worth (generally, individuals who own specified investments worth at least $5 million) and is not making or proposing to make a public offering of its securities. The latter means that private funds are heavy users of the '33 Act exemptions provided by Rules 506(b) and (c) of Reg D, studied in Chapter 5.

Although the term *hedge fund* might suggest a cautious approach to investing, quite the opposite is often true. Hedge funds are some of the most active traders in the equity and debt markets, often employing complex trading strategies to arbitrage small differences in securities or derivative positions. *See* Gemansky et al., Hedge Funds: A Dynamic Industry in Transition, 7 Ann. Rev. Fin. Econ. 483 (2015). Hedge funds have a number of regulatory advantages over mutual funds. Most importantly, they are not subject to the Investment Company Act's complicated restrictions on leveraging, diversification, and liquidity—allowing them to engage in far more risky trading strategies, including significant amounts of short selling. They also readily avoid restrictions on performance fees, leading to far greater use of high-powered incentives for hedge fund managers, who typically take a large share of the returns generated by the fund once they exceed some pre-determined benchmark. *See* Goetzmann et al., High-Water Marks and Hedge Fund Management Contracts, 58 J. Fin. 1685 (2003). Finally, hedge funds avoid the extensive public disclosure requirements imposed by the '40 Act and so can hide much about their portfolios and trading practices.

The status of hedge funds and their advisers became increasingly controversial as the hedge fund industry grew. *See* Paredes, On the Decision to Regulate Hedge Funds: The SEC's Regulatory Philosophy, Style and Mission, 2006 U. Ill. L. Rev. 975. In 2010, the Dodd-Frank Act eliminated what had been a "private adviser" exemption from the Investment Advisers Act for those with relatively few clients, thereby bringing hedge fund advisers into the SEC's regulatory regime to the extent that they have more than $150 million in assets under management. As a result of being registered investment advisers, private fund advisers are subject to SEC inspection, which increases their compliance risk considerably. Recently, the SEC has brought quite a number of enforcement actions against abusive practices in the hedge fund world that call into question the savvy of investors in those funds. *E.g., In re Clean Energy Capital LLC,* SEC Release No. 3955 (Oct. 17, 2014) (adviser allocated millions of dollars of expenses to funds, including salaries and bonuses). On the uneasy approach to mandatory disclosure, given how private funds deem their strategies highly proprietary, *see* Kaal, Private Fund Disclosure Under the Dodd Frank Act, 9 Brook. J. Corp., Fin. & Com. L. 428 (2015).

By and large, hedge fund investors have been wealthy individuals and institutions, but press reports about the extraordinary returns some funds have generated have whetted the appetite of more and more retail investors. This poses an increasingly competitive threat to the mutual fund industry, especially as a number of "funds of hedge funds" have emerged that offer investors the opportunity to invest as little as $25,000 in a registered mutual fund that simply turns around and invests in a pool of unregistered hedge fund securities. There are also readily available means for non-qualified investors to invest indirectly in the startup firms that rely on private financing, whether through mutual funds that make large stake investments in private companies, or by investing in "business development companies," which receive special statutory exemptions under the '40 Act enabling them to more aggressively provide startup financing. For a survey of investment vehicles open to public investors that seek the outsized returns that sometimes come from getting in on the early stages of issuer capital-raising, *see* Kim, A Typology of Public and Private Equity, 44 Fla. St. U. L. Rev. 1435 (2018). On how much this kind of risky retail investing should be encouraged, *see* Schwartz, Should Mutual Funds Invest in Startups? A Case Study of Fidelity Magellan Fund's Investment in Unicorns (and Other Startups) and the Regulatory Implications, 95 N.C. L. Rev. 1341 (2017).

||20||

Transnational Fraud and the Reach of U.S. Securities Laws

Transactions in securities frequently cross American borders. According to the Treasury Department, as of March 2019, American investors held more than $11 trillion in foreign securities. Globalized securities markets, massive transnational movements of capital, and internationalization of investment portfolios are relatively recent, and presumably irreversible, developments not considered in the crafting of the domestic legislation. We have seen in previous chapters that the SEC has taken a substantial number of steps to define the scope of the disclosure and regulatory requirements of the federal securities laws with respect to foreign entities and conduct that occurs primarily abroad. The reach of the antifraud provisions of the securities acts, however, remains a matter for the courts to resolve. This chapter explores the extent to which the antifraud provisions of the securities acts have been, and can be, applied on an extraterritorial basis.

A. The Extraterritorial Application of U.S. Securities Laws

1. In General

What are the limits of a nation's power under international law to regulate *unilaterally* transactions occurring, to a substantial extent, outside of its boundaries? There are, of course, practical enforcement limitations on the ability of a state to regulate extraterritorially; as a British court once rather indelicately put it, "Can the island of Tobago pass a law to bind the rights of the whole world? Would the world submit to such an assumed jurisdiction?" *Buchanan v. Rucker*, 103 Eng. Rep. 546, 547 (1808). Although applicable international law norms are a matter of some controversy, there is general agreement that laws may have *some* extraterritorial reach. The problem is in defining how much.

Prior to the 2010 decision of the Supreme Court in *Morrison v. National Australia Bank, Ltd.*, 561 U.S. 247 (2010), excerpted below, the federal circuit courts framed the issue of Section 10(b)'s reach in terms of "subject matter jurisdiction," and evaluated either whether substantial conduct had occurred in the United States or whether there were effects on the United States from conduct abroad. The leading case was *Bersch v. Drexel Firestone, Inc.*, 519 F.2d 974 (2d Cir.), *cert. denied*, 423 U.S. 1018 (1975), which involved a class action on behalf of thousands of plaintiffs, almost all of whom were citizens of foreign countries. In what became the classic framework for the extraterritorial application of securities law, the Second Circuit concluded the antifraud provisions of the federal securities laws may be applied to redress losses from sales of securities (1) to U.S. residents whether or not acts (or culpable failures to act) of material importance occurred in this country, and (2) to Americans resident abroad if, but only if, acts (or culpable failures to act) of material importance in the United States significantly contributed thereto. As to sales of securities to foreigners outside the United States, the securities laws applied only if acts (or culpable failures to act) within the United States directly caused such losses. This came to be known as the "conduct and effects test," and was the standard for assessing the extraterritorial application of the U.S. securities laws, until *Morrison* led to its undoing.

2. Limiting the Reach of Securities Law: The *Morrison* Decision

Morrison v. National Australia Bank Ltd.
561 U.S. 247 (2010)

Justice SCALIA delivered the opinion of the Court.

We decide whether §10(b) of the Securities Exchange Act of 1934 provides a cause of action to foreign plaintiffs suing foreign and American defendants for misconduct in connection with securities traded on foreign exchanges.

I

Respondent National Australia Bank Limited (National) was, during the relevant time, the largest bank in Australia. Its Ordinary Shares—what in America would be called "common stock"—are traded on the Australian Stock Exchange Limited and on other foreign securities exchanges, but not on any exchange in the United States. There are listed on the New York Stock Exchange, however, National's American Depositary Receipts (ADRs), which represent the right to receive a specified number of National's Ordinary Shares. . . .

[I]n February 1998, National bought respondent HomeSide Lending, Inc., a mortgage servicing company headquartered in Florida. HomeSide's business was to receive fees for servicing mortgages (essentially the administrative tasks associated with collecting mortgage payments. . . .) How valuable each of the rights is depends, in part, on the likelihood that the mortgage to which it applies will be fully repaid before it is due, terminating the need for servicing. HomeSide calculated the present value of its mortgage-servicing rights by using valuation models designed to take this likelihood into account. It recorded the value of its assets, and the numbers appeared in National's financial statements.

From 1998 until 2001, National's annual reports and other public documents touted the success of HomeSide's business, and [officers of Homeside and National] did the same in public statements. But on July 5, 2001, National announced that it was writing down the value of HomeSide's assets by $450 million; and then again on September 3, by another $1.75 billion. The prices of both Ordinary Shares and ADRs slumped. After downplaying the July write-down, National explained the September write-down as the result of a failure to anticipate the lowering of prevailing interest rates (lower interest rates lead to more refinancings, *i.e.*, more early repayments of mortgages), other mistaken assumptions in the financial models, and the loss of goodwill. According to the complaint, however, HomeSide [officers] had manipulated HomeSide's financial models to make the rates of early repayment unrealistically low in order to cause the mortgage-servicing rights to appear more valuable than they really were. The complaint also alleges that National [was] aware of this deception by July 2000, but did nothing about it.

As relevant here, petitioners, . . . all Australians, purchased National's Ordinary Shares in 2000 and 2001, before the write-downs. They sued . . . for alleged violations of §§10(b) and 20(a) of the Securities and Exchange Act of 1934. They sought to represent a class of foreign purchasers of National's Ordinary Shares during a specified period up to the September write-down.

Respondents moved to dismiss for lack of subject-matter jurisdiction under Federal Rule of Civil Procedure 12(b)(1) and for failure to state a claim under Rule 12(b)(6). The District Court granted the motion on the former ground, finding no jurisdiction because the acts in this country were, "at most, a link in the chain of an alleged overall securities fraud scheme that culminated abroad." . . . The Court of Appeals for the Second Circuit affirmed on similar grounds. The acts performed in the United States did not "compris[e] the heart of the alleged fraud." 547 F.3d at 175-176. . . .

II

Before addressing the question presented, we must correct a threshold error in the Second Circuit's analysis. It considered the extraterritorial reach of §10(b) to raise a question of subject-matter jurisdiction, wherefore it affirmed the District Court's dismissal under Rule 12(b)(1). In this regard it was following Circuit precedent. . . .

But to ask what conduct §10(b) reaches is to ask what conduct §10(b) prohibits, which is a merits question. Subject-matter jurisdiction, by contrast, "refers to a tribunal's '"power to hear a case."'" . . . It presents an issue quite separate from the question whether the allegations the plaintiff makes entitle him to relief. . . . The District Court here had jurisdiction under 15 U.S.C. §78aa[3] to adjudicate the question whether §10(b) applies to National's conduct.

---

3. Section 78aa provides: "The district courts of the United States . . . shall have exclusive jurisdiction of violations of [the Exchange Act] or the rules and regulations thereunder, and of all suits in equity and actions at law brought to enforce any liability or duty created by [the Exchange Act] or the rules and regulations thereunder."

. . . As we have done before in situations like this, . . . we proceed to address whether petitioners' allegations state a claim.

III

A

It is a "longstanding principle of American law 'that legislation of Congress, unless a contrary intent appears, is meant to apply only within the territorial jurisdiction of the United States.'" This principle represents a canon of construction, or a presumption about a statute's meaning, rather than a limit upon Congress's power to legislate. . . . It rests on the perception that Congress ordinarily legislates with respect to domestic, not foreign matters. . . . When a statute gives no clear indication of an extraterritorial application, it has none.

Despite this principle of interpretation, long and often recited in our opinions, the Second Circuit believed that, because the Exchange Act is silent as to the extraterritorial application of §10(b), it was left to the court to "discern" whether Congress would have wanted the statute to apply. . . .

[C]ommentators have criticized the unpredictable and inconsistent application of §10(b) to transnational cases. . . . Some have challenged the premise underlying the Courts of Appeals' approach, namely that Congress did not consider the extraterritorial application of §10(b) (thereby leaving it open to the courts, supposedly, to determine what Congress would have wanted). . . .

The criticisms seem to us justified. The results of judicial-speculation-made-law—divining what Congress would have wanted if it had thought of the situation before the court—demonstrate the wisdom of the presumption against extraterritoriality. Rather than guess anew in each case, we apply the presumption in all cases, preserving a stable background against which Congress can legislate with predictable effects.

B

Rule 10b-5, the regulation under which petitioners have brought suit, was promulgated under §10(b), and "does not extend beyond conduct encompassed by §10(b)'s prohibition." *United States v. O'Hagan*, 521 U.S. 642, 651 (1997). Therefore, if §10(b) is not extraterritorial, neither is Rule 10b-5. . . .

[T]here is no affirmative indication in the Exchange Act that §10(b) applies extraterritorially, and we therefore conclude that it does not.

IV

A

Petitioners argue that the conclusion that §10(b) does not apply extraterritorially does not resolve this case. They contend that they seek no more than domestic application anyway, since Florida is where HomeSide and its senior executives engaged in the deceptive conduct of manipulating HomeSide's financial models; their complaint also alleged that Race and Hughes made misleading public statements there. This is less an answer to the presumption against extraterritorial application than it is an assertion—a quite valid assertion—that that presumption here (as often) is not self-evidently dispositive, but its application requires further analysis. For it is a rare case of prohibited extraterritorial application that lacks *all* contact with the territory of the United States. But the presumption against extraterritorial application would be a craven watchdog indeed if it retreated to its kennel whenever *some* domestic activity is involved in the case. . . .

[W]e think that the focus of the Exchange Act is not upon the place where the deception originated, but upon purchases and sales of securities in the United States. Section 10(b) does not punish deceptive conduct, but only deceptive conduct "in connection with the purchase or sale of any security registered on a national securities exchange or any security not so registered." 15 U.S.C. §78j(b). Those purchase-and-sale transactions are the objects of the statute's solicitude. . . . And it is in our view only transactions in securities listed on domestic exchanges, and domestic transactions in other securities, to which §10(b) applies. . . .

With regard to securities *not* registered on domestic exchanges, the exclusive focus on *domestic* purchases and sales[10] is strongly confirmed by §30(a) and (b). . . . The former extends the normal scope of the Exchange Act's prohibitions to acts effecting, in violation of rules prescribed by the Commission, a "transaction" in a United States security "on an exchange not within or subject to the jurisdiction of the United States." §78dd(a). And the latter specifies that the Act does not apply to "any person insofar as he transacts a business in securities without the jurisdiction of the United States," unless he does so in violation of regulations promulgated by the Commission "to prevent evasion [of the Act]." §78dd(b). Under both provisions it is the foreign location of the *transaction* that establishes (or reflects the presumption of) the Act's inapplicability, absent regulations by the Commission. . . .

Finally, we reject the notion that the Exchange Act reaches conduct in this country affecting exchanges or transactions abroad . . . : The probability of incompatibility with the applicable laws of other countries is so obvious that if Congress intended such foreign application "it would have addressed the subject of conflicts with foreign laws and procedures." 499 U.S., at 256. Like the United States, foreign countries regulate their domestic securities exchanges and securities transactions occurring within their territorial jurisdiction. And the regulation of other countries often differs from ours as to what constitutes fraud, what disclosures must be made, what damages are recoverable, what

---

10. That is in our view the meaning which the presumption against extraterritorial application requires for the words "purchase or sale, of . . . any security not so registered" in §10(b)'s phrase "in connection with the purchase or sale of any security registered on a national securities exchange *or any security not so registered*" (emphasis added). Even without the presumption against extraterritorial application, the only alternative to that reading makes nonsense of the phrase, causing it to cover all purchases and sales of registered securities, and all purchases and sales of nonregistered securities—a thought which, if intended, would surely have been expressed by the simpler phrase "all purchases and sales of securities."

discovery is available in litigation, what individual actions may be joined in a single suit, what attorney's fees are recoverable, and many other matters. . . . The Commonwealth of Australia, the United Kingdom of Great Britain and Northern Ireland, and the Republic of France have filed *amicus* briefs in this case. So have (separately or jointly) such international and foreign organizations as the International Chamber of Commerce, the Swiss Bankers Association, the Federation of German Industries, the French Business Confederation, the Institute of International Bankers, the European Banking Federation, the Australian Bankers' Association, and the Association Francaise des Entreprises Privees. They all complain of the interference with foreign securities regulation that application of §10(b) abroad would produce, and urge the adoption of a clear test that will avoid that consequence. The transactional test we have adopted—whether the purchase or sale is made in the United States, or involves a security listed on a domestic exchange—meets that requirement.

B

The Solicitor General suggests a different test, which petitioners also endorse: "[A] transnational securities fraud violates [§]10(b) when the fraud involves significant conduct in the United States that is material to the fraud's success." Neither the Solicitor General nor petitioners provide any textual support for this test. The Solicitor General sets forth a number of purposes such a test would serve: achieving a high standard of business ethics in the securities industry, ensuring honest securities markets and thereby promoting investor confidence, and preventing the United States from becoming a "Barbary Coast" for malefactors perpetrating frauds in foreign markets. But it provides no textual support for the last of these purposes, or for the first two as applied to the foreign securities industry and securities markets abroad. It is our function to give the statute the effect its language suggests, however modest that may be; not to extend it to admirable purposes it might be used to achieve.

If, moreover, one is to be attracted by the desirable consequences of the "significant and material conduct" test, one should also be repulsed by its adverse consequences. While there is no reason to believe that the United States has become the Barbary Coast for those perpetrating frauds on foreign securities markets, some fear that it has become the Shangri-La of class-action litigation for lawyers representing those allegedly cheated in foreign securities markets. . . .

Section 10(b) reaches the use of a manipulative or deceptive device or contrivance only in connection with the purchase or sale of a security listed on an American stock exchange, and the purchase or sale of any other security in the United States. This case involves no securities listed on a domestic exchange, and all aspects of the purchases complained of by those petitioners who still have live claims occurred outside the United States. Petitioners have therefore failed to state a claim on which relief can be granted. We affirm the dismissal of petitioners' complaint on this ground.

Justice SOTOMAYOR took no part in the consideration or decision of this case.

Justice STEVENS, with whom Justice GINSBURG joins, concurring in the judgment.

. . . I would adhere to the general approach that has been the law in the Second Circuit, and most of the rest of the country, for nearly four decades.

I

[T]he text and history of §10(b) are famously opaque on the question of when, exactly, transnational securities frauds fall within the statute's compass. As those types of frauds became more common in the latter half of the 20th century, the federal courts were increasingly called upon to wrestle with that question. The Court of Appeals for the Second Circuit, located in the Nation's financial center, led the effort. . . . Relying on opinions by Judge Henry Friendly, the Second Circuit eventually settled on a conduct-and-effects test. . . .

The Second Circuit's test became the "north star" of §10(b) jurisprudence, ante, at 8, not just regionally but nationally as well. . . .

In light of this history, the Court's critique of the decision below for applying "judge-made rules" is quite misplaced. This entire area of law is replete with judge-made rules, which give concrete meaning to Congress' general commands. . . .

II

The Court's other main critique of the Second Circuit's approach. . .is that the Second Circuit has "disregard[ed]" the presumption against extraterritoriality. It is the Court, however, that misapplies the presumption. . . .

[T]he real question in this case is how much, and what kinds of, *domestic* contacts are sufficient to trigger application of §10(b). In developing its conduct-and-effects test, the Second Circuit endeavored to derive a solution from the Exchange Act's text, structure, history, and purpose. . . . [I]n my view, the Second Circuit has done the best job of discerning what sorts of transnational frauds Congress meant in 1934—and still means today—to regulate. . . .

Imagine, for example, an American investor who buys shares in a company listed only on an overseas exchange. That company has a major American subsidiary with executives based in New York City; and it was in New York City that the executives masterminded and implemented a massive deception which artificially inflated the stock price—and which will, upon its disclosure, cause the price to plummet. Or, imagine that those same executives go knocking on doors in Manhattan and convince an unsophisticated retiree, on the basis of material misrepresentations, to invest her life savings in the company's doomed securities. Both of these investors would, under the Court's new test, be barred from seeking relief under §10(b). . . . Indeed, the Court's rule turns §10(b) jurisprudence (and the presumption against extraterritoriality) on its head, by withdrawing the statute's application from cases in which there is *both* substantial wrongful conduct that occurred in the United States *and* a substantial injurious effect on United States markets and citizens.

III

In my judgment, if petitioners' allegations of fraudulent misconduct that took place in Florida are true, then respondents may have violated §10(b), and could potentially be held accountable in an enforcement proceeding brought by the Commission. But it does not follow that shareholders who have failed to allege that the bulk or the heart of the fraud occurred in the United States, or that the fraud had an adverse impact on American investors or markets, may maintain a private action to recover damages they suffered abroad. Some cases involving foreign securities transactions have extensive links to, and ramifications for, this country; this case has Australia written all over it. Accordingly, for essentially the reasons stated in the Court of Appeals' opinion, I would affirm its judgment.

The Court instead elects to upend a significant area of securities law based on a plausible, but hardly decisive, construction of the statutory text. In so doing, it pays short shrift to the United States' interest in remedying frauds that transpire on American soil or harm American citizens, as well as to the accumulated wisdom and experience of the lower courts. I happen to agree with the result the Court reaches in this case. But "I respectfully dissent," once again, "from the Court's continuing campaign to render the private cause of action under §10(b) toothless." *Stoneridge*, 552 U.S., at 175 (Stevens, J., dissenting).

Shortly after *Morrison* was decided, Congress passed the Dodd-Frank Wall Street Reform and Consumer Protection Act of 2010. Section 929P of that Act provides that federal courts "shall have jurisdiction of an action or proceeding brought or instituted by the [Securities and Exchange] Commission or the United States alleging a violation" of Section 10(b) if conduct within the United States constitutes "significant steps in furtherance of the violation" or if conduct abroad has a "foreseeable substantial effect within the United States." A parallel provision contains similar language with respect to cases brought under Section 17(a) of the Securities Act. These sections were based on versions of the bill drafted while *Morrison* was pending, but before it was decided. In light of *Morrison*'s conclusion that federal courts have—and always have had—jurisdiction over Section 10(b) claims, regardless of whether they include an extraterritorial component, the provisions raise the question whether Congress intended to restore the conduct-and-effects test in actions brought by the government, or whether instead the provisions simply confer jurisdiction on federal courts (jurisdiction that *Morrison* says courts already had). *See SEC v. Scoville*, 913 F.3d 1204 (10th Cir. 2019); *SEC v. Tourre*, 2013 U.S. Dist. LEXIS 78297 (S.D.N.Y. 2013) (both concluding that Dodd-Frank expands the securities laws' coverage for government actions); *see also* discussion in Painter, The Dodd-Frank Extraterritorial Jurisdiction Provision: Was It Effective, Needed or Sufficient?, 1 Harv. Bus. L. Rev. 195 (2011).

In addition, Section 929Y of Dodd-Frank directed the SEC to solicit public comment and conduct a study on whether private rights of action should be similarly extended. It took nearly 18 months for the study to be completed. *See SEC Staff Study on the Cross-Border Scope of the Private Right of

Action Under Section 10(b) of the Securities Exchange Act of 1934 (April 2012). The study was notable for its lack of specific recommendations and avoidance of hard positions. It prompted a particularly critical response from then-Commissioner Aguilar:

> The Study should have recommended that Congress enact for private litigants a standard that is identical to the standard set forth in Section 929P of the Dodd-Frank Act—the standard for SEC and DOJ actions. The harm that has resulted and continues to result to investors is significant, and Congress should act to rectify this with haste. . . .

Commissioner Luis A. Aguilar, Dissenting Statement Regarding the Study on the Cross-Border Scope of the Private Right of Action Under Section 10(b) of the Securities Exchange Act of 1934 as required by Section 929Y of the Dodd-Frank Wall Street Reform and Consumer Protection Act (Apr. 11, 2012).

NOTES AND QUESTIONS

1. *Choosing the Forum.* Why wasn't the *Morrison* suit filed in Australia? Does Australia or the United States have the greater interest in regulating the disclosures of NAB? Can you define what "greater interest" might mean? And in evaluating whether to apply Section 10(b), should the U.S. court have evaluated the "quality" of Australia's antifraud law?

2. *Foreign Responses.* In answering the questions posed above, consider the very positive foreign responses to *Morrison*. Urging restraint on the application of U.S. law extraterritorially, the United Kingdom, France, and Australia had filed amicus briefs in the case. Following the decision, a U.K. official observed that the decision strikes "a reasonable balance between avoiding conflict with the interests of other jurisdictions and providing the U.S. authorities with the necessary powers to pursue cross-border securities fraud." In response to the SEC's request for comments, the French government declared its full support for *Morrison* and noted the case "is in accordance with the principles of comity and international law."

The Australian government commented that the decision is "soundly based [and] adapted for consistent application" and urged the SEC not to recommend an extension of private rights. Apparently content with Dodd-Frank's expansion of extraterritorial jurisdiction in SEC actions, it added:

> Of particular concern to the Australian Government is that extraterritorial actions by private plaintiffs would almost always be actions for money damages that would necessarily be subject to a jury trial, even though they involved complex business facts that occurred in a distant locale where the jurors had no personal experience. By contrast, extraterritorial civil actions authorised under Section 929P of the Dodd-Frank Act would often be brought by the Commission seeking an injunction, or an injunction coupled with the ancillary equitable remedy of disgorgement; and, as such, these equitable cases would be tried only by a Federal Judge.

3. *Crosslisting.* *Morrison*'s statement that Section 10(b) reaches "the purchase or sale of a security listed on an American stock exchange" prompted some plaintiffs to argue they may pursue Section 10(b) claims relating to securities listed on U.S. exchanges even if their own trades were executed elsewhere. Their arguments have not been successful. For example, in *City of Pontiac Policemen's & Firemen's Ret. Sys. v. UBS AG*, 752 F.3d 173 (2d Cir. 2014), the Second Circuit acknowledged that some language in *Morrison* supports the argument that listing on the U.S. exchange is dispositive without regard to where the securities are purchased, but it concluded that this is not the result intended by the case:

> *Morrison* emphasized that "the focus of the Exchange Act is . . . upon purchases and sales of securities in the United States". . . . *Morrison*'s emphasis on transactions in securities listed on domestic exchanges, makes clear that the focus of both prongs was domestic transactions of any kind, with the domestic listing acting as a proxy for a domestic transaction. Perhaps most tellingly, in rejecting this Circuit's "conduct and effects" test in favor of a bright-line rule, *Morrison* rejected our prior holding that "the Exchange Act [applies] to transactions regarding stocks traded in the United States which are effected outside the United States."

Id. at 180.

4. *The Choice* **Morrison** *Gives Investors, and Do They Really Care?* By tying a private right of action to the purchase of a security on a U.S. exchange, *Morrison* effectively gives investors the option of being able to bring Section 10(b) claims by purchasing cross listed securities only on U.S. exchanges (e.g., directly, if the shares themselves are listed, or through exchanged-traded ADRs). How meaningful is this protection, and should we expect investors to respond to *Morrison* by directing that their orders be executed through U.S. exchanges? Professor Robert Bartlett has analyzed institutional investor trading data before and after *Morrison* and found no significant changes in trading behavior, which suggests that institutional investors have placed little if any value on preserving their ability to assert private Section 10(b) claims. *See* Bartlett, Do Institutional Investors Value the Rule 10b-5 Private Right of Action? Evidence from Investors' Trading Behavior following *Morrison v. National Australia Bank Ltd.*, 44 J. Legal Stud. 183 (2015). Are there other explanations?

5. *Crosslisting and Valuation Premiums: Are Foreign Issuers Getting a Free Pass?* Why do foreign issuers crosslist their securities on U.S. exchanges? One explanation points to the bonding effect of a U.S. listing that enables issuers from countries with weak legal and regulatory regimes effectively to rent a stronger securities law framework and thereby bypass their own inadequate local regulatory systems. *See, e.g.*, Ribstein, Crosslisting and Regulatory Competition, 1 Rev. L. & Econ. 97 (2005). This, in turn, allows the foreign issuers to enjoy a premium on market valuation and lower costs of capital. A study of SEC enforcement actions against issuers in the pre-*Morrison* period from 2000 to 2008, however, reveals a sharp disparity in the levels of SEC enforcement efforts against domestic and foreign issuers:

[T]he empirical evidence shows that, particularly at the very beginning of the twenty-first century, and at the time the bonding hypothesis was developed, the SEC gave foreign issuers a free pass. Between 2000 and 2008, it brought enforcement actions against them at a rate lower than the rate for domestic issuers and focused either on high-profile, hard to miss [Foreign Corrupt Practices Act] cases or low-profile, easy to enforce infractions.

Shnitser, Note, A Free Pass for Foreign Firms? An Assessment of SEC and Private Enforcement Against Foreign Issuers, 119 Yale L.J. 1638, 1693 (2010). The author concludes that foreign issuers face a weak "second tier" securities law regime that calls into question the valuation premium for crosslisting in U.S. markets. Id. at 1676.

6. *Personal Jurisdiction Distinguished.* *Morrison* noted that lower courts have incorrectly treated the extraterritorial issue as one of subject matter jurisdiction (sometimes referred to as jurisdiction to prescribe law). Also distinguishable are cases raising the question of whether a court has personal jurisdiction over one or more of the parties. Grounded in the Due Process Clause of the Fifth Amendment, personal jurisdiction is necessary in order for a court to have the power to issue a binding judgment affecting the rights of the parties. Consent and minimum contacts are commonly used to establish personal jurisdiction over a foreign defendant. *See, e.g., Pinker v. Roche Holdings, Ltd.,* 292 F.3d 361 (3d Cir. 2002) (foreign issuer's sponsoring of American Depository Receipts for trading in the United States was a direct solicitation of investment from the American markets and sufficient to establish personal jurisdiction over the defendant in a securities fraud action).

PROBLEMS

Consider the effect of *Morrison* on a claim filed under each of the following scenarios.

20-1. Rio Pinto is a multinational iron ore mining company headquartered in Australia. Rio Pinto's shares are listed on the Australian Securities Exchange, but it also has sponsored ADRs that are listed on the New York Stock Exchange. In a series of meetings in Melbourne and in San Francisco, CALPERS spoke with Rio Pinto's top officers, who made various representations concerning the company's future earnings based largely on binding long-term contracts it has with iron ore purchasers. Impressed with what it learned, CALPERS purchased Rio Pinto's ADRs. Shortly thereafter, Rio Pinto cut its earnings forecasts, citing a weakening market for iron ore. The disclosure caused an immediate drop in Rio Pinto stock and ADR prices. On further inquiry, CALPERS has learned that the so-called binding contracts never existed, and it now wishes to pursue a 10(b) claim.

20-2. Same facts as in Problem 20-1, except CALPERS purchased Rio Pinto stock on the Australian exchange by placing an order with the San Francisco office of Merrill Lynch.

20-3. Same facts as in Problem 20-1, except the transaction was structured as a private placement that was closed in Melbourne following negotiations in

San Francisco. The purchase price was paid via a wire transfer of funds from New York.

3.   *Morrison* Applied

Absolute Activist Value Master Fund Ltd. v. Ficeto
677 F.3d 60 (2d Cir. 2012)

KATZMANN, Circuit Judge:

This case requires us to determine whether foreign funds' purchases and sales of securities issued by U.S. companies brokered through a U.S. broker-dealer constitute "domestic transactions" pursuant to *Morrison v. National Australia Bank Ltd.* . . .

BACKGROUND

A.   THE COMPLAINT

[Plaintiffs-appellants are nine Cayman Islands hedge funds (the "Funds") that invested in a variety of asset classes on behalf of hundreds of investors around the world, including many investors in the United States. Each of the Funds engaged Absolute Capital Management Holdings Limited ("ACM") to act as its investment manager. The defendants included employees and officers of ACM and registered broker-dealers, including a broker-dealer incorporated and based in California with offices in Beverly Hills.

The complaint alleges that the defendants used their control over the Funds to engage in a variation on the classic "pump and dump" scheme. They caused the Funds to purchase billions of shares issued by thinly capitalized U.S.-based companies (the "U.S. Penny Stock Companies") directly from those companies, and then caused the Funds to trade the shares among themselves to create the illusion of volume. After inflating the prices of the U.S. Penny Stocks, defendants profited by causing the Funds to purchase defendants' own holdings of U.S. Penny Stocks that they had acquired for pennies (or less). While the defendants reaped enormous profits, the Funds allegedly suffered losses in the amount of $195,916,216.]

DISCUSSION

. . .

A.   THE *MORRISON* DECISION

. . . The case at hand does not concern the first prong of *Morrison*—whether a transaction involves a security listed on a domestic exchange. Rather, we must interpret *Morrison*'s second prong and determine under what circumstances the purchase or sale of a security that is not listed on a domestic exchange should be considered "domestic" within the meaning of *Morrison*. . . . [We] hold that transactions involving securities that are not traded on a domestic exchange are domestic if irrevocable liability is incurred or title passes within the United States. . . .

C.   DOMESTIC PURCHASES AND SALES

1.   The Meaning of a Domestic Transaction

While *Morrison* holds that §10(b) can be applied to domestic purchases or sales, it provides little guidance as to what constitutes a domestic purchase or sale. To determine the meaning of a domestic purchase or sale, we first consider how these terms are defined in the Exchange Act. "The terms 'buy' and 'purchase' each include any contract to buy, purchase, or otherwise acquire." 15 U.S.C. §78c(a)(13). Similarly, "[t]he terms 'sale' and 'sell' each include any contract to sell or otherwise dispose of." Id. §78c(a)(14). . . . [T]hese definitions suggest that the "purchase" and "sale" take place when the parties become bound to effectuate the transaction. . . .

Given that the point at which the parties become irrevocably bound is used to determine the timing of a purchase and sale, we similarly hold that the point of irrevocable liability can be used to determine the locus of a securities purchase or sale. Thus, in order to adequately allege the existence of a domestic transaction, it is sufficient for a plaintiff to allege facts leading to the plausible inference that the parties incurred irrevocable liability within the United States: that is, that the purchaser incurred irrevocable liability within the United States to take and pay for a security, or that the seller incurred irrevocable liability within the United States to deliver a security. . . .

However, we do not believe this is the only way to locate a securities transaction. After all, a "sale" is ordinarily defined as "[t]he transfer of property or title for a price." Black's Law Dictionary 1454 (9th ed. 2009). . . . Thus, a sale of securities can be understood to take place at the location in which title is transferred. . . . Accordingly, to sufficiently allege a domestic securities transaction in securities not listed on a domestic exchange, we hold that a plaintiff must allege facts suggesting that irrevocable liability was incurred or title was transferred within the United States. . . .

2.   Whether the Complaint Adequately Alleges Domestic Transactions

Having explained what constitutes a domestic transaction, we now turn to whether the complaint alleges facts giving rise to the plausible inference that irrevocable liability was incurred or title was transferred within the United States. The Funds principally argue that because the [offerings were] *direct* sales by U.S. companies to the Funds, the complaint sufficiently alleges the existence of domestic purchases. However, upon careful review of the complaint, we conclude that the allegations do not sufficiently allege that purchases or sales took place in the United States.

[T]he sole allegation that affirmatively states that the transactions took place in the United States only does so in conclusory fashion: "The fraudulent transactions that Defendants carried out through [California-based broker] took place in the United States." Absent factual allegations suggesting that the Funds became irrevocably bound within the United States or that title was transferred within the United States, including, but not limited to, facts concerning the formation of the contracts, the placement of purchase orders, the passing of title, or the exchange of money, the mere assertion that transactions "took place in the United States" is insufficient to adequately plead the existence of domestic transactions. The complaint alleges that investors subscribed to the Funds by wiring money to a bank located in New York. However, this allegation, even if true, is inapposite as the case before us was brought by the Funds themselves and is based on the Funds' purchases and sales of U.S. Penny Stocks rather than individual investors' subscriptions to the Funds. Similarly, allegations that the Funds were heavily marketed in the United States and that United States investors were harmed by the defendants' actions, while potentially satisfying the now-defunct conduct and effects test, *see Morrison*, 547 F.3d at 171, do not satisfy the transactional test announced in *Morrison*. . . .

Finally, while the complaint alleges that the U.S. Penny Stocks were issued by United States companies and were registered with the SEC, these facts do not demonstrate that the purchases and sales were "made in the United States.". . .

For a sampling of the extensive commentary on *Morrison*, *see* Beyea, *Morrison v. National Australia Bank* and the Future of Extraterritorial Application of the U.S. Securities Laws, 72 Ohio St. L.J. 537 (2011) (critical of limiting private causes of action in the wake of the 2008 financial crisis); Buxbaum, Investor Suits in the Era of the Roberts Court, 75 Law & Contemp. Prob. 161 (2012) (critical of diminishing prospects for foreign investors to recover losses through U.S. courts); Florey, State Law, U.S. Power, Foreign Disputes: Understanding the Extraterritorial Effects of State Law in the Wake of *Morrison v. National Australia Bank*, 92 B.U. L. Rev. 535 (2012) (arguing *Morrison* and the presumption against extraterritoriality fail to address the proper role of state law in regulating fraud); Fox, Securities Class Actions Against Foreign Issuers, 64 Stan. L. Rev. 1173 (2012) (evaluating whether it is ever appropriate that a foreign issuer be subject to the U.S. fraud-on-the-market private damages class action liability regime, and, if so, by what kinds of claimants and under what circumstances).

NOTES AND QUESTIONS

1. What Is a U.S. Exchange? OTC Trades and **Morrison.**   The first prong of *Morrison*'s framework allows for application of Section 10(b) for the purchase or sale of a security "listed on an American stock exchange." What does this mean? In *United States v. Georgiou*, 777 F.3d 125 (3d Cir.), *cert. denied*, 136 S. Ct. 401 (2015), the Third Circuit considered whether Section 10(b) covers offshore manipulative securities trading in U.S. public companies, the stocks of which were not listed on U.S. exchanges but were quoted on pink sheets and traded through the U.S. OTC market. The court concluded that the OTC market is not "an American stock exchange" for purposes of *Morrison*:

> Given that a "national securities exchange" is explicitly listed in Section 10(b)—to the exclusion of the OTC markets—and coupled with the absence of the Pink Sheets and the OTCBB on the list of registered national security exchanges on the SEC Webpage on Exchanges, we are persuaded that those exchanges are not national securities exchanges within the scope of *Morrison*.

Id. at 135; *see also Stoyas v. Toshiba Corporation*, 896 F.3d 933 (9th Cir. 2018). Not all courts would agree. *See, e.g., United States v. Isaacson*, 752 F.3d 1291, 1299 (11th Cir. 2014), *cert. denied*, 135 S. Ct. 990 (2015) (accepting expert testimony that the OTC Bulletin Board and pink sheets are "similar" to the NYSE and Nasdaq for purposes of *Morrison*).

Although the first prong of *Morrison* was not satisfied in *Georgiou*, the second prong—a domestic transaction in securities—was satisfied because the trades were made through market makers in the United States. Borrowing from *Absolute Activist*, the court reasoned: "Therefore, some of the relevant transactions required the involvement of a purchaser or seller working with a market maker and committing to a transaction in the United States, incurring irrevocable liability in the United States, or passing title in the United States." *Georgiou*, 777 F.3d at 136.

2.   Is a Domestic Transaction Itself Sufficient to Justify Application of Section 10(b)?

Absolute Activist involved a rather straightforward application of *Morrison* to a conventional purchase of securities. But what about purchases of securities in the United States whose value derives from references to foreign securities?

In *Parkcentral Global Hub Ltd. v. Porsche Auto. Holdings SE*, 763 F.3d 198 (2d Cir. 2014), a group of hedge funds executed in the United States securities-based swap agreements relating to the stock of Volkswagen, AG, a German corporation with stock traded only on foreign exchanges. The hedge funds took positions in the swap agreements betting that the price of Volkswagen stock was going to decline. As things turned out, the stock rose in value because of a subsequent takeover of Volkswagen by Porsche. Faced with substantial losses, the hedge funds then brought suit in the United States charging Porsche with making false statements prior to the takeover concealing its intention to acquire Volkswagen.

The issue thus presented was whether a Section 10(b) claim may be asserted by parties to swap agreements executed in the United States when the agreements related solely to stock of a foreign corporation traded only on foreign exchanges. The Second Circuit concluded that it may not. Noting *Morrison*'s concern with potentially incompatible regulation by domestic and foreign regulatory authorities, the court reasoned that the status of the swap agreement as a domestic transaction cannot be dispositive:

> If the domestic execution of the plaintiffs' agreements could alone suffice to invoke §10(b) liability with respect to the defendants' alleged conduct in this case, then it would subject to U.S. securities laws conduct that occurred in a foreign country, concerning securities in a foreign company, traded entirely on foreign exchanges, in the absence of any congressional provision addressing the

incompatibility of U.S. and foreign law nearly certain to arise. That is a result *Morrison* plainly did not contemplate and that the Court's reasoning does not, we think, permit.

[W]e conclude that, while a domestic transaction or listing is necessary to state a claim under §10(b), a finding that these transactions were domestic would not suffice to compel the conclusion that the plaintiffs' invocation of §10(b) was appropriately domestic.

Id. at 215-216.

Consider, however, the case of unsponsored ADRs. These are created by an American third-party depository institution, potentially without the consent or involvement of the foreign issuer of the underlying shares. The American institution issues the ADRs while maintaining custody of the associated shares of subject company. In *Stoyas v. Toshiba Corporation*, 896 F.3d 933 (9th Cir. 2018), the Ninth Circuit rejected *Parkcentral* in that context, holding that the foreign issuer's involvement or lack of involvement with a U.S.-based purchase of unsponsored ADRs was not relevant to the question of whether the claim concerns a domestic purchase or sale for *Morrison* purposes. It might, however, be relevant to the question whether the foreign issuer's alleged fraud was accomplished *in connection with* a domestic securities transaction, as Section 10(b) also requires.

Courts have also confronted the converse situation in the context of foreign derivative contracts referencing U.S. securities. In one recurring pattern, persons abroad have used inside information to purchase such contracts from their local brokers. Though the contracts themselves are clearly foreign, the brokers often hedge their own exposure, either by purchasing the underlying security on a U.S. exchange, or by purchasing their own derivative contracts that ultimately result in a purchase of the underlying security by the counterparty. Several district courts have held that the hedge creates enough of a domestic connection to bring the original derivative contract within Section 10(b)'s ambit (without, as might be expected, resorting to the conduct-and-effects test of Section 929P, described above). *See, e.g., SEC v. One or More Unknown Traders in the Secs. of Fortress Inv. Group, LLC*, 2018 U.S. Dist. LEXIS 167164 (D.N.J. Sept. 27, 2018); *SEC v. Sabrdaran*, 2015 U.S. Dist. LEXIS 25051 (N.D. Cal. Mar. 2, 2015). For a discussion of complex legal issues associated with these contracts, *see* Note, At the Water's Hedge: International Insider-Trading Enforcement After *Morrison*, 68 Duke L.J. 1003 (2019).

3.　International Class Action Settlements.　*Morrison* may block foreign purchasers from pursuing securities claims under U.S. law, but what if defendants prefer to resolve all claims against them in a global settlement, rather than face litigation in multiple jurisdictions?

In *In re Petrobras Securities Litigation*, 317 F. Supp. 3d 858 (S.D.N.Y. 2018), the district court approved a settlement that potentially included foreign purchasers. Following *Morrison*'s lead, the court held that extraterritoriality was a merits determination rather than a jurisdictional requirement, and thus disputes over extraterritoriality could be waived by defendants in connection with a settlement.

Global settlements may also be available outside of the United States. In 2010 (the same year *Morrison* was decided), the Amsterdam Court of Appeal issued a much anticipated decision in the *Converium* case. The decision allows use of the Dutch collective-settlement statute (adopted in 2005) to settle complex, multi-jurisdictional securities cases. The court asserted jurisdiction over the case even though the claims were not brought under Dutch law, the alleged wrongdoing took place outside the Netherlands, the parties potentially liable were not domiciled in the Netherlands, and only a handful of the claimants were domiciled in the Netherlands. Several high-profile securities class actions involving non-U.S. purchases have been settled using the Dutch procedure, including claims against Royal Dutch Shell and Ageas (formerly Fortis). For a discussion of the policy issues raised by use of global settlement procedures, *see* Coffee, Global Settlements: Promise and Peril (Apr. 9, 2019), Colum. L. & Econ. Working Paper No. 604, *https://ssrn.com/abstract=3369199.*

4. *The Reach of* Morrison. How far does *Morrison*'s presumption against territoriality reach? Consider in this regard the plight of Khaled Asadi, a U.S.-based employee of G.E. Energy. While on temporary assignment in Jordan, Asadi observed and reported to his supervisor conduct he believed violated the Foreign Corrupt Practices Act. Not long thereafter, he received a negative performance review that contrasted with ten previous positive reviews. GE pressured Asadi to resign and, in the midst of negotiations on his severance, terminated him. Asadi then brought suit under the Dodd-Frank whistleblower provisions. Relying on *Morrison* and the presumption against extraterritorial application, the court concluded that Dodd-Frank's whistleblower provisions do not have extraterritorial reach. *See Asadi v. G.E. Energy (USA),* 2012 U.S. Dist. LEXIS 89746 (June 28, 2012). The lower court's opinion was affirmed by the Fifth Circuit on other grounds (Asadi did not qualify as a whistleblower because he did not report the information to the SEC). *See Asadi v. G.E. Energy (USA), L.L.C.,* 720 F.3d 620 (5th Cir. 2013). In another case, the Second Circuit reached the same conclusion as the *Asadi* lower court and held that Dodd-Frank's whistleblower anti-retaliation provisions do not apply extraterritorially. *See Liu Meng-Lin v. Siemens AG,* 763 F.3d 175 (2d Cir. 2014). The Department of Labor, however, interprets the whistleblower protections of Sarbanes-Oxley to apply to employees who report misconduct observed while working overseas, so long as the misconduct itself has a significant domestic effect. *See Blanchard v. Exelis Systems Corp./Vectrus Systems Corp.,* ARB Case No. 15-031 (Aug. 29, 2017).

5. Morrison *and Criminal Liability Under Section 10(b).* *Morrison* left open the question whether limits on extraterritorial application of Section 10(b) apply in prosecutions seeking to establish criminal rather than civil liability under the section. In *United States v. Vilar,* 729 F.3d 62, 72 (2d Cir. 2013), *cert. denied,* 134 S. Ct. 2684 (2014), the Second Circuit stated that "we have no problem concluding that *Morrison*'s holding applies equally to criminal actions." In so ruling, the court pointed to the general presumption that criminal statutes are not applied extraterritorially, adding that Section 10(b) is no exception. Although the Second Circuit may have had "no problem" in applying *Morrison* to criminal prosecutions, the Eleventh Circuit is more hesitant and passed when given the opportunity to follow *Vilar,* noting that in the case before it *Morrison*'s requirement of a "U.S. nexus" was satisfied. *See United States v. Isaacson,* 752 F.3d 1291, 1299 (11th Cir. 2014), *cert. denied,* 135 S. Ct. 990 (2015).

Also consider Section 929P of Dodd-Frank discussed immediately following the *Morrison* decision. Recall that this provision provides that courts will have extraterritorial jurisdiction to hear cases brought by the government if conduct within the United States constitutes "significant steps in furtherance of the violation" or if conduct abroad has a "foreseeable substantial effect within the United States." As noted, there is continuing uncertainty as to whether Section 929P simply confers jurisdiction on federal courts or more broadly defines the substantive reach of Section 10(b) in actions brought by the government. If the latter, then *Vilar* diminishes in importance and becomes simply a statement of pre–Dodd-Frank case law.

*6. **Morrison** and Section 11.*   Section 11 of the '33 Act provides a private right of action to "any person acquiring such security" if "any part of the registration statement, when such part became effective, contained an untrue statement of a material fact or omitted to state a material fact required to be stated therein or necessary to make the statements therein not misleading." 15 U.S.C. §77k(a). Suppose an issuer registers its securities for sale in the United States but some portion of the offering trades abroad. May foreign purchasers bring claims under Section 11? Courts say no. *See, e.g., In re SMART Techs., Inc.*, 295 F.R.D. 50 (S.D.N.Y. 2013) (applying *Morrison*'s presumption against extraterritoriality to the "any person acquiring" language); *In re Vivendi Universal, S.A. Sec. Litig.*, 842 F. Supp. 2d 522 (S.D.N.Y. 2012).

*7. **Then What of Section 17(A)?***   Section 17(a) of the '33 Act is broader than Section 10(b) in that it reaches not just a sale but also an offer of securities. How, then, is *Morrison* to be applied when the alleged fraud is in the offer rather than the sale? The issue was addressed in *SEC v. Tourre*, 2013 U.S. Dist. LEXIS 78297 (S.D.N.Y. 2013), where the question for summary judgment purposes was whether certain marketing activities that took place in the United States were sufficient to render the fraud actionable under Section 17(a). In concluding that *Morrison* did not bar the SEC's Section 17(a) claims, the court emphasized the "key" distinction between Section 10(b)'s prohibition of fraud "in connection with the purchase or sale of any security" and Section 17(a)'s prohibition of fraud "in the offer or sale" of any securities: "Section 17(a)'s proscription extends beyond consummated transactions. . . . This means that a domestic offer may be actionable regardless of whether it results in a sale." Id. at *20-21.

PROBLEMS

20-4.   Credit Suisse Group (CSG) is a Swiss-based global investment banking firm that heavily invested in U.S. mortgage-backed securities. The credit crisis caused huge financial losses for CSG. Plaintiffs are American residents who purchased shares of CSG on the SIX Swiss Exchange; shares of CSG also are listed on the NYSE as ADRs. Plaintiffs claim CSG's financial statements were materially misleading in failing to disclose the extent of losses and necessary asset write-downs. They further claim they were induced to buy shares by overly optimistic statements of company officials and investment professionals targeted to

American investors. Does *Morrison* bar their claims in U.S. courts? *See Cornwell v. Credit Suisse Grp.*, 729 F. Supp. 2d 620 (S.D.N.Y. 2010).

20-5. Quail, a cruise ship operator, alleges that various parties conspired to induce it to purchase stock of a company that owned the M/V Pacific (better known as the eponymous Love Boat from its television days of the 1970s and 1980s) by fraudulently misrepresenting the vessel's deteriorating and defective condition. The misrepresentations included falsified inspections for the vessel. Although the misrepresentations were made while all parties were overseas, the closing for the stock purchase (privately negotiated and not on an exchange) took place at the offices of a Miami law firm. Quail files a complaint alleging securities fraud, and the defendants, citing *Morrison*, move to dismiss. What result? *See Quail Cruises Ship Mgmt. Ltd. v. Agencia de Viagens CVC Tur Limitada*, 645 F.3d 1307 (11th Cir. 2011).

20-6. French promoters form a Delaware company for the purpose of investing in New York real estate. They plan to sell interests in the company to European residents and citizens. A French investor is interested in the venture. The promoters and the investor travel to New York to inspect the property. Various misrepresentations are made by the promoters to the investor. The misrepresentations were contained in the offering materials, which were prepared in French and were repeated when the investor visited the United States. For the most part, negotiations took place in France, and all documents were signed in that country. May the investor pursue a Section 10(b) claim in U.S. court? May the SEC pursue a Section 10(b) claim? A Section 17(a) claim? *See AVC Nederland, B.V. v. Atrium Inv. P'ship*, 740 F.2d 148 (2d Cir. 1984) (pre-*Morrison*).

4. Choice of Law Options: The Relevance of Foreign Law in Securities Litigation

Parties to a transaction can, and often do, specify the jurisdiction whose laws will be applied to their relationship. Ordinarily, however, this is impossible when it comes to matters of "public" rather than "private" law because of its character as a policy tool. Imagine, for example, parties purporting to specify that a particular jurisdiction's criminal laws would not apply; the clause would be unenforceable because the criminal laws of a particular jurisdiction concern the interests of the state, not the parties.

Traditionally, U.S. securities law has been treated as "public" law. This can be seen in the variety of provisions that begin with "It shall be unlawful," for example, Securities Exchange Act Section 10(b), as well as the express prohibitions against contracts waiving application of the acts. *See* Securities Act Section 15; Securities Exchange Act Section 29(a). Additionally, regulation of insider trading, regulation of broker-dealers, prohibitions against bribing foreign government officials, and proxy solicitation rules are among the many parts of securities law driven by public interest concerns (i.e., protection of markets and the investing public) and therefore may plausibly be regarded as public law. Yet in many areas, securities law is quietly being "privatized" to an extent sufficient to undermine its status as public law. Often this is accomplished by allowing the parties to specify a particular forum for disputes, and then to further specify the law to be applied in that forum. As early as 1973, the Supreme Court found enforceable a contract (involving the sale of a foreign business to a U.S. buyer) calling for arbitration under Illinois law, even though claims were asserted under Section 10(b). *See Scherk v. Alberto-Culver Co.,* 417 U.S. 506 (1974) (emphasizing the special needs of parties engaged in international business transactions). *See generally* Hillman, Cross-Border Investment, Conflict of Laws, and the Privatization of Securities Law, 55 Law & Contemp. Probs. 331 (1992); Licht, Stock Exchange Mobility, Unilateral Recognition, and the Privatization of Securities Regulation, 41 Va. J. Int'l L. 583 (2001). And as was discussed in Chapter 18, more recent developments have assigned to the realm of arbitration most disputes involving brokers.

In the pre-*Morrison* case excerpted below, the Seventh Circuit addressed Section 10(b), Section 11, and Section 12 claims brought by Americans who had purchased British securities on British soil. The contracts included a choice of law clause selecting British law as the rule of decision, a forum selection clause selecting British courts with respect to some defendants, and an arbitration clause with respect to others.

Bonny v. The Society of Lloyd's
3 F.3d 156 (7th Cir. 1993), *cert. denied,* **510 U.S. 1113 (1994)**

Lay, Senior Circuit Judge. . . . [Plaintiffs] argue that the forum selection and choice of law clauses should be held void because together they violate public policy by prospectively waiving plaintiffs' Securities Act remedies. Plaintiffs rely on *Mitsubishi Motors Corp. v. Soler Chrysler-Plymouth, Inc.,* 473 U.S. 614 (1984), where the Supreme Court stated in dicta that forum selection and choice of law provisions which operate as prospective waivers of statutory antitrust claims would not be enforced as against public policy. Plaintiffs argue that they are being deprived of all substantive rights under the federal securities laws and should therefore be relieved of their agreement on public policy grounds. . . .

The presumptive validity of a forum selection clause can be overcome if the resisting party can show it is "unreasonable under the circumstances." *M/S Bremen* [*v. Zapata Off-Shore Co.,*] 407 U.S. [1,] 10 [(1972)]. The Supreme Court has construed this exception narrowly: forum selection and choice of law clauses are "unreasonable" (1) if their incorporation into the contract was the result of fraud, undue influence or overweening bargaining power; (2) if the selected forum is so "gravely difficult and inconvenient that [the complaining party] will for all practical purposes be deprived of its day in court"; or (3) if enforcement of the clauses would contravene a strong public policy of the forum in which the suit is brought, declared by statute or judicial decision.

Plaintiffs have not met their burden in proving the clauses unreasonable. There is no evidence in the record that the forum selection clause was tainted by fraud, undue influence or overwhelming bargaining power. Moreover, plaintiffs do not argue that they would suffer severe physical and financial hardship by being compelled to litigate in England.

As to the third factor, we have serious concerns that Lloyd's clauses operate as a prospective waiver of statutory remedies for securities violations. By including the anti-waiver provisions in the securities laws, Congress made clear that the public policy of these laws should not be thwarted. The complaint in this case asserts that defendants violated provisions of the 1933 Securities Acts in dealing with American citizens. To allow Lloyd's to avoid liability for putative violations of the 1933 Act would contravene important American policies unless remedies available in the selected forum do not subvert the public policy of that Act. This is the fundamental question we face here.

In the present case, we are satisfied that several remedies in England vindicate plaintiffs' substantive rights while not subverting the United States' policies of insuring full and fair disclosure by issuers and deterring exploitation of United States investors. English law affords plaintiffs a cause of action for fraud similar to that available for the claims they have brought under Rule 10b-5. Plaintiffs can bring claims for common law fraud and rescission of their contract made in reliance on the misrepresentation. In addition, several of the specific Lloyd's agreements require disclosure of material information to American investors with failure to do so giving rise to liability for breach of contract. Moreover, under their contracts, Member's Agents owe a fiduciary duty to Names which provides a further basis for suit. Finally, Section 47 of the Financial Services Act creates penalties for misleading statements or omissions made knowingly or recklessly. Although Section 47 provides criminal sanctions, injured persons can obtain compensation pursuant to Section 61 of the Act, which permits the court, upon the application of the Secretary of State, to order injunctions to restrain violations of §47 and to make remedial orders. While Section 61 does not create a private right of action, upon a finding of criminal liability under §47, plaintiffs could potentially receive some compensation for their injuries. More importantly, such criminal penalties serve as an important deterrent against exploitation of United States investors. . . .

We conclude that the available remedies and potential damage recoveries suffice to deter deception of American investors and to induce the disclosure of material information to investors. . . . [T]he fact that an international transaction may be subject to laws and remedies different or less favorable than those of the United States is not alone a valid basis to deny enforcement of forum selection, arbitration and choice of law clauses. . . .

NOTES AND QUESTIONS

1. Adequacy of Foreign Law. Are you persuaded by *Bonny*'s discussion of the adequacy of English law? In another case involving Lloyd's, the Second Circuit offered its own comparative analysis:

> We are concerned in the present case that the Roby Names' contract clauses may operate "in tandem" as a prospective waiver of the statutory remedies for securities violations. . . .

[T]he available remedies are adequate and the potential recoveries substantial. . . . Moreover, together with the contractual obligations imposing certain fiduciary and similar duties on Members' and Managing Agents, we believe that the available remedies and potential damages recoveries suffice to deter deception of American investors. . . .

While we do not doubt that the United States securities laws would provide the [plaintiffs] with a greater variety of defendants and a greater chance of success due to lighter scienter and causation requirements, we are convinced that there are ample and just remedies under English law. Moreover, we cannot say that the policies underlying our securities laws will be offended by the application of English law. . . .

Roby v. Corp. of Lloyd's, 996 F.2d 1353, 1364-1366 (2d Cir.), *cert. denied*, 510 U.S. 945 (1993); *see also Riley v. Kingsley Underwriting Agencies, Ltd.*, 969 F.2d 953, 958 (10th Cir.), *cert. denied*, 506 U.S. 1021 (1992) ("The fact that an international transaction may be subject to laws and remedies different or less favorable than those of the United States is not a valid basis to deny enforcement. . . . English law does not preclude Riley from pursuing an action for fraud. . . . We have been shown nothing to suggest that an English court would not be fair."). What are *Bonny* and *Roby* suggesting about the suitability of, say, New York law to resolve investment disputes? In a domestic investment, could the parties stipulate choice of forum (arbitration) and choice of law (New York)? *Cf. Shell v. R.W. Sturge, Ltd.*, 55 F.3d 1227 (6th Cir. 1995) (English law as adequate as Ohio securities law in protecting the interests of investors). Are international cases different? If the distinction between international and domestic investments is important, as it presumably is, has it been blurred by developments (discussed in Chapter 18) favorable to the arbitration of purely domestic claims between brokers and their clients?

Bonny and *Roby* are representative of a number of circuit court decisions dealing with efforts of disgruntled investors to upset contractual choice of law provisions. For the most part, the investors have been unsuccessful. *See, e.g., Allen v. Lloyd's of London*, 94 F.3d 923 (4th Cir. 1996); *Richards v. Lloyd's of London*, 135 F.3d 1289 (1998); *Lipcon v. Underwriters at Lloyd's, London*, 148 F.3d 1285 (11th Cir. 1998). For commentary on the *Lloyd's* cases, *see* Cox, Choice of Law Rules for International Securities Transactions?, 66 U. Cin. L. Rev. 1179, 1187 (1998) (expressing concern over unknowing waivers as well as allowing "private agreements [to] drive out wiser and more broadly formulated public law"); Peterson, Choice of Law and Forum Clauses and the Recognition of Foreign Country Judgments Revisited Through the Lloyd's of London Cases, 60 La. L. Rev. 1259 (2000) (arguing the cases cannot be reconciled with the anti-waiver provisions of the securities acts); Ribstein & O'Hara, Corporations and the Market for Law, 2008 U. Ill. L. Rev. 661, 710-711 (concluding the cases reflect a competitive international regulatory market that threatens the continuation of U.S. domination of securities regulation).

Should *Morrison* affect courts' willingness to enforce choice of law clauses? Prior to *Morrison*, companies like Lloyd's faced considerable uncertainty regarding the law that governed their international transactions; even executing a contract in England provided no guarantee that American law would not apply. Thus, courts expressed some sympathy for international firms simply trying to ensure some uniformity in their affairs. *See Bonny*, supra ("the elimination of all such uncertainties by agreeing in advance on a forum acceptable to both parties is an indispensable element in international trade, commerce, and contracting" (quoting *Zapata*, 407 U.S. at 13-14)). After *Morrison*, however, the application of American law is far more predictable. Does that lessen the need for such clauses? *Cf.* Kaal & Painter, Forum Competition and Choice of Law Competition in Securities Law after *Morrison v. National Australia Bank*, 97 Minn. L. Rev. 132 (2012) (arguing *Morrison's* emphasis on geographic determinants should allow for greater options on choice of law, which in turn may lead to greater competition among jurisdictions seeking to provide substantive rules attractive to parties in securities transactions).

  2. Adequacy Beyond Substantive Law. A starting point for comparing investor protection laws is substantive provisions of foreign law. Procedural law and other nonsubstantive aspects of a legal system, of course, may also affect the ability to vindicate substantive rights.

  For example, is it relevant to the adequacy inquiry that most foreign legal systems require the loser to pay the winner's litigation costs? Or that it may be impossible to retain legal counsel on a contingent fee basis? Or that class actions may not be available? As to the latter, recall the earlier noted *Converium* case, the 2010 decision in which the Amsterdam Court of Appeal approved use of the Dutch collective-settlement procedure as a means of providing a structure to facilitate global securities class action settlements; the existence of such an option for investors may make U.S. judges more comfortable in dismissing claims.

  Note that a foreign tribunal's standard of due process is relevant when U.S. courts are asked to enforce foreign judgments. In *Society of Lloyds v. Ashenden*, 233 F.3d 473 (7th Cir. 2000), Lloyds sought to enforce judgments it had obtained from English courts. The Seventh Circuit rejected a "retail" approach under which the foreign proceedings would be judged strictly by American standards of due process. Noting that it "is not open to doubt" that England has a civilized legal system, the court added:

> We need not consider what kind of evidence would suffice to show that a foreign legal system "does not provide impartial tribunals or procedures compatible with the requirements of due process of law" if the challenged judgment had been rendered by Cuba, North Korea, Iran, Iraq, Congo, or some other nation whose adherence to the rule of law and commitment to the norm of due process are open to serious question, . . . as England's are not.

Id. at 477.

  3. Limits on Contractual Choice of Law. What are the limits on contractual choice of law and forum if the chosen foreign law provides adequate protection for investors? Assume, for example, the prospectus in a global public offering prominently discloses that any claims asserted by investors against the issuer or underwriters must be brought in British courts and will be resolved under English law? Does *Bonny* extend this far? Or is a distinction to be drawn between transactions that affect the organized securities markets and transactions that are privately negotiated? *See* Hillman, Cross-Border Investment, Conflict of Laws, and the Privatization of Securities Law, 55 Law & Contemp. Probs. 331 (1992) (arguing for such a distinction). Chapter 4 discusses the policy implications of permitting issuers to select the law that will be applied to their transactions.

PROBLEM

20-7. Blinkpoint is a wireless communication company in need of significant funds to expand its product line. The company is incorporated in Belize but has extensive business operations in the United States. To raise additional funds, Blinkpoint proposes to have a public offering in the United States of preferred stock. It expects the offering will be well received by American investors. Blinkpoint wishes to avoid the burdens of registration under U.S. law, and to this end it includes a very clear statement on the cover of the offering statements that Belize law will govern all aspects of the offering of the preferred stock. It also requires investors in the offering to sign an agreement affirming their consent to this choice of law. Assuming that Blinkpoint fully complies with Belize law, will Section 5 of the '33 Act apply to this offering?

B.   *Enforcement Challenges Presented by an Internationalized Securities Market*

1.   Unilateral Enforcement Efforts

a.   *Discovery Sanctions*

Historically, the SEC has faced significant enforcement problems in collecting information needed to prosecute individuals who violate federal securities laws (particularly those dealing with insider trading). These problems are particularly acute when the trading takes place through financial institutions outside of the United States that are protected by secrecy or blocking laws of their home nations, which were not developed with securities cases in mind, but which significantly limit the ability of the SEC to obtain information needed for prosecution. Secrecy laws protect the confidentiality of information possessed by financial institutions, while blocking laws prohibit the disclosure or removal of documents from a country. *See generally* Kauffman, Note, Secrecy and Blocking Laws: A Growing Problem as the Internationalization of Securities Markets Continues, 18 Vand. J. Transnat'l L. 809 (1985).

Faced with the significant obstacles posed by secrecy and blocking laws, one response of the SEC has been to utilize the discovery process provided by Rule 37 of the Federal Rules of Civil Procedure, which permits the use of court-ordered sanctions against U.S. subsidiaries of foreign financial institutions. For example, in *SEC v. Banca della Svizzera Italiana*, 92 F.R.D. 111 (S.D.N.Y. 1981), the SEC was investigating the purchase of options on the stock of a U.S. corporation shortly before the announcement of a tender offer for the stock of the corporation. The purchases under review were made through a Swiss bank (SBI), which apparently did business in the United States through a subsidiary. Relying on Switzerland's bank secrecy laws, SBI refused to comply with the SEC's discovery requests or respond to its interrogatories. Finding jurisdiction because of the U.S. subsidiary and the presence of a strong national interest, the federal district court ordered SBI to produce the requested information. Faced with a possible fine of $50,000 per day for noncompliance with the U.S. court order, the bank secured the consent of its customers to release the information to the SEC.

The strategy employed by the SEC in *Banca della Svizzera Italiana* has serious limitations. "Persuasion" via court-imposed sanctions may enjoy some success when the obstacles to disclosure are secrecy laws, which are designed to protect the interests of customers of financial institutions and are therefore waivable by the parties protected. Blocking laws, on the other hand, protect national, rather than individual, interests and therefore are not waivable by private parties. The Public Company Accounting Oversight Board (PCAOB) maintains a list of issuers audited by firms in foreign jurisdictions whose authorities block access to audit information. *See* PCAOB, Issuers That Are Audit Clients of PCAOB-Registered Firms from Non-U.S. Jurisdictions Where the PCAOB Is Denied Access to Conduct Inspections, *https://pcaobus.org/International/Inspections/Pages/IssuerClientsWithoutAccess.aspx.*

In December 2018, the SEC and PCAOB released a joint statement decrying policies in various international jurisdictions that deny access to critical financial and audit data regarding companies listed in the United States. The statement singled out China in particular for its laws restricting SEC and PCAOB access to books and records and audit work papers. *See* SEC Chairman Jay Clayton, SEC Chief Accountant Wes Bricker, and PCAOB Chairman William D. Duhnke III, Statement on the Vital Role of Audit Quality and Regulatory Access to Audit and Other Information Internationally—Discussion of Current Information Access Challenges with Respect to U.S.-Listed Companies with Significant Operations in China (Dec. 7, 2018). In June 2019, a bipartisan group of U.S. lawmakers proposed legislation that would, among other things, place limits on the ability of foreign issuers to list on American exchanges if their home jurisdiction denies the SEC and PCAOB the ability to inspect their auditors. *See* EQUITABLE Act, S. 1731, 116th Cong., 1st Sess. (2019).

b. The Reach for Assets

In transnational securities fraud cases, the success of litigation may depend upon the adeptness of plaintiffs in locating and attaching assets of culpable defendants. The courts of most nations are empowered to provide varying types of provisional remedies that freeze assets pending disposition of litigation. In the United States, these remedies take the form of prejudgment attachments, sequestration orders, appointments of receivers, and the like. For example, foreign nationals who trade on U.S. exchanges often place their orders with local brokerages who then fulfill them via U.S.-based clearing accounts. When the SEC identifies suspicious trading from these accounts, it may swiftly seek, and receive, a federal court order freezing the relevant U.S.-based assets. *See, e.g.,*

SEC Litigation Release No. 24462 (Apr. 29, 2019) (freeze of U.S.-based assets held by unknown persons operating out of Cyprus and the U.K. who engaged in suspicious trades of Anadarko Petroleum before it announced a takeover bid by Chevron); SEC Litigation Release No. 23760 (Feb. 28, 2017) (freeze of U.S.-based assets held by unknown persons operating out of Singapore and the U.K. who engaged in suspicious trades of Fortress Investment Group before it announced a takeover bid by Softbank Group). The SEC was even able to obtain a U.S. court order to freeze assets held in Zurich because the account was maintained at a subsidiary of Goldman Sachs, a U.S. financial institution. *See SEC v. Certain Unknown Traders in the Securities of H.J. Heinz Company*, Docket No. 1:13-cv-01080 (Feb. 15, 2013).

The SEC may also apply directly to foreign authorities to obtain asset freezes. In 2008, the SEC secured an order from the High Court of Justice in London freezing the U.K. assets of Glenn Manterfield, a U.K. citizen resident in Sheffield. *See* SEC Litigation Release No. 20585 (May 19, 2008).

Does *Morrison*'s direction that U.S. securities laws do not apply extraterritorially also mean that provisional remedies may not extend to assets that are located offshore, even when the charged misconduct is domestic? At least one court has concluded *Morrison* does not limit the Commission's authority to seek equitable extraterritorial relief to protect investors who are the victims of U.S.-based securities laws violations. *See SEC v. Illarramendi*, 2011 U.S. Dist. LEXIS 65919 (D. Conn. June 26, 2011).

2.   **Bilateral and Multilateral Enforcement Efforts**

Bilateral and multilateral efforts keyed to cooperative exchanges of information and mutual support among regulators may offer a more promising basis for effective enforcement of securities laws than do "go it alone" unilateral actions that reach well beyond national boundaries.

In 2003, the International Organization of Securities Commissions (IOSCO) began utilizing the Multilateral Memorandum of Understanding Concerning Consultation and Cooperation and the Exchange of Information ("MMOU") as a means of promoting multilateral cooperation among the various enforcement agencies. The MMOU provides for the exchange of basic information in investigating cross-border violations, including bank, brokerage, and client identification records. An "Enhanced MMOU" was promulgated in 2016 that expands the scope of information to be exchanged to include items such as ISP and telephone records and audit work papers, and to permit compelled testimony. The MMOUs describe procedures for requesting information, maintaining the confidentiality of nonpublic information, and include reasons for not providing assistance, the most important of which are the existence of a pending criminal action, a conflict with domestic law, and (per the Enhanced MMOU) "on grounds of public or national interest." Regulatory bodies from more than 123 countries have signed the original MMOU, and in May 2019, the SEC became one of eleven regulatory bodies (including the U.S. CFTC) to sign the Enhanced MMOU. Though the MMOU lacks the force of international law, one study concluded that firms incorporated in signatory countries experience improved share liquidity, suggesting that investors perceive—and value—the increased oversight the MMOU promises. *See* Silvers, Cross-Border Cooperation Between Securities Regulators (May 2, 2019), *https://ssrn.com/abstract=3381887.*

Prior to the promulgation of the MMOU, the SEC relied on bilateral MOUs negotiated with individual countries, and today views these arrangements as a supplement to the information-sharing mechanisms delineated in the MMOUs. Bilateral cooperation was given further impetus in the Insider Trading and Securities Fraud Enforcement Act of 1988, which authorized the SEC to conduct investigations on behalf of foreign governments and to give wide-ranging aid—including the issuance of subpoenas—without regard to whether the investigated conduct would violate the U.S. securities laws if it occurred here.

For a discussion of bilateral and multilateral enforcement models and an explanation of why bilateral relationships may be better suited for participating jurisdictions that have developed financial markets, *see* Verdier, Mutual Recognition in International Finance, 52 Harv. Int'l L.J. 55 (2011).

Table of Cases

Principal cases are indicated by italics.

Index